Hislop's
Official International
Price Guide
to
Fine Art

Hislop's
Official International
Price Guide
to
Fine Art

Edited by
Duncan Hislop

House of Collectibles

The Crown Publishing Group, New York

 House of Collectibles is a registered trademark and the H colophon is a trademark of Random House, Inc.

Published by: House of Collectibles
                 The Crown Publishing Group
                 New York, New York

Distributed by the Crown Publishing Group, a division of Random House, Inc. New York, and simultaneously in Canada by Random House of Canada Limited, Toronto.

www.randomhouse.com

Printed in the United States of America

Cover art by Fitz Hugh Lane (1804-1865), American, "*View of West Beach, Beverly, Massachusetts, Sunset,*" $3,852,500. Image courtesy of Skinner, Inc., Auctioneers and Appraisers, Boston and Bolton, Massachusetts.

ISSN: 1537-5889

ISBN: 0-609-80874-5

10 9 8 7 6 5 4 3 2 1

First Edition: April 2002

Contents

INTRODUCTION

Buying, collecting and selling pictures are activities that are not only exciting and interesting, but can be financially rewarding. Not that every purchase you make will be a winner. Nearly everyone trading in pictures sometimes makes a mistake. The credo is "you win some and you lose some" and losing is probably superior to winning as a learning experience. As time goes on, the wins should increasingly exceed the losses.

Success depends on acquiring practical experience. This book is designed to help you make rapid progress toward your goal, whether it be to buy something beautiful or stimulating, to collect, to invest or to trade profitably.

VALUE AND PRICE

Value is an interesting and complicated concept. The value of something may, for example, depend on scarcity, beauty or usefulness. It may be psychologically valuable because it seems unobtainable. In contrast, when you have bought something, you sometimes wonder why you did so. John Updike put it starkly: "Possession diminishes perception of value immediately." Oscar Wilde makes a telling distinction between value and price in his definition of a cynic as "a man who knows the price of everything and the value of nothing." There are many things that are priceless. A child's painting may be cherished by the parents, who would not part with it for anything.

But in the more general run of things, Samuel Butler's precept that "For what is worth anything but so much money as it will bring" is a sensible guide. The price a picture commands depends on many factors. Robert Wraight has said: "A painting has no intrinsic worth. It is a luxury commodity for which a market is deliberately created and maintained by financially interested parties." This was illustrated by a charcoal drawing described as "English School, 18th Century" estimated to achieve at auction about 1,500 dollars. It was then discovered that the work was likely to be by Gainsborough, for which a considerable market has been created -a superb artist and a scarcity value depending on the fact that an artist can paint only a limited number of pictures and when he is dead there are no more. It actually sold for about 150,000 dollars. It was the same picture with the same aesthetic value both before and after the discovery, but the highly marketable name made all the difference.
Similar striking differences in price arise when there are doubts as to whether a picture

1

has actually been painted by the artist. There are two versions of what purport to be Vincent Van Gogh's painting "Sunflowers," one of which is claimed to be by the artist and one of which is not. It is known that his neighbor, Dr. Gachet, sometimes copied his paintings, and one might have been painted by him. Seen together, it is impossible for anyone other than an expert to tell the difference. The genuine one is worth $60 million, the other perhaps ten thousand times less.

Pictures are commodities, and the prices they command are determined by supply and demand, fashion and marketing. At serious prices, the name of the artist is what determines the price, which is why prices in this guide are listed by artist.
It would be nice to believe that prices are somehow correlated with some sort of virtue, like the skill of the artist, the spiritual content or a mind-blowing message. However, the millions of dollars paid for some sorts of modern art, which seem, to many observers, to be either rubbish or a joke or both, emphasizes the importance of fashion and marketing of names. Even when one can appreciate the qualities of a beautiful and inspiring painting, it is difficult to understand how it can be worth millions of dollars. But that is how it is, and this book reflects how the market values the work of many artists.

Is there a "right" price?

If you are faced with having to give advice on the value of some painting by an unknown artist, what do you say? You can see that they might be priced at, say, $150 each in a local art society exhibition, and some might sell at that price. However, put the same pictures into a picture auction and they probably wouldn't sell at all.

Another picture by a known artist is brought in for valuation. It looks genuine. The artist's name appears in the price books and his oil paintings have sold in the range $1,000 to $6,000. It is typical of the artist, skillfully painted, with convincing figures, horses and careful architectural depiction. It could well fetch upward of $3,000 at auction. This argues for a price of $6,000 retail at the very least and probably a good deal more in a fashionable gallery. If the valuation is for insurance, then to be on the safe side one might argue for $7,500. All these ways of expressing price are used on the television program "*The Antiques Road Show*", which can cause confusion as to what is the "real" price.

Probably the most dependable price is the auction price. But even then, if you examine the prices that a particular popular artist has achieved over a year at auction, you will see a wide range. For example, Andy Warhol's works on paper vary in price from $960 for a black felt-tip sketch to $2,500,000 for a portrait of Natalie Wood. Not only the name of the artist affects the price of a picture, but so do other considerations such as size, subject and the quality of the image.

The price of a picture can vary from one location to another, which is exploited by some picture traders who will buy a picture at one auction to sell at a profit at another. Prices can depend on the time of the year, the sentiment in the economy and on who is actually at the auction. Nevertheless, in spite of all these factors, most auction houses manage to estimate the prices pictures will fetch with surprising accuracy. But they are not infallible, and there are often negative surprises when pictures do not reach the estimated prices, and a few positive ones when the prices go way beyond the estimates. For paintings by known artists whose works appear regularly at auction, the prices achieved, such as those given in this book, are the best guide to estimate the price of a picture.

Why do people buy pictures?

Some pictures are bought to furnish a room, when colors, shades and brightness are important. The term "furnishing picture" is often used in a dismissive way to reduce expectations when an optimistic vendor brings a picture into an auction house for valuation, but it is a reasonable description of a wide range of pictures that are used to enhance a room. Another reason for buying is the appeal of the subject of a picture. A number of these are recognized as being "commercial" in the trade; examples are familiar landscapes or buildings, animals of any sort-wild, domestic, farm-cottages with children outside, seascapes, beaches with children.

Many pictures are bought by collectors who want pictures of a particular artist or school or of specialist subjects - for example, hunting dogs, tabby cats, moonlit scenes, Victorian sailing boats in difficulties. People may collect pictures as investments in the hope that, when they come to sell, the price of the picture will have gone up. Then there is the trader who hopes to find a bargain and to sell it again fairly quickly to make a quick profit.

The price that you are willing to pay for a picture depends on which of the above categories apply to you. If you are a furnishings picture buyer and you spot exactly the right picture to set off your interior design, you will probably not be too concerned about the price. This is probably true of the "I like it, I want it" viewpoint of the buyer of an attractive or striking subject. These buyers accept the frequently given advice "buy what you like, what moves you, what appeals to you, back your own judgment."

This is not bad advice provided you are not concerned whether the price you are paying is at least what you are likely to get back when you come to sell. The implication is that if it is worth it to you, the price is right. These buyers frequently buy from galleries and exhibitions and pay in the range $100 to $50,000. They may say "I have seen this artist fetching this sort of price in galleries and the price is on the up," but they have no way of knowing whether they are buying at the right price unless the work of the artist has an auction record, which often it doesn't. Nevertheless, from time to time an artist promoted by a gallery may become very successful, her or his exhibitions selling out at the private view and soon achieving an enviable auction performance. There are exceptions to every generality, and it is clearly a good idea to try to spot such artists.

Collectors are in a different category. They are generally well informed about their specialty and they use price guides to check the prices they are prepared to pay. Sometimes the needs of the collection will override purely commercial considerations.

Investors and traders are very price conscious. The former in the long run, and the latter in the short run, aim to buy cheaply and sell dearly. They need to know the market price of what they want to buy and sell and what prospective purchasers are likely to be prepared to pay. The price guide is one of their essential tools.

How to trade profitably in pictures

One good piece of advice is to avoid trying to buy and sell everything. Be a specialist. Don't deal in "unknowns." Choose a niche. For example, home in on a very small number of artists, living or dead, of repute, whose pictures frequently turn up at auctions. Get to know the work of these artists - the subjects they have painted, the style, the way they apply paint, their history. There are other sorts of specialties - a particular "school" of painters or a type of painting. Choose what really interests you, so that any time you spend on research is not only valuable but enjoyable. Above all, buy pictures that people are buying, so that you will find it easy to sell them.

Check the prices that are being asked or estimated, with the prices similar pictures have fetched at auctions, by using price guides. Check the artists out in the various biographical books covering your chosen artist(s). Select the gallery or auction where you see the opportunity to buy a picture for a price that will enable you to make a profit when you come to sell it.

Market trends

Broadly, the volume and value of the art market tend to follow the economic cycles. This can be seen in Fig.1, which shows the turnover in dollars (millions) and the number of lots sold in the International Art Auction Market from 1980 to 2000. There is a steady growth to 1986 and then a rapid buildup to the peak of 1990, which was fueled by the international boom at that time. This turnover was out of line with the longer-term trend from 1983. The fall after the boom showed the figures in 1992 resuming this longer-term trend. Subsequent years reflect the strength of the U.S. and international economies over the last few years. It is possible that a flattening of U.S. growth over the next year or two might be reflected in a steadying of the growth of the art market.

Fig.1

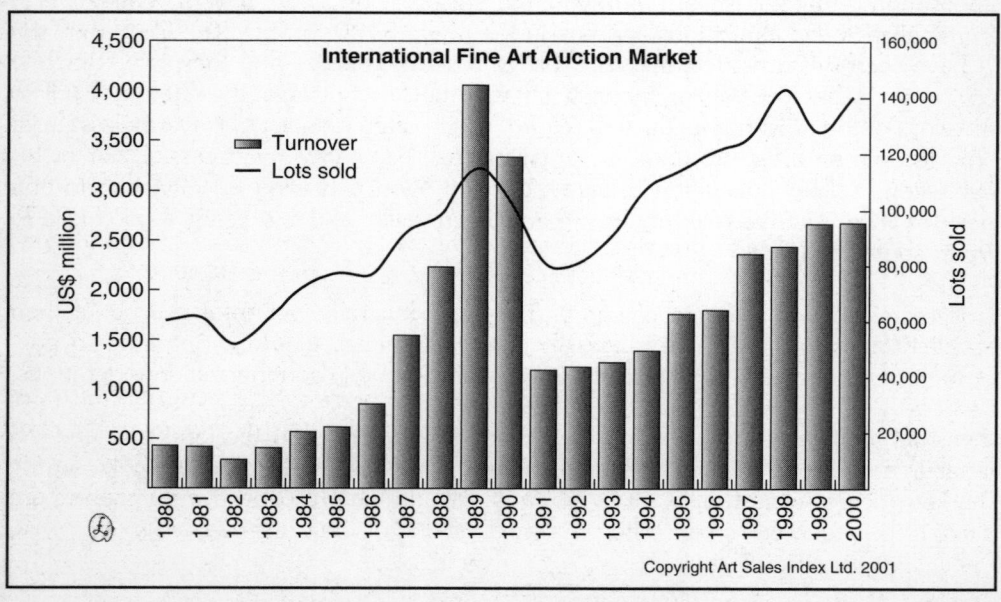

Copyright Art Sales Index Ltd. 2001

4

The U.S. Art Auction Index from 1980 to 2000 is shown in Fig.2. This index shows the average price for each year divided by $6,680 (the average for 1957/79), expressed as a percentage. It is interesting to see that it follows the pattern of turnover (Fig. 1) and that in the boom period, the price per lot at least doubled.

Fig.2

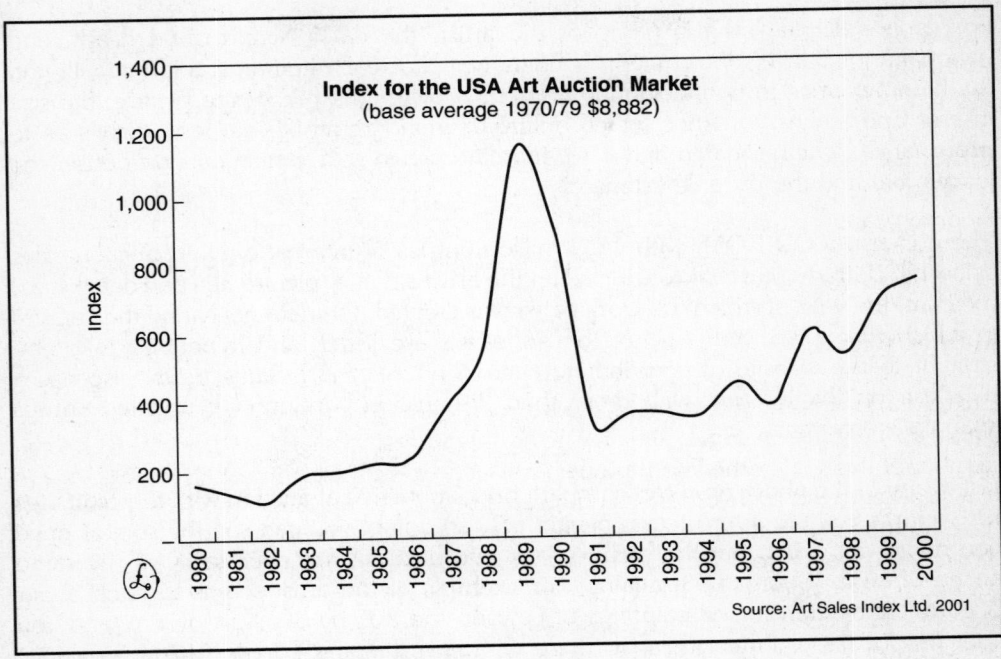

Index for the USA Art Auction Market
(base average 1970/79 $8,882)

Source: Art Sales Index Ltd. 2001

Those who can remember the fifites can recall pictures that she or he could have bought then for a few hundred dollars, which now sell for a hundred thousand dollars or more. They may also have pictures they bought then that are not worth much more now. Certainly, the experience has been that "good" pictures are a sound long-term investment.

However, like shares, prices are sensitive to interest rates. While prices are going up, the interest cost of holding stock can be ignored. However, if interest rates go up, people start to sell and prices can begin to tumble. The obvious but often ignored advice is to buy when the market is depressed and sell when it is buoyant.

Price books and CD ROMs

A price guide book, like this one, gives information on the results of picture auctions. The price recorded is the hammer price. This book lists the artists alphabetically. For an idea of what this book contains and how to use it, please see the section "About This Book" on page 29.

Another publication in two volumes, which provides much more information and lists each lot sold of each artist, is *The Art Sales Index*. The latest 2000/2001 edition provides information on 143,750 works in oils, acrylic, tempera, gouache, watercolor, pastel, crayon, drawing, chalk, charcoal, prints, sculpture and miniatures. It provides information on the hammer prices at auction that individual artists and their works have achieved.

For each artist, it lists the name of the artist, the dates of birth and death, and nationality or ? if this information is unknown. For each item (lot) sold you will find the hammer price in pound sterling and U.S. dollars, the title of the picture, the size in cms and inches, whether signed, initialed, monogrammed, etc, any details as to provenance, whether dated and if so, the date, when sold, which auction house, the lot number and the pre sale estimate.

There is also a CD ROM, with 1.23 million entries of international art auction sales since 1990, thirty search fields, including the artist's name, picture title and detail, size, medium, the year in which the work of art was created, the nationality and the century in which the artist lived. Auction house details are listed, and hyperlinks take you straight to the website of contributing auction houses. *Art Sales Index* also has a database on the Internet with more than 2.4 million continuously updated entries spanning forty years.

Using any of the above, you can compare prices obtained at auction with the estimates for pictures you are interested in buying. By so doing, you can see the sort of price you might get if you put the picture back into auction, not necessarily at the same auction house, if you sold it again. For example, if the artist seems to fetch about $5,000 at auction for oil paintings of cows in the 20" by 30" sort of size, and you spot one of his pictures similar to these with an estimate of $1,500 in a provincial auction house, it looks like an opportunity at least to double your money.

Estimating a price

You can estimate the price for a picture using price guide books. If you use this book, you will be able to get an idea of the range of prices and the median (see page 29). To refine the estimate, you will need to consult a more detailed price book, such as the *Art Sales Index*. Then you can have regard to size and subject. Both show prices for various media, so you must be careful that you are not, for example, confusing oils for watercolors. Also bear in mind that there is a lower value below which a picture will not appear in the list. In this guide, the lower value is $1,000 for oils, watercolors and miniatures. It is important to see where a picture was sold. A good price achieved in Germany may not be a good indicator of the price that might have been achieved had it been sold in the U.S. or the United Kingdom.

If you are going to buy at auction, most auctioneers will have estimated a "hammer" price, based on the auction house's experience and after consulting the price books. However, you may discover that the auctioneer's estimate is well below what your research in the price books suggest it ought to be. This may be because the auctioneer does not think it is a very good example of the artist's work; after all, artists do have "bad" days, or it may be a mistake or an intentionally low estimate to attract bidders.

There will always be some pictures that do not have a signature, or the signature is illegible and the artist is unknown. They are generally listed as "in the style of" some artist, or "School of painters", or as "American School," "English School," etc. Such pictures are often opportunities to buy if, for example, you can recognize the style, the way it is painted and hence the artist. Sometimes there is an illegible signature that, again, you might realize you have seen somewhere before and hence get a bargain.

RESEARCHING

The skill of spotting something that no one else has is cultivated by looking at many pictures and reading about them. You may become a specialist in a particular artist or niche or try to spread your expertise over a wide field. Either way, the more you see and learn, the more likely you are to spot the "sleeper" or "snip" that no one else has seen, and that the auctioneer has not realized is valuable and get it knocked down to you for a bargain price.

The price books are an initial guide as to what to pay for a picture. However, they need to be supplemented by further information. A picture you may be drawn to at auction may be signed by an artist that does not appear in any of the price books. It is very useful to be able to see what is known about him or her.

The biographical books

These books enable you to discover whether the artist has exhibited and what type of pictures he or she painted. One that is widely used for British painters, which often come up at auction, is *British Artists, 1880-1940*, volume 5 of *The Dictionary of British Art* published by the Antique Collectors Club Ltd. It is a list of 41,000 artists that exhibited at the forty-nine main exhibition centers in the U.K. in the period, and gives the type of art in which the artist specialized, biographical details and when and where she or he exhibited. Another useful two-volume publication is Volume 4, *Victorian Painters* by Christopher Wood, with 11,000 short essays covering the period 1837 to 1901 with 47 color plates and 750 black-and-white illustrations in the second volume.

Two general dictionaries of artists are Benezit, in French, and Thieme-Becker, in German.

Benezit, "Dictionnaire Critique et Documentaire des Peintres, Sculpteurs et Graveurs" is a fourteen-volume set, 13,500 pages, providing details of international artists active up to 1998.

Thieme-Becker, "Allgemeines Lexikon der bildenden Künstler von der Antike bis zur Gegenwart," is a nineteen-volume set and is claimed to be the largest biographical dictionary of artists from early history to the beginning of the twentieth century. It is supplemented by a further six volumes, "Allgemeines Lexikon der bildenen Künstler des XX Jahrhunderts", bringing it up to the late twentieth century.
A mention in any of the above is a reassurance that the artist actually existed, that the signature, if it is genuine, is of an artist of some substance, but not necessarily of value.

Galleries, museums and libraries

If you have decided to concentrate on one artist or several or a school, then you will probably want to do some research on them. A literature search can be done at most public libraries and the relevant books can often be borrowed, or at least perused within the gallery library. The prodigious *Grove Dictionary of Art* in thirty-four volumes, published by the Grove Hale Press 1996, which is available in many good libraries, is a must for any serious student.

Another important source is the Archives of American Art, which is a bureau of the Smithsonian Institution that preserves original documents, diaries, letters and photographs of artists. The main offices are in Washington, D.C., with regional offices in New York City, Boston, Detroit and San Francisco. In London there is a remarkable library open to the public. This is the Witt Library of the Courtauld Institute of Art, located in Somerset House at the Aldwych end of the Strand. It is a collection of photographs, reproductions and cuttings mostly in black-and-white but some in color of paintings, drawings and engravings of Western art from about 1200 A.D. to the present day. The library contains 1.8 million reproductions of the work of more than 66,000 artists.

Catalogue subscriptions

Nearly all auction houses issue catalogues, ranging from plain photocopied sheets to the beautifully illustrated paperback books produced by the major houses such as Sotheby's and Christie's, which are of considerable value and cost. Most auction houses are eager for you to subscribe, so that catalogues are posted to you ahead of sales. If you are a good customer of an auction house, you may receive catalogues free. If you have pictures for sale at a particular auction, you will automatically be sent a catalogue for that sale. There is also a trade in old catalogues, which often appear on stalls at fairs.

Many galleries, both private and public, issue catalogues for which a charge is usual. A catalogue issued in connection with a major exhibition may be a definitive document for a particular artist or group and well worth acquiring. Catalogues, particularly those with color illustration, are good, relatively cheap sources of information, providing the opportunity to study many artists' works and to note the subjects they painted and the colors they used, as well as being able to spot signatures and monograms.

The Internet

The internet is the open door to museums, art galleries, auction houses and dealer's galleries. It is not quite as good as a personal visit, but it provides the opportunity to trawl the world for information. It is a wonderful tool for you to do research, whether it is to seek information about an artist, an epoch or a particular picture.

Access to more than 1,000 websites involved with art and antiques is provided by www.antiquestradegazette.com. Each site is listed in one of eleven directories arranged by subject area and searchable by category and keyword.

To start your Internet journey, just enter "galleries" into the search facility of any of the main search engines. List after list will appear, giving details of establishments in a country or a specific district or town.

It is rewarding to visit the Smithsonian American Art Museum (search for the National Museum of American Art). You can browse through 4,000 images of the collection by subject. Under "Art Inventory," you can search the Inventory of American Painting and Sculpture. You can also consult the Institution Research Information Centre for specialized biographies. In the Study Center there are 360,000 art works.

There are art galleries in most capital cities in the world that can be reached through the Internet.

A very useful site is www.askart.com, which has a comprehensive database about American artists. If you enter the name of the artist, the site provides you with a list of relevant books and periodicals, museums in which the artist's work is exhibited, dealers in the artist, a biography and an image library. Nagel's Art Sales Price Research is another free service that can be reached through the www.ibidlive.com website. The Auction Index has many categories. You can enter an artist's name and the system will find a catalogue entry. Both of these sites are well worth exploring.

Internet auctions

There are two main types of Internet auction. In one, the auction takes place over a period of a week or two. In the other, it is in real time, and it is as if you are in the auction room able to bid. It takes a little perseverance to register and get into a position to bid or submit a picture, but it is very much more convenient and cheaper than traveling long distances.

Sotheby's (www.sothebys.com) is typical of the auctioneers who allow bidding to continue over a number of days. On its website, for each lot (picture) you can see an illustration, estimate, the current bid and the time remaining for you to bid. The hammer falls when the time runs out. The website also provides auction results for each sale, by lot number, with illustrations and details together with the price, including buyer's premium.

A major player in the online league is www.ebay.com. At any time there are about 14,000 pictures for sale. Each picture has a description and illustration. Details can be enlarged, and often the reverse of the picture can be viewed. eBay has a very good system of rating the integrity and efficiency of sellers. This is based on purchasers' reports. Each seller has a star, the color of which reflects the excellence or otherwise of his or her service. The rating extends from 10 to more than 10,000 points. There is a range of colors - 10/99 is yellow, 100/499 is turquoise and there is a shooting star for over 10,000. Joining and bidding is free. The commission for a successful sale is 2.5% (compare Sotheby's commission of 15%).

To enter a picture, you have to decide the description (forty-five characters) to be used, the opening bid and the reserve. You are obligated to complete the transaction, whether buyer or seller, once the equivalent of the hammer has fallen. Each picture has to be photographed front and verso. eBay and Sotheby's offer pro-formas to assist the entry process. Some facility with Internet technology is desirable. To the uninitiated, nothing seems to happen quite like the instructions say, and frequently there is a communication block when some undefined computer word is used. However, once you know how, it is simple.

A recent lawsuit result suggests that eBay is legally considered to be a "service" rather than a "contents" provider, which means that a claim for compensation, after buying an item that subsequently turns out to be a fake, is likely to fail. It was also reported that three men had been charged with allegedly using more than forty user names to inflate bids on paintings in one case, again allegedly, from 35 cents to $135,505.

Jim Franses in the *Antique Trade Gazette* Internet handbook says that "buying and selling on eBay is a tactical game which takes a long time to learn." He also points out that the seller is known from the start of bidding and is available to the purchaser by e-mail so that it becomes possible to establish good relationships speedily.

A facility to attend online real-time auctions can be found at www.Auctionroom.com. No payment is settled online, but directly with the auction house after the sale. All items are guaranteed by the auction house. Another online auction site is www.ibidlive.com. This site has a simulation to enable you to become familiar with the process of bidding at a live auction.

Most of the conditions and considerations that apply to auctions in the physical world, and which are discussed later, apply to Internet auctions. The auctioneers take very little, if any, legal responsibility for default by either seller or buyer. For example, eBay makes it clear that the " site acts as a venue." It is not involved in the actual transaction between buyer and seller and by implication takes no responsibility. Nevertheless, some Internet auctioneers will provide condition reports, and the success of Internet auctions depends on trust, integrity and a good positive experience for clients.

If you make payments over the Internet, it is usual to pay by credit card. There are a number of precautions that should be observed. The retailer's contact street address and ordinary telephone number should be available to you and should be noted. Use only companies that have an encryption certificate and use secure transaction technology. Make sure you are dealing with a legitimate business by telephoning the company. Keep copies of the trader's terms and conditions and returns policy. Never disclose your card's PIN number to anyone.

Buying on the Internet involves the matter of packing, delivery and insurance. There are international couriers and professional packers that are used by many of the more important auction houses, who also arrange and charge for insurance.

DIFFERENT TYPES OF PICTURES

As a collector, occasional trader or full-time dealer, you may specialize in one of the categories briefly described here.

Oil paintings

Oil paint consists of pigments mixed with oils, such as linseed oil or poppy oil. Pigment mixed with egg yolk is called tempera. The medium acrylic can be used as though it is a watercolor or an oil paint. It is an emulsion of pigments, water, and clear, non-yellowing acrylic resins, and it has the advantage that it dries quickly and does not darken with time.

Works on paper

Drawings

Over the years, drawings have been done using a variety of materials: pencil, pen-and-ink, charcoal, chalks and crayons. Pastels are drawn or painted with sticks of dry color.

Watercolors

Watercolors are painted with pigments, some of which are translucent and can be manipulated to some extent, and some of which dye the paper. Gouaches are painted with opaque pigments mixed with gum. Some watercolors are "heightened" with white gouache, and other colored gouaches may be used. The term "mixed media" covers combinations of the above.

Prints

Three elements are involved in making a print. These are: paper, an inked surface and an image that is transferred from the inked surface onto the paper. The idea of printing is to make a number of copies, and this multiplicity of copies distinguishes a print from an original, one-off. There are numerous printing processes with many variations, each one of which is a specialty.

The most common prints are mechanical prints, which can be seen everywhere, from flea markets to prestigious stores. Many prints are of watercolors, and some are so good that it is easy to mistake them for the real thing, especially if they are under glass. Inspection with a magnifying glass will generally reveal the myriad of small dots of color. Some mechanical prints are numbered and signed by the artist and thereby assume some enhanced value.

There are other processes that can simulate oil paintings, so that you may think you can feel the paint. Oleographs, one such process, have been printed for more than a hundred years. You are most likely to be faced with the need to tell the difference between the real thing and a reproduction, at yard and garage sales, flea markets, junk stores, and antique shops. It can work both ways; you may be taken in, but it is just possible that you might buy a print for a few dollars and, either by luck or good judgment, discover that it is an original worth thousands of dollars.

Silk screen prints are often produced by contemporary artists in limited, numbered and signed editions. They are made by using a finely meshed screen, often made of silk, and stencils to transfer the image to the paper. The artist generally supervises the printing, which may involve numerous colors, so there is some input into them apart from the original image, and they are to some extent one-offs.

Lithographs are prints, generally in color these days, although early ones were printed in black-and-white and colored by hand. Many famous artists have used lithography, and some of their work commands high prices. It is sometimes difficult to distinguish an original.

Wood and linocuts are produced from wooden blocks or pieces of lino and are known as relief or surface prints. Some are by famous artists such as Thomas Beckwith in the eighteenth century, and more recently Kandinsky and Picasso.

Intaglio processes include line engraving, etching, aquatint, drypoint and mezzotint. They involve incising a design into a metal plate, which is inked and pressed onto paper, forcing the paper into the incisions to take up the ink.

The important thing to note is that the edge of the metal plate makes an indentation all around and close to the paper's edge. Not infrequently, prints are sold that are worthless mechanical prints of intaglio prints, which do not show the indentation. Many are framed and backed to look like old prints to deceive the buyer.

CONDITION, RESTORATION, FRAMING AND FAKES

Condition

There are two parts to a picture, an image and a support, the most common being wood, fabric and paper. Wood can split and become infested with wood-boring insects. Fabrics are treated with sizing materials that, with age, become brittle and can grow mold. Paper is made from cotton or linen rags or from ground-up wood fiber pulp, which can discolor and on which mold can grow.

It is sensible for the inexperienced to avoid pictures that are damaged, or exhibit obvious blemishes. With prints, it is important to have a clear dense print and, if it is colored, for the color not to be faded. Prints may be torn, stained or have spots of mold. They may be trimmed to fit into a frame. All such faults may make the print worthless and, at best, costly to restore. Similar considerations apply to drawings and watercolors. Oil paintings can suffer physical damage (often from careless handling and stacking), when the corner of a frame may press against the canvas of an adjoining picture. Paint can crack and come away from the canvas. Frames and stretchers can be riddled with woodworm. Wooden panels often warp and crack.

Restoration

Oil paintings

Often oil paintings have just accumulated dirt, which can be removed very carefully with water or proprietary liquids. Any such mild cleaning should be done very carefully, a little at a time, looking carefully for any signs of paint being removed. If this occurs, the procedure should be stopped immediately.

Restoration often involves removing varnish without damaging the original paint. Doing so can often transform a dark brown painting into a fresh-looking colored one.

Frequently acetone is used diluted with white spirit. Tears can be repaired, and blemishes are often touched up. Where the paint is loose on canvas, the painting can be lined.

Problems occur when the artist has used too much linseed oil, which causes the paint to dry very slowly and become shriveled. The painting can never be fully restored to its original state but instead has to be retouched. Too much restoration can detract from the value of a painting, and the terms "original" condition or "unrestored" is often used to explain why a picture has attracted competitive bidding at an auction.

Most prestigious galleries seem to clean oil paintings, so the colors are bright and fresh. It would appear that buyers like this, but insensitive cleaning can detract from the value of a painting.

If you intend to use a restorer, it is advisable to use someone recommended by a person or an institute that is professionally knowledgeable about restoration. Regrettably, a poor, unskilled or inexperienced restorer can damage a picture irreparably. Good restorers are generally very busy, so they may hold a picture for months, which is something to consider when you buy, if you want to sell the picture quickly.

If you are buying from a dealer, you can inquire how much restoration has been carried out on the picture you are considering. You can ask to use an ultraviolet lamp, which will show up recently applied paint. If there is much overpainting, it may be a picture to avoid.

Watercolors

Foxed watercolors can usually be restored satisfactorily. So-called "burn marks," tannin marks from wood that has been used as a backing, are more difficult to remove, and pictures with such marks should generally be avoided. Gouaches are also difficult to restore. Some restorers will touchup or paint over faded watercolors. When buying, this is something to look out for, because such retouching detracts from the originality of the painting.

Prints

Surface dirt can be removed with a soft eraser. Foxing, a stain caused by mold, requires expert treatment. A paper conservator, who is an expert in the structure of paper, should be consulted for the restoration of valuable prints.

Framing

A frame can often say something about the picture it surrounds. Most amateur paintings are framed cheaply. An elaborate gold-leaf frame is often a good sign to corroborate the genuineness of an old painting. However, there are many reproduction pseudo gold frames, housing apparently old pictures with convincing craquelure, that were painted only yesterday. Sometimes, particularly at the lower end of the market, a frame may be worth more than the painting.

Forgeries

There are many unsigned paintings around, both amateur and professional, and some of these will acquire signatures, the effect of which is misleadingly to increase the conceived value of them. These are deliberate forgeries and they are to be found everywhere, so it is necessary to be wary. The more famous forgeries were and still are painted specially to deceive, and there are many examples of these being bought by international museums for millions of dollars. See Christopher Wright's book "*The Art of the Forger.*"

A deception, which is not illegal, is putting a name on a frame or mount to suggest that something is other than it actually is. Many examples of this occur in sale rooms. Fakes often seem to be too perfect. Tell-tale signs are whether the varnish has any crackle on the surface, whether the brushstrokes look right or whether the signature of an oil painting is in a different color from any that has been used elsewhere in the painting.

When using this book, it is essential to take care to make sure that what seems a bargain is genuine. At auction, it is generally made clear if there are doubts as to authenticity, and these need to be considered very carefully. Because a name means money, it is only too tempting to buy a signature. Authenticity requires many more clues, such as the subject, the way the paint is applied, the colors and paints used, the sort of canvas and so on.

BUYING AT AUCTION

Why buy at auction?

Many people buy at auction because they think that it will be cheaper than buying from a gallery and that they may spot something that no one else has seen and so get a bargain. It is possible to see pictures that were sold at auction subsequently appearing in a gallery, with a massive markup. I remember buying two pictures at an auction for $1,100, then selling them to a dealer for $1,900, who then sold them to a gallery for $2,800. When I visited the gallery by chance, I saw they were on sale for $7,800. You can compare gallery prices with the auction prices in this book to check the difference. There are arguments in favor of buying from galleries, and these are discussed in a later section.

At auction, you are on your own and if you are not careful, you may pay too much or buy a faded or damaged picture or a forgery. You are competing with experts, and it is not unknown for dealers to bid you up to a price that is more than the picture is worth. Nevertheless, there is the excitement of an auction, a wide choice of pictures to see and the opportunity to buy a bargain. Provided you are aware of the many errors you can make and know how to avoid them, it is possible to buy and subsequently sell profitably. Above all, be clear why you are buying and how and where you are going to sell what you have bought.

The catalogue

If you are going to buy at auction, the first thing to do is to get hold of a catalogue. This provides a list of what is for sale. Each picture is numbered, and the sequence of numbers is the sequence in which the pictures will be sold. The sequence often seems to be arbitrary. There does not seem to be a sequence in terms of price, either. However, it is often the practice to put the important items at the end of the catalogue, and so, of the sale, presumably to ensure that as many buyers as possible stay to the end. Sometimes the catalogue separates prints, watercolors and oils.

For each item or lot, the artist's name, if it is known, the title of the picture and often the size is given. In many catalogues, a range of prices is provided as a guide to what the picture is expected to fetch. Some catalogues have lavish illustrations, with every lot portrayed in color to emphasize the importance of the sale. Less prestigious sales may have photocopied lists with some illustrations. Others have no illustrations at all. It is useful to have the catalogue in advance of the sale. This may well happen if you are a regular buyer or seller at a particular auction and/or you subscribe.

One bonus of having a picture for sale at auction is that you get the catalogue free. With a catalogue in advance, you are able to search through it, to find any artists or subjects in which you are interested, research prices and biographical details, and, compare your idea of prices with the estimates.

In the auction catalogue, beware the spelling mistake. This may be accidental or it may be a way of indicating that the picture has not been painted by the person whose signature is on the painting. Either way, if you are interested in buying this picture, it is essential to seek the auctioneer's understanding of the position before the sale and, if appropriate, to get the catalogue entry altered and signed.

Viewing

Viewing days will generally be one or two days immediately before the sale. It is often possible to view on the day of the sale. The trade often do this, and it can be quite busy, with dealers taking pictures off the wall to look at their backs and others moving steps around to look at high-up pictures. The occasional member of the trade will even view a picture while it is held up for sale, perhaps to demonstrate his expertise. If you can view on the day before the sale, it gives you ample time to check each picture you are interested in for the condition, signature, and the way the painting is painted. You also have time to check the price books, CDs or phone-in service and to consult the biographical books. You can have a final second look at any pictures you are not sure of, or you might see something you have missed. Some provincial sales do not have the estimates in the catalogue, but there may be a list hung up in the sale room, from which you can enter the estimates into your catalogue.

When you first enter the sale room, it is useful to have a preliminary look around to see if something immediately stands out. Is this one of the pictures you have already marked in the catalogue, or something new? You can then check up on the pictures you have identified as being interesting. Finally, you should try to look at everything, especially the boxes of prints and folios of watercolors that seem to be of no account. Sometimes there is a treasure lurking there. Also pursue the ones you cannot find, which are generally in a cupboard or cabinet and which will be revealed by a porter or assistant on request. Follow the old adage "Leave no stone unturned." Incidentally, it is helpful if the pictures are displayed in the same sequence as they occur in the catalogue, but this rarely happens.

Looking at pictures is a skill that can be developed with practice, but it is a lifelong learning process. It is best to be on one's own. Having a companion may seem to be advantageous in that you can get a second opinion, but the presence of someone else is distracting and reduces the ability to focus and to be able to carry on an intelligent conversation with oneself. By all means, when you have seen all you want to see, seek advice if you need to do so. However, it is important to be discreet: otherwise you may draw attention to a possible bargain or "sleeper" as it is called in the trade that you have spotted and which you hope to get for very much less than it is worth. Viewing is often an oscillation between looking at the catalogue and at the picture. At the back of some catalogues there is an index of artists in alphabetical order, which is helpful if you are interested only in a few artists.

There will be some pictures that you like. You could see them on your wall. They would be pleasant to live with. Or they make a statement about you. This is all right if you are going to keep them, but may not be if you are hoping to sell them profitably. If you are buying to sell, you have to look through the eyes of your customers. So you will probably finish up with, say, twenty or thirty pictures that require more detailed scrutiny.

The image

Examine the image carefully. Is it interesting, beautiful, arresting? Is it dark or light? Does it evoke pleasurable feelings? Is it of an important place - Venice, Paris, Valetta Harbour, for example? Is it well painted? Are there dull areas, where the artist has not taken much trouble? Is it technically correct, for example, as to perspective? Are the images ones that the public frequently buy? These include country scenes with animals or pretty girls. Images of children or young girls or boys are popular, but so are old folk with character. Most animals and some birds are eagerly sought after. People have a nostalgia for the past - hay making, a village fair, the seaside promenade. Pictures, often Victorian, that tell a story have a following.

On the negative side, many landscapes, although at first sight attractive, are often boring and "ten-a-penny." Be aware that some, if not many, of the pictures in an auction are there because they have been in a gallery for years and have not sold. These are clearly ones to avoid.

Size and shape

There is a limited market for large pictures, which demand not only substantial wall space but a room big enough to allow the viewer to get far enough away from them to appreciate them properly. They also cause problems in transporting them to and from auctions if they do not sell. However, there is a market for them in places like boardrooms, churches, public art galleries and museums. Very small pictures (miniatures) are a specialist market, but are very popular, not least because they take up so little space.

Most people can accommodate pictures up to about 20" by 30". Most are rectangular. When the vertical height is less than the horizontal, the picture is termed "landscape," when the vertical height is greater than the horizontal, it is called "portrait." However, the portrait shape may fit modern wall spaces better than the landscape one. There are many other shapes, square, circular, semicircular or lunette and oval, that fit in with most furnishing arrangements.

Condition

Not looking carefully, hard and long is the reason many poor buying decisions are made.

Oil paintings

Look for dirt, brown varnish, cracks, tears and "bloom," a sort of mildew. Is it on canvas, board or wood panel? If the latter, look for cracks or badly filled-in cracks. Look at the back of the picture. Has it been lined? Look for over-painting, take the picture off the wall and look with your eye close to the canvas. At the same time, look for inscriptions and labels. Again, estimate the cost of cleaning and restoration.

Unless there is a very good reason to the contrary, it is best to buy pictures that are in good condition. Restoration is costly, especially when you take into account the cost of transporting the picture to and from the restorer and the often long delay in getting the picture back and therefore being able to sell it. However, if the picture is only dirty, a surreptitious smudge with a wetted finger end may reveal how bright the painting might be if cleaned properly.

Works on paper

Look for foxing (brown circular mold marks), burn marks (which are usually vertical brown colored bands), scuffing (actual physical damage to the surface), fading, tears, creases, where the painting has been folded. Make a comparison with adjoining watercolors, wormholes. If you can, estimate the cost of restoration.

Aesthetic appeal and commercial value

Aesthetic appeal may be defined as the value placed on a painting for its own beauty. The problem with this definition is that "Beauty is in the eye of the beholder." It is a matter of taste. Whether this is an important consideration depends on who is the ultimate recipient of the picture. What might seem exquisite to an older person may seem to be mundane to a younger one, and vice versa.

The commercial value may have little to do with aesthetics. This is certainly true of much highly priced modern art, where the main consideration seems to be on some notion of originality. With the right name an idea, however unexceptional, seems to be worth telephone numbers, even if the execution of the art work is by someone else. This is a conventional phenomenon that may vaporize like some of the dot.coms have. Otherwise, commercially, the name is probably the most important consideration, so that the authenticity of an attribution is paramount.

The frame

The frame may mislead. There is a market in old frames and there are people who deal exclusively in them. If you have a genuine old painting that has been put into a modern frame, it may give the impression of not being quite right and so might not fetch the price it deserves. It would be sensible and legitimate to reframe it in an old frame where its integrity would be evident. However, oils recently painted in ninteenth century style and subject matter are also put into either genuine old frames or simulated old frames, and are often bought as genuine ninteenth century oils. With watercolors, it is often possible to see that the painting is in its original frame and that the nails and backing paper have not been disturbed. This is very reassuring. Even so, there is a market for old nails and old paper, and therefore a need for caution, if the watercolor is expensive.

Attribution and forgeries

At auction, the usual convention used in the catalogue to indicate that, in the opinion of the auction house, the picture is by the artist stated, is to give the full recognized name of the artist, forenames as well as surname, and possibly the date of birth and death. For example "Samuel John Lamorna Birch (1855-1969)." Sometimes initials with following asterisk and the surname have the same implication. The term "signed" generally means the signature is that of the artist. The practical value of this is that if the painting so designated subsequently turns out to be a deliberate forgery, then the sale is rescinded and the purchase price refunded.

There are generally time limits, which vary from one auction house to another, within which the auctioneer has to be informed in writing that the item is believed to be a forgery, and often a longer period within which the lot has to be returned. It has to be in the same condition as when it was bought, and the buyer has to produce evidence that the item is a forgery. This is an important safeguard, the terms of which are generally stated in the catalogue or otherwise in the auction room. They should be noted in case advantage needs to be taken of them. Clearly you should try to avoid buying a forgery, but if you buy a picture by a well-known artist and have doubts as to its authenticity, perhaps, because it was cheap and the trade did not seem to be bidding for it, take it to a gallery that specializes in the artist and check it out. As there are time limits to be observed, this should be done as expeditiously as possible.

If the forenames of the artist, or the initials with following asterisks and the surname, are not given, this indicates that in the opinion of the auction house there may be some degree of uncertainty as to whether the painting is the work of the named artist, and the degrees of increasing uncertainty are indicated by a series of phrases. "Attributed to" indicates that it is probably the work of the artist. The initials of the artist and surname can indicate that in the auctioneer's opinion it is a work of the period of the artist, which may be wholly or partly his/her work. Just the surname of the artist implies that the work is unlikely to be by the artist, but is in his style and painted by a follower or a member of his school. One of the ways money can be made is to have knowledge superior to that of the auctioneer, to be convinced that what he is unsure about is the real thing. One of the ways of losing money is to get this wrong.

The word "after" associated with the name of the artist indicates a copy. "Bears signature" generally indicates doubt as to whether the signature is that of the artist. Similarly "dated" usually means that the painting was painted at that date. "Bears a date" indicates some doubt as to the date. All these indications are "in the opinion of the auction house" and it is usually made clear in the small print that they should not to be taken as statements or representations of fact.

It essential to know whether a painting is "right," whether the signature or monogram has been put on by the artist. There are so many unsigned pictures around that it is inevitable that some will acquire signatures. Viewing the painting with the aid of an ultraviolet lamp may disclose additions to the picture of a much later date than the original, including a signature. You can consult books of signatures and monograms, which are useful in identifying something the auctioneer has missed or which has been labeled "indistinctly signed." They may not help in spotting a forged signature, because the forger has access to the same books.

Provenance

A useful safeguard is to know where a picture has come from. There is often such information in some catalogues, and sometimes the back of the picture will provide a clue. Many galleries put a stock or exhibition label on the back of the picture or the frame, and some give stock numbers, Agnew's go back over a hundred years. Frame makers' labels are frequently to be found, and they may provide a starting point for research.

Estimates

Many catalogues give estimates for each lot as a lower and higher figure. These are estimates of the price range within which the auctioneers believe the picture will sell. The question is whether the estimate is realistic. Most of them will have been based on the auction house's own records and examination of price data sources, books, CDs and database services. Sometimes they will seem too low. There may be several possible reasons for this, the auctioneer has set it low to attract bargain hunters to the sale, it may be a private lot with no reserve, or the auctioneer has made a mistake. Sometimes it will seem too high. The picture may be exceptional or it may be that the vendor who has put the picture in the sale has insisted on an unrealistically high price. If you compare the estimates with the prices actually achieved at any sale you attend, you will find that many prices fall within the estimates, but there will be a sizable number that do not reach the estimate and do not sell, and a smaller number that sell well above the top estimate.

You can check the price books. Make sure the picture you are considering is of the same type as that which appears in the price books. If there are no entries, it may be that the artist's pictures have not been sold at auction for the period covered by the price data source or that they have not achieved the minimum price to be included in the price book. Even if there are entries for the artist, it is possible that some, if not many, of his/her paintings have sold under the minimum price and therefore do not appear.

Reserves

The reserve is the lowest price that the vendor has authorized the auctioneer to sell at. This amount is generally discussed and agreed with the auctioneer, who does not want to waste time and money trying to sell a picture with too high a reserve. It is sometimes argued that the picture will achieve the right price if the reserve is too low, or even if there is no reserve at all. This is not necessarily true. Often there is only one bidder for a picture and the sale is then made at the agreed reserve price. When this happens, the seller must wonder whether the reserve was set too low.

Some auction houses will consider that there is no reserve unless one has been agreed in writing. Most indicate in their conditions of sale that the auctioneer has discretion to sell at 10% less than the agreed reserve. It is important, therefore, to decide whether you agree with this if you are the vendor, or whether you insist that the reserve is firm.

If the reserve is not agreed with the auctioneer, there is not only the danger that your picture may be sold too cheaply, but if you have insisted on a higher reserve than the auctioneer is willing to accept and the picture does not sell, there may be a considerable buying-in fee to pay. The reserve may be the lower of the two estimates, but need not necessarily be so. The reserve is not known to the buyers at an auction, but is often guessed to be 10% below the lowest estimate, sometimes correctly. Some auction houses will not accept a reserve higher than the bottom estimate.

Commission bids

A commission bid is a bid made by the auctioneer on your behalf. It is a way of buying if you cannot attend the sale. There is generally no charge made for this service. You make the bid on a form that the auction house provides, giving your personal details and the sale number and date, the lot number and the price you are prepared to have bid. Your bid will have to be at or above the reserve, which you do not know. The lowest figure for a commission bid will probably be the lowest of the estimates.

If you want to have a good chance of buying a picture, you will make your bid high. If the bidding on the day does not reach your bid, you should secure the picture for whatever the next bid is, after all the other bidding has ceased. For example, your high commission bid is $1,000. On the day, the highest of all the other bids is $800. The next bid, which is yours, will be say $850 and this is the price you will pay.

There is sometimes a problem, if you cannot attend the sale, when you spot a "sleeper," i.e. a picture that you recognize as being valuable, but which has a very low estimate. Say you think it is worth $4,000. The estimate in the catalogue is $200. Do you put in a low commission bid of, perhaps, $300, or a high one of $3,000? The low bid may be insufficient if someone else has spotted the sleeper. The high bid may seem to be safe enough if you do not mind paying $3,000, because if no one else is aware of the picture's worth, you will get it for $200. However your high bid might alert the auctioneer that he has underestimated the picture and so he might revise the estimate, alerting others by so doing. Probably, the best compromise is to leave a bid that you think will just not alert the auctioneer to revise the estimate.

When you leave a commission bid, it is best not to leave a round number, but the next bid up. This is because people often set a round number as their maximum bid. For example, if you want to leave $400, actually leave $420, which will see off anyone who has decided to drop out at $400. You can leave a commission bid even if you are going to attend the sale. You may wish to do this to avoid other's seeing that you are bidding. If the bidding goes above your commission bid and you decide you want the picture, you can then enter the bidding.

Telephone bids

If you are undecided whether to bid after you have viewed, and then on the morning of the sale regret that you have not done so, you can generally telephone or e-mail a commision bid before the start of the sale. Alternatively, you can arrange for the auction house to telephone you while the auction is in progress, just before the lot you are interested in comes up. Someone at the auction house will let you know how the bidding is progressing and when the bidding stops. At this point you can decide whether to make a bid. This will not necessarily get you the picture, as the previous bidder may bid again. However, with luck, he or she may give up once they hear there is another bidder.

THE DAY OF THE SALE

Make a note of the starting time of the sale. If the lot you wish to buy is going to be later in the sale, you can calculate when this is due, if you know how many lots per hour the auctioneer sells. Some auctioneers will sell sixty lots in an hour, others one hundred and twenty or more. You can generally find out the appropriate rate when you view. It is sensible to add twenty minutes or so to your calculated time and check whether the lot numbers run consecutively, or whether there are some gaps that will affect your calculations.

Before the sale, you have to register. If you are going to settle with cash, there is no problem, but if you intend to pay by check, you need to find out whether this is acceptable. Some auction houses may want to contact your bank before releasing your purchases. Credit cards are not accepted by some auction houses. When you register, you will probably be given a number or a numbered paddle, but some provincial houses just expect you to call out your name, and if you attend sales regularly, the auctioneer will have remembered it.

The sale

The actual sale is a sort of theater. On exhibition are the works of many artists representing thousands of years of experience and effort. Attending the sale are many highly knowledgeable men and women. Decisions whether or not to buy have to be made in a matter of seconds. Although it is very exciting, most of the participants, who will be traders or gallery owners, display a laid-back nonchalance conveying that they are hardened professionals. If you are not one of these, you will find your heart beating faster as the lot you intend to bid for approaches.

If you attend the sale from the beginning, you can mark down the prices for each lot and compare them with the auctioneer's estimates or your own. You will have marked up your catalogue with the pictures you wish to buy and the price you are prepared to pay. Some lots will go beyond what you have marked as your buying price.

Avoid the temptation to chase after them. It may be that some dealer buys all the pictures that you have decided you want. It requires discipline not to get so exasperated that you become determined to beat him or her. Such dealers are generally buying for prestigious retailers or private clients, who do not mind what they pay. If you beat them, you will probably pay too much. The same indiscretions can occur at provincial sales if the local trade try to push you up or thwart your attempts to buy.

The auctioneer takes bids from the floor, but also bids on behalf of commission clients. He or she may also bid on behalf of the vendor up to the reserve price. Doing so beyond the reserve price, sometimes referred to as "bidding off the wall," gives the false impression to the beginner that he is bidding against someone else in the room. This is clearly an illegitimate practice. The bidding for some pictures does not reach the agreed reserve, and so they are unsold and are said to be "bought-in." In most auctions, at least 20% to 30% of the lots do not sell, and the percentage can be much higher. This will surprise you if you have not attended many auctions, because the auctioneer often tries to conceal the fact that there has not been a sale. It is often possible after the end of the sale to negotiate for some of the unsold lots.

Bidding prices go up in intervals, which are custom and practice in the auction house. A familiar pattern is $5 intervals up to $50, $10 up to $200, $20 and $30 intervals up to $500 - for example, $220, $250, $280. Then $50 up to $1,000, $100 up to $2,000 and so on. It is useful to know the intervals so that you can work out when to enter the bidding to finish up with a final bid, which is the one beyond an even number. If your final bid is $320, you might enter the bidding at $220 so that the sequence will be: you $220, Miss Blank $250, you $280, Miss Blank $300, you $320.

Sleepers

A sleeper is a bargain, a picture whose true identity and value is unrecognized, except by the buyer. It is what everyone is looking for, and if found, it is hoped that no one else has spotted it. This search for the sleeper explains the noncommittal way the cognoscente examine the various lots, often commenting that "there is a lot of rubbish about." Sleepers exist because of oversight or lack of knowledge. They are there at most auctions. Beware, however, of what appear to be sleepers, planted by the unscrupulous with "old" paper backs, nails, cracks, dirt and dark varnish. One of the most famous sleepers was bought at auction for about $260, sold at another auction for $550,000 and, it is alleged subsequently sold to the Getty Foundation for something like $9,000,000. This example is quoted in Philip Mould's book "*Sleepers: in search of lost Old Masters.*"

Buyer's Premium

Most auction houses charge a commission to the seller and buyer. Some major auction houses charge 15% up to $50,000 and 10% thereafter, but Sotheby's charges 20% for the first $15,000. There are exceptions where no buyer's premium is charged. Many provincial auction houses charge a commission between these figures.

It is important to take account of the buyer's commission when you decide to buy and also when you look at prices in the price books, which exclude buyer's commission.

Taxes

It is important to be aware of the sales tax or any other tax - such as value-added tax in Europe, which may apply to the sales commission or buyer's premium and also to other charges such as insurance, storage or delivery. These extra charges can make a significant difference to the profit you hope to realize when trading.

Withdrawals, revised descriptions, estimates and extra lots

These are all changes or corrections that occur from time to time, and their effect can vary from mild irritation to considerable waste of money and time if it means you have traveled a long way only to find that what you were hoping to buy has in some way been subject to alteration. The sleeper you spotted has also been spotted by someone else, perhaps the vendor or the auctioneer's superiors, and withdrawn from the sale. The picture catalogued as "attributed to XYZ" has the description revised to read "by XYZ." You knew it was "by XYZ" all the time but hoped no one else did. Of course, the estimate is revised upward.

You do not know these bits of bad news until you turn up at the sale, excited at the thought of the bargain you are going to acquire. Clearly, auction houses do not like sleepers to occur, because it means that the vendor has been ill served and might sue.

Extra lots are new lots, not described in the catalogue, that present you with the temptation to take decisions without having had the opportunity to do necessary research. It is as well to treat these with caution.

Conditions of sale

These are often set out in the catalogue or posted somewhere in the sale room. Most auction houses make it clear that their role is to act only as agents. They take no responsibility for any faults or defects. Everything they say are statements of opinion, not to be relied upon. They have absolute discretion to settle any dispute.

Once the hammer has fallen, the purchaser is totally responsible for the lot and is unlikely to be compensated for any subsequent damage. There is generally a time limit for payment after the sale and if this is exceeded, storage charges may be incurred.

Although the conditions of sale may appear onerous and too much in the auctioneer's favor, it is generally the experience that if you make friends with the auctioneer's staff and do business with them, there is some flexibility in the application of the rules.

SELLING AT AUCTION

Why do you want to sell?

It may be that you wish to sell because you want something different on your walls. There is no urgency and you are not too concerned how much your pictures will fetch. Alternatively, you may want money urgently, and as much of it as possible. You may be an investor who wants to see a good profit to cover the years of interest tied up, or you may be a trader looking for a quick profit.

To whom are you selling?

There are several possible potential customers for the pictures you put into auction, private persons looking for specific colors, artists, subjects etc.; gallery owners seeking pictures of popular subjects that will sell; dealers or runners looking for the same things as the gallery owners, but at a discount. It is largely a matter of luck who might buy your pictures, but ideally what you hope for are two private bidders with strong wills and plenty of money. However, most of the pictures at auction are bought by the trade.

If you are aiming for the private buyer, the painting should be clean, in good condition, in a good quality and undamaged frame. These factors are also relevant to the gallery owner, but less so, as most galleries do framing and simple restoration, so that as long as the painting is undamaged, condition is not so important. If it is for the trade, you do not bother to reframe or restore your pictures, don't even clean the glass. The private buyer is most probably unconcerned with the artist's name, but wants a nice picture. The gallery owner may be concerned with particular artists that his clients wish to buy. The trade mostly buys names and commercial subjects. What the market is looking for are pictures that are "fresh to the market" and "in unrestored condition," these are genuine paintings in their original frames from a private source, which have not been restored.

Which auction house?

There are a number of aspects to consider when deciding which auction house to use to sell your picture. Not least is the auctioneer's advice as to the price the picture will be expected to achieve. If you take a good picture around a number of auction houses, and ask for estimates of what hammer price it is likely to achieve at a sale, you will be surprised at the wide range of figures you will be given. Some of the variation may be due to differences of opinion as to whether or not the painting is by the artist whose signature is on the painting; some will be due to the differences of expertise and experience of those examining the picture. If you appear to be a private seller and not of the trade and apparently a novice, you may be persuaded that your picture is of little value. It is therefore essential to get several opinions, unless you have enough experience to be fairly certain of the proper price at which to set the reserve.

It is clearly helpful if your picture is by an artist listed in the price books. It is not necessarily sensible to put the picture with the auction house that gives you the highest estimate. What you want to do is sell the picture. It is costly in time, effort and travel expenses to find that the bidding does not quite reach your reserve. At the next sale you put it into, the picture will not be fresh to the trade and so you will have to reduce the reserve and again it might not sell. Better to agree on a reserve sufficiently low to get a sale, but not too low. The argument may be used that a low reserve and estimate will attract buyers, and that anyway the picture will find its true value from the bidding. However, you will often find that there is only one bidder interested in your picture and when the bidding reaches your reserve, your picture is knocked down.

When you agree on a reserve, it will probably be automatically subject to "auctioneer's discretion," which means you give the auctioneer the right to sell at a percentage, usually 10% below the agreed reserve. If you do not want to do this, you must insist that the reserve is firm and not subject to discretion. Be aware that most auction houses specify in their "conditions" that all goods are put up for sale without reserve, unless written instructions as to reserves are submitted before the sale.

Commissions and charges

Sales commission is what the auctioneer charges you for selling your picture. It is expressed as a percentage of the hammer price and can vary from about 7.5% to 20%. The charge is generally reduced for high-value items. Some auctioneers reduce the commission for genuine members of the trade. Some make a minimum charge, some a handling charge of so much per item. Sometimes the charge includes insurance and an illustration charge. Away from the big auction houses, it is often possible to negotiate charges.

Insurance charges are levied as a matter of course, unless instructions are given to the contrary. They generally cover for theft, but often with the proviso "following forcible entry" and fire and water damage, but not for the ever-present possibility of accidental breakage or damage.

If your picture does not sell, you may be charged for "buying-in." If you have agreed the reserve price, then the buying-in charge should be modest. Often it is possible to negotiate that there will be no buying-in charge at all. If you have insisted on a reserve higher than the auctioneer agrees to, the buying-in charge may be penal, which is a good reason for avoiding this situation.

If your picture has not sold, you may decide to remove it from the auctioneers, and if so, make sure you do this quickly or you may incur storage charges. Most auction houses will propose to offer your bought-ins at another sale, possibly somewhere else, perhaps a little downmarket and with a lower reserve. This may involve you in having to pay further selling commission.

Many auctioneers stipulate that they have the right to illustrate any lot. It is important that you have a say in this. An illustration charge can be quite high, $80 to $300 or more for a color illustration. It is difficult to decide whether to agree to an illustration unless you can negotiate that only if the picture sells will you pay for the illustration. Otherwise you have to balance the illustration cost against the possible higher price it may generate. At the top end of the market, all pictures are illustrated.

Finally, read the small print and decide on all the above aspects and put your intentions clearly in writing on the auctioneer's "instructions to sell" form.

BUYING FROM AND SELLING TO A GALLERY

It is a good idea to visit as many galleries as possible to see what is selling and what prices are being charged. Many galleries sell contemporary originals or prints by relatively unknown artists, and unless you like backing outsiders or are unaffected by mercenary considerations, it will be advisable not to buy. However, it is useful to note names and subjects, which may turn up at bargain prices at auction.

Quality, authenticity, framing, subject, image and the "name" are all important when buying from a gallery. At private views when the wine flows, there is an inferred pressure to buy, otherwise why would you be there? Reference may be made to an artist you are not familiar with, to the effect that similar pictures have been on sale elsewhere at much higher prices. It is difficult but essential not to be persuaded by sales talk, but to be hardheaded and objective.

Generally, it will cost more to buy the same picture from a dealer than at auction. But this is only the beginning of the comparison. In doing so, you must have regard to the buyer's premium at auction and the retailer's sales tax. Also, the gallery picture may have been reframed and restored or cleaned. The gallery takes responsibility for the condition and authenticity of the painting so that you can take back anything that is not quite right. There is also the convenience compared with attending an auction on a particular day that may not be convenient at a place that is possibly far away. The gallery may have financial arrangements that are helpful. What is more, you may not have got the picture at auction as cheaply as the experienced gallery buyer did.

Be sure to get a detailed description, with the full name of the artist (forenames as well as surname) and "signed by," not "bears a signature" or "attributed to" and with no spelling mistakes, on the bill of sale accompanying your purchase. There is usually scope for negotiating the price downward. Many gallery owners have considerable expertise, and, over a period of years, buying quality pictures from such a source can be very profitable.

Many of the galleries that sell "names" will be prepared to buy from you if everything is right, including the price. Most will not make an offer, but will ask you how much you want. Generally, they will not want to pay much more than the auction price. The profitability of a gallery depends on turning over stock as quickly as possible, so the price you are likely to achieve will depend on whether they believe that they can sell the picture quickly. If you buy at auction with the intention of selling to a gallery, the hammer price needs to be considerably less than the gallery would expect it to be. You also need to step into the shoes of the gallery owner so that you buy the pictures he can sell readily. This means establishing a good relationship and gaining a good understanding of the way the gallery works.

Some galleries will take your picture on a "sale or return" arrangement; the picture is said to be "on consignment." If the picture sells, you pay a commission, which will vary from about 20% to 50% or more. The idea looks more attractive than in practice it often turns out to be. However, a profitable arrangement can sometimes be established with a gallery that is short of funds and therefore unable adequately to finance stock.

OTHER PLACES TO BUY AND SELL PICTURES

Fairs

There are numerous fairs varying widely in prestige and the quality of goods on offer. At many of the run-of-the-mill fairs, much selling and buying seems to go on within the trade before the fair officially opens. Otherwise the customer is often an untutored member of the general public, who will buy on impulse with little regard to price or value. Having a stand at a fair is thus an alternative to having a gallery, with the possibility of dealing with less discerning buyers. It is also a way of developing a client list by persuading those visiting your stand to sign the visitors' book.

Antiques shops and dealers

Many antique shops buy and sell pictures. The term "furnishing pictures" comes to mind, but there is always the possibility that there is an undiscovered gem waiting to be unearthed. There are also antique centers, where a hundred or so dealers and units are gathered together, some are art dealers. You need to assess the expertise and integrity of the dealers in such places. Most are selling to the non-expert public, who are just wanting to buy something pleasing but not necessarily valuable. However, it is generally possible to pick out and make friends with dealers with knowledge on whom you can rely.

Shops with bric-a-brac or even "junk" may have something of interest. Some good finds have often been made at such places. It is probably not worthwhile to make it a major activity to trawl such outlets, but as a diversion on holidays or weekends it can be fun.

Pictures are also bought and sold through advertisements in home-furnishing magazines and local papers by private persons or dealers in disguise. Usually, most of what is on offer is either overpriced or of little value. These outlets may be worthwhile to try if you have pictures to sell that are known to be popular in a particular place.

Buying direct from the artist

Although most artists sell through galleries or agents, some do sell from their own studios. The advantage of buying directly from the artist is that you can discuss with her or him the range of work and can gain an understanding of how the artist paints. It is always possible that you can buy more cheaply this way.

An alternative is to become an agent for a new and as yet undiscovered artist. This can be interesting and exciting, with the possible cachet of having set a genius on the road to fame. However, it can also be an expensive and financially unrewarding venture. The budding artist is generally impecunious, so that you may have to carry the cost of framing, arranging exhibitions and even supplying materials. This can run into thousands of dollars. If you have found an artist of great promise, you might make a fortune, provided she or he repays you by staying with you.

TAKING CARE OF PICTURES

It is amazing how pictures survive being abandoned in lofts or roof spaces, only to be discovered a generation later, having appreciated substantially in value in the meantime.

Works on paper are more vulnerable than oils. Direct sunlight wreaks havoc. Unmounted works on paper can get creased or kinked. They should have a backing mount board made of pure rag fiber and acid free. Archival quality boards should ideally be used with a pH value of not less than 8. The picture should be framed with a glass front and a firm backing. Even framed watercolors can deteriorate in cold spaces where dampness is the enemy.

Oil paintings are quite durable, but are safer framed and under glass. Dampness can encourage the growth of mold on oil paintings under glass.

The obvious necessity of having secure fixings on which to hang pictures is sometimes overlooked, and it is possible to wake in the morning to find the picture on the floor with the frame and possibly the picture damaged. Another source of damage is the rusting of what appears to be brass wire used for hanging.

Handling

Perhaps the best advice when handling pictures it to use two hands. This is especially true of unmounted watercolors or prints, which can so easily be kinked. But it is also true of the frames of oil paintings, evidence of which can be seen in many auction rooms. It is dangerous, for the painting, to put it on the floor and prop it against a wall. This frequently occurs when someone is paying the bill after an auction.

Packing pictures is a job requiring skill and thought. For transport by car, it is best to wrap the pictures and separate them with cardboard or similar material. The stacking should ensure that there is no possibility on movement. Hooks and eyes should be removed. For transport by carrier or van, pictures should be wrapped in bubble wrap, with special precautions taken with the corners.

ABOUT THIS BOOK

This book contains the summarized prices for fine art and sculpture that sold at public auction during 2000. It covers 81,102 works by 24,105 artists, sculptors and miniaturists. The information is shown on separate lines for oil paintings, watercolors and drawings, prints, miniatures and sculpture for each artist:

a) the number of works sold
b) total value of works sold
c) lowest price
d) median price
e) highest price

The name of the artist is shown in full or as modified by the general usage of auctioneers.

Also shown for each artist:
a) full name
b) dates of birth and death or ? if unknown
c) nationality or ? if unknown

Sources of information

The index is compiled from catalogues, price lists and other information provided by auctioneers. ASI takes great care in extracting information accurately. However, ASI cannot be held responsible for errors unwittingly made, nor for unknowingly reproducing incorrect information. The price a picture reaches at auction can be influenced by many factors: condition, subject matter and size are just a few. We recommend additional research when buying and selling fine art, such as consulting reference books and obtaining advice from experienced sources.

Media

Media covered by *Art Sales Index Ltd* are:
a) oil paintings, including tempera and acrylic
b) watercolors and drawings, including collages, gouache, pen, pastel, crayon, pencil, charcoal, ink and chalk
c) sculpture and three-dimensional works

Price Recorded

The price recorded by ASI is the "hammer price," which is called out at auction and at which the lot is "knocked down" to the bidder. There may be occasions where a lot may consist of more than one item.

Many auctioneers levy an additional charge to the buyer of 5% to 15%. This is known as the "buyer's premium" and is **not** included in the price recorded by ASI. The seller must expect deductions to be made to the knockdown price to account for the auctioneer's commission.

Bought-in pictures

Pictures offered for sale at auction usually have a "reserve" placed on them by the owner in order that they not be sold at a price that the owner considers to be below their real value. This is not the same as the "estimate," which is provided by the auctioneer as a guide for the buyer. Pictures that do not reach the reserve are known as "bought-in." It is the policy of ASI to record only actual sales. "Bought-in" prices are **not** recorded. The majority of auctioneers do not include "bought-in" prices in their price lists. However, there might be occasions when some auctioneers inadvertently include bought-in prices on their printed price lists.

Median Price

No statistical device can fairly reflect the "value" of an artist's work but that is not what we are trying to do in this publication: rather, it is to show the current level of availability and demand as demonstrated by auction prices. It is possible to draw some conclusions that indicate a typical level of their performance at auction. ASI considers that the most satisfactory way to do this is to show the **median**, together with the highest and lowest prices, and, in addition, to show the total number and value of works sold. The median is **not** an average. (The average may be found by dividing the total turnover by the number of lots sold.) The median is the middle figure of any range of figures. It comes close to being a "typical" price because it eliminates the freakish highest price and the freakish lowest price. For example, in the range of numbers: 5, 12, 13, 18, **21**, 27, 33, 37, 104 the middle one, "21" is the **median**.

The same rule applies to auction prices in the example shown below:

Name	No.	Total Sales Value	lowest	Prices median	highest
PICASSO, Pablo (1881-1973) Spanish					
oil	98	950,200	2,000	3,800	190,000

Average price is $9,700 but the median is $3,800.

When there is an even number of prices and therefore no actual median, the middle two prices are added together and divided by two to arrive at artificial median.

RECORD PRICES ACHIEVED DURING 2000

AELST, Willem van and PICART, Jean Michel (17th C) Dutch/Flemish
$558,700   £370,000   Tulips, roses. lilies and other flowers in a basket on blue velvet (115x159cm-45x63in) lit. 7-Jul-00 Christie's, London

ALLORI, Alessandro (1535-1607) Italian
$290,000   £177,914   Flight to Egypt (34x37cm-13x15in) copper. 28-Jan-00 Sotheby's, NY

ALSLOOT, Denis van (c.1570-1628) Dutch
$588,000   £400,000   View of the abbey of Groenendael near Brussels in winter (45x86cm-18x34in) s.d.1621 panel prov. 14-Dec-00 Sotheby's, London

AMIET, Cuno (1868-1961) Swiss
$522,615   £330,769   Studio in autumn (81x108cm-32x43in) mono.d.1906 board prov.exhib.lit. 21-Mar-00 Christie's, Zurich

ANDRE, Carl (1935-) American
$360,000   £243,243   Aluminium-magnesium alloy square (x200cm-x79in) aluminium magnesium 50 plates exec 1969 prov.exhib.lit. 17-May-00 Sotheby's, NY

ANSDELL, Richard (1815-1885) British
$394,200   £270,000   The auld farmer's New Year's gift to his auld mare Maggie (112x142cm-44x56in) s.d.1851 lit.exhib. 30-Aug-00 Sotheby's, London

ARCIMBOLDO, Giuseppe (1527-1593) Italian
$1,300,000   £797,546   Reversible anthropomorphic portrait of a man composed of fruit (56x42cm-22x17in) panel. 28-Jan-00 Sotheby's, NY

BALEN, Hendrik van and BRUEGHEL, Jan (younger-studio) (17th C) Flemish
$265,299   £167,910   Adam et Eve; La creation d'Adam; Cain et Abel; L'arche de Noe, et divers (116x166cm-46x65in) two s.d.1642 set of six painted with Brueghel studio. 23-Mar-00 Tajan, Paris

BALTHUS (1908-2001) French
$2,800,000   £1,854,305   Nu aux bras leves (151x83cm-59x33in) s.d.1951 prov.exhib.lit. 10-May-00 Sotheby's, NY

BARCELO, Miguel (1957-) Spanish
$407,700   £270,000   El segundo (198x135cm-78x53in) s.i.d.90 verso oil pigment glue seaweed prov.exhib. 27-Jun-00 Christie's, London

BARLACH, Ernst (1870-1938) German
$432,000   £300,000   Der singende Mann (49cm-19in) s. gold pat. bronze st.f. H.Noak c. 1930 prov.exhib.lit. 17-Oct-00 Christie's, London

BAUGNIET, Charles (1814-1886) Flemish
$500,000   £328,947   Blind man's buff (89x127cm-35x50in) s.d.1875 panel prov.lit. 1-May-00 Christie's, Rockefeller NY

BENIVIENI, Lippo di (?) Italian?
$261,800   £185,675   Madonna. Saint John the Evangelist. The prophet Daniel. The prophet Eliah. Angels (40x21cm-16x8in) tempera board set of six prov.exhib.lit. 22-Nov-00 Finarte, Milan

BENSON, Ambrosius (attrib) (?-1550) Flemish
$1,440,600   £980,000   Portrait of lady in dark costume and white headdress, holding cat (81x66cm-32x26in) panel prov.lit. 13-Dec-00 Christie's, London

BIDAULD, Jean Joseph Xavier (1758-1846) French
$250,000   £153,374   View of the Isola di Sora (24x32cm-9x13in) s.d.1789 i.verso exhib. 28-Jan-00 Sotheby's, NY

BLAKELOCK, Ralph Albert (1847-1919) American
$3,200,000   £2,162,162   Indian encampment along the Snake River (121x213cm-48x84in) s.d.1871 prov.exhib.lit. 24-May-00 Sotheby's, NY

BLOEMAERT, Hendrick (1601-1672) Dutch
$411,600   £280,000   Allegory of winter (106x85cm-42x33in) s.d.1631. 14-Dec-00 Sotheby's, London

BOLOGNESE SCHOOL, 13th C Italian
$338,350   £234,964   Crucifixion (30x21cm-12x8in) board lit.18-Oct-00 Semenzato, Venice

BONVICINO, Alessandro (1498-1554) Italian
$412,490   £274,994   Venus and Cupid (118x210cm-46x83in) prov.lit.exhib. 31-May-00
    Finarte, Milan

BONVICINO, Alessandro (studio) (1498-1554) Italian
$260,000   £159,509   The Visitation (75x95cm-30x37in) prov.exhib.lit. 27-Jan-00
    Christie's, Rockefeller NY

BORDONE, Paris (1500-1571) Italian
$600,000   £405,405   Holy Family with Saint John the Baptist in a landscape (102x153cm-
    40x60in) panel prov.exhib.lit. 26-May-00 Christie's, Rockefeller NY

BOSSCHAERT, Ambrosius (elder) (1573-1621) Flemish
$2,642,500   £1,750,000   Still life of a bouquet of flowers, butterfly, dragonfly, sprig of
    rosemary on a ledge (30x20cm-12x8in) mono.verso copper.
    6-Jul-00 Sotheby's, London

BOTH, Jan (1618-1652) Dutch
$1,963,000   £1,300,000   Italianate evening landscape, muleteer and goatherds on wooded path
    (138x173cm-54x68in) s. prov.exhib.lit. 7-Jul-00 Christie's, London

BOTTICELLI, Sandro (studio) (1440-1510) Italian
$483,200   £320,000   Madonna and Child with four Angels (97cm-38in circular) tempera
    on panel tondo prov.exhib.lit. 7-Jul-00 Christie's, London

BOUGUEREAU, William Adolphe (1825-1905) French
$3,200,000   £2,105,263   La charite (196x117cm-77x46in) s.d.1878 prov.exhib.lit. 1-May-00
    Christie's, Rockefeller NY

BOYD, Arthur Merric Bloomfield (1920-1999) Australian
$511,600   £336,576   Dreaming bridegroom I (122x152cm-48x60in) s. oil tempera
    prov.exhib.lit. 2-May-00 Sotheby's, Melbourne

BRAY, Dirck de (17th C) Dutc
$632,100   £430,000   Still life of peonies, columbine, morning gloy and other flowers in a
    vase upon marble ledge (62x44cm-24x17in) s.d.1671 panel.
    14-Dec-00 Sotheby's, London

BREITNER, Georg Hendrik (1857-1923) Dutch
$290,770   £200,528   Paleisstraat - singelbrug (75x115cm-30x45in) s. painted c.1897
    exhib. 24-Oct-00 Christie's, Amsterdam

BRESCIANINO, Andrea del (1485-1525) Italian
$323,400   £220,000   Venus with sacred and prophane love (68x149cm-27x59in) panel
    prov.lit. 13-Dec-00 Christie's, London

BROCQUY, Louis le (1916-) Irish
$1,554,000   £1,050,000   Travelling woman with newspaper (83x115cm-33x45in) s. s.i.on
    stretcher board. 18-May-00 Sotheby's, London

BRONZINO, Angelo (attrib) (1503-1572) Italian
$1,366,180   £968,921   Etude de Christ pour une Pieta (31x21cm-12x8in) pierre noire.
    20-Nov-00 Piasa, Paris

BRUCE, Patrick Henry (1880-1937) American
$1,100,000   £769,231   Still Life (60x91cm-24x36in) oil pencil painted c.1919 prov.exhib.lit.
    30-Nov-00 Sotheby's, NY

BRUEGHEL, Jan (elder-attrib) (1568-1625) Flemish
$271,800   £180,000   Wooded landscape with peasants crossing a river, a village beyond
    (18x25cm-7x10in) indis sig.d. copper. 7-Jul-00 Christie's, London

BRUEGHEL, Jan (younger) and BALEN, Hendrik van (17th C) Flemish
$724,800   £480,000   The four elements (61x108cm-24x43in) panel. 6-Jul-00 Sotheby's, London

BRUSKIN, Grisha (1945-) Russian
$380,000   £265,734   Logies, part 1 (242x401cm-95x158in) s. thirty-five panels exhib.
    7-Nov-00 Christie's East, NY

BUCHET, Gustave (1888-1963) Swiss
$825,200   £569,106   Autumn (73x99cm-29x39in) s.d.1935 lit. 7-Dec-00 Sotheby's, Zurich

BUECKELAER, Joachim (1530-1573) Flemish
$3,969,000   £2,700,000   Four elements, greengrocer's stall. Earth, fishmonger's stall. Water,
                                poultry stall. Kitchen scene (157x214cm-62x84in) s.d.1569 set of
                                four. 13-Dec-00 Christie's, London

BUGATTI, Rembrandt (1885-1916) Italian
$521,070   £327,715   Lion et lionne de Nubie (45x135x22cm-18x53x9in) s. num. 3 black
                                pat. bronze f.st. AA Hebrard exhib. lit. 23-Feb-00 Delorme &
                                Fraysse, Paris #141/R

BUNKER, Dennis M (1861-1890) American
$2,600,000   £1,756,757   The brook, Medfield (63x76cm-25x30in) s.d.1889 prov.exhb.
                                24-May-00 Sotheby's, NY

BUTTERSWORTH, James E (1817-1894) American
$260,000   £181,818   Yachting off Castle Garden (63x76cm-25x30in) s. prov. 30-Nov-00
                                Sotheby's, NY

CAILLEBOTTE, Gustave (1848-1894) French
$13,000,000   £8,609,273   L'homme au balcon, boulevard Haussmann (116x89cm-46x35in)
                                s.d.1880 prov.exhib.lit. 8-May-00 Christie's, Rockefeller NY

CALDER, Alexander (1898-1976) American
$3,800,000   £2,676,056   Stegosaurus (406x434x243cm-160x171x96in) painted sheet metal
                                prov.exhib. 14-Nov-00 Sotheby's, NY

CARR, Emily M (1871-1945) Canadian
$620,780   £411,111   War canoes, Alert Bay (63x80cm-25x31in) s.d.1912 prov.exhib.lit.
                                10-May-00 Heffel, Vancouver

CARRACCI, Agostino (circle) (1557-1602) Italian
$538,680   £363,971   The Entombment (107x143cm-42x56in) prov. 16-May-00 AB
                                Stockholms Auktionsverk

CARRACCI, Lodovico (1555-1619) Italian
$4,750,000   £2,914,111   The Pieta (95x173cm-37x68in) prov.lit. 27-Jan-00 Christie's,
                                Rockefeller NY

CASAS, Ramon (1866-1932) Spanish
$255,000   £170,000   Escena de caza - The hunter (68x99cm-27x39in) s. prov.exhib.lit.
                                22-Jun-00 Sotheby's, London

CASTIGLIONE, Giovanni Benedetto (1616-1670) Italian
$1,328,800   £880,000   Pagan sacrifice (43x75cm-17x30in) prov.exhib.lit. 7-Jul-00 Christie's,
                                London

CAVALCANTI, Emiliano di (1897-1976) Brazilian
$800,000   £567,376   Mulher deitada com peixes e frutas (110x195cm-43x77in) s. prov.
                                21-Nov-00 Christie's, Rockefeller NY

CESARI, Giuseppe (1568-1640) Italian
$350,000   £214,724   Perseus and Andromeda (15x22cm-6x9in) oil on lapis lazuli.
                                27-Jan-00 Christie's, Rockefeller NY

CHATELET, Claude Louis (1753-1794) French
$350,000   £236,486   Pyramid at the Chateau de Maupertuis (86x115cm-34x45in)
                                s.indis.d.1785 prov.exhib. 23-May-00 Christie's, Rockefeller NY

CRESPI, Giuseppe Maria (1665-1747) Italian
$453,000   £300,000   Madonna and Child (51x41cm-20x16in) lit. 7-Jul-00 Christie's, London

CZACHORSKI, Ladislaus von (1850-1911) Polish
$295,460   £203,762   Elegant young lady seated at table with vase of roses (92x57cm-
                                36x22in) s.d.1891. 10-Dec-00 Agra, Warsaw

DALI, Salvador (1904-1989) Spanish
$3,770,000   £2,600,000   Ma femme nue regardant son propre corps devenir marches
                                (60x51cm-24x20in) s.d.1945 panel prov.exhib.lit. 4-Dec-00
                                Sotheby's, London

DANDINI, Cesare (1595-1658) Italian
$679,500   £450,000   Tobias and the Angel (220x168cm-87x66in) 6-Jul-00 Sotheby's, London

DAWSON, Henry (1811-1878) British
$264,550   £185,000   New House of Parliament, Westminster (180x272cm-71x107in)
                                 s.d.57 prov.exhib.lit. 28-Nov-00 Phillips, London

DELAUNAY, Robert (1885-1941) French
$4,200,000   £2,781,457   Les fenetres simultanees (92x86cm-36x34in) s.i.d.4.1912
                                 prov.exhib.lit. 10-May-00 Sotheby's, NY

DELEN, Dirk van (1605-1671) Dutch
$545,960   £371,402   Nature morte a la tulipe (38x28cm-15x11in) s.d.1637 oak panel
                                 prov.exhib.lit. 20-Dec-00 Tajan, Paris

DEMACHY, Pierre Antoine (1723-1807) French
$380,000   £256,757   Clearing of the Colonnade du Louvre and demolition of the Hotel
                                 Rouille (235x310cm-93x122in) s.d.1767 sold with a dr by French
                                 School, 18th C prov. 23-May-00 Christie's, Rockefeller NY

DENIS, Maurice (1870-1943) French
$467,090   £322,129   Les communiantes, la promenade au jardin (50x90cm-20x35in) s.
                                 10-Dec-00 Thierry & Lannon, Brest

DEWING, Maria Richards Oakey (1845-1927) American
$1,050,000   £709,459   Rose garden (61x103cm-24x41in) s.d.1901 prov.exhib.lit.
                                 24-May-00 Sotheby's, NY

DIXON, Maynard (1875-1946) American
$1,200,000   £833,333   Pony boy (91x183cm-36x72in) s.d.1920 i.stretcher prov.exhib.lit.
                                 30-Oct-00 Christie's, Los Angeles

DOMENICHINO (1581-1641) Italian
$3,000,000   £1,840,491   Rebuke of Adam and Eve (122x172cm-48x68in) i. prov.lit.
                                 28-Jan-00 Sotheby's, NY

DOU, Gerard (1613-1675) Dutch
$340,000   £208,589   Old Hermit (18x13cm-7x5in) mono. panel prov.lit. 28-Jan-00
                                 Sotheby's, NY

DRAPER, Herbert James (1864-1920) British
$1,144,000   £800,000   Mountain mist (126x119cm-50x47in) s. exhib.lit. 30-Nov-00
                                 Christie's, London

DRYSDALE, Sir George Russell (1912-1981) Australian
$719,050   £476,190   Billy Grace at Cattle Creek (75x126cm-30x50in) s. exhib. 28-Jun-00
                                 Christie's, Melbourne

DURRIE, George Henry (1820-1863) American
$440,000   £297,297   On the road to Boston (55x76cm-22x30in) s.d.1861 prov.
                                 24-May-00 Sotheby's, NY

ECKERSBERG, Christoffer Wilhelm (1783-1853) Danish
$425,980   £269,608   Model reclining on bed (22x27cm-9x11in) exhib.prov. 29-Feb-00
                                 Rasmussen, Copenhagen

ECKERSBERG, Johan Fredrik (1822-1870) Norwegian
$276,350   £174,908   Landscape from Romsdalen (81x117cm-32x46in) s.d.1867 lit.
                                 10-Apr-00 Blomqvist, Oslo

ERNST, Rudolph (1854-1932) Austrian
$350,000   £243,056   Flower maidens (72x92cm-28x36in) s. panel exhib. 18-Oct-00
                                 Christie's, Rockefeller NY

ESTES, Richard (1932-) American
$420,000   £295,775   Gourmet treats (91x122cm-36x48in) s. prov.exhib.lit. 15-Nov-00
                                 Christie's, Rockefeller NY

FABRIS, Pietro (18th C) Italian
$392,600   £260,000   Mediterranean port scene with fishermen drawing their catch
                                 (103x157cm-41x62in) d.1777. 6-Jul-00 Sotheby's, London

FANTIN-LATOUR, Henri (1836-1904) French
$3,200,000   £2,237,762   Bouquet de fleurs (51x62cm-20x24in) s.d.89 prov.exhib.lit. 8-Nov-00
                                 Christie's, Rockefeller NY

FISCHL, Eric (1948-) American
$900,000   £608,108   Noonwatch (165x254cm-65x100in) s.i.d.1983 verso prov.exhb.lit.
                               16-May-00 Christie's, Rockefeller NY

FLANAGAN, Barry (1941-) British
$332,200   £220,000   Drummer (244x173x91cm-96x68x36in) num.5/7 bronze prov.exhib.
                               29-Jun-00 Sotheby's, London

FLAVIN, Dan (1933-1996) American
$300,000   £211,268   Alternate diagonals of March (x366cm-x144in) red gold fluorescent
                               light prov.exhib. 14-Nov-00 Sotheby's, NY

FLEMISH SCHOOL, 16th C Flemish
$475,000   £291,411   Holy Family with St Catherine and St Barbara. Christ and male donor
                               (116x170cm-46x67in) panel triptych painted outer wings double-
                               sided. 28-Jan-00 Sotheby's, NY

FONTANA, Annibale (1540-c.1587) Italian
$1,543,500   £1,050,000   Dragon (73cm-29in) s.d.1582 bronze lit.13-Dec-00 Sotheby's, London

FORBES, Stanhope Alexander (1857-1947) British
$1,650,000   £1,100,000   Seine boat (114x157cm-45x62in) s.d.1904 prov.exhib.lit. 6-Jun-00
                               Phillips, London

FORTUNY Y MARSAL, Mariano (1838-1874) Spanish
$480,000   £320,000   Fantasia Arabe en Tanger - Arab fantasia (51x62cm-20x24in)
                               s.d.1866 prov.exhib.lit. 22-Jun-00 Sotheby's, London

GALLEN-KALLELA, Akseli Valdemar (1865-1931) Finnish
$353,130   £223,500   Valkoisia ruusuja, konginkangas - white roses (62x58cm-24x23in)
                               s.d.1906 prov. 7-Apr-00 Sotheby's, London

GARBER, Daniel (1880-1958) American
$500,000   £349,650   Late afternoon - September (107x117cm-42x46in) s. painted 1915
                               prov.exhib.lit. 30-Nov-00 Sotheby's, NY

GIACOMETTI, Alberto (1901-1966) Swiss
$13,000,000   £9,090,910   Grande femme debout I (268cm-106in) s.num.5/6 brown pat. bronze
                               conceived 1960. 8-Nov-00 Christie's, Rockefeller NY

GIACOMETTI, Augusto (1877-1947) Swiss
$850,770   £538,462   Mary with Infant Jesus (119x139cm-47x55in) prov.exhib.lit.
                               21-Mar-00 Christie's, Zurich

GIACOMETTI, Giovanni (1868-1934) Swiss
$353,660   £243,902   Boys in sunshine (91x100cm-36x39in) mono.d.1910 s.i.d.verso
                               lit.exhib. 5-Dec-00 Christie's, Zurich

GIAMBOLOGNA (after) (c.1529-1608) Italian
$310,200   £220,000   Figure of a reclining nymph (21x35cm-8x14in) bronze reddish lacquer
                               prov.lit. 22-Nov-00 Sotheby's, London

GIERYMSKI, Aleksander (1850-1901) Polish
$299,530   £203,762   Autumn park landscape (69x95cm-27x37in) s. prov.lit.exhib.
                               14-Dec-00 Unicum, Warsaw

GIORDANO, Luca (attrib) (1632-1705) Italian
$662,380   £456,817   Judgement of Solomon (94x112cm-37x44in) prov. 5-Dec-00
                               Bukowskis, Stockholm

GOBER, Robert (1954-) American
$750,000   £528,169   Deep basin sink (66x74x61cm-26x29x24in) s.i.d.1984 verso plaster
                               wire enamel semi-gloss paint prov.exhib. 14-Nov-00 Sotheby's, NY

GONZALEZ-TORRES, Felix (1957-1996) American?
$1,500,000   £1,056,338   Untitled, Blood (cm-in) plastic beads metal rod prov.lit.exhib.
                               16-Nov-00 Christie's, Rockefeller NY

GRECO, El (1541-1614) Spanish
$5,285,000   £3,500,000   Christ on the cross (83x52cm-33x20in) s. prov. 6-Jul-00 Sotheby's, London

HAMILTON, Hugh Douglas (1739-1808) British
$486,200   £340,000   Portrait of Arthur Hill, 2nd Marquess of Downshire, wearing yellow
                               frock coat (95x64cm-37x25in) pastel prov.exhib.lit. 30-Nov-00
                               Christie's, London

HARRIS, Lawren Phillips (1910-) Canadian
$348,430   £235,426   Lake, North Labrador (81x102cm-32x40in) s. s i. stretcher verso
                                prov. exhib. 24-May-00 Sotheby's, Toronto

HARTLEY, Marsden (1877-1943) American
$2,000,000   £1,398,601   Abstraction (119x100cm-47x39in) painted 1913 prov.lit. 30-Nov-00
                                Sotheby's, NY

HECKEL, Erich (1883-1970) German
$1,584,000   £1,100,000   Dangast village landscape (70x80cm-28x31in) init.d.09 prov.exhib.lit.
                                18-Oct-00 Sotheby's, London

HEEM, Jan Jansz de (1650-1695) Dutch
$367,500   £250,000   Silver tazza and a basket laden with fruit, silver platters with fruit
                                (83x108cm-33x43in) s. prov.exhib. 13-Dec-00 Christie's, London

HEPWORTH, Dame Barbara (1903-1975) British
$420,000   £278,146   Family of man, ultimate form (300cm-118in) s. num.4/4 green pat
                                bronze prov.lit. 11-May-00 Sotheby's, NY

HICKS, George Elgar (1824-1914) British
$528,500   £350,000   Infant orphan election at the London Tavern - polling (36x48cm-
                                14x19in) s.d.1865 prov.exhib.lit. 15-Jun-00 Sotheby's, London

HILL, Thomas (1829-1908) American
$310,000   £216,783   Yosemite Valley (92x152cm-36x60in) s.d.1869 i.on stretcher prov.
                                30-Nov-00 Sotheby's, NY

HIRST, Damien (1965-) British
$680,000   £478,873   In love- out of love (121x244cm-48x96in) gloss household paint
                                butterflies diptych prov.lit. 13-Nov-00 Phillips, NY

HODGES, William (1744-1797) British
$499,800   £340,000   Matavie Bay in the Island of Otaheite, now Tahiti (50x61cm-20x24in)
                                i. on stretcher. 14-Dec-00 Sotheby's, London

HONE, Nathaniel I (1718-1784) British
$325,600   £220,000   Portrait of Captain Robert Boyle Walsingham, MP, with view of
                                Louisbourg, Canada (239x147cm-94x58in) mono.i.d.1760
                                prov.exhib.lit. 19-May-00 Christie's, London

HONTHORST, Gerrit van (studio) (1590-1656) Dutch
$343,200   £240,000   Portrait of King Frederick V of Bohemia. Portrait of Elisabeth Stuart,
                                Queen of Bohemia (213x129cm-84x51in) pair prov.exhib.lit.
                                1-Dec-00 Christie's, London

HULSDONCK, Jacob van (1582-1647) Flemish
$690,900   £470,000   Still life of wild strawberries and carnation in a Ming bowl, cherries
                                and redcurrants on a ledge (28x36cm-11x14in) s. copper
                                prov.exhib.lit. 14-Dec-00 Sotheby's, London

HXU WEI (1521-1593) Chinese
$255,090   £177,148   Flowers of the four seasons (30x519cm-12x204in) s. ink handscroll
                                with poem by Qing Teng Dao Shi. 30-Oct-00 Christie's, Hong Kong

JANSSON, Eugène (1862-1915) Swedish
$266,230   £168,500   Varkvall - spring evening (73x60cm-29x24in) s. prov.lit. 7-Apr-00
                                Sotheby's, London

JAWLENSKY, Alexej von (attrib) (1864-1941) Russian
$260,000   £172,185   Abstract head (35x25cm-14x10in) s. board prov.lit. 11-May-00
                                Sotheby's, NY

JUDD, Donald (1928-1994) American
$740,000   £521,127   Untitled (457x102x79cm-180x40x31in) st.sig.st.f.Bernstein Bros.
                                steel red plexiglas prov.lit. 14-Nov-00 Sotheby's, NY

KALF, Willem (1619-1693) Dutch
$470,400   £320,000   Still life of peeled lemon, roemer, wine glass and knife, rug upon a
                                draped table (51x44cm-20x17in) s.d.1660 prov.lit. 14-Dec-00
                                Sotheby's, London

KAYAMA, Matazo (1927-) Japanese
$450,000   £298,013   Jaku - solitude (120x88cm-47x35in) s. col ink. 10-May-00 Christie's,
                                          Rockefeller NY

KESSEL, Jan van I (1626-1679) Flemish
$1,500,000   £1,013,514   Study of butterflies, spiders, lizards, a beetle, an ant, grasshopper and
                                          other insects (40x50cm-16x20in) copper prov. 25-May-00
                                          Sotheby's, NY

KLEIN, Yves (1928-1962) French
$6,100,000   £4,295,775   RE I (200x165cm-79x65in) pigment synthetic resin sponge
                                          prov.exhib.lit. 15-Nov-00 Christie's, Rockefeller NY

KLINE, Franz (1910-1962) American
$2,300,000   £1,619,718   Black sienna (234x172cm-92x68in) s.d.60 verso prov.exhib.
                                          15-Nov-00 Christie's, Rockefeller NY

KNIGHT, Daniel Ridgway (1839-1924) American
$360,000   £251,748   Coming from the garden (74x61cm-29x24in) s.i. prov.exhib.
                                          29-Nov-00 Christie's, Rockefeller NY

KOCH, Pyke (1901-1991) Dutch
$293,130   £204,986   Daphne (28x28cm-11x11in) i. verso oil tempera panel prov.exhib.lit.
                                          30-Nov-00 Christie's, Amsterdam

KOISO, Ryohei (1902-1988) Japanese
$250,000   £165,563   Ningen no kozu - composition with human figures (91x65cm-
                                          36x26in) s.d.1952 s.i.on stretcher exhib. 10-May-00 Christie's,
                                          Rockefeller NY

KROYER, Peder Severin (1851-1909) Danish
$996,600   £660,000   Marie i Haven (58x48cm-23x19in) s.d.95 panel prov. 27-Jun-00
                                          Christie's, London

KUSTODIEV, Boris (1878-1927) Russian
$458,250   £325,000   Village fair (71x111cm-28x44in) s.d.1919 i.verso prov. 23-Nov-00
                                          Sotheby's, London

LAFARGE, John (1835-1910) American
$1,900,000   £1,328,671   Last Valley - Paradise Rocks (83x107cm-33x42in) prov.exhib.lit.
                                          29-Nov-00 Christie's, Rockefeller NY

LANE, Fitz Hugh (1804-1865) American
$3,600,000   £2,432,433   The golden rule (62x92cm-24x36in) lit. 25-May-00 Christie's,
                                          Rockefeller NY

LANG SHINING (1688-1766) Italian/Chinese
$1,020,370   £708,592   Deer in an autumn forst (121x65cm-48x26in) s. ink col silk hanging
                                          scroll lit. 30-Oct-00 Christie's, Hong Kong

LARKIN, William (attrib) (17th C) British
$302,000   £200,000   Portrait of a gentleman, probably Sir Francis Nethersole, wearing
                                          embroidered doublet (56x44cm-22x17in) i. panel prov.exhib.
                                          15-Jun-00 Sotheby's, London

LAUGE, Achille (1861-1944) French
$334,580   £210,430   Route aux environs de Cailhau (40x50cm-16x20in) s.d.93 prov.
                                          31-Mar-00 Laurin Guilloux Buffetaud Tailleur, Paris

LAVERY, Sir John (attrib) (1856-1941) British
$769,600   £520,000   Played (35x30cm-14x12in) s.d.1885 i.verso panel prov. 19-May-00
                                          Christie's, London

LEGER, Fernand (after) (1881-1955) French
$340,000   £237,762   La partie de campagne (194x194cm-76x76in) s.num.1/1 glazed
                                          ceramic tile granite prov.exhib. 9-Nov-00 Christie's, Rockefeller NY

LEIGHTON, Edmund Blair (1853-1922) British
$966,400   £640,000   God speed (160x116cm-63x46in) s.d.1900 exhib. lit. 14-Jun-00
                                          Christie's, London

LEIGHTON, Lord Frederic (1830-1896) British
$1,812,000   £1,200,000   Bracelet (153x60cm-60x24in) prov.exhib.lit.14-Jun-00 Phillips, London

LEVITAN, Isaac Ilyitch (1860-1900) Russian
$271,800   £180,000   Marshes in the evening (137x71cm-54x28in) s.d.1882 prov.exhib.
                                                 10-May-00 Sotheby's, London

LHERMITTE, Léon (1844-1925) French
$850,000   £559,211   La famille (256x348cm-101x137in) s.d.1908 prov.lit.exhib.
                                                 1-May-00 Christie's, Rockefeller NY

LIEBERMANN, Max (1847-1935) German
$1,087,540   £734,824   Tennis court in Noordwijk (65x80cm-26x31in) s.d.1911
                                                 prov.exhib.lit. 26-May-00 Villa Grisebach, Berlin

LIMOSIN, Leonard (c.1505-c.1575) French
$494,600   £311,070   Sibylles, Prophetes et Saints (22x10cm-9x4in) paint on enamel plates
                                                 twenty lit. 29-Mar-00 Couturier & Nicolay, Paris

LIPPI, Filippino (1457-1504) Italian
$906,000   £600,000   The rest on the Flight into Egypt (85cm-33in circular) panel tondo
                                                 prov.exhib.lit. 7-Jul-00 Christie's, London

LONG, Edwin (1829-1891) British
$700,000   £460,526   An ancient custom (100x138cm-39x54in) s.d.1876 prov.exhib.lit.
                                                 1-May-00 Christie's, Rockefeller NY

LOO, Carle van (1705-1765) French
$250,000   £153,374   Venus requesting Vulcan to make arms for Aeneas (129x98cm-
                                                 51x39in) s. prov.exhib.lit. 27-Jan-00 Christie's, Rockefeller NY

LOTTO, Lorenzo (attrib) (1480-1556) Italian
$300,000   £184,049   Portrait of a lawyer (85x69cm-33x27in) s.i.d.A.D. MDXXXXI
                                                 prov.exhib.lit. 28-Jan-00 Sotheby's, NY

MACKE, August (1887-1914) German
$3,744,000   £2,600,000   Market in Tunis (57x51cm-22x20in) painted 1914 prov.exhib.lit.
                                                 17-Oct-00 Christie's, London

MADRAZO Y GARRETA, Raimundo de (1841-1920) Spanish
$250,000   £173,611   Pierrette (200x95cm-79x37in) s. prov.exhib. 18-Oct-00 Christie's,
                                                 Rockefeller NY

MAEDA, Seison (1885-1977) Japanese
$480,000   £317,881   Nasu no Yoichi - the archer Nasu no Yoichi (65x87cm-26x34in) col
                                                 ink gold. 10-May-00 Christie's, Rockefeller NY

MAILLOL, Aristide (1861-1944) French
$2,800,000   £1,958,042   L'air (x239cm-x94in) s.st.f.Rudier num.6/6 lead prov.exhib.lit.
                                                 9-Nov-00 Sotheby's, NY

MALEVICH, Kasimir (1878-1935) Russian
$15,500,000   £10,264,902   Suprematist composition (80x80cm-31x31in) painted 1919-20
                                                 prov.exhib.lit. 11-May-00 Phillips, NY

MANSHIP, Paul Howard (1885-1966) American
$850,000   £574,324   Celestial sphere (68cm-27in) i.d.1934 gilt bronze st.f.Priessmann
                                                 Bauer prov.lit. 25-May-00 Christie's, Rockefeller NY

MARDEN, Brice (1938-) American
$1,700,000   £1,197,183   For pearl (244x250cm-96x98in) s.i.d.1970 verso oil wax
                                                 prov.exhib.lit. 14-Nov-00 Sotheby's, NY

MARILHAT, Prosper (1811-1847) French
$408,800   £280,000   Vue de la Place de L'Esbekieh et du Quartier Copte, au Caire
                                                 (107x161cm-42x63in) s.d.1833 prov.exhib.lit. 12-Oct-00
                                                 Sotheby's, London

MARIN, John (1870-1953) American
$550,000   £384,615   Related to St. Paul's New York (66x76cm-26x30in) s.d.28
                                                 prov.exhib.lit. 30-Nov-00 Sotheby's, NY

MARTIN, Agnes (1912-) American/Canadian
$1,300,000   £878,378   Drift of summer (183x183cm-72x72in) s.i.d.65 verso acrylic graphite
                                                 prov.exhib.lit. 18-May-00 Phillips, NY

MARTINI, Arturo (1889-1947) Italian
$250,460   £176,378   Woman in the sun (43x148x68cm-17x58x27in) s. bronze exec.1930-
                                   33 prov.exhib.lit. 15-Nov-00 Finarte, Milan

MASTER OF THE ACQUAVELLA STILL LIFE (17th C) Italian
$800,000   £490,798   Basket of fruit and two children (82x126cm-32x50in) painted with
                                   Bartolomeo Cavarozzi prov.exhib.lit. 28-Jan-00 Sotheby's, NY

MASTER OF THE DEATH OF SAINT NICHOLAS OF MUNSTER (15th C)
$3,200,000   £1,963,190   Calvary (129x200cm-51x79in) s. panel prov.exhib.lit. 27-Jan-00
                                   Christie's, Rockefeller NY

MASTER OF THE MAGDALEN LEGEND (15th C) Flemish
$453,000   £300,000   The Virgin and Child (42x31cm-17x12in) panel prov.exhib.lit.
                                   7-Jul-00 Christie's, London

MATISSE, Henri (1869-1954) French
$15,500,000   £10,839,162   La robe persane (81x65cm-32x26in) s.d.40 prov.exhib.lit. 9-Nov-00
                                   Sotheby's, NY

METZINGER, Jean (1883-1956) French
$550,000   £384,615   Homme assis devant la table (100x73cm-39x29in) s. prov.lit.exhib.
                                   10-Nov-00 Sotheby's, NY

MICHELANGELO (1475-1564) Italian
$11,174,000   £7,400,000   The risen Christ (23x21cm-9x8in) red blk chk pen ink double-sided
                                   prov.exhib.lit. 4-Jul-00 Christie's, London

MIERIS, Willem van (1662-1747) Dutch
$275,000   £168,712   Violinist making merry in a tavern (31x27cm-12x11in) s.d.1703
                                   panel prov.lit. 28-Jan-00 Sotheby's, NY

MIR Y TRINXET, Joaquin (1873-1940) Spanish
$330,000   £220,000   El abismo - the abyss (172x95cm-68x37in) s. i.verso prov.exhib.lit.
                                   22-Jun-00 Sotheby's, London

MITCHELL, Joan (1926-1992) American
$750,000   £528,169   Monongehela (183x198cm-72x78in) s.prov.14-Nov-00 Sotheby's, NY

MODIGLIANI, Amedeo (1884-1920) Italian
$14,200,000   £9,930,071   Fillette assise en robe (93x61cm-37x24in) s. prov.exhib.lit. 9-Nov-00
                                   Sotheby's, NY

MOHOLY-NAGY, Laszlo (1895-1946) American/Hungarian
$981,500   £650,000   A XI (132x115cm-52x45in) i.d.1923 verso prov.exhib.lit. 28-Jun-00
                                   Christie's, London

MORALES, Luis de (c.1509-1586) Spanish
$604,000   £400,000   Christ the Man of Sorrows (49x35cm-19x14in) panel. 7-Jul-00
                                   Christie's, London

MORGAN, Frederick (1856-1927) British
$880,000   £578,947   May 1 (86x117cm-34x46in) s. prov.exhib. 1-May-00 Christie's,
                                   Rockefeller NY

MORISOT, Berthe (1841-1895) French
$4,000,000   £2,797,203   Cache-cache (46x55cm-18x22in) s. prov.exhib.lit. 9-Nov-00
                                   Sotheby's, NY

MUCHA, Alphonse (1860-1939) Czechoslovakian
$320,000   £210,526   Winter tale (124x99cm-49x39in) s.d.1917. 1-May-00 Christie's,
                                   Rockefeller NY

MUNTER, Gabriele (1877-1962) German
$600,000   £397,351   Kind mit puppe (69x48cm-27x19in) s.d.1909 s.i.verso board
                                   prov.exhib. 10-May-00 Christie's, Rockefeller NY

McCARTAN, Edward (1879-1947) American
$700,000   £472,973   Diana (211cm-83in) s.d.1928 green pat. bronze cast Roman Bronze
                                   Works provlit. 24-May-00 Sotheby's, NY

NAIVEU, Matthys (1647-1721) Dutch
$617,400   £420,000   Elegant interior with a gentleman paying court to a lady (55x65cm-
                                   22x26in) s. 13-Dec-00 Christie's, London

NATTIER, Jean Marc (1685-1766) French
$580,000   £402,778   La Force, personification of Fortitude, said to be Duchesse de
                          Chateauroux (131x114cm-52x45in) s.d.1743 prov.lit. 2-Nov-00
                          Christie's, Rockefeller NY

NEVINSON, Christopher Richard Wynne (1889-1946) British
$257,400   £180,000   Sunday evening, punts on the Thames at Henley (61x76cm-24x30in)
                          s. painted c.1924 prov.exhib. 30-Nov-00 Christie's, London

NOGUCHI, Isamu (1904-1988) American
$580,000   £408,451   Cronos (215x76x60cm-85x30x24in) s.num.1/6 d.1947-62 cast
                          bronze prov.exhib.lit. 14-Nov-00 Sotheby's, NY

NOLAN, Sidney (1917-1992) Australian
$719,050   £476,190   Death of Constable Scanlon (90x120cm-35x47in) s. s i.verso ripolin
                          board prov.exhib. 28-Jun-00 Christie's, Melbourne

NUSSBAUM, Felix (1904-1944) German
$1,584,000   £1,100,000   Self portrait in camp. Still life (52x41cm-20x16in) s.d.1940 c.1939
                          verso panel double-sided prov.exhib.lit.18-Oct-00 Sotheby's, London

OGGIONO, Marco (1470-1530) Italian
$375,000   £230,061   Madonna and Child with the infant St John the Baptist (99x78cm-
                          39x31in) panel prov.lit. 28-Jan-00 Sotheby's, NY

OLSEN, John (1928-) Australian
$263,650   £174,603   Salute to Cerberus (182x244cm-72x96in) s.d.65 board exhib.lit.
                          28-Jun-00 Christie's, Melbourne

O'CONOR, Roderic (1860-1940) Irish
$480,000   £320,000   Nature morte, Faience (54x65cm-21x26in) s.21-Jun-00 Sotheby's, London

O'NEILL, Henry Nelson (1817-1880) British
$755,000   £500,000   Home again (135x107cm-53x42in) s.d.1859 prov.exhib.lit.
                          14-Jun-00 Christie's, London

PALMER, Samuel (1805-1881) British
$1,020,000   £680,000   Oak tree and beech, Lullingstone Park (29x47cm-11x19in) s. pencil
                          pen ink W/C htd bodycol prov.exhib.lit. 8-Jun-00 Christie's, London

PARK, David (1911-1960) American
$450,000   £310,345   Flower seller (132x121cm-52x48in) s.d.56 prov. 5-Dec-00 Christie's, L.A.

PERCEVAL, John (1923-2000) Australi
$299,600   £198,413   Scudding swans (88x119cm-35x47in) s.d.59 board exhib.lit.
                          28-Jun-00 Christie's, Melbourne

PESELLINO, Francesco (1422-1457) Italian
$482,740   £335,235   The triumph of Fame, Time and Religion (42x176cm-17x69in)
                          tempera board lit. 18-Oct-00 Semenzato, Venice

PICASSO, Pablo (1881-1973) Spanish
$50,000,000 £34,965,036 Femme aux bras croises (81x58cm-32x23in) painted 1901-1902
                          prov.exhib.lit. 8-Nov-00 Christie's, Rockefeller NY

RAE, Henrietta (1859-1928) British
$743,600   £520,000   Hylas and water nymphs (142x223cm-56x88in) s. prov.exhib.lit.
                          30-Nov-00 Christie's, London

RAPHAEL, Joseph (1869-1950) American
$350,000   £231,788   The artist's home, Uccle, Belgium (79x99cm-31x39in) s. prov.
                          14-Jun-00 Butterfields, San Francisco

RAY, Charles (1953-) American
$2,000,000   £1,408,451   Male mannequin (187x69x47cm-74x27x19in) fibreglass one of 3
                          prov.lit.exhib. 16-Nov-00 Christie's, Rockefeller NY

REDFIELD, Edward (1869-1965) American
$320,000   £223,776   Spring at Point Pleasant (66x81cm-26x32in) s.d.1934 i.on stretcher
                          prov. 29-Nov-00 Christie's, Rockefeller NY

REDMOND, Granville (1871-1935) American
$380,000   £262,069   Californian poppies (46x76cm-18x30in) s. 24-Oct-00 Christie's, L.A.

REEKERS, Hendrik (1815-1854) Dutch
$331,800   £210,000   Flowers in a copper ewer with various fruits on a marble ledge (76x60cm-30x24in) s. panel. 6-Apr-00 Christie's, London

REGGIANINI, Vittorio (1858-1939) Italian
$260,000   £180,556   The birthday (66x91cm-26x36in) s.18-Oct-00 Christie's, Rockefeller NY

REMBRANDT (1606-1669) Dutch
$26,460,000   £18,000,000   Portrait Aeltje Pietersdr, Uylenburgh, wife of Johannes Cornelisz (74x56cm-29x22in) s.i.d.1632 panel oval 13-Dec-00 Christie's, London

REYNOLDS, Sir Joshua (1723-1792) British
$2,265,000   £1,500,000   The Archers, double portrait of John Dyke Acland and Thomas Townsend, Viscount Sydney (239x184cm-94x72in) prov. 14-Jun-00 Christie's, London

ROBERTS, Thomas (1748-1778) Irish
$606,800   £410,000   Sheet water at Carton Park, Co. Kildare with Duke and Duchess (112x152cm-44x60in) prov.exhib.lit. 19-May-00 Christie's, London

ROMERO DE TORRES, Julio (1879-1930) Spanish
$570,000   £380,000   La gracia - Grace (203x218cm-80x86in) s. prov.lit. 22-Jun-00 Sotheby's, London

RORBYE, Martinus (1803-1848) Danish
$525,000   £350,000   Turkish notary drawing up marriage contract (95x130cm-37x51in) init.d.1837 prov.exhib.lit. 21-Jun-00 Christie's, London

ROSA, Fabian de la (1869-1937) Philippin
$366,070   £249,027   Women working in a rice field (65x96cm-26x38in) s.i.d.1902 prov. 1-Oct-00 Christie's, Singapore

ROSSETTI, Dante Gabriel (1828-1882) British
$3,624,000   £2,400,000   Pandora (94x66cm-37x26in) mono.i.d.1869 pastel two joined sheets prov.exhib.lit. 14-Jun-00 Christie's, London

ROTHKO, Mark (1903-1970) American
$13,000,000   £8,783,784   Yellow over purple (176x151cm-69x59in) s.d.1956 village prov.exhib.lit. 17-May-00 Sotheby's, NY

RUBENS, Sir Peter Paul (1577-1640) Flemish
$7,500,000   £4,601,227   Portrait of a man as the God Mars (83x66cm-33x26in) panel prov.exhib.lit. 28-Jan-00 Sotheby's, NY

SAEKI, Yuzo (1898-1928) Japanese
$650,000   £430,464   Garage - jidoshagoya (53x73cm-21x29in) painted c.1925 exhib. 10-May-00 Christie's, Rockefeller NY

SAIVE, Jean de II (1597-?) Flemish
$453,000   £300,000   Fruit and vegetable stall in a town market (173x228cm-68x90in) indis sig. prov.exhib. 7-Jul-00 Christie's, London

SANCHEZ, Tomas (1948-) Cuban
$280,000   £186,667   Nubes sobre laguna (196x242cm-77x95in) s.d.96 i.verso prov. 1-Jun-00 Christie's, Rockefeller NY

SARACENI, Carlo (1585-1620) Italian
$324,930   £224,090   Le deluge universel (115x96cm-45x38in) prov. 6-Dec-00 Piasa, Paris

SARTO, Andrea del (1487-1530) Italian
$1,000,000   £613,497   Madonna and Child (85x62cm-33x24in) panel prov. 28-Jan-00 Sotheby's, NY

SAUPIQUE, Georges Laurent (1889-?) French
$644,420   £457,038   L'Afrique du Nord. les Antilles. L'Afrique noire. L'Indochine (185cm-73in) s.i. marble bronze four. 22-Nov-00 Tajan, Paris

SAVERY, Jacob (16/17th C) Dutch
$377,500   £250,000   Season of spring, panoramic landscape, winter yielding to summer (41x67cm-16x26in) i. panel prov.exhib. 6-Jul-00 Sotheby's, London

SAVERY, Roeland (1576-1639) Dutch
$332,200   £220,000   Orpheus charming the animals (56x100cm-22x39in) s. panel prov.lit. 6-Jul-00 Sotheby's, London

SCHALCKEN, Godfried (1643-1706) Dutch
$775,000   £475,460   Lady gazing at a mirror beneath a canopy in a wooded landscape (37x29cm-15x11in) panel prov. 28-Jan-00 Sotheby's, NY

SCHOLZ, Georg (1890-1945) German
$259,200   £180,000   Nightly noise (57x51cm-22x20in) s.d.1919 s.i.d.1919 stretcher prov.exhib.lit. 18-Oct-00 Sotheby's, London

SCHOONOVER, Frank E (1877-1972) American
$250,000   £174,825   Northern mist (79x92cm-31x36in) s.d.16 prov.exhib.lit. 29-Nov-00 Christie's, Rockefeller NY

SEGHERS, Daniel (1590-1661) Flemish
$352,800   £240,000   Still life of a rose, tulips and orange blossom in glass vase with red admiral butterfly (31x19cm-12x7in) s. copper prov. 14-Dec-00 Sotheby's, London

SHISHKIN, Ivan Ivanovich (1832-1898) Russian
$271,800   £180,000   River Kama, near Yelabuga (195x120cm-77x47in) s.d.1895. 10-May-00 Sotheby's, London

SIEMIRADZKI, Hendrik (1843-1902) Polish
$265,000   £184,028   Departure of Caterina Cornaro, Queen of Cyprus (208x293cm-82x115in) s.i.d.1878. 31-Oct-00 Sotheby's, NY

SISLEY, Alfred (1839-1899) French
$3,200,000   £2,119,205   Un jardin a Louveciennes, chemin de l'Etarche (64x46cm-25x18in) s.d.73 prov.exhib.lit. 11-May-00 Phillips, NY

SLOAN, John (1871-1951) American
$2,000,000   £1,351,351   Bleeker Street, Saturday night (67x81cm-26x32in) s. prov.exhib.lit. 24-May-00 Sotheby's, NY

SOULACROIX (1825-1879) French
$284,400   £180,000   Three for tea (81x62cm-32x24in) s. 6-Apr-00 Christie's, London

SPITZWEG, Carl (1808-1885) German
$1,078,900   £733,945   Young man offering flowers to young woman in street (48x28cm-19x11in) s.rhombus prov.lit. 27-Sep-00 Neumeister, Munich

STILL, Clyfford (1904-1980) American
$1,550,000   £1,047,297   Untitled (175x109cm-69x43in) s.d.1947 i.verso. 17-May-00 Sotheby's, NY

THEOFILOS (1867-1934) Greek
$328,490   £221,951   Villa courtyard, Mytilene (180x165cm-71x65in) prov.lit. 24-May-00 Christie's, Athens

TIDEMAND, Adolph (1814-1876) Norwegian
$444,780   £300,526   The youngest son's leaving (52x59cm-20x23in) s.d.1867 lit. 25-May-00 Grev Wedels Plass, Oslo

TIEPOLO, Giovanni Battista (1696-1770) Italian
$2,000,000   £1,226,994   Alexander and Campaspe in the studio of Apelles (42x54cm-17x21in) prov.exhib.lit. 27-Jan-00 Christie's, Rockefeller NY

TJUPURRULA, Johnny Warrangula (1932-) Australian
$263,650   £174,603   Water dreaming at Kalipinypa (80x75cm-31x30in) synthetic polymer powder paint board prov. 26-Jun-00 Sotheby's, Melbourne

TOLEDO, Francisco (1940-) Mexican
$400,000   £283,688   Plano de Juchitan (142x189cm-56x74in) oil natural pigments c.1961 prov.lit. 21-Nov-00 Christie's, Rockefeller NY

TUCKER, Albert (1914-1999) Australian
$359,520   £238,095   Last days of Leichhardt (121x152cm-48x60in) s.d.64 oil sand board exhib. 28-Jun-00 Christie's, Melbourne

TUKE, Henry Scott (1858-1929) British
$282,000   £200,000   The midday rest (103x134cm-41x53in) s.d.1906 prov. 21-Nov-00 Phillips, London

TUSCAN SCHOOL, 14th C Italian
$301,710   £209,522   The Virgin mourning. Saint John mourning (160cm-63in) polychrome wood lit. 18-Oct-00 Semenzato, Venice

UBERTINI, Francesco (1494-1557) Italian
$573,300   £390,000   Madonna and Child with Saint John the Baptist seated among rocks, village beyond with shepherds (146x114cm-57x45in) panel prov. 13-Dec-00 Christie's, London

VALLOTTON, Felix (1865-1925) Swiss
$1,473,580   £1,016,260   On the beach (42x48cm-17x19in) s.d.99 board on panel prov.lit.exhib. 5-Dec-00 Christie's, Zurich

VASARI, Giorgio (1511-1574) Italian
$520,000   £319,018   The Pieta (192x136cm-76x54in) panel prov. 27-Jan-00 Christie's, Rockefeller NY

VERELST, Pieter (c.1618-1668) Dutch
$279,300   £190,000   Head of a young boy (36x33cm-14x13in) init.d.1648 panel. 13-Dec-00 Christie's, London

VERNET, Joseph (attrib) (1714-1789) French
$338,150   £223,938   Harbour (89x138cm-35x54in) 11-May-00 Stuker, Bern

VIGNALI, Jacopo (1592-1664) Italian
$256,700   £170,000   Head of a young woman wearing a coral necklace (32x22cm-13x9in) i. col chk prov.exhib.lit. 5-Jul-00 Sotheby's, London

WATERHOUSE, John William (1849-1917) British
$9,060,000   £6,000,000   St Cecilia (123x201cm-48x79in) prov.exhib.lit. 14-Jun-00 Christie's, London

WATTEAU, Jean Antoine (1684-1721) French
$3,234,000   £2,200,000   Le Conteur, artist from the Commedia dell Arte in landscape (34 x 27cm-13x11in) panel prov.exhib.lit. 13-Dec-00 Christie's, London

WHEATLEY, Francis (1747-1801) British
$330,000   £227,586   Equestrian portrait Sir Henry Pigot (76x65cm-30x26in) s.d.1782 prov.lit. 6-Dec-00 Christie's, Rockefeller NY

WHISTLER, James Abbott McNeill (1834-1903) American
$2,600,000   £1,756,757   Harmony in grey, Chelsea in ice (45x61cm-18x24in) prov.exhib.lit. 25-May-00 Christie's, Rockefeller NY

WILLIAMS, Frederick Ronald (1927-1982) Australian
$251,670   £166,667   Green cloud and owl (183x153cm-72x60in) s.d.66 exhib.lit. 28-Jun-00 Christie's, Melbourne

WITTE, Emanuel de (1617-1692) Dutch
$317,100   £210,000   Interior of a church with a congregation listening to a sermon (57x51cm-22x20in) s.d.1671 prov. 7-Jul-00 Christie's, London

WRIGHT, John Michael (1617-1694) British
$437,900   £290,000   Portrait of Lord Mungo Murray in highland dress holding flintlock gun with sword at his side (217x151cm-85x59in) prov.exhib.lit. 14-Jun-00 Christie's, London

WYETH, Newell Convers (1882-1945) American
$570,000   £398,601   Chadda Ford Hills (109x122cm-43x48in) s. prov. 29-Nov-00 Christie's, Rockefeller

YEPES, Tomas (1600-1674) Spanish
$1,211,980   £807,985   Roses dans vase orne du lion de Leon. Oillets a la piece d'orfevrerie (87x75cm-34x30in) pair. 19-Jun-00 Neuilly St James, Neuilly

ZAO-WOU-KI (1920-) Chinese
$252,510   £171,773   Untitled (200x162cm-79x64in) prov.lit. 15-Dec-00 Laurence Calmels, Paris

ZARRAGA, Angel (1886-1946) Mexican
$260,000   £173,333   Novia (220x180cm-87x71in) s. painted c.1910 prov.exhib.lit. 1-Jun-00 Christie's, Rockefeller NY

ZONARO, Fausto (1854-1929) Italian
$390,000   £260,000   Dervish ceremony (100x201cm-39x79in) s.d.1910 prov. lit. 21-Jun-00 Christie's, London

THE $1,000,000 CLUB

for artists whose work has sold for over $1 million during 2000

ARCIMBOLDO, Giuseppe (1527-1593) Italian
$1,300,000   £797,546   Reversible anthropomorphic portrait of a man composed of fruit.
                              28-Jan-00 Sotheby's, NY

BACON, Francis (1909-1992) British
$4,077,000   £2,700,000   Study for a portrait - man screaming. 28-Jun-00 Christie's, London
$6,000,000   £4,225,352   Portrait of George Dyer talking. 15-Nov-00 Christie's, Rockefeller NY

BALTHUS (1908-2001) French
$2,800,000   £1,854,305   Nu aux bras leves. 10-May-00 Sotheby's, NY

BASQUIAT, Jean Michel (1960-1988) American
$1,250,000   £880,282   Life like son of Barney Hill. 16-Nov-00 Christie's, Rockefeller NY

BECKMANN, Max (1884-1950) German
$1,728,000   £1,200,000   Bar, brown. 18-Oct-00 Sotheby's, London

BELLOTTO, Bernardo (1720-1780) Italian
$1,812,000   £1,200,000   The Castelvecchio and the Ponte Scaligero, Verona. 7-Jul-00
                              Christie's, London

BENSON, Ambrosius (attrib) (?-1550) Flemish
$1,440,600   £980,000   Portrait of lady wearing dark costume and a white headdress, holding
                              a cat. 13-Dec-00 Christie's, London

BENSON, Frank W (1862-1951) American
$1,650,000   £1,114,865   The gray room. 25-May-00 Christie's, Rockefeller NY
$2,300,000   £1,554,054   Eleanor and Benny. 24-May-00 Sotheby's, NY

BLAKELOCK, Ralph Albert (1847-1919) American
$3,200,000   £2,162,162   Indian encampment along the Snake River. 24-May-00 Sotheby's, NY

BONNARD, Pierre (1867-1947) French
$1,300,000   £860,927   Fleurs avec poterie. 8-May-00 Christie's, Rockefeller NY
$3,900,000   £2,582,781   Nu sur fond jaune. 10-May-00 Sotheby's, NY

BOSSCHAERT, Ambrosius (elder) (1573-1621) Flemish
$2,642,500   £1,750,000   Still life of a bouquet of flowers, butterfly, dragonfly, sprig of
                              rosemary on a ledge. 6-Jul-00 Sotheby's, London

BOTH, Jan (1618-1652) Dutch
$1,963,000   £1,300,000   An Italianate evening landscape with a muleteer and goatherds on a
                              wooded path. 7-Jul-00 Christie's, London

BOUGUEREAU, William Adolphe (1825-1905) French
$3,200,000   £2,105,263   La charite. 1-May-00 Christie's, Rockefeller NY

BRANDT, Edgar (1880-1960) French
$1,700,000   £1,133,334   L'oasis. 8-Jun-00 Christie's, Rockefeller NY

BRAQUE, Georges (1882-1963) French
$2,800,000   £1,958,042   Paysage a la ciotat. 9-Nov-00 Sotheby's, NY

BROCQUY, Louis le (1916-) Irish
$1,554,000   £1,050,000   Travelling woman with newspaper. 18-May-00 Sotheby's, London

BRONZINO, Angelo (attrib) (1503-1572) Italian
$1,366,180   £968,921   Etude de Christ pour une Pieta'. 20-Nov-00 Piasa, Paris

BRUCE, Patrick Henry (1880-1937) American
$1,100,000   £769,231   Painting - still life. 30-Nov-00 Sotheby's, NY

BRUEGHEL, Jan (elder) (1568-1625) Flemish
$1,102,500   £750,000   Extensive landscape, figures on path. 14-Dec-00 Sotheby's, London
$1,396,500   £950,000   Broad landscape with travellers. 14-Dec-00 Sotheby's, London
$1,700,000   £1,042,945   Village street, carts, villagers and gentlefolk. 28-Jan-00 Sotheby's, NY

BUECKELAER, Joachim (1530-1573) Flemish
$3,969,000   £2,700,000   Four elements, greengrocer's stall. Earth, fishmonger's stall. Water,
                              poultry stall. Kitchen scene. 13-Dec-00 Christie's, London

BUNKER, Dennis M (1861-1890) American
$2,600,000   £1,756,757   The brook, Medfield. 24-May-00 Sotheby's, NY

CAILLEBOTTE, Gustave (1848-1894) French
$13,000,000   £8,609,273   L'homme au balcon, boulevard Haussmann. 8-May-00 Christie's, Rockefeller NY

CALDER, Alexander (1898-1976) American
$1,050,000   £739,437   Untitled. 14-Nov-00 Sotheby's, NY
$1,087,200   £720,000   Mobile au plomb. 28-Jun-00 Christie's, London
$3,800,000   £2,676,056   Stegosaurus. 14-Nov-00 Sotheby's, NY

CANALETTO (1697-1768) Italian
$1,500,000   £920,245   Church of the Redentore, Venice with sandalos and gondolas. 27-Jan-00 Christie's, Rockefeller NY
$1,500,000   £920,245   Church of St. Giorgio Maggiore, Venice with sandalos and gondolas. 27-Jan-00 Christie's, Rockefeller NY
$1,984,500   £1,350,000   Piazza San Marco, Venice, looking towards the Procuratie Nuove and the Church of San Geminiano. 13-Dec-00 Christie's, London
$6,000,000   £3,680,982   Grand Canal, Venice, looking from the Campo di San Vio. 27-Jan-00 Christie's, Rockefeller NY
$10,290,000   £7,000,000   Campo Santi Giovanni e Paolo, Venice, west end of the church and the Scuola di San Marco. 13-Dec-00 Christie's, London

CARRACCI, Lodovico (1555-1619) Italian
$4,750,000   £2,914,111   The Pieta. 27-Jan-00 Christie's, Rockefeller NY

CASSATT, Mary (1844-1926) American
$1,100,000   £743,243   Lydia seated on a porch crocheting. 24-May-00 Sotheby's, NY
$1,800,000   £1,258,741   En bateau, le bain. 9-Nov-00 Sotheby's, NY
$2,700,000   £1,888,112   Katharine Kelso Cassatt. 29-Nov-00 Christie's, Rockefeller NY

CASTIGLIONE, Giovanni Benedetto (1616-1670) Italian
$1,328,800   £880,000   Pagan sacrifice. 7-Jul-00 Christie's, London

CEZANNE, Paul (1839-1906) French
$1,650,000   £1,092,715   Chemin a l'entree de la foret. 8-May-00 Christie's, Rockefeller NY
$2,800,000   £1,958,042   Les deux vases de fleurs. 8-Nov-00 Christie's, Rockefeller NY
$3,322,000   £2,200,000   Tasse, verre et fruits, II. 27-Jun-00 Sotheby's, London
$4,600,000   £3,046,358   Environs de Gardanne. 11-May-00 Phillips, NY
$7,750,000   £5,419,581   La Cote au Galet, a Pontoise. 6-Nov-00 Phillips, NY
$16,610,000   £11,000,000   Nature morte aux fruits et pot de gingembre. 28-Jun-00 Christie's, London

CHAGALL, Marc (1887-1985) French/Russian
$1,100,000   £728,477   Autoportrait. 10-May-00 Sotheby's, NY
$1,200,000   £839,161   Fleurs. 9-Nov-00 Sotheby's, NY
$1,250,000   £827,815   Le violoniste. 9-May-00 Christie's, Rockefeller NY

CHIRICO, Giorgio de (1888-1978) Italian
$1,000,000   £699,301   Les philosophes grecs. 6-Nov-00 Phillips, NY

CHURCH, Frederic Edwin (1826-1900) American
$3,800,000   £2,567,568   Mount Newport on Mount Desert Island. 25-May-00 Christie's, Rockefeller NY

COURBET, Gustave (1819-1877) French
$2,000,000   £1,324,503   Portrait de Mademoiselle Jacquet. 11-May-00 Phillips, NY

CRANACH, Lucas (elder) (1472-1553) German
$1,736,500   £1,150,000   Portrait of a young lady wearing a red and orange dress and wide brimmed plumed hat. 6-Jul-00 Sotheby's, London
$2,328,670   £1,605,976   Venus et l'Amour voleur de miel. 4-Dec-00 Rieunier, Bailly-Pommery, Mathias, Paris

DALI, Salvador (1904-1989) Spanish
$1,200,000   £794,702   Galatee. 9-May-00 Christie's, Rockefeller NY
$1,400,000   £927,152   Chair de poule rhinocerontique. 10-May-00 Sotheby's, NY
$3,770,000   £2,600,000   Ma femme nue regardant son propre corps devenir marches. 4-Dec-00 Sotheby's, London

DEGAS, Edgar (1834-1917) French

$1,500,000	£1,048,951	Jeune danseuse nue. 9-Nov-00 Sotheby's, NY
$1,800,000	£1,192,053	Scene de ballet. 8-May-00 Christie's, Rockefeller NY
$2,700,000	£1,788,080	Danseuses bleutees - la repetition au foyer de la dans. 8-May-00 Christie's, Rockefeller NY
$2,700,000	£1,888,112	Apres le bain - femme s'essuyant les cheveux. 8-Nov-00 Christie's, Rockefeller NY
$3,800,000	£2,516,556	Le petit dejeuner apres le bain - jeune femme s'essuyant. 8-May-00 Christie's, Rockefeller NY
$4,800,000	£3,178,808	Preparation pour la classe. 10-May-00 Sotheby's, NY
$10,570,000	£7,000,000	Petite danseuse de quatorze ans. 27-Jun-00 Sotheby's, London

DELAUNAY, Robert (1885-1941) French

$2,718,000	£1,800,000	Homme a tulipe. 28-Jun-00 Christie's, London
$4,200,000	£2,781,457	Les fenetres simultanees. 10-May-00 Sotheby's, NY

DELVAUX, Paul (1897-1994) Belgian

$2,869,000	£1,900,000	Les promeneuses. 28-Jun-00 Christie's, London

DEWING, Maria Richards Oakey (1845-1927) American

$1,050,000	£709,459	Rose garden. 24-May-00 Sotheby's, NY

DIEBENKORN, Richard (1922-1993) American

$1,150,000	£761,589	Round table. 9-May-00 Christie's, Rockefeller NY

DIXON, Maynard (1875-1946) American

$1,200,000	£833,333	Pony boy. 30-Oct-00 Christie's, Los Angeles

DOMENICHINO (1581-1641) Italian

$3,000,000	£1,840,491	Rebuke of Adam and Eve. 28-Jan-00 Sotheby's, NY

DONGEN, Kees van (1877-1968) French/Dutch

$1,812,000	£1,200,000	Marchandes d'herbes. 28-Jun-00 Christie's, London
$1,887,500	£1,250,000	La dame au jabot. 27-Jun-00 Sotheby's, London

DRAPER, Herbert James (1864-1920) British

$1,144,000	£800,000	Mountain mist. 30-Nov-00 Christie's, London

DYCK, Sir Anthony van (1599-1641) Flemish

$1,029,000	£700,000	Bridled grey stallion, with saddle cloth and partially plaited mane. 13-Dec-00 Christie's, London

ERNST, Max (1891-1976) German

$1,300,000	£909,091	Gypsy Rose Lee. 8-Nov-00 Christie's, Rockefeller NY

FANTIN-LATOUR, Henri (1836-1904) French

$3,200,000	£2,237,762	Bouquet de fleurs. 8-Nov-00 Christie's, Rockefeller NY

FONTANA, Annibale (1540-c.1587) Italian

$1,543,500	£1,050,000	Dragon. 13-Dec-00 Sotheby's, London

FORBES, Stanhope Alexander (1857-1947) British

$1,650,000	£1,100,000	Seine boat. 6-Jun-00 Phillips, London

FRAGONARD, Jean Honore (1732-1806) French

$3,381,000	£2,300,000	Girl playing with a dog and a cat, said to be Marie Madeleine Colombe. 13-Dec-00 Christie's, London
$4,704,000	£3,200,000	Girl holding a dove said to be a portrait of Marie Catherine Colombe. 13-Dec-00 Christie's, London

FRANCIS, Sam (1923-1994) American

$2,000,000	£1,324,503	Untitled. 9-May-00 Christie's, Rockefeller NY

FRIESEKE, Frederick Carl (1874-1939) American

$1,100,000	£743,243	On the river. 24-May-00 Sotheby's, NY

GAUGUIN, Paul (1848-1903) French

$1,236,510	£777,676	Paysage de Pont Aven. Oie, Canard, bol et nature morte de fruits. 31-Mar-00 Piasa, Paris
$2,600,000	£1,721,854	Pecheur et baigneurs sur l'Aven. 10-May-00 Sotheby's, NY
$4,800,000	£3,178,808	Le toit bleu or ferme au pouldu. 8-May-00 Christie's, Rockefeller NY

GENTILESCHI, Orazio (1562-1647) Italian

$3,322,000	£2,200,000	The Holy Family with infant Saint John the Baptist in a landscape. 6-Jul-00 Sotheby's, London

GIACOMETTI, Alberto (1901-1966) Swiss
$1,150,000   £804,196   Femme debout. 9-Nov-00 Sotheby's, NY
$2,567,000   £1,700,000   Femme de Venise IV. 27-Jun-00 Sotheby's, London
$4,100,000   £2,715,232   La place. 10-May-00 Sotheby's, NY
$13,000,000   £9,090,910   Grande femme debout I. 8-Nov-00 Christie's, Rockefeller NY

GOGH, Vincent van (1853-1890) Dutch
$1,300,000   £860,927   L'avenue au parc de Voyer-d'Argenson a Asnieres. 8-May-00
                             Christie's, Rockefeller NY
$1,600,000   £1,059,603   L'entree de parc de Voyer-d'Argenson a Asnieres. 8-May-00
                             Christie's, Rockefeller NY
$4,200,000   £2,781,457   Flowers in a vase. 10-May-00 Sotheby's, NY

GONZALEZ, Julio (1876-1942) Spanish
$1,400,000   £927,152   Tete de jeune fille. 11-May-00 Phillips, NY

GONZALEZ-TORRES, Felix (1957-1996) American?
$1,500,000   £1,056,338   Untitled, Blood. 16-Nov-00 Christie's, Rockefeller NY

GORKY, Arshile (1904-1948) American
$2,000,000   £1,408,451   Khorkom. 14-Nov-00 Sotheby's, NY

GRECO, El (1541-1614) Spanish
$1,400,000   £858,896   Saint Paul. 27-Jan-00 Christie's, Rockefeller NY
$1,764,000   £1,200,000   Flight into Egypt. 13-Dec-00 Christie's, London
$5,285,000   £3,500,000   Christ on the cross. 6-Jul-00 Sotheby's, London

GRIS, Juan (1887-1927) Spanish
$1,200,000   £794,702   La casserole. 9-May-00 Christie's, Rockefeller NY

HARTLEY, Marsden (1877-1943) American
$2,000,000   £1,398,601   Abstraction. 30-Nov-00 Sotheby's, NY

HASSAM, Childe (1859-1935) American
$1,400,000   £979,021   Winter nightfall in the city. 30-Nov-00 Sotheby's, NY

HEADE, Martin Johnson (1819-1904) American
$1,350,000   £912,162   Magnolias on a wooden table. 25-May-00 Christie's, Rockefeller NY

HECKEL, Erich (1883-1970) German
$1,584,000   £1,100,000   Dangast village landscape. 18-Oct-00 Sotheby's, London

HODLER, Ferdinand (1853-1918) Swiss
$1,165,340   £776,892   The monk. 29-May-00 Sotheby's, Zurich
$1,296,750   £894,309   Le Grammont. 5-Dec-00 Christie's, Zurich
$1,296,750   £894,309   Happy woman. 5-Dec-00 Christie's, Zurich

HOMER, Winslow (1836-1910) American
$1,250,000   £844,595   How many eggs. 24-May-00 Sotheby's, NY
$1,400,000   £945,946   Farmyard wall. 24-May-00 Sotheby's, NY
$1,700,000   £1,148,649   Girl reading under a oak tree. 25-May-00 Christie's, Rockefeller NY
$2,600,000   £1,756,757   Uncle Ned at home. 24-May-00 Sotheby's, NY

KESSEL, Jan van I (1626-1679) Flemish
$1,500,000   £1,013,514   Study of butterflies, spiders, lizards, a beetle, an ant, grasshopper and
                             other insects. 25-May-00 Sotheby's, NY

KIRCHNER, Ernst Ludwig (1880-1938) German
$1,224,000   £850,000   Alpleben. 17-Oct-00 Christie's, London
$2,232,000   £1,550,000   Zwei akte auf blauem sofa. 17-Oct-00 Christie's, London

KLEIN, Yves (1928-1962) French
$1,900,000   £1,283,784   RE 40. 17-May-00 Sotheby's, NY
$6,100,000   £4,295,775   RE I. 15-Nov-00 Christie's, Rockefeller NY

KLINE, Franz (1910-1962) American
$2,300,000   £1,619,718   Black sienna. 15-Nov-00 Christie's, Rockefeller NY

KOONING, Willem de (1904-1997) American/Dutch
$1,250,000   £844,595   Untitled VI. 17-May-00 Sotheby's, NY
$1,736,500   £1,150,000   Untitled XVII. 29-Jun-00 Sotheby's, London
$2,400,000   £1,690,141   Monumental woman. 15-Nov-00 Christie's, Rockefeller NY
$4,100,000   £2,887,324   Woman, blue eyes. 15-Nov-00 Christie's, Rockefeller NY

KOONS, Jeff (1955-) American
$1,550,000   £1,047,297   Woman in tub. 16-May-00 Christie's, Rockefeller NY

LAFARGE, John (1835-1910) American
$1,900,000   £1,328,671   Last Valley - Paradise Rocks. 29-Nov-00 Christie's, Rockefeller NY

LANE, Fitz Hugh (1804-1865) American
$3,600,000   £2,432,433   The golden rule. 25-May-00 Christie's, Rockefeller NY

LANG SHINING (1688-1766) Italian/Chinese
$1,020,370   £708,592   Deer in an autumn forst. 30-Oct-00 Christie's, Hong Kong

LAVERY, Sir John (1856-1941) British
$1,332,000   £900,000   Woman and her dog, Grez-sur Loing. 18-May-00 Sotheby's, London

LEGER, Fernand (1881-1955) French
$1,600,310   £1,134,969   Les trois figures. 24-Nov-00 Villa Grisebach, Berlin
$1,736,500   £1,150,000   Deux femmes tenant un pot de fleurs. 28-Jun-00 Christie's, London
$2,300,000   £1,523,179   Composition no.1. 10-May-00 Sotheby's, NY

LEIGHTON, Lord Frederic (1830-1896) British
$1,812,000   £1,200,000   Bracelet. 14-Jun-00 Phillips, London

LIEBERMANN, Max (1847-1935) German
$1,087,540   £734,824   Tennis court in Noordwijk. 26-May-00 Villa Grisebach, Berlin

MACKE, August (1887-1914) German
$3,744,000   £2,600,000   Market in Tunis. 17-Oct-00 Christie's, London

MAGRITTE, René (1898-1967) Belgian
$1,208,000   £800,000   L'art de la conversation IV. 27-Jun-00 Sotheby's, London
$1,800,000   £1,192,053   L'automate. 10-May-00 Sotheby's, NY

MAILLOL, Aristide (1861-1944) French
$1,900,000   £1,328,671   La nuit. 8-Nov-00 Christie's, Rockefeller NY
$2,800,000   £1,958,042   L'air. 9-Nov-00 Sotheby's, NY

MALEVICH, Kasimir (1878-1935) Russian
$15,500,000   £10,264,902   Suprematist composition. 11-May-00 Phillips, NY

MANET, Edouard (1832-1883) French
$19,000,000   £13,286,715   Jeune fille dans un jardin. 9-Nov-00 Sotheby's, NY

MARDEN, Brice (1938-) American
$1,400,000   £945,946   Rain forest. 17-May-00 Sotheby's, NY
$1,700,000   £1,197,183   For pearl. 14-Nov-00 Sotheby's, NY

MARTIN, Agnes (1912-) American/Canadian
$1,100,000   £774,648   Untitled number 6. 15-Nov-00 Christie's, Rockefeller NY
$1,300,000   £878,378   Drift of summer. 18-May-00 Phillips, NY

MASTER OF THE DEATH OF SAINT NICHOLAS OF MUNSTER (15th C)
$3,200,000   £1,963,190   Calvary. 27-Jan-00 Christie's, Rockefeller NY

MATISSE, Henri (1869-1954) French
$1,262,950   £895,706   Fenetre ouverte, Etretat. 24-Nov-00 Villa Grisebach, Berlin
$2,450,000   £1,622,517   Etude pour nu rose. 9-May-00 Christie's, Rockefeller NY
$2,800,000   £1,854,305   Jeune femme fardee a l'orientale ou la bayadere. 10-May-00
                                          Sotheby's, NY
$4,500,000   £3,146,853   Les glaieuls. 6-Nov-00 Phillips, NY
$6,795,000   £4,500,000   Danseuse dans le fauteuil, sol en damier. 27-Jun-00 Sotheby's, London
$12,750,000   £8,443,709   La serpentine femme a la stele - l'araignee. 10-May-00 Sotheby's, NY
$15,500,000   £10,839,162   La robe persane. 9-Nov-00 Sotheby's, NY

MICHELANGELO (1475-1564) Italian
$11,174,000   £7,400,000   The risen Christ. 4-Jul-00 Christie's, London

MILLAIS, Sir John Everett (1829-1896) British
$1,208,000   £800,000   The brown boy - Master Liddell, son of Charles Liddell Esq.
                                          15-Jun-00 Sotheby's, London

MIRO, Joan (1893-1983) Spanish
$1,500,000   £993,378   Le Baiser. 11-May-00 Phillips, NY
$1,500,000   £1,048,951   Femme et oiseaux dans la nuit. 8-Nov-00 Christie's, Rockefeller NY
$1,900,000   £1,258,278   Le serpent a coquelicots trainant sur un champ de violettes peuple
                                          par des lezards en deuil. 9-May-00 Christie's, Rockefeller NY

MODIGLIANI, Amedeo (1884-1920) Italian

$1,500,000	£1,048,951	Paysage du Midi. 9-Nov-00 Sotheby's, NY
$1,800,000	£1,258,741	Portrait du photographe Dilewski. 8-Nov-00 Christie's, Rockefeller NY
$2,200,000	£1,456,954	Portrait de femme au corsage bleu. 9-May-00 Christie's, Rockefeller NY
$2,900,000	£1,920,530	La jeune fille a la rose. 10-May-00 Sotheby's, NY
$4,200,000	£2,937,063	Paul Guillaume. 9-Nov-00 Sotheby's, NY
$4,800,000	£3,356,644	Fillette assise. 8-Nov-00 Christie's, Rockefeller NY
$5,700,000	£3,774,835	La Rousse au pendentif. 10-May-00 Sotheby's, NY
$14,200,000	£9,930,071	Fillette assise en robe. 9-Nov-00 Sotheby's, NY

MONET, Claude (1840-1926) French

$1,000,000	£699,301	Voiliers. 8-Nov-00 Christie's, Rockefeller NY
$1,057,000	£700,000	La falaise d'Aval, la porte et L'Aigille. 27-Jun-00 Sotheby's, London
$1,100,000	£769,231	Bennecourt. 8-Nov-00 Christie's, Rockefeller NY
$1,500,000	£993,378	Falaise pres de Fecamp. 8-May-00 Christie's, Rockefeller NY
$1,500,000	£1,048,951	Iris. 8-Nov-00 Christie's, Rockefeller NY
$1,500,000	£1,048,951	Pommiers sur la cote de Chantemesle. 9-Nov-00 Sotheby's, NY
$2,100,000	£1,390,729	Camille assise sur la plage a Trouville. 10-May-00 Sotheby's, NY
$2,200,000	£1,456,954	La Gorge de Varengeville. 10-May-00 Sotheby's, NY
$2,250,000	£1,573,427	Aux petites dalles. 9-Nov-00 Sotheby's, NY
$2,600,000	£1,721,854	Effet de neige a Limetz. 10-May-00 Sotheby's, NY
$2,750,000	£1,821,192	Moulin en Hollande. 8-May-00 Christie's, Rockefeller NY
$3,926,000	£2,600,000	Pont Japonais. 28-Jun-00 Christie's, London
$4,600,000	£3,216,783	Antibes vue de la Salis. 9-Nov-00 Sotheby's, NY
$5,200,000	£3,636,364	Matinee sur la Seine. 9-Nov-00 Sotheby's, NY
$6,040,000	£4,000,000	Paysage de printemps. 28-Jun-00 Christie's, London
$6,200,000	£4,105,960	Le bassin aux nympheas. 8-May-00 Christie's, Rockefeller NY
$6,400,000	£4,475,525	Les peupliers. 8-Nov-00 Christie's, Rockefeller NY
$7,600,000	£5,033,113	Nympheas. 10-May-00 Sotheby's, NY
$15,100,000	£10,000,000	La plage a Trouville. 27-Jun-00 Sotheby's, London
$19,000,000	£12,582,783	Nympheas. 8-May-00 Christie's, Rockefeller NY
$22,000,000	£14,569,538	Le portail - soleil. 10-May-00 Sotheby's, NY

MORANDI, Giorgio (1890-1964) Italian

$1,102,000	£760,000	Still life. 25-Oct-00 Sotheby's, London

MORISOT, Berthe (1841-1895) French

$1,200,000	£794,702	Derriere la jalousie. 10-May-00 Sotheby's, NY
$4,000,000	£2,797,203	Cache-cache. 9-Nov-00 Sotheby's, NY

MUNNINGS, Sir Alfred (1878-1959) British

$1,050,000	£724,138	Sybil Harker on Saxa, with the Norwich staghounds. 6-Dec-00 Christie's, Rockefeller NY
$1,430,000	£1,000,000	Lord Astor's High Stakes with Sir Gordon Richards up at Newmarket. 30-Nov-00 Sotheby's, London
$1,812,000	£1,200,000	Arturo von Schroeders on a polo pony in a landscape. 14-Jun-00 Christie's, London
$2,750,000	£1,896,552	Gypsies arriving at Epsom. 6-Dec-00 Christie's, Rockefeller NY

NUSSBAUM, Felix (1904-1944) German

$1,584,000	£1,100,000	Self portrait in the camp. Still life. 18-Oct-00 Sotheby's, London

OSTADE, Isaac van (1621-1649) Dutch

$1,479,800	£980,000	Peasants drinking outside a vine laden inn, horseman on a piebald and boy carring a brace. 7-Jul-00 Christie's, London

PALMER, Samuel (1805-1881) British

$1,020,000	£680,000	Oak tree and beech, Lullingstone Park. 8-Jun-00 Christie's, London

PICASSO, Pablo (1881-1973) Spanish

$1,000,000	£699,301	Portrait de Marie Therese Walter. 9-Nov-00 Sotheby's, NY
$1,132,500	£750,000	Paysage. 29-Jun-00 Christie's, London
$2,100,000	£1,468,532	Femme dans un fauteuil, bust. 8-Nov-00 Christie's, Rockefeller NY
$2,265,000	£1,500,000	Tete de femme - Fernande. 27-Jun-00 Sotheby's, London
$2,400,000	£1,589,404	Femme assise, portrait de Francoise Gilot. 11-May-00 Phillips, NY
$3,000,000	£1,986,755	Femme dans un fauteuil. 10-May-00 Sotheby's, NY
$3,200,000	£2,237,762	L'atelier. 9-Nov-00 Sotheby's, NY
$3,400,000	£2,251,656	Le peintre et son modele. 9-May-00 Christie's, Rockefeller NY

... PICASSO, Pablo (1881-1973) Spanish

$4,000,000	£2,649,007	Nu couche et femme se lavant les pieds. 11-May-00 Phillips, NY
$4,100,000	£2,715,232	Buste de femme a la frange. 9-May-00 Christie's, Rockefeller NY
$4,300,000	£2,847,682	Buste de femme assise sur une chaise. 9-May-00 Christie's, Rockefeller NY
$4,500,000	£3,146,853	Femme a la collerette. 9-Nov-00 Sotheby's, NY
$5,750,000	£4,020,979	Les amants. 8-Nov-00 Christie's, Rockefeller NY
$7,200,000	£5,034,965	Le repos. 9-Nov-00 Sotheby's, NY
$9,000,000	£5,960,265	Compotier et guitare. 10-Nov-00 Sotheby's, NY
$26,000,000	£17,218,544	Nature morte aux tulips. 9-May-00 Christie's, Rockefeller NY
$50,000,000	£34,965,036	Femme aux bras croises. 8-Nov-00 Christie's, Rockefeller NY

PISSARRO, Camille (1830-1903) French

$1,200,000	£839,161	Route de Versailles a Saint-Germain a Louveciennes. 8-Nov-00 Christie's, Rockefeller NY
$1,400,000	£927,152	Port du Havre, maree haute. 11-May-00 Phillips, NY
$1,750,000	£1,223,776	Chaumieres a Auvers, pres de Pontoise. 9-Nov-00 Sotheby's, NY
$2,200,000	£1,456,954	Paysage a Osny pres l'abreuvoir. 8-May-00 Christie's, Rockefeller NY
$2,300,000	£1,608,392	Fete de Septembre, Pontoise. 6-Nov-00 Phillips, NY
$2,718,000	£1,800,000	Jardins potagers, Pontoise. 27-Jun-00 Sotheby's, London
$3,000,000	£2,097,902	Paysage avec rochers, Montfoucault. 9-Nov-00 Sotheby's, NY

POLKE, Sigmar (1941-) German

$1,500,000	£1,013,514	Zwei Frauen. 16-May-00 Christie's, Rockefeller NY

POST, Frans (1612-1680) Dutch

$2,600,000	£1,595,092	Brazilian landscape with natives on a road approaching a village. 28-Jan-00 Sotheby's, NY

PRENDERGAST, Maurice (1859-1924) American

$1,500,000	£1,048,951	Balloon. 30-Nov-00 Sotheby's, NY

RAY, Charles (1953-) American

$2,000,000	£1,408,451	Male mannequin. 16-Nov-00 Christie's, Rockefeller NY

REMBRANDT (1606-1669) Dutch

$2,300,000	£1,411,043	Ramparts near the bulwark beside city gate, St Anthonispoort, Amsterdam. 28-Jan-00 Christie's, Rockefeller NY
$3,400,000	£2,085,890	The bulwark De Rose and windmill De Smeerpot, Amsterdam. 28-Jan-00 Christie's, Rockefeller NY
$26,460,000	£18,000,000	Portrait of lady aged 62, perhaps Aeltje Pietersdr, Uylenburgh, wife of Johannes Cornelisz. 13-Dec-00 Christie's, London

RENOIR, Pierre Auguste (1841-1919) French

$1,000,000	£662,252	Femme assise. 10-May-00 Sotheby's, NY
$1,000,000	£699,301	Jardin a Alger. 9-Nov-00 Christie's, Rockefeller NY
$1,000,000	£662,252	Portrait de Gabrielle - jeune fille aux fleurs. 10-May-00 Sotheby's, NY
$1,057,000	£700,000	Jeune fille blonde. 28-Jun-00 Christie's, London
$1,100,000	£728,477	Madeleine au corsage blanc et bouquet de fleurs. 8-May-00 Christie's, Rockefeller NY
$1,200,000	£839,161	Femme au chapeau fleurs. 6-Nov-00 Phillips, NY
$1,200,000	£839,161	Etude de femme. 8-Nov-00 Christie's, Rockefeller NY
$1,300,000	£909,091	Nature morte, fleurs et fruits. 6-Nov-00 Phillips, NY
$1,400,000	£979,021	Tete d'enfant. 8-Nov-00 Christie's, Rockefeller NY
$1,500,000	£993,378	Tete de jeune fille. 8-May-00 Christie's, Rockefeller NY
$1,500,000	£1,048,951	Fille au chapeau aux eglantines. 6-Nov-00 Phillips, NY
$1,600,000	£1,118,881	Portrait de Pierre Renoir en costume marin. 8-Nov-00 Christie's, Rockefeller NY
$1,600,000	£1,059,603	Nature morte, le plat de prunes. 8-May-00 Christie's, Rockefeller NY
$5,200,000	£3,636,364	Jeune fille assise en costume Orientale. 8-Nov-00 Christie's, Rockefeller NY
$6,100,000	£4,265,735	Femmes dans un jardin. 6-Nov-00 Phillips, NY
$8,000,000	£5,298,014	Berthe Morisot et sa fille, Julie Manet. 8-May-00 Christie's, Rockefeller NY

REYNOLDS, Sir Joshua (1723-1792) British

$2,265,000	£1,500,000	The Archers, double portrait of John Dyke Acland and Thomas Townsend, Viscount Sydney. 14-Jun-00 Christie's, London

RICHTER, Gerhard (1932-) German
$1,208,000   £800,000   Korsika. 27-Jun-00 Christie's, London
$1,350,000   £912,162   Schaedel 545-3. 16-May-00 Christie's, Rockefeller NY
$1,500,000   £1,013,514   Apfelbaum. 18-May-00 Phillips, NY
$4,500,000   £3,169,014   Der Kongress, Professor Zander. 15-Nov-00 Christie's, Rockefeller NY

RODIN, Auguste (1840-1917) French
$1,100,000   £728,477   Faunesse debout. 10-May-00 Sotheby's, NY
$1,150,000   £761,589   Eve apres le peche. 8-May-00 Christie's, Rockefeller NY
$1,600,000   £1,059,603   L'eternel printemps, premier etat. 8-May-00 Christie's, Rockefeller NY
$2,500,000   £1,655,629   Le baiser. 8-May-00 Christie's, Rockefeller NY

ROSSETTI, Dante Gabriel (1828-1882) British
$3,624,000   £2,400,000   Pandora. 14-Jun-00 Christie's, London

ROTHKO, Mark (1903-1970) American
$1,000,000   £704,225   Composition. 15-Nov-00 Christie's, Rockefeller NY
$3,000,000   £2,112,676   Black in deep red. 15-Nov-00 Christie's, Rockefeller NY
$10,000,000   £7,042,254   Blue, red and green. 14-Nov-00 Sotheby's, NY
$13,000,000   £8,783,784   Yellow over purple. 17-May-00 Sotheby's, NY

RUBENS, Sir Peter Paul (1577-1640) Flemish
$1,900,000   £1,283,784   Virgin and Child enthroned adored by eight Saints. 26-May-00
       Christie's, Rockefeller NY
$4,228,000   £2,800,000   Diana and her nymphs hunting a modello. 7-Jul-00 Christie's, London
$7,500,000   £4,601,227   Portrait of a man as the God Mars. 28-Jan-00 Sotheby's, NY

RUSSELL, Charles M (1864-1926) American
$1,000,000   £666,667   Meat for wild men. 29-Jul-00 Coeur d'Alene, Hayden

SARTO, Andrea del (1487-1530) Italian
$1,000,000   £613,497   Madonna and Child. 28-Jan-00 Sotheby's, NY

SCHIELE, Egon (1890-1918) Austrian
$1,250,000   £874,126   Frau in gruner bluse mit muff. 8-Nov-00 Christie's, Rockefeller NY
$9,360,000   £6,500,000   Portrait of the art dealer Guido Arnot. 18-Oct-00 Sotheby's, London

SEURAT, Georges (1859-1891) French
$1,000,000   £662,252   La haie - la clairiere. 10-May-00 Sotheby's, NY

SISLEY, Alfred (1839-1899) French
$1,057,000   £700,000   Gelee blanche- ete de Saint-Martin. 28-Jun-00 Christie's, London
$1,300,000   £909,091   Le pont de Sevres. 8-Nov-00 Christie's, Rockefeller NY
$1,510,000   £1,000,000   Bords du Loing, Saint-Mammes. 28-Jun-00 Christie's, London
$1,800,000   £1,192,053   La Seine a Bougival. 8-May-00 Christie's, Rockefeller NY
$3,200,000   £2,119,205   Un jardin a Louveciennes, chemin de l'Etarche. 11-May-00 Phillips, NY

SLOAN, John (1871-1951) American
$2,000,000   £1,351,351   Bleeker street, Saturday night. 24-May-00 Sotheby's, NY

SPITZWEG, Carl (1808-1885) German
$1,078,900   £733,945   Young man offering flowers to young woman in narrow street.
       27-Sep-00 Neumeister, Munich

STAEL, Nicolas de (1914-1955) French
$1,350,000   £950,704   Atelier vert, coin d'atelier. 15-Nov-00 Christie's, Rockefeller NY

STELLA, Frank (1936-) American
$1,300,000   £915,493   Nothing happening. 14-Nov-00 Sotheby's, NY

STILL, Clyfford (1904-1980) American
$1,550,000   £1,047,297   Untitled. 17-May-00 Sotheby's, NY

STUBBS, George (1724-1806) British
$3,171,000   £2,100,000   Tristram Shandy, bay racehorse held by groom, in an extensive
       landscape. 14-Jun-00 Christie's, London
$3,575,000   £2,500,000   Euston, dappled grey racehorse, property of William Wildman, with
       jockey up in a landscape. 30-Nov-00 Sotheby's, London

TIEPOLO, Giovanni Battista (1696-1770) Italian
$2,000,000   £1,226,994   Alexander and Campaspe in the studio of Apelles. 27-Jan-00
       Christie's, Rockefeller NY

TITIAN (c.1488-1576) Italian

$3,322,000	£2,200,000	Portrait of Giacomo Doria wearing black robes. 7-Jul-00 Christie's, London

TOULOUSE-LAUTREC, Henri de (1864-1901) French

$2,100,000	£1,468,532	Le cotier de la compagnie des omnibus. 8-Nov-00 Christie's, Rockefeller NY
$3,775,000	£2,500,000	Helene V. 27-Jun-00 Sotheby's, London
$8,500,000	£5,629,139	L'abandon ou les deux amies. 10-May-00 Sotheby's, NY

TROY, Jean François de (1679-1752) French

$3,322,000	£2,200,000	Retour du bal. 4-Jul-00 Phillips, London

TWOMBLY, Cy (1929-) American

$2,600,000	£1,721,854	Untitled. 9-May-00 Christie's, Rockefeller NY

VALLOTTON, Felix (1865-1925) Swiss

$1,195,220	£796,813	Coucher de soleil. 29-May-00 Sotheby's, Zurich
$1,473,580	£1,016,260	On the beach. 5-Dec-00 Christie's, Zurich

VELDE, Willem van de (younger) (1633-1707) Dutch

$2,058,000	£1,400,000	Wijdschip close hauled in a fresh breeze, with other shipping. 13-Dec-00 Christie's, London

VUILLARD, Edouard (1868-1940) French

$1,000,000	£662,252	Les enfants. 8-May-00 Christie's, Rockefeller NY
$1,026,800	£680,000	Maurice Gangnat and his son Philippe in an interior. 27-Jun-00 Sotheby's, London
$2,700,000	£1,888,112	Place Vintimille. 8-Nov-00 Christie's, Rockefeller NY

WARHOL, Andy (1928-1987) American

$1,000,000	£662,252	40 two dollar bills. 9-May-00 Christie's, Rockefeller NY
$1,700,000	£1,197,183	Flowers. 13-Nov-00 Phillips, NY
$2,500,000	£1,689,189	Natalie Wood. 17-May-00 Sotheby's, NY
$2,500,000	£1,760,563	Marilyn. 14-Nov-00 Sotheby's, NY
$4,000,000	£2,816,902	Liz. 15-Nov-00 Christie's, Rockefeller NY
$4,200,000	£2,957,747	Group of five, Campbell's Soup cans. 15-Nov-00 Christie's, Rockefeller NY

WATERHOUSE, John William (1849-1917) British

$2,265,000	£1,500,000	Ophelia. 14-Jun-00 Phillips, London
$9,060,000	£6,000,000	St Cecilia. 14-Jun-00 Christie's, London

WATTEAU, Jean Antoine (1684-1721) French

$3,234,000	£2,200,000	Le Conteur, artist from the Commedia dell Arte in a landscape. 13-Dec-00 Christie's, London

WHISTLER, James Abbott McNeill (1834-1903) American

$2,600,000	£1,756,757	Harmony in grey, Chelsea in ice. 25-May-00 Christie's, Rockefeller NY

YEATS, Jack Butler (1871-1957) Irish/British

$1,258,000	£850,000	The women of the west. 18-May-00 Sotheby's, London

SUMMARIZED SALE RESULTS

BY MEDIA FOR THE TWELVE MONTHS

JANUARY TO DECEMBER 2000

Name	No.	Total Sales Value	lowest	Prices median	highest
AABYE, Jorgen (1868-1959) Danish					
oil	1	1,150		1,150	
AAE, Arvid (1877-1913) Swedish					
oil	1	4,826		4,826	
AAGAARD, C F (1833-1895) Danish					
oil	6	14,042	1,690	2,104	3,614
AAGAARD, Carl Frederic (1833-1895) Danish					
oil	10	50,339	1,850	3,334	19,000
AALAND, H P (?) Danish?					
oil	1	1,331		1,331	
AAMUND, Susanne (1943-) Danish					
oil	1	1,003		1,003	
AARONS, George (1896-1980) American					
3D	1	3,750		3,750	
AARTMANN, Nicolaas (1713-1793) Dutch					
wc/d	1	2,357		2,357	
ABACCHI, T (1831-1905) Italian					
3D	1	11,100		11,100	
ABADES, Juan Martinez (1862-1920) Spanish					
oil	7	58,217	2,048	9,117	14,518
ABAKANOWICZ, Magdalena (1930-) Polish					
3D	1	48,000		48,000	
ABALLEA, Martine (20th C) French					
3D	1	1,607		1,607	
ABART, Franz (1769-1863) Swiss					
3D	2	2,632	1,094	1,316	1,538
ABATTUCI, Pierre (1871-1942) Belgian					
oil	1	1,824		1,824	
ABBASI, Shaykh (fl.1650-1683) Persian					
wc/d	1	21,000		21,000	
ABBEMA, Louise (1858-1927) French					
oil	5	46,418	2,938	3,312	20,000
ABBEY, Edwin Austin (1852-1911) American					
wc/d	1	3,750		3,750	
ABBOTT, C (19th C) Australian?					
wc/d	1	1,323		1,323	
ABBOTT, John White (1763-1851) British					
wc/d	2	222,559	1,359	111,280	221,200
ABBOTT, Lemuel Francis (1760-1803) British					
oil	3	43,252	6,342	12,750	24,160
ABBOTT, Yarnell (1870-1938) American					
oil	1	2,600		2,600	
ABBOUD, Chafik (1926-) Lebanese					
oil	5	32,245	1,141	8,555	9,981
ABEAUVAIN, Pinson (18th C) German?					
oil	1	1,212		1,212	
ABEL, Ernst Heinrich (c.1737-?) German					
oil	1	3,409		3,409	
ABEL-TRUCHET (1857-1918) French					
oil	4	28,059	2,800	6,368	12,523
ABELA, Eduardo (1891-1965) Cuban					
oil	2	5,500	1,000	2,750	4,500
ABELENDA ESCUDERO, Alfonso (1931-) Spanish					
oil	1	3,989		3,989	
wc/d	1	1,816		1,816	
ABELLO PRAT, Joan (1922-) Spanish					
oil	1	2,829		2,829	
wc/d	1	1,076		1,076	

Name	No.	Total Sales Value	lowest	Prices median	highest
ABELS, Jacobus Theodorus (1803-1866) Dutch					
oil	1	1,075		1,075	
ABELS, Peter Josef (1954-) German					
3D	1	1,081		1,081	
ABERCROMBIE, John Brown (1843-1929) British					
oil	1	1,740		1,740	
ABERDAM, Alfred (1894-1963) Polish					
oil	4	4,576	1,033	1,072	1,400
ABERG, Pelle (1909-1964) Swedish					
oil	33	76,537	1,014	1,721	9,359
wc/d	1	2,408		2,408	
ABERLI, Johann Ludwig (1723-1786) Swiss					
wc/d	1	7,906		7,906	
ABERNATHY, J (19th C) ?					
oil	1	1,480		1,480	
ABIDINE, Dino (1913-) French					
oil	1	11,541		11,541	
wc/d	1	2,656		2,656	
ABILDGAARD, Nicolai Abraham (1743-1809) Danish					
oil	1	39,444		39,444	
ABRAHAMSEN, Emil (1875-1964) Norwegian					
oil	1	1,392		1,392	
ABRAHAMSSON, Erik (1871-1907) Swedish					
oil	1	1,558		1,558	
ABREU BASTOS, Anton (1927-) Spanish					
oil	1	1,041		1,041	
ABRIL, Ben (1923-1995) American					
oil	1	1,300		1,300	
ABSOLON, John (1815-1895) British					
wc/d	2	2,764	1,026	1,382	1,738
ABT, Otto (1903-1982) Swiss					
oil	1	2,308		2,308	
ACCARD, Eugène (1824-1888) French					
oil	1	6,617		6,617	
ACCARDI, Carla (1924-) Italian					
oil	5	20,690	1,745	2,773	10,676
wc/d	2	20,702	10,230	10,351	10,472
ACCONCI, Vito (1940-) American					
3D	1	3,500		3,500	
ACEBAL Y DIGORAS, Arturo (1912-1978) Argentinian					
3D	1	2,279		2,279	
ACEVES, Tomas (19th C) Spanish					
oil	2	14,880	4,380	7,440	10,500
ACHEFF, William (1947-) American					
oil	1	35,000		35,000	
ACHEN, Georg (1860-1912) Danish					
oil	4	21,788	1,199	3,742	13,106
ACHENBACH, Andreas (1815-1910) German					
oil	5	50,598	3,182	6,364	27,323
wc/d	2	2,277	1,100	1,139	1,177
ACHENBACH, Oswald (1827-1905) German					
oil	19	533,550	1,400	14,359	120,000
ACHILLES, August (19th C) German?					
oil	1	1,181		1,181	
ACKE, J A G (1859-1924) Swedish					
oil	1	1,919		1,919	
ACKE, Johan Axel Gustaf (1859-1924) Swedish					
oil	2	11,562	2,772	5,781	8,790

Name	No.	Total Sales Value	Prices lowest	median	highest
ACKER, Florimond van (1858-1940) Belgian					
oil	1	14,554		14,554	
ACKER, Johannes Baptista van (1794-1863) Flemish					
wc/d	1	2,538		2,538	
ACKER, van (?) ?					
oil	1	1,664		1,664	
ACKERBERG, A (19th C) Danish?					
oil	1	3,048		3,048	
ACKERMANN (?) ?					
oil	1	4,046		4,046	
ACKERMANN, Gerald (1876-1960) British					
wc/d	7	13,429	1,200	1,885	3,108
ACKERMANN, Max (1887-1975) German					
oil	3	10,299	1,413	2,831	6,055
wc/d	13	69,548	1,099	3,418	22,136
ACKERMANN, R (?) German?					
oil	1	1,024		1,024	
ACKROYD, Norman (1938-) American					
oil	1	1,223		1,223	
ACORES, Augusto (19/20th C) American					
wc/d	1	1,900		1,900	
ACOSTA LEON, Angel (1932-1964) Cuban					
oil	1	7,000		7,000	
wc/d	1	1,188		1,188	
ACS, Agostos (1889-1947) Hungarian					
oil	1	1,387		1,387	
ADAM, Albrecht (1786-1862) German					
oil	1	17,875		17,875	
ADAM, Benno (1812-1892) German					
oil	3	35,731	1,859	3,872	30,000
ADAM, Edmond (1868-1938) French					
oil	1	6,825		6,825	
ADAM, Edouard (jnr) (1868-1938) French					
oil	3	10,681	2,385	2,546	5,750
ADAM, Edouard (1847-1929) French					
oil	2	13,661	1,661	6,831	12,000
ADAM, Emil (1843-1924) German					
oil	3	10,552	2,364	2,972	5,216
ADAM, Eugen (1817-1880) German					
oil	1	2,394		2,394	
ADAM, Franz (1815-1886) German					
oil	1	1,275		1,275	
ADAM, Joseph Denovan (1842-1896) British					
oil	2	8,774	4,350	4,387	4,424
wc/d	3	12,969	2,940	5,024	5,024
ADAM, Joseph and Joseph Denovan (19th C) British					
oil	1	3,020		3,020	
ADAM, Otto (1901-1973) German					
oil	3	5,371	1,150	1,346	2,875
ADAM, P H (19/20th C) Irish?					
oil	1	1,160		1,160	
ADAM, Patrick William (1854-1929) British					
oil	9	60,905	2,409	5,110	17,520
ADAM, Richard Benno (1873-1937) German					
oil	1	1,302		1,302	
ADAM, William (1846-1931) American					
oil	1	3,250		3,250	
ADAMI, Valerio (1935-) Italian					
oil	19	159,267	3,494	7,370	18,441

Name	No.	Total Sales Value	Prices lowest	Prices median	highest
wc/d	8	15,039	1,309	1,625	3,342

ADAMS, Alfred (?) British
| wc/d | 1 | 1,184 | | 1,184 | |

ADAMS, C J (1857-1931) British
| wc/d | 2 | 5,404 | 1,232 | 2,702 | 4,172 |

ADAMS, Charles James (1857-1931) British
| wc/d | 7 | 21,717 | 1,287 | 2,086 | 5,700 |

ADAMS, Charles Partridge (1858-1942) American
| oil | 2 | 8,250 | 2,250 | 4,125 | 6,000 |
| wc/d | 1 | 3,250 | | 3,250 | |

ADAMS, Douglas (1853-1920) British
| oil | 1 | 1,650 | | 1,650 | |

ADAMS, Franklin (20th C) American
| oil | 1 | 2,250 | | 2,250 | |

ADAMS, Herbert (1858-1945) American
| 3D | 2 | 34,000 | 4,000 | 17,000 | 30,000 |

ADAMS, John Clayton (1840-1906) British
| oil | 6 | 59,671 | 2,054 | 10,050 | 20,300 |

ADAMS, M E (?) ?
| wc/d | 1 | 1,590 | | 1,590 | |

ADAMS, Norman (1927-) British
| wc/d | 1 | 1,130 | | 1,130 | |

ADAMS, Sarah (1958-) British
| oil | 1 | 4,440 | | 4,440 | |

ADAMS, Scott (20th C) American?
| wc/d | 1 | 1,200 | | 1,200 | |

ADAMS, Stephen (1953-) British
| oil | 1 | 4,260 | | 4,260 | |

ADAMS, Wayman (1883-1959) American
| oil | 1 | 6,750 | | 6,750 | |

ADAMSKI, Hans Peter (1947-) German?
| oil | 1 | 2,438 | | 2,438 | |

ADAMSON, A E (19th C) ?
| wc/d | 1 | 1,176 | | 1,176 | |

ADAMSON, Harry Curieux (20th C) American
| oil | 1 | 17,000 | | 17,000 | |

ADAMSSON, Bo Ake (1941-) Swedish
| oil | 1 | 3,455 | | 3,455 | |

ADAN, Louis Émile (1839-1937) French
| oil | 3 | 12,347 | 1,547 | 1,800 | 9,000 |

ADCOCK, Liliane (20th C) Belgian?
| oil | 1 | 1,138 | | 1,138 | |

ADDAMS, Charles (1912-1988) American
| wc/d | 4 | 17,450 | 2,200 | 4,625 | 6,000 |

ADLER, Edmund (1871-1957) German
| oil | 7 | 83,470 | 2,000 | 16,000 | 22,120 |

ADLER, Jankel (1895-1949) Polish
| oil | 5 | 59,998 | 6,000 | 6,000 | 21,998 |
| wc/d | 2 | 14,920 | 2,920 | 7,460 | 12,000 |

ADLER, Jules (1865-1952) French
| oil | 1 | 2,226 | | 2,226 | |

ADLER, Rose (20th C) ?
| wc/d | 1 | 13,103 | | 13,103 | |

ADLIVANKIN, Samuil Yakovlevich (1897-1966) Russian
| wc/d | 1 | 12,000 | | 12,000 | |

ADNET, Françoise (1924-) French
| oil | 1 | 1,490 | | 1,490 | |

ADNET, Jacques (1900-1984) French
| 3D | 1 | 1,359 | | 1,359 | |

Name	No.	Total Sales Value	lowest	Prices median	highest
ADOLFS, Gerard Pieter (1897-1968) Dutch					
oil	4	6,515	1,308	1,660	1,888
ADOLPH (?) ?					
3D	1	3,180		3,180	
ADOMEIT, George G (1879-1967) American					
oil	1	1,750		1,750	
ADRIAENSSEN, Alexander (1587-1661) Flemish					
oil	1	15,100		15,100	
ADRIAENSSEN, Vincent (1595-1675) Flemish					
oil	1	10,990		10,990	
ADRIAN-NILSSON, Gosta (1884-1965) Swedish					
oil	8	206,351	1,355	27,794	55,773
wc/d	21	70,567	1,059	2,839	13,547
ADRIATIC SCHOOL, 16th/17th C					
oil	1	9,060		9,060	
ADRIATIC SCHOOL, 18th C					
oil	1	4,710		4,710	
ADRION, Lucien (1889-1953) French					
oil	15	54,348	1,070	2,508	12,720
ADULKAR, Vasudeo Sitaram (1907-) Indian					
oil	1	1,500		1,500	
ADZAK, Roy (1927-1987) British					
wc/d	1	2,921		2,921	
AEBI, Ernst (1896-?) Swiss					
oil	1	1,807		1,807	
AECKERLIN, Christian (1884-?) German					
3D	1	1,400		1,400	
AELST, Pieter Coecke van (1502-1550) Flemish					
oil	1	37,407		37,407	
AELST, Willem van (1626-1683) Dutch					
oil	1	205,800		205,800	
AELST, Willem van and PICART, Jean Michel (17th C) Dutch/Flemish					
oil	1	558,700		558,700	
AELST, van (16/17th C) Flemish/Dutch					
oil	1	1,400		1,400	
AEMISEGGER-GIEZENDANNER, Anna Barbara (1831-1905) Swiss					
oil	1	6,484		6,484	
wc/d	1	11,789		11,789	
AENDA, G (?) ?					
3D	1	1,300		1,300	
AERENS, Robert (1883-1969) Belgian					
oil	1	2,146		2,146	
AERNI, Franz Theodor (1853-1918) German					
oil	2	12,018	2,480	6,009	9,538
AERS, Marguerite (1918-1995) Belgian					
oil	3	4,443	1,167	1,234	2,042
AERTS, Hendrick (16th C) Flemish					
oil	1	20,385		20,385	
AERTSEN, Pieter (1507-1575) Dutch					
oil	3	105,150	24,480	24,480	55,000
AERTTINGER, Carl August (1803-1876) German					
oil	1	15,000		15,000	
AESCHBACHER, Arthur (1923-) Swiss					
wc/d	2	2,140	1,021	1,070	1,119
AESCHBACHER, Hans (1906-) Swiss					
3D	1	2,824		2,824	
AFFLECK, William (1869-1909) British					
wc/d	2	3,715	1,570	1,858	2,145

Name	No.	Total Sales Value	Prices lowest	Prices median	highest
AFFORTUNATI, Aldo (1906-) Italian					
oil	1	1,730		1,730	
AFRICAN SCHOOL, 19th C					
3D	1	19,791		19,791	
AFRICANO, Nicholas (1948-) American					
3D	1	12,000		12,000	
AFRO (1912-1976) Italian					
oil	5	246,698	9,220	30,088	120,000
wc/d	6	316,586	7,201	33,916	152,250
AGAM, Yaacov (1928-) Israeli					
3D	1	1,066		1,066	
oil	3	43,600	1,600	12,000	30,000
wc/d	2	3,923	1,933	1,962	1,990
AGAR, Eileen (1904-1991) British					
wc/d	4	6,026	1,106	1,290	2,340
AGASSE, Jacques Laurent (1767-1849) Swiss					
oil	4	104,083	13,673	25,225	39,960
AGAZZI, Ermenegildo (1866-1945) Italian					
oil	1	3,200		3,200	
AGAZZI, Rinaldo (1857-1939) Italian					
oil	1	3,709		3,709	
AGERSNAP, Hans (1857-1925) Danish					
oil	1	1,008		1,008	
AGGER, Knud (1895-1973) Danish					
oil	1	1,114		1,114	
AGLIETTI, Romeo (19/20th C) Italian					
oil	2	5,460	2,730	2,730	2,730
AGLIO, Agostino (1777-1857) Italian					
oil	3	6,192	1,454	1,738	3,000
AGNELLILA, R (19/20th C) Swiss?					
oil	1	1,776		1,776	
AGNETTI, Vincenzo (1926-) Italian					
oil	2	4,194	1,848	2,097	2,346
AGOSTINI, E (fl.1871-1898) Italian					
oil	1	1,964		1,964	
AGOSTINI, Max Michel (1914-1997) French					
oil	3	4,355	1,374	1,488	1,493
AGOSTINI, Tony (1916-1990) Italian					
oil	3	3,777	1,113	1,355	1,355
AGOSTINO, Guido (19th C) Italian					
oil	1	2,546		2,546	
AGRASOT Y JUAN, Joaquim (1837-1919) Spanish					
oil	3	17,178	2,594	3,989	10,595
wc/d	3	12,595	2,024	2,024	8,547
AGRESTI (?) Italian					
oil	1	1,469		1,469	
AGRESTI, R (19th C) French					
oil	1	2,370		2,370	
AGRICOLA, Carl Joseph (1779-1852) German					
wc/d	1	1,753		1,753	
AGRICOLA, Eduard (1800-?) German					
oil	1	8,030		8,030	
AGRICOLA, Rudolf Alexander (1912-) Russian					
3D	1	1,262		1,262	
AGTERBERG, Chris (1883-1948) Dutch					
oil	1	4,087		4,087	
AGUAYO, Fermin (1926-1977) Spanish					
oil	2	3,009	1,063	1,505	1,946

Name	No.	Total Sales Value	lowest	Prices median	highest
AGUELI, Ivan (1869-1917) Swedish					
oil	2	42,001	16,042	21,001	25,959
AGUIAR GARCIA, Jose (1898-1976) Cuban					
oil	1	6,991		6,991	
AGUILAR MORE, Ramon (1924-) Spanish					
oil	1	1,906		1,906	
AGUTTE, Georgette (1867-1922) French					
oil	1	3,850		3,850	
AH, Quah (?) ?					
wc/d	1	2,250		2,250	
AHEARN, John (1951-) American					
3D	1	1,366		1,366	
AHL, Henry Hammond (1869-1953) American					
oil	1	7,000		7,000	
AHLERS-HESTERMANN, Friedrich (1883-1973) German					
oil	2	5,125	1,550	2,563	3,575
AHLGRENSSON, Bjorn (1872-1918) Swedish					
oil	4	13,265	1,156	3,209	5,692
AHNERT, Artur (1885-?) Swiss					
oil	1	1,253		1,253	
AHRENDTS, Carl Eduard (1822-1898) Dutch					
oil	1	1,832		1,832	
AHRENDTS, Conrad (1855-1901) German					
oil	1	1,133		1,133	
AHRENS, Max (1898-1967) German					
oil	1	1,505		1,505	
AI XUAN (20th C) Chinese					
oil	1	7,000		7,000	
AICHELE, Paul (19/20th C) German					
3D	2	17,571	2,451	8,786	15,120
AID, George-Charles (1872-1938) American					
oil	1	5,000		5,000	
AIGEN, Karl (1685-1762) Austrian					
oil	1	16,366		16,366	
AIKMAN, George W (1831-1906) British					
oil	2	4,320	1,562	2,160	2,758
AIKMAN, William (1682-1731) British					
oil	1	1,015		1,015	
AILLAUD, Gilles (1928-) French					
oil	2	12,608	5,731	6,304	6,877
AIMETTI, Carlo (1901-) Italian					
oil	1	1,070		1,070	
AIRY, Anna (1882-1964) British					
oil	1	5,434		5,434	
AISTROP, E (19/20th C) British					
oil	12	24,709	1,216	2,273	2,860
AITKEN, James (fl.1880-1935) British					
wc/d	5	7,352	1,073	1,482	1,872
AITKEN, James A (1846-1897) British					
oil	1	2,983		2,983	
AITKEN, John Ernest (1881-1957) British					
wc/d	13	31,782	1,248	2,496	5,863
AIVAZOFFSKI, Ivan (1817-1900) Russian					
oil	20	1,174,332	2,265	26,330	428,502
wc/d	2	5,099	1,812	2,550	3,287
AIZAVEROL, G (20th C) ?					
wc/d	1	1,670		1,670	
AIZELIN (19th C) French					
3D	1	1,241		1,241	

Name	No.	Total Sales Value	lowest	Prices median	highest
AIZELIN, Eugène (1821-1902) French					
3D	5	10,189	1,138	1,961	3,528
AIZENBERG, Nina Evseevna (1902-) Russian					
wc/d	1	2,800		2,800	
AIZPIRI, Paul (1919-) French					
oil	11	101,245	2,578	8,558	15,037
wc/d	2	11,012	5,121	5,506	5,891
AJDUKIEWICZ, Thaddeus von (1852-1916) Polish					
oil	2	70,160	3,000	35,080	67,160
AJMONE, Giuseppe (1923-) Italian					
oil	3	6,675	1,745	2,094	2,836
AJMONE, Lidio (1884-1945) Italian					
oil	7	18,892	1,333	1,839	5,240
AKEN, Frans van (18th C) Dutch					
oil	1	9,060		9,060	
AKEN, Jan van (18th C) Flemish					
wc/d	1	1,323		1,323	
AKERS, Benjamin Paul (1825-1861) American					
3D	1	2,500		2,500	
AKERS, Vivian Milner (1886-1966) American					
oil	1	3,000		3,000	
AKIN, Louis B (1868-1913) American					
oil	1	6,000		6,000	
AKKERINGA, Johannes Evert Hendrik (1861-1942) Dutch					
oil	6	134,675	2,360	23,499	44,554
wc/d	1	1,963		1,963	
AKKERMAN, Ben (1920-) Dutch					
oil	2	14,440	4,095	7,220	10,345
ALARCON, Jose (19th C) Spanish					
oil	2	4,337	2,153	2,169	2,184
ALARCON, Jose Maria (19th C) Spanish					
oil	1	4,152		4,152	
ALASTAIR (20th C) German					
wc/d	1	9,500		9,500	
ALAUX, Guillaume (?-1913) French					
oil	1	1,963		1,963	
ALAUX, Gustave (1887-1965) French					
oil	3	25,996	3,675	11,056	11,265
ALBA, Jose Mariano (17/18th C) European					
wc/d	1	1,600		1,600	
ALBACETE, Alfonso (1950-) Spanish					
oil	2	8,631	1,886	4,316	6,745
ALBANI, Francesco (1578-1660) Italian					
oil	2	292,170	22,170	146,085	270,000
wc/d	1	2,600		2,600	
ALBANI, Francesco (school) (1578-1660) Italian					
oil	1	4,812		4,812	
ALBERS, Hermann (20th C) ?					
wc/d	1	4,125		4,125	
ALBERS, Josef (1888-1976) American					
oil	20	604,934	1,252	23,500	70,000
wc/d	3	6,673	1,063	1,709	3,901
ALBERT, Ernest (1857-1946) American					
oil	1	1,200		1,200	
ALBERT, Ernest (1900-1976) Belgian					
oil	2	2,574	1,231	1,287	1,343
ALBERT, Gustaf (1866-1905) Swedish					
oil	2	15,718	3,298	7,859	12,420

Name	No.	Total Sales Value	lowest	Prices median	highest
ALBERT, Jos (1886-1981) Belgian					
oil	5	32,864	1,880	4,310	18,189
ALBERT-LEFEUVRE, Louis Étienne Marie (19th C) French					
3D	1	1,100		1,100	
ALBERTI, C (19th C) German					
oil	1	3,867		3,867	
ALBERTI, Cherubino (1553-1615) Italian					
wc/d	1	1,413		1,413	
ALBERTI, Giuseppe Vizzotto (19th C) Italian					
oil	1	12,784		12,784	
wc/d	2	4,380	1,606	2,190	2,774
ALBERTINI, Oreste (1887-1953) Italian					
oil	4	36,907	4,852	7,710	16,636
ALBERTIS, Sebastiano de (1828-1897) Italian					
oil	2	25,939	3,643	12,970	22,296
wc/d	2	11,236	1,605	5,618	9,631
ALBERTO (19th C) Italian					
oil	1	1,296		1,296	
ALBERTO, Pietro (1929-) Italian					
oil	2	3,653	1,724	1,827	1,929
ALBERTS, Willem Jacobus (1912-) Dutch					
oil	1	1,770		1,770	
ALBIKER, Karl (1878-1961) German					
3D	1	1,709		1,709	
ALBINET, Jean Paul (1954-) French					
oil	1	2,191		2,191	
ALBOTTO, Francesco (1722-1758) Italian					
oil	2	56,400	19,536	28,200	36,864
ALBRECHT, Carl (1862-1926) German					
oil	1	1,495		1,495	
ALBRECHT-SERVESTA, Herman (1871-?) German					
oil	1	3,226		3,226	
ALBRIGHT, Adam Emory (1862-1957) American					
oil	5	51,200	2,200	12,000	20,000
ALBRIGHT, Gertrude Partington (1883-1959) American					
oil	2	14,000	7,000	7,000	7,000
ALBRIGHT, Henry James (1887-1951) American					
oil	1	2,000		2,000	
ALCACER, Jose Antonio (1939-) Spanish					
oil	1	1,716		1,716	
ALCAIN, Alfredo (1936-) Spanish					
oil	1	1,229		1,229	
ALCALDE, Juan (1918-) Spanish					
oil	3	4,448	1,069	1,412	1,967
ALCANTARA, Antonio (1918-) Venezuelan					
oil	2	4,305	1,720	2,153	2,585
ALCAYDE Y MONTOYA, Julia (1885-1939) Spanish					
oil	1	6,328		6,328	
ALCHIMOWITZ, Kasimir (1840-?) Polish					
oil	1	7,295		7,295	
ALCOLEA, Carlos (1949-1992) Spanish					
oil	1	21,732		21,732	
ALCORLO BARRERA, Manuel (1935-) Spanish					
oil	1	1,126		1,126	
ALDEGREVER, Heinrich (1502-1558) German					
wc/d	1	140,000		140,000	
ALDEHUELA, Luis (?) Spanish?					
oil	1	2,406		2,406	

Name	No.	Total Sales Value	lowest	Prices median	highest
ALDERSON, Dorothy Margaret and Elizabeth Mary (20th C) British					
wc/d	2	3,129	1,549	1,565	1,580
ALDHAM, Harriet Kate (fl.1867-1876) British					
oil	1	1,587		1,587	
ALDI, Pietro (1852-1888) Italian					
oil	1	14,600		14,600	
ALDIN, Cecil (1870-1935) British					
oil	1	3,190		3,190	
wc/d	7	26,639	1,392	2,573	7,550
ALDINE, Marc (1917-) Italian					
oil	2	54,000	27,000	27,000	27,000
ALDRICH, George Ames (1872-1941) American					
oil	4	21,500	2,500	4,000	11,000
ALDRIDGE, Frederick James (1850-1933) British					
oil	2	3,220	1,440	1,610	1,780
wc/d	8	17,033	1,020	2,256	4,134
ALDRIDGE, John Arthur Malcolm (1905-1983) British					
oil	2	2,883	1,050	1,442	1,833
ALDRIDGE, R L (fl.1866-1887) British					
oil	1	1,454		1,454	
ALDRIN, Anders Gustave (1899-1970) American					
oil	1	1,300		1,300	
ALECHINSKY, Pierre (1927-) Belgian					
3D	2	11,135	2,371	5,568	8,764
oil	22	674,655	1,898	21,336	151,000
wc/d	19	154,099	1,922	5,603	35,651
ALEF, Thorwald (1896-1974) Swedish					
3D	1	2,010		2,010	
ALEGIANI, Francesco (19th C) Italian					
oil	3	8,090	1,600	2,482	4,008
ALEGRE, Agustin (1936-) Spanish					
oil	1	1,068		1,068	
ALERS, Rudolf (1812-?) German					
oil	1	2,741		2,741	
ALEXANDER, Charles (fl.1868-1894) British					
oil	1	3,976		3,976	
ALEXANDER, Clifford Grear (1870-1954) American					
oil	1	1,000		1,000	
ALEXANDER, Douglas (1871-1945) British					
oil	1	2,669		2,669	
ALEXANDER, Edwin (1870-1926) British					
wc/d	4	16,115	2,755	3,780	5,800
ALEXANDER, George (19/20th C) British					
oil	1	2,960		2,960	
ALEXANDER, John (1945-) American					
oil	1	1,000		1,000	
ALEXANDER, John White (1856-1915) American					
oil	1	20,000		20,000	
ALEXANDER, Lena (fl.1905-1936) British					
wc/d	1	1,501		1,501	
ALEXANDROVA, Kosinseva (1898-1978) ?					
oil	1	1,890		1,890	
ALEXANDROVNA, Grand Duchess Olga (1882-1960) Russian					
oil	5	6,845	1,008	1,385	1,769
ALFEREZ, Enrique (1901-) American/Mexican					
wc/d	1	1,000		1,000	
ALFIERI, Attilio (1904-1992) Italian					
oil	1	1,996		1,996	

Name	No.	Total Sales Value	Prices lowest	Prices median	highest
ALFONSO, Carlos (20th C) South American?					
oil	1	20,000		20,000	
ALFONZO, Carlos Jose (1950-1991) Cuban					
wc/d	2	7,500	3,500	3,750	4,000
ALFRED, W S (19th C) British					
oil	1	3,500		3,500	
ALFREDSON, Albert (20th C) American					
oil	1	2,000		2,000	
ALHAZIAN, Ohannes (19/20th C) Turkish					
oil	1	1,501		1,501	
ALINARI, Luca (1943-) Italian					
oil	11	18,524	1,061	1,780	2,301
wc/d	1	2,400		2,400	
ALINOVI, Giuseppe (1811-1848) Italian					
wc/d	1	2,938		2,938	
ALISON, David (1882-1955) British					
oil	1	3,504		3,504	
ALISON, Henry Young (1889-1972) British					
oil	1	3,234		3,234	
ALKARA, Ovadia (1939-) Israeli					
oil	1	3,200		3,200	
ALKEMA, Wobbe (1900-) Dutch					
oil	3	34,811	4,310	4,753	25,748
wc/d	1	6,338		6,338	
ALKEN, Henry (19th C) British					
wc/d	1	7,104		7,104	
ALKEN, Henry (jnr) (1810-1894) British					
oil	8	99,673	2,300	7,350	35,520
ALKEN, Henry (snr) (1785-1851) British					
oil	4	48,843	1,233	10,220	27,170
wc/d	3	6,795	1,510	2,567	2,718
ALLAIS, Pierre (?-1782) French					
oil	1	28,979		28,979	
ALLAN, Archibald Russell Watson (1878-1959) British					
oil	1	1,264		1,264	
wc/d	1	1,580		1,580	
ALLAN, Robert Weir (1852-1942) British					
oil	2	7,446	3,504	3,723	3,942
wc/d	8	16,776	1,106	1,989	3,675
ALLAN, Vernon (19th C) British					
oil	1	1,399		1,399	
ALLARD-L'OLIVIER, Fernand (1883-1933) Belgian					
oil	10	30,241	1,448	2,677	7,547
ALLASON, Silvio (1845-1912) Italian					
oil	1	2,994		2,994	
ALLBON, Charles Frederick (1856-1926) British					
wc/d	1	1,467		1,467	
ALLEBE, Augustus (1838-1927) Dutch					
wc/d	1	5,739		5,739	
ALLEGRAIN, Christophe Gabriel (1710-1795) French					
3D	1	1,536		1,536	
ALLEGRAIN, Étienne (1653-1736) French					
oil	2	36,401	12,401	18,201	24,000
ALLEGRE, Raymond (1857-?) French					
oil	2	8,632	2,312	4,316	6,320
ALLEGRINI, Flaminio (17th C) Italian					
wc/d	1	3,624		3,624	
ALLEGRINI, Francesco (1587-1663) Italian					
wc/d	1	3,454		3,454	

Name	No.	Total Sales Value	Prices lowest	median	highest
ALLEN, Charles Curtis (1886-1950) American					
oil	1	1,400		1,400	
ALLEN, Harry Epworth (1894-1958) British					
oil	1	5,499		5,499	
ALLEN, James E (1894-1964) American					
oil	1	4,250		4,250	
ALLEN, Joe (20th C) ?					
oil	1	2,008		2,008	
ALLEN, Junius (1898-1962) American					
oil	1	4,000		4,000	
ALLERT, Henrik (1937-) Swedish?					
3D	1	1,420		1,420	
ALLINGHAM, H (1848-1926) British					
wc/d	1	2,765		2,765	
ALLINGHAM, Helen (1848-1926) British					
wc/d	18	188,658	1,548	8,729	22,500
ALLINGTON, Edward (1951-) British					
3D	1	1,152		1,152	
ALLINSON, Adrian (1890-1959) British					
oil	8	18,206	1,080	1,888	5,100
ALLIOT, Lucien Charles Edouard (1877-1967) French					
3D	2	3,762	1,329	1,881	2,433
ALLIS, C Harry (1876-1938) American					
oil	1	12,000		12,000	
ALLISON, John William (?-1934) British					
wc/d	1	2,114		2,114	
ALLO, H J (?) ?					
oil	1	3,663		3,663	
ALLOM, Thomas (1804-1872) British					
oil	1	4,170		4,170	
wc/d	2	14,660	7,110	7,330	7,550
ALLONGE, Auguste (1833-1898) French					
oil	3	25,885	1,549	2,336	22,000
wc/d	4	6,774	1,018	1,524	2,708
ALLORI, Alessandro (1535-1607) Italian					
oil	4	471,731	40,000	70,866	290,000
ALLORI, Cristofano (1577-1621) Italian					
wc/d	1	3,995		3,995	
ALLOSIA, Giuseppe (1910-1983) Italian					
wc/d	1	1,080		1,080	
ALLSBURG, Chris van (1949-) ?					
wc/d	1	8,500		8,500	
ALLUAUD, Eugène (1866-?) French					
oil	1	4,166		4,166	
ALMA-TADEMA (19th C) British					
oil	1	67,500		67,500	
ALMA-TADEMA, Lady Laura (1852-1909) British					
oil	2	229,500	3,000	114,750	226,500
ALMA-TADEMA, Sir Lawrence (1836-1912) British					
oil	4	131,060	16,060	23,750	67,500
ALMARAZ, Carlos (1941-1989) ?					
oil	1	7,000		7,000	
ALMAVIVA, Marco (1934-) Italian					
oil	1	1,077		1,077	
ALMOG, Ditti (1959-) Israeli					
wc/d	1	4,000		4,000	
ALOISE (1886-1964) Swiss					
wc/d	1	5,703		5,703	

Name	No.	Total Sales Value	lowest	Prices median	highest
ALOISI, Baldassarre (1577-1638) Italian					
oil	1	24,568		24,568	
ALONSO PALACIOS, Vicente (1955-) Spanish					
oil	1	1,161		1,161	
wc/d	1	1,546		1,546	
ALONSO, Carlos (1929-) Argentinian					
wc/d	1	1,500		1,500	
ALONSO, Rafael (1924-1995) Spanish					
wc/d	1	1,557		1,557	
ALONSO-PEREZ, Carlos (19/20th C) Spanish					
oil	3	5,434	1,716	1,716	2,002
ALONSO-PEREZ, Mariano (1857-1930) Spanish					
oil	2	20,459	4,576	10,230	15,883
ALONZO, Angel (1923-1994) Spanish					
wc/d	1	1,400		1,400	
ALONZO, Dominique de (19/20th C) French					
3D	1	2,300		2,300	
ALOTT, Robert (1850-1910) Austrian					
oil	2	24,167	4,214	12,084	19,953
ALPERIZ (19/20th C) ?					
oil	1	2,549		2,549	
ALPERIZ, Nicolas (1869-1928) Spanish					
oil	1	9,000		9,000	
ALPINE SCHOOL, 15th C					
oil	1	10,331		10,331	
ALPUY, Julio (1919-) Uruguayan					
oil	7	20,043	1,800	2,600	4,500
ALSDORFF, Christian (fl.1789-1821) American					
wc/d	1	5,000		5,000	
ALSHETZ, Simon (20th C) American					
oil	1	3,800		3,800	
ALSINA, J (19/20th C) French					
oil	1	4,089		4,089	
ALSINA, Jacques (19/20th C) French					
oil	1	2,289		2,289	
ALSINA, Ramon Marti (1826-1895) Spanish					
oil	3	6,562	1,344	1,344	3,874
ALSLOOT, Denis van (c.1570-1628) Dutch					
oil	2	984,900	396,900	492,450	588,000
ALT, Franz (1821-1914) Austrian					
oil	1	1,785		1,785	
wc/d	2	3,467	1,634	1,734	1,833
ALT, Jacob (1789-1872) German					
oil	1	11,962		11,962	
ALT, Otmar (1940-) German					
oil	1	3,985		3,985	
ALT, Rudolf von (1812-1905) Austrian					
oil	2	69,780	34,890	34,890	34,890
wc/d	2	66,532	17,520	33,266	49,012
ALT, Theodor (1846-1937) Austrian					
oil	3	7,349	1,129	2,233	3,987
ALTAMURA, Alessandro (1855-?) Italian					
oil	1	1,082		1,082	
wc/d	1	1,468		1,468	
ALTAMURA, Jean (1852-1878) Greek					
oil	1	7,788		7,788	
ALTAMURA, Saverio (1826-1897) Italian					
oil	2	6,942	2,196	3,471	4,746
wc/d	1	6,650		6,650	

Name	No.	Total Sales Value	lowest	Prices median	highest
ALTEN, Mathias Joseph (1871-1938) German					
oil	3	17,500	2,250	4,250	11,000
ALTENBOURG, Gerhard (1926-1989) German					
oil	1	4,325		4,325	
wc/d	4	20,076	1,698	5,513	7,565
ALTENKIRCH, Otto (1875-1945) German					
oil	5	10,312	1,545	1,903	3,187
ALTHAUS, Fritz (fl.1881-1914) British					
wc/d	2	2,987	1,359	1,494	1,628
ALTHEIM, Wilhelm (1871-1914) German					
oil	1	2,212		2,212	
ALTHERR, Heinrich (1878-1947) Swiss					
oil	1	1,367		1,367	
ALTINK, Jan (1885-1975) Dutch					
oil	6	56,702	4,741	6,571	21,787
wc/d	6	52,543	1,584	6,239	19,806
ALTMANN, Alexandre (1885-1950) Russian					
oil	8	38,675	1,167	3,069	14,805
ALTMANN, Gerard (1877-1940) Dutch					
oil	4	6,093	1,090	1,370	2,263
ALTMEIER, Hans (1906-) German					
oil	1	1,366		1,366	
ALTOON, John (1925-1969) American					
wc/d	2	5,100	2,500	2,550	2,600
ALTORF, Johan Coenraad (1876-1955) Dutch					
3D	1	81,897		81,897	
ALTSON, Abbey (1864-c.1949) British					
oil	2	16,673	4,898	8,337	11,775
ALTZAR, Anders (1886-1939) Swedish					
oil	1	1,206		1,206	
ALVAR, Sunol (1935-) Spanish					
oil	4	8,592	1,318	1,674	3,926
ALVAREZ CATALA, Luis (1836-1901) Spanish					
oil	1	36,000		36,000	
ALVAREZ DE SOTOMAYOR, Maria Rosario (1921-) Spanish					
oil	1	1,427		1,427	
ALVAREZ DIAZ, Emilio (1879-1952) Argentinian					
oil	3	4,547	1,397	1,613	1,613
ALVAREZ FERNANDEZ, Jose (19th C) Spanish					
oil	2	2,551	1,257	1,276	1,294
ALVAREZ, Mabel (1891-1985) American					
oil	6	33,100	1,000	3,175	15,000
ALVAREZ, Pedro (1967-) Cuban					
oil	1	5,000		5,000	
ALVAREZ, Policarpo (19th C) Spanish					
oil	1	1,151		1,151	
ALVAREZ-DUMONT, Eugenio (1864-1927) Spanish					
oil	2	12,465	4,943	6,233	7,522
ALVARO DI PIERO (fl.1411-1434) Portuguese					
oil	1	120,800		120,800	
AMABLE-PETIT (1846-?) French					
wc/d	5	6,877	1,139	1,431	1,606
AMADIO, M (20th C) Italian					
3D	1	1,200		1,200	
AMADIO, Vittorio (1934-) Italian					
oil	1	1,844		1,844	
AMAN-JEAN, Edmond François (1860-1935) French					
3D	1	1,383		1,383	
oil	3	12,978	2,926	3,500	6,552

Name	No.	Total Sales Value	lowest	Prices median	highest
AMAND, Jacques François (1730-1769) French					
wc/d	1	3,797		3,797	
AMANDOLA, L (20th C) Italian					
oil	1	3,000		3,000	
AMANSHOFFNER, J M (18th C) German					
oil	1	2,215		2,215	
AMAT, Josep (1901-1991) Spanish					
oil	1	1,482		1,482	
AMATO, Luigi (20th C) Italian					
oil	1	5,849		5,849	
AMAURY-DUVAL, Eugène Emmanuel (1808-1885) French					
oil	1	10,000		10,000	
AMBERG, Wilhelm (1822-1899) German					
oil	3	22,856	4,144	8,000	10,712
AMBILLE, Paul (1930-) French					
oil	3	5,825	1,309	1,309	3,116
AMBROGIANI, Pierre (1907-1985) French					
oil	28	95,422	1,096	3,255	10,125
wc/d	1	1,520		1,520	
AMBROS, Raphael von (1855-1895) Czechoslovakian					
oil	1	43,800		43,800	
AMEGLIO, Mario (1897-1970) French					
oil	11	16,818	1,021	1,298	2,604
AMELIN, Albin (1902-1975) Swedish					
oil	8	67,612	1,809	9,421	14,049
wc/d	3	3,723	1,180	1,206	1,337
AMELL Y JORDA, M (19th C) Spanish					
oil	1	1,446		1,446	
AMENOFF, Gregory (1948-) American					
oil	1	2,500		2,500	
AMERICAN SCHOOL					
oil	2	36,000	8,000	18,000	28,000
wc/d	1	19,000		19,000	
AMERICAN SCHOOL, 17th C					
oil	1	3,100		3,100	
AMERICAN SCHOOL, 18th C					
oil	1	5,000		5,000	
AMERICAN SCHOOL, 18th/19th C					
3D	1	31,000		31,000	
oil	1	3,250		3,250	
AMERICAN SCHOOL, 19th C					
3D	6	59,300	2,800	10,250	19,000
oil	65	631,378	2,000	4,750	180,000
wc/d	11	73,350	3,100	4,500	20,000
AMERICAN SCHOOL, 19th/20th C					
3D	1	5,500		5,500	
oil	4	22,550	2,800	3,875	12,000
AMERICAN SCHOOL, 20th C					
3D	4	35,500	5,000	9,250	12,000
oil	8	34,150	3,000	3,675	8,000
AMERLING, Friedrich von (1803-1887) Austrian					
oil	5	13,740	1,495	2,584	4,984
AMEZAGA, Eduardo (1911-) Uruguayan					
oil	1	2,200		2,200	
AMEZAGA, Rafael (1928-) Spanish					
oil	1	1,171		1,171	
AMICI, Aurelio (19th C) Italian					
oil	1	2,146		2,146	
AMICK, Robert Wesley (1879-1969) American					
oil	2	12,300	2,300	6,150	10,000

Name	No.	Total Sales Value	lowest	Prices median	highest
AMIET, Cuno (1868-1961) Swiss					
3D	1	1,841		1,841	
oil	39	2,164,038	2,332	23,577	522,615
wc/d	16	88,301	1,210	2,839	20,916
AMIGO, Juan (17th C) Spanish					
oil	1	12,000		12,000	
AMIGONI, Jacopo (1675-1752) Italian					
oil	2	443,770	18,770	221,885	425,000
AMISANI, Giuseppe (1881-1941) Italian					
oil	1	2,898		2,898	
AMLING, Franz (1853-1894) German					
oil	2	4,675	1,486	2,338	3,189
AMMANN, Marguerite (1911-1962) Swiss					
wc/d	1	3,327		3,327	
AMORGUSTI, Antonio (20th C) Spanish					
3D	1	1,405		1,405	
AMOROS Y BOTELLA, Antonio (1849-1925) Spanish					
oil	1	8,000		8,000	
AMOROSI, Antonio (1660-1736) Italian					
oil	3	17,854	3,183	6,421	8,250
AMORSOLO, Fernando (1892-1972) Philippino					
oil	11	230,500	6,000	13,000	52,500
wc/d	1	1,751		1,751	
AMSDEN, William King (20th C) American					
oil	1	1,400		1,400	
AMUCHASTEGUI, Axel (1921-) Argentinian					
wc/d	2	9,530	2,130	4,765	7,400
AMUNDARAIN, Susana (20th C) South American					
oil	1	1,090		1,090	
ANASTASI, Auguste (1820-1889) French					
oil	2	3,986	1,993	1,993	1,993
wc/d	1	4,890		4,890	
ANATOL (1931-) German					
3D	2	2,692	1,346	1,346	1,346
wc/d	1	1,346		1,346	
ANCHER, Anna (1859-1935) Danish					
oil	13	264,136	1,763	18,468	58,381
ANCHER, Michael (1849-1927) Danish					
oil	35	247,509	2,060	5,885	38,947
ANDALUCIAN SCHOOL, 17th C Spanish					
3D	1	4,274		4,274	
ANDALUCIAN SCHOOL, 17th/18th C Spanish					
3D	1	6,991		6,991	
ANDALUCIAN SCHOOL, 19th C Spanish					
oil	1	3,496		3,496	
ANDALUCIAN SCHOOL, 20th C Spanish					
oil	1	2,876		2,876	
ANDER, Ture (1881-1959) Swedish					
oil	2	4,020	1,019	2,010	3,001
ANDERS, Ernst (1845-1911) German					
oil	3	20,061	3,770	7,900	8,391
ANDERSEN, Cilius (1865-1913) Danish					
oil	2	13,798	4,266	6,899	9,532
ANDERSEN, Mogens (1916-) Danish					
oil	7	13,388	1,025	1,549	3,587
ANDERSEN, Robin Christian (1890-1969) Austrian					
oil	1	2,696		2,696	
ANDERSEN, Roy H (1930-) American					
oil	2	145,000	50,000	72,500	95,000
wc/d	1	40,000		40,000	

Name	No.	Total Sales Value	lowest	Prices median	highest
ANDERSEN-LUNDBY, Anders (1841-1923) Danish					
oil	23	162,730	1,043	8,172	17,280
ANDERSON, A (?) ?					
oil	1	3,718		3,718	
ANDERSON, Abraham Archibald (1847-1940) American					
oil	1	5,500		5,500	
ANDERSON, Clayton (1964-) Canadian					
oil	1	1,342		1,342	
ANDERSON, Harry (1906-1996) American					
wc/d	3	9,050	2,500	2,800	3,750
ANDERSON, James Bell (1886-1938) British					
oil	1	1,208		1,208	
ANDERSON, John MacVicar (1835-1915) British					
oil	1	71,500		71,500	
ANDERSON, Ronald Lee (1886-1926) American					
oil	1	2,600		2,600	
ANDERSON, Sophie (1823-1903) British					
oil	3	54,052	6,000	15,010	33,042
ANDERSON, Stanley (1884-?) British					
wc/d	4	8,893	1,595	1,668	3,888
ANDERSON, Theo (20th C) British?					
oil	1	1,420		1,420	
ANDERSON, Victor C (1882-1937) American					
oil	2	7,200	2,200	3,600	5,000
ANDERSON, William (1757-1837) British					
oil	7	59,801	3,260	8,150	18,000
wc/d	2	10,010	4,004	5,005	6,006
ANDERSSON, Marten (1934-) Swedish					
oil	2	26,593	12,042	13,297	14,551
wc/d	1	3,591		3,591	
ANDERSSON, Nils (1817-1865) Swedish					
oil	4	9,115	1,136	1,732	4,515
ANDOE, Joe (1955-) American					
oil	2	6,500	2,000	3,250	4,500
ANDORFF, Paul (1849-?) German					
oil	1	1,963		1,963	
ANDRADA, Elsa (1920-) Uruguayan					
oil	1	2,017		2,017	
ANDRADE, Angel (1866-1936) Spanish					
oil	1	4,490		4,490	
ANDRE, Albert (1869-1954) French					
oil	14	244,085	2,700	14,500	42,000
wc/d	1	4,380		4,380	
ANDRE, Carl (1935-) American					
3D	7	1,044,000	24,000	120,000	360,000
wc/d	1	2,037		2,037	
ANDRE, Charles Hippolyte (1850-?) French					
oil	2	2,304	1,152	1,152	1,152
ANDRE, F (?) ?					
oil	1	8,915		8,915	
ANDRE, Jean (1662-1753) French					
3D	1	2,826		2,826	
ANDRE, Jules (1807-1869) French					
oil	1	1,019		1,019	
ANDREA, Cornelis (1914-) Dutch					
oil	2	3,282	1,641	1,641	1,641
ANDREA, Pat (1942-) Dutch					
oil	2	10,322	3,856	5,161	6,466

Name	No.	Total Sales Value	lowest	Prices median	highest
ANDREAS, George (1938-) Greek					
oil	1	1,535		1,535	
ANDREASSON, Folke (1902-1948) Swedish					
oil	3	4,251	1,310	1,318	1,623
ANDREIS, Alex de (19/20th C) Belgian					
oil	5	23,732	1,300	2,114	15,855
ANDREONI, Cesare (1903-1961) Italian					
oil	1	6,037		6,037	
ANDREOTTI, F (1847-1930) Italian					
oil	1	17,000		17,000	
ANDREOTTI, Federico (1847-1930) Italian					
oil	11	337,122	4,236	28,000	102,700
ANDREOTTI, Libero (1875-?) Italian					
3D	4	47,493	1,970	12,104	21,315
ANDREWS, Benny (1930-) American					
oil	1	1,700		1,700	
ANDREWS, George H (1816-1898) British					
oil	2	5,106	2,000	2,553	3,106
wc/d	2	5,330	2,041	2,665	3,289
ANDRIES, Alex de (?) ?					
oil	1	2,512		2,512	
ANDRIESSE, Erik (1957-1993) Dutch?					
oil	2	8,715	2,773	4,358	5,942
ANDRIESSEN, Anthony (1746-1813) Dutch					
wc/d	1	1,571		1,571	
ANDRIESSEN, Juriaan (1742-1819) Dutch					
oil	1	18,000		18,000	
ANDRIESSEN, Mari Silvester (1897-?) Dutch					
3D	1	1,638		1,638	
ANDRIEUX, Clement-Auguste (1829-?) French					
oil	1	2,449		2,449	
ANDRINGA, Martinus von (1864-1918) Dutch					
oil	1	2,096		2,096	
ANESI, Paolo (1697-1773) Italian					
oil	2	115,700	15,700	57,850	100,000
ANFRIE, Charles (1833-?) French					
3D	4	5,183	1,038	1,234	1,677
ANGE (?) ?					
wc/d	1	2,213		2,213	
ANGELI, Filippo (1600-1640) Italian					
oil	4	120,816	1,743	22,900	73,273
wc/d	1	1,528		1,528	
ANGELI, Franco (1935-1988) Italian					
oil	8	16,522	1,157	1,566	4,822
wc/d	28	45,914	1,034	1,358	5,236
ANGELIS, Pietro de (fl.c.1750-1800) Italian					
wc/d	2	5,799	1,804	2,900	3,995
ANGELIS, S de (1856-?) Italian					
wc/d	2	4,740	2,370	2,370	2,370
ANGELL, Helen Cordelia (1847-1884) British					
wc/d	2	9,942	4,290	4,971	5,652
ANGELO (?) ?					
oil	1	2,115		2,115	
ANGELVY, G (19th C) French					
oil	1	1,600		1,600	
ANGERER, Max (1877-1955) Swiss					
oil	2	2,233	1,079	1,117	1,154
ANGILLIS, Pieter (1685-1734) Flemish					
oil	2	13,805	5,285	6,903	8,520

Name	No.	Total Sales Value	lowest	Prices median	highest
ANGLADA-CAMARASA, Herman (1873-1959) Spanish					
oil	10	813,497	1,056	32,718	420,000
ANGLO-AMERICAN SCHOOL, 18th C					
oil	1	3,750		3,750	
ANGLO-AMERICAN SCHOOL, 19th C					
oil	2	25,000	11,000	12,500	14,000
ANGLO-CHINESE SCHOOL, 19th C					
oil	3	11,963	2,900	4,134	4,929
wc/d	1	47,000		47,000	
ANGLO-DUTCH SCHOOL, 17th C					
oil	4	52,804	3,768	13,528	21,980
ANGLO-DUTCH SCHOOL, 18th C					
oil	2	17,760	2,960	8,880	14,800
ANGLO-FLEMISH SCHOOL, 18th C					
oil	1	6,280		6,280	
ANGLO-INDIAN SCHOOL, 19th C					
oil	1	6,795		6,795	
ANGLO-ITALIAN SCHOOL, 17th C					
3D	1	22,050		22,050	
ANGLO-ITALIAN SCHOOL, 18th/19th C					
3D	1	5,292		5,292	
ANGLO-NETHERLANDISH SCHOOL, 18th C					
3D	1	4,228		4,228	
ANGO, Robert (18th C) French					
wc/d	3	4,549	1,021	1,528	2,000
ANGOLO DEL MORO, Marco (fl.1565-1586) Italian					
oil	1	3,028		3,028	
ANGRAND, Charles (1854-1926) French					
oil	1	4,468		4,468	
wc/d	2	8,787	3,600	4,394	5,187
ANGUISSOLA, Sofonisba (1527-c.1625) Italian					
oil	1	15,398		15,398	
ANGUS, John (1821-?) Flemish					
oil	1	5,674		5,674	
ANGUS, Maria L (fl.1887-1910) British					
wc/d	1	9,000		9,000	
ANISFELD, Boris (1878-1973) Russian					
wc/d	1	3,775		3,775	
ANIVITTI, Filippo (1876-1955) Italian					
oil	2	5,570	2,070	2,785	3,500
wc/d	1	1,731		1,731	
ANKARCRONA, Gustaf (1869-1933) Swedish					
oil	1	1,741		1,741	
ANKARCRONA, Henrik (1831-1917) Swedish					
oil	5	17,030	1,449	2,938	6,312
ANKEL, Julia Pietra S (20th C) Swiss?					
oil	1	1,153		1,153	
ANKELEN, Eugen (1858-1942) German					
oil	1	2,179		2,179	
ANKER, Albert (1831-1910) Swiss					
3D	1	3,242		3,242	
oil	8	1,134,425	1,131	118,196	437,538
wc/d	22	217,490	1,129	3,487	61,890
ANLAZUKIN (19th C) ?					
oil	1	1,499		1,499	
ANNA, Vito de (1720-1769) Italian					
oil	1	10,000		10,000	
ANNELER, Karl (1886-1957) Swiss					
oil	1	4,373		4,373	

Name	No.	Total Sales Value	lowest	Prices median	highest
ANNEN, Anna Margrit (1951-) Swiss					
oil	1	3,344		3,344	
ANNENKOFF, Yuri (1889-1974) Russian					
wc/d	1	1,269		1,269	
ANNER, Emil (1870-1925) German					
oil	1	1,019		1,019	
ANNIGONI, Pietro (1910-1988) Italian					
oil	3	16,717	3,567	4,698	8,452
wc/d	7	21,216	1,111	1,714	10,283
ANQUETIN, L (1861-1932) French					
oil	1	3,707		3,707	
ANQUETIN, Louis (1861-1932) French					
oil	2	19,687	2,909	9,844	16,778
wc/d	2	8,803	2,636	4,402	6,167
ANREITER, Alois von (1803-1882) Austrian					
wc/d	1	3,650		3,650	
ANSCOMBE, R (fl.1950s) British					
oil	1	3,256		3,256	
ANSDELL, R (1815-1885) British					
oil	1	1,043		1,043	
ANSDELL, Richard (1815-1885) British					
oil	13	839,985	1,800	37,180	394,200
ANSDELL, Richard and CRESWICK, Thomas (19th C) British					
oil	1	52,500		52,500	
ANSDELL, W (19th C) British?					
oil	1	1,108		1,108	
ANSELMO, Giovanni (1921-) Italian					
oil	1	24,650		24,650	
ANSELMO, Pompeo di (16th C) Italian					
oil	1	90,000		90,000	
ANSHUTZ, Thomas Pollock (1851-1912) American					
wc/d	1	8,500		8,500	
ANSINGH, Lizzy (1875-1959) Dutch					
oil	3	9,383	2,052	2,970	4,361
ANSINGH, Theresa (1883-1968) Dutch					
oil	1	1,358		1,358	
ANSLO, Pieter Laurensz van (c.1623-1680) Dutch					
oil	1	4,853		4,853	
ANSON, Mark (19th C) British					
oil	1	1,284		1,284	
ANTEN, Djef (1851-1913) Belgian					
oil	1	1,653		1,653	
ANTES, Horst (1936-) German					
3D	4	17,490	3,883	4,369	4,870
oil	3	38,343	11,325	11,325	15,641
wc/d	16	180,971	1,419	4,376	54,435
ANTHONISSEN, Arnoldus van (?-1632) Dutch					
oil	1	21,655		21,655	
ANTHONISSEN, Hendrick van (1606-?) Dutch					
oil	1	18,465		18,465	
ANTHONISSEN, Louis Joseph (1849-1913) Belgian					
oil	2	29,064	12,000	14,532	17,064
ANTHONY, Henry Mark (1817-1886) British					
oil	2	2,942	1,034	1,471	1,908
ANTHONY, J (?) ?					
oil	1	1,450		1,450	
ANTIGNA, Alexandre (1817-1878) French					
oil	2	7,631	3,378	3,816	4,253

Name	No.	Total Sales Value	lowest	Prices median	highest
ANTOINE, Marguerite (1907-1989) ?					
oil	1	2,144		2,144	
ANTOLINEZ Y SARABIA, Francisco (1644-1700) Spanish					
oil	7	92,450	2,355	7,478	55,000
ANTOLINEZ Y SARABIA, Francisco and PEREZ, Bartolome (17th C) Spanish					
oil	2	33,384	15,742	16,692	17,642
ANTOLINEZ, Jose (1635-1675) Spanish					
oil	1	3,095		3,095	
ANTONI, Janine (1964-) American					
3D	2	193,000	13,000	96,500	180,000
ANTONI, M (19th C) Austrian					
wc/d	1	1,025		1,025	
ANTONIANI, Pietro (1740-1805) Italian					
oil	2	103,090	50,240	51,545	52,850
ANTONIO, Cristobal de (19th C) Spanish					
oil	1	1,257		1,257	
ANTONIO, Ranieri Carlo (18/19th C) Italian					
oil	1	4,340		4,340	
ANTONISSEN, H J (1737-1794) Flemish					
oil	1	6,620		6,620	
ANTONISSEN, Henri Joseph (1737-1794) Flemish					
oil	1	2,109		2,109	
ANTRAL, Louis Robert (1895-1940) French					
oil	3	5,752	1,212	1,914	2,626
ANTRO, Alexandre van (19th C) Belgian?					
oil	3	20,745	2,144	6,491	12,110
ANTWERP SCHOOL, 16th C Flemish					
oil	8	156,234	3,594	15,901	50,000
ANTWERP SCHOOL, 16th/17th C Flemish					
oil	2	13,139	4,499	6,570	8,640
ANTWERP SCHOOL, 17th C Flemish					
3D	1	46,019		46,019	
oil	9	234,755	3,200	4,704	150,000
ANUSZKIEWICZ, Richard (1930-) American					
oil	3	10,700	2,500	4,200	4,200
ANY, Criss (20th C) ?					
wc/d	1	3,245		3,245	
ANZINGER, Siegfried (1953-) Austrian					
oil	1	3,398		3,398	
wc/d	2	3,428	1,009	1,714	2,419
AOUAD, Farid (20th C) ?					
oil	1	5,703		5,703	
AOYAMA, Yoshio (1894-?) Japanese					
oil	1	7,000		7,000	
APELLANIZ, Jesus (1898-1969) Spanish					
oil	2	6,189	1,688	3,095	4,501
APFELBAUM, Polly (1955-) American					
wc/d	1	3,500		3,500	
APOL, Adrianus (1780-1862) ?					
oil	1	3,707		3,707	
APOL, Armand-Adrien-Marie (1879-1950) Belgian					
oil	6	11,880	1,234	1,339	4,741
APOL, Louis (1850-1936) Dutch					
oil	15	142,348	1,168	5,092	57,284
wc/d	4	9,297	1,108	1,948	4,293
APOLLINAIRE, Guillaume (1880-1918) French					
wc/d	1	4,225		4,225	
APPARUTI, Albert Leon (19th C) French					
oil	1	1,462		1,462	

Name	No.	Total Sales Value	Prices lowest	median	highest
APPEL, Charles P (1857-1936) American					
oil	2	4,600	1,600	2,300	3,000
APPEL, Karel (1921-) Dutch					
3D	9	70,213	1,769	4,741	17,000
oil	55	1,102,489	2,155	8,340	151,000
wc/d	31	291,065	1,386	6,795	60,345
APPEL, Karl (1866-1937) German					
3D	1	20,000		20,000	
oil	3	56,723	1,079	15,644	40,000
wc/d	1	9,815		9,815	
APPENZELLER, Charles Felix (1892-1964) Swiss					
oil	2	4,311	1,516	2,156	2,795
APPERLEY, George Owen Wynne (1884-1960) British					
oil	1	2,048		2,048	
wc/d	10	17,989	1,031	1,625	2,786
APPIAN, Adolphe (1818-1898) French					
oil	7	20,684	1,582	2,326	6,419
APPIAN, Louis (1862-1896) French					
oil	2	4,068	1,690	2,034	2,378
APPIANI, Andrea (1754-1817) Italian					
wc/d	1	2,222		2,222	
APPLE, Monique (20th C) French					
wc/d	1	1,180		1,180	
APPLEYARD, Joseph (1908-1960) British					
oil	1	2,400		2,400	
APPS, Paul (1958-) British					
oil	1	2,220		2,220	
APSHOVEN, Thomas van (1622-1664) Flemish					
oil	1	5,252		5,252	
APSITIS, Aleksander Petrovic (1880-1944) Russian					
oil	1	2,509		2,509	
AQUINO, Luis (1895-1968) Argentinian					
oil	1	5,000		5,000	
ARA, Krishna Hawlaji (1914-1985) Indian					
oil	1	11,250		11,250	
ARAGONESE SCHOOL, 15th C Spanish					
oil	1	16,843		16,843	
ARAGONESE SCHOOL, 16th C Spanish					
oil	3	90,188	7,920	17,507	64,761
ARAKAWA, Shusaku (1936-) Japanese					
wc/d	1	10,625		10,625	
ARALICA, Stojan (1883-?) Yugoslavian					
oil	1	2,127		2,127	
ARAPOVA, Yuliya (20th C) Russian					
oil	1	8,736		8,736	
ARAUJO, Carlos (1950-) Brazilian					
oil	1	2,400		2,400	
ARBARELLO, Luigi (1860-1923) Italian					
oil	1	3,956		3,956	
ARBORELIUS, Olof (1842-1915) Swedish					
oil	8	44,491	1,741	3,621	19,187
ARBUS, Andre (1903-1969) French					
3D	12	47,291	1,180	3,468	8,116
ARBUTHNOT, Malcolm (1874-1967) British					
oil	1	1,350		1,350	
ARCHIPENKO, Alexander (1887-1964) American/Russian					
3D	15	962,974	1,307	25,485	370,000
wc/d	2	16,000	6,500	8,000	9,500
ARCHIZOOM ASSOCIATI (fl.1966-1974) Italian					
3D	1	14,500		14,500	

Name	No.	Total Sales Value	lowest	Prices median	highest
ARCIMBOLDO, Giuseppe (1527-1593) Italian					
oil	1	1,300,000		1,300,000	
ARDEN, Henri (1858-1917) Belgian					
oil	2	4,555	1,661	2,278	2,894
ARDISSONE, Yolande (1872-?) French					
oil	5	11,400	1,400	2,000	3,400
ARDIZZONE, Edward (1900-1979) British					
oil	1	6,900		6,900	
wc/d	11	31,370	1,029	2,448	5,040
ARDON, Mordecai (1896-1992) Israeli					
oil	11	702,000	14,000	50,000	155,000
wc/d	1	14,000		14,000	
ARELLANO Y CAMPOS, Manuel (19th C) Spanish					
oil	1	2,391		2,391	
ARELLANO, Juan de (1614-1676) Spanish					
oil	5	343,061	22,480	59,155	145,198
ARENDS, Hermanus and SEVERDONCK, Franz van (19th C) Belgian					
oil	1	1,775		1,775	
ARENDS, Jan (1738-1805) Dutch					
wc/d	1	1,886		1,886	
ARENIUS, Olof (1701-1766) Swedish					
oil	1	42,434		42,434	
ARENTSZ, Arent (1586-1635) Dutch					
oil	1	235,200		235,200	
ARENTZ, Kurt (1934-) German					
3D	1	1,729		1,729	
ARGENTI, Antonio (19/20th C) Italian					
3D	1	2,850		2,850	
ARGUELLES, Gonzalo (?) Spanish?					
oil	1	1,065		1,065	
ARGYROS, Oumbertos (1877-1963) Greek					
oil	1	5,548		5,548	
ARIAS, Francisco (1912-1977) Spanish					
oil	5	12,075	1,482	1,882	4,163
ARIAS, J (?) Spanish					
oil	1	3,318		3,318	
ARIAS-MISSON, Alain (1938-) Belgian?					
3D	1	1,745		1,745	
ARICO, Rodolfo (1930-) Italian					
oil	1	1,164		1,164	
ARIENTI, Stefano (1961-) Italian					
wc/d	1	4,501		4,501	
ARIKHA, Avigdor (1929-) Israeli					
oil	6	202,000	5,500	15,250	135,000
wc/d	7	87,550	3,000	5,600	58,000
ARIMOTO, Toshio (1946-1985) Japanese					
oil	1	140,000		140,000	
ARIOLA, Fortunato (1827-1872) American?					
oil	2	20,000	10,000	10,000	10,000
ARIYOSHI, H (19th C) Japanese					
oil	1	2,503		2,503	
ARIZMENDI, Jose Sanz (1885-1929) Spanish					
oil	1	7,584		7,584	
ARKHIPOV, Sergei (1897-?) Russian					
oil	1	3,948		3,948	
ARKWRIGHT, Elizabeth (19th C) British					
oil	1	1,311		1,311	
ARKWRIGHT, Emily (?) British?					
oil	1	1,233		1,233	

Name	No.	Total Sales Value	Prices lowest	median	highest
ARLINGSSON, Erling (1904-1982) Swedish					
oil	5	10,818	1,393	2,197	2,829
ARMAN, Fernandez (1928-1998) American/French					
3D	121	818,052	1,009	3,351	42,312
oil	13	143,300	1,213	5,916	40,000
wc/d	13	74,683	1,267	2,866	17,707
ARMAN, Jean Edmond (1860-1936) French					
wc/d	1	4,037		4,037	
ARMAN, Leopold (20th C) ?					
wc/d	1	3,400		3,400	
ARMANDO (1929-) Dutch					
oil	5	22,213	1,742	4,068	6,897
wc/d	1	1,268		1,268	
ARMENISE, Raffaello (1852-1925) Italian					
oil	1	1,784		1,784	
ARMESTO, Alvarez Primitivo (19th C) Spanish					
oil	1	2,159		2,159	
ARMET Y PORTANEL, Jose (1843-1911) Spanish					
oil	4	62,910	3,451	11,211	37,038
ARMFIELD, Diana (1920-) British					
wc/d	1	1,278		1,278	
ARMFIELD, Edward (19th C) British					
oil	12	29,045	1,057	1,800	4,500
ARMFIELD, Edwin (?) British?					
oil	1	2,205		2,205	
ARMFIELD, G (fl.1840-1875) British					
oil	1	2,408		2,408	
ARMFIELD, George (fl.1840-1875) British					
oil	19	68,262	1,200	3,146	12,000
ARMFIELD, Maxwell (1882-1972) British					
oil	4	7,148	1,106	1,596	2,850
ARMFIELD, Stuart (1916-) British					
oil	2	3,125	1,421	1,563	1,704
ARMIN, Emil (1883-1971) American					
oil	1	1,200		1,200	
ARMINGTON, Caroline (1875-1939) American/Canadian					
oil	2	7,800	1,300	3,900	6,500
ARMINGTON, Frank Milton (1876-1941) Canadian					
oil	1	1,350		1,350	
ARMITAGE, Kenneth (1916-) British					
3D	1	10,000		10,000	
ARMLEDER, John M (1948-) Swiss					
3D	3	13,855	2,552	3,403	7,900
oil	2	15,950	7,975	7,975	7,975
wc/d	2	2,897	1,439	1,449	1,458
ARMODIO (1938-) Italian					
oil	1	4,203		4,203	
ARMOR, C (1844-?) American					
oil	1	1,200		1,200	
ARMOUR, George Denholm (1864-1949) British					
oil	3	27,844	1,029	9,295	17,520
wc/d	2	9,635	2,385	4,818	7,250
ARMOUR, Mary (1902-2000) British					
oil	12	106,868	1,908	6,308	21,170
wc/d	1	4,108		4,108	
ARMSTRONG, Alixe Jean Shearer (1894-?) British					
oil	1	1,170		1,170	
ARMSTRONG, John (1893-1973) British					
oil	9	48,086	1,450	4,740	12,495

Name	No.	Total Sales Value	lowest	Prices median	highest
ARMSTRONG, Rolf (1881-1960) American					
wc/d	4	37,500	7,000	9,250	12,000
ARMSTRONG, William (1822-1914) Canadian/Irish					
wc/d	3	5,117	1,599	1,599	1,919
ARNAL, François (1924-) French					
oil	5	9,418	1,671	1,901	2,044
ARNALD, George (1763-1841) British					
oil	2	12,570	1,845	6,285	10,725
ARNAUD, Federico (1970-) Uruguayan					
3D	1	1,200		1,200	
ARNAUD, Moise (19/20th C) French					
oil	1	1,197		1,197	
ARNEGGER, A (19/20th C) Austrian					
oil	1	2,445		2,445	
ARNEGGER, Alois (1879-1967) Austrian					
oil	19	58,642	1,106	2,323	11,000
ARNEGGER, G (1905-) Austrian					
oil	1	1,708		1,708	
ARNEGGER, Gottfried (1905-) Austrian					
oil	3	8,888	1,000	3,650	4,238
ARNESEN, Vilhelm (1865-1948) Danish					
oil	11	27,423	1,033	2,015	6,045
ARNESON, Robert (1930-1992) American					
3D	1	3,500		3,500	
ARNO (20th C) ?					
3D	1	1,228		1,228	
ARNO, Giovanni Domenico (19th C) Italian					
oil	1	2,473		2,473	
ARNO, Peter (1904-1968) American					
wc/d	2	5,450	2,200	2,725	3,250
ARNOLD, Christian (1889-1960) German					
wc/d	7	12,895	1,274	1,698	2,681
ARNOLD, Jay (20th C) American					
oil	1	1,300		1,300	
ARNOLD, R (18/19th C) British					
oil	1	4,500		4,500	
ARNOLD, Reginald Ernest (1853-1938) British					
oil	1	5,000		5,000	
ARNOLDI, Charles (1946-) American					
oil	4	31,750	2,250	7,250	15,000
ARNTZENIUS, Floris (1864-1925) Dutch					
oil	11	237,436	2,052	3,317	137,731
wc/d	4	28,132	2,626	7,014	11,478
ARNTZENIUS, Paul (1883-1965) Dutch					
oil	2	3,669	1,249	1,835	2,420
ARNZ, Albert (1832-1914) German					
oil	1	27,413		27,413	
AROCH, Arieh (1908-1974) Russian					
oil	1	25,000		25,000	
wc/d	1	20,000		20,000	
AROSENIUS, Ivar (1878-1909) Swedish					
wc/d	7	19,684	1,101	2,257	5,305
ARP, Jean (1887-1966) French					
3D	22	2,052,446	1,181	28,100	700,000
oil	4	366,451	11,511	56,670	241,600
wc/d	12	83,113	1,413	5,310	23,140
ARPA, Z (?) Spanish					
oil	1	3,180		3,180	

Name	No.	Total Sales Value	lowest	Prices median	highest
ARPINO, Carlo (1866-1922) Italian					
oil	1	1,731		1,731	
ARPS, Bernardus (1865-1938) Dutch					
oil	1	4,143		4,143	
ARRANZ BRAVO, Eduard (1941-) Spanish					
oil	1	1,073		1,073	
ARRAS SCHOOL, 15th C					
oil	1	12,080		12,080	
ARREDONDO AVENDANO, Eduardo (1872-?) Spanish					
oil	1	4,916		4,916	
ARREDONDO Y CALMACHE, Ricardo (1850-1911) Spanish					
oil	1	8,104		8,104	
ARRI, Bruno (?) French?					
3D	1	1,430		1,430	
ARROYO, Edouard (1937-) Spanish					
3D	1	2,497		2,497	
oil	6	37,350	1,055	5,622	10,476
wc/d	10	27,372	1,127	2,115	5,971
ARRUE Y VALLE, Jose (1885-1977) Spanish					
wc/d	1	3,496		3,496	
ARRUE, Alberto (1878-1944) Spanish					
wc/d	1	1,207		1,207	
ARRUE, Ramiro (1892-1971) Spanish					
oil	2	41,474	7,232	20,737	34,242
ARSENIUS, John (1818-1903) Swedish					
oil	2	4,466	1,306	2,233	3,160
ARSENIUS, Karl Georg (1855-1908) Swedish					
oil	2	5,381	1,656	2,691	3,725
ARSON, Alphonse Alexandre (1822-c.1880) French					
3D	1	1,619		1,619	
ART DECO SCHOOL, 20th C					
3D	2	8,692	3,000	4,346	5,692
ART-LANGUAGE (fl.1968) British					
oil	1	9,540		9,540	
wc/d	2	17,003	2,400	8,502	14,603
ARTAN, Louis (1837-1890) Belgian					
oil	6	24,001	1,198	3,495	7,986
ARTER, Charles John (1860-1923) American					
oil	1	3,500		3,500	
ARTETA Y ERRASTI, Aureliano (1870-1940) Spanish					
wc/d	1	2,788		2,788	
ARTHUR-BERTRAND, Yvette (20th C) French					
oil	1	1,121		1,121	
ARTHURS, Stanley Massey (1877-1950) American					
oil	1	3,100		3,100	
ARTIGAU, Francesc (1940-) Spanish					
oil	1	1,398		1,398	
ARTIGUE, Albert (fl.1875-1901) French					
oil	1	1,368		1,368	
wc/d	1	3,950		3,950	
ARTS, Dorus (1901-1961) Dutch					
oil	1	1,055		1,055	
ARTSCHWAGER, Richard (1923-) American					
3D	5	48,328	1,328	10,000	18,000
oil	4	294,325	11,325	31,500	220,000
wc/d	2	69,000	4,000	34,500	65,000
ARTUR, Gilbert (1838-1894) French					
oil	1	4,038		4,038	
ARTZ, Constant (1870-1951) Dutch					
oil	20	71,389	1,358	3,340	6,106

Name	No.	Total Sales Value	lowest	Prices median	highest
wc/d	2	3,746	1,709	1,873	2,037
ARTZ, David Adolf Constant (1837-1890) Dutch					
oil	4	45,759	1,377	7,844	28,694
wc/d	2	5,823	1,413	2,912	4,410
ARUNDALE, Francis Vyvyan Jago (1807-1853) British					
wc/d	1	2,860		2,860	
ARUS, Joseph Raoul (1848-1921) French					
oil	1	4,987		4,987	
ARVEN, Florence (1952-) French?					
oil	1	1,100		1,100	
ARYA, Badri Nath (1936-) Indian					
wc/d	6	35,520	1,050	3,675	19,500
ARZADUN, Carmelo de (?) ?					
oil	8	16,765	1,265	1,850	4,500
ASCH, Pieter Jansz van (1603-1678) Dutch					
oil	1	2,355		2,355	
ASCHENBRENNER, Lennart (1943-) Swedish					
oil	5	8,521	1,555	1,687	1,785
ASCHMANN, Johann Jakob (1747-1809) Swiss					
wc/d	3	27,351	7,258	7,258	12,835
ASCIONE, Aniello (17/18th C) Italian					
oil	1	12,120		12,120	
ASH, Thomas Morris (fl.1882-1891) British					
oil	1	1,066		1,066	
ASHBURNER, William F (fl.1900-1932) British					
wc/d	5	8,979	1,492	1,738	2,364
ASHTON, Ethel V (20th C) American					
wc/d	1	1,600		1,600	
ASHTON, Federico (1840-1904) Italian					
oil	2	13,052	5,664	6,526	7,388
wc/d	1	1,133		1,133	
ASHTON, James (1860-1935) Australian					
oil	1	1,431		1,431	
ASHTON, William (18th C) British					
wc/d	1	1,141		1,141	
ASIAN SCHOOL, 19th C					
3D	1	50,501		50,501	
ASKENAZY, Maurice (1888-1961) American					
oil	1	7,000		7,000	
ASKEVOLD, Anders Monsen (1834-1900) Norwegian					
oil	3	15,569	1,219	3,922	10,428
ASLUND, Acke (1881-1958) Swedish					
oil	5	8,820	1,083	1,708	2,713
wc/d	1	1,059		1,059	
ASLUND, Elis (1872-1956) Swedish					
oil	1	2,190		2,190	
ASO, Saburo (1913-) Japanese					
oil	1	1,105		1,105	
ASOMA, Tudashi (20th C) Japanese					
oil	1	2,034		2,034	
ASP, Louis (1848-1922) Swedish					
oil	1	1,068		1,068	
ASPETTI, Tiziano (c.1565-1607) Italian					
3D	1	7,127		7,127	
ASPEVIG, Clyde (20th C) American					
oil	4	76,500	14,000	18,750	25,000
ASPINWALL, Reginald (1858-1921) British					
oil	6	16,527	1,512	2,536	5,024
wc/d	4	8,898	1,238	1,679	4,266

Name	No.	Total Sales Value	lowest	Prices median	highest
ASSCHE, Henri van (1774-1841) Belgian					
oil	1	2,940		2,940	
ASSE, Genevieve (1923-) French					
oil	1	1,221		1,221	
ASSELBERGS, Alphonse (1839-1916) Belgian					
oil	1	1,374		1,374	
ASSELBERGS, Jan (1937-) Dutch					
wc/d	2	3,622	1,811	1,811	1,811
ASSELIN, Maurice (1882-1947) French					
oil	2	2,041	1,015	1,021	1,026
ASSENDELFT, Cornelis van (1870-1945) German					
oil	1	2,617		2,617	
wc/d	1	2,155		2,155	
AST, Balthasar van der (1590-1656) Dutch					
oil	5	1,480,506	75,360	190,046	600,000
ASTE, Jean Louis (1864-?) French					
3D	1	2,897		2,897	
ASTI, Angelo (1847-1903) French					
oil	2	6,672	2,000	3,336	4,672
ASTOIN, Marie (1924-) French					
oil	5	8,578	1,139	1,756	2,308
ASTUDIN, Nicolai (1848-1925) German					
oil	3	5,982	1,066	1,734	3,182
ASTURIANO, Andres (17th C) Spanish					
oil	1	3,095		3,095	
ATALAYA, Enrique (1851-1914) Spanish					
oil	2	2,131	1,063	1,066	1,068
wc/d	2	9,141	3,226	4,571	5,915
ATAMIAN, Charles Garabed (1872-1947) Turkish					
oil	1	5,819		5,819	
ATASHKER, Farideh (1962-) ?					
oil	1	4,325		4,325	
ATHERTON, John (1900-1952) American					
oil	3	25,500	2,000	3,500	20,000
ATILA, Ede Kardy (1931-1987) French					
oil	1	1,284		1,284	
ATKINS, Samuel (fl.1787-1808) British					
wc/d	4	28,225	2,771	7,365	10,725
ATKINS, William Edward (1842-1910) British					
wc/d	1	1,716		1,716	
ATKINSON, George Mounsey Wheatley (1806-1884) British					
oil	1	21,190		21,190	
ATKINSON, Herbert (19/20th C) British					
oil	1	1,136		1,136	
ATKINSON, John (1863-1924) British					
oil	3	6,191	1,305	1,740	3,146
wc/d	11	30,322	1,359	2,826	6,040
ATKINSON, William Edwin (1862-1926) Canadian					
oil	1	1,950		1,950	
ATL, Dr (1875-1964) Mexican					
oil	1	70,000		70,000	
ATLAN, Jean (1913-1960) French					
oil	15	502,745	10,237	30,932	69,460
wc/d	8	50,680	3,790	5,453	12,263
ATOYAN, Armen (1922-) Armenian					
oil	1	1,764		1,764	
ATTANASIO, Natale (1846-1924) Italian					
wc/d	1	2,064		2,064	

Name	No.	Total Sales Value	lowest	Prices median	highest
ATTARDI, Ugo (1923-) Italian					
3D	1	1,658		1,658	
oil	5	16,675	1,767	3,617	3,965
ATTERSEE, Christian Ludwig (1940-) Austrian					
oil	3	11,137	1,992	3,320	5,825
wc/d	4	7,764	1,455	1,868	2,574
ATTWELL, Mabel Lucie (1879-1964) British					
wc/d	1	3,770		3,770	
ATYEO, Brian (1950-) Canadian					
wc/d	1	1,000		1,000	
AUBE, Paul (1837-1916) French					
3D	2	5,258	1,600	2,629	3,658
AUBERJONOIS, René (1872-1957) Swiss					
oil	9	98,016	1,864	6,685	27,823
wc/d	10	16,557	1,033	1,596	3,342
AUBERT, Jean Ernest (1824-1906) French					
oil	1	2,400		2,400	
AUBERTIN, Bernard (1934-) French					
3D	1	1,157		1,157	
oil	3	4,049	1,083	1,218	1,748
wc/d	1	1,028		1,028	
AUBLET, Albert (1851-1938) French					
oil	6	203,471	1,022	3,817	96,664
wc/d	1	2,596		2,596	
AUBREY, Charles (1873-?) New Zealander					
oil	1	1,924		1,924	
AUBROECK, Karel (1894-1986) Belgian					
3D	1	1,791		1,791	
AUBRY, Émile (1880-1964) French					
oil	3	11,683	3,491	3,549	4,643
AUBRY, Étienne (1745-1781) French					
oil	1	58,357		58,357	
AUDOUIN, Louis (1883-1968) French					
oil	1	2,578		2,578	
AUDUBON, John James (1785-1851) American/French					
wc/d	1	6,250		6,250	
AUDY, Jonny (19th C) French					
oil	1	3,322		3,322	
wc/d	1	1,804		1,804	
AUERBACH, Arnold (1898-1978) British					
oil	1	3,045		3,045	
AUERBACH, Frank (1931-) British/German					
oil	2	158,550	45,300	79,275	113,250
wc/d	5	26,502	2,226	5,760	9,300
AUERBACH-LEVY, William (1889-1964) American					
oil	1	2,200		2,200	
AUFRAY, Joseph (1836-?) French					
oil	3	11,467	2,750	4,293	4,424
wc/d	1	1,065		1,065	
AUGSBURG SCHOOL, 16th C German					
3D	1	7,976		7,976	
oil	1	6,280		6,280	
AUGUST, Carl E (19th C) American					
oil	1	1,500		1,500	
AUGUSTIN, Ludwig (20th C) German					
oil	2	3,275	1,100	1,638	2,175
AULT, George C (1891-1948) American					
oil	2	62,000	26,000	31,000	36,000
wc/d	2	25,000	8,000	12,500	17,000

Name	No.	Total Sales Value	lowest	Prices median	highest
AUMONIER, James (1832-1911) British					
oil	1	1,985		1,985	
AURELI, Giuseppe (1858-1929) Italian					
wc/d	4	7,858	1,558	1,950	2,400
AURILI, Richard (1854-?) Italian?					
3D	1	25,000		25,000	
AURIOL, Charles Joseph (1778-1834) Swiss					
oil	1	2,033		2,033	
AURIOUST, Gabrielle (19th C) French?					
wc/d	1	1,947		1,947	
AURRENS, Henri (1873-?) French					
oil	1	5,192		5,192	
AUSLEGER, Rudolf (1897-?) German					
wc/d	2	3,483	1,328	1,742	2,155
AUSTEN, Alexander (fl.1891-1909) British					
oil	1	1,533		1,533	
AUSTEN, H (19th C) British					
oil	1	1,364		1,364	
AUSTIN, C (?) ?					
oil	2	3,059	1,272	1,530	1,787
AUSTIN, Charles Percy (1883-1948) American					
oil	1	2,500		2,500	
AUSTRIAN SCHOOL					
3D	1	1,900		1,900	
AUSTRIAN SCHOOL, 15th C					
oil	2	14,843	6,868	7,422	7,975
AUSTRIAN SCHOOL, 16th C					
3D	2	20,203	3,111	10,102	17,092
AUSTRIAN SCHOOL, 17th C					
3D	2	14,787	3,864	7,394	10,923
AUSTRIAN SCHOOL, 18th C					
3D	4	11,252	2,379	2,799	3,276
oil	6	28,565	3,418	3,961	7,500
AUSTRIAN SCHOOL, 19th C					
oil	4	42,072	2,273	3,840	32,120
wc/d	2	9,289	3,750	4,645	5,539
AUSTRIAN SCHOOL, 20th C					
3D	4	11,028	1,470	2,763	4,032
AUSTRIAN, Ben (1870-1921) American					
oil	3	30,644	7,000	11,644	12,000
AUSTRO-HUNGARIAN SCHOOL, 18th C					
oil	1	5,455		5,455	
AUTHOUART, Daniel (?) French?					
wc/d	2	3,818	1,854	1,909	1,964
AUTIO, Rudy (1926-) American					
oil	1	1,000		1,000	
AUWERA, Louis van der (1882-1965) Belgian					
oil	1	2,144		2,144	
AUZOU, Pauline (1775-1835) French					
oil	1	2,205		2,205	
wc/d	5	10,731	1,764	2,058	2,646
AVATI, James (1912-) American					
oil	2	7,500	1,500	3,750	6,000
AVED, Jacques-Andre-Joseph-Camelot (1702-1766) French					
oil	2	38,243	3,243	19,122	35,000
AVELLANEDA, Manuel (1938-) Spanish					
oil	1	1,368		1,368	
AVENDANO FERNANDEZ, Donato (1840-) Spanish					
oil	1	3,608		3,608	

Name	No.	Total Sales Value	lowest	Prices median	highest
AVERCAMP, Hendrick (1585-1634) Dutch					
wc/d	1	149,286		149,286	
AVERIN, Alexandre (1952-) Russian					
oil	4	5,639	1,008	1,329	1,875
AVERLY, S (?) ?					
oil	1	1,056		1,056	
AVERY, Milton (1885-1965) American					
oil	6	371,500	6,500	60,000	120,000
wc/d	13	360,600	2,600	6,000	110,000
AVI, Kenan (1951-) Israeli					
3D	1	1,671		1,671	
AVIA, Amalia (1930-) Spanish					
oil	6	17,094	1,613	2,800	4,290
AVIGNON SCHOOL, 17th C French					
3D	1	8,026		8,026	
AVNER, Herve (1954-) French?					
oil	1	1,701		1,701	
wc/d	1	1,191		1,191	
AVNI, Aaron (1906-1951) Israeli					
oil	1	2,700		2,700	
AVRAMIDIS, Joannis (1922-) Austrian					
3D	1	13,592		13,592	
AW, Meinrad von (1712-?) German					
oil	1	1,936		1,936	
AXELSON, Axel (1854-1892) Swedish					
oil	1	1,407		1,407	
AYALA, Josefa de (1630-1684) Spanish					
oil	1	147,495		147,495	
AYLING, Albert W (?-1905) British					
wc/d	1	1,387		1,387	
AYLING, George (1887-1960) British					
oil	1	2,370		2,370	
AYME, Alix (1894-1989) French					
wc/d	1	2,302		2,302	
AYOTTE, Leo (1909-1976) Canadian					
oil	4	7,944	1,349	1,696	3,198
AYRES, Gillian (1930-) British					
oil	1	10,875		10,875	
wc/d	1	1,326		1,326	
AYRTON, Michael (1921-1975) British					
3D	5	30,526	5,396	6,320	7,110
oil	3	17,367	2,844	3,948	10,575
wc/d	9	20,146	1,014	1,716	6,000
AZAMBRE, Étienne (19/20th C) French					
oil	1	1,974		1,974	
AZEGLIO, Massimo de (1798-1866) Italian					
oil	1	4,082		4,082	
AZEMA, Louis (1876-1963) French					
oil	1	1,218		1,218	
AZENE, Aryeh (1934-) Israeli					
oil	1	2,000		2,000	
AZPARREN, Jose Luis (1955-) Spanish					
oil	1	1,010		1,010	
AZUELOS, Samuel (20th C) Israeli?					
oil	1	3,562		3,562	
AZZINARI, Franco (1949-) Italian					
oil	2	2,827	1,405	1,414	1,422
AZZOLINI, Giovanni Bernardino (c.1572-c.1645) Italian					
oil	1	5,005		5,005	

Name	No.	Total Sales Value	lowest	Prices median	highest
BAADE, Knud Andreassen (1808-1879) Norwegian					
oil	1	22,650		22,650	
BAADER, Johann (1709-1779) German					
oil	1	1,108		1,108	
BAAGOE, Carl (1829-1902) Danish					
oil	6	18,317	1,084	1,856	6,384
BAAR, Hugo (1873-1912) German?					
oil	1	30,020		30,020	
BABB, Stanley Nicholson (19/20th C) British					
3D	1	2,352		2,352	
BABOULENE, Eugène (1905-1994) French					
oil	8	23,737	1,296	2,759	4,641
BACCARD, Joseph (1843-?) French					
oil	1	2,400		2,400	
BACCARINI, Lino (1893-) Italian					
oil	1	1,539		1,539	
BACCI, Baccio Maria (1888-1974) Italian					
oil	2	6,982	3,491	3,491	3,491
BACCI, Edmondo (1913-) Italian					
oil	4	6,900	1,500	1,700	2,000
BACCIARELLI, Marcello (1731-1818) Italian					
wc/d	2	17,873	8,036	8,937	9,837
BACH, Alois (1809-1893) German					
oil	2	3,209	1,591	1,605	1,618
BACH, Andreas (1886-?) German					
oil	1	1,177		1,177	
BACH, Elvira (1951-) German					
oil	3	14,088	1,500	3,734	8,854
wc/d	1	1,683		1,683	
BACH, Michael (1953-) German?					
oil	1	2,163		2,163	
BACH, Paul (1866-1919) German					
oil	2	2,524	1,068	1,262	1,456
BACHE, Otto (1839-1927) Danish					
oil	8	73,248	1,033	4,239	37,075
BACHELET, Émile Just (1892-?) French					
3D	1	1,707		1,707	
BACHELIN, Auguste (1830-1890) Swiss					
oil	4	14,361	1,749	2,458	7,696
BACHEM, Bele (1916-) German					
oil	1	2,727		2,727	
BACHER, Otto Henry (1856-1909) American					
oil	1	28,000		28,000	
BACHINSKI, Walter Joseph Gerard (1939-) Canadian?					
wc/d	1	2,844		2,844	
BACHMANN, Adolphe (19/20th C) Swiss					
oil	1	3,819		3,819	
BACHMANN, Alfred (1863-1954) German					
oil	2	28,905	4,243	14,453	24,662
BACHMANN, Edwin (1900-) Swiss					
oil	1	1,105		1,105	
BACHMANN, Hans (1852-1917) Swiss					
oil	4	6,022	1,149	1,428	2,018
BACHMANN, Otto (1915-1996) Swiss					
oil	1	1,068		1,068	
BACK, Robert (1922-) ?					
oil	1	8,305		8,305	
BACKER (?) ?					
oil	1	1,800		1,800	

Name	No.	Total Sales Value	lowest	Prices median	highest
BACKER, Jacob Adriaensz (1608-1651) Dutch					
oil	1	13,951		13,951	
wc/d	1	2,265		2,265	
BACKER, Jacob de (1560-c.1590) Flemish					
oil	1	26,000		26,000	
BACKER, Philips de (17th C) Belgian					
oil	1	9,420		9,420	
BACKSTROM, Barbro (1939-1990) Swedish					
3D	10	96,357	1,229	4,445	37,130
BACKUS, Albert (1906-1996) American					
oil	1	5,000		5,000	
BACKVIS, François (1857-1926) Belgian					
oil	3	7,197	1,157	1,389	4,651
BACON, Francis (1909-1992) British					
oil	2	10,077,000	4,077,000	5,038,500	6,000,000
BACON, I Lewis (1853-1910) American					
oil	1	3,750		3,750	
BACON, John Henry Frederick (1868-1914) British					
oil	1	47,400		47,400	
BADALOCCHIO, Sisto (1581-1647) Italian					
oil	1	29,400		29,400	
BADEN, Hans Jurriaens van (1604-1663) Dutch					
oil	1	3,910		3,910	
BADGER, Frances (19/20th C) American					
oil	1	1,900		1,900	
BADGER, S F M (19/20th C) American					
oil	2	24,500	11,500	12,250	13,000
BADIALI, Carla (20th C) Italian					
oil	1	11,796		11,796	
BADILE, Antonio (1516-1560) Italian					
oil	1	8,000		8,000	
BADIN, J J (19th C) French					
oil	1	3,014		3,014	
BADIN, Jean Jules (1843-?) French					
oil	1	10,500		10,500	
BADMIN, Stanley Roy (1906-1989) British					
wc/d	2	4,424	2,212	2,212	2,212
BAECHLER, Donald (1956-) American					
oil	7	233,264	1,964	14,000	130,000
wc/d	7	95,419	1,549	10,570	32,500
BAECK, Johan (1600-1655) Dutch					
oil	1	8,355		8,355	
BAEDER, John (1938-) American					
wc/d	1	15,000		15,000	
BAEGERT, Jan (fl.1476-1515) German					
oil	2	38,707	15,938	19,354	22,769
BAELLIEUR, Cornelis de (17th C) Flemish					
oil	2	11,404	3,854	5,702	7,550
BAELLIEUR, Cornelis de and DANIELS, Andries (17th C) Flemish					
oil	1	44,216		44,216	
BAERDEMAEKER, Felix de (1836-1878) Belgian					
oil	1	2,318		2,318	
BAERENTZEN, Emilius (1799-1868) Danish					
oil	2	5,875	2,896	2,938	2,979
BAERTLING, Olle (1911-1981) Swedish					
oil	13	184,097	2,176	13,046	51,322
BAERWIND, Rudi (1910-1982) German					
oil	2	3,418	1,307	1,709	2,111

Name	No.	Total Sales Value	Prices lowest	median	highest
BAES, Émile (1889-1954) Belgian					
oil	5	11,087	1,150	1,880	4,508
BAES, Firmin (1874-1945) Belgian					
oil	2	15,458	1,058	7,729	14,400
wc/d	10	28,643	1,065	2,312	8,588
BAES, Lionel (1839-1913) Belgian					
oil	1	1,368		1,368	
BAETS, Marc (18th C) Flemish					
oil	4	53,529	4,914	12,277	24,061
BAEZA, Manuel (1915-1986) Spanish					
oil	1	1,526		1,526	
BAGARIA, Luis (1882-1940) Spanish					
wc/d	1	1,125		1,125	
BAGG, Henry Howard (1852-1928) American					
oil	1	1,000		1,000	
BAGGE, Eva (1871-1964) Swedish					
oil	4	6,890	1,206	1,687	2,311
wc/d	1	1,129		1,129	
BAGLIONE, Cavaliere Giovanni (1571-1644) Italian					
wc/d	1	1,013		1,013	
BAGSHAWE, Joseph Richard (1870-1909) British					
wc/d	1	1,015		1,015	
BAHAMONTES-AGUDO, Jose (19th C) Spanish					
oil	1	6,745		6,745	
BAHIEU, Jules G (19th C) Belgian					
oil	1	1,000		1,000	
BAHIEU, Jules J (1860-?) Belgian					
oil	1	1,218		1,218	
BAIERL, Theodor (1881-1932) German					
oil	1	7,450		7,450	
BAIJ, Ramkinkar (1910-1980) Indian					
oil	1	3,600		3,600	
wc/d	2	6,200	2,600	3,100	3,600
BAIJOT-GOMARD, Marie Ange (20th C) French					
wc/d	1	1,101		1,101	
BAIL (?) ?					
oil	1	1,528		1,528	
BAIL, Antoine Jean (1830-1918) French					
oil	1	3,476		3,476	
BAIL, Franck Antoine (1858-1924) French					
oil	2	12,281	3,976	6,141	8,305
BAIL, Joseph (1862-1921) French					
oil	6	50,331	4,082	6,937	20,000
BAILEY, Frederick Victor (20th C) British					
oil	2	3,286	1,582	1,643	1,704
BAILLY, Alice (1872-1938) Swiss					
oil	3	5,328	1,108	1,568	2,652
wc/d	2	7,613	1,129	3,807	6,484
BAILLY, David (1584-c.1657) Dutch					
wc/d	1	57,380		57,380	
BAILY, Edward Hodges (1788-1867) British					
3D	1	2,160		2,160	
BAIN, Donald (1904-1979) British					
oil	4	6,675	1,186	1,461	2,567
BAIN, Walter (20th C) British					
wc/d	1	1,422		1,422	
BAIRD, Annie (20th C) New Zealander					
oil	1	3,200		3,200	

Name	No.	Total Sales Value	lowest	Prices median	highest
BAIRD, Nathaniel Hughes (1865-c.1930) British					
oil	1	1,672		1,672	
wc/d	3	4,974	1,057	1,208	2,709
BAIRD, William Baptiste (1847-1917) American					
oil	9	41,156	1,178	4,000	10,000
BAISCH, Hermann (1846-1894) German					
oil	7	29,034	1,475	2,696	9,905
BAITLER, Zoma (1908-1994) Uruguayan					
oil	7	10,200	1,100	1,500	1,800
BAIXERAS Y VERDAGUER, Dionisio (1862-1943) Spanish					
wc/d	1	1,294		1,294	
BAJ, Enrico (1924-) Italian					
3D	2	9,942	1,868	4,971	8,074
oil	18	182,414	1,328	4,196	50,750
wc/d	8	55,586	1,773	4,890	17,966
BAK, Samuel (1933-) Israeli					
oil	11	140,891	1,500	13,578	34,000
wc/d	4	7,739	1,358	1,969	2,444
BAKALOWICZ, Ladislaus (1833-1904) Polish					
oil	1	4,238		4,238	
BAKE, Sophie Christina van den Wall (1866-1915) Dutch					
oil	1	2,020		2,020	
BAKER, Elisha Taylor (1827-1890) American					
oil	1	10,000		10,000	
BAKER, George Herbert (1878-1943) American					
oil	2	14,000	7,000	7,000	7,000
BAKER, Gladys M (1889-?) British					
oil	1	3,500		3,500	
BAKER, Samuel Henry (1824-1909) British					
oil	1	1,087		1,087	
wc/d	1	1,390		1,390	
BAKHUYZEN, Alexandre H (1826-1878) Dutch					
oil	1	2,903		2,903	
BAKHUYZEN, Gerardina Jacoba van de Sande (1826-1895) Dutch					
oil	2	50,638	2,220	25,319	48,418
BAKHUYZEN, Hendrick van de Sande (1795-1860) Dutch					
oil	3	87,762	17,216	19,627	50,919
BAKHUYZEN, Julius Jacobus van de Sande (1835-1925) Dutch					
oil	2	4,211	2,065	2,106	2,146
BAKHUYZEN, Ludolf (1631-1708) Dutch					
oil	5	409,374	16,345	36,929	196,300
BAKKER-KORFF, Alexander Hugo (1824-1882) Dutch					
wc/d	1	1,134		1,134	
BAKST, Léon (1866-1924) Russian					
wc/d	16	109,906	1,410	6,852	11,325
BAKSTEEN, Dirk (1886-1971) Dutch					
oil	5	9,374	1,109	1,880	3,110
BALACA, Ricardo (1844-1880) Portuguese					
oil	2	4,482	2,109	2,241	2,373
BALAGUER, Julio (1957-) Spanish					
oil	4	8,752	1,621	2,210	2,711
BALANDE, G (1880-1971) French					
oil	1	2,145		2,145	
BALANDE, Gaston (1880-1971) French					
oil	9	30,164	1,178	2,341	7,295
BALASCH MATEU, Mateo (1870-1936) Spanish					
oil	1	1,301		1,301	
BALDAUGH, Anni (1886-1953) American					
oil	1	2,750		2,750	

Name	No.	Total Sales Value	lowest	Prices median	highest
BALDERO, Giorgio (19th C) Italian					
oil	1	2,184		2,184	
BALDERO, L G (?) ?					
oil	1	4,183		4,183	
BALDESSARI, John (1931-) American					
oil	4	76,000	13,000	18,500	26,000
BALDESSARI, Roberto Iras (1894-1965) Italian					
oil	3	65,672	11,647	12,617	41,408
wc/d	3	33,725	1,571	10,802	21,352
BALDI, Giovanni (18th C) Italian					
3D	1	2,193		2,193	
BALDI, Lazzaro (1624-1703) Italian					
wc/d	2	9,182	2,182	4,591	7,000
BALDINO, Richard (20th C) Italian?					
oil	2	2,662	1,297	1,331	1,365
BALDOCK, Charles E (fl.1890-1905) British					
wc/d	1	1,573		1,573	
BALDOCK, James Walsham (c.1822-1898) British					
oil	1	5,005		5,005	
BALDRY, Harry (fl.1887-1890) British					
oil	1	1,332		1,332	
BALDUCCI, Giovanni (?-1603) Italian					
wc/d	1	5,836		5,836	
BALDWYN, C H C (fl.1887-1912) British					
wc/d	1	1,421		1,421	
BALE, Charles Thomas (fl.1866-1875) British					
oil	10	34,321	1,087	2,155	14,112
BALE, Edwin (1838-1923) British					
wc/d	1	4,862		4,862	
BALE, T C (19th C) British					
oil	1	2,250		2,250	
BALEN, Hendrik van (1575-1632) Flemish					
oil	1	11,077		11,077	
BALENCIAGA, Narciso (1905-1935) Spanish					
oil	1	1,453		1,453	
BALESTRA, Angelo (1803-1881) Italian					
oil	1	17,687		17,687	
BALESTRA, Antonio (1666-1740) Italian					
oil	3	112,742	7,542	30,200	75,000
BALESTRIERI, Lionello (1872-1958) Italian					
oil	3	9,013	1,115	3,491	4,407
wc/d	1	1,365		1,365	
BALET, Jan (20th C) ?					
oil	1	1,900		1,900	
BALETTI BIANCHI, Romeo (1903-1958) Uruguayan					
oil	1	1,425		1,425	
BALFOUR-BROWNE, Vincent (1880-1963) British					
wc/d	4	15,259	1,034	2,400	9,425
BALINK, Hendricus (1882-1963) American					
wc/d	1	12,000		12,000	
BALINT, Endre (1914-) Hungarian					
oil	1	7,110		7,110	
BALJEU, Joost (1925-1991) Dutch					
3D	1	11,091		11,091	
oil	1	16,379		16,379	
BALKA, Miroslaw (1958-) Polish					
3D	1	12,835		12,835	
BALKAN, Adele (20th C) American					
wc/d	1	1,058		1,058	

Name	No.	Total Sales Value	lowest	Prices median	highest
BALKANSKI, N (?) ?					
oil	1	2,500		2,500	
BALKE, Theodore Charles (1875-1951) French					
oil	4	12,450	1,933	2,641	5,235
BALKENHOL, Stephan (1957-) German					
3D	8	393,070	9,515	38,640	105,000
oil	1	65,000		65,000	
BALL, Alfred (?) British					
wc/d	1	1,580		1,580	
BALL, Thomas (1819-1911) American					
3D	1	26,000		26,000	
BALL, Wilfred Williams (1853-1917) British					
wc/d	2	2,354	1,050	1,177	1,304
BALLA, Giacomo (1871-1958) Italian					
oil	7	101,738	8,483	12,602	30,088
wc/d	16	432,949	1,440	20,361	65,450
BALLAGH, Robert (1943-) Irish					
oil	1	1,231		1,231	
BALLARD, Brian (1943-) Irish					
oil	6	9,811	1,008	1,507	2,610
BALLAVOINE, Jules Frederic (1855-1901) French					
oil	2	24,168	9,000	12,084	15,168
BALLE, Mogens (1921-1988) Danish					
oil	18	29,152	1,000	1,386	4,066
BALLESIO, Federico (19th C) Italian					
wc/d	3	4,900	1,500	1,500	1,900
BALLESIO, Francesco (1860-1923) Italian					
wc/d	1	18,000		18,000	
BALLESTER, Rosalie (1949-) French					
wc/d	1	1,201		1,201	
BALLIN, Auguste (1842-?) French					
oil	1	1,305		1,305	
BALLINGALL, Alexander (fl.1880-1910) British					
wc/d	4	11,688	1,258	3,185	4,088
BALLINGER, Harry Russell (1892-1994) American					
oil	1	1,600		1,600	
BALLOT, Clementine (1879-1964) French					
oil	1	1,005		1,005	
BALLUE, Pierre Ernest (1855-1928) French					
oil	1	1,694		1,694	
BALMER, George (1806-1846) British					
oil	1	1,963		1,963	
BALMER, Paul Friedrich Wilhelm (1865-1922) Swiss					
oil	3	4,313	1,129	1,384	1,800
BALOUN (20th C) French					
3D	1	5,418		5,418	
BALSAMO, Vincenzo (1935-) Italian					
oil	2	4,147	1,552	2,074	2,595
BALSGAARD, Carl Vilhelm (1812-1893) Danish					
oil	5	18,674	1,220	2,840	8,701
BALTHUS (1908-2001) French					
oil	4	2,943,599	1,659	70,970	2,800,000
wc/d	17	555,965	1,219	5,285	192,826
BALUNIN, Mikhail Abramovich (1875-c.1939) Russian					
oil	2	12,835	5,587	6,418	7,248
BALUSCHEK, Hans (1870-1935) German					
wc/d	2	7,831	1,211	3,916	6,620
BALWE, Arnold (1898-1983) German					
oil	8	95,496	3,188	10,075	21,779

Name	No.	Total Sales Value	lowest	Prices median	highest
BAMA, James E (1926-) American					
oil	3	64,500	4,500	25,000	35,000
BAMBER, Bessie (fl.1900-1910) British					
oil	6	17,272	1,131	2,258	6,594
BAMBERGER, Fritz (1814-1873) German					
oil	3	20,029	5,538	5,844	8,647
wc/d	2	2,563	1,196	1,282	1,367
BAMBINI, Nicolo (1651-1736) Italian					
oil	1	10,990		10,990	
BAN, Gerbrand (1613-1652) Dutch					
oil	1	15,700		15,700	
BANANA, Charly (1953-) German					
wc/d	1	1,553		1,553	
BANCROFT, Elias (?-1924) British					
oil	2	2,234	1,008	1,117	1,226
wc/d	1	1,650		1,650	
BAND, Max (1900-1974) Israeli?					
oil	1	1,100		1,100	
BANDEIRA, Antonio (1922-1967) Brazilian					
oil	2	11,116	4,113	5,558	7,003
wc/d	1	4,600		4,600	
BANDINELLI, Baccio (1493-1560) Italian					
wc/d	2	72,500	27,500	36,250	45,000
BANDINI, Giovanni di Benedetto (1540-1599) Italian					
wc/d	1	19,110		19,110	
BANDO, Toshio (1890-1973) Japanese					
oil	4	7,095	1,422	1,670	2,334
BANDUEL (?) ?					
3D	1	2,400		2,400	
BANE, E (19th C) ?					
oil	1	3,000		3,000	
BANG, Christian (1868-?) Danish					
oil	1	32,000		32,000	
BANKS, Thomas J (19th C) British					
oil	1	6,090		6,090	
BANNER, A (19th C) ?					
oil	1	2,054		2,054	
BANNER, Alfred (fl.1878-1914) British					
oil	3	3,970	1,050	1,350	1,570
BANTING, John (1902-1970) British					
oil	1	2,508		2,508	
BANTING, Sir Frederick Grant (1891-1941) Canadian					
oil	4	15,591	1,678	2,555	8,803
BANTZER, Carl (1857-1941) German					
oil	1	2,589		2,589	
BARABINO, Nicolo (1832-1891) Italian					
oil	1	1,115		1,115	
BARANOFF-ROSSINE, Vladimir (1888-1942) Russian					
oil	1	7,071		7,071	
BARATTA, A and TAGLIAFICO, J B (18th C) Italian					
wc/d	1	9,432		9,432	
BARATTI, Filippo (19/20th C) Italian					
oil	1	5,738		5,738	
BARBA, Juan (20th C) Spanish					
oil	1	1,012		1,012	
BARBARIN, Thomas de (1821-1892) French					
wc/d	1	2,208		2,208	
BARBARINI, Emil (1855-1930) Austrian					
oil	4	11,271	1,519	2,633	4,487

Name	No.	Total Sales Value	lowest	Prices median	highest
BARBARINI, Franz (1804-1873) Austrian					
oil	2	5,876	1,452	2,938	4,424
wc/d	1	1,845		1,845	
BARBARINI, Gustav (1840-1909) Austrian					
oil	2	4,081	1,936	2,041	2,145
BARBARO, Giovanni (?) Italian?					
wc/d	2	2,999	1,043	1,500	1,956
BARBASAN, Mariano (1864-1924) Spanish					
oil	3	31,461	1,835	4,302	25,324
BARBEAU, Marcel (1925-) Canadian					
oil	1	1,622		1,622	
wc/d	1	1,000		1,000	
BARBELLA, Constantino (1852-1925) Italian					
3D	1	14,000		14,000	
BARBER, Alfred R (fl.1879-1893) British					
oil	1	16,790		16,790	
BARBER, George (1910-) American?					
oil	1	1,500		1,500	
BARBER, Joel (20th C) American					
wc/d	1	4,200		4,200	
BARBER, Thomas Stanley (fl.1891-1899) British					
oil	1	1,050		1,050	
BARBERA, C la (19th C) ?					
oil	1	1,667		1,667	
BARBERI, Giuseppe (1682-1767) Italian					
wc/d	1	5,285		5,285	
BARBERO, Ernesto (20th C) Italian					
wc/d	1	1,379		1,379	
BARBIER, Andre (1883-1970) French					
oil	2	4,701	1,164	2,351	3,537
BARBIER, Georges (1882-1932) French					
wc/d	1	5,050		5,050	
BARBIER, Jean Jacques le (1738-1826) French					
oil	1	11,122		11,122	
wc/d	2	3,264	1,460	1,632	1,804
BARBIER, Louis le (younger) (1743-?) French					
wc/d	1	2,139		2,139	
BARBIERS, Pieter II (1798-1848) Dutch					
oil	1	5,507		5,507	
BARBISAN, Giovanni (1914-1988) Italian					
oil	2	14,500	6,390	7,250	8,110
BARBIZON SCHOOL, 19th C French					
oil	1	3,000		3,000	
BARBLAN, Oscar (1909-1987) Swiss					
oil	1	1,141		1,141	
BARBOT, Prosper (1798-1878) French					
wc/d	1	2,596		2,596	
BARBUDO, Salvador Sanchez (1858-1917) Spanish					
oil	5	94,163	5,680	17,727	42,198
wc/d	1	1,168		1,168	
BARBUT-DAVRAY, Luc (1863-?) French					
oil	1	3,712		3,712	
BARCALA, Washington (20th C) ?					
oil	1	1,393		1,393	
BARCELO, Miguel (1957-) Spanish					
oil	3	635,726	11,054	216,972	407,700
wc/d	9	1,043,520	5,051	98,150	365,700
BARCLAY, Edgar (1842-1913) British					
oil	1	3,002		3,002	

Name	No.	Total Sales Value	lowest	Prices median	highest
BARCLAY, John Rankin (1884-1962) British					
oil	2	6,009	1,329	3,005	4,680
BARCLAY, McClelland (1891-1943) American					
3D	1	1,200		1,200	
oil	8	43,450	1,150	2,850	17,000
BARDASANO BAOS, Jose (1910-1979) Spanish					
oil	1	1,307		1,307	
BARDELLINI, Pietro (1728-1806) Italian					
oil	4	33,762	3,917	7,892	14,061
BARDILL, Ralph William (1876-1935) British					
wc/d	2	3,127	1,027	1,564	2,100
BARDONE, Guy (1927-) French					
oil	2	2,492	1,084	1,246	1,408
BARDWELL, Thomas (1704-1767) British					
oil	4	59,624	9,664	14,410	21,140
BARE, Esnault (19th C) French					
oil	1	1,668		1,668	
BAREAU, Georges (1866-1931) French					
3D	2	5,177	1,177	2,589	4,000
BAREFORD, David (20th C) American					
oil	2	4,400	2,000	2,200	2,400
BARELIER, Andre (20th C) French?					
3D	1	4,647		4,647	
BARENGER, James (jnr) (1780-1831) British					
oil	1	28,120		28,120	
BARET (19th C) French					
3D	1	2,112		2,112	
BARETTA, Michele (1916-1987) Italian					
oil	10	18,647	1,009	1,590	4,310
BARGHEER, Eduard (1901-1979) German					
oil	9	43,836	1,553	3,128	9,457
wc/d	37	88,548	1,151	1,905	6,311
BARGIS, Stefano (1916-1999) Italian					
oil	1	1,758		1,758	
BARILE, Xavier J (1891-1981) American					
oil	1	1,000		1,000	
BARILLI, Aristide (20th C) Italian?					
oil	1	1,941		1,941	
BARILLOT, E (19th C) ?					
3D	1	4,898		4,898	
BARISANI, Renato (1918-) Italian					
3D	1	3,601		3,601	
BARISON (19th C) British					
oil	1	3,000		3,000	
BARISON, Giuseppe (1853-1930) Italian					
oil	2	18,316	6,090	9,158	12,226
BARJOLA, Juan (1919-) Spanish					
oil	3	47,016	12,646	14,044	20,326
BARKER OF BATH, Benjamin (1776-1838) British					
oil	1	1,673		1,673	
BARKER OF BATH, Thomas (1769-1847) British					
oil	4	29,175	2,610	6,110	14,345
BARKER OF THIRSK, Thomas (19th C) British					
oil	1	1,125		1,125	
BARKER, Clive (1940-) British					
3D	2	5,100	2,400	2,550	2,700
BARKER, Edmund (1940-) British					
oil	1	1,776		1,776	

Name	No.	Total Sales Value	Prices lowest	median	highest
BARKER, J (19th C) British					
oil	1	3,000		3,000	
BARKER, J S (fl.1858) British					
oil	1	1,036		1,036	
BARKER, John (19th C) British					
oil	2	20,514	1,274	10,257	19,240
BARKER, John Joseph (fl.1835-1866) British					
oil	1	3,861		3,861	
BARKER, Joseph (fl.1843-1848) British					
oil	1	1,099		1,099	
BARKER, Lucette E (fl.1853-1874) British					
oil	1	7,250		7,250	
BARKER, Theodore (fl.1909-1916) British					
oil	1	1,015		1,015	
BARKER, Wright (1864-1941) British					
oil	6	133,790	3,300	5,820	60,000
BARLACH, Ernst (1870-1938) German					
3D	19	1,105,427	1,903	21,600	432,000
wc/d	3	12,137	2,413	2,574	7,150
BARLAND, Adam (fl.1843-1875) British					
oil	4	7,685	1,272	1,848	2,717
BARLE, Maurice (1903-) French					
oil	1	1,258		1,258	
BARLIUK (20th C) ?					
oil	1	2,000		2,000	
BARLOW, John Noble (1861-1924) American/British					
oil	2	2,900	1,300	1,450	1,600
BARNABA, L (?) ?					
oil	1	2,431		2,431	
BARNABE, Duilio (1914-1961) Italian					
oil	5	11,219	1,050	1,623	4,500
BARNARD, Edward Herbert (1855-1909) American					
oil	1	3,750		3,750	
BARNEKOW, Brita (1868-1936) Danish					
oil	1	1,192		1,192	
BARNES, Archibald George (1887-1934) British					
oil	1	5,700		5,700	
BARNES, E C (19th C) British					
oil	2	7,758	3,650	3,879	4,108
BARNES, Edward Charles (19th C) British					
oil	8	36,874	1,001	4,488	8,500
BARNES, F D (fl.1914) British					
oil	1	6,578		6,578	
BARNES, H (?) ?					
oil	1	1,145		1,145	
BARNES, James (19/20th C) British					
oil	1	1,000		1,000	
BARNES, Joseph H (fl.1867-1887) British					
wc/d	1	1,205		1,205	
BARNES, Samuel John (1847-1901) British					
oil	1	1,185		1,185	
BARNETT, Thomas P (1870-1929) American					
oil	1	1,000		1,000	
BARNEY, Frank A (1862-?) American					
oil	1	6,500		6,500	
BARNEY, Matthew (1967-) American					
oil	1	82,000		82,000	
wc/d	1	20,000		20,000	

Name	No.	Total Sales Value	lowest	Prices median	highest
BARNI, Roberto (1939-) Italian					
oil	2	3,565	1,165	1,783	2,400
BARNITZ, Alexander M (1824-1903) American					
oil	1	1,750		1,750	
BARNOIN, Henri Alphonse (1882-1935) French					
oil	18	117,064	1,653	5,683	17,600
wc/d	1	5,373		5,373	
BARNS-GRAHAM, Wilhelmina (1912-) British					
wc/d	1	4,056		4,056	
BARNSLEY, James MacDonald (1861-1929) Canadian					
oil	1	1,659		1,659	
BAROCCI, Federico (1526-1612) Italian					
wc/d	1	90,600		90,600	
BAROJA, Ricardo (1871-1953) Spanish					
wc/d	1	2,245		2,245	
BARON Y CARRILLO, Manuel (19th C) Spanish					
oil	1	53,362		53,362	
BARON, Henri Charles Antoine (1816-1885) French					
oil	3	33,488	1,798	15,334	16,356
wc/d	1	1,015		1,015	
BARON, Theodor (1840-1899) Belgian					
oil	6	13,137	1,083	1,450	6,246
BARONE, Adolfo C (1861-?) Italian					
oil	1	5,236		5,236	
BARONS, D (18th C) Irish					
oil	1	2,300		2,300	
BAROTTE, Léon (20th C) French					
oil	1	1,053		1,053	
BARR, Allan (fl.1912-1921) British					
oil	1	1,350		1,350	
BARR, G R (19th C) ?					
oil	1	1,846		1,846	
BARR, W (1867-1933) American					
oil	1	1,343		1,343	
BARR, William (1867-1933) American					
oil	2	4,591	2,175	2,296	2,416
BARRABAND, Jacques (1767-1809) French					
wc/d	23	1,072,874	3,950	26,335	131,676
BARRADAS, Rafael (1890-1929) Uruguayan					
wc/d	2	10,200	4,000	5,100	6,200
BARRAGAN, Luis (20th C) South American					
oil	1	3,200		3,200	
BARRALET, John James (1747-1815) British					
wc/d	1	9,420		9,420	
BARRATT, Watson (1884-1962) American					
oil	1	1,100		1,100	
wc/d	1	1,000		1,000	
BARRAU, Laureano (1864-1957) Spanish					
oil	4	54,882	2,529	10,608	31,137
BARRAUD, Aime (1902-1954) Swiss					
oil	6	19,551	1,516	3,055	4,956
BARRAUD, Francis (1856-1924) British					
oil	1	15,800		15,800	
BARRAUD, François (1899-1934) Swiss					
oil	3	70,812	2,842	3,133	64,837
BARRAUD, Henry (1811-1874) British					
oil	1	1,359		1,359	
BARRAUD, Maurice (1889-1954) Swiss					
oil	11	79,313	3,344	4,715	17,259

Name	No.	Total Sales Value	lowest	Prices median	highest
wc/d	1	1,554		1,554	
BARRAUD, W (1810-1850) British					
oil	1	9,000		9,000	
BARRAUD, William (1810-1850) British					
oil	3	28,505	4,650	8,000	15,855
BARRE, A (19th C) ?					
3D	1	3,142		3,142	
BARRE, E (?) ?					
oil	1	1,287		1,287	
BARRÉ, Martin (1924-1993) French					
oil	9	66,502	5,413	6,688	10,541
BARREDA, B de (c.1800-1890) Spanish					
oil	1	1,629		1,629	
BARREDA, Enrique D (1880-1953) Peruvian					
oil	1	2,190		2,190	
BARREDA, Ernesto (1927-) Chilean					
oil	1	7,000		7,000	
BARREIRO, Jose Maria (1940-) Spanish					
oil	2	3,020	1,438	1,510	1,582
BARRERA, Francisco (17th C) Spanish					
oil	1	10,275		10,275	
BARRERA, Manuel (19th C) Spanish					
oil	1	12,100		12,100	
BARRET, George (18/19th C) British					
oil	1	162,800		162,800	
BARRET, George (jnr) (1767-1842) British					
wc/d	1	1,125		1,125	
BARRET, George and GILPIN, Sawrey (18th C) British					
oil	1	60,400		60,400	
BARRET, Marius-Antoine (1865-1929) French					
oil	1	2,918		2,918	
BARRETO, Lia Menna (1959-) Brazilian					
3D	1	2,000		2,000	
BARRETT, Charles (20th C) British					
oil	1	1,036		1,036	
BARRETT, Joseph (20th C) American					
oil	1	1,000		1,000	
BARRETT, Thomas (19th C) British					
oil	1	1,205		1,205	
BARRETT, William S (1854-1927) American					
oil	1	7,000		7,000	
BARRIAS, E (19/20th C) French					
3D	2	18,414	3,500	9,207	14,914
BARRIAS, Félix (1822-1907) French					
oil	1	6,111		6,111	
BARRIAS, Louis Ernest (1841-1905) French					
3D	7	157,661	2,355	10,800	105,000
BARRIAT, Charles (1821-?) French					
oil	2	3,293	1,084	1,647	2,209
BARRIGUES, Prosper de (1760-1850) Portuguese					
oil	1	1,638		1,638	
BARRINGTON, Arthur (?) ?					
wc/d	1	2,265		2,265	
BARRIOS, Armando (1920-) Venezuelan					
oil	1	45,130		45,130	
BARRIOS, Rafael (1947-) Venezuelan					
3D	3	6,545	1,600	1,900	3,045
BARRISH, Barbara (20th C) American					
3D	1	1,400		1,400	

Name	No.	Total Sales Value	lowest	Prices median	highest
BARRON Y CARRILLO, Manuel (1814-1884) Spanish					
oil	3	52,343	8,629	19,425	24,289
BARROW, Jane (fl.1890-1897) British					
oil	1	4,828		4,828	
BARRY, Claude-Francis (1883-1970) British					
oil	2	4,612	1,422	2,306	3,190
BARRY, François Pierre Bernard (1813-1905) French					
oil	1	3,279		3,279	
BARRY, Moyra A (1886-1960) Irish					
oil	1	1,125		1,125	
BARRY, Robert (1936-) American					
oil	6	25,362	1,228	4,572	7,500
BARRY, William (19th C) British					
oil	1	4,060		4,060	
BARTA, Ladislas (1902-) Hungarian					
oil	1	1,933		1,933	
BARTEL, A (18th C) ?					
3D	1	1,530		1,530	
BARTELLETTI, Aldo (20th C) Italian					
3D	1	10,570		10,570	
BARTELS, Hans von (1856-1913) German					
wc/d	2	9,851	4,554	4,926	5,297
BARTELS, Rudolf (1872-1946) German					
oil	2	3,799	1,788	1,900	2,011
BARTEZAGO, Luigi (1820-1905) Italian					
oil	2	3,078	1,539	1,539	1,539
BARTH, A (20th C) German					
oil	1	1,895		1,895	
BARTH, Carl (1896-1976) German					
oil	2	3,233	1,000	1,617	2,233
BARTH, Carl Wilhelm (1847-1919) Norwegian					
oil	1	1,259		1,259	
BARTH, Ferdinand (1842-1892) German					
oil	1	1,045		1,045	
BARTH, Paul Basilius (1881-1955) Swiss					
oil	8	20,063	1,016	2,515	4,781
BARTHALOT, Marius (1861-?) French					
oil	1	3,651		3,651	
BARTHELEMY, Camille (1890-1961) Belgian					
oil	9	65,933	1,065	3,105	18,241
wc/d	1	1,278		1,278	
BARTHELEMY, L (19/20th C) French					
3D	1	1,824		1,824	
BARTHELEMY, Marguerite (20th C) French					
oil	1	1,151		1,151	
BARTHOLDI, Frederic Auguste (1834-1904) French					
3D	3	5,389	1,251	1,673	2,465
oil	1	6,573		6,573	
BARTHOLOME, Albert (1848-1928) French					
3D	2	8,805	1,317	4,403	7,488
BARTHOLOME, E (?) French?					
oil	1	2,200		2,200	
BARTHOLOMEW, James H (1962-) British					
oil	1	3,749		3,749	
BARTHOLOMEW, Valentine (1799-1879) British					
wc/d	2	2,519	1,106	1,260	1,413
BARTLE, K (19th C?) British?					
oil	1	1,021		1,021	

Name	No.	Total Sales Value	lowest	Prices median	highest
BARTLETT, Dana (1878-1957) American					
oil	6	21,300	1,900	4,000	4,750
BARTLETT, Jennifer (1941-) American					
wc/d	2	9,500	4,000	4,750	5,500
BARTLETT, William H (1858-1932) British					
oil	5	47,777	5,400	9,295	13,050
BARTLETT, William Henry (1809-1854) British					
oil	1	15,000		15,000	
BARTNING, Ludwig (1876-?) German					
oil	1	1,486		1,486	
BARTOLENA, Giovanni (1866-1942) Italian					
oil	5	24,835	1,273	1,745	12,939
BARTOLI, Jacques (1920-) French					
oil	2	3,600	1,400	1,800	2,200
BARTOLINI, Frederico (19/20th C) Italian					
wc/d	1	7,500		7,500	
BARTOLINI, Philippo (1861-1908) Italian					
wc/d	2	9,307	3,307	4,654	6,000
BARTOLINI, Ubaldo (1944-) Italian					
oil	1	2,656		2,656	
BARTOLO, Andrea di (fl.1389-1428) Italian					
oil	2	220,166	54,066	110,083	166,100
BARTOLO, Taddeo di (1363-1422) Italian					
oil	1	91,140		91,140	
BARTOLOMMEO, Fra (1472-1517) Italian					
oil	2	67,006	33,503	33,503	33,503
BARTON, Donald Blagge (1903-1990) American					
oil	2	2,400	1,200	1,200	1,200
BARTON, Harry (20th C) American?					
wc/d	1	1,100		1,100	
BARTON, Rose Maynard (1856-1929) British					
wc/d	4	29,344	3,000	6,512	13,320
BARTSCH, C-F (1829-1908) Danish					
oil	1	1,787		1,787	
BARTSCH, Carl-Frederick (1829-1908) Danish					
oil	1	1,072		1,072	
BARTSCH, Gustav (1821-?) German					
oil	1	7,900		7,900	
BARTSCH, Reinhold (20th C) German					
oil	1	1,365		1,365	
BARUCCI, Pietro (1845-1917) Italian					
oil	7	76,400	3,000	8,000	21,817
wc/d	1	1,741		1,741	
BARUCCO, Felice (1830-1906) Italian					
oil	1	1,977		1,977	
BARWELL, Frederick Bacon (?-1897) British					
oil	1	79,000		79,000	
BARWICK, John (fl.1835-1870) British					
oil	1	9,540		9,540	
BARYE (?) French					
3D	5	14,736	1,331	1,712	5,703
BARYE, A (19th C) French					
3D	1	2,160		2,160	
BARYE, Alfred (1839-1882) French					
3D	5	14,768	1,200	2,826	5,506
BARYE, Alfred and GUILLEMIN, Émile (19th C) French					
3D	1	2,500		2,500	
BARYE, Antoine-Louis (1796-1875) French					
3D	100	971,116	1,088	3,909	164,850

Name	No.	Total Sales Value	lowest	Prices median	highest
oil	2	24,442	7,916	12,221	16,526
wc/d	1	1,047		1,047	
BARZAGHI-CATTANEO, Antonio (1837-1922) Swiss					
oil	2	51,323	1,323	25,662	50,000
BARZAGLI, Massimo (1960-) Italian					
oil	1	2,230		2,230	
wc/d	1	6,327		6,327	
BARZANTI, P (19/20th C) Italian					
3D	1	4,737		4,737	
BARZANTI, Peter (19/20th C) Italian					
3D	1	2,173		2,173	
BAS, Edward le (1904-1966) British					
oil	3	12,250	3,120	3,130	6,000
BASCHENIS, Evaristo (1617-1677) Italian					
oil	1	10,325		10,325	
BASCHINDJAGHIAN, Gevork Zacharovich (1857-1925) Russian					
oil	1	5,640		5,640	
BASELITZ, Georg (1938-) German					
oil	7	1,340,252	43,252	190,000	320,000
wc/d	9	152,336	3,775	7,550	90,000
BASHKIRTSEFF, Maria (1860-1884) Russian					
wc/d	2	3,308	1,196	1,654	2,112
BASIANO, Jesus (1889-1966) Spanish					
oil	1	1,613		1,613	
BASKIN, Leonard (1922-2000) American					
3D	3	24,600	2,600	6,000	16,000
wc/d	1	2,400		2,400	
BASKINE, Maurice (20th C) French					
wc/d	1	2,772		2,772	
BASQUIAT, Jean Michel (1960-1988) American					
oil	45	10,134,881	10,000	180,000	1,250,000
wc/d	8	228,543	5,000	28,425	60,000
BASQUIAT, Jean Michel and WARHOL, Andy (20th C) American					
oil	1	50,000		50,000	
BASSANO, Francesco (15/16th C) Italian					
oil	1	12,960		12,960	
BASSANO, Francesco (younger) (1549-1592) Italian					
oil	1	15,840		15,840	
BASSANO, Francesco (younger-school) (1549-1592) Italian					
oil	1	4,273		4,273	
BASSANO, Gerolamo (1566-1621) Italian					
oil	1	102,900		102,900	
BASSANO, Giambattista (1553-1613) Italian					
oil	1	10,080		10,080	
BASSANO, Jacobo (1515-1592) Italian					
oil	1	44,314		44,314	
wc/d	1	6,078		6,078	
BASSANO, Jacobo (school) (1515-1592) Italian					
oil	1	4,301		4,301	
BASSANO, Leandro (1557-1622) Italian					
oil	3	126,190	10,990	30,200	85,000
BASSET, Urbin (?) French					
3D	1	1,775		1,775	
BASSETTI, Marcantonio (1588-1630) Italian					
wc/d	1	1,309		1,309	
BASSI, Adele (19th C) ?					
oil	1	2,546		2,546	
BASSOT, Ferdinand (19th C) French					
oil	2	11,884	2,884	5,942	9,000

Name	No.	Total Sales Value	lowest	Prices median	highest
BASTERT, Nicolaas (1854-1939) Dutch					
oil	6	20,822	1,273	2,384	8,417
wc/d	1	1,697		1,697	
BASTET, T (?) French					
oil	1	8,147		8,147	
BASTET, Victorien Antoine (1853-1905) French					
3D	1	54,360		54,360	
BASTIANINI, Giulio (19th C) Italian					
3D	1	15,686		15,686	
BASTIEN LEPAGE, Jules (1848-1884) French					
oil	2	18,854	7,928	9,427	10,926
BASTIEN, A (1873-1955) Belgian					
oil	2	2,616	1,149	1,308	1,467
BASTIEN, Alfred (1873-1955) Belgian					
oil	15	27,749	1,034	1,597	4,292
BASTIEN, D (19th C) French?					
oil	1	1,149		1,149	
BASTIN, Ernest (c.1870-?) Belgian					
3D	1	2,440		2,440	
BATAILLE, Henry (1872-1922) French					
oil	1	1,382		1,382	
BATALLA, Daniel (20th C) South American?					
oil	1	1,110		1,110	
BATCHELDER, Stephen (1849-1932) British					
wc/d	13	28,337	1,044	1,470	4,998
BATCHELLER, Frederick S (1837-1889) American					
oil	2	11,500	4,000	5,750	7,500
BATCHELOR, Roland (1889-1990) British					
wc/d	4	6,001	1,029	1,414	2,145
BATEMAN OF KENDAL, James (1893-1959) British					
oil	1	35,250		35,250	
wc/d	1	6,768		6,768	
BATEMAN, H M (1887-1970) British					
wc/d	1	2,592		2,592	
BATEMAN, Henry Mayo (1887-1970) British					
wc/d	17	92,716	1,176	5,372	12,324
BATEMAN, Herbert J (fl.1907-1916) British					
wc/d	1	1,208		1,208	
BATEMAN, Robert (1842-1922) British					
wc/d	1	21,450		21,450	
BATEMAN, Robert (1930-) Canadian					
oil	3	33,279	1,333	11,946	20,000
wc/d	2	4,003	1,846	2,002	2,157
BATES, David (c.1841-1921) British					
oil	26	139,517	1,136	4,233	14,220
wc/d	4	7,951	1,369	1,830	2,923
BATES, Frederick-Davenport (1867-1930) British					
oil	1	4,968		4,968	
BATES, Maxwell (1906-1980) Canadian					
oil	1	4,698		4,698	
BATET, François (1923-) Spanish/French					
oil	3	19,736	2,114	3,322	14,300
BATHNER, H (19th C) German					
oil	1	1,580		1,580	
BATONI, Pompeo (1708-1787) Italian					
oil	2	257,950	67,950	128,975	190,000
wc/d	3	17,377	1,942	2,600	12,835
BATT, Arthur (19th C) British					
oil	3	7,474	1,963	2,079	3,432

Name	No.	Total Sales Value	Prices lowest	median	highest
BATTAGLIA, Alessandro (1870-1940) Italian					
oil	2	26,412	1,497	13,206	24,915
BATTAGLIOLI, Francesco (18th C) Italian					
oil	1	51,340		51,340	
BATTAILLE, Jan (1808-1957) Belgian					
oil	1	1,410		1,410	
BATTERMANN, Jan (1909-) Dutch					
oil	1	1,377		1,377	
BATTIGLIO, Eugenio (19/20th C) Italian					
3D	1	1,284		1,284	
BATTIN, Louis (19th C) French					
oil	1	1,908		1,908	
BATTY, Lt Col Robert (1789-1848) British					
oil	2	16,398	5,586	8,199	10,812
BATZ, Eugen (1905-) German					
wc/d	1	1,587		1,587	
BAUCHANT, Andre (1873-1958) French					
oil	22	145,328	1,063	4,137	21,395
BAUD-BOVY, Auguste (1848-1899) Swiss					
oil	3	7,354	1,864	2,621	2,869
BAUDESSON, Nicolas (1611-1680) French					
oil	2	45,870	12,412	22,935	33,458
BAUDISCH, Gudrun (1907-1982) Austrian					
3D	1	4,898		4,898	
BAUDIT, Amedee (1825-1890) French					
oil	2	15,700	2,700	7,850	13,000
BAUDIT, Louis (1870-1960) Swiss					
oil	1	1,898		1,898	
BAUDOIN, F (?) French					
oil	1	9,000		9,000	
BAUDOUIN, Pierre-Antoine (1723-1769) French					
wc/d	1	8,000		8,000	
BAUDOUIN, Raphael (1870-1956) Belgian					
oil	3	11,335	2,820	2,820	5,695
BAUDRY, A (?) French					
wc/d	4	9,553	1,228	1,774	4,777
BAUDRY, Leon Georges (1898-1978) French					
3D	1	1,478		1,478	
BAUDRY, Paul (1828-1886) French					
oil	1	1,100		1,100	
BAUER, Carl Franz (1879-1954) Austrian					
wc/d	1	1,178		1,178	
BAUER, Gustav (1874-1933) Austrian					
oil	1	1,092		1,092	
BAUER, John (1882-1918) Swedish					
oil	2	15,898	6,351	7,949	9,547
wc/d	7	25,544	1,035	3,105	6,831
BAUER, Maria (1870-1945) Austrian					
oil	1	1,132		1,132	
BAUER, Marius Alexander Jacques (1867-1932) Dutch					
oil	4	30,434	5,092	7,002	11,339
wc/d	6	27,255	1,231	2,830	11,478
BAUER, Rudolf (1889-1967) Polish					
oil	2	81,000	31,000	40,500	50,000
wc/d	2	2,800	1,200	1,400	1,600
BAUER, Wilhelm-Gottfried (1779-1853) German					
oil	1	4,276		4,276	
BAUERLE, C W F (1831-1912) German					
oil	1	3,566		3,566	

Name	No.	Total Sales Value	lowest	Prices median	highest
BAUERLE, Carl Wilhelm Friedrich (1831-1912) German					
oil	5	24,728	1,413	4,290	10,000
BAUERNFEIND, Gustav (1848-1904) Austrian					
oil	2	230,658	10,220	115,329	220,438
BAUFFE, Victor (19th C) Dutch					
oil	3	9,026	2,037	2,257	4,732
BAUGNIET, Charles (1814-1886) Flemish					
oil	2	529,610	29,610	264,805	500,000
BAUGNIET, Marcel Louis (1896-1995) Belgian					
oil	5	18,928	1,753	3,135	8,517
wc/d	2	4,142	1,007	2,071	3,135
BAUKEMA, Sieger (1852-1936) German					
oil	1	2,334		2,334	
BAUKNECHT, Philipp (1884-1933) German					
wc/d	1	2,733		2,733	
BAULLERY, Nicolas (1560-1630) French					
oil	1	30,200		30,200	
BAUM, Otto (1900-1977) German					
3D	2	8,759	2,777	4,380	5,982
BAUM, Paul (1859-1932) German					
oil	2	104,509	4,325	52,255	100,184
wc/d	1	2,624		2,624	
BAUM, Walter Emerson (1884-1956) American					
oil	23	185,947	1,000	5,500	37,500
wc/d	1	1,750		1,750	
BAUMANN, E J (19th C) Danish					
oil	1	1,569		1,569	
BAUMANN, Ida (1864-?) Swiss					
oil	1	7,000		7,000	
BAUMBACH, Marx (1859-1915) German					
3D	1	2,458		2,458	
BAUMBERGER, Otto (1889-1961) Swiss					
oil	1	2,915		2,915	
BAUMEISTER, Willi (1889-1955) German					
oil	9	695,782	17,733	67,961	126,720
wc/d	5	53,020	2,913	7,969	27,180
BAUMER, Lewis (1870-1963) British					
oil	1	2,248		2,248	
BAUMGARTEN, M (20th C) German?					
oil	1	1,771		1,771	
BAUMGARTL, Moritz (1934-) Czechoslovakian					
oil	1	2,271		2,271	
BAUMGARTNER, A (19/20th C) European					
oil	3	4,101	1,036	1,226	1,839
BAUMGARTNER, Fritz (1929-) German					
wc/d	1	1,456		1,456	
BAUMGARTNER, Johann Wolfgang (1712-1761) German					
wc/d	1	4,126		4,126	
BAUMGARTNER, Peter (1834-1911) German					
oil	2	18,633	4,114	9,317	14,519
BAUMGARTNER, Thomas (1892-1962) German					
oil	1	1,463		1,463	
BAUR, Johann Wilhelm (1607-c.1640) Austrian					
wc/d	1	19,000		19,000	
BAURIEDL, Otto (1879-1956) German					
wc/d	1	1,374		1,374	
BAURSCHEIT, Jan Pieter van (elder) (1669-1728) Flemish					
3D	2	25,061	7,696	12,531	17,365

Name	No.	Total Sales Value	lowest	Prices median	highest
BAVARIAN SCHOOL, 16th C German					
3D	2	21,993	6,055	10,997	15,938
oil	1	8,650		8,650	
BAVARIAN SCHOOL, 17th C German					
3D	1	5,497		5,497	
BAVARIAN SCHOOL, 19th C German					
oil	2	12,150	2,245	6,075	9,905
BAVARIAN-TYROLEAN SCHOOL, 16th C German/Austrian					
3D	1	27,273		27,273	
BAWA, Manjit (1941-) Indian					
wc/d	1	1,500		1,500	
BAWDEN, Edward (1903-1989) British					
wc/d	7	19,342	1,199	2,198	5,436
BAXTER, Charles (1809-1879) British					
oil	2	20,612	7,097	10,306	13,515
BAY SALA (1912-) Spanish					
oil	1	3,432		3,432	
BAYARD (19/20th C) ?					
oil	1	8,456		8,456	
BAYART, Paul Leon (1861-1921) Belgian					
oil	1	2,445		2,445	
BAYE, Adolphe (19th C) French					
oil	1	2,400		2,400	
BAYENS, Han (1876-1945) Dutch					
oil	1	2,617		2,617	
BAYENS, Hans (1924-) Dutch					
wc/d	1	2,371		2,371	
BAYER, August von (1803-1875) German					
oil	1	1,136		1,136	
BAYER, Herbert (1900-1985) German					
3D	2	10,400	2,400	5,200	8,000
oil	5	23,307	1,107	4,500	8,000
BAYER, Joseph (19th C) German					
oil	1	1,264		1,264	
BAYER, Peter (1871-1919) German					
oil	1	6,731		6,731	
BAYES, Alfred Walter (1832-1909) British					
oil	3	7,210	1,422	2,538	3,250
BAYEU Y SUBIAS, Francisco (1734-1795) Spanish					
oil	1	14,381		14,381	
BAYLE, Luc Marie (20th C) French					
wc/d	1	1,338		1,338	
BAYLINSON, Abraham S (1882-1950) American					
oil	1	2,000		2,000	
BAYLISS, Margaret E (fl.1928-1938) British					
wc/d	1	2,860		2,860	
BAYNE, Walter McPherson (fl.1832-1858) British					
oil	1	1,200		1,200	
BAYNES, Keith (1887-1977) British					
oil	1	4,230		4,230	
BAYNES, Pauline Diana (1922-) British					
wc/d	1	1,305		1,305	
BAYON SALADO, Juan (1903-) Spanish					
oil	2	2,321	1,092	1,161	1,229
BAYROS, Franz von (1866-1924) Austrian					
wc/d	1	1,455		1,455	
BAYSER-GRATRY, Margueritte de (20th C) French					
3D	1	2,137		2,137	

| Name | No. | Total Sales Value | | Prices | |
			lowest	median	highest
BAZAINE, Jean (1904-1995) French					
oil	2	46,400	5,800	23,200	40,600
wc/d	5	9,778	1,314	2,047	2,424
BAZILE, Castera (1923-1965) Haitian					
oil	1	5,500		5,500	
BAZIN, Charles Louis (1802-1859) French					
oil	1	8,580		8,580	
BAZIOTES, William (1912-1963) American					
wc/d	1	10,000		10,000	
BAZIRAY (18th C) French?					
oil	3	74,144	8,555	27,091	38,498
BAZZANTI, P (19/20th C) Italian					
3D	1	5,150		5,150	
BAZZARO, Ernesto (1859-1937) Italian					
oil	1	13,473		13,473	
BAZZARO, Leonardo (1853-1937) Italian					
oil	7	67,459	4,013	6,880	20,687
BAZZI, Giovanni Antonio (1477-1549) Italian					
oil	1	34,318		34,318	
BEACH, Ernest G (1865-c.1934) British					
wc/d	1	1,764		1,764	
BEACH, Thomas (1738-1806) British					
oil	2	6,426	2,198	3,213	4,228
BEADLE, James Princep (1863-1947) British					
oil	1	3,636		3,636	
BEAL, Gifford (1879-1956) American					
oil	2	11,000	5,500	5,500	5,500
wc/d	1	1,800		1,800	
BEAL, Reynolds (1867-1951) American					
oil	2	110,000	45,000	55,000	65,000
wc/d	5	11,800	1,800	2,600	2,600
BEALE, Mary (1632-1697) British					
oil	1	12,640		12,640	
BEAR, George Telfer (1874-1973) British					
oil	1	1,284		1,284	
BEARD, James Henry (1812-1893) American					
oil	1	1,500		1,500	
BEARD, William Holbrook (1824-1900) American					
oil	5	52,600	2,600	7,500	28,000
BEARDEN, Romare (1914-1988) American					
oil	1	20,000		20,000	
wc/d	6	81,350	3,600	6,500	38,000
BEARDSLEY, Jefferson (1833-1895) American					
oil	1	2,800		2,800	
BEARE, George (18th C) British					
oil	1	3,212		3,212	
BEATON, Penelope (1886-1963) British					
oil	2	6,297	1,740	3,149	4,557
BEATON, Sir Cecil (1904-1980) British					
wc/d	11	21,224	1,063	1,800	3,160
BEATTIE, Arthur (?) British					
oil	1	4,530		4,530	
BEATTY, John William (1869-1941) Canadian					
oil	7	29,355	1,170	1,896	15,541
BEAU, Alcide le (1872-1943) French					
oil	3	18,276	3,535	6,475	8,266
BEAUCE, Jean (1818-1875) French					
oil	1	1,193		1,193	

Name	No.	Total Sales Value	lowest	Prices median	highest
BEAUCLERK, Lady Diana (1734-1808) British					
wc/d	1	4,740		4,740	
BEAUDIN, Andre (1895-1979) French					
oil	6	24,155	1,741	2,765	10,619
wc/d	2	3,753	1,317	1,877	2,436
BEAUDUIN, Jean (1851-1916) Belgian					
oil	2	9,095	1,595	4,548	7,500
BEAUFRERE, Adolphe (1876-1960) French					
oil	26	112,085	1,056	2,411	19,304
wc/d	2	3,790	1,240	1,895	2,550
BEAUJEUX, R de (19th C) French					
oil	1	6,279		6,279	
BEAULIEU, Henri de (1819-1884) French					
oil	1	6,128		6,128	
BEAULIEU, Paul Vanier (1910-1995) Canadian					
oil	8	37,932	1,519	3,241	12,610
wc/d	2	2,390	1,187	1,195	1,203
BEAUME, Émile Marie (1888-1967) French					
oil	1	1,258		1,258	
BEAUME, Joseph (1796-1885) French					
oil	3	6,570	1,166	2,783	2,783
BEAUMONT, A (?) ?					
oil	1	1,208		1,208	
BEAUMONT, Arthur Edwaine (1890-1978) American					
wc/d	3	7,200	1,700	2,000	3,500
BEAUMONT, D (?) ?					
oil	1	1,300		1,300	
BEAUMONT, Ernest (1871-1933) American					
oil	1	1,600		1,600	
BEAUPUY, Louis (1896-1974) French					
oil	1	1,258		1,258	
BEAUQUESNE, Wilfrid Constant (1847-1913) French					
oil	3	14,580	1,770	3,750	9,060
BEAUREGARD, Charles G (c.1856-d.1919) Canadian/American					
oil	1	1,250		1,250	
BEAVIS, Richard (1824-1896) British					
oil	4	11,307	1,590	2,246	5,226
BECAN, Bernard (1890-1943) French					
oil	2	4,880	1,885	2,440	2,995
BECCARD, Louis (19th C) French?					
oil	1	5,313		5,313	
BECERRA, Milton (1951-) Venezuelan					
wc/d	1	1,060		1,060	
BECH, Poul Anker (1942-) Danish					
oil	1	1,668		1,668	
BECHI, Luigi (1830-1919) Italian					
oil	3	193,744	25,000	52,744	116,000
BECHSTEDT, Johann Caspar (1735-1801) German					
oil	2	4,368	2,093	2,184	2,275
BECHSTEIN, Lothar (1884-1936) German					
oil	1	2,943		2,943	
BECHTEL, David B (19th C) American					
oil	1	4,500		4,500	
BECHTOLD, Erwin (1925-) German					
oil	1	11,395		11,395	
BECHTOLD, J C (18th C) ?					
oil	2	4,518	2,163	2,259	2,355
BECK, Dunbar D (1902-1986) American					
oil	1	1,800		1,800	

Name	No.	Total Sales Value	Prices lowest	Prices median	highest
BECK, Jacob Samuel (1715-1778) German					
oil	2	31,961	12,835	15,981	19,126
BECK, Julia (1853-1935) Swedish					
oil	5	43,159	1,804	5,869	24,172
BECKENKAMP, Kaspar Benedikt (1747-1828) German					
oil	2	19,886	2,379	9,943	17,507
BECKER, Carl (1862-1926) German					
oil	2	4,632	1,788	2,316	2,844
wc/d	1	3,750		3,750	
BECKER, Carl Ludwig Friedrich (1820-1900) German					
oil	2	6,419	3,200	3,210	3,219
BECKER, Curt Georg (1904-1972) German					
oil	1	2,094		2,094	
BECKER, Frederick W (1888-1953) American					
oil	1	2,750		2,750	
BECKER, Harry (1865-1928) British					
oil	2	7,056	3,234	3,528	3,822
wc/d	4	7,603	1,267	2,052	2,232
BECKER, Howard Daniel (1914-1995) American					
oil	1	3,000		3,000	
BECKER, J (18/19th C) German					
oil	1	2,318		2,318	
BECKER, Ludwig Hugo (1833-1868) German					
oil	1	2,215		2,215	
BECKER, Peter (1828-1904) German					
wc/d	2	11,537	4,325	5,769	7,212
BECKMAN, Ford (1952-) American					
oil	1	1,843		1,843	
BECKMANN, Max (1884-1950) German					
oil	2	1,972,800	244,800	986,400	1,728,000
wc/d	4	54,363	1,500	10,498	31,867
BECKMANN-TUBE, Minna (1881-1964) German					
oil	2	3,984	1,992	1,992	1,992
BECKWITH, James Carroll (1852-1917) American					
oil	5	91,500	4,500	16,000	30,000
BECQUEREL, Andre-Vincent (19/20th C) French					
3D	3	4,014	1,085	1,113	1,816
BECVAR, Karel (1955-) Czechoslovakian					
3D	1	1,209		1,209	
BEDA, Francesco (1840-1900) Italian					
oil	1	20,040		20,040	
BEDA, Giulio (1879-1954) Italian					
oil	1	1,458		1,458	
BEDFORD, Ella M (fl.1882-1908) British					
oil	1	3,625		3,625	
BEDIA, Jose (1959-) Cuban					
oil	2	39,000	17,000	19,500	22,000
BEDINI, Paolo (1844-1924) Italian					
oil	1	17,380		17,380	
BEECHAM, Tom (1926-2000) American					
oil	2	11,500	5,000	5,750	6,500
BEECHEY, Captain Richard Brydges (1808-1895) British					
oil	2	105,600	22,000	52,800	83,600
BEECHEY, Sir William (1753-1839) British					
oil	5	113,760	2,256	13,114	44,330
BEECQ, Jan Karel Donatus van (1638-1722) Dutch					
oil	1	6,080		6,080	
BEECROFT, Vanesa (1969-) American					
oil	3	33,000	8,000	12,000	13,000

Name	No.	Total Sales Value	lowest	Prices median	highest
wc/d	2	7,000	2,500	3,500	4,500
BEEK, Bernardus Antonie van (1875-1941) Dutch					
oil	1	1,015		1,015	
BEEK, Jurrien (1879-1965) Dutch					
oil	1	1,075		1,075	
BEELDMAKER, Adriaen Cornelisz (1625-1701) Dutch					
oil	1	1,557		1,557	
BEELT, Cornelis (fl.1660-1702) Dutch					
oil	1	2,768		2,768	
BEEN, Daniel (1885-1976) Dutch					
oil	1	1,301		1,301	
BEENFELDT, Ulrich F (1714-1782) Danish					
oil	1	1,978		1,978	
BEER, Dick (1893-1938) Swedish					
oil	1	1,706		1,706	
BEER, Jan de (1475-1542) Flemish					
oil	1	42,280		42,280	
BEER, John (fl.1895-1915) British					
wc/d	4	13,385	1,101	2,072	8,140
BEER, Willem S de (1941-) South African					
oil	2	5,964	1,420	2,982	4,544
BEERBOHM, Sir Max (1872-1956) British					
wc/d	8	47,983	1,029	4,214	15,750
BEERNAERT, Euphrosine (1831-1901) Flemish					
oil	1	1,775		1,775	
BEERNAERT, Jacques (18th C) Flemish					
oil	1	17,507		17,507	
BEERS, Jan van (1852-1927) Belgian					
oil	5	26,489	2,847	3,796	11,881
BEERS, Julie Hart (1835-1913) American					
oil	3	24,600	1,200	2,400	21,000
BEERSTRATEN, Jan Abrahamsz (1622-1666) Dutch					
wc/d	1	5,285		5,285	
BEERT, Osias I (c.1570-1624) Flemish					
oil	1	367,500		367,500	
BEEST, Albertus van (1820-1860) Dutch					
oil	2	18,000	5,000	9,000	13,000
BEETHOLME, George Law (19th C) British					
oil	1	1,296		1,296	
BEFANI, Achille Formis (1832-1906) Italian					
oil	3	14,857	3,694	3,825	7,338
BEGA, Cornelis Pietersz (1620-1664) Dutch					
oil	1	8,000		8,000	
BEGARAT, Eugène (1943-) French					
oil	1	1,368		1,368	
BEGAS, Oskar (1828-1883) German					
oil	2	22,815	9,685	11,408	13,130
BEGAS-PARMENTIER, Louise (1850-?) Austrian					
oil	1	1,226		1,226	
BEGAY, Harrison (1917-) American					
wc/d	1	2,500		2,500	
BEGBIE, David (20th C) ?					
3D	1	1,269		1,269	
BEGEYN, Abraham (1637-1697) Dutch					
oil	2	14,823	7,273	7,412	7,550
BEGGROF, Alexandre (1841-1914) Russian					
oil	1	57,380		57,380	
wc/d	1	5,760		5,760	

Name	No.	Total Sales Value	lowest	Prices median	highest
BEHAN, John (20th C) Irish					
3D	2	6,660	2,960	3,330	3,700
BEHLER, Will (20th C) American					
oil	1	1,500		1,500	
BEHN, Fritz (1878-1970) Austrian					
3D	1	2,681		2,681	
BEHNES, William (1794-1864) British					
3D	1	1,350		1,350	
BEHR, Carel Jacobus (1812-1895) Dutch					
oil	1	4,088		4,088	
BEICH, Joachim Franz (1665-1748) German					
oil	5	16,668	1,510	2,647	6,292
BEINASCHI, Giovan Battista (1636-1688) Italian					
oil	3	34,966	6,480	7,920	20,566
wc/d	1	8,232		8,232	
BEINKE, Fritz (1842-1907) German					
oil	2	3,314	1,555	1,657	1,759
BEITHAN, Emil (1878-?) Belgian					
wc/d	2	7,768	2,589	3,884	5,179
BEJARANO, Manuel C (1827-1891) Spanish					
oil	3	54,865	7,030	22,335	25,500
BEKAERT, Piet (1939-) Belgian					
oil	2	6,197	2,862	3,099	3,335
BEKLEMISCHEFF, Sergei Vasilevich (1870-1920) Russian					
oil	1	8,486		8,486	
BELAIR, Pierre de (1892-?) French					
oil	1	5,548		5,548	
BELANGER, Louis (1736-1816) French					
wc/d	3	66,204	6,110	7,594	52,500
BELARSKI, Rudolph (1900-1983) American					
oil	1	3,750		3,750	
BELAY, Pierre de (1890-1947) French					
oil	19	93,456	1,242	5,098	9,093
wc/d	9	21,444	1,218	2,172	4,197
BELCASTRO, Alfredo (1893-1961) Italian					
oil	1	1,098		1,098	
BELDER, Joseph de (1871-1927) Belgian					
oil	2	2,494	1,006	1,247	1,488
BELES, L (19th C) Dutch					
oil	1	4,813		4,813	
BELGIAN SCHOOL					
oil	3	24,587	2,893	2,893	18,801
BELGIAN SCHOOL, 16th C					
3D	1	14,298		14,298	
BELGIAN SCHOOL, 19th C					
oil	4	8,124	1,021	1,995	3,114
BELGIAN SCHOOL, 20th C					
3D	1	4,274		4,274	
oil	1	7,250		7,250	
BELGRANO, Jose Denis (1844-1917) Spanish					
oil	3	9,440	2,729	3,200	3,511
BELIMBAU, Adolfo (1845-1938) Italian					
oil	1	2,182		2,182	
BELIYE, Alexander (1874-1934) British					
wc/d	1	5,358		5,358	
BELKAMP, Jan van (c.1610-1653) Dutch					
oil	1	4,530		4,530	
BELKNAP, Zedekiah (1781-1858) American					
oil	1	8,500		8,500	

Name	No.	Total Sales Value	lowest	Prices median	highest
BELL, Arthur George (1849-1916) British					
wc/d	1	1,207		1,207	
BELL, David C (1950-) British					
oil	1	3,942		3,942	
BELL, Graham (1910-1943) British					
oil	1	2,465		2,465	
BELL, John (1812-1895) British					
3D	1	34,560		34,560	
BELL, John Charles (fl.1857-1868) British					
oil	1	3,000		3,000	
BELL, Larry (1939-) American					
wc/d	1	5,000		5,000	
BELL, Lilian Russell (fl.1899-1933) British					
wc/d	3	5,720	1,430	2,145	2,145
BELL, Robert Anning (1863-1933) British					
wc/d	1	3,146		3,146	
BELL, Stuart H (1823-1896) British					
oil	2	3,237	1,510	1,619	1,727
BELL, Thomas Currie (fl.1892-1925) British					
wc/d	1	4,290		4,290	
BELL, Vanessa (1879-1961) British					
oil	7	143,408	2,288	8,250	87,420
wc/d	1	2,100		2,100	
BELL-SMITH, Frederick Marlett (1846-1923) Canadian/British					
oil	4	13,920	1,040	2,179	8,486
wc/d	9	17,470	1,009	1,946	3,186
BELLA, Stefano Della (1610-1664) Italian					
wc/d	6	87,719	1,309	3,165	72,480
BELLA, Vincenzo la (1872-?) Italian					
oil	1	1,527		1,527	
BELLANGE, Eugène (1837-?) French					
oil	1	1,746		1,746	
BELLANGE, Hippolyte (1800-1866) French					
oil	2	6,233	2,578	3,117	3,655
BELLANGER, René-Charles (1895-1964) French					
oil	1	1,200		1,200	
BELLANGER-ADHEMAR, Paul (1868-1925) French					
oil	1	1,788		1,788	
BELLANO, Bartolommeo (1434-1496) Italian					
3D	1	11,320		11,320	
BELLANY, John (1942-) British					
oil	4	48,657	8,232	11,760	16,905
wc/d	2	11,376	3,160	5,688	8,216
BELLE, Alexis Simon (1674-1734) French					
oil	1	15,771		15,771	
wc/d	1	11,638		11,638	
BELLE, C E van (19th C) Belgian					
oil	1	1,300		1,300	
BELLE, Charles Ernest de (1873-1939) Canadian/Hungarian					
oil	1	10,619		10,619	
BELLE, Karel van (1884-1959) Belgian					
oil	2	10,508	1,278	5,254	9,230
BELLE, Marcel (1871-1948) French					
oil	2	151,230	1,230	75,615	150,000
BELLEFLEUR, Léon (1910-) Canadian					
oil	3	12,408	2,005	4,646	5,757
BELLEGARDE (1927-) French					
oil	1	1,975		1,975	

Name	No.	Total Sales Value	lowest	Prices median	highest
BELLEGARDE, Claude (1927-) French					
oil	2	2,248	1,069	1,124	1,179
BELLEGHEM, Aime van (1922-1996) Belgian					
oil	1	1,003		1,003	
BELLENGE, Michel Bruno (1726-1793) French					
oil	1	8,106		8,106	
BELLERMANN, Ferdinand (1814-1889) German					
oil	1	5,593		5,593	
BELLET DU POISAT, Jean Pierre Joseph Alfred (1823-1883) French					
wc/d	1	1,141		1,141	
BELLET, Pierre (19/20th C) French					
oil	1	1,455		1,455	
BELLEVOIS, Jacob Adriaensz (1621-1675) Dutch					
oil	1	7,346		7,346	
BELLI, Benito (19th C) ?					
oil	1	1,676		1,676	
BELLI, Luigi (1848-?) Italian					
3D	1	17,000		17,000	
BELLIAZZI, Raffaele (1835-1914) Italian					
3D	1	1,145		1,145	
BELLINGHAM-SMITH, Elinor (1906-) British					
oil	1	1,422		1,422	
BELLINI, B (18th C) Italian					
oil	1	1,550		1,550	
BELLINI, C (19th C) Italian					
oil	1	1,848		1,848	
BELLINI, Emmanuel (1904-1989) French					
oil	4	8,614	1,927	2,184	2,320
BELLINI, Giovanni (1430-1516) Italian					
oil	1	573,800		573,800	
BELLINI, Giovanni (school) (1430-1516) Italian					
oil	1	9,332		9,332	
BELLIS, Hubert (1831-1902) Belgian					
oil	12	26,767	1,003	1,958	4,294
BELLMER, Hans (1902-1975) French/Polish					
3D	4	68,078	1,456	7,936	50,750
oil	1	15,473		15,473	
wc/d	9	48,986	1,112	4,641	16,711
BELLO, Bruno di (1938-) Italian					
wc/d	1	1,561		1,561	
BELLOD, Guillermo (1940-) Spanish					
oil	1	1,022		1,022	
BELLOLI, Andrei Franzowitsch (1820-1881) Russian					
wc/d	1	2,553		2,553	
BELLON, Jean (1944-) French					
oil	1	1,400		1,400	
BELLONI, Giorgio (1861-1944) Italian					
oil	7	58,601	2,618	5,172	26,122
BELLONI, Jose (1882-1965) Uruguayan					
3D	2	3,400	1,600	1,700	1,800
BELLONI, Serge (1925-) Italian					
oil	1	1,164		1,164	
BELLOTTO, Bernardo (1720-1780) Italian					
oil	2	2,429,400	617,400	1,214,700	1,812,000
BELLOWS, Albert F (1829-1883) American					
oil	3	10,850	2,100	4,000	4,750
BELLOWS, George (1882-1925) American					
oil	4	1,194,000	24,000	185,000	800,000
wc/d	1	5,500		5,500	

Name	No.	Total Sales Value	lowest	Prices median	highest
BELLUCCI, Antonio (1654-1726) Italian					
oil	1	25,714		25,714	
BELLYNCK, Hubert Émile (1859-?) French					
oil	1	1,354		1,354	
BELMON, Gaston (1907-1995) French					
oil	6	10,397	1,018	1,392	3,666
wc/d	4	6,453	1,031	1,294	2,835
BELMONDO, Paul (1898-1982) French?					
3D	1	7,901		7,901	
BELOFF, Angelina (1884-1969) Russian					
oil	1	32,826		32,826	
BELONOG, Anatoli (1946-) Russian					
oil	11	25,194	1,187	2,211	3,719
BELOT, A (?) ?					
oil	1	1,068		1,068	
BELOV, Victor (1925-) Russian					
oil	1	3,528		3,528	
BELPAUME, Maurice (1890-) French					
oil	1	1,267		1,267	
BELTRAME, Achille (1871-1945) Italian					
oil	1	1,714		1,714	
BELTRAN-MASSES, Frederico (1885-1949) Spanish					
oil	8	26,297	1,016	2,254	7,706
BELVEDERE, Andrea (1642-1732) Italian					
oil	2	51,055	6,955	25,528	44,100
BEMELMANS, Ludwig (1898-1963) American					
oil	6	180,000	5,500	24,250	60,000
wc/d	5	52,886	2,200	4,000	32,000
BEMIS, Harriet (19/20th C) American					
oil	1	1,300		1,300	
BEMMEL, Georg Christoph Gottlieb von I (1738-1794) German					
oil	1	1,315		1,315	
BEMMEL, Jacob Gerritz van (1628-1673) Flemish?					
oil	1	5,040		5,040	
BEMMEL, Karl Sebastian von (1743-1796) German					
oil	1	4,945		4,945	
wc/d	2	4,750	1,672	2,375	3,078
BEMMEL, Peter von (1685-1754) German					
oil	3	11,275	1,961	1,961	7,353
BEMMEL, Wilhelm von (1630-1708) Dutch					
oil	1	12,000		12,000	
wc/d	1	2,469		2,469	
BEN (1935-) Swiss					
3D	3	5,205	1,482	1,482	2,185
oil	15	38,083	1,197	2,427	6,291
wc/d	3	10,394	1,928	2,564	5,902
BEN-TRE, Howard (20th C) American					
3D	1	15,000		15,000	
BEN-ZVI, Asaf (1953-) Israeli					
oil	1	8,000		8,000	
BEN-ZVI, Zeev (1904-1952) Israeli					
3D	1	3,200		3,200	
BENARD, Hubert Eugène (1834-?) French					
oil	1	3,988		3,988	
BENARD, Jean Baptiste (?-1789) French					
oil	3	36,000	10,000	12,000	14,000
BENATI, Davide (1949-) Italian					
wc/d	1	2,415		2,415	
BENAVENT-CALATAYUD, Jose (1858-?) Spanish					
oil	1	8,000		8,000	

Name	No.	Total Sales Value	lowest	Prices median	highest
BENAVIDES, Pablo (1918-) Venezuelan					
oil	1	2,300		2,300	
BENCOVICH, Federico (1675-1753) Dalmatian					
oil	1	21,980		21,980	
wc/d	1	7,852		7,852	
BENDALL, Claude D (1891-1970) British/French					
wc/d	9	13,904	1,185	1,343	2,370
BENDALL, Mildred (1891-1977) British/French					
oil	5	30,505	3,925	5,400	10,150
BENDEMANN, Eduard Julius Friedrich (1811-1889) German					
oil	1	13,956		13,956	
BENDEMANN, Rudolf (1851-1884) German					
oil	1	2,458		2,458	
BENDINI, Vasco (1922-) Italian					
oil	1	3,709		3,709	
wc/d	1	1,964		1,964	
BENDRE, Narayan Shridhar (1910-1992) Indian					
oil	3	64,500	16,000	22,500	26,000
BENDTSEN, Folmer (1907-1993) Swedish					
oil	8	10,629	1,023	1,252	1,789
BENDZ, Wilhelm (1804-1832) Danish					
oil	1	16,781		16,781	
wc/d	1	5,290		5,290	
BENEDETTO, Enzo (1905-) Italian					
oil	1	9,706		9,706	
BENEDIT, Luis F (1937-) Argentinian					
wc/d	1	4,000		4,000	
BENEDITO-VIVES, Manuel (1875-1963) Spanish					
oil	4	20,184	2,422	3,447	10,868
wc/d	2	3,329	1,613	1,665	1,716
BENEKER, Gerrit Albertus (1882-1934) American					
oil	1	2,800		2,800	
BENFATTO, Luigi (1559-1611) Italian					
oil	1	23,550		23,550	
BENGAL SCHOOL, 20th C Indian					
oil	2	11,500	4,500	5,750	7,000
wc/d	1	3,150		3,150	
BENGLIS, Linda (1941-) American					
3D	1	6,342		6,342	
oil	1	11,000		11,000	
BENGSTON, Billy Al (1934-) American					
oil	1	3,000		3,000	
wc/d	2	7,500	2,000	3,750	5,500
BENGTSSON, Dick (1936-1989) Swedish					
wc/d	1	2,730		2,730	
BENIVIENI, Lippo di (?) Italian?					
oil	1	261,801		261,801	
BENJAMIN, Karl (1925-) American					
oil	2	4,700	1,200	2,350	3,500
BENLLIURE Y GIL, Jose (1855-1937) Spanish					
oil	4	94,379	21,000	21,075	30,000
wc/d	1	1,026		1,026	
BENLLIURE Y GIL, Mariano (1862-1947) Spanish					
3D	2	127,153	6,353	63,577	120,800
BENN (1905-) Polish					
oil	1	1,571		1,571	
BENN, Ben (1884-1983) American					
oil	3	7,000	1,200	2,800	3,000
BENN, Benejou (1905-1989) Polish					
oil	1	1,196		1,196	

Name	No.	Total Sales Value	lowest	Prices median	highest
BENNASSAR, Joan (1950-) Spanish					
oil	1	1,087		1,087	
BENNER, Emmanuel (1836-1896) French					
oil	3	7,026	1,092	2,279	3,655
BENNER, Emmanuel Michel (1873-1965) French					
oil	2	4,571	1,709	2,286	2,862
BENNER, Gerrit (1897-1981) Dutch					
oil	8	166,091	11,207	21,121	30,172
wc/d	7	50,048	1,584	9,483	10,776
BENNER, Jean (1796-1849) French					
oil	1	17,400		17,400	
BENNER, Jean (1836-1909) French					
oil	1	7,758		7,758	
BENNETT, Alfred (19th C) British					
oil	1	1,806		1,806	
BENNETT, Frank Moss (1874-1953) British					
oil	17	229,997	1,413	9,420	70,000
BENNETT, William (1811-1871) British					
wc/d	3	3,088	1,018	1,020	1,050
BENNETT, William James (1787-1844) American					
oil	1	1,500		1,500	
BENNEWITZ VON LOFEN, Karl (elder) (1826-1895) German					
oil	2	3,224	1,246	1,612	1,978
BENOIS, Albert Nikolaievitch (1852-1936) Russian					
wc/d	1	1,661		1,661	
BENOIS, Alexander (1870-1960) Russian					
wc/d	29	128,048	1,138	3,102	18,120
BENOIS, Nadia (1896-1975) Russian					
oil	1	1,152		1,152	
BENOIST, Marie Guilhelmine (1768-1826) French					
oil	1	54,155		54,155	
BENOIT, A (19th C) French					
oil	1	2,139		2,139	
BENOIT-LEVY, Jules (1866-c.1925) French					
oil	1	2,550		2,550	
BENOUVILLE, Francois Léon (1821-1859) French					
oil	1	3,000		3,000	
wc/d	1	1,414		1,414	
BENOUVILLE, Jean-Achille (1815-1891) French					
oil	2	10,681	5,187	5,341	5,494
BENRATH, Frederic (1930-) French					
oil	1	1,284		1,284	
BENSA, Alexander von (1820-1902) Austrian					
oil	4	20,288	2,585	4,244	9,216
BENSA, Ernesto (19th C) Italian					
wc/d	1	1,364		1,364	
BENSELL, George F (1837-1879) American					
oil	2	5,250	2,000	2,625	3,250
BENSING, Frank S (1893-1983) American					
oil	1	2,200		2,200	
BENSO, Giulio (1601-1668) Italian					
wc/d	1	10,570		10,570	
BENSON, Ambrosius (?-1550) Flemish					
oil	1	37,500		37,500	
BENSON, Frank W (1862-1951) American					
oil	3	4,390,000	440,000	1,650,000	2,300,000
wc/d	5	237,050	1,050	42,500	95,000
BENT, Jan van der (1650-1690) Dutch					
oil	1	24,160		24,160	

Name	No.	Total Sales Value	lowest	Prices median	highest
BENTABOLE, Louis (?-1880) French					
oil	2	3,823	1,564	1,912	2,259
BENTLEY, Charles (1806-1854) British					
wc/d	4	9,498	1,216	2,041	4,200
BENTLEY, John W (1880-1951) American					
oil	1	1,600		1,600	
BENTON, Fletcher (1931-) American					
3D	1	5,000		5,000	
oil	1	9,500		9,500	
wc/d	1	4,500		4,500	
BENTON, Thomas Hart (1889-1975) American					
oil	8	584,000	24,000	61,250	150,000
wc/d	4	51,000	8,000	13,000	17,000
BENTUM, Rik van (1936-) Dutch					
wc/d	1	2,065		2,065	
BENTZEN, Axel (1893-1952) Danish					
oil	2	2,053	1,023	1,027	1,030
BENTZEN, Edvard Harald (1833-1914) Danish					
3D	1	1,192		1,192	
BENVENISTI, L (19th C) Italian					
oil	1	1,123		1,123	
BENVENUTI, Giambattista (1488-1525) Italian					
oil	1	32,000		32,000	
BENVENUTI, Pietro (1769-1844) Italian					
oil	1	42,598		42,598	
BENWELL, Joseph Austin (fl.1865-1886) British					
wc/d	2	10,251	1,350	5,126	8,901
BENZ, Achilles (1766-1852) Swiss					
oil	1	1,089		1,089	
BEOTHY-STEINER, Anne (20th C) ?					
wc/d	1	1,068		1,068	
BER (18th C) ?					
oil	1	6,480		6,480	
BERALDO, Franco (1944-) Italian					
wc/d	1	1,294		1,294	
BERANGER, Antoine (1785-1867) French					
oil	1	38,220		38,220	
BERANGER, Maurice (20th C) American					
oil	1	1,300		1,300	
BERARD, Christian (1902-1949) French					
oil	8	53,653	1,021	6,393	12,220
wc/d	9	26,621	1,021	2,457	5,106
BERARD, Evremond de (19th C) French					
oil	1	2,204		2,204	
BERASSIT, F (19th C) Russian?					
oil	1	1,094		1,094	
BERATON, Jose (1747-1796) Spanish					
oil	1	2,816		2,816	
BERAUD, Jean (1849-1936) French					
oil	6	144,638	1,200	18,319	50,000
wc/d	1	3,867		3,867	
BERAUD, Louis (20th C) French					
oil	1	22,000		22,000	
BERBERIAN, Ovanes (20th C) American					
oil	1	1,700		1,700	
BERCHEM (1620-1683) Dutch					
oil	1	2,658		2,658	
wc/d	1	2,826		2,826	
BERCHEM, Nicolaes (1620-1683) Dutch					
oil	5	154,529	3,418	19,631	66,440

Name	No.	Total Sales Value	lowest	Prices median	highest
wc/d	3	15,586	1,200	1,815	12,571
BERCHEM, Nicolaes (school) (1620-1683) Dutch					
oil	3	14,449	1,751	4,666	8,032
BERCHERE, Narcisse (1819-1891) French					
oil	4	21,776	3,549	4,603	9,022
wc/d	1	1,817		1,817	
BERCHMANS, Émile Edouard (1843-1914) Belgian					
oil	1	1,580		1,580	
BERCKHEYDE, Gerrit Adriaensz (1638-1698) Dutch					
oil	1	16,000		16,000	
wc/d	1	39,286		39,286	
BERCKHEYDE, Job Adriaensz (1630-1693) Dutch					
oil	1	11,391		11,391	
BERDANIER, Paul F (1879-?) American					
oil	1	1,100		1,100	
BERDUSAN, Vicente (fl.1650) Spanish					
oil	1	1,421		1,421	
BERENGER, J (?) British?					
oil	1	2,256		2,256	
BERENTS, Jacob (1679-1748) German					
wc/d	1	5,107		5,107	
BERENTZ, Christian (1658-1722) German					
oil	3	232,390	22,390	50,000	160,000
BERESTEYN, Claes van (1629-1684) Dutch					
wc/d	1	90,357		90,357	
BERG, Adrian (1929-) British					
oil	2	3,708	1,022	1,854	2,686
BERG, Anna Carolina van den (1873-1942) Dutch					
oil	1	3,182		3,182	
BERG, Anton van den (?) Dutch					
oil	1	3,000		3,000	
BERG, Bertil (1935-) Swedish					
oil	2	2,464	1,146	1,232	1,318
BERG, Christian (1893-1976) Swedish					
3D	4	19,307	1,966	4,631	8,080
BERG, Else (1877-1942) Dutch					
oil	2	7,370	3,409	3,685	3,961
BERG, Franciscus Johannes Gybertus van den (20th C) Dutch					
oil	1	6,249		6,249	
BERG, Frans (1892-1949) Swedish					
oil	1	1,708		1,708	
BERG, Freek van den (1918-2000) Dutch					
oil	2	5,166	1,205	2,583	3,961
BERG, George Louis (1870-1941) American					
oil	1	2,200		2,200	
BERG, Hans (19th C) Scandinavian					
oil	1	4,170		4,170	
BERG, Jan van den (1932-) Dutch					
oil	1	1,449		1,449	
BERG, Jos van den (1905-1978) Dutch					
oil	1	1,513		1,513	
BERG, Julius (1820-1883) Swedish					
oil	1	4,175		4,175	
BERG, Simon van den (1812-1891) Dutch					
oil	1	1,148		1,148	
BERG, Werner (1904-1981) Austrian					
oil	1	31,877		31,877	
BERG, Willem van den (1886-1970) Dutch					
oil	9	27,403	1,000	2,200	8,150

Name	No.	Total Sales Value	lowest	Prices median	highest
wc/d	1	2,038		2,038	
BERGA BOADA, Jose (1872-1923) Spanish					
oil	1	1,271		1,271	
BERGAMESE SCHOOL, 16th C Italian					
oil	1	7,350		7,350	
BERGAMESE SCHOOL, 17th C Italian					
oil	2	5,361	2,523	2,681	2,838
BERGAMINI, Francesco (1815-1883) Italian					
oil	4	16,263	1,730	2,977	8,580
BERGANDER, Rudolf (1909-1970) German					
oil	1	1,079		1,079	
BERGDORFF, Ferdinand (1881-1975) American					
oil	1	1,200		1,200	
BERGE, Edward (1876-1924) American					
3D	1	6,000		6,000	
BERGEN, Carl von (1853-1933) German					
oil	2	8,002	2,229	4,001	5,773
BERGEN, Claus (1885-1964) German					
oil	1	9,464		9,464	
wc/d	1	1,733		1,733	
BERGEN, Dirck van (1645-1690) Dutch					
oil	1	3,800		3,800	
BERGENSTRAHLE, Marie Louise de Geer (1944-) Swedish					
3D	3	5,632	1,092	1,529	3,011
oil	3	5,428	1,147	1,747	2,534
wc/d	4	7,565	1,130	1,562	3,312
BERGER, Einar (1893-1960) Norwegian					
oil	1	1,501		1,501	
BERGER, Ernst (1857-1919) Austrian					
oil	1	3,011		3,011	
BERGER, Hans (1882-1977) Swiss					
oil	5	12,922	1,073	2,390	5,677
BERGER, Henri and WALTER, Amalric (20th C) ?					
3D	1	1,595		1,595	
BERGER, Jason (1923-) American					
oil	1	1,000		1,000	
BERGER, Johan Christian (1803-1871) Swedish					
oil	1	4,176		4,176	
BERGER, Johann (?) ?					
wc/d	1	4,434		4,434	
BERGER, Mathieu (1807-?) French					
oil	1	11,000		11,000	
BERGERET, Denis Pierre (1846-1910) French					
oil	5	59,977	1,425	5,431	43,000
BERGEVIN, Edouard de (1861-1925) French					
oil	1	1,010		1,010	
BERGEY, Earle K (1901-1952) American					
oil	2	4,600	2,000	2,300	2,600
BERGH, Edvard (1828-1880) Swedish					
oil	2	14,944	2,817	7,472	12,127
BERGH, Gillis de (c.1600-1669) Dutch					
oil	1	10,398		10,398	
BERGH, Jan van (c.1587-c.1650) Flemish					
wc/d	1	13,590		13,590	
BERGH, Nicolaas van den (1725-1774) Flemish					
oil	1	25,536		25,536	
BERGH, Rickard (1858-1919) Swedish					
oil	5	33,229	1,206	4,036	20,700

Name	No.	Total Sales Value	Prices lowest	median	highest
BERGHE, Frits van den (1883-1939) Belgian					
oil	1	56,945		56,945	
BERGHE, Wilhelm Jan van der (1828-1901) Dutch					
oil	1	3,925		3,925	
BERGMAN (?) ?					
3D	5	14,262	2,431	2,826	4,000
BERGMAN, Anna-Eva (1909-1987) Swedish/French					
oil	2	2,784	1,179	1,392	1,605
wc/d	2	5,053	2,353	2,527	2,700
BERGMAN, Franz (19/20th C) Austrian					
3D	9	28,260	1,185	2,775	5,372
BERGMAN, Karl (1891-1965) Swedish					
oil	2	2,460	1,155	1,230	1,305
BERGMAN, Oskar (1879-1963) Swedish					
oil	7	15,258	1,088	1,806	3,950
wc/d	13	30,191	1,088	2,257	4,864
BERGMANN, Max (1884-1955) German					
oil	7	19,004	1,196	2,163	5,611
BERGMULLER, Johan Georg (1688-1762) German					
wc/d	1	1,081		1,081	
BERGNER, Yosl (1920-) Israeli					
oil	12	62,600	1,300	5,250	13,000
wc/d	2	2,900	1,400	1,450	1,500
BERGSTROM, Alfred (1869-1930) Swedish					
oil	4	33,409	2,822	5,982	18,623
BERGT, Michael (1956-) American					
oil	2	4,000	2,000	2,000	2,000
BERGUE, Tony Francis de (1820-1893) French					
oil	1	2,934		2,934	
BERJON, Antoine (1754-1843) French					
wc/d	1	60,400		60,400	
BERJONNEAU, Jehan (1890-1972) French					
oil	1	1,630		1,630	
BERK (?) ?					
oil	1	1,586		1,586	
BERKE, Hubert (1908-1979) German					
oil	1	5,313		5,313	
BERKELEY, Stanley (?-1909) British					
oil	1	1,450		1,450	
BERKEMEIER, Ludolph (1864-1931) Dutch					
oil	1	1,831		1,831	
BERKES, Antal (1874-1938) Hungarian					
oil	3	3,732	1,002	1,230	1,500
BERKHOLZ, G (fl.1866-1872) German					
oil	1	1,212		1,212	
BERKHOUT, A (19th C) ?					
oil	1	2,988		2,988	
BERKHOUT, N (19th C) Dutch					
oil	1	3,902		3,902	
BERKS, Robert (1922-) American					
3D	1	5,250		5,250	
BERLAND, Ruben (1955-) Cuban					
oil	1	12,000		12,000	
BERLANT, Tony (1941-) American					
3D	1	10,000		10,000	
wc/d	2	34,000	6,000	17,000	28,000
BERLIN SCHOOL, 18th C German					
oil	1	2,732		2,732	

Name	No.	Total Sales Value		Prices	
			lowest	median	highest
BERLIN SCHOOL, 19th C German					
3D	1	7,354		7,354	
oil	1	4,500		4,500	
BERLIN, Sven Paul (1911-) British					
3D	1	3,648		3,648	
wc/d	1	1,900		1,900	
BERLIT, Rudiger (1883-1939) German					
oil	1	1,486		1,486	
BERLOT, Jean Baptiste (1775-?) French					
oil	1	6,142		6,142	
BERMAN, Eugene (1899-1972) American/Russian					
oil	1	3,915		3,915	
wc/d	5	7,538	1,000	1,438	2,000
BERMAN, Saul (1899-1972) American					
oil	2	8,000	3,000	4,000	5,000
BERMANN, Cipri Adolf (1862-?) German					
3D	1	1,609		1,609	
BERMUDEZ, Cundo (1914-) Cuban					
oil	2	61,000	26,000	30,500	35,000
wc/d	3	33,000	7,000	10,000	16,000
BERMUDEZ, Henry (20th C) ?					
oil	1	1,650		1,650	
BERMUDEZ, Jorge (1883-1926) Argentinian					
oil	1	1,300		1,300	
BERNACHIN (19/20th C) French?					
oil	1	1,033		1,033	
BERNARD, Adolphe (1812-1890) Belgian					
oil	1	1,097		1,097	
BERNARD, Albert (1849-1934) French					
wc/d	1	1,494		1,494	
BERNARD, Émile (1868-1941) French					
oil	30	447,118	1,055	6,347	105,700
wc/d	3	17,873	1,129	8,189	8,555
BERNARD, François (1814-?) French					
oil	1	55,000		55,000	
BERNARD, J (?) ?					
oil	1	1,489		1,489	
BERNARD, Joseph (1864-1933) French					
oil	2	10,126	1,937	5,063	8,189
BERNARD, Joseph Antoine (1866-1931) Austrian					
3D	1	10,425		10,425	
BERNARD, Louis Michel (1885-1962) French					
oil	1	3,003		3,003	
BERNARDI, Joseph (1826-1907) German					
oil	1	2,773		2,773	
BERNARDIN (19/20th C) ?					
3D	1	1,761		1,761	
BERNASCONI, Ugo (1874-1960) Argentinian					
oil	1	2,495		2,495	
BERNATZIK, Wilhelm (1853-1906) Austrian					
oil	1	21,600		21,600	
BERNDORF (19/20th C) ?					
3D	1	3,312		3,312	
BERNDTSON, Gunnar Fredrik (1854-1895) Finnish					
oil	1	5,038		5,038	
BERNE-BELLECOUR, Étienne Prosper (1838-1910) French					
oil	5	145,134	1,700	5,434	110,000
BERNEKER, Louis Frederick (1876-1937) American					
oil	2	4,700	1,900	2,350	2,800

Name	No.	Total Sales Value	Prices lowest	median	highest
BERNER, Eugen Friedrich (19th C) German					
oil	1	2,301		2,301	
BERNESE SCHOOL, 16th C Swiss					
wc/d	1	45,300		45,300	
BERNESE SCHOOL, 19th C Swiss					
oil	1	6,015		6,015	
BERNHARD, Pieter Gerardus (1813-1880) Dutch					
oil	2	8,051	3,260	4,026	4,791
BERNI, Antonio (1905-1981) Argentinian					
oil	1	420,000		420,000	
BERNIER, Camille (1823-1903) French					
oil	3	7,499	1,000	1,050	5,449
BERNIER, Georges (1862-1918) Belgian					
oil	2	2,893	1,391	1,447	1,502
BERNIER, Pascal (1960-) ?					
3D	1	7,248		7,248	
BERNINGER, Edmund (1843-?) German					
oil	3	34,336	1,981	6,355	26,000
BERNINGER, John E (20th C) American					
oil	3	4,200	1,100	1,200	1,900
BERNINGHAUS, J Charles (1905-1971) American					
oil	1	1,400		1,400	
BERNINGHAUS, Oscar E (1874-1952) American					
oil	5	189,319	11,000	37,000	90,000
wc/d	1	22,500		22,500	
BERNO, Simone (1950-) French					
oil	1	1,804		1,804	
BERNSTEIN, Theresa F (1890-?) American					
oil	4	15,750	2,000	4,375	5,000
BEROUD, Louis (1852-1910) French					
oil	1	10,000		10,000	
BERRESFORD, Virginia (1904-) American					
oil	2	13,500	5,000	6,750	8,500
BERRETTONI, Nicolo (1637-1682) Italian					
oil	1	14,582		14,582	
BERROCAL, Miguel (1933-) Spanish					
3D	30	66,941	1,004	1,758	7,000
BERROU, P (19th C) ?					
oil	1	1,220		1,220	
BERRUER, Pierre Francois (1733-1797) French					
3D	1	8,640		8,640	
BERRUETA, Vicente (1867-1909) Spanish					
oil	2	5,687	1,969	2,844	3,718
BERSANI, Stefano (1872-1914) Italian					
oil	2	5,424	1,484	2,712	3,940
BERSTAMM, Leopold Bernard (1859-c.1910) Russian					
3D	1	1,359		1,359	
BERTA, Alfredo (?) ?					
oil	1	1,800		1,800	
BERTA, Eduardo (1867-1931) Swiss					
oil	2	12,201	3,552	6,101	8,649
BERTASIOLY (19/20th C) Continental					
oil	1	1,800		1,800	
BERTEA, Ernesto (1836-1904) Italian					
oil	1	1,996		1,996	
BERTELLI, S (19th C) Italian?					
wc/d	1	2,289		2,289	
BERTELSEN, Aage (1873-1945) Danish					
oil	1	2,067		2,067	

Name	No.	Total Sales Value	Prices lowest	median	highest
BERTELSEN, Albert (1921-) Danish					
oil	2	4,721	2,306	2,361	2,415
wc/d	2	2,455	1,090	1,228	1,365
BERTELSMANN, Walter (1877-1963) Dutch					
oil	1	1,195		1,195	
BERTHELSEN, Christian (1839-1909) Danish					
oil	6	17,726	1,105	3,122	5,290
BERTHELSEN, Johann (1883-1969) American					
oil	18	97,637	1,287	5,100	19,000
wc/d	1	1,600		1,600	
BERTHET, Pierre (Guincamp) French					
oil	1	1,300		1,300	
BERTHIER (?) French					
3D	1	6,289		6,289	
BERTHIER, Paul (19th C) French					
3D	1	2,542		2,542	
BERTHOLLE, Jean (1909-1996) French					
oil	2	5,026	2,032	2,513	2,994
BERTHOME-SAINT-ANDRE (1905-1977) French					
oil	1	2,037		2,037	
BERTHOME-SAINT-ANDRE, Louis (1905-1977) French					
oil	1	1,710		1,710	
BERTHON (19th C) French					
oil	1	1,600		1,600	
BERTHOT, Jake (1939-) American					
oil	1	2,500		2,500	
BERTHOUD, Alfred-Henri (1848-1906) Swiss					
oil	2	3,944	1,149	1,972	2,795
BERTHOUD, Léon (1822-1892) Swiss					
oil	1	1,228		1,228	
BERTHOUD, Paul François (1870-?) French					
3D	2	13,868	5,652	6,934	8,216
oil	1	2,341		2,341	
BERTHOUX, Guillaume Francis (20th C) French					
3D	1	1,015		1,015	
BERTI, Antonio (1904-1990) Italian					
3D	1	2,007		2,007	
BERTI, Vinicio (1921-1991) Italian					
oil	1	2,096		2,096	
wc/d	2	2,269	1,091	1,135	1,178
BERTIN, Jean-Victor (1775-1842) French					
oil	6	170,194	3,759	21,135	80,000
BERTIN, Nicolas (1668-1736) French					
oil	1	13,230		13,230	
BERTINI, Gianni (1922-) Italian					
oil	1	1,861		1,861	
wc/d	3	3,658	1,034	1,314	1,314
BERTINI, L (?) Italian					
oil	1	2,087		2,087	
BERTLING, Carl (1835-?) German					
oil	1	3,574		3,574	
BERTOIA, Harry (1915-1978) American					
3D	9	139,595	4,095	13,000	40,000
BERTOLA, Louis (1891-) French/Italian					
3D	1	1,911		1,911	
BERTOLETTI, Nino (1890-?) Italian					
oil	1	1,309		1,309	
BERTOLOTTI, Cesare (1855-?) Italian					
oil	1	9,851		9,851	

Name	No.	Total Sales Value	lowest	Prices median	highest
BERTRAM, Abel (1871-1954) French					
oil	12	27,610	1,262	1,848	5,596
BERTRAND, Elise (19th C) French					
oil	1	9,000		9,000	
BERTRAND, Eugène (19/20th C) French					
oil	1	3,678		3,678	
BERTRAND, Gaston (1910-1994) Belgian					
oil	1	7,940		7,940	
BERTRAND, Paulin Andre (1852-1940) French					
oil	1	1,971		1,971	
BERTRAND, Pierre-Philippe (1884-1975) French					
oil	1	1,045		1,045	
BERTRAND, S (20th C) ?					
3D	1	1,751		1,751	
BERTUCHI NIETO, Mariano (1885-1955) Spanish					
oil	1	9,716		9,716	
wc/d	1	2,200		2,200	
BERTUCHI, Mariano (1885-1920) Italian					
oil	1	9,872		9,872	
wc/d	2	2,134	1,067	1,067	1,067
BERTUZZI, Francesco (19/20th C) Italian					
3D	1	4,032		4,032	
BERTUZZI, Nicola (1710-1777) Italian					
oil	1	5,876		5,876	
BERUETE, Aureliano de (1845-1911) Spanish					
oil	2	129,788	9,662	64,894	120,126
BERZON, A (18th C) ?					
oil	1	1,090		1,090	
BESCHEY, Balthasar (1708-1776) Flemish					
oil	3	12,625	2,052	5,024	5,549
BESCHEY, Jacob Andries (1710-1786) Flemish					
oil	1	13,854		13,854	
BESCHEY, Jan Frans (1717-1799) Flemish?					
oil	1	2,245		2,245	
BESCHEY, Karel (1706-1776) Flemish					
oil	2	52,727	7,456	26,364	45,271
BESCO, Donald (?) Canadian					
oil	1	1,306		1,306	
BESJI, G (19th C) Italian					
3D	1	1,600		1,600	
BESNARD, Albert (1849-1934) French					
oil	3	13,051	1,752	2,921	8,378
BESNARD, Pierre (fl.1658-1682) French					
oil	1	5,187		5,187	
BESS, Forrest (1911-1977) American					
oil	2	38,000	19,000	19,000	19,000
BESSA, Pancrace (1772-c.1835) French					
wc/d	1	1,092		1,092	
BESSE, Raymond (1899-1969) French					
oil	1	1,611		1,611	
BESSI, Giovanni (fl.1731-1748) Italian					
3D	1	4,109		4,109	
BESSIRE, Dale Phillip (1892-1974) American					
oil	1	10,000		10,000	
BEST, Arthur W (1859-1935) American					
oil	1	3,000		3,000	
BEST, Hans (1874-1942) German					
oil	1	2,179		2,179	

Name	No.	Total Sales Value	lowest	Prices median	highest
BEST, Harry Cassie (1863-1936) American					
oil	3	6,350	1,500	1,600	3,250
BESTIEU, Jean Jacques (1754-1842) French					
oil	1	1,459		1,459	
BETHKE, Hermann (1825-1895) German					
oil	1	2,206		2,206	
BETHUNE, Gaston (1857-1897) French					
wc/d	1	1,050		1,050	
BETLEN, Guyla (1879-) Rumanian					
3D	1	3,140		3,140	
BETTENCOURT, Pierre (1917-) French					
wc/d	3	12,114	3,093	3,894	5,127
BETTS, Anna Whelan (19/20th C) American					
oil	1	1,100		1,100	
BETTS, Louis (1873-1961) American					
oil	1	4,000		4,000	
BEUCHOT, Jean Baptiste (1821-?) French					
oil	1	6,000		6,000	
BEUCKER, Pascal de (1861-1945) ?					
oil	2	2,628	1,128	1,314	1,500
BEUERLIN, Wilhelm (19th C) Italian					
oil	1	2,905		2,905	
BEUL, Henri de (1845-1900) Belgian					
oil	3	16,147	2,383	4,077	9,687
BEUL, Laurent de (1821-1872) Belgian					
oil	1	3,053		3,053	
BEULAS, José (1921-) Spanish					
oil	10	56,446	2,146	4,302	14,629
BEURDEN, Alfons van (1878-1962) Belgian					
3D	1	3,941		3,941	
oil	2	19,746	4,256	9,873	15,490
BEURDEN, Alphonse van (1854-1938) Flemish					
3D	1	1,420		1,420	
BEURMANN, Emil (1862-1951) Swiss					
oil	1	1,547		1,547	
BEUYS, Joseph (1921-1986) German					
3D	10	187,471	3,155	7,834	85,000
oil	3	5,253	1,000	1,031	3,222
wc/d	11	95,476	1,019	2,552	34,000
BEUYS, Joseph and HAFNER, Jonas (20th C) German					
wc/d	1	4,254		4,254	
BEUYS, Joseph and PAIK, Nam June (20th C) German/American					
3D	1	4,369		4,369	
BEVAN, Irvine (fl.1908-1915) British					
wc/d	2	6,302	3,002	3,151	3,300
BEVAN, Robert (1865-1925) British					
oil	2	39,480	9,480	19,740	30,000
wc/d	3	18,188	1,440	2,448	14,300
BEVAN, Tony (1951-) British					
oil	2	111,120	34,800	55,560	76,320
wc/d	1	22,650		22,650	
BEWICK, Pauline (1935-) Irish					
wc/d	2	6,660	2,960	3,330	3,700
BEYER, J (19th C) German					
oil	1	2,376		2,376	
BEYER, J C W (18th C) German					
3D	2	3,100	1,514	1,550	1,586
BEYER, Max Otto (19th C) German					
oil	1	25,642		25,642	

Name	No.	Total Sales Value	Prices lowest	median	highest
BEYEREN, Abraham van (1620-1690) Dutch					
oil	1	30,000		30,000	
BEYNON, Jan (1830-1877) Indonesian					
oil	2	59,758	18,364	29,879	41,394
BEYSCHLAG, Robert (1838-1903) German					
oil	1	3,320		3,320	
BEZEM, Naphtali (1924-) Israeli					
oil	4	11,200	2,200	2,500	4,000
wc/d	4	5,900	1,100	1,300	2,200
BEZNER, Max (20th C) German					
3D	1	1,053		1,053	
BEZOMBES, Roger (1913-1994) French					
oil	3	92,964	3,300	21,355	68,309
BEZZI, Angelo (19th C) Italian					
3D	1	2,826		2,826	
BEZZI, Bartolomeo (1851-1925) Italian					
oil	1	6,880		6,880	
BEZZUOLI, Giuseppe (1784-1855) Italian					
oil	1	3,000		3,000	
BHATTACHARJEE, Bikash (1940-) Indian					
wc/d	1	2,850		2,850	
BHATTACHARYA, Chittoprasad (1915-1978) Indian					
wc/d	1	3,000		3,000	
BIALINITSKI-BIROULIA, Vitold (1872-1957) Russian					
oil	2	13,472	5,922	6,736	7,550
BIANCHI, Mose (1840-1904) Italian					
oil	6	214,932	3,678	29,328	78,036
wc/d	1	14,460		14,460	
BIANCHI, Mose di Giuseppe (1836-1893) Italian					
oil	1	2,197		2,197	
BIANCHI, Nina (fl.1843-1863) Italian					
wc/d	1	4,381		4,381	
BIANCHINI, V (?) Italian					
oil	1	1,500		1,500	
BIANCO, Remo (1922-1990) Italian					
oil	1	2,815		2,815	
wc/d	2	6,327	1,745	3,164	4,582
BIANCONI, Fulvio (20th C) Italian					
wc/d	1	1,228		1,228	
BIASI DA TEULADA, Giuseppe (1885-1945) Italian					
oil	4	52,297	8,407	9,631	24,628
wc/d	1	9,890		9,890	
BIASI, Guido (1933-) Italian					
oil	1	1,025		1,025	
BIBERMAN, Edward (1904-1986) American					
oil	1	2,000		2,000	
BIBIENA, Francesco Galli (1659-1739) Italian					
oil	1	120,000		120,000	
BICCI DI LORENZO (1373-1452) Italian					
oil	1	20,580		20,580	
BICKERSTAFF, Frank (20th C) American					
oil	1	1,800		1,800	
BICKNELL, Frank Alfred (1866-1943) American					
oil	6	42,650	2,900	6,250	14,000
BICKNELL, William H W (1860-1947) American					
oil	1	9,500		9,500	
BIDA, Alexandre (1823-1895) French					
wc/d	1	1,414		1,414	

Name	No.	Total Sales Value	Prices lowest	median	highest
BIDART, L (20th C) French					
3D	1	2,043		2,043	
BIDAU, Eugène (fl.1867-1900) French					
oil	1	60,000		60,000	
BIDAULD, Jean Joseph Xavier (1758-1846) French					
oil	6	480,667	4,278	65,525	250,000
BIDAULT, Jean Pierre Xavier (1743-1813) French					
oil	2	24,000	5,000	12,000	19,000
BIDDLE, George (1885-1973) American					
wc/d	2	4,400	1,400	2,200	3,000
BIDDLE, Laurence (1888-?) British					
oil	7	12,532	1,001	1,199	3,625
BIDLO, Mike (1955-) American					
oil	3	78,160	14,000	24,160	40,000
wc/d	1	28,000		28,000	
BIDON, Daniel (19/20th C) ?					
oil	1	2,856		2,856	
BIE, Eugène de (20th C) Belgian					
oil	2	3,114	1,437	1,557	1,677
BIEDERMANN, J C (19th C) ?					
oil	1	1,861		1,861	
BIEDERMANN, Johann Jakob (1763-1830) Swiss					
oil	3	61,971	15,959	22,050	23,962
wc/d	3	6,122	1,818	2,045	2,259
BIEDERMANN-ARENDTS, Hermine (1855-?) German					
oil	1	1,000		1,000	
BIEDERMEIER SCHOOL, 19th C German					
oil	1	2,275		2,275	
BIEGAS, Boleslas (1877-1954) Polish					
3D	1	4,898		4,898	
oil	6	14,151	1,804	1,933	4,228
BIEGEL, Peter (1913-1988) British					
oil	1	4,672		4,672	
BIEHLER, Sepp (1907-1973) German					
oil	1	1,596		1,596	
wc/d	1	1,337		1,337	
BIEL, Antonie (1830-1880) German					
oil	1	4,200		4,200	
BIELEFELD, Bruno (1879-?) German					
oil	1	2,784		2,784	
BIELER, André Charles (1896-1989) Canadian					
oil	2	2,912	1,175	1,456	1,737
BIELER, Ernest (1863-1948) Swiss					
oil	6	146,553	9,115	14,991	58,943
wc/d	3	41,333	2,431	15,325	23,577
BIELING, Hermann Friedrich (1887-1964) Dutch					
oil	5	10,479	1,493	1,723	3,036
wc/d	1	1,810		1,810	
BIENABE ARTIA, Bernardino (1889-1987) Spanish					
oil	1	1,479		1,479	
BIENFAIT, Aline (1941-) Belgian					
3D	1	1,473		1,473	
BIERGE, Roland (1922-) French					
oil	1	1,474		1,474	
BIERMANN, Edouard (1803-1892) German					
wc/d	2	2,553	1,229	1,277	1,324
BIERMANN, Gottlieb (1842-1908) German					
oil	1	4,740		4,740	
BIERSTADT, Albert (1830-1902) American/German					
oil	19	2,099,000	9,500	50,000	850,000

Name	No.	Total Sales Value	lowest	Prices median	highest
wc/d	2	37,000	12,000	18,500	25,000
BIERUMA-OOSTING, Jeanne (1898-1995) Dutch					
oil	1	1,811		1,811	
BIESE, Karl (1863-1930) German					
wc/d	1	1,319		1,319	
BIESEBROECK, Jules van (1873-1965) Belgian					
oil	5	39,689	1,287	3,444	26,285
wc/d	1	3,082		3,082	
BIESEBROECK, van (1873-?) Belgian					
oil	1	2,677		2,677	
BIESSY, Marie Gabriel (1854-1935) French					
oil	1	3,800		3,800	
BIESZCZAD, Severin (1852-1923) European					
oil	1	2,146		2,146	
BIEVRE, Marie de (1865-?) Belgian					
oil	1	20,000		20,000	
BIGARI, Vittori (1692-1776) Italian					
wc/d	2	10,911	4,116	5,456	6,795
BIGATTI, Pasqualino (18th C) Italian?					
wc/d	1	2,567		2,567	
BIGAUD, Wilson (1931-) Haitian					
oil	3	4,460	1,049	1,611	1,800
BIGAUX, Louis Felix (1850-?) French					
oil	1	1,044		1,044	
BIGG, William Redmore (1755-1828) British					
oil	1	2,544		2,544	
BIGGI, Gastone (1925-) Italian					
wc/d	1	1,309		1,309	
BIGGS, Walter (1886-?) American					
wc/d	1	10,000		10,000	
BIGOT, Raymond (1872-1953) French					
3D	1	4,026		4,026	
BIHAN, le (19th C) ?					
oil	1	8,000		8,000	
BIKANER SCHOOL, 18th C Indian					
oil	1	4,200		4,200	
BILAS, Peter (1952-) British					
oil	1	20,520		20,520	
BILBAO Y MARTINEZ, Gonzalo (1860-1938) Spanish					
oil	6	26,547	1,686	2,898	13,444
BILCOQ, Marie Marc Antoine (1755-1838) French					
oil	1	3,279		3,279	
BILDERS, Johannes Wernardus (1811-1890) Dutch					
oil	2	8,308	3,872	4,154	4,436
BILHAUT, Elisabeth Gabrielle (20th C) French					
oil	1	1,457		1,457	
BILIBIN, Alexander (1903-1972) Russian					
oil	1	4,369		4,369	
BILIBIN, Ivan (1876-1942) Russian					
wc/d	1	8,305		8,305	
BILIVERTI, Giovanni (1576-1666) Italian					
oil	2	182,437	5,000	91,219	177,437
BILL, Jakob (1942-) Swiss					
oil	1	5,016		5,016	
BILL, Max (1908-1994) Swiss					
3D	8	300,754	2,419	27,740	125,330
oil	3	38,684	10,166	14,585	14,585
wc/d	3	7,298	1,184	1,638	4,476

Name	No.	Total Sales Value	lowest	Prices median	highest
BILLAUD, Eugene (1888-1964) French					
oil	1	1,168		1,168	
BILLE, Carl (1815-1898) Danish					
oil	11	87,971	1,332	2,306	42,821
wc/d	2	3,181	1,558	1,591	1,623
BILLE, Edmond (1878-?) Swiss					
oil	1	5,010		5,010	
BILLE, Ejler (1910-) Danish					
3D	1	6,703		6,703	
oil	3	66,675	13,947	18,135	34,593
BILLE, Vilhelm (1864-1908) Danish					
oil	5	17,113	1,104	2,075	8,662
BILLET, Étienne (1821-?) French					
oil	1	8,437		8,437	
BILLET, Pierre (1837-1922) French					
oil	1	12,000		12,000	
BILLGREN, Ernst (1957-) Swedish					
3D	1	4,014		4,014	
oil	8	38,663	1,104	5,337	7,863
wc/d	2	11,918	5,897	5,959	6,021
BILLGREN, Ola (1940-) Swedish					
oil	15	353,682	2,408	5,419	132,126
wc/d	3	27,867	1,769	3,713	22,385
BILLING, Frederick W (1835-1914) American					
oil	1	4,500		4,500	
BILLINGS, Henry (1901-1987) American					
oil	1	1,200		1,200	
BILLOIN, Charles (1813-1869) Belgian					
oil	2	3,598	1,359	1,799	2,239
BILLOTTE, L (19th C) French					
oil	1	2,445		2,445	
BILLOTTE, René (1846-1915) French					
oil	1	2,800		2,800	
BILQUIN, Jean (1938-) Belgian					
oil	1	1,013		1,013	
BILS, Claude (1884-1968) French					
oil	2	2,816	1,163	1,408	1,653
BIMBI, Bartolomeo (1648-1725) Italian					
oil	1	26,122		26,122	
BINARD, Henri (1862-1939) Belgian					
oil	1	2,859		2,859	
BINDER, Alois (19th C) German					
oil	1	1,967		1,967	
BINDER, Friedrich Gustav (1897-1990) German					
oil	1	7,316		7,316	
BINDER, Jacob (19/20th C) German					
oil	1	1,600		1,600	
BINDER, Tony (1868-1944) British					
oil	2	11,800	2,320	5,900	9,480
BINDLEY, Frank (fl.1872-1887) British					
oil	2	4,128	1,590	2,064	2,538
BINDSEIL, J (19th C) Canadian?					
oil	1	1,471		1,471	
BINET, George (1865-1949) French					
oil	10	39,059	1,713	3,559	7,250
BINET, Louis (1744-1800) French					
wc/d	1	13,091		13,091	
BINET, Victor (?) French					
oil	1	3,073		3,073	

Name	No.	Total Sales Value	lowest	Prices median	highest
BINET, Victor Jean Baptiste Barthelemy (1849-1924) French					
oil	2	16,268	7,000	8,134	9,268
BINGLEY, James George (1841-1920) British					
wc/d	8	11,545	1,128	1,199	2,288
BINJE, Franz (1835-1900) Belgian					
oil	1	2,156		2,156	
BINKS, Reuben Ward (fl.1924-1948) British					
oil	1	1,800		1,800	
wc/d	30	59,352	1,000	1,550	8,500
BINKS, Thomas (1799-1852) British					
oil	1	4,402		4,402	
BINNING, Bertram Charles (1909-1976) Canadian					
oil	1	9,750		9,750	
wc/d	1	2,389		2,389	
BINOIT, Peter (17th C) German					
oil	2	786,380	21,980	393,190	764,400
BINYON, Edward (1830-1876) British					
oil	1	1,134		1,134	
BINZ, Hermann (1876-?) German					
3D	1	1,538		1,538	
BIONDA, Mario (1913-1985) Italian					
oil	6	8,676	1,262	1,401	1,670
BIONDI, Nicola (1866-1929) Italian					
oil	1	1,669		1,669	
BIOT, Charles Jerome (1754-1838) Belgian					
oil	1	9,456		9,456	
BIOT, Gustave Joseph (1833-1905) Belgian					
oil	1	1,030		1,030	
BIOULES, Vincent (1938-) French?					
oil	1	2,918		2,918	
BIR, Rosette (20th C) French					
3D	1	1,212		1,212	
BIRCH, Lionel (1858-1930) British					
oil	1	1,152		1,152	
BIRCH, Samuel John Lamorna (1869-1955) British					
oil	33	172,947	1,043	3,335	19,500
wc/d	17	44,210	1,290	2,058	8,085
BIRCH, Thomas (1779-1851) American					
oil	1	13,000		13,000	
BIRCHALL, William Minshall (1884-?) British					
wc/d	7	12,058	1,108	1,230	3,200
BIRD, Cyril Kenneth (1887-1965) British					
wc/d	1	1,099		1,099	
BIRD, Edward (1772-1819) British					
oil	1	25,120		25,120	
BIRGER, Hugo (1854-1887) Swedish					
oil	3	70,713	2,277	8,039	60,397
BIRGER-ERICSON, Birger (1904-1994) Swedish					
oil	4	8,471	1,004	1,323	4,805
BIRKEMOSE, Jens (1943-) Danish					
oil	5	12,896	1,025	2,691	4,943
BIRKHOLM, Jens (1869-1915) Danish					
oil	2	3,275	1,461	1,638	1,814
BIRKLE, Albert (1900-1986) Austrian/German					
oil	2	92,398	13,198	46,199	79,200
wc/d	1	4,320		4,320	
BIRLEY, Sir Oswald (1880-1952) British					
oil	3	3,525	1,110	1,168	1,247

Name	No.	Total Sales Value	lowest	Prices median	highest
BIRMANN, Peter (1758-1844) Swiss					
wc/d	2	6,723	2,735	3,362	3,988
BIRNEY, William Verplanck (1858-1909) American					
oil	2	6,630	2,100	3,315	4,530
BIRNIE, Johan (1866-1958) Dutch					
oil	1	1,723		1,723	
BIROLLI, Renato (1906-1959) Italian					
oil	4	40,600	5,672	7,865	19,199
wc/d	1	2,560		2,560	
BIRREN, Joseph P (1864-1933) American					
oil	1	5,500		5,500	
BIRTLES, Harry (fl.1880-1905) British					
wc/d	2	3,827	1,034	1,914	2,793
BISCARRA, Carlo Felice (1825-?) Italian					
oil	2	3,565	1,148	1,783	2,417
BISCARRA, Cesare (1866-1943) Italian					
3D	2	6,126	1,884	3,063	4,242
BISCHOFF, Elmer Nelson (1916-1991) American					
oil	2	53,500	6,000	26,750	47,500
wc/d	1	3,500		3,500	
BISCHOFF, Franz A (1864-1929) American					
oil	17	538,750	3,500	20,000	110,000
BISEO, Cesare (1843-1909) Italian					
wc/d	2	4,512	2,201	2,256	2,311
BISGAARD, J (19th C) Scandinavian					
oil	1	1,322		1,322	
BISHOP, Isabel (1902-1988) American					
oil	1	42,000		42,000	
wc/d	1	1,500		1,500	
BISHOP, Richard (1887-1975) American					
oil	1	10,000		10,000	
BISI, Giuseppe (1787-1869) Italian					
oil	1	2,693		2,693	
BISI, Luigi (1814-1886) Italian					
wc/d	1	1,273		1,273	
BISI, Satyendranath (20th C) Indian					
wc/d	1	2,100		2,100	
BISMOUTH, Maurice (1885-1965) French					
oil	4	8,716	1,024	2,240	3,213
BISOGNO, Vincenzo (1866-?) Italian					
wc/d	1	1,200		1,200	
BISON, Giuseppe Bernardino (1762-1844) Italian					
oil	6	198,139	8,104	22,661	82,904
wc/d	9	29,898	1,383	2,682	8,305
BISSCHOP, Christoffel (1828-1904) Dutch					
oil	2	26,952	1,493	13,476	25,459
BISSCHOP, Jan de (1628-1671) Dutch					
wc/d	5	43,574	1,650	10,570	16,610
BISSCHOPS, Charles (1894-1975) Belgian					
oil	3	3,673	1,021	1,352	1,352
BISSEN, Rudolf (1846-1911) Danish					
oil	1	1,008		1,008	
BISSEN, Vilhelm Christian Gottlieb (1836-1913) Danish					
3D	1	1,887		1,887	
BISSIER, Jules (1893-1965) German					
oil	4	37,404	2,214	8,170	18,850
wc/d	6	43,239	2,610	5,602	13,557
BISSIERE, Roger (1884-1964) French					
oil	5	28,857	1,843	4,297	11,109
wc/d	2	4,976	1,414	2,488	3,562

Name	No.	Total Sales Value	lowest	Prices median	highest
BISSON, Edouard (1856-?) French					
oil	1	4,800		4,800	
BISTAGNE, Paul (1850-1886) French					
oil	1	2,883		2,883	
BISTOLFI, Leonardo (1859-1933) Italian					
3D	4	13,287	1,376	3,726	4,459
oil	2	4,197	1,669	2,099	2,528
BISTTRAM, Emil (1895-1976) American					
oil	2	19,000	7,000	9,500	12,000
wc/d	2	9,700	2,200	4,850	7,500
BISWAS, Nikhil (?) Indian					
wc/d	1	1,080		1,080	
BITKER, Colette (1929-) Belgian					
oil	1	1,073		1,073	
BITRAN, Albert (1929-) French					
3D	1	1,192		1,192	
oil	5	11,098	1,192	1,814	3,836
BITTER, Ary (1883-1960) French					
3D	3	13,345	3,130	3,600	6,615
BITTER, Theo (1916-1994) Dutch					
oil	3	17,457	2,155	2,371	12,931
BITTERLI, Fritz (1909-) Swiss					
oil	1	1,043		1,043	
BIUSSE, C A S (19th C) British					
wc/d	1	2,198		2,198	
BIVA, Henri (1848-1928) French					
oil	1	10,000		10,000	
BIVA, Paul (1851-1900) French					
oil	3	41,000	6,500	13,500	21,000
BIZARD, Suzanne (1873-1963) French					
3D	1	2,160		2,160	
BIZER, Emil (1881-1957) German					
wc/d	1	1,090		1,090	
BJERG, Johannes C (1886-1955) Danish					
3D	3	22,341	5,365	7,367	9,609
BJERKE-PETERSEN, Vilhelm (1909-1957) Danish					
oil	8	14,157	1,055	1,365	3,819
BJORCK, Oscar (1860-1929) Swedish					
oil	4	15,725	1,430	4,120	6,055
wc/d	1	1,099		1,099	
BJORK, Jakob (1726-1793) Swedish					
oil	4	16,546	2,612	4,276	5,382
BJORKLUND-RASMUSSEN, Poul (1909-1984) Danish					
oil	1	1,150		1,150	
BJORN, Christian Aleth (1859-1945) Danish					
oil	1	11,000		11,000	
BJULF, Soren Christian (1890-1958) Danish					
oil	18	29,737	1,000	1,228	3,750
BJURSTROM, Tor (1888-1966) Swedish					
oil	10	27,648	1,318	2,452	5,132
BLAADEREN, Gerrit Willem van (1873-1935) Dutch					
oil	1	13,864		13,864	
BLAAS, Eugen von (1843-1932) Austrian					
oil	11	1,545,571	7,300	93,220	440,000
wc/d	2	9,123	3,975	4,562	5,148
BLAAS, Julius von (1845-1922) Austrian					
oil	3	15,444	1,472	2,972	11,000
BLACAS, Beatrix de (1841-?) French					
wc/d	1	1,180		1,180	

Name	No.	Total Sales Value	lowest	Prices median	highest
BLACHE, Christian (1838-1920) Danish					
oil	12	28,828	1,016	1,411	5,801
BLACK, Andrew (1850-1916) British					
oil	1	2,300		2,300	
BLACK, Olive Parker (1868-1948) American					
oil	6	26,400	2,400	4,500	7,500
BLACKADDER, Elizabeth (1931-) British					
oil	1	14,600		14,600	
wc/d	20	131,412	1,368	4,160	15,750
BLACKBURN, Arthur (19/20th C) British					
oil	1	1,908		1,908	
BLACKBURN, Joseph (1700-?) American					
oil	1	5,000		5,000	
BLACKHAM, Warren (19th C) British					
oil	2	3,710	1,154	1,855	2,556
BLACKLOCK, Thomas Bromley (1863-1903) British					
oil	7	32,812	1,501	4,200	10,290
BLACKLOCK, William Kay (1872-?) British					
oil	5	40,976	2,201	5,250	23,430
wc/d	3	8,833	1,050	1,817	5,966
BLACKMAN, Walter (1847-1928) American					
oil	4	10,075	1,300	2,638	3,500
BLACKSHAW, Basil (1932-) British					
oil	7	174,240	1,296	19,240	78,650
wc/d	5	22,845	1,275	1,430	17,280
BLAGOVESHCHENSKY, Nikolai Dimitrevich (1868-?) Russian					
oil	1	6,345		6,345	
BLAIR, John (1850-1934) British					
wc/d	4	6,005	1,001	1,342	2,320
BLAIR, Mary Robinson (1911-1979) American					
wc/d	1	1,200		1,200	
BLAIRAT, Marcel (19th C) French					
oil	1	5,155		5,155	
BLAIS, Jean Charles (1956-) French					
oil	11	102,650	1,553	9,384	21,905
wc/d	11	54,337	1,038	2,596	21,606
BLAKE (?) ?					
oil	1	1,872		1,872	
BLAKE, Benjamin (?-1830) British					
oil	2	3,495	1,278	1,748	2,217
BLAKE, Leo (1887-1976) American					
oil	1	1,500		1,500	
BLAKE, Peter (1932-) British					
oil	4	150,900	9,300	13,050	115,500
wc/d	5	56,260	5,510	8,250	20,300
BLAKE, Quentin (1932-) British					
wc/d	1	1,430		1,430	
BLAKE, William (1757-1827) British					
wc/d	1	4,000		4,000	
BLAKELOCK, Ralph Albert (1847-1919) American					
oil	12	3,560,550	2,300	5,250	3,200,000
wc/d	1	1,000		1,000	
BLAMPIED, Edmund (1886-1966) British					
oil	6	36,664	4,000	4,410	12,690
wc/d	4	16,651	2,812	4,060	5,720
BLANC, Pierre (20th C) Swiss					
3D	1	1,284		1,284	
BLANCH, Arnold (1896-1968) American					
oil	1	6,500		6,500	

Name	No.	Total Sales Value	lowest	Prices median	highest
BLANCH, Xavier (1918-) Spanish					
oil	2	3,445	1,629	1,723	1,816
BLANCHARD, Antoine (1910-1988) French					
oil	20	152,151	3,750	6,940	17,365
BLANCHARD, Maria (1881-1932) Spanish					
oil	4	182,947	34,980	47,095	53,777
wc/d	5	97,460	7,524	11,224	47,703
BLANCHARD, Remy (1958-1993) French					
oil	3	6,625	1,179	2,489	2,957
BLANCHARD, Theophile Clement (1820-1849) French					
oil	1	2,500		2,500	
BLANCHE, J E (1861-1942) French					
oil	2	51,063	7,295	25,532	43,768
BLANCHE, Jacques Émile (1861-1942) French					
oil	7	152,008	2,422	5,106	109,192
BLANCHET, Alexandre (1882-1961) Swiss					
oil	1	2,762		2,762	
BLANCHET, Louis Gabriel (1705-1772) French					
wc/d	1	4,750		4,750	
BLANCHON, Emile Henri (1845-) French					
oil	1	35,000		35,000	
BLANCO, Antonio (1927-1999) Philippino					
oil	1	3,160		3,160	
BLANCO, Venancio (20th C) Italian?					
3D	1	2,200		2,200	
BLAND, Emily Beatrice (1864-1951) British					
oil	3	5,840	1,296	2,016	2,528
BLANES VIALE, Pedro (1879-1926) Uruguayan					
oil	2	125,000	55,000	62,500	70,000
BLANES, Juan Manuel (1830-1901) Uruguayan					
oil	4	38,280	1,400	8,950	18,980
wc/d	1	6,000		6,000	
BLANT, Julien le (1851-?) French					
oil	1	18,000		18,000	
BLARENBERGHE, Louis Nicolas van (1716-1794) French					
wc/d	1	9,060		9,060	
BLARENBERGHE, Louis Nicolas van and Henri Joseph van (18th C) French					
wc/d	1	9,114		9,114	
BLAS, Olleroy (20th C) Italian					
wc/d	1	1,258		1,258	
BLAS, U (19th C) Italian					
wc/d	1	2,574		2,574	
BLASHFIELD, Edwin Howland (1848-1936) American					
oil	2	31,000	13,000	15,500	18,000
BLASI, August (1903-1979) Swiss					
3D	1	1,105		1,105	
BLAT, Ismael (1901-1987) Spanish					
oil	2	10,283	2,373	5,142	7,910
BLATAS, Arbit (1908-) American/Lithuanian					
oil	1	5,500		5,500	
BLAU, Tina (1845-1916) Austrian					
oil	1	23,426		23,426	
BLAVIER, G (20th C) French					
3D	1	3,346		3,346	
BLAZEBY, J (19th C) British					
oil	1	6,040		6,040	
BLECHEN, Karl (1798-1840) German					
oil	2	33,143	13,206	16,572	19,937

Name	No.	Total Sales Value	Prices lowest	median	highest
BLECKNER, Ross (1949-) American					
oil	17	386,090	7,000	15,000	65,250
wc/d	6	25,450	3,200	3,500	7,000
BLES, David Joseph (1821-1899) Dutch					
oil	1	2,200		2,200	
BLES, Herri met de (1480-1550) Flemish					
oil	1	61,740		61,740	
BLES, Joseph (1825-1875) Dutch					
oil	2	12,469	5,582	6,235	6,887
BLESS, Johan Peder (1825-1880) Danish					
oil	1	4,051		4,051	
BLEULER, Johann Heinrich (1758-1823) Swiss					
wc/d	10	38,323	1,964	3,780	6,574
BLEULER, Johann Ludwig (1792-1850) Swiss					
wc/d	11	37,378	1,450	2,454	5,729
BLEULER, Johann-Heinrich (younger) (1787-1857) Swiss					
wc/d	1	1,437		1,437	
BLEUMNER, Oscar F (1864-1938) American					
wc/d	1	1,300		1,300	
BLIECK, Maurice (1876-1922) Belgian					
oil	2	3,487	1,358	1,744	2,129
BLINKS, Thomas (1860-1912) British					
oil	4	90,118	2,201	15,359	57,200
wc/d	1	2,200		2,200	
BLISS, Douglas Percy (1900-1984) British					
oil	2	3,906	1,554	1,953	2,352
BLOC, Andre (1896-1966) French					
3D	1	4,113		4,113	
BLOCH, Carl (1834-1890) Danish					
oil	1	1,575		1,575	
BLOCH, Marjorie (1956-) Irish					
oil	1	1,233		1,233	
BLOCH, Martin (19/20th C) ?					
oil	2	5,630	1,400	2,815	4,230
BLOCK, Emiel de (1941-) Belgian					
3D	1	3,085		3,085	
BLOCK, Eugène Francois de (1812-1893) Belgian					
oil	1	5,821		5,821	
wc/d	1	1,073		1,073	
BLOCK, Joseph (1863-1923) German					
oil	1	2,600		2,600	
BLOCKHAUER, Harmen (17th C) Dutch					
wc/d	1	24,765		24,765	
BLODGETT, Walton (1908-) American					
wc/d	1	1,500		1,500	
BLOEMAERT, Abraham (1564-1651) Dutch					
oil	1	21,600		21,600	
wc/d	8	153,631	1,289	5,928	83,050
BLOEMAERT, Hendrick (1601-1672) Dutch					
oil	1	411,600		411,600	
BLOEMEN, Jan Frans van (1662-1749) Flemish					
oil	6	214,721	2,327	30,610	90,000
BLOEMEN, Jan Frans van (school) (1662-1749) Flemish					
oil	2	8,482	3,482	4,241	5,000
BLOEMEN, Pieter van (1657-1720) Flemish					
oil	6	80,060	1,963	5,640	46,661
wc/d	1	4,530		4,530	
BLOEMERS, Arnoldus (c.1786-1844) Dutch					
oil	3	42,612	2,869	5,896	33,847

Name	No.	Total Sales Value	Prices lowest	median	highest
BLOK, van der (19th C) ?					
oil	1	2,544		2,544	
BLOMMAERT, Maximilian (17/18th C) Flemish					
oil	1	40,360		40,360	
BLOMMERS, Bernardus Johannes (1845-1914) Dutch					
oil	6	141,850	1,231	23,812	57,388
wc/d	6	33,052	1,336	4,634	14,851
BLONDAL, Gunnlaugur (1893-1962) Icelandic					
wc/d	1	1,860		1,860	
BLONDEL, Émile (1893-1970) French					
oil	1	1,053		1,053	
BLONDEL, Merry Joseph (1781-1853) French					
oil	2	33,061	10,561	16,531	22,500
BLOOS, Richard (1878-1957) German					
oil	1	10,090		10,090	
BLOOT, Pieter de (1602-1658) Dutch					
oil	2	83,214	40,000	41,607	43,214
BLOSSFELDT, Karl (1865-1932) German					
3D	1	5,911		5,911	
BLOT, Eugene (1830-1899) French					
3D	1	12,583		12,583	
BLOUIN, Georges (c.1920-) French					
oil	2	4,858	1,958	2,429	2,900
BLOW, Sandra (1925-) British					
wc/d	3	20,105	1,080	4,680	14,345
BLUEMNER, Oscar (1867-1938) American					
wc/d	3	10,000	1,600	2,400	6,000
BLUHM, Norman (1920-) American					
oil	7	34,222	2,767	3,200	13,000
wc/d	3	3,679	1,000	1,128	1,551
BLUHM, Oscar (19/20th C) German					
wc/d	1	1,273		1,273	
BLUM, Clarence (1897-?) Swedish?					
3D	1	2,277		2,277	
BLUM, Felix (19th C) German					
wc/d	1	1,000		1,000	
BLUM, Hans (1858-?) German					
oil	1	1,384		1,384	
BLUM, Ludwig (1891-1975) Israeli					
oil	9	86,536	3,836	9,000	18,000
BLUM, Maurice (1832-1909) French					
oil	1	1,851		1,851	
BLUME, Edmund (1844-?) German					
oil	1	1,230		1,230	
BLUMENFELD, E (20th C) ?					
oil	1	1,638		1,638	
BLUMENSCHEIN, Helen Greene (1909-) American					
wc/d	1	2,000		2,000	
BLYHOOFT, Jacques Zacharias (17th C) Dutch					
wc/d	1	2,161		2,161	
BLYK, Frans Jacobus van den (1806-1876) Dutch					
wc/d	1	2,595		2,595	
BLYTH, Robert Burn (?) British					
oil	1	1,113		1,113	
BLYTH, Robert Henderson (1919-1970) British					
oil	1	9,702		9,702	
BO, Giacinto (?-1912) Italian					
oil	6	14,959	1,835	2,523	3,218

Name	No.	Total Sales Value	lowest	Prices median	highest
BOBAK, Molly Lamb (1922-) Canadian					
oil	3	10,720	1,208	3,207	6,305
BOBELDIJK, Felicien (1876-1964) Dutch					
wc/d	1	1,963		1,963	
BOBERG, Jorgen (1940-) Swedish					
oil	1	1,311		1,311	
BOBYCHEV (20th C) Russian					
oil	1	2,417		2,417	
BOCCACCINO, Giovanni di Agostino (15/16th C) Italian					
oil	1	15,000		15,000	
BOCCHETTI, Gaetano (1888-1992) Italian					
oil	1	1,318		1,318	
BOCCHI, Faustino (1659-1742) Italian					
oil	3	104,946	4,926	45,300	54,720
BOCH, A (?) ?					
oil	1	5,807		5,807	
BOCH, Anna (1848-1933) Belgian					
oil	4	46,510	2,518	5,360	33,273
BOCHMANN, Gregor von (elder) (1850-1930) German					
oil	7	33,540	1,475	6,256	7,975
BOCHNER, Mel (1940-) American					
wc/d	2	7,750	3,750	3,875	4,000
BOCION, François (1828-1890) Swiss					
oil	1	24,308		24,308	
wc/d	1	3,586		3,586	
BOCK, Arthur (1875-?) German					
3D	1	1,500		1,500	
BOCK, Ludwig (1886-1955) German					
oil	2	3,560	1,609	1,780	1,951
BOCK, Th E A de (1851-1904) Dutch					
oil	1	1,080		1,080	
BOCK, Theophile Emile Achille de (1851-1904) Dutch					
oil	10	33,760	1,358	2,507	7,000
BOCKLIN, Arnold (1827-1901) Swiss					
oil	2	161,238	23,788	80,619	137,450
BOCKSTIEGEL, Peter August (1889-1951) German					
oil	1	28,371		28,371	
wc/d	4	8,414	1,683	2,164	2,404
BODDINGTON, Edwin H (1836-1905) British					
oil	4	8,664	1,354	2,055	3,200
BODDINGTON, Henry John (1811-1865) British					
oil	8	113,385	4,260	8,150	55,000
BODDY, William James (c.1831-1911) British					
wc/d	1	1,264		1,264	
BODENMULLER, Friedrich (1845-1913) German					
oil	1	1,200		1,200	
BODENSEE SCHOOL, 15th C German					
3D	1	10,380		10,380	
BODINI, Floriano (1933-) Italian					
3D	3	18,358	4,726	4,905	8,727
BODMER (20th C) ?					
oil	1	2,229		2,229	
BODMER, Karl (1809-1893) Swiss					
oil	1	3,606		3,606	
wc/d	1	1,298		1,298	
BOECHER, August (20th C) German					
oil	1	1,000		1,000	
BOECK, Felix de (1898-1995) Belgian					
oil	12	29,834	1,149	1,824	6,100

Name	No.	Total Sales Value	Prices lowest	median	highest
BOECKL, Herbert (1894-1966) Austrian					
oil	1	2,083		2,083	
BOEHM, A (?) ?					
oil	1	1,314		1,314	
BOEHM, Eduard (1830-1890) German/Austrian					
oil	6	9,201	1,162	1,676	1,898
BOEHM, Emil (1873-?) German					
oil	1	1,707		1,707	
BOEHM, Sir Joseph Edgar (1834-1890) British					
3D	1	2,880		2,880	
BOEHM-HENNES, Leonie (20th C) Austrian?					
3D	1	1,639		1,639	
BOEHME, Karl Theodor (1866-1939) German					
oil	2	4,784	1,988	2,392	2,796
BOEL, John Henry (19/20th C) British					
oil	2	2,266	1,027	1,133	1,239
BOEL, Pieter (1622-1674) Flemish					
oil	2	27,996	1,996	13,998	26,000
BOENDERMAKER, Kees (1904-) Dutch					
oil	1	1,188		1,188	
BOERO, Jacques (19th C) Italian					
3D	1	5,920		5,920	
BOERS, Frans Henri (1904-1988) Dutch					
oil	1	2,371		2,371	
BOERS, Sebastian Theodorus Voorn (1828-1893) Dutch					
oil	2	5,795	1,652	2,898	4,143
BOERS, Willy (1905-) Dutch					
wc/d	2	4,092	1,075	2,046	3,017
BOERVE, Jean de (?) French?					
oil	1	2,043		2,043	
BOESEN, A V (1812-1857) Danish					
oil	1	1,162		1,162	
BOESEN, August Vilhelm (1812-1857) Danish					
oil	1	5,424		5,424	
BOESEN, Johannes (1847-1916) Danish					
oil	2	5,658	1,866	2,829	3,792
BOETTI, Alighiero e (1940-1994) Italian					
oil	2	110,548	40,948	55,274	69,600
wc/d	21	546,987	1,758	3,826	174,000
BOETTO, Giulio (1894-1967) Italian					
oil	5	15,664	1,192	1,379	8,714
BOEVER, Jean François de (1872-1949) Belgian					
oil	3	4,817	1,075	1,305	2,437
BOEYERMANS, Theodore (1620-1678) Flemish					
oil	1	42,146		42,146	
BOFILL, Antoine (19/20th C) Spanish					
3D	1	1,300		1,300	
BOGAARD, Willem Jacobus (1842-1891) Belgian?					
oil	1	4,659		4,659	
BOGAERT, Andre (1920-1986) Belgian					
3D	1	1,880		1,880	
BOGAERT, Bram (1921-) Dutch					
3D	3	14,111	2,239	3,582	8,290
oil	5	49,919	1,196	12,534	18,801
wc/d	11	64,528	1,144	5,003	18,801
BOGAERT, Gaston (1918-) Belgian					
oil	5	7,138	1,186	1,220	2,145
BOGAERT, Hendrik (17th C) Dutch					
oil	1	4,530		4,530	

Name	No.	Total Sales Value	lowest	Prices median	highest
BOGAERT, Hendrik Hendricksz (1635-1719) Dutch					
oil	1	5,107		5,107	
BOGAERTS, Jan (1878-1962) Dutch					
oil	4	44,390	3,169	11,429	18,364
BOGDANI, Jakob (1660-1724) Hungarian					
oil	1	31,400		31,400	
BOGDANOFF-BJELSKI, Nikolai (1868-1945) Russian					
oil	3	25,923	3,149	9,060	13,714
wc/d	1	1,129		1,129	
BOGDANOVE, Abraham J (1888-1946) American					
oil	1	1,900		1,900	
BOGDANOVICH, Borislav (20th C) Russian?					
oil	1	1,900		1,900	
BOGERT, George H (1864-1944) American					
oil	1	1,200		1,200	
BOGGILD, Mogens (20th C) ?					
3D	1	3,060		3,060	
BOGGIO, Emilio (1857-1920) French/Venezuelan					
oil	2	21,785	7,745	10,893	14,040
wc/d	3	3,880	1,020	1,170	1,690
BOGGS, Frank Myers (1855-1926) French/American					
oil	9	108,777	1,425	6,559	45,000
wc/d	5	9,388	1,355	1,818	2,600
BOGH, Carl Henrik (1827-1893) Danish					
oil	5	16,968	1,313	2,383	8,564
BOGH, Elisabeth (1865-1910) Danish					
oil	1	1,687		1,687	
BOGHOSIAN, Varujan (1926-) American					
3D	1	2,600		2,600	
BOGLIONE, Marcello (1891-1957) Italian					
oil	1	1,103		1,103	
BOGMAN, Hermanus Charles Christiaan (1861-1921) Dutch					
oil	2	2,990	1,190	1,495	1,800
BOGO, Christian (1882-1945) Danish					
oil	1	4,560		4,560	
BOGOLIUBOV, Alexei Petrovich (1824-1896) Russian					
oil	3	31,978	2,828	6,500	22,650
BOGOMAZOV, Alexander (1880-1930) Russian					
wc/d	1	8,000		8,000	
BOHATSCH, Erwin (1951-) Austrian					
oil	1	1,615		1,615	
BOHEMEN, Kees van (1928-1986) Dutch					
oil	3	26,500	1,940	11,884	12,676
wc/d	5	9,706	1,109	1,724	3,961
BOHEMIAN SCHOOL, 17th C					
3D	1	2,277		2,277	
BOHEMIAN SCHOOL, 18th C					
3D	3	11,365	3,168	3,643	4,554
BOHM, Alfred (1850-1885) German					
oil	1	1,133		1,133	
BOHM, C Curry (1894-1972) American					
oil	1	8,500		8,500	
BOHM, Karl (1868-?) German					
oil	1	3,435		3,435	
BOHM, Max (1868-1923) American					
oil	1	6,300		6,300	
BOHMER, Heinrich (1852-?) German					
oil	2	2,581	1,276	1,291	1,305

Name	No.	Total Sales Value	lowest	Prices median	highest
BOHRDT, Hans (1857-1945) German					
oil	1	1,609		1,609	
BOHRES, T (19th C) Dutch?					
wc/d	1	3,077		3,077	
BOHRINGER, Volker (1912-) German					
oil	2	16,128	6,048	8,064	10,080
BOHRMANN, Karl (1928-) German					
oil	2	4,029	1,124	2,015	2,905
BOHROD, Aaron (1907-1992) American					
oil	1	10,000		10,000	
BOHUN, P (19th C) ?					
oil	1	3,480		3,480	
BOILAUGES, Fernand (1891-?) French					
oil	1	1,623		1,623	
BOILLY, Jules (1796-1874) French					
oil	1	10,035		10,035	
wc/d	1	1,746		1,746	
BOILLY, Louis Léopold (1761-1845) French					
oil	31	861,915	1,028	4,800	600,000
wc/d	6	267,159	1,898	4,873	241,910
BOILPELIER, Emile (19th C) French					
wc/d	1	9,117		9,117	
BOIS, P Dv (19th C) ?					
3D	1	1,144		1,144	
BOIS-VIVES, Anselme (1899-1969) French?					
oil	1	1,428		1,428	
BOISROND, François (1959-) French					
oil	13	29,707	1,244	1,971	4,095
BOISSARD (19th C) French					
oil	1	4,777		4,777	
BOISSEAU, E A (1842-1923) French					
3D	1	4,523		4,523	
BOISSEAU, Émile Andre (1842-1923) French					
3D	3	48,863	1,880	4,983	42,000
BOISSEREE, Frederick (fl.1876-1877) British					
wc/d	1	1,138		1,138	
BOISSIEU, Jean Jacques de (1736-1810) French					
wc/d	3	24,380	2,416	2,964	19,000
BOISSONNADE, Henry Paul Marc (19/20th C) French					
3D	1	6,795		6,795	
BOIT, Edward Darley (1840-c.1915) American					
oil	1	1,101		1,101	
BOITARD, François (c.1670-c.1715) French					
wc/d	1	1,200		1,200	
BOIVIN, Émile (1846-1920) French					
oil	1	1,378		1,378	
wc/d	1	2,336		2,336	
BOIZOT, Simon Louis (1743-1809) French					
3D	3	56,567	1,300	19,246	36,021
BOK, Hannes Vajn (1914-1964) American					
oil	2	14,500	6,000	7,250	8,500
BOKET, Edmund (19th C) German					
oil	1	1,000		1,000	
BOKKENHEUSER, Borge (1910-1976) Danish					
oil	1	1,530		1,530	
BOKKENHEUSER, F (19th C) Danish					
oil	1	1,019		1,019	
BOKLIN, Per Erik (1913-) Swedish					
wc/d	2	3,818	1,907	1,909	1,911

Name	No.	Total Sales Value	lowest	Prices median	highest
BOKLUND, Johan-Kristofer (1817-1880) Swedish					
oil	1	1,300		1,300	
BOKS, Evert Jan (1838-?) Dutch					
oil	1	9,581		9,581	
BOKS, Martinus (1849-1895) Dutch					
oil	1	1,175		1,175	
BOL, Ferdinand (1616-1680) Dutch					
oil	1	11,385		11,385	
BOLAND, C H D (19/20th C) Belgian					
oil	2	4,759	2,276	2,380	2,483
BOLDING, Cornelis (1897-?) Dutch					
oil	1	1,951		1,951	
BOLDINI, Giovanni (1842-1931) Italian					
oil	7	427,708	3,871	21,457	237,017
wc/d	7	110,084	1,549	7,755	43,677
BOLDISZAR, I (20th C) Hungarian					
oil	1	1,213		1,213	
BOLDIZSAR (19/20th C) Polish					
oil	1	1,160		1,160	
BOLDUC, Blanche (1906-) Canadian					
oil	2	4,387	1,009	2,194	3,378
BOLE, Jeanne (fl.1870-1883) French					
oil	1	11,067		11,067	
BOLEN, F (19/20th C) Danish?					
oil	1	1,033		1,033	
BOLENS, Ernest (1881-1959) Swiss					
oil	2	4,618	1,242	2,309	3,376
BOLIN, Gustave (1920-) Swedish					
oil	5	9,324	1,094	1,610	3,658
wc/d	1	2,188		2,188	
BOLL, Reinholdt Fredrik (1825-1897) Norwegian					
oil	1	1,906		1,906	
BOLLE, Martin (1912-1968) Belgian					
oil	1	1,075		1,075	
BOLLER, Louis Jakob (1862-1896) German					
oil	1	1,486		1,486	
BOLLES, Enoch (20th C) American					
oil	2	12,500	5,500	6,250	7,000
BOLOGNESE SCHOOL, 13th C Italian					
oil	1	338,348		338,348	
BOLOGNESE SCHOOL, 16th C Italian					
oil	4	81,921	3,234	16,844	45,000
wc/d	1	3,140		3,140	
BOLOGNESE SCHOOL, 17th C Italian					
oil	22	159,363	2,176	4,392	26,000
wc/d	3	13,892	3,624	4,530	5,738
BOLOGNESE SCHOOL, 17th/18th C Italian					
oil	1	22,727		22,727	
BOLOGNESE SCHOOL, 18th C Italian					
3D	2	5,099	2,439	2,550	2,660
oil	5	61,511	2,311	5,387	35,000
BOLONACHI, Constantin (1837-1907) Greek					
oil	2	229,220	105,120	114,610	124,100
BOLOTOWSKY, Ilya (1907-1981) American/Russian					
oil	3	8,948	1,974	1,974	5,000
BOLTANSKI, Christian (1944-) French					
3D	4	209,000	23,000	33,000	120,000
BOLTE, Georg Friedrich (1814-?) German					
oil	1	1,721		1,721	

Name	No.	Total Sales Value	Prices lowest	median	highest
BOLTON, Stuart (20th C) British					
wc/d	1	2,431		2,431	
BOLZE, Carl (1832-1913) Austrian					
oil	1	1,557		1,557	
BOMAR, Walter (20th C) American					
oil	1	1,500		1,500	
BOMBERG, David (1890-1957) British					
oil	5	117,495	3,000	16,500	60,630
wc/d	6	48,388	1,911	5,451	22,000
BOMBLED, Karel Frederik (1822-1902) Dutch					
oil	1	4,832		4,832	
BOMBOIS, Camille (1883-1970) French					
oil	14	271,468	3,000	14,040	50,000
BOMMEL, Elias Pieter van (1819-1890) Dutch					
oil	7	68,553	1,967	3,872	22,709
BOMMELS, Peter (1951-) German					
oil	5	9,418	1,165	1,942	3,010
BOMPARD, Maurice (1857-1936) French					
oil	8	29,860	1,658	3,445	6,000
BOMPARD, Pierre (1890-1962) French					
oil	1	1,584		1,584	
BOMPIANI, Roberto (1821-1908) Italian					
oil	1	4,198		4,198	
BOMPIANI-BATTAGLIA, Clelia (1847-1927) Italian					
wc/d	1	1,898		1,898	
BON, Angelo Del (1898-1952) Italian					
oil	7	16,752	1,278	2,230	3,858
BONAIRE, N (19/20th C) ?					
oil	1	1,300		1,300	
BONALINI, Giuseppe (1869-1938) Italian					
oil	1	1,285		1,285	
BONALUMI, Agostino (1935-) Italian					
oil	8	26,640	1,877	2,983	5,672
BONAMICI, Louis (1878-1966) Italian					
oil	5	15,915	1,600	2,200	6,750
BONATO, Victor (1934-) German					
3D	1	1,034		1,034	
wc/d	1	2,048		2,048	
BONAVIA, Carlo (fl.1740-1756) Italian					
oil	2	167,579	16,379	83,790	151,200
BONAVIA, Carlo (school) (18th C) Italian					
wc/d	1	12,743		12,743	
BONCOMPAIN, Pierre (1938-) French					
oil	1	2,042		2,042	
BONCQUET, Henri (1868-1908) Belgian					
3D	1	1,097		1,097	
BOND, Jenny (19th C) British					
oil	1	2,556		2,556	
BOND, Terence James (1946-) British					
wc/d	1	3,297		3,297	
BOND, William Joseph J C (1833-1926) British					
oil	12	23,200	1,125	1,680	3,624
BONDE, Peter (1958-) Danish					
oil	2	5,164	2,582	2,582	2,582
BONDLE, W B (19th C) British					
oil	1	1,128		1,128	
BONDUEL, Léon (19th C) French					
3D	1	2,307		2,307	

Name	No.	Total Sales Value	lowest	Prices median	highest
BONE, Sir Muirhead (1876-1953) British					
wc/d	4	4,945	1,066	1,287	1,305
BONEH, Schmuel (20th C) Israeli					
oil	1	1,000		1,000	
BONER, Alice (1889-1981) Swiss/Indian					
oil	1	8,250		8,250	
BONESI, Giovanni Girolamo (1653-1725) Italian					
wc/d	1	2,718		2,718	
BONEVARDI, Marcelo (1929-1994) Argentinian					
3D	1	3,500		3,500	
oil	4	27,900	1,100	6,900	13,000
BONFANTI, Antonio (17th C) Italian					
oil	1	3,039		3,039	
BONFANTI, Arturo (1905-1978) Italian					
oil	1	1,180		1,180	
BONFANTINI, Sergio (1910-1989) Italian					
oil	3	3,639	1,133	1,220	1,286
BONFILS, Gaston (1855-1946) French					
oil	1	5,966		5,966	
BONFILS, Robert (1886-1972) French					
oil	2	6,615	1,197	3,308	5,418
BONGART, Sergei R (1918-1985) American/Russian					
oil	2	8,550	1,800	4,275	6,750
BONGHI, A (19th C) Italian					
oil	1	1,200		1,200	
BONHEUR, Auguste (1824-1884) French					
oil	2	4,821	1,900	2,411	2,921
BONHEUR, Ferdinand (19th C) French					
oil	5	14,776	1,455	2,483	4,753
BONHEUR, I (1827-1901) French					
3D	1	1,367		1,367	
BONHEUR, Isidore (1827-1901) French					
3D	8	39,317	1,151	4,567	9,420
BONHEUR, Juliette Peyrol (1830-1891) French					
oil	2	5,526	1,233	2,763	4,293
BONHEUR, Rosa (1822-1899) French					
3D	5	15,395	2,160	2,662	4,293
oil	13	183,556	1,337	12,110	42,600
wc/d	12	30,366	1,032	2,646	4,238
BONHOMME, Francois Ignace (1809-1881) French					
wc/d	1	2,618		2,618	
BONHOMME, Léon (1870-1924) French					
oil	1	1,329		1,329	
BONI, A (19/20th C) Italian					
3D	1	6,280		6,280	
BONIFAZI, Adriano (19th C) Italian					
oil	2	6,654	3,250	3,327	3,404
BONIFAZIO DI PITATI (1487-1553) Italian					
oil	1	2,799		2,799	
BONIN, A (19/20th C) French					
oil	1	1,706		1,706	
BONINGTON, Richard Parkes (1802-1828) British					
oil	1	10,220		10,220	
wc/d	4	44,190	1,600	12,000	18,590
BONIROTE, Pierre (1811-1891) French					
oil	1	2,190		2,190	
BONIS, N (20th C) French					
oil	1	2,859		2,859	

Name	No.	Total Sales Value	lowest	Prices median	highest
BONITO, Giuseppe (1705-1789) Italian					
oil	1	88,200		88,200	
BONITO, Giuseppe and RUIZ, Tommaso (18th C) Italian					
oil	1	76,649		76,649	
BONIVENTO, Eugenio (1880-1956) Italian					
oil	4	7,401	1,187	1,731	2,752
wc/d	1	1,410		1,410	
BONNAR, James King (1885-1961) American					
oil	2	4,600	2,100	2,300	2,500
BONNARD, Pierre (1867-1947) French					
3D	2	9,932	3,160	4,966	6,772
oil	21	9,500,206	5,500	226,500	3,900,000
wc/d	25	182,310	1,078	3,277	55,870
BONNARDEL, A F (1867-1942) French					
oil	1	1,076		1,076	
BONNARDEL, Alexandre François (1867-1942) French					
oil	1	1,105		1,105	
BONNAT, Léon (1833-1922) French					
oil	2	11,192	1,442	5,596	9,750
BONNEFOI, A (?) ?					
oil	1	2,683		2,683	
BONNEFOI, Christian (20th C) French?					
oil	1	1,154		1,154	
BONNEFOIT, Alain (1939-) French					
oil	6	21,747	2,168	3,520	5,148
BONNEMAISON, Jules de (1809-?) French					
oil	1	1,782		1,782	
BONNEN, Peter (1945-) Danish					
3D	1	1,162		1,162	
BONNER, A (19/20th C) British					
oil	1	1,200		1,200	
BONNET, Anne (1908-1960) Belgian					
oil	2	10,621	4,926	5,311	5,695
wc/d	1	1,054		1,054	
BONNET, Louis Marin (1736-1793) French					
wc/d	1	2,633		2,633	
BONNET, Rudolf (1895-1978) Dutch					
wc/d	1	9,366		9,366	
BONNETT, F M (20th C) ?					
oil	1	6,320		6,320	
BONNIER, Olle (1925-) Swedish					
oil	4	65,566	1,004	1,172	62,218
BONNOTTE, Ernest Lucien (20th C) French					
oil	1	2,535		2,535	
BONNOTTE, J (20th C) ?					
wc/d	2	5,724	1,908	2,862	3,816
BONO, Primitif (fl.1920-1940) Italian					
oil	1	1,022		1,022	
BONOMI, Giovanni (19th C) Italian					
oil	1	3,076		3,076	
BONTA, Marcos (20th C) South American					
oil	1	1,015		1,015	
BONTJES VAN BEEK, Olga (1896-?) German					
oil	1	1,317		1,317	
BONVICINO, Alessandro (1498-1554) Italian					
oil	1	412,491		412,491	
BONVIN, François (1817-1887) French					
oil	1	28,000		28,000	
wc/d	2	33,241	1,237	16,621	32,004

Name	No.	Total Sales Value	lowest	Prices median	highest
BONVOISIN, Catherine Helie (1788-c.1836) French					
oil	1	12,967		12,967	
BONZANIGO, Giuseppe Maria (1725-1820) Italian					
3D	1	12,538		12,538	
BONZI, Pietro Paolo (16th C) Italian					
oil	3	70,672	10,290	17,280	43,102
BOOGAARD, Willem Jacobus (1842-1887) Dutch					
oil	5	15,044	1,064	3,480	4,050
BOOK, Max Mikael (1953-) Swedish					
oil	4	8,808	1,583	2,308	2,609
wc/d	6	13,474	1,088	1,935	4,522
BOOK, R (20th C) American					
oil	1	4,000		4,000	
BOON, Jan (1882-) Dutch					
oil	2	14,572	7,244	7,286	7,328
BOONEN, Arnold (1669-1729) Dutch					
oil	1	22,050		22,050	
BOOSTROM, Harry (1917-1996) Swedish?					
oil	1	4,586		4,586	
BOOTH, Franklin (1874-1948) American					
wc/d	1	4,750		4,750	
BOOTH, James W (1867-1953) British					
oil	4	19,763	1,445	2,769	12,780
wc/d	3	5,629	1,769	1,769	1,988
BOOTH, Kate E (fl.1850-1870) British					
wc/d	2	2,330	1,131	1,165	1,199
BOOTH, Raymond C (1929-) British					
oil	1	1,670		1,670	
wc/d	1	1,177		1,177	
BOOTY, Frederick William (1840-1924) British					
wc/d	3	3,248	1,057	1,133	1,133
BOQUET, Jean (1908-1976) Belgian					
oil	2	2,831	1,180	1,416	1,651
BOR, Jan (1910-) Dutch					
oil	2	33,274	4,753	16,637	28,521
BORCHERT, Erich (20th C) German					
wc/d	2	8,064	2,304	4,032	5,760
BORDELET (19th C) ?					
oil	1	2,097		2,097	
BORDIGNON, Noe (1841-1920) Italian					
oil	1	4,250		4,250	
BORDONE, Paris (1500-1571) Italian					
oil	3	810,240	30,240	180,000	600,000
BORDONI, Enrico (1904-1969) Italian					
oil	1	1,800		1,800	
BORDUAS, Paul Emile (1905-1960) Canadian					
oil	4	63,723	4,197	10,023	39,480
wc/d	1	6,637		6,637	
BOREIN, Edward (1872-1945) American					
wc/d	77	1,036,950	1,000	4,000	90,000
BOREN, James (1921-1990) American					
oil	1	2,200		2,200	
wc/d	2	18,800	2,800	9,400	16,000
BORENSTEIN, Samuel (1908-1969) Canadian					
oil	2	8,697	3,900	4,349	4,797
wc/d	1	1,648		1,648	
BORES, Francisco (1898-1972) Spanish					
oil	40	689,183	2,485	12,394	73,097
wc/d	8	27,290	1,196	3,092	5,846

Name	No.	Total Sales Value	lowest	Prices median	highest
BORG, Axel (1847-1916) Swedish					
oil	1	6,222		6,222	
BORG, Carl Oscar (1879-1947) American					
oil	4	180,609	10,609	37,500	95,000
wc/d	13	89,000	2,000	5,500	18,000
BORGEAUD, Georges (1913-1997) Swiss					
oil	3	13,287	3,376	4,081	5,830
BORGEAUD, Marius (1861-1924) Swiss					
oil	2	112,728	53,785	56,364	58,943
BORGELLA, Frederic (19th C) French					
oil	3	6,013	1,368	1,752	2,893
BORGES SALAS, Francisco (1901-1984) Spanish					
wc/d	5	30,932	3,093	3,867	12,888
BORGES, Jacobo (1931-) Venezuelan					
oil	1	2,900		2,900	
BORGET, Auguste (1809-1877) French					
wc/d	1	3,003		3,003	
BORGHESE, Franz (1941-) Italian					
oil	13	21,972	1,042	1,495	3,344
BORGHI, Ambrogio (1849-1887) Italian					
3D	1	11,325		11,325	
BORGIANI, Orazio (?-1616) Italian					
oil	2	130,400	60,400	65,200	70,000
BORGLUM, John Gutzon (1867-1941) American					
3D	1	3,000		3,000	
BORGLUM, Solon Hannibal (1868-1922) American					
3D	1	8,000		8,000	
BORGOGNONE (school) (15/16th C) Italian					
3D	1	64,652		64,652	
BORGONOVO, Giovanni (1881-?) Italian					
oil	1	12,314		12,314	
BORGS (?) ?					
3D	1	1,516		1,516	
BORIE, Adolphe (1877-1934) American					
oil	1	3,500		3,500	
BORIONE, Bernard Louis (1865-?) French					
oil	4	13,499	1,263	2,614	7,008
BORIONS, W (19th C) French					
oil	1	2,976		2,976	
BORISSOFF, J (20th C) Russian?					
oil	1	1,035		1,035	
BORJE, Gideon (1891-1969) Swedish					
oil	2	9,044	1,819	4,522	7,225
BORJESON, Agnes (1827-1900) Swedish					
oil	1	1,226		1,226	
BOROFSKY, Jonathan (1942-) American					
3D	1	22,000		22,000	
wc/d	2	3,945	1,210	1,973	2,735
BORRA, Pompeo (1898-1973) Italian					
oil	3	6,656	1,314	1,484	3,858
BORRANI, Odoardo (1833-1905) Italian					
oil	1	5,110		5,110	
BORRAS Y ABELLA, Vicente (19th C) Spanish					
oil	1	2,840		2,840	
BORRAS, Jorge (1952-) French					
3D	2	3,233	1,510	1,617	1,723
BORRAS, Juan II (20th C) ?					
oil	1	1,075		1,075	

Name	No.	Total Sales Value	lowest	Prices median	highest
BORREL, Ramon (1876-1963) Spanish					
oil	1	7,307		7,307	
BORRELL VIDAL, Felix (1875-) Spanish					
oil	1	1,804		1,804	
BORRELL, Juli (1877-1957) Spanish					
oil	1	3,413		3,413	
wc/d	1	1,266		1,266	
BORROW, William H (fl.1863-1893) British					
oil	1	1,087		1,087	
BORSELEN, Jan Willem van (1825-1892) Dutch					
oil	7	143,613	2,231	13,182	65,770
wc/d	1	7,386		7,386	
BORSELEN, Pieter van (1802-1873) Dutch					
oil	1	2,181		2,181	
BORSSOM, Anthonie van (1630-1677) Dutch					
oil	1	25,000		25,000	
wc/d	1	95,000		95,000	
BORTMAN, Alan (20th C) American?					
oil	1	2,200		2,200	
BORTOLINI, Mattia (1696-1750) Italian					
wc/d	1	3,457		3,457	
BORTOLUZZI, Camillo (1868-1933) Italian					
oil	2	8,037	2,206	4,019	5,831
BORTOLUZZI, P (20th C) ?					
wc/d	1	1,471		1,471	
BORY, Jean François (1938-) French					
3D	1	3,491		3,491	
BORZINO, Leopoldina Zanetti (1826-1902) Italian					
oil	1	3,000		3,000	
BOS, Caspar van den (1634-?) Dutch					
oil	1	4,543		4,543	
BOS, Henk (1901-) Dutch					
oil	8	15,050	1,300	1,550	3,011
BOSA, Louis (1905-1981) American/Italian					
oil	4	7,900	1,200	1,850	3,000
BOSBOOM, Herman (1920-) Dutch					
wc/d	7	14,774	2,052	2,052	2,462
BOSBOOM, Johannes (1817-1891) Dutch					
oil	4	39,488	4,302	10,093	15,000
wc/d	8	22,531	1,021	1,660	7,652
BOSCH, Edouard van den (1828-1878) Belgian					
oil	2	4,556	1,221	2,278	3,335
BOSCH, Ernst (1834-?) German					
oil	3	26,114	1,088	1,341	23,685
BOSCHETTI, Benedetto (19th C) Italian					
3D	1	1,184		1,184	
BOSCHETTI, Gaetano (1888-?) Italian					
oil	1	1,385		1,385	
BOSCOVITS, Fritz (younger) (1871-1965) Swiss					
oil	1	1,309		1,309	
BOSE, Atul (20th C) Indian					
oil	1	3,000		3,000	
BOSE, Nandalal (1882-1966) Indian					
wc/d	1	24,000		24,000	
BOSELLI, Felice (1650-1732) Italian					
oil	5	71,316	6,465	13,886	24,763
BOSER, Friedrich (1809-1881) German					
oil	1	2,600		2,600	

Name	No.	Total Sales Value	lowest	Prices median	highest
BOSHAMER, Johan Hendrik (1775-?) Dutch					
oil	1	5,891		5,891	
BOSIO, Jean François (1764-1827) French					
oil	1	5,100		5,100	
wc/d	1	6,692		6,692	
BOSMA, Wim (1902-) Dutch					
oil	3	6,783	1,807	2,395	2,581
BOSMAN, Richard (1944-) American					
oil	1	6,500		6,500	
BOSQUE GARCIA, Sergio (1943-) Spanish					
oil	1	1,338		1,338	
BOSS, Eduard (1873-1958) Swiss					
oil	1	1,864		1,864	
BOSSCHAERT, Ambrosius (elder) (1573-1621) Flemish					
oil	1	2,642,500		2,642,500	
BOSSCHAERT, Jean Baptiste (1667-1746) Flemish					
oil	1	38,900		38,900	
BOSSCHE, Balthasar van den (1681-1715) Flemish					
oil	4	28,656	2,653	7,242	11,520
BOSSENROTH, Karl (1869-1935) German					
oil	1	1,028		1,028	
BOSSHARD, Rodolphe-Theophile (1889-1960) Swiss					
oil	15	105,801	2,259	3,831	28,685
BOSSI, Giuseppe (19th C) Italian					
wc/d	2	3,414	1,086	1,707	2,328
BOSSI, Pietro (19th C) Italian					
oil	1	5,545		5,545	
BOSSO, Francesco (1864-1933) Italian					
oil	1	1,098		1,098	
wc/d	1	1,098		1,098	
BOSSOLI, Carlo (1815-1884) Italian					
oil	4	23,835	3,732	5,742	8,620
wc/d	9	124,813	1,098	2,636	81,003
BOSSUET, François Antoine (1798-1889) Belgian					
oil	1	4,470		4,470	
wc/d	1	1,057		1,057	
BOSTIK, Vaclav (1913-) Czechoslovakian					
oil	1	2,308		2,308	
BOSTON, Joseph H (1860-1954) American					
oil	2	2,600	1,200	1,300	1,400
BOTELLO (20th C) Spanish					
wc/d	1	5,500		5,500	
BOTELLO, Angel (1913-1986) Spanish					
oil	2	15,750	3,750	7,875	12,000
BOTERO, Fernando (1932-) Colombian					
3D	6	1,170,000	80,000	155,000	420,000
oil	4	730,000	60,000	205,000	260,000
wc/d	8	448,390	10,150	31,120	150,000
BOTH, Jan (1618-1652) Dutch					
oil	1	1,963,000		1,963,000	
BOTHAMS, Walter (c.1850-1914) British					
wc/d	1	1,570		1,570	
BOTKE, Cornelius (1887-1954) American					
oil	2	11,800	2,800	5,900	9,000
BOTKE, Jessie Arms (1883-1971) American					
oil	9	271,500	5,000	13,000	70,000
wc/d	11	27,550	1,100	2,200	6,500
BOTKIN, Michael Petrovitch (1839-1914) Russian					
oil	1	1,661		1,661	

Name	No.	Total Sales Value	lowest	Prices median	highest
BOTT, Francis (1904-1998) German					
oil	11	36,936	1,028	2,595	9,223
wc/d	3	5,381	1,183	1,516	2,682
BOTTANI, Giuseppe (1717-1784) Italian					
wc/d	1	2,216		2,216	
BOTTESINI, A (19th C) Italian?					
oil	1	2,550		2,550	
BOTTGER, Herbert (1898-1954) German					
oil	2	4,267	1,992	2,134	2,275
BOTTICINI, Francesco (1446-1497) Italian					
wc/d	1	90,000		90,000	
BOTTIN, Camille (1890-1944) Belgian					
oil	1	1,507		1,507	
BOTTINELLI, Antonio (1827-1898) Italian					
3D	1	11,840		11,840	
BOTTOMLEY, Edwin (1865-1929) British					
wc/d	1	1,410		1,410	
BOTTOMLEY, John William (1816-1900) German					
oil	1	2,850		2,850	
BOU, Emile (1908-1989) Algerian					
oil	1	1,947		1,947	
BOUCART, Gaston H (1878-1962) French					
oil	1	1,776		1,776	
BOUCHARD, Lorne Holland (1913-1978) Canadian					
oil	1	3,264		3,264	
BOUCHARD, Louis Henri (1875-1960) French					
3D	2	7,572	2,964	3,786	4,608
BOUCHARD, Marie Cecile (1920-) Canadian					
oil	1	1,023		1,023	
BOUCHARD, Simone Mary (1912-1945) Canadian					
oil	2	8,839	3,198	4,420	5,641
BOUCHARDON, Edme (1698-1762) French					
wc/d	1	2,182		2,182	
BOUCHAUD, Étienne (1898-1989) French					
oil	1	2,535		2,535	
BOUCHE, A de (19/20th C) ?					
oil	1	1,000		1,000	
BOUCHE, Georges (1874-1941) French					
oil	4	11,184	1,567	2,600	4,417
BOUCHE, Louis (1896-1969) American					
oil	1	2,250		2,250	
BOUCHE, M (19th C) French					
oil	1	1,567		1,567	
BOUCHEIX, François (1940-) French					
oil	1	14,225		14,225	
BOUCHER (school) (18th C) French					
wc/d	1	2,047		2,047	
BOUCHER, Alfred (1850-1934) French					
3D	6	38,495	2,206	4,557	18,059
BOUCHER, François (1703-1770) French					
oil	2	1,156,000	250,000	578,000	906,000
wc/d	14	727,556	2,400	17,705	302,000
BOUCHER, François (school) (18th C) French					
oil	1	20,000		20,000	
BOUCHER, Germaine (20th C) French					
oil	2	2,759	1,307	1,380	1,452
BOUCHER, Guillaume (19th C) French					
oil	1	4,000		4,000	

Name	No.	Total Sales Value	lowest	Prices median	highest
BOUCHERLE, Pierre (1894-1988) French/Tunisian					
oil	2	6,113	2,990	3,057	3,123
BOUCHET, Auguste (?-1937) French					
oil	1	9,000		9,000	
BOUCHOR, Joseph Felix (1853-1937) French					
oil	2	6,030	2,000	3,015	4,030
BOUDET, Leon Rene Lucien (20th C) French					
3D	1	2,186		2,186	
BOUDET, Pierre (1925-) French					
oil	13	34,114	1,120	2,032	8,437
BOUDEWYNS, Adriaen Frans (1644-1711) Flemish					
oil	2	7,327	2,617	3,664	4,710
wc/d	1	1,176		1,176	
BOUDEWYNS, Adriaen Frans and BOUT, Pieter (17/18th C) Flemish					
oil	1	33,458		33,458	
BOUDIN, E (1824-1898) French					
oil	1	6,687		6,687	
BOUDIN, Eugène (1824-1898) French					
oil	30	1,935,985	9,268	62,693	140,000
wc/d	26	206,115	1,045	4,816	39,954
BOUDRY, A (?) Belgian					
oil	1	1,043		1,043	
BOUDRY, Alois (1851-1938) Belgian					
oil	1	1,433		1,433	
BOUESSO, Daniel (?) ?					
3D	1	4,543		4,543	
BOUGH, Sam (1822-1878) British					
oil	9	84,691	1,125	2,860	29,200
wc/d	6	23,584	1,103	3,371	10,220
BOUGHTON, George Henry (1833-1905) American/British					
oil	4	30,900	2,400	7,750	13,000
BOUGUEREAU, Elizabeth Gardner (1837-1922) American					
oil	2	270,000	120,000	135,000	150,000
BOUGUEREAU, William Adolphe (1825-1905) French					
oil	11	6,131,550	22,000	330,000	3,200,000
wc/d	1	4,481		4,481	
BOUGUEREAU, William Adolphe and ITASSE, Adolphe (1825-1905) French					
3D	1	3,761		3,761	
BOUHOT, Étienne (1780-1862) French					
oil	2	60,303	2,115	30,152	58,188
BOUILLE, Christian (20th C) French					
wc/d	1	1,854		1,854	
BOUILLE, Émile (20th C) French?					
oil	1	2,735		2,735	
BOUILLION, Michel de (17th C) Flemish					
oil	1	11,910		11,910	
BOUKERCHE, Miloud (?-1979) Algerian					
oil	1	6,613		6,613	
BOULANGER, François Jean Louis (1819-1873) Belgian					
oil	1	27,471		27,471	
BOULANGER, Graciela Rodo (1935-) Bolivian					
oil	1	8,500		8,500	
BOULANGER, Gustave Clarence Rodolphe (1824-1888) French					
oil	1	140,000		140,000	
BOULANGER, Louis Rene (1860-1917) French					
oil	1	4,672		4,672	
BOULANGER, Louis Vercelli (1806-1867) French					
oil	1	3,651		3,651	

Name	No.	Total Sales Value		Prices	
			lowest	median	highest
BOULARD, Auguste (1825-1897) French					
oil	1	1,329		1,329	
BOULAY, A (19th C) ?					
oil	1	2,600		2,600	
BOULAYE, Antoine de la (1849-?) French					
oil	1	45,430		45,430	
BOULENGER, Hippolyte (1837-1874) Belgian					
oil	3	16,329	5,000	5,323	6,006
BOULEZ, Jules (1889-1960) Belgian					
oil	3	3,960	1,048	1,398	1,514
BOULIER, Lucien (1882-1963) French					
oil	1	1,166		1,166	
BOULINEAU, N Abel (1839-) French					
oil	1	1,168		1,168	
BOULLEY, J (18th C) ?					
oil	1	1,106		1,106	
BOULLOGNE, Louis de (18th C) French					
wc/d	1	1,898		1,898	
BOULOGNE, Valentin de (1591-1634) French					
oil	1	24,723		24,723	
BOULY, E (19th C) ?					
oil	2	6,208	1,978	3,104	4,230
BOUMAN, Johannes (1602-c.1626) German					
oil	1	27,930		27,930	
BOUMEESTER, Christine (1904-1971) Dutch					
oil	1	1,928		1,928	
BOUNDEY, Burton Shepard (1879-1962) American					
oil	1	1,000		1,000	
BOUNIEU, Michel Honore (1740-1814) French					
oil	2	13,646	4,803	6,823	8,843
BOURAINE (20th C) ?					
3D	3	7,147	1,430	2,717	3,000
BOURAINE, Antoine (20th C) French					
3D	1	1,063		1,063	
BOURAINE, M (20th C) French					
3D	1	2,385		2,385	
BOURAINE, Marcel (20th C) French					
3D	3	6,520	1,300	1,898	3,322
BOURBON, Louis de (1845-1909) French					
wc/d	1	2,356		2,356	
BOURCE, Henri Jacques (1826-1899) Belgian					
oil	2	18,136	3,582	9,068	14,554
BOURDELIN, Emile (?) French					
wc/d	1	1,353		1,353	
BOURDELLE, Émile Antoine (1861-1929) French					
3D	17	258,734	3,412	9,511	60,000
wc/d	3	7,943	1,494	2,175	4,274
BOURET, Eutrope (1833-1906) French					
3D	5	8,542	1,250	1,452	2,742
BOURGAIN, Gustave (?-1921) French					
wc/d	2	9,928	4,380	4,964	5,548
BOURGAULT, Medard (1897-1967) Canadian					
3D	1	2,409		2,409	
BOURGEOIS, Amedee (1798-1837) French					
oil	1	2,476		2,476	
BOURGEOIS, Arthur (?) French					
3D	1	2,164		2,164	
BOURGEOIS, Eugène (1855-1909) French					
oil	1	1,500		1,500	

Name	No.	Total Sales Value	lowest	Prices median	highest
BOURGEOIS, Louise (1911-) American/French					
3D	4	149,000	6,000	36,500	70,000
wc/d	2	46,000	16,000	23,000	30,000
BOURGES, Pauline Elise Leonide (1838-1910) French					
oil	1	3,884		3,884	
BOURGINON, J (17th C) Dutch					
oil	2	31,367	10,570	15,684	20,797
BOURMANCE (19th C) ?					
oil	1	15,330		15,330	
BOURNE, J (?) ?					
oil	1	1,450		1,450	
BOURNICHON, François Edouard (1816-1896) French					
oil	1	1,082		1,082	
BOURRON (20th C) ?					
3D	1	1,157		1,157	
BOUT, Pieter (1658-1719) Flemish					
oil	6	197,953	2,727	29,480	66,150
BOUT, Pieter and BOUDEWYNS, Adriaen Frans (17/18th C) Flemish					
oil	3	57,148	6,734	8,134	42,280
BOUTELLE, De Witt Clinton (1817-1884) American					
oil	2	17,500	5,500	8,750	12,000
BOUTEN, Armand (20th C) ?					
wc/d	1	2,160		2,160	
BOUTER, Cornelis (1888-1966) Dutch					
oil	15	51,551	1,067	2,717	6,750
BOUTER, Pieter (1887-1968) Dutch					
oil	1	1,148		1,148	
BOUTERWEK, Frederich (1806-1867) German					
oil	1	1,377		1,377	
BOUTET DE MONVEL, Bernard (1884-1949) French					
oil	2	19,977	7,089	9,989	12,888
wc/d	1	1,167		1,167	
BOUTHOORN, Willy Leo (1916-) Dutch					
oil	2	3,168	1,584	1,584	1,584
BOUTIN, Christophe (1957-) French					
wc/d	1	1,028		1,028	
BOUTON, Charles Marie (1781-1853) French					
oil	1	5,896		5,896	
BOUTTATS, Frederik (elder) (?-1661) Flemish					
oil	1	25,685		25,685	
BOUTTATS, Jacob (17th C) Flemish					
oil	2	45,760	21,838	22,880	23,922
BOUTTATS, Johann Baptist (18th C) Flemish					
oil	1	17,640		17,640	
BOUVAL, M (1863-1920) French					
3D	3	10,106	1,812	2,288	6,006
BOUVAL, Maurice (1863-1920) French					
3D	4	60,327	1,302	10,673	37,680
BOUVARD (19/20th C) French					
oil	3	16,969	3,600	6,000	7,369
BOUVARD, Antoine (?-1956) French					
oil	30	528,737	4,500	16,773	39,000
BOUVARD, Auguste (20th C) French					
oil	1	1,800		1,800	
BOUVARD, Joseph Antoine (1840-1920) French					
oil	1	5,586		5,586	
BOUVARD, Noël (1912-1975) French					
oil	9	94,308	3,300	11,440	21,150

Name	No.	Total Sales Value	Prices lowest	median	highest
BOUVET, Henry (1859-1945) French					
oil	1	1,152		1,152	
BOUVIE, F A (20th C) French?					
oil	1	1,916		1,916	
BOUVIER, Arthur (1837-1921) Belgian					
oil	1	1,145		1,145	
BOUVIER, Augustus Jules (c.1827-1881) British					
wc/d	5	23,595	2,160	2,955	10,080
BOUVIER, James (snr) (?) ?					
wc/d	1	1,749		1,749	
BOUVIER, Joseph (fl.1839-1888) British					
wc/d	1	2,100		2,100	
BOUVIER, M (19/20th C) ?					
oil	1	1,100		1,100	
BOUVIER, Pierre-Louis (1766-1836) Swiss					
oil	1	14,442		14,442	
BOUVIER, Pietro (1839-1927) Italian					
oil	1	2,955		2,955	
BOUVIOLLE, Maurice (1893-1971) French					
oil	1	1,031		1,031	
BOUY, Gaston (1866-?) French					
oil	2	3,326	1,400	1,663	1,926
wc/d	3	6,298	1,269	2,400	2,629
BOUYS, André (1656-1740) French					
oil	1	11,000		11,000	
BOUYSSOU, Jacques (1926-1997) French					
oil	9	27,511	1,309	2,437	8,500
BOVAR, J P (fl.1806-1812) French					
wc/d	1	7,901		7,901	
BOVEDA, Carlos (1933-) Spanish					
oil	1	1,038		1,038	
BOVERI, E de (19th C) French					
oil	1	1,068		1,068	
BOVIN, Karl (1907-1985) Danish					
oil	2	3,856	1,028	1,928	2,828
BOWEN, Christine (?) British?					
wc/d	1	1,430		1,430	
BOWEN, Denis (1921-) British					
oil	1	1,128		1,128	
BOWEN, Owen (1873-1967) British					
oil	19	40,186	1,050	1,908	3,976
BOWER, Edward (17th C) British					
oil	2	38,324	11,154	19,162	27,170
BOWERS, Stephen J (fl.1874-1891) British					
wc/d	1	1,350		1,350	
BOWES, David (20th C) American?					
oil	2	4,682	2,182	2,341	2,500
BOWKETT (19th C) British					
oil	1	1,102		1,102	
BOWKETT, Jane Maria (fl.1860-1885) British					
oil	2	11,610	2,130	5,805	9,480
BOWLEY, Edward O (fl.1843-1870) British					
oil	1	4,819		4,819	
BOWLEY, W (19th C) British					
oil	1	2,000		2,000	
BOWNER, M (19/20th C) ?					
oil	1	1,040		1,040	
BOWNESS, William (1809-1867) British					
oil	1	1,304		1,304	

Name	No.	Total Sales Value	lowest	Prices median	highest
BOWYER, William (1926-) British					
oil	1	1,692		1,692	
BOX, Garstang (?) British					
wc/d	1	1,043		1,043	
BOXER, Stanley (1926-) American					
oil	1	1,100		1,100	
BOYADJIAN, Micheline (1923-) Belgian					
oil	1	1,669		1,669	
BOYCE, George Price (1826-1897) British					
wc/d	2	25,024	2,114	12,512	22,910
BOYCOTT-BROWN, Hugh (1909-) British					
oil	6	7,079	1,008	1,185	1,460
BOYD, E S (?) Irish					
wc/d	1	1,178		1,178	
BOYD, Jamie (1948-) Australian					
oil	1	1,138		1,138	
BOYD, Walter Scott (fl.1883-1899) British					
oil	1	3,677		3,677	
BOYDEN, Dwight Frederick (1860-1933) American					
oil	1	2,600		2,600	
BOYDEN, S (19th C) American					
oil	1	3,500		3,500	
BOYE, Abel Dominique (1864-1934) French					
oil	1	5,955		5,955	
BOYER, Trevor (1948-) British					
oil	4	8,700	1,026	1,862	3,950
BOYER, V and LENORDEZ, Pierre (19th C) French					
3D	1	2,809		2,809	
BOYLE, George A (fl.1884-1899) British					
oil	2	10,639	1,099	5,320	9,540
BOYS, Justyn J (fl.1909) British					
oil	1	1,520		1,520	
BOYS, Thomas Shotter (1803-1874) British					
wc/d	4	21,018	2,700	5,609	7,500
BOZE, Honore (1830-1908) British					
oil	3	48,035	5,111	10,474	32,450
BOZE, Joseph (1744-1826) French					
wc/d	3	22,066	3,500	6,110	12,456
BOZZATO, Attilio (19th C) Italian					
oil	1	2,720		2,720	
BRAAKENSIEK-DEKKER, Anna Maria (1890-?) Dutch					
oil	1	1,268		1,268	
BRABANT SCHOOL, 15th C Belgian					
3D	2	24,245	4,281	12,123	19,964
BRABANT SCHOOL, 16th C Belgian					
3D	1	4,495		4,495	
BRABAZON, Hercules Brabazon (1821-1906) British					
wc/d	75	352,755	1,027	2,860	19,750
BRABO, Albert (1894-1964) ?					
oil	2	4,060	1,305	2,030	2,755
BRACHO, Gabriel (1915-1994) Venezuelan					
oil	1	2,200		2,200	
BRACHT, Eugen (1842-1921) Swiss					
oil	6	31,028	2,492	3,432	10,000
BRACK, Emil (1860-1905) German					
oil	1	34,739		34,739	
BRACKETT, Sidney Lawrence (1852-1910) American					
oil	1	1,500		1,500	

Name	No.	Total Sales Value	Prices lowest	median	highest
BRACKLE, Jakob (1897-1987) German					
oil	7	15,334	1,496	1,923	3,073
BRACKMAN, David (19th C) British					
oil	1	12,160		12,160	
wc/d	1	3,040		3,040	
BRACKMAN, Robert (1898-1980) American					
oil	3	8,200	1,600	2,800	3,800
BRACONNIER, Stéphane (1958-) French					
oil	3	7,461	2,408	2,512	2,541
BRADFORD, William (1827-1892) American					
oil	5	158,000	8,000	30,000	50,000
BRADLEY, Basil (1842-1904) British					
oil	2	25,883	7,008	12,942	18,875
BRADLEY, Cuthbert (1861-1943) British					
oil	1	1,430		1,430	
BRADLEY, Helen (1900-1979) British					
oil	14	646,596	4,116	39,330	119,850
wc/d	9	195,710	1,740	17,250	50,240
BRADLEY, Martin (1931-) British					
oil	1	2,575		2,575	
BRADLEY, William (19/20th C) British					
wc/d	1	2,114		2,114	
BRADSHAW, Constance (?-1961) British					
oil	1	3,322		3,322	
BRADSHAW, George Fagan (1887-1960) British					
wc/d	1	1,208		1,208	
BRADWAY, Florence Dell (1897-) American					
oil	1	3,750		3,750	
BRAEKEL, A (20th C) Belgian					
oil	1	1,730		1,730	
BRAEKELEER, Adrien de (1818-1904) Belgian					
oil	1	6,165		6,165	
BRAEKELEER, F de (19th C) Belgian					
oil	1	7,883		7,883	
BRAEKELEER, Ferdinand de (19th C) Belgian					
oil	2	9,583	3,727	4,792	5,856
BRAEKELEER, Ferdinand de (elder) (1792-1883) Belgian					
oil	4	44,557	1,419	14,519	14,708
BRAEKELEER, Henri de (1840-1888) Belgian					
oil	3	7,840	1,030	1,526	5,284
BRAITH, Anton (1836-1905) German					
oil	7	104,033	1,591	6,818	44,892
wc/d	2	3,826	1,756	1,913	2,070
BRAKEL, Simon van (?) ?					
oil	1	2,341		2,341	
BRAKENBURGH, Richard (1650-1702) Dutch					
oil	2	22,641	11,022	11,321	11,619
BRAMBILLA, Ferdinando (1838-1921) Italian					
oil	1	2,495		2,495	
BRAMER, Leonard (1596-1674) Dutch					
wc/d	3	20,253	1,324	3,929	15,000
BRAMLEY, Frank (1857-1915) British					
oil	6	34,708	1,368	4,648	10,575
BRANCACCIO, Carlo (1861-1920) Italian					
oil	14	194,566	2,861	6,993	44,911
BRANCUSI, Constantin (1876-1957) Rumanian					
3D	2	957,692	7,692	478,846	950,000
BRANDANI, Enrico (1914-) Italian					
oil	1	1,600		1,600	

Name	No.	Total Sales Value	Prices lowest	Prices median	highest
BRANDEIS, Antonietta (1849-1920) Bohemian					
oil	17	179,582	1,600	7,584	31,600
BRANDELIUS, Gustaf (1833-1884) Swedish					
oil	1	2,299		2,299	
BRANDENBURG, Wilhelm (1824-1901) German					
oil	1	3,476		3,476	
BRANDES, Hans Heinrich Jurgen (1803-1868) German					
oil	1	5,075		5,075	
BRANDI, Domenico (1683-1736) Italian					
oil	5	28,521	1,493	3,000	11,466
BRANDI, Giacinto (1623-1691) Italian					
oil	1	5,785		5,785	
BRANDIEN, Carl W (20th C) American					
oil	1	1,200		1,200	
BRANDIS, August (1862-1947) German					
oil	1	1,168		1,168	
BRANDISH-HOLTE, Augustus (19th C) British					
oil	1	3,634		3,634	
BRANDON, E (19th C) ?					
oil	1	3,565		3,565	
BRANDON, Frederic (20th C) French					
oil	1	5,111		5,111	
BRANDRIFF, George Kennedy (1890-1936) American					
oil	2	14,200	3,200	7,100	11,000
BRANDS, Eugène (1913-) Dutch					
oil	13	55,113	1,109	3,879	11,091
wc/d	13	26,448	1,188	1,584	4,741
BRANDT, Carl (1852-1930) Swedish					
oil	10	21,052	1,204	1,796	4,740
BRANDT, Edgar (1880-1960) French					
3D	4	1,709,673	1,106	4,284	1,700,000
BRANDT, Fritz (1853-1905) Canadian/German					
oil	1	1,178		1,178	
BRANDT, Heinrich Carl (1724-1787) Austrian					
oil	1	1,594		1,594	
BRANDT, I H (1850-1926) Danish					
oil	5	9,769	1,020	2,324	2,622
BRANDT, Johannes Herman (1850-1926) Danish					
oil	1	1,697		1,697	
BRANDT, Josef von (1841-1915) Polish					
oil	1	2,755		2,755	
BRANDT, Otto (1828-1892) German					
oil	2	5,332	2,045	2,666	3,287
BRANDT, Warren (1918-) American					
oil	1	1,600		1,600	
BRANDTNER, Fritz (1896-1969) Canadian					
oil	1	4,897		4,897	
BRANEGAN, John F (19th C) British					
wc/d	1	1,410		1,410	
BRANGWYN (1867-1956) British					
wc/d	1	4,640		4,640	
BRANGWYN, Sir Frank (1867-1956) British					
oil	12	132,582	2,700	7,500	42,300
wc/d	6	26,526	1,500	2,723	10,500
BRANSOM, Paul (1885-1979) American					
wc/d	2	6,350	2,100	3,175	4,250
BRANSON, J (19th C) British					
oil	1	1,316		1,316	

Name	No.	Total Sales Value	lowest	Prices median	highest
BRANWHITE, Charles (1817-1880) British					
oil	1	4,710		4,710	
wc/d	1	1,073		1,073	
BRAQUAVAL, Louis (1856-1919) French					
oil	2	5,360	1,510	2,680	3,850
BRAQUE, Georges (1882-1963) French					
oil	21	6,769,960	24,000	160,000	2,800,000
wc/d	4	149,983	30,200	36,347	47,089
BRASCASSAT, Jacques Raymond (1804-1867) French					
oil	4	58,567	1,847	4,840	47,040
wc/d	1	1,031		1,031	
BRASCH, Hans (1882-?) German					
oil	2	9,388	4,001	4,694	5,387
BRASCH, Wenzel Ignaz (?-1761) Czechoslovakian					
oil	1	4,598		4,598	
BRASEN, Hans (1849-1930) Danish					
oil	4	6,847	1,235	1,794	2,079
BRASHER, Gordon E (20th C) British					
oil	1	1,036		1,036	
BRASILIER, Andre (1929-) French					
oil	10	116,838	8,000	10,666	17,400
wc/d	1	3,171		3,171	
BRASS, Aldo (1870-1943) Italian?					
oil	1	2,699		2,699	
BRASS, Italico (1870-1943) Italian					
oil	3	44,803	5,066	18,960	20,777
BRASSEUR, Georges (1880-1950) Belgian					
wc/d	1	1,553		1,553	
BRAT, Vladimir (1965-) Russian					
oil	3	4,147	1,287	1,430	1,430
BRATBY, Jean (20th C) British					
oil	1	2,256		2,256	
BRATBY, John (1928-1992) British					
oil	22	67,703	1,050	2,074	9,480
wc/d	2	2,273	1,103	1,137	1,170
BRATE, Fanny (1861-1940) Swedish					
oil	2	33,405	4,060	16,703	29,345
BRAU, C (20th C) French					
3D	1	1,309		1,309	
BRAUD, Stephane (20th C) French					
oil	2	3,210	1,459	1,605	1,751
BRAUER, Erich (1929-) Austrian					
oil	1	17,096		17,096	
wc/d	2	8,038	2,992	4,019	5,046
BRAUN, Adam (1748-1827) Austrian					
oil	1	6,646		6,646	
BRAUN, Heinz (20th C) German					
wc/d	1	2,355		2,355	
BRAUN, Ludwig (1836-1916) German					
oil	4	68,833	3,409	19,304	26,816
BRAUN, Maurice (1877-1941) American					
oil	24	515,750	2,250	12,500	110,000
BRAUN, Reinhold (1821-1884) German					
oil	3	7,863	1,771	2,905	3,187
BRAUN, Wilhelm (1873-1937) Austrian					
oil	1	2,400		2,400	
BRAUNER, Victor (1903-1966) French/Rumanian					
oil	12	859,170	20,774	56,594	200,000
wc/d	26	165,131	1,086	4,677	45,300

Name	No.	Total Sales Value	lowest	Prices median	highest
BRAUWER, Cyriel de (1914-1989) Belgian					
3D	4	8,086	1,880	1,938	2,330
BRAUX, René de (19/20th C) French?					
oil	1	1,094		1,094	
BRAVO, Claudio (1936-) Chilean					
oil	4	547,981	10,220	158,881	220,000
wc/d	4	146,547	12,424	39,562	55,000
BRAY, Dirck de (17th C) Dutch					
oil	2	970,200	338,100	485,100	632,100
BRAY, F H de (20th C) ?					
oil	1	1,097		1,097	
BRAY, Jan de (1627-1697) Dutch					
wc/d	1	1,964		1,964	
BRAYER, Yves (1907-1990) French					
oil	33	253,289	3,158	7,506	13,268
wc/d	28	72,046	1,024	2,208	11,682
BRAZDA, Oskar (1888-?) Czechoslovakian					
oil	1	2,170		2,170	
BRAZZA SAVORGNAN, Ascani di (1793-1877) Italian					
oil	3	112,552	32,430	36,246	43,876
BREAKSPEARE, W A (1856-1914) British					
oil	1	1,079		1,079	
BREAKSPEARE, William A (1856-1914) British					
oil	4	12,576	2,320	3,044	3,976
BREANSKI, A de (snr) (1852-1928) British					
oil	3	16,074	1,933	2,291	11,850
BREANSKI, Alfred Fontville de (1877-1945) British					
oil	51	237,681	1,200	3,692	16,060
BREANSKI, Alfred de (snr) (1852-1928) British					
oil	48	927,638	1,184	12,510	108,040
BREANSKI, Arthur de (20th C) British					
oil	1	2,820		2,820	
BREANSKI, Gustave de (19th C) British					
oil	13	40,984	1,399	2,934	7,500
BRECHT, George (1926-) American					
wc/d	1	13,282		13,282	
BRECK, John Leslie (1860-1899) American					
oil	4	379,500	22,000	58,750	240,000
BRECKENRIDGE, Hugh Henry (1870-1937) American					
oil	1	8,000		8,000	
BREDA, Carl Fredrik von (1759-1818) Swedish					
oil	2	3,535	1,608	1,768	1,927
BREDA, J A van (fl.1797) Dutch?					
wc/d	1	1,896		1,896	
BREDA, Johan Fredrik von (1788-1835) Swedish					
oil	1	1,242		1,242	
BREDA, Lukas von (1676-1752) Swedish					
oil	1	4,657		4,657	
BREDAEL, Alexandre van (1663-1720) Flemish					
oil	1	36,929		36,929	
BREDAEL, Jan Frans van (18th C) Flemish					
oil	3	91,789	3,085	3,219	85,485
BREDAEL, Jan Frans van (elder) and MOUCHERON, Frederic de (a (18th C) Flemish					
oil	1	4,250		4,250	
BREDAEL, Jan Peter van (younger) (1683-1735) Flemish					
oil	1	4,040		4,040	
BREDAEL, Joseph van (1688-1739) Flemish					
oil	3	47,124	11,014	17,270	18,840

Name	No.	Total Sales Value	lowest	Prices median	highest
BREDAEL, Peeter van (1629-1719) Flemish					
oil	2	61,511	9,925	30,756	51,586
BREDAL, Niels (19th C) Danish					
oil	1	2,099		2,099	
BREDOW (19/20th C) German					
oil	1	1,349		1,349	
BREDOW, Adolf (1875-?) German					
3D	1	1,796		1,796	
oil	1	1,055		1,055	
BREDSDORFF, Axel (1883-1947) Danish					
oil	1	1,162		1,162	
BREDT, Ferdinand Max (1860-1921) German					
oil	2	207,245	2,245	103,623	205,000
BREE, Anthony de (1856-1921) British					
oil	1	2,431		2,431	
BREED, Dirk (1920-) Dutch					
oil	1	1,549		1,549	
BREEDAM, Camiel van (1936-) Belgian					
3D	1	1,542		1,542	
BREEDVELD, Hendrik (1918-) Dutch					
oil	2	2,553	1,208	1,277	1,345
BREEN, Adam van (17th C) Dutch					
oil	1	362,400		362,400	
BREENBERG, Bartholomaus (1599-1659) Dutch					
oil	3	165,849	11,520	29,379	124,950
BREGNO, Jens Jacob (1877-1946) Danish					
3D	5	11,633	1,005	2,050	4,528
BREGOLI, L (fl.1898-1918) ?					
oil	2	3,147	1,259	1,574	1,888
BREIDWISER, Theodor (1847-1930) Austrian					
oil	1	1,215		1,215	
BREINLINGER, Hans (1888-1963) Swiss					
oil	10	16,502	1,118	1,603	2,439
wc/d	1	1,366		1,366	
BREITBACH, Carl (1833-1904) German					
oil	4	30,098	3,337	7,150	12,461
BREITNER, Georg Hendrik (1857-1923) Dutch					
oil	6	532,450	1,609	30,042	290,765
wc/d	3	80,447	8,486	21,042	50,919
BREIVIK, Bard (1948-) Norwegian					
3D	1	2,419		2,419	
BREKELENKAM, Quiryn Gerritsz van (1620-1668) Dutch					
oil	2	228,820	8,820	114,410	220,000
BREKER, Arno (1900-1991) German					
3D	5	9,231	1,453	1,750	2,913
wc/d	1	1,231		1,231	
BREL, Jose Maria (1841-1894) Spanish					
oil	1	1,294		1,294	
BRELING, Heinrich (1849-1914) German					
oil	3	6,790	1,000	1,050	4,740
BREM, Rolf (1926-) Swiss					
3D	4	6,197	1,350	1,569	1,717
BREMAN, Co (1865-1938) Dutch					
wc/d	1	6,897		6,897	
BREMMER, Hendricus Petrus (1871-1956) Dutch					
oil	1	6,466		6,466	
BRENAN, James Butler (1825-1889) Irish					
oil	1	20,160		20,160	

Name	No.	Total Sales Value	lowest	Prices median	highest
BRENDEKILDE, Hans Andersen (1857-1942) Danish					
oil	16	287,369	1,356	5,052	187,500
BRENDEL, Walter L (1923-) German					
wc/d	2	2,823	1,040	1,412	1,783
BRENDSTRUP, Thorald (1812-1883) Danish					
oil	1	2,220		2,220	
BRENET, Albert (1903-) French					
oil	1	1,954		1,954	
BRENNEMAN, George W (1856-1906) American					
oil	1	1,410		1,410	
BRENNER, Carl Christian (1838-1888) American					
oil	1	1,300		1,300	
BRENNIR, Carl (1850-1920) British					
oil	2	3,420	1,290	1,710	2,130
BRENTANO, Al (19th C) Italian					
oil	1	2,288		2,288	
BRENTEL, Friedrich (1580-1651) German					
wc/d	3	105,855	6,795	9,060	90,000
BRERETON, James Joseph (1954-) British					
oil	2	4,872	2,288	2,436	2,584
BRESCIAN SCHOOL, 16th C Italian					
oil	1	6,528		6,528	
BRESCIAN SCHOOL, 17th/18th C Italian					
oil	1	3,732		3,732	
BRESCIANI, L (20th C) Italian					
3D	1	8,640		8,640	
BRESCIANINO, Andrea del (1485-1525) Italian					
oil	1	323,400		323,400	
BRESLAU, Marie-Louise-Catharine (1856-1928) Swiss					
oil	1	5,000		5,000	
BRESLAUR, C (19th C) German					
oil	1	2,658		2,658	
BRESSON, Rene (20th C) French					
oil	1	1,760		1,760	
BREST, Ferdinand Fabius (1823-1900) French					
oil	2	50,354	9,022	25,177	41,332
BREST, Germain-Fabius (1823-1900) French					
oil	4	86,503	8,030	21,737	35,000
BRET-CHARBONNIER, Claudia Julia (1863-1951) French					
oil	2	19,093	1,093	9,547	18,000
BRETLAND, Thomas (1802-1874) British					
oil	1	2,414		2,414	
BRETON, Andre (1896-1966) French					
wc/d	1	21,750		21,750	
BRETON, Émile Adelard (1831-1902) French					
oil	1	2,812		2,812	
BRETON, Jules Adolphe (1827-1906) French					
oil	3	71,166	2,883	8,283	60,000
wc/d	1	8,000		8,000	
BRETON, Louis le (1909-1957) French					
wc/d	1	6,111		6,111	
BRETON, Luc Francois (1731-1800) French					
3D	1	5,760		5,760	
BRETT, Dorothy (1883-1977) British/American					
oil	1	4,200		4,200	
BRETT, John (1830-1902) British					
oil	7	62,031	1,800	7,150	15,730
BRETT, John Edward (19th C) British					
wc/d	1	1,110		1,110	

Name	No.	Total Sales Value	Prices lowest	Prices median	highest
BRETTE, Pierre (1905-1961) French					
wc/d	1	1,760		1,760	
BRETZ, Julius (1870-1953) German					
oil	1	1,058		1,058	
BREU, Max (?) German?					
oil	1	1,318		1,318	
BREUER, Henri Joseph (1860-1932) American					
oil	1	13,000		13,000	
BREUIL, Georges (1904-1997) French					
oil	1	3,820		3,820	
BREVAL, Henri de (19th C) French					
oil	1	1,197		1,197	
BREVEGLIERI, Cesare (1902-1948) Italian					
oil	2	12,271	4,853	6,136	7,418
BREVOORT, James Renwick (1832-1918) American					
oil	2	4,300	2,000	2,150	2,300
BREWER, Henry Charles (1866-1950) British					
wc/d	3	7,770	1,410	1,749	4,611
BREWER, Nicholas Richard (1857-1949) American					
oil	1	7,500		7,500	
BREWERTON, George Douglas (1827-1901) American					
oil	1	12,000		12,000	
wc/d	1	1,300		1,300	
BREWSTER, Anna Richards (1870-1952) American					
oil	1	1,900		1,900	
BREYDEL, Karel (1678-1733) Flemish					
oil	3	21,641	5,652	5,909	10,080
BREYER, Robert (1866-1941) German					
oil	1	1,430		1,430	
BREYTENBACH, Breyten (1936-) Dutch					
wc/d	1	1,132		1,132	
BRIANCHON, Maurice (1899-1979) French					
oil	15	214,116	3,233	11,067	51,645
wc/d	5	19,127	1,069	4,368	5,596
BRIANTE, Ezelino (1901-1970) Italian					
oil	8	12,943	1,120	1,577	2,279
BRIATA, Georges (1933-) French					
oil	1	1,490		1,490	
BRICARD, A (19th C) French?					
oil	1	2,774		2,774	
BRICHER, Alfred Thompson (1837-1908) American					
oil	18	761,250	1,000	27,500	160,000
wc/d	4	29,100	2,600	5,750	15,000
BRICHERASIO, Sofia (1869-1950) Italian					
oil	1	1,651		1,651	
BRICHTA, Frank F (fl.1888-1898) British					
oil	1	1,963		1,963	
BRIDELL, Frederick Lee (1831-1863) British					
oil	1	1,341		1,341	
BRIDGEFORD, Thomas (1812-1878) British					
oil	1	5,250		5,250	
BRIDGEHOUSE, W (?) British?					
oil	1	1,088		1,088	
BRIDGES, Fidelia (1834-1923) American					
oil	1	5,500		5,500	
BRIDGMAN, Frederick Arthur (1847-1928) American					
oil	21	1,080,804	2,159	18,500	598,600
BRIDGMAN, George Brandt (1864-1943) Canadian					
wc/d	2	2,800	1,300	1,400	1,500

Name	No.	Total Sales Value	lowest	Prices median	highest
BRIEDE, Johan (1885-1980) Dutch					
oil	1	2,717		2,717	
BRIELMAN, Jacques-Alfred (?-1892) French					
oil	1	1,911		1,911	
BRIERLY, Sir Oswald Walter (1817-1894) British					
wc/d	2	2,212	1,106	1,106	1,106
BRIET, Arthur (1867-1939) Dutch					
oil	3	4,266	1,273	1,358	1,635
BRIGANTI, Nicholas P (1895-1989) American					
oil	2	4,250	1,000	2,125	3,250
BRIGDEN, Frederick Henry (1871-1956) Canadian					
oil	2	3,068	1,501	1,534	1,567
BRIGGS, Austin (1909-1973) American					
oil	1	2,900		2,900	
BRIGGS, Raymond (1934-) British					
wc/d	1	2,567		2,567	
BRIGHT, H (1814-1873) British					
oil	1	2,186		2,186	
wc/d	1	1,958		1,958	
BRIGHT, Harry (fl.1867-1892) British					
wc/d	1	2,265		2,265	
BRIGHT, Henry (1814-1873) British					
oil	10	54,216	2,862	4,132	14,600
wc/d	1	1,284		1,284	
BRIGHT, Henry Barnabus (1824-1876) British					
wc/d	3	6,272	1,296	1,816	3,160
BRIGNONI, Sergio (1903-) Swiss					
oil	5	16,335	1,458	2,372	5,305
BRIL, Paul (1554-1626) Flemish					
oil	2	415,000	95,000	207,500	320,000
wc/d	2	4,328	1,094	2,164	3,234
BRIL, Paul (school) (1554-1626) Flemish					
oil	2	8,222	3,264	4,111	4,958
BRILL, Reginald C (1902-1974) British					
oil	2	26,649	3,609	13,325	23,040
wc/d	1	3,000		3,000	
BRILLAUD, Francois Eugène (?-1920) French					
oil	1	1,935		1,935	
BRIN, Émile-Quentin (1863-?) French					
oil	1	1,440		1,440	
BRINA, Francesco (16th C) Italian					
oil	2	21,857	7,727	10,929	14,130
BRINCKMANN, Enrique (1938-) Spanish					
oil	2	6,980	3,484	3,490	3,496
BRINCKMANN, Philip Hieronymus (1709-1761) German					
oil	1	7,785		7,785	
BRINDEAU DE JARNY, Louis Edouard (1867-1943) French					
oil	2	3,345	1,298	1,673	2,047
BRINDESI, Jean (19th C) ?					
wc/d	1	4,511		4,511	
BRINDISI, Remo (1918-1996) Italian					
oil	12	26,996	1,155	1,976	4,363
wc/d	1	4,665		4,665	
BRING, Maj (1880-1971) ?					
oil	1	1,254		1,254	
BRION, Gustave (1824-1877) French					
oil	1	3,663		3,663	
BRIOUX, Henri Lionel (19th C) Italian					
oil	2	4,655	1,855	2,328	2,800

Name	No.	Total Sales Value	lowest	Prices median	highest
BRISBOIS, Patrice (1945-) French					
3D	1	1,975		1,975	
BRISCOE, Arthur (1873-1943) British					
oil	3	21,284	4,564	6,080	10,640
wc/d	2	10,447	4,256	5,224	6,191
BRISCOE, F D (1844-1903) American					
oil	1	1,050		1,050	
BRISCOE, Franklin D (1844-1903) American					
oil	9	48,300	1,800	2,800	14,700
BRISGAND, Gustave (?-1950) French					
wc/d	1	2,525		2,525	
BRISIGHELLA, Carlo (17/18th C) Italian					
oil	1	15,044		15,044	
BRISPOT, Henri (1846-1928) French					
oil	1	1,711		1,711	
BRISSOT DE WARVILLE, Felix-Saturnin (1818-1892) French					
oil	5	13,839	1,996	2,696	3,987
BRISTOW, Edmund (1787-1876) British					
oil	10	36,166	1,000	2,939	9,000
BRITISH SCHOOL, 18th C					
oil	1	3,500		3,500	
wc/d	1	4,750		4,750	
BRITISH SCHOOL, 19th C					
oil	9	44,715	3,400	5,000	6,283
BRITISH SCHOOL, 19th/20th C					
oil	1	4,750		4,750	
BRITISH SCHOOL, 20th C					
3D	1	3,848		3,848	
BRITTAIN, Miller Gore (1912-1968) Canadian					
oil	1	7,054		7,054	
wc/d	3	7,350	1,438	1,460	4,452
BRITTAN, Charles Edward (snr) (1837-1888) British					
wc/d	1	1,963		1,963	
BRITTAN, Charles Edward (19/20th C) British					
wc/d	1	1,924		1,924	
BRITTON, Harry (1878-1958) Canadian					
oil	1	1,117		1,117	
BRIULLOV, Karl Pavlovich (1799-1852) Russian					
wc/d	1	17,625		17,625	
BRIZARD, Suzanne (20th C) French					
3D	1	1,394		1,394	
BRIZIO, Francesco (1574-1623) Italian					
wc/d	1	1,500		1,500	
BROCA, Alex de (19/20th C) French					
oil	1	3,245		3,245	
BROCAS, Henry (snr) (1762-1837) British					
wc/d	1	4,576		4,576	
BROCHART, Constant Joseph (1816-1899) French					
wc/d	1	8,500		8,500	
BROCK, R H (fl.1896-1925) British					
oil	1	1,970		1,970	
BROCK, Richard H (fl.1896-1925) British					
oil	2	16,640	4,060	8,320	12,580
BROCKER, Ernst (1893-1963) German					
oil	1	1,189		1,189	
BROCKHURST, Gerald Leslie (1890-1978) British					
oil	1	17,760		17,760	
wc/d	1	3,300		3,300	

Name	No.	Total Sales Value	Prices lowest	median	highest
BROCKHUSEN, Theo von (1882-1919) German					
oil	3	39,962	8,650	9,948	21,364
BROCONY, G (19th C) French					
3D	1	1,816		1,816	
BROCOS, Modesto (1852-1936) Brazilian, Spanish					
oil	1	1,525		1,525	
BROCQUY, Louis le (1916-) Irish					
oil	2	1,820,400	266,400	910,200	1,554,000
wc/d	3	51,060	11,100	11,840	28,120
BRODAUF, Friedrich (1872-1939) German					
3D	1	1,366		1,366	
BRODERICK, Laurence (1935-) British					
3D	1	1,136		1,136	
BRODWOLF, Jurgen (1932-) Swiss					
3D	4	13,276	2,271	2,879	5,247
BRODZKY, Horace (1885-1969) Australian					
oil	1	1,050		1,050	
BROE, Vern (20th C) American					
oil	1	1,000		1,000	
BROECK, Clemence van den (1843-1922) Belgian					
oil	1	4,271		4,271	
BROECK, Crispin van den (1524-1588) Flemish					
wc/d	1	1,510		1,510	
BROECK, Elias van den (1650-1708) Dutch					
oil	2	78,417	38,220	39,209	40,197
BROEDELET, Hetty (1877-1966) Dutch					
oil	2	3,621	1,405	1,811	2,216
BROGE, Alfred (1870-1955) Danish					
oil	3	6,457	1,850	2,194	2,413
BROITMAN, Yekuda (1956-) ?					
oil	1	3,947		3,947	
BROKMANN-KNUDSEN, Henry (1868-1933) American/Danish					
oil	1	1,191		1,191	
BROMBO, Angelo (1893-1962) Italian					
oil	1	1,468		1,468	
BROMEIS, August (1813-1881) German					
oil	2	2,626	1,313	1,313	1,313
BROMLEY, John (18th C) British					
wc/d	1	3,260		3,260	
BROMLEY, John M (fl 1876-1904) British					
wc/d	1	1,125		1,125	
BROMLEY, John Mallord (fl.1876-1904) British					
oil	1	2,100		2,100	
BROMLEY, William (19th C) British					
oil	4	25,734	2,829	3,945	15,015
wc/d	1	3,600		3,600	
BROMPTON, Richard (1734-1782) British					
oil	1	2,451		2,451	
BROMS, Birgit (1924-) Swedish					
oil	1	8,039		8,039	
BRON, Jean Louis Henri (1884-1959) Dutch					
oil	1	1,359		1,359	
BRONDY, Matteo (19th C) French					
oil	2	7,749	2,336	3,875	5,413
wc/d	3	5,788	1,241	1,516	3,031
BRONKHORST, Marcel Louis (19/20th C) French					
3D	1	2,351		2,351	
BRONNIKOFF, Feodor Andrejewitsch (1827-1902) Russian					
oil	2	4,238	2,031	2,119	2,207

Name	No.	Total Sales Value	lowest	Prices median	highest
BROOD, Herman (1946-) Dutch					
oil	2	4,675	2,298	2,338	2,377
BROODTHAERS, Marcel (1924-1976) Belgian					
3D	2	321,186	1,186	160,593	320,000
wc/d	2	4,644	1,285	2,322	3,359
BROOK, Alexander (1898-1980) American					
oil	1	2,500		2,500	
BROOK, Peter (20th C) British					
oil	2	2,400	1,125	1,200	1,275
BROOKE, Edward Adveno and HERRING, Benjamin (jnr) (19th C) British					
oil	1	1,440		1,440	
BROOKE, Leonard Leslie (1862-1940) British					
wc/d	1	1,595		1,595	
BROOKER, Bertram (1888-1955) Canadian					
oil	3	12,865	1,175	2,399	9,291
BROOKER, Harry (1848-1940) British					
oil	3	35,680	5,909	6,771	23,000
BROOKER, William (1918-1983) British					
oil	2	16,950	6,750	8,475	10,200
BROOKES, Samuel Marsden (1816-1892) American					
oil	1	6,500		6,500	
BROOKING, Charles (1723-1759) British					
oil	1	7,550		7,550	
BROOKING, E (20th C) ?					
oil	1	1,359		1,359	
BROOKS, James (1906-1992) American					
oil	2	10,000	5,000	5,000	5,000
wc/d	2	3,500	1,600	1,750	1,900
BROOKS, Kim (1936-) British					
oil	2	21,868	1,988	10,934	19,880
wc/d	1	1,136		1,136	
BROOKS, N A (fl.1880-1914) American					
oil	1	1,136		1,136	
BROOKS, Nicholas Alden (fl.1880-1914) American					
oil	1	8,000		8,000	
BROOKS, T and CHAESE, E (19th C) British					
oil	1	1,015		1,015	
BROOKS, Thomas (1818-1891) British					
oil	2	20,140	6,280	10,070	13,860
BROOME, G J (fl.1867-1873) British					
oil	1	1,181		1,181	
BROOME, William (1838-1892) British					
oil	2	4,054	1,354	2,027	2,700
BROOS, Jean-Jacques (19th C) Flemish					
oil	1	5,250		5,250	
wc/d	1	1,501		1,501	
BROOSS (19th C) ?					
oil	1	1,105		1,105	
BROSE, Carl (1880-?) German					
3D	1	2,610		2,610	
BROSE, Moris (20th C) American					
3D	1	3,000		3,000	
BROSSARD DE BEAULIEU, François (1727-1806) French					
oil	1	3,491		3,491	
BROSSE, Eugène (1855-?) French					
oil	1	2,023		2,023	
BROTAT, Joan (1920-1990) Spanish					
oil	6	14,966	1,742	2,255	3,764

Name	No.	Total Sales Value	Prices lowest	Prices median	highest
BROTO, Jose Manuel (20th C) ?					
oil	3	32,001	1,068	11,241	19,692
BROUGH, Robert (1872-1905) British					
oil	1	4,640		4,640	
BROUTY, Charles (20th C) French					
wc/d	2	5,335	2,207	2,668	3,128
BROUWER, Adriaen (school) (1606-1638) Flemish					
oil	2	4,116	1,516	2,058	2,600
BROUWER, Berend Jan (1872-1936) Dutch					
oil	1	3,140		3,140	
BROUWN, Stanley (20th C) German?					
wc/d	1	5,596		5,596	
BROWERE, Albertus del Orient (1814-1887) American					
oil	1	1,800		1,800	
BROWN, Alexander Kellock (1849-1922) British					
oil	1	1,859		1,859	
BROWN, Benjamin Chambers (1865-1942) American					
oil	2	51,500	1,500	25,750	50,000
BROWN, Cecil (1868-1926) British					
oil	2	78,000	3,000	39,000	75,000
wc/d	1	1,100		1,100	
BROWN, Cecily (20th C) American?					
oil	2	130,000	55,000	65,000	75,000
wc/d	2	6,050	2,420	3,025	3,630
BROWN, Charlotte Harding (1873-1951) American					
wc/d	1	4,000		4,000	
BROWN, Christopher (20th C) American					
oil	1	7,000		7,000	
BROWN, Don (1962-) British					
3D	1	3,020		3,020	
BROWN, E (19th C) British					
oil	1	12,870		12,870	
BROWN, Ford Madox (1821-1893) British					
oil	1	63,420		63,420	
BROWN, Francis F (1891-1971) American					
oil	1	1,100		1,100	
BROWN, General Rodney (19th C) British					
wc/d	1	1,350		1,350	
BROWN, George Loring (1814-1889) American					
oil	3	44,772	9,500	13,272	22,000
BROWN, Glenn (1966-) American					
oil	1	28,690		28,690	
BROWN, Grafton Tyler (1841-1918) American					
oil	2	54,500	12,000	27,250	42,500
BROWN, Harley (1939-) Canadian					
wc/d	1	6,500		6,500	
BROWN, Harrison B (1831-1915) American					
oil	5	34,300	1,400	6,800	17,000
BROWN, Harry (20th C) American					
wc/d	1	4,500		4,500	
BROWN, Henry Harris (1864-1948) British					
oil	1	2,840		2,840	
BROWN, J G (19th C) British					
oil	1	8,500		8,500	
BROWN, James (1951-1991) American					
3D	1	5,500		5,500	
oil	7	89,033	2,214	7,526	34,730
wc/d	7	29,376	2,596	3,200	7,323

Name	No.	Total Sales Value	lowest	Prices median	highest
BROWN, Joe (1909-1985) American					
3D	2	21,000	7,000	10,500	14,000
BROWN, John Appleton (1844-1902) American					
oil	2	7,550	3,750	3,775	3,800
BROWN, John Arnesby (1866-1955) British					
oil	6	30,555	1,950	4,086	11,025
BROWN, John George (1831-1913) American					
oil	12	276,400	4,400	23,500	45,000
wc/d	2	11,800	2,300	5,900	9,500
BROWN, John Lewis (1829-1890) French					
oil	3	9,329	2,067	3,512	3,750
BROWN, Lancelot (1715-1783) British					
wc/d	1	4,108		4,108	
BROWN, Lucy Madox (1843-1894) British					
wc/d	2	19,305	9,295	9,653	10,010
BROWN, M H (19/20th C) British					
oil	1	3,160		3,160	
BROWN, Roger (1941-1997) American					
oil	1	14,500		14,500	
BROWN, Samuel John Milton (1873-1965) British					
wc/d	5	7,764	1,050	1,440	2,445
BROWN, T Bryant (19/20th C) British					
oil	1	7,248		7,248	
BROWN, Taylor (?) British?					
oil	1	1,628		1,628	
BROWN, Thomas Austen (1857-1924) British					
oil	2	7,178	3,528	3,589	3,650
BROWN, W M (?) ?					
oil	1	3,375		3,375	
BROWN, Walter Francis (1853-1929) American					
oil	2	2,900	1,000	1,450	1,900
BROWN, William (19th C) British					
oil	1	2,500		2,500	
BROWN, William Beattie (1831-1909) British					
oil	3	14,604	2,544	5,292	6,768
BROWN, William Fulton (1873-1905) British					
wc/d	1	2,145		2,145	
BROWN, William Marshall (1863-1936) British					
oil	2	10,304	1,544	5,152	8,760
wc/d	2	4,200	1,959	2,100	2,241
BROWN, William Mason (1828-1898) American					
oil	5	101,500	6,500	28,000	30,000
BROWNE, Belmore (1880-1954) American/Canadian					
oil	3	18,250	4,250	5,500	8,500
wc/d	1	6,500		6,500	
BROWNE, Byron (1907-1961) American					
wc/d	1	1,300		1,300	
BROWNE, George (1918-1958) American					
oil	1	4,667		4,667	
BROWNE, George Elmer (1871-1946) American					
oil	3	12,500	2,000	5,000	5,500
BROWNE, Harold Putnam (1894-1931) American					
oil	1	1,200		1,200	
BROWNE, J (?) ?					
oil	1	3,624		3,624	
BROWNE, Madame Henriette (1829-1901) French					
oil	3	146,460	18,960	37,500	90,000
BROWNE, Matilda (1869-1947) American					
oil	1	2,300		2,300	

Name	No.	Total Sales Value	Prices lowest	median	highest
BROWNE, Nassau Blair (?-1940) Irish					
oil	1	1,057		1,057	
BROWNELL, Charles de Wolf (1822-1909) American					
oil	1	64,000		64,000	
BROWNELL, Franklin (1856-1946) Canadian					
oil	1	15,928		15,928	
BROWNING, Amy Katherine (1882-1978) British					
oil	2	3,286	1,390	1,643	1,896
BROWNLOW, Emma (1858-1933) British					
oil	1	1,416		1,416	
BROWNLOW, H (19th C) British					
oil	1	4,000		4,000	
BROWNRIDGE, William Roy (1932-) Canadian					
oil	1	1,667		1,667	
BROWNSCOMBE, Jennie (1850-1936) American					
oil	1	8,000		8,000	
BROZIK, Wenceslas (1851-1901) Bohemian					
oil	2	53,000	15,000	26,500	38,000
BRUANDET, Lazare (1755-1804) French					
oil	1	2,026		2,026	
BRUCE, Edward (1879-1943) American					
oil	2	8,500	3,000	4,250	5,500
BRUCE, Patrick Henry (1880-1937) American					
oil	1	1,100,000		1,100,000	
BRUCE, Peter (1949-) British					
oil	1	2,840		2,840	
wc/d	1	1,704		1,704	
BRUCE, William Blair (1859-1906) Canadian					
oil	1	1,648		1,648	
BRUCK, Lajos (1846-1910) Hungarian					
oil	4	26,352	1,450	4,951	15,000
BRUCKMAN, Loki (1903-) Dutch					
oil	1	3,500		3,500	
BRUDER, Anton (1899-?) German					
wc/d	1	1,307		1,307	
BRUEGHEL, Abraham (1631-1690) Flemish					
oil	1	29,094		29,094	
BRUEGHEL, Jan (elder) (1568-1625) Flemish					
oil	8	5,829,709	18,695	743,100	1,700,000
BRUEGHEL, Jan (elder) and CLERCK, Hendrick de (16/17th C) Flemish					
oil	1	13,590		13,590	
BRUEGHEL, Jan (elder) and FRANCKEN, Frans (younger) (17th C) Flemish					
oil	1	65,940		65,940	
BRUEGHEL, Jan (elder-school) (1568-1625) Flemish					
oil	1	14,858		14,858	
BRUEGHEL, Jan (school) (16/17th C) Flemish					
oil	1	1,278		1,278	
BRUEGHEL, Jan (younger) (1601-1678) Flemish					
oil	6	1,069,661	7,930	58,690	617,400
BRUEGHEL, Jan (younger) and BALEN, Hendrik van (17th C) Flemish					
oil	1	724,800		724,800	
BRUEGHEL, Jan Pieter (1628-?) Flemish					
oil	1	42,280		42,280	
BRUEGHEL, Pieter (younger) (1564-1637) Flemish					
oil	8	3,012,182	117,600	347,634	850,000
BRUELL, Will (1922-) German					
3D	1	1,699		1,699	
BRUESTLE, George M (1871-1939) American					
oil	1	1,400		1,400	

Name	No.	Total Sales Value	lowest	Prices median	highest
BRUGAIROLLES, Victor (1869-1936) French					
oil	1	3,488		3,488	
BRUGES SCHOOL, 15th C Belgian					
oil	1	16,485		16,485	
BRUGGEN, Coosje van and OLDENBURG, Claes (20th C) American					
wc/d	1	11,000		11,000	
BRUGGER, Arnold (1888-1975) Swiss					
oil	1	3,498		3,498	
BRUGNER, Colestin (1824-1887) German					
oil	4	7,578	1,138	1,759	2,922
BRUGNOLI, Emanuele (1859-1944) Italian					
oil	5	17,717	1,833	3,567	5,723
wc/d	3	4,542	1,058	1,335	2,149
BRUHLMANN, Hans Ernst (1878-1911) Swiss					
oil	2	31,198	12,967	15,599	18,231
BRULE, Elmo A (1917-) American					
oil	1	3,750		3,750	
BRUMERI, Francesco (19/20th C) Italian					
oil	1	1,471		1,471	
BRUN, Guillaume Charles (1825-1908) French					
oil	1	11,000		11,000	
BRUN, Marguerite (19th C) Dutch?					
oil	1	1,501		1,501	
BRUN, Pierre (?) French?					
3D	1	1,882		1,882	
BRUNATI, Gabriele (1852-1925) Italian					
oil	1	9,000		9,000	
BRUNEAU, Florimont (1877-1956) Belgian					
oil	1	1,067		1,067	
BRUNEAU, Odette (1891-1984) French					
oil	6	21,574	2,190	3,505	5,511
BRUNEL DE NEUVILLE, A A (1852-1941) French					
oil	1	1,395		1,395	
BRUNEL DE NEUVILLE, Alfred Arthur (1852-1941) French					
oil	36	120,653	1,119	2,690	10,270
wc/d	1	2,800		2,800	
BRUNEL, Alexandre (19th C) French					
oil	1	1,365		1,365	
BRUNELLESCHI, E (19/20th C) Italian					
oil	1	12,456		12,456	
BRUNERY, François (1849-1926) Italian					
oil	7	120,094	2,000	11,000	36,340
BRUNERY, Marcel (20th C) French					
oil	2	86,280	42,280	43,140	44,000
BRUNET, Alexandre (19th C) French					
oil	1	6,572		6,572	
BRUNI, Bruno (1935-) Italian					
3D	2	3,397	1,349	1,699	2,048
wc/d	1	1,609		1,609	
BRUNIN, Charles (1841-1887) Belgian					
3D	2	4,351	1,331	2,176	3,020
BRUNIN, Léon (1861-1949) Belgian					
oil	4	10,187	1,553	2,437	3,760
BRUNING, Peter (1929-1970) German					
oil	5	178,439	26,563	35,418	43,606
wc/d	3	13,965	3,783	4,427	5,755
BRUNNER, Ferdinand (1870-1945) Austrian					
oil	2	6,482	1,870	3,241	4,612

Name	No.	Total Sales Value	lowest	Prices median	highest
BRUNNER, Hans (1813-1888) German					
oil	1	3,388		3,388	
BRUNNER, Hattie K (1890-1982) American					
wc/d	3	9,000	1,600	3,100	4,300
BRUNNER, Julienne (?) ?					
oil	1	2,226		2,226	
BRUNNER-LACOSTE, Émile Henri (1838-1881) French					
oil	1	2,660		2,660	
BRUNONI, Serge (1930-) Canadian					
oil	3	4,144	1,141	1,436	1,567
BRUNOW, C (19th C) German					
oil	1	2,550		2,550	
BRUNTON, Violet (1878-1951) British					
oil	3	10,364	2,682	2,682	5,000
wc/d	1	1,500		1,500	
BRUS, Gunter (1938-) Austrian					
oil	1	1,852		1,852	
wc/d	4	7,963	1,066	1,434	4,029
BRUS, Johannes (1942-) German					
3D	1	4,206		4,206	
BRUSAFERRO, Girolamo (1700-1760) Italian					
wc/d	2	4,306	1,033	2,153	3,273
BRUSASORCI, Domenico (1516-1567) Italian					
oil	1	27,500		27,500	
BRUSASORCI, Felice (1540-1605) Italian					
wc/d	1	109,552		109,552	
BRUSCHAT, G (19/20th C) German					
oil	1	2,245		2,245	
BRUSEWITZ, Gustaf (1812-1899) Swedish					
oil	2	10,056	1,155	5,028	8,901
BRUSH, George de Forest (1855-1941) American					
oil	1	26,000		26,000	
BRUSKIN, Grisha (1945-) Russian					
oil	1	380,000		380,000	
BRUSSE, Mark (1937-) Dutch					
3D	2	6,042	1,414	3,021	4,628
BRUSSELMANS, Jean (1884-1953) Belgian					
oil	3	52,267	4,292	13,270	34,705
wc/d	4	9,906	1,096	2,367	4,077
BRUSSELS SCHOOL, 15th C Belgian					
3D	2	230,427	3,028	115,214	227,399
BRUTT, Ferdinand (1849-1936) German					
oil	1	1,900		1,900	
BRUYCKER, François Antoine de (1816-1882) Belgian					
oil	2	7,627	2,525	3,814	5,102
BRUYCKER, Jules de (1870-1945) Belgian					
wc/d	2	4,429	1,819	2,215	2,610
BRUYERE, Elise (1776-1842) French					
oil	1	4,239		4,239	
BRUYN, Barthel (elder) (1493-1555) German					
oil	1	20,761		20,761	
BRUYN, Frans de (19th C) ?					
oil	1	1,641		1,641	
BRUYN, Jacques de (?) Belgian?					
oil	1	2,289		2,289	
BRUYNE, Dees de (1940-) Belgian					
oil	2	2,298	1,149	1,149	1,149
wc/d	1	1,186		1,186	

Name	No.	Total Sales Value	Prices lowest	Prices median	highest
BRUYNE, Gustaaf de (1914-1981) Belgian					
oil	2	12,766	4,178	6,383	8,588
wc/d	1	1,429		1,429	
BRYANT, Alice (20th C) American					
oil	1	1,800		1,800	
BRYANT, H C (fl.1860-1880) British					
oil	1	57,200		57,200	
BRYANT, Henry (1812-1881) American					
oil	1	28,979		28,979	
BRYANT, Henry C (fl.1860-1880) British					
oil	1	3,915		3,915	
BRYCE, Gordon (1943-) British					
oil	1	2,132		2,132	
BRYEN, Camille (1907-1977) French					
oil	3	15,467	1,947	6,142	7,378
wc/d	2	2,712	1,141	1,356	1,571
BRYERS, Duane (1911-) American					
oil	2	4,632	1,000	2,316	3,632
BRYGGE, Hans (1885-1959) Danish					
oil	1	2,343		2,343	
BRYMNER, William (1855-1925) Canadian					
oil	1	2,568		2,568	
BUBARNIK, A Gyula (20th C) Hungarian					
oil	1	1,413		1,413	
BUCAILLE, Max (1906-1992) French					
wc/d	1	2,900		2,900	
BUCCI, Anselmo (1887-1955) Italian					
oil	1	4,853		4,853	
BUCHANAN, George F (fl.1848-1864) British					
oil	2	3,904	1,304	1,952	2,600
BUCHANAN, Hugh (1958-) British					
wc/d	2	4,704	1,470	2,352	3,234
BUCHANAN, Peter Ronald (20th C) British					
wc/d	1	5,285		5,285	
BUCHANAN, Peter S (fl.1860-1911) British					
oil	1	1,087		1,087	
BUCHE, Josef (1848-1917) Austrian					
oil	2	3,492	1,364	1,746	2,128
BUCHER, Carl (1935-) Swiss					
oil	1	1,016		1,016	
BUCHET, Gustave (1888-1963) Swiss					
oil	5	1,017,956	9,115	76,626	825,203
wc/d	7	54,544	1,996	7,073	14,736
BUCHHEISTER, Carl (1890-1964) German					
oil	3	41,627	1,776	10,725	29,126
wc/d	1	1,760		1,760	
BUCHHOLZ, Erich (1891-1972) German					
3D	1	35,922		35,922	
BUCHMANN, Helen (1843-) German					
oil	1	1,385		1,385	
BUCHNER, F (?) ?					
oil	1	1,463		1,463	
BUCHNER, Georg (1858-1914) German					
oil	1	1,518		1,518	
BUCHNER, Gustav Johann (1880-1951) German					
oil	1	1,481		1,481	
BUCHNER, Hans (1856-1941) German					
oil	1	3,002		3,002	

Name	No.	Total Sales Value	Prices lowest	median	highest
BUCHS, Raymond (1878-1958) Swiss					
oil	1	5,247		5,247	
BUCHSER, Frank (1828-1890) Swiss					
oil	7	106,982	4,183	9,562	28,685
BUCK, Adam (1759-1833) British					
wc/d	1	3,432		3,432	
BUCK, Claude (1890-1974) American					
oil	7	21,150	1,100	2,750	6,500
BUCK, Evariste de (1892-1974) Belgian					
oil	1	6,410		6,410	
BUCK, Rafael de (1902-1986) Belgian					
oil	1	1,259		1,259	
BUCK, William H (1840-1888) American					
oil	3	83,000	17,000	22,000	44,000
BUCKEN, Peter (1831-1915) German					
oil	1	2,159		2,159	
BUCKLER, John (1770-1851) British					
wc/d	1	3,796		3,796	
BUCKLER, William (fl.1836-1856) British					
wc/d	2	5,738	2,567	2,869	3,171
BUCKLEY, Charles F (fl.1841-1869) British					
wc/d	3	38,118	1,510	9,438	27,170
BUCKLEY, John Michael (1891-1958) American					
oil	1	1,000		1,000	
BUCKLIN, William Savery (1851-1928) American					
oil	1	1,700		1,700	
wc/d	1	1,000		1,000	
BUCKNER, Richard (1812-1883) British					
oil	2	7,798	1,363	3,899	6,435
BUDDENBERG, Wilhelm (1890-?) German					
oil	1	1,171		1,171	
BUDELOT, Philippe (18/19th C) French					
oil	4	22,683	1,897	2,438	15,911
BUDNICK, Sydney Jonas (1921-1994) American					
3D	1	11,000		11,000	
BUDTZ-MOLLER, Carl (1882-1953) Danish					
oil	2	5,730	2,250	2,865	3,480
BUECKELAER, Joachim (1530-1573) Flemish					
oil	2	3,994,000	25,000	1,997,000	3,969,000
BUEHR, Karl Albert (1866-1952) American					
oil	5	40,500	1,100	2,600	19,000
BUEL, Hubert (1915-1984) American					
wc/d	1	1,300		1,300	
BUENO FERRER, Pascual (1930-) Spanish					
oil	1	3,106		3,106	
BUENO, Antonio (1918-1984) Italian					
oil	15	152,921	3,927	9,969	17,361
wc/d	8	13,593	1,038	1,716	2,473
BUENO, Javier (19th C) Spanish					
oil	1	3,372		3,372	
BUENO, Pedro (1910-1993) Spanish					
oil	3	9,459	1,748	2,013	5,698
BUENO, Xavier (1915-1979) Spanish					
oil	15	172,365	5,598	10,775	24,112
wc/d	2	5,390	2,218	2,695	3,172
BUESEM, Jan Jansz (1600-c.1649) Dutch					
oil	1	32,000		32,000	
BUFANO, Beniamino (1888-1970) American					
3D	1	2,750		2,750	

Name	No.	Total Sales Value	lowest	Prices median	highest
BUFF, Conrad (1886-1975) American					
oil	4	11,850	1,600	3,125	4,000
BUFFET, Bernard (1928-1999) French					
oil	51	1,719,043	8,000	28,931	100,000
wc/d	32	379,734	1,460	9,384	50,000
BUFFET, François (1789-1843) French					
oil	1	1,832		1,832	
BUFILL, Jose Llovera (1846-1896) Spanish					
oil	2	11,826	5,769	5,913	6,057
wc/d	1	1,370		1,370	
BUGAREL, Emile (19th C) French					
oil	1	1,518		1,518	
BUGATTI, Rembrandt (1885-1916) Italian					
3D	22	3,630,281	23,850	116,404	521,067
wc/d	1	9,576		9,576	
BUHLER, Augustus W (1853-1920) American					
oil	1	1,300		1,300	
BUHLER, Robert (1916-1989) British					
oil	2	5,530	2,054	2,765	3,476
BUHLMANN, Johann Rudolf (1802-1890) Swiss					
oil	1	3,950		3,950	
BUHOT, Felix (1847-1898) French					
wc/d	1	7,865		7,865	
BUI XUAN PHAI (1920-1988) Vietnamese					
oil	3	13,643	1,899	5,179	6,565
BUISSERET, Louis (1888-1956) Belgian					
oil	2	6,052	1,581	3,026	4,471
BUITEVELD, J (18th C) ?					
oil	1	16,732		16,732	
BUKOVAC, B (19th C) Hungarian					
oil	1	12,325		12,325	
BUKOVAC, Ivanka (20th C) Czechoslovakian					
oil	1	1,617		1,617	
BUKOVAC, Vlacho (1855-1923) Yugoslavian					
oil	2	30,367	8,367	15,184	22,000
BUKOVETSKY, Evgeniy Iosipovich (1866-1948) Russian					
oil	1	1,155		1,155	
BULCKE, Émile (1875-1963) Belgian					
oil	1	1,087		1,087	
BULL, Charles Livingston (1874-1932) American					
wc/d	1	1,200		1,200	
BULL-HEDLUND, Bertil (1893-1950) Swedish					
oil	2	7,749	2,129	3,875	5,620
BULLEID, George Lawrence (1858-1933) British					
wc/d	1	6,040		6,040	
BULMAN, Orville (20th C) American					
oil	7	31,450	2,200	4,500	6,500
BUNBURY, H W (1750-1811) British					
wc/d	1	1,325		1,325	
BUNBURY, Henry William (1750-1811) British					
wc/d	1	1,359		1,359	
BUNCE, William Gedney (1840-1916) British					
oil	1	1,100		1,100	
BUNDY, Edgar (1862-1922) British					
oil	5	70,270	3,600	10,360	38,610
wc/d	5	12,279	1,088	2,325	4,108
BUNING, Johan (1893-1963) Dutch					
oil	1	3,169		3,169	

Name	No.	Total Sales Value	lowest	Prices median	highest
BUNKE, Franz (1857-1939) German					
oil	2	3,451	1,655	1,726	1,796
BUNKER, Dennis M (1861-1890) American					
oil	4	3,370,000	150,000	310,000	2,600,000
BUNNY, Rupert Charles Wulsten (1864-1947) Australian					
oil	4	81,269	1,570	22,492	34,716
BUNTZEN, Heinrich (1802-1892) Danish					
oil	1	3,508		3,508	
BUONO, Léon Giuseppe (1888-1975) Italian					
oil	2	3,099	1,494	1,550	1,605
BURAGLIO, Pierre (1939-) French					
oil	1	6,911		6,911	
BURAIMOH, Jimoh (1943-) Nigerian					
wc/d	3	4,160	1,058	1,269	1,833
BURBANK, Elbridge Ayer (1858-1949) American					
oil	1	3,250		3,250	
wc/d	1	1,500		1,500	
BURBURE, Louis de (1837-?) Belgian					
oil	1	5,324		5,324	
BURCH, Jacques Hippolyte van der (c.1786-1856) French					
wc/d	1	7,369		7,369	
BURCHFIELD, Charles (1893-1967) American					
wc/d	11	1,242,300	1,800	60,000	460,000
BURDE, Paul (1819-1874) German					
oil	1	1,475		1,475	
BURDEN, Chris (1946-) American					
3D	1	15,000		15,000	
wc/d	1	10,000		10,000	
BUREAU, Léon (1866-1906) French					
3D	7	13,906	1,321	1,898	3,171
BUREN, Daniel (1938-) French					
wc/d	1	21,626		21,626	
BURGARITSKI, Joseph (1836-1890) Austrian					
oil	1	2,681		2,681	
BURGDORFF, Ferdinand (1883-1975) American					
oil	3	7,300	1,500	2,800	3,000
BURGER, Anton (1824-1905) German					
oil	2	20,564	5,844	10,282	14,720
BURGER, Walter (1923-) Swiss					
oil	1	1,118		1,118	
BURGER-WILLING, Willi Hans (1882-1969) German					
oil	1	1,000		1,000	
BURGERMAN, J (?) ?					
oil	1	2,528		2,528	
BURGESS, Arthur James Wetherall (1879-1957) Australian					
oil	1	4,983		4,983	
wc/d	1	1,256		1,256	
BURGESS, Eliza Mary (1873-?) British					
wc/d	1	1,826		1,826	
BURGESS, George Henry (1831-1905) American					
oil	1	3,500		3,500	
BURGESS, James Howard (1817-1890) British					
wc/d	3	7,854	1,692	1,692	4,424
BURGESS, John (jnr) (1814-1874) British					
wc/d	1	1,302		1,302	
BURGESS, John Bagnold (1830-1897) British					
oil	3	23,700	1,200	10,500	12,000
BURGESS, John Cart (1798-1863) British					
wc/d	2	2,558	1,020	1,279	1,538

Name	No.	Total Sales Value	lowest	Prices median	highest
BURGESS, William (18/19th C) British					
oil	2	6,042	1,138	3,021	4,904
BURGH, Hendrick van der (1627-c.1669) Dutch					
oil	2	30,032	3,120	15,016	26,912
BURGH, Hendrik Adam van der (1798-1877) Dutch					
oil	1	1,970		1,970	
BURGH, Pieter Daniel van der (1805-1879) Dutch					
oil	1	2,453		2,453	
BURGH, van der (?) Dutch					
oil	1	1,349		1,349	
BURGHARDT, A (19th C) ?					
oil	1	13,500		13,500	
BURGHARDT, Gustav (fl.1935) German					
oil	2	4,359	1,500	2,180	2,859
BURGIN, Victor (1941-) American					
wc/d	1	4,530		4,530	
BURGMEIER, Max (1881-1947) Swiss					
oil	1	1,105		1,105	
BURGUNDIAN SCHOOL, 15th C French					
3D	1	4,949		4,949	
BURI, Max (1868-1915) Swiss					
oil	1	27,985		27,985	
BURI, Samuel (1935-) Swiss					
oil	2	5,676	2,598	2,838	3,078
wc/d	2	2,383	1,155	1,192	1,228
BURKE, Augustus (c.1838-1891) British					
oil	1	10,176		10,176	
BURKEL, Heinrich (1802-1869) German					
oil	10	140,907	2,922	10,836	30,902
BURKENROAD, Flora S (1873-?) American					
oil	1	1,400		1,400	
BURKHARDT, Hans Gustav (1904-1994) American/Swiss					
oil	1	2,700		2,700	
BURLEIGH, C H H (1875-1956) British					
oil	1	1,908		1,908	
BURLISON, Clement (1815-1899) British					
oil	1	2,226		2,226	
BURLIUK, David (1882-1967) American/Russian					
oil	19	47,495	1,100	2,200	6,345
wc/d	3	9,250	1,100	1,100	7,050
BURMAN, Sakti (1935-) Indian					
oil	1	5,000		5,000	
BURMANN, Fritz (1892-1945) German					
oil	1	69,120		69,120	
BURMEISTER, Paul (1847-?) German					
oil	1	2,662		2,662	
BURMESTER, Georg (1864-1936) German					
oil	5	25,662	2,875	5,100	7,500
BURN, Thomas F (fl.1861-1872) British					
oil	1	1,095		1,095	
BURNAND, Eugène (1850-1921) Swiss					
oil	1	1,472		1,472	
wc/d	1	2,274		2,274	
BURNE-JONES, Sir Edward Coley (1833-1898) British					
oil	1	362,400		362,400	
wc/d	20	166,793	1,021	4,753	28,600
BURNET, James M (1788-1816) British					
oil	1	3,020		3,020	

Name	No.	Total Sales Value	Prices lowest	median	highest
BURNETT, Calvin (1921-) American					
oil	1	1,400		1,400	
BURNIER, Richard (1826-1884) Dutch					
oil	2	5,035	2,239	2,518	2,796
BURNITZ, Karl-Peter (1824-1886) German					
oil	1	1,935		1,935	
BURNS, Colin W (1944-) British					
oil	11	124,817	2,058	11,000	24,000
wc/d	2	6,588	1,590	3,294	4,998
BURNS, William H (20th C) Irish					
oil	1	1,233		1,233	
BURON, Henri Lucien Joseph (1880-1969) French					
oil	1	1,066		1,066	
wc/d	1	1,130		1,130	
BURPEE, William P (1846-?) American					
oil	1	1,100		1,100	
wc/d	2	5,000	1,000	2,500	4,000
BURR, Alexander Hohenlohe (1837-1899) British					
oil	1	20,300		20,300	
BURR, John (1831-1893) British					
oil	3	8,801	2,556	3,045	3,200
BURRA, Edward (1905-1976) British					
wc/d	9	350,030	5,760	40,040	82,500
BURRELL, James (fl.1859-c.1865) British					
oil	1	6,000		6,000	
BURRELL-SMITH, L (19th C) British					
wc/d	1	1,425		1,425	
BURRI, Alberto (1915-1995) Italian					
oil	3	512,018	36,240	203,978	271,800
wc/d	3	130,253	18,326	37,750	74,177
BURRILL, Edward (19th C) American					
oil	1	1,100		1,100	
BURROUGHS, A Leicester (fl.1881-1916) British					
oil	1	3,976		3,976	
BURROUGHS, William and CONDO, George (20th C) American					
oil	2	3,000	1,000	1,500	2,000
BURROWS, Harold Longmore (1889-1965) American					
wc/d	1	1,600		1,600	
BURROWS, Robert (1810-1883) British					
oil	2	4,839	1,214	2,420	3,625
BURSSENS, Jan (1925-) Belgian					
oil	2	3,152	1,542	1,576	1,610
BURT, Charles Thomas (1823-1902) British					
oil	4	10,483	1,185	2,516	4,266
BURTON, Richmond (1960-) American					
oil	1	2,000		2,000	
BURTON, Sir Frederick William (1816-1900) British					
oil	1	2,190		2,190	
wc/d	4	93,916	1,570	9,173	74,000
BURWOOD, G Vemply (19/20th C) British					
oil	1	6,080		6,080	
BURY, Pol (1922-) Belgian					
3D	1	4,000		4,000	
BURZI, Ettore (1872-1937) Italian					
oil	1	1,615		1,615	
BUSA, Peter (1914-) American					
oil	1	1,100		1,100	
BUSCAGLIONE, Giuseppe (1868-1928) Italian					
oil	5	8,485	1,142	1,651	2,390

Name	No.	Total Sales Value	lowest	Prices median	highest
BUSCH, Wilhelm (1832-1908) German					
3D	1	2,591		2,591	
oil	11	99,242	4,458	7,785	20,761
BUSCHELBERGER, Anton (1869-1934) German					
3D	1	2,958		2,958	
BUSCIONI, Umberto (1931-) Italian					
oil	1	3,491		3,491	
BUSCO, L (?) ?					
3D	1	5,133		5,133	
BUSH, Jack (1909-1977) Canadian					
oil	3	37,983	5,400	14,000	18,583
BUSH, Norton (1834-1894) American					
oil	3	32,250	2,250	5,000	25,000
BUSHBY, Thomas (1861-1918) British					
wc/d	3	10,977	1,020	3,807	6,150
BUSIERI, Giovanni Battista (1698-1757) Italian					
oil	2	31,075	11,925	15,538	19,150
wc/d	1	12,835		12,835	
BUSIRI-VICI, Andrea (1817-?) Italian					
wc/d	1	2,037		2,037	
BUSOM, Simo (1927-) Spanish					
oil	1	1,026		1,026	
BUSSCHE, Joseph Emanuel van den (1837-1903) Belgian					
oil	2	3,780	1,429	1,890	2,351
BUSSON, Charles (1822-1908) French					
oil	1	3,000		3,000	
BUSSON, Georges (1859-1933) French					
3D	1	3,651		3,651	
oil	1	3,441		3,441	
wc/d	1	2,308		2,308	
BUSSON, Marcel (1913-) French?					
oil	2	4,133	1,378	2,067	2,755
BUSSY, M de (20th C) ?					
wc/d	1	1,408		1,408	
BUSSY, Simon (1869-1954) French					
wc/d	9	47,682	1,088	3,335	15,274
BUTAKOV, Maksim Kharitonovich (1916-) Russian					
oil	1	4,530		4,530	
BUTER, Bernhard (1883-1959) German					
oil	1	1,500		1,500	
BUTHAUD, René (1866-?) French					
oil	2	3,290	1,645	1,645	1,645
BUTHE, Michael (1944-1994) German					
oil	1	14,572		14,572	
wc/d	3	13,760	2,277	2,831	8,652
BUTLER, Horacio (1897-1983) Argentinian					
wc/d	1	1,800		1,800	
BUTLER, Howard Russell (1856-1934) American					
oil	1	4,750		4,750	
BUTLER, James (1931-) British					
3D	1	3,744		3,744	
BUTLER, Joseph Nikolaus (1822-1885) Swiss					
oil	1	4,254		4,254	
BUTLER, Mildred Anne (1858-1941) British					
wc/d	5	37,126	2,960	6,660	11,544
BUTLER, Reg (1913-1981) British					
3D	1	18,000		18,000	
BUTLER, Theodore E (1861-1936) American					
oil	2	40,000	16,000	20,000	24,000

Name	No.	Total Sales Value	lowest	Prices median	highest
BUTTERFIELD, Deborah (20th C) American					
3D	2	78,500	31,000	39,250	47,500
BUTTERSACK, Bernhard (1858-1925) German					
oil	3	5,120	1,500	1,500	2,020
BUTTERSWORTH, James E (1817-1894) American					
oil	8	855,890	13,430	92,500	260,000
BUTTERSWORTH, Thomas (1768-1842) British					
oil	13	214,932	4,379	12,000	76,960
wc/d	3	19,072	2,002	4,200	12,870
BUTTERWORTH, Ninetta (1922-) British					
oil	2	4,478	1,478	2,239	3,000
BUTTI, Argelia (19th C) Italian?					
oil	1	1,716		1,716	
BUTTNER, G H (19th C) German					
oil	1	5,024		5,024	
BUTTNER, Hans (19th C) German?					
oil	1	6,132		6,132	
BUTTNER, Helena (1861-?) Hungarian					
oil	1	1,397		1,397	
BUTTON, Albert Prentice (1872-?) American					
wc/d	2	2,400	1,200	1,200	1,200
BUX, Allah (1895-1978) Indian					
oil	3	46,110	5,760	18,750	21,600
BUXTON, Alfred Isaac (19th C) ?					
oil	1	1,300		1,300	
BUXTON, E (20th C) British					
oil	1	1,600		1,600	
BUXTON, R H (1871-?) British					
wc/d	1	1,422		1,422	
BUYS, Bob (1912-) Dutch					
oil	1	1,721		1,721	
BUYS, Jacob (1724-1801) Dutch					
oil	1	5,893		5,893	
BUZON, Marius de (1879-1958) French					
oil	2	4,482	1,038	2,241	3,444
BUZZI, A (19th C) Italian					
oil	1	2,624		2,624	
wc/d	1	1,500		1,500	
BUZZI, Achille (19th C) Italian					
wc/d	1	1,058		1,058	
BUZZI, F (19/20th C) Italian					
wc/d	1	1,125		1,125	
BUZZI, Federigo (19/20th C) Italian					
wc/d	1	1,287		1,287	
BYARS, James Lee (1932-1997) American					
3D	1	30,200		30,200	
wc/d	3	33,524	2,524	15,000	16,000
BYLANDT, Alfred Edouard van (1829-1890) Dutch					
oil	1	4,253		4,253	
BYLANDT, Alfred de (fl.1853-1884) British					
oil	1	2,849		2,849	
BYLERT, Jan van (1603-1671) Dutch					
oil	1	32,970		32,970	
BYLES, William Hounsom (1872-c.1924) British					
oil	1	2,812		2,812	
BYRNE, John (1786-1847) British					
oil	1	1,386		1,386	
BYRON, E (?) British					
oil	1	1,275		1,275	

Name	No.	Total Sales Value	Prices lowest	median	highest
BYRON, Michael (1954-) American					
3D	2	12,500	4,500	6,250	8,000
BYSS, Johann Rudolf (1660-1738) Swiss					
oil	1	23,922		23,922	
CABAILLOT, Louis Simon (1810-?) French					
oil	1	1,800		1,800	
CABALLERO Y VILLAROEL, Jose (1842-?) Spanish					
oil	1	6,969		6,969	
CABALLERO, Alfredo (1958-) Cuban					
oil	1	2,500		2,500	
CABALLERO, Jose Luis (1916-1991) Spanish					
oil	3	13,990	2,786	3,989	7,215
wc/d	16	24,720	1,023	1,460	2,589
CABALLERO, Jose Luis and VIUDES, Vincente (20th C) Spanish					
wc/d	6	7,111	1,143	1,143	1,396
CABALLERO, Manuel (1924-1993) Spanish					
oil	1	1,505		1,505	
CABALLERO, Maximo (1867-1951) Spanish					
oil	3	41,457	11,263	15,000	15,194
CABANAS-OTEIZA, Angel (19/20th C) Spanish					
oil	1	4,314		4,314	
CABANEL, Alexandre (1823-1889) French					
oil	2	51,353	1,353	25,677	50,000
wc/d	1	1,103		1,103	
CABANES, Felix (18th C) French					
oil	2	39,888	19,944	19,944	19,944
CABANYES, Alejandro de (1877-1972) Spanish					
oil	1	4,840		4,840	
CABAT, Louis (1812-1893) French					
oil	2	16,255	6,000	8,128	10,255
CABEL, Adrian van der (c.1631-1705) Dutch					
oil	4	35,830	4,032	7,911	15,976
CABIANCA, Vincenzo (1827-1902) Italian					
oil	4	50,144	1,111	8,910	31,214
CABIE, Louis Alexandre (1853-1939) French					
oil	5	7,502	1,066	1,372	2,112
CABRAL Y AGUADO, Manuel (1827-c.1890) Spanish					
oil	1	47,774		47,774	
CABRERA MORENO, Servando (1932-1981) Cuban					
oil	2	10,500	4,500	5,250	6,000
CABRERA, Miguel (1695-1768) Mexican					
oil	2	14,090	4,886	7,045	9,204
CABUTTI, Camillo Filippo (1863-1922) Italian					
oil	1	6,591		6,591	
CACCIA, Guglielmo (1568-1625) Italian					
oil	1	10,775		10,775	
CACCIAPUOTI, Guido (1892-1953) Italian					
3D	1	1,835		1,835	
CACCIARELLI, U (?) Italian?					
oil	1	2,660		2,660	
CACCIARELLI, Victor (19th C) Italian					
oil	1	14,500		14,500	
wc/d	2	4,690	2,320	2,345	2,370
CACHOUD, François-Charles (1866-1943) French					
oil	4	6,230	1,130	1,550	2,000
CADELL, Florence St John (fl.1900-1940) British					
oil	1	3,775		3,775	
CADELL, Francis Campbell Boileau (1883-1937) British					
oil	9	410,580	11,680	42,300	81,760

Name	No.	Total Sales Value	lowest	Prices median	highest
wc/d	4	39,084	6,204	9,090	14,700
CADENASSO, Giuseppe (1858-1918) American					
oil	1	4,100		4,100	
wc/d	1	2,500		2,500	
CADENHEAD, James (1858-1927) British					
oil	1	1,343		1,343	
CADES, Giuseppe (1750-1799) Italian					
wc/d	1	9,060		9,060	
CADMAN, Dorothy A (fl.1914-1927) British					
oil	1	1,278		1,278	
CADMAN, Michael (1920-) British					
oil	1	1,170		1,170	
CADMUS, Paul (1904-1999) American					
oil	1	1,800		1,800	
wc/d	5	84,750	3,000	17,000	35,000
CADORET, Michel (1912-1985) French					
oil	1	3,168		3,168	
CADORIN, Guido (1892-1978) Italian					
oil	1	2,080		2,080	
CADY, Walter Harrison (1877-1970) American					
wc/d	2	5,500	2,000	2,750	3,500
CAESAR, Doris (1892-1971) American					
3D	1	9,000		9,000	
CAFFE, Daniel Ferdinand (1793-?) German					
wc/d	1	1,178		1,178	
CAFFE, Nino (1909-1975) Spanish					
oil	3	10,575	1,966	2,099	6,510
CAFFI, Ippolito (1809-1866) Italian					
oil	2	33,778	3,758	16,889	30,020
wc/d	3	9,896	2,041	3,773	4,082
CAFFI, Margherita (c.1650-1710) Italian					
oil	3	106,303	20,160	22,650	63,493
CAFFIERI (?) ?					
3D	1	1,162		1,162	
CAFFIERI, Hector (1847-1932) British					
wc/d	5	13,387	1,100	2,960	4,440
CAFFYN, Walter Wallor (?-1898) British					
oil	9	57,276	1,328	4,284	18,000
CAGE, John (1912-1992) American					
wc/d	8	45,425	1,063	3,646	13,369
CAGLI, Corrado (1910-1976) Italian					
oil	3	15,669	3,625	3,625	8,290
wc/d	5	8,473	1,222	1,447	2,500
CAGNACCI, Guido (1601-1681) Italian					
oil	1	3,265		3,265	
CAGNACCIO DI SAN PIETRO (1897-1946) Italian					
oil	1	5,013		5,013	
CAGNONE, Angelo (1941-) Italian					
oil	2	2,400	1,170	1,200	1,230
CAGNONI, Amerino (1853-1923) Italian					
oil	1	2,080		2,080	
CAHANNE, P (?) French?					
oil	1	1,309		1,309	
CAHEN-MICHEL, Lucien (1888-1979) French					
oil	1	3,412		3,412	
CAHILL, William Vincent (1878-1924) American					
oil	2	9,300	2,800	4,650	6,500
CAHN, Marcelle (1895-1981) French					
oil	1	1,160		1,160	

Name	No.	Total Sales Value	Prices lowest	median	highest
CAHN, Miriam (1949-) Swiss					
wc/d	3	15,799	3,342	5,165	7,292
CAHOON, Charles D (1861-1951) American					
oil	1	1,055		1,055	
CAHOON, Ralph (1910-1982) American					
oil	10	269,500	9,500	20,500	50,000
CAHOURS, Henry Maurice (1889-1974) French					
oil	2	2,710	1,130	1,355	1,580
CAILLARD, Christian (1899-1985) French					
oil	2	3,036	1,141	1,518	1,895
CAILLE, Léon Emile (1836-1907) French					
oil	1	7,500		7,500	
CAILLEBOTTE, Gustave (1848-1894) French					
oil	5	14,468,904	60,704	483,200	13,000,000
CAILTEUX, Math (20th C) French					
3D	1	1,885		1,885	
CAIN, Auguste (1822-1894) French					
3D	6	16,621	1,774	2,424	4,339
CAIN, Peter (1958-1997) American					
oil	1	11,000		11,000	
wc/d	1	2,400		2,400	
CAIRO, Francesco del (1607-1665) Italian					
oil	1	16,636		16,636	
CAJES, Eugenio (school) (1575-1634) Italian					
oil	1	9,779		9,779	
CALABRIA, Ennio (1937-) Italian					
oil	5	8,068	1,260	1,456	2,025
wc/d	1	1,134		1,134	
CALAME, Alexandre (1810-1864) Swiss					
oil	16	218,100	1,149	8,270	72,500
wc/d	5	6,503	1,062	1,154	1,749
CALAME, Arthur (1843-1919) Swiss					
oil	2	21,307	5,769	10,654	15,538
CALAME, Charles Edouard (1815-1852) French					
oil	1	4,026		4,026	
CALANDRA, Davide (1856-1915) Italian					
3D	1	2,868		2,868	
CALANDRUCCI, Giacinto (1646-1707) Italian					
wc/d	2	9,461	1,911	4,731	7,550
CALAU, Benjamin (1724-1785) German					
oil	2	3,574	1,787	1,787	1,787
CALBET, Antoine (1860-1944) French					
oil	4	18,569	1,218	3,426	10,500
wc/d	2	5,512	1,854	2,756	3,658
CALCAGNADORO, Antonino (1876-1935) Italian					
oil	2	4,016	1,959	2,008	2,057
CALCAGNO, C (?) Italian					
oil	1	1,121		1,121	
CALDAS, Waltercio (1946-) Brazilian					
3D	1	18,000		18,000	
oil	1	55,000		55,000	
CALDECOTT, Randolph (1846-1886) British					
oil	1	4,530		4,530	
CALDER, Alexander (1898-1976) American					
3D	37	15,125,145	23,000	163,788	3,800,000
oil	5	344,232	5,236	15,000	300,000
wc/d	52	510,870	1,700	8,599	27,377
CALDERARA, Antonio (1903-1978) Italian					
oil	6	51,397	2,926	7,671	17,749
wc/d	5	11,234	1,240	2,233	3,738

Name	No.	Total Sales Value	Prices lowest	median	highest
CALDERINI, Marco (1850-c.1941) Italian					
oil	6	11,395	1,379	1,886	2,477
CALDERON, Charles-Clement (1870-1906) French					
oil	4	21,831	2,572	5,380	8,500
CALDERON, Fernando (1926-) Spanish					
oil	1	1,022		1,022	
CALDERON, Philip Hermogenes (1833-1898) Spanish					
oil	2	28,640	2,900	14,320	25,740
CALES, Abbe Pierre (1870-1961) French					
oil	8	17,874	1,706	2,293	2,771
CALIFANO, John (1864-1946) American/Italian					
oil	3	5,400	1,200	2,000	2,200
CALIGO, Domenico (19th C) Italian					
wc/d	2	21,274	5,764	10,637	15,510
CALKIN, Lance (1859-?) British					
oil	1	42,900		42,900	
CALLCOTT, Sir Augustus Wall (1779-1844) British					
oil	2	6,316	2,416	3,158	3,900
CALLCOTT, William J (19th C) British					
wc/d	1	2,608		2,608	
CALLERY, Mary (20th C) American					
3D	1	3,200		3,200	
CALLET, Antoine François (1741-1823) French					
oil	1	31,519		31,519	
CALLIAS, Horace de (?-1921) French					
oil	1	16,000		16,000	
CALLISTER, Alfred James (?) British					
wc/d	1	2,145		2,145	
CALLOT, Henri Eugène (1875-1956) French					
oil	1	1,791		1,791	
CALLOT, Jacques (1592-1635) French					
wc/d	1	166,100		166,100	
CALLOW, F (?) British					
oil	1	1,679		1,679	
CALLOW, George D (fl.1858-1873) British					
oil	1	4,000		4,000	
CALLOW, J (19th C) British					
oil	1	8,208		8,208	
CALLOW, John (1822-1878) British					
oil	7	45,056	2,190	4,440	14,112
wc/d	5	16,122	1,444	1,885	6,006
CALLOW, R V (19th C) British					
oil	1	7,912		7,912	
CALLOW, William (1812-1908) British					
wc/d	23	139,224	1,264	3,575	28,600
CALLOWHILL, Scott (fl.1876-1890) British					
oil	2	2,455	1,106	1,228	1,349
CALMETTES, Pierre (1874-?) French					
oil	1	15,000		15,000	
CALOGERO, Jean (1922-) Italian					
oil	2	6,634	1,200	3,317	5,434
CALOSCI, Arturo (1855-1926) Italian					
oil	1	1,745		1,745	
CALRAET, Abraham van (1642-1722) Dutch					
oil	2	31,796	7,796	15,898	24,000
CALRAET, Barend van (1649-1737) Dutch					
oil	1	6,565		6,565	
CALS, Adolphe Felix (1810-1880) French					
oil	9	34,677	1,107	2,757	12,833

Name	No.	Total Sales Value	lowest	Prices median	highest
wc/d	1	1,031		1,031	
CALSINA, Ramon (1901-) Spanish					
oil	1	2,445		2,445	
CALTHROP, Claude Andrew (1845-1893) British					
oil	1	1,727		1,727	
CALVAERT, Dionisio (1540-1619) Flemish					
oil	1	30,200		30,200	
wc/d	1	6,055		6,055	
CALVERT, Edward (1799-1883) British					
wc/d	1	2,000		2,000	
CALVERT, Frederick (c.1785-1845) British					
oil	5	14,557	1,081	3,000	4,500
CALVERT, Henry (1798-1869) British					
oil	3	31,331	5,680	9,796	15,855
CALVERT, S W (19th C) British					
oil	1	1,057		1,057	
CALVERT, Samuel (19th C) British					
oil	1	4,290		4,290	
CALVES, Marie (1883-1957) French					
oil	4	6,141	1,024	1,458	2,202
CALVET, Gregoire (19th C) French					
3D	1	1,900		1,900	
CALVI, Ercole (1824-1900) Italian					
oil	2	18,337	7,635	9,169	10,702
CALVI, Giuseppe (19/20th C) Continental					
oil	1	1,605		1,605	
CALVI, Pietro (1833-1884) Italian					
3D	1	7,536		7,536	
CALVO, Carmen (20th C) Spanish?					
oil	1	1,537		1,537	
wc/d	1	2,586		2,586	
CALYO, Nicolino (1799-1884) American					
oil	1	17,000		17,000	
wc/d	1	7,500		7,500	
CALZADA, Dionisio and DIAZ Y GONZALEZ, Vicente (19th C) Spanish					
oil	1	1,048		1,048	
CALZOLARI, Pier Paolo (1943-) Italian					
3D	1	46,400		46,400	
wc/d	1	9,706		9,706	
CAMACHO, Jorge (1934-) Cuban					
oil	6	25,549	1,177	2,437	14,589
CAMARGO, Sergio de (1930-1990) Brazilian					
3D	3	55,000	6,000	15,000	34,000
CAMARLENCH, Ignacio Pinazo (1849-1916) Spanish					
oil	2	21,748	4,368	10,874	17,380
CAMARON TORRA, Vicente (1803-1864) Spanish					
oil	1	2,178		2,178	
CAMARON Y BORONAT, Jose (1730-1803) Spanish					
oil	1	4,602		4,602	
CAMARON, Maria Elena (19/20th C) Spanish					
oil	1	4,062		4,062	
CAMBELLOTTI, Duilio (1876-1960) Italian					
3D	1	2,306		2,306	
CAMBIASO, Domenico (1811-1894) Italian					
wc/d	2	3,655	1,297	1,828	2,358
CAMBIASO, Luca (1527-1585) Italian					
wc/d	4	24,751	1,103	5,824	12,000
CAMBIASO, Luca (school) (1527-1585) Italian					
wc/d	1	3,200		3,200	

Name	No.	Total Sales Value	lowest	Prices median	highest
CAMBIER, Guy (1923-) French					
oil	1	1,605		1,605	
CAMBOS, Jean Jules (1828-1917) French					
3D	1	3,634		3,634	
CAMBOUR, Claude (?) French					
oil	1	1,200		1,200	
CAMENISCH, Paul (1893-1970) Swiss					
wc/d	1	1,210		1,210	
CAMENZIND, Balz (1907-) ?					
oil	1	2,250		2,250	
CAMERON, Douglas (?) British					
oil	6	11,763	1,029	1,704	3,796
CAMERON, Duncan (1837-1916) British					
oil	3	8,677	1,027	1,080	6,570
CAMERON, Hugh (1835-1918) British					
oil	2	7,773	3,657	3,887	4,116
CAMERON, Katherine (1874-1965) British					
wc/d	3	6,486	1,027	1,544	3,915
CAMERON, Mary (c.1865-1921) British					
oil	1	28,120		28,120	
CAMERON, Sir David Young (1865-1945) British					
oil	7	31,952	2,646	4,380	5,928
wc/d	5	15,203	1,764	2,205	6,320
CAMILLE, F (?) ?					
oil	1	3,160		3,160	
CAMIN, Joaquin Rubio (1926-) Spanish					
oil	2	17,810	3,292	8,905	14,518
CAMINO, Giuseppe (1818-1890) Italian					
oil	1	12,383		12,383	
CAMMARANO, Michele (1849-1920) Italian					
oil	1	1,845		1,845	
CAMMILLI, E (19/20th C) French					
3D	1	1,385		1,385	
CAMMILLIERI DE MARSEILLES, Nicolas (1780-1855) French					
wc/d	1	1,501		1,501	
CAMOIN, Charles (1879-1965) French					
oil	39	752,544	1,701	13,515	110,000
wc/d	4	28,036	1,804	2,966	20,300
CAMOS, Honore (1906-) French					
oil	1	1,228		1,228	
CAMOYANO (?) Spanish					
oil	1	1,638		1,638	
CAMP DE MARBAIS, van (?) Belgian?					
oil	1	2,422		2,422	
CAMP, C van (19th C) Belgian					
oil	1	2,373		2,373	
CAMP, Camille van (19th C) Belgian					
oil	2	3,797	1,006	1,899	2,791
CAMP, Jeffery (1923-) British					
oil	3	7,258	1,200	1,738	4,320
CAMP, Joseph Rodefer de (1858-1923) American					
oil	2	81,500	34,000	40,750	47,500
CAMPAGNA, Girolamo (1550-c.1623) Italian					
3D	1	15,517		15,517	
CAMPAGNE, Pierre Étienne Daniel (1851-?) French					
3D	1	2,000		2,000	
CAMPAGNOLA, Domenico (1484-1550) Italian					
wc/d	2	26,400	2,400	13,200	24,000

| Name | No. | Total Sales Value | | Prices | |
			lowest	median	highest
CAMPBELL, Elmer Simms (1906-1974) American					
wc/d	1	1,600		1,600	
CAMPBELL, George (1917-1979) British					
oil	10	60,091	1,152	6,597	11,775
CAMPBELL, Hugh (20th C) American					
oil	1	3,500		3,500	
CAMPBELL, James (?-1903) British					
oil	1	1,058		1,058	
CAMPBELL, John Henry (1755-1828) Irish					
wc/d	4	15,118	1,184	2,897	8,140
CAMPBELL, John Reed (fl.1945) American					
oil	1	2,400		2,400	
CAMPBELL, L (?) ?					
oil	1	1,500		1,500	
CAMPBELL, Laurence A (20th C) American					
oil	1	3,300		3,300	
CAMPBELL, Reginald Henry (1877-?) British					
oil	1	1,117		1,117	
CAMPBELL, Tom (1865-1943) British					
oil	1	1,838		1,838	
CAMPENDONK, Heinrich (1889-1957) German					
oil	3	398,414	53,563	136,800	208,051
wc/d	3	70,979	3,010	13,592	54,377
CAMPESTRINI, Ernesto Alcide (1897-1983) Italian					
oil	1	1,450		1,450	
CAMPI, Antonio (1531-1591) Italian					
wc/d	1	14,000		14,000	
CAMPI, Giacomo (1846-?) Italian					
wc/d	1	1,184		1,184	
CAMPI, Vincenzo (1536-1591) Italian					
oil	1	17,259		17,259	
wc/d	1	1,234		1,234	
CAMPIGLI, Massimo (1895-1971) Italian					
oil	18	1,281,725	6,763	60,744	161,444
wc/d	2	11,027	2,025	5,514	9,002
CAMPION, George Bryant (1796-1870) British					
wc/d	2	5,720	1,430	2,860	4,290
CAMPION, Oliver (1928-) British					
oil	1	1,015		1,015	
CAMPO, Federico del (19/20th C) Peruvian					
oil	3	365,960	78,000	97,960	190,000
CAMPO, Frederik Willem del (1803-1890) Dutch					
wc/d	1	9,241		9,241	
CAMPO, J (19th C) Spanish					
oil	1	4,559		4,559	
CAMPO, Santiago del (1928-) Spanish					
oil	1	1,790		1,790	
CAMPOS, Alain (1955-) French					
oil	1	1,164		1,164	
CAMPOS, Florencio Molina (20th C) South American					
oil	1	11,000		11,000	
wc/d	4	10,000	1,000	1,000	7,000
CAMPOS, Manuel de Maria (fl.1840-1880) Spanish					
oil	1	15,000		15,000	
CAMPRIANI, Alceste (1848-1933) Italian					
oil	4	28,867	2,705	5,497	15,168
CAMRADT, Frederik Christian (1762-1844) Danish					
oil	1	1,854		1,854	

Name	No.	Total Sales Value	Prices lowest	median	highest
CAMUS, Blanche (19/20th C) French					
oil	2	9,701	1,751	4,851	7,950
CAMUS, Gustave (1914-1984) Belgian					
oil	7	10,749	1,149	1,305	2,146
CAMUS, Jean Marie (1877-1955) French					
3D	1	1,080		1,080	
CANAILLIONI, Leon (?) ?					
oil	1	4,278		4,278	
CANALETTO (1697-1768) Italian					
oil	8	21,875,126	4,215	1,500,000	10,290,001
wc/d	4	431,940	48,320	111,810	160,000
CANALS Y LLAMBI, Ricardo (1876-1931) Spanish					
oil	1	105,000		105,000	
CANALS, Antonio (1940-) Spanish					
oil	1	2,900		2,900	
CANAVERAL Y PEREZ, Alfonso (?) Spanish					
oil	1	6,777		6,777	
CANDA, Charles (19th C) ?					
oil	1	9,000		9,000	
CANDID, Peter (1548-1628) Flemish					
oil	1	2,500		2,500	
CANDIDO, Sal (19th C) Italian					
oil	1	33,496		33,496	
CANE, Louis (1943-) French					
3D	10	77,530	1,928	3,549	31,369
oil	7	16,164	1,702	2,525	2,951
wc/d	1	4,147		4,147	
CANELLA, Carlo (1800-1879) Italian					
oil	1	24,951		24,951	
CANELLA, Giuseppe (1788-1847) Italian					
oil	5	124,617	11,376	25,642	39,404
wc/d	2	4,264	1,309	2,132	2,955
CANIFF, Milton (1907-1988) American					
wc/d	1	1,800		1,800	
CANINO, Vincenzo (?) Italian					
oil	1	1,571		1,571	
CANNATA, Antonio (1895-1960) Italian					
oil	1	1,567		1,567	
CANNAVACCIUOLO, Maurizio (1954-) Italian					
oil	2	4,581	1,745	2,291	2,836
CANNEEL, Eugène (1882-1966) Belgian					
3D	5	7,287	1,027	1,374	1,996
CANNEY, Michael (1923-) British					
oil	2	2,721	1,029	1,361	1,692
CANNICCI, Nicolo (1846-1906) Italian					
wc/d	1	4,682		4,682	
CANNICIONI, Léon Charles (1879-1957) French					
oil	2	7,839	3,707	3,920	4,132
CANO DE CASTRO, Manuel (1891-?) Costa Rican					
oil	1	1,000		1,000	
CANO, Alonso (1601-1667) Spanish					
3D	1	20,326		20,326	
oil	2	28,492	14,246	14,246	14,246
wc/d	2	98,653	20,133	49,327	78,520
CANO, Alonso (school) (1601-1667) Spanish					
oil	1	2,000		2,000	
CANOGAR, Rafael (1934-) Spanish					
oil	4	35,151	6,764	9,085	10,218
CANOVA, Antonio (1757-1822) Italian					
3D	1	126,188		126,188	

Name	No.	Total Sales Value	lowest	Prices median	highest
CANOVA, Antonio (school) (1757-1822) Italian					
3D	1	2,175		2,175	
CANOVAS, Fernando (1960-) Argentinian					
oil	1	20,000		20,000	
CANTA, Johannes Antonius (1816-1888) Dutch					
oil	1	3,189		3,189	
CANTAGALLINA, Remigio (1582-1628) Italian					
oil	1	1,317		1,317	
wc/d	3	7,217	1,193	1,774	4,250
CANTARINI, Simone (1612-1648) Italian					
oil	1	58,800		58,800	
wc/d	2	7,895	1,100	3,948	6,795
CANTATORE, Domenico (1906-1998) Italian					
oil	11	80,380	3,139	6,545	15,237
wc/d	6	19,900	1,350	1,721	11,781
CANTI, E (19th C) Italian					
oil	1	3,931		3,931	
CANTINEAU, Virgile (1864-?) Belgian					
oil	1	3,993		3,993	
CANTRE, Jozef (1890-1957) Belgian					
3D	2	2,348	1,003	1,174	1,345
CANU, Yvonne (1921-) French					
oil	2	5,600	2,400	2,800	3,200
CANUTI, Domenico Maria (1620-1684) Italian					
oil	1	2,216		2,216	
wc/d	1	4,750		4,750	
CANZI, A E (1813-1866) Austrian					
oil	1	2,159		2,159	
CAP, Constant (1842-?) Belgian					
oil	1	7,000		7,000	
CAPA, Joaquin (1941-) Spanish					
oil	1	2,904		2,904	
CAPACCI, Bruno (1906-1993) French					
oil	1	1,602		1,602	
CAPDEVIELLE, Louis (1850-1905) French					
oil	1	3,200		3,200	
CAPDEVILA MASSANA, Manuel (1910-) Spanish					
oil	1	1,882		1,882	
CAPDEVILLA PUIG, Genis (1860-?) Spanish					
oil	2	11,411	1,344	5,706	10,067
CAPEINICK, Jean (1838-1890) Belgian					
oil	4	34,477	1,801	3,838	25,000
CAPELAIN, John le (c.1814-1848) British					
wc/d	3	4,206	1,144	1,335	1,727
CAPELAN, Carlos (1948-) Uruguayan					
oil	1	13,000		13,000	
wc/d	1	9,500		9,500	
CAPELLAN, Tony (1959-) Dominican					
wc/d	1	5,500		5,500	
CAPELLE, Jan van de (1624-1679) Dutch					
oil	1	7,500		7,500	
CAPMARTIN, E (19th C) ?					
wc/d	4	5,698	1,095	1,424	1,756
CAPOBIANCHI, V (19th C) Italian					
oil	1	1,069		1,069	
CAPOBIANCHI, Vincentius (19th C) Italian					
oil	1	43,500		43,500	
CAPOGROSSI, Costanza Mennyey (20th C) Italian					
wc/d	1	3,135		3,135	

Name	No.	Total Sales Value	Prices lowest	median	highest
CAPOGROSSI, Giuseppe (1900-1972) Italian					
oil	5	93,573	5,932	11,647	55,050
wc/d	2	19,240	1,350	9,620	17,890
CAPON, Georges (c.1890-1980) French					
oil	1	6,600		6,600	
CAPONE, Gaetano (1845-1920) Italian					
oil	3	5,919	1,600	1,861	2,458
wc/d	1	1,000		1,000	
CAPP, Al (1909-) American					
wc/d	1	1,150		1,150	
CAPPEL, F (?) British					
oil	1	1,659		1,659	
CAPPELLI, Giovanni (1923-1994) Italian					
oil	3	3,928	1,078	1,173	1,677
CAPPELLI, Pietro (?-1724) Italian					
oil	1	26,690		26,690	
CAPPIELLO, Leonetto (1875-1942) French					
wc/d	1	1,298		1,298	
CAPRILE, Vincenzo (1856-1936) Italian					
oil	10	36,851	1,240	3,507	6,371
wc/d	2	3,354	1,376	1,677	1,978
CAPRON, Jean Pierre (1921-1997) French					
oil	1	2,400		2,400	
CAPSONI, Aurelio (?) Italian					
3D	1	1,468		1,468	
CAPULETO, Francisco (1928-) Spanish					
wc/d	1	1,452		1,452	
CAPULETTI, Jose Manuel (1925-1978) Spanish					
oil	5	14,250	1,269	2,793	4,995
wc/d	4	4,951	1,143	1,206	1,396
CAPURRO, Sara (20th C) ?					
oil	2	3,050	1,500	1,525	1,550
CAPUTO, Ulisse (1872-1948) Italian					
oil	16	83,486	1,338	1,861	24,231
CARABAIN, Emile (19/20th C) Belgian					
oil	1	5,075		5,075	
CARABAIN, J (1834-1892) Belgian					
oil	1	4,953		4,953	
CARABAIN, Jacques (1834-1892) Belgian					
oil	11	134,175	3,375	10,531	30,020
CARABAIN, V (?) Belgian					
oil	1	2,067		2,067	
CARABAIN, Victor (19/20th C) Belgian					
oil	1	2,621		2,621	
CARABIN, Rupert (1862-1932) French					
3D	3	9,172	2,067	2,176	4,929
CARACCIOLO, Giovanni Battista (1570-1637) Italian					
wc/d	1	2,203		2,203	
CARADEC, L (20th C) French					
oil	1	1,476		1,476	
CARADEC, Louis (1936-) French					
oil	1	2,572		2,572	
CARADOSSI, Vittorio (1861-?) Italian					
3D	1	150,000		150,000	
CARAN D'ACHE, Emile Poire (1858-1909) French					
wc/d	1	1,460		1,460	
CARASSI, Antoine (?) Italian?					
wc/d	1	1,000		1,000	

Name	No.	Total Sales Value	Prices lowest	median	highest
CARAUD, Joseph (1821-1905) French					
oil	4	68,778	2,218	14,530	37,500
CARAVAGGIO (1573-1610) Italian					
oil	3	21,166	5,966	7,850	7,850
CARAVANNIEZ, Alfred (1855-?) French					
3D	1	10,000		10,000	
CARAZO MARTINEZ, Jose (1891-1958) Spanish					
oil	1	1,747		1,747	
CARBAAT, Jan (1866-1925) ?					
oil	1	2,268		2,268	
CARBASIUS, F (19/20th C) Dutch					
3D	1	1,561		1,561	
CARBASIUS, Françoise Charlotte (1885-1984) Dutch					
3D	1	15,510		15,510	
CARBONERO, Jose Moreno (1860-1942) Spanish					
oil	2	10,146	4,646	5,073	5,500
CARBONI, Giovanni Bernardo (1616-1683) Italian					
oil	2	28,237	8,166	14,119	20,071
CARD, Stephan J (20th C) American					
oil	1	2,800		2,800	
CARDEN, Claude (fl.1892-1915) ?					
oil	1	7,975		7,975	
CARDENAS, Augustin (1927-) Cuban					
3D	10	92,985	1,854	3,528	38,000
CARDI, Lodovico (1559-1613) Italian					
oil	2	53,273	11,683	26,637	41,590
wc/d	1	5,000		5,000	
CARDINAL-SCHUBERT, Joanne (1942-) Canadian					
wc/d	1	1,076		1,076	
CARDINAUX, Emile (1877-1936) Swiss					
oil	1	6,484		6,484	
CARDON, Claude (fl.1892-1920) British					
oil	5	20,993	1,996	3,976	8,460
wc/d	1	1,214		1,214	
CARDONA, Jose (19/20th C) Spanish					
3D	2	2,493	1,193	1,247	1,300
CARDONA, Juan (1877-c.1957) Spanish					
wc/d	1	2,413		2,413	
CARDOZO, Eduardo (1965-) Uruguayan					
oil	1	1,200		1,200	
CARDOZO, Maria Fernanda (1963-) Colombian					
3D	1	6,500		6,500	
CARDUCHO, Vicente (1578-1638) Italian					
wc/d	2	5,275	1,022	2,638	4,253
CAREL, Isidore Francois (19/20th C) French					
oil	1	1,964		1,964	
CARELLI, Conrad (1869-?) British					
wc/d	1	1,369		1,369	
CARELLI, Consalve (1818-1900) Italian					
oil	8	61,368	3,956	6,021	16,193
wc/d	8	17,653	1,497	1,897	3,898
CARELLI, G (19th C) Italian					
wc/d	1	1,058		1,058	
CARELLI, Gabrielli (1820-1880) Italian					
wc/d	5	6,765	1,034	1,296	1,812
CARELLI, Giuseppe (1858-1921) Italian					
oil	9	33,766	1,492	3,900	6,182
CARENA, Felice (1879-1966) Italian					
oil	6	72,501	8,680	10,748	20,071

Name	No.	Total Sales Value	lowest	Prices median	highest
CARESME, Jacques Philippe (1734-1796) French					
oil	1	2,188		2,188	
wc/d	2	12,350	2,137	6,175	10,213
CAREY, Joseph William (1859-1937) British					
wc/d	6	20,353	1,325	3,603	5,920
CARGALEIRO, Manuel (1927-) Portuguese					
oil	6	108,766	5,582	17,288	30,987
wc/d	15	70,844	2,166	4,252	8,853
CARGILL, R G (19th C) American					
oil	1	2,400		2,400	
CARGNEL, Vittore Antonio (1872-1931) Italian					
oil	1	2,201		2,201	
CARIANI, V J (1891-1969) American					
oil	1	4,500		4,500	
CARIANI, Veraldo J (1891-1969) American					
oil	1	3,000		3,000	
CARIBBEAN SCHOOL, 19th C					
wc/d	1	12,500		12,500	
CARIFFA, Francis (1890-1975) French					
oil	3	9,038	2,207	2,707	4,124
CARIGIET, Alois (1902-1985) Swiss					
oil	3	46,135	11,294	14,800	20,041
wc/d	5	19,139	2,341	4,254	5,920
CARINI, G (19th C) Italian					
wc/d	1	11,033		11,033	
CARIOT, Gustave (1872-1950) French					
oil	3	5,859	1,499	1,827	2,533
CARIS, Johann Wilhelm (1747-1830) German					
oil	1	1,282		1,282	
CARISS, Henry T (1840-1903) American					
oil	1	28,000		28,000	
CARL-ROSA (1855-1913) French					
oil	1	1,153		1,153	
CARL-ROSA, Mario (1855-1913) French					
oil	1	1,431		1,431	
CARLANDI, Onorato (1848-1939) Italian					
wc/d	11	19,557	1,134	1,399	3,498
CARLEBUR, F (19th C) Dutch					
wc/d	2	3,346	1,630	1,673	1,716
CARLEBUR, François II (1821-1893) Dutch					
oil	1	1,193		1,193	
wc/d	1	1,658		1,658	
CARLES (1969-) Spanish?					
oil	1	1,422		1,422	
CARLES, Arthur B (1882-1952) American					
oil	3	191,500	24,000	72,500	95,000
wc/d	1	1,800		1,800	
CARLEVARIS, Luca (1665-1731) Italian					
oil	2	1,066,400	302,000	533,200	764,400
CARLIER, Émile Joseph Nestor (1849-1927) French					
3D	1	1,522		1,522	
CARLIER, M (19/20th C) French					
oil	1	1,021		1,021	
CARLIER, Max (1872-1938) Belgian					
oil	5	10,523	1,148	1,639	4,436
CARLIER, Modeste (1820-1878) Belgian					
oil	3	5,516	1,437	2,036	2,043
CARLIN, James (1909-) American					
oil	1	1,300		1,300	

Name	No.	Total Sales Value	Prices lowest	median	highest
CARLINI, Giulio (1830-1887) Italian					
oil	1	45,000		45,000	
CARLO, C (19th C) Italian					
oil	2	2,700	1,200	1,350	1,500
CARLO, Chiostri (19th C) Italian					
oil	1	1,400		1,400	
CARLONE, Carlo (1686-1776) Italian					
oil	1	6,480		6,480	
CARLROSA, Mario Cornilleau Raoul (20th C) ?					
oil	1	1,240		1,240	
CARLSEN, Carl (1855-1917) Danish					
oil	3	6,586	1,549	1,939	3,098
CARLSEN, Dines (1901-1966) American					
oil	3	34,250	5,000	5,250	24,000
CARLSEN, E (19th C) Danish?					
oil	1	4,000		4,000	
CARLSEN, Emil (1853-1932) American/Danish					
oil	9	153,100	1,100	6,500	65,000
CARLSON, George (1940-) American					
3D	4	45,750	4,750	6,750	27,500
wc/d	2	18,500	3,500	9,250	15,000
CARLSON, John F (1875-1947) American					
oil	4	13,250	1,500	3,375	5,000
CARLSON, Ken (20th C) British?					
oil	2	60,500	18,000	30,250	42,500
CARLSSON, Harry (1913-) Danish					
oil	1	3,531		3,531	
CARLSTROM, Gustaf (1896-1964) Swedish					
oil	7	13,394	1,088	1,529	4,135
CARLSUND, Otto (1897-1948) Swedish					
oil	1	8,080		8,080	
wc/d	3	9,842	2,417	2,730	4,695
CARLTON, Frederick (19th C) British					
oil	3	6,098	1,570	1,859	2,669
CARLTON, Thomas (18th C) Irish					
oil	1	2,664		2,664	
CARMASSI, Arturo (1925-) Italian					
oil	1	3,273		3,273	
CARMELO DE ARZADUN (1888-1968) Uruguayan					
oil	1	2,301		2,301	
CARMI, Eugenio (1920-) Italian					
wc/d	1	1,964		1,964	
CARMICHAEL, Franklin (1890-1945) Canadian					
oil	2	83,633	33,857	41,817	49,776
wc/d	1	37,375		37,375	
CARMICHAEL, J W (1800-1868) British					
oil	1	2,160		2,160	
CARMICHAEL, John Wilson (1800-1868) British					
oil	25	341,564	2,717	10,570	50,050
wc/d	6	32,938	1,345	2,632	12,720
CARMIENCKE, Johan-Herman (1810-1867) Danish/American					
oil	2	10,675	1,675	5,338	9,000
CARMONTELLE, Louis Carrogis (1717-1806) French					
wc/d	2	24,364	4,364	12,182	20,000
CARNELLI, J (?) ?					
oil	1	15,000		15,000	
CARNICERO, Tomas (19th C) Spanish					
oil	1	4,091		4,091	

Name	No.	Total Sales Value	lowest	Prices median	highest
CARNIER, H (?) ?					
oil	1	1,510		1,510	
CARNIER, Henri (1843-1901) German					
oil	3	5,587	1,191	1,429	2,967
CARO, Anita de (1900-?) French					
3D	1	1,031		1,031	
CARO, Anthony (1924-) British					
3D	7	129,084	8,216	18,000	36,000
CARO, Antonio (19th C) Mexican					
3D	1	15,000		15,000	
CARO, Baldassare de (1689-c.1755) Italian					
oil	4	25,544	5,598	6,533	7,000
CARO, Lorenzo de (18th C) Italian					
oil	2	16,934	7,874	8,467	9,060
CARO-DELVAILLE, Henri (1876-1926) French					
oil	1	13,000		13,000	
CAROLUS, Jean (1814-1897) Belgian					
oil	7	129,728	1,684	17,625	48,000
CAROLUS-DURAN (1838-1917) French					
oil	1	1,455		1,455	
CAROLUS-DURAN, Émile Auguste (1838-1917) French					
oil	3	59,239	6,239	24,000	29,000
CARON, Henri Paul Edmond (1860-?) French					
oil	1	1,215		1,215	
CARON, J (19/20th C) French					
oil	1	1,791		1,791	
CARON, Marcel (1890-1961) Belgian					
oil	1	2,782		2,782	
CAROSELLI, Angelo (1585-1652) Italian					
oil	3	123,162	10,500	12,662	100,000
CAROSI, Alberto (1891-1968) Italian					
oil	1	2,385		2,385	
CARPACCIO, Vittore (1450-1522) Italian					
wc/d	2	304,360	54,360	152,180	250,000
CARPEAUX (1827-1875) French					
3D	2	7,201	3,137	3,601	4,064
CARPEAUX, J B (1827-1875) French					
3D	1	1,367		1,367	
CARPEAUX, Jean Baptiste (1827-1875) French					
3D	30	193,345	1,250	4,776	21,884
oil	1	4,353		4,353	
wc/d	4	9,382	1,233	2,290	3,505
CARPENTER, Fred Green (1882-1965) American					
oil	2	2,500	1,100	1,250	1,400
CARPENTER, Margaret (1793-1872) British					
oil	1	9,295		9,295	
CARPENTER, Mildred Bailey (1894-?) American					
wc/d	1	1,500		1,500	
CARPENTERO, Fritz (?) ?					
oil	1	1,165		1,165	
CARPENTERO, H (19/20th C) ?					
oil	1	1,065		1,065	
CARPENTERO, Henri Joseph Gommarus (1820-1874) Belgian					
oil	1	5,014		5,014	
CARPENTERO, Jean Charles (1774-1823) Belgian					
oil	1	1,165		1,165	
CARPENTIER, Evariste (1845-1922) Belgian					
oil	2	29,406	1,507	14,703	27,899

Name	No.	Total Sales Value	lowest	Prices median	highest
CARPI, Girolamo da (1501-1556) Italian					
oil	1	105,700		105,700	
wc/d	1	3,054		3,054	
CARPIONI (1613-1679) Italian					
oil	1	1,800		1,800	
CARPIONI, Giulio (1613-1679) Italian					
oil	1	10,570		10,570	
wc/d	1	3,054		3,054	
CARR, Emily M (1871-1945) Canadian					
oil	11	1,109,196	19,247	45,500	620,778
wc/d	3	109,973	5,973	48,750	55,250
CARR, Samuel S (1837-1908) American					
oil	2	65,000	3,000	32,500	62,000
CARR, Tom (1912-1977) British					
wc/d	3	8,259	1,275	3,600	3,600
CARR, Tom (1909-1999) British					
oil	3	29,975	3,335	5,920	20,720
wc/d	5	20,903	1,450	1,885	9,360
CARRA, Carlo (1881-1966) Italian					
oil	7	495,277	34,907	43,634	194,113
wc/d	8	67,394	1,396	6,827	20,944
CARRACCI, Agostino (1557-1602) Italian					
wc/d	2	14,832	4,832	7,416	10,000
CARRACCI, Annibale (1560-1609) Italian					
oil	1	3,912		3,912	
wc/d	1	10,570		10,570	
CARRACCI, Annibale (school) (1560-1609) Italian					
oil	2	54,244	10,499	27,122	43,745
CARRACCI, Antonio (1583-1618) Italian					
oil	1	51,840		51,840	
CARRACCI, Antonio (school) (1583-1618) Italian					
oil	1	2,675		2,675	
CARRACCI, Lodovico (1555-1619) Italian					
oil	2	4,795,538	45,538	2,397,769	4,750,000
CARRADE, Michel (1923-) French					
oil	1	1,911		1,911	
CARRAND, Louis (1821-1899) French					
oil	1	3,537		3,537	
CARRASCO, Françoise (20th C) ?					
3D	1	2,336		2,336	
CARRE, Léon (1878-?) French					
oil	2	14,095	4,095	7,048	10,000
wc/d	1	1,933		1,933	
CARREE, Michiel (1657-1747) Dutch					
oil	2	8,901	4,135	4,451	4,766
CARRENO, Mario (1913-) Cuban					
oil	1	32,263		32,263	
wc/d	3	57,500	4,000	8,500	45,000
CARRENTALLA (18/19th C) Italian					
oil	1	4,250		4,250	
CARRERA, Maria (1934-) Spanish					
oil	1	1,076		1,076	
CARRICK, John Mulcaster (1833-?) British					
oil	8	39,490	1,287	3,073	17,160
CARRICK, William (1879-?) British					
oil	1	2,220		2,220	
CARRIER, A (19th C) French					
3D	2	4,692	1,700	2,346	2,992
CARRIER-BELLEUSE (19/20th C) French					
3D	2	5,660	2,419	2,830	3,241

Name	No.	Total Sales Value	lowest	Prices median	highest
CARRIER-BELLEUSE, A (1824-1887) French					
3D	5	21,018	1,944	3,000	9,109
CARRIER-BELLEUSE, Albert (1824-1887) French					
3D	31	159,130	1,131	3,935	16,014
wc/d	1	1,167		1,167	
CARRIER-BELLEUSE, Louis (1848-1913) French					
3D	2	6,428	2,567	3,214	3,861
oil	1	2,897		2,897	
wc/d	1	2,100		2,100	
CARRIER-BELLEUSE, Pierre (1851-1932) French					
oil	1	3,770		3,770	
wc/d	1	2,480		2,480	
CARRIERA, Rosalba (1675-1757) Italian					
wc/d	3	63,126	12,956	16,170	34,000
CARRIERE, Eugène (1849-1906) French					
oil	14	67,061	1,031	2,771	13,000
CARRIES, Jean (1855-1894) French					
3D	2	41,905	15,150	20,953	26,755
CARRILLO, S (20th C) ?					
oil	1	2,160		2,160	
CARRINGTON, Dora (1893-1932) British					
oil	1	8,460		8,460	
wc/d	1	1,350		1,350	
CARRINGTON, Leonora (1917-) British					
oil	4	540,000	70,000	105,000	260,000
wc/d	3	10,688	1,180	2,508	7,000
CARRINO, Nicola (1932-) Italian					
oil	1	3,154		3,154	
CARROL, Robert (1934-) American					
oil	1	1,121		1,121	
CARROLL, Lawrence (1954-) American					
oil	2	11,500	1,500	5,750	10,000
CARROLL, W J (19/20th C) British					
oil	2	3,601	1,177	1,801	2,424
CARROLL, William Joseph (19/20th C) British					
oil	2	8,595	1,485	4,298	7,110
CARSE, Alexander (c.1770-1843) British					
oil	1	5,110		5,110	
CARSON, Robert Taylor (1919-) British					
oil	5	7,342	1,087	1,470	1,776
CARSTENS, C (19th C) Finnish					
oil	1	1,000		1,000	
CARSTENS, Julius Viktor (1849-1908) German					
oil	1	5,672		5,672	
CARTE, Antoine (1886-1954) Belgian					
oil	4	90,968	3,216	16,329	55,094
wc/d	4	59,153	1,852	8,899	39,503
CARTER, Carol (20th C) American					
oil	1	1,000		1,000	
CARTER, Clarence Holbrook (1904-2000) American					
oil	1	4,000		4,000	
CARTER, Dennis Malone (1827-1881) American					
oil	1	19,000		19,000	
CARTER, Frank Thomas (1853-1934) British					
oil	1	2,054		2,054	
CARTER, George (1737-1796) British					
oil	1	5,550		5,550	
CARTER, Henry Barlow (1803-1867) British					
wc/d	5	11,272	1,080	1,551	3,900

Name	No.	Total Sales Value	lowest	Prices median	highest
CARTER, Pruett A (1891-1955) American					
oil	3	12,500	2,750	3,750	6,000
CARTER, R (?) British					
oil	1	2,709		2,709	
CARTER, Sydney (1874-1945) British					
oil	1	2,000		2,000	
CARTER, V H B (fl.1860-1895) British					
oil	1	6,520		6,520	
CARTIER (?) French					
3D	2	3,745	1,606	1,873	2,139
CARTIER, Karl (1855-1925) French					
oil	1	1,672		1,672	
wc/d	1	2,730		2,730	
CARTIER, T (20th C) French					
3D	1	4,062		4,062	
CARTIER, Thomas (1879-?) French					
3D	2	2,254	1,017	1,127	1,237
CARTON, Jean (1912-1988) French					
3D	2	13,500	6,750	6,750	6,750
CARTOTTO, Ercole (1889-1946) American/Italian					
oil	1	5,500		5,500	
CARUELLE D'ALIGNY, Theodore (1798-1871) French					
oil	1	2,826		2,826	
wc/d	2	3,491	1,600	1,746	1,891
CARUNCHO, Luis (1929-) Spanish					
wc/d	1	1,686		1,686	
CARUS, Carl Gustav (1789-1869) German					
oil	1	104,669		104,669	
CARUSO, Bruno (1927-) Italian					
oil	3	6,421	1,440	2,182	2,799
CARVIS, O R (?) ?					
oil	1	1,420		1,420	
CARY, William de la Montagne (1840-1922) American					
oil	1	3,200		3,200	
CARZOU, Jean (1907-2000) French					
oil	3	12,406	2,596	4,310	5,500
wc/d	3	5,387	1,167	1,659	2,561
CASABOLO, N (20th C) ?					
oil	1	1,102		1,102	
CASADO, Hernandez (20th C) Spanish					
oil	1	1,557		1,557	
CASAGEMAS, Carles (1880-1901) Spanish					
oil	1	19,460		19,460	
CASAGRANDE, Peter (1946-) German					
oil	1	2,308		2,308	
wc/d	1	1,815		1,815	
CASALI, Andrea (1720-1784) Italian					
oil	1	10,213		10,213	
CASAMADA, Alberto Rafols (1923-) Spanish					
oil	3	11,988	1,278	2,422	8,288
CASANOVA Y ESTORACH, Antonio (1847-1896) Spanish					
oil	1	2,515		2,515	
wc/d	1	1,028		1,028	
CASANOVA, Carlo (1871-1950) Italian					
oil	1	2,080		2,080	
CASANOVA, Francesco Giuseppe (1727-1802) Italian					
oil	5	109,291	8,250	12,835	59,660
wc/d	2	4,958	1,818	2,479	3,140
CASANOVA, Jose (1933-) Spanish					
oil	1	6,660		6,660	

Name	No.	Total Sales Value	lowest	Prices median	highest
CASANOVAS Y ASTORZA, Enrique (19th C) Spanish					
oil	1	1,688		1,688	
CASAS, Jesus Maria de las (1854-1926) Venezuelan					
oil	3	7,675	1,760	2,985	2,985
CASAS, Ramon (1866-1932) Spanish					
oil	4	468,458	48,003	82,728	255,000
wc/d	1	18,731		18,731	
CASATI, A (?) Italian?					
oil	1	1,993		1,993	
CASCELLA, Andrea (1920-1990) Italian					
3D	1	4,000		4,000	
CASCELLA, Basilio (1860-1950) Italian					
oil	1	2,967		2,967	
wc/d	1	1,309		1,309	
CASCELLA, Michele (1892-1989) Italian					
oil	28	301,566	2,340	7,390	31,424
wc/d	5	12,792	1,980	2,395	3,743
CASCELLA, Pietro (1921-) Italian					
3D	1	4,305		4,305	
CASCELLA, Tommaso (1890-1968) Italian					
wc/d	1	1,640		1,640	
CASCIARO, Giuseppe (1861-1943) Italian					
oil	5	16,443	2,077	3,295	4,500
wc/d	11	22,546	1,049	1,978	3,448
CASCIARO, Guido (1900-1963) Italian					
oil	1	1,142		1,142	
CASE, Edmund E (1840-1919) American					
oil	1	2,500		2,500	
CASENELLI, Victor (20th C) American					
wc/d	1	1,500		1,500	
CASER, Ettore (20th C) Italian					
oil	2	2,700	1,000	1,350	1,700
CASH, H (20th C) ?					
3D	1	1,139		1,139	
CASILE, Alfred (1847-1909) French					
oil	10	44,270	1,382	4,532	7,521
CASILEAR, John W (1811-1893) American					
oil	1	11,000		11,000	
CASISSA, Nicola (?-1730) Italian					
oil	5	154,997	9,000	13,710	93,620
CASLEY, Leonard (20th C) British					
wc/d	2	4,986	2,346	2,493	2,640
CASNEDI, Raffaele (1822-1892) Italian					
oil	1	19,169		19,169	
CASORATI, Daphne Maugham (1897-1984) Italian					
oil	1	2,109		2,109	
CASORATI, Felice (1883-1963) Italian					
oil	9	684,600	7,418	36,007	342,730
wc/d	4	31,609	5,823	6,465	12,857
CASPAR, Karl (1879-1956) German					
oil	1	7,286		7,286	
CASPAR-FILSER, Maria (1878-1968) German					
oil	6	50,364	2,824	8,790	14,072
CASSAS, Louis-François (1756-1827) French					
wc/d	4	109,245	5,211	31,577	40,880
CASSATT, Mary (1844-1926) American					
oil	4	6,350,000	750,000	1,450,000	2,700,000
wc/d	11	1,027,836	2,629	14,741	650,000
CASSE, R L (20th C) French?					
oil	1	1,140		1,140	

Name	No.	Total Sales Value	lowest	Prices median	highest
CASSEL, Pol (20th C) ?					
oil	1	51,840		51,840	
CASSELL, F (?) ?					
oil	1	4,082		4,082	
CASSELL, Frank (?) British					
oil	1	1,176		1,176	
CASSIDY, Ira Diamond Gerald (1879-1934) American					
oil	2	82,500	2,500	41,250	80,000
wc/d	2	8,450	3,200	4,225	5,250
CASSIE, James (1819-1879) British					
oil	1	10,150		10,150	
CASSIERS, H (1858-1944) Belgian					
oil	1	2,434		2,434	
wc/d	2	3,570	1,331	1,785	2,239
CASSIERS, Henry (1858-1944) Belgian					
oil	1	2,017		2,017	
wc/d	3	5,595	1,111	1,600	2,884
CASSIGNEUL, Jean Pierre (1935-) French					
oil	7	119,204	4,986	14,622	38,000
wc/d	1	2,112		2,112	
CASSINARI, Bruno (1912-1992) Italian					
oil	14	126,804	2,773	7,636	18,791
wc/d	5	7,802	1,309	1,449	1,833
CASSINELLI, H (19th C) ?					
oil	1	1,711		1,711	
CASSIOLI, Amos (1832-1891) Italian					
oil	1	46,728		46,728	
CASSIOLI, Giuseppe (1865-?) Italian					
wc/d	1	1,126		1,126	
CASSON, A J (1898-1992) Canadian					
oil	4	52,681	8,053	11,409	21,811
wc/d	1	5,704		5,704	
CASSON, Alfred Joseph (1898-1992) Canadian					
oil	15	260,351	2,611	8,628	99,552
wc/d	2	21,525	3,650	10,763	17,875
CASSON, Sir Hugh (1910-) British					
wc/d	2	2,345	1,058	1,173	1,287
CASTAGNINO, Juan Carlos (1908-1972) Argentinian					
oil	1	3,400		3,400	
CASTAN, Gustave-Eugène (1823-1892) Swiss					
oil	17	81,395	1,242	2,947	14,146
CASTAN, Pierre Jean Edmond (1817-?) French					
oil	2	13,006	2,220	6,503	10,786
CASTANEDA, Alfredo (1938-) Mexican					
oil	2	87,000	42,000	43,500	45,000
CASTANEDA, Felipe (1933-) Mexican					
3D	1	2,750		2,750	
CASTEDO, Julian (1899-?) Spanish					
oil	1	2,293		2,293	
CASTEELS, Peter II (fl.1690-1699) Flemish					
oil	1	1,285		1,285	
CASTEELS, Peter III (1684-1749) Flemish					
oil	3	162,202	20,516	46,686	95,000
CASTEL, Maurice (1927-) French					
oil	1	1,964		1,964	
CASTEL, Moshe (1909-1992) Israeli					
oil	6	100,500	4,000	13,500	40,000
wc/d	6	54,200	2,400	5,600	20,000
CASTELL, Anton (1810-1867) German					
oil	1	5,981		5,981	

Name	No.	Total Sales Value	lowest	Prices median	highest
CASTELLANI, Enrico (1930-) Italian					
oil	4	97,568	1,929	18,820	58,000
CASTELLANO, Carmelo (20th C) ?					
oil	1	2,207		2,207	
CASTELLANOS, Carlos Alberto (1881-1945) Uruguayan					
oil	3	4,250	1,000	1,450	1,800
CASTELLI (?) ?					
oil	1	3,894		3,894	
CASTELLI, Luciano (1951-) Swiss					
oil	5	16,029	1,169	1,717	9,060
wc/d	1	6,147		6,147	
CASTELLO, Bernardo (1557-1629) Italian					
oil	1	2,912		2,912	
CASTELLO, Felice (1602-1656) Spanish					
oil	1	28,762		28,762	
CASTELLO, Jacopo da (1637-1712) Flemish/Italian					
oil	1	26,000		26,000	
CASTELLO, Valerio (1625-1659) Italian					
wc/d	1	9,060		9,060	
CASTELLON, Federico (1914-1971) American					
wc/d	1	2,600		2,600	
CASTELLS CAPURRO, Enrique (20th C) South American					
oil	1	3,500		3,500	
CASTELUCHO, Claudio (1870-1927) Spanish					
oil	1	1,088		1,088	
CASTIGLIONE, Francesco (?-1716) Italian					
wc/d	1	1,266		1,266	
CASTIGLIONE, Giovanni Benedetto (1616-1670) Italian					
oil	2	2,063,800	735,000	1,031,900	1,328,800
CASTIGLIONE, Giovanni Francesco (1641-1710) Italian					
oil	1	12,842		12,842	
CASTIGLIONE, Giuseppe (1829-1908) Italian					
oil	2	25,114	9,827	12,557	15,287
wc/d	2	11,000	2,000	5,500	9,000
CASTIGLIONI, Giani (1917-) Swiss?					
oil	1	1,538		1,538	
CASTIGLIONI, Livio and FRATTINI, Gianfran (20th C) ?					
3D	1	2,500		2,500	
CASTILIAN SCHOOL, 17th C Spanish					
3D	1	8,440		8,440	
CASTILLO Y SAAVEDRA, Antonio del (1603-1667) Spanish					
oil	2	66,977	32,788	33,489	34,189
CASTILLO, Jorge (1933-) Spanish					
oil	31	71,945	1,003	1,665	10,690
wc/d	3	3,759	1,165	1,297	1,297
CASTILLO, Jose del (1737-1793) Spanish					
wc/d	1	1,083		1,083	
CASTILLO, Marcos (1897-1966) Venezuelan					
oil	1	3,290		3,290	
CASTRES, Edouard (1838-1902) Swiss					
oil	6	32,169	1,025	2,265	21,911
CASTRO CIRES, Raimundo (1894-1970) Spanish					
oil	1	2,052		2,052	
CASTRO LENERO, Miguel (20th C 1954-) Mexican					
oil	1	5,500		5,500	
CASTRO, Humberto (1957-) Cuban					
oil	2	9,097	1,097	4,549	8,000
CASTRO, Sergio de (1922-) Argentinian					
oil	3	5,576	1,710	1,804	2,062

Name	No.	Total Sales Value	lowest	Prices median	highest
wc/d	3	4,210	1,289	1,289	1,496
CATALAN SCHOOL, 15th C Spanish					
oil	1	6,416		6,416	
CATARSINI, Alfredo (1899-1993) Italian					
oil	2	14,008	3,233	7,004	10,775
CATEL, Franz Ludwig (1778-1856) German					
oil	1	40,871		40,871	
CATELIN, Bernard (1919-) French					
oil	1	20,951		20,951	
CATHELIN, Bernard (1919-) French					
oil	18	175,695	2,800	9,918	18,000
wc/d	2	3,294	1,614	1,647	1,680
CATLIN, George (1796-1872) American					
oil	1	40,000		40,000	
CATLOW, G S (fl.1884-1916) British					
wc/d	1	1,230		1,230	
CATS, Jacob (1741-1799) Dutch					
wc/d	3	5,991	1,029	1,029	3,929
CATTANEO, Achille (1872-1931) Italian					
oil	5	9,955	1,338	2,077	2,463
CATTELAN, Maurizo (1960-) Italian					
3D	5	552,620	26,100	78,520	240,000
CATTERMOLE, George (1800-1868) British					
wc/d	2	2,804	1,304	1,402	1,500
CATTI, Aurelio (19th C) Italian					
oil	6	26,411	1,145	1,979	16,215
wc/d	5	8,959	1,335	1,908	2,473
CATTON, Charles (18/19th C) British					
oil	1	3,454		3,454	
CATY, H (20th C) Belgian?					
oil	1	5,406		5,406	
CAUCHIE, Paul (1875-1952) Belgian					
oil	1	1,395		1,395	
CAUCHOIS, Eugène-Henri (1850-1911) French					
oil	31	140,852	1,263	3,722	13,500
CAUDRON, Jacques-Eugène (1818-1865) French					
3D	1	2,783		2,783	
CAUER, C (19th C) German?					
3D	1	1,065		1,065	
CAUER, Emil (19th C) German					
3D	1	1,882		1,882	
CAUER, Hannah (1902-1989) German					
3D	1	1,822		1,822	
CAULAERT, Jean van (20th C) French					
oil	1	1,083		1,083	
CAULFIELD, Patrick (1936-) British					
oil	1	2,272		2,272	
CAULLERY, Louis de (16/17th C) French/Flemish					
oil	6	353,580	5,009	24,298	225,480
CAULLET, Albert (1875-1950) Belgian					
oil	1	1,359		1,359	
CAUQUIE, H (19th C) French					
3D	1	2,087		2,087	
CAUVET, Gilles Paul (1731-1788) Italian					
wc/d	1	1,000		1,000	
CAUVY, Léon (1874-1933) French					
oil	5	44,582	1,929	8,542	18,000
wc/d	1	1,547		1,547	

Name	No.	Total Sales Value	Prices lowest	median	highest
CAUWER, Émile Pierre Joseph de (1828-1873) Belgian					
oil	2	18,641	8,491	9,321	10,150
CAUWER, Leopold de (19th C) German					
oil	1	1,573		1,573	
CAVAEL, Rolf (1898-1979) German					
oil	17	56,057	1,068	2,878	7,767
wc/d	12	28,300	1,211	1,803	5,727
CAVAILLES (1901-1977) French					
oil	1	1,854		1,854	
CAVAILLES, Jules (1901-1977) French					
oil	13	81,367	1,013	5,667	16,610
wc/d	2	8,500	3,000	4,250	5,500
CAVALCANTI, Emiliano di (1897-1976) Brazilian					
oil	3	962,000	42,000	120,000	800,000
wc/d	1	85,000		85,000	
CAVALLA, R (?) ?					
oil	1	1,184		1,184	
CAVALLERI, Vittorio (1860-1938) Italian					
oil	4	16,588	1,379	1,642	11,925
CAVALLI, Emanuele (1904-1981) Italian					
oil	3	15,703	1,575	5,401	8,727
CAVALLINO, Bernardo (1622-1654) Italian					
oil	1	352,800		352,800	
CAVALLUCCI, Antonio (1752-1795) Italian					
oil	1	5,760		5,760	
CAVE, Jules-Cyrille (1859-?) French					
oil	1	4,800		4,800	
CAVE, Peter le (fl.1769-1810) British					
oil	1	1,335		1,335	
wc/d	1	1,335		1,335	
CAVE, William (fl.1794) British?					
oil	1	2,355		2,355	
CAVELIER, Pierre Jules (1814-1896) French					
3D	3	4,961	1,420	1,493	2,048
CAVIN, Marylin (20th C) French					
wc/d	1	1,188		1,188	
CAWSE, John (1779-1862) British					
oil	1	1,173		1,173	
CAWSTON, Mick (1959-) British					
oil	1	1,716		1,716	
CAWTHORN (?) ?					
oil	1	1,600		1,600	
CAWTHORNE, Neil (1936-) British					
oil	11	31,805	1,287	3,322	5,434
CAYON, Henri-Felix (1878-?) French					
oil	1	2,578		2,578	
CAZABON, Michel J (1814-?) French					
wc/d	2	38,639	13,649	19,320	24,990
CAZAUX, Edouard (1889-1974) French					
3D	16	52,353	1,302	1,960	7,232
wc/d	2	2,603	1,157	1,302	1,446
CAZES, Pierre-Jacques (1676-1754) French					
oil	1	1,326		1,326	
CAZIN, Jean Charles (1841-1901) French					
oil	9	67,389	1,798	5,841	16,000
CAZZANIGA, Giancarlo (1930-) Italian					
oil	1	1,166		1,166	
CEBALLOS, Rufino (1907-1970) Spanish					
oil	1	2,711		2,711	

Name	No.	Total Sales Value	Prices lowest	Prices median	highest
CECCHI, Adriano (1850-1936) Italian					
oil	1	3,428		3,428	
CECCOBELLI, Bruno (1952-) Italian					
3D	1	1,600		1,600	
oil	1	1,484		1,484	
wc/d	4	8,989	1,254	2,169	3,397
CECCONI (?) Italian					
oil	1	1,240		1,240	
CECCONI, Alberto (1897-1971) Italian					
oil	1	1,198		1,198	
CECCONI, Eugenio (1842-1903) Italian					
oil	1	8,472		8,472	
CECIONI, Adriano (1836-1886) Italian					
3D	2	2,580	1,023	1,290	1,557
wc/d	1	2,230		2,230	
CEDERGREN, Per Vilhelm (1823-1896) Swedish					
oil	2	4,153	1,444	2,077	2,709
CEDERHOLM, Axel Fredrik (1780-1828) Swedish					
wc/d	1	3,482		3,482	
CEDERSTROM, Ture Nikolaus (1843-1924) Swedish					
oil	2	6,206	1,206	3,103	5,000
CEDOV, A (?) Russian					
oil	1	6,111		6,111	
CEESEPE (1958-) Spanish					
oil	2	3,276	1,582	1,638	1,694
CEI, Cipriano (1867-1922) Italian					
oil	1	5,500		5,500	
CELADA DA VIRGILIO, Ugo (1895-1995) Italian					
oil	12	29,709	1,833	2,387	3,617
CELEBRANO, Francesco (1729-1814) Italian					
oil	1	3,515		3,515	
CELERIER, Edouard (19/20th C) French					
oil	1	2,780		2,780	
CELIBERTI, Giorgio (1929-) Italian					
oil	3	9,340	1,408	2,581	5,351
wc/d	2	3,172	1,017	1,586	2,155
CELIE, Pieter (1942-) Dutch					
3D	2	2,090	1,045	1,045	1,045
CELIS, Agustin (1932-) Spanish					
oil	1	1,365		1,365	
CELLA, Ezio (20th C) ?					
oil	1	2,047		2,047	
CELLI (19/20th C) Italian					
oil	1	1,800		1,800	
CELMINS, Vija (1939-) American					
oil	1	300,000		300,000	
CELOMMI, Pasquale (1860-?) Italian					
oil	1	4,500		4,500	
CELOMMI, Raffaello (19/20th C) Italian					
oil	2	6,676	2,861	3,338	3,815
CELOS, Julien (1884-?) Belgian					
oil	5	7,721	1,186	1,391	2,060
CEMIN, Saint Clair (1951-) American					
3D	4	68,772	3,932	18,075	28,690
CENAC, Marc (20th C) French					
oil	1	2,948		2,948	
CENDALI, Pietro (1893-?) Italian					
3D	1	1,147		1,147	

Name	No.	Total Sales Value	lowest	Prices median	highest
CENTENO VALLENILLA, Pedro (1904-1982) Venezuelan					
oil	1	7,510		7,510	
CENTRAL ITALIAN SCHOOL, 14th C					
3D	1	105,599		105,599	
CENTRAL ITALIAN SCHOOL, 15th C					
3D	1	43,102		43,102	
oil	1	13,000		13,000	
CENTRAL ITALIAN SCHOOL, 16th C					
oil	1	3,140		3,140	
CERACCHINI, Gisberto (1899-1982) Italian					
oil	1	8,922		8,922	
CERAMANO (19/20th C) Belgian					
oil	1	1,854		1,854	
CERAMANO, Charles Ferdinand (1829-1909) Belgian					
oil	7	26,945	2,368	3,057	8,031
CEREZO, Mateo (1635-1685) Spanish					
oil	3	42,120	5,273	8,085	28,762
CERF, Ivan (1883-1963) Belgian					
oil	2	3,093	1,289	1,547	1,804
CERIA, Edmond (1884-1955) French					
oil	7	12,843	1,097	1,653	3,249
CERNY, Charles (1892-1965) French/Czech					
oil	1	2,250		2,250	
CEROLI, Mario (1938-) Italian					
3D	3	7,814	1,034	2,417	4,363
wc/d	2	4,166	1,254	2,083	2,912
CERQUOZZI, Michelangelo and ANGELUCCIO (17th C) Italian					
oil	1	32,000		32,000	
CERRINI, Giandomenico (1609-1681) Italian					
oil	2	60,000	10,000	30,000	50,000
CERUTI, Giacomo (1698-1767) Italian					
oil	1	12,960		12,960	
CESAR and FOLON (20th C) French					
wc/d	1	2,734		2,734	
CESAR, Baldaccini (1921-1998) French					
3D	67	661,324	1,078	6,171	80,529
oil	2	21,362	9,660	10,681	11,702
wc/d	19	52,982	1,009	1,408	7,083
CESARI, Giuseppe (1568-1640) Italian					
oil	3	523,650	45,300	128,350	350,000
wc/d	2	6,287	2,205	3,144	4,082
CESARI, Roberto (?) Italian?					
oil	4	6,545	1,334	1,514	2,184
CESBRON, Achille (1849-1915) French					
oil	2	3,834	1,571	1,917	2,263
CESETTI, Giuseppe (1902-1990) Italian					
oil	14	55,071	1,401	3,430	10,908
wc/d	1	1,440		1,440	
CESI, Bartolomeo (1556-1629) Italian					
wc/d	1	13,000		13,000	
CESTARO, Jacopo (18th C) Italian					
oil	1	24,000		24,000	
CESTERO, Sebastian (1931-1998) Spanish					
oil	2	3,464	1,716	1,732	1,748
CEYTAIRE, Jean-Pierre (1946-) French					
oil	4	19,057	1,289	3,822	10,124
CEZANNE, Paul (1839-1906) French					
oil	8	37,293,227	220,000	3,061,000	16,610,001
wc/d	7	1,526,562	109,312	220,000	340,000

Name	No.	Total Sales Value	lowest	Prices median	highest
CHABANIAN, Arsene (1864-1949) French					
wc/d	1	1,996		1,996	
CHABAS, Maurice (1862-1947) French					
oil	3	10,768	1,263	2,656	6,849
wc/d	1	1,047		1,047	
CHABAS, Paul (1869-1937) French					
oil	2	4,632	1,632	2,316	3,000
CHABAUD, Auguste (1882-1955) French					
oil	17	89,258	1,211	3,239	30,074
wc/d	1	1,286		1,286	
CHABOT, Andre (20th C) French					
3D	1	1,107		1,107	
CHABRY, Leonce (1832-1883) French					
oil	1	3,520		3,520	
CHACON, Sigfredo (20th C) South American?					
oil	1	1,005		1,005	
wc/d	1	1,440		1,440	
CHADWICK, Emma (1855-1932) Swedish					
oil	2	6,199	2,587	3,100	3,612
CHADWICK, Ernest Albert (1876-1955) British					
wc/d	6	12,141	1,362	1,654	3,087
CHADWICK, Lynn (1914-) British					
3D	21	539,733	1,975	13,500	130,000
wc/d	5	10,100	1,300	2,400	2,499
CHADWICK, Tom (1914-1942) British					
oil	1	23,970		23,970	
CHADWICK, William (1879-1962) American/British					
oil	2	5,250	1,000	2,625	4,250
CHAFFANEL, Eugène (19/20th C) French					
oil	1	2,578		2,578	
CHAGALL, Marc (1887-1985) French/Russian					
3D	2	137,421	57,862	68,711	79,559
oil	43	15,747,463	21,750	302,000	1,250,000
wc/d	45	3,755,258	1,709	50,000	300,000
CHAHNAZAR, Kouyoumdjian (20th C) Armenian					
oil	2	2,950	1,400	1,475	1,550
CHAIGNEAU, Jean Ferdinand (1830-1906) French					
oil	3	6,702	1,328	2,450	2,924
CHAIGNEAU, Paul (20th C) French					
oil	4	10,388	1,595	2,691	3,412
CHAILLOUX, Max Serge (19/20th C) ?					
oil	1	1,677		1,677	
CHAILLOUX, Robert (1913-) French					
oil	4	5,308	1,050	1,098	2,000
CHAISSAC, Gaston (1910-1964) French					
3D	1	90,219		90,219	
oil	4	155,580	13,649	40,588	60,755
wc/d	16	182,947	1,215	8,780	30,377
CHALFANT, Jefferson David (1856-1931) American					
oil	1	1,000		1,000	
wc/d	2	5,700	1,900	2,850	3,800
CHALIAPIN, Boris (1904-1982) Russian					
wc/d	1	1,000		1,000	
CHALLE, Charles Michelange (1718-1778) French					
oil	1	24,000		24,000	
CHALLENER, Frederick (1869-1959) Canadian					
oil	1	3,152		3,152	
CHALLIE, Jean Laurent (1880-1943) French					
oil	1	5,800		5,800	

Name	No.	Total Sales Value	lowest	Prices median	highest
CHALLIOUX, Robert (1913-) French					
oil	1	1,200		1,200	
CHALMERS, George Paul (1833-1878) British					
oil	1	2,528		2,528	
CHALMERS, Hector (c.1849-1943) British					
oil	1	2,250		2,250	
CHALMERS, John (19th C) British					
oil	1	2,265		2,265	
CHALMERS, Sir George (?-1791) British					
oil	2	14,172	3,300	7,086	10,872
CHALON, Alfred Edward (1780-1860) British					
wc/d	1	1,649		1,649	
CHALON, Charles (19th C) ?					
oil	1	1,010		1,010	
CHALON, Henry Bernard (1770-1849) British					
oil	1	11,700		11,700	
CHALON, Louis (1866-?) French					
3D	2	24,004	6,004	12,002	18,000
CHALOU (1942-) French					
oil	1	1,313		1,313	
CHAMAILLARD, Ernest (1862-1930) French					
oil	1	6,889		6,889	
CHAMBAS, Jean Paul (1947-) French					
oil	2	2,975	1,426	1,488	1,549
wc/d	1	2,571		2,571	
CHAMBERLAIN, J I (?) ?					
oil	1	1,724		1,724	
CHAMBERLAIN, John (1927-) American					
3D	7	281,410	9,540	42,000	60,000
CHAMBERS, C Bosseron (1882-?) American					
oil	1	1,700		1,700	
CHAMBERS, George (19th C) British					
oil	3	19,409	3,423	4,576	11,410
wc/d	1	1,575		1,575	
CHAMBERS, George (jnr) (fl.1848-1868) British					
oil	4	23,391	3,097	6,215	7,869
CHAMBERS, George (snr) (1803-1840) British					
oil	1	15,000		15,000	
CHAMBERS, John (1852-1928) British					
oil	1	1,250		1,250	
CHAMBERS, T (19th C) ?					
oil	1	1,404		1,404	
CHAMBLIN, E (18th C) French					
oil	1	2,844		2,844	
CHAMPAGNE, Horace (1937-) Canadian					
wc/d	4	4,799	1,009	1,099	1,593
CHAMPAIGNE, Philippe de (1602-1674) Flemish					
oil	2	400,000	160,000	200,000	240,000
CHAMPEIL, Jean Baptiste Antoine (1866-1913) French					
3D	1	7,488		7,488	
CHAMPION, Theo (1887-1952) German					
oil	4	9,167	1,653	1,777	3,883
CHAMPNEY, Benjamin (1817-1907) American					
oil	5	28,300	1,700	4,000	15,000
CHAMPNEY, James Wells (1843-1903) American					
wc/d	1	2,211		2,211	
CHANASE, Dane (1898-1976) American					
oil	1	2,500		2,500	

Name	No.	Total Sales Value	lowest	Prices median	highest
CHANDRA, Avinash (1931-) British					
wc/d	1	1,350		1,350	
CHANTEREAU, Jerome François (?-1757) French					
wc/d	1	1,031		1,031	
CHANTEROU, R (20th C) Belgian					
oil	1	1,842		1,842	
CHANTREY, Sir Francis (1781-1842) British					
3D	1	87,580		87,580	
oil	1	5,960		5,960	
CHAPELAIN-MIDY, Roger (1904-1992) French					
oil	5	18,556	1,297	3,322	7,123
CHAPELET, Roger (1902-1995) French					
oil	1	1,954		1,954	
wc/d	3	11,333	1,895	3,146	6,292
CHAPELLIER, Jose (1946-) Belgian					
oil	1	3,833		3,833	
CHAPERON, Philippe Marie (1823-1907) French					
wc/d	1	1,365		1,365	
CHAPIN, Bryant (1859-1927) American					
oil	2	2,500	1,000	1,250	1,500
CHAPIN, Francis (1899-1965) American					
oil	2	3,300	1,500	1,650	1,800
CHAPIN, James Ormsbee (1887-1975) American					
oil	1	1,000		1,000	
CHAPIN, Lucy Grosvenor (?-1939) American					
oil	1	2,600		2,600	
CHAPIRO, Jacques (1887-1972) Russian					
oil	2	5,089	1,489	2,545	3,600
CHAPLIN, Arthur (1869-?) French					
oil	2	8,546	2,546	4,273	6,000
CHAPLIN, Charles (1825-1891) French					
oil	7	83,162	2,634	8,000	25,000
wc/d	2	6,824	3,412	3,412	3,412
CHAPMAN, Conrad Wise (1842-1910) American					
oil	2	17,000	8,000	8,500	9,000
CHAPMAN, Dinos and Jake (20th C) British					
3D	4	62,449	4,095	17,177	24,000
CHAPMAN, George (1908-1993) British					
oil	2	5,148	2,145	2,574	3,003
CHAPMAN, James (?) British					
oil	1	2,567		2,567	
CHAPMAN, John Linton (1839-1905) American					
oil	1	1,800		1,800	
CHAPMAN, Minerva Josephine (1858-1947) American					
oil	2	3,524	1,024	1,762	2,500
CHAPOTON, Gregoire (1845-?) French					
oil	1	1,538		1,538	
CHAPOVAL, Youla (1919-1951) French/Russian					
oil	4	26,503	2,596	7,279	9,350
CHAPPE, Jean (c.1660-?) French					
oil	1	4,077		4,077	
CHAPPEL, Edouard (1859-1946) Belgian					
oil	2	2,303	1,050	1,152	1,253
CHAPPELL, Reuben (1870-1940) British					
oil	1	3,775		3,775	
CHAPUIS, Pierre Marie Alfred (1863-1942) French					
oil	1	1,127		1,127	
wc/d	1	1,480		1,480	

Name	No.	Total Sales Value	Prices lowest	median	highest
CHAPUROT, Aristide (fl.1848-1850) French					
wc/d	1	2,533		2,533	
CHAPUY, Andre (?-1941) French					
oil	1	1,176		1,176	
CHARASSON, Eugene (20th C) French					
oil	1	1,970		1,970	
CHARAVEL, Paul (1877-1961) French					
oil	1	1,378		1,378	
CHARBONNET, Marie Nathalie Loew (1845-1924) American					
oil	1	7,000		7,000	
CHARCHOUNE (1888-1975) Russian					
oil	1	2,852		2,852	
CHARCHOUNE, Serge (1888-1975) Russian					
oil	21	51,710	1,013	1,568	8,874
wc/d	2	3,276	1,638	1,638	1,638
CHARDERON, Francine (19/20th C) French					
oil	1	4,095		4,095	
CHARDIGNY, Jules (?-1892) French					
oil	2	4,073	1,309	2,037	2,764
CHARDIN, Jean Baptiste Simeon (1699-1779) French					
oil	2	905,700	105,700	452,850	800,000
wc/d	1	5,697		5,697	
CHARIGNY, Andre Auguste (1902-) French					
oil	1	1,194		1,194	
CHARLEMAGNE, Paul (1892-1972) French					
oil	1	1,082		1,082	
CHARLEMONT, Eduard (1848-1906) Austrian					
oil	1	1,364		1,364	
CHARLES, James (1851-1906) British					
oil	5	13,196	1,716	2,850	3,124
CHARLET, Frans (1862-1928) Belgian					
oil	2	6,401	1,901	3,201	4,500
CHARLET, Nicolas Toussaint (1792-1845) French					
oil	1	3,259		3,259	
wc/d	2	8,582	2,618	4,291	5,964
CHARLOT, Jean (1898-1979) Mexican/French					
oil	2	11,300	1,800	5,650	9,500
CHARLOT, Louis (1878-1951) French					
oil	3	5,098	1,168	1,442	2,488
CHARLOT, Paul (1906-1985) French					
oil	7	14,773	1,386	2,100	3,273
CHARLTON, Alan (1948-) British					
oil	1	12,080		12,080	
CHARLTON, John (1849-1917) British					
oil	4	31,652	1,057	5,298	20,000
wc/d	1	1,087		1,087	
CHARMAISON, Raymond Louis (1876-1955) French					
oil	1	1,024		1,024	
CHARMAN, Rodney (1944-) American					
oil	1	2,717		2,717	
CHARMY, Emilie (1877-1974) French					
oil	1	1,561		1,561	
CHAROL, Dorothea (1889-1963) Russian					
3D	1	2,869		2,869	
CHARPENTIER, Alexandre (1856-1909) French					
3D	1	3,899		3,899	
CHARPENTIER, Auguste (1813-1880) French					
oil	1	9,346		9,346	

Name	No.	Total Sales Value	Prices lowest	median	highest
CHARPENTIER, Felix (1858-1924) French					
3D	4	14,303	1,273	3,118	6,795
CHARPENTIER, Georges (19th C) French					
3D	1	1,694		1,694	
CHARPENTIER, Michel (20th C) French					
3D	1	1,053		1,053	
CHARPENTIER-MIO, Maurice (1881-1976) French					
3D	1	1,975		1,975	
CHARPIN, Albert (1842-1924) French					
oil	1	6,000		6,000	
CHARRETON, Victor (1864-1937) French					
oil	10	117,770	3,616	6,899	29,644
CHARRIET (20th C) French					
oil	1	2,190		2,190	
CHARTRAN, Theobald (1849-1907) French					
oil	1	2,708		2,708	
CHARTRAND, Esteban (1824-1884) Cuban					
oil	1	18,000		18,000	
CHASE, Harry (1853-1889) American					
oil	3	20,000	2,000	8,500	9,500
CHASE, Louisa (1951-) American					
oil	1	5,000		5,000	
CHASE, Marian (1844-1905) British					
wc/d	1	2,940		2,940	
CHASE, William Merritt (1849-1916) American					
oil	7	1,836,000	26,000	170,000	780,000
wc/d	1	19,000		19,000	
CHASHNIK, Ilya Grigorevich (1902-1929) Russian					
wc/d	1	40,000		40,000	
CHASSAGNAC, Emil (20th C) ?					
oil	1	1,079		1,079	
CHASSEPOT (20th C) French?					
3D	1	1,297		1,297	
CHASSERIAU, Theodore (1819-1856) French					
oil	1	8,500		8,500	
wc/d	1	1,673		1,673	
CHATAUD, Marc Alfred (1833-1908) French					
oil	1	7,316		7,316	
wc/d	2	2,259	1,033	1,130	1,226
CHATEIGNON, Ernest (1851-?) French					
oil	1	3,455		3,455	
CHATELET, Claude Louis (1753-1794) French					
oil	3	512,650	22,650	140,000	350,000
wc/d	8	53,832	1,460	2,903	32,000
CHATELIN, Ambroise (19th C) French					
oil	1	7,900		7,900	
CHATILLON, Pierre (1885-1974) Swiss					
wc/d	1	1,049		1,049	
CHATTAWAY, William (1927-) British					
3D	1	5,413		5,413	
CHATTERTON, Clarence K (1880-1973) American					
oil	1	5,500		5,500	
CHAUDET, Jeanne Elisabeth (1767-1832) French					
oil	1	16,711		16,711	
CHAUVEAU, Pascal (1962-) French					
oil	1	3,292		3,292	
CHAUVIN, Pierre Athanase (1774-1832) French					
oil	2	160,183	30,000	80,092	130,183

Name	No.	Total Sales Value	Prices lowest	median	highest
CHAVANIS (20th C) ?					
wc/d	2	2,855	1,356	1,428	1,499
CHAVAZ, Albert (1907-1990) Swiss					
oil	2	4,993	2,332	2,497	2,661
CHAVET, Victor Joseph (1822-1906) French					
oil	3	6,266	1,224	2,400	2,642
CHAVEZ LOPEZ, Gerardo (1937-) Peruvian					
oil	1	1,428		1,428	
wc/d	3	5,460	1,240	1,608	2,612
CHAVIGNAUD, Georges (1865-1944) Canadian					
wc/d	1	1,652		1,652	
CHEADLE, Henry (1852-1910) British					
oil	4	16,180	1,000	3,300	8,580
CHECA Y SANZ, Ulpiano (1860-1916) Spanish					
wc/d	1	9,648		9,648	
CHECA, Felipe (1844-1907) Spanish					
oil	3	9,812	1,056	1,056	7,700
CHECA, Jose Luis (1950-) Spanish					
oil	12	16,991	1,055	1,452	1,852
CHEEK, Carl (20th C) British?					
oil	1	1,413		1,413	
CHEESWRIGHT, Ethel S (1874-?) British					
wc/d	10	16,343	1,051	1,308	2,850
CHEKRYGIN, Vassilii Nikolaevich (1897-1922) Russian					
wc/d	1	2,115		2,115	
CHELIUS, Adolf (1856-1923) German					
oil	4	9,337	1,709	2,093	3,418
CHELMINSKI, Jan van (1851-1925) Polish					
oil	2	21,393	5,393	10,697	16,000
CHELMONSKI, Josef (1850-1914) Polish					
oil	1	35,000		35,000	
CHEMIAKIN, Mikhail (1943-) Russian					
3D	13	68,568	2,288	3,718	11,440
wc/d	4	36,356	1,240	8,504	18,108
CHEMIN, Joseph Victor (1825-1901) French					
3D	1	5,760		5,760	
CHEN WENBO (1969-) Chinese					
oil	2	14,174	6,142	7,087	8,032
CHENAVARD, Paul (19th C) French					
wc/d	1	3,098		3,098	
CHENEY, Russell (1881-1945) American					
oil	2	4,100	1,400	2,050	2,700
CHEREBAEV, Vladimir (20th C) Russian					
oil	1	1,100		1,100	
CHEREMETEFF, Vassily (1830-?) Russian					
oil	1	1,460		1,460	
CHERET, Jules (1836-1933) French					
3D	1	2,580		2,580	
oil	5	18,090	1,736	2,961	6,075
wc/d	4	14,439	1,016	3,457	6,509
CHERKI, Sabine (20th C) French?					
3D	1	1,148		1,148	
CHERON, Louis (1660-1715) French					
wc/d	1	2,058		2,058	
CHERRY, Kathryn (1880-1931) American					
oil	4	16,600	2,300	2,650	9,000
CHERUBINI, Carlo (20th C) Italian					
oil	2	2,938	1,414	1,469	1,524

Name	No.	Total Sales Value	lowest	Prices median	highest
CHESSA, Mauro (1933-) Italian					
oil	1	1,454		1,454	
CHESTRET, Caroline Levache de (19th C) French					
wc/d	1	2,274		2,274	
CHEVALIER, Eugene Adolphe (19th C) French					
oil	1	40,000		40,000	
CHEVALIER, Henry (?) French					
oil	1	3,222		3,222	
CHEVALIER, Nicholas (1828-1902) Australian					
wc/d	2	14,553	2,793	7,277	11,760
CHEVALIER, Peter (1953-) German					
oil	2	4,551	1,153	2,276	3,398
CHEVALIER, Robert Magnus (fl.1876-1911) British					
oil	1	5,720		5,720	
CHEVINS, Hugh (20th C) British					
oil	1	2,250		2,250	
CHEVIOT, Lilian (fl.1894-1930) British					
oil	5	26,114	2,114	3,250	11,000
CHEVOLLEAU, Jean (1924-1996) French					
oil	3	5,999	1,273	1,829	2,897
CHEVRE, Paul Romain (19th C) French					
3D	2	7,399	3,651	3,700	3,748
CHIA, Sandro (1946-) Italian					
3D	7	38,160	1,964	4,089	15,000
oil	9	216,455	1,848	30,200	42,280
wc/d	14	115,274	1,165	5,338	41,452
CHIALIVA, Luigi (1842-1914) Swiss					
oil	5	141,884	5,314	21,858	55,000
wc/d	1	7,584		7,584	
CHIARI, Giuseppe Bartolomeo (1654-1727) Italian					
oil	1	48,320		48,320	
CHICHARRO Y AGUERA, Eduardo (1873-1949) Spanish					
oil	1	4,302		4,302	
CHICHESTER, Cecil (1891-1963) American					
oil	2	2,900	1,300	1,450	1,600
CHICHESTER, N (19th C) British?					
oil	1	1,435		1,435	
CHIERICI, Gaetano (1838-1920) Italian					
oil	2	175,607	15,607	87,804	160,000
CHIESA, Pietro (1876-1959) Swiss					
oil	1	1,538		1,538	
CHIESA, Renato (1947-) Italian					
wc/d	1	1,929		1,929	
CHIGHINE, Alfredo (1914-1974) Italian					
oil	3	29,329	8,847	9,853	10,629
CHIGOT, Eugène (1860-1927) French					
oil	5	16,857	1,064	2,369	5,925
CHIHULY, Dale (20th C) American?					
3D	2	5,750	2,250	2,875	3,500
CHILD, Jane Bridgham Curtis (1868-?) American					
wc/d	1	9,790		9,790	
CHILDE, Elias (fl.1798-1848) British					
oil	1	8,216		8,216	
CHILLIDA, Eduardo (1924-) Spanish					
3D	3	695,250	43,500	198,750	453,000
wc/d	6	148,119	2,427	24,556	57,554
CHILONE, Vincenzo (1758-1839) Italian					
oil	2	73,590	5,896	36,795	67,694

Name	No.	Total Sales Value	lowest	Prices median	highest
CHIMENTI, Jacopo (1554-1640) Italian					
wc/d	1	3,926		3,926	
CHIMIELINSKI, Vladislav (?) Russian?					
oil	1	1,385		1,385	
CHIMOT, Edouard (20th C) French					
wc/d	1	1,136		1,136	
CHINESE SCHOOL					
3D	4	36,226	4,144	9,981	12,120
oil	2	97,307	2,536	48,654	94,771
CHINESE SCHOOL, 16th C					
3D	2	17,250	4,250	8,625	13,000
CHINESE SCHOOL, 17th/18th C					
3D	2	27,374	5,729	13,687	21,645
wc/d	1	2,435		2,435	
CHINESE SCHOOL, 18th C					
3D	3	31,346	4,456	4,500	22,390
oil	1	19,925		19,925	
wc/d	2	23,100	2,100	11,550	21,000
CHINESE SCHOOL, 18th/19th C					
wc/d	2	13,080	5,250	6,540	7,830
CHINESE SCHOOL, 19th C					
3D	3	25,736	5,774	5,774	14,176
oil	25	309,023	3,000	9,000	37,000
wc/d	1	9,456		9,456	
CHINESE SCHOOL, 8th/9th C					
3D	1	5,000		5,000	
CHINET, Charles (1891-1978) Swiss					
oil	4	8,974	1,581	2,203	2,988
CHING, Raymond (1939-) New Zealander					
wc/d	3	5,474	1,136	1,924	2,414
CHINI, Galileo (1873-1956) Italian					
oil	3	43,579	7,345	13,710	22,524
CHINNERY, George (1774-1852) British					
oil	1	26,640		26,640	
wc/d	9	36,505	1,350	1,500	14,300
CHINTREUIL, Antoine (1816-1873) French					
oil	3	7,219	1,317	1,402	4,500
CHIPARUS (1888-1950) Rumanian					
3D	5	45,300	1,510	6,795	22,650
CHIPARUS, D (1888-1950) Rumanian					
3D	8	44,952	2,145	3,411	17,490
CHIPARUS, Demetre (1888-1950) Rumanian					
3D	45	1,021,696	1,063	8,822	169,237
CHIRICO, Giacomo di (1845-1884) Italian					
oil	1	3,493		3,493	
CHIRICO, Giorgio de (1888-1978) Italian					
3D	9	317,844	1,833	10,322	150,000
oil	34	5,855,046	9,060	79,270	1,000,000
wc/d	10	276,927	1,297	12,618	166,750
CHIRINO, Martin (1925-) Spanish					
wc/d	1	1,694		1,694	
CHITTENDEN, Alice B (1859-1934) American					
oil	2	7,800	1,300	3,900	6,500
CHIURAZZI (18th C) Italian?					
3D	3	22,572	2,844	6,048	13,680
CHIUSO, Tommaso (18th C) Italian					
wc/d	1	3,171		3,171	
CHIVOT, C (?) French					
3D	1	2,772		2,772	

Name	No.	Total Sales Value	Prices lowest	median	highest
CHIZMARICK, Steven (1898-?) American					
oil	1	1,500		1,500	
CHMIELINSKI, W T (19/20th C) Polish					
oil	1	2,800		2,800	
CHOCARNE-MOREAU (1855-1931) French					
oil	2	8,226	3,565	4,113	4,661
CHOCARNE-MOREAU, Paul Charles (1855-1931) French					
oil	3	13,630	1,697	3,133	8,800
CHODOWIECKI, Daniel (1726-1801) German					
oil	2	7,650	1,650	3,825	6,000
wc/d	4	10,338	1,125	2,507	4,200
CHONG SON (1676-1759) Chinese					
wc/d	1	2,500		2,500	
CHOQUET, René (fl.1896-1939) French					
oil	1	4,740		4,740	
CHOUBRAC, Alfred (1853-1902) French					
oil	1	2,698		2,698	
CHOULANT, Ludwig Theodor (1827-1900) German					
wc/d	1	1,800		1,800	
CHOULTSE, Ivan Fedorovich (1874-1939) Russian					
oil	12	86,219	2,310	6,634	13,590
CHOUPPE, Jean Henri (1817-1894) French					
oil	1	1,646		1,646	
wc/d	1	1,422		1,422	
CHOWDHURY, Jogen (1939-) Indian					
oil	1	5,000		5,000	
wc/d	1	2,250		2,250	
CHRETIEN, René Louis (1867-1942) French					
oil	3	15,884	3,442	3,442	9,000
CHRIS, J E (19/20th C) British					
oil	1	1,400		1,400	
CHRIST, Pieter Casper (1822-1888) Dutch					
oil	1	1,721		1,721	
CHRISTENSEN, Antonore (1849-1926) Danish					
oil	3	13,092	1,059	1,072	10,961
CHRISTENSEN, Godfred (1845-1928) Danish					
oil	9	16,675	1,044	1,084	5,224
CHRISTENSEN, Kay (1899-1981) Danish					
oil	11	19,648	1,073	1,476	4,068
CHRISTIANSEN, Nils H (1850-1922) Danish					
oil	3	4,498	1,036	1,168	2,294
CHRISTIANSEN, Poul S (1855-1933) Danish					
oil	2	3,067	1,530	1,534	1,537
CHRISTIANSEN, Professor Hans (1866-1945) German					
oil	2	7,576	2,115	3,788	5,461
CHRISTIANSEN, Rasmus (1863-1940) Danish					
oil	3	22,409	1,569	2,968	17,872
CHRISTIANSEN, Ursula Reuter (1943-) Danish					
oil	1	1,177		1,177	
CHRISTIE, James Elder (1847-1914) British					
oil	4	25,272	2,844	6,714	9,000
CHRISTO (1935-) American/Bulgarian					
3D	6	105,783	1,212	1,633	70,000
oil	3	131,200	23,200	28,000	80,000
wc/d	22	676,788	2,385	25,632	100,000
CHRISTOFFERSEN, Frede (1919-1987) Danish					
oil	3	4,060	1,177	1,281	1,602
CHRISTOFFERSEN, Uffe (1947-) Danish					
oil	1	2,441		2,441	

Name	No.	Total Sales Value	lowest	Prices median	highest
CHRISTOFOROU, John (1921-) British					
oil	7	12,552	1,152	1,463	3,689
CHRISTOPHE (?) ?					
oil	1	1,875		1,875	
CHRISTY, F Earl (20th C) American					
wc/d	1	4,000		4,000	
CHRISTY, Howard Chandler (1872-1952) American					
oil	2	9,727	1,727	4,864	8,000
wc/d	2	8,800	2,800	4,400	6,000
CHRYSTIE, E P (19th C) American?					
wc/d	1	1,600		1,600	
CHU TEH CHUN (1920-) Chinese					
oil	6	67,465	7,475	10,228	19,109
wc/d	2	4,957	1,993	2,479	2,964
CHUANG CHE (1934-) Chinese					
oil	1	2,000		2,000	
CHUGHTAI, Abdur Rahman (1894-1975) Indian					
wc/d	10	249,220	5,040	23,000	45,000
CHUPYATOV, Leonid Terentevich (1890-1941) Russian					
oil	1	3,775		3,775	
CHURCH, Frederic Edwin (1826-1900) American					
oil	1	3,800,000		3,800,000	
CHURCH, Frederick Stuart (1842-1923) American					
oil	5	41,750	2,250	3,500	19,000
wc/d	1	2,750		2,750	
CHURCHILL, Martin (1954-) British					
oil	1	1,440		1,440	
CHURCHILL, William W (1858-1926) American					
oil	1	6,750		6,750	
CHURCHYARD, Thomas (1798-1865) British					
oil	1	1,050		1,050	
wc/d	2	3,289	1,144	1,645	2,145
CHWALA, Adolf (1836-1900) Czechoslovakian					
oil	3	8,084	1,932	2,552	3,600
CHWALA, Adolf and OSTERSETZER, Carl (19th C) Czech/Austrian					
oil	1	1,364		1,364	
CHWALA, Fritz (1872-1936) Austrian					
oil	1	1,387		1,387	
CIAMPELLI, Agostini (1578-1640) Italian					
wc/d	1	2,058		2,058	
CIANGOTTINI, Giovanni (1912-) Italian					
oil	1	1,260		1,260	
CIANI, Cesare (1854-1925) Italian					
oil	2	3,078	1,526	1,539	1,552
CIAPPA, Carlo (19/20th C) Italian					
oil	1	1,286		1,286	
CIAPPA, Frederico (fl.1830-1840) Italian					
oil	1	1,200		1,200	
CIARDI, Beppe (1875-1932) Italian					
oil	10	113,949	1,747	9,100	26,588
CIARDI, C (19th C) Italian					
oil	1	1,266		1,266	
wc/d	1	1,811		1,811	
CIARDI, Emma (1879-1933) Italian					
oil	11	105,447	2,752	10,902	18,960
CIARDI, Guglielmo (1842-1917) Italian					
oil	7	185,326	6,864	11,923	55,740
wc/d	1	1,294		1,294	
CIARDIELLO, Carmine (1871-?) Italian					
oil	3	7,538	1,160	1,896	4,482

Name	No.	Total Sales Value	Prices lowest	median	highest
CIARROCCHI, Arnoldo (1916-) Italian					
oil	2	6,479	3,135	3,240	3,344
CIBO, Gherardo (16th C) Italian					
wc/d	1	9,060		9,060	
CICCOTELLI, Beniamino (1937-) Italian					
oil	2	2,199	1,078	1,100	1,121
CICERI (?) ?					
wc/d	1	2,546		2,546	
CICERI, Eugène (1813-1890) French					
oil	2	13,398	1,398	6,699	12,000
wc/d	4	8,461	1,230	1,841	3,549
CICERI, Pierre Luc Charles (1782-1868) French					
wc/d	1	1,626		1,626	
CICOGNA, Giammaria (1813-1849) Italian					
oil	1	2,836		2,836	
CIDONCHA, Rafael (1952-) Spanish					
oil	2	4,331	1,537	2,166	2,794
wc/d	1	1,956		1,956	
CIENFUEGOS BROWN, Gonzalo (1949-) Chilean					
oil	1	38,000		38,000	
CIGNANI, Carlo (1628-1719) Italian					
wc/d	1	23,405		23,405	
CIGNANI, Carlo (school) (1628-1719) Italian					
oil	1	26,830		26,830	
CIGNAROLI, Pietro (1665-1720) Italian					
oil	1	9,420		9,420	
CIGNAROLI, Scipione (school) (1715-1766) Italian					
oil	1	7,500		7,500	
CIGNAROLI, Vittorio Amedeo (c.1747-1793) Italian					
oil	1	51,414		51,414	
CIKOVSKY, Nicolai (1894-1984) American					
oil	1	2,500		2,500	
CILFONE, Gianni (1908-) American/Italian					
oil	1	1,200		1,200	
CIMA, Luigi (1860-1938) Italian					
oil	1	5,664		5,664	
CIMIOTTI, Emil (1927-) German					
3D	2	16,065	5,340	8,033	10,725
CIMIOTTI, Gustave (1875-1969) American					
oil	1	2,250		2,250	
CINOT, Franck (?-1890) French					
oil	2	9,000	3,500	4,500	5,500
CINOTTI, Guido (1870-1932) Italian					
oil	2	6,729	1,784	3,365	4,945
CIOCCHINI, Cleto (1899-1974) Argentinian					
oil	1	1,200		1,200	
CIOCHINI, Cleto (?) ?					
oil	1	3,000		3,000	
CIOTTA, C (19th C) Italian					
oil	1	2,664		2,664	
CIOTTA, F (19th C) Italian					
oil	1	1,817		1,817	
CIPOLLA, F (1854-?) Italian					
oil	1	7,000		7,000	
CIPOLLA, Fabio (1854-?) Italian					
oil	1	11,364		11,364	
CIPPER, Giacomo Francesco (c.1670-1738) Italian					
oil	1	44,100		44,100	

Name	No.	Total Sales Value	lowest	Prices median	highest
CIPRIANI, A (19th C) Italian					
3D	6	13,258	1,020	1,606	5,145
CIPRIANI, Giovanni Battista (1727-1785) Italian					
wc/d	1	2,200		2,200	
CIPRIANI, Giovanni Pinotti (19/20th C) French					
3D	1	4,511		4,511	
oil	1	2,037		2,037	
CIPRIANI, Nazzarreno (1843-1925) Italian					
wc/d	1	2,000		2,000	
CIRINO, Antonio (1889-1983) American					
oil	1	1,500		1,500	
CIROU, Paul (19/20th C) French					
oil	2	10,437	3,867	5,219	6,570
CITROEN, Paul (1896-1983) Dutch					
oil	4	17,910	1,721	2,335	11,520
wc/d	1	13,500		13,500	
CITTADINI, Tito (20th C) ?					
oil	2	10,103	1,800	5,052	8,303
CIVITALI, Matteo (1436-1501) Italian					
3D	2	220,173	69,317	110,087	150,856
CIVITARESE, Goffredo (1938-) Italian					
oil	2	2,605	1,121	1,303	1,484
CLAESZ, Pieter (1590-1661) Dutch					
oil	2	356,800	151,000	178,400	205,800
CLAEUW, Jacques Grief (?-1676) Dutch					
oil	1	40,320		40,320	
CLAEYS, Albert (1889-1967) Belgian					
oil	2	7,384	3,302	3,692	4,082
CLAGETT, Jean (20th C) French					
3D	2	4,500	1,265	2,250	3,235
CLAGHORN, Joseph C (1869-1947) American					
oil	1	1,000		1,000	
CLAIR, Charles (1860-1930) French					
oil	4	9,386	1,378	2,235	3,539
CLAIRIN, Georges (1843-1919) French					
oil	4	114,018	7,500	26,079	54,360
wc/d	1	1,197		1,197	
CLAIRIN, Pierre Eugène (1897-1980) French					
oil	2	2,622	1,268	1,311	1,354
CLAISSE, Genevieve (1935-) French					
oil	2	5,526	1,500	2,763	4,026
wc/d	4	6,188	1,033	1,268	2,619
CLAPP, William H (1879-1954) Canadian					
oil	10	45,346	1,400	3,375	12,696
CLARA, Jose (1878-?) Spanish					
3D	1	2,876		2,876	
oil	1	1,026		1,026	
CLARA, Luigi (1875-1925) Italian					
oil	1	1,297		1,297	
CLARE, George (1835-c.1890) British					
oil	13	42,011	1,073	2,600	9,060
CLARE, Oliver (1853-1927) British					
oil	38	107,085	1,058	2,646	6,750
CLARE, Vincent (1855-1930) British					
oil	23	98,422	1,088	4,405	8,700
wc/d	3	5,880	1,008	1,440	3,432
CLARENBACH, Max (1880-1952) German					
oil	9	40,739	1,000	4,098	8,342
CLARK, Albert (19th C) British					
oil	4	9,126	1,011	1,964	4,187

Name	No.	Total Sales Value	lowest	Prices median	highest
CLARK, Albert James (fl.1892-1909) British					
oil	1	3,432		3,432	
CLARK, Allan (1896-1950) American					
3D	1	6,000		6,000	
CLARK, Alson Skinner (1876-1949) American					
oil	10	172,400	2,200	11,000	55,000
CLARK, Alson Skinner and PARKER, Lawton S (19/20th C) American					
oil	1	55,000		55,000	
CLARK, Benton (1895-1964) American					
oil	1	4,000		4,000	
CLARK, C Myron (20th C) American					
oil	2	4,400	1,200	2,200	3,200
wc/d	1	1,400		1,400	
CLARK, Dixon (1849-1944) British					
oil	2	5,194	1,476	2,597	3,718
wc/d	1	1,001		1,001	
CLARK, Eliot (1883-1980) American					
oil	1	1,600		1,600	
wc/d	1	1,000		1,000	
CLARK, Frederick Albert (fl.1888-1909) British					
oil	3	6,500	1,716	2,217	2,567
CLARK, J (?) British					
oil	1	1,207		1,207	
CLARK, James (fl.1858-1909) British					
oil	2	6,350	2,400	3,175	3,950
CLARK, James (1858-1943) British					
oil	2	2,576	1,226	1,288	1,350
CLARK, Joseph (1834-1926) British					
oil	2	6,902	3,002	3,451	3,900
CLARK, Joseph Dixon (jnr) (1878-1966) British					
oil	2	2,507	1,178	1,254	1,329
CLARK, Lygia (1920-1988) Brazilian					
3D	3	100,000	12,000	38,000	50,000
oil	1	9,483		9,483	
CLARK, Matt (1903-) American					
oil	1	5,000		5,000	
wc/d	1	2,800		2,800	
CLARK, Norman (1913-) British					
oil	1	1,050		1,050	
CLARK, Octavius T (1850-1921) British					
oil	5	9,345	1,141	1,859	2,500
CLARK, Paraskeva (1898-1986) Canadian					
oil	1	3,356		3,356	
CLARK, R (?) ?					
3D	1	2,400		2,400	
CLARK, Roland (?) ?					
oil	2	13,300	3,800	6,650	9,500
CLARK, S (?) ?					
oil	1	2,942		2,942	
CLARK, S J (19/20th C) British					
oil	4	16,073	1,320	3,117	8,520
CLARK, S Joseph (19th C) British					
oil	1	4,500		4,500	
CLARK, Samuel James (19th C) British					
oil	1	3,456		3,456	
CLARK, Stanley (?) ?					
oil	1	2,370		2,370	
CLARK, W A (19/20th C) British					
oil	1	1,272		1,272	

Name	No.	Total Sales Value	lowest	Prices median	highest
CLARK, Walter (1848-1917) American					
oil	1	2,500		2,500	
CLARK, William Albert (20th C) British					
oil	3	8,825	2,717	3,000	3,108
CLARKE, Frederick (fl.1834-1870) British					
oil	1	2,050		2,050	
CLARKE, George Row (fl.1858-1889) British					
wc/d	1	1,185		1,185	
CLARKE, Harry (1889-1931) British					
wc/d	1	4,290		4,290	
CLARKE, James (19th C) British					
oil	1	2,320		2,320	
CLARKE, Margaret (1888-1961) Irish					
oil	1	14,800		14,800	
CLARKE, P (?) British					
oil	1	1,208		1,208	
CLARKE, R E (fl.1825-1848) British					
oil	1	1,872		1,872	
CLARKE, W H (1882-1924) British					
oil	1	1,081		1,081	
CLARKE, William Hanna (1882-1924) British					
oil	1	5,009		5,009	
CLARKSON, Edward (fl.1835-1860) American					
oil	1	3,000		3,000	
CLARKSON, R (fl.1880-1914) British					
oil	1	3,950		3,950	
CLAROT (20th C) ?					
oil	1	1,449		1,449	
CLAROT, René (1882-1972) Belgian					
oil	1	1,508		1,508	
CLARY, James (20th C) American					
oil	1	5,000		5,000	
CLARY, Jean Eugène (1856-1930) French					
oil	3	3,957	1,168	1,240	1,549
CLARY-BAROUX, A A (1865-1933) French					
oil	1	1,211		1,211	
CLARY-BAROUX, Albert Adolphe (1865-1933) French					
oil	1	1,422		1,422	
CLATWORTHY, Robert (1928-) British					
3D	1	2,400		2,400	
CLAUDE, Eugène (1841-1923) French					
oil	2	6,356	2,431	3,178	3,925
CLAUDE, Jean Maxime (1824-1904) French					
oil	2	11,874	5,819	5,937	6,055
CLAUDEL, Camille (1864-1943) French					
3D	8	1,109,000	13,000	125,500	270,000
CLAUDIUS, Wilhelm (1854-1942) German					
oil	2	5,359	2,668	2,680	2,691
wc/d	1	3,414		3,414	
CLAUDOT, Jean-Baptiste-Charles (1733-1805) French					
oil	1	18,000		18,000	
CLAUS, Émile (1849-1924) Belgian					
oil	11	433,775	8,429	24,000	138,000
wc/d	1	6,909		6,909	
CLAUS, Hugo (1929-) Belgian					
wc/d	1	1,724		1,724	
CLAUS, William A J (1862-?) American					
oil	1	3,000		3,000	

Name	No.	Total Sales Value	Prices lowest	median	highest
CLAUSADES, Pierre de (1910-1976) French					
oil	8	10,283	1,044	1,299	1,586
CLAUSEN, Franciska (1899-1986) Danish					
wc/d	4	30,414	2,111	5,435	17,433
CLAUSEN, Sir George (1852-1944) British					
oil	5	425,190	4,740	27,000	343,200
CLAVE (1913-) Spanish					
3D	1	1,219		1,219	
oil	1	20,075		20,075	
wc/d	1	6,131		6,131	
CLAVE, Antoni (1913-) Spanish					
3D	6	66,596	2,935	5,516	30,852
oil	25	658,334	1,510	19,630	72,340
wc/d	27	173,049	1,063	3,989	18,120
CLAVE, Pelegrin (1810-1880) Spanish					
oil	1	1,885		1,885	
CLAVO, Javier (1918-1994) Spanish					
oil	4	9,786	1,249	1,740	5,058
CLAXTON, Adelaide (fl.1860-1876) British					
wc/d	1	2,574		2,574	
CLAY, Elizabeth C Fisher (fl.1927-1938) American/British					
oil	1	5,220		5,220	
CLAYES, Alice des (1890-?) Canadian					
oil	3	13,078	1,062	1,216	10,800
CLAYES, Berthe des (1877-1968) Canadian					
oil	1	2,257		2,257	
wc/d	1	1,306		1,306	
CLAYS, Paul Jean (1819-1900) Belgian					
oil	8	26,822	1,021	3,075	10,000
CLAYTON, Harold (1896-1979) British					
oil	8	150,615	4,260	19,890	36,000
CLAYTON, J Hughes (fl.1891-1929) British					
wc/d	7	10,608	1,021	1,233	2,265
CLAYTON, William J M (20th C) British					
oil	1	4,500		4,500	
CLEAR, G (19th C) British?					
oil	1	1,520		1,520	
CLEARY, Manon (20th C) American					
wc/d	1	1,000		1,000	
CLEAVES, Helen E (1878-) American					
oil	1	1,000		1,000	
CLEEMPUT, Jean van (1881-?) Belgian					
oil	1	1,216		1,216	
CLEENEWERCK, Henry (19th C) French					
oil	1	7,300		7,300	
CLELAND-HURA, D J (20th C) American					
oil	3	9,114	2,072	2,072	4,970
CLEMENS, Curt (1911-1947) Swedish					
oil	2	5,948	1,727	2,974	4,221
CLEMENS, Gustaf Adolf (1870-1918) Danish					
oil	1	6,454		6,454	
CLEMENS, Paul Lewis (1911-) American					
oil	1	2,500		2,500	
CLEMENT, Charles (1889-1972) Swiss					
oil	1	1,691		1,691	
CLEMENT, Felix Auguste (1826-1888) French					
oil	1	1,102		1,102	
CLEMENT, Gad Frederick (1867-1933) Danish					
oil	1	5,250		5,250	

Name	No.	Total Sales Value	lowest	Prices median	highest
CLEMENT, Hans (?) ?					
oil	1	1,429		1,429	
CLEMENTE, Francesco (1952-) Italian					
oil	4	316,560	60,000	66,570	120,000
wc/d	17	627,617	3,491	17,400	150,000
CLEMENTS, George Henry (1854-1935) American					
wc/d	1	1,800		1,800	
CLEMINSON, R (19th C) British					
oil	1	1,230		1,230	
CLEMINSON, Robert (19th C) British					
oil	15	39,474	1,020	1,868	5,550
CLERCK, Hendrick de (1570-1629) Flemish					
oil	1	124,950		124,950	
CLERCK, Jan de (1881-1962) Belgian					
oil	1	1,761		1,761	
CLERCQ, Alphonse de (1868-1945) Belgian					
oil	1	2,218		2,218	
CLERCQ, Pieter Jan de (1891-1964) Belgian					
oil	2	3,664	1,300	1,832	2,364
CLERGET, Adele (19th C) French					
wc/d	1	1,898		1,898	
CLERGET, Alexandre (1856-?) French					
3D	1	4,250		4,250	
CLERICI, Fabrizio (1913-1993) Italian					
oil	1	1,780		1,780	
CLERICI, Leone (19/20th C) ?					
3D	1	5,530		5,530	
CLERISSEAU, Charles Louis (1721-1820) French					
wc/d	1	4,500		4,500	
CLERMONT, Jean François (1717-1807) French					
wc/d	1	2,750		2,750	
CLESINGER, Jean Baptiste (1814-1883) French					
3D	14	271,212	1,691	3,406	200,000
CLESSE, Louis (1889-1961) Belgian					
oil	17	42,032	1,109	1,553	11,130
CLEVE, Joos van (1485-1540) Dutch					
oil	1	4,926		4,926	
CLEVE, Marten van (1527-1581) Flemish					
oil	2	64,408	2,063	32,204	62,345
CLEVE-JONAND, Agnes (1876-1951) Swedish					
oil	15	94,705	1,092	5,678	16,379
wc/d	3	4,674	1,044	1,337	2,293
CLEVELEY, John (jnr) (1747-1786) British					
wc/d	2	8,288	2,114	4,144	6,174
CLIFFE, Henry (1919-1983) British					
oil	5	6,988	1,021	1,185	2,198
wc/d	1	1,015		1,015	
CLIFFORD, Edward (1844-1907) British					
wc/d	1	7,200		7,200	
CLIFFORD, Henry Charles (1861-?) British					
oil	1	1,444		1,444	
CLIMENT, Elena (20th C) Mexican					
oil	1	15,000		15,000	
CLINT, Alfred (1807-1883) British					
oil	1	1,106		1,106	
CLINT, George (1770-1854) British					
oil	1	2,072		2,072	
CLODION (1738-1814) French					
3D	13	76,489	1,198	4,133	19,791

Name	No.	Total Sales Value	lowest	Prices median	highest
CLOSTERMAN, Johann Baptist (1660-1713) German					
oil	1	9,000		9,000	
CLOT, René Jean (1913-1997) French					
oil	1	1,365		1,365	
CLOUARD, Albert (1866-1952) French					
oil	1	3,520		3,520	
CLOUET (school) (16th C) French					
wc/d	1	10,183		10,183	
CLOUET, Felix (?-1882) French					
oil	1	3,647		3,647	
CLOUET-D'ORVAL, Francis (c.1840-?) French					
oil	1	1,012		1,012	
CLOUGH, George L (1824-1901) American					
oil	1	10,000		10,000	
CLOUGH, Prunella (1919-) British					
oil	3	20,974	1,704	9,000	10,270
wc/d	1	1,326		1,326	
CLOUGH, Tom (1867-1943) British					
oil	1	1,144		1,144	
wc/d	8	17,339	1,216	2,397	3,000
CLOWES, Daniel (1774-1829) British					
oil	5	43,744	3,575	7,865	17,168
CLOWES, H (1799-1871) British					
oil	1	3,624		3,624	
CLUYSENAAR, Alfred Jean Andre (1837-1902) Belgian					
oil	1	5,739		5,739	
CLYMER, John Ford (1907-1989) American					
oil	9	394,500	8,500	45,000	95,000
CLYNE, Thora (1937-) British					
oil	1	2,416		2,416	
COAST, Oscar Regan (1851-1931) American					
oil	1	1,977		1,977	
COATES, Edmund C (1816-1871) American					
oil	3	9,500	2,000	3,000	4,500
COATES, Tom (1941-) British					
oil	2	5,313	1,413	2,657	3,900
COATS, Randolph (1891-?) American					
oil	1	6,000		6,000	
COBAS, B (19th C) Italian					
oil	1	2,836		2,836	
COBB, David (19th C) British?					
oil	1	2,282		2,282	
COBBAERT, Jan (1909-1995) Belgian					
oil	6	14,872	1,053	2,717	3,322
wc/d	1	1,343		1,343	
COBBETT, Edward John (1815-1899) British					
oil	7	16,909	1,716	2,360	3,318
COBELLE, Charles (1902-) French					
wc/d	1	1,000		1,000	
COBIANCHI, Ignio (fl.1880-1901) French					
oil	1	2,799		2,799	
COBLITZ, Louis (19th C) French					
oil	1	1,242		1,242	
COBO, Chema (1952-) Spanish					
wc/d	2	2,373	1,076	1,187	1,297
COBURN, Frank (1866-1931) American					
oil	15	87,950	1,900	4,250	13,000
wc/d	1	3,250		3,250	

Name	No.	Total Sales Value	lowest	Prices median	highest
COBURN, Frederick Simpson (1871-1960) Canadian					
oil	10	71,876	1,416	8,825	13,274
COCCORANTE, Leonardo (1680-1750) Italian					
oil	3	123,750	16,000	37,750	70,000
COCHELET, Louise (19th C) French					
wc/d	1	4,200		4,200	
COCHIN, Charles-Nicolas (18th C) French					
wc/d	10	36,534	1,676	2,562	9,280
COCHIN, Charles-Nicolas and DELAFOSSE, Jean Charles (18th C) French					
wc/d	1	1,021		1,021	
COCK, Cesar de (1823-1904) Flemish					
oil	2	10,168	1,898	5,084	8,270
COCK, Gilbert de (1928-) Belgian					
oil	2	2,924	1,462	1,462	1,462
COCK, Xavier de (1818-1896) Flemish					
oil	1	11,195		11,195	
COCKBURN, Edwin (fl.1837-1868) British					
oil	1	4,108		4,108	
COCKERELL, Charles Robert (1788-1863) British					
wc/d	2	4,214	1,068	2,107	3,146
COCKRAM, George (1861-1950) British					
wc/d	1	1,430		1,430	
COCKRILL, Maurice (1936-) British					
oil	7	17,052	1,027	1,323	6,300
COCKX, Philibert (1879-1949) Belgian					
oil	1	1,294		1,294	
COCTEAU (19/20th C) French					
wc/d	1	1,431		1,431	
COCTEAU, Jean (1889-1963) French					
3D	2	5,733	2,158	2,867	3,575
oil	2	5,273	1,273	2,637	4,000
wc/d	46	140,093	1,106	1,850	27,298
COCTEAU, Jean and MORETTI, Lucien Philippe (20th C) French					
wc/d	1	3,704		3,704	
CODAZZI, Niccolo (1648-1693) Italian					
oil	1	10,570		10,570	
CODAZZI, Viviano (1603-1672) Italian					
oil	1	33,161		33,161	
CODAZZI, Viviano (school) (1603-1672) Italian					
oil	1	6,792		6,792	
CODDE, Pieter (1599-1678) Dutch					
oil	4	147,290	20,580	31,955	62,800
CODDE, Pieter (school) (1599-1678) Dutch					
oil	1	3,169		3,169	
CODDRON, Oscar (1881-1960) Belgian					
oil	1	14,260		14,260	
CODINA Y LANGLIN, Victoriano (1844-1911) Spanish					
oil	1	5,065		5,065	
CODNER, Maurice Frederick (1888-?) British					
oil	1	1,450		1,450	
COE, Sue (20th C) American					
oil	1	13,000		13,000	
COELENBIER, Jan (1630-1677) Dutch					
oil	2	18,800	2,960	9,400	15,840
COELLO, Claudio (1630-1693) Spanish					
oil	1	25,813		25,813	
COENE, Constantinus Fidelio (1780-1841) Flemish					
oil	5	58,448	1,567	10,831	23,797

Name	No.	Total Sales Value	lowest	Prices median	highest
COENE, Jean Baptiste (1805-1850) Belgian					
oil	1	6,488		6,488	
COENE, Jean Henri de (1798-1866) Flemish					
oil	2	6,605	1,541	3,303	5,064
COESERMANS, Johannes (fl.1661) Dutch					
oil	1	5,000		5,000	
COESSIN DE LA FOSSE, Charles Alexandre (1829-?) French					
oil	1	9,481		9,481	
COESTER, Oskar (20th C) ?					
oil	2	10,455	5,000	5,228	5,455
wc/d	1	1,609		1,609	
COFFIN, W A (1855-1925) American					
oil	1	1,200		1,200	
COFFIN, William A (1855-1925) American					
oil	1	6,000		6,000	
COFFIN, William Haskell (1878-1941) American					
oil	1	3,250		3,250	
COGELS, Joseph Carl (1786-1831) Flemish					
wc/d	1	1,026		1,026	
COGEN, Felix (1838-1907) Belgian					
oil	2	8,350	2,550	4,175	5,800
COGHLAN, J (19th C) British?					
oil	1	2,718		2,718	
COGNATA, Giovanni la (20th C) Italian					
oil	1	1,236		1,236	
COGNEE, Philippe (1957-) French					
wc/d	1	3,099		3,099	
COHELEACH, Guy Joseph (20th C) American					
oil	1	6,500		6,500	
COHEN, Elaine Lustig (1927-) American					
oil	1	2,800		2,800	
COHEN, Larry (20th C) American					
oil	2	6,750	3,250	3,375	3,500
COHEN-GAN, Pinchas (1942-) Israeli					
wc/d	1	1,300		1,300	
COHN, Paul (19th C) German					
oil	1	2,083		2,083	
COIELLI, A (19th C) Italian					
oil	1	3,851		3,851	
COIGNARD, James (1925-1997) French					
3D	1	1,117		1,117	
oil	6	16,005	1,033	2,873	3,879
wc/d	10	15,817	1,005	1,317	2,676
COIGNET, Jules Louis Philippe (1798-1860) French					
oil	2	6,311	2,626	3,156	3,685
COINCHON, Jacques Antoine Theodore (1814-1881) French					
3D	1	1,783		1,783	
COKE, Edward Thomas (fl.1807-1888) British					
wc/d	1	4,576		4,576	
COKE-SMYTH, Frederick (fl.1835-1867) British					
wc/d	1	1,422		1,422	
COKER, Peter (1926-) British					
oil	1	11,376		11,376	
COL, D (19th C) ?					
oil	1	8,642		8,642	
COL, Jan David (1822-1900) Belgian					
oil	3	37,606	1,331	1,936	34,339
COLACICCHI, Giovanni (1900-1993) Italian					
oil	1	2,301		2,301	

Name	No.	Total Sales Value	lowest	Prices median	highest
COLACICCO, Salvatore (1935-) British/Italian					
oil	3	5,686	1,144	1,824	2,718
COLATRELLA, Marie Odile (20th C) French?					
oil	1	1,032		1,032	
COLBY, George E (1859-?) American					
oil	1	3,000		3,000	
COLE, George (1810-1883) British					
oil	7	121,710	1,562	8,500	72,000
COLE, George Vicat (1833-1893) British					
oil	6	62,389	2,826	9,353	22,650
wc/d	2	6,062	1,057	3,031	5,005
COLE, Herbert (1867-1930) British					
oil	1	1,065		1,065	
COLE, James (19th C) British					
oil	1	3,256		3,256	
COLE, James William (19th C) British					
oil	5	22,020	1,200	5,032	6,040
COLE, John Vicat (1903-) British					
oil	2	3,537	1,275	1,769	2,262
COLE, Joseph Foxcroft (1837-1892) American					
oil	2	3,200	1,000	1,600	2,200
COLE, Joseph Greenleaf (1803-1858) American					
oil	1	7,500		7,500	
COLE, Philip Tennyson (fl.1880-1930) British					
wc/d	2	4,498	1,908	2,249	2,590
COLE, Rex Vicat (1870-1940) British					
oil	3	7,079	1,080	1,917	4,082
COLE, Thomas (1801-1848) American					
oil	1	7,500		7,500	
COLEBROOKE, Robert H (1762-1808) British					
wc/d	1	3,300		3,300	
COLEMAN, Charles Caryl (1840-1928) American					
oil	4	402,584	5,000	78,792	240,000
COLEMAN, Edward (?-1867) British					
oil	1	1,422		1,422	
COLEMAN, Enrico (1846-1911) Italian					
oil	1	1,286		1,286	
wc/d	1	1,471		1,471	
COLEMAN, Francesco (1851-?) Italian					
oil	2	3,501	1,616	1,751	1,885
COLEMAN, Glenn O (1887-1932) American					
oil	1	2,200		2,200	
COLEMAN, Henry (?) British					
wc/d	1	4,769		4,769	
COLEMAN, John (?) British					
oil	1	2,250		2,250	
COLEMAN, Loring W (20th C) American					
oil	1	1,100		1,100	
COLEMAN, Michael (1946-) American					
oil	2	33,500	11,000	16,750	22,500
wc/d	4	32,250	4,750	6,750	14,000
COLEMAN, W S (1829-1904) British					
wc/d	1	1,027		1,027	
COLEMAN, William Stephen (1829-1904) British					
oil	6	74,000	5,250	13,500	19,000
wc/d	3	18,229	1,029	3,160	14,040
COLERIDGE, F G (fl.1866-1914) British					
wc/d	3	4,698	1,389	1,450	1,859

Name	No.	Total Sales Value	lowest	Prices median	highest
COLERIDGE, Stephen (1854-1936) British					
oil	1	1,435		1,435	
COLETTE and DONGEN, Kees van (20th C) French					
wc/d	1	48,221		48,221	
COLETTI, Nando (1907-1979) Italian					
oil	1	2,310		2,310	
COLEY, Alice Mary (1882-) British					
oil	1	1,187		1,187	
COLIN, Francois (1798-1864) French					
wc/d	1	1,400		1,400	
COLIN, G (19th C) French					
3D	1	8,580		8,580	
COLIN, Georges (1876-?) French					
3D	2	5,429	1,313	2,715	4,116
COLIN, Gustave (1828-1910) French					
oil	6	17,222	2,075	2,643	4,202
COLIN, P G P (18th C) Flemish					
oil	1	11,195		11,195	
COLIN, Paul (1892-1985) French					
oil	1	1,141		1,141	
wc/d	1	9,148		9,148	
COLIN, Paul Alfred (1838-1916) French					
oil	2	10,844	2,844	5,422	8,000
COLIN, Paul-Émile (1867-1949) French					
wc/d	1	2,358		2,358	
COLINET, C J R (fl.1913-1945) French					
3D	3	12,393	1,370	4,228	6,795
COLINET, Claire Jeanne Roberte (fl.1913-1945) French					
3D	7	28,679	1,427	3,800	9,295
COLINSON, J (?) British					
oil	1	1,425		1,425	
COLKETT, Samuel David (1806-1863) British					
oil	5	15,347	1,208	2,900	5,720
COLLA, Ettore (1896-1968) Italian					
3D	3	108,312	1,784	48,528	58,000
COLLADO, Pedro (1874-?) Spanish					
oil	1	1,600		1,600	
COLLAMARINI, René (1904-1983) French					
3D	2	6,763	1,975	3,382	4,788
COLLANTES, Francisco (1599-1656) Spanish					
oil	1	13,130		13,130	
COLLE, Michel-Auguste (1872-1949) French					
oil	1	10,000		10,000	
COLLETTE, Aubrey (1920-1992) British?					
wc/d	1	13,500		13,500	
COLLIER, A L (?) ?					
oil	1	1,185		1,185	
COLLIER, Alan Caswell (1911-1990) Canadian					
oil	5	8,828	1,241	1,784	2,611
COLLIER, Arthur Bevan (fl.1855-1899) British					
oil	1	1,896		1,896	
COLLIER, Evert (1640-1706) Dutch					
oil	5	289,796	12,488	51,512	130,000
COLLIER, Thomas Frederick (fl.1848-1874) British					
wc/d	3	5,388	1,470	1,470	2,448
COLLIGNON, Georges (1923-) Belgian					
oil	9	31,670	1,288	3,549	5,695
wc/d	1	1,671		1,671	

Name	No.	Total Sales Value	Prices lowest	median	highest
COLLIN, Alberic (1886-1962) Belgian					
3D	7	42,158	1,395	4,658	15,014
COLLINA, Giuliano (1938-) Italian					
oil	1	1,256		1,256	
COLLINS, Alfred (fl.1851-1882) British					
oil	2	4,102	1,558	2,051	2,544
COLLINS, Cecil (1908-1989) British					
oil	2	6,670	2,900	3,335	3,770
wc/d	2	12,630	3,335	6,315	9,295
COLLINS, Charles (1851-1921) British					
oil	5	9,967	1,352	2,067	2,643
wc/d	3	6,155	1,267	1,988	2,900
COLLINS, H (19th C) British					
oil	1	4,564		4,564	
COLLINS, Henry (1782-1824) British					
oil	1	21,750		21,750	
COLLINS, William (1788-1847) British					
oil	5	12,902	1,287	1,483	5,877
COLLINS, William Wiehe (1862-1952) British					
oil	1	1,136		1,136	
COLLIS, Peter (1911-) Irish					
wc/d	1	1,015		1,015	
COLLOMB, Fernand (1902-1981) French					
oil	2	4,277	1,761	2,139	2,516
COLLOMB, Paul (1921-) French					
oil	1	2,600		2,600	
COLLS, Ebenezer (1812-1887) British					
oil	3	8,082	2,115	2,115	3,792
COLLYER, Margaret (fl.1897-1903) British					
oil	1	2,002		2,002	
COLLYER, Nora Frances Elisabeth (1889-?) Canadian					
oil	2	4,204	1,593	2,102	2,611
COLMAN OF BRISTOL, Samuel (1780-1845) British					
oil	1	25,740		25,740	
COLMAN, Roi Clarkson (1884-1945) American					
oil	2	2,700	1,100	1,350	1,600
COLMAN, Samuel (1832-1920) American					
oil	2	30,000	2,500	15,000	27,500
COLMEIRO, Manuel (1901-1999) Spanish					
oil	1	18,567		18,567	
wc/d	4	5,218	1,103	1,364	1,452
COLMENAREZ, Asdrubal (1936-) South American					
wc/d	2	2,180	1,030	1,090	1,150
COLMO, Giovanni (1867-1947) Italian					
oil	1	1,582		1,582	
COLMORE, Nina (1889-?) British					
oil	2	3,609	1,178	1,805	2,431
COLN, David von (1689-1763) Swedish					
oil	1	15,576		15,576	
COLNOT, Arnout (1887-1983) Dutch					
oil	5	9,641	1,149	1,477	4,357
COLOGNE SCHOOL, 14th C German					
3D	1	20,367		20,367	
COLOGNE SCHOOL, 15th C German					
oil	1	13,840		13,840	
COLOMBE, Chretien C (?) ?					
oil	1	3,135		3,135	
COLOMBI, Plinio (1873-1951) Swiss					
oil	2	5,457	2,215	2,729	3,242

Name	No.	Total Sales Value	lowest	Prices median	highest
COLOMBO (?) ?					
3D	1	1,254		1,254	
COLOMBO, Ambrogio (1821-?) Italian					
3D	1	2,400		2,400	
COLOMBO, Gianni (1937-1993) Italian					
3D	1	29,000		29,000	
oil	1	15,950		15,950	
wc/d	1	3,622		3,622	
COLOMBO, Giovanni Battista Innocenzo (1717-1793) Italian					
oil	1	127,425		127,425	
COLOMBO, Grange (?) ?					
3D	1	3,454		3,454	
COLOMBO, Joe (20th C) Italian?					
3D	1	10,150		10,150	
COLONIA, Adam de (1634-1685) Dutch					
oil	2	8,265	2,505	4,133	5,760
COLONIA, Adriaan (1668-1701) Dutch					
oil	1	1,833		1,833	
COLONIAL SCHOOL, 17th C					
oil	1	3,608		3,608	
COLONIAL SCHOOL, 18th/19th C					
oil	1	9,428		9,428	
COLONIAL SCHOOL, 19th C					
oil	2	16,512	7,632	8,256	8,880
COLOT, Robert (1927-1993) Belgian					
oil	2	4,072	1,437	2,036	2,635
COLQUHOUN, Robert (1914-1962) British					
oil	1	21,170		21,170	
COLSON, Charles Jean Baptiste (1810-?) French					
oil	1	3,800		3,800	
COLSON, Guillaume François (1785-1850) French					
oil	1	27,298		27,298	
COLSON, Jean François (1733-1803) French					
oil	2	44,530	6,530	22,265	38,000
COLUCCI, Gio (1892-1974) Italian?					
3D	1	1,702		1,702	
oil	2	11,092	1,119	5,546	9,973
COLUCCI, Vincenzo (1898-1970) Italian					
oil	1	1,959		1,959	
COLUNGA, Alejandro (1948-) Mexican					
oil	1	8,000		8,000	
COLVILLE, Alex (1920-) Canadian					
wc/d	1	14,601		14,601	
COLYN, David (c.1582-?) Dutch					
oil	1	52,920		52,920	
COMBAS, Robert (1957-) French					
3D	2	3,610	1,127	1,805	2,483
oil	58	385,604	1,093	4,039	25,603
wc/d	9	20,425	1,018	1,739	6,889
COMBAZ, Ghisbert (1869-1941) Belgian					
oil	1	2,581		2,581	
COMBER, Melanie (1970-) British					
oil	1	4,935		4,935	
COMBET-DESCOMBES, Pierre (1885-1966) French					
oil	1	1,267		1,267	
COMENSOLI, Mario (1922-1993) Italian					
oil	2	4,731	1,458	2,366	3,273
wc/d	3	4,527	1,066	1,093	2,368
COMERRE, Léon (1850-1916) French					
oil	4	99,446	2,436	26,120	44,770

Name	No.	Total Sales Value	Prices lowest	Prices median	highest
COMFORT, Charles Fraser (1900-) Canadian					
oil	4	8,710	1,659	2,115	2,821
COMINS, Eben F (1875-1949) American					
oil	1	18,000		18,000	
COMMERE, Jean Yves (1920-1986) French					
oil	2	5,590	2,593	2,795	2,997
COMMUNAL, Joseph (1876-1962) French					
oil	1	1,501		1,501	
COMOLERA, Melanie de (fl.1816-1854) French					
oil	1	4,113		4,113	
COMOLLI, Gigi (1893-1976) Italian					
oil	2	4,392	1,929	2,196	2,463
COMOY, M E G (19th C) ?					
oil	1	2,525		2,525	
COMPAGNO, Scipione (1624-1685) Italian					
oil	1	17,457		17,457	
COMPANY SCHOOL, 19th C					
wc/d	3	23,100	3,300	3,300	16,500
COMPARD, Émile (1900-1977) French					
oil	5	7,928	1,151	1,354	2,437
COMPERET, Alexis (1856-1906) American					
oil	1	1,600		1,600	
COMPIGNE (18th C) French					
wc/d	2	6,230	1,622	3,115	4,608
COMPRIS, Maurice (1885-1939) American					
oil	1	2,900		2,900	
COMPTE-CALIX, François Claudius (1813-1880) French					
oil	1	9,000		9,000	
COMPTON, Charles (1828-1884) British					
oil	1	1,988		1,988	
COMPTON, Edward Harrison (1881-1960) British					
oil	14	33,779	1,076	1,948	6,000
wc/d	7	11,537	1,028	1,227	4,211
COMPTON, Edward Theodore (1849-1921) British					
oil	3	23,990	3,188	4,091	16,711
wc/d	8	23,199	1,597	2,555	5,324
COMPTON, Edward Thomas (19/20th C) British					
wc/d	1	11,778		11,778	
CONCA, Sebastiano (1676-1764) Italian					
oil	1	19,000		19,000	
CONCONI, Luigi (1852-1917) Italian					
oil	3	33,019	3,054	3,210	26,755
wc/d	2	4,830	1,284	2,415	3,546
CONDAMY, Charles Fernand de (1855-?) French					
oil	1	6,500		6,500	
wc/d	4	7,216	1,354	1,709	2,444
CONDO, George (1957-) American					
oil	16	248,551	1,200	12,500	40,000
wc/d	2	11,000	3,000	5,500	8,000
CONDOPOULOS, Alecos (1905-1975) Greek					
wc/d	1	6,570		6,570	
CONDY, Nicholas (1793-1857) British					
oil	1	12,225		12,225	
wc/d	3	8,525	1,335	1,470	5,720
CONDY, Nicholas Matthew (1816-1851) British					
oil	3	31,556	6,006	7,550	18,000
wc/d	3	4,884	1,271	1,650	1,963
CONE, Marvin D (1891-1964) American					
oil	4	205,500	14,000	23,250	145,000

Name	No.	Total Sales Value	lowest	Prices median	highest
CONEJO, Andres (1913-) Spanish					
oil	1	1,124		1,124	
CONGNET, Gillis (1538-1599) Dutch					
oil	1	9,456		9,456	
CONGNET, Michiel (fl.1640-1641) Flemish					
oil	1	5,024		5,024	
CONGO SCHOOL Africa					
3D	1	50,501		50,501	
CONINCK, David de (1636-1699) Flemish					
oil	4	148,593	17,783	37,428	55,954
CONLLIE, F (19th C) American					
oil	1	1,000		1,000	
CONNARD, Philip (1875-1958) British					
oil	3	7,536	2,160	2,496	2,880
CONNAWAY, Jay Hall (1893-1970) American					
oil	1	3,250		3,250	
CONNER, Charles (1857-1905) American					
oil	1	2,250		2,250	
CONNER, John Anthony (1892-1971) American					
oil	4	5,500	1,200	1,350	1,600
CONNER, Paul (1881-1968) American					
oil	1	1,300		1,300	
CONNOLLY, Howard (20th C) American					
oil	1	3,000		3,000	
CONOLLY, Thurloe (20th C) British?					
oil	1	1,106		1,106	
CONOR, W (1881-1968) Irish					
oil	1	7,150		7,150	
CONOR, William (1881-1968) Irish					
oil	4	173,900	9,620	37,740	88,800
wc/d	11	122,809	2,341	6,960	38,880
CONRAD, Carl Emanuel (1810-1873) German					
wc/d	1	2,307		2,307	
CONRAD, Charles (1912-) Belgian					
3D	3	6,113	1,159	2,320	2,634
CONRADE, Alfred Charles (1863-1955) British					
wc/d	2	3,336	1,080	1,668	2,256
CONROY, Stephen (1964-) British					
wc/d	1	1,824		1,824	
CONSADORI, Silvio (1909-1996) Italian					
oil	4	7,827	1,159	2,121	2,495
CONSAGRA, Pietro (1920-) Italian					
3D	4	15,374	1,620	3,376	7,003
oil	1	1,800		1,800	
CONSEIL, Napoleon (1837-1871) French					
oil	1	4,280		4,280	
CONSTABLE, Jane Bennett (1865-?) British					
oil	1	1,208		1,208	
CONSTABLE, John (1776-1837) British					
oil	5	1,880,600	34,760	290,000	915,200
wc/d	10	861,990	7,110	83,050	178,180
CONSTABLE, John (school) (1776-1837) British					
oil	1	1,714		1,714	
CONSTABLE, Lionel (1828-1884) British					
oil	2	10,428	4,108	5,214	6,320
CONSTANCE SCHOOL, 15th C German					
oil	1	11,781		11,781	
CONSTANS, Charles Louis (18/19th C) French					
oil	1	36,344		36,344	

Name	No.	Total Sales Value	lowest	Prices median	highest
CONSTANT (1920-) Dutch					
3D	2	22,579	5,942	11,290	16,637
oil	2	21,525	4,869	10,763	16,656
wc/d	4	30,443	1,495	7,578	13,793
CONSTANT, Benjamin (1845-1902) French					
oil	2	25,331	11,682	12,666	13,649
CONSTANT, Eugene (19th C) French					
oil	1	4,525		4,525	
CONSTANT, George (1892-1978) American					
wc/d	2	3,100	1,200	1,550	1,900
CONSTANTIN, Jean Antoine (1756-1844) French					
oil	1	2,211		2,211	
wc/d	2	4,746	1,247	2,373	3,499
CONSTANTINE, G Hamilton (1875-1967) British					
wc/d	12	23,155	1,072	1,914	2,812
CONSTANTINI, Giuseppe (19th C) Italian					
oil	1	3,239		3,239	
CONTE (16/17th C) Italian					
oil	1	2,861		2,861	
CONTE, Domenico (?) ?					
oil	1	6,594		6,594	
CONTE, Meiffren (1630-1705) French					
oil	2	55,240	23,520	27,620	31,720
CONTE, T (?) ?					
wc/d	1	1,176		1,176	
CONTENOT, H D (20th C) French					
3D	3	7,452	1,313	2,395	3,744
CONTESSE, Gaston Louis Joseph (1870-1946) French					
3D	1	1,809		1,809	
CONTI, Francesco (1681-1760) Italian					
wc/d	1	1,065		1,065	
CONTI, P (?) Italian					
3D	1	2,285		2,285	
CONTI, Regina (1890-1960) Swiss					
oil	6	8,765	1,049	1,469	1,976
CONTINENTAL SCHOOL					
3D	2	8,800	3,300	4,400	5,500
oil	2	5,750	2,000	2,875	3,750
CONTINENTAL SCHOOL, 16th C					
3D	1	18,182		18,182	
CONTINENTAL SCHOOL, 17th C					
oil	2	7,248	2,248	3,624	5,000
CONTINENTAL SCHOOL, 17th/18th C					
3D	1	7,727		7,727	
oil	2	7,488	3,500	3,744	3,988
CONTINENTAL SCHOOL, 18th C					
3D	4	11,269	2,451	2,534	3,750
oil	8	40,547	2,248	3,671	11,000
CONTINENTAL SCHOOL, 18th/19th C					
oil	2	33,600	3,600	16,800	30,000
CONTINENTAL SCHOOL, 19th C					
3D	10	57,152	2,451	3,618	16,928
oil	22	162,381	1,185	4,515	27,740
wc/d	2	5,682	2,727	2,841	2,955
CONTINENTAL SCHOOL, 19th/20th C					
3D	2	8,250	3,250	4,125	5,000
oil	4	13,950	3,200	3,350	4,000
CONTINENTAL SCHOOL, 20th C					
3D	3	9,976	3,000	3,476	3,500
oil	3	17,289	4,431	6,042	6,816

Name	No.	Total Sales Value	lowest	Prices median	highest
CONTRERAS Y MUNOZ, Jose Marcelo (1827-1890) Spanish					
oil	2	11,980	4,070	5,990	7,910
CONTWAY, Jay (20th C) American					
3D	1	2,152		2,152	
CONWAY, Fred (1900-1972) American					
oil	1	1,000		1,000	
CONZ, Gustav (1832-?) German					
oil	1	3,750		3,750	
CONZ, Walter (1872-1947) German					
oil	2	5,899	1,282	2,950	4,617
COOK OF PLYMOUTH, William (fl.1870-1880) British					
wc/d	1	1,256		1,256	
COOK, Beryl (1926-) British					
oil	6	79,695	7,755	11,280	24,000
COOK, Ebenezer Wake (1843-1926) British					
wc/d	2	6,227	1,491	3,114	4,736
COOK, Gordon (1927-1985) American					
wc/d	1	2,400		2,400	
COOK, Herbert Moxon (1844-c.1920) British					
wc/d	1	1,284		1,284	
COOK, Howard (1901-1980) American					
wc/d	1	5,000		5,000	
COOK, J (?) ?					
oil	1	1,030		1,030	
COOK, John A (1870-1936) American					
wc/d	1	1,200		1,200	
COOK, May Elizabeth (1881-1951) American					
3D	1	4,200		4,200	
COOK, Otis (1900-1980) American					
oil	3	9,000	1,000	4,000	4,000
COOK, Samuel (1806-1859) British					
wc/d	1	1,787		1,787	
COOK, William (fl.1877-1879) British					
wc/d	1	1,661		1,661	
COOKE, Arthur Claude (1867-?) British					
oil	1	7,500		7,500	
COOKE, Dorothea (1908-) American					
wc/d	1	2,000		2,000	
COOKE, E C V (?) ?					
oil	1	1,738		1,738	
COOKE, Edward William (1811-1880) British					
oil	6	429,380	2,880	25,725	185,900
wc/d	2	15,376	4,576	7,688	10,800
COOKE, W E (19th C) British					
oil	1	1,081		1,081	
COOKESLEY, Margaret Murray (?-1927) British					
oil	2	3,049	1,099	1,525	1,950
COOKSEY, May Louise Greville (1878-1943) British					
oil	1	1,037		1,037	
COOL, Thomas Simon (1831-1870) Dutch					
oil	1	1,650		1,650	
COOLE, Brian (19th C) British					
oil	2	4,000	1,500	2,000	2,500
COOLIDGE, Cassius M (1844-1934) American					
oil	1	26,000		26,000	
COOMANS, Auguste (1855-?) Belgian					
oil	1	4,294		4,294	
COOMANS, Heva (19th C) Belgian					
oil	2	39,500	9,500	19,750	30,000

Name	No.	Total Sales Value	lowest	Prices median	highest
COOMANS, Pierre Olivier Joseph (1816-1889) Belgian					
oil	1	1,100		1,100	
COOMBS, Delbert Dana (1850-1938) American					
oil	1	2,500		2,500	
COOMBS, Edith Grace (?) Canadian					
oil	1	4,469		4,469	
COOP, Hubert (1872-1953) British					
wc/d	3	11,706	1,691	2,431	7,584
COOPER, A D M (1865-1924) American					
oil	1	1,500		1,500	
COOPER, Abraham (1787-1868) British					
oil	2	7,977	1,977	3,989	6,000
COOPER, Alfred Egerton (1883-1974) British					
wc/d	1	2,114		2,114	
COOPER, Alfred Heaton (1864-1929) British					
wc/d	2	4,526	1,998	2,263	2,528
COOPER, Astley D M (1865-1924) American					
oil	5	13,650	1,600	3,250	3,500
COOPER, Colin Campbell (1856-1937) American					
oil	5	45,050	1,600	3,250	35,000
wc/d	4	5,800	1,000	1,400	2,000
COOPER, Edwin (1785-1833) British					
oil	2	12,835	5,285	6,418	7,550
COOPER, Gerald (1898-1975) British					
oil	4	23,862	4,512	6,150	7,050
COOPER, Henry (19/20th C) British					
oil	3	4,071	1,065	1,444	1,562
COOPER, S (19/20th C) British					
oil	1	1,410		1,410	
COOPER, T S (1803-1902) British					
oil	1	1,140		1,140	
COOPER, Teal (19th C) British?					
oil	1	1,553		1,553	
COOPER, Thomas George (1836-1901) British					
wc/d	2	3,341	1,430	1,671	1,911
COOPER, Thomas Sidney (1803-1902) British					
oil	30	517,238	1,200	10,575	63,000
wc/d	6	15,394	1,214	2,125	4,582
COOPER, Thomas Sidney and LEE, Frederick Richard (19th C) British					
oil	1	52,500		52,500	
COOPER, William Heaton (1903-) British					
wc/d	9	15,745	1,241	1,695	2,304
COOPER, William Sidney (1854-1927) British					
oil	3	9,322	1,230	3,352	4,740
wc/d	4	7,880	1,016	1,365	4,134
COOPSE, Pieter (?-1677) Dutch					
oil	1	10,146		10,146	
COOSEMANS, Alexander (1627-1689) Flemish					
oil	1	35,189		35,189	
COPE, Arthur Stockdale (1857-?) British					
oil	1	1,976		1,976	
COPE, Charles West (1811-1890) British					
oil	4	19,223	3,000	4,362	7,500
COPE, George (1855-1929) American					
oil	1	6,500		6,500	
COPELAND, Charles (1858-1945) American					
oil	1	1,200		1,200	
COPLAND, J (20th C) ?					
oil	1	1,275		1,275	

Name	No.	Total Sales Value	Prices lowest	median	highest
COPLEY (?) ?					
oil	1	4,750		4,750	
COPLEY, John Singleton (1738-1815) American					
oil	1	260,000		260,000	
COPLEY, William Nelson (1919-1996) American					
oil	6	52,174	6,256	8,124	12,621
wc/d	4	6,883	1,406	1,500	2,427
COPMANN, Peter (1794-1850) Danish					
oil	1	1,826		1,826	
COPPEDGE, Fern Isabel (1888-1951) American					
oil	6	153,700	4,200	18,250	65,000
COPPENOLLE, Edmon van (1846-1914) Belgian					
oil	5	16,339	1,063	4,108	6,000
COPPENS, Omer (1864-1926) Belgian					
oil	3	4,436	1,109	1,109	2,218
COPPI, Jacopo (1523-1591) Italian					
oil	1	26,000		26,000	
COPPINI, Fausto Eliseo (1870-1945) Italian					
oil	1	3,000		3,000	
COPPINI, Paolo (20th C) ?					
oil	1	1,400		1,400	
COPPOLA, Andrew (1941-1992) American					
3D	1	9,000		9,000	
COPPOLA-CASTALDO, Francesco (c.1845-1916) Italian					
oil	1	1,318		1,318	
COQUES, Gonzales (1614-1684) Flemish					
oil	2	51,642	6,342	25,821	45,300
CORA, H (20th C) Austrian					
oil	1	1,254		1,254	
CORA, Vladimir (20th C) Mexican					
oil	1	2,750		2,750	
CORAZZO, Alexander (1908-1971) French/American					
oil	1	3,000		3,000	
CORBELLI, Edgardo (1935-1980) Italian?					
oil	1	1,098		1,098	
CORBELLINI, Luigi (1901-1968) French					
oil	4	5,786	1,100	1,343	2,000
CORBET, Edith (fl.1891-1916) British					
oil	1	1,256		1,256	
CORBETT, Julian S (fl.1882) British					
oil	1	4,440		4,440	
CORBIERE, R de la (?) French?					
oil	1	1,240		1,240	
CORBINEAU, Charles August (1835-1901) French					
oil	1	1,866		1,866	
CORBINO, Jon (1905-1964) American					
oil	2	3,200	1,000	1,600	2,200
CORBOULD, Alfred (fl.1831-1875) British					
oil	2	23,085	5,720	11,543	17,365
CORBOULD, Aster R C (1812-1882) British					
oil	1	2,794		2,794	
CORBOULD, Edward Henry (1815-1905) British					
oil	1	21,195		21,195	
wc/d	2	7,004	2,608	3,502	4,396
CORBUSIER, le (1887-1965) French					
oil	2	177,947	18,447	88,974	159,500
wc/d	25	201,190	1,038	7,369	32,500
CORCHON DAQUIN, Jose Maria (19th C) Spanish					
oil	1	1,103		1,103	

Name	No.	Total Sales Value	lowest	Prices median	highest
CORCOS, Vittorio (1859-1933) Italian					
oil	1	22,000		22,000	
CORCY, V (19th C) ?					
oil	1	1,650		1,650	
CORDA, Mauro (1960-) French					
3D	1	2,047		2,047	
CORDEN, William (19th C) British					
oil	1	1,001		1,001	
CORDERO, Francisco (19th C) Mexican					
oil	2	3,539	1,388	1,770	2,151
CORDERO, Horacio (1945-) Spanish					
3D	1	1,548		1,548	
CORDEY, Frederic (1854-1911) French					
oil	1	1,500		1,500	
CORDIER, Charles Henri Joseph (1827-1905) French					
3D	1	8,352		8,352	
CORDINGLEY, Ricard (?) French?					
oil	1	1,746		1,746	
CORDIVIOLA, Luis Adolfo (1892-1967) Argentinian					
oil	1	4,800		4,800	
CORDONNIER, F (19/20th C) French					
oil	1	5,400		5,400	
CORDREY, John (fl.1765-1825) British					
oil	2	9,020	3,020	4,510	6,000
CORINTH, L (1858-1925) German					
wc/d	1	1,748		1,748	
CORINTH, Lovis (1858-1925) German					
oil	7	767,545	15,100	53,883	374,400
wc/d	10	98,115	1,072	3,788	57,600
CORINTIN (?) ?					
oil	1	2,368		2,368	
CORLEY, Philip (1944-) American/Irish					
oil	3	5,200	1,300	1,700	2,200
CORMON, Fernand (1854-1924) French					
oil	4	54,566	2,376	2,735	46,720
CORNEAU, Alfred (19th C) French					
3D	1	6,660		6,660	
CORNEILLE (1922-) Dutch					
3D	12	31,513	1,109	2,259	4,800
oil	8	108,407	3,571	11,184	30,172
wc/d	33	129,975	1,032	2,306	20,690
CORNEILLE DE LYON (?-1574) Flemish					
oil	2	360,150	161,700	180,075	198,450
CORNEILLE, Jean Baptiste (1649-1695) French					
oil	1	4,567		4,567	
CORNEILLE, Michel (17th C) French					
oil	1	120,000		120,000	
CORNEILLE, Michel (younger) (1642-1708) French					
oil	1	22,000		22,000	
CORNEILLE, Michel (younger-school) (1642-1708) French					
oil	1	17,000		17,000	
CORNEILLE, Pierre (1922-) French					
oil	1	21,725		21,725	
CORNELISSEN, Remy (1913-1990) Belgian					
3D	1	1,610		1,610	
CORNELISZ, Cornelis van Haarlem (1562-1638) Dutch					
oil	4	131,308	12,256	34,700	49,652
CORNELIUS, Jean Georges (1880-1963) French					
oil	1	3,169		3,169	

Name	No.	Total Sales Value	Prices lowest	median	highest
CORNELL, Joseph (1903-1972) American					
3D	8	512,200	32,000	56,100	125,000
wc/d	6	149,500	9,500	24,250	42,000
CORNIK, F (19/20th C) Austrian					
3D	1	1,600		1,600	
CORNISH, Norman (1919-) British					
oil	1	1,359		1,359	
wc/d	3	12,918	2,248	2,550	8,120
CORNOYER, Paul (1864-1923) American					
oil	7	148,700	3,400	5,000	85,000
CORNU, Jean Jean (1819-1876) French					
oil	1	3,526		3,526	
CORNU, Pierre (1895-1996) French					
oil	5	6,936	1,140	1,382	1,778
CORNU, Vital (1851-?) French					
3D	2	12,808	2,518	6,404	10,290
CORNWALL, W H (19th C) British					
oil	1	13,590		13,590	
CORNWELL, Dean (1892-1960) American					
oil	7	109,300	1,800	10,000	40,000
CORONA, Poul (1872-1945) Danish					
oil	2	2,675	1,191	1,338	1,484
CORONA, Vittorio (1901-1966) Italian					
oil	1	5,401		5,401	
wc/d	1	8,250		8,250	
CORONADO, Manuel (20th C) Spanish					
oil	2	6,591	2,900	3,296	3,691
CORONEL, Rafael (1932-) Mexican					
oil	3	37,000	6,000	14,000	17,000
COROT (1796-1875) French					
wc/d	1	29,230		29,230	
COROT, C (1850-?) French					
oil	1	1,580		1,580	
COROT, Jean Baptiste Camille (1796-1875) French					
oil	22	4,027,517	25,000	110,750	581,885
wc/d	9	275,626	1,193	8,728	196,386
CORPAATO (1950-) Swiss					
oil	1	1,516		1,516	
CORPER, M (19th C) ?					
oil	1	1,896		1,896	
CORPORA, Antonio (1909-) Italian					
oil	16	52,175	1,890	2,717	5,549
wc/d	4	8,671	1,187	2,151	3,182
CORRADI, Alfonso (1889-1972) Italian					
oil	1	3,235		3,235	
CORRADI, Konrad (1813-1878) Swiss					
wc/d	1	4,482		4,482	
CORRADINI, Antonio (1668-1752) Italian					
3D	1	27,167		27,167	
CORREDOYRA DE CASTRO, Jesus Rodriguez (1889-1939) Spanish					
oil	4	28,088	3,822	6,097	12,073
CORREGGIO (1494-1534) Italian					
oil	2	7,590	2,566	3,795	5,024
CORREGGIO, Joseph (1810-1891) German					
oil	2	3,984	1,992	1,992	1,992
CORREGGIO, Ludwig (1846-1920) German					
oil	2	3,113	1,090	1,557	2,023
CORRENS, Erich (1821-1877) German					
oil	1	1,258		1,258	

Name	No.	Total Sales Value	lowest	Prices median	highest
CORRODI, Heinrich (1762-1833) Swiss					
oil	2	3,745	1,099	1,873	2,646
CORRODI, Hermann David Salomon (1844-1905) Italian					
oil	9	164,161	2,469	14,000	52,369
CORRODI, Salomon (1810-1892) Swiss					
wc/d	5	20,709	1,884	3,586	7,865
CORSI DI BOSNASCO, Giacinto (1829-1909) Italian					
oil	1	1,115		1,115	
CORSI, Carlo (1879-1966) Italian					
oil	1	1,028		1,028	
CORSI, Nicolas de (1882-1956) Italian					
oil	7	22,704	1,845	2,285	9,481
CORT, Hendrik Frans de (1742-1810) Dutch					
oil	2	31,675	9,555	15,838	22,120
CORTAZZO, Oreste (1836-?) Italian					
oil	2	12,418	2,918	6,209	9,500
CORTE, Gabriel de la (1648-1694) Spanish					
oil	1	41,625		41,625	
CORTELLINI Y HERNANDEZ, Angel Maria (1820-1882) Spanish					
oil	1	12,073		12,073	
CORTES (?) ?					
oil	1	23,697		23,697	
CORTES Y CORDERO, Antonio (1826-1908) Spanish					
oil	1	1,358		1,358	
CORTES, A (?) ?					
oil	2	13,490	6,745	6,745	6,745
CORTES, Andre (1815-1880) Spanish					
oil	4	24,568	1,350	2,736	17,746
CORTES, Andres (1810-1879) Spanish					
oil	1	16,650		16,650	
CORTES, Antonio (19th C) Spanish					
oil	2	3,441	1,400	1,721	2,041
CORTES, E (19th C) French					
oil	3	83,740	22,120	30,020	31,600
CORTES, Edouard (1882-1969) French					
oil	55	1,505,995	4,392	25,000	85,000
wc/d	11	128,471	2,621	12,300	13,800
CORTESE, Federico (1829-1913) Italian					
oil	1	2,077		2,077	
CORTIER, Amedee (1921-1976) Belgian					
oil	3	7,726	1,253	1,253	5,220
CORTIJO, Francisco (1936-) Spanish					
oil	1	2,033		2,033	
CORTONA, Pietro da (1596-1669) Italian					
oil	1	23,550		23,550	
wc/d	1	10,570		10,570	
CORVER, J (19th C?) Dutch?					
oil	3	4,820	1,339	1,339	2,104
CORVI, Domenico (1721-1803) Italian					
oil	1	28,800		28,800	
wc/d	1	1,434		1,434	
CORYN, Celest E (20th C) American					
oil	1	18,000		18,000	
COSCHELL, Moritz (1875-?) Austrian					
oil	1	1,071		1,071	
COSENZA, Giuseppe (1847-1922) Italian					
oil	3	7,344	1,538	1,908	3,898
COSGROVE, Stanley Morel (1911-) Canadian					
oil	10	30,193	1,524	2,936	4,314

Name	No.	Total Sales Value	lowest	Prices median	highest
wc/d	3	5,015	1,083	1,950	1,982
COSOLA, Demetrio (1851-1895) Italian					
oil	2	24,769	10,978	12,385	13,791
COSSAAR, Jan (1874-1966) Dutch					
oil	1	17,701		17,701	
COSSARD, Adolphe Auguste Edouard (1880-1952) French					
oil	1	2,866		2,866	
wc/d	1	1,092		1,092	
COSSIERS, Jan (1600-1671) Flemish					
oil	1	41,626		41,626	
COSSIO, Pancho (1898-1970) Spanish					
oil	2	23,473	2,013	11,737	21,460
COSSMANN, Hermann Maurice (1821-1890) French					
oil	1	6,121		6,121	
COSSON (19/20th C) French					
oil	1	2,213		2,213	
COSSON, Marcel (1878-1956) French					
oil	38	137,140	1,474	2,967	12,634
COSTA (?) ?					
oil	1	2,750		2,750	
COSTA, Emanuele (1833-1913) French/Italian					
wc/d	3	5,212	1,038	1,077	3,097
COSTA, Giovanni (1833-1903) Italian					
oil	4	51,129	1,160	8,900	32,169
wc/d	1	1,027		1,027	
COSTA, John da (1866-1931) British					
oil	1	3,624		3,624	
COSTA, Lorenzo (1460-1535) Italian					
oil	1	18,180		18,180	
COSTA, Nino Giovanni (1826-1903) Italian					
oil	2	43,847	21,457	21,924	22,390
COSTAL, V (?) European					
oil	1	2,162		2,162	
COSTANTINI, Egidio (1912-) Italian					
3D	1	4,091		4,091	
COSTANTINI, Ernani (20th C) Italian					
oil	1	1,130		1,130	
COSTANTINI, Giuseppe (c.1843-1893) Italian					
oil	1	19,780		19,780	
COSTANZI, Placido (1690-1759) Italian					
oil	2	35,330	16,610	17,665	18,720
COSTETTI, Giovanni (1875-1949) Italian					
oil	2	19,464	6,243	9,732	13,221
COSTIGAN, John E (1888-1972) American					
oil	1	15,000		15,000	
wc/d	1	3,750		3,750	
COSTIGLIOLO, Jose P (20th C) Uruguayan					
oil	1	1,200		1,200	
COSWAY, Richard (1742-1821) British					
oil	1	15,800		15,800	
wc/d	2	11,934	5,184	5,967	6,750
COSYNS, Gies (1920-1997) Belgian					
oil	1	1,048		1,048	
COT, Pierre Auguste (1837-1883) French					
oil	1	32,500		32,500	
COTARD-DUPRE, Therese Marthe François (1877-?) French					
oil	1	12,000		12,000	
COTELLE, Jean (younger) (1642-1708) French					
oil	1	18,639		18,639	

Name	No.	Total Sales Value	lowest	Prices median	highest
COTES, Francis (1726-1770) British					
wc/d	4	23,187	3,750	6,321	6,795
COTHARIN, Kate Leah (1866-?) American					
wc/d	1	2,400		2,400	
COTMAN, J S (1782-1842) British					
wc/d	1	4,500		4,500	
COTMAN, John Joseph (1814-1878) British					
wc/d	2	2,084	1,034	1,042	1,050
COTMAN, John Sell (1782-1842) British					
oil	3	39,183	1,145	3,718	34,320
wc/d	7	35,290	1,600	2,860	12,000
COTMAN, Miles Edmund (1810-1858) British					
wc/d	2	2,922	1,422	1,461	1,500
COTT, J (19th C) British?					
oil	1	1,088		1,088	
COTTAAR, Piet (1878-1950) Dutch					
oil	1	1,657		1,657	
COTTAVOZ, Andre (1922-) French					
oil	16	29,859	1,031	1,805	2,985
COTTET, Charles (1863-1924) French					
oil	5	90,309	1,378	4,062	75,500
COTTON, John Wesley (1860-1931) Canadian					
oil	2	21,000	10,000	10,500	11,000
COTTON, William (1880-1958) American					
oil	1	4,400		4,400	
COUBINE, Othon (1883-1969) Czechoslovakian					
oil	2	10,546	4,705	5,273	5,841
COUCH, Shane (1963-) British					
oil	1	12,160		12,160	
COUDARD, Edouard Emile Elie (20th C) French					
oil	1	1,106		1,106	
COUDER, Alexandre (1808-1879) French					
oil	1	11,602		11,602	
COUDRAY, Georges Charles (fl.1883-1903) French					
3D	1	1,176		1,176	
COUGHTRY, John Graham (1931-) Canadian					
oil	1	11,283		11,283	
COULDERY, Horatio H (1832-1893) British					
oil	4	20,421	3,171	4,500	8,250
COULENTIANOS, Costas (20th C) French					
3D	1	2,951		2,951	
COULON, George (1854-1922) American					
oil	1	5,000		5,000	
COULSON, Gerald (19/20th C) British					
oil	1	1,185		1,185	
COULTER, William Alexander (1849-1936) American					
oil	4	18,900	1,900	5,500	6,000
COUMONT, Charles (1822-1889) Flemish					
oil	2	6,429	1,080	3,215	5,349
COUNHAYE, Charles (1884-1971) Belgian					
oil	1	3,105		3,105	
COUPE, Louise (1877-1915) Belgian					
oil	1	2,755		2,755	
COUR, Janus la (1837-1909) Danish					
oil	9	30,865	1,192	2,000	8,340
COURANT, Maurice (1847-1925) French					
oil	2	2,559	1,247	1,280	1,312
COURBET, Gustave (1819-1877) French					
3D	1	42,280		42,280	

Name	No.	Total Sales Value	lowest	Prices median	highest
oil	16	2,815,825	4,260	30,134	2,000,000
COURBET, Gustave and PATA, Cherubino (19th C) French					
oil	2	33,140	12,000	16,570	21,140
COURDOUAN, Vincent-Joseph-François (1810-1893) French					
oil	4	26,274	1,706	6,279	12,011
wc/d	3	7,030	2,116	2,184	2,730
COURIGER (18th C) French					
3D	1	5,316		5,316	
COURMES, Alfred (1898-1993) French					
oil	2	51,443	4,390	25,722	47,053
wc/d	1	4,829		4,829	
COURT, Franklin van (1903-) American					
oil	1	2,000		2,000	
COURT, Joseph-Desire (1797-1865) French					
oil	1	1,285		1,285	
COURTEN, Comte Angelo de (1848-1925) Italian					
oil	1	5,250		5,250	
COURTENS, Alfred (1889-1967) Belgian					
3D	1	1,160		1,160	
COURTENS, Franz (1854-1943) Belgian					
oil	17	92,630	1,006	4,807	18,053
COURTENS, Hermann (1884-1956) Belgian					
oil	3	11,655	1,531	3,904	6,220
COURTICE, Rody Kenny (1895-?) Canadian					
oil	1	1,514		1,514	
COURTIER, Prosper le (1851-1924) French					
3D	1	5,000		5,000	
COURTOIS, Jacques (1621-1676) French					
oil	3	82,740	3,000	13,590	66,150
COURTOIS, Jacques (school) (1621-1676) French					
oil	4	35,581	5,000	9,458	11,665
COUSE, E Irving (1866-1936) American					
oil	13	522,900	2,400	30,000	140,000
wc/d	1	2,600		2,600	
COUSIN, Camille (1861-1899) French					
oil	1	1,141		1,141	
COUSIN, Charles (19/20th C) French					
oil	2	2,521	1,028	1,261	1,493
COUSIN, Charles Louis Auguste (1807-1887) French					
oil	1	2,163		2,163	
COUSIN, Jean I (1490-1560) French					
wc/d	1	2,047		2,047	
COUSTOU (17/18th C) French					
3D	1	1,218		1,218	
COUSTURIER, Lucie (1876-1925) French					
oil	1	10,000		10,000	
COUTAUD, Lucien (1904-1977) French					
oil	5	10,777	1,167	1,923	3,627
wc/d	4	19,953	1,033	4,845	9,230
COUTTS, Alice Gray (1880-1973) American					
oil	1	4,750		4,750	
COUTTS, Gordon (1868-1937) British/American					
oil	5	16,150	1,900	3,000	6,000
COUTTS, Hubert (1851-1921) British					
wc/d	1	2,920		2,920	
COUTURE, Thomas (1815-1879) French					
oil	1	6,050		6,050	
wc/d	1	4,124		4,124	

Name	No.	Total Sales Value	lowest	Prices median	highest
COUTURIER, Philibert Léon (1823-1901) French					
oil	3	29,425	1,580	5,000	22,845
COUTURIER, Robert (1905-) French					
3D	2	4,239	2,112	2,120	2,127
COUTY, Jean (1907-1991) French					
oil	4	15,901	1,547	1,797	10,612
COUVEN, F W von (1786-1866) German					
oil	1	2,248		2,248	
COUVER, Jan van (1836-1909) Dutch					
oil	5	9,431	1,082	1,885	2,600
COUVERCHEL, Alfred (1834-1867) French					
oil	1	3,694		3,694	
COUWENBERG, Christiaan van (1604-1667) Dutch					
oil	1	15,100		15,100	
wc/d	1	7,528		7,528	
COVARRUBIAS, Miguel (1904-1957) Mexican					
wc/d	3	9,200	1,600	2,600	5,000
COVENTRY, Gertrude Mary (1886-1964) British					
oil	1	2,844		2,844	
COVENTRY, Keith (1958-) British					
oil	4	40,470	7,250	9,665	13,590
COVENTRY, Robert McGown (1855-1914) British					
oil	4	4,899	1,106	1,177	1,440
wc/d	1	1,580		1,580	
COWARD, Sir Noel (1899-1973) British					
oil	2	12,458	4,970	6,229	7,488
wc/d	1	4,800		4,800	
COWEN, William (1797-1860) British					
wc/d	6	9,189	1,012	1,396	2,336
COWIE, Andrew B (19th C) British					
oil	1	7,399		7,399	
COWIE, James (1886-1956) British					
wc/d	2	42,630	16,905	21,315	25,725
COWLES, Russell (1887-1979) American					
oil	1	1,300		1,300	
COWPER, Frank Cadogan (1877-1958) British					
oil	1	128,700		128,700	
COX, D (1783-1859) British					
wc/d	1	3,624		3,624	
COX, David (jnr) (1809-1885) British					
wc/d	3	9,746	1,500	3,476	4,770
COX, David (1783-1859) British					
oil	6	38,366	2,370	6,293	10,512
wc/d	36	136,673	1,106	2,591	12,750
COX, Fannie (19th C) British?					
oil	1	3,124		3,124	
COX, Garstin (1892-1933) British					
oil	2	3,450	1,200	1,725	2,250
wc/d	1	1,208		1,208	
COX, Jan (1919-1980) Belgian					
oil	1	11,389		11,389	
wc/d	1	1,186		1,186	
COX, Kenyon C (1856-1919) American					
oil	2	21,500	4,500	10,750	17,000
COX, Palmer (1840-1924) American					
wc/d	2	7,300	1,800	3,650	5,500
COYPEL, Antoine (1661-1722) French					
oil	2	18,536	5,306	9,268	13,230
wc/d	1	17,000		17,000	

Name	No.	Total Sales Value	lowest	Prices median	highest
COYPEL, Charles Antoine (1694-1752) French					
oil	3	630,000	50,000	160,000	420,000
wc/d	3	65,266	3,266	26,000	36,000
COYPEL, Noel Nicolas (1690-1734) French					
oil	1	57,380		57,380	
COYSEVOX, Antoine (1640-1720) French					
3D	3	66,118	4,000	12,469	49,649
COZENS, John Robert (1752-1799) British					
wc/d	1	36,000		36,000	
COZZARELLI, Guidoccio di Giovanni (1450-c.1516) Italian					
oil	1	75,000		75,000	
COZZENS, Frederick Schiller (1846-1928) American					
wc/d	1	3,200		3,200	
CRABB, William (1811-1876) British					
oil	1	1,185		1,185	
CRABEELS, Florent (1829-1896) Flemish					
oil	4	36,080	1,268	1,879	31,055
CRABETH, Wouter II (1593-1644) Dutch					
oil	1	8,978		8,978	
CRACO, Juan (?) ?					
3D	1	2,835		2,835	
CRADOCK, Marmaduke (1660-1717) British					
oil	2	14,603	2,592	7,302	12,011
CRAESBEECK, Joos van (1606-1654) Flemish					
oil	2	18,809	4,109	9,405	14,700
wc/d	1	1,057		1,057	
CRAEYVANGER, Gijsbertus (1810-1895) Dutch					
oil	1	2,678		2,678	
CRAFFONARA, Aurelio (1875-1945) Italian					
wc/d	1	3,790		3,790	
CRAFT, Percy R (1856-1934) British					
oil	3	4,789	1,140	1,595	2,054
CRAHAY, Albert (1881-1914) Belgian					
oil	1	1,567		1,567	
CRAIG, Charles (1846-1931) American					
oil	6	72,950	3,200	11,500	25,000
CRAIG, J H (1878-1944) Irish					
oil	3	18,055	3,140	7,065	7,850
CRAIG, J Humbert (1878-1944) Irish					
oil	25	219,772	3,190	4,608	47,360
wc/d	1	1,238		1,238	
CRAIG, James Stevenson (fl.1854-1870) British					
oil	1	4,266		4,266	
CRAIG, Thomas (19th C) ?					
oil	1	1,300		1,300	
CRAIG, Thomas Bigelow (1849-1924) American					
oil	4	8,500	1,500	2,000	3,000
CRAIG, William Marshall (fl.1788-1828) British					
wc/d	3	9,757	2,607	3,146	4,004
CRAIG-MARTIN, Michael (1941-) Irish					
oil	2	7,000	3,500	3,500	3,500
CRALI, Tullio (1910-) Italian					
oil	2	25,072	2,749	12,536	22,323
CRAMER, Helene (1844-1916) German					
oil	1	1,366		1,366	
CRAMER, Konrad (1888-1963) American					
oil	1	35,000		35,000	
CRAMER, Peter (1726-1782) Danish					
oil	1	1,134		1,134	

Name	No.	Total Sales Value	Prices lowest	median	highest
CRANACH, L (younger) (1515-1586) German					
oil	1	210,000		210,000	
CRANACH, Lucas (elder) (1472-1553) German					
oil	7	5,282,693	8,978	422,800	2,328,665
CRANCH, Christopher Pearse (1813-1892) American					
oil	1	4,250		4,250	
CRANE, Bruce (1857-1937) American					
oil	7	38,950	1,500	4,000	14,000
CRANE, Walter (1845-1915) British					
wc/d	4	44,505	3,020	5,643	30,200
CRANS, Johannes Marinus Schmidt (1830-1908) Dutch					
oil	1	3,798		3,798	
CRANSTON, Meg (20th C) American					
3D	1	1,600		1,600	
CRAPELET, Louis-Amable (1822-1867) French					
oil	1	45,430		45,430	
wc/d	1	1,038		1,038	
CRAS, Monique (1910-) French					
oil	1	4,193		4,193	
wc/d	1	1,174		1,174	
CRASH (1961-) American					
oil	1	2,073		2,073	
CRAWFORD, C (19th C) British					
oil	1	2,556		2,556	
CRAWFORD, C P (19th C) British					
oil	1	1,159		1,159	
CRAWFORD, Edmund Thornton (1806-1885) British					
oil	6	21,757	1,264	2,551	8,758
CRAWFORD, Esther Mabel (1872-1958) American					
oil	1	2,250		2,250	
CRAWFORD, J (19/20th C) British					
oil	1	1,738		1,738	
CRAWFORD, Ralston (1906-1978) American					
oil	1	24,000		24,000	
CRAWFORD, Robert C (1842-1924) British					
oil	1	1,110		1,110	
CRAWHALL, Joseph (1861-1913) British					
wc/d	1	24,090		24,090	
CRAWSHAW, Lionel Townsend (1864-1949) British					
oil	1	1,988		1,988	
CRAWSHAW, T (19th C) British?					
oil	1	3,000		3,000	
CRAXTON, John (1922-) British					
oil	1	13,965		13,965	
wc/d	6	22,295	1,501	2,139	10,010
CRAYER, Gaspar de (1584-1669) Flemish					
oil	1	37,440		37,440	
CREDICO, Robert di (20th C) French					
oil	1	4,377		4,377	
CREEFT, Jose de (1884-1982) American/Spanish					
3D	2	3,300	1,600	1,650	1,700
CREHAY, Gerard Antoine (1844-1936) Belgian					
oil	1	1,561		1,561	
CREIXAMS, Pierre (1893-1965) Spanish					
oil	15	35,092	1,045	2,026	4,501
CREMA, Giovanni Battista (1883-1964) Italian					
oil	3	49,731	3,100	7,631	39,000
CREMER, Jan (1940-) Dutch					
oil	1	1,293		1,293	

Name	No.	Total Sales Value	Prices lowest	median	highest
wc/d	1	2,155		2,155	
CREMONA, Italo (1905-) Italian					
oil	1	1,877		1,877	
CREMONESE SCHOOL, 16th C Italian					
oil	1	5,314		5,314	
CREMONESE SCHOOL, 18th C Italian					
oil	1	13,759		13,759	
CREMONESE, Antonio (1947-) Italian					
oil	1	1,262		1,262	
CREMONINI, Leonardo (1925-) Italian					
oil	4	58,759	2,898	16,329	23,203
CREPIN, Joseph (20th C) French					
oil	1	7,739		7,739	
CREPIN, Louis Philippe (1772-1851) French					
oil	2	5,276	2,596	2,638	2,680
CRESPELLE, Emile (1831-) French					
oil	1	11,496		11,496	
CRESPI, Daniele (1590-1630) Italian					
wc/d	1	5,285		5,285	
CRESPI, Giuseppe Maria (1665-1747) Italian					
oil	5	625,195	3,419	33,220	453,000
wc/d	1	5,065		5,065	
CRESPO RIVERA, Tomas (1932-) Spanish					
3D	1	1,479		1,479	
CRESTI, Domenico (1558-1638) Italian					
wc/d	2	5,500	1,000	2,750	4,500
CRESTY, Marguerite (1841-?) French					
oil	1	7,500		7,500	
CRESWICK, Thomas (1811-1869) British					
oil	11	76,770	1,034	4,205	21,000
CRETAN SCHOOL, 16th C					
oil	1	3,709		3,709	
CRETAN-VENETIAN SCHOOL, 16th C					
oil	1	5,005		5,005	
CRETEN-GEORGES (1887-1966) Belgian					
oil	2	2,870	1,015	1,435	1,855
CRETI, Donato (1671-1749) Italian					
wc/d	3	5,046	1,058	1,519	2,469
CREVEL, René (20th C) French					
oil	1	2,980		2,980	
CREVILLE (18th C) French					
oil	1	1,355		1,355	
CRIDLAND, Helen (fl.1886-1909) British					
oil	1	17,000		17,000	
CRILEY, Theodore Morrow (1880-1930) American					
oil	1	6,000		6,000	
CRIPA, Roberto (1921-1972) Italian					
oil	1	7,038		7,038	
CRIPPA, Roberto (1921-1972) Italian					
oil	19	65,797	1,068	3,381	6,932
wc/d	25	91,549	1,408	3,017	10,254
CRISCONIO, Luigi (1893-1946) Italian					
oil	1	1,861		1,861	
CRISS, Francis (1901-1973) American					
oil	1	2,500		2,500	
wc/d	1	4,000		4,000	
CRISTALL, Joshua (1767-1847) British					
wc/d	2	3,641	1,113	1,821	2,528

Name	No.	Total Sales Value	lowest	Prices median	highest
CRIVELLI, Angelo Maria (17/18th C) Italian					
oil	1	22,050		22,050	
CRIVELLI, Giovanni (?-1760) Italian					
oil	2	32,000	16,000	16,000	16,000
CROAK, James (20th C) American?					
3D	1	1,595		1,595	
CROATTO, Bruno (1875-1945) Italian					
oil	1	1,908		1,908	
CROCE, Achille della (19th C) Italian					
3D	1	3,454		3,454	
CROCE, Johann Nepomuk della (1736-1819) Austrian					
oil	1	2,955		2,955	
CROCETTI, Venanzo (1913-) Italian					
3D	1	11,092		11,092	
CROCICCHI, Luca (1958-) Italian					
oil	2	4,628	2,155	2,314	2,473
CROCKER, Charles Matthew (1877-1950) American					
oil	1	1,500		1,500	
CROCKER, W H (20th C) American					
oil	1	1,000		1,000	
CROCKFORD, Duncan (1920-1991) Canadian					
oil	3	6,862	1,110	1,698	4,054
CRODEL, Charles (1894-1973) French					
oil	1	1,634		1,634	
CRODEL, Paul Eduard (1862-1928) German					
oil	1	2,697		2,697	
CROEGAERT, Georges (1848-1923) Belgian					
oil	7	155,030	2,862	13,590	72,500
CROFT, Arthur (1828-?) British					
wc/d	1	1,440		1,440	
CROFT, Marianne Dalton (fl.1804-1814) British					
oil	1	3,450		3,450	
CROFTS, Ernest (1847-1911) British					
oil	3	21,164	4,500	5,254	11,410
CROIN, Joseph (1894-1949) Dutch					
oil	3	4,838	1,093	1,652	2,093
CROISSANT, Michael (1928-) German					
3D	2	11,172	4,916	5,586	6,256
CROLA, Georg Heinrich (1804-1879) German					
oil	1	2,594		2,594	
CROME, John (1768-1821) British					
oil	1	1,305		1,305	
CROME, John Berney (1794-1842) British					
oil	3	8,048	1,088	3,335	3,625
CROME, William Henry (1806-1873) British					
oil	2	5,095	1,981	2,548	3,114
CROMPTON, James Shaw (1853-1916) British					
wc/d	1	1,024		1,024	
CROMWELL, Joane (1889-1966) American					
oil	2	6,800	1,300	3,400	5,500
CRONE, Robert (c.1718-1779) Irish					
oil	1	12,780		12,780	
CRONQVIST, Lena (1938-) Swedish					
3D	2	7,207	1,856	3,604	5,351
oil	7	32,554	2,176	3,440	10,597
CROOK, Pamela Jane (1945-) British					
oil	1	8,690		8,690	
CROOKS, Ron (1925-) American					
oil	1	1,200		1,200	

Name	No.	Total Sales Value	lowest	Prices median	highest
CROOS, Anthony Jansz van der (1606-1662) Dutch					
oil	3	24,120	1,500	11,131	11,489
CROOS, Jacob van der (17th C) Dutch					
oil	1	5,082		5,082	
CROOS, Pieter van der (1610-1677) Dutch					
oil	1	3,953		3,953	
CROPSEY, Jasper Francis (1823-1900) American					
oil	13	818,500	16,000	40,000	150,000
wc/d	9	88,500	3,000	7,000	28,000
CROS, Charles (1842-1888) French					
wc/d	1	6,055		6,055	
CROSBIE, William (1915-1999) British					
oil	5	23,193	2,920	4,557	6,525
wc/d	2	5,986	2,774	2,993	3,212
CROSIO, Luigi (1835-1915) Italian					
oil	2	19,122	6,896	9,561	12,226
CROSS, Henri Edmond (1856-1910) French					
oil	8	1,955,233	1,038	144,275	550,000
wc/d	6	70,096	1,069	3,786	48,000
CROSS, Henry H (1837-1918) American					
oil	3	5,400	1,700	1,700	2,000
CROSSE, Malcolm (20th C) British					
wc/d	1	1,065		1,065	
CROSSLAND, James Henry (1852-1939) British					
oil	3	8,503	1,950	3,003	3,550
CROTTI, Jean (1878-1958) French					
oil	3	14,765	3,537	5,444	5,784
wc/d	2	4,260	1,222	2,130	3,038
CROTTY, Thomas (20th C) American					
wc/d	1	1,200		1,200	
CROUCH, William (fl.1817-1850) British					
wc/d	2	2,508	1,073	1,254	1,435
CROWE, Victoria (1945-) British					
oil	1	2,736		2,736	
wc/d	1	2,736		2,736	
CROWELL, Tom (20th C) British					
oil	1	1,347		1,347	
CROWLEY, Donald (20th C) American					
oil	1	32,500		32,500	
CROWN PRINCESS MARGARETA (1851-1920) Swedish					
oil	1	1,524		1,524	
CROWTHER, Henry (19/20th C) British?					
oil	1	2,800		2,800	
CROXFORD, Agnes McIntyre (19th C) British					
oil	1	2,212		2,212	
CROZIER, William (1930-) British					
oil	6	12,046	1,050	1,773	3,454
wc/d	3	10,361	1,185	3,848	5,328
CRUICKSHANK, William (1848-1922) British					
wc/d	3	5,599	1,316	1,963	2,320
CRUIKSHANK, George (1792-1878) British					
wc/d	1	1,875		1,875	
CRUISE, Boyd (1909-1988) American					
wc/d	3	16,500	4,000	4,250	8,250
CRUST, Theobald (19th C) German?					
oil	1	1,420		1,420	
CRUZ HERRERA, Jose Herrerilla (1890-1972) Spanish					
oil	4	100,681	1,911	4,276	90,219
CRUZ-DIEZ, Carlos (1923-) Venezuelan					
oil	4	22,430	2,500	5,860	8,210

Name	No.	Total Sales Value	lowest	Prices median	highest
wc/d	1	4,142		4,142	
CSAKY (20th C) French/Hungarian					
3D	1	4,537		4,537	
CSAKY, Josef (1888-1971) French/Hungarian					
3D	8	39,812	2,139	4,300	7,956
wc/d	4	5,685	1,197	1,496	1,496
CSOK, Istvan (1865-1961) Hungarian					
oil	1	1,760		1,760	
CSOKA, L (20th C) Hungarian					
oil	1	2,370		2,370	
CSUZY, Karoly (19th C) ?					
oil	1	12,578		12,578	
CUARTIELLES, R (19th C) Spanish					
oil	1	1,688		1,688	
CUBELLS Y RUIZ, Enrique Martinez (1874-1947) Spanish					
oil	13	372,421	2,220	23,154	106,631
CUBELLS, Salvador Martinez (1845-1914) Spanish					
oil	3	45,117	5,800	13,928	25,389
CUBLEY, Henry Hadfield (fl.1882-1904) British					
oil	2	3,406	1,208	1,703	2,198
CUCCHI, Enzo (1949-) Italian					
oil	3	121,134	32,500	45,000	45,000
wc/d	4	31,195	1,901	3,322	22,650
CUCUEL, Edward (1875-1951) American					
oil	17	655,890	2,000	24,828	150,000
CUDENNEC, Patrice (20th C) French					
oil	1	1,218		1,218	
CUECO, Henri (1929-) French?					
wc/d	1	2,006		2,006	
CUENI, August (1883-1966) Swiss					
oil	1	1,719		1,719	
CUEVAS, Jose Luis (1934-) Mexican					
3D	1	3,000		3,000	
CUEVAS, Raymond (1932-) American					
oil	1	2,500		2,500	
CUEVAS, Telesforo (1850-1933) Spanish					
wc/d	1	2,346		2,346	
CUGUEN, Victor Louis (1882-) French					
oil	1	1,800		1,800	
CUILLOT, R (19th C) French					
oil	1	1,736		1,736	
CUIRBLANC, Berthe (fl.1868-1874) French					
oil	1	4,238		4,238	
CUITT, George (18/19th C) British					
oil	1	2,370		2,370	
CUITT, George (elder) (1743-1818) British					
oil	2	37,160	1,410	18,580	35,750
CUIXART, Modest (1925-) Spanish					
oil	2	45,646	2,146	22,823	43,500
wc/d	1	3,771		3,771	
CULL, Alma Burlton (fl.1906-1927) British					
wc/d	2	7,466	2,250	3,733	5,216
CULLBERG, Erland (1931-) Swedish					
oil	7	8,974	1,066	1,201	1,624
CULLEN, Maurice Galbraith (1866-1934) Canadian					
oil	6	158,188	3,186	15,344	92,915
CULLIN, Isaac (fl.1881-1920) British					
oil	2	43,115	1,675	21,558	41,440

Name	No.	Total Sales Value	lowest	Prices median	highest
CULVER, Charles (1908-1967) American					
wc/d	2	3,500	1,000	1,750	2,500
CULVERHOUSE, J M (1820-1892) Dutch					
oil	1	3,732		3,732	
CULVERHOUSE, Johann Mongels (1820-1892) Dutch					
oil	4	59,008	1,444	13,782	30,000
CUMBERWORTH, Charles (1811-1852) French					
3D	1	1,615		1,615	
CUMBO, Ettore (1833-?) Italian					
oil	6	29,442	1,331	4,630	8,428
CUMING, Frederick G R (1930-) British					
oil	12	25,629	1,026	1,481	6,300
CUMMING, James (1922-1991) British					
oil	2	4,178	1,898	2,089	2,280
CUMMINGS, E E (19/20th C) British?					
oil	3	4,800	1,300	1,500	2,000
CUNAEUS, Conradyn (1828-1895) Dutch					
oil	3	21,315	4,526	6,789	10,000
wc/d	1	1,291		1,291	
CUNDALL, Charles (1890-1971) British					
oil	5	26,150	1,692	1,846	14,800
CUNEO, Cyrus (1878-1916) American/British					
oil	1	26,000		26,000	
CUNEO, Jose (1887-1977) Uruguayan					
oil	4	19,100	3,500	3,800	8,000
CUNEO, Rinaldo (1877-1935) American					
oil	2	13,000	1,000	6,500	12,000
CUNEO, Terence (1907-1996) British					
oil	10	145,363	1,170	4,001	79,000
CUNHA, Hector da (1915-1996) Spanish/Uruguayan					
wc/d	1	3,226		3,226	
CUNNINGHAM, Earl (1893-1977) American					
oil	1	2,750		2,750	
CUNNINGHAM, John (1926-1999) British					
oil	4	29,935	6,525	7,325	8,760
CUNNINGHAM, William (?) British?					
wc/d	1	1,716		1,716	
CUNZ, Martha (1876-?) Swiss					
oil	2	3,124	1,474	1,562	1,650
CUPRIEN, Frank W (1871-1948) American					
oil	7	62,700	1,000	2,800	35,000
CURDON, Claude (?) ?					
oil	1	4,401		4,401	
CURNOCK, J J (1839-1891) British					
wc/d	1	3,339		3,339	
CURNOCK, James (1812-1862) British					
oil	2	2,633	1,284	1,317	1,349
CURNOCK, James Jackson (1839-1891) British					
wc/d	1	1,050		1,050	
CURNOE, Greg (1936-) Canadian					
wc/d	1	1,593		1,593	
CURRADI, Francesco (1570-1661) Italian					
oil	2	24,654	6,632	12,327	18,022
CURRAN, Charles Courtney (1861-1942) American					
oil	10	424,000	3,000	21,000	180,000
wc/d	2	38,600	6,600	19,300	32,000
CURRIE, Claude (?) ?					
oil	1	1,428		1,428	

Name	No.	Total Sales Value	lowest	Prices median	highest
CURRIE, Sidney (fl.1892-1930) British					
oil	1	1,617		1,617	
CURRIER, J Frank (1843-1909) American					
wc/d	1	1,900		1,900	
CURRIN, John (1962-) American					
oil	5	420,900	45,300	85,000	130,000
wc/d	4	87,500	6,500	13,000	55,000
CURRY, Robert F (1872-1945) American					
oil	4	5,118	1,090	1,197	1,634
CURSARO, Enzo (1953-) Italian					
oil	1	5,647		5,647	
CURSITER, Stanley (1887-1976) British					
oil	9	115,848	1,350	7,350	43,500
wc/d	3	27,447	1,397	5,510	20,540
CURTER, J (20th C) ?					
oil	1	1,272		1,272	
CURTIS, David (20th C) American					
oil	1	1,378		1,378	
CURTIS, George (1816-?) American					
oil	2	114,500	4,500	57,250	110,000
CURTIS, Leland (1897-?) American					
oil	1	7,000		7,000	
wc/d	1	1,200		1,200	
CURTY, Joseph Emmanuel (1750-1813) Swiss					
wc/d	1	5,127		5,127	
CURZON, Paul Alfred de (1820-1895) French					
oil	1	1,855		1,855	
CUSACHS Y CUSACHS, Jose (1851-1908) Spanish					
oil	4	469,881	28,881	104,250	232,500
wc/d	1	2,178		2,178	
CUST, Arthur (1840-1911) British					
wc/d	1	15,015		15,015	
CUSTIS, Eleanor Parke (1897-1983) American					
wc/d	1	2,600		2,600	
CUTLER, Carl Gordon (1873-1945) American					
oil	2	6,000	3,000	3,000	3,000
CUTLER, Charles Gordon (1914-) American					
3D	1	2,100		2,100	
CUTSEM, van (20th C) Belgian					
3D	1	1,395		1,395	
CUYLENBORCH, Abraham van (1620-1658) Dutch					
oil	2	9,589	2,182	4,795	7,407
CUYP, Aelbert (1620-1691) Dutch					
oil	1	21,779		21,779	
CUYP, Aelbert (school) (1620-1691) Dutch					
oil	1	3,200		3,200	
CUYP, Benjamin Gerritsz (1612-1652) Dutch					
oil	4	38,639	6,564	8,857	14,361
CUYP, Jacob Gerritsz (1594-1651) Dutch					
oil	2	12,163	5,989	6,082	6,174
CUZCO SCHOOL, 18th C South American					
oil	2	10,862	2,862	5,431	8,000
CUZNETZOTT, A (19th C) ?					
oil	1	1,140		1,140	
CYETNH (20th C) Russian					
oil	1	1,472		1,472	
CYR, Georges (1880-1964) French					
oil	1	7,075		7,075	

Name	No.	Total Sales Value	Prices lowest	median	highest
CZACHORSKI, Ladislaus von (1850-1911) Polish					
oil	1	137,731		137,731	
CZECH, Emil (1862-1929) Austrian					
oil	2	3,300	1,600	1,650	1,700
CZERMAK, Jaroslav (1831-1878) Czechoslovakian					
oil	1	2,500		2,500	
CZERNOTZKY, Ernst (1869-1939) Austrian					
oil	1	2,000		2,000	
CZERNY, Ludwig (1821-1889) Austrian					
oil	1	1,200		1,200	
CZOBEL, Bela (1883-1974) Hungarian					
oil	1	1,771		1,771	
CZOK, Maria (1947-) Lebanese					
oil	1	2,025		2,025	
DA, Tony (?) American					
wc/d	1	4,750		4,750	
DAALHOFF, Hermanus Antonius van (1867-1953) Dutch					
oil	1	2,334		2,334	
DABHOLKAR, R P (?) Indian?					
wc/d	1	2,400		2,400	
DABO, Leon (1868-1960) American					
oil	6	37,600	2,100	4,125	18,000
DABRA, F L (19/20th C) German					
oil	1	2,567		2,567	
DABREU, J (?) French?					
oil	1	1,253		1,253	
DACK, F van den (?) ?					
oil	1	2,292		2,292	
DADAMAINO (1935-) Italian					
3D	1	4,145		4,145	
wc/d	1	3,139		3,139	
DADD, Frank (1851-1929) British					
wc/d	2	5,058	2,355	2,529	2,703
DADE, Ernest (1864-1935) British					
wc/d	6	20,917	2,041	2,908	5,966
DADO, Miodrag Djuric (1933-) Yugoslavian					
oil	9	44,238	2,037	3,666	10,919
wc/d	1	2,268		2,268	
DAEL, Jan Frans van (1764-1840) Dutch					
oil	3	1,144,972	210,681	330,000	604,291
DAELE, Casimir van den (1818-1880) Belgian					
oil	2	4,838	1,429	2,419	3,409
DAELEMANS, F (?) ?					
oil	1	1,006		1,006	
DAENS, Antoine (20th C) Belgian					
oil	2	2,134	1,012	1,067	1,122
DAENS, S (17th C) Flemish					
oil	1	7,867		7,867	
DAEPP, Arnold Hans (1886-1949) Swiss					
oil	1	1,166		1,166	
DAEYE, Hippolyte (1873-1952) Belgian					
oil	2	11,033	1,629	5,517	9,404
D'AGAR, Jacob (1642-1715) French					
oil	2	3,029	1,480	1,515	1,549
DAGGY, Augustus Smith (1858-1942) American					
oil	1	1,100		1,100	
DAGNAC-RIVIERE, Charles (1864-1945) French					
oil	4	7,656	1,460	1,809	2,578

Name	No.	Total Sales Value	lowest	Prices median	highest
DAGNAN, Isidore (1794-1873) French					
oil	5	21,987	1,956	3,894	6,846
DAGNAN-BOUVERET (1852-1929) French					
wc/d	1	1,220		1,220	
DAGNAUX, Albert Marie (1861-1933) French					
oil	1	15,000		15,000	
DAGNEAU, Henry (19th C) French					
oil	1	6,300		6,300	
DAHL, Hans (1849-1937) Norwegian					
oil	8	107,840	2,285	12,612	31,049
DAHL, Hans Andreas (1881-1919) Norwegian					
oil	1	8,838		8,838	
DAHL, J (1825-1890) Danish					
oil	1	1,392		1,392	
DAHL, Johan Christian Clausen (1788-1857) Norwegian					
oil	3	133,347	9,876	46,215	77,256
DAHL, Johan Vilhelm Ludvig (1818-1885) Danish					
oil	1	4,060		4,060	
DAHL, Michael (1656-1743) Swedish					
oil	3	48,772	6,342	18,120	24,310
DAHL, Peter (1934-) Swedish/Norwegian					
3D	1	1,209		1,209	
oil	11	164,631	1,310	4,805	100,351
wc/d	1	1,407		1,407	
DAHL, Sigwald Johannes (1827-1902) Norwegian					
oil	3	11,563	1,524	2,348	7,691
DAHLEN, F von (19th C) ?					
oil	1	1,162		1,162	
DAHLEN, Reiner (1836-1874) German					
oil	1	1,609		1,609	
DAHLGREEN, Charles W (1864-1955) American					
oil	1	3,750		3,750	
DAHLSKOG, Evald (1894-1950) Swedish					
oil	2	4,853	1,240	2,427	3,613
DAHM, Helen (1878-1968) Swiss					
oil	1	2,849		2,849	
wc/d	1	3,831		3,831	
DAHMEN, Karl-Fred (1917-1981) German					
3D	4	9,246	1,349	2,223	3,452
wc/d	6	17,056	1,349	2,544	4,323
DAHN, Walter (1954-) German					
oil	4	24,271	3,883	6,553	7,282
wc/d	1	9,709		9,709	
DAHN-FRIES, Sophie (1835-1898) German					
oil	1	7,360		7,360	
DAILLION (19th C) French					
3D	1	1,444		1,444	
DAILLION, Horace (1854-1937) French					
3D	1	1,150		1,150	
DAINGERFIELD, Elliott (1859-1932) American					
oil	1	6,250		6,250	
DAINI, Augusto (1860-1920) Italian					
oil	1	5,217		5,217	
DAINTREY, Adrian (1902-1988) British					
oil	2	2,968	1,230	1,484	1,738
DAIWAILLE, A J and VERBOECKHOVEN, E (19th C) Dutch/Belgian					
oil	1	6,864		6,864	
DAJOU (19th C) French					
oil	1	3,504		3,504	

Name	No.	Total Sales Value	lowest	Prices median	highest
DAKON, S T (20th C) Austrian?					
3D	1	2,703		2,703	
DALBE (18th C) ?					
wc/d	1	4,251		4,251	
DALBERT, Yolande (19th/20th C) French					
oil	1	2,119		2,119	
DALBONO, Eduardo (1843-1915) Italian					
oil	2	7,868	1,868	3,934	6,000
wc/d	3	6,973	1,240	2,293	3,440
DALBY OF YORK, David (1794-1836) British					
oil	1	10,725		10,725	
DALBY, John (fl.1826-1853) British					
oil	4	87,764	6,660	21,312	38,480
DALEN, Patricia van (1955-) Venezuelan					
oil	1	1,830		1,830	
DALENS, Dirk (elder) (1600-1676) Dutch					
oil	1	6,552		6,552	
DALENS, Dirk II (1659-1688) Dutch					
oil	1	36,240		36,240	
DALGAS, Carlo (1820-1851) Danish					
oil	3	14,055	3,574	4,766	5,715
D'ALHEIM, Duenes (19/20th C) French?					
oil	1	3,813		3,813	
D'ALHEIM, Jean (1840-1894) Russian					
oil	1	2,400		2,400	
DALI, Salvador (1904-1989) Spanish					
3D	72	1,591,442	1,031	2,273	700,000
oil	10	7,778,323	66,440	260,942	3,770,000
wc/d	37	904,175	1,354	10,632	159,500
DALL, Hans (1862-1920) Danish					
oil	1	2,502		2,502	
DALLAIRE, Jean Philippe (1916-1965) Canadian					
oil	2	19,825	7,300	9,913	12,525
wc/d	6	23,304	2,005	4,273	4,677
DALLEVES, Raphy (1878-1940) Swiss					
wc/d	2	12,638	2,915	6,319	9,723
DALLIN, Cyrus Edwin (1861-1944) American					
3D	2	30,750	2,750	15,375	28,000
DALLINGER VON DALLING, Alexander Johann (1783-1844) Austrian					
oil	2	5,696	1,709	2,848	3,987
DALL'OCA BIANCA, Angelo (1858-1942) Italian					
oil	4	37,399	1,848	11,231	13,090
DALMATIAN SCHOOL, 17th C European					
oil	1	7,644		7,644	
DALOU (19th C) French					
3D	1	2,423		2,423	
DALOU, Aime Jules (1838-1902) French					
3D	29	163,038	1,056	1,861	40,770
DALPAYRAT, Pierre Adrien (1844-?) French					
3D	1	2,406		2,406	
DALSGAARD, Christen (1824-1907) Danish					
oil	1	2,118		2,118	
DALSGAARD, Sven (1914-1999) Danish					
3D	1	2,840		2,840	
oil	5	10,352	1,220	1,666	4,013
wc/d	2	2,254	1,030	1,127	1,224
DALVIT, Oskar (1911-1975) Swiss					
oil	1	3,242		3,242	
DALY, Kathleen (1898-1995) Canadian					
oil	5	21,258	1,195	2,821	11,283

Name	No.	Total Sales Value	lowest	Prices median	highest
wc/d	2	3,318	1,493	1,659	1,825
DALY, Thomas Aquinas (20th C) American					
wc/d	1	3,750		3,750	
DAM VAN ISSELT, Lucie van (1871-1949) Dutch					
oil	2	4,457	1,967	2,229	2,490
DAM, Willem van (1895-1964) Dutch					
oil	1	1,664		1,664	
DAMART, Henriette (19/20th C) French					
oil	1	1,102		1,102	
D'AMATI, Cadducini (?) Italian					
wc/d	1	1,192		1,192	
D'AMBEL, P (?) French?					
oil	1	1,933		1,933	
DAMBERG, Alexander Konstantinovitch (1843-?) Finnish					
oil	1	1,366		1,366	
DAMBEZA, Léon (1865-?) French					
oil	1	1,200		1,200	
D'AMBROSI, Jasper (1926-1985) American					
3D	1	1,200		1,200	
DAMERON, Émile Charles (1848-1908) French					
oil	1	1,019		1,019	
DAMIANI, Jorge (1931-) Italian					
oil	2	3,200	1,000	1,600	2,200
wc/d	1	1,900		1,900	
DAMIANO, Bernard (20th C) ?					
oil	1	1,082		1,082	
DAMM, Johan Frederik (1820-1894) Danish					
oil	1	7,744		7,744	
DAMMAN, Hans (1867-1942) German					
3D	1	1,463		1,463	
DAMMAN, Y (19th C) Belgian					
oil	1	1,150		1,150	
DAMME, Frans van (1858-1925) Belgian					
oil	4	9,949	1,102	1,993	4,862
DAMME-SYLVA, Émile van (1853-1935) Belgian					
oil	3	5,817	1,412	1,561	2,844
DAMOISELET, Florentin and HUILLIOT, Claude (17th C) French					
oil	1	33,000		33,000	
DAMOYE, Pierre Emmanuel (1847-1916) French					
oil	17	88,215	1,775	3,987	9,532
DAMSCHROEDER, Jan Jac Matthys (1825-1905) German					
oil	1	2,285		2,285	
DANBY, Francis (1793-1861) British					
oil	1	3,376		3,376	
DANBY, J G (19th C) British					
oil	1	1,200		1,200	
DANBY, James Francis (1816-1875) British					
oil	4	35,382	3,218	9,082	14,000
DANBY, Ken (1940-) Canadian					
oil	1	2,742		2,742	
wc/d	4	8,902	1,599	1,974	3,356
DANBY, Thomas (1818-1886) British					
oil	1	4,434		4,434	
DANCE, Nathaniel (1734-1811) British					
oil	1	2,800		2,800	
D'ANCONA, Edward (20th C) American					
oil	1	6,500		6,500	
D'ANCONA, Vito (1825-1884) Italian					
oil	1	19,871		19,871	

Name	No.	Total Sales Value	lowest	Prices median	highest
DANDINI, Cesare (1595-1658) Italian					
oil	2	714,171	34,671	357,086	679,500
DANDINI, Pietro (1646-1712) Italian					
wc/d	1	5,000		5,000	
DANDOY, Jan Baptist (17th C) Belgian					
oil	1	14,519		14,519	
DANDRE BARDON, Michel (1700-1778) French					
wc/d	2	22,310	2,191	11,155	20,119
DANEKES, Andreas (1788-1855) Dutch					
oil	1	2,546		2,546	
DANGER, Henri (1857-1937) French					
oil	1	10,000		10,000	
DANIELI, Giovanni (1824-1890) Italian					
oil	1	2,403		2,403	
DANIELL, Thomas (1749-1840) British					
oil	1	11,440		11,440	
DANIELL, Thomas and William (18th C) British					
wc/d	2	5,574	2,574	2,787	3,000
DANIELL, William (1769-1837) British					
oil	3	89,340	5,148	5,148	78,650
wc/d	5	17,577	1,287	2,574	6,000
DANIELS, A (1580-?) Flemish					
oil	1	5,100		5,100	
DANIELS, Alfred (1924-) British					
oil	1	2,250		2,250	
DANIELS, George Fisher (1821-?) American					
oil	1	30,000		30,000	
DANIELS, René (1950-) Dutch					
oil	1	40,948		40,948	
DANIELS, William (1813-1880) British					
oil	1	5,285		5,285	
DANIELSEN, Jakob (1888-1938) Danish					
wc/d	1	1,743		1,743	
DANIELSON-GAMBOGI, Elin (1861-1919) Finnish					
oil	1	3,813		3,813	
DANIELSZ, Hendrick (17th C) Flemish					
oil	1	12,131		12,131	
DANIOTH, Heinrich (1896-1953) German					
oil	2	10,098	4,325	5,049	5,773
DANISH SCHOOL, 18th C					
oil	1	3,356		3,356	
DANISH SCHOOL, 19th C					
oil	5	33,753	2,740	5,686	15,320
DANISH SCHOOL, 19th/20th C					
oil	1	6,381		6,381	
DANKMEYER, Carel Bernardus (1861-1923) Dutch					
oil	2	2,926	1,291	1,463	1,635
DANLOUX, Henri Pierre (1753-1809) French					
oil	4	37,303	8,616	9,344	10,022
wc/d	1	5,738		5,738	
DANNHAUSER, Johan Eduard (1869-?) German					
3D	1	1,288		1,288	
DANS, Maria Antonia (1932-1988) Spanish					
oil	3	8,319	1,379	3,087	3,853
wc/d	7	9,766	1,013	1,553	1,977
DANSAERT, Léon (1830-1909) Belgian					
oil	5	37,240	2,135	3,833	15,730
DANTAN, Edouard Joseph (1848-1897) French					
oil	3	12,564	1,713	1,713	9,138

Name	No.	Total Sales Value	lowest	Prices median	highest
DANTI, Gino (1881-1968) Italian					
oil	1	2,448		2,448	
DANTI, Ignazio (1536-1586) Italian					
oil	1	162,465		162,465	
DANTI, Vincenzo (1530-1576) Italian					
3D	1	9,339		9,339	
DANTU, Georges (19/20th C) French					
oil	1	1,168		1,168	
DANTZIG, Rachel Margaretha van (1878-1949) Dutch					
3D	1	1,717		1,717	
DANUBE SCHOOL, 15th C European					
oil	1	42,280		42,280	
DANUBE SCHOOL, 16th C European					
oil	1	8,305		8,305	
DANZIGER, Itzhak (1916-1977) Israeli					
wc/d	2	4,100	1,600	2,050	2,500
DARANIYAGALA, Justin Pieris (1903-1967) Sri Lankan					
oil	1	4,500		4,500	
wc/d	1	3,300		3,300	
DARBANVILLE, Marie (?) ?					
wc/d	1	1,021		1,021	
DARBOUR, Marguerite Mary (19/20th C) French					
oil	1	2,967		2,967	
DARDEL, Ingrid von (1922-1962) Swedish					
wc/d	1	3,265		3,265	
DARDEL, Nils (1888-1943) Swedish					
oil	2	68,378	5,659	34,189	62,719
wc/d	4	7,440	1,005	1,789	2,857
DAREY, Louis (1863-1914) French					
oil	1	1,573		1,573	
DARGELAS, Andre Henri (1828-1906) French					
oil	4	57,348	9,068	11,500	25,280
DARGENT, Edouard van (1824-1889) French					
oil	1	6,613		6,613	
DARGIE, Sir William (1912-) Australian					
oil	1	1,125		1,125	
DARGOUGE, Georges Edmond (1897-) French					
oil	1	4,874		4,874	
D'ARIENZO, Miguel A (1950-) Argentinian					
oil	1	19,000		19,000	
DARLEY, Felix O C (1822-1888) American					
wc/d	1	3,000		3,000	
DARLING, Louis (1916-1970) American					
oil	1	9,000		9,000	
DARLING, William (1856-1933) American					
oil	2	10,000	2,500	5,000	7,500
DARNAUT, Hugo (1851-1937) Austrian					
oil	2	47,648	22,727	23,824	24,921
DARNEL, Jacques (20th C) French					
oil	1	1,392		1,392	
DARPY, Lucien Gilbert (1875-?) French					
wc/d	1	3,951		3,951	
DARROW, Whitney (jnr) (1909-) American					
wc/d	2	3,400	1,500	1,700	1,900
DARRU, Louise (19th C) French					
oil	1	7,387		7,387	
DARSTAD, V (19/20th C) ?					
oil	1	1,700		1,700	

Name	No.	Total Sales Value	lowest	Prices median	highest
D'ARTHOIS, Jacques (1613-1686) Flemish					
oil	3	17,699	4,469	5,145	8,085
DARTNELL, George Russell (19th C) British					
wc/d	1	1,128		1,128	
DARVASSY, V (19th C) ?					
oil	1	1,590		1,590	
DAS, Arup (1927-) Indian					
oil	1	2,600		2,600	
DASBURG, Andrew (1887-1979) American					
wc/d	3	57,000	12,000	20,000	25,000
D'ASCANIO, Corradino (1891-1981) Italian					
3D	1	8,990		8,990	
DASGUPTA, Dharmanarayan (1939-) Indian					
oil	1	1,200		1,200	
DASSELBORNE, Lucien (1873-1952) Belgian					
oil	2	5,240	2,540	2,620	2,700
D'ASSIA, Enrico (20th C) ?					
wc/d	1	1,551		1,551	
D'ASTE, J (20th C) French					
3D	1	3,105		3,105	
D'ASTE, Joseph (20th C) Italian					
3D	3	4,789	1,210	1,220	2,359
D'ASTINIERES, Comte Eugène Nicolas (1841-1918) French					
3D	1	4,250		4,250	
DASTUGUE, Maxime (19th C) French					
oil	1	1,138		1,138	
DATAS, Alberto (20th C) Spanish					
oil	3	6,911	1,721	2,076	3,114
DATSENKO, Lidya (1946-) Russian					
oil	1	1,275		1,275	
DAUBIGNY, Charles François (1817-1878) French					
oil	15	261,703	1,188	11,476	50,000
wc/d	2	4,691	1,891	2,346	2,800
DAUBIGNY, Karl (1846-1886) French					
oil	14	54,141	1,185	2,798	8,000
wc/d	1	4,510		4,510	
DAUCHEZ, Andre (1870-1943) French					
oil	3	6,580	1,276	1,354	3,950
wc/d	1	2,678		2,678	
DAUDELIN, Charles (1920-) Canadian					
oil	1	3,304		3,304	
DAUGHERTY, James (1889-1974) American					
wc/d	2	6,400	2,400	3,200	4,000
DAUGHTERS, Robert (1929-) American					
oil	2	11,500	5,000	5,750	6,500
DAUMIER, H (1808-1879) French					
3D	1	1,223		1,223	
DAUMIER, Honore (1808-1879) French					
3D	10	159,270	5,017	7,254	98,150
wc/d	8	202,630	1,500	8,933	116,377
DAUMILLER, Gustav Adolf (1876-?) German					
3D	1	1,424		1,424	
DAUPHIN, Eugène Baptiste Emile (1857-1930) French					
oil	1	6,000		6,000	
D'AURIA, Vittorio (20th C) Italian					
oil	1	3,200		3,200	
DAUSSY, Raymond (1919-) French					
oil	1	2,884		2,884	

Name	No.	Total Sales Value	lowest	Prices median	highest
DAUX, Charles Edmond (1855-?) French					
oil	1	5,235		5,235	
DAUZATS, Adrien (1804-1868) French					
oil	1	1,283		1,283	
wc/d	1	6,837		6,837	
D'AVENNES, Emile Prisse (19th C) French					
wc/d	1	1,431		1,431	
DAVERNY, G (?) ?					
3D	1	2,567		2,567	
DAVID (?) ?					
oil	1	4,231		4,231	
wc/d	1	1,092		1,092	
DAVID, Hermine (1886-1971) French					
oil	2	7,154	1,459	3,577	5,695
wc/d	1	1,817		1,817	
DAVID, Jacques-Louis (1748-1825) French					
wc/d	5	154,031	1,481	21,140	100,000
DAVID, Jose Maria (20th C) ?					
3D	4	28,513	2,188	4,523	17,280
DAVID, L (19th C) French					
3D	1	1,553		1,553	
DAVIDSON, Allan Douglas (1873-1932) British					
oil	3	4,093	1,027	1,533	1,533
DAVIDSON, Bessie (1879-1965) Australian					
oil	1	2,628		2,628	
DAVIDSON, Daniel Pender (1885-1933) British					
oil	1	1,080		1,080	
DAVIDSON, George (19/20th C) British					
oil	1	3,675		3,675	
DAVIDSON, J (?) ?					
oil	1	2,306		2,306	
DAVIDSON, Jo (1883-1952) American					
3D	1	2,592		2,592	
DAVIDSON, Rowland (20th C) British					
oil	8	12,340	1,088	1,342	2,592
DAVIDSON, Thomas (19th C) British					
oil	1	2,145		2,145	
DAVIE, Alan (1920-) British					
oil	7	94,491	3,770	6,525	27,180
wc/d	7	19,576	1,725	2,573	4,530
DAVIE, Karen (1965-) American					
oil	2	24,500	8,500	12,250	16,000
wc/d	1	4,250		4,250	
DAVIES, Arthur B (1862-1928) American					
oil	7	30,450	1,250	4,000	8,000
wc/d	3	5,200	1,300	1,600	2,300
DAVIES, Arthur E (1893-1965) British					
wc/d	1	1,058		1,058	
DAVIES, Edward (1843-1912) British					
wc/d	1	1,073		1,073	
DAVIES, G (19/20th C) ?					
oil	1	1,900		1,900	
DAVIES, H (19th C) British					
oil	1	1,884		1,884	
DAVIES, James Hey (1844-1930) British					
oil	2	6,600	2,400	3,300	4,200
DAVIES, Llewellyn (1950-) South African					
3D	1	7,100		7,100	
DAVIES, Norman Prescott (1862-1915) British					
oil	1	6,000		6,000	

Name	No.	Total Sales Value	lowest	Prices median	highest
DAVIES, William (1826-1910) British					
oil	1	10,744		10,744	
DAVILA Y ZEA, Luis (19th C) Spanish					
oil	1	2,301		2,301	
DAVILA, Jose Antonio (1935-) Venezuelan					
oil	1	1,900		1,900	
DAVIS, Arthur A (fl.1877-1905) British					
oil	1	3,796		3,796	
DAVIS, B (?) ?					
oil	1	1,272		1,272	
DAVIS, Cecil Clark (1877-?) American					
oil	1	4,250		4,250	
DAVIS, Charles Harold (1856-1933) American					
oil	3	47,950	4,750	5,200	38,000
DAVIS, Frederick William (1862-1919) British					
oil	1	4,108		4,108	
DAVIS, Gene (1920-1985) American					
oil	3	8,700	2,400	2,900	3,400
DAVIS, Harry (?) British					
wc/d	1	1,027		1,027	
DAVIS, Henry William Banks (1833-1914) British					
oil	3	26,966	2,826	11,000	13,140
DAVIS, J Valentine (1854-1930) British					
oil	1	1,627		1,627	
DAVIS, Jack (1924-) American					
wc/d	1	1,500		1,500	
DAVIS, Richard Barrett (1782-1854) British					
oil	2	15,040	3,600	7,520	11,440
DAVIS, Stuart (1894-1964) American					
oil	1	85,000		85,000	
wc/d	2	62,000	12,000	31,000	50,000
DAVIS, W H (19th C) British					
oil	1	2,067		2,067	
DAVIS, William (1812-1873) British					
oil	2	13,738	1,413	6,869	12,325
DAVIS, William Henry (?-1865) British					
oil	3	13,784	1,590	2,198	9,996
DAVIS, William M (1829-1920) American					
oil	1	1,000		1,000	
DAVIS, Willis E (1855-1910) American					
oil	1	10,000		10,000	
DAVISON, Colin (20th C) British?					
oil	1	5,510		5,510	
DAVISSON, Homer Gordon (1866-1957) American					
oil	3	11,300	1,300	3,500	6,500
DAVOL, Joseph B (1864-1923) American					
oil	1	1,200		1,200	
DAVRINGHAUSEN, Heinrich Maria (1894-1970) German					
oil	2	4,096	2,039	2,048	2,057
wc/d	1	1,359		1,359	
DAWS, Frederick Thomas (1878-?) British					
oil	1	1,600		1,600	
DAWSON, Alfred (fl.1860-1894) British					
oil	2	3,381	1,431	1,691	1,950
DAWSON, Henry (1811-1878) British					
oil	6	298,843	1,727	7,883	264,550
DAWSON, Henry Thomas (fl.1860-1896) British					
oil	2	15,800	2,512	7,900	13,288

Name	No.	Total Sales Value	lowest	Prices median	highest
DAWSON, Manierre (1887-1969) American					
oil	1	20,000		20,000	
DAWSON, Montague (1895-1973) British					
oil	30	1,290,906	1,199	37,500	120,000
wc/d	7	117,967	1,103	15,984	39,520
DAWSON, S (?) British?					
oil	2	4,537	1,737	2,269	2,800
DAWSON, Verne (20th C) American?					
oil	1	2,000		2,000	
DAWSON-WATSON, Dawson (1864-1939) American/British					
oil	4	72,300	4,500	8,900	50,000
DAXHELET, Paul (1905-1993) Belgian					
oil	7	9,808	1,048	1,424	1,952
DAY, Foreshaw (1837-1903) Canadian					
oil	3	18,476	1,958	2,581	13,937
DAY, G (20th C) American					
oil	1	2,700		2,700	
DAY, G F (19th C) British					
oil	2	9,625	3,625	4,813	6,000
DAY, James Francis (1863-1942) American					
oil	2	20,000	3,000	10,000	17,000
wc/d	1	4,000		4,000	
DAYES, Edward (1763-1804) British					
wc/d	6	56,435	1,099	1,835	44,240
DAYEZ, Georges (1907-1991) French					
oil	4	9,511	1,940	2,186	3,200
D'AZEGLIO, Massimo (1798-1866) Italian					
oil	2	3,140	1,397	1,570	1,743
DEACON, Richard (1949-) British					
3D	2	46,000	14,000	23,000	32,000
DEAK EBNER, Lajos (1850-1934) Hungarian					
oil	1	3,718		3,718	
DEAK, Adrienne (1895-?) Hungarian					
oil	5	10,706	1,224	1,580	3,498
DEAKIN, Edwin (1838-1923) American					
oil	6	39,500	3,500	5,000	11,000
DEALY, Jane M (fl.1880-1931) British					
wc/d	1	14,220		14,220	
DEAN, Walter Lofthouse (1854-1912) American					
oil	1	1,300		1,300	
DEANE, William Wood (1825-1873) British					
wc/d	1	2,755		2,755	
DEARDEN, Harold (1888-1969) British					
oil	1	1,034		1,034	
DEARLE, John H (fl.1853-1891) British					
wc/d	1	1,738		1,738	
DEARMAN, John (?-1857) British					
oil	4	18,918	2,567	3,676	9,000
DEARN, Raymond (?) British					
oil	2	4,459	2,028	2,230	2,431
DEARTH, Henry Golden (1864-1918) American					
oil	1	6,500		6,500	
DEBAT-PONSAN, Edouard-Bernard (1847-1913) French					
oil	4	10,416	1,246	1,808	5,457
DEBAUSSY, J (19th C) ?					
oil	1	5,093		5,093	
DEBAY, Auguste Hyacinth (1804-1865) French					
oil	1	13,629		13,629	

Name	No.	Total Sales Value	lowest	Prices median	highest
DEBELLE, Charles Ernest (?) Canadian?					
wc/d	1	1,203		1,203	
DEBON, Francois Hippolyte (1807-1872) French					
oil	1	6,006		6,006	
DEBRE, Olivier (1920-1999) French					
oil	32	240,045	2,057	6,597	24,220
wc/d	4	14,590	2,185	2,514	7,378
DEBRUS, Alexandre (19th C) French					
oil	1	2,038		2,038	
DEBUCOURT, Philibert Louis (1755-1832) French					
oil	1	1,638		1,638	
DEBUT, Jean-Didier (1824-1893) French					
3D	3	4,673	1,022	1,855	1,855
DEBUT, Marcel (1865-1933) French					
3D	5	13,302	1,463	1,946	6,000
DECAISNE, Henri (1799-1852) Belgian					
oil	2	3,923	1,793	1,962	2,130
DECAMP, G (19th C) French					
oil	1	1,133		1,133	
DECAMP, Ralph Earll (1858-1936) American					
oil	1	5,500		5,500	
DECAMPS, Alexandre Gabriel (1803-1860) French					
oil	2	6,311	2,774	3,156	3,537
wc/d	6	34,983	1,256	3,164	17,872
DECAMPS, Maurice (1892-1953) French					
oil	6	14,944	1,224	2,613	4,134
DECARIS, Albert (1901-1988) French					
oil	1	4,050		4,050	
DECCAN SCHOOL, 17th C Indian					
oil	1	6,000		6,000	
DECK, Theodore (?) ?					
3D	1	10,333		10,333	
DECKER, Albert (1817-1871) French					
wc/d	1	1,772		1,772	
DECKER, Cornelis (1651-1709) Dutch					
oil	1	4,436		4,436	
DECKER, Jos de (1912-) Belgian					
3D	1	2,226		2,226	
DECKER, Joseph (1853-1924) American					
oil	1	100,000		100,000	
DECKER, Robert M (1847-?) American					
oil	1	1,500		1,500	
DECKERS, Émile (1885-1968) Belgian					
oil	4	89,702	3,247	20,728	45,000
wc/d	1	3,867		3,867	
DECOUX (20th C) French					
3D	2	4,610	1,430	2,305	3,180
DECOUX, Michel (1837-1924) Belgian					
3D	1	1,442		1,442	
DEDREUX-DORCY, Pierre Joseph (1789-1874) French					
wc/d	1	1,323		1,323	
DEFAUT, Amelie M (19th C) French					
oil	1	2,000		2,000	
DEFAUX (19th C) French					
oil	1	1,597		1,597	
DEFAUX, Alexandre (1826-1900) French					
oil	12	55,709	1,690	3,146	17,941
DEFER, Jean Joseph Jules (1803-?) French					
oil	1	1,776		1,776	

Name	No.	Total Sales Value	lowest	Prices median	highest
DEFLANS, G C (?) ?					
oil	1	3,140		3,140	
DEFOSSEZ (20th C) ?					
oil	1	1,180		1,180	
DEFOSSEZ, Alfred (20th C) ?					
oil	1	1,767		1,767	
DEFRANCE, Leonard (1735-1805) Flemish					
oil	1	8,635		8,635	
DEFREES, T (19th C) American					
oil	1	1,413		1,413	
DEFREGGER, Franz von (1835-1921) German					
oil	20	262,031	2,960	12,481	29,905
wc/d	3	13,750	2,215	2,339	9,196
DEGAS, Edgar (1834-1917) French					
3D	20	17,183,035	14,130	281,000	10,570,000
oil	3	2,825,503	40,503	85,000	2,700,000
wc/d	39	18,872,047	8,030	75,070	4,800,000
DEGEN, Dismar (c.1730-c.1751) Dutch					
oil	1	2,697		2,697	
DEGODE, Wilhelm (1862-1931) German					
oil	1	1,122		1,122	
DEGOTTEX, Jean (1918-1988) French					
oil	11	57,663	2,596	3,599	17,981
wc/d	8	31,746	1,783	3,792	8,555
DEGOUVE DE NUNCQUES, William (1867-1935) Belgian					
wc/d	1	1,145		1,145	
DEGREEF, Amedee (1878-1968) Belgian					
oil	1	3,261		3,261	
DEGREEF, Jean (1852-1894) Belgian					
oil	6	9,619	1,144	1,489	2,395
DEGROSSI, Adelchi (19th C) Italian					
wc/d	3	5,173	1,145	1,500	2,528
DEHNE, Pia (1964-) German					
wc/d	1	2,163		2,163	
DEHNER, Dorothy (20th C) American					
3D	1	9,000		9,000	
DEHODENCQ, Alfred (1822-1882) French					
oil	1	4,062		4,062	
wc/d	3	6,535	1,095	2,483	2,957
DEHOY, Charles (1872-1940) Belgian					
oil	2	2,815	1,113	1,408	1,702
DEIKER, Carl Friedrich (1836-1892) German					
oil	6	26,060	1,230	3,484	9,805
DEIKER, Johannes Christian (1822-1895) German					
oil	1	1,644		1,644	
DEINEKA, Alexander (1899-1969) Russian					
oil	1	19,630		19,630	
DEITERS, Hans (1868-?) German					
oil	1	1,276		1,276	
DEITERS, Heinrich (1840-1916) German					
oil	1	4,903		4,903	
DEJOINER, Luther Evans (1886-1954) American					
oil	1	3,750		3,750	
DEJUINNE, François Louis (1786-1844) French					
oil	1	15,476		15,476	
DEKEN, Albert de (1915-) Belgian					
oil	6	13,370	1,880	2,089	2,716
DEKKER, Hendrik Adriaan Christian (1836-1905) Dutch					
oil	1	1,244		1,244	

Name	No.	Total Sales Value	lowest	Prices median	highest
DEKKER, Henk (1897-1957) Dutch					
oil	3	3,644	1,118	1,190	1,336
DEKKERS, Ad (1938-) Dutch					
3D	1	6,466		6,466	
wc/d	1	2,366		2,366	
DEKKERT, Eugène (1865-1956) German					
oil	1	1,471		1,471	
DELABORDE, Henri (1811-1899) French					
oil	1	8,324		8,324	
DELABRIERE, P E (1829-1912) French					
3D	2	6,804	1,304	3,402	5,500
DELABRIERE, Paul Edouard (1829-1912) French					
3D	3	7,698	1,638	2,290	3,770
DELACOU, Yvonne (20th C) French?					
3D	3	12,649	1,489	1,489	9,644
DELACROIX, Eugène (1798-1863) French					
oil	6	172,842	1,391	22,815	60,571
wc/d	20	545,210	1,909	12,624	189,113
DELAHAUT, Jo (1911-1992) Belgian					
oil	1	1,113		1,113	
wc/d	1	1,305		1,305	
DELAHOGUE, Alexis-Auguste (1867-1936) French					
oil	4	12,393	1,298	3,406	4,283
DELAMAIN, Paul (1821-1882) French					
oil	1	4,000		4,000	
DELAMARE, Guillaume (18th C) French					
oil	1	2,392		2,392	
DELAMARRE, L (18th C) French					
oil	1	4,073		4,073	
DELAMOTTE, William (1775-1863) British					
oil	1	4,530		4,530	
wc/d	2	3,430	1,300	1,715	2,130
DELANEY, A (20th C) British					
oil	1	3,322		3,322	
DELANEY, Arthur (1927-1987) British					
oil	6	31,875	2,610	6,136	6,552
DELANO, Gerard Curtis (1890-1972) American					
oil	5	124,250	4,250	17,000	55,000
wc/d	1	15,000		15,000	
DELAPLANCHE, Eugène (1836-1891) French					
3D	2	6,597	1,433	3,299	5,164
DELAPORTE, Maurice Eugène (1878-1964) French					
oil	1	1,105		1,105	
DELAPUENTE, Fernando (1909-1975) Spanish					
wc/d	1	2,279		2,279	
DELAROCHE, Eugene (19th C) French					
oil	1	1,600		1,600	
DELAROCHE, Paul (1797-1856) French					
oil	1	6,040		6,040	
wc/d	1	3,675		3,675	
DELATOUR, Alexandre (1780-1858) Belgian					
wc/d	1	1,460		1,460	
DELATTRE, Joseph (1858-1912) French					
oil	2	3,200	1,510	1,600	1,690
DELAUNAY (?) French					
oil	1	2,037		2,037	
DELAUNAY, Jules (?-1906) French					
oil	1	1,073		1,073	
DELAUNAY, Robert (1885-1941) French					
oil	3	6,968,628	50,628	2,718,000	4,200,000

Name	No.	Total Sales Value	lowest	Prices median	highest
wc/d	2	45,472	10,472	22,736	35,000

DELAUNAY, Sonia (1885-1979) French/Russian
oil	3	160,582	4,368	61,214	95,000
wc/d	17	136,744	1,005	4,356	28,000

DELAVALLEE, Henri (1862-1943) French
wc/d	1	4,975		4,975	

DELAVALLEE, Jean Gabriel Henri (1887-?) French
oil	1	4,200		4,200	

DELAVILLE, Louis (1763-1841) French
3D	1	11,776		11,776	

DELAYE, Charles Claude (1793-?) French
oil	1	1,850		1,850	

DELAYE, Theophile Jean (20th C) French
wc/d	1	3,222		3,222	

DELBOVE, Raoul (?) Belgian
oil	1	1,602		1,602	

DELDERENE, Léon (1864-1921) Belgian
oil	2	4,057	1,132	2,029	2,925

DELEN, Dirk van (1605-1671) Dutch
oil	2	634,161	88,200	317,081	545,961

DELERIVE, Nicolas Louis Albert (18th C) French
oil	1	1,176		1,176	

DELESCLUZE, Edmond (1905-1993) Belgian
oil	1	1,341		1,341	

DELESTRE, Eugène (1862-1919) French
oil	1	1,462		1,462	

DELFGAAUW, Gerard Johannes (1882-1947) Dutch
oil	16	48,958	1,100	1,612	15,610

DELFOSSE, Eugène (1825-1865) Belgian
oil	1	3,085		3,085	

DELFOSSE, Georges Marie Joseph (1869-1939) Canadian
oil	2	2,424	1,002	1,212	1,422

DELFS, Moritz (1823-1906) German
oil	1	1,963		1,963	

DELFT SCHOOL, 17th C Dutch
oil	1	5,114		5,114	

DELGADO RAMOS, Alvaro (1922-) Spanish
oil	9	32,527	1,966	2,286	8,190
wc/d	2	2,891	1,328	1,446	1,563

DELHAYE, Jose (1921-) Belgian
oil	1	1,916		1,916	

DELHOMMEAU, Charles (1883-?) French
3D	2	10,631	2,730	5,316	7,901

DELIGNY, Claude Felix Theodore (1798-1863) French
oil	1	7,369		7,369	

DELIOTTI, Walter (20th C) Uruguayan?
3D	1	2,000		2,000	
oil	8	11,663	1,025	1,369	2,000

DELL, John H (1836-1888) British
oil	1	2,145		2,145	

DELL'ACQUA, Cesare Felix Georges (1821-1904) Italian
oil	1	11,974		11,974	
wc/d	1	43,800		43,800	

DELLEANI, Lorenzo (1840-1908) Italian
oil	10	113,549	4,459	9,739	35,120

DELLEPIANE, David (1866-c.1925) French/Italian
oil	1	45,000		45,000	

DELMOTTE, Marcel (1901-1984) Belgian
oil	6	12,297	1,109	1,858	3,323

Name	No.	Total Sales Value	lowest	Prices median	highest
DELOR, Jean Marie (19th C) French					
oil	1	1,605		1,605	
DELORME, H E (19th C) French					
oil	1	7,000		7,000	
DELORME, Marguerite (1876-1946) French					
oil	1	4,271		4,271	
DELORME, Raphael (1886-1962) French					
oil	1	5,586		5,586	
DELORT, Charles Edouard (1841-1895) French					
oil	1	19,000		19,000	
wc/d	1	1,359		1,359	
DELPEREE, Émile (1850-1896) Belgian					
oil	1	1,006		1,006	
DELPRAT, Helene (20th C) French					
oil	2	2,711	1,281	1,356	1,430
DELPY, Hippolyte Camille (1842-1910) French					
oil	30	175,925	1,139	5,159	18,000
DELPY, Jacques-Henry (1877-1957) French					
oil	11	32,254	1,269	2,302	7,110
DELPY, Lucien Victor (1898-1966) French					
oil	6	17,801	2,166	3,091	3,970
wc/d	2	2,453	1,049	1,227	1,404
DELSAUX, Willem (1862-1945) Belgian					
oil	2	6,227	1,358	3,114	4,869
DELSER, Johann (1725-1801) Austrian					
oil	1	1,812		1,812	
DELTIL, Jean Julien (1791-1863) French					
oil	1	1,164		1,164	
DELTOMBE, Paul (1878-1971) French					
oil	1	2,736		2,736	
DELVAUX, Edouard (1806-1862) Belgian					
oil	1	1,780		1,780	
DELVAUX, Paul (1897-1994) Belgian					
oil	6	4,010,160	7,265	268,025	2,869,000
wc/d	20	195,026	1,068	4,619	66,440
DELVIN, Jean Joseph (1853-1922) Belgian					
oil	1	1,371		1,371	
DELVOYE, Wim (1965-) Dutch?					
3D	2	41,200	11,000	20,600	30,200
oil	1	2,707		2,707	
DEMACHY, Pierre Antoine (1723-1807) French					
oil	5	432,981	2,983	8,998	380,000
DEMAKIS (19th C) ?					
oil	1	2,961		2,961	
DEMAREST, Suzanne (1900-1985) French					
oil	1	1,800		1,800	
DEMARNE, Jean Louis (1744-1829) French					
oil	8	98,961	2,658	8,372	33,015
DEMAY, Jean François (1798-1850) French					
oil	1	1,033		1,033	
DEMETZ, K (?) German					
oil	1	1,288		1,288	
DEMETZ, Karl (1909-1986) German					
oil	2	4,159	1,706	2,080	2,453
DEMIN, Giovanni (1786-1859) Italian					
wc/d	1	1,415		1,415	
DEMING, Edwin Willard (1860-1942) American					
oil	2	4,400	1,900	2,200	2,500

Name	No.	Total Sales Value	lowest	Prices median	highest
DEMME, Paul (1866-1953) Swiss					
wc/d	2	3,043	1,228	1,522	1,815
DEMONGIN, V (20th C) French					
oil	1	2,957		2,957	
DEMONT (19th C) French?					
oil	1	1,898		1,898	
DEMONT-BRETON, Virginie (1859-1935) French					
oil	1	85,000		85,000	
DEMUTH, Charles (1883-1935) American					
wc/d	9	799,500	16,000	55,000	350,000
DENARDE, M (19th C) Continental					
oil	1	2,717		2,717	
DENCKER, August (19/20th C) German?					
oil	1	1,400		1,400	
DENECHEAU, Seraphin (1831-1912) French					
3D	1	24,159		24,159	
DENEUX, Gabriel Charles (1856-?) French					
oil	1	1,300		1,300	
DENIERE and CARRIER-BELLEUSE, Albert (19th C) French					
3D	1	3,234		3,234	
DENIES, Isaak (1647-1690) Dutch					
oil	1	10,800		10,800	
DENIS, Maurice (1870-1943) French					
oil	18	904,666	2,272	13,846	467,087
wc/d	10	96,778	1,451	4,512	35,048
DENIS, Riccardo R (?) Italian					
oil	1	4,002		4,002	
DENIS, Simon Joseph Alexander Clement (1755-1813) Flemish					
oil	2	20,154	10,000	10,077	10,154
DENIS-VALVERANE, Louis (1870-?) French					
oil	9	25,455	1,092	1,433	12,284
wc/d	1	2,184		2,184	
DENISE, Alexandre (19th C) French					
oil	1	2,724		2,724	
DENMARK (1950-) Belgian					
wc/d	1	1,030		1,030	
DENNER, Balthasar (1685-1749) German					
oil	4	22,308	2,437	3,382	13,107
DENNERY, Gustave Lucien (1863-?) French					
wc/d	1	1,418		1,418	
DENNY, Robin (1930-) British					
oil	1	1,413		1,413	
DENON, Vivant Dominique (1747-1825) French					
wc/d	1	1,493		1,493	
DENT, Rupert Arthur (fl.1884-1909) British					
oil	1	1,988		1,988	
DENTE, Girolamo (1510-?) Italian					
oil	2	17,282	5,065	8,641	12,217
DENTON, Kenneth (20th C) ?					
oil	1	1,141		1,141	
D'ENTRAYGUES, Charles Bertrand (1851-?) French					
oil	4	47,800	6,800	8,500	24,000
DENTS, D M (20th C) British?					
oil	1	1,115		1,115	
DENZEL, Anton (1888-?) German					
oil	1	1,058		1,058	
DEPERO, Fortunato (1892-1960) Italian					
3D	1	19,199		19,199	
oil	1	15,272		15,272	

Name	No.	Total Sales Value	lowest	Prices median	highest
wc/d	6	14,631	1,026	1,256	5,776
D'EPINAY, Prosper (1830-1914) French					
3D	1	14,915		14,915	
DEPPE, Gustav (1913-) German					
wc/d	1	1,202		1,202	
DEPRE, E (19th C) ?					
oil	1	2,140		2,140	
DERAIN, Andre (1880-1954) French					
oil	19	322,474	4,135	14,000	61,364
wc/d	11	27,353	1,095	1,833	6,000
DERBRE, Louis (1925-) French?					
3D	2	3,293	1,547	1,647	1,746
DEREUX, Philippe (1918-) French					
wc/d	1	1,159		1,159	
DERICKX, Louis (1835-1895) Belgian					
oil	1	3,205		3,205	
DERKERT, Siri (1888-1973) Swedish					
oil	2	2,750	1,044	1,375	1,706
wc/d	2	3,198	1,457	1,599	1,741
DEROME, Albert Thomas (1885-1959) American					
oil	2	12,000	5,500	6,000	6,500
wc/d	1	1,000		1,000	
DEROME, Jasmin (1976-) French					
3D	1	1,203		1,203	
DERUET, Claude (1588-1660) French					
oil	1	22,339		22,339	
DESAN, Charles (19th C) ?					
oil	1	1,507		1,507	
DESAN, Karel (19th C) French					
oil	1	1,963		1,963	
DESBOIS, Jules (1851-1935) French					
3D	7	23,610	1,157	1,975	12,185
DESBOUTIN, Marcelin Gilbert (1823-1902) French					
oil	1	2,676		2,676	
DESCAMPS (18/19th C) French					
3D	1	2,069		2,069	
DESCHAMPS, Gabriel (1919-) French					
oil	2	14,380	1,738	7,190	12,642
DESCHAMPS, Louis Henri (1846-1902) French					
oil	1	1,500		1,500	
DESCHWANDEN, Melchior Paul von (1811-1881) Swiss					
oil	1	1,924		1,924	
DESCHWANDEN, Theodor von (1826-1861) Swiss					
oil	1	1,139		1,139	
DESCOMPS, Joe (1869-1950) French					
3D	4	9,828	1,400	2,563	3,356
DESCOURS, Michel Hubert (1707-1775) French					
oil	2	10,432	2,400	5,216	8,032
DESFONTAINES, A B (19th C) French					
oil	1	1,702		1,702	
DESFONTAINES, F B (?) ?					
oil	1	5,393		5,393	
DESFRICHES, Aignan (1715-1800) French					
wc/d	3	6,111	1,228	1,661	3,222
DESHAYES, Charles Felix Edouard (1831-1895) French					
oil	4	8,191	1,102	2,050	2,990
DESHAYES, Eugène (1828-1890) French					
oil	5	14,181	1,834	2,067	4,308

Name	No.	Total Sales Value	Prices lowest	median	highest
DESHAYS DE COLLEVILLE, Jean Baptiste (1729-1765) French					
oil	1	13,820		13,820	
wc/d	1	2,400		2,400	
DESIDERIO, Vincent (20th C) American?					
oil	1	4,070		4,070	
DESIRE-LUCAS, Louis-Marie (1869-1949) French					
oil	8	24,065	1,476	3,011	4,960
wc/d	1	1,929		1,929	
DESMAREES, George (1697-1776) Swedish					
oil	2	16,137	5,324	8,069	10,813
DESMEDT, Jos (1894-?) Belgian					
oil	2	2,236	1,022	1,118	1,214
DESNOS, Ferdinand (1901-1958) French					
oil	1	1,296		1,296	
DESNOYER, François (1894-1972) French					
oil	6	18,336	1,167	2,675	5,755
D'ESPAGNAT, Georges (1870-1950) French					
oil	35	444,748	1,697	9,580	45,000
DESPAGNE, Artus (fl.1823-1835) French					
oil	1	1,975		1,975	
DESPIAU, Charles (1874-1946) French					
3D	6	24,012	1,710	3,934	7,604
oil	1	1,024		1,024	
wc/d	2	3,586	1,549	1,793	2,037
DESPORTES, Alexandre-François (1661-1743) French					
oil	4	932,245	49,830	236,472	409,471
DESPOSETA, L (19th C) French					
oil	1	10,220		10,220	
D'ESPOSITO, G (19/20th C) ?					
wc/d	2	4,675	2,067	2,338	2,608
D'ESPOSITO, Giacomo (19/20th C) Italian					
wc/d	1	1,549		1,549	
DESPRAS, T (19/20th C) ?					
oil	1	6,644		6,644	
DESPRES, J (19th C) French?					
oil	1	1,896		1,896	
DESPRET, Georges (1862-1952) French					
3D	2	17,524	1,460	8,762	16,064
DESPREZ, D (19th C) French					
oil	1	3,160		3,160	
DESPREZ, Louis Jean (1743-1804) French					
wc/d	2	3,700	1,306	1,850	2,394
DESPUJOLS, Jean (1886-1965) French					
oil	4	17,485	3,501	3,706	6,315
DESRUELLES, Felix (1865-?) French					
3D	1	2,030		2,030	
DESSERPRIT, Roger (1923-1985) French					
3D	2	7,946	3,857	3,973	4,089
DESSINGH, R (?) ?					
oil	1	3,125		3,125	
DESSOULAVY, Thomas (fl.1839-1853) British					
oil	1	12,410		12,410	
DESTEE, Jos (19/20th C) ?					
3D	1	2,918		2,918	
D'ESTIENNE, Henri (1872-1949) French					
oil	2	2,843	1,418	1,422	1,425
wc/d	2	20,037	3,504	10,019	16,533
DESTREE, Johannes Josephus (1827-1888) Belgian					
oil	2	4,411	1,506	2,206	2,905

Name	No.	Total Sales Value	lowest	Prices median	highest
DESURMONT (19/20th C) ?					
3D	1	3,222		3,222	
DESVALLIERES, Georges (1861-1950) French					
oil	2	5,247	2,350	2,624	2,897
DESVARREUX-LARPENTEUR, James (1847-1937) American					
oil	1	3,792		3,792	
DESVIGNES, Emily (fl.1880-1890) British					
oil	2	2,543	1,108	1,272	1,435
DETAILLE, Edouard (1848-1912) French					
oil	1	1,955		1,955	
wc/d	1	3,915		3,915	
DETHOMAS, Maxime (1867-?) French					
wc/d	2	4,027	1,328	2,014	2,699
DETMOLD, Edward Julian (1883-1957) British					
wc/d	4	7,468	1,305	1,849	2,465
DETMOLD, Henry E (1854-1924) British					
oil	1	1,208		1,208	
DETRAIT, Jacques (1948-) French					
oil	1	1,282		1,282	
DETROY, Léon (1857-1955) French					
oil	1	1,069		1,069	
DETTHOW, Eric (1888-1952) Swedish					
oil	6	12,832	1,062	1,776	4,026
DETTI, Cesare Auguste (1847-1914) Italian					
oil	7	190,704	3,049	5,500	150,000
wc/d	2	8,182	3,624	4,091	4,558
DETTMANN, Ludwig Julius Christian (1865-1944) German					
oil	1	1,605		1,605	
DETTMANN, Walter (20th C) German					
oil	1	1,184		1,184	
DEUCHERT, Heinrich (1840-?) German					
oil	2	9,083	2,215	4,542	6,868
DEULLY, Eugène Auguste Francois (1860-?) French					
oil	1	1,504		1,504	
DEURS, Caroline van (1860-1932) Danish					
oil	1	1,059		1,059	
DEUSKAR, Gopal Damodar (1911-1994) Indian					
oil	1	5,040		5,040	
DEUSSER, August (1870-1942) German					
oil	2	2,366	1,002	1,183	1,364
DEUTSCH, Ludwig (1855-1935) French					
oil	2	136,225	16,225	68,113	120,000
DEUX, Fred (1924-) French					
wc/d	5	7,116	1,018	1,180	2,188
DEVADE, Marc (1943-1983) French					
oil	3	10,855	3,190	3,412	4,253
wc/d	1	2,057		2,057	
DEVAL, Pierre (1897-1993) French					
oil	4	10,103	1,901	2,185	3,832
wc/d	1	1,998		1,998	
DEVAMBEZ, Andre (1867-1943) French					
oil	6	49,470	1,233	1,319	34,047
DEVAS, Anthony (1911-1958) British					
oil	6	12,914	1,092	1,861	4,108
wc/d	1	1,350		1,350	
DEVE, Eugène (1826-1867) French					
oil	1	1,805		1,805	
DEVEDEUX, Louis (1820-1874) French					
oil	3	8,373	1,460	2,755	4,158

Name	No.	Total Sales Value	lowest	Prices median	highest
DEVENTER, Willem Anthonie van (1824-1893) Dutch					
oil	1	56,880		56,880	
DEVERIA, Achille (1800-1857) French					
wc/d	1	1,355		1,355	
DEVERIA, Eugène (1808-1865) French					
oil	3	6,352	1,408	1,944	3,000
DEVILLE-CHABROLLE, Marie Paule (1952-) French					
3D	1	3,077		3,077	
DEVINA, J (19th C) ?					
wc/d	1	1,059		1,059	
DEVIS, Anthony (1729-1817) British					
wc/d	2	8,400	1,200	4,200	7,200
DEVIS, Arthur (1711-1787) British					
oil	3	163,210	9,060	75,500	78,650
DEVOLDER, Roland (1938-) Belgian					
oil	1	1,083		1,083	
DEVOLL, Frederick Usher (1873-1941) American					
oil	3	26,500	5,000	7,500	14,000
DEVOS, Léon (1897-1974) Belgian					
oil	4	9,970	1,618	2,411	3,472
DEVOTO, John (18th C) British					
oil	1	10,570		10,570	
DEWASNE, Jean (1921-) French					
oil	1	6,070		6,070	
wc/d	3	17,615	2,994	5,942	8,679
DEWHURST, Wynford (1864-1941) British					
oil	2	14,490	1,740	7,245	12,750
DEWING, Maria Richards Oakey (1845-1927) American					
oil	1	1,050,000		1,050,000	
DEWING, Thomas W (1851-1938) American					
oil	2	303,000	23,000	151,500	280,000
DEWS, J Steven (1949-) British					
oil	3	188,480	39,520	45,600	103,360
DEXEL, Walter (1890-1973) German					
oil	5	50,460	4,469	12,396	15,534
DEY, Manishi (20th C) Indian					
oil	2	2,100	1,050	1,050	1,050
DEY, Mukul (20th C) Indian					
wc/d	1	1,800		1,800	
DEYNUM, Guilliam van (17th C) Flemish					
oil	3	155,666	40,770	47,386	67,510
DEYROLLE, Jean (1911-1967) French					
oil	11	44,653	2,006	3,497	7,150
wc/d	1	1,212		1,212	
DEYROLLE, Theophile-Louis (1844-1923) French					
oil	4	13,073	1,929	2,822	5,500
DEZAUNAY, Émile (1854-1940) French					
oil	6	15,982	1,151	2,342	4,603
wc/d	3	6,078	1,405	2,193	2,480
D'HAESE, Reinhoud (1928-) Belgian					
3D	7	26,635	2,239	3,873	5,262
D'HALHEIM, Jean (1840-1894) French					
oil	1	2,816		2,816	
D'HAVELOOSE, Marnix (1885-1973) Belgian					
oil	1	1,712		1,712	
DHERMAND (?) ?					
wc/d	1	2,422		2,422	
D'HUART, A B (20th C) French?					
oil	1	2,012		2,012	

Name	No.	Total Sales Value	lowest	Prices median	highest
DI TIANA (20th C) ?					
3D	1	1,353		1,353	
DI TIANA, Fontenay (20th C) ?					
3D	1	3,422		3,422	
DIAGO, Roberto (1920-1957) Cuban					
oil	3	88,500	4,000	4,500	80,000
DIAS, Antonio (20th C) Brazilian					
3D	1	30,000		30,000	
oil	1	35,000		35,000	
DIAZ CANEJA, Juan Manuel (1905-) Spanish					
oil	1	10,227		10,227	
DIAZ CASTILLA, Luciano (1940-) Spanish					
oil	6	9,353	1,124	1,474	2,286
DIAZ DE LA PENA, Narcisse-Virgile (1807-1876) French					
oil	32	477,591	1,166	6,121	138,700
wc/d	2	2,421	1,021	1,211	1,400
DIAZ PARDO, Isaac (20th C) Mexican					
oil	1	1,427		1,427	
DIBBETS, Jan (1941-) Dutch					
wc/d	1	2,718		2,718	
DIBDIN, Thomas Colman (1810-1893) British					
wc/d	2	3,722	1,354	1,861	2,368
DICK, Sir William Reid (1879-1961) British					
3D	3	14,944	2,250	4,530	8,164
DICK, Walter (1950-) Swiss?					
wc/d	1	1,089		1,089	
DICKERT, Adolf (1878-?) German					
oil	1	2,884		2,884	
DICKEY, Robert L (1861-1944) American					
wc/d	1	3,000		3,000	
DICKGIESSER, Fritz (1952-) German					
wc/d	1	3,244		3,244	
DICKINSON, Edwin (1891-1978) American					
wc/d	1	12,000		12,000	
DICKINSON, Preston (1891-1930) American					
wc/d	1	15,000		15,000	
DICKMEIS, Gerhard (1918-1978) German					
oil	1	1,422		1,422	
DICKSEE, Frank (1853-1928) British					
oil	5	73,409	1,199	4,290	45,000
wc/d	1	1,950		1,950	
DICKSEE, Thomas Francis (1819-1895) British					
oil	3	39,812	1,812	18,000	20,000
DICKSON, Charles (19/20th C) British					
wc/d	1	3,473		3,473	
DICKSON, William (fl.1881-1904) British					
oil	1	1,050		1,050	
DICREDICO, Robert (20th C) ?					
oil	1	1,947		1,947	
DIDAY, François (1802-1877) Swiss					
oil	3	11,200	1,937	3,287	5,976
DIDDAERT, Henri (fl.1845-1866) Belgian					
oil	1	3,600		3,600	
DIDIER, Clovis François Auguste (1858-?) French					
oil	1	18,000		18,000	
DIDIER, Jules (1831-1892) French					
oil	1	2,353		2,353	
DIDIER, Luc (1954-) French					
oil	3	3,732	1,015	1,309	1,408

Name	No.	Total Sales Value	Prices lowest	median	highest
DIDIER-POUGET, William (1864-1959) French					
oil	7	23,584	1,127	4,211	6,000
DIEBENKORN, Richard (1922-1993) American					
oil	1	1,150,000		1,150,000	
wc/d	4	250,500	13,000	51,250	135,000
DIEDERICH, Wilhelm Hunt (1884-1953) American					
3D	3	95,300	1,800	3,500	90,000
DIEDERICHS, Peter (1923-1982) German					
oil	1	1,162		1,162	
DIEFENBACH, Karl Wilhelm (1851-1931) German					
oil	1	5,920		5,920	
wc/d	1	1,864		1,864	
DIEFFENBACH, Anton Heinrich (1831-1914) German					
oil	2	7,750	2,250	3,875	5,500
DIEFFENBACHER, August Wilhelm (1858-1940) German					
wc/d	1	1,593		1,593	
DIEGHEM, J H van (19th C) Dutch					
oil	1	1,133		1,133	
DIEGHEM, Jacob van (19th C) Dutch					
oil	6	15,157	1,138	2,770	3,770
DIEHL, Arthur (1870-1929) American					
oil	5	9,500	1,100	1,900	3,000
DIEHL, Hugo von (1821-1883) German					
oil	1	3,372		3,372	
DIEHLE, Alwin (1854-?) German					
oil	1	1,151		1,151	
DIELEMAN, Piet (1956-) Dutch?					
oil	1	1,078		1,078	
wc/d	1	2,802		2,802	
DIELS, Jef (20th C) Belgian					
oil	1	2,330		2,330	
DIEMER, Michael Zeno (1867-1939) German					
oil	4	44,776	2,100	9,938	22,800
DIEMER, Zeno (19/20th C) German					
oil	5	29,744	3,928	5,217	8,712
DIENZIO, B (19th C) Italian?					
oil	1	2,334		2,334	
DIEPENBECK, Abraham van (1596-1675) Flemish					
oil	1	1,257		1,257	
DIERA, G L (20th C) ?					
oil	2	3,858	1,929	1,929	1,929
DIES, Albert-Christophe (1755-1822) German					
wc/d	1	2,163		2,163	
DIEST, Adriaen van (1655-1704) Dutch					
oil	2	21,095	5,896	10,548	15,199
DIEST, Willem van (1610-1673) Dutch					
oil	1	44,153		44,153	
DIESTE, Hermann (20th C) German					
oil	1	4,692		4,692	
DIETER, Hans (1881-?) German					
oil	8	22,032	1,038	1,301	9,000
DIETERLE, Marie (1856-1935) French					
oil	2	23,000	11,000	11,500	12,000
DIETLER, Johann Friedrich (1804-1874) Swiss					
oil	1	9,116		9,116	
wc/d	1	1,233		1,233	
DIETMANN, Erik (1937-) Swedish					
3D	4	19,145	1,785	3,562	10,237
oil	3	4,564	1,028	1,028	2,442
wc/d	1	1,706		1,706	

Name	No.	Total Sales Value	lowest	Prices median	highest
DIETRICH, Adelheid (1827-?) German					
oil	3	180,600	40,600	60,000	80,000
DIETRICH, Adolf (1877-1957) Swiss					
oil	28	1,714,268	8,841	39,370	237,000
wc/d	2	4,834	1,297	2,417	3,537
DIETRICH, Christian Wilhelm Ernst (1712-1774) German					
oil	11	95,959	1,330	5,586	27,500
DIETRICH, Thomas Mueller (1912-) American					
oil	1	2,100		2,100	
DIETZ, Feodor (1813-1870) German					
oil	1	1,571		1,571	
DIETZ, Herman R (1860-1923) American					
oil	1	1,500		1,500	
DIETZSCH, Barbara Regina (1706-1783) German					
wc/d	1	2,114		2,114	
DIETZSCH, Johann Christoph (1710-1769) German					
wc/d	1	2,222		2,222	
DIETZSCH, Margareta Barbara (1716-1795) German					
wc/d	1	3,800		3,800	
DIEUDONNE, Emmanuel de (19th C) French					
oil	3	114,761	2,261	4,500	108,000
DIEVENBACH, Hendricus Anthonius (1872-1946) Dutch					
oil	3	4,783	1,431	1,450	1,902
DIEZ, Julius (1870-1957) German					
oil	1	1,636		1,636	
DIEZ, Samuel (1803-1873) Swiss					
oil	1	2,451		2,451	
DIEZ, Wilhelm von (1839-1907) German					
oil	2	6,033	1,080	3,017	4,953
DIEZLER, Jakob (1789-1855) German					
oil	1	7,976		7,976	
DIGHTON, Denis (1792-1827) British					
wc/d	1	1,430		1,430	
DIGHTON, Joshua (fl.1820-1840) British					
oil	1	2,736		2,736	
DIGHTON, Robert (1752-1814) British					
wc/d	3	12,742	2,160	4,862	5,720
DIGNAM, Mary Ella Williams (1860-1938) Canadian					
oil	1	1,659		1,659	
DIGNIMONT, Andre (1891-1965) French					
oil	1	1,106		1,106	
wc/d	1	1,584		1,584	
DIJSSELHOF, Gerrit Willem (1866-1924) Dutch					
oil	3	4,087	1,273	1,308	1,506
DIKE, Philip Latimer (1906-1990) American					
oil	1	5,000		5,000	
DIKMEN, Tiraje (20th C) ?					
oil	1	3,647		3,647	
DILL, Laddie John (1943-) American					
wc/d	1	2,000		2,000	
DILL, Ludwig (1848-1940) German					
oil	12	39,665	1,079	2,825	7,104
wc/d	1	2,329		2,329	
DILL, Otto (1884-1957) German					
oil	9	92,836	1,330	5,046	40,372
wc/d	3	4,582	1,170	1,682	1,730
DILLEN, Peter Martinus (1890-?) Dutch					
oil	1	2,732		2,732	

Name	No.	Total Sales Value	lowest	Prices median	highest
DILLENS, Adolphe Alexander (1821-1877) Belgian					
oil	2	5,952	2,289	2,976	3,663
DILLENS, Albert (1844-?) Belgian					
oil	2	6,595	2,507	3,298	4,088
DILLENS, Hendrick Joseph (1812-1872) Belgian					
oil	1	4,924		4,924	
DILLER, Burgoyne (1906-1965) American					
wc/d	2	9,700	4,200	4,850	5,500
DILLEY, Ramon (1933-) French					
oil	2	3,188	1,496	1,594	1,692
D'ILLIERS, Gaston (1876-1952) French					
3D	2	5,164	2,066	2,582	3,098
DILLIS, Johann Georg von (1759-1841) German					
wc/d	7	13,354	1,050	1,364	4,059
DILLON, Frank (1823-1909) British					
wc/d	3	8,317	2,054	2,765	3,498
DILLON, Gerard (1917-1971) Irish					
oil	3	73,704	7,104	22,200	44,400
wc/d	5	30,808	4,176	5,624	8,880
DIMITRIJEVIC, Braco (20th C) ?					
oil	1	1,133		1,133	
DINE, Jim (1935-) American					
3D	1	27,489		27,489	
oil	3	141,000	36,000	40,000	65,000
wc/d	13	162,934	2,600	10,000	34,000
DINET, Étienne (1861-1929) French					
oil	8	352,206	6,490	25,311	123,996
wc/d	8	24,019	2,320	2,587	5,111
DING, Henri Marius (1844-1898) French					
3D	1	7,301		7,301	
DINGLE, Kim (1951-) American?					
oil	2	30,000	13,000	15,000	17,000
DINGLE, Thomas (19th C) British					
oil	1	1,020		1,020	
DINGLI, Charles Caruana (1876-1950) Maltese					
wc/d	3	23,373	5,088	7,950	10,335
DINOU, Julien (1895-) Swiss					
oil	1	2,148		2,148	
DINSDALE, John Bentham (19th C) British					
oil	2	5,000	2,200	2,500	2,800
DIOGG, Felix Maria (1764-1834) Swiss					
oil	1	1,822		1,822	
DIP, A Abbiati (19th C) American?					
wc/d	1	1,020		1,020	
DIRCKINCK-HOLMFELD, H (1835-1912) Danish					
oil	1	1,162		1,162	
DIRKS, Andreas (1866-1922) German					
oil	6	10,865	1,208	1,719	2,944
DIRR, Johann Georg (1723-1779) German					
3D	1	6,364		6,364	
DISCART, Jean (19th C) French					
oil	1	226,500		226,500	
DISCHER, Fritz (1880-?) German					
oil	1	1,352		1,352	
DISCHLER, Hermann (1866-1935) German					
oil	5	10,721	1,117	2,127	4,081
DISCOVOLO, Antonio (1874-1956) Italian					
oil	1	7,834		7,834	

Name	No.	Total Sales Value	Prices lowest	median	highest
DISLER, Martin (1949-1996) Swiss					
oil	3	5,322	1,480	1,942	1,942
wc/d	3	7,135	1,226	1,783	4,126
DITTMANN, Edmund (19th C) German					
oil	1	1,253		1,253	
DIULGHEROFF, Nicolas (1901-1982) Italian/Bulgarian					
oil	1	1,350		1,350	
D'IVERNOIS, Jean François Jules (1823-1884) Swiss					
oil	1	1,367		1,367	
DIVO, Louis (19/20th C) Austrian					
oil	1	1,183		1,183	
DIX, Otto (1891-1969) German					
oil	4	276,283	6,466	12,509	244,800
wc/d	45	582,786	1,365	7,281	100,800
DIXON, A (?) British					
oil	1	1,793		1,793	
DIXON, Alfred (1842-1919) British					
oil	2	8,886	1,386	4,443	7,500
DIXON, Annie (1817-1901) British					
wc/d	1	2,465		2,465	
DIXON, Charles Edward (1872-1934) British					
oil	3	15,657	1,712	6,080	7,865
wc/d	31	170,738	1,001	4,530	15,730
DIXON, James (1887-1970) British?					
oil	5	29,288	1,241	3,775	10,360
wc/d	2	11,067	1,447	5,534	9,620
DIXON, Maynard (1875-1946) American					
oil	6	1,675,000	30,000	47,500	1,200,000
wc/d	15	157,450	1,400	4,250	44,000
DIXON, Nellie Gertrude (fl.1900-1932) British					
oil	1	6,750		6,750	
DIXON, Paul B (1956-) South African					
wc/d	1	1,480		1,480	
DIZIANI, Antonio (1737-1797) Italian					
oil	1	12,217		12,217	
DIZIANI, Gaspare (1689-1767) Italian					
oil	1	10,990		10,990	
wc/d	4	21,211	2,037	2,792	13,590
DJOCJA (20th C) Javanese					
oil	1	2,304		2,304	
DMITRIENKO, Pierre (1925-1974) French					
oil	5	20,263	1,027	4,705	7,700
DMITRIEV, Vladimir Vladimirovich (1900-1948) Russian					
oil	2	67,680	25,380	33,840	42,300
wc/d	1	8,178		8,178	
DOBBELMAN, Theo (1906-) Dutch					
3D	1	1,075		1,075	
DOBBIN, John (1815-1888) British					
wc/d	3	5,522	1,335	1,937	2,250
DOBBIN, John and COOPER, Abraham (19th C) British					
wc/d	1	1,073		1,073	
DOBELI, Johann Othmar (1874-1922) Swiss					
oil	1	1,615		1,615	
DOBELL, Sir William (1899-1970) Australian					
oil	1	2,765		2,765	
DOBIE, Beatrix Charlotte (1887-?) New Zealander					
oil	1	4,022		4,022	
DOBOUJINSKY, Mstislav (1875-1957) Russian					
wc/d	6	27,095	1,000	1,600	16,610

Name	No.	Total Sales Value	Prices lowest	Prices median	highest
DOBROWSKY, Josef (1889-1964) Austrian					
wc/d	2	2,665	1,165	1,333	1,500
DOBSON, Frank (1886-1963) British					
wc/d	2	4,822	2,212	2,411	2,610
DOBSON, Henry John (1858-1928) British					
oil	5	12,014	1,015	1,100	5,372
wc/d	3	5,087	1,147	1,294	2,646
DOBSON, Henry Raeburn (1901-) British					
oil	2	5,379	1,291	2,690	4,088
DOBSON, Robert (fl.1860-1901) British					
wc/d	1	1,001		1,001	
DOBSON, William Charles Thomas (1817-1898) British					
oil	3	10,058	1,316	2,400	6,342
wc/d	1	3,102		3,102	
DOBUJINSKY, Mstislav Valerianovitch (1875-1957) Russian-American					
wc/d	3	5,700	1,000	1,200	3,500
DOCHARTY, A Brownlie (1862-1940) British					
oil	2	5,624	1,274	2,812	4,350
DODD, Howell (20th C) American					
oil	1	2,100		2,100	
DODD, Lamar (?) ?					
oil	1	8,500		8,500	
DODD, Louis (1943-) British					
oil	3	26,407	5,720	7,852	12,835
DODD, Robert (1748-1816) British					
oil	2	60,800	22,800	30,400	38,000
DODDS, Peggy (1900-) American					
oil	1	3,200		3,200	
DODEIGNE, Eugène (1923-) French					
3D	4	8,704	1,638	2,005	3,057
wc/d	1	2,135		2,135	
DODGE, William de Leftwich (1867-1935) American					
oil	1	1,600		1,600	
DODIYA, Atul (1959-) Indian					
oil	1	6,000		6,000	
DOES, Simon van der (1653-1717) Dutch					
oil	1	6,280		6,280	
DOGARTH, Oskar Robert (1898-1961) Austrian					
oil	2	2,656	1,038	1,328	1,618
DOHANOS, Stevan (1907-1994) American					
oil	1	14,000		14,000	
wc/d	1	3,000		3,000	
DOHMEN, M (19th C) ?					
oil	1	2,158		2,158	
DOIG, Peter (1959-) British					
oil	4	324,240	8,000	88,120	140,000
DOIGNEAU, Edouard Edmond de (1865-1954) French					
oil	2	5,511	2,067	2,756	3,444
wc/d	3	5,124	1,653	1,667	1,804
DOITCH, Erich (20th C) Austrian					
oil	1	2,414		2,414	
DOKOUPIL, Jiri Georg (1954-) Czechoslovakian					
3D	1	1,068		1,068	
oil	8	44,679	1,682	4,139	17,000
wc/d	6	26,359	1,133	4,163	9,000
DOLAN, Patrick (1926-1980) British					
oil	2	2,942	1,178	1,471	1,764
DOLCHI, Charles (?) ?					
oil	1	1,343		1,343	

Name	No.	Total Sales Value	lowest	Prices median	highest
DOLCI, Carlo (1616-1686) Italian					
oil	1	3,164		3,164	
DOLE, William (1917-1983) American					
wc/d	3	13,000	2,000	3,000	8,000
DOLICE, Leon (1892-1960) American					
wc/d	2	2,400	1,000	1,200	1,400
DOLL, Anton (1826-1887) German					
oil	14	102,025	1,727	5,250	13,373
wc/d	1	1,552		1,552	
DOLLA, Noel (1945-) French					
oil	1	2,629		2,629	
DOLLMAN, John Charles (1851-1934) British					
oil	2	20,674	2,370	10,337	18,304
DOLLOND, W Anstey (fl.1880-1911) British					
wc/d	3	23,356	1,776	8,580	13,000
DOLPH, John Henry (1835-1903) American					
oil	2	4,450	1,200	2,225	3,250
DOMBA, R (?) ?					
oil	1	1,480		1,480	
DOMBROWSKI, Carl Ritter von (1872-?) German					
oil	1	1,100		1,100	
DOMBURG, Antoon (1882-1954) Dutch					
oil	1	3,000		3,000	
DOMELA, Cesar (1900-1992) Dutch					
3D	1	1,031		1,031	
DOMENCHIN DE CHAVANNE, Pierre Salomon (1673-1744) French					
oil	2	22,356	4,756	11,178	17,600
DOMENICHINO (1581-1641) Italian					
oil	1	3,000,000		3,000,000	
DOMENICI, Carlo (1898-1981) Italian					
oil	9	17,392	1,153	1,784	2,676
DOMENICO DI MICHELINO (1417-1491) Italian					
oil	1	161,700		161,700	
DOMENJOZ, Raoul (1896-1978) Swiss					
oil	1	1,166		1,166	
DOMERGUE (1889-1962) French					
oil	1	3,850		3,850	
DOMERGUE, Jean Gabriel (1889-1962) French					
oil	65	341,313	1,382	4,569	19,548
wc/d	3	6,102	1,175	1,933	2,994
DOMINGO Y FALLOLA, Roberto (1867-1956) Spanish					
oil	1	2,786		2,786	
wc/d	6	36,238	2,810	5,000	12,655
DOMINGO Y MARQUES, Francisco (1842-1920) Spanish					
oil	9	248,417	1,186	4,171	197,198
DOMINGO, Roberto (1883-1956) Spanish					
wc/d	2	8,160	2,245	4,080	5,915
DOMINGUEZ (?) ?					
wc/d	1	1,751		1,751	
DOMINGUEZ BECQUER, Joaquin (1819-1879) Spanish					
oil	1	18,519		18,519	
DOMINGUEZ, Oscar (1906-1958) Spanish					
3D	1	10,384		10,384	
oil	29	1,113,288	2,044	17,997	361,633
wc/d	17	165,648	1,219	4,293	65,523
DOMINICIS, Achille de (19th C) Italian					
oil	1	2,911		2,911	
wc/d	1	2,065		2,065	
DOMINICIS, Gino de (1947-1998) Italian					
oil	1	10,352		10,352	

Name	No.	Total Sales Value	lowest	Prices median	highest
wc/d	2	14,498	4,853	7,249	9,645
DOMINIQUE, John August (1893-?) American					
oil	1	2,800		2,800	
DOMINIQUE, S (20th C) French					
oil	1	1,700		1,700	
DOMINQUE, Maurice (1918-) Canadian					
wc/d	1	1,023		1,023	
DOMMERSASS, W (?) ?					
oil	1	2,854		2,854	
DOMMERSEN, Cornelis Christian (1842-1928) Dutch					
oil	5	48,265	2,753	8,486	18,125
DOMMERSEN, Pieter Christian (1834-1908) Dutch					
oil	22	180,703	1,630	5,886	22,120
DOMMERSEN, W (1850-1927) Dutch					
oil	1	1,716		1,716	
DOMMERSEN, William (1850-1927) Dutch					
oil	12	35,479	1,378	2,562	8,030
DOMSCHKE, Carl (1812-1881) German					
oil	1	1,205		1,205	
DONADUM, S (?) ?					
wc/d	1	1,144		1,144	
DONAHEY, William (20th C) American					
wc/d	1	2,000		2,000	
DONALDSON, Andrew (1790-1846) British					
wc/d	1	1,352		1,352	
DONALDSON, David (20th C) British					
wc/d	1	1,292		1,292	
DONAT, Friederich Reginald (1830-1907) Belgian					
oil	2	5,988	2,366	2,994	3,622
DONCK, G (17th C) Flemish					
oil	1	27,930		27,930	
DONCRE, Guillaume-Dominique (1743-1820) French					
oil	1	4,422		4,422	
DONDUCCI, Giovanni Andrea (1575-1655) Italian					
oil	1	69,460		69,460	
DONGEN, Kees van (1877-1968) French/Dutch					
oil	21	6,969,017	1,382	89,685	1,887,500
wc/d	20	302,627	1,373	4,477	75,000
DONGHI, Antonio (1897-1963) Italian					
oil	1	19,290		19,290	
wc/d	1	4,501		4,501	
DONINI, Emilio (1825-?) Italian					
oil	1	2,193		2,193	
DONNAY, Auguste (1862-1921) Belgian					
oil	2	31,831	1,885	15,916	29,946
wc/d	2	8,134	3,425	4,067	4,709
DONNER, Diego (1959-) Uruguayan					
wc/d	1	2,200		2,200	
DONNITHORNE, Peter (20th C) British					
oil	1	1,100		1,100	
DONNY, D (1798-1861) Flemish					
oil	1	2,265		2,265	
DONOHO, Gaines Ruger (1857-1916) American					
oil	1	16,000		16,000	
DONSHEA, Clement H (fl.1920) American					
oil	1	3,000		3,000	
DOOMER, Lambert (1623-1700) Dutch					
oil	1	11,489		11,489	

Name	No.	Total Sales Value	Prices lowest	median	highest
DOOMS, Vic (1912-) Belgian					
oil	2	4,252	1,610	2,126	2,642
DOOREN, Edmond van (1895-1965) ?					
oil	1	1,277		1,277	
DOOREN, Émile van (20th C) Belgian					
oil	1	3,246		3,246	
DOOREN, H van (19/20th C) ?					
oil	1	2,039		2,039	
DOORN, Adriaan van (1825-1903) Dutch					
oil	1	1,058		1,058	
DOOYEWAARD, Jacob (1876-1969) Dutch					
oil	3	4,693	1,093	1,700	1,900
DOOYEWAARD, Willem (1892-1980) Dutch					
oil	2	15,395	4,683	7,698	10,712
wc/d	1	3,226		3,226	
DOQUIN, A M (20th C) ?					
wc/d	1	4,898		4,898	
DORAZIO, Piero (1927-) Italian					
oil	31	132,163	1,222	2,960	14,558
wc/d	3	9,085	1,184	1,845	6,056
DORBAY (18th C) French					
oil	1	2,311		2,311	
DORCHIN, Yaacov (1946-) Israeli					
3D	1	3,600		3,600	
DORE, Armand (1824-1882) French					
oil	1	5,000		5,000	
DORE, Genevieve (1907-1936) French					
oil	1	1,719		1,719	
DORE, Gustave (1832-1883) French					
3D	2	40,000	18,000	20,000	22,000
oil	6	289,337	4,089	17,423	204,735
wc/d	5	58,482	1,425	3,501	43,821
D'ORGEIX, Christian (20th C) French					
wc/d	1	1,167		1,167	
DORIGNY, Michel (1617-1665) French					
oil	1	244,392		244,392	
DORING, Adam Lude (1925-) German					
3D	1	1,196		1,196	
oil	1	1,026		1,026	
D'ORLEANS, Duke Ferdinand Philippe Louis Charles Henri (1810-1842) French					
wc/d	1	1,387		1,387	
D'ORLEANS, François (1818-1900) French					
wc/d	4	80,902	1,964	6,742	65,455
D'ORLEANS, Marie Christine (1813-1839) French					
3D	1	1,073		1,073	
wc/d	2	2,880	1,440	1,440	1,440
DORNBACH, Hans (1900-1992) Dutch					
wc/d	1	1,240		1,240	
DORNE, Martin van (1736-1808) Flemish					
oil	2	63,837	18,887	31,919	44,950
DORNER, Helmut (1952-) German					
3D	1	16,000		16,000	
DORNER, Johann Jakob (younger) (1775-1852) German					
oil	3	19,475	3,545	4,965	10,965
wc/d	1	1,365		1,365	
DORPH, Anton (1831-1914) Danish					
oil	4	10,210	1,212	2,047	4,905
DORPH, Bertha (1875-1960) Danish					
oil	2	4,708	1,059	2,354	3,649

Name	No.	Total Sales Value	lowest	Prices median	highest
DORRIES, Bernhard (1898-1978) German					
wc/d	1	1,730		1,730	
D'ORSAY, Count Alfred Guillaume Gabriel (1801-1852) French					
3D	1	13,546		13,546	
DORSCH, Ferdinand (1875-1938) German					
oil	2	9,731	1,081	4,866	8,650
DORSEY, W (20th C) American					
oil	1	1,100		1,100	
DORSEY, William (1942-) American					
oil	4	6,850	1,200	1,700	2,250
DORSSELAER, E van (?) Belgian?					
oil	1	1,450		1,450	
D'OSZE (19th C) ?					
oil	1	1,454		1,454	
DOTREMONT, Christian (1922-1979) Belgian					
oil	1	20,969		20,969	
wc/d	5	21,114	2,589	3,093	8,189
DOTTORI, Gerardo (1884-1977) Italian					
oil	1	27,176		27,176	
wc/d	1	28,146		28,146	
DOU, Gerard (1613-1675) Dutch					
oil	2	406,861	66,861	203,431	340,000
DOU, Gerard (school) (1613-1675) Dutch					
oil	1	2,088		2,088	
DOUCET, Jacques (1924-1994) French					
oil	7	45,180	1,092	4,634	15,274
wc/d	8	14,949	1,005	1,704	2,662
DOUGHERTY, Paul (1877-1947) American					
wc/d	1	4,000		4,000	
DOUGLAS (19th C) ?					
oil	1	3,326		3,326	
DOUGLAS, Andrew A (1870-1935) British					
oil	1	1,470		1,470	
DOUGLAS, Edward Algernon Stuart (1850-c.1920) British					
oil	3	19,946	2,114	4,832	13,000
DOUGLAS, Edwin (1848-1914) British					
oil	3	66,180	13,430	17,000	35,750
wc/d	1	1,304		1,304	
DOUGLAS, James (1858-1911) British					
wc/d	2	3,510	1,492	1,755	2,018
DOUGLAS, R (?) ?					
oil	1	1,359		1,359	
DOUGLAS, Sir William Fettes (1822-1891) British					
oil	3	11,764	2,610	3,234	5,920
DOUGLAS, William (1780-1832) British					
oil	1	6,435		6,435	
DOUMET, Zacharie Felix (1761-1818) French					
wc/d	5	94,473	2,058	10,335	57,380
DOUNTCHEV, Serguei (1916-) Russian					
oil	1	2,793		2,793	
DOUST, Jacob van (19th C) Dutch					
oil	1	2,800		2,800	
DOUTRELEAU (19/20th C) French					
wc/d	1	1,422		1,422	
DOUTRELEAU, Agathe (19th C) French					
oil	1	1,006		1,006	
DOUTRELEAU, Pierre (1938-) French					
oil	1	1,909		1,909	

Name	No.	Total Sales Value	lowest	Prices median	highest
DOUVEN, Jac (1908-) Belgian					
oil	1	1,424		1,424	
DOUW, Simon Johannes van (1630-1677) Flemish					
oil	1	7,071		7,071	
DOUZETTE, Louis (1834-1924) German					
oil	4	8,975	1,822	2,259	2,636
DOVA, Gianni (1925-1991) Italian					
oil	13	53,301	1,493	2,836	13,621
wc/d	4	9,508	1,456	2,306	3,441
DOVASTON, Margaret (1884-?) British					
oil	1	9,480		9,480	
DOVE, Arthur G (1880-1946) American					
oil	1	80,000		80,000	
wc/d	1	22,000		22,000	
DOVERA, Achille (1838-1895) Italian					
oil	1	8,207		8,207	
wc/d	1	1,731		1,731	
DOW, Arthur W (1857-1922) American					
oil	2	104,000	4,000	52,000	100,000
DOWELL, Charles R (?-1935) British					
oil	1	1,716		1,716	
DOWINAR, B M (19th C) British?					
oil	1	6,520		6,520	
DOWLING, Blewid (19th C) British					
oil	1	2,568		2,568	
DOWNES, Rackstraw (1939-) American					
oil	3	112,000	5,000	42,000	65,000
DOWNIE, John P (1871-1945) British					
wc/d	1	1,838		1,838	
DOWNIE, Patrick (1854-1945) British					
oil	4	22,545	1,073	4,531	12,410
wc/d	2	3,536	1,352	1,768	2,184
DOWNING, Delapoer (fl.1886-1902) British					
oil	1	3,792		3,792	
DOWNING, Joe (1925-) ?					
oil	1	2,997		2,997	
DOWNMAN, John (1750-1824) British					
oil	2	145,900	69,460	72,950	76,440
wc/d	5	22,908	1,450	5,056	7,536
DOWNS, Edgar (1876-1963) British					
oil	1	6,300		6,300	
DOYEN, Gabriel François (1726-1806) French					
oil	3	85,596	1,796	3,800	80,000
wc/d	1	3,797		3,797	
DOYLE, Charles Altamont (1832-1893) British					
wc/d	1	7,865		7,865	
DOYLE, Richard (1824-1883) British					
wc/d	3	34,285	1,885	2,200	30,200
D'OYLY, Maj Gen Sir Charles Walters (1822-1900) British					
oil	1	3,300		3,300	
DOZE, Melchior Jean Marie (1827-1913) French					
oil	1	2,500		2,500	
DOZIER, Otis (1904-1987) American					
oil	1	5,500		5,500	
DRABKIN, Stella (1906-1976) American					
oil	1	2,000		2,000	
DRACHMANN, Holger (1846-1908) Danish					
oil	14	39,183	1,162	2,661	4,518
DRAGON, J (20th C) ?					
oil	1	5,100		5,100	

Name	No.	Total Sales Value	lowest	Prices median	highest
DRAHONET, Alexandre Jean Dubois (1791-1834) French					
wc/d	1	3,797		3,797	
DRAINS, Geo A (20th C) French					
wc/d	1	5,787		5,787	
DRAKE, Peter (20th C) American					
oil	1	1,100		1,100	
DRAPER, F (19th C) British					
wc/d	1	1,430		1,430	
DRAPER, Herbert James (1864-1920) British					
oil	2	1,173,000	29,000	586,500	1,144,000
DRAVER, Orrin (20th C) American					
oil	1	1,100		1,100	
DREBER, Heinrich (1822-1875) German					
oil	2	7,725	2,741	3,863	4,984
DRECHSLER, Johann Baptist (1756-1811) Austrian					
oil	1	9,806		9,806	
DREI, Ercole (1886-1973) Italian					
3D	2	7,230	3,498	3,615	3,732
DRENKHAHN, Reinhard (20th C) German					
oil	2	2,316	1,019	1,158	1,297
DREUX, Alfred de (1810-1860) French					
oil	6	210,105	2,037	29,296	86,977
wc/d	4	77,516	1,761	3,841	68,073
DREW, Clement (1806-1889) American					
oil	4	11,750	1,900	2,550	4,750
DREW, George W (1875-1968) American					
oil	2	4,200	2,000	2,100	2,200
DREWES, Werner (1899-1985) American					
oil	3	15,250	1,500	4,000	9,750
DREYER, Dankvart (1816-1852) Danish					
oil	7	29,210	1,883	2,436	8,936
DRIAN, Étienne (1885-1961) French					
oil	1	2,164		2,164	
DRIBEN, Peter (c.1903-1968) American					
oil	2	13,250	3,750	6,625	9,500
DRIELENBURGH, Willem van (1635-1677) Flemish					
oil	1	7,536		7,536	
DRIESSCHE, Jan van den (1954-) Belgian					
wc/d	1	1,780		1,780	
DRIESSCHE, Lucien van den (1926-1991) Belgian					
oil	1	2,373		2,373	
DRIESTEN, Arend Jan van (1878-1969) Dutch					
oil	4	7,053	1,268	1,761	2,264
wc/d	2	4,582	1,738	2,291	2,844
DRING, William (1904-1990) British					
oil	1	1,008		1,008	
DRINKWATER, Milton (19/20th C) British					
wc/d	2	2,408	1,139	1,204	1,269
DRIVER, Sue (1957-) British					
oil	1	1,628		1,628	
DRIVIER, Leon-Ernest (1878-1951) French					
wc/d	1	1,273		1,273	
DROESE, Felix (1950-) German					
oil	1	1,891		1,891	
wc/d	1	1,195		1,195	
DROGKAMP, Charles (20th C) American					
oil	1	2,400		2,400	
DROHAN, Walter (1932-) Canadian					
oil	1	1,135		1,135	

Name	No.	Total Sales Value	lowest	Prices median	highest
DROLLING, Martin (1752-1817) French					
oil	4	30,881	3,520	7,116	13,130
DROLLING, Michel Martin (1786-1851) French					
oil	1	4,422		4,422	
DROOCHSLOOT, Cornelis (1630-1673) Dutch					
oil	4	63,269	9,834	13,056	27,324
DROOCHSLOOT, Joost Cornelisz (1586-1666) Dutch					
oil	13	273,555	3,000	20,410	55,860
DROUAIS, François Hubert (1727-1775) French					
oil	1	220,000		220,000	
DROUET-CORDIER, Suzanne (1885-1973) French					
oil	1	4,133		4,133	
DROUGGE, Mauritz (1874-1949) Norwegian					
oil	1	1,039		1,039	
DROUIN, J (19th C) French					
oil	1	3,926		3,926	
DROUOT (?) French					
3D	1	2,314		2,314	
DROUOT, E (1859-1945) French					
3D	1	2,343		2,343	
DROUOT, Edouard (1859-1945) French					
3D	13	33,042	1,007	1,968	7,089
DROWN, William Staples (?-1915) American					
oil	1	4,200		4,200	
DRUILLET (20th C) French					
oil	1	2,921		2,921	
wc/d	1	1,606		1,606	
DRUKS, Michael (1940-) Israeli					
oil	2	4,100	2,000	2,050	2,100
wc/d	1	1,350		1,350	
DRUMAUX, Angelina (1881-1959) Luxembourger					
oil	1	3,246		3,246	
DRUMMOND, B M (fl.1840-1855) British					
oil	1	2,084		2,084	
DRUMMOND, J (19th C) British					
wc/d	1	1,974		1,974	
DRUMMOND, Malcolm (1880-1945) British					
oil	1	7,540		7,540	
DRUMMOND, N (?) ?					
oil	1	2,698		2,698	
DRURY, Alfred (1856-1944) British					
3D	2	7,556	2,516	3,778	5,040
DRUYF, Dirck (c.1620-?) Dutch					
wc/d	1	1,257		1,257	
DRYDEN, Helen (1887-?) American					
wc/d	1	2,300		2,300	
DRYSDALE, Alexander John (1870-1934) American					
oil	32	126,000	1,100	2,200	38,000
DUASSUT, Curtius (fl.1889-1903) British					
wc/d	2	2,775	1,185	1,388	1,590
DUBACH, Margaretha (1938-) Swiss					
3D	1	2,552		2,552	
DUBASTY, Adolphe Henri (1814-1884) French					
oil	1	1,368		1,368	
DUBBELS, Hendrik (1620-1676) Dutch					
oil	2	43,092	21,140	21,546	21,952
DUBEN, Anders Gustav von (1785-1846) Swedish					
wc/d	1	1,809		1,809	

Name	No.	Total Sales Value	lowest	Prices median	highest
DUBLIN, Jacques (1901-1978) Swiss					
oil	1	1,924		1,924	
DUBOIS (?) ?					
oil	1	13,546		13,546	
DUBOIS DE PACE, Marguerite (1883-) French					
oil	1	1,273		1,273	
DUBOIS, A (?) French					
oil	1	3,216		3,216	
DUBOIS, François (1790-1871) French					
oil	1	2,755		2,755	
DUBOIS, Guillam (1620-1680) Dutch					
oil	1	5,692		5,692	
DUBOIS, Henri Pierre Hippolyte (1837-1909) French					
oil	1	4,214		4,214	
DUBOIS, P (?) ?					
3D	2	5,897	1,246	2,949	4,651
DUBOIS, Paul (1830-1887) American					
3D	1	2,000		2,000	
DUBOIS, Paul (1858-1938) Belgian					
3D	1	1,278		1,278	
DUBOIS, Paul (1829-1905) French					
3D	9	25,537	1,547	2,300	5,494
DUBOIS, Paul-Elie (1886-1949) French					
oil	4	55,280	1,979	3,287	46,728
DUBOIS, Paulus (16th C) Flemish					
oil	1	2,828		2,828	
DUBOIS, Raphael (1888-?) Belgian					
oil	2	4,445	1,667	2,223	2,778
DUBOIS, Simon (1632-1708) Dutch					
oil	1	2,697		2,697	
DUBOURG, Alexandre (?) French?					
oil	2	5,514	1,923	2,757	3,591
DUBOURG, Henri (18/19th C) French					
oil	1	1,000		1,000	
DUBOURG, Louis Alexandre (c.1825-1891) French					
oil	1	1,182		1,182	
DUBOUT, Albert (1905-1978) French					
3D	2	3,029	1,443	1,515	1,586
wc/d	10	17,594	1,009	1,515	2,884
DUBOVSKOY, Nicolay Nikanorovich (1859-1918) Russian					
oil	1	12,080		12,080	
DUBRAY, Vital-Gabriel (1832-1892) French					
3D	1	5,495		5,495	
DUBREUIL, C F (1828-1880) French					
oil	1	3,988		3,988	
DUBREUIL, Cheri François (1828-1880) French					
oil	6	50,681	1,698	7,300	15,000
DUBREUIL, Victor (19th C) French					
oil	3	80,045	2,252	6,500	71,293
DUBUC, Jean Louis (1946-) French					
oil	1	2,765		2,765	
DUBUC, Roland (1924-1998) Swiss					
oil	5	5,893	1,057	1,103	1,328
DUBUCAND, Alfred (1828-1894) French					
3D	14	45,199	1,580	2,638	5,964
DUBUFE, Edouard Louis (1820-1883) French					
oil	2	29,915	7,301	14,958	22,614
DUBUFE, Edouard Marie Guillaume (1853-1909) French					
wc/d	1	5,133		5,133	

Name	No.	Total Sales Value	lowest	Prices median	highest
DUBUFFET, Jean (1901-1985) French					
3D	2	365,000	125,000	182,500	240,000
oil	16	3,194,134	5,841	77,184	981,500
wc/d	21	1,023,024	1,596	18,749	317,100
DUBUIS, Fernand (1908-1991) Swiss					
oil	1	2,033		2,033	
DUBUISSON, Alexandre (1805-1870) French					
oil	3	9,128	1,956	2,608	4,564
DUBUTZ, Edouard (19th C) French					
wc/d	1	1,018		1,018	
DUC (?) ?					
oil	1	1,033		1,033	
DUC, Antoine (17th C) ?					
oil	1	1,389		1,389	
DUCA, Alfred Milton (1920-1997) American					
oil	2	2,600	1,200	1,300	1,400
DUCAMP, P (19/20th C) ?					
oil	1	1,897		1,897	
DUCAT, R (?) ?					
oil	1	1,166		1,166	
DUCE, Alberto (1919-) Spanish?					
oil	1	1,661		1,661	
DUCERCEAU, Jacques Androuet (1510-?) French					
wc/d	1	1,000		1,000	
DUCHAMP, Marcel (1887-1968) French					
3D	3	173,695	4,095	69,600	100,000
DUCHAMP, Suzanne (1889-1963) French					
oil	1	2,213		2,213	
wc/d	1	1,317		1,317	
DUCHAMP-VILLON, Raymond (1876-1918) French					
3D	2	90,105	5,105	45,053	85,000
DUCHATEAU, Hugo (1938-) Belgian					
wc/d	1	3,302		3,302	
DUCHEMIN, Daniel (1866-?) French					
oil	1	2,837		2,837	
DUCHEMIN, Emma (19th C) ?					
oil	1	1,269		1,269	
DUCHOISELLE (19th C) French					
3D	1	3,500		3,500	
DUCHOW, Achim (1948-) German					
oil	1	7,597		7,597	
DUCK, Jacob (1600-1660) Dutch					
oil	3	89,452	26,671	26,671	36,110
DUCKORT, Joseph (19th C) Dutch?					
oil	1	2,370		2,370	
DUCLERE, Teodoro (1816-1867) Italian					
oil	3	45,711	11,662	13,272	20,777
wc/d	3	3,165	1,055	1,055	1,055
DUCMELIC, Zdravko (1923-) Argentinian					
wc/d	1	1,400		1,400	
DUCQ, Jean le (19th C) Dutch					
oil	1	14,134		14,134	
DUCROS, Abraham Louis Rodolphe (1748-1810) Swiss					
oil	1	3,200		3,200	
wc/d	3	25,931	2,145	2,646	21,140
DUCROS, Abraham Louis Rodolphe and VOLPATO, Giovanni (18th C) Swiss/Italian					
wc/d	2	13,271	6,142	6,636	7,129
DUCROT, Jean (19th C) ?					
oil	1	1,573		1,573	

Name	No.	Total Sales Value	lowest	Prices median	highest
DUDA, Gary (1951-) American					
oil	1	2,300		2,300	
DUDANT, Roger (1929-) Belgian					
oil	1	1,288		1,288	
DUDLEY, Arthur (fl.1890-1907) British					
wc/d	2	2,141	1,060	1,071	1,081
DUDLEY, Charles (19/20th C) British					
oil	1	1,481		1,481	
DUDLEY, Frank V (1868-1957) American					
oil	5	89,300	1,800	2,800	47,500
DUDNIK, R (20th C) Russian					
oil	1	1,176		1,176	
DUDOVICH, Marcello (1878-1962) Italian					
wc/d	2	3,998	1,017	1,999	2,981
DUDREVILLE, Leonardo (1885-1974) Italian					
oil	1	3,601		3,601	
DUEREN, Jan van (17th C) Dutch					
oil	1	4,413		4,413	
DUESSEL, Henry A (19th C) American/German					
oil	2	5,500	1,000	2,750	4,500
DUEZ, Ernest Ange (1846-1896) French					
oil	1	10,831		10,831	
DUFAU, Helene (1869-1937) French					
oil	2	3,323	1,507	1,662	1,816
DUFAUX, Alexandre (?) Swiss?					
oil	1	6,343		6,343	
DUFAUX, Camille (?) French					
oil	1	1,640		1,640	
DUFAUX, Frederic II (1852-1943) Swiss					
oil	2	2,525	1,242	1,263	1,283
DUFAUX, Henri (1878-?) French					
oil	1	11,739		11,739	
DUFEU, Edouard (1840-1900) French					
oil	4	10,803	1,064	2,404	4,932
DUFF, Graham (20th C) British					
oil	1	1,573		1,573	
DUFF, John (1925-) Canadian					
3D	1	5,500		5,500	
DUFFAUD, Jean Baptiste (1853-1927) French					
oil	1	1,105		1,105	
DUFFIELD, Mary Elizabeth (1819-1914) British					
wc/d	5	7,808	1,305	1,580	1,812
DUFFIELD, William (1816-1863) British					
oil	2	31,900	7,150	15,950	24,750
DUFLOS, Robert Louis Raymond (1898-?) French					
wc/d	1	1,061		1,061	
DUFOUR, Jos (1925-) Belgian					
oil	1	1,305		1,305	
DUFOUR, Jules (1812-1871) French					
oil	1	1,812		1,812	
DUFRAIS, Simon (20th C) British					
oil	1	10,640		10,640	
DUFRENE, François (1930-1992) French					
oil	2	4,759	2,307	2,380	2,452
wc/d	1	1,402		1,402	
DUFRESNAY VILLEYEGU (19th C) French?					
oil	1	7,000		7,000	
DUFRESNE, Charles (1876-1938) French					
oil	12	44,983	1,033	1,760	15,682

Name	No.	Total Sales Value	lowest	Prices median	highest
wc/d	4	20,239	1,993	5,108	8,030
DUFRESNE, Francois (1930-1982) French					
oil	1	2,320		2,320	
DUFSTROM, Eric (20th C) American					
oil	1	1,000		1,000	
DUFTAS, Robert (?) British?					
oil	1	1,709		1,709	
DUFY, Jean (1888-1964) French					
oil	26	452,365	3,250	15,500	35,000
wc/d	43	275,981	1,568	5,009	20,000
DUFY, Raoul (1877-1953) French					
oil	33	2,705,894	19,182	66,700	196,300
wc/d	82	2,458,901	1,027	16,495	230,000
DUGDALE, Thomas Cantrell (1880-1952) British					
wc/d	1	1,073		1,073	
DUGHET, Gaspard (1615-1675) French					
oil	8	135,875	5,000	16,192	31,400
DUGHET, Gaspard (school) (1615-1675) French					
oil	3	12,567	2,100	4,374	6,093
DUGMORE, Arthur Radclyffe (1870-1955) American					
oil	3	13,200	1,200	6,000	6,000
DUGOURC, Jean Demosthene (1749-1825) French					
wc/d	2	9,347	2,801	4,674	6,546
DUGRENOT, Jean (20th C) French					
oil	1	1,676		1,676	
DUHEM, Marie Genevieve (1871-1918) French					
oil	1	2,135		2,135	
DUJARDIN, Karel (1622-1678) Dutch					
oil	2	4,430	1,297	2,215	3,133
wc/d	1	2,840		2,840	
DUKE, Alfred (?-1905) British					
oil	3	21,593	3,020	6,795	11,778
DUKES, Charles (fl.1829-1865) British					
oil	1	5,005		5,005	
DULAC, Edmund (1882-1953) British/French					
wc/d	1	9,860		9,860	
DULIN, Pierre (1669-1748) French					
wc/d	1	4,832		4,832	
DULMEN KRUMPELMAN, Erasmus Bernhard van (1897-1987) Dutch					
oil	2	6,893	3,118	3,447	3,775
wc/d	1	1,559		1,559	
DULONG, Jean Louis (1800-1868) French					
oil	1	8,900		8,900	
DUMAIGE, Étienne-Henri (1830-1888) French					
3D	7	61,972	1,088	1,480	45,300
DUMAS, Marlene (1953-) Dutch					
wc/d	6	21,090	1,664	3,190	7,500
DUMEE (19th C) French					
oil	1	2,031		2,031	
DUMINIL, Frank (1933-) French					
oil	1	1,056		1,056	
DUMITRESCO, Natalie (1915-1997) French					
oil	24	57,533	1,069	1,506	5,500
DUMMER, Erich (1889-1929) German					
oil	1	1,171		1,171	
DUMMER, H Boylston (1878-1945) American					
oil	1	1,300		1,300	
DUMOND, Frank Vincent (1865-1951) American					
oil	1	5,250		5,250	

Name	No.	Total Sales Value	Prices lowest	median	highest
DUMONSTIER, Daniel (1574-1646) French					
wc/d	1	16,000		16,000	
DUMONT, Augustin Alexandre (1801-1884) French					
3D	1	2,175		2,175	
DUMONT, C (19/20th C) French					
oil	1	3,793		3,793	
DUMONT, François (1850-?) Belgian					
oil	2	5,763	1,963	2,882	3,800
DUMONT, Jean Claude (1805-1874) French					
oil	1	3,988		3,988	
DUMONT, L (19th C) French					
oil	1	2,592		2,592	
DUMONT, P (1884-1936) French					
oil	1	2,845		2,845	
DUMONT, Pierre (1884-1936) French					
oil	14	44,508	1,230	2,715	8,638
DUMOULIN, J (?) French					
oil	1	1,275		1,275	
DUMOULIN, Romeo (1883-1944) Belgian					
oil	2	14,778	2,687	7,389	12,091
wc/d	1	1,876		1,876	
DUNAND, Jean (1877-1942) Swiss					
3D	4	90,447	14,082	19,876	36,613
wc/d	1	29,572		29,572	
DUNAND, Pierre (20th C) French					
wc/d	1	2,137		2,137	
DUNBAR, George (20th C) American					
oil	1	1,100		1,100	
DUNBAR, Harold (1882-1953) American					
oil	1	2,300		2,300	
DUNBAR, P (19th C) British					
oil	1	1,184		1,184	
DUNCAN, Darwin (1905-) American					
oil	1	1,300		1,300	
DUNCAN, Edward (1803-1882) British					
oil	5	44,985	2,250	5,985	18,850
wc/d	12	47,933	1,057	2,607	11,850
DUNCAN, James D (1806-1881) Canadian					
wc/d	1	4,314		4,314	
DUNCAN, Robert (20th C) American					
oil	4	36,000	7,000	8,000	13,000
DUNCANSON, Robert S (1821-1872) American					
oil	2	310,000	110,000	155,000	200,000
DUNDAS, Agnes (19th C) British					
oil	1	1,178		1,178	
DUNDAS, G (19th C) American					
wc/d	2	4,300	1,500	2,150	2,800
DUNER, Sten (1931-) Swedish					
oil	1	4,221		4,221	
DUNGEROW, W (19th C) American					
oil	1	1,700		1,700	
DUNHAM, Carroll (1949-) American					
oil	2	62,500	7,500	31,250	55,000
wc/d	3	38,000	7,000	15,000	16,000
DUNINGTON, Albert (1860-c.1928) British					
oil	1	1,562		1,562	
DUNKEL, Joachim (1925-) German					
3D	2	2,941	1,427	1,471	1,514

Name	No.	Total Sales Value	Prices lowest	median	highest
DUNKER, Balthasar Anton (1746-1807) German					
wc/d	2	3,244	1,108	1,622	2,136
DUNLOP, R O (1894-1973) British					
oil	1	1,176		1,176	
DUNLOP, Ronald Ossory (1894-1973) British					
oil	16	34,795	1,073	1,546	5,056
DUNN, Harvey (1884-1952) American					
oil	3	61,000	19,000	19,000	23,000
DUNN, Joseph (1806-1860) British					
oil	1	2,717		2,717	
DUNOUY, Alexandre Hyacinthe (1757-1841) French					
oil	3	58,574	3,574	20,000	35,000
DUNOYER DE SEGONZAC, Andre (1884-1974) French					
oil	5	29,443	1,523	3,200	16,000
wc/d	38	182,937	1,018	2,615	32,000
DUNSELMAN, Jan (1863-1931) Dutch					
oil	1	1,249		1,249	
DUNSTAN, Bernard (1920-) British					
oil	17	67,650	1,727	3,190	10,152
wc/d	5	10,632	1,425	1,875	3,102
DUNTLEY (?) ?					
oil	1	2,561		2,561	
DUNTON, W Herbert (1878-1936) American					
oil	2	45,000	15,000	22,500	30,000
DUNTZE, Johannes Bertholomaus (1823-1895) German					
oil	6	38,104	3,187	3,918	12,600
DUPAGNE, Adrien (1889-1980) Belgian					
oil	2	3,000	1,220	1,500	1,780
DUPAGNE, Arthur (1895-1961) Belgian					
3D	1	2,725		2,725	
DUPAS, Jean (1882-1964) French					
wc/d	2	141,212	70,606	70,606	70,606
DUPLESSI-BERTAUX, Jean (1747-1819) French					
oil	1	5,040		5,040	
DUPOINT, F (19/20th C) French					
oil	1	1,034		1,034	
DUPON, Josue (1864-1935) Belgian					
3D	1	1,109		1,109	
DUPONT, Gainsborough (1755-1797) British					
oil	2	26,920	2,920	13,460	24,000
DUPONTIER, S (?) ?					
oil	1	1,800		1,800	
DUPORT, F A (19/20th C) French					
oil	1	3,825		3,825	
DUPPA, Bryan Edward (fl.1832-1853) Irish					
oil	1	1,668		1,668	
DUPRA, Giorgio Domenico (1689-1770) Italian					
oil	1	9,500		9,500	
DUPRAT, Albert Ferdinand (1882-?) Italian					
oil	2	4,238	2,112	2,119	2,126
DUPRAY, Henry-Louis (1841-1909) French					
oil	4	17,983	2,100	4,223	7,437
DUPRE, J (19th C) French					
oil	1	3,017		3,017	
DUPRE, Jules (1811-1889) French					
oil	35	216,422	1,824	4,052	32,000
wc/d	1	1,382		1,382	
DUPRE, Julien (1851-1910) French					
oil	9	161,815	1,458	12,000	60,000

Name	No.	Total Sales Value	lowest	Prices median	highest
DUPRE, Victor (1816-1879) French					
oil	23	106,445	1,130	3,374	17,941
DUPUIS, Francois Joseph (1842-1921) Belgian					
3D	1	4,659		4,659	
DUPUIS, Maurice (1882-1959) French					
oil	2	4,136	1,001	2,068	3,135
DUPUIS, P (?) French					
oil	1	2,054		2,054	
DUPUIS, Pierre (1610-1682) French					
oil	1	320,037		320,037	
DUPUIS, Pierre (1833-?) French					
oil	1	1,430		1,430	
DUPUY DELAROCHE, Alexandre Amedee (1819-?) French					
oil	1	3,665		3,665	
DUPUY, L (19th C) French					
oil	1	1,834		1,834	
DUPUY, Louis (19/20th C) French					
oil	3	9,079	1,638	2,043	5,398
DUPUY, Paul Michel (1869-1949) French					
oil	1	1,415		1,415	
DUQUENNE, Jules Alfred (1874-1950) French					
oil	4	5,325	1,167	1,386	1,386
DUQUESNE, Albert Charles (1891-1972) French					
wc/d	1	1,298		1,298	
DUQUESNOY, François (school) (1594-1643) Flemish					
3D	1	15,014		15,014	
DURA, Alberto (1888-1971) Uruguayan					
oil	1	1,700		1,700	
DURAN, Carolus (1837-1917) French					
oil	1	6,040		6,040	
wc/d	1	2,804		2,804	
DURANCAMPS, Rafael (1891-1979) Spanish					
oil	19	241,118	2,248	12,038	25,960
wc/d	4	6,061	1,370	1,442	1,807
DURAND, Asher Brown (1796-1886) American					
oil	2	11,244	1,244	5,622	10,000
DURAND, Francisque (1810-?) French					
oil	1	1,679		1,679	
DURAND, Godefroy (1832-?) French					
oil	1	1,160		1,160	
DURAND, Simon (1838-1896) Swiss					
oil	2	4,420	2,210	2,210	2,210
DURAND-BRAGER, Jean Baptiste Henri (1814-1879) French					
oil	7	35,424	1,347	1,801	16,512
wc/d	1	2,066		2,066	
DURANTE, Conte Giorgio (1685-1755) Italian					
oil	1	2,826		2,826	
DURBAN, Arne (1912-1993) Norwegian					
3D	1	1,546		1,546	
DURBEC, Arnaud (19/20th C) French					
oil	1	2,482		2,482	
DURDEN, James (1878-1964) British					
oil	1	2,528		2,528	
DUREL, Gaston (1879-1954) French					
oil	2	3,072	1,514	1,536	1,558
wc/d	1	1,022		1,022	
DURENNE (?) French					
oil	1	2,983		2,983	

Name	No.	Total Sales Value	lowest	Prices median	highest
DURER (school) (16th C) German					
wc/d	1	1,611		1,611	
DURER, Albrecht (1471-1528) German					
oil	2	8,619	2,990	4,310	5,629
DURET, Francisque-Joseph (1804-1864) French					
3D	12	25,061	1,168	1,920	3,651
DURET-DUJARRIC, Isabelle (1949-) French					
oil	3	28,260	4,740	12,080	12,080
wc/d	2	6,110	2,002	3,055	4,108
DUREY, René (1890-1959) French					
oil	1	2,481		2,481	
DURIG, Rolf (1926-) Swiss					
oil	4	6,308	1,108	1,376	2,449
DURINGER, Daniel (1720-1786) French?					
wc/d	1	3,024		3,024	
DURINGER, Henri (1892-1980) French					
oil	2	2,263	1,095	1,132	1,168
DURRIE, George Henry (1820-1863) American					
oil	5	511,000	11,000	15,000	440,000
DURRIE, John (1818-1898) American					
oil	1	2,400		2,400	
DURST, Auguste (1842-1930) French					
oil	1	1,963		1,963	
DUSART, Cornelis (1660-1704) Dutch					
oil	1	2,527		2,527	
wc/d	3	12,571	3,536	4,321	4,714
DUSS, Carlos (1932-1990) Swiss					
oil	3	3,555	1,089	1,143	1,323
DUSSELDORF SCHOOL, 19th C German					
oil	3	16,871	2,453	6,000	8,418
DUTCH SCHOOL					
oil	1	2,837		2,837	
DUTCH SCHOOL, 16th C					
oil	2	24,383	7,260	12,192	17,123
DUTCH SCHOOL, 16th/17th C					
oil	2	9,572	3,536	4,786	6,036
DUTCH SCHOOL, 17th C					
oil	70	501,651	1,396	4,784	31,680
wc/d	6	52,153	3,128	8,144	20,948
DUTCH SCHOOL, 17th/18th C					
oil	13	103,469	2,476	3,317	29,794
DUTCH SCHOOL, 18th C					
oil	24	129,369	2,469	3,678	19,639
wc/d	1	7,000		7,000	
DUTCH SCHOOL, 18th/19th C					
oil	5	28,399	2,997	3,715	15,003
DUTCH SCHOOL, 19th C					
3D	1	3,144		3,144	
oil	29	197,281	2,462	3,750	68,849
wc/d	1	2,357		2,357	
DUTCH SCHOOL, 20th C					
oil	1	7,244		7,244	
DUTCH-GERMAN SCHOOL, 18th C					
oil	1	2,469		2,469	
DUTCH-ITALIAN SCHOOL, 16th/17th C					
oil	1	5,324		5,324	
DUTEURTRE, Pierre Eugène (1911-) French					
oil	3	5,200	1,500	1,800	1,900
DUTTON, Thomas G (c.1819-1891) British					
wc/d	1	1,812		1,812	

Name	No.	Total Sales Value	lowest	Prices median	highest
DUVAL, Beatrice (1880-1973) French?					
oil	1	1,947		1,947	
wc/d	2	2,985	1,103	1,493	1,882
DUVAL, Edward J (fl.1876-1916) British					
wc/d	1	1,128		1,128	
DUVAL, Étienne (1824-1914) Swiss					
oil	3	9,261	1,805	3,222	4,234
DUVAL, Eugene Stanislas Guillaume (1845-?) French					
oil	1	13,500		13,500	
DUVAL, Eustace François (fl.1784-1836) French					
oil	2	10,202	3,137	5,101	7,065
DUVAL, G (20th C) French					
oil	1	2,036		2,036	
DUVAL, Henri Philippe Adolphe (19th C) Belgian					
oil	1	4,118		4,118	
DUVAL, Jean F (1776-1854) Swiss					
oil	1	1,144		1,144	
DUVAL, R (20th C) Spanish					
oil	2	4,630	1,824	2,315	2,806
DUVAL-GOZLAN, Léon (1853-1941) French					
oil	2	4,049	1,741	2,025	2,308
DUVAL-LECAMUS, Pierre (1790-1854) French					
oil	2	95,532	28,517	47,766	67,015
DUVALL, John (1816-1892) British					
oil	1	1,544		1,544	
DUVENECK, Frank (1848-1919) American					
oil	2	22,000	4,000	11,000	18,000
DUVENT, Charles Jules (1867-1940) French					
wc/d	1	1,800		1,800	
DUVERGER, Theophile Emmanuel (1821-1886) French					
oil	4	102,523	1,413	19,305	62,500
DUVERGNE, Paul (19th C) French					
oil	1	3,400		3,400	
DUVIEUX, Henri (?-1882) French					
oil	13	43,566	1,323	2,658	7,310
wc/d	1	1,897		1,897	
DUVILLIER, René (1919-) French					
oil	1	1,053		1,053	
DUVIVIER, Thomas Germain Joseph (1735-1814) French					
oil	1	17,000		17,000	
DUWE, Harald (1926-1984) German					
oil	2	2,596	1,230	1,298	1,366
DUWEE, Henri Joseph (19th C) Belgian					
oil	1	1,191		1,191	
DUYNEN, Isaac van (?-1688) Flemish					
oil	1	7,386		7,386	
DUYSTER, Willem Cornelisz (1600-1635) Dutch					
oil	1	8,000		8,000	
DUYTS, Gustave den (1850-1897) Belgian					
wc/d	1	1,824		1,824	
DUYTS, Jan de (1629-1676) Flemish					
oil	1	15,500		15,500	
DWYER, G (19th C) Continental					
oil	1	4,200		4,200	
DYBRIS, Freddie (1922-1993) Danish					
oil	1	1,153		1,153	
DYCK, Abraham van (1635-1672) Dutch					
oil	4	188,065	14,915	37,500	98,150

Name	No.	Total Sales Value	lowest	Prices median	highest
DYCK, Floris van (1575-1651) Dutch					
oil	1	110,250		110,250	
DYCK, Paul (1917-) American					
oil	1	4,000		4,000	
wc/d	1	7,000		7,000	
DYCK, Philip van (1680-1753) Flemish					
oil	1	2,724		2,724	
DYCK, Sir Anthony van (1599-1641) Flemish					
oil	5	2,583,609	1,609	453,000	1,029,000
DYCK, Sir Anthony van (school) (1599-1641) Flemish					
oil	1	1,749		1,749	
DYCK, Victor van (19/20th C) ?					
oil	1	3,594		3,594	
DYE, Charlie (1906-1972) American					
oil	5	115,500	13,000	20,000	42,500
wc/d	1	27,500		27,500	
DYE, Clarkson (1869-1955) American					
oil	1	20,000		20,000	
DYER, Lawrence A (1949-) Canadian					
oil	1	1,354		1,354	
DYER, Lowell (19th C) British					
oil	1	4,800		4,800	
DYF (1899-1985) French					
oil	1	2,164		2,164	
DYF, Marcel (1899-1985) French					
oil	57	552,172	1,948	8,779	30,764
DYKE, Samuel P (19th C) American					
oil	2	4,200	1,200	2,100	3,000
DYKSTRA, Johan (1896-1978) Dutch					
oil	1	20,598		20,598	
wc/d	5	13,449	1,585	2,371	3,961
DYXHOORN, Pieter Arnout (1810-1839) Dutch					
oil	1	4,659		4,659	
DZIERSK, Udo (1961-) German					
oil	1	3,460		3,460	
DZIGURSKI, Alex (1911-1995) American					
oil	9	20,750	1,300	2,500	3,000
DZUBAS, Friedel (1915-1994) American/German					
oil	2	27,300	1,300	13,650	26,000
EADIE, Robert (1877-1954) British					
oil	1	5,800		5,800	
wc/d	1	1,029		1,029	
EAKINS, Susan (1851-1938) American					
oil	1	1,300		1,300	
EAKINS, Thomas (1844-1916) American					
3D	1	5,500		5,500	
oil	1	48,000		48,000	
EARDLEY, Joan (1921-1963) British					
oil	6	199,110	5,840	15,435	118,900
wc/d	5	42,121	2,265	8,700	15,950
EARL, George (19th C) British					
oil	3	70,252	9,540	23,532	37,180
EARL, Maud (?-1943) British					
oil	5	52,780	1,200	6,250	21,450
wc/d	2	13,476	3,476	6,738	10,000
EARL, Percy (fl.1909-1930) British					
oil	1	33,173		33,173	
EARL, Thomas (fl.1824-1831) British					
oil	2	8,265	2,265	4,133	6,000

Name	No.	Total Sales Value	lowest	Prices median	highest
EARL, Thomas P (fl.1900-1930) British					
oil	2	3,616	1,216	1,808	2,400
EARLE, Charles (?-1893) British					
wc/d	3	4,930	1,160	1,740	2,030
EARLE, Wesley (19th C) American?					
oil	1	5,000		5,000	
EARLY and PRUITT (20th C) American					
3D	1	3,200		3,200	
EARLY, Miles J (1886-?) American					
oil	2	4,500	1,500	2,250	3,000
EARP, H (snr) (1831-1914) British					
oil	1	2,774		2,774	
EARP, Henry (19th C) British					
oil	1	1,848		1,848	
wc/d	1	1,193		1,193	
EARP, Henry (snr) (1831-1914) British					
oil	2	4,488	1,015	2,244	3,473
wc/d	5	7,177	1,106	1,480	1,650
EAST EUROPEAN SCHOOL, 18th C					
oil	1	5,966		5,966	
EAST, H (?) British					
oil	1	1,008		1,008	
EAST, Sir Alfred (1849-1913) British					
oil	7	42,428	2,041	5,000	10,010
EATON, Charles Warren (1857-1937) American					
oil	4	16,800	1,500	3,650	8,000
EBBE, Axel (1868-1941) Swedish					
3D	2	2,607	1,204	1,304	1,403
EBEL, Fritz Carl Werner (1835-1895) German					
oil	3	12,721	2,764	4,720	5,237
EBERHARD, Heinrich (1884-1973) German					
oil	1	1,178		1,178	
EBERL, François (1887-1962) French					
oil	1	1,237		1,237	
EBERLE, Abastenia St Leger (1878-1942) American					
3D	1	3,200		3,200	
EBERLE, Adolf (1843-1914) German					
oil	5	38,630	2,844	8,991	10,795
EBERLE, Robert (1815-1860) Swiss					
oil	2	5,545	2,476	2,773	3,069
EBERLEIN, G H (1847-1926) German					
3D	1	1,511		1,511	
EBERLEIN, Gustav Heinrich (1847-1926) German					
3D	1	1,019		1,019	
EBERLEIN, Otto (19th C) ?					
oil	1	5,465		5,465	
EBERT, Anton (1845-1896) German					
oil	1	2,689		2,689	
EBERT, Carl (1821-1885) German					
oil	5	24,293	1,219	2,944	14,365
EBERT, Charles H (1873-1959) American					
oil	2	42,500	7,500	21,250	35,000
EBERZ, Josef (1880-1942) German					
oil	3	57,530	14,078	16,003	27,449
wc/d	5	20,241	1,456	2,524	8,252
ECCARDT, John Giles (?-1779) German					
oil	1	37,180		37,180	
ECHEGARAY Y GARCIA, Martin (20th C) Spanish					
wc/d	1	1,297		1,297	

Name	No.	Total Sales Value	lowest	Prices median	highest
ECHENA, Jose (1845-1909) Spanish					
oil	1	21,000		21,000	
ECHEVARRIA, Jose Luis (20th C) Spanish					
oil	1	3,520		3,520	
ECHEVERRIA, Federico de (1911-) Spanish?					
oil	3	11,766	2,389	3,657	5,720
ECHTLER, Adolf (1843-1914) German					
oil	1	1,219		1,219	
ECKARDT, Christian (1832-1914) Danish					
oil	2	11,481	1,219	5,741	10,262
ECKELBOOM, Hendrik Daniel (1806-1847) Dutch					
oil	1	2,229		2,229	
ECKENBRECHER, T von (1842-1921) German					
oil	1	1,170		1,170	
ECKENBRECHER, Themistocles von (1842-1921) German					
oil	9	43,086	1,162	2,178	23,360
ECKENFELDER, Friedrich (1861-1938) German					
oil	3	5,765	1,500	1,796	2,469
ECKERSBERG, C W (1783-1853) Danish					
wc/d	1	1,622		1,622	
ECKERSBERG, Christoffer Wilhelm (1783-1853) Danish					
oil	11	1,318,752	3,700	103,268	425,980
wc/d	4	16,148	1,787	4,053	6,256
ECKERSBERG, Christoffer Wilhelm (school) (1783-1853) Danish					
oil	2	6,497	1,850	3,249	4,647
ECKERSBERG, Erling (1808-1889) Danish					
wc/d	1	6,196		6,196	
ECKERSBERG, Johan Fredrik (1822-1870) Norwegian					
oil	1	24,490		24,490	
ECKERT, Heinrich Ambros (1807-1840) German					
oil	1	7,273		7,273	
EDE, Basil (1931-) British					
wc/d	5	7,848	1,406	1,628	1,846
EDE, Frederick Charles Vipond (1865-1907) American					
oil	1	2,259		2,259	
EDELFELT, Albert (1854-1905) Finnish					
oil	3	199,947	24,411	69,836	105,700
EDELMANN, Yrjo (1941-) Swedish					
oil	7	21,560	1,843	2,394	5,604
EDGAR, Edmund (1801-?) Australian					
oil	1	4,000		4,000	
EDGAR, Norman (?) ?					
oil	2	5,292	2,205	2,646	3,087
EDGE, John William (19th C) British					
wc/d	1	1,650		1,650	
EDLICH, Stephen (1944-) American					
oil	2	6,500	1,500	3,250	5,000
EDMONDSON, William J (1868-1966) American					
oil	1	1,400		1,400	
EDOUART, Augustin (1789-1861) French					
wc/d	1	4,200		4,200	
EDRIDGE, Henry (1769-1821) British					
wc/d	2	6,510	2,718	3,255	3,792
EDUARD, Jean Marie (1847-1916) Swiss					
oil	1	11,008		11,008	
EDWARDS, Henrietta (1849-1931) Canadian					
oil	1	1,318		1,318	
EDWARDS, J W (20th C) British					
oil	1	2,808		2,808	

Name	No.	Total Sales Value	lowest	Prices median	highest
EDWARDS, Lionel (1878-1966) British					
oil	1	7,222		7,222	
wc/d	19	162,286	1,359	4,380	65,000
EDY-LEGRAND, Edouard Léon Louis (1892-1970) French					
wc/d	1	10,952		10,952	
EDZARD, Dietz (1893-1963) German					
oil	17	72,906	1,000	3,295	10,730
EECKHOUDT, Jean van den (1875-1946) Belgian					
oil	2	5,426	2,207	2,713	3,219
EECKHOUT, Gerbrand van den (1621-1674) Dutch					
oil	3	241,236	4,844	9,892	226,500
wc/d	1	17,286		17,286	
EECKHOUT, Jakob Joseph (1793-1861) Flemish					
oil	1	16,048		16,048	
EEKMAN, Nicolaas (1889-1973) Belgian					
oil	5	12,820	1,264	1,836	5,695
EELSINGH, Stien (1903-1964) Dutch?					
wc/d	1	2,185		2,185	
EEMANS, Marc (1907-1998) Belgian					
wc/d	1	1,787		1,787	
EERELMAN, Otto (1839-1926) Dutch					
oil	5	91,634	2,950	12,243	34,433
wc/d	3	34,245	2,296	9,759	22,190
EERTVELT, Andries van (1590-1652) Flemish					
oil	1	9,554		9,554	
EGAN, Eloise (20th C) American					
oil	1	1,900		1,900	
EGEA LOPEZ, Alberto (1901-1958) Venezuelan					
oil	1	2,840		2,840	
EGELL, Augustin (1731-1785) German					
wc/d	2	7,388	3,694	3,694	3,694
EGERSDORFER, Andreas (1866-?) German					
oil	2	2,859	1,359	1,430	1,500
EGERSDORFER, Konrad (1868-?) German					
wc/d	1	3,386		3,386	
EGG, Augustus Leopold (1816-1863) British					
oil	1	3,750		3,750	
EGGENHOFER, Nick (1897-1985) American					
oil	1	2,600		2,600	
wc/d	4	13,400	1,600	2,650	6,500
EGGENSCHWILER, Franz (1930-) Swiss					
3D	2	2,856	1,033	1,428	1,823
oil	1	1,226		1,226	
EGGER, Jean (1897-1934) Austrian					
oil	2	38,900	16,379	19,450	22,521
EGGER-LIENZ, Albin (1868-1926) Austrian					
oil	1	79,200		79,200	
EGGERMONT, Jacques (1919-) Belgian					
oil	1	1,880		1,880	
EGGERS, Johan Peter (1855-1907) Swedish					
oil	1	1,256		1,256	
EGGINTON, Frank (1908-1990) British					
oil	1	2,373		2,373	
wc/d	21	45,409	1,284	2,016	3,848
EGGINTON, Wycliffe (1875-1951) British					
wc/d	6	8,923	1,001	1,253	2,220
EGGLESTON, Benjamin (1867-1937) American					
oil	1	3,250		3,250	
EGLAU, Otto (1917-) German					
oil	1	1,026		1,026	

Name	No.	Total Sales Value	lowest	Prices median	highest
EGLER, Willi (1887-?) German					
oil	1	1,319		1,319	
EGLEY, William Maw (c.1827-1916) British					
wc/d	1	1,350		1,350	
EGMONT, Justus van (1601-1674) Flemish					
oil	1	18,000		18,000	
EGNELL, Allan (1884-1960) Swedish					
oil	1	1,036		1,036	
EGORNOV, Alexander Semenovich (1858-1902) Russian					
oil	1	7,550		7,550	
EGYPTIAN SCHOOL					
3D	1	39,561		39,561	
EHHARDT, Edris (20th C) American					
3D	1	1,200		1,200	
EHMSEN, Heinrich (1886-1964) German					
oil	1	2,681		2,681	
wc/d	2	9,936	2,016	4,968	7,920
EHRENBERG, Paul (1876-1949) German					
oil	1	1,300		1,300	
EHRENBERG, Wilhelm von (1630-1676) Dutch					
oil	1	10,222		10,222	
EHRENSTRAHL, David Klocker von (1629-1698) German					
oil	3	48,118	4,063	14,673	29,382
EHRENSTRAHL, David Klocker von (school) (1629-1698) German					
oil	2	27,652	5,079	13,826	22,573
EHRET, Georg Dyonis (1710-1770) British					
wc/d	1	12,155		12,155	
EHRHARDT, Curt (1895-1972) Swiss					
oil	7	23,733	2,128	2,878	5,461
EHRHARDT, Karl Ludwig Adolf (1813-1899) German					
oil	1	3,234		3,234	
EIBNER, Friedrich (1825-1877) German					
oil	1	27,413		27,413	
EICHHORN, Albert (1811-1851) German					
oil	1	9,000		9,000	
EICHHORN, Alfred (1909-1972) Austrian					
oil	4	6,470	1,365	1,591	1,923
EICHHORN, Peter (1877-1960) German					
oil	2	2,258	1,000	1,129	1,258
EICHHORST, Franz (1885-?) German					
oil	1	2,699		2,699	
EICHINGER, Erwin (19th C) Austrian					
oil	6	13,283	1,185	1,541	4,992
EICHINGER, Otto (1922-) Austrian					
oil	4	15,454	1,444	3,450	7,110
EICHLER, Joseph Franz Maria (1724-?) German					
oil	1	8,240		8,240	
EICKEN, Elisabeth von (1862-?) German					
oil	1	1,969		1,969	
EIDSON (20th C) American?					
wc/d	1	1,500		1,500	
EIEMINO, E (18/19th C) Italian					
oil	1	2,000		2,000	
EIGENBERGER, Gary (1960-) American					
3D	1	2,840		2,840	
EILERS, Conrad (1845-1914) German					
oil	2	2,779	1,106	1,390	1,673
EILERSEN, Eiler Rasmussen (1827-1912) Danish					
oil	3	7,294	1,311	1,311	4,641

Name	No.	Total Sales Value	lowest	Prices median	highest
EILSHEMIUS, Louis M (1864-1941) American					
oil	3	3,700	1,000	1,100	1,600
EINBECK, Walter (1890-?) German					
oil	1	1,100		1,100	
EINHART, Karl (1885-1959) German					
oil	3	5,510	1,581	1,725	2,204
EISEN, Charles-Dominique-Joseph (1720-1778) French					
oil	1	43,489		43,489	
EISEN, François (1695-1778) Flemish					
oil	1	3,214		3,214	
EISENDIECK, Suzanne (1908-) German					
oil	3	7,201	1,463	1,738	4,000
EISENHUT, Ferencz (1857-1903) Hungarian					
oil	1	13,636		13,636	
EISENLOHR, Friedrich (1805-1856) German					
wc/d	3	4,547	1,231	1,463	1,853
EISENMAN, Nicole (1963-) American					
oil	1	1,800		1,800	
wc/d	4	8,900	1,400	1,750	4,000
EISENSCHER, Yaacov (1896-1980) Israeli					
oil	6	20,700	2,000	3,250	5,400
EISENSCHITZ, Willy (1889-1974) French					
oil	18	111,691	1,100	4,964	23,582
wc/d	4	4,926	1,002	1,126	1,625
EISLER, Georg (1928-1998) Austrian					
oil	1	1,621		1,621	
EISMOND, Jozef (19th C) Polish?					
oil	1	3,715		3,715	
EITNER, Ernst (1867-1955) German					
oil	1	3,575		3,575	
EJSMOND, Franz von (1859-1931) Polish					
oil	1	11,964		11,964	
EKELS, Jan (younger) (1759-1793) Dutch					
oil	1	44,100		44,100	
EKELUND, Poul (1920-1976) Danish					
oil	5	6,071	1,025	1,039	1,765
EKENAES, Jahn (1847-1920) Norwegian					
oil	1	35,000		35,000	
EKLUND, Sten (1942-) Swedish					
oil	1	3,111		3,111	
EKLUNDH, Claes (1944-) Swedish					
wc/d	1	1,152		1,152	
EKMAN, Emil (1880-1951) Swedish					
oil	1	1,201		1,201	
EKSTAM, Alfred (1878-1935) Danish					
oil	1	1,806		1,806	
EKSTROM, Fredrik af (1852-1915) Swedish					
oil	1	1,084		1,084	
EKSTROM, Per (1844-1935) Swedish					
oil	29	130,250	1,239	4,289	10,882
EKVALL, Emma (1838-1925) Swedish					
oil	6	36,852	1,442	2,691	19,147
EKVALL, Knut (1843-1912) Swedish					
oil	7	21,388	1,741	3,312	4,176
ELAND, Leonardus Joseph (1884-1952) Dutch					
oil	1	1,073		1,073	
ELDH, Carl (1873-1955) Swedish					
3D	7	14,854	1,129	1,741	3,819

Name	No.	Total Sales Value	lowest	Prices median	highest
ELDRED, Lemeul D (1848-1921) American					
oil	1	11,000		11,000	
ELFFERS, Dick (1919-1991) Dutch					
wc/d	1	1,573		1,573	
ELGOOD, G S (1851-1943) British					
wc/d	1	1,146		1,146	
ELGOOD, George Samuel (1851-1943) British					
wc/d	8	15,245	1,125	2,206	2,516
ELGUEA, Carmelo Ortiz de (1944-) Spanish					
oil	1	1,115		1,115	
ELIAS, Alfred (19th C) British					
oil	2	2,352	1,130	1,176	1,222
ELIAS, Étienne (1936-) Belgian					
oil	1	1,386		1,386	
ELIAS, Nicolaes (1590-1656) Dutch					
oil	1	90,600		90,600	
ELIE, Madame (19th C) French					
wc/d	1	7,536		7,536	
ELIM, Frank (20th C) French					
oil	2	2,972	1,313	1,486	1,659
ELIN, Felix (20th C) ?					
oil	1	1,600		1,600	
ELIOT, Maurice (1864-?) French					
oil	1	1,422		1,422	
ELIOTT, Harry (1882-1959) ?					
wc/d	3	7,243	1,595	1,993	3,655
ELISCHER, Hans (?-1935) Austrian/German					
3D	1	3,146		3,146	
ELLE, Louis (elder) (1612-1689) French					
oil	4	91,049	6,379	24,335	36,000
ELLENRIEDER, Maria (1791-1863) Swiss					
wc/d	1	1,268		1,268	
ELLERBY, Thomas (19th C) British					
oil	1	10,010		10,010	
ELLIGER, Ottmar I (1633-1679) Swedish					
oil	1	30,774		30,774	
ELLIOT, Kate E (fl.1881-1886) British					
oil	1	1,034		1,034	
ELLIOTT, Robinson (1814-1894) British					
oil	1	2,184		2,184	
ELLIS, A (18/19th C) ?					
oil	1	1,421		1,421	
ELLIS, Arthur (1856-?) British					
oil	1	2,574		2,574	
ELLIS, Edwin (1841-1895) British					
oil	2	3,129	1,141	1,565	1,988
ELLIS, Fremont F (1897-1985) American					
oil	9	189,194	1,694	9,000	70,000
ELLIS, Gordon (1920-1978) British					
oil	2	6,320	3,020	3,160	3,300
ELLIS, Joseph F (1783-1848) British					
oil	2	16,065	7,065	8,033	9,000
wc/d	1	1,793		1,793	
ELLIS, Stephen (1951-) American					
oil	2	6,225	2,600	3,113	3,625
ELLIS, Tristram (1844-1922) British					
wc/d	3	10,035	2,628	3,637	3,770
ELLIS, Walter E (?) British					
oil	2	5,340	1,548	2,670	3,792

Name	No.	Total Sales Value	lowest	Prices median	highest
ELLSWORTH, Clarence (1885-1961) American					
oil	1	1,200		1,200	
ELMORE, Alfred (1815-1881) British					
oil	1	5,434		5,434	
ELSHEIMER, Adam (1574-1620) German					
oil	1	3,657		3,657	
wc/d	1	10,607		10,607	
ELSHOLTZ, Ludwig (1805-1850) German					
oil	1	1,552		1,552	
ELSLEY, Arthur John (1861-1952) British					
oil	5	1,739,750	47,400	377,500	750,000
ELTEN, Hendrik Dirk Kruseman van (1829-1904) Dutch					
oil	3	7,895	2,011	2,601	3,283
ELUARD, Paul (20th C) French					
wc/d	1	20,064		20,064	
ELVGREN, Gil (1914-1980) American					
oil	3	99,000	15,000	40,000	44,000
ELWELL, D Jerome (1847-1912) American					
oil	1	2,750		2,750	
ELWELL, Frederick William (1870-1958) British					
oil	5	18,157	1,139	1,580	11,100
ELWERT, A (19th C) American					
oil	1	1,400		1,400	
EMANUEL, Anund (1859-1941) Swedish					
oil	1	1,573		1,573	
EMBDE, August von der (1780-1862) German					
oil	1	11,394		11,394	
EMBIL, Miguel (19th C) Cuban					
3D	1	3,140		3,140	
EME, Andre (1931-) French					
oil	1	1,096		1,096	
EMERSON, William C (1865-?) American					
oil	1	2,600		2,600	
EMETT, Rowland (1906-1990) British					
wc/d	9	10,838	1,015	1,133	1,670
EMILIAN SCHOOL, 16th C Italian					
oil	3	29,481	5,504	8,727	15,250
wc/d	2	10,322	3,322	5,161	7,000
EMILIAN SCHOOL, 17th C Italian					
3D	1	2,495		2,495	
oil	7	54,247	3,491	5,192	21,312
EMILIAN SCHOOL, 17th/18th C Italian					
oil	1	2,495		2,495	
EMILIAN SCHOOL, 18th C Italian					
oil	3	16,403	2,588	6,421	7,394
EMIN, Tracey (1963-) British					
wc/d	2	2,567	1,208	1,284	1,359
EMMENEGGER, Hans (1866-1940) Swiss					
oil	3	12,501	1,253	5,624	5,624
EMMERIK, Govert van (1808-1882) Dutch					
oil	3	8,205	1,744	2,784	3,677
EMMERSON, Henry H (1831-1895) British					
oil	1	7,500		7,500	
EMMS, John (1843-1912) British					
oil	16	395,988	2,567	12,750	125,000
EMOKPAE, Erhabor (1934-1984) Nigerian					
3D	1	1,100		1,100	
EMPIRE SCHOOL, 19th C					
3D	1	3,735		3,735	

Name	No.	Total Sales Value	lowest	Prices median	highest
EMPOLI, V (19th C) Italian					
oil	1	7,300		7,300	
EMPRESS OF PRUSSIA, Victoria (1840-1901) British					
oil	1	33,220		33,220	
EMSLIE, Alfred Edward (1848-1918) British					
oil	1	10,725		10,725	
wc/d	1	1,431		1,431	
ENDE, Felix von (1856-?) German					
oil	1	26,000		26,000	
ENDE, Hans am (1864-1918) German					
oil	6	28,037	1,950	5,050	7,273
wc/d	2	4,046	1,773	2,023	2,273
ENDER, Axel Hjalmar (1853-1920) Norwegian					
oil	1	12,415		12,415	
ENDER, Johann Nepomuk (1793-1854) Austrian					
oil	1	25,918		25,918	
ENDER, Thomas (1793-1875) Austrian					
oil	2	26,646	5,712	13,323	20,934
wc/d	2	5,074	2,018	2,537	3,056
ENDRES, Louis John (1896-1989) American					
wc/d	2	3,927	1,447	1,964	2,480
ENGEL VON DER RABENAU, Carl (1817-1870) German					
oil	1	2,234		2,234	
ENGEL, Otto Heinrich (1866-1949) German					
oil	2	15,008	7,150	7,504	7,858
ENGEL, Werner Emil (1880-1941) Swiss					
oil	1	1,615		1,615	
ENGELEN, Peter (1962-) ?					
3D	1	1,509		1,509	
ENGELEN, Piet van (1863-1923) Belgian					
oil	2	8,573	2,621	4,287	5,952
ENGELHARD, Heinrich (19th C) American?					
wc/d	1	7,750		7,750	
ENGELHARDT, Georg (1823-1883) German					
oil	1	2,234		2,234	
ENGELHARDT, Maja Lisa (1956-) Danish					
oil	1	1,311		1,311	
ENGELHART, Catherine Caroline (1845-1926) Danish					
oil	1	6,641		6,641	
ENGELS, L (20th C) Belgian					
oil	1	2,911		2,911	
ENGELS, Leo (1882-1952) Belgian					
oil	1	2,575		2,575	
ENGELSBERG, Léon (1908-1999) Israeli					
oil	2	16,500	8,000	8,250	8,500
ENGELSTED, Malthe (1852-1930) Danish					
oil	1	3,813		3,813	
ENGELUND, Svend (1908-) Danish					
oil	5	8,664	1,027	1,803	2,404
ENGHART, G (?) ?					
oil	1	2,198		2,198	
ENGL, Hugo (1852-?) Austrian					
oil	1	1,133		1,133	
ENGLAND, E S (19/20th C) ?					
oil	1	1,080		1,080	
ENGLEHART, John Joseph (1867-1915) American					
oil	3	5,500	1,000	1,800	2,700
ENGLISH COLONIAL SCHOOL					
oil	1	14,049		14,049	

Name	No.	Total Sales Value	lowest	Prices median	highest
ENGLISH COLONIAL SCHOOL, 19th C					
oil	1	29,820		29,820	
ENGLISH MARINE SCHOOL, 19th C					
oil	2	14,896	6,080	7,448	8,816
ENGLISH NAIVE SCHOOL, 18th C					
oil	1	4,544		4,544	
ENGLISH PROVINCIAL SCHOOL, 18th C					
oil	1	3,926		3,926	
ENGLISH PROVINCIAL SCHOOL, 19th C					
oil	1	5,076		5,076	
wc/d	2	15,477	3,552	7,739	11,925
ENGLISH SCHOOL					
3D	1	9,554		9,554	
oil	3	31,561	3,813	5,548	22,200
ENGLISH SCHOOL, 16th C					
oil	1	3,718		3,718	
ENGLISH SCHOOL, 17th C					
3D	2	9,536	3,750	4,768	5,786
oil	8	120,171	6,006	11,318	39,260
wc/d	1	6,000		6,000	
ENGLISH SCHOOL, 17th/18th C					
oil	5	51,325	2,940	2,940	38,610
ENGLISH SCHOOL, 18th C					
oil	37	361,339	2,000	6,123	138,920
wc/d	2	160,139	10,000	80,070	150,139
ENGLISH SCHOOL, 18th/19th C					
oil	3	21,323	3,926	4,647	12,750
ENGLISH SCHOOL, 19th C					
3D	4	23,270	3,616	6,052	7,550
oil	78	451,293	1,800	4,407	50,050
wc/d	5	30,339	4,527	5,005	9,750
ENGLISH SCHOOL, 19th/20th C					
3D	1	7,056		7,056	
oil	1	7,500		7,500	
wc/d	1	6,520		6,520	
ENGLISH SCHOOL, 20th C					
oil	2	8,512	4,060	4,256	4,452
ENGLISH, Frank F (1854-1922) American					
wc/d	3	5,200	1,000	1,200	3,000
ENGLISH, James (1916-1988) British					
oil	1	1,305		1,305	
ENGLUND, Lars (1933-) Swedish					
3D	3	5,148	1,180	1,958	2,010
ENGSTROM, Albert (1869-1940) Swedish					
oil	1	3,967		3,967	
wc/d	2	4,489	2,006	2,245	2,483
ENGSTROM, Leander (1886-1927) Swedish					
oil	1	24,084		24,084	
wc/d	1	1,806		1,806	
ENHUBER, Karl von (1811-1867) German					
oil	3	7,932	1,648	3,102	3,182
ENJOLRAS, Delphin (1857-1945) French					
oil	10	146,807	5,351	8,706	37,700
wc/d	7	95,785	1,638	5,686	37,500
ENKAOUA, Daniel (1962-) Israeli					
oil	6	52,000	5,500	9,500	11,000
ENNEKING, John J (1841-1916) American					
oil	14	149,300	1,900	6,750	65,000
wc/d	1	2,000		2,000	
ENNEKING, Joseph Elliot (1881-1942) American					
oil	3	23,000	1,200	1,800	20,000

Name	No.	Total Sales Value	Prices lowest	median	highest
ENNESS, Augustus William (1876-1948) British					
oil	6	13,732	1,200	1,440	4,710
ENNION, Eric (1900-1981) British					
wc/d	1	1,160		1,160	
ENOCK, Arthur Henry (fl.1869-1910) British					
wc/d	2	2,696	1,256	1,348	1,440
ENOTRIO (1920-1989) Argentinian					
oil	2	2,374	1,120	1,187	1,254
ENRIQUEZ, Carlos (1900-1957) Cuban					
oil	1	48,000		48,000	
ENRIQUEZ, Nicolas (fl.1738-1770) Mexican					
oil	1	14,789		14,789	
ENSOR, James (1860-1949) Belgian					
oil	5	152,349	2,140	22,714	97,594
wc/d	9	46,957	1,253	3,342	15,411
ENWONWU, Ben (1921-1994) Nigerian					
oil	1	1,974		1,974	
ENZINGER, Hans (1889-1972) Austrian					
oil	1	1,043		1,043	
EPP, Rudolf (1834-1910) German					
oil	7	29,142	1,603	3,500	9,796
EPPENS, Hans (1905-1988) Swiss					
oil	1	1,224		1,224	
EPPER, Ignaz (1892-1969) Swiss					
oil	1	1,019		1,019	
wc/d	6	16,875	1,210	1,905	8,165
EPPLE, Emil (1877-?) German					
3D	1	2,226		2,226	
EPSTEIN, Henri (1892-1944) Polish/French					
oil	4	20,314	3,704	4,606	7,399
EPSTEIN, Sir Jacob (1880-1959) British/American					
3D	13	90,404	2,844	5,640	20,540
wc/d	18	58,336	1,400	2,619	16,920
EQUIPO CRONICA (20th C) Spanish					
3D	1	4,646		4,646	
oil	1	18,999		18,999	
wc/d	3	44,904	10,020	17,442	17,442
EQUIPO REALIDAD (20th C) Spanish					
wc/d	1	1,405		1,405	
ERARD, Charles II (1606-1689) French					
oil	1	117,600		117,600	
ERBE, Paul (1894-1972) German					
oil	1	2,273		2,273	
ERBEN, Ulrich (1940-) German					
oil	3	6,703	1,068	2,391	3,244
ERBLAD, F (19th C) ?					
oil	2	3,200	1,300	1,600	1,900
ERBSLOH, Adolf (1881-1947) German					
oil	2	207,608	43,252	103,804	164,356
ERDELY, Francis de (1904-1959) American/Hungarian					
oil	4	25,000	4,000	5,000	11,000
ERDTMANN, Elias (1862-1945) Swedish					
oil	1	1,959		1,959	
ERICKSON, George T (1924-) American					
oil	1	1,600		1,600	
ERICKSON, Oscar B (1883-1968) American					
oil	1	2,000		2,000	
ERICSON, Johan (1849-1925) Swedish					
oil	7	31,045	1,206	3,519	11,851

Name	No.	Total Sales Value	Prices lowest	median	highest
ERIKSEN, Edvard (1876-1959) Danish					
3D	2	46,901	17,433	23,451	29,468
ERIKSSON, Christian (1858-1935) Swedish					
3D	2	4,159	1,345	2,080	2,814
ERIKSSON, Liss (1919-2000) Swedish					
3D	1	2,010		2,010	
ERIXSON, Sven (1899-1970) Swedish					
oil	22	129,526	1,197	3,469	33,116
wc/d	7	15,192	1,034	2,117	3,919
ERLER, Fritz (1868-1940) German					
oil	1	3,049		3,049	
ERLER-SAMADEN, Erich (1870-1946) German					
oil	2	5,945	2,510	2,973	3,435
ERNI, Hans (1909-) Swiss					
oil	3	14,044	2,000	5,629	6,415
wc/d	7	11,580	1,025	1,749	2,565
ERNST, Helge (1916-1990) Danish					
oil	3	4,453	1,162	1,549	1,742
wc/d	1	1,811		1,811	
ERNST, Max (1891-1976) German					
3D	15	511,341	6,142	24,000	173,584
oil	33	5,786,336	14,563	81,894	1,300,000
wc/d	22	505,509	2,396	15,922	64,275
ERNST, Otto (1884-1967) Swiss					
oil	1	1,038		1,038	
ERNST, R (?) ?					
wc/d	1	6,131		6,131	
ERNST, Rita (1956-) Swiss					
oil	1	2,118		2,118	
ERNST, Rudolph (1854-1932) Austrian					
oil	8	672,225	1,730	38,566	350,000
wc/d	2	17,399	7,733	8,700	9,666
EROLI, Erulo (1854-1916) Italian					
wc/d	1	1,468		1,468	
ERPIKUM, Léon Vuilleminot (19th C) French					
oil	1	1,481		1,481	
ERRO, Gudmundur (1932-) Icelandic					
oil	32	233,719	1,355	4,875	61,702
wc/d	11	19,166	1,160	1,690	2,535
ERTE, Romain de Tirtoff (1892-1990) Russian					
3D	11	27,373	1,500	2,400	5,349
wc/d	23	54,023	1,000	1,653	11,280
ERWIN, E (19th C) British					
oil	1	1,191		1,191	
ES, Jacob van (1596-1666) Flemish					
oil	1	19,630		19,630	
ESBENS, Emile Étienne (1821-?) French					
oil	2	5,547	1,547	2,774	4,000
ESCARDO, Daniel (1957-) Uruguayan					
3D	1	2,100		2,100	
ESCH, Anna Barbara von (1706-1773) Swiss					
oil	1	9,419		9,419	
ESCHBACH, Paul Andre Jean (1881-1961) French					
oil	2	3,411	1,276	1,706	2,135
ESCHER, Johann Heinrich (18th C) Swiss					
wc/d	1	1,793		1,793	
ESCHKE, Hermann (1823-1900) German					
oil	1	1,437		1,437	
ESCUDIER, Charles-Jean-Auguste (1848-?) French					
oil	3	7,085	1,005	2,938	3,142

Name	No.	Total Sales Value	Prices lowest	median	highest
ESHUYS, Hendrikus Jacobus (1888-1967) Dutch					
wc/d	1	1,635		1,635	
ESKILSON, Per (1820-1872) Swedish					
oil	1	1,469		1,469	
ESPERLING, Joseph (1707-1775) Swiss					
oil	1	3,685		3,685	
ESPINOS, Benito (1748-1818) Spanish					
oil	2	14,699	5,495	7,350	9,204
ESPINOZA, Eugenio (20th C) ?					
oil	1	1,150		1,150	
ESPINOZA, Manuel (1937-) Venezuelan					
oil	3	5,900	1,440	1,440	3,020
ESPLANDIU, Juan (1901-1978) Spanish					
wc/d	2	2,198	1,076	1,099	1,122
ESPOSITO, Gaetano (1858-1911) Italian					
oil	4	11,716	2,285	2,848	3,735
ESPOY, Angel (1879-1963) American					
oil	14	60,650	1,700	3,875	9,000
ESPRIT, Anne Marie (19/20th C) French					
oil	1	2,531		2,531	
ESQUIVEL, Antonio Maria de (1806-1857) Spanish					
oil	5	60,449	2,000	4,065	46,019
ESSELENS, Jacob (1626-1687) Dutch					
oil	1	13,234		13,234	
ESSEN, Jan van (17th C) Flemish					
oil	1	103,829		103,829	
ESSEN, Johannes Cornelis (1854-1936) Dutch					
oil	2	23,358	1,358	11,679	22,000
ESSIG, George E (1838-?) American					
oil	1	1,600		1,600	
ESTES, Richard (1932-) American					
oil	4	920,000	40,000	230,000	420,000
wc/d	1	1,700		1,700	
ESTEVE, Agustin (1753-1809) Spanish					
oil	1	5,550		5,550	
ESTEVE, Maurice (1904-) French					
oil	2	26,315	12,120	13,158	14,195
wc/d	9	85,064	3,713	6,910	21,928
ESTEVE, Miguel (fl.1507-1530) Spanish					
oil	1	13,590		13,590	
ESTRADA, Adolfo (1927-) Spanish?					
oil	1	2,420		2,420	
ESTRADA, Angel (1933-) Spanish					
oil	1	1,859		1,859	
ESTRANY, Raphael (1884-1958) French					
oil	2	4,094	1,210	2,047	2,884
ETHOFER, Theodor J (1849-1915) Austrian					
oil	1	4,614		4,614	
ETIENNE (19th C) French					
3D	2	42,291	19,477	21,146	22,814
ETIENNE-MARTIN (1913-1995) French					
3D	3	111,944	1,028	8,548	102,368
ETNIER, Stephen (1903-1984) American					
oil	9	101,800	1,800	7,000	35,000
ETROG, Sorel (1933-) Canadian/Rumanian					
3D	5	28,249	1,535	4,646	12,793
ETTY, William (1787-1849) British					
oil	7	66,429	1,950	6,435	37,180

Name	No.	Total Sales Value	Prices lowest	median	highest
EUGEN (1865-1947) Swedish					
oil	4	49,760	4,020	7,069	31,603
wc/d	1	1,449		1,449	
EUGENIA, Alonso (?) Spanish					
oil	1	3,226		3,226	
EUGENIO DA VENEZIA (1900-1992) Italian					
oil	1	1,622		1,622	
EUN NIM RO (1946-) Korean					
oil	1	2,779		2,779	
EURICH, Richard (1903-1992) British					
oil	6	57,623	1,057	5,371	31,020
EUROPEAN SCHOOL					
3D	4	21,004	4,436	4,536	7,496
oil	2	7,684	2,684	3,842	5,000
EUROPEAN SCHOOL, 15th C					
3D	3	16,025	2,248	6,019	7,758
EUROPEAN SCHOOL, 16th C					
3D	2	36,794	2,849	18,397	33,945
EUROPEAN SCHOOL, 16th/17th C					
3D	1	4,832		4,832	
EUROPEAN SCHOOL, 17th C					
3D	4	84,946	4,374	7,699	65,174
oil	2	9,748	3,919	4,874	5,829
EUROPEAN SCHOOL, 18th C					
3D	4	19,332	2,837	4,173	8,150
oil	12	60,401	2,810	3,958	13,839
EUROPEAN SCHOOL, 18th/19th C					
oil	1	8,691		8,691	
EUROPEAN SCHOOL, 19th C					
3D	6	41,664	3,011	5,232	18,250
oil	16	80,113	1,000	5,008	15,981
EUROPEAN SCHOOL, 19th/20th C					
oil	1	3,868		3,868	
EUROPEAN SCHOOL, 20th C					
3D	1	4,527		4,527	
oil	2	12,364	2,364	6,182	10,000
EVANS OF ETON, Samuel (1829-1904) British					
wc/d	1	6,040		6,040	
EVANS OF ETON, William (1798-1877) British					
wc/d	3	15,113	2,860	5,005	7,248
EVANS, Bernard (1848-1922) British					
wc/d	1	1,154		1,154	
EVANS, Cerith Wyn (1959-) British					
3D	1	4,530		4,530	
EVANS, De Scott (1847-1898) American					
oil	1	7,000		7,000	
EVANS, Frank MacNamara (?) British					
wc/d	2	3,675	1,275	1,838	2,400
EVANS, Frederick M (1859-1929) British					
wc/d	6	22,358	1,500	2,436	10,428
EVANS, J (19th C) American?					
oil	1	1,900		1,900	
EVANS, Marjorie (c.1850-1907) British					
oil	1	2,544		2,544	
EVANS, William E (fl.1889-1897) British					
oil	1	1,523		1,523	
EVE, Jean (1900-1968) French					
oil	4	10,245	1,760	2,475	3,535
EVEN, Jean (19th C) French					
wc/d	3	3,237	1,033	1,047	1,157

Name	No.	Total Sales Value	lowest	Prices median	highest
EVENEPOEL, Henri (1872-1899) Belgian					
oil	1	33,100		33,100	
wc/d	1	2,253		2,253	
EVENO, Edouard (fl.1930) French					
oil	2	4,504	2,047	2,252	2,457
wc/d	3	14,741	1,092	4,777	8,872
EVERARD, J (19th C) Dutch					
oil	1	1,410		1,410	
EVERDINGEN, A van (1832-1912) Dutch					
oil	1	3,219		3,219	
EVERDINGEN, Allart (1621-1675) Dutch					
oil	1	105,840		105,840	
EVEREN, Jay van (1875-1947) American?					
oil	1	6,500		6,500	
EVERGOOD, Phillip (1901-1973) American					
oil	3	13,050	2,800	4,250	6,000
EVERITT, W H (19th C) British					
wc/d	1	1,256		1,256	
EVERS, Ivar Elis (1866-?) American					
oil	1	1,400		1,400	
EVERSEN, Adrianus (1818-1897) Dutch					
oil	12	457,726	4,974	20,069	210,000
wc/d	1	8,417		8,417	
EVERSEN, Johannes Hendrik (1906-1995) Dutch					
oil	7	103,352	1,967	12,678	28,275
EVES, Reginald Grenville (1876-1941) British					
oil	1	5,148		5,148	
EVOLA, Giulio (1898-1974) Italian					
oil	2	51,440	14,558	25,720	36,882
EVRARD, Adele (1792-1889) Flemish					
oil	2	3,500	1,000	1,750	2,500
EVRARD, G (20th C) ?					
oil	1	1,885		1,885	
EWBANK, John Wilson (1799-1847) British					
oil	1	1,387		1,387	
EWBANK, T J (?-1863) British					
oil	1	8,690		8,690	
EWEN, William Paterson (1925-) Canadian					
wc/d	1	1,362		1,362	
EWING, G (?) Continental					
wc/d	1	4,500		4,500	
EXNER, Julius (1825-1910) Danish					
oil	10	174,903	1,134	5,084	88,170
EXTER, Alexandra (1882-1949) Russian					
oil	1	84,600		84,600	
EXTER, Julius (1863-1939) German					
oil	2	18,965	8,511	9,483	10,454
EYBL, Franz (1806-1880) Austrian					
oil	1	2,844		2,844	
EYCK, Charles (1897-1983) Dutch					
oil	1	2,495		2,495	
EYCKEN, Charles van den (19th C) Belgian					
oil	1	3,551		3,551	
EYCKEN, Charles van den (jnr) (1859-1923) Belgian					
oil	4	18,542	1,065	3,239	11,000
EYCKEN, Charles van den (snr) (1809-1891) Belgian					
oil	3	9,832	1,043	1,831	6,958
EYCKEN, Felix van den (19th C) Belgian					
oil	1	3,335		3,335	

Name	No.	Total Sales Value	lowest	Prices median	highest
EYCKEN, Jean Baptiste van (1809-1853) Belgian					
oil	1	7,783		7,783	
EYCKEN, Marie van den (19th C) Belgian					
oil	1	1,177		1,177	
EYDEN, William A (1893-1982) American					
oil	1	1,200		1,200	
EYRE, Ivan Kenneth (1935-) Canadian					
oil	3	75,722	22,194	23,500	30,028
EYSKENS, Felix (1882-1968) Belgian					
oil	2	3,330	1,186	1,665	2,144
EYTON, Anthony (1923-) British					
oil	2	8,296	2,016	4,148	6,280
wc/d	1	1,278		1,278	
EYVEAU, Pietro (1855-) Italian					
oil	1	2,898		2,898	
EZDORF, Christian (1801-1851) German					
oil	1	19,940		19,940	
EZQUERRA, Joaquin Antonio (1660-1733) Spanish					
oil	4	31,639	6,328	8,054	9,204
FABBI, Fabio (1861-1946) Italian					
oil	11	361,656	2,500	22,000	90,000
wc/d	5	20,761	1,109	4,321	6,490
FABBIANI, Juan Vicente (1910-) Venezuelan					
oil	3	5,955	1,045	1,400	3,510
FABBRI, Agenore (1911-1998) Italian					
3D	2	3,928	1,964	1,964	1,964
FABELO, Roberto (1950-) Cuban					
oil	1	10,000		10,000	
wc/d	1	10,000		10,000	
FABER DU FAUR, Hans von (1863-1949) German					
wc/d	2	2,457	1,091	1,229	1,366
FABER DU FAUR, Otto von (1828-1901) German					
oil	5	35,708	1,744	2,991	26,280
FABER, Hermann (1832-1913) German/American					
wc/d	1	1,300		1,300	
FABER, Will (1901-1987) German/Spanish					
oil	2	3,327	1,662	1,664	1,665
FABRE, Edmond (1812-1880) French?					
wc/d	1	1,125		1,125	
FABRE, François-Xavier (1766-1837) French					
oil	1	35,046		35,046	
FABRE, François-Xavier (school) (1766-1837) French					
oil	1	1,300		1,300	
FABRE, Jan (1958-) Belgian					
wc/d	2	7,520	3,760	3,760	3,760
FABRES Y COSTA, Antonio (1854-1936) Spanish					
oil	4	133,237	2,021	9,824	111,569
wc/d	1	1,425		1,425	
FABRI-CANTI, Jose (1910-1994) French					
oil	4	5,321	1,038	1,266	1,752
FABRIS, Pietro (18th C) Italian					
oil	2	406,184	13,584	203,092	392,600
FABRY, Ana (1963-) Argentinian					
wc/d	1	18,000		18,000	
FACCINCANI, Athos (1951-) Italian					
oil	12	18,650	1,038	1,417	2,495
FACCINI, Pietro (1560-1602) Italian					
oil	1	18,720		18,720	
wc/d	1	1,812		1,812	

Name	No.	Total Sales Value	Prices lowest	median	highest
FACCIOLI, Raffaele (1846-1916) Italian					
oil	1	3,428		3,428	
FACHNLEIN, Louis (19th C) French					
oil	1	9,828		9,828	
FADER, Fernando (1882-1935) Argentinian					
oil	1	70,000		70,000	
FAED, J (19th C) British					
oil	1	1,185		1,185	
FAED, James (jnr) (1847-1920) British					
oil	1	3,386		3,386	
FAED, James (snr) (1821-1911) British					
wc/d	1	3,770		3,770	
FAED, John (1820-1902) British					
oil	4	64,560	6,570	18,270	21,450
FAED, Thomas (1826-1900) British					
oil	4	33,276	3,504	7,900	13,972
FAED, William C (fl.1880-1897) British					
oil	1	1,422		1,422	
FAES, Pieter (1750-1814) Belgian					
oil	1	51,450		51,450	
FAFARD, Joseph (1942-) Canadian					
3D	1	1,460		1,460	
FAGAN, Robert (1745-1816) British					
oil	1	118,400		118,400	
FAGEL, Léon (1851-1913) French					
3D	2	5,681	1,442	2,841	4,239
FAGERBERG, Carl (1878-1948) Swedish					
3D	1	1,727		1,727	
FAGERLIN, Ferdinand (1825-1907) Swedish					
oil	2	42,804	16,930	21,402	25,874
FAGUAYS, Pierre le (1892-?) French					
3D	9	44,269	1,553	3,942	13,533
FAGUAYS, le (20th C) French					
3D	2	7,550	1,812	3,775	5,738
FAHEY, Edward Henry (1844-1907) British					
oil	1	7,000		7,000	
FAHEY, James (1804-1885) British					
oil	1	4,050		4,050	
FAHLCRANTZ, Carl Johan (1774-1861) Swedish					
oil	2	4,634	2,176	2,317	2,458
FAHLSTROM, Oyvind (1928-1976) Swedish					
oil	5	312,073	4,215	21,853	180,632
wc/d	3	9,976	1,747	3,011	5,218
FAHNER, F (19th C) German					
oil	1	1,382		1,382	
FAHNLE, Hans (1903-1968) German					
oil	2	2,850	1,312	1,425	1,538
FAHR-EL-NISSA-ZEID (1904-) Turkish					
oil	3	12,680	1,425	4,274	6,981
FAHRBACH, Carl Ludwig (1835-1902) German					
oil	3	12,132	1,138	3,958	7,036
FAHRINGER, Carl (1874-1952) Austrian					
oil	2	10,261	3,265	5,131	6,996
FAHRNER, Kurt (1932-1977) Swiss					
oil	1	3,950		3,950	
FAILLE, Louis de la (20th C) ?					
oil	1	1,590		1,590	
FAIRCLOUGH, Wilfred (1907-1996) British					
oil	1	1,065		1,065	

Name	No.	Total Sales Value	lowest	Prices median	highest
FAIRFAX, T (20th C) ?					
oil	1	1,050		1,050	
FAIRHURST, Angus and HIRST, Damien (20th C) British					
oil	1	2,900		2,900	
FAIRLIE, Helene (?-1916) British					
oil	1	3,256		3,256	
FAIRMAN, James (1826-1904) American					
oil	1	7,500		7,500	
FAIRNINGTON, Mark (1957-) British					
oil	1	2,265		2,265	
FAIS, Eunice (20th C) American					
oil	1	1,500		1,500	
FAISTENBERGER, Anton (1663-1708) Austrian					
oil	1	11,374		11,374	
FAIT, Carlo (1877-?) Italian					
3D	1	1,157		1,157	
FAIVRE, Abel (?) French					
oil	1	5,869		5,869	
FAIVRE, Antoine Jean Étienne (1830-1905) French					
oil	1	9,500		9,500	
FAKEYE, Lamidi (1928-) Nigerian					
3D	1	4,230		4,230	
FALAT, Julian (1853-1929) Polish					
oil	1	10,647		10,647	
FALCHETTI, A (19/20th C) Italian					
oil	1	1,047		1,047	
FALCHETTI, Alberto (19/20th C) Italian					
oil	1	2,836		2,836	
FALCHETTI, Giuseppe (1843-1918) Italian					
oil	5	24,148	1,098	3,498	9,194
FALCINI, Carlo (19th C) Italian					
oil	1	2,067		2,067	
FALCONE, Aniello (1607-1656) Italian					
oil	1	44,100		44,100	
FALCONER, Douglas (?) British					
oil	2	2,930	1,450	1,465	1,480
FALCONET, Étienne Maurice (1716-1791) French					
3D	1	52,647		52,647	
FALENS, Carel van (1683-1733) Dutch					
oil	2	19,830	2,596	9,915	17,234
FALERO, Luis Riccardo (1851-1896) Spanish					
oil	1	16,862		16,862	
FALGUIERE, Alexandre (1831-1900) French					
3D	10	62,976	1,185	2,975	33,580
FALK, Hans (1918-) Swiss					
oil	1	3,901		3,901	
wc/d	2	2,249	1,023	1,125	1,226
FALK, Lars-Erik (1922-) Swedish					
3D	1	1,180		1,180	
oil	3	3,538	1,081	1,081	1,376
FALKEISEN, Johann-Jakob (1804-1883) Swiss					
oil	2	26,151	4,251	13,076	21,900
FALKENSTEIN, Claire (1908-1997) American					
oil	1	6,000		6,000	
FALL, George (c.1848-1925) British					
wc/d	2	2,173	1,065	1,087	1,108
FALTER, John P (1910-1982) American					
oil	4	56,500	9,000	11,250	25,000

Name	No.	Total Sales Value	lowest	Prices median	highest
FANART, Clement-Alphonse-Antonin (1831-1903) French					
oil	1	3,658		3,658	
FANELLI-SEMAH, Louis Joseph (1804-1875) French					
oil	1	1,100		1,100	
FANFANI, Paolo (1823-?) Italian					
3D	1	18,720		18,720	
FANNER, Alice (1865-1930) British					
oil	2	21,087	3,087	10,544	18,000
FANROSE (20th C) ?					
3D	1	3,224		3,224	
FANTIN-LATOUR, Henri (1836-1904) French					
oil	14	6,454,512	3,625	132,500	3,200,000
wc/d	1	3,995		3,995	
FANTIN-LATOUR, Theodore (1805-1872) French					
oil	1	7,584		7,584	
wc/d	4	12,530	1,053	2,889	5,700
FANTIN-LATOUR, Victoria (1840-1926) French					
oil	3	86,000	9,000	17,000	60,000
wc/d	1	7,250		7,250	
FANTUZZI, Eliano (1909-1987) Italian					
oil	1	1,070		1,070	
FARASYN, E (1858-1938) Belgian					
oil	2	4,429	1,620	2,215	2,809
FARASYN, Edgard (1858-1938) Belgian					
oil	7	34,502	1,170	3,342	15,411
FARASYN, Edward (19th C) ?					
oil	1	3,021		3,021	
FARELLI, Giacomo (1624-1706) Italian					
oil	1	8,324		8,324	
FARGE, Pierre (19/20th C) French					
oil	1	4,753		4,753	
FARGEOT, Ferdinand (1880-1957) French					
oil	1	9,981		9,981	
FARGES, Pierre (1900-) French					
oil	1	4,838		4,838	
FARGUE, Maria Margaretha la (1743-1813) Dutch					
oil	1	10,080		10,080	
FARGUE, Paulus Constantin la (1732-1782) Dutch					
wc/d	1	2,946		2,946	
FARINA (?) ?					
oil	1	6,880		6,880	
FARINATI, Paolo (1524-1606) Italian					
wc/d	2	8,600	1,600	4,300	7,000
FARLOW, Harry (1882-?) American					
oil	1	4,000		4,000	
FARMER, Henry (19/20th C) British					
oil	1	1,738		1,738	
FARNDON, Walter (1876-1964) American					
oil	10	71,000	2,500	6,500	12,000
FARNETI, Stefano (1855-?) Italian					
oil	1	5,841		5,841	
FARNHAM, Sally James (1876-1943) American					
3D	1	1,400		1,400	
FARNY, Henry F (1847-1916) American					
wc/d	5	535,000	10,000	65,000	320,000
FARQUHARSON, David (1839-1907) British					
oil	15	91,218	1,058	6,320	20,540
FARQUHARSON, John (1865-1931) British					
wc/d	1	1,590		1,590	

Name	No.	Total Sales Value	lowest	Prices median	highest
FARQUHARSON, Joseph (1846-1935) British					
oil	14	316,420	1,284	8,058	84,680
FARR, Helen (20th C) American					
oil	3	5,900	1,500	2,000	2,400
FARRE, Henri (1871-1934) American					
oil	1	1,200		1,200	
FARREN, R (1832-?) British					
oil	1	2,400		2,400	
FARREN, Robert (1832-?) British					
oil	1	1,422		1,422	
FARRERAS, Francisco (1927-) Spanish					
3D	1	3,260		3,260	
oil	2	3,360	1,600	1,680	1,760
FARRIER, Robert (1796-1879) British					
oil	1	2,400		2,400	
FARUFFINI, Federico (1831-1869) Italian					
oil	1	12,400		12,400	
FASANOTTI, Gaetano (1831-1882) Italian					
wc/d	1	1,070		1,070	
FASCE, Gianfranco (1927-) Italian					
oil	1	1,689		1,689	
FASOLI (?) ?					
oil	1	5,364		5,364	
FASSBENDER, Josef (1903-1974) German					
wc/d	1	1,346		1,346	
FASSIANOS, A (1935-) Greek					
oil	3	9,857	1,831	2,112	5,914
FASSIANOS, Alecos (1935-) Greek					
oil	3	12,098	2,320	3,504	6,274
wc/d	5	54,953	1,459	3,562	40,880
FASSIN, Nicholas de (1728-1811) Flemish					
oil	1	9,821		9,821	
FATOSSY (20th C) ?					
3D	1	2,000		2,000	
FATTORI, Giovanni (1825-1908) Italian					
oil	3	40,387	5,101	16,326	18,960
wc/d	3	35,561	9,396	13,061	13,104
FAUCONNET, Pierre (1882-1920) French					
wc/d	1	1,500		1,500	
FAUCONNIER, Henri le (1881-1946) French					
oil	3	5,013	1,101	1,775	2,137
wc/d	2	4,862	2,145	2,431	2,717
FAUDACQ, Louis Marie (1840-1914) French					
wc/d	1	3,344		3,344	
FAUERHOLDT, Viggo (1832-1883) Danish					
oil	3	8,216	1,637	2,519	4,060
FAUGERON, Adolphe (1866-?) French					
oil	1	1,199		1,199	
FAULKNER, Charles (fl.1874-1891) British					
oil	1	2,100		2,100	
FAULKNER, John (c.1830-1888) British					
oil	1	4,736		4,736	
wc/d	5	8,666	1,058	1,058	2,900
FAURE DE BROUSSE, Vincent Desire (19th C) French					
3D	1	2,953		2,953	
FAURE, Amandus (1874-1931) German					
oil	2	2,668	1,000	1,334	1,668
FAUSTIN, Celestin (1948-1981) Haitian					
oil	1	1,547		1,547	

Name	No.	Total Sales Value	lowest	Prices median	highest
FAUSTINI, Modesto (1839-1892) Italian					
oil	1	28,000		28,000	
FAUSTMAN, Mollie (1883-1966) Swedish					
oil	1	1,407		1,407	
FAUTRIER, Jean (1898-1964) French					
3D	1	7,025		7,025	
oil	9	1,134,642	32,462	79,750	483,200
wc/d	11	63,053	1,065	4,929	18,120
FAUX-FROIDURE, Eugenie-Juliette (1886-?) French					
wc/d	1	2,017		2,017	
FAVELLE, Robert (19th C) ?					
oil	1	2,368		2,368	
FAVEN, Antti (1882-1948) Finnish					
oil	4	6,632	1,060	1,535	2,484
FAVIER, Philippe (1957-) French					
oil	2	9,009	3,728	4,505	5,281
wc/d	4	5,004	1,028	1,268	1,440
FAVIN, Roger (20th C) French					
3D	1	1,482		1,482	
FAVORY, Andre (1888-1937) French					
oil	6	12,602	1,638	2,107	2,579
FAVRETTO, G (1849-1887) Italian					
oil	1	4,641		4,641	
FAVRETTO, Giacomo (1849-1887) Italian					
oil	1	11,376		11,376	
FAWCETT, Robert (1903-1967) American					
wc/d	1	3,000		3,000	
FAWSSETT, Constance Mary (fl.1897-1898) British					
oil	1	1,181		1,181	
FAY, Hans (1888-1957) German					
oil	3	8,778	1,073	3,609	4,096
FAZIO, Gano di (fl.1302-1318) Italian					
3D	1	134,012		134,012	
FEARNLEY, Thomas (1802-1842) Norwegian					
oil	1	15,168		15,168	
wc/d	1	55,300		55,300	
FEBVRE, Edouard (20th C) French					
oil	2	6,168	2,648	3,084	3,520
FECHENBACH, Hermann (20th C) Israeli					
oil	1	1,201		1,201	
FECHIN, Nicolai (1881-1955) American/Russian					
oil	5	370,000	25,000	70,000	125,000
wc/d	1	7,000		7,000	
FECTEAU, Marcel (1927-) Canadian					
oil	1	1,252		1,252	
FEDDEN, Mary (1915-) British					
oil	50	393,682	2,256	6,998	20,445
wc/d	27	97,145	1,305	3,476	8,532
FEDDER, Otto (1873-1919) German					
oil	4	8,282	1,564	1,989	2,741
FEDDERSEN, Hans Peter (younger) (1848-1941) Danish					
oil	3	21,208	1,547	9,036	10,625
FEDDON (20th C) British?					
oil	1	3,322		3,322	
FEDELER, Carl (1837-1897) German					
oil	1	8,000		8,000	
FEDERICO, Cavalier Michele (1884-1966) Italian					
oil	6	10,660	1,000	1,699	3,250
FEDERLE, Karl Aegidius (1781-1840) German					
oil	1	1,427		1,427	

Name	No.	Total Sales Value	lowest	Prices median	highest
FEDI, Pio (1816-1892) Italian					
3D	1	7,248		7,248	
FEDIER, Franz (1922-) Swiss					
oil	1	1,331		1,331	
FEDOTOV, Pavel Andreevich (1815-1852) Russian					
oil	1	10,570		10,570	
FEENEY, Patrick M (fl.1867-1911) British					
oil	1	2,272		2,272	
FEER, Anneke van der (1902-1956) Dutch					
oil	1	1,090		1,090	
FEHDMER, Eugène (19/20th C) Belgian					
oil	1	2,193		2,193	
FEHDMER, Richard (1860-?) German					
oil	1	1,682		1,682	
wc/d	2	3,002	1,501	1,501	1,501
FEHR, Friedrich (1862-1927) German					
oil	1	1,550		1,550	
FEHRLE, Jakob Wilhelm (1884-1974) German					
3D	4	8,411	1,367	2,230	2,585
FEIBUSCH, Hans (1898-?) German					
oil	1	1,305		1,305	
FEID, Josef (1806-1870) Austrian					
oil	1	6,978		6,978	
FEIFFER, Jules (1929-) American?					
wc/d	1	2,400		2,400	
FEILER, Paul (1918-) British					
oil	3	39,480	7,755	11,985	19,740
wc/d	2	7,242	1,950	3,621	5,292
FEININGER, Lyonel (1871-1956) American/German					
oil	4	1,648,527	70,927	320,800	936,000
wc/d	38	700,261	2,500	10,013	180,000
FEININGER, Theodore Lux (1910-) American					
oil	1	3,204		3,204	
FEITAMA, Sybrand (1694-1758) Dutch					
wc/d	1	1,099		1,099	
FEITELSON, Lorser (1898-1978) American					
oil	1	8,000		8,000	
FEITO, Luis (1929-) Spanish					
oil	19	109,718	1,638	4,302	15,813
wc/d	2	4,185	1,717	2,093	2,468
FELBER, Carl (1880-1932) Swiss					
oil	3	3,669	1,002	1,002	1,634
FELDBAUER, Max (1869-1948) German					
oil	2	9,199	1,913	4,600	7,286
FELDHUSEN, Anna (1867-?) German					
oil	1	1,282		1,282	
FELDHUTTER, Ferdinand (1842-1898) German					
oil	2	8,207	1,273	4,104	6,934
FELDMANN, Peter (1790-1871) German					
wc/d	1	1,341		1,341	
FELDMANN, Wilhelm (1859-1932) German					
oil	1	1,081		1,081	
FELEZ, Mariano (?) ?					
oil	1	4,930		4,930	
FELGENTREFF, Paul (1854-1933) German					
oil	3	7,230	1,139	1,596	4,495
FELIPE, Antonio de (1965-) Spanish					
oil	1	1,403		1,403	

Name	No.	Total Sales Value	lowest	Prices median	highest
FELIX, Eugen (1837-1906) American					
oil	1	13,000		13,000	
FELIX, Maurice (1895-?) French					
oil	1	2,100		2,100	
FELIX, Nelson (1954-) Brazilian					
3D	1	16,000		16,000	
FELIXMULLER, Conrad (1897-1977) German					
oil	2	403,200	187,200	201,600	216,000
wc/d	5	422,933	3,676	83,520	227,520
FELL, Sheila (1931-1979) British					
oil	1	8,352		8,352	
FELLI, Paolo and SPADOLINI, Pierluigi (20th C) ?					
3D	1	1,500		1,500	
FELLINI, Federico (1920-1993) Italian					
wc/d	1	2,202		2,202	
FELON, Joseph (1818-1896) French					
oil	1	51,000		51,000	
FELSER, Anton (19th C) Austrian					
oil	1	3,188		3,188	
FENASSE, Paul (1899-1976) French					
oil	4	42,947	1,817	2,393	36,344
FENETTY, F M (1854-1915) American/Italian					
oil	2	4,000	1,200	2,000	2,800
FENETTY, Frederick M (1854-1915) American/Italian					
oil	1	8,000		8,000	
FENGER, Johan Gustav (19/20th C) Danish					
oil	1	1,363		1,363	
FENNESSY, Rena (?) ?					
oil	1	1,480		1,480	
FENOSA, Apelles (1899-1989) Spanish					
3D	15	34,999	1,154	2,139	4,511
FENOUIL, Herve (20th C) French					
oil	1	2,730		2,730	
FENSON, R (19/20th C) British?					
oil	2	2,409	1,060	1,205	1,349
FENWICK, Thomas (?-1850) British					
oil	1	2,212		2,212	
FENZONI, Ferrau (1562-1645) Italian					
wc/d	1	180,000		180,000	
FER, Edouard (1887-1959) French					
oil	1	2,185		2,185	
FERAT, Serge (1881-1958) Russian					
oil	3	14,251	3,056	4,195	7,000
wc/d	1	6,090		6,090	
FERAUD, Albert (1921-) French					
3D	6	10,112	1,027	1,552	2,852
FERAUD, Vincent (1800-?) French					
oil	1	1,593		1,593	
FERBER, E (19th C) ?					
oil	1	1,000		1,000	
FERG, Franz de Paula (1689-1740) Austrian					
oil	1	26,671		26,671	
FERGOLA, Salvatore (1799-1877) Italian					
oil	1	2,051		2,051	
FERGUSON, Henry Augustus (1842-1911) American					
oil	1	4,200		4,200	
FERGUSON, Nancy Maybin (20th C) American					
oil	2	16,500	2,500	8,250	14,000

Name	No.	Total Sales Value	lowest	Prices median	highest
FERGUSSON, John Duncan (1874-1961) British					
oil	14	832,209	4,964	36,100	182,500
wc/d	36	219,846	1,103	4,102	30,450
FERMARIELLO, Sergio (20th C) Italian					
oil	1	3,709		3,709	
FERNAND-DUBOIS, Émile (1869-?) French					
3D	1	1,080		1,080	
FERNANDEZ ACEVEDO, Manuel (1744-1800) Spanish					
oil	1	8,949		8,949	
FERNANDEZ GRANELL, Mario (1915-1991) Spanish					
oil	1	2,595		2,595	
FERNANDEZ MARTIN, Trinidad (1937-) Spanish					
oil	3	11,751	1,882	3,764	6,105
FERNANDEZ Y GONZALEZ, Domingo (1862-c.1918) Spanish					
oil	1	1,171		1,171	
FERNANDEZ, F (19/20th C) ?					
wc/d	1	1,073		1,073	
FERNANDEZ, Francisco (1897-?) Venezuelan					
oil	1	2,120		2,120	
FERNANDEZ, Louis (1900-1973) French					
oil	2	26,944	5,106	13,472	21,838
FERNANDEZ-MURO, Jose Antonio (1920-) Argentinian					
wc/d	1	4,005		4,005	
FERNE, Hortense (1885-1976) American					
oil	1	4,750		4,750	
FERNELEY, Claude Lorraine (1822-1892) British					
oil	1	8,758		8,758	
FERNELEY, John (jnr) (1815-1862) British					
oil	7	71,718	4,832	7,097	25,160
FERNELEY, John (snr) (1781-1860) British					
oil	8	716,312	3,900	55,911	220,000
FERNEZ, Louis (1900-1983) French					
oil	2	3,359	1,057	1,680	2,302
FERNIER, Robert (1895-1977) French					
oil	1	1,519		1,519	
FERRAND, Ennemond (1829-1892) French					
oil	1	1,600		1,600	
FERRANDIZ Y BADENES, Bernardo (1835-1890) Spanish					
oil	3	48,226	2,589	16,060	29,577
FERRANT Y FISCHERMANS, Alejandro (1843-1917) Spanish					
oil	1	3,164		3,164	
FERRANT Y LLAUSAS, Luis (1806-1868) Spanish					
oil	1	8,053		8,053	
FERRANT, Angel (1891-1961) Spanish					
3D	1	5,915		5,915	
FERRANTE, Mario de (1898-1992) Italian					
oil	3	7,600	2,200	2,500	2,900
FERRARESE SCHOOL, 16th C Italian					
oil	3	68,454	2,979	5,589	59,886
FERRARI, Antoine (1910-1996) French					
oil	2	3,135	1,425	1,568	1,710
FERRARI, Arturo (1861-1932) Italian					
oil	1	7,394		7,394	
FERRARI, Carlo (1813-1871) Italian					
oil	1	85,800		85,800	
FERRARI, G (?) Italian					
3D	1	2,164		2,164	
FERRARI, Gaudenzio (1484-1546) Italian					
wc/d	1	1,500		1,500	

Name	No.	Total Sales Value	Prices lowest	median	highest
FERRARI, Giovanni Battista (1829-1906) Italian					
oil	1	2,400		2,400	
FERRARI, Gregorio de (1647-1726) Italian					
oil	1	196,300		196,300	
wc/d	1	2,182		2,182	
FERRARI, Guiseppe (1773-1864) Italian					
3D	1	2,229		2,229	
FERRARI, Lorenzo de (1680-1744) Italian					
wc/d	1	7,000		7,000	
FERRAZZI, Ferruccio (1891-?) Italian					
oil	2	46,170	3,732	23,085	42,438
FERREN, John (1905-1970) American					
oil	1	3,000		3,000	
FERRER CARBONELL, Juan (1892-?) Spanish					
oil	1	1,397		1,397	
FERRER Y CABRERA, Emilio (20th C) Spanish					
oil	1	2,876		2,876	
FERRER, Jose (19/20th C) Spanish					
oil	1	1,076		1,076	
FERRERO, Alberto (1883-1963) Italian					
oil	3	9,631	1,758	2,299	5,574
FERRETTI, Gian Domenico (1692-1766) Italian					
oil	1	47,772		47,772	
FERRETTINI ROSSOTTI, Emilia (19/20th C) Italian					
oil	1	1,098		1,098	
FERRI, Antonio (?) Spanish					
oil	2	2,575	1,194	1,288	1,381
FERRI, Ciro (1634-1689) Italian					
oil	1	120,000		120,000	
wc/d	2	32,630	13,000	16,315	19,630
FERRIER, Gabriel (1847-1914) French					
oil	1	10,500		10,500	
wc/d	2	2,525	1,228	1,263	1,297
FERRIERE, Robert (20th C) French					
oil	1	1,400		1,400	
FERRIERES, Louis François Georges Comte de (1837-1907) French					
3D	1	3,555		3,555	
FERRON, Marcelle (20th C) ?					
oil	2	3,897	1,123	1,949	2,774
FERRONI, Egisto (1835-1912) Italian					
oil	2	18,292	3,577	9,146	14,715
FERRONI, Gianfranco (1927-) Italian					
oil	2	12,618	1,710	6,309	10,908
wc/d	4	30,115	5,492	8,167	8,863
FERRUCCI, Matteo (17th C) Italian					
3D	1	91,140		91,140	
FERRY, Jules Jean (1844-?) French					
oil	1	1,100		1,100	
FERVILLE-SUAN, Charles (19th C) French					
3D	2	5,863	1,113	2,932	4,750
FERWERDA, Barend (1880-1958) Dutch					
oil	1	1,308		1,308	
FERY, John (1859-1934) American/Hungarian					
oil	3	24,300	2,300	8,000	14,000
FESER, Albert (19/20th C) German					
oil	6	10,134	1,122	1,483	2,924
FESTA, Tano (1938-1988) Italian					
oil	25	80,342	1,260	2,400	10,813
wc/d	10	30,611	1,553	2,658	8,727

Name	No.	Total Sales Value	lowest	Prices median	highest
FETT, William (1918-) American					
wc/d	1	1,300		1,300	
FETTING, Rainer (1949-) German					
3D	1	8,738		8,738	
oil	12	190,590	6,000	12,686	31,553
wc/d	1	7,969		7,969	
FEUBURE, Carl le (1847-1911) German					
oil	2	2,747	1,007	1,374	1,740
FEUCHERE, Jean-Jacques (1807-1852) French					
3D	4	25,132	1,738	6,261	10,872
FEUERBACH, Anselm (1829-1880) German					
oil	3	19,392	1,775	6,331	11,286
FEUILLATTE, Raymond (1901-1971) French					
oil	1	1,414		1,414	
FEVRE, Pierre (1889-1975) French?					
wc/d	1	3,250		3,250	
FEY, C (?) German					
oil	1	3,792		3,792	
FEY, Carl (19th C) German					
oil	1	1,090		1,090	
FEYEN, Eugène (1826-1895) French					
oil	5	41,834	1,269	2,369	28,152
FEYEN, Leon Arie (?) German?					
oil	2	4,319	1,966	2,160	2,353
FEYEN-PERRIN, François Nicolas Augustin (1826-1888) French					
oil	6	12,181	1,161	1,917	3,064
FEYERABEND, Erich (20th C) ?					
oil	1	2,250		2,250	
FEYZEAU, Maurice (19th C) ?					
oil	1	6,133		6,133	
FIAMBERTI, Tommaso (?-c.1524) Italian					
3D	1	168,096		168,096	
FIAMMINGO, A (c.1523-1601) Italian					
wc/d	1	17,000		17,000	
FIAMMINGO, Paolo (1540-1596) Flemish					
oil	1	220,000		220,000	
FIASCHI, E (19th C) Italian					
3D	2	4,229	1,400	2,115	2,829
FIASCHI, P C E (19/20th C) Italian					
3D	1	3,420		3,420	
FIASCHI, P E (19/20th C) Italian					
3D	1	14,700		14,700	
FIASELLA, Domenico (1589-1669) Italian					
oil	2	61,354	30,200	30,677	31,154
FICHEFET, Georges (1864-1954) Belgian					
oil	1	1,073		1,073	
FICHEL, Benjamin Eugène (1826-1895) French					
oil	2	10,496	3,386	5,248	7,110
FICHET, Pierre (1927-) French					
oil	2	2,400	1,160	1,200	1,240
FICHTNER, Hugo de (1872-?) French					
oil	1	1,200		1,200	
FICUS, Andre Hans (1919-) German					
oil	1	1,363		1,363	
FIDANI, Orazio (1610-1656) Italian					
oil	1	25,225		25,225	
FIDANZA, Giuseppe (1750-c.1820) Italian					
wc/d	1	11,357		11,357	

Name	No.	Total Sales Value	lowest	Prices median	highest
FIDLER, Harry (1856-1935) British					
oil	2	3,166	1,136	1,583	2,030
FIDLER, Laura B S (?-1936) British					
oil	1	1,081		1,081	
FIEBIG (19/20th C) ?					
oil	1	1,497		1,497	
FIEDLER, Arnold (1900-) ?					
oil	1	1,650		1,650	
FIEDLER, Bernhard (1816-1904) German					
oil	1	1,460		1,460	
FIEDLER, Herbert (1891-1962) Dutch					
oil	2	4,914	1,466	2,457	3,448
FIELD, Charles (18th C) British					
oil	1	6,864		6,864	
FIELD, E Loyal (1856-1914) American					
oil	1	3,100		3,100	
FIELDING (?) British					
oil	1	4,057		4,057	
FIELDING, Anthony Vandyke Copley (1787-1855) British					
oil	2	5,006	1,106	2,503	3,900
wc/d	12	59,219	1,692	3,840	10,500
FIELDING, Newton Limbird Smith (1799-1856) British					
wc/d	1	1,580		1,580	
FIELDING, R (19th C) British					
oil	1	1,152		1,152	
FIELDING, Thales (1793-1837) British					
wc/d	2	5,230	2,512	2,615	2,718
FIELDS, Chester (20th C) American					
3D	1	13,500		13,500	
FIELER, Jacomo (19th C) ?					
oil	1	1,889		1,889	
FIENE, Ernest (1894-1965) American/German					
oil	4	14,000	1,400	3,550	5,500
FIERAVINO, Francesco (17th C) Italian					
oil	1	73,500		73,500	
FIERROS, Dionisio (1827-1894) Spanish					
oil	2	13,262	5,465	6,631	7,797
FIESSI, Angelo (1891-) Italian					
oil	1	1,153		1,153	
FIETELSON, Lorser (1898-1978) ?					
oil	1	19,000		19,000	
FIETZ, Gerhard (1910-1997) German					
oil	3	10,071	1,419	2,670	5,982
wc/d	2	2,264	1,068	1,132	1,196
FIGARI, Pedro (1861-1938) Uruguayan					
oil	13	297,574	2,493	18,000	50,000
FIGINO, Giovanni Ambrogio (1548-1608) Italian					
wc/d	1	1,133		1,133	
FILARSKI, Dirk Herman Willem (1885-1964) Flemish					
oil	13	68,748	1,109	6,034	13,468
FILDES, Lady Fanny (19/20th C) British					
oil	1	3,792		3,792	
FILDES, Sir Luke (1843-1927) British					
oil	1	1,287		1,287	
FILIGER, Charles (1863-1928) French					
oil	1	5,280		5,280	
wc/d	1	3,927		3,927	
FILIP, Konrad (1874-?) ?					
oil	1	1,129		1,129	

Name	No.	Total Sales Value	lowest	Prices median	highest
FILIPKIEWICZ, Stefan (1879-1944) Polish					
oil	1	2,613		2,613	
FILIPPELLI, Cafiero (1889-1973) Italian					
oil	8	18,589	1,338	2,274	3,694
FILIPPI, Fernando de (1940-) Italian					
oil	1	1,561		1,561	
FILIPPINI, Antonio (?-1710) Italian					
wc/d	1	3,020		3,020	
FILIPPINI, Francesco (1853-1895) Italian					
oil	2	33,463	1,115	16,732	32,348
FILKUKA, Anton (1888-1957) Austrian					
oil	2	2,372	1,080	1,186	1,292
FILLA, Emil (1882-1953) Czechoslovakian					
3D	1	2,721		2,721	
oil	1	105,700		105,700	
FILLANS, James (1808-1852) British					
3D	1	5,198		5,198	
FILLIA (1904-1936) Italian					
oil	2	42,483	1,975	21,242	40,508
FILLIARD, Ernest (1868-1933) French					
wc/d	5	11,805	1,178	2,000	3,849
FILLON, Arthur (1900-1974) French					
oil	2	3,355	1,282	1,678	2,073
FILONOV, Pavel (1883-1941) Russian					
wc/d	1	60,400		60,400	
FILOQUE, T (17th C) Swedish					
oil	1	33,735		33,735	
FILOSA, Giovanni B (1850-1935) Italian					
oil	1	13,140		13,140	
wc/d	1	3,121		3,121	
FILOSINI, C (19th C) Italian					
oil	1	4,500		4,500	
wc/d	1	5,000		5,000	
FINALE, Moises (1957-) Cuban					
wc/d	5	7,170	1,171	1,390	1,756
FINART, Noel Dieudonne (1797-1852) French					
oil	1	10,270		10,270	
wc/d	1	2,292		2,292	
FINCK, Adolphe David (1802-?) French					
wc/d	1	1,353		1,353	
FINCK, Hazel (1894-1977) American					
oil	2	16,000	3,000	8,000	13,000
FINETTI, F (19/20th C) Italian/American					
oil	1	1,700		1,700	
FINGESTEN, Michel (1884-1943) German?					
wc/d	1	1,251		1,251	
FINI, Leonor (1908-1996) Italian					
3D	1	34,192		34,192	
oil	10	120,294	1,481	7,642	40,770
wc/d	8	11,217	1,006	1,312	1,947
FINK, August (1846-1916) German					
oil	2	6,393	1,516	3,197	4,877
FINK, Waldemar (1893-1948) Swiss					
oil	1	1,468		1,468	
FINKELNBURG, Augusta (20th C) American					
oil	1	1,000		1,000	
FINNIE, John (1829-1907) British					
oil	2	10,048	1,413	5,024	8,635
FINOT and WALTER, Amalric (19th C) French					
3D	1	5,465		5,465	

Name	No.	Total Sales Value	lowest	Prices median	highest
FINOT, B (19th C) French					
oil	1	2,755		2,755	
FIODOROV (20th C) Russian					
oil	1	1,112		1,112	
FIOT (?) French					
3D	1	2,578		2,578	
FIOT, Maximilien Louis (1886-1953) French					
3D	2	7,338	2,730	3,669	4,608
FIRFIRES, Nicholas S (1917-1990) American					
oil	1	4,800		4,800	
FIRLE, Walter (1859-1929) German					
oil	1	2,693		2,693	
FISCHER, Adam (1888-1968) Danish					
3D	1	18,596		18,596	
FISCHER, Anton Otto (1882-1962) American					
oil	10	43,000	1,200	3,500	9,000
FISCHER, August (1854-1921) Danish					
oil	5	7,836	1,044	1,549	2,383
FISCHER, Egon (1935-) Danish					
3D	1	4,121		4,121	
FISCHER, Ernst Albert (1853-1932) German					
oil	1	54,826		54,826	
wc/d	1	4,657		4,657	
FISCHER, Hans (19th C) Danish					
oil	1	1,017		1,017	
FISCHER, Hans Christian (1849-1886) Danish					
oil	1	2,502		2,502	
FISCHER, Harriet (1895-1981) Danish					
oil	1	1,559		1,559	
FISCHER, Heinrich (1820-1886) Swiss					
oil	1	1,215		1,215	
FISCHER, Johann Georg Paul (1786-1875) German					
wc/d	4	9,152	2,002	2,288	2,574
FISCHER, Johann Thomas (1603-1685) German					
wc/d	1	15,714		15,714	
FISCHER, Lothar (1933-) German					
3D	6	25,384	1,820	3,037	8,252
FISCHER, Otto (1870-?) German					
wc/d	1	1,292		1,292	
FISCHER, Paul (1860-1934) Danish					
oil	39	883,592	1,000	10,000	154,902
wc/d	2	4,596	1,549	2,298	3,047
FISCHER, Vilhelm Theodor (1857-1928) Danish					
oil	3	4,970	1,192	1,259	2,519
FISCHER-KOYSTRAND, Carl (1861-1918) Austrian					
oil	1	4,147		4,147	
FISCHETTI, Fedele (1734-1789) Italian					
oil	1	79,121		79,121	
FISCHHOF, Georg (1859-1914) Austrian					
oil	1	1,500		1,500	
FISCHL, Eric (1948-) American					
oil	7	1,992,500	32,500	240,000	900,000
wc/d	2	17,300	8,500	8,650	8,800
FISCHLI, Peter and WEISS, David (20th C) Swiss					
3D	2	81,180	17,760	40,590	63,420
FISH, Anne (20th C) American					
wc/d	2	2,400	1,100	1,200	1,300
FISH, Janet (1938-) American					
oil	1	25,000		25,000	

Name	No.	Total Sales Value	lowest	Prices median	highest
FISHER, Anna S (?-1942) American					
oil	1	4,500		4,500	
FISHER, Ellen Thayer and THAYER, Abbott H (19/20th C) American					
wc/d	1	1,600		1,600	
FISHER, Harrison (1875-1934) American					
wc/d	1	7,500		7,500	
FISHER, Hugo Antoine (1854-1916) American					
wc/d	1	1,988		1,988	
FISHER, Hugo Melville (1876-1946) American					
oil	1	1,000		1,000	
FISHER, Larry (?) ?					
oil	2	6,500	3,000	3,250	3,500
FISHER, Percy Harland (1867-1944) British					
oil	1	3,000		3,000	
wc/d	1	1,500		1,500	
FISHER, Randi (1920-) Swedish					
oil	2	7,314	2,509	3,657	4,805
FISHER, Rowland (1885-1969) British					
oil	3	4,742	1,397	1,470	1,875
FISHER, T (18th C) ?					
oil	1	2,114		2,114	
FISHER, William Mark (1841-1923) British/American					
oil	5	11,530	1,350	1,800	4,851
wc/d	1	2,220		2,220	
FISKE, Joseph Winn (1832-?) American					
3D	1	6,000		6,000	
FISSETTE, Leopold (1814-1889) German					
oil	1	1,775		1,775	
FISSORE, Daniele (1947-) Italian					
oil	5	7,023	1,032	1,422	1,689
FITLER, William Crothers (1857-1915) American					
oil	2	6,150	1,900	3,075	4,250
FITTON, James (1899-1982) British					
oil	3	30,290	1,170	10,270	18,850
FITZGERALD, Florence (?-1927) British					
wc/d	1	2,072		2,072	
FITZGERALD, Frederick R (19/20th C) British					
wc/d	2	2,402	1,201	1,201	1,201
FITZGERALD, James (1899-?) American					
oil	1	15,000		15,000	
wc/d	1	8,500		8,500	
FITZGERALD, John Austen (1832-1906) British					
oil	3	389,580	18,000	128,480	243,100
wc/d	1	37,180		37,180	
FITZGERALD, Lionel Lemoine (1890-1956) Canadian					
wc/d	4	11,581	1,235	2,718	4,911
FITZGERALD, Lloyd (1941-) Canadian					
oil	2	5,437	2,399	2,719	3,038
FITZGERALD, Peggy (fl.1930-1940) British					
oil	1	3,408		3,408	
FITZI, Johann Ulrich (1798-1855) Swiss					
wc/d	1	6,429		6,429	
FIUME, Salvatore (1915-1997) Italian					
oil	20	127,621	1,941	6,401	10,142
FIX-MASSEAU, P-F (1869-1937) French					
3D	1	1,282		1,282	
FIX-MASSEAU, Pierre-Felix (1869-1937) French					
3D	3	13,746	3,277	4,975	5,494

Name	No.	Total Sales Value	lowest	Prices median	highest
FJAESTAD, Gustaf (1868-1948) Swedish					
oil	6	91,026	3,950	9,073	44,504
wc/d	1	6,003		6,003	
FJELLSTROM, Per Ericsson (1719-1790) Swedish					
oil	2	2,389	1,035	1,195	1,354
FLACHERON, Gregoire-Isidore (1806-1873) French					
oil	1	1,482		1,482	
FLACK, Audrey (1931-) American					
oil	1	15,000		15,000	
FLAGG, H Peabody (1859-1937) American					
oil	1	1,000		1,000	
FLAGG, James Montgomery (1877-1960) American					
oil	1	8,000		8,000	
wc/d	3	6,000	1,600	2,000	2,400
FLAIG, Waldemar (1892-1932) German					
oil	1	2,040		2,040	
FLAMAND, G (19/20th C) French?					
3D	1	5,966		5,966	
FLAMENG, François (1856-1923) French					
oil	5	67,719	5,273	13,000	28,000
FLAMENG, Marie Auguste (1843-1893) French					
oil	1	3,200		3,200	
FLANAGAN, Barry (1941-) British					
3D	5	711,200	16,000	85,000	332,200
FLANAGAN, Francis (fl.1897-1927) American					
oil	1	3,800		3,800	
FLANDIN, Eugène Napoleon (1803-1876) French					
oil	1	16,355		16,355	
FLANDRIN, Jean Hippolyte (1809-1864) French					
wc/d	1	1,022		1,022	
FLANDRIN, Jules (1871-1947) French					
oil	1	1,014		1,014	
FLANDRIN, Paul Jean (1811-1902) French					
oil	1	3,637		3,637	
FLANNAGAN, John B (1895-1942) American					
3D	2	44,000	22,000	22,000	22,000
FLANNINGAN, Lucy (c.1900-) American					
wc/d	1	1,800		1,800	
FLASCHI (18th C) ?					
3D	2	12,114	6,057	6,057	6,057
FLASSCHOEN, Gustave (1868-1940) Belgian					
oil	7	19,900	1,020	2,642	5,796
FLATHER, Donald M (1903-1990) Canadian					
oil	6	17,613	1,599	2,477	5,525
FLAUBERT, Paul (1928-) French					
oil	1	2,667		2,667	
FLAVIN, Dan (1933-1996) American					
3D	12	996,850	25,000	48,750	300,000
FLAXMAN, John (1755-1826) British					
wc/d	1	3,000		3,000	
FLEISCHMANN, Adolf (1892-1969) German					
oil	2	23,167	4,495	11,584	18,672
wc/d	7	31,111	1,269	3,871	8,937
FLEMING, Alexander M (1878-1929) Canadian					
oil	1	1,128		1,128	
FLEMING, John (1792-1845) British					
oil	2	8,618	4,238	4,309	4,380
FLEMISH SCHOOL					
oil	4	12,330	2,532	2,792	4,215

Name	No.	Total Sales Value	lowest	Prices median	highest
FLEMISH SCHOOL, 14th C					
oil	1	53,470		53,470	
FLEMISH SCHOOL, 15th/16th C					
oil	1	5,809		5,809	
FLEMISH SCHOOL, 16th C					
3D	4	38,829	2,568	9,523	17,215
oil	15	586,453	1,239	6,488	475,000
FLEMISH SCHOOL, 16th/17th C					
3D	2	35,082	15,120	17,541	19,962
oil	3	14,866	3,420	4,657	6,789
FLEMISH SCHOOL, 17th C					
3D	7	49,178	3,087	4,312	17,539
oil	99	753,698	1,007	5,718	58,955
wc/d	2	11,813	2,357	5,907	9,456
FLEMISH SCHOOL, 17th/18th C					
oil	7	69,745	2,752	3,545	27,228
FLEMISH SCHOOL, 18th C					
3D	2	8,911	2,568	4,456	6,343
oil	43	288,278	2,400	4,966	38,170
wc/d	1	4,073		4,073	
FLEMISH SCHOOL, 18th/19th C					
oil	1	5,267		5,267	
FLEMISH SCHOOL, 19th C					
oil	3	18,823	2,681	4,634	11,508
FLEMISH-FRENCH SCHOOL, 16th C					
wc/d	1	8,119		8,119	
FLEMISH-ITALIAN SCHOOL, 17th C					
oil	1	2,773		2,773	
FLERS, Camille (1802-1868) French					
oil	2	4,265	2,099	2,133	2,166
FLETCHER, Edwin (1857-1945) British					
oil	6	10,394	1,050	1,469	3,423
FLETCHER, William Blandford (1858-1936) British					
oil	2	5,160	1,410	2,580	3,750
FLEURY, Charles (20th C) French					
oil	1	3,466		3,466	
FLEURY, François-Antoine (1804-1858) French					
oil	1	10,186		10,186	
FLEURY, J (?) ?					
oil	1	1,144		1,144	
FLEURY, J V de (19th C) British					
oil	1	5,100		5,100	
FLEURY, Jules Amedee Louis (1845-?) French					
oil	1	2,044		2,044	
FLEURY, R (?) ?					
oil	1	1,304		1,304	
FLEXOR, Samson (1907-) French					
oil	1	14,298		14,298	
FLICK, Carl (1904-1976) American					
oil	3	5,100	1,100	1,500	2,500
FLICKEL, Paul Franz (1852-1903) German					
oil	2	3,574	1,211	1,787	2,363
FLIGHT, Graham (20th C) American					
oil	2	2,500	1,100	1,250	1,400
FLINCK, Govaert (1615-1660) Dutch					
oil	3	93,450	14,400	25,670	53,380
FLINT, Francis Russell (1915-1977) British					
oil	1	1,491		1,491	
FLINT, Leroy (1909-) American					
oil	1	3,025		3,025	

Name	No.	Total Sales Value	lowest	Prices median	highest
FLINT, Sir William Russell (1880-1969) British					
oil	3	205,744	10,744	75,000	120,000
wc/d	64	565,650	1,400	5,163	60,000
FLINTOE, Johan (1786-1870) Danish					
wc/d	1	18,262		18,262	
FLOCH, Josef (1895-1977) American/Austrian					
oil	7	49,760	1,500	5,434	15,000
FLOCH, Lionel (20th C) French					
oil	2	5,044	1,389	2,522	3,655
FLOCKENHAUS, Heinz (1856-1919) German					
oil	1	2,245		2,245	
FLODBERG, Gilbert (1938-) Canadian					
oil	1	1,834		1,834	
FLODMAN, Carl (1863-1888) Swedish					
oil	3	6,133	1,693	2,070	2,370
FLOGNY, Eugène Victor de (1825-?) French					
oil	1	4,109		4,109	
FLOQUET FAMILY (17th C) Flemish					
oil	1	7,065		7,065	
FLORA, Paul (1922-) Austrian					
wc/d	3	3,467	1,040	1,189	1,238
FLOREANI, Roberto (1956-) Italian					
wc/d	1	2,400		2,400	
FLORENTINE SCHOOL Italian					
3D	1	4,410		4,410	
wc/d	1	90,000		90,000	
FLORENTINE SCHOOL, 14th C Italian					
oil	2	39,492	12,132	19,746	27,360
FLORENTINE SCHOOL, 15th C Italian					
3D	2	57,810	14,708	28,905	43,102
oil	3	60,186	6,342	14,143	39,701
wc/d	1	3,000		3,000	
FLORENTINE SCHOOL, 16th C Italian					
3D	4	289,033	9,913	45,185	188,750
oil	5	40,289	5,440	6,048	15,076
wc/d	4	37,301	3,000	8,846	16,610
FLORENTINE SCHOOL, 16th/17th C Italian					
3D	5	99,565	12,068	22,844	24,137
wc/d	1	6,040		6,040	
FLORENTINE SCHOOL, 17th C Italian					
3D	3	50,255	6,465	16,610	27,180
oil	7	81,941	3,322	6,000	40,390
FLORENTINE SCHOOL, 17th/18th C Italian					
wc/d	1	4,634		4,634	
FLORENTINE SCHOOL, 18th C Italian					
wc/d	1	8,456		8,456	
FLORENTINE SCHOOL, 19th C Italian					
oil	1	11,791		11,791	
FLORES, Pedro (1897-1967) Spanish					
oil	1	4,335		4,335	
FLORIDIA, Emanuele (1932-) Italian					
oil	1	1,399		1,399	
FLORIS, Frans (16/17th C) Flemish					
oil	1	12,534		12,534	
FLOUR, Adrien Jules (1864-1921) French					
oil	1	1,164		1,164	
FLOUTIER, Louis (20th C) French					
oil	3	10,479	1,367	4,163	4,949
FLOWERS, Alfred (19-20th C) ?					
wc/d	1	1,176		1,176	

Name	No.	Total Sales Value	Prices lowest	median	highest
FLOYD, Donald H (1892-1965) British					
oil	2	2,088	1,001	1,044	1,087
FLOYD, Harry (fl.1884-1917) British					
oil	1	1,113		1,113	
FLUCK, Johann Peter (1902-1954) Swiss					
oil	2	2,998	1,016	1,499	1,982
FLUMIANI, Ugo (1876-1938) Italian					
oil	1	1,784		1,784	
FLURY, Burckhardt (1862-1928) Swiss					
oil	1	1,210		1,210	
wc/d	1	1,350		1,350	
FOCACCI, Emma (20th C) Italian					
oil	1	1,025		1,025	
FOCARDI, Piero (1889-?) Italian					
oil	3	50,048	1,665	19,702	28,681
FOCARDI, Ruggero (1864-1934) Italian					
oil	2	8,382	2,182	4,191	6,200
FOCHT, Frederic (1879-?) French					
3D	1	3,180		3,180	
FODOR, Mihaly (19th C) British					
oil	1	2,304		2,304	
FOGELIN, Anders (1933-1982) Swedish					
oil	1	1,260		1,260	
FOGG, Howard (1917-1996) American					
wc/d	2	18,500	7,500	9,250	11,000
FOGGIA, Mario Moretti (1882-?) Italian					
oil	4	8,071	1,098	1,878	3,218
FOHR, Karl Philipp (1795-1818) German					
wc/d	1	15,455		15,455	
FOISIL, Edith (20th C) French					
oil	1	2,198		2,198	
FOKKE, Jan (1745-1812) Dutch					
wc/d	1	1,533		1,533	
FOLCHI, P (19th C) Italian					
wc/d	1	13,118		13,118	
FOLDI, Augusto (20th C) ?					
oil	1	1,183		1,183	
FOLEY, Barry (20th C) British					
3D	1	1,208		1,208	
FOLEY, Henry (19th C) British					
3D	1	1,658		1,658	
oil	1	1,000		1,000	
FOLEY, John Henry (1818-1874) British					
3D	1	3,256		3,256	
oil	1	1,600		1,600	
FOLINSBEE, John F (1892-1972) American					
oil	2	7,100	1,100	3,550	6,000
FOLKERTS, Poppe (1875-?) German					
oil	4	23,704	2,732	5,215	10,543
FOLLENWEIDER, Rudolf (1774-1847) Swiss					
wc/d	1	1,911		1,911	
FOLLINI, Carlo (1848-1938) Italian					
oil	11	66,284	1,605	6,152	12,383
FOLLMER, Frank (20th C) American					
wc/d	1	1,000		1,000	
FOLLOWFIELD, W H (?) ?					
oil	1	1,898		1,898	
FOLON, Jean Michel (1934-) Belgian					
wc/d	7	15,891	1,391	2,144	3,520

Name	No.	Total Sales Value	lowest	Prices median	highest
FOLTYN (20th C) French?					
oil	1	5,914		5,914	
FOLTZ, Philipp von (1805-1877) German					
oil	2	4,877	1,994	2,439	2,883
FOMSGAARD, Jes (20th C) Danish					
wc/d	1	3,174		3,174	
FONGUEUSE, Maurice (20th C) French					
oil	1	1,100		1,100	
FONSECA, Gonzalo (1922-1997) Uruguayan					
oil	7	63,421	2,105	6,200	30,000
FONTAINE, Charles la (19th C) French					
oil	1	9,036		9,036	
FONTAINE, Gabrielle (19th C) French					
wc/d	1	4,156		4,156	
FONTAINE, Pierre François Leonard (1762-1853) French					
wc/d	1	4,400		4,400	
FONTAINE, Thomas Sherwood la (1915-) British					
oil	1	2,860		2,860	
FONTAINE, Victor (1837-1884) Belgian					
oil	2	11,550	3,550	5,775	8,000
FONTAINEBLEAU SCHOOL French					
wc/d	1	3,750		3,750	
FONTAINEBLEAU SCHOOL, 16th C French					
oil	2	19,881	4,062	9,941	15,819
wc/d	1	3,867		3,867	
FONTANA, Annibale (1540-c.1587) Italian					
3D	1	1,543,500		1,543,500	
FONTANA, Lavinia (school) (1552-1614) Italian					
oil	1	12,000		12,000	
FONTANA, Lucio (1899-1968) Italian					
3D	20	1,008,003	2,097	11,999	507,500
oil	15	2,949,183	2,701	120,800	936,200
wc/d	34	4,310,159	1,063	10,424	650,000
FONTANA, Prospero (1512-1597) Italian					
wc/d	1	1,335		1,335	
FONTANA, Riccardo (19/20th C) Italian					
3D	1	2,752		2,752	
FONTANAROSA, Lucien (1912-1975) French					
oil	13	30,072	1,018	1,996	6,444
FONTANE, A (?) ?					
oil	1	3,800		3,800	
FONTANESI, Antonio (1818-1882) Italian					
oil	2	52,904	15,379	26,452	37,525
FONTEBASSO, Francesco (1709-1769) Italian					
oil	2	19,291	1,171	9,646	18,120
wc/d	4	15,132	1,134	3,375	7,248
FONTENAY, Jean Baptiste Belin de (1653-1715) French					
oil	4	177,156	13,406	25,250	113,250
FONTEYN, Adriaen Lucasz (1626-1661) Dutch					
oil	1	1,231		1,231	
FONTINELLE, Jean de la (20th C) French					
3D	1	1,831		1,831	
FONVILLE, Horace-Antoine (1832-1910) French					
oil	2	9,761	1,096	4,881	8,665
FOOTE, Will Howe (1874-1965) American					
oil	1	4,500		4,500	
FOPPIANI, Gustavo (1925-1986) Italian					
oil	1	1,100		1,100	

Name	No.	Total Sales Value	lowest	Prices median	highest
FORABOSCO, Gerolamo (1605-1679) Italian					
oil	1	21,838		21,838	
FORAIN, Jean Louis (1852-1931) French					
oil	13	204,139	2,004	10,950	50,915
wc/d	7	25,688	1,037	2,336	11,922
FORBES, Alexander (1802-1839) British					
oil	2	11,588	2,528	5,794	9,060
FORBES, Elizabeth Adela (1859-1912) British					
oil	1	26,100		26,100	
wc/d	4	38,845	4,930	10,583	12,750
FORBES, Helen K (1891-1945) American					
oil	1	2,500		2,500	
FORBES, J (19th C) ?					
oil	1	1,500		1,500	
FORBES, Maud Stanhope (fl.1903-1940) British					
oil	1	1,450		1,450	
FORBES, Stanhope Alexander (1857-1947) British					
oil	17	2,512,089	2,844	29,200	1,650,000
FORBES, Vivian (1891-1937) British					
oil	1	1,349		1,349	
FORCELLA, Nicola (19th C) Italian					
oil	1	3,943		3,943	
FORD, Henry Chapman (1828-1894) American					
oil	1	25,000		25,000	
FOREAU, Louis Henri (1866-1938) French					
oil	1	1,586		1,586	
FOREST, Roy de (1930-) American					
oil	1	12,000		12,000	
FORESTIER, Amedee (?) ?					
oil	1	1,305		1,305	
FORG, Gunther (1952-) German					
3D	2	4,066	1,153	2,033	2,913
oil	4	64,629	6,040	14,771	29,047
wc/d	9	89,079	1,748	5,006	27,180
FORGIOLI, Attilio (1933-) Italian					
oil	1	1,959		1,959	
FORKUN, Roy (20th C) American					
oil	1	1,300		1,300	
FORNARA, Carlo (1871-1968) Italian					
oil	1	18,659		18,659	
wc/d	3	25,525	4,145	9,163	12,217
FORNARO D'ATERNO, A (1936-) Italian					
oil	1	9,472		9,472	
FORNENBURGH, Jan Baptist van (c.1600-1649) Dutch					
oil	2	120,657	20,657	60,329	100,000
FORNER, Raquel (1902-1990) Argentinian					
oil	1	1,136		1,136	
FORNES ISERN, Pablo (1930-) Spanish					
oil	1	2,241		2,241	
FORNS BADA, Carlos (1956-) French					
oil	1	2,806		2,806	
FORNS Y ROMANS, Rafael (1868-1939) Spanish					
oil	1	1,137		1,137	
FORREST, Archie (20th C) British					
oil	1	3,020		3,020	
FORREST, William S (fl.1840-1866) British					
3D	1	3,000		3,000	
FORRESTALL, Thomas de Vany (1936-) Canadian					
oil	1	1,896		1,896	

Name	No.	Total Sales Value	Prices lowest	median	highest
FORSBERG, Nils (elder) (1842-1934) Swedish					
oil	2	3,352	1,155	1,676	2,197
FORSSLUND, Jonas (1754-1809) Swedish					
wc/d	2	3,933	1,656	1,967	2,277
FORSTER, George (1817-1896) American					
oil	1	3,500		3,500	
FORSTER, George E (19th C) American					
oil	3	26,000	6,000	10,000	10,000
FORSTNER, A (?) German?					
oil	1	1,214		1,214	
FORSYTH, Richard (fl.1956) British					
oil	1	1,029		1,029	
FORSYTH, William (1854-1935) American					
oil	2	7,000	3,500	3,500	3,500
FORSYTHE, Victor Clyde (1885-1962) American					
oil	2	3,100	1,500	1,550	1,600
FORT, Theodore (19th C) French					
oil	1	1,275		1,275	
FORTE, Gaetano (1797-1866) Italian					
oil	1	10,106		10,106	
FORTE, Vicente (20th C) South American					
oil	1	1,000		1,000	
FORTESCUE, William B (1850-1924) British					
oil	3	10,504	3,322	3,432	3,750
FORTEZA, Nicolas (1918-) Spanish					
oil	1	1,742		1,742	
FORTI, Ettore (19th C) Italian					
oil	1	50,000		50,000	
FORTIN, Marc-Aurele (1888-1970) Canadian					
oil	7	44,618	1,453	4,009	16,592
wc/d	8	45,696	1,514	6,443	9,595
FORTINI, Edouard (19th C) Italian					
oil	1	8,000		8,000	
FORTSCH, Sebastian (1753-1803) German					
oil	1	1,016		1,016	
FORTUNATO, Franco (1946-) Italian					
oil	1	1,201		1,201	
FORTUNATO, P (20th C) Italian					
oil	2	2,300	1,100	1,150	1,200
FORTUNEY (1878-1950) French					
wc/d	2	5,123	1,459	2,562	3,664
FORTUNEY, Louis (1878-1950) French					
wc/d	1	1,097		1,097	
FORTUNIO (20th C) Italian?					
oil	1	2,054		2,054	
FORTUNY Y MADRAZO, Mariano (1871-1949) Spanish					
oil	1	5,309		5,309	
FORTUNY Y MARSAL, Mariano (1838-1874) Spanish					
oil	2	484,305	4,305	242,153	480,000
wc/d	5	56,063	1,210	11,447	18,000
FORTUNY, Mariano (19th C) Spanish					
wc/d	2	75,786	30,200	37,893	45,586
FORUP, Carl Christian (1883-1939) Danish					
oil	2	2,808	1,008	1,404	1,800
FOSCHI, Francesco (?-1780) Italian					
oil	1	29,400		29,400	
FOSS, Harald (1843-1922) Danish					
oil	1	1,668		1,668	

Name	No.	Total Sales Value	lowest	median	highest
FOSS, Olivier (1920-) French/American					
oil	1	1,400		1,400	
FOSSATI, Emilio (20th C) Italian					
oil	1	2,200		2,200	
FOSSE, Jean Baptiste Adolphe la (1810-1879) French					
oil	1	1,000		1,000	
FOSTA, Bianca (19th C) Italian					
oil	1	4,523		4,523	
FOSTER, Ben (1852-1926) American					
oil	4	12,500	1,500	3,400	4,200
FOSTER, H K (19th C) American					
oil	1	1,343		1,343	
FOSTER, Hattie B (19th C) American					
oil	1	1,141		1,141	
FOSTER, Myles Birket (1825-1899) British					
oil	1	2,900		2,900	
wc/d	25	235,291	1,109	8,580	27,170
FOSTER, R John (1908-) American					
oil	1	4,250		4,250	
FOSTER, W P H (?) British?					
oil	1	1,382		1,382	
FOSTER, Will (1882-1953) American					
oil	5	14,850	2,500	3,000	3,600
FOSTER, William Gilbert (1855-1906) British					
oil	2	12,871	1,021	6,436	11,850
FOSTER, William Harden (1886-1941) American					
oil	1	2,800		2,800	
FOTINSKY, Serge (fl.1912-1940) Russian					
oil	2	11,874	4,777	5,937	7,097
FOUACE, Guillaume Romain (1827-1895) French					
oil	2	10,723	3,992	5,362	6,731
FOUBERT, Émile (1840-1910) French					
oil	4	21,694	1,197	5,249	10,000
FOUCHET, B (?) French?					
oil	2	5,026	1,804	2,513	3,222
FOUGSTEDT, Arvid (1888-1949) Swedish					
oil	4	15,185	1,863	3,931	5,460
wc/d	2	6,566	1,560	3,283	5,006
FOUGSTEDT, Nils (20th C) Swedish					
3D	1	1,560		1,560	
FOUJITA (1886-1968) French/Japanese					
wc/d	2	16,699	1,069	8,350	15,630
FOUJITA, Tsuguharu (1886-1968) French/Japanese					
oil	19	1,353,555	4,960	40,770	350,000
wc/d	42	533,939	1,066	9,500	47,772
FOULONGONE, Alfred (1821-1897) French					
oil	1	4,740		4,740	
FOUQUERAY, Charles (1872-1956) French					
oil	1	4,133		4,133	
FOURMOIS, Theodore (1814-1871) Belgian					
oil	13	32,474	1,006	1,810	4,571
FOURNIER, Alexis Jean (1865-1948) American					
oil	4	19,500	4,000	4,750	6,000
FOURNIER, Alfred Victor (19/20th C) French					
oil	1	1,610		1,610	
FOURNIER, Jean Simon (18th C) French?					
oil	2	130,000	35,000	65,000	95,000
FOWERAKER, A Moulton (1873-1942) British					
wc/d	9	18,539	1,422	1,950	2,808

Name	No.	Total Sales Value	lowest	Prices median	highest
FOWLER, Robert (1853-1926) British					
wc/d	2	4,426	1,170	2,213	3,256
FOWLER, Trevor Thomas (1830-1871) American					
oil	1	1,500		1,500	
FOWLES, Arthur W (c.1815-1878) British					
oil	4	56,694	2,574	13,475	27,170
FOX, Charles James (1860-?) British					
oil	1	1,250		1,250	
FOX, George (19th C) British					
oil	2	3,369	1,065	1,685	2,304
FOX, H C (1860-?) British					
wc/d	2	2,340	1,020	1,170	1,320
FOX, Henry Charles (1860-1929) British					
wc/d	22	35,824	1,001	1,242	3,768
FOX, R Atkinson (1860-?) Canadian					
oil	1	1,300		1,300	
FOYATIER, Denis (1793-1863) French					
3D	1	3,308		3,308	
FRACANZANO, Cesare (1605-1653) Italian					
oil	2	6,909	1,323	3,455	5,586
FRACANZANO, Francesco (1612-1656) Italian					
oil	1	6,280		6,280	
FRAGIACOMO, Pietro (1856-1922) Italian					
oil	8	39,174	1,561	4,188	10,090
FRAGONARD, Alexandre Evariste (1780-1850) French					
oil	1	8,240		8,240	
FRAGONARD, Jean Honore (1732-1806) French					
oil	8	10,938,500	73,500	670,000	4,704,000
wc/d	7	222,311	1,401	10,000	130,000
FRAGUIER, Gabriel Auguste Claire Armand de (1803-1873) French					
oil	2	8,044	1,933	4,022	6,111
FRAIA, G (?) Italian					
oil	1	2,400		2,400	
FRAICHOT, Claude Joseph II (18th C) French					
oil	1	6,200		6,200	
FRAILE, Alfonso (1930-1988) Spanish					
oil	3	11,017	1,355	2,133	7,529
wc/d	3	32,677	6,745	10,218	15,714
FRAMPTON, Meredith (1894-1984) British					
oil	1	1,534		1,534	
FRAMPTON, Sir George James (1860-1928) British					
3D	5	87,650	2,355	13,590	42,280
FRAN-BARO (1926-) French					
oil	4	7,676	1,282	2,003	2,389
FRANC-LAMY, Pierre (1855-1919) French					
oil	1	3,160		3,160	
FRANCAIS, François Louis (1814-1897) French					
oil	1	7,000		7,000	
FRANCALANCIA, Riccardo (1886-1965) Italian					
oil	2	8,624	3,273	4,312	5,351
FRANCE, Charles (19th C) British					
oil	1	2,556		2,556	
FRANCE, Charles and LOWCOCK, Charles Frederick (19th C) British					
oil	1	1,343		1,343	
FRANCES Y PASCUAL, Placido (1840-?) Spanish					
oil	1	18,286		18,286	
FRANCESCHI, Louis Julien (1825-1893) French					
3D	1	3,963		3,963	

Name	No.	Total Sales Value	lowest	Prices median	highest
FRANCESCHI, Mariano de (1849-1896) Italian					
oil	1	1,413		1,413	
wc/d	1	1,700		1,700	
FRANCESCHINI, Marco Antonio (1648-1729) Italian					
oil	2	263,250	113,250	131,625	150,000
FRANCESCHINI, Vincenzo (1812-1885) Italian					
wc/d	1	1,009		1,009	
FRANCESCO DI GIORGIO (1439-1502) Italian					
oil	1	105,700		105,700	
FRANCESE, Franco (1920-1996) Italian					
oil	3	6,140	1,318	1,966	2,856
wc/d	3	3,290	1,017	1,017	1,256
FRANCHERE, Joseph-Charles (1866-1921) Canadian					
oil	3	15,697	2,406	6,275	7,016
FRANCHEVILLE, Clemence Andree Lenique de (1875-) French					
oil	1	1,000		1,000	
FRANCHI, Alessandro (1838-1914) Italian					
oil	1	4,000		4,000	
FRANCIA, A (19/20th C) French					
wc/d	1	1,237		1,237	
FRANCIA, François Louis Thomas (1772-1839) French					
oil	1	2,567		2,567	
wc/d	3	9,701	1,049	4,424	4,424
FRANCIA, Giacomo (1486-1557) Italian					
oil	2	77,246	37,986	38,623	39,260
FRANCIS, John F (1808-1886) American					
oil	3	204,300	2,100	2,200	200,000
FRANCIS, Mark (1962-) British					
oil	10	103,026	2,595	11,300	19,000
FRANCIS, Sam (1923-1994) American					
oil	33	4,281,362	3,856	27,180	2,000,000
wc/d	17	511,608	4,363	16,824	143,450
FRANCISCO, J Bond (1863-1931) American					
oil	2	5,150	1,400	2,575	3,750
FRANCISCO, Pietro de (19th C) Italian					
oil	1	4,933		4,933	
FRANCK, Albert Jacques (1899-1973) Canadian					
oil	5	15,679	1,625	2,167	6,305
wc/d	1	1,062		1,062	
FRANCKE (19/20th C) ?					
oil	1	2,578		2,578	
FRANCKE, Carl Ludwig (1797-1846) German					
oil	1	1,000		1,000	
FRANCKE-NAUTSCHUTZ, Rudolf (1860-?) German					
oil	1	1,258		1,258	
FRANCKEN, Ambrosius (16/17th C) Flemish					
oil	1	7,507		7,507	
FRANCKEN, Frans (16/17th C) Flemish					
oil	1	12,985		12,985	
FRANCKEN, Frans (school) (16/17th C) Flemish					
oil	1	1,761		1,761	
FRANCKEN, Frans I (1542-1616) Flemish					
oil	2	40,414	3,295	20,207	37,119
FRANCKEN, Frans II (1581-1642) Flemish					
oil	15	860,913	2,259	21,000	203,660
FRANCKEN, Frans II (school) (1581-1642) Flemish					
oil	1	4,652		4,652	
FRANCKEN, Hieronymus (16/17th C) Flemish					
oil	1	11,407		11,407	

Name	No.	Total Sales Value	lowest	Prices median	highest
FRANCKEN, Hieronymus II (1578-1623) Flemish					
oil	2	31,269	7,550	15,635	23,719
FRANCKEN, Ruth (20th C) ?					
wc/d	1	1,092		1,092	
FRANCKEN, Thomas (1574-1626) Belgian					
oil	1	5,715		5,715	
FRANCO Y CORDERO, Jose (19th C) Spanish					
oil	6	20,925	1,415	3,663	4,843
FRANCO Y SALINAS, Luis (1850-1899) Spanish					
oil	2	15,328	5,110	7,664	10,218
FRANCO, Giovanni Battista (c.1498-1580) Italian					
wc/d	3	26,527	1,727	2,800	22,000
FRANCO, Siron (1947-) Brazilian					
oil	2	26,000	12,000	13,000	14,000
FRANCO-FLEMISH SCHOOL, 15th C					
wc/d	1	27,500		27,500	
FRANCO-FLEMISH SCHOOL, 16th C					
oil	3	29,032	4,320	8,712	16,000
FRANCO-FLEMISH SCHOOL, 17th C					
3D	1	14,400		14,400	
oil	3	25,493	3,140	9,793	12,560
FRANCO-FLEMISH SCHOOL, 18th C					
3D	2	16,911	5,586	8,456	11,325
FRANCO-GERMAN SCHOOL, 15th C					
3D	1	13,391		13,391	
FRANCOIS, Celestin (19th C) Belgian					
oil	1	3,549		3,549	
FRANCOIS, Joseph Charles (1851-1940) Belgian					
oil	9	36,115	1,150	1,602	10,300
FRANCOLIN, Robert (20th C) French					
oil	1	1,062		1,062	
FRANCONIAN SCHOOL, 15th/16th C German					
3D	1	39,260		39,260	
FRANCONIAN SCHOOL, 17th C German					
3D	1	3,189		3,189	
FRANCONIAN SCHOOL, 18th C German					
oil	1	2,595		2,595	
FRANCUCCI, Innocenzo (1494-1550) Italian					
oil	1	23,294		23,294	
FRANCX, François (18th C) ?					
wc/d	1	1,058		1,058	
FRANDZEN, Eugene M (1893-1972) American					
oil	1	5,000		5,000	
FRANGI, Giovanni (1959-) Italian					
oil	1	1,484		1,484	
FRANGIAMORE, Salvatore (1853-1915) Italian					
oil	1	15,000		15,000	
FRANGIPANE, Niccolo (1555-1600) Italian					
oil	1	21,653		21,653	
FRANK WILL (1900-1951) French					
oil	11	36,045	1,019	3,032	7,302
wc/d	19	37,411	1,012	1,625	3,685
FRANK, Edvard (1909-1972) German					
wc/d	2	2,214	1,000	1,107	1,214
FRANK, Ellen (fl.1889-1912) British					
oil	1	2,147		2,147	
FRANK, Friedrich (1871-1945) Austrian					
wc/d	3	7,761	1,737	1,796	4,228

Name	No.	Total Sales Value	Prices lowest	Prices median	highest
FRANK, Gerson (20th C) American					
3D	1	1,600		1,600	
FRANK, Johan Willem (1720-1761) Dutch					
oil	1	3,128		3,128	
FRANK, Josef (1873-?) Austrian					
oil	1	1,000		1,000	
FRANK, Lucien (1857-1920) Belgian					
oil	13	77,855	1,191	3,771	31,100
wc/d	4	13,599	2,537	3,313	4,436
FRANK, Mary (1933-) American					
3D	1	4,750		4,750	
FRANKE, Albert (1860-1924) German					
oil	1	1,184		1,184	
FRANKE, Carl (19th C) German?					
oil	1	3,187		3,187	
FRANKE, Hanny (1890-1973) German					
oil	4	5,595	1,154	1,264	1,913
FRANKEL, Clemens (1872-1944) German					
oil	1	1,283		1,283	
FRANKEN, Marianne (1884-1945) Dutch					
oil	1	1,015		1,015	
FRANKEN, Paul von (1818-1884) German					
oil	1	8,532		8,532	
FRANKENTHAL SCHOOL, 16th C German					
3D	1	4,983		4,983	
wc/d	1	4,597		4,597	
FRANKENTHAL SCHOOL, 17th C German					
oil	1	2,234		2,234	
FRANKENTHALER, Helen (1928-) American					
oil	9	475,500	12,000	45,000	115,000
wc/d	1	4,060		4,060	
FRANQUELIN, Jean Augustin (1798-1839) French					
oil	2	48,000	13,000	24,000	35,000
FRANQUIN, Andre (20th C) Belgian?					
wc/d	1	1,606		1,606	
FRANS, Paul (20th C) French					
oil	1	1,047		1,047	
FRANSE, Cornelis (1924-1982) Dutch					
3D	1	2,773		2,773	
FRANZ, Ettore Roesler (1845-1907) Italian					
wc/d	10	65,224	1,001	6,022	15,669
FRANZEN, John E (1942-) Swedish					
wc/d	1	1,613		1,613	
FRANZIS-SLUSING (20th C) German					
oil	1	2,366		2,366	
FRAPIN (19th C) ?					
3D	1	1,818		1,818	
FRAPPA, Jose (1854-1904) French					
oil	2	8,120	1,800	4,060	6,320
FRASCHETTI, Giuseppe (?) Italian					
oil	1	2,857		2,857	
FRASER, Alec (fl.1902-1912) British					
oil	2	4,002	1,208	2,001	2,794
FRASER, Alexander (jnr) (1828-1899) British					
oil	3	9,830	1,740	2,352	5,738
FRASER, Alexander (snr) (1786-1865) British					
oil	1	5,313		5,313	
FRASER, Alexander (19th C) British					
oil	2	21,938	1,638	10,969	20,300

Name	No.	Total Sales Value		Prices	
			lowest	median	highest
FRASER, Alexander C (19th C) British					
oil	1	5,292		5,292	
FRASER, Donald Hamilton (1929-) British					
oil	4	26,715	1,015	5,725	14,250
FRASER, George Gordon (1859-1895) British					
wc/d	1	1,057		1,057	
FRASER, James Earle (1876-1953) American					
3D	4	14,400	1,300	1,800	9,500
FRASER, John (20th C) ?					
oil	5	8,246	1,080	1,278	2,934
FRASER, John Arthur (1839-1898) Canadian/British					
wc/d	1	2,275		2,275	
FRASER, Robert Winchester (1848-1906) British					
wc/d	3	4,261	1,185	1,264	1,812
FRASER, Robert Winter (fl.1880-1904) British					
wc/d	1	1,444		1,444	
FRASER, Thomas Douglas (1883-1955) American					
oil	1	5,000		5,000	
FRASSON, Tonio (1922-) Swiss					
oil	1	1,025		1,025	
FRATIN, Christopher (1800-1864) French					
3D	14	42,677	1,088	2,841	6,708
FRAU, Jose (1898-1976) Spanish					
oil	5	28,014	1,927	4,152	12,378
FRAZER, W M (1864-1961) British					
oil	2	2,289	1,021	1,145	1,268
FRAZER, William Miller (1864-1961) British					
oil	26	83,789	1,057	2,440	8,760
FRAZETTA, Frank (1928-) American					
oil	1	2,400		2,400	
FRAZIER, Luke (20th C) American					
oil	1	20,000		20,000	
FRECKLETON, Harry (1890-1979) British					
oil	1	1,260		1,260	
FREDDIE, W (1909-1995) Danish					
wc/d	1	1,025		1,025	
FREDDIE, Wilhelm (1909-1995) Danish					
oil	19	141,271	1,883	4,612	30,218
wc/d	2	6,064	1,417	3,032	4,647
FREDENTHAL, David (1914-1958) American					
wc/d	1	1,500		1,500	
FREDERIC, Léon (1856-1940) Belgian					
wc/d	2	2,783	1,331	1,392	1,452
FREDERICKS, Ernest (1877-1927) American					
oil	1	1,600		1,600	
FREDERICKS, Marshall Maynard (1908-1998) American					
3D	13	127,000	2,250	9,000	21,000
FREDERIKS, S (fl.c.1812) Dutch					
oil	1	1,992		1,992	
FREDOU, Jean Martial (1711-1795) French					
wc/d	6	25,970	1,455	4,737	7,274
FREDOUILLE, Felix Maurice (1896-?) French					
oil	1	1,653		1,653	
FREDRIKS, Johannes Hendrik (1751-1822) Dutch					
oil	1	135,408		135,408	
FREEBAIRN, Robert (1765-1808) British					
oil	2	22,930	6,320	11,465	16,610
FREEDMAN, C (20th C) British					
3D	1	1,450		1,450	

Name	No.	Total Sales Value	Prices lowest	median	highest
FREEMAN, Dick (1932-1991) Canadian					
oil	6	9,181	1,235	1,401	2,205
FREEMAN, William Philip Barnes (1813-1897) British					
oil	1	2,385		2,385	
FREEZOR, G M (fl.1861-1879) British					
oil	1	1,275		1,275	
FREIXANES, Jose (1953-) Spanish					
oil	1	3,813		3,813	
FREJO GUTIERREZ, Emilio (1956-) Spanish					
oil	1	1,686		1,686	
FRELINGHUYSEN, Suzy (1911-1988) American					
oil	1	32,000		32,000	
FREMIET, E (1824-1910) French					
3D	2	13,416	3,126	6,708	10,290
FREMIET, Emmanuel (1824-1910) French					
3D	49	246,761	1,200	3,354	27,091
wc/d	1	1,160		1,160	
FREMIET, Ernest and MULLER, Emile (20th C) ?					
3D	1	7,594		7,594	
FREMIN, R (18th C) ?					
3D	1	9,329		9,329	
FREMION, Joel A (1952-) American					
wc/d	1	4,000		4,000	
FREMONT (19/20th C) French					
3D	1	10,676		10,676	
FREMY, Antoine Alexandre Auguste (1816-1885) French					
wc/d	1	1,338		1,338	
FRENCH COLONIAL SCHOOL, 18th C					
oil	1	4,051		4,051	
FRENCH PROVINCIAL SCHOOL, 18th C					
oil	1	3,243		3,243	
FRENCH SCHOOL					
3D	8	88,759	2,730	7,880	33,653
oil	10	45,477	2,869	3,885	8,357
FRENCH SCHOOL, 12th C					
3D	1	90,600		90,600	
FRENCH SCHOOL, 14th C					
3D	6	112,155	2,890	10,474	52,850
FRENCH SCHOOL, 15th C					
3D	4	76,113	3,210	15,718	41,467
oil	1	105,840		105,840	
wc/d	1	5,982		5,982	
FRENCH SCHOOL, 16th C					
3D	8	50,649	2,245	3,330	17,507
oil	2	59,889	14,589	29,945	45,300
wc/d	1	7,274		7,274	
FRENCH SCHOOL, 16th/17th C					
3D	1	2,874		2,874	
wc/d	1	15,100		15,100	
FRENCH SCHOOL, 17th C					
3D	19	732,096	3,593	13,578	436,769
oil	47	561,125	2,578	6,274	151,000
wc/d	12	79,229	2,783	4,614	21,821
FRENCH SCHOOL, 17th/18th C					
3D	3	34,484	8,385	12,080	14,019
oil	6	24,389	2,748	3,665	7,146
wc/d	1	11,671		11,671	
FRENCH SCHOOL, 18th C					
3D	28	877,938	1,800	16,810	190,000
oil	115	965,436	2,458	5,539	44,991
wc/d	13	136,914	3,473	7,350	25,251

Name	No.	Total Sales Value	Prices lowest	median	highest
FRENCH SCHOOL, 18th/19th C					
3D	3	19,899	3,020	3,340	13,539
oil	7	26,824	1,211	3,412	6,666
FRENCH SCHOOL, 19th C					
3D	56	568,049	1,400	5,325	105,700
oil	113	773,888	1,564	5,111	45,000
wc/d	20	179,934	2,951	5,405	38,792
FRENCH SCHOOL, 19th/20th C					
3D	2	32,411	3,611	16,206	28,800
oil	3	12,517	1,845	4,380	6,292
FRENCH SCHOOL, 20th C					
3D	3	11,483	3,140	3,633	4,710
oil	7	67,816	3,721	8,728	26,580
wc/d	1	3,214		3,214	
FRENCH, Annie (1872-1965) British					
wc/d	9	69,942	1,896	5,840	25,280
FRENCH, F (?) ?					
oil	1	1,144		1,144	
FRENCH, Frederick (19th C) British					
oil	1	1,700		1,700	
FRENCH, Michael (1951-) Canadian					
oil	1	9,291		9,291	
FRENCH, Percy (1854-1920) Irish					
wc/d	21	176,197	1,087	6,360	74,000
FRENCH-GERMAN SCHOOL, 16th C					
3D	1	3,085		3,085	
FRERE, Charles Edouard (1837-1894) French					
oil	1	12,000		12,000	
FRERE, Charles Theodore (1814-1888) French					
oil	18	180,187	1,573	7,782	24,820
wc/d	3	5,667	1,791	1,929	1,947
FRERE, Edouard (1819-1886) French					
oil	3	91,160	27,000	31,600	32,560
FRERICHS, William C A (1829-1905) American					
oil	2	16,700	2,500	8,350	14,200
FRERIKS, Otto (20th C) ?					
oil	1	1,570		1,570	
FRESNAYE, Roger de la (1885-1925) French					
3D	1	10,125		10,125	
oil	1	15,000		15,000	
wc/d	17	58,532	1,028	3,067	9,492
FREUD, Lucian (1922-) British/German					
oil	1	362,400		362,400	
wc/d	3	30,195	3,000	9,815	17,380
FREUDENBERGER, Sigmund (1745-1801) Swiss					
wc/d	2	3,874	1,458	1,937	2,416
FREUDENTHAL, Peter (1938-) Swedish					
oil	2	2,751	1,004	1,376	1,747
FREUDWEILER, Heinrich (1755-1795) Swiss					
oil	4	43,419	2,917	9,793	20,916
FREUND, Fritz (1859-1942) German					
oil	1	4,661		4,661	
FREUND, Rudolf (20th C) German					
wc/d	1	1,200		1,200	
FREUNDLICH, Otto (1878-1943) German					
oil	1	39,791		39,791	
wc/d	1	25,086		25,086	
FREVILLE, Noel de (1803-?) German					
oil	1	1,136		1,136	

Name	No.	Total Sales Value	Prices lowest	median	highest
FREY, Alice (1895-1981) Belgian					
oil	3	7,531	1,661	2,127	3,743
wc/d	1	1,459		1,459	
FREY, Anna de (?-1808) Dutch					
wc/d	1	1,793		1,793	
FREY, Johann Jakob (1813-1865) Swiss					
oil	4	22,583	2,026	5,697	9,163
FREY-MOOCK, Adolf (1881-1954) German					
oil	6	13,039	1,268	1,594	4,965
FREY-SURBECK, Marguerite (1886-1981) Swiss					
oil	1	1,108		1,108	
FREYBERG, Conrad (1842-?) German					
oil	1	6,340		6,340	
FREYMAN, A (?) ?					
oil	1	4,228		4,228	
FREYMUTH, Alphons (1940-) Dutch					
oil	1	2,361		2,361	
FRIAS Y ESCALANTI, Juan Antonio de (1630-1670) Spanish					
oil	1	20,133		20,133	
FRIBERG, Emil (19/20th C) Swedish?					
oil	1	2,380		2,380	
FRIBERG, Roj (1934-) Swedish					
wc/d	1	1,306		1,306	
FRIDELL, Axel (1894-1935) Swedish					
oil	3	27,100	1,861	2,308	22,931
FRIDERICIA, William (20th C) ?					
oil	1	2,664		2,664	
FRIE, Peter (1947-) Swedish?					
oil	5	19,133	2,162	3,914	6,422
wc/d	1	1,305		1,305	
FRIED, Pal (1893-1976) Hungarian/American					
oil	11	17,166	1,038	1,600	2,450
wc/d	2	2,200	1,000	1,100	1,200
FRIEDENSON, Arthur (1872-1955) British					
oil	4	7,781	1,491	1,867	2,556
FRIEDERICI, Walter (1874-?) German					
oil	1	2,724		2,724	
FRIEDLANDER, Friedrich (1825-1901) Austrian					
oil	2	5,868	2,248	2,934	3,620
FRIEDLANDER, Julius (1810-1861) Danish					
oil	2	5,090	1,191	2,545	3,899
FRIEDLINGER, John (20th C) ?					
oil	1	1,200		1,200	
FRIEDMAN, Arnold (1874-1946) American					
oil	2	20,000	5,000	10,000	15,000
FRIEDMAN, Tom (1965-) American					
3D	4	131,000	10,000	23,000	75,000
FRIEDRICH, Caspar David (1774-1840) German					
wc/d	1	1,560		1,560	
FRIEND, Donald Stuart Leslie (1915-1989) Australian					
wc/d	1	2,485		2,485	
FRIEND, Washington F (1820-1886) British					
wc/d	1	1,115		1,115	
FRIER, Harry (c.1849-1919) British					
wc/d	3	5,128	1,233	1,450	2,445
FRIERS, Julian (?) British?					
oil	1	3,190		3,190	
FRIERS, Rowel (?) ?					
oil	1	1,015		1,015	

Name	No.	Total Sales Value	lowest	Prices median	highest
FRIES, Bernhard (1820-1879) German					
oil	2	17,119	1,169	8,560	15,950
FRIES, Charles Arthur (1854-1940) American					
oil	4	25,000	4,000	5,000	11,000
FRIES, Ernst (1801-1833) German					
wc/d	3	7,381	1,594	2,568	3,219
FRIES, Hanny (1918-) Swiss					
oil	1	2,723		2,723	
FRIES, Pia (1955-) Swiss					
oil	1	1,081		1,081	
FRIESEKE, Frederick Carl (1874-1939) American					
oil	9	2,093,500	7,500	50,000	1,100,000
wc/d	1	12,000		12,000	
FRIESZ, Émile Othon (1879-1949) French					
oil	36	859,594	1,964	6,887	286,900
wc/d	10	35,209	1,365	3,528	6,825
FRIGERIO, R (19/20th C) ?					
oil	1	3,066		3,066	
FRIGOLI, Marlene (20th C) Italian?					
oil	1	2,320		2,320	
FRIIS, Hans Gabriel (1838-1892) Danish					
oil	1	2,600		2,600	
FRILLI, A (19th C) Italian					
3D	4	7,890	1,650	1,896	2,449
FRILLI, Antonio (19/20th C) Italian					
3D	4	223,707	3,297	25,205	170,000
FRILLY, A (?) ?					
3D	1	1,220		1,220	
FRIND, August (1852-1924) Austrian					
oil	1	1,272		1,272	
FRINGBUTH, F (?) ?					
oil	1	1,049		1,049	
FRINK, Elizabeth (1930-1993) British					
3D	19	479,282	2,397	17,380	117,000
wc/d	10	83,660	3,792	7,225	13,585
FRIPP, Alfred Downing (1822-1895) British					
wc/d	2	8,232	1,872	4,116	6,360
FRIPP, George Arthur (1813-1896) British					
oil	2	11,190	1,440	5,595	9,750
wc/d	5	20,673	1,359	3,473	7,150
FRIPP, Thomas William (1864-1931) Canadian/British					
wc/d	1	1,009		1,009	
FRISCH, J C (1738-1815) German					
oil	1	4,000		4,000	
FRISCHE, Heinrich Ludwig (1831-1901) German					
oil	2	7,082	2,179	3,541	4,903
FRISENDAHL, Carl (1886-1948) Swedish					
3D	1	1,606		1,606	
FRISHMUTH, Harriet Whitney (1880-1980) American					
3D	7	159,250	3,250	16,000	65,000
FRISIA, Donato (1883-1953) Italian					
oil	1	1,996		1,996	
FRISON, Jehan (1882-1961) Belgian					
oil	14	22,874	1,053	1,362	3,222
FRITH, W P (1819-1909) British					
oil	1	1,908		1,908	
wc/d	1	2,250		2,250	
FRITH, William Powell (1819-1909) British					
oil	5	87,205	2,100	25,000	30,615
wc/d	1	1,125		1,125	

Name	No.	Total Sales Value	Prices lowest	Prices median	highest
FRITSCH, Ernst (1892-?) German					
oil	1	7,282		7,282	
wc/d	2	4,390	1,553	2,195	2,837
FRITSCH, Katarina (1956-) American?					
3D	1	17,301		17,301	
FRITZ, Andreas (1828-1906) Danish					
oil	2	2,749	1,327	1,375	1,422
FRITZ, Charles (20th C) American					
oil	1	42,500		42,500	
FRITZ, Max (1849-?) German					
oil	3	8,349	1,927	2,922	3,500
FRITZEL, Wilhelm (1870-1943) German					
oil	3	4,259	1,197	1,341	1,721
FRITZSCH, Claudius Ditlev (1763-1841) Danish					
oil	2	40,472	6,910	20,236	33,562
FRIZE, Bernard (1949-) French					
wc/d	1	1,478		1,478	
FRODING, Jonas (1905-1959) Swedish					
3D	1	1,305		1,305	
FRODMAN-CLUZEL, Boris (20th C) Swedish/Russian					
3D	5	25,707	2,422	3,950	11,572
FROHLICH, Bernard (1823-1885) Austrian					
oil	1	1,700		1,700	
FROLICH, Lorenz (1820-1908) Danish					
oil	4	16,390	1,331	3,751	7,557
FROLICHER, Otto (1840-1890) Swiss					
oil	7	24,837	1,049	2,988	8,972
FROM, Einar (1872-1972) Norwegian					
oil	1	1,700		1,700	
FROMANGER, Gerard (1939-) French					
oil	8	79,483	3,099	8,189	18,306
FROMENT-MEURICE, Jacques Charles (1864-1948) French					
3D	2	5,598	2,355	2,799	3,243
FROMENTIN, Eugène (1820-1876) French					
oil	6	67,236	1,623	8,239	24,221
wc/d	3	6,261	1,287	2,200	2,774
FROMME, Ludwig (19/20th C) ?					
oil	1	2,364		2,364	
FROMUTH, Charles Henry (1861-1937) American					
wc/d	4	10,558	2,098	2,600	3,261
FROSSARD, L (?) ?					
oil	1	1,000		1,000	
FROST, A B (1851-1928) American					
wc/d	1	1,500		1,500	
FROST, Arthur Burdett (1851-1928) American					
wc/d	6	27,500	1,500	3,500	9,000
FROST, James (fl.1766-1783) British					
oil	1	4,228		4,228	
FROST, John (1890-1937) American					
oil	1	47,500		47,500	
FROST, M H (19th C) British					
oil	1	1,500		1,500	
FROST, Terry (1915-) British					
oil	35	280,509	1,065	6,300	22,500
wc/d	1	2,686		2,686	
FRUHTRUNK, Gunther (1923-1983) German					
oil	5	82,218	5,825	13,067	37,632
FRY, Anthony (1927-) British					
oil	2	6,240	3,120	3,120	3,120

Name	No.	Total Sales Value	Prices lowest	median	highest
FRY, John Hemming (1861-1946) American					
oil	2	3,900	1,000	1,950	2,900
FRY, Roger (1866-1934) British					
oil	1	6,345		6,345	
FUCHS, Bernard (1932-) American					
oil	4	21,500	4,000	5,000	7,500
FUCHS, Ernst (1930-) Austrian					
3D	2	6,841	2,274	3,421	4,567
wc/d	2	2,283	1,043	1,142	1,240
FUEGER, Friedrich Heinrich (1751-1818) German					
oil	2	21,432	2,492	10,716	18,940
FUERTES, Louis Agassiz (1874-1927) American					
wc/d	26	112,600	2,000	3,875	16,000
FUGER, A (19th C) ?					
oil	1	1,926		1,926	
FUGERE, H (1872-?) French					
3D	1	1,749		1,749	
FUHR, Franz Xaver (1898-1973) German					
oil	6	73,787	2,776	10,314	21,944
wc/d	14	22,195	1,073	1,462	2,146
FUHRICH, Josef von (1800-1876) Austrian					
oil	1	6,978		6,978	
wc/d	1	14,747		14,747	
FUHRMANN, Arend (20th C) Swiss?					
oil	2	3,065	1,505	1,533	1,560
FUHRMANN, Rudolf (1909-1977) German					
wc/d	4	16,416	2,304	4,176	5,760
FUJISHIMA, Takeji (1867-1943) Japanese					
oil	1	30,000		30,000	
FUKUDA, Heihachiro (1892-1974) Japanese					
wc/d	1	60,000		60,000	
FULDE, Edward (19/20th C) American					
oil	1	5,528		5,528	
FULLER, Arthur Davenport (1889-1967) American					
oil	1	8,000		8,000	
FULLER, George (1822-1884) American					
oil	1	6,000		6,000	
FULLER, Richard Henry (1822-1871) American					
oil	1	1,600		1,600	
FULLERTON, Emma W (19th C) American					
oil	1	2,500		2,500	
FULLEYLOVE, John (1845-1908) British					
wc/d	2	4,587	1,287	2,294	3,300
FULLJAMES, Penelope (1942-) British					
oil	2	6,084	2,960	3,042	3,124
FULLWOOD, John (1854-1931) British					
oil	1	1,106		1,106	
FULOP, Karoly (1893-1963) American					
3D	2	8,000	3,250	4,000	4,750
FULTON, David (1848-1930) British					
oil	2	10,272	1,582	5,136	8,690
FULTON, Fitch Burt (1879-1955) American					
oil	1	2,250		2,250	
FULTON, Samuel (1855-1941) British					
oil	7	26,298	1,421	4,108	6,040
FUNI, Achille (1890-1972) Italian					
oil	1	3,956		3,956	
wc/d	1	1,575		1,575	

Name	No.	Total Sales Value	lowest	Prices median	highest
FUNK, Emil (fl.1854-1864) German					
oil	1	10,238		10,238	
FURET, François (1842-1909) Swiss					
oil	1	10,000		10,000	
FURNEAUX, Charles (1835-1913) American					
oil	1	13,000		13,000	
FURSE, Charles Wellington (1868-1904) British					
oil	2	3,987	1,431	1,994	2,556
FUSARO, Jean (1925-) French					
oil	4	10,854	2,051	2,554	3,696
wc/d	2	3,570	1,716	1,785	1,854
FUSSELL, Charles Lewis (1840-1909) American					
oil	1	1,700		1,700	
FUSSLI, Johann Heinrich (1741-1825) Swiss					
oil	2	160,385	30,385	80,193	130,000
wc/d	9	376,937	5,285	13,500	137,450
FUSSLI, Johann Melchior and PREISSLER, Johann Daniel (18th C) Swiss/German					
wc/d	2	3,020	1,510	1,510	1,510
FUSSMANN, Klaus (1938-) German					
oil	11	44,382	2,163	3,641	8,495
wc/d	12	27,383	1,170	2,108	4,791
FUSTIER, Georges (1892-1982) Swiss					
oil	2	15,448	6,484	7,724	8,964
FUTTERER, Joseph (1871-1930) German					
oil	1	1,117		1,117	
FYT, Jan (1609-1661) Flemish					
oil	2	57,252	23,405	28,626	33,847
wc/d	1	2,909		2,909	
GAAL, Ferenc (1891-1956) Hungarian					
oil	1	2,581		2,581	
GABAIN, Ethel (1883-1950) British					
oil	1	1,580		1,580	
GABANI, Giuseppe (1849-1899) Italian					
wc/d	1	1,099		1,099	
GABBIANI, Antonio Domenico (1652-1726) Italian					
oil	1	18,000		18,000	
wc/d	2	4,000	1,778	2,000	2,222
GABE, Nicolas Edward (1814-1865) French					
oil	2	2,709	1,030	1,355	1,679
GABINI, Alfonso (19th C) ?					
oil	1	2,371		2,371	
GABL, Alois (1845-1893) Swiss					
oil	1	12,975		12,975	
GABREILLE, P (19/20th C) French					
3D	1	2,826		2,826	
GABRIEL, François (?-1993) French					
oil	3	6,000	1,800	2,000	2,200
GABRIEL, Isabelle (1902-1990) French					
oil	1	2,500		2,500	
GABRIEL, P J C (1828-1903) Dutch					
wc/d	1	1,072		1,072	
GABRIEL, Paul Joseph Constantin (1828-1903) Dutch					
oil	10	124,750	1,231	9,026	55,162
GABRINI, Pietro (1865-1926) Italian					
oil	2	8,093	3,893	4,047	4,200
wc/d	4	7,004	1,000	1,502	3,000
GABRON, Guilliam (1619-1678) Belgian					
oil	1	53,060		53,060	
GACHET, Niclaus (1736-1817) Swiss					
wc/d	1	1,129		1,129	

Name	No.	Total Sales Value	lowest	Prices median	highest
GACHET, Paul (c.1828-1909) French					
oil	2	5,806	1,875	2,903	3,931
GAD, Mogens (1887-1931) Danish					
oil	1	1,560		1,560	
GADAN, Antoine (1854-1934) French					
oil	3	13,922	4,089	4,381	5,452
GADBOIS, Louis (?-1826) French					
wc/d	1	6,795		6,795	
GADDI, Angelo di Taddeo (c.1345-1396) Italian					
oil	1	51,063		51,063	
GADDI, Taddeo (?-1366) Italian					
oil	1	625,000		625,000	
GADE, Hari Ambados (1917-) Indian					
oil	1	2,700		2,700	
GADEGAARD, Paul (1920-1996) Danish					
oil	11	34,172	1,084	2,243	8,181
wc/d	1	1,715		1,715	
GADEGAARD, Paul and SCHWALBE, Ole (20th C) Danish					
oil	1	11,612		11,612	
GADENNE, Charles (1925-) French					
3D	1	1,623		1,623	
GADO, Bertil (1916-) Swedish					
oil	1	1,206		1,206	
GAEL, Barent (c.1620-1703) Dutch					
oil	7	88,043	2,691	7,696	39,286
GAERTNER, Carl (1898-1952) American					
oil	3	6,650	1,250	1,400	4,000
GAERTNER, J P E (1801-1877) German					
oil	1	24,400		24,400	
GAERTNER, Johann Philipp Eduard (1801-1877) German					
wc/d	1	2,904		2,904	
GAETA, Enrico (1840-1887) Italian					
oil	2	5,022	1,313	2,511	3,709
GAGARIN, Prince Grigori Grigorievich (1810-1893) Russian					
wc/d	1	4,379		4,379	
GAGE, Merrell Robert (1892-1981) American					
3D	1	3,250		3,250	
GAGEN, Robert Ford (1847-1926) Canadian					
oil	1	1,327		1,327	
wc/d	1	2,399		2,399	
GAGEY, Andre (20th C) French					
oil	2	19,750	7,110	9,875	12,640
GAGGIOTTI-RICHARDS, Mrs E (1825-1912) Italian					
wc/d	1	1,376		1,376	
GAGINI, Antonello (1478-1536) Italian					
3D	1	13,302		13,302	
GAGLIARDINI, Julien Gustave (1846-1927) French					
oil	4	14,429	1,731	3,722	5,255
GAGLIARDO, Alberto Helios (1893-1987) Italian					
oil	1	7,631		7,631	
GAGNEAU, Paul Léon (?-c.1910) French					
oil	1	11,265		11,265	
GAGNEREAUX, Benigne (1756-1795) French					
oil	1	147,000		147,000	
GAGNEUX, Paul (?-1892) French					
oil	1	11,000		11,000	
GAGNIERE (19th C) French					
oil	1	10,311		10,311	

Name	No.	Total Sales Value	lowest	Prices median	highest
GAGNON, Clarence A (1881-1942) Canadian					
oil	4	340,832	3,318	79,161	179,193
wc/d	2	5,037	1,787	2,519	3,250
GAIDAN, Louis (1847-1925) French					
oil	2	53,515	13,515	26,758	40,000
GAIGHER, Horazio (1870-1938) ?					
oil	1	1,500		1,500	
GAIL, Wilhelm (1804-1890) German					
oil	1	1,486		1,486	
GAILLANT, Gilbert (1870-1956) French					
oil	1	10,366		10,366	
GAILLARD, Franz (1861-1932) Belgian					
oil	1	2,033		2,033	
GAILLARDOT, Pierre (1910-) French					
oil	1	1,514		1,514	
wc/d	1	1,927		1,927	
GAILLIARD, Franz (1861-1932) Belgian					
oil	3	17,091	1,065	2,202	13,824
GAILLIARD, Jean Jacques (1890-1976) Belgian					
oil	3	6,267	1,065	1,459	3,743
GAILLOIT, V (20th C) French					
oil	1	1,721		1,721	
GAINSBOROUGH, Thomas (1727-1788) British					
oil	9	738,390	28,600	57,200	244,900
wc/d	11	544,905	3,600	18,000	278,850
GAISSER, Jakob Emmanuel (1825-1899) German					
oil	4	10,699	1,506	2,423	4,347
GAISSER, Max (1857-1922) German					
oil	5	43,410	1,463	4,108	32,120
GAITIS, Yannis (1923-1984) Greek					
oil	1	5,110		5,110	
GAITONDE, Vasudeo S (1924-) Indian					
oil	1	26,000		26,000	
GAJARDO, Jose Vicente (20th C) Chilean					
3D	1	5,500		5,500	
GAL, Menchu (1923-) Spanish					
oil	2	8,476	2,371	4,238	6,105
wc/d	1	2,163		2,163	
GALAND, Léon (1872-1960) French					
oil	2	5,731	2,331	2,866	3,400
GALANTE, Francesco (1884-1972) Italian					
oil	1	2,417		2,417	
GALANTE, Nicola (1883-1969) Italian					
oil	1	6,465		6,465	
GALBUSERA, Giovacchino (1871-1942) Italian					
oil	4	10,981	1,632	2,698	3,953
GALE, William (1823-1909) British					
oil	2	7,658	1,088	3,829	6,570
wc/d	1	13,585		13,585	
GALEA, L M (1847-1917) Maltese					
wc/d	1	1,343		1,343	
GALEA, Luigi M (1847-1917) Maltese					
oil	6	35,002	1,908	5,512	9,858
GALEOTA-RUSSO, Leopoldo (1868-1938) Italian					
oil	2	5,925	1,937	2,963	3,988
GALEY, Gaston-Pierre (1880-1959) French					
wc/d	1	2,186		2,186	
GALIBERT, Pierre (19th C) French					
oil	1	2,967		2,967	

Name	No.	Total Sales Value	lowest	Prices median	highest
GALICIA, Cesar (1957-) Spanish					
oil	1	6,268		6,268	
GALIEN-LALOUE (1854-1941) French					
oil	1	30,656		30,656	
GALIEN-LALOUE, E (1854-1941) French					
oil	1	2,727		2,727	
wc/d	2	3,781	1,394	1,891	2,387
GALIEN-LALOUE, Eugène (1854-1941) French					
oil	28	122,508	1,113	3,053	20,474
wc/d	64	1,031,378	2,687	14,000	85,342
GALINDO, Florencio (1947-) Spanish					
oil	1	1,967		1,967	
GALL, François (1912-1987) French					
oil	31	125,200	1,000	2,662	10,000
wc/d	3	3,869	1,068	1,300	1,501
GALLAGHER, Sears (1869-1955) American					
oil	1	7,500		7,500	
wc/d	1	2,600		2,600	
GALLAIT, Louis (1810-1887) Belgian					
oil	2	2,272	1,064	1,136	1,208
GALLAND, Gilbert (1870-?) French					
oil	1	6,490		6,490	
GALLAND, Henri (19/20th C) French					
oil	1	3,950		3,950	
GALLAND, Pierre Victor (1822-1892) French					
oil	1	1,700		1,700	
GALLAND, Semerand (?) Haitian					
oil	1	1,288		1,288	
GALLANY (19th C) ?					
oil	1	2,226		2,226	
GALLARD, Michel de (1921-) French					
oil	3	10,334	1,897	3,310	5,127
GALLARD-LEPINAY, Paul Charles Emmanuel (1842-1885) French					
oil	1	2,991		2,991	
GALLARDO, Gustavo (1891-?) Spanish					
oil	1	3,648		3,648	
GALLE, Claude (1759-1815) French					
3D	1	25,264		25,264	
GALLE, Hieronymus (17/18th C) Flemish					
oil	1	30,200		30,200	
GALLEBAERT, Maria van (?) Belgian?					
oil	1	1,102		1,102	
GALLEGO MARQUINA, Jesus (1900-1987) Spanish					
oil	1	1,147		1,147	
GALLEGOS Y ARNOSA, Jose (1859-1917) Spanish					
oil	6	238,741	4,591	38,200	81,303
GALLEGOS, Fernando (1440-c.1507) Spanish					
oil	2	264,226	46,019	132,113	218,207
GALLELLI, Massimiliano (1863-1956) Italian					
oil	1	12,000		12,000	
GALLEN-KALLELA, Akseli Valdemar (1865-1931) Finnish					
oil	3	401,298	15,168	33,000	353,130
GALLETTI, L (19th C) Italian?					
oil	1	2,482		2,482	
GALLEZ, A (19th C) British?					
oil	1	7,436		7,436	
GALLI, Leopold (19th C) ?					
oil	1	7,950		7,950	

Name	No.	Total Sales Value	lowest	Prices median	highest
GALLI, Luigi (1820-1906) Italian					
wc/d	1	1,581		1,581	
GALLIAC, Louis (1849-1931) French					
oil	3	4,544	1,059	1,676	1,809
GALLIAN, Octave (1855-?) French					
oil	1	1,392		1,392	
GALLIANI, Omar (1954-) Italian					
oil	4	9,115	1,479	2,509	2,618
GALLIS, Pieter (1633-1697) Dutch					
oil	1	10,000		10,000	
GALLIZIO, Pinot (1902-1964) Italian					
oil	1	1,847		1,847	
GALLO, Frank (1933-) American					
3D	1	1,700		1,700	
GALLO, Giuseppe (1954-) Italian					
wc/d	1	3,927		3,927	
GALLOCHE, Louis (1670-1761) French					
wc/d	2	32,000	12,000	16,000	20,000
GALLON, R (19th C) British					
oil	1	2,100		2,100	
GALLON, Robert (1845-1925) British					
oil	14	121,833	1,099	6,775	34,500
GALLOTTI, Alessandro (1879-1961) Italian					
oil	1	1,848		1,848	
GALLUCCI, Sandro (1897-?) Italian					
oil	1	1,026		1,026	
GALOFRE Y GIMENEZ, Baldomero (1849-1902) Spanish					
oil	9	223,746	3,657	18,822	82,500
wc/d	3	13,420	1,334	3,554	8,532
GALOYER (1944-) French					
3D	1	1,489		1,489	
GALT, J (19/20th C) British					
oil	1	2,212		2,212	
GALTA, W della (19th C) Italian					
wc/d	1	2,942		2,942	
GALVANO, Albino (1907-1991) Italian					
oil	3	4,149	1,236	1,338	1,575
GAMAIN, Louis Honore Frederic (1803-1871) French					
oil	1	3,745		3,745	
GAMARRA, Jose (1934-) Uruguayan					
oil	3	27,819	1,712	2,107	24,000
GAMBA, Enrico (1831-1883) Italian					
oil	2	9,427	2,836	4,714	6,591
wc/d	1	1,249		1,249	
GAMBA, Francesco (1818-1887) Italian					
oil	1	26,000		26,000	
GAMBARD, Henri Augustin (1819-1882) French					
oil	1	3,500		3,500	
GAMBLE, John M (1863-1957) American					
oil	7	467,080	6,000	41,080	170,000
wc/d	1	7,500		7,500	
GAMBOGI, G (19th C) Italian					
3D	1	1,988		1,988	
GAMEIRO, Roque (19th C) Portuguese					
wc/d	1	2,251		2,251	
GAMMELL, Robert Hale Ives (1893-1981) American					
oil	1	5,000		5,000	
GAMMON, Reg (1894-1997) British					
oil	1	1,800		1,800	

Name	No.	Total Sales Value	lowest	Prices median	highest
GAMOISSE (18th C) French					
wc/d	1	4,673		4,673	
GAMP, Botho von (1894-1977) German					
oil	8	12,875	1,108	1,601	2,093
GAMPENRIEDER, Karl (1860-1930) German					
oil	1	1,573		1,573	
GANDARA, Antonio de la (1862-1917) French					
oil	1	14,200		14,200	
wc/d	1	1,963		1,963	
GANDINI DEL GRANO, Giorgio (c.1489-1538) Italian					
oil	1	21,000		21,000	
wc/d	1	22,500		22,500	
GANDOLFI, Gaetano (1734-1802) Italian					
oil	1	92,000		92,000	
wc/d	4	10,222	1,134	2,128	4,832
GANDOLFI, Mauro (1764-1834) Italian					
oil	1	4,242		4,242	
GANDOLFI, Ubaldo (1728-1781) Italian					
wc/d	3	21,510	2,182	7,248	12,080
GANDON, Adolphe (1828-1889) French					
oil	1	3,400		3,400	
GANDY, William (1660-1729) British					
oil	1	5,005		5,005	
GANNAM, John (1907-1965) American					
wc/d	1	2,100		2,100	
GANSO, Emil (1895-1941) American					
oil	1	1,500		1,500	
GANTNER, Bernard (1928-) French					
oil	4	6,684	1,086	1,413	2,772
GANTO, C (19th C) Italian					
oil	2	6,022	3,011	3,011	3,011
GANTZ, Justinian (1802-1862) British					
wc/d	3	9,900	1,500	3,600	4,800
GANZ, Henry F W (19/20th C) British					
oil	1	1,378		1,378	
GARABETIAN, Cricor (20th C) French					
oil	1	1,916		1,916	
GARAT, Francis (19th C) French					
oil	2	10,352	2,852	5,176	7,500
wc/d	1	2,866		2,866	
GARATE Y CLAVERO, Juan Jose (1870-1939) Spanish					
oil	2	7,619	1,778	3,810	5,841
wc/d	3	3,496	1,076	1,210	1,210
GARATE, Cecilia (20th C) ?					
oil	1	3,775		3,775	
GARAUD, Gustave Cesaire (1847-1914) French					
oil	1	1,168		1,168	
GARBER, Daniel (1880-1958) American					
oil	1	500,000		500,000	
GARBO, Raffaellino del (c.1476-1524) Italian					
oil	1	72,000		72,000	
GARBUZ, Yair (1945-) Israeli					
wc/d	2	2,900	1,200	1,450	1,700
GARCEMENT, Alfred (1830-?) French					
oil	1	1,442		1,442	
GARCIA BARRENA, Carmelo (1926-) Spanish					
oil	1	2,958		2,958	
GARCIA CUERVAS, Carlos (1916-) Spanish					
oil	1	1,398		1,398	

Name	No.	Total Sales Value	lowest	Prices median	highest
GARCIA DEL MORAL, Amalio (1922-1995) Spanish					
oil	1	1,299		1,299	
GARCIA ERGUIN, Ignacio (1934-) Spanish					
oil	1	1,665		1,665	
GARCIA OCHOA, Luis (1920-) Spanish					
oil	1	4,004		4,004	
GARCIA RAMON, Leopoldo (1876-1958) Spanish					
oil	1	10,575		10,575	
GARCIA Y HISPALETO, Manuel (1836-1898) Spanish					
wc/d	2	2,052	1,026	1,026	1,026
GARCIA Y RAMOS, Jose (1852-1912) Spanish					
oil	5	159,059	2,157	16,500	107,300
GARCIA Y RAMOS, Juan (1856-1911) Spanish					
wc/d	1	1,760		1,760	
GARCIA Y RODRIGUEZ (1863-1925) Spanish					
oil	1	13,140		13,140	
GARCIA Y RODRIGUEZ, Manuel (1863-1925) Spanish					
oil	12	115,055	2,118	4,507	28,000
wc/d	2	2,600	1,300	1,300	1,300
GARCIA Y SALMERON, Cristobal (c.1603-1666) Spanish					
oil	1	5,115		5,115	
GARCIA, Diego (?) ?					
oil	1	4,071		4,071	
GARCIA, Gloria (1945-) ?					
oil	1	1,265		1,265	
GARCIA, Juan (19th C) Spanish					
oil	1	2,020		2,020	
GARCIA, Juan Gil (1879-1931) Cuban					
oil	5	14,909	2,109	2,800	3,500
GARCIA-SEVILLA, Ferran (1949-) Spanish					
oil	3	16,952	2,422	3,800	10,730
GARDANNE, Auguste (19th C) French					
oil	1	5,127		5,127	
GARDELL-ERICSON, Anna (1853-1939) Swedish					
wc/d	19	36,070	1,005	1,632	4,285
GARDEN, William Fraser (1856-1921) British					
wc/d	11	77,957	1,287	4,134	28,440
GARDET, G (1863-1939) French					
3D	1	2,809		2,809	
GARDET, Georges (1863-1939) French					
3D	8	47,724	1,142	2,432	23,520
GARDETTE, Louis (19th C) French					
oil	1	4,108		4,108	
GARDIELLO, G (19/20th C) Italian					
oil	1	2,873		2,873	
GARDIER, Raoul du (1871-1952) French					
oil	1	5,323		5,323	
GARDINER, Gerald (1902-) British					
oil	1	1,099		1,099	
GARDINER, Stanley (1888-1952) British					
oil	1	2,356		2,356	
GARDNER, Charles R (1901-) American					
oil	1	1,500		1,500	
GARDNER, Daniel (1750-1805) British					
wc/d	4	46,332	3,146	9,438	24,310
GARDNER, Derek George Montague (1914-) British					
wc/d	1	1,284		1,284	
GARDNER, William Biscombe (c.1847-1919) British					
wc/d	1	1,057		1,057	

Name	No.	Total Sales Value	lowest	Prices median	highest
GARDOT (19/20th C) French					
oil	1	1,569		1,569	
GARE, W (18/19th C) ?					
oil	1	1,600		1,600	
GARELLA, Antonio (19/20th C) Italian					
3D	2	66,963	1,963	33,482	65,000
GARF, Salomon (1879-?) Dutch					
oil	1	2,667		2,667	
wc/d	1	2,557		2,557	
GARGALLO, Pablo (1881-1934) Spanish					
3D	4	327,404	36,076	75,664	140,000
wc/d	1	2,024		2,024	
GARGIULIO, Domenico (1612-1679) Italian					
wc/d	1	2,164		2,164	
GARGIULLO, E (?) Italian					
oil	1	1,047		1,047	
GARI, A (20th C) French					
3D	1	8,500		8,500	
GARIBALDI, Joseph (1863-?) French					
oil	1	3,147		3,147	
GARIN, Louis (1888-1959) French					
oil	3	15,642	1,625	6,499	7,518
GARINEI, Michele (1871-1960) Italian					
oil	1	1,322		1,322	
GARLAND, H (19th C) British					
oil	1	1,661		1,661	
GARLAND, Henry (fl.1854-1900) British					
oil	7	26,365	1,200	2,400	7,400
GARLAND, J Valentine (?) British					
oil	1	8,154		8,154	
GARLAND, Valentine Thomas (1868-1914) British					
oil	3	13,599	2,475	5,724	5,724
GARMAN, Ed (20th C) American					
oil	1	13,000		13,000	
GARNELO Y ALDA, Jose (1866-1945) Spanish					
oil	3	44,984	1,430	21,777	21,777
GARNER, Charles S (jnr) (1890-1933) American					
oil	2	7,250	2,000	3,625	5,250
GARNERAY, Ambroise Louis (1783-1857) French					
oil	1	5,528		5,528	
wc/d	2	4,227	1,547	2,114	2,680
GARNERAY, Hippolyte (1787-1858) French					
oil	1	2,184		2,184	
GARNIER, Antoine (1869-1948) French					
oil	1	1,621		1,621	
GARNIER, J (?) ?					
3D	1	2,145		2,145	
GARNIER, Michel (18th C) French					
oil	1	36,240		36,240	
GARNIER, Pierre (1847-?) French					
oil	1	7,283		7,283	
GARNSEY, Julian (1887-?) American					
wc/d	1	1,100		1,100	
GAROUSTE, Gerard (1946-) French					
oil	4	98,766	18,029	24,331	32,075
GARRATT, Arthur Paine (1873-?) British					
oil	1	3,500		3,500	
GARRI, Giorgio (?-1731) Italian					
oil	1	6,152		6,152	

Name	No.	Total Sales Value	Prices lowest	median	highest
GARRIDO, Eduardo Léon (1856-1949) Spanish					
oil	10	153,123	1,452	8,261	54,596
GARRIDO, Leandro Ramon (1868-1909) Spanish					
oil	1	3,404		3,404	
GARROS, Catherine (20th C) French					
oil	1	1,756		1,756	
GARSIDE, Thomas H (1906-1980) Canadian					
oil	1	1,044		1,044	
GARSON, Etta Corbett (1898-1968) American					
oil	1	3,400		3,400	
GARSTIN, Alethea (1894-1978) British					
oil	3	14,500	2,755	3,045	8,700
GARSTIN, Norman (1847-1926) British/Irish					
oil	3	15,370	3,480	5,220	6,670
wc/d	4	9,546	1,776	2,290	3,190
GARTHWAITE, William (1821-1889) British					
oil	1	3,775		3,775	
GARTMEIER, Hans (1910-1986) Swiss					
oil	4	6,441	1,073	1,696	1,976
GARTNER, Fritz (1882-?) German					
oil	1	1,318		1,318	
GARTNER, L (?) ?					
oil	1	1,139		1,139	
GARZI, Luigi (1638-1721) Italian					
oil	2	37,915	14,915	18,958	23,000
GARZI, Luigi (school) (1638-1721) Italian					
oil	1	5,133		5,133	
GARZOLINI, Giuseppe (1850-1938) Italian					
oil	1	1,316		1,316	
GASCHKA, Rudolf (1953-) German?					
wc/d	1	1,298		1,298	
GASCROFT, N (20th C) British?					
wc/d	1	1,817		1,817	
GASIOROWSKI, Gerard (1930-1986) French					
oil	1	4,340		4,340	
GASPARD, Léon (1882-1964) French					
3D	1	30,000		30,000	
oil	8	467,750	3,250	16,000	240,000
GASPARI, Luciano (1913-) Italian					
oil	4	6,832	1,081	1,278	3,195
GASPARINI, Bruna (1937-) Italian					
oil	2	4,051	1,236	2,026	2,815
GASPARINI, Luigi (1779-?) Italian					
oil	1	6,280		6,280	
GASSER, Henry (1909-1981) American					
wc/d	1	1,500		1,500	
GASTALDI, Andrea (1826-1889) Italian					
oil	1	3,577		3,577	
GASTEIGER, Anna Sophie (1878-1954) German					
oil	5	16,469	1,709	3,702	4,356
GASTIGLIONE, G (?) Italian					
oil	1	4,215		4,215	
GASTINEAU, Henry (1791-1876) British					
wc/d	1	2,288		2,288	
GASTO, Pedro (1908-1997) Spanish					
oil	6	15,476	1,547	2,474	4,067
GASTYNE, Marco de (1889-?) French					
oil	1	3,988		3,988	

Name	No.	Total Sales Value	Prices lowest	median	highest
GAT, Eliahu (1919-1987) Israeli					
oil	2	5,600	2,600	2,800	3,000
GATE, Simon (1883-1945) ?					
oil	2	6,733	2,311	3,367	4,422
GATEHOUSE, C (20th C) British					
oil	2	3,115	1,340	1,558	1,775
GATEHOUSE, Charles E (20th C) British					
oil	2	2,302	1,015	1,151	1,287
GATHER, Christa (1960-) German					
oil	1	1,125		1,125	
GATTA, Saverio della (?-1829) Italian					
oil	1	3,491		3,491	
wc/d	6	39,920	1,205	2,887	17,160
GATTI (?) Italian					
wc/d	1	1,580		1,580	
GATTI, Arturo (1878-) Italian					
oil	1	1,681		1,681	
GATZ, Volker (1955-) German					
oil	1	1,298		1,298	
GAUBAULT, Alfred Émile (19th C) French					
oil	1	1,184		1,184	
GAUCI, E S (19/20th C) British					
oil	1	1,590		1,590	
GAUD, Léon (1844-1908) Swiss					
oil	1	1,253		1,253	
GAUDENZI, Pietro (1880-1955) Italian					
wc/d	1	14,970		14,970	
GAUDEZ, Adrien Étienne (1845-1902) French					
3D	7	19,158	1,329	2,500	4,710
GAUDIER-BRZESKA, Henri (1891-1915) French					
wc/d	10	16,038	1,000	1,500	2,184
GAUDISSARD, Émile (1872-?) French					
oil	1	2,336		2,336	
GAUDOT, A (fl.1793) French					
wc/d	1	6,500		6,500	
GAUERMANN, Friedrich (1807-1862) Austrian					
oil	1	6,055		6,055	
GAUFFIER, Louis (1761-1801) French					
oil	1	28,000		28,000	
GAUFFRIAUX, E (?) French					
oil	1	1,171		1,171	
GAUGUIN, Paul (1848-1903) French					
3D	6	152,980	6,000	23,405	55,000
oil	4	7,734,568	24,568	1,455,000	4,800,000
wc/d	12	1,904,026	8,462	38,500	1,236,505
GAUGUIN, Pola (1883-1961) Danish					
oil	1	3,763		3,763	
GAUL, Arrah Lee (20th C) American					
oil	1	1,500		1,500	
GAUL, August (1869-1921) German					
3D	12	38,472	1,293	2,124	8,621
GAUL, Gilbert (1855-1919) American					
oil	5	52,500	2,500	5,500	25,000
GAUL, Winfred (1928-) German					
oil	2	11,314	1,366	5,657	9,948
GAULD, David (1865-1936) British					
oil	5	36,173	3,212	5,840	12,835
GAULLI, Giovanni Battista (1639-1709) Italian					
wc/d	1	15,000		15,000	

Name	No.	Total Sales Value	lowest	Prices median	highest
GAULT, Jacques Joseph de (18th C) French					
oil	1	16,000		16,000	
GAUMONT (19th C) ?					
oil	1	1,855		1,855	
GAUPP, Gustav Adolf (1844-1918) German					
oil	1	1,257		1,257	
GAUQUIE, H (1858-1927) French					
3D	1	1,285		1,285	
GAUQUIE, Henri (1858-1927) French					
3D	1	7,920		7,920	
GAUSE, Wilhelm (1853-1916) German					
oil	1	2,040		2,040	
wc/d	1	1,300		1,300	
GAUSSEN, Adolphe-Louis (1871-1954) French					
oil	2	4,873	1,069	2,437	3,804
GAUSSON, Leo (1860-1944) French					
oil	4	16,590	1,507	2,856	9,371
GAUTHERIN, Jacques (1929-) French					
3D	1	2,917		2,917	
GAUTHIER, Charles Gabriel (1802-1858) French					
oil	1	2,600		2,600	
GAUTHIER, Lucien (?) French?					
wc/d	1	2,239		2,239	
GAUTIER, Jean Rodolphe (1764-1820) Swiss					
wc/d	1	3,658		3,658	
GAUVREAU, Pierre (1922-) Canadian					
oil	1	5,945		5,945	
GAVIN, Robert (1827-1883) British					
oil	2	2,920	1,264	1,460	1,656
GAW, William Alexander (1891-1973) American					
oil	4	12,400	1,400	3,250	4,500
GAWELL, Oskar (1888-1955) Austrian					
wc/d	1	1,942		1,942	
GAY, A du (19/20th C) French					
oil	1	4,903		4,903	
GAY, August (1890-1949) American					
oil	2	60,000	20,000	30,000	40,000
GAY, Edward (1837-1928) American					
oil	10	44,550	1,700	3,500	10,000
wc/d	1	1,100		1,100	
GAY, Edward and TAIT, Arthur Fitzwilliam (19th C) American					
oil	1	4,000		4,000	
GAY, George Howell (1858-1931) American					
wc/d	2	2,000	1,000	1,000	1,000
GAY, Nikolai Nikolajewitsch (1831-1894) Russian					
oil	1	8,305		8,305	
GAY, Walter (1856-1937) American					
oil	2	74,000	14,000	37,000	60,000
wc/d	1	1,746		1,746	
GAY, Winkworth Allen (1821-1910) American					
oil	4	15,400	1,800	2,300	9,000
GAYA, Ramon (1910-) Spanish					
wc/d	2	33,330	1,067	16,665	32,263
GAYRARD, Joseph Raymond Paul (1807-1855) French					
3D	2	9,434	1,884	4,717	7,550
GAZZERA, Romano (1908-1985) Italian					
oil	1	1,386		1,386	
GEAR, Mabel (1900-) British					
oil	2	7,115	2,765	3,558	4,350

Name	No.	Total Sales Value	lowest	Prices median	highest
wc/d	5	7,634	1,020	1,200	2,800
GEAR, William (1915-1997) British					
oil	20	79,298	1,570	3,311	9,165
GEBAUER, C D (1777-1831) German					
oil	1	1,013		1,013	
GEBAUER, Christian David (1777-1831) German					
oil	1	1,233		1,233	
GEBHARDT, Eduard K F von (1838-1925) German					
oil	3	7,141	1,668	2,741	2,741
GEBLER, Otto Friedrich (1838-1917) German					
oil	4	24,816	3,922	5,227	10,440
GEBURSCH, Theo (1890-1958) German					
oil	1	1,716		1,716	
GECELLI, Johannes (1925-) German					
oil	1	4,854		4,854	
GECHTER (19th C) French					
3D	1	3,346		3,346	
GECHTER, Jean François Theodore (1796-1844) French					
3D	3	12,742	2,007	3,247	7,488
GECHTOFF, G (20th C) Russian?					
oil	1	1,510		1,510	
GECHTOFF, Leonid (19/20th C) American					
oil	1	1,000		1,000	
GEDDES, Norman Bel (1893-1958) American					
3D	1	4,000		4,000	
GEDLEK, Ludwig (1847-?) Austrian					
oil	6	48,448	1,624	8,056	12,500
GEE, John (20th C) American					
oil	1	1,300		1,300	
GEEFS, Guillaume (1805-1883) Belgian					
3D	1	2,997		2,997	
GEEL, Johannes Ludovicus van (1787-1852) Belgian					
3D	1	3,297		3,297	
GEELEN, Guido (1961-) Dutch					
3D	1	4,357		4,357	
GEELHOED, Johannes Jeremias (1821-1880) Dutch					
wc/d	1	1,963		1,963	
GEERING, Johanna (1885-?) German					
oil	1	1,001		1,001	
GEERTSEN, Ib (1919-) Danish					
oil	2	2,794	1,207	1,397	1,587
GEETS, W (19/20th C) Belgian					
wc/d	1	3,546		3,546	
GEETS, Willem (1838-1919) Belgian					
oil	4	21,575	1,321	4,410	11,435
GEFFCKEN, Walter (1872-1950) German					
oil	1	4,250		4,250	
GEGERFELT, Wilhelm von (1844-1920) Swedish					
oil	18	81,123	1,140	2,695	14,490
GEHR, Ferdinand (1896-1996) Swiss					
oil	5	44,596	2,795	7,827	20,988
wc/d	14	85,867	1,025	4,990	13,409
GEIDEL-LIEBING, Lotte (1891-?) German?					
oil	1	1,865		1,865	
GEIGENBERGER, Otto (1881-1946) German					
wc/d	1	1,133		1,133	
GEIGER, Caspar Augustin (1847-1924) German					
oil	1	2,067		2,067	

Name	No.	Total Sales Value	lowest	Prices median	highest
GEIGER, Ernst (1876-1965) Swiss					
oil	7	87,869	1,089	10,165	26,236
GEIGER, Rupprecht (1908-) German					
3D	1	33,716		33,716	
GEIRNAERT, Jozef (1791-1859) Belgian					
oil	2	10,029	2,487	5,015	7,542
GEISER, Karl (1898-1957) Swiss					
3D	1	5,469		5,469	
GEISSER, Johann Josef (1824-1894) Swiss					
oil	1	1,166		1,166	
GEISSER, V (19th C) Swiss					
oil	1	1,519		1,519	
GEIST, Carl Friedrich Wilhelm (1870-?) German					
oil	1	1,079		1,079	
GELDEREN, Simon van (1905-1986) Belgian					
oil	2	2,158	1,045	1,079	1,113
GELDORP, Gortzius (1553-1618) Flemish					
oil	2	9,895	3,064	4,948	6,831
GELENG, Otto (19th C) German					
oil	2	14,417	1,417	7,209	13,000
GELIBERT, Jules-Bertrand (1834-1916) French					
oil	4	14,061	1,095	3,640	5,686
GELIBERT, Paul Jean Pierre (1802-1882) French					
oil	2	6,067	2,047	3,034	4,020
GELISSEN, Maximilien Lambert (1786-1867) Belgian					
oil	1	2,262		2,262	
GELLEE, Claude (c.1600-1682) French					
oil	1	3,641		3,641	
wc/d	2	66,690	28,690	33,345	38,000
GEMICKE, Joakim (1959-) Swedish					
oil	2	3,211	1,204	1,606	2,007
GEMITO, Vincenzo (1852-1929) Italian					
3D	11	56,713	1,031	1,758	28,798
wc/d	2	6,677	1,908	3,339	4,769
GEMPT, Bernard de (1826-1879) Dutch					
oil	3	48,043	3,489	4,600	39,954
GEN-PAUL (1895-1975) French					
oil	34	251,395	1,194	4,385	28,514
wc/d	47	108,951	1,049	1,924	4,986
GENBERG, Anton (1862-1939) Swedish					
oil	9	14,271	1,206	1,500	2,613
GENDEBIEN, Louis (1882-1946) Belgian					
oil	1	1,557		1,557	
GENEAU, Alain (1935-) French					
oil	3	3,900	1,100	1,100	1,700
GENERALIC, Josip (1936-) Yugoslavian					
oil	1	1,749		1,749	
GENET, Alexandre (1799-) French					
oil	1	1,595		1,595	
GENEVA SCHOOL, 18th C Swiss					
oil	1	3,637		3,637	
GENEVA SCHOOL, 20th C Swiss					
oil	1	3,160		3,160	
GENEVIEVE (1918-) French					
3D	1	3,598		3,598	
oil	1	2,512		2,512	
GENGEMBRE, Joseph Z (19th C) French					
oil	1	2,048		2,048	

Name	No.	Total Sales Value	Prices lowest	median	highest
GENILLION, Jean Baptiste François (1750-1829) French					
oil	2	57,000	25,000	28,500	32,000
wc/d	1	2,320		2,320	
GENIN, Lucien (1894-1958) French					
oil	8	26,823	1,823	3,016	5,121
wc/d	12	22,717	1,003	1,569	3,234
GENIN, Robert (1884-1939) French					
oil	1	1,298		1,298	
GENIS, René (1922-) French					
oil	5	9,530	1,024	1,200	3,806
GENISSON, J V (1805-1860) Belgian					
oil	1	11,379		11,379	
GENKINGER, Fritz (1934-) German					
oil	1	1,538		1,538	
GENN, Robert (1936-) Canadian					
oil	1	1,038		1,038	
GENNADIOS, Cleonice (19th C) Greek					
oil	1	20,735		20,735	
GENNARELLI, Amedeo (20th C) Italian					
3D	2	16,415	5,431	8,208	10,984
GENNARI, Bartolomeo (1594-1661) Italian					
oil	2	5,764	2,217	2,882	3,547
GENNARI, Cesare (1637-1688) Italian					
oil	1	11,082		11,082	
GENOELS, Abraham (1640-1723) Flemish					
oil	1	10,213		10,213	
wc/d	1	1,179		1,179	
GENOESE SCHOOL, 17th C Italian					
3D	3	133,473	7,760	9,339	116,374
oil	14	162,125	2,693	5,625	53,380
GENOESE SCHOOL, 18th C Italian					
3D	1	4,945		4,945	
oil	3	45,769	3,448	9,463	32,858
GENOUD, Nanette (1907-) Swiss					
oil	1	1,129		1,129	
GENOVES, Juan (1930-) Spanish					
oil	3	11,340	1,126	1,334	8,880
wc/d	3	3,489	1,008	1,147	1,334
GENSTHALER, J (19th C) German?					
oil	1	1,033		1,033	
GENTH, Lillian (1876-1953) American					
oil	2	8,000	1,000	4,000	7,000
GENTILESCHI, Orazio (1562-1647) Italian					
oil	2	3,394,000	72,000	1,697,000	3,322,000
GENTILINI, Franco (1909-1981) Italian					
oil	10	208,641	3,578	14,836	52,618
wc/d	5	30,560	1,543	3,601	18,326
GENTILS, Vic (1919-1997) Belgian					
3D	8	45,321	1,186	2,493	17,795
GENTZ, Ismael (1862-1914) German					
oil	2	27,130	1,668	13,565	25,462
GENTZ, Karl Wilhelm (1822-1890) German					
oil	2	50,382	13,000	25,191	37,382
GENZKEN, Isa (1948-) German?					
oil	2	4,368	2,184	2,184	2,184
GENZMER, Berthold (1858-?) German					
oil	1	2,587		2,587	
GEOFFROY, Henry Jules Jean (1853-1924) French					
oil	4	34,675	1,175	7,988	17,524

Name	No.	Total Sales Value	lowest	Prices median	highest
GEORGE, Ernest (1839-1922) British					
wc/d	4	4,634	1,130	1,144	1,216
GEORGE, H P (?) Swiss					
oil	1	2,306		2,306	
GEORGE, Jean Philippe (1818-1888) Swiss					
oil	1	1,094		1,094	
GEORGE-JULLIARD, Jean Philippe (1818-1888) Swiss					
oil	1	1,516		1,516	
GEORGES, Charles E (19/20th C) British					
wc/d	1	1,011		1,011	
GEORGES, Claude (1929-1988) French					
wc/d	1	2,139		2,139	
GEORGES, Jean Louis (1860-1894) French					
oil	1	8,340		8,340	
GEORGESCU, Niculai Florin (1946-1985) Rumanian					
oil	1	1,117		1,117	
GEORGI, Edwin (1896-1964) American					
wc/d	2	7,000	1,500	3,500	5,500
GEORGI, Friedrich Otto (1819-1874) German					
oil	4	13,008	2,581	3,114	4,200
GERALIS, Apostolos (1886-1983) Greek					
oil	2	28,470	8,030	14,235	20,440
GERALIS, Loucas (1875-1958) Greek					
oil	1	5,840		5,840	
GERANZANI, Cornelio (1880-1955) Italian					
oil	3	27,749	2,473	10,969	14,307
GERARD, Baron François (1770-1837) French					
oil	2	250,366	20,366	125,183	230,000
wc/d	3	34,160	1,455	17,000	17,000
GERARD, Gustave (?) ?					
wc/d	1	2,058		2,058	
GERARD, Henry (19th C) French					
oil	1	3,359		3,359	
GERARD, Lucien (1852-1935) Belgian					
oil	6	21,560	1,800	2,420	10,010
GERARD, Marguerite (1761-1837) French					
oil	4	248,028	49,136	55,656	87,580
GERARD, Theodore (1829-1895) Belgian					
oil	6	58,156	1,054	4,069	24,650
GERBAUD, Abel (1888-1954) French					
oil	1	1,110		1,110	
GERBER, Theo (1928-) Swiss					
oil	1	1,059		1,059	
GERCHMAN, Rubens (1942-) Brazilian					
oil	1	35,000		35,000	
GERDES, Ludwig (1954-) German					
oil	1	1,550		1,550	
GERELL, Greta (1898-1982) Swedish					
oil	2	7,782	1,449	3,891	6,333
GERHARD, A (19th C) Continental					
oil	1	2,250		2,250	
GERHARD, Ernst (1867-?) German					
oil	1	2,955		2,955	
GERHARD, Johan Friedrich (c.1695-1748) Danish					
oil	1	5,444		5,444	
GERHARDINGER, Constantin (1888-1970) German					
oil	4	6,320	1,275	1,541	1,963
GERICAULT, Theodore (1791-1824) French					
wc/d	14	919,959	2,764	29,704	363,678

Name	No.	Total Sales Value	lowest	Prices median	highest
GERICKE, Paul (1876-?) German					
oil	1	1,481		1,481	
GERINI, Lorenzo di Niccolo (15th C) Italian					
oil	2	250,000	110,000	125,000	140,000
GERINI, Niccolo di Pietro (?-1415) Italian					
oil	1	241,600		241,600	
GERLE, Aron (1860-1930) Swedish					
oil	1	1,306		1,306	
GERMAIN, Jacques (1915-) French					
oil	11	33,154	1,086	2,716	5,787
GERMAIN, Jean-Baptiste (1841-1910) French					
3D	1	1,600		1,600	
GERMAN LLORENTE, Bernardo (1680-1759) Spanish					
oil	2	25,347	9,779	12,674	15,568
GERMAN SCHOOL					
3D	1	7,727		7,727	
oil	1	1,596		1,596	
GERMAN SCHOOL, 14th C					
3D	1	31,818		31,818	
GERMAN SCHOOL, 15th C					
3D	1	19,811		19,811	
oil	3	26,521	6,128	7,642	12,751
GERMAN SCHOOL, 15th/16th C					
oil	2	6,923	3,456	3,462	3,467
GERMAN SCHOOL, 16th C					
3D	8	39,635	2,311	3,654	9,625
oil	12	98,915	2,786	6,384	22,154
wc/d	1	5,000		5,000	
GERMAN SCHOOL, 16th/17th C					
oil	3	38,018	3,609	4,209	30,200
GERMAN SCHOOL, 17th C					
3D	9	60,228	3,211	6,200	14,858
oil	14	140,381	2,880	6,614	55,084
wc/d	1	4,000		4,000	
GERMAN SCHOOL, 17th/18th C					
oil	1	3,927		3,927	
GERMAN SCHOOL, 18th C					
3D	8	213,162	2,273	3,549	184,845
oil	50	452,195	2,163	4,431	83,050
wc/d	3	19,586	5,247	6,142	8,197
GERMAN SCHOOL, 18th/19th C					
3D	1	5,880		5,880	
oil	4	17,247	2,451	3,561	7,675
wc/d	1	2,366		2,366	
GERMAN SCHOOL, 19th C					
3D	6	37,171	3,500	4,146	16,849
oil	19	117,059	2,658	4,325	22,000
wc/d	4	10,990	2,215	2,733	3,310
GERMAN SCHOOL, 20th C					
3D	1	3,773		3,773	
oil	1	3,939		3,939	
GERMAN-AUSTRIAN SCHOOL, 18th C					
3D	1	3,354		3,354	
oil	1	2,918		2,918	
GERMANA, Mimmo (1944-1992) Italian					
oil	6	14,351	1,055	1,856	5,454
wc/d	1	1,396		1,396	
GERMASCHEFF, Michail (1868-1930) Russian					
oil	2	10,925	5,285	5,463	5,640
GERNAY, P N (19th C) Belgian					
oil	1	5,114		5,114	

Name	No.	Total Sales Value	lowest	Prices median	highest
GERNES, Poul (1925-) Danish					
oil	1	1,281		1,281	
GERNEZ, Paul Elie (1888-1948) French					
oil	8	62,843	3,279	5,947	14,893
wc/d	11	28,266	1,053	3,137	3,723
GEROME, J L (1824-1904) French					
3D	1	13,234		13,234	
GEROME, Jean Léon (1824-1904) French					
3D	12	354,990	2,188	10,500	130,000
oil	6	1,316,589	1,289	290,000	390,000
wc/d	2	14,608	5,548	7,304	9,060
GEROME, M (?) French					
oil	1	1,039		1,039	
GERRITS, Gerrit Jacobus (1893-1965) Dutch					
oil	1	4,310		4,310	
GERRY, Samuel Lancaster (1813-1891) American					
oil	4	14,909	1,600	2,905	7,500
GERSHUNI, Moshe (1936-) Israeli					
oil	2	6,600	3,000	3,300	3,600
wc/d	1	1,400		1,400	
GERSTL, Richard (1883-1908) Austrian					
oil	1	3,212		3,212	
GERSTNER, Karl (c.1930-) Swiss					
oil	1	5,555		5,555	
GERTLER, Mark (1891-1939) British					
oil	1	27,550		27,550	
GERVAIS, Lise (1933-1998) Canadian					
oil	2	4,085	1,846	2,043	2,239
GERVASI, Frank (1895-1985) American					
oil	1	2,000		2,000	
GERVEX, Henri (1852-1929) French					
oil	6	98,050	1,591	11,555	52,757
wc/d	2	4,050	1,166	2,025	2,884
GERWING, Hans (20th C) ?					
3D	1	1,269		1,269	
GERZSO, Gunther (1915-2000) Mexican					
oil	3	123,000	29,000	34,000	60,000
GESELSCHAP, Eduard (1814-1878) Dutch					
oil	2	10,131	5,000	5,066	5,131
GESELSCHAP, Friedrich (1835-1898) German/Italian					
wc/d	1	1,171		1,171	
GESNE, Jean Victor Albert de (1834-1903) French					
oil	2	3,713	1,663	1,857	2,050
GESSA Y ARIAS, Sebastian (1840-1920) Spanish					
oil	3	11,683	2,613	4,424	4,646
GESSI, Francesco (1588-1649) Italian					
oil	1	21,600		21,600	
GESSNER, Conrad (1764-1826) Swiss					
oil	1	7,218		7,218	
GESSNITZER, C (19th C) German?					
oil	1	8,991		8,991	
GESTEL, Leo (1881-1941) Dutch					
oil	1	9,483		9,483	
wc/d	20	96,185	1,268	4,124	12,676
GEUDENS, Albert (?) Belgian					
oil	1	2,343		2,343	
wc/d	1	1,044		1,044	
GEULLEBERT, M (?) French					
oil	1	3,685		3,685	

Name	No.	Total Sales Value	lowest	Prices median	highest
GEYER, Hermann (1934-) German					
oil	1	1,502		1,502	
GEYER, Wilhelm (1900-1968) German					
oil	1	1,538		1,538	
GEYMULLER, Betty (1799-1866) Austrian					
oil	2	10,143	2,691	5,072	7,452
GEYP, Adriaan Marinus (1855-1926) Dutch					
oil	4	7,172	1,067	1,744	2,617
GHEDUZZI, Augusto (1883-1969) Italian					
oil	1	1,845		1,845	
GHEDUZZI, Cesare (1894-1944) Italian					
oil	14	28,743	1,011	1,745	4,292
GHEDUZZI, Giuseppe (1889-1957) Italian					
oil	5	16,256	2,752	3,218	3,992
GHEDUZZI, Mario (1891-1970) Italian					
oil	1	1,494		1,494	
GHEDUZZI, Ugo (1853-1925) Italian					
oil	2	6,046	1,120	3,023	4,926
GHENT, Peter (1856-1911) British					
oil	2	5,652	2,669	2,826	2,983
GHERARDI, Antonio (1644-1702) Italian					
oil	1	8,922		8,922	
GHERRI-MORO, Bruno (1899-1967) Italian					
oil	1	1,049		1,049	
GHESQUIERRE, Napoleon François (1812-1862) Belgian					
oil	1	1,791		1,791	
GHEZZI, Pier Leone (1674-1755) Italian					
wc/d	3	8,845	1,527	1,527	5,738
GHIBERTI, Lorenzo (1378-1455) Italian					
3D	1	245,679		245,679	
GHIGLIA, Oscar (1876-1945) Italian					
oil	2	82,049	6,243	41,025	75,806
GHIGLIA, Paulo (1905-1979) Italian					
oil	2	2,399	1,159	1,200	1,240
GHIGLIA, Valentino (1903-1960) Italian					
oil	3	4,671	1,065	1,153	2,453
GHIGLION-GREEN, Maurice (1913-) French					
oil	3	5,681	1,359	1,359	2,900
GHIKA, Nicolas (1906-1994) Greek					
oil	1	8,030		8,030	
wc/d	4	27,957	3,575	7,081	10,220
GHISOLFI, Giovanni (1632-1683) Italian					
oil	3	146,652	12,262	28,690	105,700
GHITTONI, Francesco (1855-1928) Italian					
oil	1	5,418		5,418	
GHIVARELLO, Benedetto (1882-1955) Italian					
oil	1	1,098		1,098	
GHORPADE, M D (20th C) Indian					
wc/d	1	1,440		1,440	
GHOSE, Gopal (20th C) Indian					
wc/d	1	2,000		2,000	
GHOSH, Nibaran Chandra (19/20th C) Indian					
wc/d	1	2,016		2,016	
GIACOMETTI, Alberto (1901-1966) Swiss					
3D	20	22,364,730	12,640	50,613	13,000,000
oil	4	619,991	6,709	106,641	400,000
wc/d	16	346,764	1,117	14,516	62,202
GIACOMETTI, Alberto and Diego (20th C) Swiss					
3D	9	617,313	24,000	35,000	170,000

Name	No.	Total Sales Value	lowest	Prices median	highest
GIACOMETTI, Augusto (1877-1947) Swiss					
oil	5	1,765,445	72,923	117,886	850,769
wc/d	14	180,882	4,421	12,138	35,857
GIACOMETTI, Diego (1902-1985) Swiss					
3D	38	3,219,714	5,984	67,000	480,000
GIACOMETTI, Giovanni (1868-1934) Swiss					
oil	16	2,668,927	23,904	154,605	376,769
wc/d	9	46,566	1,025	1,815	13,147
GIACOMI, Eugenio de (1852-1917) Italian					
oil	1	17,428		17,428	
GIALLINA, Angelos (1857-1939) Greek					
wc/d	10	75,325	1,378	5,113	18,960
GIAMBATTISTA, di (19th C) Italian					
oil	2	5,246	1,908	2,623	3,338
GIANI, Felice (1760-1823) Italian					
wc/d	2	3,847	1,665	1,924	2,182
GIANI, H (19th C) Italian?					
oil	1	1,216		1,216	
GIANNACCINI, Ilio (1897-1968) Italian					
oil	1	1,933		1,933	
GIANNETTI, Raffaele (1832-1916) Italian					
oil	1	15,000		15,000	
GIANNI (?) Italian					
oil	2	19,392	1,872	9,696	17,520
GIANNI, G (19th C) Italian					
oil	1	8,460		8,460	
GIANNI, Gerolamo (1837-1887) Italian					
oil	5	69,972	5,285	5,738	46,215
GIANNI, Gian (19th C) Italian					
oil	4	29,322	2,094	6,300	14,628
GIANNI, M (19th C) Italian					
wc/d	1	1,716		1,716	
GIANNI, Maria (19th C) Italian					
wc/d	2	5,151	1,100	2,576	4,051
GIANQUINTO, Alberto (1929-) Italian					
oil	7	14,723	1,401	1,710	3,139
GIAQUINTO, Corrado (c.1690-1765) Italian					
oil	4	113,531	17,257	20,814	54,647
GIARDIELLO, Giovanni (19th C) Italian					
oil	1	1,180		1,180	
GIARDIELLO, Giuseppe (19/20th C) Italian					
oil	1	1,318		1,318	
GIBB, Robert (younger) (1845-1932) British					
wc/d	1	13,524		13,524	
GIBB, T H (19th C) British					
oil	1	1,910		1,910	
GIBBS, Charles (fl.1878-1899) British					
oil	1	1,501		1,501	
GIBBS, H (19th C) British					
oil	1	3,450		3,450	
GIBBS, Harry (fl.1880-1907) British?					
oil	1	5,850		5,850	
GIBBS, Jane (1859-?) American					
oil	1	4,800		4,800	
GIBBS, Len (1929-) Canadian					
oil	1	1,400		1,400	
GIBBS, Thomas Binney (1870-?) British					
oil	1	1,268		1,268	

Name	No.	Total Sales Value	lowest	Prices median	highest
GIBERT, Lucien (1904-1988) French					
3D	101	300,825	1,033	2,067	16,533
oil	1	1,082		1,082	
GIBERTO, Luigi Baggi (19th C) Italian					
3D	1	2,906		2,906	
GIBSON, Charles Dana (1867-1944) American					
oil	2	17,800	3,800	8,900	14,000
wc/d	1	2,800		2,800	
GIBSON, George (1904-) American/British					
wc/d	1	5,500		5,500	
GIBSON, Thomas (1680-1751) British					
oil	1	15,000		15,000	
GIBSON, William Alfred (1866-1931) British					
oil	10	41,892	1,738	3,346	10,150
GIEBEL, Heinrich (1865-1951) German					
oil	2	4,170	1,365	2,085	2,805
GIEL, Frans van (1892-1975) Belgian					
oil	1	2,716		2,716	
GIERSING, Harald (1881-1927) Danish					
oil	5	10,351	1,133	1,674	3,844
GIERYMSKI, Maksymilian (1846-1874) Polish					
oil	1	21,000		21,000	
GIES, Joseph W (1860-1935) American					
oil	1	2,800		2,800	
GIEZENDANNER, Babeli (1831-1905) German					
wc/d	1	5,591		5,591	
GIFFARD, Alexandre S (19th C) Canadian					
oil	1	5,222		5,222	
GIFFORD, Charles H (1839-1904) American					
oil	2	16,400	2,400	8,200	14,000
wc/d	2	3,100	1,200	1,550	1,900
GIFFORD, John (19th C) British					
oil	6	35,362	2,718	6,023	9,000
GIFFORD, R Swain (1840-1905) American					
oil	1	6,000		6,000	
GIFFORD, Sanford Robinson (1823-1880) American					
oil	2	228,000	8,000	114,000	220,000
GIGANTE, Ercole (19th C) Italian					
oil	5	40,578	1,376	7,538	21,257
wc/d	1	4,292		4,292	
GIGANTE, Giacinto (1806-1876) Italian					
wc/d	7	53,466	1,147	4,652	24,411
GIGER, Hans-Rudolf (1940-) Swiss					
oil	1	39,012		39,012	
wc/d	1	1,203		1,203	
GIGNOUS, Eugenio (1850-1906) Italian					
oil	4	49,716	4,198	13,748	18,022
GIGNOUS, Lorenzo (1862-c.1954) Italian					
oil	2	8,561	3,940	4,281	4,621
GIGNOUX, François Regis (1816-1882) American/French					
oil	1	4,000		4,000	
GIGOLA, Giovanni Battista (1769-1841) Italian					
wc/d	1	3,950		3,950	
GIGOTTI, Lorenzo (1908-1994) Italian					
oil	1	1,929		1,929	
GIHON, Clarence M (1871-1929) American					
oil	2	22,000	9,000	11,000	13,000
GIL SALA, Ignacio (1912-) Spanish					
oil	2	4,152	1,113	2,076	3,039

Name	No.	Total Sales Value	Prices lowest	Prices median	highest
GIL, A B (16th C) Spanish					
oil	1	18,000		18,000	
GIL, Ignacio (20th C) Spanish					
oil	3	15,170	1,200	2,307	11,663
GILADI, Aharon (1907-1993) Israeli					
oil	1	1,600		1,600	
GILARDI, Irene (1879-1951) Italian					
wc/d	1	4,586		4,586	
GILARDI, Pier Celestino (1837-1905) Italian					
oil	1	4,089		4,089	
GILARDI, Piero (1942-) Italian					
3D	6	12,568	1,222	1,811	3,826
GILBAULT, Joseph Eugène (19th C) French					
oil	1	11,000		11,000	
GILBERT and GEORGE (20th C) British					
wc/d	3	32,094	4,228	9,540	18,326
GILBERT, Albert (fl.1880-1920) British					
oil	1	6,320		6,320	
GILBERT, Alfred (1854-1934) British					
3D	1	4,424		4,424	
GILBERT, Arthur (1819-1895) British					
oil	6	22,729	1,219	3,857	7,550
GILBERT, Arthur Hill (1894-1970) American					
oil	1	3,500		3,500	
GILBERT, Dennis (1922-) British					
oil	1	1,050		1,050	
GILBERT, E (?) ?					
oil	1	1,088		1,088	
GILBERT, Ferdinand (?-1877) ?					
oil	2	3,358	1,570	1,679	1,788
GILBERT, Horace W (1855-?) British					
oil	1	1,359		1,359	
GILBERT, J (?) British?					
oil	2	6,824	2,400	3,412	4,424
GILBERT, John Graham (1794-1866) British					
oil	1	1,580		1,580	
GILBERT, Joseph Francis (1792-1855) British					
oil	1	4,824		4,824	
GILBERT, Pierre Julian (1783-1860) French					
wc/d	1	2,608		2,608	
GILBERT, Stephen (1910-) British					
oil	1	8,528		8,528	
GILBERT, Victor (1847-1933) French					
oil	7	126,404	1,314	4,200	81,069
wc/d	2	13,004	5,004	6,502	8,000
GILBERT, Vieton (20th C) French					
wc/d	1	5,118		5,118	
GILBERT, W J (fl.1835-1851) British					
oil	1	7,550		7,550	
GILCHREST, Joan (1918-) British					
oil	2	2,902	1,230	1,451	1,672
GILCHRIST, William Wallace (jnr) (1879-1926) American					
oil	1	8,500		8,500	
GILDEMEISTER, Gustav (1876-1915) German					
oil	1	25,000		25,000	
GILDOR, Jacob (1948-) Israeli					
oil	2	6,400	2,000	3,200	4,400
wc/d	1	1,476		1,476	

Name	No.	Total Sales Value	lowest	Prices median	highest
GILE, Seldon Connor (1877-1947) American					
oil	6	91,500	2,000	16,000	32,000
wc/d	2	11,500	2,500	5,750	9,000
GILES, Arthur (fl.1915-1925) British?					
oil	1	1,087		1,087	
GILES, Howard (1876-1955) American					
oil	1	2,000		2,000	
GILES, James William (1801-1870) British					
oil	4	45,983	1,351	2,741	39,150
GILES, John West (fl.1830-1865) British					
oil	1	1,144		1,144	
GILI Y ROIG, Baldomero (1837-1926) Spanish					
oil	1	2,964		2,964	
GILIBERT, Gaston (1850-1931) French					
wc/d	1	3,123		3,123	
GILIOLI, Émile (1911-1977) French					
3D	4	21,176	4,641	4,852	6,825
wc/d	2	4,111	1,328	2,056	2,783
GILJE, Cathleen (20th C) Dutch					
oil	1	1,109		1,109	
GILL, Andre (1840-1884) French					
oil	1	1,549		1,549	
GILL, Charles (1871-1918) Canadian					
oil	1	2,050		2,050	
GILL, DeLancey (1859-1940) American					
oil	1	4,250		4,250	
GILL, Edmund (1820-1894) British					
oil	5	14,819	1,128	3,140	5,434
GILL, Eric (1882-1940) British					
3D	1	8,410		8,410	
wc/d	2	6,518	1,008	3,259	5,510
GILL, J (19th C) British					
wc/d	1	1,450		1,450	
GILL, Samuel Thomas (1818-1880) Australian					
wc/d	1	3,692		3,692	
GILL, W W (19th C) British					
oil	2	2,114	1,057	1,057	1,057
GILL, William W (19th C) British					
oil	2	4,424	2,212	2,212	2,212
GILLE, Christian Friedrich (1805-1899) German					
oil	2	11,381	2,549	5,691	8,832
GILLEMANS, Jan Pauwel (17th C) Flemish					
oil	2	12,117	4,867	6,059	7,250
GILLEMANS, Jan Pauwel (elder) (1618-1675) Flemish					
oil	4	50,734	9,060	11,837	18,000
GILLEMANS, Jan Pauwel (younger) (1651-1704) Flemish					
oil	3	36,497	7,071	11,786	17,640
GILLES, Barthel (1891-1977) German					
oil	1	3,546		3,546	
wc/d	1	3,883		3,883	
GILLES, Werner (1894-1961) German					
oil	3	22,907	2,640	9,102	11,165
wc/d	6	12,862	1,135	2,042	3,546
GILLES-MURIQUE, Jeannine (1924-) French					
oil	1	1,771		1,771	
GILLESPIE, George K (1924-1996) British					
oil	16	34,606	1,015	1,595	6,594
GILLESPIE, Jessie (1888-1972) American					
wc/d	1	4,500		4,500	

Name	No.	Total Sales Value	Prices lowest	median	highest
GILLET, Edgar (20th C) French					
oil	1	1,911		1,911	
GILLET, Frederic (1814-1884) Swiss					
oil	1	5,500		5,500	
GILLET, Guillaume (1912-1987) French					
oil	1	1,638		1,638	
GILLET, Roger Edgar (1924-) French					
oil	6	10,302	1,186	1,679	2,259
GILLI, Claude (1938-) French					
3D	2	5,754	1,254	2,877	4,500
oil	2	6,729	3,249	3,365	3,480
wc/d	3	12,058	1,157	3,599	7,302
GILLIAM, Sam (1933-) American					
3D	1	8,000		8,000	
GILLIES, Sir William George (1898-1973) British					
oil	5	45,868	6,795	8,760	12,495
wc/d	12	66,426	1,103	4,876	13,050
GILLIS, Marcel (20th C) ?					
oil	1	1,191		1,191	
GILLIS, Nicolaes (1580-1632) Dutch					
oil	1	83,050		83,050	
GILLMORE, W (19/20th C) British					
oil	1	1,073		1,073	
GILLOT, Claude (1673-1722) French					
wc/d	2	66,440	22,650	33,220	43,790
GILLOT, Eugène Louis (1868-1925) French					
oil	1	2,213		2,213	
GILMAN, Harold (1876-1919) British					
oil	2	16,725	4,740	8,363	11,985
GILPIN, Sawrey (1733-1807) British					
oil	4	75,100	4,800	20,350	29,600
GILPIN, William Sawrey (1762-1843) British					
oil	1	2,826		2,826	
GILROY, John William (1868-1944) British					
oil	1	1,510		1,510	
GILSOUL, Victor (1867-1939) Belgian					
oil	6	25,035	1,048	2,203	11,975
GILSOUL-HOPPE, Ketty (1868-1939) Belgian					
wc/d	3	4,709	1,066	1,668	1,975
GIMENO Y ARASA, Francisco (1858-1927) Spanish					
oil	3	191,129	3,484	47,824	139,821
wc/d	1	1,412		1,412	
GIMIGNANI, Giacinto (1611-1681) Italian					
oil	1	57,330		57,330	
GIMMI, Wilhelm (1886-1965) Swiss					
oil	16	55,168	1,742	2,544	8,841
wc/d	4	6,001	1,043	1,519	1,920
GINDERTAEL, Roger van (1899-1982) Belgian					
wc/d	1	2,218		2,218	
GINDRA, Jozef (?) ?					
oil	1	1,221		1,221	
GINER VALLS, Luis (1900-1995) Spanish					
oil	1	1,022		1,022	
GINESI, Edna (1902-) British					
oil	1	4,740		4,740	
GINGELEN, Jacques van (1801-?) Flemish					
oil	1	3,993		3,993	
GINKEL, Johan Godfried van (1827-1863) Dutch					
oil	1	2,943		2,943	

Name	No.	Total Sales Value	lowest	Prices median	highest
GINNER, Charles (1878-1952) British					
oil	2	14,052	2,067	7,026	11,985
wc/d	2	9,130	3,600	4,565	5,530
GINNETT, Louis (1875-1946) British					
oil	1	1,138		1,138	
GINTRAC, Jean Louis (1808-1886) French					
oil	1	1,844		1,844	
GIOJA, Belisario (1829-1906) Italian					
wc/d	1	3,709		3,709	
GIOJA, Edoardo (1862-1937) Italian					
oil	1	1,240		1,240	
GIOLI, Francesco (1849-1922) Italian					
oil	5	27,797	1,224	5,351	9,810
GIOLI, Luigi (1854-1947) Italian					
oil	3	16,288	1,669	4,363	10,256
GIORDA, Patrice (1952-) French					
oil	1	2,571		2,571	
GIORDANO, Edoardo (1904-1974) Italian					
wc/d	1	1,080		1,080	
GIORDANO, Felice (1880-1964) Italian					
oil	12	29,775	1,149	2,201	5,492
GIORDANO, Luca (1632-1705) Italian					
oil	9	394,515	9,420	37,608	95,000
wc/d	4	6,019	1,026	1,386	2,222
GIORDANO, Luca (school) (1632-1705) Italian					
oil	2	7,428	3,076	3,714	4,352
GIORGETTI, Angelo (1899-1952) Swiss					
oil	1	1,096		1,096	
GIORGIONE (school) (1477-1510) Italian					
oil	1	38,133		38,133	
GIOVANELLI, G (19/20th C) Italian					
oil	1	1,106		1,106	
GIOVANNI D'EPISCOPO (18th C) Italian					
oil	1	8,714		8,714	
GIOVANNI DI SAN GIOVANNI (1592-1636) Italian					
oil	1	110,000		110,000	
GIOVANNI, Luigi di (1856-1938) Italian					
oil	2	2,400	1,050	1,200	1,350
wc/d	2	3,252	1,293	1,626	1,959
GIOVANNINI, Vincenzo (1816-?) Italian					
oil	3	35,612	8,965	10,595	16,052
GIPE, Lawrence (1962-) American?					
oil	1	5,000		5,000	
GIRALDEZ Y PENALVER, Adolfo (c.1840-1920) Spanish					
oil	4	11,869	2,431	3,146	3,146
GIRALT, Agustin (19/20th C) Spanish					
oil	1	3,934		3,934	
GIRARD (?) ?					
oil	1	2,750		2,750	
GIRARD, Eugene Leonard (1842-1917) French					
3D	1	12,110		12,110	
GIRARD, Hippolyte (19th C) French					
oil	1	1,203		1,203	
GIRARD, Karine Firmin (1959-) French					
oil	3	3,281	1,038	1,161	1,161
GIRARD, Marie Firmin (1838-1921) French					
oil	3	108,756	3,000	18,000	87,756
GIRARDET, Edouard-Henri (1819-1880) Swiss					
oil	1	1,184		1,184	

Name	No.	Total Sales Value	Prices lowest	median	highest
GIRARDET, Eugène Alexis (1853-1907) French					
oil	8	170,244	1,875	15,750	64,442
GIRARDET, Jules (1856-1946) French/Swiss					
oil	4	15,011	1,019	1,349	11,294
wc/d	1	1,813		1,813	
GIRARDET, Karl (1813-1871) Swiss					
oil	2	3,742	1,691	1,871	2,051
GIRARDET, Léon (1857-1895) French					
wc/d	1	1,000		1,000	
GIRARDET, Leopold Henri (1848-1904) Swiss					
oil	1	1,337		1,337	
GIRARDON, G (19th C) ?					
oil	1	1,273		1,273	
GIRARDOT, Ernest Gustave (fl.1860-1893) British					
oil	3	9,007	2,272	2,475	4,260
GIRARDOT, Louis Auguste (1858-1933) French					
oil	3	15,983	2,070	2,184	11,729
GIRAUD (19/20th C) French					
wc/d	2	4,015	1,679	2,008	2,336
GIRAUD, Charles (19th C) French					
oil	1	2,067		2,067	
GIRAUD, Pierre Francois Eugène (1806-1881) French					
oil	1	36,665		36,665	
GIRAUD, Sebastien Charles (1819-1892) French					
oil	2	15,613	1,741	7,807	13,872
GIRIER, Jean-Aime (1837-1912) French					
oil	1	2,164		2,164	
GIRIN, David Eugène (1848-1917) French					
oil	1	55,480		55,480	
GIRKE, Raimund (1930-) German					
oil	3	17,366	2,214	6,641	8,511
wc/d	1	1,766		1,766	
GIRODET DE ROUCY TRIOSON, Anne Louis (1767-1824) French					
oil	2	153,250	40,000	76,625	113,250
wc/d	1	17,457		17,457	
GIRON, Leon (1839-1914) French					
oil	1	2,175		2,175	
GIRONELLA, Alberto (1929-1999) Mexican					
oil	1	7,000		7,000	
GIROSI, Franco (1896-1987) Italian					
oil	1	1,845		1,845	
GIROUX, Achille (1820-1854) French					
oil	1	3,782		3,782	
GIRSCHER, Bernhard Moritz (1822-1870) German					
oil	1	3,308		3,308	
GIRTIN, Thomas (1775-1802) British					
wc/d	4	32,370	1,950	6,210	18,000
GIRTIN, Thomas and TURNER, Joseph Mallord William (19th C) British					
wc/d	2	31,460	14,300	15,730	17,160
GISCHIA, Léon (1903-1991) French					
oil	7	13,485	1,228	1,558	2,980
wc/d	1	1,983		1,983	
GISLANDER, William (1890-1937) Swedish					
oil	2	2,125	1,033	1,063	1,092
GISSING, Roland (1895-1967) Canadian					
oil	10	13,342	1,074	1,348	1,761
GISSON, Andre (1910-) French/American					
oil	27	70,318	1,000	2,400	7,900

Name	No.	Total Sales Value	lowest	Prices median	highest
GIULIANO, Bartolomeo (1829-1909) Italian					
oil	3	20,318	1,318	4,500	14,500
GIUNTA, Joseph (1911-) Canadian					
oil	2	2,125	1,002	1,063	1,123
GIUNTOTARDI, Philippe (1768-1831) Italian					
wc/d	1	1,950		1,950	
GIUSTI, Guglielmo (1824-1916) Italian					
oil	2	5,157	2,536	2,579	2,621
wc/d	1	1,670		1,670	
GIUSTO, Faust (19/20th C) Italian					
oil	3	6,490	1,709	1,897	2,884
GIVANIAN, G (19/20th C) ?					
oil	1	3,300		3,300	
GJEDSTED, Rolf (1947-) Danish					
oil	1	1,281		1,281	
GJERDEVIK, Niels Erik (1962-) Norwegian					
oil	2	2,178	1,025	1,089	1,153
GLABBEECK, Gysbert van (fl.c.1630-1648) Dutch					
oil	1	30,000		30,000	
GLACKENS, William (1870-1938) American					
oil	7	1,471,000	26,000	250,000	440,000
wc/d	4	55,300	2,000	2,900	47,500
GLADENBECK, H (20th C) German					
3D	1	1,800		1,800	
GLAIZE, Auguste Barthelemy (1807-1893) French					
oil	1	2,308		2,308	
GLANSDORFF, Hubert (1877-1964) Belgian					
oil	7	10,669	1,007	1,442	1,880
GLAOUI, Hassan el (1924-) Moroccan					
oil	1	3,292		3,292	
GLARNER, Fritz (1899-1972) American/Swiss					
oil	1	1,474		1,474	
wc/d	1	6,000		6,000	
GLASKER, Horst (1949-) German?					
oil	1	1,427		1,427	
GLASS, Hamilton (19/20th C) British					
wc/d	1	1,074		1,074	
GLASS, James William (1825-1857) American					
oil	1	1,200		1,200	
GLASS, William Mervyn (1885-1965) British					
oil	3	24,592	6,342	8,030	10,220
GLATTFELDER, Hansjorg (1939-) Swiss					
3D	1	4,124		4,124	
oil	2	7,815	2,250	3,908	5,565
GLAUBER, Johannes (1646-1726) Dutch					
oil	1	11,496		11,496	
GLAZEBROOK, Hugh de (1855-1937) British					
oil	2	3,179	1,223	1,590	1,956
GLEASON, Joe Duncan (1881-1959) American					
oil	2	14,500	7,000	7,250	7,500
GLEHN, Jane de (1873-1961) British					
oil	1	5,640		5,640	
GLEHN, Wilfred Gabriel de (1870-1951) British					
oil	10	115,025	2,800	13,040	17,490
wc/d	2	3,096	1,332	1,548	1,764
GLEICH, John (1879-?) German					
oil	3	29,236	1,858	2,716	24,662
GLEICHEN, Lady Helena (1873-1947) British					
oil	1	2,983		2,983	

Name	No.	Total Sales Value	lowest	Prices median	highest
GLEICHMANN, Otto (1887-1963) German					
wc/d	2	14,298	6,925	7,149	7,373
GLEIM, Eduard (1812-1899) German					
oil	2	2,538	1,189	1,269	1,349
GLEIZE, Claude (?-1892) French					
oil	1	1,524		1,524	
GLEIZES, Albert (1881-1953) French					
oil	17	1,009,531	2,760	52,850	178,598
wc/d	23	290,996	1,238	5,063	75,000
GLEN, Robert (20th C) American					
3D	1	2,750		2,750	
GLENAVY, Lady Beatrice (1883-1970) British					
3D	1	14,800		14,800	
oil	1	12,714		12,714	
GLENDENING, Alfred (19th C) British					
oil	1	1,800		1,800	
GLENDENING, Alfred Augustus (19th C) British					
oil	16	149,040	1,354	8,080	25,670
wc/d	5	19,327	2,341	4,000	5,500
GLENDENING, Alfred Augustus (jnr) (1861-1907) British					
oil	5	38,450	1,238	7,400	15,000
GLENDENING, Alfred Augustus (snr) (?-c.1910) British					
oil	1	21,140		21,140	
GLENNIE, Arthur (1803-1890) British					
wc/d	1	1,264		1,264	
GLENNIE, George F (fl.1861-1882) British					
wc/d	1	1,422		1,422	
GLICENSTEIN, Enoch-Henryk (1870-1942) American					
wc/d	1	1,000		1,000	
GLICK, C (19/20th C) ?					
oil	1	2,000		2,000	
GLIENKE, Ferdinand August (1854-?) German					
oil	1	1,000		1,000	
GLIKSBERG, Haim (1904-1970) Israeli					
oil	1	9,500		9,500	
wc/d	1	2,500		2,500	
GLINDONI, Henry Gillard (1852-1913) British					
oil	2	9,898	1,378	4,949	8,520
wc/d	2	3,537	1,034	1,769	2,503
GLINZ, Theo (1890-1962) Swiss					
oil	10	31,646	1,118	1,573	12,702
GLOCKENDON, Nikolaus (elder) (16th C) German					
oil	1	22,650		22,650	
GLOCKNER, Hermann (1889-1987) German					
wc/d	1	7,282		7,282	
GLOECKNER, Michael (1915-1989) German/American					
oil	2	2,100	1,000	1,050	1,100
GLOEDE, C (19th C) Dutch?					
oil	1	1,932		1,932	
GLORIE, Raymond (1918-) Belgian					
3D	1	1,824		1,824	
GLOVER, Ablade (1934-) Ghanean					
oil	4	5,993	1,199	1,481	1,833
GLOVER, John (1767-1849) British					
oil	1	9,060		9,060	
wc/d	5	23,360	2,054	3,160	8,294
GLOVER, Kenneth (?) British?					
oil	1	1,189		1,189	
GLUCK, Anselm (1950-) Austrian					
oil	1	2,038		2,038	

Name	No.	Total Sales Value	lowest	Prices median	highest
GLUCKLICH, Simon (1863-1943) German					
oil	1	54,045		54,045	
GLUCKMANN, Grigory (1898-1973) American/Russian					
oil	2	5,250	2,000	2,625	3,250
GLUCKSTEIN, Hannah (1895-1976) British					
oil	1	82,500		82,500	
GLYDE, Henry George (1906-1998) Canadian					
oil	6	11,608	1,007	1,578	4,062
GMELIN, Johann (1810-1854) German					
oil	2	27,670	13,107	13,835	14,563
GNOLI, Domenico (1933-1970) Italian					
oil	4	449,823	27,005	80,909	261,000
wc/d	3	10,566	1,959	3,322	5,285
GOBAUT, Gaspard (1814-1882) French					
wc/d	4	61,322	1,712	10,825	37,960
GOBBAERTS, Jan (?) ?					
oil	1	1,651		1,651	
GOBBI, Enrico (19th C) Italian					
oil	2	2,248	1,015	1,124	1,233
GOBER, Robert (1954-) American					
3D	5	1,135,000	20,000	70,000	750,000
wc/d	1	48,000		48,000	
GOBERT, Pierre (1662-1744) French					
oil	2	44,309	16,379	22,155	27,930
GOBILLARD, Paule (1869-1946) French					
oil	3	89,038	26,188	26,188	36,009
GOBL, Camilla (1871-1965) Austrian					
oil	1	1,456		1,456	
GOBRON, Roger (1899-1985) Belgian					
oil	1	1,153		1,153	
GODCHAUX (?) ?					
3D	1	3,750		3,750	
GODCHAUX, A (19th C) French					
oil	4	9,667	1,354	2,364	3,586
GODCHAUX, Alfred (1835-1895) French					
oil	2	6,067	2,112	3,034	3,955
GODCHAUX, Emil (1860-?) Austrian?					
oil	3	3,813	1,038	1,063	1,712
GODCHAUX, Roger (1878-?) French					
3D	6	25,174	2,047	4,708	6,142
oil	2	18,981	4,981	9,491	14,000
GODECHARLE, Gilles Lambert (1750-1835) Belgian					
3D	1	2,246		2,246	
GODEFROID, Marie Eleonore (1778-1849) French					
oil	1	18,000		18,000	
GODET, Henri (1863-1937) French					
3D	1	2,572		2,572	
GODET, Julius (fl.1844-1894) British					
oil	1	1,553		1,553	
GODFRINON, Ernest (1878-1927) Belgian					
oil	4	13,840	1,165	1,386	9,903
GODINEAU, Jacobus Ludovicus (1811-1873) Flemish					
oil	1	2,911		2,911	
GODLEVSKY, Ivan (1908-) Russian					
oil	1	1,713		1,713	
GODOY Y CASTRO, Federico (1869-1939) Spanish					
oil	1	6,000		6,000	
GODWARD, John William (1858-1922) British					
oil	6	1,362,000	60,000	260,000	360,000

Name	No.	Total Sales Value	lowest	Prices median	highest
GODWIN, Mary (1887-1960) British					
oil	1	1,178		1,178	
GODWIN, Ted (1933-) Canadian					
oil	1	1,000		1,000	
GOEBEL, Carl (1824-1899) Austrian					
wc/d	1	2,700		2,700	
GOEBEL, Hermann (1885-1945) German					
oil	2	3,639	1,716	1,820	1,923
GOEBEL, Rod (1946-1993) American					
oil	1	6,500		6,500	
GOEJE-BARBIERS, M G de (18/19th C) Dutch					
oil	1	1,065		1,065	
GOENEUTTE, Norbert (1854-1894) French					
oil	1	5,914		5,914	
GOERG, Edouard (1893-1969) French					
oil	13	88,399	2,350	3,958	35,000
GOETZ, Edouard (20th C) French					
oil	1	1,309		1,309	
GOETZ, Gottfried Bernhard (1708-1774) German					
wc/d	2	2,767	1,182	1,384	1,585
GOETZ, Henri (1909-1989) French					
oil	9	18,502	1,119	1,638	3,793
wc/d	12	19,840	1,267	1,493	2,828
GOFF, Frederick E J (1855-1931) British					
wc/d	9	15,515	1,113	1,670	3,312
GOFF, Lloyd Lozes (1918-1982) American					
oil	3	5,600	1,200	1,400	3,000
GOFFINON, Aristide (1881-1952) Belgian					
oil	3	5,457	1,214	1,595	2,648
GOGARTEN, Heinrich (1850-1911) German					
oil	3	5,187	1,463	1,573	2,151
GOGH, Vincent van (1853-1890) Dutch					
oil	6	8,637,000	377,500	989,750	4,200,000
GOGO, Felix (19/20th C) Belgian					
oil	1	1,936		1,936	
GOGUEN, Jean (1928-1989) Canadian					
wc/d	1	2,043		2,043	
GOHLER, Hermann (1874-?) German					
oil	3	4,010	1,143	1,307	1,560
GOINGS, Ralph (1928-) American					
oil	2	49,200	4,200	24,600	45,000
GOLA, Emilio (1852-1923) Italian					
wc/d	1	2,395		2,395	
GOLDBERG, Gustav Adolf (1848-1911) German					
oil	1	1,800		1,800	
GOLDBERG, Michael (1924-) American					
oil	1	3,200		3,200	
GOLDFARB, Walter (1964-) Brazilian					
oil	1	12,000		12,000	
GOLDIE, Charles Alphonse (20th C) British					
wc/d	4	6,873	1,027	1,817	2,212
GOLDING, Tomás (1909-) Venezuelan					
oil	9	19,399	1,030	2,440	3,590
GOLDSCHEIDER (19/20th C) Austrian					
3D	3	6,704	1,397	2,328	2,979
GOLDSCHEIDER, A (20th C) ?					
3D	1	1,133		1,133	
GOLDSCHEIDER, Friedrich (1845-1897) Austrian/French					
3D	5	11,626	1,302	2,019	4,484

Name	No.	Total Sales Value	lowest	Prices median	highest
GOLDSCHMIDT, Gertrudis (1912-1994) Venezuelan					
3D	2	52,000	10,000	26,000	42,000
GOLDSCHMIDT, Hilde (1897-1980) Austrian?					
oil	1	2,536		2,536	
GOLDSTEIN, Jack (1945-) Canadian					
oil	1	1,500		1,500	
GOLDSWORTHY, Andy (1956-) British					
oil	1	3,020		3,020	
GOLLER, Bruno (1901-) German					
wc/d	1	1,505		1,505	
GOLLINGS, William Elling (1878-1932) American					
oil	4	134,500	7,000	33,750	60,000
wc/d	3	16,244	2,500	6,000	7,744
GOLLNER, Herman (1830-1906) German					
oil	1	3,173		3,173	
GOLTZIUS, Hendrik (1558-1616) Dutch					
oil	1	2,225		2,225	
wc/d	1	440,000		440,000	
GOLUB, Leon Albert (1922-) American					
oil	4	75,000	12,000	14,000	35,000
GOMEZ MARTIN, Enrique (19th C) Spanish					
oil	2	4,701	1,969	2,351	2,732
GOMEZ MORENO Y GONZALEZ, Manuel (?-1918) Spanish					
oil	1	15,010		15,010	
GOMEZ Y GIL, Guillermo (1862-1942) Spanish					
oil	2	3,542	1,575	1,771	1,967
GONDOUIN, Emmanuel (1883-1934) French					
wc/d	1	5,106		5,106	
GONIN, Francesco (1808-1889) Italian					
oil	2	55,328	4,228	27,664	51,100
GONSCHIOR, Kuno (1935-) German					
oil	1	3,985		3,985	
GONTCHAROVA, Natalia (1881-1962) Russian					
oil	6	72,654	1,103	8,263	31,393
wc/d	11	39,431	1,501	2,866	14,345
GONTIER (?) French					
oil	1	1,697		1,697	
GONTIER, C (19th C) French					
oil	1	3,565		3,565	
GONTIER, Pierre Camille (1840-?) French					
oil	1	11,850		11,850	
GONZAGA, Giovanfrancesco (1921-) Italian					
oil	11	18,103	1,121	1,548	2,815
GONZAGA, Pietro di Gottardo (1751-1831) Italian					
wc/d	1	16,000		16,000	
GONZALES, Eva (1849-1883) French					
oil	1	32,000		32,000	
GONZALES, Xavier (1898-1993) American					
oil	1	1,800		1,800	
GONZALEZ ALACREU, Juan (1937-) Spanish					
oil	1	2,933		2,933	
wc/d	1	3,813		3,813	
GONZALEZ CAMACHO, Fernando (1925-) Spanish					
oil	1	2,323		2,323	
GONZALEZ FERNANDEZ, Lazaro (18/19th C) Spanish					
oil	1	2,564		2,564	
GONZALEZ GONZALEZ, Pedro (1927-) Spanish					
oil	2	4,901	1,943	2,451	2,958

Name	No.	Total Sales Value	lowest	Prices median	highest
GONZALEZ SUAREZ, Antonio (1915-1975) Spanish					
wc/d	1	1,405		1,405	
GONZALEZ VELAZQUEZ, Zacarias (1763-1834) Spanish					
oil	2	38,964	16,763	19,482	22,201
GONZALEZ, Jose (?) Spanish					
oil	1	1,588		1,588	
GONZALEZ, Juan Antonio (1842-1914) Spanish					
oil	4	21,427	2,054	3,687	12,000
GONZALEZ, Julio (1876-1942) Spanish					
3D	3	1,660,681	55,000	205,681	1,400,000
oil	1	105,700		105,700	
wc/d	6	64,480	2,528	6,244	36,240
GONZALEZ, Modesto (19th C) Argentinian					
oil	1	5,200		5,200	
GONZALEZ, Pedro Angel (1901-1981) Venezuelan					
oil	2	12,000	4,390	6,000	7,610
GONZALEZ, Rafael Ramón (1894-1975) Portuguese					
oil	1	1,230		1,230	
GONZALEZ, Simon (19/20th C) French/Chilean					
3D	1	2,239		2,239	
GONZALEZ-TORRES, Felix (1957-1996) American?					
3D	4	2,050,000	50,000	250,000	1,500,000
GONZALO, Alberto (1954-) Spanish					
oil	1	1,037		1,037	
GONZALVO Y PEREZ, Pablo (1830-1896) Spanish					
oil	1	10,679		10,679	
GOOD, John Willis (19th C) British					
3D	3	22,810	4,530	7,920	10,360
GOODALL, Edward Alfred (1819-1908) British					
oil	1	1,471		1,471	
wc/d	6	19,815	1,029	1,167	12,000
GOODALL, F (1822-1904) British					
wc/d	1	1,650		1,650	
GOODALL, Frederick (1822-1904) British					
oil	17	102,808	1,000	3,991	22,500
GOODALL, John Edward (fl.1877-1891) British					
wc/d	1	2,250		2,250	
GOODALL, John Strickland (1908-) British					
wc/d	4	5,496	1,287	1,287	1,570
GOODALL, Walter (1830-1889) British					
wc/d	1	2,250		2,250	
GOODAN, Till P (1896-1958) American					
oil	1	1,500		1,500	
GOODE, Joe (1937-) American					
oil	4	12,800	1,800	3,000	5,000
GOODIN, Walter (1907-1992) British					
oil	4	4,677	1,022	1,078	1,500
GOODMAN, Maude (1860-1938) British					
oil	2	8,300	3,300	4,150	5,000
GOODMAN, Robert Gwelo (1871-1939) British					
oil	3	7,295	1,133	3,002	3,160
GOODNOUGH, Robert (1917-) American					
oil	1	4,500		4,500	
GOODWIN, Albert (1845-1932) British					
oil	1	1,800		1,800	
wc/d	46	295,198	1,034	3,380	37,180
GOODWIN, Arthur C (1866-1929) American					
oil	5	42,750	3,250	9,000	13,000
wc/d	5	33,200	2,500	3,000	17,000

Name	No.	Total Sales Value	lowest	Prices median	highest
GOODWIN, Betty (1923-) Canadian					
oil	1	7,571		7,571	
GOODWIN, Harry (?-1925) British					
wc/d	3	4,175	1,015	1,015	2,133
GOODWIN, Phillip R (1882-1935) American					
oil	1	80,000		80,000	
GOODWIN, Richard Labarre (1840-1910) American					
oil	2	7,400	3,200	3,700	4,200
GOODWIN, S L (19th C) British					
oil	1	1,400		1,400	
GOODWIN, Sidney (1867-1944) British					
wc/d	4	5,252	1,110	1,331	1,480
GOOL, Jan van (1685-1763) Dutch					
oil	3	25,948	4,000	9,948	12,000
GOPAR, Juan (1958-) Spanish?					
wc/d	1	2,346		2,346	
GORANSSON, Ake (1902-1942) Swedish					
oil	8	84,930	3,385	6,109	37,632
GORBATOFF, Konstantin (1876-1945) Russian					
oil	11	118,548	2,500	11,325	24,160
wc/d	2	4,538	1,510	2,269	3,028
GORBERTI, N (19th C) French?					
oil	1	7,436		7,436	
GORBITZ, Johan (1782-1853) Norwegian					
oil	1	1,162		1,162	
GORDER, Luther Emerson van (1861-1931) American					
oil	1	7,500		7,500	
GORDIGIANI, Edoardo (1866-1961) Italian					
oil	3	4,924	1,222	1,743	1,959
GORDIGIANI, Michele (1835-1909) Italian					
oil	3	21,883	1,109	1,774	19,000
GORDIJN, Araun (1947-) Dutch					
oil	1	2,802		2,802	
GORDILLO, Gun (20th C) ?					
3D	2	3,342	1,420	1,671	1,922
GORDILLO, Luis (1939-) Spanish					
oil	1	35,794		35,794	
GORDON, Arthur (19th C) British					
oil	4	8,126	1,329	1,959	2,880
GORDON, Sir John Watson (1788-1864) British					
oil	1	20,735		20,735	
GORDON, William (20th C) American					
wc/d	1	1,300		1,300	
GORDON-CUMMING, Constance Frederika (1837-1924) British					
wc/d	1	1,359		1,359	
GORDON-FRAZER, Charles (?-1899) British/Australian					
oil	1	3,624		3,624	
GORDY, Robert (20th C) American					
wc/d	3	6,700	2,000	2,300	2,400
GORE, Frederick (1913-) British					
oil	7	42,916	2,058	5,880	10,270
GORE, Spencer (1878-1914) British					
oil	2	45,750	14,250	22,875	31,500
GORE, William Crampton (1871-1946) Irish					
oil	3	12,284	3,700	4,144	4,440
GORE, William Henry (fl.1880-1916) British					
oil	1	1,287		1,287	
GORGE, Paul Eugène (1856-1941) Belgian					
oil	1	1,284		1,284	

Name	No.	Total Sales Value	lowest	Prices median	highest
GORI, A (17/18th C) Italian					
3D	1	6,280		6,280	
GORI, Alessandro (17th C) Italian					
oil	1	7,302		7,302	
GORI, G (20th C) French					
3D	2	4,293	1,908	2,147	2,385
GORIN, Jean (1899-1981) French					
3D	1	7,084		7,084	
oil	1	1,443		1,443	
GORKY, Arshile (1904-1948) American					
oil	2	2,035,000	35,000	1,017,500	2,000,000
wc/d	4	483,000	23,000	30,000	400,000
GORMAN, R C (1933-) American					
3D	1	3,000		3,000	
GORMLEY, Anthony (1950-) British					
3D	1	52,850		52,850	
oil	1	2,718		2,718	
wc/d	1	4,512		4,512	
GORNER (19th C) Austrian					
oil	1	6,500		6,500	
GORNIK, April (1953-) American					
oil	1	11,000		11,000	
wc/d	1	3,000		3,000	
GORP, Henri Nicolas van (1756-1819) French					
oil	5	25,418	1,460	2,800	10,000
GORSON, Aaron Henry (1872-1933) American					
oil	5	49,000	5,500	6,500	16,000
GORTER, Arnold Marc (1866-1933) Dutch					
oil	7	49,498	2,147	5,739	15,303
GORUS, Pieter (1881-1941) Belgian					
oil	2	5,504	2,422	2,752	3,082
GORY, Affortunato (1895-1925) ?					
3D	5	37,211	2,354	3,647	20,540
GOS, Albert (1852-1942) Swiss					
oil	5	6,697	1,096	1,139	1,749
GOS, François (1880-1975) Swiss					
oil	1	1,139		1,139	
GOSE, Jean François (1827-?) French					
oil	1	2,173		2,173	
GOSLING, William (1824-1883) British					
wc/d	3	4,985	1,043	1,256	2,686
GOSSE, Sylvia (1881-1968) British					
oil	3	12,225	2,256	3,624	6,345
GOSSELIN, Ferdinand Jules Albert (1862-1931) French					
oil	1	2,500		2,500	
GOSSELIN-PARELLE, Maurice (1876-1931) French					
oil	1	1,408		1,408	
GOSSIN, Louis (19th C) French					
3D	1	1,671		1,671	
GOTCH, Thomas Cooper (1854-1931) British					
oil	2	17,715	8,175	8,858	9,540
wc/d	3	9,811	1,672	2,217	5,922
GOTH, Moricz (1873-1944) Hungarian					
oil	1	2,796		2,796	
GOTH, Sarika (1900-) Hungarian					
oil	2	3,356	1,635	1,678	1,721
GOTHEIN, Werner (1890-?) German					
oil	1	18,145		18,145	
GOTSCH, Friedrich Karl (1900-1984) Danish					
oil	2	25,558	4,363	12,779	21,195

Name	No.	Total Sales Value	lowest	Prices median	highest
wc/d	3	5,029	1,390	1,455	2,184
GOTTLIEB, Adolph (1903-1974) American					
oil	4	280,000	20,000	30,000	200,000
wc/d	4	53,500	5,500	13,000	22,000
GOTTLIEB, Harry (1895-?) American					
oil	2	5,000	1,750	2,500	3,250
wc/d	1	1,700		1,700	
GOTTSCHALK, Albert (1866-1906) Danish					
oil	7	17,286	1,059	1,668	5,362
GOTTWALD, Frederick C (1860-1941) American					
oil	1	1,400		1,400	
GOTZ, Josef Matthias (1696-1760) German					
3D	1	3,146		3,146	
GOTZ, Karl Otto (1914-) German					
oil	2	4,563	1,942	2,282	2,621
wc/d	7	40,605	1,413	3,274	20,229
GOTZLOFF, Carl (1799-1866) German					
oil	3	78,376	14,953	17,445	45,978
GOUBIE, Jean Richard (1842-1899) French					
oil	2	11,798	3,380	5,899	8,418
GOUDIACHVILI, Lado (1896-?) Russian					
oil	1	6,769		6,769	
wc/d	4	12,898	1,365	3,344	4,845
GOUDIE, Alexander (1933-) British					
oil	1	2,844		2,844	
wc/d	1	1,354		1,354	
GOUDT, Hendrik (1585-1630) Dutch					
wc/d	2	5,343	1,414	2,672	3,929
GOUDY, Frederic William (1865-1947) American					
oil	1	6,000		6,000	
GOUGH, J (19th C) British					
oil	2	7,375	2,375	3,688	5,000
GOUIN, G (?) ?					
oil	1	3,940		3,940	
GOULARD, V (19th C) French					
oil	6	18,000	2,500	2,750	4,000
GOULD, Alexander Carruthers (1870-1948) British					
oil	1	1,340		1,340	
GOULD, David (fl.1885-1930) British					
oil	2	14,400	5,400	7,200	9,000
GOULD, Debenham (?) British?					
oil	1	1,200		1,200	
GOULD, Joseph J (1880-1935) American					
wc/d	1	3,750		3,750	
GOULD, Walter (1829-1893) American					
oil	1	9,000		9,000	
GOULLIN, Francis (19th C) French					
oil	1	1,673		1,673	
GOUNARO, Georges (c.1889-1977) Greek/French					
oil	1	4,814		4,814	
GOUNAROPOULOS, Georges (1889-1977) Greek					
oil	2	85,410	6,570	42,705	78,840
GOUNOD, François Louis (1758-1823) French					
oil	1	3,995		3,995	
GOUPIL, Léon (1834-1890) French					
oil	1	2,361		2,361	
GOURDON, L (?) French?					
oil	1	1,092		1,092	

Name	No.	Total Sales Value	lowest	Prices median	highest
GOURDON, René (19th C) French					
oil	1	1,171		1,171	
GOURGUE, Enguerrand-Jean (1930-) Haitian					
oil	1	1,400		1,400	
GOUWE, Adriaan Herman (1875-1965) Dutch					
oil	6	29,686	2,163	4,701	8,621
GOUWELOOS, Charles (1867-?) Belgian					
oil	1	1,296		1,296	
GOUWELOOS, Jean (1868-1943) Belgian					
oil	5	27,674	1,109	1,391	16,121
GOVAERTS, Hendrik (1669-1720) Flemish					
oil	1	8,290		8,290	
GOVAERTS, Jean (1898-1985) Belgian					
wc/d	1	1,191		1,191	
GOW, James (?-1886) British					
oil	1	3,466		3,466	
GOW, Mary L (1851-1929) British					
wc/d	1	3,625		3,625	
GOWEN, Elwyn George (1895-1945) American					
oil	1	2,500		2,500	
GOWING, Lawrence (1918-1991) British					
oil	2	10,570	3,020	5,285	7,550
GOYA Y LUCIENTES, Francisco Jose de (1746-1828) Spanish					
oil	1	450,000		450,000	
wc/d	1	850,000		850,000	
GOYEN, Jan van (1596-1656) Dutch					
oil	16	2,638,052	4,545	107,675	661,500
wc/d	11	217,614	3,339	10,570	66,786
GOZZARD, J Walter (1888-1950) British					
oil	1	1,430		1,430	
GRAAT, Barend (1628-1709) Flemish					
oil	1	3,000		3,000	
GRABACH, John R (1886-1981) American					
oil	4	25,150	2,250	2,950	17,000
GRABAR, Igor (1872-1960) Russian					
oil	3	29,445	6,040	9,060	14,345
GRABMAYER, Franz (1927-) German					
wc/d	1	1,275		1,275	
GRABWINKLER, Paul (1880-1946) Austrian					
oil	1	1,050		1,050	
GRACE, A L (19th C?) British					
oil	2	6,658	1,728	3,329	4,930
GRACHEV (19th C) Russian					
3D	1	5,922		5,922	
GRACIA, Manuel de (1937-) Spanish					
oil	1	1,493		1,493	
GRADA, Raffaele de (1885-1957) Italian					
oil	9	38,520	1,452	3,397	9,220
GRADL, Hermann (1883-1964) German					
oil	4	7,901	1,040	2,047	2,767
GRAEB, Karl Georg Anton (1816-1884) German					
oil	2	7,927	1,946	3,964	5,981
GRAEF, Gustav (1821-1895) German					
oil	1	5,418		5,418	
GRAEF, Timotheus de (17th C) Dutch					
oil	1	8,635		8,635	
GRAEFLE, Albert (1807-1889) German					
oil	1	4,800		4,800	

Name	No.	Total Sales Value	lowest	Prices median	highest
GRAEFNER, L (19/20th C) German					
3D	1	1,139		1,139	
GRAEME, Colin (fl.1858-1910) British					
oil	14	46,414	1,000	2,400	8,000
GRAESER, Camille (1892-?) French?					
3D	1	1,776		1,776	
oil	2	3,552	1,776	1,776	1,776
GRAEVENITZ, Fritz von (1892-1959) German					
3D	1	1,867		1,867	
GRAF, Carl C (1892-1947) American					
oil	2	10,000	4,500	5,000	5,500
GRAF, Diogo (1896-1966) Swiss					
oil	1	1,845		1,845	
GRAF, Emil (1901-1980) Swiss					
oil	1	2,762		2,762	
GRAF, Gerhard (1883-1960) German					
oil	3	6,522	1,151	1,832	3,539
GRAF, Oskar (1870-1958) German					
oil	1	2,234		2,234	
GRAF, Philip (1874-?) German					
oil	4	6,257	1,053	1,613	1,978
GRAF-REINHART, Anna Emilia (1809-1884) Dutch					
wc/d	1	1,963		1,963	
GRAFAELI, Felo (20th C) Italian					
3D	1	1,532		1,532	
GRAFF, Anton (1736-1813) German/Swiss					
oil	10	65,156	2,420	3,950	17,445
GRAFISEN, Philipp (19/20th C) ?					
oil	1	1,480		1,480	
GRAFTON, G (19/20th C) ?					
oil	1	1,305		1,305	
GRAFTON, Robert W (1876-1936) American					
oil	6	55,800	1,300	5,250	34,000
GRAHAM, Dan (1942-) American					
3D	1	11,000		11,000	
GRAHAM, David (?) ?					
oil	1	1,223		1,223	
GRAHAM, Florence (fl.1881-1905) British					
wc/d	1	1,073		1,073	
GRAHAM, George (1881-1949) British					
oil	2	4,628	1,628	2,314	3,000
GRAHAM, James Lillie (1873-?) Canadian					
oil	3	5,688	1,151	1,151	3,386
wc/d	1	1,761		1,761	
GRAHAM, John D (c.1881-1961) American/Russian					
oil	1	35,000		35,000	
GRAHAM, Peter (1836-1921) British					
oil	2	6,622	3,168	3,311	3,454
GRAHAM, Robert (1938-) American					
3D	4	13,138	1,500	3,069	5,500
GRAHAM, Robert Alexander (1873-1946) American					
oil	2	14,500	4,500	7,250	10,000
GRAHAM, Rodney (1949-) Canadian					
wc/d	1	6,000		6,000	
GRAHAM, Thomas Alexander (1840-1906) British					
oil	1	3,750		3,750	
GRAHAM, William (1841-1910) American					
oil	1	9,000		9,000	

Name	No.	Total Sales Value	Prices lowest	median	highest
GRAILLY, Victor de (1804-1889) French					
oil	1	4,120		4,120	
GRAMATTE, Walter (19/20th C) ?					
wc/d	1	4,837		4,837	
GRAMMATICA, Antiveduto (1571-1626) Italian					
oil	1	8,256		8,256	
GRAN, Enrique (1928-) Spanish					
oil	2	6,682	1,569	3,341	5,113
GRANCHI-TAYLOR, Achille (1857-1921) French					
oil	1	1,110		1,110	
GRANDE, Giovanni (1887-1937) Italian					
oil	1	1,186		1,186	
GRANDGERARD, Lucien Henri (1880-1965) French					
oil	1	1,721		1,721	
GRANDI, Francesco (1831-1891) Italian					
oil	1	4,603		4,603	
GRANDI, Giuseppe (1843-1897) Italian					
3D	2	2,884	1,284	1,442	1,600
GRANDI, Mario Dario (1918-1971) Argentinian					
oil	1	1,800		1,800	
GRANDIO, Constantino (1923-1977) Spanish					
oil	5	16,878	1,804	2,555	6,189
GRANDMAISON, Nickola de (1892-1978) Canadian/Russian					
oil	1	1,110		1,110	
wc/d	10	71,723	1,959	5,771	15,667
GRANDMAISON, Oreste de (1932-1985) Canadian					
oil	2	2,312	1,071	1,156	1,241
GRANELL, Eugenio F (1912-) Spanish					
oil	4	18,069	2,237	3,070	9,623
wc/d	3	5,180	1,137	1,897	2,146
GRANELLO, G (19/20th C) Italian					
oil	1	1,038		1,038	
GRANER Y ARRUFI, Luis (1863-1929) Spanish					
oil	4	46,810	2,555	9,878	24,500
wc/d	1	2,371		2,371	
GRANER Y VINUELAS, Antonio (19th C) Spanish					
oil	1	2,429		2,429	
GRANERI, Giovanni Michele (school) (18th C) Italian					
oil	1	4,822		4,822	
GRANET, François Marius (1775-1849) French					
oil	5	45,474	3,422	5,987	18,954
wc/d	1	2,336		2,336	
GRANGE, Remy de la (19/20th C) American					
oil	1	4,000		4,000	
GRANIE, Joseph (1866-1915) French					
oil	1	1,196		1,196	
GRANITSCH, Susanna (1869-?) Austrian					
oil	1	2,385		2,385	
GRANSTON, J H (19th C) British					
oil	1	11,440		11,440	
GRANT, Alistair (1925-) British					
oil	1	4,050		4,050	
GRANT, Carleton (fl.1885-1899) British					
oil	1	1,500		1,500	
GRANT, Clement Rollins (1849-1893) American					
oil	1	1,800		1,800	
GRANT, Donald (1930-) British					
oil	6	15,436	1,422	2,136	5,920

Name	No.	Total Sales Value	lowest	Prices median	highest
GRANT, Duncan (1885-1978) British					
oil	23	164,307	1,015	5,400	31,600
wc/d	10	30,313	1,001	3,223	5,700
GRANT, Frederick M (1886-1959) American					
oil	3	14,300	2,800	5,500	6,000
GRANT, Gordon (1875-1962) American					
oil	2	28,500	2,500	14,250	26,000
wc/d	1	1,700		1,700	
GRANT, William James (1829-1866) British					
oil	1	5,680		5,680	
GRAPHITO, Speedy (20th C) ?					
oil	1	1,824		1,824	
GRARD, Georges (1901-1984) Belgian					
3D	2	31,530	8,346	15,765	23,184
GRASS, Adolf (19th C) ?					
oil	1	4,211		4,211	
GRASS, Hans (1935-) German					
oil	1	2,206		2,206	
GRASS-MICK, Augustin (1873-1963) French					
oil	1	1,382		1,382	
GRASSEL, Franz (1861-1948) German					
oil	1	4,356		4,356	
GRASSET, Adele (19th C) French					
oil	1	8,754		8,754	
GRASSET, Eugène (1841-1917) Swiss					
wc/d	1	1,855		1,855	
GRASSI, Nicola (1662-1748) Italian					
oil	2	16,600	4,105	8,300	12,495
wc/d	1	7,550		7,550	
GRASSIS, Giuseppe (1870-1949) Italian					
oil	1	2,636		2,636	
GRASSY, Giuseppe (1755-1838) Austrian					
oil	1	2,921		2,921	
GRATALOUP (20th C) French?					
wc/d	1	1,455		1,455	
GRATE, Eric (1896-1983) Swedish					
3D	6	18,128	1,529	2,794	5,897
wc/d	1	1,727		1,727	
GRATHWOL, Ray Anthony (1900-1992) American					
oil	4	10,200	1,800	1,950	4,500
GRATZ, Theodor (1859-1947) German					
oil	1	4,784		4,784	
GRAU SANTOS, Julian (1937-) Spanish					
oil	8	16,221	1,110	2,193	2,786
wc/d	1	1,676		1,676	
GRAU, Enrique (1920-) Colombian					
oil	2	9,500	3,500	4,750	6,000
wc/d	1	4,500		4,500	
GRAU, Xavier (20th C) French?					
oil	1	5,339		5,339	
GRAU-SALA, Emile (1911-1975) Spanish					
oil	52	847,694	2,500	15,963	35,807
wc/d	20	73,502	1,087	2,816	10,165
GRAUBNER, Gotthard (1930-) German					
3D	1	6,796		6,796	
oil	1	2,913		2,913	
wc/d	2	5,900	1,575	2,950	4,325
GRAUSS, Geert (1882-1929) Dutch					
oil	1	1,377		1,377	

Name	No.	Total Sales Value	lowest	Prices median	highest
GRAVE, Josua de (17/18th C) Dutch					
wc/d	2	15,179	6,679	7,590	8,500
GRAVES, Abbott Fuller (1859-1936) American					
oil	6	164,100	1,100	15,000	80,000
GRAVES, Morris (1910-) American					
oil	1	18,000		18,000	
wc/d	9	137,500	2,000	18,000	26,000
GRAVES, Nancy (1940-1995) American					
3D	1	7,500		7,500	
oil	1	5,000		5,000	
wc/d	1	6,000		6,000	
GRAVINA, Antonio (1934-) Italian?					
oil	1	4,720		4,720	
GRAY, Cleve (1918-) American					
oil	1	5,000		5,000	
GRAY, Douglas Stannus (1890-1959) British					
oil	4	8,216	1,580	1,580	3,476
GRAY, George (18/19th C) British					
oil	2	3,085	1,044	1,543	2,041
GRAY, Harold (1894-1968) American					
wc/d	1	1,700		1,700	
GRAY, Henry Percy (1869-1952) American					
oil	1	22,500		22,500	
wc/d	12	137,500	5,000	9,500	19,000
GRAY, Henry Peters (1819-1877) American					
oil	1	1,700		1,700	
GRAY, Jack L (1927-1981) American					
wc/d	1	1,700		1,700	
GRAY, James (?-1947) British					
wc/d	1	1,184		1,184	
GRAY, Jessie D (fl.1881-1893) British					
oil	1	1,108		1,108	
GRAY, John (?-1957) British					
oil	1	2,119		2,119	
GRAY, Kate (fl.1870-1987) British					
oil	1	4,379		4,379	
GRAY, Monica F (fl.1898-1919) British					
oil	2	3,100	1,300	1,550	1,800
GRAY, Norah Neilson (1882-1931) British					
wc/d	1	4,640		4,640	
GRAYBACH, John R (20th C) American					
oil	1	4,500		4,500	
GRAZIANI, Ercole (17/18th C) Italian					
oil	1	78,520		78,520	
GRAZIANI, Francesco (17th C) Italian					
oil	4	51,872	6,676	13,090	19,017
GRAZIANI, Pietro (18th C) Italian					
oil	1	2,669		2,669	
GREACEN, Edmund William (1877-1949) American					
oil	2	7,100	1,600	3,550	5,500
GREACEN, Nan (1909-) American					
oil	1	1,800		1,800	
GREASON, William (1884-?) American					
oil	3	4,400	1,300	1,500	1,600
GREATHEAD, Bernard (fl.1780-1810) British					
oil	1	3,180		3,180	
GREAVES, Walter (1846-1930) British					
oil	1	1,000		1,000	

Name	No.	Total Sales Value	lowest	Prices median	highest
GREAVES, William (fl.1882-1920) British					
oil	3	5,912	1,420	1,420	3,002
GREBE, Fritz (1850-?) German					
oil	1	1,969		1,969	
GREBER, Henri Léon (1855-1941) French					
3D	1	1,882		1,882	
GRECO, Alberto (1931-1965) ?					
wc/d	7	24,170	1,017	2,813	6,078
GRECO, El (1541-1614) Spanish					
oil	3	8,449,000	1,400,000	1,764,000	5,285,000
GRECO, Emilio (1913-1995) Italian					
3D	5	167,033	14,558	28,000	70,000
wc/d	2	5,476	2,676	2,738	2,800
GRECO, Emilio (1932-) Italian					
oil	2	2,350	1,100	1,175	1,250
GRECO, Gennaro (1663-1714) Italian					
oil	3	39,140	9,140	13,000	17,000
GREEK SCHOOL, 17th C					
oil	1	2,981		2,981	
GREEN (?) ?					
oil	1	1,498		1,498	
GREEN, Alfred H (fl.1844-1862) British					
oil	5	11,732	1,168	2,550	3,454
GREEN, Anthony (1939-) British					
oil	2	3,397	1,551	1,699	1,846
GREEN, Charles (1840-1898) British					
wc/d	4	11,973	1,193	1,615	7,550
GREEN, Dennis (1942-) British					
wc/d	1	1,057		1,057	
GREEN, E F (19th C) British					
oil	1	7,850		7,850	
GREEN, Elizabeth Shippen (1871-1954) American					
wc/d	1	15,000		15,000	
GREEN, Gregory (1959-) American					
3D	1	2,265		2,265	
GREEN, N E (fl.1880-1896) British					
wc/d	1	1,169		1,169	
GREEN, Roland (1896-1972) British					
wc/d	1	1,200		1,200	
GREEN, Tony (20th C) American					
wc/d	1	1,600		1,600	
GREEN, William (1760-1823) British					
wc/d	1	1,011		1,011	
GREENAWAY, Kate (1846-1901) British					
wc/d	2	4,548	2,100	2,274	2,448
GREENBAUM, Joseph (1864-1940) American					
oil	2	5,000	2,000	2,500	3,000
GREENE, Mark (1916-1986) American					
oil	1	1,400		1,400	
GREENE, Walter L (19/20th C) American					
oil	1	4,500		4,500	
GREENHAM, Peter (1909-1992) British					
oil	4	7,927	1,021	2,157	2,664
GREENHAM, Robert Duckworth (1906-1975) British					
oil	2	9,647	2,397	4,824	7,250
GREENOUGH, Horatio (1805-1852) American					
3D	1	161,700		161,700	
GREENWOOD, Ethan Allen (1779-1856) American					
oil	2	4,800	2,100	2,400	2,700

Name	No.	Total Sales Value	lowest	Prices median	highest
GREENWOOD, Joseph H (1857-1927) American					
oil	3	10,550	1,250	2,800	6,500
GREENWOOD, Marion (1909-1970) American					
oil	1	6,750		6,750	
GREENWOOD, Orlando (1892-1989) British					
oil	1	1,392		1,392	
GREENWOOD, Parker (fl.1880-c.1904) British					
oil	2	16,454	1,454	8,227	15,000
GREER, Blanche F (1883-?) American					
wc/d	1	2,000		2,000	
GREGOIRE (19th C) French					
oil	1	3,634		3,634	
GREGOIRE, C (20th C) ?					
oil	1	1,043		1,043	
GREGOIRE, Jean-Louis (1840-1890) French					
3D	5	17,223	1,073	2,420	8,318
GREGOIRE, L (?) ?					
3D	1	2,330		2,330	
GREGOOR, Gillis Smak (1770-1843) Dutch					
oil	2	9,760	1,964	4,880	7,796
GREGOR, Harold (1929-) American					
oil	1	15,000		15,000	
GREGORI, Gino (1906-1973) Italian					
oil	1	1,272		1,272	
GREGORY, Angela (1903-1990) American					
3D	1	4,500		4,500	
oil	1	3,600		3,600	
GREGORY, Edith Marian (20th C) British					
oil	1	1,898		1,898	
GREGORY, Edward James (1850-1909) British					
oil	1	63,420		63,420	
wc/d	2	10,780	2,200	5,390	8,580
GREGORY, George (1849-1938) British					
oil	6	21,082	1,036	3,398	5,865
GREGORY, J (19th C) British					
oil	1	1,275		1,275	
GREIFFENHAGEN, Maurice (1862-1931) British					
oil	1	2,538		2,538	
GREINER, Otto (1869-1916) German					
oil	1	2,234		2,234	
GREIS, Otto (1913-) German					
oil	1	1,456		1,456	
wc/d	2	6,310	1,456	3,155	4,854
GREIVE, Johan Conrad (jnr) (1837-1891) Dutch					
oil	1	1,951		1,951	
GRELLET, François (1838-1908) French					
oil	1	4,640		4,640	
GREMLICH, Adolf (1915-1971) German					
oil	2	5,713	2,215	2,857	3,498
GRENET DE JOIGNY, Dominique Adolphe (1821-1885) French					
oil	3	5,178	1,125	1,425	2,628
GRENIER, Henri (20th C) French					
wc/d	1	1,057		1,057	
GRENNESS, Johannes (1875-1963) Danish					
oil	1	1,191		1,191	
GRESLEY, Frank (1855-1936) British					
wc/d	3	4,239	1,087	1,352	1,800
GRESLEY, Harold (1892-1967) British					
wc/d	2	2,415	1,192	1,208	1,223

Name	No.	Total Sales Value	lowest	Prices median	highest
GRESLEY, James S (1829-1908) British					
wc/d	2	2,812	1,390	1,406	1,422
GRETHE, Carlos (1864-1913) German					
oil	2	2,887	1,189	1,444	1,698
GRETZNER, Harold (1902-1977) American					
wc/d	4	5,100	1,000	1,250	1,600
GREUZE, Anne Genevieve (1762-1842) French					
oil	1	2,618		2,618	
GREUZE, Jean-Baptiste (1725-1805) French					
oil	10	737,259	1,666	47,500	260,000
wc/d	5	86,806	1,482	15,100	38,021
GREVENBROECK, Alessandro (18th C) Italian					
oil	2	85,474	42,737	42,737	42,737
GREVENBROECK, Orazio (17/18th C) Dutch					
oil	4	91,200	6,064	9,318	66,501
GREVILLE, R K (fl.1844-1852) British					
oil	1	1,272		1,272	
GREY, Gregor (fl.1880-1911) British					
oil	1	8,880		8,880	
GREY, Roger de (1918-) British					
oil	1	1,584		1,584	
GRIBBLE, Bernard Finegan (1873-1962) British					
oil	2	5,106	1,106	2,553	4,000
wc/d	1	1,026		1,026	
GRICE, Jeremy le (1936-) British					
oil	1	1,278		1,278	
GRIDEL, Joseph Emile (1839-1901) French					
oil	1	3,367		3,367	
GRIEBEL, Otto (1895-?) German					
wc/d	1	66,240		66,240	
GRIEKEN, Jef van (1950-) Belgian					
oil	2	4,209	1,567	2,105	2,642
GRIER, Louis Monro (1864-1920) British/Australian					
oil	3	9,815	1,133	3,002	5,680
GRIERSON, Charles MacIver (1864-1939) British					
oil	1	5,100		5,100	
wc/d	4	6,406	1,058	1,416	2,516
GRIESHABER, Helmut A P (1909-1981) German					
wc/d	5	40,516	2,564	4,389	23,501
GRIEVE, Walter Graham (1872-1937) British					
oil	1	1,057		1,057	
GRIFFIER, Jan (elder) (1652-1718) Dutch					
oil	1	21,054		21,054	
GRIFFIER, Jan (elder) and LINGELBACH, Johannes (17th C) Dutch					
oil	1	18,120		18,120	
GRIFFIER, Jan (younger) (fl.1738-1773) British					
oil	1	29,400		29,400	
GRIFFIER, Robert (1688-1750) British					
oil	1	26,425		26,425	
GRIFFIN, Thomas Bailey (19th C) American					
oil	5	7,300	1,000	1,700	1,700
GRIFFIN, Thomas Bartholomew (19th C) American					
oil	1	2,000		2,000	
GRIFFING, Robert (20th C) American					
oil	1	75,000		75,000	
GRIFFITH, Beatrice Fox (1890-?) American					
3D	1	1,700		1,700	
GRIFFITH, Ella N (19/20th C) American					
oil	1	7,500		7,500	

Name	No.	Total Sales Value	Prices lowest	median	highest
GRIFFITH, Louis Oscar (1875-1956) American					
oil	3	20,000	5,000	7,000	8,000
GRIFFITH, William Alexander (1866-1940) American					
oil	1	2,000		2,000	
wc/d	3	61,700	1,700	5,000	55,000
GRIGELY, Joseph (1956-) French					
wc/d	1	1,775		1,775	
GRIGIOTTI, Francesco (17th C) Italian					
wc/d	1	2,716		2,716	
GRIGNASCHI, Giovanni (1839-1905) Italian					
oil	1	1,500		1,500	
GRIGORIEV, Boris (1886-1939) Russian					
oil	2	28,690	7,550	14,345	21,140
wc/d	4	10,683	1,269	2,945	3,525
GRIMALDI, Giovanni Francesco (1606-1680) Italian					
wc/d	3	19,781	4,228	7,248	8,305
GRIMELUND, Johannes Martin (1842-1917) Norwegian					
oil	1	4,395		4,395	
GRIMM, Arthur (1883-1948) German?					
oil	3	13,665	3,958	4,837	4,870
GRIMM, Ludwig Emil (1790-1863) German					
wc/d	3	5,816	1,135	1,608	3,073
GRIMM, Paul (1892-1974) American					
oil	45	150,850	1,100	3,000	11,000
GRIMM, Pierre (1898-1979) French/Russian					
oil	1	1,212		1,212	
GRIMM, Samuel Hieronymus (1733-1794) Swiss					
wc/d	2	6,776	1,342	3,388	5,434
GRIMM, Walter O (1894-1919) American/German					
wc/d	1	1,135		1,135	
GRIMMER, Abel (1573-1619) Flemish					
oil	3	316,850	30,200	51,450	235,200
GRIMMER, Jacob (1526-1589) Flemish					
oil	7	710,881	6,211	83,050	235,200
GRIMSHAW, Arthur (1868-1913) British					
oil	2	19,559	4,544	9,780	15,015
GRIMSHAW, Atkinson (1836-1893) British					
oil	10	946,055	26,455	105,960	200,200
wc/d	2	133,500	60,000	66,750	73,500
GRIMSHAW, Louis (1870-1943) British					
oil	1	61,910		61,910	
GRINNELL, George Victor (1878-1946) American					
oil	1	1,100		1,100	
GRIPENHOLM, Ulf (1943-) Swedish					
oil	3	5,624	1,365	1,638	2,621
GRIPS, Charles Joseph (1825-1920) Belgian					
oil	1	12,080		12,080	
GRIS, Jeanne Aubert (1881-) French					
oil	1	1,249		1,249	
GRIS, Juan (1887-1927) Spanish					
oil	3	1,694,510	237,810	256,700	1,200,000
wc/d	8	312,887	1,239	30,136	120,000
GRISCHOW, O E (19th C) German					
oil	1	1,264		1,264	
GRISELLI, Orlando Italo (1880-1958) Italian					
3D	1	2,385		2,385	
GRISON, François Adolphe (1845-1914) French					
oil	3	65,793	3,586	4,665	57,542

Name	No.	Total Sales Value	Prices lowest	median	highest
GRISOR, Dominique (1947-) French					
oil	1	1,107		1,107	
GRISOT, Pierre (1911-1995) French					
oil	7	9,142	1,056	1,293	1,671
GRISSEMANN, E (20th C) German?					
oil	1	2,617		2,617	
GRISTER (?) ?					
oil	1	2,794		2,794	
GRITCHENKO, Alexis (1883-1977) Russian					
oil	1	2,100		2,100	
GRITTEN, Henry C (1818-1873) British					
oil	1	2,500		2,500	
GRIVEAU, Lucien (1858-?) Italian					
oil	1	2,600		2,600	
GRIVOLAS, Antoine (1843-1902) French					
oil	1	6,644		6,644	
GROB, Konrad (1828-1904) Swiss					
oil	1	1,283		1,283	
GROBE, German (1857-1938) German					
oil	4	12,260	2,151	2,581	4,947
GROBON, Jean Michel (1770-1853) French					
oil	1	11,552		11,552	
GROEBER, Hermann (1865-1935) German					
oil	1	2,396		2,396	
GROEBER, Paul A (fl.1880-1910) German					
oil	1	8,000		8,000	
GROEN, Hendrik Pieter (1886-1964) Dutch					
oil	2	3,447	1,395	1,724	2,052
GROENEWEGEN, Adrianus Johannes (1874-1963) Dutch					
oil	1	2,357		2,357	
wc/d	3	6,898	1,559	2,581	2,758
GROENEWEGEN, Gerrit (1754-1826) Dutch					
wc/d	1	5,107		5,107	
GROESCHEL, Rudolf (1891-1985) German					
oil	2	3,415	1,452	1,708	1,963
GROLIG, Curt Victor Clemens (1805-1863) German					
oil	1	13,777		13,777	
GROLL, Albert Lorey (1866-1952) American					
oil	3	10,800	1,000	3,800	6,000
GROLL, Henriette (20th C) French?					
oil	1	1,094		1,094	
GROLL, Theodor (1857-1913) German					
oil	1	7,369		7,369	
GROLLERON, Paul Louis Narcisse (1848-1901) French					
oil	2	34,000	7,000	17,000	27,000
GROLLIER, Marquise de (1742-1828) ?					
oil	1	6,416		6,416	
GROMAIRE, Marcel (1892-1971) French					
oil	11	212,969	3,568	14,589	57,862
wc/d	26	45,587	1,006	1,415	4,000
GRONLAND, René (1849-1892) German					
oil	1	2,703		2,703	
GRONLAND, Theude (1817-1876) German					
oil	1	3,792		3,792	
GROOME, William H C (fl.1881-1914) British					
oil	1	2,293		2,293	
wc/d	2	2,789	1,073	1,395	1,716
GROOMS, Red (1937-) American					
3D	4	102,600	3,600	32,000	35,000

Name	No.	Total Sales Value	lowest	Prices median	highest
oil	2	25,800	3,800	12,900	22,000
GROOT, Frans Breuhaus de (1796-1875) Dutch					
oil	3	21,473	2,727	3,443	15,303
GROOT, Joseph de (1828-1899) Dutch					
oil	1	2,006		2,006	
GROOTE, A de (19/20th C) ?					
oil	3	3,883	1,106	1,267	1,510
GROOTVELT, Jan Hendrik van (1808-1855) Dutch					
oil	3	10,260	2,458	3,571	4,231
GROPEANO, Nicolas (1865-1936) Rumanian					
wc/d	1	2,549		2,549	
GROS, Antoine Jean (1771-1835) French					
oil	2	15,485	6,425	7,743	9,060
GROSCH, Gustav (20th C) German					
oil	1	1,154		1,154	
GROSE, D C (1865-1890) American					
oil	1	1,500		1,500	
GROSE, Daniel C (1865-1890) American					
oil	2	6,200	1,600	3,100	4,600
GROSJEAN, Henry (1864-1948) French					
oil	1	2,500		2,500	
GROSPERIN, Claude (1936-) French					
oil	1	1,433		1,433	
GROSPIETSCH, Florian (1789-1830) German					
wc/d	1	4,256		4,256	
GROSS, Anthony (1905-1984) British					
oil	1	1,264		1,264	
wc/d	1	2,175		2,175	
GROSS, Chaim (1904-1991) American					
3D	8	31,900	1,500	2,800	14,000
wc/d	2	4,700	1,500	2,350	3,200
GROSS, F (?) ?					
wc/d	1	3,102		3,102	
GROSS, George (20th C) American					
oil	1	2,800		2,800	
wc/d	1	4,250		4,250	
GROSSMANN, M (19/20th C) ?					
wc/d	1	2,601		2,601	
GROSSMANN, Rudolf (1882-1941) German					
oil	1	3,629		3,629	
GROSSO, Alfonso (1893-1983) Spanish					
oil	3	24,799	5,273	6,552	12,974
GROSSO, Giacomo (1860-1938) Italian					
oil	2	4,000	1,793	2,000	2,207
GROSZ, August Ignatz (1847-1917) Austrian					
oil	1	1,083		1,083	
GROSZ, George (1893-1959) American/German					
oil	5	74,084	6,488	6,488	43,200
wc/d	34	332,935	1,100	5,685	54,720
GROUMELLEC, Loic le (1958-) French					
oil	3	7,797	1,093	1,244	5,460
wc/d	1	1,086		1,086	
GROUX, Henry de (1867-1930) Belgian					
oil	2	3,056	1,498	1,528	1,558
wc/d	1	1,070		1,070	
GROVE, Nordahl (1822-1885) Danish					
oil	2	2,811	1,300	1,406	1,511
GROVES, Mary (fl.1884-1904) British					
oil	1	1,034		1,034	

Name	No.	Total Sales Value	lowest	Prices median	highest
GROVES, Robert E (?-1944) British					
wc/d	1	6,000		6,000	
GROVES, Thomas (fl.1881-1894) British					
oil	1	1,716		1,716	
GRUAU, René (1910-) French?					
oil	1	12,888		12,888	
wc/d	2	2,621	1,165	1,311	1,456
GRUBACS, Carlo (19th C) German					
oil	3	52,932	7,632	21,895	23,405
wc/d	2	12,469	2,041	6,235	10,428
GRUBACS, Giovanni (1829-1919) Italian					
oil	2	33,280	7,900	16,640	25,380
GRUBAS, Marco (1839-1910) Italian					
oil	1	4,000		4,000	
GRUBER, Francis (1912-1948) French					
oil	7	106,319	2,866	12,185	43,483
wc/d	1	2,535		2,535	
GRUBER, Franz (1878-1945) German					
oil	1	1,090		1,090	
GRUBICY DE DRAGON, Vittore (1851-1920) Italian					
oil	1	6,584		6,584	
GRUN, Jules Alexandre (1868-1934) French					
oil	2	6,845	2,845	3,423	4,000
GRUN, Maurice (1869-1947) French					
oil	5	17,148	1,146	3,119	6,050
GRUNBERG, T R (fl.1900) German?					
oil	1	1,219		1,219	
GRUNBERG, Wolfgang (?) German					
oil	5	7,652	1,471	1,471	1,619
GRUND, Johann (1808-1887) Austrian					
oil	1	1,924		1,924	
GRUND, Norbert Joseph Carl (1717-1767) Czechoslovakian					
oil	2	7,712	2,880	3,856	4,832
GRUNDER, Mariann (1926-) Swiss					
3D	1	1,468		1,468	
GRUNDMANN, B (1726-1798) German					
3D	2	8,227	2,000	4,114	6,227
GRUNENWALD, Agnes (19th C) German					
oil	1	1,861		1,861	
GRUNENWALD, Jakob (1822-1896) German					
oil	2	34,910	1,241	17,455	33,669
GRUNEWALD, Isaac (1889-1946) Swedish					
oil	40	499,156	1,318	8,830	65,294
wc/d	17	36,853	1,114	1,788	4,805
GRUNFELD, Thomas (1956-) German					
3D	1	30,200		30,200	
wc/d	1	3,398		3,398	
GRUNSWEIGH, Nathan (1880-?) Polish					
oil	1	1,186		1,186	
GRUPPE, Charles Paul (1860-1940) American					
oil	14	50,422	1,500	2,850	9,500
wc/d	3	5,000	1,500	1,700	1,800
GRUPPE, Emile A (1896-1978) American					
oil	54	528,850	1,000	9,750	25,000
GRUPPE, Robert C (20th C) American					
oil	1	1,100		1,100	
GRUST, F G (19/20th C) Dutch					
oil	1	1,600		1,600	
GRUTTEFIEN, Elisabeth (19th C) German					
oil	1	1,088		1,088	

Name	No.	Total Sales Value	lowest	Prices median	highest
GRUTZKE, Johannes (1937-) German					
oil	1	3,643		3,643	
wc/d	4	9,203	1,040	2,422	3,320
GRUTZNER, Eduard von (1846-1925) German					
oil	12	190,050	4,953	9,914	71,100
GRUYERE, Theodore Charles (1814-1885) French					
3D	1	190,000		190,000	
GRUYTER, Jacob Willem (1856-1908) Dutch					
oil	2	6,149	1,485	3,075	4,664
GRUYTER, Willem (jnr) (1817-1880) Dutch					
oil	1	4,880		4,880	
wc/d	2	5,548	1,722	2,774	3,826
GRYEFF, Adriaen de (1670-1715) Flemish					
oil	5	51,620	1,603	8,578	24,160
GRZIMEK, Waldemar (1918-1984) Polish					
3D	1	6,055		6,055	
GSCHOSMANN (1901-) German					
oil	1	2,700		2,700	
GSCHOSMANN, Ludwig (1901-) German					
oil	8	19,768	1,045	1,497	6,055
GSELL, Georg (1673-1740) Swiss					
oil	1	4,924		4,924	
GSELL, Laurent (1860-1944) French					
oil	1	1,055		1,055	
GU JIANLONG (1606-?) Chinese					
wc/d	1	6,300		6,300	
GUACCIMANNI, Vittorio (1859-1938) Italian					
oil	1	2,438		2,438	
GUARANA, Jacopo (1720-1808) Italian					
oil	3	20,208	2,904	2,904	14,400
GUARDI, Francesco (1712-1793) Italian					
oil	5	6,222,850	32,340	117,910	5,100,000
wc/d	3	114,559	1,309	15,100	98,150
GUARDI, Francesco (school) (1712-1793) Italian					
oil	2	7,100	3,500	3,550	3,600
GUARDI, Giacomo (1764-1835) Italian					
oil	3	155,728	6,792	16,636	132,300
wc/d	6	73,357	3,822	10,811	22,500
GUARDI, Giovanni Antonio (1698-1760) Italian					
wc/d	1	18,120		18,120	
GUARIENTI, Carlo (1923-) Italian					
oil	2	7,378	3,273	3,689	4,105
wc/d	5	13,413	1,157	1,449	6,278
GUARLOTTI, Giovanni (1869-1954) Italian					
oil	4	8,609	1,098	1,917	3,678
GUASCONE, Felice (?-1830) Italian					
oil	1	2,218		2,218	
GUASTALLA, Roberto (1855-1912) Italian					
oil	5	27,661	2,861	6,200	7,631
GUAYASAMIN, Oswaldo (1919-1999) Ecuadorian					
oil	2	49,500	7,500	24,750	42,000
wc/d	3	16,633	2,017	2,406	12,210
GUBLER, Max (1898-1973) Swiss					
oil	14	337,688	5,328	22,911	43,726
GUCCILLATO, V (19th C) Italian					
3D	1	1,800		1,800	
GUCCIONE, Piero (1925-) Italian					
oil	4	41,465	5,018	8,843	18,762
wc/d	8	63,913	1,586	8,808	15,860

Name	No.	Total Sales Value	lowest	Prices median	highest
GUCHT, Rob van de (20th C) Belgian?					
oil	1	11,739		11,739	
GUDE, Hans Fredrik (1825-1903) Norwegian					
oil	6	352,694	9,576	44,308	179,330
GUDIN, Fidel (19th C) French					
oil	1	1,694		1,694	
GUDIN, Henriette (1825-?) French					
oil	14	61,353	2,109	4,322	6,905
GUDIN, Theodore (1802-1880) French					
oil	10	103,604	1,070	2,892	50,267
wc/d	11	18,955	1,031	1,224	3,995
GUDNASON, Svavar (1909-1988) Icelandic					
oil	1	1,794		1,794	
GUDNI, Georg (1961-) Icelandic					
oil	2	7,860	3,713	3,930	4,147
GUEDEN, Colette (20th C) French					
3D	1	2,078		2,078	
GUEDY, Gaston (1874-1955) French					
oil	1	82,500		82,500	
GUELDRY, Ferdinand Joseph (1858-1945) French					
oil	1	3,796		3,796	
GUELTZL, Marco de (1958-1992) ?					
3D	2	6,653	1,901	3,327	4,752
GUERARD, Bernard von (1780-1836) German					
oil	1	1,035		1,035	
GUERARD, Charles-Jean (1790-?) French					
oil	1	11,139		11,139	
GUERCINO (1591-1666) Italian					
wc/d	1	3,000		3,000	
GUERCINO, Giovanni Francesco (1591-1666) Italian					
oil	1	58,800		58,800	
wc/d	8	75,205	1,300	5,127	37,500
GUERIN, Charles (1875-1939) French					
oil	1	4,788		4,788	
GUERIN, E (19/20th C) French					
wc/d	1	2,115		2,115	
GUERIN, Ernest (1887-1952) French					
oil	1	12,980		12,980	
wc/d	5	12,022	1,061	1,914	4,822
GUERIN, Gabriel (1869-1916) French					
oil	1	2,849		2,849	
GUERIN, Jules (1866-1946) American					
oil	1	10,000		10,000	
GUERIN, Marie (19th C) French					
wc/d	1	1,264		1,264	
GUERMACHEV, Mikhail Mikhailovich (1867-1930) Russian					
oil	1	2,320		2,320	
GUERRA, Achille (1832-1903) Italian					
oil	1	16,060		16,060	
GUERRA, Evaristo (1942-) Spanish?					
oil	5	12,026	2,002	2,288	2,933
GUERRA, Isabel (?) Spanish					
oil	1	5,378		5,378	
GUERRERO GALVAN, Jesus (1910-1973) Mexican					
oil	2	21,500	4,500	10,750	17,000
GUERRERO, Jose (1914-1992) Spanish					
oil	5	79,308	6,328	20,133	26,133
wc/d	1	3,831		3,831	

Name	No.	Total Sales Value	lowest	Prices median	highest
GUERRESCHI, Giuseppe (1929-1985) Italian					
oil	1	8,472		8,472	
GUERRIER, Jacqueline (20th C) French					
oil	1	1,580		1,580	
GUERRIER, Raymond (1920-) French					
oil	5	7,655	1,000	1,300	2,355
GUERRINI, Renato (1938-) Italian					
oil	1	1,350		1,350	
GUERY, Armand (1850-1912) French					
oil	4	25,719	1,500	5,610	13,000
GUERY-COLAS, Fernand (20th C) French					
oil	1	1,350		1,350	
GUES, Alfred François (1837-?) French					
oil	1	1,454		1,454	
GUEY, Fernand (1877-?) French					
oil	2	3,760	1,880	1,880	1,880
GUEYTON (19th C) French					
3D	1	1,724		1,724	
GUFFENS, Godfried (1823-1901) Belgian					
oil	1	4,844		4,844	
GUGEL, Karl Adolf (1820-1885) German					
oil	1	3,102		3,102	
GUGGENBERGER, Thomas (1815-1882) German					
oil	1	1,486		1,486	
GUGLIELMI, Gennaro (1804-?) Italian					
oil	3	23,030	3,672	5,928	13,430
GUICHARD, Joseph Alexandre (c.1830-1877) French					
oil	1	1,337		1,337	
GUIDI, Giuseppe (19/20th C) Italian					
wc/d	1	1,450		1,450	
GUIDI, Virgilio (1892-1984) Italian					
oil	29	204,917	1,260	2,356	43,634
GUIDOTTI, Salvatore (1836-?) Italian					
oil	1	1,554		1,554	
GUIETTE, René (1893-1976) Belgian					
oil	5	11,450	1,030	1,664	5,431
wc/d	3	14,778	2,263	5,220	7,295
GUIGNER (20th C) French					
3D	1	15,100		15,100	
GUIGNERY, Louis Jules (1818-?) French					
oil	1	4,300		4,300	
GUIGNIER, Henri (20th C) French					
oil	1	3,926		3,926	
GUIGOU, Paul (1834-1871) French					
oil	4	86,032	3,412	6,310	70,000
GUIGUET, François Joseph (1860-1937) French					
oil	3	8,644	1,375	3,115	4,154
GUIJARRO, Antonio (1923-) Spanish					
oil	2	5,146	1,129	2,573	4,017
GUILBERT, Maurice (1876-1933) Belgian					
oil	2	3,541	1,159	1,771	2,382
GUILBERT, Narcisse (1878-1942) French					
oil	3	14,532	2,679	3,422	8,431
GUILBERT, Sir John (?) ?					
3D	1	1,592		1,592	
GUILLAUME, Albert (1873-1942) French					
oil	5	40,280	1,290	9,000	15,000
GUILLAUMET, Gustave (1840-1887) French					
oil	6	15,224	1,016	1,623	7,316

Name	No.	Total Sales Value	lowest	Prices median	highest
wc/d	1	4,898		4,898	

GUILLAUMIN (19/20th C) French
| oil | 1 | 49,152 | | 49,152 | |

GUILLAUMIN, Armand (1841-1927) French
| oil | 29 | 1,066,994 | 2,200 | 28,000 | 125,000 |
| wc/d | 11 | 90,556 | 1,998 | 7,500 | 18,875 |

GUILLEMER, Ernest (1839-?) French
| oil | 1 | 2,370 | | 2,370 | |

GUILLEMET (19th C) French
| oil | 1 | 1,191 | | 1,191 | |

GUILLEMET, Jean Baptiste Antoine (1843-1918) French
| oil | 8 | 29,317 | 2,195 | 3,910 | 4,829 |

GUILLEMIN, Alexandre Marie (1817-1880) French
| oil | 1 | 2,273 | | 2,273 | |

GUILLEMIN, E C H (1841-1907) French
| 3D | 1 | 2,191 | | 2,191 | |

GUILLEMIN, Émile Coriolan Hippolyte (1841-1907) French
| 3D | 4 | 24,507 | 1,338 | 6,169 | 11,000 |

GUILLEMINET (19th C) French
| oil | 1 | 2,281 | | 2,281 | |

GUILLEMINET, Claude (1821-1860) French
| oil | 8 | 22,898 | 1,752 | 2,428 | 4,655 |

GUILLEMINET, Claude (school) (1821-1860) French
| oil | 1 | 2,112 | | 2,112 | |

GUILLERY, Franz (1863-1933) German
| oil | 1 | 1,486 | | 1,486 | |

GUILLIBAUD, Barthelemy (1687-1742) Swiss
| oil | 1 | 2,499 | | 2,499 | |

GUILLON, Adolphe-Irenee (1829-1896) French
| oil | 1 | 22,955 | | 22,955 | |

GUILLONNET, O D V (1872-1967) French
| oil | 1 | 2,252 | | 2,252 | |

GUILLONNET, Octave Denis Victor (1872-1967) French
| oil | 2 | 15,999 | 6,499 | 8,000 | 9,500 |

GUILLOU, Alfred (1844-1926) French
| oil | 4 | 17,357 | 1,130 | 3,364 | 9,500 |

GUILLOUX, Charles Victor (1866-1946) French
| oil | 1 | 1,008 | | 1,008 | |

GUILMOT, Jacques (1927-) French
| 3D | 1 | 1,131 | | 1,131 | |

GUIMARD, Hector (1867-1942) French
| 3D | 1 | 9,369 | | 9,369 | |

GUINDRANT, Anthoine (1801-1843) French
| oil | 1 | 3,979 | | 3,979 | |

GUINEA, Anselmo de (1855-1906) French
| oil | 1 | 3,000 | | 3,000 | |

GUINIER, Henri Jules (1867-1927) French
| oil | 1 | 2,699 | | 2,699 | |

GUINNESS, May (1863-1955) British
| oil | 1 | 4,440 | | 4,440 | |

GUINO, Richard (1890-1973) French
| 3D | 7 | 32,967 | 1,157 | 1,433 | 23,203 |

GUINO, Richard and RENOIR, Pierre Auguste (20th C) French
| 3D | 4 | 66,343 | 5,252 | 17,000 | 27,091 |

GUINOVART, Jose (1927-) Spanish
| oil | 7 | 18,238 | 1,520 | 2,233 | 3,808 |
| wc/d | 7 | 24,278 | 1,994 | 2,613 | 7,662 |

GUION, Molly (1910-) American
| oil | 1 | 1,800 | | 1,800 | |

Name	No.	Total Sales Value	lowest	Prices median	highest
GUIOT, Jean Pierre (1935-) French					
oil	1	2,562		2,562	
GUIRAMAND, Paul (1926-) French					
oil	3	4,789	1,289	1,700	1,800
GUIRAND DE SCEVOLA (1871-1950) French					
oil	1	1,684		1,684	
wc/d	1	1,091		1,091	
GUIRAND DE SCEVOLA, Lucien (1871-1950) French					
oil	3	4,850	1,178	1,530	2,142
wc/d	1	3,988		3,988	
GUIRAUD-RIVIERE, Maurice (1881-?) French					
3D		82,388	1,808	11,060	69,520
GUIRLANDI, H (19th C) Italian					
3D	1	1,500		1,500	
GUISSON, Andre (20th C) ?					
oil	1	3,160		3,160	
GUITET, James (1925-) French					
oil	2	6,875	1,746	3,438	5,129
GUITTET, Georges Henri (1871-1902) French					
3D	2	14,564	7,089	7,282	7,475
GULBRANSSON, Olaf (1873-1958) Norwegian					
wc/d	2	5,163	2,431	2,582	2,732
GULGEE, Ismail (1926-) Indian					
oil	1	5,400		5,400	
GULIK, Franciscus Lodewijk van (1841-1899) Dutch					
oil	1	2,052		2,052	
GULLEYLOVE, John (19th C) British					
oil	1	1,103		1,103	
GULUCHE, J le (1849-?) French					
3D	1	1,426		1,426	
GULUCHE, Joseph le (1849-?) French					
3D	3	9,150	2,835	3,093	3,222
GUMERY, Adolphe (1861-1943) French					
oil	1	2,755		2,755	
GUMMESSON, Per (1858-1928) Swedish					
oil	1	2,310		2,310	
GUMSHEIMER, F (19/20th C) German					
oil	1	1,374		1,374	
GUNBOGI (?) Spanish?					
3D	1	2,854		2,854	
GUNN, A (?) ?					
oil	1	1,359		1,359	
GUNN, Herbert James (1893-1964) British					
oil	4	34,213	2,528	10,043	12,000
GUNN, W (19th C) British?					
oil	1	1,057		1,057	
GUNSTON, Audley (fl.1903-1935) British					
wc/d	1	1,580		1,580	
GUNTEN, Roger von (1933-) Swiss					
oil	1	2,000		2,000	
GUNTER, Randolph (?) ?					
wc/d	1	1,000		1,000	
GUNTERICK, L (?) ?					
oil	1	1,570		1,570	
GUNTERMANN, Wilhelm (1887-?) German					
oil	1	1,100		1,100	
GUNTHER, Erwin (1864-1927) German					
oil	3	4,575	1,238	1,455	1,882

Name	No.	Total Sales Value	lowest	Prices median	highest
GUNTHER, Georg (1886-?) German					
oil	1	1,558		1,558	
GUNTHER, Paul (?) German					
oil	1	1,136		1,136	
GUPTA, Ajit (20th C) Indian					
wc/d	1	1,296		1,296	
GUPTA, Jagdish (1924-) Indian					
wc/d	1	3,900		3,900	
GUPTA, Manindra Bhusan (1898-1968) Indian					
wc/d	1	1,728		1,728	
GURLITT, Louis (1812-1897) German					
oil	2	8,630	1,065	4,315	7,565
GURSCHNER, Herbert (1901-1975) Austrian					
oil	7	37,656	1,314	5,096	9,780
wc/d	2	9,782	2,774	4,891	7,008
GURVICH, Jose (1927-1974) Lithuanian					
oil	12	82,380	1,300	7,165	13,000
wc/d	3	19,500	2,000	7,500	10,000
GUSEV, Vladimir (1957-) Russian					
oil	17	31,127	1,050	1,425	3,476
GUSSMANN, Otto (1869-1926) German					
oil	1	1,707		1,707	
GUSSONI, Vittorio (1893-1968) Italian					
oil	1	2,799		2,799	
GUSSOW, Ulrich (20th C) German?					
oil	1	1,045		1,045	
GUSTAVSSON, Mats (1951-) Swedish					
wc/d	3	3,921	1,037	1,355	1,529
GUSTON, Philip (1913-1980) American					
oil	4	880,000	30,000	205,000	440,000
wc/d	3	77,650	3,800	21,000	52,850
GUTFREUND, Otto (1889-1927) Czechoslovakian					
3D	2	8,855	3,542	4,428	5,313
GUTH, Hella (1912-) Czechoslovakian					
oil	1	1,367		1,367	
GUTHRIE, James (1859-1930) British					
oil	2	3,094	1,036	1,547	2,058
GUTHRIE, Kathleen (1905-1981) British					
oil	1	1,115		1,115	
GUTIERREZ (?) ?					
oil	1	2,500		2,500	
GUTIERREZ DE LA VEGA, Jose (?-1865) Spanish					
oil	1	4,646		4,646	
GUTIERREZ SOLANA, Jose (1886-1945) Spanish					
oil	3	347,360	31,638	145,183	170,539
GUTIERREZ, Ernesto (1873-1934) Spanish					
oil	2	8,260	3,764	4,130	4,496
GUTMAN, Nachum (1898-1978) Israeli					
oil	3	195,000	40,000	60,000	95,000
wc/d	4	29,500	5,000	6,000	12,500
GUTMANN, Bernhard (1869-1936) American					
oil	2	28,800	4,800	14,400	24,000
GUTTENBRUNN, Ludwig (18th C) German					
oil	1	1,350		1,350	
GUTTERIA, R (19th C) ?					
oil	1	2,626		2,626	
GUTTUSO, Renato (1912-1987) Italian					
oil	21	470,151	2,669	17,453	108,750
wc/d	17	66,848	1,061	2,099	15,455

Name	No.	Total Sales Value	lowest	Prices median	highest
GUY, Graham (20th C) British					
oil	1	1,029		1,029	
GUY, James Meikle (1909-1963) American					
oil	1	7,500		7,500	
GUY, Louis (1824-1886) French					
oil	1	1,064		1,064	
GUY, Seymour (1824-1910) American					
oil	2	71,850	24,350	35,925	47,500
GUYOMARD, Gerard (1936-) French					
oil	9	25,107	1,514	2,139	5,733
GUYOT, Georges Lucien (1885-1973) French					
3D	5	22,794	1,251	2,804	9,691
oil	2	2,422	1,140	1,211	1,282
wc/d	4	15,923	1,337	4,795	5,133
GUYOT, J (19th C) ?					
oil	1	1,132		1,132	
GUYOT, J L (19th C) ?					
oil	1	1,963		1,963	
GUYS, Constantin (1802-1892) French					
wc/d	12	36,788	1,031	1,471	18,911
GUZMAN, Enrique (1952-) Mexican					
3D	1	3,200		3,200	
GUZMAN, Federico (1964-) Spanish					
oil	1	1,958		1,958	
GUZMAN, Manuel Rodriguez de (1818-1867) Spanish					
oil	3	55,113	14,051	17,598	23,464
GUZZONE, Sebastiano (1856-1890) Italian					
oil	1	3,915		3,915	
GWILYM, R A (19th C) British?					
oil	1	2,880		2,880	
GWYNNE-JONES, Allan (1892-1982) British					
oil	2	9,870	4,230	4,935	5,640
GYBORSON, Indiana (20th C) American					
oil	2	2,700	1,200	1,350	1,500
GYNSELLYNCZ, J (?) ?					
oil	1	1,491		1,491	
GYSELAER, Nicolas de (1590-1654) Dutch					
oil	1	2,234		2,234	
GYSELMAN, Warner (1827-?) Dutch					
oil	1	3,250		3,250	
GYSELS, Philips (fl.1650) Dutch					
oil	1	20,160		20,160	
GYSIS, Nicolas (1842-1901) Greek					
oil	3	1,124,200	58,400	394,200	671,600
HAAG (?) ?					
oil	1	3,700		3,700	
HAAG, Axel Herman (19th C) Swedish					
wc/d	1	1,059		1,059	
HAAG, Carl (1820-1915) German					
oil	1	1,374		1,374	
wc/d	88	469,997	1,020	3,600	37,500
HAAG, F (19th C) ?					
oil	1	2,355		2,355	
HAAG, J (?) ?					
oil	1	1,661		1,661	
HAAGREN (19th C) ?					
oil	1	2,250		2,250	
HAALA, Anton (19th C) Austrian					
oil	1	1,734		1,734	

Name	No.	Total Sales Value	lowest	Prices median	highest
HAALAND, Lars Laurits (1855-1938) Norwegian					
oil	1	4,000		4,000	
HAAN, Willem Jacob de (1913-1967) Dutch					
oil	1	3,565		3,565	
HAANEN, Adriana (1814-1895) Dutch					
oil	5	77,849	3,053	21,042	24,868
wc/d	1	1,018		1,018	
HAANEN, Cecil van (1844-1914) Dutch					
oil	1	5,000		5,000	
HAANEN, Elisabeth Alida (1809-1845) Dutch					
oil	1	10,712		10,712	
HAANEN, Georg Gillis van (1807-1876) Dutch					
oil	2	9,912	4,243	4,956	5,669
HAANEN, Remi van (1812-1894) Dutch					
oil	3	12,127	2,422	3,105	6,600
HAARLEM SCHOOL, 17th C Dutch					
oil	4	54,704	2,750	12,387	27,180
HAAS, Johannes Hubertus Leonardus de (1832-1908) Flemish					
oil	3	11,877	3,582	3,826	4,469
wc/d	1	5,233		5,233	
HAAS, Mauritz F H de (1832-1895) Dutch					
oil	6	109,174	5,500	17,837	35,000
HAAS, William F de (1830-1880) Dutch					
oil	1	60,000		60,000	
HAASE, Carl Friedrich Moritz Emil von (1844-?) German					
oil	1	3,372		3,372	
HAASE, Hermann Georg (1864-1912) German					
3D	1	3,848		3,848	
HAAXMAN, Pieter Alardus (1814-1887) Dutch					
oil	1	2,487		2,487	
HABENSCHADEN, Sebastian (1813-1868) German					
oil	1	1,568		1,568	
HABERLE, John (1856-1933) American					
oil	1	8,000		8,000	
HABERMANN, Hugo von (1849-1929) German					
oil	2	2,942	1,000	1,471	1,942
wc/d	1	1,591		1,591	
HABERT, François (17th C) French?					
oil	2	199,976	48,976	99,988	151,000
HACCOU, Johannes Cornelis (1798-1839) Dutch					
wc/d	1	2,554		2,554	
HACHE, C (19th C) French					
oil	1	1,343		1,343	
HACKAERT, Jan (1629-1699) Dutch					
wc/d	2	3,261	1,375	1,631	1,886
HACKER, Adolf (1908-) German					
oil	1	1,058		1,058	
HACKER, Arthur (1858-1919) British					
oil	3	50,208	1,908	6,300	42,000
HACKER, Horst (1842-1906) German					
oil	2	3,034	1,307	1,517	1,727
HACKERT, Carl Ludwig (1740-1800) German					
oil	1	7,975		7,975	
HACKERT, Georg Abraham (1755-1805) German					
wc/d	1	7,550		7,550	
HACKERT, Jacob Philippe (1737-1807) German					
oil	5	494,215	25,120	124,606	148,926
wc/d	27	137,200	1,047	4,189	13,353

Name	No.	Total Sales Value	lowest	Prices median	highest
HACKING, Grant (1964-) South African					
oil	3	3,604	1,136	1,136	1,332
HADDEN, N (19/20th C) British					
oil	1	1,073		1,073	
HADDON, David W (fl.1884-1914) British					
oil	8	16,622	1,016	1,767	3,476
HADDON, Trevor (1864-1941) British					
oil	6	17,178	1,740	3,207	3,525
HADENGUE, Louis Michel (19th C) French					
oil	2	27,874	13,430	13,937	14,444
HADLEY, Michael (20th C) American					
oil	1	1,200		1,200	
HAECKE, Joseph (1811-?) German					
oil	1	5,100		5,100	
HAEFLIGER, Leopold (1929-1989) Swiss					
oil	10	27,566	1,184	2,080	7,976
HAEHNEL, Julius Heinrich (1823-1909) German					
3D	2	4,488	2,133	2,244	2,355
HAEN, Dirck de (1832-1886) Belgian					
oil	1	4,500		4,500	
HAER, Adolf de (1892-1945) German					
oil	1	45,000		45,000	
HAERNING, August (1874-1961) Danish					
oil	1	4,350		4,350	
HAES, Carlos de (1829-1898) Spanish					
oil	5	90,578	3,813	6,594	46,019
HAESE, Gunter (1924-) German					
3D	2	12,396	6,198	6,198	6,198
HAFFNER, Léon (1881-1972) French					
wc/d	3	9,789	2,432	3,478	3,879
HAFFTEN, Karl von (1834-1884) German					
oil	1	1,783		1,783	
HAFSTROM, Jan (1937-) Swedish					
3D	2	2,327	1,147	1,164	1,180
oil	1	3,110		3,110	
HAGARTY, Parker (1859-1934) British					
oil	1	1,110		1,110	
HAGBORG, August (1852-1925) Swedish					
oil	12	64,275	2,080	4,431	19,187
HAGBORG, Otto (19th C) British					
oil	1	2,211		2,211	
HAGEDORN, Karl (1889-1969) British					
oil	1	5,530		5,530	
wc/d	2	2,185	1,015	1,093	1,170
HAGEL, Frank (20th C) American					
oil	1	6,500		6,500	
HAGEMAN, Victor (1868-1938) Belgian					
oil	1	2,687		2,687	
HAGEMANS, M (19/20th C) Belgian					
wc/d	1	1,507		1,507	
HAGEMANS, Maurice (1852-1917) Belgian					
oil	4	20,739	1,687	2,340	14,372
wc/d	9	21,309	1,055	1,855	5,349
HAGEMANS, Paul (1884-1959) Belgian					
oil	14	30,256	1,065	1,931	5,270
HAGEMEISTER, Karl (1848-1933) German					
oil	1	5,398		5,398	
wc/d	3	10,394	1,942	3,575	4,877

Name	No.	Total Sales Value	Prices lowest	median	highest
HAGEN, Johann van der (1676-1745) Dutch					
oil	1	14,130		14,130	
HAGEN, Theodor (1842-1919) German					
oil	5	10,940	1,471	1,539	4,469
HAGENAUER (20th C) Austrian					
3D	7	46,801	2,416	5,056	14,300
HAGENAUER, Franz (1906-1986) Austrian					
3D	3	16,205	1,220	2,875	12,110
HAGER, Albert (1857-1940) Belgian					
3D	1	3,456		3,456	
HAGER, Marie (20th C) German?					
oil	1	1,636		1,636	
HAGER, Philipp (?) Swiss					
wc/d	1	1,153		1,153	
HAGERBAUMER, David (1921-) American					
wc/d	1	2,250		2,250	
HAGERUP, Nels (1864-1922) American					
oil	2	5,313	1,500	2,657	3,813
HAGG, Jacob (1839-1931) Swedish					
oil	1	26,118		26,118	
HAGGIN, Ben Ali (1882-1951) American					
oil	1	22,000		22,000	
HAGHE, Louis (1806-1885) Belgian					
wc/d	6	19,551	1,650	2,704	6,235
HAGHE, M M (19th C) British					
oil	1	1,285		1,285	
HAGN, Ludwig von (1819-1898) German					
oil	1	3,106		3,106	
HAGN, Richard von (1850-c.1890) German					
oil	3	4,231	1,000	1,475	1,756
HAGREEN, Philip (20th C) British					
oil	1	1,425		1,425	
HAGUE, Joshua Anderson (1850-1916) British					
oil	3	10,595	1,649	3,976	4,970
HAGUE, Raoul (1905-) American					
3D	1	2,049		2,049	
HAHN, Friedemann (1949-) German					
oil	1	7,969		7,969	
HAHN, Karl Wilhelm (1829-1887) German					
oil	1	3,000		3,000	
HAHNISCH, Anton (1817-1897) Austrian					
wc/d	1	2,693		2,693	
HAIER, Joseph (1816-1891) Austrian					
oil	2	11,332	1,332	5,666	10,000
HAIG, Axel Herman (1835-1921) Swedish					
wc/d	1	2,500		2,500	
HAIG, J Hermiston (fl.1887-1919) British					
oil	1	5,200		5,200	
HAIGH, Alfred Grenfell (1870-1963) British					
oil	1	3,020		3,020	
HAINES, Frederick Stanley (1879-1960) Canadian					
oil	9	21,910	1,044	1,726	7,964
HAINES, Richard (1906-1984) American					
oil	1	2,500		2,500	
HAINES, William Henry (1812-1884) British					
oil	1	54,060		54,060	
HAINS, Raymond (1926-) French					
wc/d	9	81,604	3,386	8,189	21,699

Name	No.	Total Sales Value	Prices lowest	median	highest
HAIQ, F E (19th C) British					
wc/d	1	1,502		1,502	
HAJDU, Étienne (1907-) French					
3D	1	4,340		4,340	
HAJEK, Otto Herbert (1927-) Czechoslovakian					
3D	3	8,950	2,776	2,776	3,398
wc/d	3	6,594	1,682	2,136	2,776
HALAPY, Janus (1893-1960) Hungarian					
oil	1	2,252		2,252	
HALAUSKA, Ludwig (1827-1882) German					
oil	2	28,842	2,742	14,421	26,100
HALBACH, David (20th C) American					
wc/d	2	4,300	1,700	2,150	2,600
HALBART, Gustave (1846-1913) Belgian					
oil	1	2,364		2,364	
HALBERG-KRAUSS, Fritz (1874-1951) German					
oil	20	40,976	1,364	1,845	3,715
HALD, Edward (1883-1980) Swedish					
wc/d	1	1,206		1,206	
HALDANKAR, Sawalaram Laxman (1882-1969) Indian					
wc/d	4	6,300	1,200	1,350	2,400
HALDEY, A J (19th C) British					
oil	1	8,500		8,500	
HALE, Lilian Westcott (1881-1963) American					
oil	2	27,500	3,500	13,750	24,000
HALE-SANDERS, T (19/20th C) British					
oil	1	2,512		2,512	
HALEY, John C (1905-1991) American					
oil	3	6,000	1,500	1,500	3,000
HALFNIGHT, Richard William (1855-1925) British					
oil	1	1,737		1,737	
HALK, H (19/20th C) Danish?					
oil	1	1,311		1,311	
HALL (?) ?					
oil	1	1,430		1,430	
HALL, Clifford (1904-1973) British					
oil	3	4,232	1,248	1,404	1,580
HALL, Edward (1922-1991) British					
oil	1	1,125		1,125	
HALL, Frederick (1860-1948) British					
oil	12	107,877	1,463	4,692	29,230
HALL, George Henry (1825-1913) American					
oil	6	89,500	2,000	6,750	38,000
HALL, Harry (1814-1882) British					
oil	4	7,523	1,057	1,821	2,824
HALL, Jan Jacob Teyler van (1794-1851) Dutch					
oil	2	2,396	1,188	1,198	1,208
HALL, Jessie (?-1915) British					
oil	1	1,240		1,240	
HALL, Maja van (1937-) Dutch?					
3D	1	1,293		1,293	
HALL, Norman Philip (1885-?) American					
oil	1	2,500		2,500	
HALL, Patrick (1906-1992) British					
wc/d	1	1,074		1,074	
HALL, Peter Adolphe (1739-1793) Swedish					
wc/d	1	4,515		4,515	
HALL, Thomas P (fl.1837-1867) British					
oil	2	9,786	3,150	4,893	6,636

Name	No.	Total Sales Value	Prices lowest	median	highest
HALLAM, Joseph Sydney (1898-1953) Canadian					
oil	1	1,439		1,439	
HALLATZ, Emil (1837-1888) German					
oil	1	1,210		1,210	
HALLE, Charles Edward (1846-1914) British					
oil	1	9,815		9,815	
HALLE, Claude Guy (1652-1736) French					
oil	1	5,285		5,285	
HALLE, Noel (1711-1781) French					
oil	1	3,661		3,661	
HALLE, William (1912-) British					
oil	1	2,850		2,850	
HALLER, Anna (1872-1924) Swiss					
oil	1	3,508		3,508	
HALLER, G (?) ?					
oil	1	1,472		1,472	
HALLER, Hermann (1880-1950) Swiss					
3D	3	15,635	1,312	1,945	12,378
HALLET, Andre (1890-1959) Belgian					
oil	11	18,366	1,019	1,593	3,549
HALLETT, Allen (20th C) ?					
3D	1	2,072		2,072	
HALLETT, Hendricks (1847-1921) American					
oil	2	13,700	1,700	6,850	12,000
wc/d	1	1,300		1,300	
HALLEY, Peter (1953-) American					
oil	6	249,828	2,114	47,700	75,000
HALLIDAY, Alan (1952-) British					
wc/d	1	1,065		1,065	
HALLMAN, Magnus (1745-1822) Swedish					
oil	1	2,131		2,131	
HALLSTROM, Eric (1893-1946) Swedish					
oil	13	81,807	1,005	2,730	29,483
wc/d	7	18,307	1,417	2,107	6,824
HALLSTROM, Gunnar A (1875-1943) Swedish					
oil	2	2,675	1,004	1,338	1,671
HALLSTROM, Staffan (1914-1976) Swedish					
oil	6	39,773	1,143	4,949	19,797
wc/d	3	10,241	1,201	2,609	6,431
HALNON, Frederick James (1881-?) British					
3D	2	3,549	1,435	1,775	2,114
HALONEN, Pekka (1865-1933) Finnish					
oil	1	40,764		40,764	
HALPEN, Francis (19th C) British					
oil	1	1,340		1,340	
HALPERT, Samuel (1884-1930) American					
oil	1	7,000		7,000	
HALS, Dirck (1591-1656) Dutch					
oil	1	47,143		47,143	
HALS, Harmen (1611-1669) Dutch					
oil	2	24,025	1,256	12,013	22,769
HALSALL, William Formby (1841-1919) American					
oil	1	5,000		5,000	
HALSE, George (19th C) British					
3D	1	5,024		5,024	
HALSWELLE, Keeley (1832-1891) British					
oil	4	42,941	1,352	5,785	30,020
HALSZEL, Johann Baptist (1710-1777) German					
oil	1	10,910		10,910	

Name	No.	Total Sales Value	Prices lowest	median	highest
HAM, Jean Baptiste (1771-1802) Dutch					
oil	1	2,753		2,753	
HAMAK, Herbert (1952-) German?					
3D	1	1,207		1,207	
HAMANAKA (20th C) ?					
3D	1	22,795		22,795	
HAMBIDGE, Jay (1867-1924) Canadian					
wc/d	1	1,800		1,800	
HAMBLING, Maggi (1945-) British					
wc/d	1	1,278		1,278	
HAMBOURG, Albert (?) French					
oil	1	3,707		3,707	
HAMBOURG, Andre (1909-1999) French					
oil	21	157,567	1,933	6,220	27,298
HAMBRESIN, Albrecht (1850-1937) Belgian					
3D	1	1,501		1,501	
HAMBUCHEN, Wilhelm (1869-1939) German					
oil	3	6,016	1,081	1,500	3,435
HAMEL, Jack (1890-1951) Dutch					
oil	1	3,233		3,233	
HAMEL, Theophile (1817-1870) Canadian					
oil	1	2,438		2,438	
HAMEL, Willem (1860-1924) Dutch					
oil	1	1,180		1,180	
HAMERS, Flip (1909-1995) Dutch					
oil	1	1,721		1,721	
HAMILTON (?) ?					
oil	1	7,978		7,978	
HAMILTON, Ann (1956-) American					
3D	1	24,000		24,000	
HAMILTON, Charles (19th C) British					
oil	1	4,228		4,228	
HAMILTON, Eva H (1880-1959) British					
oil	6	47,656	4,736	7,400	14,800
HAMILTON, F (20th C) ?					
oil	1	1,045		1,045	
HAMILTON, Hamilton (1847-1928) American/British					
oil	1	6,500		6,500	
HAMILTON, Helen (19/20th C) American					
oil	2	7,750	3,250	3,875	4,500
HAMILTON, Hugh Douglas (1739-1808) British					
wc/d	7	743,084	3,160	7,104	486,200
HAMILTON, James (1819-1878) American					
oil	1	12,000		12,000	
HAMILTON, James (1853-1894) British					
oil	1	2,288		2,288	
HAMILTON, James Whitelaw (1860-1932) British					
oil	4	13,491	1,147	3,852	4,640
HAMILTON, Johann Georg de (1672-1737) Flemish					
oil	3	14,463	4,368	4,911	5,184
HAMILTON, Ken (20th C) Irish					
oil	4	7,136	1,088	1,872	2,304
HAMILTON, Letitia (1878-1964) British					
oil	8	81,248	4,710	8,420	22,200
HAMILTON, Mary Riter (1873-1954) Canadian					
oil	2	4,194	1,510	2,097	2,684
HAMILTON, Philipp Ferdinand de (1664-1750) Flemish					
oil	2	84,812	4,812	42,406	80,000

Name	No.	Total Sales Value	lowest	Prices median	highest
HAMILTON, Richard (1922-) British					
wc/d	2	5,280	2,000	2,640	3,280
HAMILTON, Richard and ROTH, Dieter (20th C) British/German					
wc/d	1	11,546		11,546	
HAMILTON, Vereker (fl.1886-1914) British					
oil	1	7,975		7,975	
HAMILTON-RENWICK, Lionel (1919-) British					
oil	2	2,276	1,029	1,138	1,247
HAMLET-GRIFFITS, Charles (1848-?) French					
oil	1	2,800		2,800	
HAMMAN (?) ?					
oil	1	2,600		2,600	
HAMMAN, Edouard-Michel-Ferdinand (1850-?) French					
oil	1	2,140		2,140	
HAMME, Alexis van (1818-1875) Belgian					
oil	8	136,726	1,594	18,414	33,946
HAMME, Peter van (1880-1936) German					
oil	1	1,788		1,788	
HAMMEE, Antoine van (1836-1903) Flemish					
oil	2	4,410	1,092	2,205	3,318
HAMMER, William (1821-1889) German					
oil	1	2,316		2,316	
HAMMERSHOI, Svend (1873-1948) Danish					
oil	3	4,735	1,162	1,668	1,905
HAMMERSHOI, Vilhelm (1864-1916) Danish					
oil	5	189,887	2,621	18,562	100,725
wc/d	1	1,110		1,110	
HAMMERSTAD, John Olsen (1842-1925) American					
oil	1	1,400		1,400	
HAMMITT, Clawson S (1857-1927) American					
oil	2	4,000	1,600	2,000	2,400
HAMMOND, Arthur Henry Knighton (1875-1970) British					
oil	2	3,241	1,141	1,621	2,100
wc/d	6	7,661	1,036	1,240	1,800
HAMMOND, John A (1843-1939) Canadian					
oil	8	15,344	1,235	1,632	3,264
HAMMOND, Miss Gertrude Demain (1862-1953) British					
wc/d	1	1,036		1,036	
HAMMOND, R J (fl.1882-1911) British					
oil	3	9,174	1,208	3,700	4,266
HAMMOND, Robert John (fl.1882-1911) British					
oil	4	9,586	1,276	2,125	4,060
HAMPE, Ernest Wilhelm (1806-1862) German					
oil	1	1,300		1,300	
HAMPE, Guido (1839-1902) German					
oil	3	5,698	1,226	2,000	2,472
HAMPEL, Charlotte (1863-?) Austrian					
oil	1	6,826		6,826	
HAMPEL, Sigmund Walter (1868-1949) Austrian					
oil	1	3,800		3,800	
HAMSLEY, W (19th C) ?					
oil	1	1,151		1,151	
HAMZA, Hans (1879-1945) Austrian					
oil	1	6,500		6,500	
HAMZA, Johann (1850-1927) German					
oil	3	75,651	6,364	19,937	49,350
HAN DYNASTY Chinese					
3D	1	16,000		16,000	

Name	No.	Total Sales Value	Prices lowest	median	highest
HANAN, A (20th C) American					
oil	1	2,800		2,800	
HANBRIDGE, J E (19/20th C) British					
oil	1	5,500		5,500	
HANCOCK, Charles (1795-1868) British					
oil	4	15,690	1,152	2,739	9,060
HAND, Thomas (?-1804) British					
oil	1	1,501		1,501	
HANDACHER, V (19th C) German					
oil	1	3,778		3,778	
HANDLER, Richard (1932-) Austrian					
oil	5	11,078	1,079	1,818	4,200
HANDLOW, Frank (?) ?					
oil	1	11,000		11,000	
HANEL, Georg (1879-?) German					
oil	2	7,127	2,904	3,564	4,223
HANFIELD, C (?) British?					
wc/d	1	1,467		1,467	
HANFSTANGL, Ernst (1840-1897) German					
oil	3	5,666	1,594	1,717	2,355
HANFT, Willy (1888-?) German					
oil	1	1,190		1,190	
HANGEN, Heijo (1927-) German					
oil	1	1,107		1,107	
HANGER, Max (1874-1955) German					
oil	6	7,870	1,000	1,213	1,816
HANGK, Gustav von (1804-1861) ?					
oil	1	6,297		6,297	
HANICOTTE, Augustin (1870-1957) French					
oil	1	2,854		2,854	
HANKA, Carl Apati (19th C) ?					
oil	2	9,329	3,498	4,665	5,831
HANNAUX, Emmanuel (1855-1934) French					
3D	4	34,277	1,912	7,183	18,000
HANNEY, Clifford (1890-1990) British					
oil	1	12,720		12,720	
HANNIS, W (19th C) American					
oil	1	4,000		4,000	
HANNO, Fritz (19th C) German					
oil	1	1,424		1,424	
HANNOCK, Stephen (20th C) American?					
oil	1	6,490		6,490	
HANRIOT, Jules-Armand (1853-1877) French					
oil	1	4,527		4,527	
HANS, Josefus Gerardus (1826-1891) Dutch					
oil	4	21,730	1,132	4,555	11,489
HANSCH, Anton (1813-1876) Austrian					
oil	2	7,389	3,489	3,695	3,900
HANSEN, Adolf Heinrich (1859-1925) Danish					
oil	1	1,118		1,118	
HANSEN, Armin Carl (1886-1957) American					
oil	4	26,465	1,215	4,625	16,000
wc/d	1	8,000		8,000	
HANSEN, Constantin (1804-1880) Danish					
oil	2	4,565	1,077	2,283	3,488
wc/d	1	7,244		7,244	
HANSEN, Gaylen (1921-) American					
oil	1	3,000		3,000	

Name	No.	Total Sales Value	Prices lowest	median	highest
HANSEN, Hans (1874-1948) Danish					
oil	1	1,193		1,193	
HANSEN, Harald (1890-1967) Danish					
oil	3	3,616	1,040	1,191	1,385
HANSEN, Heinrich (1821-1890) Danish					
oil	8	32,015	1,566	2,968	9,861
HANSEN, Henrik Asor (1862-1929) Norwegian					
oil	2	8,576	3,694	4,288	4,882
HANSEN, Herman Wendelborg (1854-1924) American					
wc/d	2	17,500	5,500	8,750	12,000
HANSEN, J T (1848-1912) Danish					
oil	1	1,430		1,430	
wc/d	1	1,013		1,013	
HANSEN, Jakob (20th C) Danish					
oil	1	1,276		1,276	
HANSEN, Johannes (1903-) Danish					
3D	1	10,947		10,947	
HANSEN, Jorgen Teik (1947-) Danish					
oil	1	1,226		1,226	
HANSEN, Josef Theodor (1848-1912) Danish					
oil	5	45,168	1,399	6,429	26,790
HANSEN, Niels Christian (1834-1922) Danish					
oil	3	22,697	2,169	4,528	16,000
HANSEN, Peter (1868-1928) Danish					
oil	5	10,608	1,790	2,026	2,740
HANSEN, Sigvard (1859-1938) Danish					
oil	5	10,568	1,013	1,489	4,832
HANSON, Rolf (1953-) Swedish					
oil	4	21,155	2,211	4,066	10,812
HANSTEEN, Nils (1855-1912) Norwegian					
oil	2	7,299	2,784	3,650	4,515
HANTAI (1922-) French					
oil	1	19,791		19,791	
HANTAI, Simon (1922-) French					
oil	11	531,492	5,582	35,646	105,614
HAPASKA, Siobhan (1963-) British?					
3D	1	5,800		5,800	
HAQUETTE, Georges Jean Marie (1854-1906) French					
oil	2	5,401	1,901	2,701	3,500
wc/d	1	1,000		1,000	
HARD, R (19th C) British					
oil	1	4,290		4,290	
HARDER, Hans Georg (1792-1873) Danish					
oil	1	1,016		1,016	
HARDERS, Johannes (1871-1950) German					
oil	1	2,875		2,875	
HARDIE, Charles Martin (1858-1916) British					
oil	4	12,036	1,524	3,212	4,088
HARDING, Charles T (19th C) British					
oil	1	4,576		4,576	
HARDING, Chester (1792-1866) American					
oil	1	2,342		2,342	
HARDING, Edward J (1804-1870) Irish					
wc/d	1	3,848		3,848	
HARDING, George Perfect (1780-1853) British					
oil	1	1,077		1,077	
HARDING, James Duffield (1798-1863) British					
oil	2	8,596	2,556	4,298	6,040
wc/d	4	5,714	1,185	1,238	2,054

Name	No.	Total Sales Value	lowest	Prices median	highest
HARDING, Samuel A (20th C) British					
wc/d	1	4,004		4,004	
HARDORFF, Herman Rudolf (1816-1907) German					
oil	1	2,718		2,718	
HARDRICK, John W (1891-1968) American					
oil	6	13,900	1,000	1,850	5,000
HARDS, Charles G (fl.1883-1891) British					
oil	1	5,655		5,655	
HARDWICK, Melbourne H (1857-1916) American					
oil	1	20,000		20,000	
HARDY, Anna Eliza (1839-1934) American					
oil	1	1,500		1,500	
HARDY, Cyril (19th C) British					
oil	1	1,222		1,222	
HARDY, David (fl.1855-1870) British					
oil	2	4,593	2,175	2,297	2,418
HARDY, Dorofield (fl.1882-1920) British					
oil	3	6,627	1,974	2,115	2,538
HARDY, Dudley (1865-1922) British					
oil	1	1,113		1,113	
wc/d	3	4,462	1,187	1,187	2,067
HARDY, Frederick Daniel (1826-1911) British					
oil	6	85,295	1,727	6,464	45,760
wc/d	1	1,216		1,216	
HARDY, Heywood (1843-1933) British					
oil	15	506,856	1,208	21,140	71,500
HARDY, James (jnr) (1832-1889) British					
oil	4	229,720	24,820	46,950	111,000
wc/d	2	5,119	1,115	2,560	4,004
HARDY, James (snr) (1801-1879) British					
oil	1	4,640		4,640	
HARDY, Janes (20th C) British					
oil	1	1,034		1,034	
HARDY, M Dorothy (19/20th C) British					
wc/d	1	1,817		1,817	
HARDY, Nina (fl.1890-1929) British					
oil	1	7,110		7,110	
HARDY, Norman H (c.1864-1914) British					
wc/d	1	3,354		3,354	
HARDY, Thomas Bush (1842-1897) British					
oil	1	12,768		12,768	
wc/d	75	230,940	1,022	2,288	15,730
HARE, John Knowles (1882-1947) American					
oil	1	1,400		1,400	
HARE, Julius (1859-1932) British					
oil	1	2,925		2,925	
HARE, St George (1857-1933) British					
oil	2	32,020	10,570	16,010	21,450
HARGENS, Charles (1893-) American					
oil	1	1,050		1,050	
HARGITT, Edward (1835-1895) British					
oil	3	6,370	1,200	1,470	3,700
wc/d	1	1,716		1,716	
HARING, Keith (1958-1990) American					
3D	5	201,180	1,180	12,000	90,000
oil	13	796,249	6,249	40,000	210,000
wc/d	21	338,399	1,079	9,583	65,000
HARING, Keith and LA2 (20th C) American					
3D	1	42,000		42,000	
wc/d	1	11,345		11,345	

Name	No.	Total Sales Value	Prices lowest	median	highest
HARITONOFF, Nicholas B (1880-1944) American					
oil	1	4,000		4,000	
HARKE, Evelyn (fl.1899-1914) British					
oil	1	2,256		2,256	
HARLAMOFF, Alexis (1842-1915) Russian					
oil	4	120,688	2,088	16,640	85,320
HARLES, Victor Joseph (1894-1975) American					
oil	1	1,000		1,000	
HARLOW, George Henry (1787-1819) British					
oil	3	25,754	5,134	6,320	14,300
wc/d	1	5,250		5,250	
HARMAN, Jean C (1897-?) American					
oil	2	3,800	1,400	1,900	2,400
HARMAR, Fairlie (1876-1945) British					
oil	1	1,125		1,125	
HARMER, Alexander F (1856-1925) American					
wc/d	1	14,000		14,000	
HARMER, Fairlie (?) British?					
oil	1	3,000		3,000	
HAROUARD, Emile A (19th C) French					
oil	1	1,817		1,817	
HARPER, Henry Andrew (1835-1900) British					
wc/d	1	3,816		3,816	
HARPER, William St John (1851-1910) American					
oil	2	17,500	8,000	8,750	9,500
HARPIGNIES, Henri (1819-1916) French					
oil	25	295,678	1,086	3,785	140,000
wc/d	22	44,672	1,003	1,845	5,004
HARPLEY, Sydney (1927-) British					
3D	1	1,080		1,080	
HARRADEN, Richard Bankes (1778-1862) British					
oil	2	85,930	10,010	42,965	75,920
HARRINGTON, Charles (?-1943) British					
wc/d	2	4,898	1,106	2,449	3,792
HARRINGTON, J O (19th C) American					
oil	2	4,400	1,500	2,200	2,900
HARRIS, C Gordon (1891-) American					
oil	1	1,200		1,200	
HARRIS, Edwin (1855-1906) British					
oil	7	68,823	2,844	8,250	16,920
HARRIS, F H Howard (fl.1882-1901) British					
wc/d	1	1,870		1,870	
HARRIS, George Walter (fl.1864-1893) British					
oil	1	2,031		2,031	
HARRIS, H (19th C) British					
oil	1	2,500		2,500	
HARRIS, Henry (1852-1926) British					
oil	2	3,235	1,015	1,618	2,220
HARRIS, Lawren Phillips (1910-) Canadian					
oil	3	359,889	4,158	7,300	348,431
HARRIS, Lawren Stewart (1885-1970) Canadian					
oil	22	417,311	2,762	5,435	67,162
HARRIS, Martin Hayward (1959-) British					
3D	2	17,520	5,680	8,760	11,840
HARRIS, Robert (1849-1919) Canadian					
oil	9	15,950	1,007	1,439	3,198
HARRIS, Sam Hyde (1889-1977) American					
oil	15	61,600	2,500	4,000	6,000

Name	No.	Total Sales Value	lowest	Prices median	highest
HARRIS, William E (1856-1929) British					
oil	1	1,296		1,296	
HARRISON (?) ?					
oil	1	3,565		3,565	
HARRISON, Birge (1854-1929) American					
oil	2	41,750	4,250	20,875	37,500
HARRISON, Charles Harmony (1842-1902) British					
wc/d	6	11,189	1,029	1,446	4,134
HARRISON, Clifford (20th C) British					
oil	1	3,700		3,700	
HARRISON, F C (20th C) British					
oil	1	1,580		1,580	
HARRISON, Gerald E (20th C) British?					
oil	1	1,278		1,278	
HARRISON, John Cyril (1898-1985) British					
wc/d	8	16,168	1,001	1,678	3,504
HARRISON, Ted (1926-) Canadian					
oil	1	1,327		1,327	
HARRISON, Thomas Alexander (1853-1930) American					
oil	2	10,390	4,390	5,195	6,000
HARROWING, Walter (fl.1877-1904) British					
oil	2	5,095	1,773	2,548	3,322
HARSING, Wilhelm (1861-?) German					
oil	1	1,385		1,385	
HART, Frederick (20th C) American					
3D	6	21,600	3,000	3,200	4,800
HART, George Overbury (1868-1933) American					
wc/d	1	2,500		2,500	
HART, James MacDougal (1828-1901) American					
oil	11	92,403	1,700	6,000	20,000
HART, Salomon Alexander (1806-1881) British					
oil	1	42,920		42,920	
HART, T G J (20th C) British					
oil	1	1,073		1,073	
HART, Thomas Gray (1797-1881) British					
wc/d	2	3,950	1,343	1,975	2,607
HART, William MacDougal (1823-1894) American					
oil	7	31,250	1,100	4,250	7,500
wc/d	1	1,500		1,500	
HARTA, Felix Albrecht (1884-1970) Hungarian/Austrian					
oil	1	4,356		4,356	
HARTENKAMPF, Gottlieb Theodor Kempf von (1871-1964) Austrian					
oil	1	3,388		3,388	
HARTIG, Carl Christoph (1888-?) Swiss					
oil	3	97,950	2,175	2,175	93,600
HARTIG, Hans (1873-?) German					
oil	1	1,644		1,644	
HARTIGAN, Grace (1922-) American					
oil	1	2,200		2,200	
HARTING, Lloyd (1901-1976) American					
oil	1	4,250		4,250	
wc/d	1	1,100		1,100	
HARTINGER, Anton (1806-1890) Austrian					
wc/d	1	1,486		1,486	
HARTLAND, Henry Albert (1840-1893) Irish					
oil	1	4,396		4,396	
HARTLEY, Alex (1963-) British					
3D	1	4,060		4,060	

Name	No.	Total Sales Value	lowest	Prices median	highest
HARTLEY, Marsden (1877-1943) American					
oil	5	2,525,000	40,000	80,000	2,000,000
wc/d	3	95,300	2,800	37,500	55,000
HARTMANN, Erich (1886-?) German					
oil	3	11,374	2,396	3,706	5,272
HARTMANN, F (?) ?					
oil	1	4,245		4,245	
HARTMANN, Johann Jacob (1680-1730) Czechoslovakian					
oil	1	28,282		28,282	
HARTMANN, L (1835-1902) German					
oil	1	1,452		1,452	
HARTMANN, Ludwig (1835-1902) German					
oil	1	2,105		2,105	
HARTMANN, Werner (1903-1981) Swiss					
3D	1	1,783		1,783	
oil	3	4,254	1,094	1,215	1,945
wc/d	1	1,226		1,226	
HARTRATH, Lucie (1868-1962) American					
oil	2	36,000	16,000	18,000	20,000
HARTSON, Walter C (1866-?) British					
oil	1	1,500		1,500	
HARTUNG, H (?) ?					
oil	1	3,208		3,208	
HARTUNG, Hans (1904-1989) French/German					
oil	25	880,156	1,594	25,670	202,507
wc/d	28	267,878	1,382	8,250	34,180
HARTUNG, Heinrich (1851-1919) German					
oil	1	7,820		7,820	
HARTUNG, Johann (19th C) German					
oil	1	1,463		1,463	
HARTUNG, Karl (1908-1967) German					
3D	2	11,560	1,820	5,780	9,740
HARTWICH, Emil Hermann (1801-1879) German					
oil	1	9,323		9,323	
HARTWICH, Herman (1853-1926) American					
oil	2	5,719	2,469	2,860	3,250
HARTWIG, Heinie (1937-) American					
oil	2	2,200	1,100	1,100	1,100
HARTZ, Lauritz (1903-1987) Danish					
oil	2	2,497	1,105	1,249	1,392
HARTZ, Louis (1869-1935) Dutch					
oil	1	1,171		1,171	
HARVEY, Eli (1860-1957) American					
3D	3	14,500	3,000	3,500	8,000
HARVEY, G (20th C) American					
oil	1	4,200		4,200	
HARVEY, George Wainwright (1855-1930) American					
oil	1	3,700		3,700	
HARVEY, Harold (1874-1941) British					
oil	9	184,800	2,220	13,500	63,420
wc/d	1	1,846		1,846	
HARVEY, Marion Roger Hamilton (1886-1971) British					
wc/d	2	2,859	1,342	1,430	1,517
HARVEY, Nelly (19/20th C) British					
oil	1	1,137		1,137	
wc/d	1	1,491		1,491	
HARVEY, Paul (1878-1948) American					
oil	1	6,500		6,500	
HARVEY, R (?) ?					
oil	1	2,831		2,831	

Name	No.	Total Sales Value	Prices lowest	median	highest
HARVEY, Seymour Garstin (fl.1896-1906) British					
oil	1	9,060		9,060	
HARWOOD, John (fl.1818-1829) British					
oil	1	32,970		32,970	
HASCH, Carl (1834-1897) Austrian					
oil	6	21,430	1,981	3,452	6,000
HASELEER, Frans (1804-1890) Belgian					
oil	1	14,220		14,220	
HASELTINE, Herbert (1877-1962) American					
3D	1	16,000		16,000	
HASELTINE, William Stanley (1835-1900) American					
oil	4	159,500	3,000	18,250	120,000
HASEMANN, Wilhelm Gustav Friederich (1850-1913) German					
oil	1	11,131		11,131	
HASENCLEVER, Johann Peter (1810-1853) German					
oil	1	17,445		17,445	
wc/d	1	1,458		1,458	
HASENPFLUG, Carl George Adolph (1802-1858) German					
oil	3	25,641	1,259	4,486	19,896
HASKEW, Danny (?) American?					
3D	1	3,000		3,000	
HASLUND, Otto (1842-1917) Danish					
oil	2	6,424	1,420	3,212	5,004
HASS, Sigfred (1848-1908) Danish/German					
oil	2	8,942	3,400	4,471	5,542
HASSALL, John (1868-1948) British					
wc/d	1	1,988		1,988	
HASSAM, Childe (1859-1935) American					
oil	13	4,865,000	40,000	210,000	1,400,000
wc/d	6	399,000	18,000	43,500	140,000
HASSE, Ernst (1819-1860) German					
oil	1	1,274		1,274	
HASSELBERG, Per (1850-1894) Swedish					
3D	1	1,872		1,872	
HASSELGREN, Gustaf Erik (1781-1827) Swedish					
oil	1	3,721		3,721	
HASSELHORST, Johann Heinrich (1825-1904) German					
oil	1	1,486		1,486	
HASSELQUIST, Thekla (1850-?) Scandinavian					
oil	1	2,011		2,011	
HASSELT, Willem van (1882-1963) Dutch					
oil	2	2,094	1,024	1,047	1,070
HASTIE, Grace H (fl.1874-1927) British					
wc/d	2	2,612	1,222	1,306	1,390
HASTINGS, T Mitchell (20th C) American					
wc/d	1	1,200		1,200	
HASUI, Kawase (1883-1957) Japanese					
wc/d	4	8,800	1,800	2,300	2,400
HATFIELD, J A (19th C) British					
3D	1	6,227		6,227	
HATHAWAY, George M (1852-1903) American					
oil	2	3,300	1,100	1,650	2,200
HATOUM, Mona (1952-) Lebanese					
3D	2	217,580	87,580	108,790	130,000
HATTAB, Kamel (1947-) ?					
oil	1	1,185		1,185	
HATVANY, Christa Winsloe (20th C) ?					
3D	1	5,210		5,210	

Name	No.	Total Sales Value	Prices lowest	median	highest
HATZIS, Vassilios (1870-1915) Greek					
oil	2	15,330	3,650	7,665	11,680
HAUBERG, Peter Christian (1844-?) Danish					
oil	1	3,250		3,250	
HAUBTMANN, Michael (1843-1921) German/Czech					
oil	1	4,545		4,545	
HAUDEBOURT-LESCOT, Antoinette (1784-1845) French					
oil	2	26,713	7,713	13,357	19,000
HAUEISEN, Albert (1872-1954) German					
oil	5	17,136	1,560	3,489	5,483
HAUG, Kristian (1862-1953) Norwegian					
oil	2	4,106	1,164	2,053	2,942
HAUG, Robert von (1857-1922) German					
oil	3	4,603	1,238	1,500	1,865
HAUGEN-SORENSEN, Arne (1932-) Danish					
oil	5	25,402	1,614	4,472	9,609
HAUGHTON, Moses (jnr) (c.1772-1848) British					
oil	1	2,860		2,860	
HAUPT, Karl Hermann (20th C) German					
wc/d	1	7,282		7,282	
HAUPTMANN, Ivo (1886-1973) German					
oil	2	9,115	1,591	4,558	7,524
wc/d	3	4,097	1,324	1,324	1,414
HAUPTMANN, Karl (1880-1947) German					
oil	6	27,860	2,578	4,928	6,373
HAUSCHILD, Max (1810-1895) German					
oil	1	2,469		2,469	
HAUSCHILD, Wilhelm (1827-?) German					
wc/d	1	1,164		1,164	
HAUSDORF, Georg (20th C) German					
oil	1	3,000		3,000	
HAUSEN, Werning (?) German?					
3D	1	1,059		1,059	
HAUSER, John (1859-1913) American					
oil	1	7,500		7,500	
wc/d	1	15,000		15,000	
HAUSHOFER, Alfred (1872-1943) German					
wc/d	3	10,949	2,179	3,147	5,623
HAUSHOFER, Maximilian (1811-1866) Austrian					
oil	1	26,619		26,619	
HAUSMANN, Gustav (1827-1899) German					
oil	1	1,257		1,257	
HAUSMANN, Heinz (1959-) German					
wc/d	1	1,427		1,427	
HAUSMANN, Wilhelm (1906-1980) German					
3D	1	1,463		1,463	
oil	1	3,028		3,028	
HAUSNER, Xenia (1951-) Austrian					
oil	1	17,423		17,423	
HAUSSER, Johann (16/17th C) German					
oil	1	12,000		12,000	
HAUSSMAN, Raoul (1886-1970) German?					
wc/d	2	35,775	4,323	17,888	31,452
HAUSTRAETE, Gaston (1878-1949) Belgian					
oil	7	11,695	1,021	1,580	2,310
HAUSWIRTH, Johann Jakob (1809-1871) Swiss					
wc/d	1	16,324		16,324	
HAUTOT, Rachel (1882-?) French					
3D	1	1,289		1,289	

Name	No.	Total Sales Value	lowest	Prices median	highest
HAVARD, James (1937-) American					
oil	1	2,991		2,991	
HAVE, Henrik (20th C) Danish					
oil	1	1,059		1,059	
HAVELL, Alfred C (1855-1928) British					
oil	1	3,473		3,473	
HAVELL, Robert (jnr) (1793-1878) British					
oil	1	5,500		5,500	
HAVELL, William (1782-1857) British					
oil	3	11,762	1,287	2,610	7,865
HAVEN, Franklin de (1856-1934) American					
oil	2	3,600	1,600	1,800	2,000
HAVERKAMP, J van (1874-1954) ?					
oil	1	3,993		3,993	
HAVERKAMP, S C (20th C) Dutch					
oil	1	5,324		5,324	
HAVERMANN, Hendrik Johannes (1857-1928) Dutch					
wc/d	1	1,071		1,071	
HAVERO, Bert Hage (1923-) Swedish					
oil	3	11,955	1,073	2,340	8,542
HAVERS, Alice (1850-1890) British					
oil	2	24,228	4,228	12,114	20,000
HAVET, Henri-Charles-Julien (1862-1913) French					
oil	1	3,120		3,120	
HAVSTEEN, Theodora (19th C) Danish					
oil	1	1,508		1,508	
HAVSTEEN-MIKKELSEN, Sven (1912-1999) Danish					
oil	9	20,501	1,473	1,743	4,985
HAWKINS, Louis Welden (1849-1910) British					
oil	5	42,998	1,263	2,320	35,730
wc/d	1	2,864		2,864	
HAWKS, Rachel Marshall (1879-) American					
3D	1	10,000		10,000	
HAWKSETT, Emile (19th C) Irish					
oil	1	1,000		1,000	
HAWKSWORTH, Joseph Haslam (1827-1908) British?					
oil	1	1,170		1,170	
HAWLEY, Hughson (1850-1936) American					
wc/d	1	16,000		16,000	
HAWTHORNE, Charles W (1872-1930) American					
oil	2	210,000	40,000	105,000	170,000
wc/d	1	3,000		3,000	
HAY, Bernard (1864-?) British/Italien					
oil	6	27,706	1,368	4,149	8,030
HAY, Peter Alexander (1866-1952) British					
wc/d	1	1,500		1,500	
HAYAKAWA, Miki (1904-1953) American					
oil	1	12,000		12,000	
HAYAMI, Gyoshu (1894-1935) Japanese					
wc/d	1	75,000		75,000	
HAYDEN, Charles Henry (1856-1901) American					
oil	1	2,500		2,500	
HAYDEN, Frank (1934-1996) American					
3D	1	1,300		1,300	
HAYDEN, Henri (1883-1970) French					
oil	10	28,691	1,083	2,353	6,927
wc/d	2	4,986	1,510	2,493	3,476
HAYDON, Benjamin Robert (1786-1846) British					
oil	1	31,460		31,460	

Name	No.	Total Sales Value	lowest	Prices median	highest
HAYE, Reinier de la (1640-1684) Dutch					
oil	1	2,880		2,880	
HAYEK, Hans von (1869-1940) Austrian					
oil	1	2,255		2,255	
HAYES, C W (?) ?					
oil	1	1,413		1,413	
HAYES, Charles (19th C) British?					
oil	1	1,425		1,425	
HAYES, Claude (1852-1922) British					
oil	3	7,353	1,122	1,207	5,024
wc/d	4	4,968	1,125	1,201	1,441
HAYES, Colin (1919-) British					
oil	2	3,353	1,178	1,677	2,175
HAYES, E (19th C) British					
oil	1	5,053		5,053	
HAYES, Edwin (1820-1904) British					
oil	12	35,961	1,009	2,935	5,168
wc/d	4	6,758	1,323	1,570	2,220
HAYES, F William (1848-1918) British					
oil	2	8,816	3,266	4,408	5,550
HAYES, Frank (19th C) British					
oil	1	2,574		2,574	
HAYES, Gabriel (1909-1978) Irish					
oil	1	29,600		29,600	
HAYES, John (1786-1866) British					
oil	1	21,000		21,000	
HAYET, Louis (1854-1940) French					
oil	2	5,746	2,334	2,873	3,412
wc/d	1	2,730		2,730	
HAYLLAR, James (1829-1920) British					
wc/d	1	9,750		9,750	
HAYMAN, F (1708-1776) British					
oil	1	1,314		1,314	
HAYMAN, Francis (1708-1776) British					
oil	1	9,362		9,362	
HAYNES, Frederick (fl.1860-1880) British					
oil	1	8,816		8,816	
HAYNES, John William (fl.1852-1882) British					
oil	1	4,640		4,640	
HAYS, George Arthur (1854-?) American					
oil	1	2,000		2,000	
HAYTER, Sir George (1792-1871) British					
oil	2	5,400	1,144	2,700	4,256
HAYTER, Stanley William (1901-1988) British					
oil	3	6,166	1,000	2,508	2,658
HAYWARD, Alfred Robert (1875-1971) British					
oil	2	6,400	2,900	3,200	3,500
HAYWARD, Arthur (1889-1971) British					
oil	1	8,150		8,150	
HAYWARD, F Harold (1867-1945) American					
oil	1	1,900		1,900	
HAYWARD, H C (?) British					
oil	1	1,157		1,157	
HAZARD, Arthur Merton (1872-1930) American					
oil	1	2,000		2,000	
HAZELHUST, Ernest William (1866-1949) British					
wc/d	1	1,027		1,027	
HAZELTON, Mary Brewster (1868-1953) American					
oil	3	13,750	2,000	5,000	6,750

Name	No.	Total Sales Value	lowest	Prices median	highest
HAZELZET, D J (1889-1953) Dutch					
oil	1	2,052		2,052	
HAZLEDINE, Alfred (1876-1954) Belgian					
oil	4	8,104	1,275	1,624	3,582
HAZON DE SAINT-FIRMIN, Jane (19th C) French					
wc/d	1	4,500		4,500	
HAZON, Barthelemy Michel (1722-1822) ?					
wc/d	1	1,363		1,363	
HEAD, B G (fl.1867-1888) British					
oil	3	3,998	1,008	1,431	1,559
HEAD, Cecil (1906-) American					
oil	1	1,400		1,400	
HEAD, Guy (1753-1800) British					
oil	1	13,288		13,288	
HEADE, Martin Johnson (1819-1904) American					
oil	5	1,916,400	1,400	230,000	1,350,000
HEALY, George Peter Alexander (1813-1894) American					
wc/d	1	1,300		1,300	
HEAPHY, Thomas (1775-1835) British					
wc/d	2	3,124	1,420	1,562	1,704
HEARD, H Percy (fl.1886-1914) British					
oil	2	2,790	1,323	1,395	1,467
HEARNE, Thomas (1744-1817) British					
wc/d	1	3,792		3,792	
HEATH, Adrian (1920-1992) British					
oil	5	18,355	1,081	1,224	10,875
HEATH, Frank Gascoigne (1873-1936) British					
oil	2	9,185	1,917	4,593	7,268
HEATHCOTE, E S (19/20th C) British					
oil	1	1,138		1,138	
HEBBAR, Kattingeri Krishna (1911-1996) Indian					
oil	5	43,250	3,750	9,000	12,000
HEBENSTREIT, Ferdinand (16th C) German					
wc/d	1	2,076		2,076	
HEBERER, Charles (19th C) American					
oil	1	2,600		2,600	
HEBERT, Adrien (1890-1967) Canadian					
oil	1	1,321		1,321	
HEBERT, Antoine Auguste Ernest (1817-1908) French					
oil	1	9,000		9,000	
wc/d	1	1,164		1,164	
HEBERT, Louis Philippe (1850-?) Canadian					
3D	2	26,728	12,028	13,364	14,700
HEBUTERNE (20th C) French					
oil	1	1,326		1,326	
HEBUTERNE, Jeanne (?) ?					
oil	1	15,833		15,833	
wc/d	1	2,629		2,629	
HECHT, H van der (1841-1901) Belgian					
oil	1	1,852		1,852	
HECHT, Hendrick van der (1841-1901) Belgian					
oil	1	1,545		1,545	
HECK, Claes Dircksz van der (17th C) Dutch					
oil	1	32,970		32,970	
HECK, Claes Jacobsz van der (c.1580-1652) Dutch					
oil	1	25,440		25,440	
HECKE, Arthur van (1924-) French					
oil	2	2,406	1,178	1,203	1,228

Name	No.	Total Sales Value	lowest	Prices median	highest
HECKEL, August von (1824-1883) German					
oil	1	7,110		7,110	
HECKEL, Erich (1883-1970) German					
oil	6	1,727,294	9,401	36,586	1,584,000
wc/d	34	428,212	1,268	8,354	83,520
HECKEN, Abraham van den II (fl.1635-1655) Flemish					
oil	1	4,377		4,377	
HECKENDORF, Franz (1888-1962) German					
oil	11	49,257	1,552	4,310	11,348
wc/d	3	3,797	1,009	1,309	1,479
HECKER, Franz (1870-1944) German					
oil	2	8,985	2,051	4,493	6,934
HEDA, Willem Claesz (1594-1680) Dutch					
oil	1	705,600		705,600	
HEDLEY, Ralph (c.1851-1913) British					
oil	5	29,389	3,550	6,493	6,768
HEEL, Jan van (1898-1991) Dutch					
oil	9	30,675	1,770	2,557	9,483
wc/d	2	3,082	1,180	1,541	1,902
HEEM, Cornelis de (1631-1695) Dutch					
oil	3	413,336	94,286	150,000	169,050
HEEM, Jan Davidsz de (1606-1684) Dutch					
oil	2	194,766	3,666	97,383	191,100
HEEM, Jan Jansz de (1650-1695) Dutch					
oil	1	367,500		367,500	
HEEMSKERK, Egbert van (17/18th C) Dutch					
oil	3	10,649	3,295	3,385	3,969
HEEMSKERK, Egbert van (elder) (1610-1680) Dutch					
oil	4	63,120	7,200	12,960	30,000
wc/d	1	4,530		4,530	
HEEMSKERK, Egbert van (younger) (1634-1704) Dutch					
oil	3	11,508	1,570	4,396	5,542
HEEMSKERK, Jacob Eduard van Beest (1828-1894) Dutch					
oil	3	17,585	2,955	6,978	7,652
HEEMSKERK, Marten van (school) (17th C) Dutch					
oil	1	12,877		12,877	
HEEREMANS, Thomas (fl.1660-1697) Dutch					
oil	11	202,534	7,852	12,842	44,100
HEERFORDT, Anna Cathrine Christine (1839-1910) Danish					
oil	1	1,295		1,295	
HEERICH, Erwin (1922-) German					
3D	1	2,435		2,435	
wc/d	1	1,328		1,328	
HEERUP, Henry (1907-1993) Danish					
3D	2	11,933	2,324	5,967	9,609
oil	15	49,088	1,162	2,759	8,136
wc/d	3	4,494	1,473	1,473	1,537
HEFFNER, Karl (1849-1925) German					
oil	12	37,288	1,594	1,995	9,000
HEFFNER, Karl and PHILIPS, Hermann (19/20th C) German					
oil	1	15,000		15,000	
HEGEMANN, Martha (1894-1970) German					
wc/d	1	1,240		1,240	
HEGENAUER, Konrad (1734-1807) German					
3D	1	1,981		1,981	
HEGENBARTH, Emanuel (1868-1923) German					
oil	1	1,024		1,024	
HEGENBARTH, Josef (1884-1962) German					
oil	2	8,174	2,500	4,087	5,674
wc/d	7	15,524	1,068	1,553	6,731

Name	No.	Total Sales Value	Prices lowest	median	highest
HEGG, Teresa (fl.1872-1893) British					
wc/d	1	1,625		1,625	
HEICKE, Joseph (1811-1861) Austrian					
oil	1	5,309		5,309	
HEIDACKER, Stephanus (20th C) American					
oil	1	1,700		1,700	
HEIDI (20th C) ?					
oil	1	3,500		3,500	
HEIKHAUS, Gustave (1905-1999) Belgian					
oil	1	1,210		1,210	
HEIKKA, Earle E (1910-1941) American					
3D	2	8,000	1,500	4,000	6,500
HEIL, Charles Emile (1870-1953) American					
oil	2	3,600	1,500	1,800	2,100
HEIL, Daniel van (1604-1662) Flemish					
oil	1	8,134		8,134	
HEILBUTH, Ferdinand (1826-1889) French					
wc/d	1	4,558		4,558	
HEILIGER, Bernhard (1915-1995) German					
3D	2	14,336	5,825	7,168	8,511
HEILMAYER, Karl (1829-1908) German					
oil	4	9,800	1,554	2,101	4,044
HEIM, François Joseph (1787-1865) French					
oil	2	18,743	5,187	9,372	13,556
HEIM, Liane (1920-) Greek					
oil	1	1,115		1,115	
HEIMERDINGER, Friedrich (1817-1882) Italian/German					
oil	2	9,707	4,800	4,854	4,907
HEIMERL, Josef (19/20th C) Austrian					
oil	1	1,182		1,182	
HEIN, Eduard (19th C) German					
oil	1	1,366		1,366	
HEIN, Eduard (jnr) (?) ?					
oil	1	1,337		1,337	
HEIN, Franz (1863-?) German					
oil	1	4,076		4,076	
HEIN, Hendrik Jan (1822-1866) Dutch					
oil	1	2,206		2,206	
HEIN, Marie Vlielander (1871-1955) Dutch					
oil	1	3,077		3,077	
HEINDEL, Robert (1938-) American?					
oil	1	1,500		1,500	
HEINE, Johann Adalbert (1850-?) German					
oil	3	5,529	1,117	1,936	2,476
HEINE, Thomas Theodor (1867-1948) German					
wc/d	2	4,150	1,729	2,075	2,421
HEINE, Wilhelm Josef (1813-1839) German					
oil	1	12,107		12,107	
HEINEL, Eduard (1835-1895) German					
oil	1	2,400		2,400	
HEINEMANN, Fritz (1864-?) German					
3D	1	1,806		1,806	
HEINEMANN, Reinhardt (1895-?) ?					
oil	1	1,090		1,090	
HEINERTZ, Erik (1908-1965) Swedish					
wc/d	1	1,693		1,693	
HEINISCH, Karl Adam (1847-1923) German					
oil	5	17,836	1,238	4,091	4,903

Name	No.	Total Sales Value	lowest	Prices median	highest
HEINLEIN, Heinrich (1803-1885) German					
oil	3	8,433	1,124	1,981	5,328
HEINRICH, Franz (1802-1890) German					
wc/d	1	1,229		1,229	
HEINRICH-HANSEN, Adolf (1859-1925) Danish					
oil	1	1,511		1,511	
HEINS, John Theodore (snr) (1697-1756) British					
oil	5	24,581	2,130	4,082	8,635
HEINTZ, Johann (17th C) ?					
wc/d	1	4,369		4,369	
HEINTZ, Joseph (16/17th C) Swiss					
oil	1	32,348		32,348	
HEINTZ, Joseph (elder) (1564-1609) Swiss					
wc/d	1	55,000		55,000	
HEINTZ, Joseph (younger) (1600-1678) Swiss					
oil	2	281,724	32,000	140,862	249,724
HEINTZ, Richard (1871-1929) Belgian					
oil	8	43,820	1,437	6,126	10,647
HEINZE, Adolph (1887-?) American					
oil	2	3,900	1,300	1,950	2,600
HEIREMANS, P (?) ?					
oil	1	1,483		1,483	
HEISIG, Bernhard (1925-) Polish					
oil	1	84,118		84,118	
HEIZER, Michael (1944-) American					
3D	2	28,000	8,000	14,000	20,000
HEKELE, Leopoldine (19th C) German?					
oil	1	1,276		1,276	
HEKKING, Willem (1796-1862) Dutch					
wc/d	3	4,989	1,571	1,650	1,768
HEKKING, Willem (jnr) (1825-1904) Dutch					
oil	1	2,869		2,869	
HELAND, Marten Rudolf (1765-1814) Swedish					
wc/d	2	4,057	1,445	2,029	2,612
HELBERGER, Alfred Hermann (1871-1946) German					
oil	4	5,567	1,155	1,323	1,766
HELBIG, Walter (1878-1965) Swiss?					
oil	7	29,396	1,094	2,824	10,875
HELCK, Peter (1897-?) American					
wc/d	1	11,000		11,000	
HELD, Al (1928-) American					
oil	3	22,141	5,141	7,000	10,000
HELD, Alma M (1898-1988) American					
oil	1	1,500		1,500	
HELD, John (jnr) (1889-1958) American					
oil	1	9,500		9,500	
HELDER, Johannes (1842-1913) Dutch					
oil	2	5,770	1,510	2,885	4,260
HELDNER, Collette Pope (fl.1930-1970) American					
oil	6	16,250	1,000	2,300	5,250
wc/d	1	1,800		1,800	
HELDNER, Knute (1884-1952) American					
oil	5	26,600	1,200	4,000	10,500
HELDT, Werner (1904-1954) German					
oil	1	12,975		12,975	
wc/d	4	18,167	1,618	2,837	10,875
HELFER, Emile (20th C) Belgian?					
oil	1	1,899		1,899	

Name	No.	Total Sales Value	lowest	Prices median	highest
HELFFERICH, Frans (1871-1941) Dutch					
oil	3	15,656	1,641	2,134	11,881
HELION (1904-1987) French					
wc/d	1	1,760		1,760	
HELION, Jean (1904-1987) French					
oil	12	152,836	1,594	5,193	85,551
wc/d	39	127,613	1,009	3,055	8,872
HELL, Johan van (1889-1952) Dutch					
oil	1	25,748		25,748	
HELL, Ter (1954-) ?					
oil	1	3,310		3,310	
HELLEMANS, Pierre (1787-1845) Belgian					
oil	3	25,443	5,720	5,720	13,840
HELLESEN, Hanne (1801-1844) Danish					
oil	3	52,980	3,881	20,700	28,399
HELLESEN, Thorwald (1888-1937) Danish					
wc/d	1	3,494		3,494	
HELLEU, Jean (1894-?) French					
oil	2	5,683	1,911	2,842	3,772
HELLEU, Paul-Cesar (1859-1927) French					
oil	3	476,339	31,139	37,500	407,700
wc/d	17	196,521	1,365	8,000	35,000
HELLGREWE, Rudolf (1860-?) German					
oil	1	1,514		1,514	
wc/d	1	1,384		1,384	
HELLWAG, Rudolf (1867-1942) German					
oil	1	1,421		1,421	
HELMBREKER, Theodor (1633-1696) Flemish					
oil	2	20,514	4,135	10,257	16,379
HELME, Helge (1894-1987) Danish					
oil	1	1,537		1,537	
HELMER, R (?) ?					
oil	1	1,160		1,160	
HELMICK, Howard (1845-1907) American					
oil	1	2,519		2,519	
HELMONT, Lucas van Gassel (c.1480-c.1570) Flemish					
oil	2	153,100	42,312	76,550	110,788
HELMONT, Matheus van (1623-1679) Flemish					
oil	3	46,425	8,112	10,813	27,500
HELST, Bartholomeus van der (1613-1670) Dutch					
oil	3	169,930	9,930	75,000	85,000
HELST, Lodewyck van der (1642-1680) Dutch					
oil	1	3,143		3,143	
HELSTED, Axel (1847-1907) Danish					
oil	2	3,521	1,549	1,761	1,972
HELU (?) French?					
oil	1	5,155		5,155	
HEM, Piet van der (1885-1961) Dutch					
oil	13	56,440	1,231	4,293	8,911
wc/d	1	7,328		7,328	
HEMCHE, Abdelhalim (1906-1979) Algerian					
oil	1	17,911		17,911	
HEMING, Arthur (1870-1940) Canadian					
oil	1	3,318		3,318	
HEMINGWAY, Charles (fl.1932-1937) British					
oil	1	1,716		1,716	
HEMKEN, Willem de Haas (1831-1911) Dutch					
wc/d	1	1,067		1,067	

Name	No.	Total Sales Value	Prices lowest	median	highest
HEMPFING, Wilhelm (1886-1951) German					
oil	1	1,184		1,184	
HEMSLEY, William (1819-1906) British					
oil	5	29,574	1,884	3,750	16,500
HEMY, Bernard Benedict (1845-1913) British					
oil	2	2,958	1,233	1,479	1,725
HEMY, Charles Napier (1841-1917) British					
oil	5	21,317	3,454	4,530	4,983
wc/d	9	41,993	1,020	3,792	9,295
HEMY, Thomas Marie (1852-1937) British					
oil	1	1,390		1,390	
HENAULT, Antoine (19th C) French?					
oil	1	2,067		2,067	
HENDERSON, Charles Cooper (1803-1877) British					
oil	6	26,192	2,282	3,925	7,536
wc/d	1	1,020		1,020	
HENDERSON, J (?) British					
oil	1	1,141		1,141	
HENDERSON, James (1871-1951) Canadian					
oil	4	11,332	2,175	2,538	4,081
HENDERSON, Joseph (1832-1908) British					
oil	5	30,905	1,103	4,232	14,500
HENDERSON, Joseph Morris (1863-1936) British					
oil	5	10,498	1,390	1,900	2,669
HENDERSON, L (?) British					
oil	1	1,043		1,043	
HENDERSON, Thomas (19th C) British					
oil	1	6,816		6,816	
HENDERSON, William (fl.1874-1892) British					
wc/d	1	1,410		1,410	
HENDERSON, William Penhallow (1877-1943) American					
wc/d	4	8,800	1,800	2,250	2,500
HENDRICH, Hermann (1856-1931) German					
oil	1	7,000		7,000	
HENDRIKS, Gerardus (19th C) Dutch					
oil	1	4,308		4,308	
HENDRIKS, Willem (1828-1891) Dutch					
oil	2	3,418	1,704	1,709	1,714
HENKES, Gerke (1844-1927) Dutch					
oil	1	1,177		1,177	
HENLEY, A C (19th C) British					
oil	1	3,900		3,900	
HENLEY, H W (19th C) British					
oil	2	2,405	1,100	1,203	1,305
HENLEY, Henry W (fl.1871-1895) British					
oil	1	1,300		1,300	
HENLEY, W B (?) ?					
oil	1	1,050		1,050	
HENNEBICQ, Andre (1836-1904) Belgian					
oil	1	1,093		1,093	
HENNER, Jean Jacques (1829-1905) French					
oil	9	69,374	1,595	5,133	26,000
HENNESSEY, Frank Charles (1893-1941) Canadian					
oil	1	1,128		1,128	
wc/d	1	1,336		1,336	
HENNESSY, Patrick (1915-1980) Irish					
oil	1	7,500		7,500	
HENNESSY, William John (1839-1917) British					
oil	3	21,281	3,800	7,481	10,000

Name	No.	Total Sales Value	lowest	Prices median	highest
HENNIG, Albert (1907-) German					
wc/d	1	1,065		1,065	
HENNING, Amanda (19th C) Swedish?					
oil	1	1,247		1,247	
HENNING, Gerhard (1880-1967) Swedish					
3D	5	47,879	2,789	11,542	17,568
HENNINGER, Manfred (1894-1986) German					
oil	8	36,246	1,749	4,713	7,597
wc/d	4	8,131	1,117	1,371	4,273
HENNINGS, Ernest Martin (1886-1956) American					
oil	12	1,389,000	6,000	50,000	460,000
HENNINGS, Johann Friedrich (1838-1899) German					
oil	1	26,860		26,860	
HENNINGSEN, Erik (1855-1930) Danish					
oil	2	7,929	3,526	3,965	4,403
HENNINGSEN, Frants (1850-1908) Danish					
oil	2	2,177	1,072	1,089	1,105
HENNO, Louis (1907-1990) Belgian					
oil	2	3,104	1,278	1,552	1,826
HENRI, Robert (1865-1929) American					
oil	4	196,000	10,000	35,500	115,000
wc/d	3	6,700	1,100	1,600	4,000
HENRICHSEN, Carsten (1824-1897) Danish					
oil	5	10,124	1,191	1,624	3,244
HENRICHSEN-BREMSEN, Charles (1854-1924) Danish					
oil	1	1,814		1,814	
HENRICI, John H (19/20th C) American					
oil	1	2,000		2,000	
HENRIKSEN, William (1880-1964) Danish					
oil	1	2,600		2,600	
HENRION, A (1875-?) Belgian					
oil	1	1,738		1,738	
HENRION, Armand (1875-?) Belgian					
oil	3	4,425	1,050	1,200	2,175
HENRIQUES, Marie (1866-1944) Danish					
oil	1	4,379		4,379	
HENRIQUES, Sally (1815-1886) Danish					
oil	1	1,420		1,420	
HENRY, B B (?) British?					
oil	1	1,128		1,128	
HENRY, Edward Lamson (1841-1919) American					
oil	4	143,000	25,000	38,000	42,000
wc/d	1	11,000		11,000	
HENRY, Émile (1822-1920) French					
oil	1	1,740		1,740	
HENRY, George (1859-1943) British					
oil	3	191,130	2,320	69,090	119,720
wc/d	2	12,395	5,145	6,198	7,250
HENRY, Grace (1868-1953) British					
oil	3	36,555	1,775	8,140	26,640
HENRY, Harry Raymond (1882-1974) American					
oil	4	22,250	2,250	5,750	8,500
HENRY, James Levin (1855-?) British					
oil	1	1,074		1,074	
HENRY, John (1943-) American					
3D	1	1,200		1,200	
HENRY, Maurice (1907-1984) French					
oil	1	1,571		1,571	

Name	No.	Total Sales Value	lowest	Prices median	highest
HENRY, Michel (1928-) French					
oil	2	6,296	3,046	3,148	3,250
HENRY, N (19th C) ?					
oil	1	1,090		1,090	
HENRY, Paul (1876-1958) Irish					
oil	10	890,440	26,640	57,720	251,600
HENRY, R (20th C) American					
oil	1	1,600		1,600	
HENS, Frans (1856-1928) Belgian					
oil	2	4,473	1,448	2,237	3,025
HENSALL, Henry (?) British?					
wc/d	1	1,133		1,133	
HENSEL, Maurice (1890-?) French					
oil	1	2,449		2,449	
HENSELER, Ernst (1852-1940) German					
oil	1	1,639		1,639	
HENSHALL, John Henry (1856-1928) British					
wc/d	2	5,917	1,829	2,959	4,088
HENSHAW, Frederick Henry (1807-1891) British					
oil	3	19,316	4,740	7,426	7,426
HENSING, Albert (20th C) German?					
oil	1	1,154		1,154	
HENSTENBURGH, Herman (1667-1726) Dutch					
oil	1	1,397		1,397	
wc/d	3	34,229	5,729	11,000	17,500
HENTZE, Gudmund Herman Peter (1875-1948) Danish					
wc/d	1	1,209		1,209	
HENZE, Ingfried (1925-) German					
oil	1	4,650		4,650	
HENZELL, Isaac (1815-1876) British					
oil	1	4,719		4,719	
HEPPENER, Johannes Jacobus (1826-1898) Dutch					
oil	1	1,717		1,717	
HEPPLE, John Wilson and STICKS, George Blackie (19/20th C) British					
oil	1	2,041		2,041	
HEPPLE, Robert Norman (1908-1994) British					
oil	4	5,791	1,088	1,302	2,100
HEPPLE, Wilson (1854-1937) British					
oil	4	8,899	1,065	1,547	4,740
wc/d	2	4,251	2,039	2,126	2,212
HEPWORTH, Dame Barbara (1903-1975) British					
3D	6	690,070	29,610	37,500	420,000
oil	2	55,700	25,500	27,850	30,200
HERALD, James Watterson (1859-1914) British					
oil	1	15,950		15,950	
wc/d	5	15,488	2,465	2,793	4,263
HERBERT, A (19th C) ?					
oil	1	1,500		1,500	
wc/d	1	1,589		1,589	
HERBERT, Albert (19th C) British					
wc/d	1	3,300		3,300	
HERBERT, Alfred (?-1861) British					
wc/d	2	5,051	2,117	2,526	2,934
HERBERT, John Rogers (1810-1890) British					
oil	2	33,590	8,030	16,795	25,560
HERBERT, Sidney (1854-1914) British					
oil	1	2,315		2,315	
HERBERT, Wilfred V (fl.1863-1891) British					
oil	2	6,246	1,716	3,123	4,530

Name	No.	Total Sales Value	Prices lowest	median	highest
HERBERTE, Edward Benjamin (fl.1860-1893) British					
oil	4	18,915	2,600	5,298	6,520
HERBIG, Otto (1889-1971) German					
wc/d	2	2,272	1,010	1,136	1,262
HERBIN, Auguste (1882-1960) French					
oil	15	496,665	2,949	36,163	65,000
wc/d	13	99,657	1,365	7,257	12,674
HERBO, Fernand (1905-1995) French					
oil	5	10,142	1,197	2,342	2,552
wc/d	7	14,043	1,037	1,211	6,911
HERBO, Léon (1850-1907) Belgian					
oil	5	12,915	1,093	3,085	4,030
HERBOSCH, Léon (?) Belgian?					
oil	1	1,149		1,149	
HERBST, Adolf (1909-1983) Swiss					
oil	16	53,246	1,323	3,006	7,104
wc/d	1	1,003		1,003	
HERBST, Rene (1891-1982) French					
wc/d	1	1,092		1,092	
HERBST, Thomas (1848-1915) German					
oil	10	49,892	2,145	4,313	10,965
HERDIES, Oliver (1906-1994) ?					
oil	1	2,511		2,511	
HERDMAN, Robert (1828-1888) British					
wc/d	1	2,610		2,610	
HERGE (1907-1983) Belgian					
wc/d	4	54,604	2,062	7,583	37,377
HERING, G E (1805-1879) British					
oil	1	1,097		1,097	
HERING, Georg Wilhelm Richard (1884-1936) Dutch					
oil	2	3,752	1,589	1,876	2,163
HERING, George Edwards (1805-1879) British					
oil	3	16,420	2,058	5,000	9,362
HERINK, F (19th C) Belgian					
oil	1	3,500		3,500	
HERKELMAN (?) ?					
oil	1	1,573		1,573	
HERKENRATH, Peter (1900-1992) German					
oil	2	9,298	3,985	4,649	5,313
HERKOMER, H (19/20th C) ?					
wc/d	1	1,580		1,580	
HERKOMER, Hubert von (1849-1914) British					
oil	2	8,908	4,108	4,454	4,800
HERLE, F van (19th C) ?					
oil	1	2,355		2,355	
HERMAN, Hermine (1857-?) Austrian					
oil	1	2,556		2,556	
HERMAN, Josef (1911-1999) British					
oil	9	65,887	2,416	6,345	12,690
wc/d	7	8,757	1,050	1,208	1,896
HERMANJAT, Abraham (1862-1932) Swiss					
oil	3	8,050	1,166	1,719	5,165
HERMANN, Hans (1813-1890) German					
oil	2	15,470	4,862	7,735	10,608
HERMANN, Leo (19th C) French					
oil	2	6,441	2,175	3,221	4,266
HERMANN, Ludwig (1812-1881) German					
oil	8	62,437	2,596	5,721	21,980

Name	No.	Total Sales Value	lowest	Prices median	highest
HERMANNS, Ernst (1914-) German					
3D	1	3,763		3,763	
HERMANNS, Heinrich (1862-1942) German					
oil	9	40,964	1,462	4,245	11,766
HERMANS, Charles (1839-1924) Belgian					
oil	1	3,703		3,703	
HERMANSEN, O A (1849-1897) Danish					
oil	1	1,192		1,192	
HERMANSEN, Olaf August (1849-1897) Danish					
oil	2	7,998	1,998	3,999	6,000
HERMANUS, Paul (1859-1911) Belgian					
oil	1	2,427		2,427	
HERMELIN, Olof (1827-1913) Swedish					
oil	17	35,578	1,015	1,785	4,380
HERMES, Erich (1881-1971) Swiss					
oil	1	1,196		1,196	
HERMES, Gertrude (1901-1983) British					
3D	1	10,875		10,875	
HERNANDEZ COP, Francisco (1944-) Spanish					
oil	1	1,307		1,307	
HERNANDEZ MOMPO, Manuel (1927-1992) Spanish					
oil	5	41,167	3,106	6,996	15,680
wc/d	11	41,880	2,075	3,260	7,957
HERNANDEZ MONJO, Francesc (1862-1937) Spanish					
oil	3	8,312	2,457	2,816	3,039
HERNANDEZ PIJUAN, Juan (1931-) Spanish					
oil	1	8,873		8,873	
HERNANDEZ, Charles L (19th C) ?					
oil	1	5,500		5,500	
HERNANDEZ, D (1856-1932) Peruvian					
oil	1	1,100		1,100	
HERNANDEZ, Daniel (1856-1932) Peruvian					
oil	1	19,000		19,000	
HERNANDEZ, Jose (1944-) Spanish					
oil	1	2,598		2,598	
HERNANDEZ, Manuel (1928-) Colombian					
oil	1	15,466		15,466	
HERNANDEZ, Sergio (1957-) Mexican					
oil	1	9,000		9,000	
HEROLD, Georg (20th C) American?					
oil	1	6,068		6,068	
HEROLD, Jacques (1910-1987) Rumanian					
oil	1	1,740		1,740	
wc/d	2	28,559	2,626	14,280	25,933
HERON, Jean Pierre (19th C) French					
oil	1	1,388		1,388	
HERON, Patrick (1920-1999) British					
oil	3	57,105	10,575	22,560	23,970
wc/d	1	7,830		7,830	
HERP, Willem van (16/17th C) Flemish					
oil	1	7,259		7,259	
HERP, Willem van (elder) (1614-1677) Flemish					
oil	1	50,000		50,000	
HERP, Willem van (school) (17/18th C) Flemish					
oil	1	2,662		2,662	
HERPEL, Franz (1850-?) German					
oil	1	3,641		3,641	
HERPFER, Carl (1836-1897) German					
oil	4	286,500	9,500	68,500	140,000

Name	No.	Total Sales Value	Prices lowest	median	highest
HERPIN, Léon (1841-1880) French					
oil	1	1,596		1,596	
HERREGOUTS, Maximilian (fl.1674) Flemish					
oil	2	7,469	2,355	3,735	5,114
HERRERA, Carlos Maria (1875-1914) Uruguayan					
oil	1	1,400		1,400	
HERRERA, Francisco (elder) (1576-1656) Spanish					
oil	1	21,713		21,713	
HERRFELDT (1890-1965) French					
oil	1	1,707		1,707	
HERRFELDT, Marcel René von (1890-1965) French					
oil	5	17,084	1,496	1,951	9,540
HERRICK, William Salter (fl.1852-1888) British					
oil	1	2,145		2,145	
HERRIMAN, George (1880-1944) American					
wc/d	3	22,000	6,000	8,000	8,000
HERRING, Benjamin (jnr) (1830-1871) British					
oil	2	6,396	1,896	3,198	4,500
HERRING, J F (19/20th C) British					
oil	1	1,600		1,600	
HERRING, J F (jnr) (1815-1907) British					
oil	1	1,264		1,264	
HERRING, J F (snr) (1795-1865) British					
oil	1	5,005		5,005	
HERRING, James (1796-1867) American					
oil	1	26,000		26,000	
HERRING, John Frederick (jnr) (1815-1907) British					
oil	14	120,725	1,994	9,060	16,000
HERRING, John Frederick (snr) (1795-1865) British					
oil	23	1,326,457	1,950	40,040	310,800
HERRING, John Frederick (snr) and FAED, Thomas (19th C) British					
oil	1	100,100		100,100	
HERRMANN, A (19th C) ?					
oil	1	1,115		1,115	
HERRMANN, Alexander (1814-1845) German					
oil	1	1,655		1,655	
HERRMANN, Curt (1854-1929) German					
oil	2	34,997	14,167	17,499	20,830
HERRMANN, Franz (1864-?) German					
oil	1	1,079		1,079	
HERRMANN, Hans (1858-1942) German					
oil	3	12,260	1,770	1,961	8,529
wc/d	1	1,135		1,135	
HERRMANN, Hans Christian (1891-1981) German					
oil	1	2,303		2,303	
HERRMANN, Karl (1813-1881) German					
oil	1	1,658		1,658	
HERRMANN, Willy (1895-?) German					
oil	1	1,238		1,238	
HERRMANN-ALLGAU, August (?) German					
oil	1	1,978		1,978	
HERRY, Jax (19th C) ?					
oil	1	2,373		2,373	
HERSCHEL, Otto (1871-1937) German					
oil	1	1,097		1,097	
HERSENT, Louis (1777-1860) French					
oil	3	10,509	1,752	2,205	6,552
HERSEY, Dick (20th C) American					
oil	1	8,500		8,500	

Name	No.	Total Sales Value	lowest	Prices median	highest
HERSHEY, Samuel Franklin (1904-) American					
oil	1	1,800		1,800	
HERST, Auguste-Clement (1825-?) French					
oil	1	6,000		6,000	
HERTEL, Albert (1843-1912) German					
oil	2	3,390	1,197	1,695	2,193
HERTEL, O (19/20th C) German					
3D	1	1,475		1,475	
HERTER, Albert (1871-1950) American					
oil	1	4,000		4,000	
wc/d	4	22,150	3,150	5,250	8,500
HERTERICH, Johann Caspar (1843-1905) German					
oil	1	1,961		1,961	
HERTERICH, Ludwig Ritter von (1856-1932) German					
oil	1	1,711		1,711	
HERTZ, Mogens (1909-1990) Danish					
oil	3	4,870	1,452	1,452	1,881
HERTZBERG, Axel Gustaf (1832-1878) Swedish					
oil	2	3,555	1,073	1,778	2,482
HERVE, Jacques (1905-) French					
oil	1	1,532		1,532	
HERVE, Jules R (1887-1981) French					
oil	46	138,829	1,127	2,425	10,000
HERVE-MATHE, Jules Alfred (1868-1953) French					
oil	3	5,491	1,193	1,771	2,527
HERVIER, Adolphe (1818-1879) French					
oil	2	6,886	1,886	3,443	5,000
wc/d	1	1,091		1,091	
HERVIER, Eugene (?) French					
oil	1	4,332		4,332	
HERWEGEN-MANINI, Veronica Maria (1851-1933) German					
oil	1	70,585		70,585	
HERZBERG, Robert A (1886-?) American					
oil	1	4,000		4,000	
HERZIG, Edouard (1860-1926) ?					
oil	1	2,835		2,835	
HERZIG, Heinrich (1887-1964) Swiss					
oil	6	14,475	1,789	2,156	4,025
wc/d	1	1,230		1,230	
HERZOG, August (1885-?) German					
oil	2	4,353	1,740	2,177	2,613
HERZOG, Hermann (1832-1932) American/German					
oil	22	384,550	2,755	7,500	60,000
HERZOG, Lewis (1868-?) American					
oil	2	4,200	1,200	2,100	3,000
HESS, Carl (1801-1874) Austrian					
oil	1	3,489		3,489	
HESS, Florence (1891-1974) British					
oil	1	3,266		3,266	
HESS, Hildi (1911-) Swiss					
3D	1	1,823		1,823	
HESS, Ludwig (1760-1800) Swiss					
oil	1	4,800		4,800	
HESS, Marcel (1878-1948) Belgian					
oil	1	1,500		1,500	
wc/d	1	1,185		1,185	
HESS, Sara M (1880-?) American					
oil	1	1,300		1,300	

Name	No.	Total Sales Value	Prices lowest	median	highest
HESSE, Eva (1936-1970) American					
oil	2	270,000	100,000	135,000	170,000
wc/d	4	427,680	10,000	111,340	195,000
HESSE, Henri-Joseph (1781-1849) French					
oil	1	16,048		16,048	
HESSE, Hermann (1877-1962) German					
wc/d	7	15,695	1,269	2,117	3,763
HESSELBOM, Otto (1848-1913) Swedish					
oil	4	10,361	1,978	2,484	3,415
HESSLER, Otto (1858-?) German					
oil	1	1,177		1,177	
HETREAU, Remy (1913-) French					
oil	1	1,774		1,774	
HETSCH, Philippe Friedrich von (1758-1839) German					
oil	2	25,365	10,965	12,683	14,400
HETTINGA TROMP, T G M van (1872-1962) Dutch					
oil	1	1,308		1,308	
HETZ, Carl (1828-1899) German					
oil	1	3,596		3,596	
HETZEL, George (1826-1899) American					
oil	1	2,900		2,900	
HEUBNER, Hermann (1843-1915) German					
wc/d	1	1,436		1,436	
HEUDELMANS, L (19/20th C) ?					
3D	1	2,057		2,057	
HEUSCH, Jacob de (1657-1701) Dutch					
oil	1	20,000		20,000	
HEUSCHER, Johann Jakob (1843-1901) Swiss					
wc/d	1	23,577		23,577	
HEUSER, Christian (1862-1942) German					
oil	2	6,326	1,526	3,163	4,800
HEUSSER, Heinrich (1886-1943) Swiss?					
oil	1	1,224		1,224	
HEUVEL, Theodore Bernard de (1817-1906) Flemish					
oil	3	5,487	1,115	1,400	2,972
HEUVELMANS (?) ?					
3D	1	1,283		1,283	
HEUZE, Edmond (1884-1967) French					
oil	1	1,408		1,408	
HEVETT, J H (19th C) Dutch					
oil	1	3,000		3,000	
HEWARD, Prudence (1896-1947) Canadian					
oil	2	9,793	2,852	4,897	6,941
HEWES, Horace G (19th C).?					
oil	1	1,200		1,200	
HEWETT, A W (?) British?					
oil	1	1,450		1,450	
HEWTON, Randolph Stanley (1888-1960) Canadian					
oil	1	3,038		3,038	
HEY, Paul (1867-1952) German					
oil	1	1,619		1,619	
wc/d	3	5,266	1,189	1,684	2,393
HEYBOER, Anton (1924-) Dutch					
oil	1	6,338		6,338	
wc/d	1	1,207		1,207	
HEYDE, Herman Henri op der (1813-1857) Dutch					
oil	1	6,776		6,776	
HEYDEN, J C J van der (1928-) Dutch					
oil	1	2,060		2,060	

Name	No.	Total Sales Value	lowest	Prices median	highest
HEYDEN, Jan van der (1637-1712) Dutch					
oil	1	26,000		26,000	
HEYDEN, van der (17/18th C) Dutch					
oil	1	7,536		7,536	
HEYDENDAHL, Friedrich Joseph Nicolai (1844-1906) German					
oil	5	9,170	1,162	1,306	3,415
HEYDUCK, Brigitta (?) German?					
oil	1	1,108		1,108	
HEYENBROCK, Johan Coenrad Hermann (1871-1948) Dutch					
wc/d	1	1,100		1,100	
HEYER, Arthur (1872-1931) German					
oil	5	7,259	1,000	1,292	2,400
HEYERDAHL, Hans Olaf (1857-1913) Norwegian					
oil	1	43,889		43,889	
HEYERMANS, Jean Arnould (1837-1892) Belgian					
oil	3	25,455	1,533	5,922	18,000
HEYL, Marinus (1836-1931) Dutch					
oil	1	1,697		1,697	
HEYLIGERS, Antoon François (1828-1897) Dutch					
oil	2	16,912	3,327	8,456	13,585
HEYLIGERS, Hendrik (1877-1967) Dutch					
oil	1	4,119		4,119	
HEYMANS, Adriaan Josef (1839-1921) Flemish					
oil	7	34,228	1,157	3,327	11,490
HEYN, Auguste (1837-1920) German					
oil	1	4,250		4,250	
HEYN, Karl (1834-1906) German					
oil	1	4,081		4,081	
HEYRAULT, Louis Robert (19th C) French					
oil	1	27,804		27,804	
HEYRMAN, Hugo (20th C) ?					
oil	1	3,097		3,097	
HEYSEN, Sir Hans (1877-1968) Australian					
wc/d	1	12,560		12,560	
HEYSER, Friedrich Wilhelm T (1857-1921) German					
oil	1	6,488		6,488	
HIBBARD, Aldro Thompson (1886-1972) American					
oil	14	180,006	1,656	8,625	33,000
HIBBARD, Marsh (20th C) American					
oil	1	1,100		1,100	
HIBEL, Edna (1917-) American					
oil	1	2,500		2,500	
wc/d	1	1,200		1,200	
HICKEL, Joseph (1736-1807) Austrian					
oil	2	41,590	20,795	20,795	20,795
HICKEY, Thomas (1741-1824) British					
oil	1	8,700		8,700	
HICKIN, George Arthur (19th C) British					
oil	2	5,264	1,864	2,632	3,400
wc/d	1	1,057		1,057	
HICKS, David (20th C) American					
oil	1	1,036		1,036	
HICKS, Edward (1780-1849) American					
oil	1	575,000		575,000	
HICKS, Edward (school) (1780-1849) American					
oil	1	40,000		40,000	
HICKS, George Elgar (1824-1914) British					
oil	2	548,130	19,630	274,065	528,500

Name	No.	Total Sales Value	lowest	Prices median	highest
HICKS, Thomas (1823-1890) American					
oil	1	1,500		1,500	
HIDALGO (20th C) Spanish?					
oil	1	1,125		1,125	
HIDALGO DE CAVIEDES, Hipolito (1902-) Spanish					
oil	1	1,748		1,748	
HIDDEMANN, Friedrich Peter (1829-1892) German					
oil	1	2,049		2,049	
HIDER, Frank (1861-1933) British					
oil	2	2,132	1,000	1,066	1,132
HIEN, Albert (1956-) German					
3D	2	4,674	1,214	2,337	3,460
wc/d	1	3,244		3,244	
HIERCK, Huub (1917-1970) Dutch					
oil	1	1,188		1,188	
HIERSCH-MINERBI, Joachim (1834-?) Austrian					
oil	1	1,788		1,788	
HIGASHIYAMA, Kaii (1908-1999) Japanese					
wc/d	1	160,000		160,000	
HIGGINS, Victor (1884-1949) American					
oil	1	23,000		23,000	
HIGHMORE, Joseph (1692-1780) British					
oil	3	63,160	4,290	4,290	54,340
HIGUERO, Enrique Marin (1876-?) Spanish					
wc/d	6	12,103	1,613	1,893	2,564
HILAIRE, Camille (1916-1988) French					
oil	30	146,474	1,100	4,163	17,061
wc/d	16	26,874	1,083	1,596	3,248
HILAIRE, Jean Baptiste (1753-1822) French					
oil	1	28,000		28,000	
HILBERT, Georges (1900-1982) French					
3D	1	4,214		4,214	
HILDEBRAND, Adolf von (1847-1921) German					
3D	1	3,864		3,864	
HILDEBRANDT, Eduard (1818-1869) German					
oil	4	24,135	1,006	5,117	12,896
HILDEBRANDT, Ernst (1876-?) German					
oil	1	2,670		2,670	
HILDEBRANDT, Greg and Tim (20th C) American					
oil	1	4,250		4,250	
HILDEBRANDT, Howard Logan (1872-1958) American					
oil	1	70,000		70,000	
HILDER, Richard (1813-1852) British					
oil	3	7,562	1,562	1,800	4,200
HILDER, Rowland (1905-1993) British					
wc/d	7	9,858	1,001	1,250	2,416
HILDITCH, George (1803-1857) British					
oil	1	1,967		1,967	
HILES, Bartram (1872-1927) British					
oil	1	1,113		1,113	
HILGERS, Carl (1818-1890) German					
oil	8	38,432	3,000	4,247	8,937
HILKER, Georg Christian (1807-1875) Danish					
oil	1	5,712		5,712	
HILKIER, Knud Ove (1884-1953) Danish					
oil	1	1,174		1,174	
HILL, Adrian (1897-1977) British					
oil	1	1,625		1,625	

Name	No.	Total Sales Value	lowest	Prices median	highest
HILL, Carl Frederik (1849-1911) Swedish					
oil	2	27,289	7,537	13,645	19,752
wc/d	20	67,467	1,237	3,419	6,230
HILL, Derek (1916-2000) British					
oil	3	11,023	1,223	3,140	6,660
HILL, Edward (1843-1923) American					
oil	3	71,000	3,000	34,000	34,000
HILL, Edward Rufus (1852-c.1908) American					
oil	1	1,700		1,700	
HILL, Ernest F (20th C) British					
wc/d	1	1,716		1,716	
HILL, F (fl.1885) British					
oil	1	1,590		1,590	
HILL, Howard (19th C) American					
oil	3	6,150	1,300	1,350	3,500
HILL, James John (1811-1882) British					
oil	4	32,094	2,544	7,275	15,000
wc/d	1	1,014		1,014	
HILL, James Stevens (1854-1921) British					
wc/d	1	1,200		1,200	
HILL, John Henry (1839-1922) American/British					
oil	1	6,500		6,500	
wc/d	1	53,000		53,000	
HILL, John William (1812-1879) American					
wc/d	1	13,000		13,000	
HILL, Nina (1877-1970) British					
oil	1	1,420		1,420	
HILL, Rowland Henry (1873-1952) British					
oil	4	7,889	1,238	1,665	3,322
wc/d	4	5,223	1,020	1,115	1,974
HILL, T (?) ?					
oil	1	2,000		2,000	
HILL, Thomas (1829-1908) American					
oil	14	688,500	16,000	23,750	310,000
HILL, Thomas (1852-1926) British					
oil	1	1,264		1,264	
HILL, Thomas J (19th C) American					
oil	1	1,100		1,100	
HILLEGAERT, Pauwels van (c.1596-1640) Dutch					
oil	1	41,160		41,160	
wc/d	1	2,161		2,161	
HILLENIUS, Jaap (1934-) Dutch					
oil	1	2,155		2,155	
HILLER, Heinrich (19th C) German					
oil	1	2,476		2,476	
HILLER-FOELL, Maria (1880-1943) German					
oil	2	3,024	1,073	1,512	1,951
HILLESTROM, Carl Peter (1760-1812) Swedish					
wc/d	1	1,176		1,176	
HILLESTROM, Per (1733-1816) Swedish					
oil	6	100,385	3,670	16,398	33,119
wc/d	1	1,608		1,608	
HILLEVELD, Adrianus David (1838-1869) Dutch					
oil	2	14,725	3,247	7,363	11,478
HILLFON, Curt (1943-) Swedish					
oil	1	1,037		1,037	
HILLIARD, Nicholas (1547-1619) British					
oil	1	1,285		1,285	
HILLIER, H D (19th C) British					
oil	2	7,547	2,145	3,774	5,402

Name	No.	Total Sales Value	lowest	Prices median	highest
HILLIER, Tristram (1905-1983) British					
oil	2	12,496	5,680	6,248	6,816
HILLINGFORD, Robert Alexander (1825-1904) British					
oil	10	100,959	1,287	5,739	50,560
HILLS, Anna A (1882-1930) American					
oil	7	109,300	4,500	6,500	70,000
HILLS, Laura Coombs (1859-1952) American					
wc/d	9	107,750	5,250	10,000	26,000
HILLS, Robert (1769-1844) British					
oil	1	3,021		3,021	
wc/d	3	8,470	2,212	2,826	3,432
HILSOE, Hans (20th C) Danish					
oil	1	2,453		2,453	
HILTON, John William (1904-1983) American					
oil	4	8,700	1,200	1,500	4,500
HILTON, Roger (1911-1975) British					
oil	6	51,188	2,272	7,345	20,540
wc/d	19	60,437	1,378	2,880	7,110
HILTON, Rose (1931-) British					
oil	3	7,507	1,021	1,410	5,076
HILVERDINK, Eduard Alexander (1846-1891) Dutch					
oil	3	22,359	4,591	7,500	10,268
HILVERDINK, Johannes (1813-1902) Dutch					
oil	5	11,249	1,101	1,657	4,243
HILZ, Sepp (20th C) German					
oil	2	3,988	1,551	1,994	2,437
HIND, William George Richardson (1833-1888) Canadian					
wc/d	1	1,121		1,121	
HINDS, Will (20th C) American					
oil	1	1,800		1,800	
HINE, Harry T (1845-1941) British					
wc/d	1	1,184		1,184	
HINE, Henry George (1811-1895) British					
wc/d	2	2,990	1,241	1,495	1,749
HINES, Theodore (fl.1876-1889) British					
oil	6	20,705	1,829	2,188	9,750
HINEY, Harlan (?) American					
wc/d	1	3,000		3,000	
HINKLE, Clarence Keiser (1880-1960) American					
oil	2	5,400	1,600	2,700	3,800
HINRICHSEN, Lorenz V (1865-1929) Danish					
oil	1	2,509		2,509	
HINSCH, Joachim Anton (?-1800) German					
oil	1	1,457		1,457	
HINTERMEISTER, Henry (1897-?) American					
oil	2	6,500	1,500	3,250	5,000
HINTERREITER, Hans (1902-1989) Swiss					
oil	1	1,300		1,300	
HINTZ, Julius (1805-1862) German					
oil	1	1,091		1,091	
HINTZE, Johann Heinrich (1800-1860) German					
wc/d	1	7,963		7,963	
HINTZE, L (19th C) Danish					
oil	2	4,993	2,209	2,497	2,784
HINZ, Johann Georg (1630-1688) German					
oil	2	38,932	19,293	19,466	19,639
HIPPOLYTE, Joseph Gabriel (1888-) French					
oil	1	1,730		1,730	

Name	No.	Total Sales Value	lowest	Prices median	highest
HIQUILY, Philippe (1925-) French					
3D	8	46,581	2,400	5,016	8,872
HIRAYAMA, Ikuo (1930-) Japanese					
wc/d	2	280,000	130,000	140,000	150,000
HIROMASA (19th C) Chinese					
3D	1	5,688		5,688	
HIRSCH, Joseph (1910-1981) American					
oil	1	2,000		2,000	
HIRSCH, Karl Jakob (1892-?) German					
wc/d	1	20,160		20,160	
HIRSCHBERG, Carl (1854-1923) American					
oil	1	2,010		2,010	
HIRSCHFELD, Al (1903-) American					
wc/d	1	3,500		3,500	
HIRSCHFELDER, Salomon (1832-1903) German					
oil	1	1,107		1,107	
HIRSCHIG, Anton (1877-1961) Belgian					
oil	1	1,075		1,075	
HIRSCHMANN, Johann Baptist (1770-c.1829) German					
oil	1	1,500		1,500	
HIRST, Claude Raguet (1855-1942) American					
oil	1	7,750		7,750	
HIRST, Damien (1965-) British					
3D	4	1,251,000	140,000	305,500	500,000
oil	9	1,740,315	4,800	125,000	680,000
wc/d	5	23,958	1,208	3,200	8,250
HIRT, Friedrich Wilhelm (1721-1772) German					
oil	1	8,165		8,165	
HIRT, Heinrich (19th C) German					
oil	2	42,706	15,734	21,353	26,972
HIRTH DU FRENES, Rudolf (1846-1916) German					
oil	3	4,399	1,238	1,273	1,888
HIRTH, Heinrich (1841-1902) German					
oil	1	2,972		2,972	
HIS, René Charles Edmond (1877-1960) French					
oil	8	33,144	1,058	2,430	16,000
HISLOP, Margaret Ross (1894-1972) British					
oil	1	1,930		1,930	
HITCHCOCK, D Howard (1861-1943) American					
oil	1	12,000		12,000	
HITCHCOCK, George (1850-1913) American					
oil	3	20,800	4,800	6,000	10,000
HITCHCOCK, Harold (1914-) British					
wc/d	1	1,020		1,020	
HITCHENS, Alfred (1861-?) British					
oil	1	8,640		8,640	
HITCHENS, Ivon (1893-1979) British					
oil	11	290,821	9,425	22,560	48,000
HITCHENS, John (1940-) British					
oil	2	2,700	1,050	1,350	1,650
HITORFF, Jacques Ignace (1792-1867) German					
3D	1	1,378		1,378	
HITZ, Dora (1856-?) German					
wc/d	1	2,020		2,020	
HITZLER, Franz (1946-) German					
oil	2	3,957	1,093	1,979	2,864
HJERTEN, Sigrid (1885-1948) Swedish					
oil	8	448,367	24,023	32,737	158,333
wc/d	4	27,884	3,822	5,480	13,103

Name	No.	Total Sales Value	lowest	Prices median	highest
HJORTH, Bror (1894-1968) Swedish					
3D	4	8,522	1,314	2,294	2,621
oil	1	39,310		39,310	
wc/d	1	1,180		1,180	
HJORTH-NIELSEN, Soren (1901-1983) Danish					
oil	2	3,103	1,300	1,552	1,803
HJORTZBERG, Olle (1872-1959) Swedish					
oil	20	207,801	1,345	7,691	43,454
wc/d	4	7,139	1,059	1,488	3,105
HLIDDAL, Freda Taylor (1908-) American					
oil	1	3,000		3,000	
HOBART, J (19th C) British?					
oil	1	1,859		1,859	
HOBBEMA, Meindert (1638-1709) Dutch					
oil	2	324,513	24,513	162,257	300,000
HOBBY, Jess (20th C) American					
oil	1	1,000		1,000	
HOBDELL, Roy (20th C) British					
oil	1	1,123		1,123	
HOBDEN, Frank (fl.1882-1915) British					
oil	1	7,498		7,498	
HOBERL, J (19/20th C) Austrian					
oil	1	1,961		1,961	
HOBERMAN, Nicky (1967-) South African					
oil	1	5,800		5,800	
HOBLEY, Edward George (1866-1916) British					
oil	1	2,256		2,256	
HOBSON, Cecil J (1874-1918) British					
oil	1	9,948		9,948	
HOBSON, Henry E (fl.1857-1866) British					
wc/d	1	1,670		1,670	
HOCH, Franz Xaver (1869-1916) German					
oil	1	1,136		1,136	
HOCH, Hannah (1889-1979) German					
oil	4	28,561	2,435	6,920	12,287
wc/d	8	121,142	2,422	3,914	83,520
HOCHMANN, Franz Gustav (1861-?) German					
oil	1	1,040		1,040	
HOCKELMANN, Antonius (1937-) German					
oil	1	1,165		1,165	
HOCKEN, Marion Grace (1922-1987) British					
oil	2	3,704	1,590	1,852	2,114
HOCKERT, Johan (1826-1866) Swedish					
oil	1	1,197		1,197	
HOCKNER, Rudolf (1864-1942) German					
oil	7	21,755	1,564	3,205	4,469
HOCKNEY, David (1937-) British					
oil	3	555,000	25,000	240,000	290,000
wc/d	21	1,484,351	3,975	16,000	600,000
HODDER, Albert (fl.1880-1895) British					
oil	1	1,944		1,944	
HODE, Pierre (1889-1942) French					
oil	9	42,489	1,063	2,626	15,971
HODEL, Ernst (1881-1955) Swiss					
oil	6	8,833	1,038	1,210	2,413
HODGE, Francis Edwin (1883-1949) British					
oil	1	18,000		18,000	
HODGE, Spencer (1943-) British?					
oil	1	5,396		5,396	
wc/d	1	1,184		1,184	

Name	No.	Total Sales Value	lowest	Prices median	highest
HODGE, Thomas (fl.1880-1895) British					
wc/d	1	9,928		9,928	
HODGES, Gary (1954-) British					
wc/d	9	64,027	1,027	7,810	13,320
HODGES, Jim (1957-) American					
3D	1	35,000		35,000	
wc/d	1	7,000		7,000	
HODGES, William (1744-1797) British					
oil	1	499,800		499,800	
HODGKIN, Eliot (1905-1987) British					
oil	11	228,312	2,190	15,000	62,480
HODGKIN, Howard (1932-) British					
oil	2	148,900	50,750	74,450	98,150
HODGKINS, Frances (1869-1947) New Zealander					
oil	2	67,500	28,500	33,750	39,000
HODGKINSON, Lewis (19/20th C) British?					
oil	1	1,064		1,064	
HODGSON, George (1847-1921) British					
wc/d	2	3,289	1,287	1,645	2,002
HODGSON, John Evan (1831-1895) British					
oil	1	18,000		18,000	
wc/d	1	3,552		3,552	
HODGSON, Thomas Sherlock (1924-) Canadian					
wc/d	1	1,737		1,737	
HODICKE, Karl Horst (1938-) German					
oil	3	45,264	12,294	13,939	19,031
wc/d	1	2,595		2,595	
HODIENER, Hugo (1886-c.1935) German					
oil	1	2,273		2,273	
HODLER, Ferdinand (1853-1918) Swiss					
oil	16	5,328,141	3,671	139,770	1,296,748
wc/d	17	79,501	1,105	1,730	23,577
HODSON, Samuel John (1836-1908) British					
wc/d	1	4,530		4,530	
HOEBER, Arthur (1854-1915) American					
oil	2	21,500	2,500	10,750	19,000
HOECKE, Caspar van den (?-1648) Flemish					
oil	4	93,949	10,849	20,458	42,185
HOECKE, Jan van den (1611-1651) Flemish					
oil	1	72,184		72,184	
HOEF, Abraham van der (fl.1613-1649) Dutch					
oil	1	29,545		29,545	
HOEFFLER, Adolf (1826-1898) German					
oil	4	18,230	1,564	4,844	6,978
HOEFFLER, Christine (1827-1878) German					
oil	1	1,933		1,933	
HOEHME, Gerhard (1920-1990) German					
oil	3	53,186	2,234	16,990	33,962
wc/d	4	18,392	1,341	2,701	11,650
HOEK, Hans van (1947-) Dutch					
oil	5	43,535	5,172	8,621	14,655
wc/d	3	7,923	1,981	2,377	3,565
HOEK, Rudolph (20th C) Dutch?					
oil	1	1,639		1,639	
HOELLERING, Stefanie (1955-) German					
oil	1	2,273		2,273	
HOENIGER, Paul (1865-?) German					
oil	2	13,993	3,028	6,997	10,965
HOENIGSMANN, Rela (1865-?) German					
oil	3	4,062	1,189	1,373	1,500

Name	No.	Total Sales Value	Prices lowest	median	highest
HOEPFNER, Franz (19th C) German					
oil	1	2,900		2,900	
HOERLE, Heinrich (1895-1936) German					
wc/d	5	35,519	3,320	4,649	15,049
HOESE, Jean de la (1846-1917) Belgian					
oil	1	1,296		1,296	
HOESSLIN, George von (1851-1923) Hungarian					
oil	1	2,431		2,431	
HOET, Gerard (17/18th C) Dutch					
oil	1	1,426		1,426	
HOET, Gerard (elder) (1648-1733) Dutch					
oil	2	14,074	1,994	7,037	12,080
HOETGER, Bernhard (1874-1949) German					
3D	2	17,243	6,133	8,622	11,110
wc/d	2	10,359	1,136	5,180	9,223
HOEYDONCK, Paul van (1925-) Belgian					
oil	1	1,502		1,502	
HOFELICH, Friedrich Ludwig (1842-1903) German					
oil	1	2,972		2,972	
HOFER, Heinrich (1825-1878) German					
oil	3	22,025	3,636	4,903	13,486
HOFER, Ignaz (19th C) ?					
oil	1	4,886		4,886	
HOFER, Karl (1878-1955) German					
oil	21	1,108,811	8,044	45,509	158,400
wc/d	24	125,954	1,090	2,077	59,105
HOFF, Conrad (1816-1883) German					
oil	1	3,146		3,146	
HOFF, L (?) ?					
oil	1	2,000		2,000	
HOFFBAUER, Charles (1875-1957) French					
oil	2	4,300	1,700	2,150	2,600
HOFFMAN, Frank B (1888-1958) American					
oil	4	28,500	4,000	7,250	10,000
HOFFMAN, Harry Leslie (1871-1964) American					
oil	2	3,200	1,600	1,600	1,600
HOFFMAN, Malvina (1887-1966) American					
3D	2	10,960	3,460	5,480	7,500
HOFFMANN, Anker (1904-) Danish					
3D	1	1,917		1,917	
HOFFMANN, Anton (1863-1938) German					
oil	1	2,200		2,200	
HOFFMANN, Carl Heinrich (19th C) German					
oil	1	2,206		2,206	
HOFFMANN, Eugen (20th C) ?					
3D	1	7,802		7,802	
HOFFMANN, Georg (1891-1975) German					
oil	1	1,106		1,106	
HOFFMANN, Heinrich (19th C) German					
oil	1	1,199		1,199	
HOFFMANN, Heinrich Adolf (1814-1896) German					
oil	1	2,601		2,601	
HOFFMANN, Helmut (1928-1998) Germany					
oil	1	4,000		4,000	
HOFFMANN, Josef (1831-1904) Austrian					
oil	1	3,336		3,336	
HOFFMANN, O (20th C) ?					
3D	1	4,530		4,530	

Name	No.	Total Sales Value	lowest	Prices median	highest
HOFFMANN, Oskar Adolfovitch (1851-1913) Russian					
oil	1	3,948		3,948	
HOFFMANN, Werner Ernst Albert (1881-1962) German					
oil	1	1,298		1,298	
HOFFMANN, Z B (18th C) ?					
oil	1	1,242		1,242	
HOFFMANN-FALLERSLEBEN, Franz (1855-1927) German					
oil	4	5,230	1,090	1,333	1,475
HOFFMANN-JENSEN (?) ?					
3D	1	1,288		1,288	
HOFFNAS, Ferdinand Wilhelm (1769-1850) German					
wc/d	1	1,776		1,776	
HOFKER, Willem Gerard (1902-1981) Dutch					
oil	29	88,598	1,011	2,426	9,301
wc/d	21	36,958	1,011	1,617	3,842
HOFKUNST, Alfred (1942-) Austrian					
3D	3	5,408	1,458	1,519	2,431
wc/d	1	2,127		2,127	
HOFLAND, Thomas Christopher (1777-1843) British					
oil	2	24,417	1,057	12,209	23,360
HOFMANN, Eugene Ansen (19/20th C) German					
oil	1	2,610		2,610	
HOFMANN, Hans (1880-1966) American/German					
oil	14	1,388,200	11,000	37,000	450,000
wc/d	3	18,600	1,600	7,500	9,500
HOFMANN, Ludwig von (1861-1945) German					
oil	1	1,162		1,162	
wc/d	5	16,342	1,081	1,324	11,245
HOFMANN, Otto (1907-) German?					
wc/d	1	1,298		1,298	
HOFMANN, R (19/20th C) German					
oil	1	1,105		1,105	
HOFMEISTER, Johannes (1914-1990) Danish					
oil	13	23,040	1,039	1,731	2,634
HOGAN, John (1800-1858) Irish					
3D	1	16,610		16,610	
HOGARTH, William (1697-1764) British					
oil	1	52,850		52,850	
HOGENDORPS JACOB, Adrienne Jacqueline van (1857-1920) Dutch					
oil	2	5,739	2,796	2,870	2,943
HOGER, Rudolf A (1877-1930) Austrian					
oil	1	5,544		5,544	
HOGFELDT, Robert (1894-1986) Swedish					
oil	5	9,410	1,206	1,850	2,503
wc/d	7	9,699	1,034	1,306	1,742
HOGGATT, William (1880-1961) British					
oil	7	15,773	1,404	1,573	5,134
wc/d	9	25,573	1,287	2,448	5,720
HOGLEY, Stephen E (fl.1874-1893) British					
oil	1	5,966		5,966	
HOGLUND, Eric (1932-) Swedish					
3D	1	5,441		5,441	
HOGUET, Charles (1821-1870) French					
oil	4	11,595	1,136	3,067	4,325
HOHENBERG, Rosa (19/20th C) German					
oil	1	3,000		3,000	
HOHENLEITER, Francisco (1889-1968) Spanish					
oil	1	5,058		5,058	
HOHLWEIN, Ludwig (1879-1949) German					
wc/d	1	1,065		1,065	

Name	No.	Total Sales Value	lowest	Prices median	highest
HOHNECK, Adolf (1812-1878) German					
oil	1	1,716		1,716	
HOHNSTEDT, P L (1872-1957) American					
oil	1	1,400		1,400	
HOIN, Claude (1750-1817) French					
wc/d	1	1,314		1,314	
HOKUSAI, Katsushika (1760-1849) Japanese					
oil	1	1,254		1,254	
HOLBECH, N P (1804-1889) Danish					
oil	2	3,564	1,549	1,782	2,015
HOLD, Abel (1815-1891) British					
oil	5	12,982	1,106	2,190	4,230
HOLD, Tom (19th C) British					
oil	1	1,425		1,425	
HOLDER, E H (19th C) British					
oil	1	1,264		1,264	
HOLDER, Edward Henry (fl.1864-1917) British					
oil	5	10,582	1,064	2,550	2,850
HOLDING, Edgar Thomas (1870-1952) British					
wc/d	1	1,342		1,342	
HOLDREDGE, Ransome G (1836-1899) American					
oil	5	27,600	1,800	4,500	13,000
HOLDSTOCK, Alfred Worsley (1820-1901) Canadian					
wc/d	2	2,721	1,062	1,361	1,659
HOLE, William B (1846-1917) British					
oil	1	2,512		2,512	
HOLFELD, Rudolf Kurt (1872-1945) German					
oil	1	1,254		1,254	
HOLGATE, Edwin Headley (1892-1977) Canadian					
oil	5	96,031	3,186	23,892	33,556
wc/d	1	2,112		2,112	
HOLIDAY, Gilbert (1879-1937) British					
wc/d	2	37,330	16,610	18,665	20,720
HOLIDAY, Henry (1839-1927) British					
wc/d	1	1,304		1,304	
HOLLAENDER, Alphons (1845-1923) German					
oil	1	5,110		5,110	
HOLLAIN, N F J (c.1761-?) French					
oil	1	3,596		3,596	
HOLLAMS, F M (fl.1897-1929) British					
oil	1	5,724		5,724	
HOLLAMS, F Mabel (fl.1897-1929) British					
oil	20	46,529	1,113	2,146	4,800
HOLLAND, James (1800-1870) British					
oil	11	49,089	1,216	4,200	10,500
wc/d	4	67,240	8,250	16,855	25,280
HOLLAND, John (18/19th C) British					
oil	2	10,792	3,256	5,396	7,536
HOLLAND, John (jnr) (1830-1886) British					
oil	1	1,650		1,650	
HOLLAND, Philip Sidney (1855-1891) British					
oil	1	1,896		1,896	
HOLLAND, Sebastopol Samuel (fl.1877-1911) British					
oil	1	1,988		1,988	
HOLLAND, Tom (1936-) American					
wc/d	1	2,000		2,000	
HOLLANDER, Hendrik (1823-1884) Dutch					
oil	1	2,904		2,904	

Name	No.	Total Sales Value	lowest	Prices median	highest
HOLLAR (17th C) Hungarian					
wc/d	1	3,205		3,205	
HOLLAR, Wencelaus (1606-1677) Hungarian					
wc/d	2	18,750	3,020	9,375	15,730
HOLLEGHA, Wolfgang (1929-) Austrian					
oil	1	7,597		7,597	
HOLLENBERG, Felix (1868-1946) German					
oil	3	5,860	1,570	2,019	2,271
HOLLER, Carsten (1961-) German					
3D	1	5,285		5,285	
HOLLINGSWORTH, Ruth (fl.1906-1934) British					
oil	1	1,352		1,352	
HOLLINS, John (1798-1855) British					
oil	1	2,067		2,067	
HOLLYER, Eva (fl.1889-1902) British					
oil	3	10,634	1,170	2,600	6,864
wc/d	1	1,413		1,413	
HOLLYER, W P (1834-1922) British					
oil	2	2,938	1,138	1,469	1,800
HOLM, H G F (1803-1861) Danish					
wc/d	6	10,217	1,073	1,686	2,324
HOLM, Niels Peter (1890-1963) Danish					
oil	1	1,668		1,668	
HOLM, P C and PETERSEN, L (19th C) Danish/German					
oil	1	4,652		4,652	
HOLM, Peder (1798-1875) Danish					
oil	3	3,323	1,017	1,153	1,153
HOLM, Per Daniel (1835-1903) Swedish					
oil	2	2,297	1,091	1,149	1,206
HOLM, Peter Christian (1823-1888) Danish/German					
oil	1	2,265		2,265	
HOLMAN, Francis (18th C) British					
oil	1	10,570		10,570	
HOLMBERG, A (19th C) ?					
oil	1	1,282		1,282	
HOLMENS, Gerard (1934-) Belgian					
3D	1	5,695		5,695	
HOLMES, Edward (?-1893) British					
oil	2	9,300	3,000	4,650	6,300
HOLMES, John J (20th C) British					
oil	3	7,271	2,114	2,288	2,869
HOLMES, Ralph (1876-1963) American					
oil	4	5,600	1,000	1,400	1,800
HOLMES, William H (1846-1933) American					
oil	1	2,400		2,400	
HOLMLUND, Josephina (1827-1905) Swedish					
oil	2	4,945	2,088	2,473	2,857
HOLMSTEDT, J (19/20th C) Scandinavian					
oil	2	2,305	1,033	1,153	1,272
HOLMSTRAND, Cajsa (1951-) Swedish					
oil	1	1,638		1,638	
HOLMSTROM, Tora Vega (1880-1967) Swedish					
oil	1	3,048		3,048	
HOLSOE, Carl (1863-1935) Danish					
oil	35	867,170	4,154	19,739	69,836
HOLSOE, Niels (1865-1928) Danish					
oil	2	8,049	1,549	4,025	6,500
HOLST, Johannes (1880-1965) Swedish					
oil	17	69,857	1,655	3,535	10,032

Name	No.	Total Sales Value	lowest	Prices median	highest
HOLST, Laurits (1848-1934) Danish					
oil	3	7,891	1,788	2,099	4,004
HOLSTEIN, Bent (1942-) Danish					
oil	1	1,177		1,177	
HOLSTEYN, Pieter (younger) (1614-1687) Flemish					
wc/d	1	1,284		1,284	
HOLT, E F (19th C) British					
oil	1	1,136		1,136	
HOLT, Edwin Frederick (fl.1864-1897) British					
oil	4	18,997	2,200	4,399	8,000
HOLT, Frank (1911-1987) American					
oil	1	1,500		1,500	
HOLT, Geoffrey (1882-1977) American					
oil	1	1,100		1,100	
HOLTE, Arthur Brandish (fl.1883-1894) British					
oil	1	1,757		1,757	
HOLTHAUSEN, Ludwig (1807-1890) German					
wc/d	1	1,231		1,231	
HOLTL, Josef (19th C) Austrian					
oil	1	4,046		4,046	
HOLTRUP, Jan (1917-) Dutch					
oil	6	10,264	1,021	1,416	3,343
HOLTZMAN, Fanny (1895-1980) American					
oil	1	3,021		3,021	
HOLUBITSCHKA, Hansjorg (1960-) ?					
oil	1	1,644		1,644	
HOLWECK, Oskar (1924-) German					
3D	1	1,904		1,904	
HOLWEG, Gustav (1855-1890) Austrian					
oil	1	1,490		1,490	
HOLY, Adrien (1898-1978) Swiss					
oil	2	3,800	1,468	1,900	2,332
HOLYOAKE, Rowland (fl.1880-1911) British					
oil	3	5,453	1,113	2,099	2,241
HOLYOAKE, William (1834-1894) British					
oil	3	43,016	2,370	3,146	37,500
HOLZ, Albert (1884-1954) German					
oil	1	1,472		1,472	
HOLZ, Johann Daniel (1867-1945) German					
oil	5	6,987	1,167	1,355	1,727
HOLZ, Paul (1883-1938) German					
wc/d	3	6,146	1,182	1,891	3,073
HOLZEL, Adolf (1853-1934) German					
oil	1	160,875		160,875	
wc/d	6	27,912	1,262	3,128	13,636
HOLZER, Jenny (1950-) American					
3D	8	148,968	1,284	9,142	70,000
wc/d	2	7,500	3,500	3,750	4,000
HOLZHALB, Adolf Rudolf (1835-1885) German					
oil	2	5,156	1,168	2,578	3,988
HOLZHANDLER, Dora (1928-) British					
oil	1	1,138		1,138	
HOLZMAN, Shimshon (1907-1986) Israeli					
oil	2	3,700	1,300	1,850	2,400
HOM, G (?) ?					
oil	1	1,114		1,114	
HOM, Poul (1905-1994) Danish					
oil	2	2,665	1,003	1,333	1,662

Name	No.	Total Sales Value	lowest	Prices median	highest
HOMBERG, Louis Marie (20th C) French					
oil	1	1,309		1,309	
HOMER, Winslow (1836-1910) American					
oil	2	4,300,000	1,700,000	2,150,000	2,600,000
wc/d	9	3,945,500	5,500	240,000	1,400,000
HONDECOETER (17th C) Dutch					
oil	1	27,360		27,360	
HONDECOETER, Gillis Claesz de (1570-1638) Dutch					
oil	4	54,364	9,000	12,445	20,474
HONDECOETER, Gysbert Gillisz de (1604-1653) Dutch					
oil	1	57,446		57,446	
HONDECOETER, Melchior de (1636-1695) Dutch					
oil	6	644,542	2,557	55,580	266,900
HONDIUS, Abraham (1625-1695) Dutch					
oil	4	32,874	1,818	8,028	15,000
HONDIUS, Gerrit (20th C) German					
oil	9	14,450	1,000	1,200	3,250
HONDT, Lambert de (17th C) Flemish					
oil	2	7,036	1,450	3,518	5,586
HONDUIS, Gerrit (1891-1970) American					
oil	1	1,500		1,500	
HONE, Evie (1894-1955) British					
wc/d	1	1,776		1,776	
HONE, Nathaniel I (1718-1784) British					
oil	4	405,955	8,140	36,108	325,600
HONICH, Heinrich (1875-1957) German					
oil	1	1,091		1,091	
HONTHORST, Gerrit van (1590-1656) Dutch					
oil	3	168,690	29,830	59,660	79,200
HOOCH, Charles Cornelisz de (?-1638) Dutch					
oil	2	14,790	5,652	7,395	9,138
HOOCH, Pieter de (1629-1681) Dutch					
oil	3	250,240	50,240	80,000	120,000
HOOD, George Washington (1869-1949) American					
oil	2	2,400	1,100	1,200	1,300
HOOG, Bernard de (1866-1943) Dutch					
oil	20	141,044	1,530	6,732	19,894
HOOGSTRATEN, Samuel van (1627-1678) Flemish					
oil	1	21,140		21,140	
HOOK, James Clarke (1819-1907) British					
oil	2	33,520	13,500	16,760	20,020
HOOK, Sandy (1879-1960) French					
wc/d	6	19,677	1,043	1,592	10,701
HOOM, K van (?) Dutch					
oil	1	2,918		2,918	
HOOP, A May (1879-?) Austrian					
oil	1	1,549		1,549	
HOOPER, John Horace (fl.1877-1899) British					
oil	8	21,750	1,154	2,333	5,285
HOOPER, W (?) British					
oil	1	1,074		1,074	
HOPE, James (1818-1892) American					
oil	18	245,430	1,100	6,078	130,000
HOPE, Robert (1869-1936) British					
oil	1	2,528		2,528	
HOPFGARTEN, August Ferdinand (1807-1896) German					
wc/d	1	1,026		1,026	
HOPKIN, Robert (1832-1909) American					
oil	1	1,200		1,200	

Name	No.	Total Sales Value	Prices lowest	median	highest
HOPKINS, Arthur (1848-1930) British					
wc/d	2	4,089	1,106	2,045	2,983
HOPKINS, W F (18/19th C) British					
oil	1	3,766		3,766	
HOPKINS, William H (?-1892) British					
oil	2	39,635	4,424	19,818	35,211
HOPKINSON, Charles Sydney (1869-1962) American					
oil	1	17,000		17,000	
HOPKINSON, William John (1887-?) Canadian					
oil	1	1,151		1,151	
HOPPE, Erik (1897-1968) Danish					
oil	7	22,877	1,417	2,947	5,329
HOPPE, Ferdinand Bernhard (1841-1922) Dutch					
oil	1	1,495		1,495	
HOPPE, Georg (fl.1844-1860) German					
oil	1	1,325		1,325	
HOPPEN, Gerard (1885-1928) Dutch					
3D	1	3,448		3,448	
HOPPENBROUWERS, Johannes Franciscus (1819-1866) Dutch					
oil	2	9,593	1,449	4,797	8,144
HOPPER, Edward (1882-1967) American					
wc/d	7	434,000	4,000	10,000	370,000
HOPPNER, J (1758-1810) British					
oil	1	1,467		1,467	
HOPPNER, John (1758-1810) British					
oil	2	30,000	12,000	15,000	18,000
HOPWOOD, Henry Silkstone (1860-1914) British					
wc/d	3	10,150	1,154	3,600	5,396
HORACIO (1912-1972) Mexican					
oil	5	13,800	1,500	2,000	6,000
HORBERG, Pehr (1746-1816) Swedish					
oil	2	7,860	3,725	3,930	4,135
HORDYK, Gerard (1899-1958) Dutch					
oil	2	5,823	2,060	2,912	3,763
HOREL, E Albert (1876-1964) French					
oil	2	4,154	1,298	2,077	2,856
HOREMANS, Jan Josef (18th C) Flemish					
oil	5	66,345	1,296	11,760	34,661
HOREMANS, Jan Josef (elder) (1682-1759) Flemish					
oil	3	38,997	2,730	3,147	33,120
wc/d	4	11,590	1,179	2,063	6,286
HOREMANS, Jan Josef (younger) (1714-1790) Flemish					
oil	3	146,730	18,840	61,740	66,150
HOREMANS, Peter Jacob (1700-1776) Flemish					
oil	1	21,140		21,140	
HORENBANT, Joseph (1863-1956) Belgian					
oil	1	2,840		2,840	
HORLOR, George W (fl.1849-1891) British					
oil	3	8,762	1,318	3,020	4,424
HORLOR, Joseph (1809-1887) British					
oil	3	7,562	1,716	1,846	4,000
HORMANN, Theodor von (1840-1895) Austrian					
oil	2	33,551	3,646	16,776	29,905
HORMUTH-KALLMORGEN, Margarethe (1858-1916) German					
oil	1	1,219		1,219	
HORN, Josef (1902-1951) German					
oil	1	1,400		1,400	
HORN, Julius (1910-1981) Austrian					
oil	1	1,113		1,113	

Name	No.	Total Sales Value	Prices lowest	median	highest
HORN, Rebecca (1944-) German					
3D	3	29,140	1,895	11,245	16,000
HORNBROOK, Thomas L (1780-1850) British					
oil	1	6,716		6,716	
HORNE, E (?) British?					
oil	1	2,482		2,482	
HORNE, Margery (fl.1898-1901) British					
oil	1	1,500		1,500	
HORNEL, Edward Atkinson (1864-1933) British					
oil	16	478,324	6,004	21,100	84,100
HORNEMAN, Christian (1765-1844) Danish					
wc/d	2	3,876	1,287	1,938	2,589
HORNER, C (18th C) Swiss					
wc/d	1	4,064		4,064	
HORNLY, T (19th C) British					
oil	1	1,377		1,377	
HORNSTAIN, Gabriel (17th C) German					
wc/d	1	1,419		1,419	
HORNUNG, Preben (1919-1989) Danish					
oil	11	34,453	1,162	2,582	6,406
HORNUNG-JENSEN, Carl (1882-1960) Danish					
oil	1	1,191		1,191	
HORNY, Franz (1798-1824) German					
wc/d	1	127,668		127,668	
HORQUES, Manuel de (19/20th C) Spanish					
oil	2	2,288	1,085	1,144	1,203
HORRIX, Hendrikus Mattheus (1845-1932) Dutch					
oil	1	1,697		1,697	
HORSBURGH, Edith M (fl.1900-1902) British					
oil	1	1,491		1,491	
HORSLEY, John Callcott (1817-1903) British					
oil	2	2,664	1,323	1,332	1,341
HORSLEY, T J (19th C) British					
wc/d	1	1,001		1,001	
HORSPOOL, Francis L (1871-1951) American					
oil	1	2,200		2,200	
HORST, Wilhelm (1852-?) German					
oil	1	1,765		1,765	
HORSTOK, Johannes Petrus van (1745-1825) Dutch					
oil	1	8,820		8,820	
HORTEN, J (19th C) British?					
oil	1	1,421		1,421	
HORTER, Earl (1881-1940) American					
wc/d	4	12,800	1,300	2,250	7,000
HORTON, Etty (fl.1882-1905) British					
oil	3	5,934	1,278	2,288	2,368
HORTON, William Samuel (1865-1936) American					
oil	1	3,000		3,000	
wc/d	2	5,350	1,300	2,675	4,050
HORY, Elmyr de (1905-1978) French					
oil	19	53,168	1,219	2,736	4,800
wc/d	3	7,408	1,012	1,287	5,109
HOSCH, Karl (1900-1972) Swiss					
oil	1	1,242		1,242	
HOSCHEDE-MONET, Blanche (1865-1947) French					
oil	2	42,000	16,000	21,000	26,000
HOSEMANN, Theodor (1807-1875) German					
oil	2	5,234	1,924	2,617	3,310

Name	No.	Total Sales Value	Prices lowest	median	highest
HOSIASSON, Philippe (1898-1978) French					
oil	3	6,859	1,306	1,731	3,822
HOSKINS, Gayle Porter (1887-1962) American					
oil	5	43,000	6,000	9,500	10,500
wc/d	1	2,200		2,200	
HOSOTTE, Georges (1936-) French					
oil	5	11,761	1,771	2,307	2,964
wc/d	1	1,261		1,261	
HOST, Oluf (1884-1966) Danish					
oil	10	106,421	2,324	6,406	34,593
HOSTEIN, Edouard (1804-1889) French					
oil	3	58,602	3,501	22,101	33,000
HOTTINGER, Johann Konrad (1788-1828) Austrian					
wc/d	1	3,287		3,287	
HOTZENDORFF, Theodor von (1898-1974) German					
oil	1	1,612		1,612	
HOU, Axel (1860-1948) Danish					
oil	3	5,719	1,431	1,706	2,582
HOUASSE, M-A (1680-1730) French					
oil	1	14,530		14,530	
HOUASSE, René-Antoine (1645-1710) French					
wc/d	1	1,208		1,208	
HOUBEN, Henri (1858-1931) Belgian					
oil	5	39,657	1,787	5,824	14,311
HOUDON (?) French					
3D	1	2,465		2,465	
HOUDON, Jean Antoine (1741-1828) French					
3D	1	2,122		2,122	
HOUEL, Jean Pierre (1735-1813) French					
oil	1	4,228		4,228	
wc/d	3	18,296	1,256	6,040	11,000
HOUGH, William (fl.1857-1894) British					
oil	1	1,430		1,430	
wc/d	2	5,118	2,400	2,559	2,718
HOULY (18th C) ?					
oil	1	17,000		17,000	
HOUSSER, Yvonne McKague (1898-1996) Canadian					
oil	1	2,878		2,878	
HOUSTON, Bruce (20th C) American					
3D	1	1,700		1,700	
HOUSTON, George (1869-1947) British					
oil	15	94,438	1,264	3,190	32,120
wc/d	1	2,058		2,058	
HOUSTON, Ian (1934-) British					
oil	6	7,332	1,001	1,175	1,502
HOUSTON, John (1930-) British					
oil	4	19,285	1,885	5,220	6,960
HOUSTON, John Adam (1812-1884) British					
oil	1	2,700		2,700	
HOUSTON, Robert (1891-1942) British					
oil	1	6,615		6,615	
HOUTEN, Barbara van (1862-1950) Dutch					
oil	1	1,485		1,485	
HOUTHUESEN, Albert (1903-) British					
oil	4	5,852	1,058	1,410	1,974
HOVANIAN, Rachel (20th C) American?					
wc/d	1	1,100		1,100	
HOVE, Bartholomeus Johannes van (1790-1880) Dutch					
oil	2	28,740	3,872	14,370	24,868
wc/d	2	4,903	2,357	2,452	2,546

Name	No.	Total Sales Value	lowest	Prices median	highest
HOVE, Edmond van (1853-?) Belgian					
oil	1	2,140		2,140	
HOVE, Hubertus van (1814-1865) Dutch					
oil	2	7,526	1,585	3,763	5,941
HOVENDEN, Thomas (1840-1895) American/Irish					
oil	1	55,000		55,000	
HOVENER, Johannes Josephus (1936-) Dutch?					
oil	1	1,179		1,179	
HOW, Beatrice (1867-1932) British					
oil	1	2,618		2,618	
wc/d	1	1,558		1,558	
HOWARD, Henry (1769-1847) British					
oil	1	14,345		14,345	
HOWARD, Ken (1932-) British					
oil	13	44,640	1,326	2,610	8,892
wc/d	1	1,058		1,058	
HOWARD, Marion (1883-?) American					
oil	1	28,000		28,000	
HOWE, James (1780-1836) British					
oil	1	2,400		2,400	
HOWE, Theodore (19th C) American					
oil	1	1,030		1,030	
HOWE, William Henry (1846-1929) American					
oil	2	4,200	2,000	2,100	2,200
HOWELL, Felicie (1897-1968) American					
wc/d	1	4,000		4,000	
HOWES, Samuel P (1806-1881) American					
oil	1	11,000		11,000	
HOWET, Marie (1897-1984) Belgian					
oil	4	6,376	1,220	1,358	2,440
HOWIS, William (1804-1882) Irish					
oil	1	2,145		2,145	
HOWITT, John Newton (1885-1958) American					
oil	2	8,000	2,500	4,000	5,500
HOWITT, Samuel (1765-1822) British					
wc/d	1	1,208		1,208	
HOWLAND, Alfred Cornelius (1838-1909) American					
oil	1	3,000		3,000	
HOWSON, Peter (1958-) British					
oil	4	15,438	2,920	3,994	4,530
wc/d	2	3,450	1,080	1,725	2,370
HOYER, Edward (19th C) British					
oil	2	10,109	1,057	5,055	9,052
HOYLAND, John (1934-) British					
oil	7	27,258	1,058	3,624	6,750
wc/d	1	1,580		1,580	
HOYOS, Anna Mercedes (1942-) Colombian					
oil	1	5,000		5,000	
HOYRUP, Carl (1893-1961) Danish					
oil	1	1,097		1,097	
HRDLICKA, Alfred (1928-) Austrian					
3D	2	2,807	1,390	1,404	1,417
wc/d	2	2,834	1,417	1,417	1,417
HSIAO CHIN (1935-) Chinese					
oil	2	4,310	2,155	2,155	2,155
HUANG BINHONG (1864-1955) Chinese					
wc/d	2	9,250	4,500	4,625	4,750
HUANG DAZENG (19th C) Chinese					
oil	1	15,819		15,819	

Name	No.	Total Sales Value	lowest	Prices median	highest
HUANG JUNBI (1898-1991) Chinese					
wc/d	1	2,200		2,200	
HUANG ZHOU (1925-1997) Chinese					
wc/d	1	2,000		2,000	
HUBACHER, Hermann (1885-?) Swiss					
3D	3	7,590	1,074	2,390	4,126
HUBBARD, Lydia M B (1849-1911) American					
oil	1	2,000		2,000	
HUBBARD, Richard William (1817-1888) American					
oil	1	18,000		18,000	
HUBBELL, Henry Salem (1870-1949) American					
oil	1	2,181		2,181	
HUBBUCH, Karl (1891-1979) German					
oil	1	54,720		54,720	
wc/d	7	313,824	1,028	4,427	108,000
HUBER, Carl Rudolf (1839-1896) Austrian					
oil	1	4,984		4,984	
HUBER, Conrad (1752-1830) German					
oil	1	2,045		2,045	
HUBER, Ernst (1895-1960) Austrian					
oil	3	26,899	3,871	8,456	14,572
wc/d	1	3,953		3,953	
HUBER, Hans (1813-1889) Austrian					
oil	1	2,944		2,944	
HUBER, Hermann (1888-1968) Swiss					
oil	1	1,033		1,033	
HUBER, Johann Rudolf (1668-1748) Swiss					
oil	2	4,044	1,733	2,022	2,311
HUBER, Léon (1858-1928) French					
oil	3	17,585	2,385	5,700	9,500
HUBER, Wilhelm (1787-1871) German					
oil	1	1,452		1,452	
HUBER-SULZEMOOS, Hans (1873-?) German					
oil	1	1,227		1,227	
HUBERT, L (19/20th C) French					
oil	1	1,082		1,082	
HUBERTIE DE NOVARRA, Pierre (18th C) ?					
oil	1	1,144		1,144	
HUBLIN, Émile Auguste (1830-?) French					
oil	1	14,000		14,000	
HUBNER, Julius (1842-1874) German					
oil	2	15,124	1,168	7,562	13,956
HUBNER, Ulrich (1872-1932) German					
oil	3	10,860	1,097	4,758	5,005
HUC, Eugene (1891-?) French					
oil	2	19,278	6,750	9,639	12,528
HUCHTENBURGH, Jan van (1647-1733) Dutch					
oil	5	52,791	6,028	10,500	13,739
HUCLEUX, Jean Olivier (1923-) French					
wc/d	1	14,397		14,397	
HUDDESFORD, George (1749-1809) British					
oil	1	4,082		4,082	
HUDDLE, Nannie Zenobia (1860-1951) American					
oil	1	1,600		1,600	
HUDNUT, Alexander M (c.1870-?) American					
wc/d	1	4,200		4,200	
HUDSON RIVER SCHOOL, 19th C American					
oil	2	7,150	3,400	3,575	3,750

Name	No.	Total Sales Value	lowest	Prices median	highest
HUDSON, Charles Bradford (1865-1938) American					
oil	2	5,500	2,500	2,750	3,000
HUDSON, Grace Carpenter (1865-1937) American					
oil	2	6,100	2,600	3,050	3,500
HUDSON, John (19th C) British					
oil	1	2,100		2,100	
HUDSON, Robert (snr) (1826-1885) British					
oil	1	1,113		1,113	
HUDSON, Thomas (1701-1779) British					
oil	7	123,853	2,979	8,294	45,300
HUDSON, Tony (1936-1989) ?					
oil	1	2,175		2,175	
HUE DE BREVAL, Virginie (fl.1810-1822) French					
wc/d	1	1,021		1,021	
HUE, Alexandre (19th C) French					
oil	1	8,000		8,000	
HUE, Jean François (1751-1823) French					
oil	4	245,018	3,390	10,814	220,000
HUEBLER, Douglas (1924-1997) American					
oil	1	6,500		6,500	
HUEFFER, Catherine (1850-1927) British					
wc/d	1	22,650		22,650	
HUENS, Jean L (1921-) American					
wc/d	1	1,400		1,400	
HUET, François (1772-1813) French					
wc/d	1	7,500		7,500	
HUET, Jean Baptiste (1745-1811) French					
oil	3	55,138	2,578	12,560	40,000
wc/d	2	17,347	6,000	8,674	11,347
HUET, Paul (1803-1869) French					
oil	6	18,447	1,365	2,936	4,845
wc/d	41	146,355	1,176	3,624	9,996
HUF, Fritz (1888-1970) Swiss					
3D	1	1,421		1,421	
HUFFORD, Nick (20th C) American?					
oil	1	5,500		5,500	
HUG, Charles (1899-1979) Swiss					
oil	3	8,169	1,719	3,069	3,381
HUG, Fritz Rudolf (1921-1989) Swiss					
oil	2	2,248	1,038	1,124	1,210
HUGARD, Claude S (1861-?) French					
oil	1	1,072		1,072	
HUGENTOBLER, Ivan Edwin (1886-1972) Swiss					
wc/d	2	2,295	1,129	1,148	1,166
HUGGINS, J M (19th C) British					
oil	1	1,738		1,738	
HUGGINS, James Miller (fl.1836-1849) British					
oil	3	23,482	4,000	9,780	9,780
HUGGINS, William (1820-1884) British					
oil	4	29,056	1,200	6,063	15,730
wc/d	2	4,854	1,136	2,427	3,718
HUGGLER, Arnold (1894-1988) Swiss					
3D	2	3,787	1,823	1,894	1,964
HUGGLER, Hans (1877-1947) Swiss					
3D	1	1,203		1,203	
HUGHES, Arthur (1832-1915) British					
oil	2	24,310	7,150	12,155	17,160
HUGHES, David Gordon (?) Irish					
oil	1	1,080		1,080	

Name	No.	Total Sales Value	lowest	Prices median	highest
HUGHES, E J (1913-) Canadian					
wc/d	1	10,067		10,067	
HUGHES, Edward (1832-1908) British					
oil	1	1,716		1,716	
HUGHES, Edward John (1913-) Canadian					
oil	4	120,556	17,550	20,628	61,750
wc/d	2	12,608	4,158	6,304	8,450
HUGHES, Edward Robert (1851-1914) British					
wc/d	1	117,780		117,780	
HUGHES, Edwin (fl.1862-1892) British					
oil	1	1,200		1,200	
HUGHES, George H (fl.1832-1861) Canadian					
oil	1	3,518		3,518	
HUGHES, Ian (1958-) British					
oil	1	1,064		1,064	
HUGHES, J J (?-c.1909) British					
oil	2	4,365	1,131	2,183	3,234
HUGHES, John (18th C) British					
3D	1	7,104		7,104	
HUGHES, John Joseph (?-1909) British					
oil	2	2,991	1,201	1,496	1,790
HUGHES, Patrick (1939-) British					
oil	2	11,370	1,500	5,685	9,870
HUGHES, R H (20th C) British					
oil	1	3,300		3,300	
HUGHES, Robert Morson (1873-1953) British					
oil	2	3,496	1,748	1,748	1,748
HUGHES, Talbot (1869-1942) British					
oil	4	17,719	1,704	3,575	8,866
HUGHES, William (1842-1901) British					
oil	5	17,549	1,200	3,925	6,216
HUGHES-STANTON, Sir Herbert (1870-1937) British					
oil	1	3,180		3,180	
wc/d	1	2,416		2,416	
HUGIN, Karl Otto (1887-1963) German					
oil	1	3,106		3,106	
wc/d	1	1,016		1,016	
HUGNET, Georges (20th C) French					
oil	1	1,928		1,928	
wc/d	2	31,900	11,600	15,950	20,300
HUGO, Jean (1894-1984) French					
oil	3	11,325	2,265	4,228	4,832
wc/d	1	1,549		1,549	
HUGO, Valentine (1890-1968) French					
oil	1	231,391		231,391	
wc/d	3	37,108	3,685	12,855	20,568
HUGO, Victor (1802-1885) French					
wc/d	9	67,120	1,273	3,057	30,567
HUGONNET, Aloys (1879-1938) Swiss					
oil	1	1,822		1,822	
HUGREL, Honore (1880-1944) French					
oil	1	1,782		1,782	
HUGUENY, Jean (1768-1817) French					
wc/d	1	2,775		2,775	
HUGUES, Paul Jean (1891-?) French					
oil	1	2,686		2,686	
HUGUET, Victor Pierre (1835-1902) French					
oil	3	14,750	2,750	5,700	6,300
HUHN, Friedrich Wilhelm (1821-?) German					
oil	1	4,183		4,183	

Name	No.	Total Sales Value	Prices lowest	median	highest
HUIBERS, Jan Derk (1829-1919) Dutch					
oil	1	3,053		3,053	
HUIDEKOPER, Geertruida Margaretha Jacoba (1824-1884) Dutch					
oil	1	2,557		2,557	
HUILLIOT, Pierre Nicolas (1674-1751) French					
oil	3	28,824	7,075	8,100	13,649
HUILLIOT, Pierre Nicolas (school) (1674-1751) French					
oil	1	20,000		20,000	
HUISMAN, Jopie (20th C) Dutch					
wc/d	1	4,095		4,095	
HUISMANN, A (19/20th C) ?					
3D	1	3,064		3,064	
HULETT, J G (19th C) American					
oil	1	2,000		2,000	
HULINGS, Clark (1922-) American					
oil	1	80,000		80,000	
wc/d	1	5,500		5,500	
HULK, A (19th C) Dutch					
oil	1	1,010		1,010	
HULK, Abraham (19th C) Dutch					
oil	14	191,386	1,841	10,138	39,500
HULK, Abraham (jnr) (1851-1922) British					
oil	9	21,057	1,001	2,399	4,500
HULK, Abraham (snr) (1813-1897) Dutch					
oil	18	229,145	1,027	9,617	64,385
HULK, Hendrik (1842-1937) Dutch					
oil	5	17,126	1,888	3,256	5,363
HULK, J (?) ?					
oil	1	1,015		1,015	
HULK, J F (19th C) Dutch					
oil	1	4,564		4,564	
HULK, John Frederick (jnr) (1855-1913) Dutch					
oil	1	19,500		19,500	
HULK, John Frederick (snr) (1829-1911) Dutch					
oil	3	10,870	1,103	1,967	7,800
HULK, N J (?) ?					
oil	1	1,539		1,539	
HULK, William F (1852-1906) British					
oil	5	7,466	1,099	1,327	1,985
HULL, Gregory (1950-) American					
oil	2	4,500	2,000	2,250	2,500
HULL, Marie (1890-1980) American					
oil	2	21,250	4,750	10,625	16,500
wc/d	1	9,000		9,000	
HULL, William (1820-1880) British					
wc/d	2	3,289	1,264	1,645	2,025
HULLGREN, Oscar (1869-1948) Swedish					
oil	1	3,499		3,499	
HULME, Frederick William (1816-1884) British					
oil	8	89,822	1,207	10,113	20,520
HULSDONCK, Jacob van (1582-1647) Flemish					
oil	2	911,400	220,500	455,700	690,900
HULSER, Joseph (1819-1850) German					
oil	1	1,065		1,065	
HULSMAN, Johann (17th C) German					
oil	2	3,699	1,650	1,850	2,049
HULST, Frans de (1610-1661) Flemish					
oil	3	44,190	6,286	18,840	19,064

Name	No.	Total Sales Value	Prices lowest	median	highest
HULSWIT, Jan (1766-1822) Dutch					
wc/d	1	2,946		2,946	
HULTEN, Carl Otto (1916-) Swedish					
oil	3	9,471	2,803	3,156	3,512
HULTSTROM, Karl (1884-1973) Swedish?					
3D	1	3,918		3,918	
HUMBERT, J-C-F (1813-1881) Swiss					
oil	1	7,171		7,171	
HUMBERT, Jacques Fernand (1842-1934) French					
oil	2	17,640	1,640	8,820	16,000
HUMBERT, Jean-Charles-Ferdinand (1813-1881) Swiss					
oil	1	3,106		3,106	
HUMBERT, Manuel (1890-1975) Spanish					
oil	2	6,788	3,243	3,394	3,545
HUMBERT-VIGNOT, Leonie (19/20th C) French					
oil	1	1,752		1,752	
HUMBLOT, Robert (1907-1962) French					
oil	7	19,152	1,370	2,392	5,050
HUMBORG, Adolf (1847-1913) Austrian					
oil	2	7,630	2,130	3,815	5,500
HUME, Edith (fl.1862-1906) British					
oil	2	13,042	6,292	6,521	6,750
wc/d	1	1,233		1,233	
HUME, Gary (1962-) British					
oil	2	215,500	75,500	107,750	140,000
HUMMEL, Carl (1821-1907) German					
wc/d	2	2,955	1,164	1,478	1,791
HUMMEL, Theodor (1864-1939) German					
oil	1	1,942		1,942	
HUMPHREY, Jack Weldon (1901-1967) Canadian					
oil	1	3,020		3,020	
wc/d	1	1,074		1,074	
HUMPHREYS, Malcolm (1894-?) American					
oil	1	2,250		2,250	
HUMPHRISS, Charles Henry (1867-1934) British					
3D	11	77,900	2,000	6,500	16,000
HUMPHRYS, H B (fl.1840-1880) British					
oil	1	3,500		3,500	
HUNDEBERG, Jurgen von (1922-1996) German					
oil	1	2,080		2,080	
HUNDERTWASSER, Friedrich (1928-2000) Austrian					
oil	1	196,300		196,300	
wc/d	4	127,854	25,862	32,884	37,750
HUNG, Francisco (1937-) Chinese					
oil	1	1,120		1,120	
HUNGARIAN SCHOOL, 19th/20th C					
oil	2	4,151	1,468	2,076	2,683
HUNN, Tom (fl.1878-1908) British					
wc/d	3	4,086	1,099	1,223	1,764
HUNT, A (?) British					
oil	1	1,590		1,590	
HUNT, Alan M (1947-) British					
oil	4	64,184	3,124	18,460	24,140
HUNT, Alfred William (1830-1896) British					
oil	3	11,251	2,773	3,454	5,024
wc/d	33	358,695	1,287	8,690	44,240
HUNT, Bryan (1947-) American					
3D	2	20,000	5,000	10,000	15,000

Name	No.	Total Sales Value	lowest	Prices median	highest
HUNT, Cecil Arthur (1873-1965) British					
wc/d	5	9,949	1,073	2,212	2,844
HUNT, Charles (jnr) (1829-1900) British					
oil	5	35,496	2,002	3,397	21,450
HUNT, Charles (snr) (1803-1877) British					
oil	2	22,400	2,900	11,200	19,500
HUNT, Charles (19th C) British					
oil	1	5,880		5,880	
HUNT, E (1876-1953) British					
oil	2	7,026	3,455	3,513	3,571
HUNT, Edgar (1876-1953) British					
oil	16	565,334	10,744	29,315	75,920
HUNT, Edward Aubrey (1855-1922) British					
oil	7	21,198	1,500	3,423	4,681
HUNT, Geoffrey William (1948-) British					
oil	1	1,430		1,430	
HUNT, Lynn Bogue (1878-1960) American					
wc/d	2	4,600	1,100	2,300	3,500
HUNT, M (?) ?					
oil	1	1,925		1,925	
HUNT, Michael John (20th C) British?					
oil	1	1,131		1,131	
HUNT, Millson (fl.1875-1900) British					
oil	1	5,800		5,800	
HUNT, Reuben (19th C) British					
oil	1	2,175		2,175	
HUNT, Thomas (1854-1929) British					
oil	1	1,168		1,168	
HUNT, W (19th C) British?					
oil	1	1,362		1,362	
HUNT, Walter (1861-1941) British					
oil	3	91,650	18,720	20,020	52,910
HUNT, William Henry (1790-1864) British					
oil	2	5,278	1,778	2,639	3,500
wc/d	8	24,976	1,034	2,033	8,250
HUNT, William Holman (1827-1910) British					
oil	1	8,478		8,478	
HUNT, William Morris (1824-1879) American					
3D	1	35,000		35,000	
oil	1	5,000		5,000	
HUNTEN, Emil (1827-1902) German					
oil	3	11,641	3,750	3,750	4,020
HUNTEN, Franz Johann Wilhelm (1822-1887) German					
oil	1	4,938		4,938	
HUNTER, Clementine (1887-1988) American					
oil	17	41,585	1,000	2,300	6,000
HUNTER, Colin (1841-1904) British					
oil	4	15,340	1,492	2,574	8,700
HUNTER, George Leslie (1877-1931) British					
oil	13	475,763	3,160	32,340	74,260
wc/d	8	49,176	1,352	4,902	14,700
HUNTER, George Sherwood (1846-1919) British					
oil	2	4,740	2,190	2,370	2,550
HUNTER, John F (1893-1951) British					
oil	1	2,072		2,072	
HUNTER, John Young (1874-1955) British					
oil	5	7,000	1,000	1,500	1,800
HUNTER, Leslie (?-1934) British					
oil	1	55,100		55,100	

Name	No.	Total Sales Value	Prices lowest	Prices median	highest
wc/d	1	1,740		1,740	
HUNTER, M C (19th C) British					
oil	1	3,480		3,480	
HUNTER, Mary Ethel (?-c.1936) British					
oil	2	2,195	1,065	1,098	1,130
HUNTER, Mason (1854-1921) British					
oil	1	1,027		1,027	
HUNTER, Robert (fl.1745-1803) Irish					
oil	1	29,600		29,600	
HUNTINGTON, Anna Hyatt (1876-1973) American					
3D	1	9,000		9,000	
oil	2	79,000	4,000	39,500	75,000
HUNTINGTON, Daniel (1816-1906) American					
oil	2	7,500	2,000	3,750	5,500
HUNZIKER, Max (1901-1976) Swiss					
oil	1	1,730		1,730	
HUOT, Charles Edouard (1855-1930) Canadian					
oil	2	2,235	1,032	1,118	1,203
wc/d	1	1,055		1,055	
HUQUIER, L (18th C) Dutch					
wc/d	1	2,473		2,473	
HURD, Peter (1904-1984) American					
oil	2	45,300	2,800	22,650	42,500
wc/d	1	6,500		6,500	
HURIT, Eduard (20th C) ?					
oil	1	1,269		1,269	
HURLESTONE, Frederick (1801-1869) British					
oil	1	2,431		2,431	
HURLEY, Wilson (1924-) American					
oil	3	93,000	5,500	7,500	80,000
HURST, Hal (1863-1938) British					
oil	1	1,222		1,222	
HURT, Louis B (1856-1929) British					
oil	16	472,941	1,181	32,230	58,000
HURTUBISE, Jacques (1939-) Canadian					
wc/d	1	3,746		3,746	
HUSAIN, Maqbool Fida (1915-) Indian					
oil	5	47,500	4,000	11,000	11,000
wc/d	4	14,700	2,250	3,075	6,300
HUSE, Marion (1896-?) American					
oil	2	2,500	1,200	1,250	1,300
HUSKISSON, Robert (1820-1861) British					
oil	1	112,500		112,500	
HUSSEM, Willem (1900-1974) Dutch					
oil	7	35,250	2,179	5,172	7,526
HUSSMANN, Albert Heinrich (1874-1946) German					
3D	6	13,225	1,204	2,588	2,724
HUSTIN, C (20th C) ?					
wc/d	1	1,250		1,250	
HUSTON, William (19th C) American					
oil	1	3,750		3,750	
HUSZAR, Vilmos (1884-1960) Dutch					
oil	1	60,680		60,680	
HUTCHENS, Frank Townsend (1869-1937) American					
oil	1	10,000		10,000	
wc/d	2	11,000	1,500	5,500	9,500
HUTCHINSON, Nick Hely (20th C) European					
oil	1	1,650		1,650	

Name	No.	Total Sales Value	lowest	Prices median	highest
HUTCHINSON, Peter (20th C) ?					
wc/d	1	1,068		1,068	
HUTCHISON, Frederick William (1871-1953) Canadian					
oil	2	3,296	1,599	1,648	1,697
HUTCHISON, Robert Gemmell (1855-1936) British					
oil	16	196,945	1,575	11,878	29,200
wc/d	5	36,848	1,029	9,480	12,556
HUTCHISON, William Oliphant (1889-c.1971) British					
oil	1	2,054		2,054	
HUTH, Franz (1876-?) German					
wc/d	1	1,122		1,122	
HUTH, Julius (1838-1892) German					
oil	4	13,822	1,597	3,907	4,412
HUTH, Willy Robert (1890-1977) German					
oil	1	1,125		1,125	
HUTHER, Julius (1881-1954) German					
oil	5	6,628	1,002	1,437	1,655
HUTHSTEINER, Rudolf (1855-1935) German					
oil	1	4,907		4,907	
HUTTE, Axel (1951-) ?					
oil	1	9,515		9,515	
HUTTER, Schang (1934-) Swiss					
3D	1	3,623		3,623	
HUTTON, Thomas S (c.1865-1935) British					
oil	1	1,131		1,131	
wc/d	2	3,313	1,138	1,657	2,175
HUTTY, Alfred (1877-1954) American					
oil	2	35,000	5,000	17,500	30,000
wc/d	1	9,500		9,500	
HUYGENS, Constantyn (younger) (1628-1697) Dutch					
wc/d	2	33,000	2,357	16,500	30,643
HUYGENS, François Joseph (1820-1908) Belgian					
oil	4	17,295	1,734	2,432	10,697
HUYGENS, Frederik Lodewijk (1802-1887) Dutch					
oil	1	1,817		1,817	
HUYGENS, Léon (19/20th C) Belgian					
oil	1	4,034		4,034	
HUYS, Bernhard (1885-1973) German					
oil	1	1,196		1,196	
HUYS, Modeste (1875-1932) Belgian					
oil	7	225,360	4,844	33,585	70,280
HUYSMANS, Jacob (1633-1680) Flemish					
oil	2	7,158	1,908	3,579	5,250
HUYSMANS, Jacobus Carolus (1776-1859) Dutch					
oil	1	5,063		5,063	
HUYSMANS, Jan Baptist (1826-1906) Belgian					
oil	2	3,333	1,502	1,667	1,831
HUYSMANS, Jan Baptist (1654-1716) Flemish					
oil	1	7,742		7,742	
HUYSUM, Jan van (1682-1749) Dutch					
oil	2	11,643	5,387	5,822	6,256
wc/d	2	5,521	1,650	2,761	3,871
HUYSUM, Justus van (17/18th C) Dutch					
oil	1	50,000		50,000	
HYAMS, William (1878-?) British					
wc/d	1	2,114		2,114	
HYBERT, Fabrice (20th C) French?					
3D	2	25,343	3,505	12,672	21,838
oil	4	25,767	4,777	6,401	8,189
wc/d	5	66,799	1,365	7,916	46,407

Name	No.	Total Sales Value	lowest	Prices median	highest
HYDE, David (1947-) British					
oil	1	1,278		1,278	
HYDE-POWNALL, George (1876-1932) British					
oil	1	1,833		1,833	
HYDMAN-VALLIEN, Ulrika (1938-) Swedish					
oil	2	2,477	1,033	1,239	1,444
HYLAND, B A (?) ?					
oil	1	1,716		1,716	
HYLANDER, Einar (1913-1989) Swedish					
wc/d	1	3,011		3,011	
HYNAIS, Voytech (1854-1925) Czechoslovakian					
oil	1	3,595		3,595	
HYNCKES, Raoul (1893-1973) Dutch					
oil	3	47,188	2,802	9,903	34,483
HYNER, Arend (1866-1916) Dutch					
oil	1	7,386		7,386	
HYON, Georges Louis (1855-?) French					
oil	1	1,947		1,947	
HYRE, Laurent de la (1606-1656) French					
oil	2	144,706	16,379	72,353	128,327
wc/d	1	2,352		2,352	
IACOVLEFF, Alexandre (1887-1938) French					
oil	1	22,650		22,650	
wc/d	1	1,812		1,812	
IACURTO, Francesco (1908-) Canadian					
oil	1	1,205		1,205	
IAKOVLEFF, Michail Nicolaievitch (1880-1942) Russian					
oil	1	2,764		2,764	
IALENTI, Antonio (1937-) Italian					
oil	2	3,003	1,126	1,502	1,877
IANCHELEVICI, Idel (1909-1994) Belgian/Rumanian					
3D	1	2,783		2,783	
IBANEZ DE ALDECOA, Julian (1866-?) Spanish					
oil	1	1,318		1,318	
IBARROLA, Agustin (20th C) ?					
oil	1	11,367		11,367	
IBBETSON, Julius Caesar (1759-1817) British					
oil	6	42,272	1,422	5,397	20,020
wc/d	3	5,118	1,580	1,738	1,800
IBELS, Henri Gabriel (1867-1936) French					
oil	2	4,139	1,382	2,070	2,757
ICART, Louis (1888-1950) French					
3D	1	1,072		1,072	
oil	6	40,574	5,706	6,735	7,708
wc/d	5	7,362	1,007	1,500	2,000
IEPEREN, Johan Hendrik van (1909-1995) Dutch					
oil	4	8,155	1,795	2,010	2,341
IFFLAND, Franz (19th C) German					
3D	2	2,875	1,373	1,438	1,502
IGLER, Gustav (1842-1908) Hungarian					
oil	1	3,417		3,417	
IGLESIAS SANZ, Antonio (1935-) Spanish					
oil	4	5,604	1,037	1,306	1,956
IGLESIAS, Cristina (1956-) ?					
3D	1	9,060		9,060	
IGNATEV, Petr (1923-) Russian					
oil	1	5,880		5,880	
IHLE, Johann Eberhard (1727-1814) German					
oil	1	17,270		17,270	

Name	No.	Total Sales Value	lowest	Prices median	highest
IHLEE, Rudolph (1883-1968) British					
oil	4	7,705	1,050	1,733	3,190
IHLY, Daniel (1854-1910) Swiss					
oil	2	2,794	1,230	1,397	1,564
IHLY, J (19/20th C) French					
oil	1	1,166		1,166	
IHMELS-HERGET, Marlies (20th C) American?					
oil	1	2,540		2,540	
IHRAN, Manne (1877-1917) Swedish					
oil	1	1,294		1,294	
IKEMURA, Leiko (1951-) ?					
oil	1	2,486		2,486	
ILIGAN, Ralph W (20th C) American					
oil	1	2,300		2,300	
ILJIA (20th C) ?					
oil	1	1,038		1,038	
ILLIES, Arthur (1870-1952) German					
oil	4	17,119	1,581	3,576	8,387
ILLITSCH, Alexander (1860-?) Austrian					
3D	1	1,144		1,144	
ILSTED, Peter Vilhelm (1861-1933) Danish					
oil	13	207,529	2,145	4,175	55,300
wc/d	1	2,065		2,065	
IMAI, Sachiko (20th C) Japanese?					
oil	1	1,084		1,084	
IMAI, Toshimitau (1928-) Japanese					
oil	2	5,091	2,368	2,546	2,723
IMAM, Ali (1924-) Indian					
oil	1	8,250		8,250	
IMANDT, Willem (1882-1967) Dutch					
oil	1	2,422		2,422	
IMHOF, Heinrich Maximilian (1798-1869) Swiss					
3D	1	5,363		5,363	
IMHOF, Joseph A (1871-1955) American					
oil	1	4,000		4,000	
IMKAMP, Wilhelm (1906-1990) German					
oil	5	7,476	1,250	1,587	1,683
IMMENDORF, Jorg (1945-) German					
3D	1	18,598		18,598	
oil	3	39,429	2,621	4,369	32,439
wc/d	3	4,510	1,298	1,557	1,655
IMMENRAEDT, Philip Augustyn (1627-1679) Flemish					
oil	1	10,849		10,849	
IMSCHOOT, Jules van (1821-1884) Flemish					
oil	1	3,322		3,322	
INCE, Joseph Murray (1806-1859) British					
oil	1	1,350		1,350	
wc/d	3	7,780	1,214	1,510	5,056
INCHBOLD, Stanley (1856-?) British					
oil	1	1,800		1,800	
wc/d	2	10,074	1,606	5,037	8,468
INDEN, Ernst (1879-1945) German					
oil	2	2,405	1,178	1,203	1,227
INDENBAUM, Léon (20th C) Russian					
3D	1	1,055		1,055	
INDIA, Bernardino (1528-1590) Italian					
wc/d	1	18,000		18,000	
INDIAN COLONIAL SCHOOL, 18th C					
3D	1	5,040		5,040	

Name	No.	Total Sales Value	lowest	Prices median	highest
INDIAN SCHOOL, 16th C					
oil	1	14,000		14,000	
INDIAN SCHOOL, 17th C					
oil	1	6,000		6,000	
wc/d	1	5,841		5,841	
INDIAN SCHOOL, 17th/18th C					
3D	1	3,259		3,259	
INDIAN SCHOOL, 18th C					
oil	2	15,000	4,000	7,500	11,000
wc/d	3	10,969	2,675	2,943	5,351
INDIAN SCHOOL, 18th/19th C					
oil	1	7,000		7,000	
INDIAN SCHOOL, 19th C					
oil	1	5,902		5,902	
INDIAN SCHOOL, 19th/20th C					
oil	1	6,847		6,847	
INDIAN SCHOOL, 20th C					
oil	2	16,196	6,847	8,098	9,349
INDIANA, Robert (1928-) American					
3D	2	152,500	57,500	76,250	95,000
oil	3	203,907	23,907	55,000	125,000
INDO-PERSIAN SCHOOL, 18th C					
wc/d	2	6,420	3,210	3,210	3,210
INDO-PORTUGUESE SCHOOL, 17th C					
3D	1	2,893		2,893	
INDO-PORTUGUESE SCHOOL, 18th C					
3D	4	60,806	3,528	9,479	38,321
INDO-PORTUGUESE SCHOOL, 19th C					
3D	1	7,218		7,218	
INDONI, Filippo (19th C) Italian					
wc/d	8	17,984	1,300	1,731	4,250
INDUNO, Domenico (1815-1878) Italian					
oil	1	66,888		66,888	
wc/d	1	2,099		2,099	
INDUNO, Gerolamo (1827-1890) Italian					
oil	2	72,010	24,725	36,005	47,285
wc/d	1	4,769		4,769	
INGALL, Frank (20th C) British					
oil	1	2,039		2,039	
INGANNI, Amanzia Guerillot (19th C) Italian					
oil	1	3,669		3,669	
INGANNI, Angelo (1807-1880) Italian					
oil	1	40,132		40,132	
INGEMANN, Lucie (1792-1868) Danish					
oil	2	8,378	3,016	4,189	5,362
INGERLE, Rudolph (1879-1950) American					
oil	2	2,700	1,200	1,350	1,500
INGHAM, Bryan (1936-) British					
wc/d	2	5,358	2,538	2,679	2,820
INGLE, Ella B (1895-1981) American					
oil	1	1,000		1,000	
INGLIS, John (1867-?) Irish					
oil	1	4,500		4,500	
INGRES, Jean Auguste Dominique (1780-1867) French					
oil	1	2,435		2,435	
wc/d	5	396,278	4,074	22,500	338,400
INGRES, Maurice (?) ?					
oil	1	1,000		1,000	
INGUIMBERTY, Joseph (1896-1971) French					
oil	2	2,957	1,309	1,479	1,648

Name	No.	Total Sales Value	Prices lowest	Prices median	highest
INJALBERT, Jean Antoine (1845-1933) French					
3D	1	1,174		1,174	
INMAN, Henry (1801-1846) American					
oil	1	2,750		2,750	
INMAN, John O'Brien (1828-1896) American					
oil	1	1,200		1,200	
wc/d	1	1,700		1,700	
INNERST, Mark (1957-) American					
wc/d	1	5,000		5,000	
INNES, Callum (1962-) British					
oil	4	43,538	6,500	8,704	19,630
INNES, James Dickson (1887-1914) British					
wc/d	1	1,332		1,332	
INNESS, George (1825-1894) American					
oil	21	1,997,200	2,700	50,000	600,000
INNOCENTI, Camillo (1871-1961) Italian					
oil	5	27,658	1,370	1,412	21,817
INSHAW, David (1943-) British					
oil	1	5,056		5,056	
INSLEY, Albert (1842-1937) American					
oil	1	1,000		1,000	
INUKAI, Kyohei (1913-1985) American					
oil	1	4,000		4,000	
IPCAR, Dahlov (1917-) American					
oil	2	9,500	4,000	4,750	5,500
IPSEN, Ernest Ludwig (1869-1951) American					
oil	4	25,000	4,500	5,500	9,500
IPSEN, P (?) Danish					
3D	1	1,342		1,342	
IRELAND, L M C (19th C) British					
oil	1	1,233		1,233	
IRELAND, Thomas Tayler (fl.1880-c.1927) British					
wc/d	1	1,074		1,074	
IRIBARREN, Juan (1956-) Venezuelan					
oil	1	1,440		1,440	
IRISH PROVINCIAL SCHOOL, 19th C					
oil	1	1,015		1,015	
IRISH SCHOOL, 18th C					
oil	1	3,400		3,400	
IRISH SCHOOL, 19th C					
oil	2	7,913	2,800	3,957	5,113
IRMER, Carl (1834-1900) German					
oil	2	4,167	1,373	2,084	2,794
IRMINGER, Valdemar (1850-1938) Danish					
oil	3	6,423	1,134	2,393	2,896
IROLLI, Vincenzo (1860-1949) Italian					
oil	15	231,974	2,182	13,000	44,000
wc/d	3	24,596	1,835	2,988	19,773
IRVIN, Fred (1914-) American					
wc/d	2	7,000	3,000	3,500	4,000
IRVINE (20th C) American					
oil	1	4,500		4,500	
IRVINE, Sadie (1887-1970) American					
wc/d	2	5,800	1,200	2,900	4,600
IRVINE, Wilson (1869-1936) American					
oil	6	58,800	4,000	9,000	20,000
IRVING, J Thwaite (fl.1888-1893) British					
oil	1	1,230		1,230	

Name	No.	Total Sales Value	lowest	Prices median	highest
ISABEY (18/19th C) French					
wc/d	1	1,981		1,981	
ISABEY, Eugène (1803-1886) French					
oil	10	66,273	2,000	5,267	18,960
wc/d	1	2,033		2,033	
ISABEY, Jean Baptiste (1767-1855) French					
wc/d	4	112,443	9,857	9,929	82,586
ISAKSON, Karl (1878-1922) Swedish					
oil	4	53,852	2,910	10,920	29,102
ISBAK, Poul (1943-) Danish					
3D	2	2,498	1,217	1,249	1,281
ISELI, Rolf (1934-) Swiss					
oil	2	15,126	1,573	7,563	13,553
wc/d	11	41,808	1,129	3,145	8,252
ISENBART, E (?) French?					
oil	1	1,648		1,648	
ISENBART, Marie Victor Émile (1846-1921) French					
oil	2	14,272	2,824	7,136	11,448
ISENBERG, Y (20th C) ?					
wc/d	1	4,231		4,231	
ISGRO, Emilio (1936-) Spanish					
oil	1	1,800		1,800	
wc/d	1	1,440		1,440	
ISHIDA, S (1888-1960) Japanese					
oil	1	2,718		2,718	
ISHIKAWA, K (19/20th C) Japanese					
wc/d	1	1,200		1,200	
ISHIMOTO, Tadashi (1920-) Japanese					
wc/d	1	65,000		65,000	
ISMAEL, Juan (20th C) Spanish					
wc/d	1	2,053		2,053	
ISOE, Gustavo (1954-) Japanese					
oil	1	3,280		3,280	
ISRAELS, Isaac (1865-1934) Dutch					
oil	12	541,124	3,800	39,181	95,646
wc/d	10	314,141	1,205	13,400	173,973
ISRAELS, Josef (1824-1911) Dutch					
oil	8	108,424	1,156	12,500	31,824
wc/d	7	17,817	1,180	1,923	7,000
ISSUPOFF, Alessio (1889-1957) Russian					
oil	7	42,820	1,431	5,797	16,747
ISTOK, J (20th C) ?					
3D	1	2,099		2,099	
ISTRATI, Alexandre (1915-1991) Rumanian					
oil	17	36,132	1,047	2,095	3,689
ISTVANFFY, Gabrielle Rainer (1877-1964) Hungarian					
oil	2	5,600	1,100	2,800	4,500
ITALIAN SCHOOL					
3D	13	84,124	2,605	6,500	17,485
oil	6	20,747	2,245	3,456	5,065
wc/d	2	7,407	3,472	3,704	3,935
ITALIAN SCHOOL, 13th C					
oil	1	5,199		5,199	
ITALIAN SCHOOL, 15th C					
3D	2	39,270	9,704	19,635	29,566
oil	3	36,834	3,200	7,354	26,280
wc/d	1	3,400		3,400	
ITALIAN SCHOOL, 15th/16th C					
oil	1	33,556		33,556	

Name	No.	Total Sales Value	lowest	Prices median	highest
ITALIAN SCHOOL, 16th C					
3D	6	50,386	4,558	6,643	17,815
oil	14	117,179	2,831	7,448	22,789
wc/d	1	4,000		4,000	
ITALIAN SCHOOL, 16th/17th C					
oil	3	11,533	3,579	3,990	3,990
ITALIAN SCHOOL, 17th C					
3D	15	114,891	2,732	7,550	22,257
oil	97	747,957	1,605	4,245	56,433
wc/d	3	9,605	2,696	3,454	3,455
ITALIAN SCHOOL, 17th/18th C					
3D	3	32,806	4,116	6,040	22,650
oil	13	82,315	3,076	5,387	12,287
ITALIAN SCHOOL, 18th C					
3D	19	367,363	2,955	9,114	154,350
oil	84	618,341	2,293	4,868	34,981
wc/d	2	9,765	3,565	4,883	6,200
ITALIAN SCHOOL, 18th/19th C					
3D	4	17,624	2,844	3,958	6,864
oil	3	27,138	3,500	5,766	17,872
ITALIAN SCHOOL, 19th C					
3D	48	568,029	2,306	5,513	129,860
oil	47	401,224	1,000	4,082	72,679
wc/d	8	50,030	2,791	5,880	13,430
ITALIAN SCHOOL, 19th/20th C					
3D	9	125,959	2,660	15,010	24,554
oil	1	2,938		2,938	
ITALIAN SCHOOL, 20th C					
oil	1	3,819		3,819	
ITALIAN-FLEMISH SCHOOL, 17th C					
3D	3	53,645	4,410	22,055	27,180
oil	1	2,849		2,849	
wc/d	1	2,554		2,554	
ITALIAN-FLEMISH SCHOOL, 18th C					
3D	1	6,174		6,174	
oil	1	3,143		3,143	
ITALIAN-SPANISH SCHOOL, 17th C					
oil	1	2,662		2,662	
ITASSE, Adolphe (1830-1893) French					
3D	1	8,706		8,706	
ITEN, Hans (1874-1930) Swiss/British					
oil	5	21,313	1,359	4,710	7,400
ITSCHNER, Karl (1868-1953) Swiss					
oil	1	3,242		3,242	
ITTEN, Johannes (1888-1967) Swiss					
wc/d	3	8,364	2,368	2,723	3,273
ITTENBACH, Franz (1813-1879) German					
oil	2	62,975	7,975	31,488	55,000
ITURRIA, Ignacio de (1949-) Uruguayan					
oil	13	149,800	2,000	9,800	25,000
IUDICE, Giovanni (1970-) Italian					
wc/d	1	1,586		1,586	
IVACKOVIC, Djoka (20th C) ?					
oil	2	2,092	1,010	1,046	1,082
wc/d	1	2,213		2,213	
IVANOFF, Sergei Vasilievich (c.1854-1910) Russian					
oil	1	6,345		6,345	
IVARSON, Ivan (1900-1939) Swedish					
oil	19	409,926	2,293	16,481	80,805
wc/d	2	4,235	1,927	2,118	2,308

Name	No.	Total Sales Value	Prices lowest	median	highest
IVERSEN, Helen (19th C) German					
oil	1	1,366		1,366	
IVES, Hazel Beauregard (fl.1915-c.1980) American					
wc/d	2	3,300	1,500	1,650	1,800
IVES, S (19th C) American					
oil	1	1,300		1,300	
IWILL (1850-1923) French					
oil	1	2,957		2,957	
IWILL, Joseph (1850-1923) French					
oil	3	7,129	1,693	2,457	2,979
IZANT OF CROYDON, Herbert (fl.1880-1898) British					
oil	1	2,320		2,320	
IZQUIERDO, J J (20th C) Venezuelan					
oil	1	3,440		3,440	
JAAR, Alfredo (1956-) American					
3D	1	22,000		22,000	
oil	1	24,000		24,000	
JABONEAU, Albert (19th C) French					
oil	1	1,113		1,113	
JACAKI, G (20th C) ?					
oil	1	3,227		3,227	
JACANAMIJOY, Carlos (20th C) Colombian					
oil	1	4,500		4,500	
JACCARD, Christian (20th C) French					
oil	1	2,185		2,185	
JACK, John (19/20th C) British					
oil	1	3,549		3,549	
JACK, Richard (1866-1952) Canadian/British					
oil	1	12,080		12,080	
JACKLIN, Bill (1943-) British					
oil	2	9,053	2,528	4,527	6,525
JACKMAN, Oscar Theodore (1878-1940) American					
oil	1	2,500		2,500	
JACKSON, A Y (1882-1974) Canadian					
oil	4	61,408	4,698	8,222	40,267
wc/d	1	1,208		1,208	
JACKSON, Alexander Young (1882-1974) Canadian					
oil	34	587,231	4,569	9,123	195,833
wc/d	1	1,195		1,195	
JACKSON, Ashley (1940-) British					
wc/d	2	3,141	1,492	1,571	1,649
JACKSON, E M (?-1934) American					
oil	1	4,750		4,750	
JACKSON, Everett Gee (1900-) American					
oil	1	3,500		3,500	
JACKSON, Frederick Hamilton (1848-1923) British					
wc/d	1	1,350		1,350	
JACKSON, Frederick William (1859-1918) British					
oil	6	22,531	1,278	3,195	8,360
wc/d	2	2,428	1,022	1,214	1,406
JACKSON, Harry (1924-) American					
3D	7	111,750	3,250	20,000	25,000
JACKSON, James Ranalph (1882-1975) Australian					
oil	1	1,431		1,431	
JACKSON, Michael (1961-) British					
wc/d	1	4,544		4,544	
JACKSON, Ronald (1902-1992) Canadian					
oil	1	6,376		6,376	

Name	No.	Total Sales Value	lowest	median	highest
JACKSON, Samuel (1794-1869) British					
wc/d	1	6,864		6,864	
JACKSON, Samuel Phillips (1830-1904) British					
oil	1	6,194		6,194	
wc/d	7	20,417	1,316	3,552	3,718
JACKSON, William Franklin (1850-1936) American					
oil	3	8,250	2,000	3,000	3,250
JACOB, Alexandre (1876-1972) French					
oil	5	21,884	1,036	1,944	13,430
JACOB, Max (1876-1944) French					
oil	1	1,309		1,309	
wc/d	9	19,071	1,000	2,047	4,752
JACOB, Ned (1938-) American					
oil	1	9,000		9,000	
JACOBBER, Moise (1786-1863) French					
oil	1	3,962		3,962	
JACOBER, Ben (20th C) ?					
3D	1	1,571		1,571	
JACOBI, Marcus (1891-1969) Swiss					
oil	2	2,565	1,049	1,283	1,516
JACOBI, Otto Reinhard (1812-1901) German/Canadian					
oil	4	14,723	1,490	3,630	5,973
JACOBI, Rudolf (1889-1972) American					
wc/d	1	1,594		1,594	
JACOBS, François (19th C) ?					
oil	2	5,692	1,148	2,846	4,544
JACOBS, Herman (1936-) Belgian					
oil	1	2,298		2,298	
JACOBS, Jacob Albertus Michael (1812-1879) Belgian					
oil	3	13,069	1,275	4,405	7,389
JACOBS, Louis Adolphe (1855-1929) Belgian					
oil	1	1,542		1,542	
JACOBS, Michel (1877-1958) American					
oil	1	1,600		1,600	
JACOBS, Stephen (19th C) British					
oil	1	1,508		1,508	
JACOBSEN, A (19th C) ?					
oil	2	7,832	1,582	3,916	6,250
JACOBSEN, Antonio (1850-1921) American					
oil	32	365,538	2,600	9,500	27,000
JACOBSEN, David (1821-1871) Danish					
oil	1	1,889		1,889	
JACOBSEN, Egill (1910-1998) Danish					
oil	14	211,514	1,907	10,151	61,598
JACOBSEN, Georg (1887-1976) Danish					
oil	1	1,089		1,089	
JACOBSEN, Ludvig (1890-1975) Danish					
oil	1	1,020		1,020	
JACOBSEN, Robert (1912-1993) Danish					
3D	15	104,267	1,958	5,430	25,071
oil	1	2,673		2,673	
wc/d	4	6,132	1,385	1,469	1,810
JACOBSEN, Sophus (1833-1912) Norwegian					
oil	2	4,492	1,698	2,246	2,794
JACOBSON, Jacob (1818-1891) German					
oil	1	1,573		1,573	
JACOBSON, John (1958-) Swedish					
oil	1	2,064		2,064	

Name	No.	Total Sales Value	Prices lowest	Prices median	highest
JACOBSZ, Lambert (c.1598-1636) Dutch					
oil	1	26,000		26,000	
JACOMB-HOOD, George Percy (1857-1937) British					
oil	1	12,640		12,640	
JACOMIN, Alfred (1842-1913) French					
oil	1	6,771		6,771	
JACOMMETTI, Tarquinio (17th C) Italian					
oil	1	1,774		1,774	
JACOPS, Joseph (1808-?) Belgian					
oil	1	1,364		1,364	
JACOVACCI, Francesco (19th C) Italian					
oil	2	13,600	6,000	6,800	7,600
JACQUAND, Claudius (1804-1878) French					
oil	2	2,912	1,354	1,456	1,558
JACQUE, Charles Émile (1813-1894) French					
oil	23	139,363	1,199	3,250	36,000
wc/d	1	3,000		3,000	
JACQUE, Frederic (1859-?) French					
oil	1	1,306		1,306	
JACQUELIN, Marguerite (19/20th C) French					
oil	2	9,095	2,963	4,548	6,132
JACQUEMART, Alfred (1824-1896) French					
3D	3	7,015	1,728	2,198	3,089
JACQUES, François-Louis (1877-1937) Swiss					
oil	1	1,596		1,596	
JACQUES, Robin (1920-) ?					
wc/d	1	2,304		2,304	
JACQUET, Alain (1939-) French					
wc/d	1	1,902		1,902	
JACQUET, Gustave-Jean (1846-1909) French					
oil	5	71,298	4,858	10,270	40,600
wc/d	2	4,259	1,667	2,130	2,592
JACQUET, Maurice (1877-?) French					
oil	1	1,015		1,015	
JADELOT, Sophie (1820-?) French					
oil	1	2,904		2,904	
JADIN, Charles Emannuel (19th C) French					
oil	1	17,215		17,215	
JAECKEL, Henry (19th C) German					
oil	3	11,804	2,049	2,469	7,286
JAECKEL, Willy (1888-1944) German					
oil	3	14,653	3,846	5,184	5,623
wc/d	2	18,000	6,480	9,000	11,520
JAEGER, E G (20th C) German					
3D	1	1,156		1,156	
JAEGER, Ernst Gustav (1880-?) German					
3D	1	2,428		2,428	
JAEGER, Tyco Christopher (1819-1889) Norwegian					
oil	1	20,145		20,145	
JAENISCH, Hans (1907-1989) German					
oil	3	9,132	1,990	2,364	4,778
JAFFE, Shirley (20th C) American					
oil	3	8,823	1,736	2,314	4,773
JAGEMANN, Ferdinand (1780-1820) German					
wc/d	1	2,949		2,949	
JAGERSPACHER, Gustav (20th C) German					
oil	1	2,505		2,505	
JAHL, Wladyslaw Adam Alojzy (1886-1953) Polish					
oil	2	2,506	1,032	1,253	1,474

Name	No.	Total Sales Value	lowest	Prices median	highest
JAHN, Anton (1810-1841) German					
oil	1	4,907		4,907	
JAHN, Hans Emil (1834-1902) Norwegian					
oil	1	4,757		4,757	
JAHNS, Rudolf (1896-1983) German					
oil	1	2,151		2,151	
wc/d	2	33,981	2,913	16,991	31,068
JAKIMOV, Anne Marie (1889-?) German					
oil	1	2,727		2,727	
JAKOBIDES, Georg (1853-1932) Greek					
oil	1	105,120		105,120	
JAMAR, Armand (1870-1946) Belgian					
oil	8	15,917	1,253	1,689	3,574
JAMBOR, Louis (1884-1955) American					
oil	1	2,115		2,115	
JAMES, Alan Gossett (1875-1950) British					
oil	1	12,870		12,870	
JAMES, Alexander (20th C) American					
oil	1	1,500		1,500	
JAMES, D (fl.1881-1898) British					
oil	1	7,742		7,742	
JAMES, David (fl.1881-1898) British					
oil	12	81,159	1,425	6,675	15,800
JAMES, Will (1892-1942) American					
wc/d	3	21,500	5,500	6,000	10,000
JAMES, William (18th C) British					
oil	4	219,960	30,200	57,380	75,000
JAMESON, Frank (1898-1968) British					
wc/d	1	1,200		1,200	
JAMESON, Joan (fl.1933-1938) British					
oil	3	14,948	3,848	5,180	5,920
JAMIESON, Alexander (1873-1937) British					
oil	3	10,432	3,002	3,322	4,108
JAMIESON, F E (1895-1950) British					
oil	2	2,600	1,000	1,300	1,600
JAMIESON, Mitchell (1915-) American					
wc/d	1	1,000		1,000	
JAMPOLSKY, Michail (1847-?) French/Russian					
3D	1	1,716		1,716	
JAN, Elvire (1904-1996) French/Bulgarian					
oil	5	14,967	1,053	1,441	7,492
JANCO, Marcel (1895-1984) Israeli/Rumanian					
3D	1	1,328		1,328	
oil	17	182,670	2,600	6,000	32,000
wc/d	3	6,710	1,300	2,200	3,210
JANEBE (1907-) Swiss					
oil	3	4,584	1,073	1,412	2,099
JANENSCH, Gerhard Adolf (1860-1933) German					
3D	1	1,636		1,636	
JANERAND, Daniel du (1919-1990) French					
oil	1	1,053		1,053	
JANESCH, Albert (1889-1973) Austrian					
oil	1	1,593		1,593	
JANESCH, G (20th C) ?					
3D	1	1,946		1,946	
JANK, Angelo (1868-1956) German					
oil	5	9,197	1,002	1,823	3,028
JANKOWSKI, F W (19th C) Austrian					
oil	1	4,000		4,000	

Name	No.	Total Sales Value	lowest	Prices median	highest
JANKOWSKI, J Wilhelm (fl.1825-1861) Austrian					
oil	2	6,793	2,279	3,397	4,514
JANMOT, Anne François Louis (1814-1892) French					
oil	1	31,677		31,677	
wc/d	1	24,730		24,730	
JANNECK, Franz Christoph (1703-1761) Austrian					
oil	3	88,937	1,187	37,750	50,000
JANNI, Guglielmo (1892-1958) Italian					
oil	1	2,893		2,893	
JANNIOT, Alfred Auguste (1889-1969) French					
3D	4	48,028	8,449	10,235	19,109
wc/d	1	5,187		5,187	
JANNOT, Henri (1909-) French					
oil	1	1,385		1,385	
JANS, Edouard de (1855-?) Belgian					
oil	2	5,622	1,186	2,811	4,436
JANSE, Felix (?) ?					
oil	2	7,134	2,129	3,567	5,005
JANSEM, Jean (1920-) French					
oil	12	153,613	2,032	11,769	26,313
wc/d	5	15,515	1,549	3,658	4,582
JANSEN, Fritz (1892-?) German					
wc/d	1	4,528		4,528	
JANSEN, Hendrik Willebrord (1855-1908) Dutch					
oil	1	5,433		5,433	
JANSEN, Johannes Maurisz (1812-1857) Dutch					
oil	2	4,562	1,766	2,281	2,796
JANSEN, Joseph (1829-1905) German					
oil	3	7,321	1,603	2,944	2,944
JANSEN, Willem (1892-?) Dutch					
oil	2	4,116	1,782	2,058	2,334
JANSEN, Willem George Frederick (1871-1949) Dutch					
oil	5	20,117	1,937	3,512	6,789
wc/d	1	1,641		1,641	
JANSON, Johannes (1729-1784) Dutch					
oil	1	1,800		1,800	
JANSON, Johannes Christian (1763-1823) Dutch					
oil	1	2,646		2,646	
JANSSAUD, Mathurin (1857-1940) French					
wc/d	7	17,808	1,378	2,031	6,075
JANSSEN, Horst (1929-1995) German					
wc/d	30	168,949	1,079	3,251	22,330
JANSSEN, Ludovic (1888-1954) Belgian					
oil	1	1,278		1,278	
JANSSEN, Luplau (19/20th C) Danish					
oil	2	2,885	1,207	1,443	1,678
JANSSEN, W (?) ?					
oil	1	3,944		3,944	
JANSSENS, Hieronymus (1624-1693) Flemish					
oil	1	57,380		57,380	
JANSSENS, Jacques (19th C) Belgian					
oil	1	4,121		4,121	
JANSSON, Alfred (1863-1931) American/Swedish					
oil	5	15,800	1,400	2,200	7,000
JANSSON, Alvar (1922-1990) Scandinavian					
oil	1	1,693		1,693	
JANSSON, Eugène (1862-1915) Swedish					
oil	3	317,649	1,360	50,059	266,230

Name	No.	Total Sales Value	lowest	Prices median	highest
JANSSON, Rune (1918-) Swedish					
oil	1	1,507		1,507	
JANSSON, Tove (1914-) Finnish					
oil	2	15,156	2,110	7,578	13,046
wc/d	1	9,250		9,250	
JANTHUR, Richard (1883-1956) German?					
oil	1	2,745		2,745	
JANVIER, Alex (1935-) Canadian					
oil	1	1,946		1,946	
JAPANESE SCHOOL					
3D	1	11,983		11,983	
JAPANESE SCHOOL, 17th C					
wc/d	2	19,037	6,641	9,519	12,396
JAPANESE SCHOOL, 18th C					
wc/d	1	2,214		2,214	
JAPANESE SCHOOL, 19th C					
3D	4	43,156	4,020	8,658	21,821
oil	1	11,000		11,000	
JAPANESE SCHOOL, 20th C					
3D	3	18,601	6,004	6,170	6,427
JAPY, Louis Aime (1840-1916) French					
oil	10	98,811	1,600	6,204	38,000
JAQUET, Jacques (1830-1898) Belgian					
3D	1	53,737		53,737	
JAQUET, Jan Jozef (1822-1898) Belgian					
3D	2	10,340	4,396	5,170	5,944
JARAIZ, Jaime de (1934-) Spanish					
oil	1	1,430		1,430	
JARDINES, Jose Maria (1862-?) Spanish					
oil	2	8,646	3,419	4,323	5,227
JARMAN, Gerald (20th C) British?					
oil	1	1,422		1,422	
JARNEFELT, Eero (1863-1937) Finnish					
oil	1	1,730		1,730	
wc/d	1	1,962		1,962	
JAROSZ, Romain (1889-1932) French					
oil	1	2,393		2,393	
JARRETT, Charles (20th C) American					
oil	1	2,750		2,750	
JARVIS, Georgia (1944-1990) Canadian					
oil	5	8,483	1,045	1,413	3,243
JASINSKI, Zdzislaw (1863-1932) Polish					
oil	1	6,903		6,903	
JASON, Mario (20th C) American					
3D	1	1,300		1,300	
JAUDON, Valerie (1945-) American					
oil	1	3,200		3,200	
JAULMES, Gustave (1873-1959) Swiss					
oil	1	2,116		2,116	
JAUMOTTE, Gaston (1926-) Belgian					
oil	1	1,030		1,030	
JAVUREK, Karel (1815-1909) Czechoslovakian					
oil	1	4,672		4,672	
JAWLENSKY, Alexej von (1864-1941) Russian					
oil	27	4,247,785	5,674	78,203	655,200
wc/d	5	93,921	1,307	7,802	60,729
JAWLENSKY, Andreas (1902-1984) Polish					
oil	2	11,285	3,010	5,643	8,275
wc/d	2	3,153	1,262	1,577	1,891

Name	No.	Total Sales Value	lowest	Prices median	highest
JAX, Theobald (19th C) ?					
oil	1	3,000		3,000	
JAY, Cecil (1884-?) American					
oil	1	5,836		5,836	
JAZET, Paul-Léon (1848-?) French					
oil	1	4,228		4,228	
JEANCLOS, Georges (1933-) French					
3D	1	9,127		9,127	
JEANMAIRE, Edouard (1847-1916) Swiss					
oil	2	4,409	2,051	2,205	2,358
JEANNENEY, François Victor (1832-1885) French					
oil	1	4,740		4,740	
JEANNERET, Gustave (1847-1927) Swiss					
oil	1	1,805		1,805	
JEANNIN, Georges (1841-1925) French					
oil	6	14,415	1,106	2,346	4,060
JEAURAT, Étienne (1699-1789) French					
oil	2	8,817	2,918	4,409	5,899
JEDLICZKA, V (19th C) ?					
oil	1	1,366		1,366	
JEFFERSON, Joseph (1829-1905) American					
oil	2	6,900	2,400	3,450	4,500
JEFFERYS, Marcel (1872-1924) Belgian					
oil	3	31,600	2,354	14,623	14,623
JELINEK, Rudolf (1880-?) Austrian					
oil	1	1,273		1,273	
JELINK, Hendrikus Johannes (1808-1846) Dutch					
oil	1	1,180		1,180	
JELLETT, Mainie (1897-1944) Irish					
oil	1	29,600		29,600	
wc/d	1	9,620		9,620	
JENKINS, Arthur H (1871-?) British					
oil	1	1,628		1,628	
JENKINS, George Henry (1843-1914) British					
oil	3	5,588	1,570	1,584	2,434
wc/d	1	1,027		1,027	
JENKINS, Joseph John (1811-1885) British					
wc/d	2	4,123	1,425	2,062	2,698
JENKINS, Paul (1923-) American					
oil	10	39,870	1,047	3,943	8,000
wc/d	6	10,223	1,047	1,473	2,618
JENKINS, Wilfred (fl.1875-1888) British					
oil	3	20,193	1,152	2,556	16,485
JENKINSON, John (fl.1790-1823) British					
oil	1	27,710		27,710	
JENKINSON, Lady L (?) British?					
wc/d	1	1,580		1,580	
JENNER, Isaac Walter (1836-1901) Australian					
oil	2	6,325	1,109	3,163	5,216
wc/d	1	2,567		2,567	
JENNER, William (?) ?					
oil	1	1,125		1,125	
JENNEY, Neil (1945-) American					
oil	6	552,500	50,000	85,000	175,000
JENSEN, Alfred (1903-1981) American					
oil	1	38,000		38,000	
JENSEN, Alfred (1859-1935) Danish					
oil	8	18,938	1,000	1,375	7,975

Name	No.	Total Sales Value	lowest	Prices median	highest
JENSEN, Berit (1956-) Danish					
oil	1	1,033		1,033	
JENSEN, C A (1792-1870) Danish					
oil	1	1,889		1,889	
JENSEN, Christian Albrecht (1792-1870) Danish					
oil	2	66,128	5,801	33,064	60,327
JENSEN, Clay (20th C) American					
3D	1	2,000		2,000	
JENSEN, E M (1822-1915) Danish					
oil	1	1,108		1,108	
JENSEN, Gabriel (1862-1930) Danish					
oil	1	1,015		1,015	
JENSEN, George (1878-?) American					
oil	1	1,000		1,000	
JENSEN, Herman (1893-1947) Danish					
oil	1	1,342		1,342	
JENSEN, J-L (1800-1856) Danish					
oil	4	14,758	1,972	4,189	4,408
JENSEN, Johan-Laurents (1800-1856) Danish					
oil	22	356,930	2,275	11,249	76,569
JENSEN, Johan-Laurents (school) (1800-1856) Danish					
oil	19	43,008	1,259	1,787	5,809
JENSEN, Karl (1851-1933) Danish					
oil	1	11,618		11,618	
JENSEN, Louis Isak Napolean (1858-1908) Danish					
oil	2	4,607	2,025	2,304	2,582
JENSEN, Olaf Christopher (1954-) Norwegian					
oil	2	3,111	1,505	1,556	1,606
JENSEN, Olga (1877-1949) Danish					
oil	2	2,731	1,311	1,366	1,420
JENSEN, Soren Georg (1917-1982) Danish					
3D	3	8,461	1,922	2,232	4,307
JENTZSCH, Johannes Gabriel (1862-?) German					
oil	1	2,163		2,163	
JERICHAU, Harald Adolf Nikolai (1851-1878) Danish					
oil	2	4,416	2,204	2,208	2,212
JERICHAU, Holger H (1861-1900) Danish					
oil	6	14,886	1,084	2,235	4,500
JERICHAU, Jens Adolf (1890-1916) Danish					
oil	2	59,311	5,849	29,656	53,462
JERICHAU-BAUMANN, Elisabeth (1819-1881) Danish					
oil	6	29,034	1,326	3,906	10,008
JERKEN, Erik (1898-1947) Swedish					
oil	1	1,405		1,405	
JERNBERG, August (1826-1896) Swedish					
oil	4	10,462	1,449	2,766	3,482
JERNBERG, Olof (1855-1935) Swedish					
oil	4	7,785	1,420	1,490	3,386
JERNDORFF, August (1846-1906) Danish					
oil	1	10,076		10,076	
JEROME, Ambrosini (fl.1840-1871) British					
oil	1	1,590		1,590	
JERVAS, Charles (1675-1739) British					
oil	3	24,173	4,608	10,270	10,270
JERZY, Richard (20th C) American					
wc/d	1	1,000		1,000	
JESPERS, Émile Louis (1862-1918) Belgian					
3D	2	6,010	1,775	3,005	4,235

Name	No.	Total Sales Value	Prices lowest	median	highest
JESPERS, Floris (1889-1965) Belgian					
oil	58	238,243	1,045	2,227	55,133
wc/d	5	21,667	1,045	1,898	9,491
JESPERS, Oscar (1887-1970) Belgian					
3D	2	19,016	7,526	9,508	11,490
JESPERSEN, Henrik (1853-1936) Danish					
oil	2	3,830	1,889	1,915	1,941
JESS (1923-) American					
wc/d	2	37,000	12,000	18,500	25,000
JESSEN, Carl Ludwig (1833-1917) Danish/German					
oil	2	4,127	1,624	2,064	2,503
JESSEN, Thomas (1958-) German?					
oil	1	3,244		3,244	
JESSUP, Frederick (1920-) Australian					
wc/d	1	3,928		3,928	
JETELOWA, Magdalena (1946-) ?					
3D	1	1,788		1,788	
JETTEL, Eugen (1845-1901) Austrian					
oil	3	42,018	1,788	5,340	34,890
JETTMAR, Rudolf (1869-1939) Austrian					
oil	1	6,364		6,364	
wc/d	1	2,909		2,909	
JEUNE, James le (1910-1983) Irish					
oil	3	24,740	5,500	8,140	11,100
wc/d	1	1,106		1,106	
JEWELS, Mary (20th C) British?					
oil	1	5,640		5,640	
JEX, Garnet W (1895-1979) American					
oil	14	50,650	1,100	2,450	15,000
JIMENEZ Y ARANDA, Jose (1837-1903) Spanish					
oil	4	269,444	18,472	58,040	134,892
wc/d	4	11,116	2,332	2,667	3,451
JIMENEZ Y ARANDA, Luis (1845-1928) Spanish					
oil	4	30,705	2,253	6,726	15,000
wc/d	2	4,066	1,038	2,033	3,028
JIMENEZ Y MARTIN, Juan (1858-1901) Spanish					
oil	1	10,827		10,827	
JIRLOW, Lennart (1936-) Swedish					
3D	1	3,618		3,618	
oil	10	101,645	3,618	6,432	30,105
wc/d	4	19,739	1,359	5,070	8,240
JOACHIM, Jean (1905-1990) French					
3D	3	13,958	2,502	4,872	6,584
JOANOVITCH, Paul (1859-?) Austrian					
oil	1	67,160		67,160	
JOBERT, Paul (1863-?) French					
oil	1	4,847		4,847	
JOBLING, Isa (1850-1926) British					
oil	1	1,359		1,359	
wc/d	1	2,512		2,512	
JOBLING, R (1841-1923) British					
oil	1	9,106		9,106	
JOBLING, Robert (1841-1923) British					
oil	10	62,634	1,284	3,738	16,300
wc/d	1	1,738		1,738	
JOCHIMS, Reimer (1934-) German					
oil	1	2,427		2,427	
JOENSEN-MIKINES, S (1906-1979) Danish					
oil	3	11,651	2,729	3,809	5,113

Name	No.	Total Sales Value	Prices lowest	median	highest
JOENSEN-MIKINES, Samuel (1906-1979) Danish					
oil	9	32,362	1,630	3,763	5,894
JOFFRIN, Guily (1909-) French					
oil	1	1,298		1,298	
JOHANSEN, Axel (1872-1938) Danish					
oil	1	1,420		1,420	
JOHANSEN, John C (1876-1964) American					
oil	2	2,800	1,200	1,400	1,600
JOHANSEN, Svend (1890-1970) Danish					
oil	1	3,203		3,203	
JOHANSEN, Viggo (1851-1935) Danish					
oil	8	35,629	1,159	1,763	22,042
wc/d	1	1,029		1,029	
JOHANSON-THOR, Emil (1889-1958) Swedish					
oil	1	2,065		2,065	
JOHANSSON VON COLN, Anders (1663-1716) Swedish					
oil	1	26,662		26,662	
JOHANSSON, Albert (1926-1998) Swedish					
oil	6	9,484	1,037	1,570	2,075
wc/d	1	1,573		1,573	
JOHANSSON, Arvid (1862-1923) Swedish					
oil	1	1,675		1,675	
JOHANSSON, Carl (1863-1944) Swedish					
oil	6	18,427	1,077	2,462	7,400
JOHANSSON, Stefan (1876-1955) Swedish					
oil	1	5,079		5,079	
wc/d	1	2,747		2,747	
JOHANSSON, Sven-Erik (1925-) Swedish					
wc/d	1	1,693		1,693	
JOHFRA (1919-) Dutch					
oil	1	6,073		6,073	
wc/d	1	1,936		1,936	
JOHN, Augustus (1878-1961) British					
oil	8	134,489	3,750	8,730	53,580
wc/d	10	52,091	1,287	3,375	14,628
JOHN, Gwen (1876-1939) British					
wc/d	3	24,962	2,002	8,460	14,500
JOHN, Vivien (1915-1994) British					
oil	1	1,460		1,460	
JOHNAR, Rachel (19th C) German					
oil	1	8,500		8,500	
JOHNS, Jasper (1930-) American					
3D	4	82,000	15,000	20,500	26,000
wc/d	2	840,000	240,000	420,000	600,000
JOHNSON, A Hale (?) American					
oil	1	2,200		2,200	
JOHNSON, David (1827-1908) American					
oil	4	145,000	9,000	33,000	70,000
JOHNSON, Eastman (1824-1906) American					
oil	1	58,000		58,000	
JOHNSON, Edward Killingworth (1825-1923) British					
wc/d	5	23,786	1,950	5,720	6,946
JOHNSON, F Morton (1846-1921) ?					
oil	1	1,455		1,455	
JOHNSON, Frank Tenney (1874-1939) American					
oil	7	163,500	15,000	20,000	47,500
wc/d	1	55,000		55,000	
JOHNSON, Harry John (1826-1884) British					
wc/d	1	1,430		1,430	

Name	No.	Total Sales Value	lowest	Prices median	highest
JOHNSON, Harvey W (1920-) American					
oil	1	18,000		18,000	
JOHNSON, Lester (1919-) American					
oil	2	9,000	4,000	4,500	5,000
JOHNSON, Marshall (1850-1915) American					
oil	3	12,600	1,200	1,400	10,000
JOHNSON, Neville (1911-) British					
oil	2	3,925	1,884	1,963	2,041
JOHNSON, Patty (fl.1877-1904) British					
wc/d	1	1,058		1,058	
JOHNSON, Raymond (20th C) American					
oil	1	3,000		3,000	
JOHNSON, Robert Barbour (20th C) American					
wc/d	1	1,500		1,500	
JOHNSON, S Y (fl.1901-1910) British					
oil	1	1,495		1,495	
JOHNSON, Samuel Frost (1835-?) American					
oil	1	8,000		8,000	
JOHNSON, Sargent (1889-1967) American					
3D	1	40,000		40,000	
JOHNSON, Sidney Yates (fl.1901-1910) British					
oil	3	3,509	1,027	1,232	1,250
JOHNSON, Theodore (1902-) American					
oil	1	7,000		7,000	
JOHNSON, W Noel (fl.1887-1914) British					
wc/d	1	1,108		1,108	
JOHNSON, Willes (19th C) ?					
oil	1	2,550		2,550	
JOHNSTON, Alexander (1815-1891) British					
oil	1	31,400		31,400	
JOHNSTON, David (1946-) British					
oil	1	4,260		4,260	
JOHNSTON, David Claypoole (1797-1865) American					
oil	1	3,500		3,500	
JOHNSTON, Frank Hans (1888-1949) Canadian					
oil	21	85,516	1,062	3,198	14,361
wc/d	1	1,261		1,261	
JOHNSTON, Henry (fl.1834-1858) British					
wc/d	1	6,952		6,952	
JOHNSTON, Reuben le Grand (1850-1919) American					
oil	1	1,600		1,600	
JOHNSTON, Ynez (1920-) American					
oil	1	2,000		2,000	
wc/d	1	1,400		1,400	
JOHNSTONE, George Whitton (1849-1901) British					
oil	1	1,352		1,352	
JOHNSTONE, Henry James (1835-1907) British					
wc/d	1	8,866		8,866	
JOHNSTONE, Henry John (fl.1881-1900) British					
oil	1	2,431		2,431	
JOHNSTONE, William (1897-1981) British					
oil	4	20,173	1,178	5,510	7,975
JOHNSTONE, William Borthwick (1804-1868) British					
oil	1	1,470		1,470	
JOINVILLE, Antoine Victor Edmond (1801-1849) French					
oil	1	5,155		5,155	
JOIRE, Jean (1862-?) French					
3D	1	2,178		2,178	

Name	No.	Total Sales Value	Prices lowest	median	highest
JOLI, Antonio (1700-1770) Italian					
oil	2	554,600	240,000	277,300	314,600
JOLIN, Einar (1890-1976) Swedish					
oil	30	103,807	1,016	2,562	11,039
wc/d	4	11,128	1,582	2,325	4,897
JOLIN, Ellen (1854-1939) Swedish					
oil	1	3,465		3,465	
JOLLAIN, Pierre (1720-?) French					
oil	1	4,710		4,710	
JOLLEY, Martin Gwilt (1859-?) British					
oil	1	8,700		8,700	
JOLLIVET, Pierre Jules (1794-1871) French					
oil	1	3,114		3,114	
JOLLY, Andre (19/20th C) French					
oil	2	15,449	1,910	7,725	13,539
JOLY, Jules (19th C) French					
wc/d	1	2,540		2,540	
JON-AND, John (1889-1941) Swedish					
oil	3	24,635	2,914	5,441	16,280
wc/d	1	1,420		1,420	
JONAS, Henri Charles (1878-1944) Dutch					
oil	1	6,634		6,634	
JONAS, Rudolf (1822-1888) German					
oil	1	1,981		1,981	
JONAS, Siegfried (20th C) ?					
3D	1	3,245		3,245	
JONAVILLE, Pierre (1827-?) French					
oil	1	4,133		4,133	
JONCHERIE, Gabriele Germain (19th C) French					
oil	1	5,159		5,159	
JONCHERY (1873-?) French					
3D	1	2,265		2,265	
JONCHERY, Charles (1873-?) French					
3D	1	14,031		14,031	
JONES, Allen (1937-) British					
wc/d	2	4,764	1,650	2,382	3,114
JONES, Arne (1914-1976) Swedish					
3D	1	1,806		1,806	
JONES, Brian J (20th C) British					
oil	5	14,915	1,359	2,860	5,738
JONES, Charles (1836-1892) British					
oil	9	60,344	1,699	3,171	15,855
JONES, Daniel Adolphe Robert (1806-1874) Belgian					
oil	1	2,513		2,513	
JONES, David (1895-1974) British					
wc/d	8	66,738	1,125	4,800	24,960
JONES, Emma (19th C) British?					
oil	1	2,400		2,400	
JONES, Francis Coates (1857-1932) American					
oil	1	58,000		58,000	
wc/d	2	7,000	2,500	3,500	4,500
JONES, Hugh Bolton (1848-1927) American					
oil	6	80,500	1,500	13,500	22,000
wc/d	2	4,000	1,000	2,000	3,000
JONES, Joe (1909-1963) American					
oil	2	4,000	2,000	2,000	2,000
JONES, Maude Raphael (fl.1889-1900) British					
wc/d	1	1,235		1,235	

Name	No.	Total Sales Value	lowest	Prices median	highest
JONES, Paul (19th C) British					
oil	4	12,073	1,495	3,264	4,050
JONES, R (19/20th C) British					
oil	1	1,584		1,584	
JONES, Robert (fl.1906-1940) British					
oil	2	7,865	3,915	3,933	3,950
JONES, Robinson (?) ?					
oil	1	3,040		3,040	
JONES, Samuel John Egbert (fl.1820-1855) British					
oil	2	9,366	3,400	4,683	5,966
JONES, Steven (1959-) British					
oil	1	1,463		1,463	
JONES, Thomas (1742-1803) British					
oil	1	14,220		14,220	
JONG, Frans de (?-1705) Dutch					
oil	1	10,990		10,990	
JONG, Germ de (1886-1967) Dutch					
oil	1	2,852		2,852	
wc/d	1	2,586		2,586	
JONG, Jacqueline de (1939-) Dutch					
oil	3	4,767	1,192	1,192	2,383
JONG, Jan de (1863-1901) Dutch					
oil	2	3,473	1,327	1,737	2,146
JONGERE, Marinus de (1912-1978) Dutch					
oil	12	24,841	1,231	1,925	3,614
wc/d	2	2,496	1,205	1,248	1,291
JONGH, Ludolf de (1616-1679) Dutch					
oil	2	147,852	7,852	73,926	140,000
JONGH, O R de (1812-1896) Dutch					
oil	1	1,672		1,672	
JONGH, Oene Romkes de (1812-1896) Dutch					
oil	4	12,964	1,405	2,436	6,687
JONGH, Tinus de (1885-1942) Dutch					
oil	2	5,439	1,323	2,720	4,116
wc/d	1	1,454		1,454	
JONGHE, Gustave de (1829-1893) Belgian					
oil	6	74,984	2,089	10,293	28,000
JONGKIND, Johan Barthold (1819-1891) Dutch					
oil	8	470,943	1,709	27,630	240,000
wc/d	13	105,203	1,710	5,713	18,620
JONK, Nic (1928-1994) Dutch					
3D	1	1,347		1,347	
JONNAERT, Albert (1850-1943) Belgian					
oil	1	2,796		2,796	
JONNEVOLD, Carl Henrik (1856-1930) American					
oil	4	13,150	1,400	3,125	5,500
JONSON (?) Dutch					
oil	1	2,503		2,503	
JONSON, Cornelis (1593-1664) Dutch					
oil	2	12,473	1,903	6,237	10,570
JONSON, Raymond (1891-1982) American					
oil	1	32,000		32,000	
JONSON, Sven (1902-1981) Danish					
oil	26	103,119	1,256	2,993	13,046
JONSSON, Alfred (?) Swedish					
oil	1	1,555		1,555	
JONSSON, Lars (1952-) Swedish					
wc/d	1	2,015		2,015	

Name	No.	Total Sales Value	Prices lowest	median	highest
JOORS, Eugeen (1850-1910) Belgian					
oil	8	21,202	1,259	1,889	6,500
JOOSTEN, Dirk Jan Hendrik (1818-1882) Dutch					
oil	1	14,049		14,049	
JOOSTENS, Paul (1889-1960) Belgian					
oil	14	40,871	1,045	2,837	6,147
wc/d	32	59,344	1,040	1,478	5,201
JOPLING, Louise (1843-1933) British					
oil	1	1,716		1,716	
JORDAENS, Hans III (1595-1643) Flemish					
oil	1	9,091		9,091	
JORDAENS, Jacob (1593-1678) Flemish					
oil	9	833,445	1,475	40,820	286,900
wc/d	7	58,706	4,321	6,500	18,071
JORDAENS, Jacob (school) (1593-1678) Flemish					
oil	1	6,961		6,961	
JORDAINS, A (18th C) ?					
wc/d	1	13,883		13,883	
JORDAN, Carl (1826-1907) German					
oil	1	3,000		3,000	
JORDAN, Martin (20th C) British					
oil	1	1,420		1,420	
JORDENS, Jan (1883-1962) Dutch					
oil	2	8,404	2,971	4,202	5,433
JORGENSEN, Aksel (1883-1957) Danish					
oil	2	2,224	1,006	1,112	1,218
JORGENSEN, Borge (1926-) Danish					
3D	3	18,203	4,508	6,392	7,303
JORGENSEN, Christian (1860-1935) American					
oil	1	6,500		6,500	
JORGENSEN, Erling (1905-1977) Danish					
oil	1	1,281		1,281	
JORGENSEN, Willer (20th C) Danish					
oil	3	10,507	2,141	3,600	4,766
JORIS, Pio (1843-1921) Italian					
oil	2	19,992	9,500	9,996	10,492
wc/d	3	7,823	1,835	2,495	3,493
JORN, Asger (1914-1973) Danish					
oil	26	957,801	2,152	22,442	176,541
wc/d	23	102,120	1,132	3,685	13,590
JORROT (19/20th C) ?					
oil	2	6,831	1,933	3,416	4,898
JOS, Julien (?) ?					
oil	1	2,500		2,500	
JOSEPH, Julian (1882-1964) American					
wc/d	1	8,000		8,000	
JOSEPH, Lily Delissa (1864-1940) British					
oil	1	13,345		13,345	
JOSEPH, Ronald (1910-1992) American					
wc/d	1	30,000		30,000	
JOSEPH, S (20th C) British?					
oil	1	1,368		1,368	
JOSEPHI, Isaac A (?-1954) American					
oil	1	8,500		8,500	
JOSEPHSON, Ernst (1851-1906) Swedish					
oil	1	2,176		2,176	
wc/d	15	182,395	1,190	3,105	115,688
JOSSEN, Josef (1895-?) German					
oil	1	2,265		2,265	

Name	No.	Total Sales Value	lowest	Prices median	highest
JOST, Joseph (1888-?) Austrian					
oil	1	3,400		3,400	
JOTTI, Carlo (1826-1905) Italian					
oil	3	5,782	1,286	1,286	3,210
JOUAS, Charles (1866-1942) French					
wc/d	1	2,217		2,217	
JOUBERT, Léon (19th C) French					
oil	1	13,142		13,142	
JOUBIN, Georges (1888-1983) French					
oil	5	7,005	1,112	1,310	1,767
JOUCLARD, Adrienne (1882-1971) French					
oil	2	2,309	1,069	1,155	1,240
wc/d	2	4,257	2,067	2,129	2,190
JOUENNE, Michel (1933-) French					
oil	7	20,949	1,354	1,933	5,853
JOUETT, Matthew Harris (1788-1827) American					
oil	1	22,000		22,000	
JOUFFROY, Pierre (1912-) French					
oil	1	1,016		1,016	
JOULLIN, Amadee (1862-1917) American					
oil	1	24,000		24,000	
JOURDAIN, Francis (1876-1958) French					
wc/d	2	6,082	3,041	3,041	3,041
JOURDAIN, Roger Joseph (1845-1918) French					
oil	2	5,951	1,570	2,976	4,381
JOURDAN, Émile (1860-1931) French					
oil	1	23,016		23,016	
JOURDAN, Jacques Jean Raoul (1880-1916) French					
oil	1	2,019		2,019	
JOURDAN, Theodore (1833-?) French					
oil	1	3,279		3,279	
JOURNIAC, Michel (1943-) French					
3D	1	1,671		1,671	
JOUVE, Paul (1880-1973) French					
oil	8	82,400	3,867	10,854	17,381
wc/d	29	324,180	1,600	9,456	38,665
JOUVENET, Jean Baptiste (1644-1717) French					
oil	1	37,000		37,000	
wc/d	1	5,093		5,093	
JOUVET-MAGRON, Dominique (20th C) French					
oil	1	3,651		3,651	
JOVINGE, Torsten (1898-1936) Swedish					
oil	4	133,768	1,324	23,011	86,423
JOVINO, Felix (1882-) Italian					
3D	1	2,487		2,487	
JOWETT, John Marshall (fl.1900-1924) British					
wc/d	1	1,716		1,716	
JOWETT, Percy Hague (1882-1955) British					
oil	1	1,500		1,500	
JOY, George William (1844-1925) British					
oil	1	9,295		9,295	
JOY, Jessie (fl.1843-1869) British					
wc/d	1	1,749		1,749	
JOY, John Cantiloe (1806-1866) British					
wc/d	1	4,950		4,950	
JOY, William (1803-1867) British					
oil	1	2,955		2,955	
wc/d	3	10,051	1,185	4,290	4,576

Name	No.	Total Sales Value	lowest	Prices median	highest
JOYANT, J (19th C) French					
oil	1	5,267		5,267	
JOYANT, Jules Romain (1803-1854) French					
oil	1	7,900		7,900	
JUDD, Donald (1928-1994) American					
3D	19	2,673,150	3,500	80,000	740,000
JUDGE, Spencer Percival (1874-1956) Canadian					
wc/d	3	8,655	2,112	2,852	3,691
JUDSON, William Lees (1842-1928) American					
oil	5	17,602	1,100	2,302	9,500
JUEL, Jens (1745-1802) Danish					
oil	10	247,533	6,927	16,867	77,451
wc/d	1	12,463		12,463	
JUELL, Tore (1942-) Norwegian					
oil	1	1,770		1,770	
JUENGLING, Frederick (1848-1889) German					
wc/d	1	3,000		3,000	
JUGNET, Anne Marie (1958-) French					
oil	1	1,911		1,911	
JUILLARD (20th C) French?					
wc/d	2	4,161	1,533	2,081	2,628
JULES, Mervin (1912-) American					
oil	3	6,300	1,400	2,000	2,900
JULIARD, Alexander (1817-?) French					
oil	1	6,000		6,000	
JULIARD, Nicolas Jacques (1715-1790) French					
oil	2	15,099	5,822	7,550	9,277
JULIEN (?) ?					
wc/d	1	1,516		1,516	
JULIEN, Jean Pierre (1888-?) French					
oil	1	3,750		3,750	
JULIEN, René (1937-) Belgian					
oil	1	2,083		2,083	
JULIN, Johan Fredrik (1798-1843) Swedish					
wc/d	1	1,002		1,002	
JULIO, F (?) ?					
oil	1	1,804		1,804	
JULIUS, Per (1951-) Swedish					
wc/d	2	4,657	1,759	2,329	2,898
JUNCKER, H (?) ?					
oil	1	2,336		2,336	
JUNCKER, Justus (1703-1767) German					
oil	1	5,472		5,472	
JUNCKER, Wilhelm Karl (1820-1901) German					
oil	1	6,278		6,278	
JUNG, Emil Felix (1886-?) German					
oil	1	7,183		7,183	
JUNG, Simonetta (20th C) ?					
oil	2	2,662	1,331	1,331	1,331
JUNG, Theodore (1803-1865) French					
wc/d	2	2,801	1,146	1,401	1,655
JUNGBLUT, Johann (1860-1912) German					
oil	18	60,206	1,139	2,911	13,391
JUNGHANNS, Julius Paul (1876-1958) Austrian					
oil	11	33,495	1,068	2,750	6,789
JUNGHEIM, Carl (1803-1886) German					
oil	1	1,319		1,319	
JUNGMANN, Maarten Johannes Balthasar (1877-1964) Dutch					
oil	1	1,179		1,179	

Name	No.	Total Sales Value	Prices lowest	median	highest
JUNGMANN, Nico W (1872-1935) Dutch					
wc/d	3	6,633	1,343	2,370	2,920
JUNGSTEDT, Axel (1859-1933) Swedish					
oil	1	2,909		2,909	
JUNGSTEDT, Kurt (1894-1963) Swedish					
oil	1	6,230		6,230	
JUNGWIRTH, Josef (1869-1950) Austrian					
oil	2	3,850	1,350	1,925	2,500
JUNIGE, Ernst (19th C) German					
oil	1	2,041		2,041	
JUNKER (19/20th C) German					
oil	1	2,900		2,900	
JURISICH, Krista (20th C) American					
oil	1	2,750		2,750	
JURRES, Johannes Hendricus (1875-1946) Dutch					
wc/d	2	3,356	1,639	1,678	1,717
JURUTKA, Josef (19/20th C) ?					
oil	2	4,558	1,520	2,279	3,038
JURY, Anne P (1907-1995) Irish					
oil	3	3,672	1,008	1,080	1,584
JUSELIUS, Erik (1891-1948) Finnish					
oil	1	1,269		1,269	
JUSSEL, Eugen (1912-1997) Austrian					
oil	4	21,597	1,442	2,499	15,158
wc/d	1	1,228		1,228	
JUTAND, Pierre (?) South African?					
oil	1	1,084		1,084	
JUTSUM, Henry (1816-1869) British					
oil	1	2,041		2,041	
wc/d	1	2,250		2,250	
JUTZ, Adolf Gustav (1887-1945) German					
oil	1	1,002		1,002	
JUTZ, Carl (elder) (1838-1916) German					
oil	4	14,582	1,452	3,905	5,321
JUTZ, Carl (younger) (1873-1915) German					
oil	1	3,902		3,902	
JUUEL, Andreas (1817-1868) Danish					
oil	2	9,690	1,569	4,845	8,121
KAATZ, Carl Ludwig (1733-1810) German					
wc/d	1	2,882		2,882	
KABAKOV, Ilya (1933-) Russian					
wc/d	1	2,435		2,435	
KABELL, Ludwig (1853-1902) Danish					
oil	1	1,796		1,796	
KABOTIE, Fred (1900-1985) American					
wc/d	3	58,000	8,000	25,000	25,000
KABREGU, Enzo Domestico (20th C) ?					
oil	1	4,200		4,200	
KACERE, John (1920-) American					
oil	1	8,000		8,000	
wc/d	4	9,245	1,543	2,302	3,098
KACZ, Endre Komaromi (1880-1969) Hungarian					
oil	2	3,508	1,600	1,754	1,908
KADAR, Bela (1877-1955) Hungarian					
oil	2	9,204	3,106	4,602	6,098
wc/d	13	49,335	1,000	2,600	11,000
KADISHMAN, Menashe (1932-) Israeli					
3D	7	33,054	1,267	3,000	18,500
oil	7	16,604	1,000	2,000	6,000

Name	No.	Total Sales Value	lowest	Prices median	highest
KAEHRLING, Suzanne Blanche (20th C) French					
oil	1	1,947		1,947	
KAELIN, Charles Salis (1858-1929) American					
oil	6	61,300	3,500	6,400	33,000
wc/d	1	3,250		3,250	
KAEMMERER, Frederik Hendrik (1839-1902) Dutch					
oil	3	62,148	1,694	12,000	48,454
wc/d	1	1,873		1,873	
KAERCHER, Amalie (19th C) German					
oil	2	6,354	2,697	3,177	3,657
KAESBACH, R (1873-?) German					
3D	1	1,203		1,203	
KAESBACH, Rudolph (1873-?) German					
3D	1	1,337		1,337	
KAGER, Johann Matthias (1575-1634) German					
oil	1	1,981		1,981	
KAGIE, Jan (1885-1971) Dutch					
oil	1	1,722		1,722	
KAHANA, Aharon (1905-1967) Israeli					
oil	2	10,200	3,200	5,100	7,000
wc/d	3	4,300	1,000	1,100	2,200
KAHLE (20th C) American					
oil	1	1,500		1,500	
KAHLER, Carl (1855-?) Austrian					
oil	1	3,000		3,000	
KAHLO, Frida (1907-1954) Mexican					
oil	1	750,000		750,000	
wc/d	1	22,000		22,000	
KAHN, Leo (20th C) ?					
oil	1	1,502		1,502	
KAHN, Wolf (1927-) American					
oil	6	63,400	1,400	7,000	28,000
wc/d	1	2,600		2,600	
KAIGORODOV, Anatole Dmitrevich (1878-?) Russian					
oil	1	2,256		2,256	
KAISER, Richard (1868-1941) German					
oil	5	12,408	1,634	2,248	4,046
KAKS, Olle (1941-) Swedish					
oil	2	4,688	1,958	2,344	2,730
KALCKREUTH, Karl Walter Leopold von (1855-1928) German					
oil	1	3,871		3,871	
KALCKREUTH, Patrick von (1892-1970) German					
oil	8	12,154	1,038	1,541	2,230
KALCKREUTH, Stanislas von (1821-1894) German					
oil	1	1,551		1,551	
KALF, Willem (1619-1693) Dutch					
oil	1	470,400		470,400	
KALIGHAT SCHOOL, 20th C Indian					
oil	1	8,250		8,250	
KALISH, Max (1891-1945) American					
3D	5	74,500	5,000	17,500	22,500
KALLENBERG, Anders (1834-1902) Swedish					
oil	2	3,882	1,270	1,941	2,612
KALLMORGEN, Friedrich (1856-1924) German					
oil	11	47,811	1,002	3,128	10,127
KALLOS, Paul (1928-) French					
oil	3	6,287	1,548	1,710	3,029
KALLSTENIUS, Gottfried (1861-1943) Swedish					
oil	11	18,974	1,066	1,727	3,047

Name	No.	Total Sales Value	lowest	Prices median	highest
KALMAKOFF, Nicolas (1873-1955) Russian					
oil	1	7,300		7,300	
KALMAN, Peter (1877-1948) Hungarian					
oil	1	2,019		2,019	
KALMIKOFF, Nicholas (1873-1955) Russian					
wc/d	1	2,100		2,100	
KALTENMOSER, Kaspar (1806-1867) German					
oil	3	15,222	1,219	2,727	11,276
KAMINSKI, Max G (1938-) German					
oil	1	2,435		2,435	
KAMINSKI, Stan (1952-) British					
oil	3	3,492	1,036	1,036	1,420
KAMKE, Ivar (1882-1936) Swedish					
oil	2	3,504	1,201	1,752	2,303
wc/d	1	1,256		1,256	
KAMPER, Godaert (1614-1679) Dutch					
oil	1	8,635		8,635	
KAMPF, Arthur (1864-1950) German					
oil	4	8,826	1,251	2,001	3,500
KAMPF, Eugen (1861-1933) German					
oil	4	11,785	1,580	2,772	4,661
KAMPF, Max (1912-1982) Swiss					
oil	1	13,911		13,911	
KAMSETZER, Jan Baptist (1753-1795) Polish					
wc/d	1	1,022		1,022	
KANDINSKY, Wassily (1866-1944) Russian					
oil	4	1,056,214	126,214	205,000	520,000
wc/d	8	388,022	9,000	54,000	93,620
KANELBA (1897-1960) Polish					
oil	1	3,394		3,394	
KANG, K S (?) British?					
oil	1	6,042		6,042	
KANGRA SCHOOL, 19th C Indian					
wc/d	1	3,600		3,600	
KANNEMANS, Christian Cornelis (1812-1884) Dutch					
oil	2	10,897	4,784	5,449	6,113
KANNIK, Frans (1949-) Danish					
wc/d	1	2,691		2,691	
KANO SCHOOL, 19th C Japanese					
wc/d	1	3,000		3,000	
KANOLDT, Alexander (1881-1939) German					
oil	2	55,128	17,301	27,564	37,827
KANOLDT, Edmund (1845-1904) German					
oil	1	3,121		3,121	
KAP, Cornelius (?) Belgian?					
oil	1	1,113		1,113	
KAPELL, Paul (1876-1943) German					
oil	1	3,337		3,337	
KAPLAN, Hubert (1932-) German					
oil	5	15,214	1,733	1,853	5,455
KAPOOR, Anish (1954-) British/Indian					
3D	2	102,680	27,180	51,340	75,500
KAPPEL, Anders (1956-) Swedish					
oil	1	1,037		1,037	
KAPPIS, Albert (1836-1914) German					
oil	6	20,918	1,573	3,003	5,943
KAPRALIK, Jacques (20th C) American?					
wc/d	1	7,000		7,000	

Name	No.	Total Sales Value	lowest	Prices median	highest
KARAHALIOS, Constantin (20th C) ?					
oil	1	1,897		1,897	
KARCHER, Gustave (1831-1908) French					
oil	1	1,096		1,096	
KARELL, Johann (fl.1760-1780) German					
oil	1	14,600		14,600	
KARELLA, Marina (1940-) American					
3D	1	4,368		4,368	
wc/d	1	1,267		1,267	
KARFVE, Fritz (1880-1967) Swedish					
oil	1	1,213		1,213	
KARGEL, Axel (1896-1971) Swedish					
oil	5	8,608	1,204	1,861	2,285
KARGER, Karl (1848-1913) Austrian					
oil	1	4,500		4,500	
KARGL, Rudolf (1878-1942) Austrian					
wc/d	1	1,026		1,026	
KARLOWSKA, Stanislawa (1876-1952) Polish					
oil	1	3,600		3,600	
KARLSSON, C Goran (1944-) Swedish					
oil	2	3,859	1,555	1,930	2,304
wc/d	1	1,278		1,278	
KARLY, P (?) ?					
oil	1	2,416		2,416	
KAROLY, Gerna (1867-1944) Hungarian					
oil	1	1,350		1,350	
KARPATHY, Jeno (1871-?) Hungarian					
oil	1	1,924		1,924	
KARS, Georges (1882-1945) Czechoslovakian					
oil	4	22,840	2,670	3,593	12,985
KARSEN, Kaspar (1810-1896) Dutch					
oil	2	5,750	2,581	2,875	3,169
KARSSEN, A (1932-) Dutch					
oil	1	3,707		3,707	
KARSTEN, Ludvig (1876-1926) Norwegian					
oil	1	8,610		8,610	
KAS, Achille (19th C) Belgian					
oil	1	1,048		1,048	
KASELITZ, Albert Friedrich (1821-1884) German					
oil	1	1,367		1,367	
KASPER, Ludwig (1893-1945) German					
3D	2	4,854	2,184	2,427	2,670
KASS, Deborah (20th C) American					
oil	1	1,100		1,100	
KASSAK, Lajos (1887-1967) Hungarian					
oil	1	8,711		8,711	
wc/d	3	22,658	1,505	7,500	13,653
KASTRUP, Emilie (19th C) Danish					
oil	1	24,694		24,694	
KASYN, John (1926-) Canadian					
oil	12	43,320	1,014	3,790	6,528
wc/d	1	1,168		1,168	
KAT, Anne-Pierre de (1881-1968) Belgian					
oil	3	11,087	1,253	2,716	7,118
KAT, Otto Boudewijn de (1907-1995) Dutch					
oil	1	2,179		2,179	
wc/d	1	1,268		1,268	
KATCHADOURIAN, Sarkis (20th C) Iranian					
oil	1	2,500		2,500	

Name	No.	Total Sales Value	lowest	Prices median	highest
KATHELIN, Ernest (19th C) Belgian					
wc/d	1	3,212		3,212	
KATHY, Roger (1934-) Belgian					
oil	1	1,006		1,006	
KATZ, Alex (1927-) American					
oil	6	135,000	6,500	25,000	32,500
wc/d	1	21,140		21,140	
KAUBA, C (1865-1922) Austrian/American					
3D	2	14,787	6,207	7,394	8,580
KAUFFMAN (?) ?					
wc/d	1	2,437		2,437	
KAUFFMANN, Angelica (1741-1807) Swiss					
oil	3	420,100	100,100	130,000	190,000
wc/d	1	2,574		2,574	
KAUFFMANN, Angelica (school) (1741-1807) Swiss					
oil	1	10,000		10,000	
KAUFFMANN, Hermann (elder) (1808-1889) German					
oil	3	33,082	5,777	8,000	19,305
KAUFFMANN, Hugo Wilhelm (1844-1915) German					
oil	11	88,420	3,142	6,776	19,359
KAUFMANN, A (1848-1916) Austrian					
oil	1	3,089		3,089	
KAUFMANN, Adolf (1848-1916) Austrian					
oil	3	7,200	2,023	2,222	2,955
KAUFMANN, Arthur (1888-1971) German/Argentinian					
oil	1	4,489		4,489	
KAUFMANN, B (?) ?					
oil	1	1,136		1,136	
KAUFMANN, F J (18th C) German					
wc/d	1	4,431		4,431	
KAUFMANN, Isidor (1853-1921) Austrian					
oil	5	321,600	14,600	65,000	120,000
KAUFMANN, Joseph Clemens (1867-1925) Swiss					
oil	1	3,498		3,498	
KAUFMANN, Karl (1843-1901) Austrian					
oil	14	50,351	1,117	2,242	12,878
KAUFMANN, Wilhelm (1895-?) Austrian					
oil	1	3,226		3,226	
KAULA, Lee Lufkin (1865-1957) American					
oil	1	9,250		9,250	
KAULA, William J (1871-1952) American					
oil	2	15,500	2,500	7,750	13,000
wc/d	1	2,700		2,700	
KAULBACH, Friedrich (1822-1903) German					
oil	2	6,674	1,800	3,337	4,874
KAULBACH, Friedrich August von (1850-1920) German					
oil	7	46,374	1,045	4,400	16,712
KAULBACH, Hermann (1846-1909) German					
oil	4	50,931	1,288	12,822	24,000
KAULBACH, Wilhelm von (1805-1874) German					
wc/d	1	5,555		5,555	
KAULUM, Haakon Jensen (1863-1933) Norwegian					
oil	2	3,257	1,005	1,629	2,252
KAUS, Max (1891-1977) German					
oil	2	49,025	5,825	24,513	43,200
wc/d	7	14,922	1,024	2,128	3,460
KAUTZKY, Ted (?-1953) American/Hungarian					
wc/d	1	3,250		3,250	

Name	No.	Total Sales Value	lowest	Prices median	highest
KAUZMANN, Paul (1874-1951) German					
oil	1	11,176		11,176	
KAVANAGH, Joseph Malachy (1856-1918) Irish					
oil	4	16,111	1,160	2,388	10,176
KAVLI, Arne Texnes (1878-1970) Norwegian					
oil	2	71,084	6,699	35,542	64,385
KAWABATA, Ryushi (1885-1966) Japanese					
oil	1	50,000		50,000	
wc/d	4	82,000	14,000	19,000	30,000
KAWARA, On (1933-) Japanese					
3D	2	127,000	32,000	63,500	95,000
KAY, Archibald (1860-1935) British					
oil	2	11,692	5,372	5,846	6,320
KAY, James (1858-1942) British					
oil	7	59,015	1,580	4,740	19,710
wc/d	4	17,646	1,896	4,395	6,960
KAYAMA, Matazo (1927-) Japanese					
wc/d	5	1,150,000	110,000	150,000	450,000
KAYE, Otis (1885-1974) American					
oil	1	80,000		80,000	
wc/d	1	5,000		5,000	
KEARNEY, William Henry (c.1800-1858) British					
wc/d	1	1,065		1,065	
KEATING, Sean (1889-1978) Irish					
wc/d	1	11,100		11,100	
KEATING, Tom (1917-1984) British					
oil	4	9,568	1,199	2,397	3,575
KEATS, C J (?) British					
wc/d	1	1,050		1,050	
KECK, H (19/20th C) ?					
3D	2	7,834	2,114	3,917	5,720
KECK, Otto (1873-1948) German					
oil	5	9,730	1,274	1,593	3,985
KECK, Paul (1904-1973) German					
oil	1	2,011		2,011	
KEELHOFF, Frans (1820-1893) Belgian					
oil	1	7,000		7,000	
KEGHEL, Desire de (1839-1901) Belgian					
oil	2	66,761	1,761	33,381	65,000
KEIL, Bernhard (1624-1687) Danish					
oil	5	24,527	3,390	3,599	9,011
KEIL, Robert (1905-1989) Austrian					
wc/d	1	1,417		1,417	
KEIRSBILCK, Jules van (1833-1896) Belgian					
oil	1	2,596		2,596	
KEISER, Joseph (1859-?) Swiss					
oil	1	1,213		1,213	
KEISER, Karl Albert (1834-1885) German					
oil	1	9,890		9,890	
KEISERMANN, Franz (1765-1833) Swiss					
wc/d	8	52,326	2,730	5,119	14,000
KEITH, Elizabeth (1887-?) American					
oil	1	1,600		1,600	
KEITH, William (1839-1911) American					
oil	18	305,400	1,600	6,500	110,000
wc/d	1	2,500		2,500	
KEITH, William Castle (1864-1927) American					
oil	1	2,250		2,250	

Name	No.	Total Sales Value	lowest	Prices median	highest
KELDER, Toon (1894-1973) Dutch					
3D	1	1,293		1,293	
oil	7	23,157	1,259	1,981	8,207
KELETY, A (20th C) French					
3D	1	5,436		5,436	
KELETY, Alexander (20th C) French					
3D	2	49,477	23,700	24,739	25,777
KELL, Violet B (?) British					
wc/d	1	1,800		1,800	
KELLEN, David van der III (1827-1895) Dutch					
oil	1	13,578		13,578	
KELLER (?) ?					
oil	1	11,879		11,879	
KELLER, A (?) ?					
wc/d	1	1,094		1,094	
KELLER, Albert von (1844-1920) Swiss					
oil	3	9,556	1,481	2,155	5,920
KELLER, Ferdinand (1842-1922) German					
oil	4	31,754	2,100	9,465	11,185
KELLER, Friedrich von (1840-1914) German					
oil	4	26,194	2,942	3,321	16,610
KELLER, Gottfried (1819-1890) ?					
wc/d	1	5,895		5,895	
KELLER, Henry George (1870-1949) American					
wc/d	1	3,100		3,100	
KELLER, Johann Heinrich (1692-1765) Swiss					
oil	3	11,332	2,304	2,736	6,292
KELLER-HERMANN, Marie (1868-1952) Austrian					
oil	1	1,471		1,471	
KELLER-REUTLINGEN, Paul Wilhelm (1854-1920) German					
oil	5	54,257	2,023	9,427	23,700
KELLEY, Mike (1954-) American					
3D	2	131,140	21,140	65,570	110,000
oil	5	108,000	13,000	17,000	45,000
wc/d	3	155,000	40,000	55,000	60,000
KELLEY, Mike and OURSLER, Tony (20th C) American					
3D	1	4,000		4,000	
KELLIN, Nicolas Joseph (1788-1858) French					
wc/d	1	1,047		1,047	
KELLNER, Charles H (1890-?) American					
oil	1	3,500		3,500	
KELLY, David (1959-) Malawian					
oil	2	4,970	2,272	2,485	2,698
KELLY, Ellsworth (1923-) American					
3D	1	28,000		28,000	
oil	2	1,475,000	500,000	737,500	975,000
wc/d	2	85,000	20,000	42,500	65,000
KELLY, Felix (1916-1994) New Zealander					
oil	4	21,371	3,476	4,960	7,975
KELLY, H O (20th C) American					
oil	1	5,500		5,500	
KELLY, Leon (1901-1982) American					
oil	1	4,500		4,500	
wc/d	1	5,000		5,000	
KELLY, O (?) British?					
oil	1	1,359		1,359	
KELLY, Richard Barrett Talbot (1896-1971) British					
wc/d	1	1,397		1,397	
KELLY, Sir Gerald (1879-1972) British					
oil	2	13,665	4,500	6,833	9,165

Name	No.	Total Sales Value	lowest	Prices median	highest
KELLY, Walt (1913-1973) American					
wc/d	1	4,000		4,000	
KELPE, Paul (1902-) German					
oil	1	45,000		45,000	
KELS, Franz (1828-1893) German					
oil	1	2,273		2,273	
KELSEY, C (fl.1850-1860) American					
oil	1	2,000		2,000	
KELSEY, Frank (fl.1887-1923) British					
wc/d	1	3,160		3,160	
KELSY (20th C) ?					
3D	1	2,077		2,077	
KELTERBORN, Ludwig Adam (1811-1878) German					
oil	1	3,171		3,171	
KEMENEDY, Jeno (1860-1925) Hungarian					
oil	1	8,216		8,216	
KEMENY, Zoltan (1907-1965) Swiss					
3D	1	3,533		3,533	
KEMEYS, Edward (1843-1907) American					
3D	1	3,750		3,750	
KEMM, Robert (fl.1874-1885) British					
oil	8	91,553	1,055	9,436	31,638
KEMMER, Johann (1495-?) German					
oil	1	120,800		120,800	
KEMP, Jeka (19th C) British					
oil	1	1,812		1,812	
KEMP-WELCH, Lucy (1869-1958) British					
oil	8	78,915	1,050	5,912	31,020
wc/d	1	1,500		1,500	
KEMPER, Charles Jean (1913-1986) Dutch					
oil	1	1,231		1,231	
KEMPTON, Elmira (20th C) American					
oil	1	1,100		1,100	
KENDALL, Marie B (1885-1953) American					
oil	1	1,200		1,200	
KENDALL, William Sergeant (1869-1938) American					
wc/d	1	6,000		6,000	
KENDRICK, Mel (1949-) American					
3D	1	3,800		3,800	
KENDRICK, Sydney (1874-1955) British					
oil	1	1,267		1,267	
KENNEDY, Cecil (1905-1997) British					
oil	15	362,005	1,595	19,630	105,000
KENNEDY, Charles Napier (1852-1898) British					
oil	1	15,010		15,010	
KENNEDY, William (1860-1918) British					
oil	3	31,265	3,087	3,528	24,650
KENNEY, John Theodore Eardley (1911-1972) British					
oil	1	2,679		2,679	
KENNINGTON, Eric (1888-1960) British					
oil	1	5,510		5,510	
wc/d	3	11,416	1,378	2,550	7,488
KENNINGTON, Thomas Benjamin (1856-1916) British					
oil	1	13,500		13,500	
KENSETT, John Frederick (1816-1872) American					
oil	4	219,000	26,000	41,500	110,000
KENT, E J (19th C) British					
oil	1	1,595		1,595	

Name	No.	Total Sales Value	lowest	Prices median	highest
KENT, Leslie (1890-1980) British					
oil	3	3,587	1,060	1,060	1,467
KENT, Rockwell (1882-1971) American					
oil	6	484,000	16,000	75,000	170,000
wc/d	4	17,500	2,400	4,300	6,500
KENTRIDGE, William (1955-) South African?					
wc/d	2	85,000	10,000	42,500	75,000
KENWORTHY, Jonathan (1943-) British					
3D	2	47,885	16,485	23,943	31,400
KERCKHOVE, Ernest van den (1840-1879) Belgian					
oil	1	3,335		3,335	
KERELS, Henri (1896-1956) Belgian					
oil	1	1,065		1,065	
KERG, Theo (1909-) Luxembourger					
oil	1	3,292		3,292	
KERKOVIUS, Ida (1879-1970) German					
oil	8	81,603	2,523	9,609	16,383
wc/d	5	14,435	1,068	1,594	5,755
KERMADEC, Eugène Nestor le (1899-1976) French					
oil	2	8,931	3,713	4,466	5,218
KERMARREC, Joel (1939-) French					
oil	3	4,992	1,285	1,640	2,067
KERN, Anton (1710-1747) German					
oil	1	48,320		48,320	
KERN, Hermann (1839-1912) Hungarian					
oil	10	49,927	1,419	4,918	9,815
KERN, Jean (1874-?) Swiss					
oil	1	1,244		1,244	
KERN, Leonhard (1588-1662) German					
3D	3	20,387	1,865	3,950	14,572
KERN, Richard Hovenden (1821-1853) British					
wc/d	1	24,000		24,000	
KERNAN, Joseph F (1878-1958) American					
oil	1	3,000		3,000	
KERNN-LARSEN, Rita (1904-1998) Danish					
oil	1	1,281		1,281	
KERNOFF, Harry Aaron (1900-1974) British					
oil	5	126,679	1,350	5,180	103,600
KERR, David Ord (1952-) British					
oil	1	4,144		4,144	
wc/d	2	3,834	1,420	1,917	2,414
KERR, Illingsworth Holey (1905-1988) Canadian					
oil	5	8,107	1,267	1,297	2,186
KERR, Tiko (1953-) Canadian?					
oil	1	1,690		1,690	
KERRICH, Thomas (1748-1828) British					
oil	1	50,560		50,560	
wc/d	1	37,920		37,920	
KERSCHENSTEINER, Joseph (1864-1936) German					
oil	1	1,341		1,341	
KERSTEN, Wilhelm (19th C) German					
oil	1	1,865		1,865	
KERSTING, Georg Friedrich (1785-1847) Danish					
wc/d	1	1,419		1,419	
KESSEL, Ferdinand van (1648-1696) Flemish					
oil	2	8,908	1,500	4,454	7,408
KESSEL, J van (17th C) Flemish					
oil	1	15,483		15,483	

Name	No.	Total Sales Value	lowest	Prices median	highest
KESSEL, Jan Thomas van (1677-1741) Flemish					
oil	2	24,201	4,705	12,101	19,496
KESSEL, Jan van (17th C) Flemish					
oil	2	75,344	13,234	37,672	62,110
KESSEL, Jan van I (1626-1679) Flemish					
oil	14	3,396,495	10,067	47,770	1,500,000
KESSEL, Jan van II (1654-1708) Flemish					
oil	4	357,479	36,929	70,000	180,550
KESSEL, Jan van III (1641-1680) Flemish					
oil	2	73,074	10,800	36,537	62,274
KESSLER, Andreas (fl.1805-1820) American					
wc/d	1	2,000		2,000	
KESSLER, August (1826-1906) German					
oil	2	9,125	2,255	4,563	6,870
KESSLER, Jon (1957-) American					
3D	1	3,686		3,686	
KESTING, Edmund (1892-1970) German					
oil	1	26,613		26,613	
wc/d	3	61,693	13,306	21,774	26,613
KET, Dick (1902-) Dutch					
oil	1	21,552		21,552	
wc/d	1	5,172		5,172	
KETEL, Cornelis (1548-1616) Dutch					
oil	2	24,487	4,077	12,244	20,410
KETTELSEN, C (19/20th C) Scandinavian					
oil	1	1,196		1,196	
KETTEMANN, Erwin (1897-1971) German					
oil	5	5,816	1,016	1,047	1,463
KETTER, Clay (1961-) Swedish					
3D	1	7,500		7,500	
wc/d	1	15,000		15,000	
KETTLE, Tilly (1735-1786) British					
oil	7	52,701	5,285	8,000	10,010
KEUDELL, Marie von (1836-1918) German					
oil	1	3,334		3,334	
KEULEYAN-LAFON (1886-1973) French					
oil	1	1,019		1,019	
KEULLER, Vital (1866-1945) ?					
3D	2	4,178	2,089	2,089	2,089
oil	3	3,701	1,019	1,070	1,612
KEUN, Hendrik (1738-1788) Dutch					
oil	1	3,343		3,343	
KEVER (19/20th C) ?					
oil	1	4,905		4,905	
KEVER, Gerard (1956-) German					
oil	1	1,553		1,553	
KEVER, Jacob Simon Hendrik (1854-1922) Dutch					
oil	5	25,187	1,951	2,667	13,578
KEY, Geoffrey (1946-) British					
3D	1	1,088		1,088	
KEY, John Ross (1837-1920) American					
oil	2	6,300	1,300	3,150	5,000
KEY, Willem (1520-1568) Flemish					
oil	1	83,050		83,050	
KEYSER, Auguste Paul de (19th C) Belgian					
oil	1	1,067		1,067	
KEYSER, Elisabeth (1851-1898) Swedish					
oil	1	11,376		11,376	

Name	No.	Total Sales Value	Prices lowest	median	highest
KEYSER, Jean Baptiste de (1857-) Belgian					
3D	1	4,710		4,710	
KEYSER, Ragnhild (1889-1943) Norwegian					
oil	2	23,125	11,039	11,563	12,086
wc/d	1	4,586		4,586	
KEYSER, Thomas de (1596-1667) Dutch					
oil	2	100,599	10,327	50,300	90,272
KEYT, George (1901-1993) Indian					
oil	1	1,800		1,800	
wc/d	2	6,900	1,650	3,450	5,250
KHAKKAR, Bhupen (1934-) Indian					
oil	1	12,000		12,000	
KHANNA, Krishen (1925-) Indian					
oil	1	8,000		8,000	
wc/d	1	4,200		4,200	
KHASTGIR, Sudhir Ranjan (1907-1974) Indian					
oil	1	3,000		3,000	
wc/d	3	7,278	1,728	2,550	3,000
KHNOPFF, Fernand (1858-1921) Belgian					
oil	1	420,000		420,000	
wc/d	7	492,650	14,100	60,400	195,000
KHOURY, Michael (?) Canadian?					
oil	1	1,240		1,240	
KHROMOVA, Tatiana (20th C) ?					
oil	2	2,336	1,168	1,168	1,168
KIAERSKOU, F (1805-1891) Danish					
oil	2	2,550	1,102	1,275	1,448
KIAERSKOU, Frederik (1805-1891) Danish					
oil	2	5,554	2,306	2,777	3,248
KIBRIA, Mohammad (1929-) Indian					
oil	1	1,350		1,350	
KICCO (1969-) Italian					
oil	1	1,126		1,126	
KICKERT, Conrad (1882-1965) Dutch					
oil	1	1,078		1,078	
KIDD, William (1790-1863) British					
oil	1	3,160		3,160	
KIEFER, Anselm (1945-) German					
3D	1	17,000		17,000	
oil	8	686,881	24,000	80,666	196,300
wc/d	1	27,706		27,706	
KIELBERG, Ole (1911-1985) Danish					
oil	2	2,876	1,406	1,438	1,470
KIELDRUP, Anton Edvard (1826-1869) Danish					
oil	2	6,599	1,030	3,300	5,569
KIELHOLZ, Heiner (20th C) Swiss?					
oil	1	2,564		2,564	
KIEN, Josef (1903-) German					
oil	2	8,603	2,505	4,302	6,098
wc/d	3	3,360	1,002	1,138	1,220
KIENERK, Giorgio (1869-1948) Italian					
oil	1	8,918		8,918	
KIENHOLZ, Edward (1927-1994) American					
3D	4	25,388	1,880	4,254	15,000
wc/d	4	6,551	1,200	1,736	1,966
KIENHOLZ, Edward and Nancy (20th C) American					
3D	1	3,147		3,147	
KIENMAYER, Franz (20th C) German					
oil	1	4,661		4,661	

Name	No.	Total Sales Value	Prices lowest	median	highest
KIERS, George Laurens (1838-1916) Dutch					
oil	1	1,723		1,723	
KIESEL, Conrad (1846-1921) German					
oil	3	15,150	1,587	4,000	9,563
KIJNO (1921-) French					
wc/d	1	1,828		1,828	
KIJNO, Ladislas (1921-) French					
oil	18	46,807	1,018	1,507	16,048
wc/d	10	16,516	1,024	1,631	2,780
KIKOINE, Michel (1892-1968) Russian					
oil	16	99,912	1,600	4,803	15,493
wc/d	2	4,254	1,282	2,127	2,972
KILBURNE, G G (1839-1924) British					
wc/d	1	1,950		1,950	
KILBURNE, George Goodwin (1839-1924) British					
oil	8	52,585	1,058	4,191	21,140
wc/d	16	104,619	2,016	3,623	42,000
KILIAN, Lukas (1579-1637) German					
wc/d	1	1,557		1,557	
KILIMNICK, Karen (1962-) American					
wc/d	3	20,000	4,000	6,500	9,500
KILPACK, Sarah Louise (fl.1880-1909) British					
oil	5	7,023	1,001	1,413	1,716
KILPATRICK, Aaron Edward (1872-1953) American					
oil	8	52,000	2,000	5,250	16,000
KIMMICH, Wilhelm (1897-?) German					
oil	1	2,724		2,724	
KIMPE, Reimond (1885-1970) Belgian					
oil	5	40,401	5,603	6,466	13,583
KINCH, Hayter (19th C) British					
oil	1	8,305		8,305	
KINDBORG, Johan (1861-1907) Swedish					
oil	1	1,088		1,088	
wc/d	1	1,975		1,975	
KINDERMANS, Jean-Baptiste (c.1822-1876) Belgian					
oil	1	1,099		1,099	
KINDLER, A (1833-1876) German					
oil	1	1,079		1,079	
KING, Albert F (1854-1934) American					
oil	1	24,000		24,000	
KING, B (19/20th C) British					
oil	1	1,021		1,021	
KING, C (18/19th C) British					
oil	1	9,734		9,734	
KING, Emma B (20th C) American					
oil	1	4,750		4,750	
KING, George W (1836-1922) American					
oil	1	6,500		6,500	
KING, Gordon (?) British					
wc/d	1	1,095		1,095	
KING, H (?) ?					
oil	1	2,938		2,938	
KING, Henry John Yeend (1855-1924) British					
oil	16	185,035	2,300	4,873	60,000
wc/d	1	1,661		1,661	
KING, Jack (20th C) Canadian					
oil	1	1,686		1,686	
KING, John Baragwanath (1864-1939) British					
wc/d	1	1,168		1,168	

Name	No.	Total Sales Value	Prices lowest	median	highest
KING, John Gregory (1929-) British					
oil	1	1,898		1,898	
KING, Lilian Yeend (1882-?) British					
oil	1	14,000		14,000	
KING, Paul (1867-1947) American					
oil	3	9,750	2,500	2,750	4,500
KING, Percy (19th C) ?					
oil	1	1,600		1,600	
KING, W Gunning (1859-1940) British					
oil	2	23,200	10,875	11,600	12,325
KING, William J (1857-?) British					
oil	1	1,726		1,726	
KINGMAN, Eduardo (1913-1997) Ecuadorian					
oil	1	30,000		30,000	
KINGSBURGER, Sylvain (1855-1935) French					
3D	1	3,950		3,950	
KINGSTON, Steve (1951-) British					
oil	1	6,390		6,390	
KINKADE, Thomas (20th C) American					
oil	1	15,000		15,000	
wc/d	1	18,000		18,000	
KINLEY, Peter (1926-1988) British					
oil	2	6,300	1,500	3,150	4,800
KINNAIRD, F G (19th C) British					
oil	1	2,556		2,556	
KINNAIRD, Frederick Gerald (19th C) British					
oil	2	2,833	1,000	1,417	1,833
KINNAIRD, H J (fl.1880-1908) British					
oil	1	1,843		1,843	
KINNAIRD, Henry J (fl.1880-1908) British					
oil	3	7,118	1,988	2,130	3,000
wc/d	24	47,699	1,008	1,801	5,112
KINNEAR, James (fl.1880-1917) British					
wc/d	1	1,737		1,737	
KINSBURGER, Sylvain (1855-?) French					
3D	1	3,500		3,500	
KINSEY, Alberta (1875-1955) American					
oil	2	4,800	2,000	2,400	2,800
KINUTANI, Koji (1943-) Japanese					
oil	1	55,000		55,000	
KINZEL, Josef (1852-1925) Austrian					
oil	3	14,200	3,300	3,900	7,000
KIOERBOE, Carl Fredrik (1799-1876) Swedish					
oil	5	12,550	1,010	1,608	4,528
KIPPENBERGER, Martin (1953-1997) German					
3D	5	99,377	3,020	14,300	55,000
oil	9	371,759	1,417	18,166	150,000
wc/d	6	76,459	1,933	7,426	32,000
KIPS, Erich (1869-?) German					
oil	3	9,367	1,684	2,617	5,066
KIRBERG, Otto (1850-1926) German					
oil	3	8,678	1,400	3,060	4,218
KIRCHER, Alexandre (1867-?) German					
oil	1	2,581		2,581	
KIRCHNER, Albert Emil (1813-1885) German					
oil	1	3,636		3,636	
wc/d	1	1,365		1,365	
KIRCHNER, Ernst Ludwig (1880-1938) German					
oil	7	5,146,100	60,000	460,800	2,232,000
wc/d	50	731,969	1,196	10,278	100,800

Name	No.	Total Sales Value	lowest	Prices median	highest
KIRCHNER, Heinrich (1902-) German					
3D	1	1,417		1,417	
KIRCHNER, Otto (1887-1960) German					
oil	1	1,591		1,591	
KIRCHNER, Raphael (1867-1917) Austrian					
oil	1	1,095		1,095	
KIRKEBY, G (19th C) ?					
oil	1	2,011		2,011	
KIRKEBY, Per (1938-) Danish					
3D	1	1,549		1,549	
oil	5	55,395	1,787	12,172	19,630
wc/d	8	95,820	1,456	2,012	67,905
KIRKEGAARD, Anders (1946-) Danish					
oil	1	1,395		1,395	
KIRKPATRICK, Joseph (1872-c.1930) British					
wc/d	2	3,611	1,399	1,806	2,212
KIRKPATRICK, Lily (fl.1894-1902) British					
oil	1	7,436		7,436	
KIRKUP, Mary A (fl.c.1940) American					
oil	1	1,700		1,700	
KIRNER, Johann Baptist (1806-1866) German					
oil	1	1,452		1,452	
KIROUAC, Louise Lecor (1939-) Canadian					
oil	3	4,700	1,175	1,436	2,089
KISELEV, Sergei N (fl.1910-1920) Russian					
oil	1	2,557		2,557	
KISELYOV, Kiril (20th C) Russian					
oil	1	1,650		1,650	
KISLING (?) ?					
oil	1	7,414		7,414	
KISLING, Moise (1891-1953) French					
oil	34	1,632,880	8,696	33,541	170,000
wc/d	4	24,153	1,897	3,999	14,259
KISS, Jozsef (1833-1900) Hungarian					
oil	1	5,483		5,483	
KISSELEOV, Alexandre Alexandrovitch (1838-1911) Russian					
oil	1	1,340		1,340	
KITAJ, R B (1932-) American					
oil	1	45,300		45,300	
wc/d	2	94,604	4,004	47,302	90,600
KITCHELL, Hudson Mindell (1862-1944) American					
oil	2	4,200	1,800	2,100	2,400
KITE, Joseph Milner (1862-1946) British					
oil	2	4,722	2,130	2,361	2,592
KITO, Akira (1925-) Japanese					
oil	1	1,164		1,164	
KITZEL, Herbert (1928-) German					
wc/d	1	1,419		1,419	
KITZINGER, Maximiliaan Leonard (1811-1882) Dutch					
oil	1	4,740		4,740	
KJARVAL, Johannes (1885-1972) Icelandic					
oil	2	6,044	2,557	3,022	3,487
KJERNER, Esther (1873-1952) Swedish					
oil	18	43,275	1,055	2,329	5,192
KLAAS, J (?) ?					
oil	1	1,595		1,595	
KLAIBERG, F (1921-) German					
oil	1	1,128		1,128	

Name	No.	Total Sales Value	lowest	Prices median	highest
KLAPISH, Liliane (1933-) Israeli					
oil	1	8,000		8,000	
KLAPPER, Siegfried (1918-) German					
wc/d	1	1,072		1,072	
KLASEN, Peter (1935-) German					
3D	2	7,415	1,712	3,708	5,703
oil	25	102,260	1,455	4,427	9,591
wc/d	1	1,629		1,629	
KLAUER, Martin Gottlieb (1742-1801) German					
3D	1	6,285		6,285	
KLAUKE, Jurgen (1943-) German					
wc/d	4	15,144	1,107	3,034	7,969
KLEE, Paul (1879-1940) Swiss					
oil	6	687,424	28,800	87,202	300,000
wc/d	28	3,882,561	9,930	64,930	600,000
KLEIMA, Ekke Abel (1899-1958) Dutch					
oil	1	8,190		8,190	
KLEIN (?) ?					
oil	1	11,915		11,915	
KLEIN VON DIEPOLD, Leo (1865-1944) German					
oil	1	1,275		1,275	
KLEIN VON DIEPOLD, Maximilian (1873-?) German					
oil	1	1,227		1,227	
KLEIN, Bernhard (1888-?) German					
oil	1	2,184		2,184	
KLEIN, Cesar (1876-1954) German					
wc/d	1	1,171		1,171	
KLEIN, Friedrich Franz (1898-1990) Dutch					
oil	3	12,166	1,073	4,301	6,792
KLEIN, Johann Adam (1792-1875) German					
oil	1	5,538		5,538	
wc/d	2	5,918	2,880	2,959	3,038
KLEIN, Leonhard Christian (1810-1891) Danish					
oil	1	3,098		3,098	
KLEIN, Medard P (1905-) American					
oil	2	3,500	1,700	1,750	1,800
KLEIN, Paul (1909-1993) French					
oil	2	2,920	1,145	1,460	1,775
KLEIN, Philipp (1871-1907) German					
oil	1	1,382		1,382	
KLEIN, Yves (1928-1962) French					
3D	22	611,397	5,920	20,658	105,700
oil	5	381,632	2,163	42,422	244,247
wc/d	9	10,164,480	18,120	256,700	6,100,000
KLEINERTZ, Alexius (1831-1903) German					
oil	1	1,472		1,472	
KLEINMANN, Alain (1953-) French					
oil	1	1,728		1,728	
KLEINSCHMIDT, Paul (1883-1949) German					
oil	1	33,516		33,516	
wc/d	3	28,813	8,000	8,192	12,621
KLEINSMIEDE, J A (19th C) Dutch					
oil	1	1,061		1,061	
KLEINTJES, Jan (1872-1955) Dutch					
oil	2	10,193	4,087	5,097	6,106
KLEITSCH, Joseph (1885-1931) American					
oil	3	41,500	3,500	10,000	28,000
KLEMENTIEFF, Eugene (20th C) French/Russian					
oil	1	8,000		8,000	

Name	No.	Total Sales Value	lowest	Prices median	highest
KLENGEL, Johan Christian (1751-1824) German					
oil	4	27,584	3,872	6,872	9,968
KLERK, Willem de (1800-1876) Dutch					
oil	3	10,111	1,698	2,163	6,250
wc/d	1	2,750		2,750	
KLESTOVA, Irene (?) ?					
oil	1	1,725		1,725	
KLETT, Hans (1876-?) German					
3D	1	1,226		1,226	
KLEVER, Julius Sergius von (1850-1924) Russian					
oil	3	16,474	2,696	3,053	10,725
KLEVER, Yuli Yulievich (elder) (1850-1924) Russian					
oil	11	90,936	1,812	7,550	18,875
KLEY, Heinrich (1863-1945) German					
wc/d	2	10,100	2,600	5,050	7,500
KLEY, Louis (1833-1911) French					
3D	1	1,419		1,419	
KLEYN, Lodewyk Johannes (1817-1897) Dutch					
oil	6	73,571	2,185	5,231	38,189
KLEYNE, David (1754-1805) Dutch					
oil	4	25,562	4,208	5,315	10,725
KLIEMANN, Carl Heinz (1924-) German					
wc/d	1	1,009		1,009	
KLIMEK, Ludwig (1912-1992) Polish					
oil	2	2,904	1,107	1,452	1,797
KLIMSCH, Fritz (1870-1960) German					
3D	11	106,930	1,124	6,703	38,926
KLIMT, Gustav (1862-1918) Austrian					
wc/d	18	653,341	2,524	16,610	250,000
KLINCK, J D (19th C) ?					
wc/d	1	1,936		1,936	
KLINCKENBERG, Eugen (1858-?) Dutch					
oil	1	8,074		8,074	
KLINE, Franz (1910-1962) American					
oil	7	3,444,142	5,500	85,000	2,300,000
wc/d	4	138,581	12,000	15,791	95,000
KLINGELHOFER, Fritz (1832-1903) German					
oil	1	2,155		2,155	
wc/d	1	3,023		3,023	
KLINGER, Max (1857-1920) German					
3D	3	14,933	1,661	4,778	8,494
wc/d	3	5,688	1,452	1,700	2,536
KLINKENBERG, J C K (1852-1924) Dutch					
oil	1	1,585		1,585	
KLINKENBERG, Johannes Christiaan Karel (1852-1924) Dutch					
oil	7	230,641	2,700	7,652	161,243
wc/d	2	6,275	1,607	3,138	4,668
KLINT, Hilma af (1862-1944) Swedish					
wc/d	1	1,303		1,303	
KLIUN, Ivan (1873-1943) Russian					
wc/d	2	79,483	4,195	39,742	75,288
KLODT, Nikolai Aleksandrovich (1865-1918) Russian					
oil	1	2,718		2,718	
KLOETZKE, Reinhard (1821-?) German					
oil	1	2,229		2,229	
KLOMBEEK, Johann Bernard (1815-1893) Dutch					
oil	3	170,009	34,609	47,400	88,000
KLOMBEEK, Johann Bernard and VERBOECKHOVEN, Eugène (19th C) Dutch					
oil	1	30,000		30,000	

Name	No.	Total Sales Value	lowest	Prices median	highest
KLOMP, Aelbert (1618-1688) Dutch					
oil	2	11,079	4,514	5,540	6,565
KLOOS, Cornelis (1895-) Dutch					
oil	1	1,951		1,951	
KLOSS, Gene (1903-) American					
oil	1	1,200		1,200	
wc/d	3	14,000	3,000	5,500	5,500
KLOTZ, Lenz (1925-) Swiss					
oil	1	1,043		1,043	
wc/d	1	1,033		1,033	
KLOYOU, J (20th C) ?					
oil	1	1,431		1,431	
KLUGE, Constantine (1912-) French					
oil	6	25,217	2,067	3,580	8,760
KLUGE, Gustav (1947-) German					
oil	1	2,972		2,972	
wc/d	1	1,117		1,117	
KLUYVER, Pieter Lodewijk Francisco (1816-1900) Dutch					
oil	7	79,604	2,038	8,486	38,189
KNAB, Ferdinand (1834-1902) German					
oil	2	10,373	1,708	5,187	8,665
KNAP, Jan (1949-) Czechoslovakian?					
oil	1	3,676		3,676	
wc/d	1	1,125		1,125	
KNAPP, Charles R (20th C) American					
oil	1	7,500		7,500	
KNAPP, Charles W (1822-1900) American					
oil	5	23,300	1,100	4,500	8,500
KNAPP, F (?) ?					
oil	1	2,200		2,200	
KNAPP, Stephan (1921-) British					
wc/d	1	1,725		1,725	
KNAPP, X (19th C) ?					
oil	1	1,737		1,737	
KNARREN, Petrus Renier Hubertus (1826-1869) Belgian					
oil	2	31,600	10,150	15,800	21,450
KNATHS, Karl (1891-1971) American					
oil	3	17,200	4,200	6,500	6,500
KNAUS, Ludwig (1829-1910) German					
oil	2	25,154	5,217	12,577	19,937
KNAUTH, A W (1918-) American					
oil	1	1,400		1,400	
KNAYER, Immanuel (1896-1962) German					
wc/d	1	3,456		3,456	
KNEBEL, Franz (jnr) (1809-1877) Swiss					
oil	4	51,387	5,808	12,821	19,937
KNEELING, Knight (19th C) British					
oil	1	1,223		1,223	
KNEFFEL, Karin (1957-) German					
oil	1	3,676		3,676	
KNELL, Adolphus (fl.1860-1890) British					
oil	11	29,875	1,133	1,950	6,520
KNELL, William Adolphus (1805-1875) British					
oil	2	6,827	2,027	3,414	4,800
wc/d	2	5,420	2,400	2,710	3,020
KNELL, William Callcott (19th C) British					
oil	9	29,110	1,350	2,718	7,200
KNELLER, Sir Godfrey (1646-1723) British					
oil	7	88,689	4,530	6,864	26,860

Name	No.	Total Sales Value	lowest	Prices median	highest
KNELLER, Sir Godfrey (school) (1646-1723) British					
oil	1	1,600		1,600	
KNIGHT, A R (19th C) British					
oil	1	2,265		2,265	
KNIGHT, A Roland (19th C) British					
oil	14	22,855	1,060	1,350	2,718
KNIGHT, Charles (19/20th C) British					
wc/d	2	2,214	1,076	1,107	1,138
KNIGHT, Charles Parsons (1829-1897) British					
oil	1	1,271		1,271	
wc/d	1	1,284		1,284	
KNIGHT, Charles Robert (1874-1953) American					
3D	1	1,300		1,300	
KNIGHT, Dame Laura (1877-1970) British					
oil	7	331,744	10,744	39,000	113,250
wc/d	29	198,736	1,022	3,666	45,000
KNIGHT, Daniel Ridgway (1839-1924) American					
oil	14	1,698,000	8,000	102,500	360,000
wc/d	1	3,800		3,800	
KNIGHT, George (19th C) British					
oil	6	9,019	1,001	1,454	2,282
KNIGHT, Harold (1874-1961) British					
oil	3	206,445	13,395	45,000	148,050
KNIGHT, John Buxton (1843-1908) British					
oil	6	17,600	1,103	1,450	10,990
wc/d	1	1,257		1,257	
KNIGHT, Joseph (1837-1909) British					
oil	2	4,007	1,397	2,004	2,610
wc/d	1	1,397		1,397	
KNIGHT, Louis Aston (1873-1948) American					
oil	15	218,058	1,200	3,200	47,500
wc/d	1	1,042		1,042	
KNIKKER, Aris (1887-1962) Dutch					
oil	3	7,012	1,071	2,122	3,819
KNIKKER, Jan (jnr) (1911-1990) Dutch					
oil	5	6,712	1,061	1,291	1,697
KNIKKER, Jan (snr) (1889-1957) Dutch					
oil	2	6,198	1,530	3,099	4,668
KNIP, August (1819-?) Dutch					
oil	2	7,488	2,581	3,744	4,907
KNIP, Henri (1819-1897) Dutch					
wc/d	3	4,543	1,038	1,377	2,128
KNIP, Willem (1883-1967) Dutch					
oil	7	19,272	1,100	1,641	8,873
KNOBLAUCH, C (19/20th C) German					
oil	1	2,944		2,944	
KNOEBEL, Imi (1940-) German					
3D	3	6,124	1,068	1,514	3,542
oil	9	81,043	1,748	3,883	27,184
wc/d	3	57,786	2,502	8,000	47,284
KNOLLER, Martin (1725-1804) Austrian					
oil	1	1,661		1,661	
KNOOP, A (1856-1900) German					
oil	1	1,250		1,250	
KNOOP, August (1856-1900) German					
oil	3	7,434	1,170	1,200	5,064
KNOPF, Herman (1870-?) Austrian					
oil	2	5,734	1,636	2,867	4,098
KNOPFF, Fernand (1858-1921) Belgian					
oil	1	50,267		50,267	

Name	No.	Total Sales Value	Prices lowest	median	highest
KNOPPEL, Arvid (1893-1970) Swedish					
3D	2	3,834	1,247	1,917	2,587
KNOWLES, Dorothy (1927-) Canadian					
oil	3	13,211	1,208	5,277	6,726
KNOWLES, Farquhar McGillivray (1859-1932) Canadian					
oil	2	2,437	1,110	1,219	1,327
KNOWLES, Gareth P (1965-) Irish					
3D	1	1,776		1,776	
KNOWLES, George Sheridan (1863-1931) British					
oil	2	15,700	3,700	7,850	12,000
wc/d	3	12,077	2,067	2,145	7,865
KNOWLES, Joseph Edward (1907-1980) American					
oil	2	10,800	3,300	5,400	7,500
KNOX, Archibald (1864-1933) British					
wc/d	13	31,352	1,144	2,340	4,290
KNOX, Jack (20th C) British					
oil	1	1,738		1,738	
KNOX, John (1778-1845) British					
oil	1	36,250		36,250	
KNOX, Susan Ricker (1875-1959) American					
oil	2	2,500	1,000	1,250	1,500
KNOX, Wilfred (1884-1966) British					
wc/d	2	2,416	1,066	1,208	1,350
KNOX, William (1862-1925) British					
wc/d	1	1,095		1,095	
KNUDSEN, Peder (1868-1944) Danish					
oil	1	1,690		1,690	
KNUDSON, Robert L (20th C) American					
wc/d	1	1,600		1,600	
KNUPFER, Benes (1848-1910) Czechoslovakian					
oil	1	18,960		18,960	
KNUTSON-TZARA, Greta (1899-1983) Swedish					
oil	2	9,244	4,020	4,622	5,224
KNUTTEL, Graham (1954-) Irish					
oil	2	4,189	1,885	2,095	2,304
KNYFF, Jacob (1638-1681) Dutch					
oil	1	21,140		21,140	
KNYFF, Wouter (1607-1693) Dutch					
oil	3	38,707	5,107	12,000	21,600
KOBELL, Ferdinand (1740-1799) German					
wc/d	1	1,298		1,298	
KOBELL, Franz (1749-1822) German					
wc/d	3	3,518	1,068	1,219	1,231
KOBELL, J (18/19th C) Dutch					
oil	1	1,800		1,800	
KOBELL, Jan (1756-1833) Dutch					
oil	2	16,772	7,022	8,386	9,750
wc/d	1	2,182		2,182	
KOBELL, Jan Baptist (1778-1814) Dutch					
oil	2	6,101	2,940	3,051	3,161
KOBELL, Wilhelm von (1766-1855) German					
oil	2	18,238	1,733	9,119	16,505
wc/d	4	47,824	1,729	13,448	19,200
KOBERSTEIN, Hans (1864-?) German					
oil	1	1,047		1,047	
KOBKE, Christen (1810-1848) Danish					
oil	1	322,712		322,712	
KOCH, François (19/20th C) Austrian					
oil	1	22,500		22,500	

Name	No.	Total Sales Value	lowest	Prices median	highest
KOCH, Georg (1857-1926) German					
oil	4	14,889	1,427	3,140	7,183
wc/d	1	8,000		8,000	
KOCH, J (19th C) ?					
oil	1	1,559		1,559	
KOCH, John (1909-1978) American					
oil	6	116,000	1,000	5,750	70,000
KOCH, Josef Anton (1768-1839) Austrian					
oil	1	4,984		4,984	
wc/d	3	11,964	2,000	2,273	7,691
KOCH, Ludwig (1866-1934) Austrian					
oil	1	5,765		5,765	
wc/d	1	1,410		1,410	
KOCH, Pyke (1901-1991) Dutch					
oil	2	336,703	43,573	168,352	293,130
KOCH, Willi (1909-1988) Swiss					
oil	1	1,516		1,516	
KOCHANOWSKY, Roman (1856-1945) Polish					
oil	3	6,550	1,100	2,200	3,250
KOCKE, Hugo Wilhelm Georg (1874-1956) German					
oil	1	1,463		1,463	
KODRA, Ibrahim (1918-) Middle Eastern					
oil	2	2,697	1,338	1,349	1,359
KOEFOED, Hans Christian (1849-1921) Danish					
oil	1	2,118		2,118	
KOEHLER, Henry (1927-) American					
oil	2	8,100	1,600	4,050	6,500
wc/d	2	5,500	2,300	2,750	3,200
KOEHLER, Paul R (c.1866-1909) American					
wc/d	1	2,300		2,300	
KOEK-KOEK, Stephen Roberto (1887-1934) Argentinian					
oil	10	37,740	1,600	2,050	18,000
KOEKKOEK, Barend Cornelis (1803-1862) Dutch					
oil	4	450,557	6,863	109,347	225,000
wc/d	3	10,826	1,007	2,181	7,638
KOEKKOEK, Gerard (1871-1956) Dutch					
oil	1	1,358		1,358	
KOEKKOEK, H B (1849-1909) Dutch					
oil	1	1,435		1,435	
KOEKKOEK, Hendrik Barend (1849-1909) Dutch					
oil	5	26,738	4,416	5,461	6,723
KOEKKOEK, Hendrik Pieter (1843-1890) Dutch					
oil	7	26,383	1,635	4,740	4,750
KOEKKOEK, Hermanus (1815-1882) Dutch					
oil	11	149,314	1,952	6,320	63,200
KOEKKOEK, Hermanus (jnr) (1836-1909) Dutch					
oil	3	19,624	4,000	7,638	7,986
KOEKKOEK, Hermanus Willem (1867-1929) Dutch					
oil	4	31,249	2,422	4,866	19,095
KOEKKOEK, Jan Hermanus (1778-1851) Dutch					
oil	4	179,237	7,268	43,900	84,169
KOEKKOEK, Jan Hermanus Barend (1840-1912) Dutch					
oil	12	116,393	1,721	8,396	21,216
KOEKKOEK, Marinus Adrianus I (1807-1870) Dutch					
oil	7	54,764	1,211	7,214	23,360
KOEKKOEK, Marinus Adrianus II (1873-1944) Dutch					
oil	2	3,555	1,185	1,778	2,370
KOEKKOEK, Willem (1839-1895) Dutch					
oil	3	73,569	16,069	18,000	39,500

Name	No.	Total Sales Value	lowest	Prices median	highest
KOEKOEK, B C (?) ?					
wc/d	1	9,554		9,554	
KOELLA, Heinrich (1757-1789) Swiss					
wc/d	1	1,694		1,694	
KOELMAN, Johan Daniel (19th C) Dutch					
oil	1	1,268		1,268	
KOENIGER, Walter (1881-1945) American					
oil	3	9,400	2,600	3,000	3,800
KOEPPEN, Dorothea Wusten (20th C) German					
wc/d	1	10,080		10,080	
KOERLE, Pancraz (1823-1875) German					
oil	1	1,798		1,798	
KOERNER, Ernst Karl Eugen (1846-1927) German					
oil	3	9,753	1,427	2,041	6,285
KOERNER, William Henry Dethlef (1878-1938) American					
oil	2	63,000	18,000	31,500	45,000
KOESTER, Alexander (1864-1932) German					
oil	17	773,107	3,962	29,600	130,000
wc/d	3	4,775	1,045	1,254	2,476
KOETS, P (18th C) Dutch					
oil	1	1,544		1,544	
KOETS, Roelof (elder) (1592-1655) Dutch					
oil	1	5,398		5,398	
KOETS, Roelof (younger) (1655-1725) Dutch					
oil	1	13,000		13,000	
KOFFLER, T (19th C) Swiss					
wc/d	1	1,516		1,516	
KOFOED, Herman (1743-1815) ?					
oil	1	2,922		2,922	
KOGAN, Moissey (1879-1942) Russian					
3D	2	9,499	1,902	4,750	7,597
KOGAN, Nina (1887-1942) Russian					
wc/d	3	6,359	1,227	2,234	2,898
KOGL, Benedict (1892-1969) German					
oil	11	16,073	1,122	1,486	2,157
KOHLER, Fritz (1887-1971) German					
oil	1	1,000		1,000	
KOHLER, Gustav (1859-?) German					
oil	1	2,182		2,182	
KOHLHOFF, Wilhelm (1893-1971) German					
oil	1	3,244		3,244	
wc/d	4	6,809	1,135	1,702	2,270
KOHLMANN, Ejnar (1888-1968) Finnish					
oil	1	1,224		1,224	
KOHLMEYER, Ida (1912-1997) American					
oil	2	26,250	8,250	13,125	18,000
wc/d	1	8,000		8,000	
KOHLSCHEIN, Hans (1879-?) German					
oil	1	1,619		1,619	
KOHLSCHEIN, Joseph (younger) (1884-1958) German					
oil	2	2,813	1,341	1,407	1,472
wc/d	1	1,079		1,079	
KOHRL, Ludwig (1858-1927) German					
oil	2	2,245	1,107	1,123	1,138
KOISO, Ryohei (1902-1988) Japanese					
oil	3	452,000	42,000	160,000	250,000
KOISTINEN, Unto (1917-1994) Finnish					
oil	1	1,507		1,507	

Name	No.	Total Sales Value	lowest	Prices median	highest
KOIZUME, Tomohide (1944-) Japanese					
wc/d	2	22,000	7,000	11,000	15,000
KOK, Johannes Cornelis (1826-1890) Dutch					
oil	1	4,075		4,075	
KOKEN, Friedrich Hans (1883-?) German					
oil	1	1,442		1,442	
KOKEN, Paul (1853-?) German					
oil	1	2,954		2,954	
KOKINE, Mikhail (1921-) Russian					
oil	1	1,050		1,050	
KOKKEN, Henry (1860-1941) Belgian					
oil	1	1,211		1,211	
KOKOSCHKA, Oskar (1886-1980) Austrian					
oil	1	403,200		403,200	
wc/d	8	68,396	1,405	8,151	20,000
KOLAR, Jiri (1914-) Czechoslovakian					
wc/d	4	5,063	1,063	1,143	1,710
KOLARE, Nils (1930-) Swedish					
oil	1	1,223		1,223	
KOLBE, Georg (1877-1947) German					
3D	11	285,392	1,125	28,113	60,552
wc/d	6	21,971	1,100	2,694	6,796
KOLBE, Heinrich Christoph (1771-1836) German					
oil	3	46,268	1,250	1,250	43,768
KOLDEWAY, Bernard Marie (1859-1898) Dutch					
oil	1	2,038		2,038	
KOLESNICOFF, J (20th C) Russian					
wc/d	1	1,365		1,365	
KOLESNIKOFF, Stepan (1879-1955) Russian					
oil	1	1,208		1,208	
KOLESNIKOV, Ivan Feodorovich (1887-1929) Russian					
wc/d	1	3,000		3,000	
KOLLE, Helmut (1899-1931) German					
oil	1	11,165		11,165	
KOLLER, Matthias (19th C) German					
oil	1	1,080		1,080	
KOLLER, Rudolf (1828-1905) Swiss					
oil	9	96,717	1,193	9,723	22,154
KOLLORSZ, Richard Franz (1900-1983) American					
oil	1	4,250		4,250	
KOLLWITZ, Kathe (1867-1945) German					
3D	2	5,666	2,564	2,833	3,102
wc/d	9	117,505	1,073	12,097	35,000
KOLMSPERGER, Waldemar (elder) (1858-1943) German					
oil	3	13,310	1,694	5,808	5,808
wc/d	1	1,210		1,210	
KOLMSPERGER, Waldemar (younger) (1881-1954) German					
oil	2	2,420	1,065	1,210	1,355
KOLOSVARY, Sigismund (1899-1983) Hungarian					
oil	19	30,048	1,019	1,528	2,801
wc/d	1	1,146		1,146	
KONARSKI, J (19th C?) Russian?					
oil	2	2,580	1,007	1,290	1,573
KONEBERG, Johann Michael (fl.1765-1787) German					
oil	1	1,684		1,684	
KONECNY, Josef (1907-) Czechoslovakian					
oil	4	9,496	1,259	2,385	3,467
KONIG, Ferdinand (1827-1894) German					
oil	1	2,370		2,370	

Name	No.	Total Sales Value	lowest	Prices median	highest
KONIG, Fritz (1924-) German					
3D	6	36,978	1,251	6,030	10,467
wc/d	1	1,182		1,182	
KONIG, Leo von (1871-1944) German					
oil	4	44,403	4,877	10,306	18,914
KONIJNENBURG, Willem A van (1868-1943) Dutch					
oil	1	4,243		4,243	
KONINCH, S de (?) ?					
oil	1	2,566		2,566	
KONINCK, D de (17/18th C) Flemish/Dutch					
oil	1	19,630		19,630	
KONINCK, Philips de (1619-1688) Dutch					
oil	1	30,000		30,000	
wc/d	1	2,750		2,750	
KONINCK, Salomon (1609-1656) Dutch					
oil	1	117,600		117,600	
KONING, Arnold Hendrik (1860-1945) Dutch					
oil	1	1,609		1,609	
KONING, Edzard (1869-1954) Dutch					
oil	1	2,334		2,334	
KONING, Elisabeth Johanna (1816-1888) Dutch					
oil	2	4,114	1,963	2,057	2,151
KONINGH, Leendert de (elder) (1777-1849) Dutch					
oil	2	9,711	2,175	4,856	7,536
KONINGH, Leonard de (younger) (1810-1887) Dutch					
oil	1	6,998		6,998	
KONINGSBRUGGEN, Rob van (20th C) Dutch?					
oil	1	3,763		3,763	
KONO, Micao (20th C) Japanese					
oil	5	40,529	1,852	8,936	12,970
KONSTANTINOPOLSKI, Adolf (1923-) Russian					
oil	1	5,439		5,439	
KONTI, Isidore (1862-1938) Austrian/American					
3D	2	5,000	1,250	2,500	3,750
KOOGH, Adrianus van der (1796-1831) Dutch					
oil	2	13,873	2,970	6,937	10,903
KOOIMAN, Willem (1831-1881) Dutch					
oil	1	2,200		2,200	
KOOL, Willem (1608-1666) Dutch					
oil	1	4,032		4,032	
KOOLEN, A (c.1608-c.1666) Dutch					
oil	1	5,480		5,480	
KOONING, Willem de (1904-1997) American/Dutch					
oil	19	10,470,029	24,000	140,000	4,100,000
wc/d	5	2,940,500	12,000	32,500	2,400,000
KOONS, Jeff (1955-) American					
3D	13	4,681,375	1,095	230,000	1,550,000
oil	2	188,000	48,000	94,000	140,000
wc/d	2	2,586	1,086	1,293	1,500
KOORNSTRA, Metten (1912-1978) Dutch					
oil	2	4,394	1,377	2,197	3,017
KOOS, Victor (1864-1925) French					
oil	1	2,918		2,918	
KOPCKE, Arthur (1928-1977) Danish					
3D	1	2,056		2,056	
oil	2	4,168	1,409	2,084	2,759
wc/d	2	3,403	1,020	1,702	2,383
KOPFERMANN, Sigrid (1923-) German					
oil	1	2,438		2,438	

Name	No.	Total Sales Value	Prices lowest	median	highest
KOPMAN, Katharine (1870-1950) American					
wc/d	1	2,200		2,200	
KOPP, Mathilde (1836-?) German					
oil	1	1,347		1,347	
KOPPENOL, Cornelis (1865-1946) Dutch					
oil	3	7,864	1,207	2,950	3,707
wc/d	1	1,530		1,530	
KORAB, Karl (1937-) Austrian					
wc/d	4	4,584	1,081	1,146	1,211
KOREAN SCHOOL, 20th C					
wc/d	1	4,750		4,750	
KORECKI, Victor (1890-1980) Polish					
oil	2	2,484	1,084	1,242	1,400
KORN, Johan Philip (1728-1796) Swedish					
oil	1	1,242		1,242	
KORNBECK, Julius (1839-1920) German					
oil	4	6,342	1,257	1,562	1,961
KORNBECK, Peter (1837-1894) Danish					
oil	4	13,414	2,324	2,647	5,797
KORNEK, Albert Friedrich Rudolf (1813-1905) German					
oil	1	3,000		3,000	
KORNER, E (20th C) ?					
oil	1	1,510		1,510	
KORNERUP, Valdemar (1865-1924) Danish					
oil	1	1,356		1,356	
KOROMPAY, Giovanni (1904-1988) Italian					
oil	1	2,182		2,182	
KOROVINE, Alexei Konstantinovitch (1897-1950) Russian					
oil	1	7,248		7,248	
KOROVINE, Constantin (1861-1939) Russian					
oil	15	193,025	2,419	12,000	24,160
wc/d	5	23,248	1,128	5,285	6,795
KORSAKOFF-GALSTON, Alexandra (1884-1969) American/Russian					
wc/d	1	1,162		1,162	
KORSCHANN, Charles (1872-?) Czechoslovakian					
3D	1	5,652		5,652	
KORSCHGEN, Jos (19/20th C) German					
3D	1	1,500		1,500	
KORTHALS, Johannes (1916-) Dutch					
oil	3	8,039	1,015	3,122	3,902
KORTRIGHT, Guy (1877-?) British					
oil	1	1,332		1,332	
KORWAN, Franz (1865-?) German					
oil	1	3,182		3,182	
KORZOUKHIN, Alexei Ivanovich (1835-1894) Russian					
oil	1	3,020		3,020	
KOSA, Emil (jnr) (1903-1968) American					
oil	3	15,000	4,000	4,000	7,000
wc/d	2	6,300	1,800	3,150	4,500
KOSA, Emil (snr) (1876-1955) American					
oil	1	7,500		7,500	
KOSKULL, Anders Gustaf (1831-1904) Swedish					
oil	3	6,462	1,354	1,428	3,680
KOSLER, Franz Xavier (1864-?) Austrian					
oil	1	4,000		4,000	
KOSNICK-KLOSS, Jeanne (1892-1955) German					
wc/d	1	1,244		1,244	
KOSSAK, Jerzy (1886-1955) Polish					
oil	4	5,667	1,200	1,333	1,726

Name	No.	Total Sales Value	lowest	Prices median	highest
KOSSAK, Julius (1824-1899) Polish					
wc/d	1	2,750		2,750	
KOSSAK, Woiciech von (1857-1942) French					
oil	1	2,178		2,178	
KOSSOFF, Léon (1926-) British					
wc/d	4	7,027	1,349	1,632	2,414
KOSSUTH, Egon Josef (1874-?) Czechoslovakian					
oil	1	1,600		1,600	
KOSTA, Alex (1925-) Swiss?					
3D	1	4,228		4,228	
KOSTABI, Mark (1961-) American					
3D	1	1,527		1,527	
oil	18	39,814	1,126	1,811	4,692
KOSTELOV, Dmitrii (20th C) Russian					
oil	1	1,115		1,115	
KOSTER, Everhardus (1817-1892) Dutch					
oil	2	17,678	6,232	8,839	11,446
wc/d	1	2,617		2,617	
KOSTER, H (19/20th C) German					
oil	1	1,257		1,257	
KOSTER, Jo (1869-1944) Dutch					
oil	1	2,179		2,179	
KOSTER, Karl Georg (1812-1893) German					
oil	1	1,136		1,136	
KOSUTH, Joseph (1945-) American					
3D	2	168,250	55,000	84,125	113,250
wc/d	1	3,709		3,709	
KOT, Pawel (20th C) South African					
oil	1	2,516		2,516	
KOTHE, Fritz (1916-) German					
oil	3	10,275	2,163	2,885	5,227
KOTSCHENREITER, Hugo (1854-1908) German					
oil	2	3,634	1,634	1,817	2,000
KOUNELLIS, Jannis (1936-) Greek					
3D	1	30,000		30,000	
oil	7	657,353	4,853	72,500	246,500
wc/d	5	190,132	5,800	33,220	87,000
KOUPETZIAN, Aram (1928-) Russian					
oil	2	3,648	1,742	1,824	1,906
KOUSNETZOFF, Constantin (1863-1936) Russian					
oil	1	1,015		1,015	
KOVACS, Attila (1938-) Hungarian					
oil	1	1,068		1,068	
KOVERECH, Aleardo (1948-) Italian					
oil	1	2,426		2,426	
KOWALCZEWSKI, P L (1865-1910) German					
3D	1	1,048		1,048	
KOWALSKI, Ivan Ivanovitch (20th C) Russian					
oil	1	1,691		1,691	
KOWALSKY, Leopold Franz (1856-1931) Russian/French					
oil	1	9,000		9,000	
KOYANAGUI, Sei (1896-?) Japanese					
oil	2	4,258	1,751	2,129	2,507
KOZAKIEWICZ, Anton (1841-1929) Polish					
oil	1	8,760		8,760	
KOZMAN, Myron (1916-) American					
oil	1	2,100		2,100	
KRABBE, Hendrik Maarten (1868-1931) Dutch					
oil	2	19,053	3,750	9,527	15,303
wc/d	1	1,573		1,573	

Name	No.	Total Sales Value	lowest	Prices median	highest
KRAEMER, Peter (19/20th C) German					
wc/d	3	3,614	1,038	1,038	1,486
KRAEMER, Peter (jnr) (1857-1941) German					
oil	1	1,251		1,251	
wc/d	3	5,122	1,080	1,816	2,226
KRAER, Charles François (1822-1878) Italian					
oil	2	6,421	2,307	3,211	4,114
KRAFFT, Albert (19th C) German					
oil	1	3,500		3,500	
KRAFFT, Carl R (1884-1938) American					
oil	7	98,850	1,000	3,250	70,000
KRAFFT, David von (1655-1724) Swedish					
oil	1	29,345		29,345	
KRAFFT, J F (18th C) Austrian?					
oil	1	1,087		1,087	
KRAFFT, Johann Peter (1780-1856) German					
oil	1	44,858		44,858	
KRAFFT, Per (elder) (1724-1793) Swedish					
oil	2	37,342	4,740	18,671	32,602
KRAFFT, Per (younger) (1777-1863) Swedish					
oil	1	2,613		2,613	
KRAFT, Frederik (1823-1854) Danish					
oil	1	1,300		1,300	
KRAHE, Peter Joseph (1758-1840) German					
wc/d	1	1,068		1,068	
KRAJCBERG, Frans (1921-) Brazilian/Polish					
wc/d	1	5,787		5,787	
KRAKAUER, Leopold (1890-1954) Israeli					
wc/d	4	7,600	1,600	1,600	2,800
KRAMER, Franz (19th C) German					
oil	1	3,500		3,500	
KRAMER, H (?) ?					
oil	1	1,061		1,061	
KRAMER, Jacob (1892-1962) British					
oil	3	7,599	1,156	2,609	3,834
wc/d	1	1,099		1,099	
KRAMSKY, S (19/20th C) Russian					
oil	1	8,268		8,268	
KRANEWITTER, Franz Josef (1893-1974) Austrian					
3D	1	3,600		3,600	
KRANTZ, F (19th C) French					
oil	1	1,500		1,500	
KRASNER, Lee (1908-1984) American					
oil	1	160,000		160,000	
wc/d	1	22,000		22,000	
KRATSCHOWSKI, Jossif (1854-1914) Russian					
oil	2	7,248	2,416	3,624	4,832
KRATZER, Hans (19/20th C) German					
oil	1	1,329		1,329	
KRAUS, Georg Melchior (1737-1806) German					
oil	2	11,242	2,592	5,621	8,650
KRAUS, Robert Frank (1893-1950) German					
oil	1	1,339		1,339	
KRAUSE, Franz Emil (1836-1900) German					
oil	1	1,030		1,030	
KRAUSE, Karl Heinz (1924-) German					
3D	1	1,019		1,019	
KRAUSE, Lina (1857-?) German					
oil	1	1,096		1,096	

Name	No.	Total Sales Value	Prices lowest	median	highest
KRAUSE, Wilhelm August (1803-1864) German					
oil	1	2,145		2,145	
KRAUSE, William (1875-1925) German					
oil	1	1,000		1,000	
KRAUSKOPF, Bruno (1892-1960) German					
oil	7	34,535	1,942	3,641	9,753
wc/d	5	8,825	1,073	1,891	2,302
KRAUSZ, Simon Andreas (1760-1825) Dutch					
oil	1	2,581		2,581	
KRAWCZYK, Joan (1951-) Canadian					
oil	1	1,600		1,600	
KRAY, Wilhelm (1828-1889) German					
oil	1	3,001		3,001	
KREBS, A (20th C) ?					
wc/d	1	1,709		1,709	
KREBS, Walter (1900-1965) Swiss					
oil	1	1,182		1,182	
KREGTEN, Fedor van (1871-1937) Dutch					
oil	2	2,911	1,405	1,456	1,506
KREIDOLF, Ernst Konrad Theophil (1863-1956) Swiss					
wc/d	4	6,153	1,115	1,412	2,215
KREIENBUHL, Jurg (1932-) Swiss					
oil	1	1,033		1,033	
KREITMAYER, Johann Baptist (19th C) German					
oil	2	4,809	2,208	2,405	2,601
KREITZ, Willy (1903-1982) Belgian					
3D	3	4,466	1,462	1,462	1,542
KREMEGNE, Pinchus (1890-1981) Russian					
oil	21	54,978	1,197	2,356	4,752
KRENN, Edmund (1846-1902) Austrian					
oil	2	3,100	1,100	1,550	2,000
KRETZSCHMER, Johann Hermann (1811-1890) German					
oil	2	23,094	6,094	11,547	17,000
KREUGER, Nils (1858-1930) Swedish					
oil	10	96,180	1,708	7,066	28,138
wc/d	2	4,088	1,345	2,044	2,743
KREUZER, Franz (1819-1872) German					
oil	1	1,036		1,036	
KREYDER, Alexis (1839-1912) French					
oil	3	10,754	2,065	2,487	6,202
KREYFELT, Julius van (1863-?) German					
oil	1	1,170		1,170	
KRICHELDORF, Carl (1863-?) German					
oil	2	3,900	1,666	1,950	2,234
KRICKE, Norbert (1922-1984) German					
wc/d	2	2,936	1,165	1,468	1,771
KRIEBEL, Anton Maria Ludwig (1823-1890) German					
oil	1	1,207		1,207	
KRIEFF, Antonio (1928-) Spanish					
3D	1	1,279		1,279	
KRIEGEL, Willy (1901-) German					
oil	1	1,655		1,655	
KRIEGER, Joseph (1848-1914) Swiss					
oil	1	3,352		3,352	
KRIEGHOFF, Cornelius (1815-1872) Canadian					
oil	13	495,533	3,198	19,910	172,556
wc/d	1	1,460		1,460	
KRIEHUBER, Josef (1800-1876) Austrian					
wc/d	1	2,724		2,724	

Name	No.	Total Sales Value	lowest	Prices median	highest
KRIKHAAR, Herman (1930-) Dutch					
oil	1	1,205		1,205	
KRIKI (1965-) French					
3D	1	1,286		1,286	
oil	1	1,141		1,141	
KRINNER, Michaela (1915-) German					
oil	1	1,402		1,402	
KRISANAMIS, Udomsak (1966-) American?					
oil	1	16,000		16,000	
wc/d	1	10,000		10,000	
KRISTO, Bela de (1920-) ?					
oil	6	9,798	1,273	1,419	2,730
KRIZE, Yehiel (1909-1968) Israeli					
oil	2	3,300	1,300	1,650	2,000
KROGER, Diego (1958-) Uruguayan					
oil	1	1,250		1,250	
KROGH, Charlotte Sofie von (1827-1914) Danish					
oil	1	3,813		3,813	
KROHG, Christian (1852-1925) Norwegian					
oil	1	5,605		5,605	
KROJER, Tom (1942-) Danish					
oil	4	5,825	1,153	1,375	1,922
KROLL, Leon (1884-1974) American					
oil	5	185,000	10,000	35,000	72,000
wc/d	1	1,500		1,500	
KRON, Paul (1869-1936) French					
oil	1	1,092		1,092	
KRONBERG, Julius (1850-1921) Swedish					
oil	5	11,286	1,290	2,144	3,208
KRONBERG, Louis (1872-1965) American					
wc/d	2	4,100	1,100	2,050	3,000
KRONBERGER, Carl (1841-1921) Austrian					
oil	4	16,237	1,431	3,197	8,412
KRONENBERG, Fritz (20th C) German?					
oil	1	2,524		2,524	
KRONER, Christian (1838-1911) German					
oil	7	24,336	1,145	2,476	7,844
KRONER, Erwin (1889-?) German					
oil	1	1,698		1,698	
KRONER, Karl (1887-1972) German					
oil	1	1,723		1,723	
KROP, Hildo (1884-?) Dutch					
3D	3	8,620	2,586	2,586	3,448
KROPFF, Joop (1892-1979) Dutch					
oil	4	6,843	1,072	1,635	2,502
KROPSCH, Josef (1813-1854) Austrian					
oil	1	1,744		1,744	
KROTOV, Youri (1964-) Russian					
oil	29	122,817	2,016	3,744	7,900
KROUTHEN, Johan (1858-1932) Swedish					
oil	21	160,307	2,070	4,506	49,661
KROYER, Peder Severin (1851-1909) Danish					
3D	1	8,936		8,936	
oil	15	1,647,450	4,051	40,764	996,600
wc/d	1	8,901		8,901	
KRUG, P (19th C) ?					
oil	1	2,065		2,065	
KRUGER, Erich (20th C) German					
oil	1	1,026		1,026	

Name	No.	Total Sales Value	lowest	Prices median	highest
KRUGER, Eugen (1832-1876) German					
oil	1	15,473		15,473	
KRUGER, Franz (1797-1857) German					
wc/d	3	5,815	1,891	1,891	2,033
KRUGER, Hermann (1823-1909) German					
oil	1	1,159		1,159	
KRUGER, Johann Conrad (1773-1791) German?					
oil	1	4,622		4,622	
KRUGER, Karl Maximilian (1834-1880) German					
oil	1	2,129		2,129	
KRUGER, Otto (1868-?) German?					
oil	1	1,936		1,936	
KRUGER, Richard (1880-?) American					
oil	1	2,500		2,500	
KRUIF, Henri Gilbert de (1882-1944) American					
oil	1	1,300		1,300	
KRUIJFF, Cornelis de (1771-1854) Dutch					
oil	1	9,555		9,555	
KRUIZINGA, Dirk (1895-?) Dutch					
oil	2	2,756	1,032	1,378	1,724
KRUMLINDE, Olof (1856-1945) Swedish					
oil	8	15,090	1,016	1,769	3,811
KRUMMACHER, Karl (1867-1955) German					
oil	1	4,146		4,146	
KRUPPEL, Johann (19th C) German					
oil	1	1,374		1,374	
KRUSEMAN, F M (1817-1882) Dutch					
oil	2	127,670	34,567	63,835	93,103
KRUSEMAN, Frederik Marianus (1817-1882) Dutch					
oil	4	364,554	9,052	58,940	237,622
KRUSEMAN, Jan Adam (1804-1862) Dutch					
oil	2	7,011	1,111	3,506	5,900
KRUSI, Hans (1920-1995) Swiss					
oil	1	1,866		1,866	
KRUUSE, A (19th C) Norwegian					
oil	1	1,278		1,278	
KRUYDER, Herman (1881-1935) Dutch					
wc/d	3	8,860	1,188	3,362	4,310
KRUYS, Cornelis (?-1702) Dutch					
oil	1	26,185		26,185	
KRUYSEN, Johannes (1874-1938) Dutch					
oil	1	1,509		1,509	
KRYMOV, Nikolai Petrovich (1884-1958) Russian					
wc/d	1	1,510		1,510	
KRYZHITSKY, Constantin (1858-1911) Russian					
oil	2	15,960	6,795	7,980	9,165
KUBAT, Milan (20th C) Czechoslovakian					
oil	2	5,169	2,178	2,585	2,991
KUBIERSCHKY, Erich (1854-1944) German					
oil	2	2,604	1,275	1,302	1,329
KUBIN, Alfred (1877-1959) Austrian					
wc/d	52	585,154	1,210	3,150	89,280
KUCHEL, Max (1859-1933) German					
oil	3	12,086	2,000	2,212	7,874
KUCHENMEISTER, Rainer (1926-) German					
wc/d	2	2,816	1,214	1,408	1,602
KUCKEI, Peter (1938-) German					
oil	2	12,109	5,313	6,055	6,796

Name	No.	Total Sales Value	Prices lowest	median	highest
KUDO, Tetsumi (1935-) Japanese					
3D	1	11,570		11,570	
KUEHL, Gotthardt Johann (1850-1915) German					
oil	1	1,709		1,709	
wc/d	1	2,379		2,379	
KUEHNE, Max (1880-c.1968) American					
oil	7	69,000	2,100	6,000	32,500
KUGLER, August (fl.1890-1910) Austrian					
oil	1	1,400		1,400	
KUGLER, Franz Theodor (1808-1858) German					
wc/d	1	5,317		5,317	
KUGLER, K (19/20th C) German					
oil	1	1,246		1,246	
KUHFELD, Peter (1952-) British					
oil	4	9,601	2,054	2,273	3,002
KUHFUSS, Paul (1883-1960) German					
oil	1	1,081		1,081	
wc/d	2	3,183	1,298	1,592	1,885
KUHN, Bob (1920-) American					
oil	5	178,420	5,920	37,500	65,000
wc/d	1	12,000		12,000	
KUHN, Friedrich (1926-1972) Swiss					
oil	1	3,586		3,586	
KUHN, Hans (1905-1992) German					
oil	1	5,674		5,674	
wc/d	1	1,151		1,151	
KUHN, Johann Baptist (1810-1861) German					
wc/d	1	3,102		3,102	
KUHN, Walt (1877-1949) American					
oil	1	4,000		4,000	
wc/d	5	33,500	1,300	2,200	14,000
KUHNE, Lebrecht (1803-?) German					
oil	1	7,039		7,039	
KUHNE, Otil (1909-1999) German					
oil	1	4,398		4,398	
KUHNEN, Pieter Lodewyk (1812-1877) Belgian					
oil	1	3,244		3,244	
KUHNEN, Pieter Lodewyk and VERBOECKHOVEN, Eugene (19th C) Belgian					
oil	1	16,314		16,314	
KUHNERT, Wilhelm (1865-1926) German					
oil	5	32,966	1,865	3,636	16,280
wc/d	5	19,025	1,040	2,840	8,520
KUHNLE, H (19th C) American					
oil	1	1,900		1,900	
KUINDJI, Arkhip Ivanovitch (1842-1910) Russian					
oil	2	49,350	21,150	24,675	28,200
KUITCA, Guillermo (1961-) Argentinian					
3D	1	18,000		18,000	
oil	3	210,000	30,000	40,000	140,000
KUKUK, Willy (1875-1943) German					
oil	1	1,198		1,198	
KULLBERG, Isak Fredrik (1853-1917) Scandinavian					
oil	1	2,822		2,822	
KULLE, Jakob (1838-1898) Swedish					
oil	1	5,418		5,418	
KUMAR, Ram (1924-) Indian					
oil	3	15,250	4,500	5,250	5,500
KUMLIEN, Akke (1884-1949) Swedish					
oil	7	18,343	1,197	2,829	3,700

Name	No.	Total Sales Value	Prices lowest	median	highest
KUMMER, Karl Robert (1810-1889) German					
oil	1	1,366		1,366	
KUNDIG, Reinhold (1888-1984) Swiss					
oil	18	47,730	1,073	1,943	11,952
KUNDU, Pulin Krishna (20th C) Indian					
oil	1	1,500		1,500	
KUNG, Walter (1912-) Swiss					
oil	1	1,082		1,082	
KUNIYOSHI, Yasuo (1893-1953) American					
wc/d	3	28,200	3,200	9,000	16,000
KUNTZ, Roger (1926-1975) American					
oil	2	5,000	1,500	2,500	3,500
KUNZ, Emma (1892-1963) Swiss?					
3D	1	2,552		2,552	
oil	1	1,730		1,730	
wc/d	9	50,921	3,344	4,464	12,154
KUNZ, Ludwig Adam (1857-1929) Austrian					
oil	4	16,514	1,694	2,160	10,500
KUPELWIESER, Leopold (1796-1862) Austrian					
oil	1	3,240		3,240	
KUPETZKI, Johann (1667-1740) German					
oil	3	11,917	1,995	4,114	5,808
KUPFER, Johann Michael (1859-1917) Austrian					
oil	1	37,382		37,382	
KUPFERMAN, Moshe (20th C) Israeli					
oil	2	10,800	2,300	5,400	8,500
wc/d	1	2,000		2,000	
KUPHAL, Walter (1890-?) German					
oil	1	1,162		1,162	
KUPKA, Frank (1871-1957) Czechoslovakian					
oil	2	48,584	23,144	24,292	25,440
wc/d	16	189,053	1,167	7,565	49,300
KUPPERS, Friedrich (?) German?					
oil	1	1,481		1,481	
KUPPFERMAN, Moshe (1926-) French?					
wc/d	1	1,514		1,514	
KURAMATA, Shiro (20th C) ?					
3D	2	78,500	8,500	39,250	70,000
KURELEK, William (1927-1977) Canadian					
wc/d	11	99,132	2,987	7,181	20,788
KURODA, Aki (1944-) ?					
wc/d	1	2,185		2,185	
KURON, Herbert (1888-?) German					
oil	1	1,788		1,788	
KUROVSKA, Lena (1969-) Russian					
oil	1	1,764		1,764	
KURPERSHOEK, Theo (1914-1998) Dutch					
oil	3	15,128	1,259	2,966	10,903
KURRENNOY, Alexander Avvakumovich (1865-1944) Russian					
oil	1	14,805		14,805	
KURTZWORTH, Harry Muir (1887-1979) American					
oil	1	1,200		1,200	
KURZINGER, Ignaz (1777-c.1839) German					
oil	1	3,243		3,243	
KUSAMA, Yayoi (1929-) Japanese					
3D	6	46,025	2,800	6,270	21,140
oil	5	54,000	6,000	7,000	18,000
wc/d	1	5,510		5,510	
KUSHNER, Robert (1949-) American					
oil	1	1,500		1,500	

Name	No.	Total Sales Value	lowest	Prices median	highest
KUSTER, Johann Kaspar (1747-1818) Swiss					
oil	3	4,485	1,089	1,573	1,823
KUSTNER, Carl (1861-1934) German					
oil	3	4,279	1,136	1,182	1,961
KUSTODIEV, Boris (1878-1927) Russian					
oil	1	458,250		458,250	
wc/d	2	13,818	6,768	6,909	7,050
KUWASSEG, Charles Euphrasie (1838-1904) French					
oil	14	66,024	1,431	4,046	9,723
KUWASSEG, Karl-Josef (1802-1877) French					
oil	3	14,644	1,589	3,500	9,555
KUYCK, Frans van (1852-1915) Belgian					
oil	1	3,889		3,889	
KUYCK, Jean Louis van (1821-1871) Flemish					
oil	1	1,975		1,975	
KUYCK, van (19/20th C) Flemish					
oil	1	10,345		10,345	
KUYK, Laurens van (20th C) Dutch					
oil	1	2,155		2,155	
KUYPERS, Cornelis (1864-1932) Dutch					
oil	4	10,550	1,000	1,825	5,900
KUYPERS, Jan (1845-1912) Dutch					
oil	1	3,611		3,611	
KUYTEN, Harrie (1883-1952) Dutch					
oil	4	25,815	1,526	3,955	16,379
KUZNETSOV, Pavel (1878-1968) Russian					
oil	2	34,730	12,080	17,365	22,650
KVAPIL, Charles (1884-1958) Belgian					
oil	15	30,502	1,085	1,964	4,092
KVIUM, Michael (1955-) Danish					
oil	2	9,220	1,666	4,610	7,554
KWIATKOWSKI, Jean (1896-1971) Polish					
oil	1	3,689		3,689	
KWIATKOWSKI, Teofil (1809-1891) Polish					
wc/d	2	3,238	1,426	1,619	1,812
KYBER, J (19th C) ?					
oil	1	2,613		2,613	
KYHN, Knud (1880-1967) Danish					
oil	1	2,441		2,441	
KYHN, Vilhelm (1819-1903) Danish					
oil	13	69,077	1,700	3,366	19,063
KYLBERG, Carl (1878-1952) Danish					
oil	18	376,704	4,020	12,258	105,368
wc/d	1	2,621		2,621	
LAABS, Hans (1915-) Polish					
oil	2	3,074	1,419	1,537	1,655
LAANEN, Jasper van der (1592-1626) Flemish					
oil	6	134,127	14,112	22,079	33,847
LAAR, Jan Hendrik van de (1807-1874) Dutch					
oil	2	11,063	2,758	5,532	8,305
LAASNER, Hans (1864-?) German					
oil	1	1,310		1,310	
LABHARDT, Emanuel (1810-1874) Swiss					
wc/d	1	4,235		4,235	
LABILLE-GUIARD, Madame Adelaide (1749-1803) French					
oil	2	56,693	2,869	28,347	53,824
LABILOTTE (?) ?					
oil	1	1,747		1,747	

Name	No.	Total Sales Value	lowest	Prices median	highest
LABISSE, Felix (1905-1982) French					
oil	4	37,721	1,037	4,336	28,012
wc/d	3	4,897	1,353	1,353	2,144
LABITTE, Eugène-Leon (1858-1937) French					
oil	4	20,379	1,297	4,041	11,000
LABITTE, G (20th C) French					
wc/d	1	2,188		2,188	
LABO, Savinio (1899-1976) Italian					
oil	1	1,386		1,386	
LABOINTE, A (20th C) ?					
3D	1	1,738		1,738	
LABORDE, Chas (1886-1941) French					
wc/d	1	1,178		1,178	
LABORNE, Edme Émile (1837-1913) French					
oil	1	1,613		1,613	
LABOUREUR, Jean Émile (1877-1943) French					
wc/d	5	16,349	1,095	3,651	4,739
LABRA, Jose Maria de (1925-) Spanish					
wc/d	1	2,082		2,082	
LABRADOR, Juan Fernandez (fl.1629-1636) Spanish					
oil	2	41,760	20,160	20,880	21,600
LACAMERA, Fortunato (1887-1951) Argentinian					
oil	1	4,200		4,200	
LACASSE (20th C) Belgian					
oil	1	6,452		6,452	
LACASSE, Joseph (1894-1975) Belgian					
oil	3	21,438	4,869	7,165	9,404
wc/d	2	2,107	1,050	1,054	1,057
LACCETTI, Valerico (1836-1909) Italian					
oil	1	3,338		3,338	
LACEPEDE, Amelie Kautz de (1796-1860) French					
wc/d	1	1,428		1,428	
LACH, Fritz (1868-1933) Austrian					
oil	1	3,000		3,000	
LACHAISE, Eugene A (1857-1925) American					
oil	1	19,000		19,000	
LACHAISE, Gaston (1882-1935) American/French					
3D	3	96,500	4,500	12,000	80,000
wc/d	1	3,400		3,400	
LACHER, Max (1905-) German					
oil	1	1,138		1,138	
LACHEVRE, Bernard (?) ?					
oil	1	1,875		1,875	
LACHIEZE-REY, Henri (20th C) French					
oil	2	57,281	4,327	28,641	52,954
LACHMAN, Harry (1886-1974) American/French					
oil	1	6,000		6,000	
LACOMBE, Georges (1868-1916) French					
oil	2	229,799	10,849	114,900	218,950
LACOSTE (?) ?					
oil	1	1,741		1,741	
LACOSTE, Charles (1870-1959) French					
oil	2	9,238	4,074	4,619	5,164
LACOUR, Charles (20th C) French					
oil	1	2,578		2,578	
LACOURT, Madeleine (20th C) French					
wc/d	1	1,106		1,106	
LACROIX DE MARSEILLE, Charles François (1720-c.1782) French					
oil	6	189,051	12,000	27,840	65,515

Name	No.	Total Sales Value	lowest	Prices median	highest
LACROIX, Paul (fl.1858-1869) French?					
oil	3	56,000	2,000	20,000	34,000
LACROIX, Tristan (19th C) French					
oil	3	19,093	1,010	1,083	17,000
LACY, Charles J de (1860-1936) British					
oil	1	1,113		1,113	
LADATTE, Francois (1706-1787) French					
3D	1	16,610		16,610	
LADBROOKE, Henry (1800-1870) British					
oil	1	1,029		1,029	
LADBROOKE, John Berney (1803-1879) British					
oil	6	28,745	1,133	4,690	9,424
LADDEY, E (?) German					
oil	1	1,317		1,317	
LADELL, Edward (1821-1886) British					
oil	7	136,641	3,796	15,000	51,340
LADELL, Ellen (fl.1886-1898) British					
oil	1	9,060		9,060	
LADUREAU, Pierre (1882-) French					
oil	1	1,474		1,474	
LAENEN, J J (20th C) ?					
oil	1	1,055		1,055	
LAER, Alexander T van (1857-1920) American					
oil	1	3,500		3,500	
LAER, van (1751-1830) Belgian?					
3D	1	3,146		3,146	
LAERMANS, Eugène (1864-1940) Belgian					
oil	2	17,464	5,580	8,732	11,884
wc/d	3	7,139	1,508	1,508	4,082
LAESSOE, Thorald (1816-1878) Danish					
oil	5	19,237	1,625	2,962	7,153
LAEUGER, Max (20th C) German?					
3D	1	4,633		4,633	
LAEZZA, Giuseppe (?-1905) Italian					
oil	1	8,000		8,000	
LAFAGE, Raymond (1656-1690) French					
wc/d	3	14,046	1,727	3,351	8,968
LAFARGE, John (1835-1910) American					
oil	3	2,050,000	40,000	110,000	1,900,000
LAFENESTRE, Gaston Ernest (1841-?) French					
oil	1	3,179		3,179	
LAFFON, Carmen (1934-) Spanish					
oil	1	48,895		48,895	
LAFOI LEBRUN (?) French?					
oil	2	7,693	1,852	3,847	5,841
LAFON, François (19th C) French					
oil	1	1,751		1,751	
LAFON, Jacques Emile (1817-1886) French					
oil	1	2,625		2,625	
LAFONTAINE, R (?) French?					
oil	1	17,539		17,539	
LAFORCE, H de (19th C) French					
oil	1	3,965		3,965	
LAFORET, Eugene (19/20th C) ?					
oil	1	1,100		1,100	
LAFOSSE, C de (1636-1716) French					
wc/d	1	1,519		1,519	
LAFOSSE, Charles de (1636-1716) French					
wc/d	1	1,746		1,746	

Name	No.	Total Sales Value	lowest	Prices median	highest
LAFRENSEN, Nicolas (younger) (1737-1807) Swedish					
oil	1	31,400		31,400	
wc/d	1	8,762		8,762	
LAFUENTE, Ramiro (?) Spanish					
oil	1	2,707		2,707	
LAGAGE, Pierre (1911-1977) French					
oil	8	32,008	1,139	2,947	12,626
LAGAR, Celso (1891-1966) Spanish					
oil	24	262,909	1,173	11,130	34,514
wc/d	6	20,286	1,173	3,327	5,005
LAGATTA, John (1894-1977) American					
wc/d	1	3,000		3,000	
LAGERSTEDT, Georg (1892-1982) Swedish					
oil	1	1,513		1,513	
LAGNEAU, Nicolas (16/17th C) French					
wc/d	1	4,231		4,231	
LAGO RIVERA, Antonio (1916-1990) Spanish					
oil	5	45,693	1,076	1,694	38,130
LAGOUTTE, Claude (1935-) French					
wc/d	1	1,140		1,140	
LAGRANGE, Andre (1889-?) French					
oil	1	3,858		3,858	
LAGRANGE, Jacques (1917-) French					
oil	3	3,982	1,164	1,197	1,621
LAGRENEE, Jean Jacques (1739-1821) French					
oil	4	37,148	4,000	9,374	14,400
wc/d	1	2,320		2,320	
LAGRENEE, Louis Jean François (1725-1805) French					
oil	1	6,490		6,490	
wc/d	1	1,309		1,309	
LAGROST, Marguerite (?) French					
oil	1	1,220		1,220	
LAGUARDIA, Jorge (19th C) Spanish					
oil	1	1,082		1,082	
LAGUNAS MAYANDIA, Santiago (1912-1995) Spanish					
oil	2	5,222	1,423	2,611	3,799
LAGYE, Victor (1825-1896) Belgian					
oil	2	10,315	2,315	5,158	8,000
LAHARRAGUE, Carlos (1936-) Spanish					
oil	4	6,293	1,012	1,518	2,245
wc/d	1	2,933		2,933	
LAI FONG (fl.1890-1910) Chinese					
oil	6	20,588	1,580	3,611	5,652
LAIDMAN, George (?) British?					
oil	2	5,625	2,625	2,813	3,000
LAINE, Victor (1830-?) French					
oil	1	3,000		3,000	
LAING, Annie Rose (1869-1946) British					
oil	1	5,110		5,110	
LAING, James Garden (1852-1915) British					
wc/d	3	3,573	1,110	1,264	1,264
LAING, Tomson (fl.1890-1904) British					
oil	4	4,835	1,144	1,161	1,320
LAING, William Wardlaw (fl.1873-98) British					
wc/d	1	1,332		1,332	
LAIRESSE, Jan (1674-?) Dutch					
oil	1	1,190		1,190	
LAISSEMENT, Henri Adolphe (?-1921) French					
oil	2	27,100	1,100	13,550	26,000

Name	No.	Total Sales Value	lowest	Prices median	highest
LAITINI (?) ?					
oil	1	4,089		4,089	
LAJALLET, Helene (1858-?) French					
oil	1	13,000		13,000	
LAJOUE, Jacques de (1687-1761) French					
oil	12	556,240	13,000	45,000	80,000
wc/d	1	3,820		3,820	
LAKHOVSKY, Arnold Borisovich (1880-1937) Russian					
wc/d	1	2,774		2,774	
LALAGUE (20th C) French					
oil	1	2,320		2,320	
LALANNE, François-Xavier (1924-) French					
3D	1	1,026		1,026	
wc/d	1	1,760		1,760	
LALANNE, Maxime (1827-1886) French					
oil	1	7,003		7,003	
LALIBERTE, Alfred (1878-1953) Canadian					
3D	1	2,774		2,774	
oil	1	1,648		1,648	
LALL, Oscar de (1903-1971) Canadian					
oil	2	2,063	1,023	1,032	1,040
LALLEMAND, J B (1710-1805) French					
oil	1	2,755		2,755	
LALLEMAND, Jean Baptiste (1710-1805) French					
oil	3	44,730	7,740	9,060	27,930
wc/d	3	14,376	1,492	1,884	11,000
LALLIE, Jacques Etienne (18th C) French					
wc/d	1	1,282		1,282	
LAM, Wilfredo (1902-1982) Cuban					
3D	8	35,998	1,160	2,893	10,000
oil	14	947,024	1,670	49,339	226,500
wc/d	11	218,788	5,796	8,693	90,000
LAMA, Giovanni Battista (1673-c.1748) Italian					
oil	1	5,966		5,966	
LAMA, Giovanni Bernardo (1508-1579) Italian					
oil	1	5,995		5,995	
LAMAS, Menchu (1954-) Spanish					
oil	2	3,094	1,547	1,547	1,547
LAMASURE, Edwin (jnr) (1866-1916) American					
wc/d	1	1,200		1,200	
LAMAZARES, Anton (20th C) Spanish					
oil	1	4,496		4,496	
LAMB, Charles Vincent (1893-1965) Irish					
oil	4	13,412	2,016	3,626	4,144
LAMB, F Mortimer (1861-1936) American					
oil	1	1,000		1,000	
wc/d	1	1,300		1,300	
LAMB, Henry (1883-1960) British					
oil	4	15,575	1,125	2,725	9,000
wc/d	4	13,352	1,080	2,502	7,268
LAMB, Rubin G (19/20th C) American					
oil	1	2,750		2,750	
LAMBDIN, George Cochran (1830-1896) American					
oil	1	14,000		14,000	
LAMBEAUX (19th C) Belgian					
3D	1	1,296		1,296	
LAMBEAUX, Jef (1852-1908) Belgian					
3D	15	48,270	1,016	2,592	11,775
LAMBEAUX, Jules (1858-1890) Belgian					
oil	1	9,128		9,128	

Name	No.	Total Sales Value	lowest	Prices median	highest
LAMBERECHTS, Frans (1909-1988) Belgian					
3D	1	1,066		1,066	
LAMBERT (?) ?					
oil	1	1,661		1,661	
LAMBERT, Antoine Eugène (1824-1903) French					
oil	1	1,219		1,219	
LAMBERT, B (19th C) ?					
oil	2	4,952	1,152	2,476	3,800
LAMBERT, Eugène (1825-1900) French					
oil	4	26,493	3,250	5,622	12,000
LAMBERT, Georges (1919-) French					
oil	1	2,000		2,000	
LAMBERT, James (snr) (1725-1788) British					
oil	1	1,334		1,334	
LAMBERT, Kurt (1908-) German					
oil	1	1,341		1,341	
LAMBERT, Léon (1868-?) French					
3D	1	2,400		2,400	
LAMBERT-RUCKI, Jean (1888-1967) French					
3D	7	30,030	1,382	2,978	15,014
oil	2	15,442	3,158	7,721	12,284
LAMBINET, Émile (1815-1877) French					
oil	5	13,957	1,364	2,265	5,000
LAMBRAY, L (20th C) Continental					
oil	1	1,200		1,200	
LAMBRECHTS, Jan Baptist (1680-1731) Flemish					
oil	1	8,313		8,313	
LAMBRICHS, Edmond Alfonse Charles (1830-1887) Belgian					
oil	1	2,097		2,097	
LAMEE, Leontine (?) French?					
oil	1	4,239		4,239	
LAMEN, Christoffel Jacobsz van der (c.1606-1651) Flemish					
oil	2	34,184	13,130	17,092	21,054
LAMI, Eugène Louis (1800-1890) French					
wc/d	3	41,211	1,029	8,764	31,418
LAMI, Stanislas (1858-1944) French					
3D	1	11,325		11,325	
LAMME, Arie Johannes (1812-1900) Dutch					
oil	1	2,360		2,360	
LAMMEYER, Ferdinand (1899-?) German					
oil	1	1,981		1,981	
LAMMLER, Jakob (1934-1989) Swiss?					
oil	1	1,230		1,230	
LAMOISSE, Eugene (19th C) French					
oil	1	1,356		1,356	
LAMOND, William B (1857-1924) British					
oil	3	12,824	1,400	5,292	6,132
LAMONT, Joseph (20th C) French					
oil	1	1,998		1,998	
LAMORINIERE, Francois (1828-1911) Belgian					
oil	1	4,288		4,288	
LAMORINIERE, Jean Pierre François (1828-1911) Belgian					
oil	3	10,510	1,070	3,395	6,045
LAMOTTE, Alidor (1800-?) Belgian					
oil	1	1,700		1,700	
LAMOTTE, Bernard (1903-1983) French					
oil	3	8,800	1,600	2,400	4,800
LAMOUR, C H (?) ?					
oil	1	1,704		1,704	

Name	No.	Total Sales Value	lowest	Prices median	highest
LAMOURDEIEU, Raoul (1877-1963) French					
3D	1	2,265		2,265	
LAMPI, Johann Baptist (18/19th C) Italian					
oil	1	1,869		1,869	
LAMPI, Johann Baptist (elder) (1751-1830) Italian					
oil	2	8,154	3,240	4,077	4,914
LAMPLOUGH, Augustus Osborne (1877-1930) British					
wc/d	21	41,727	1,113	1,606	4,672
LAMPRECHT, Anton (1901-1984) German					
oil	1	1,089		1,089	
LAMPREY, J (?) Irish					
oil	1	2,220		2,220	
LAMSWEERDE, Clotildis Alexandrina Maria Cornelia van (1848-1913) Dutch					
oil	1	6,155		6,155	
LAN-BAR (1912-1987) Israeli					
oil	1	1,239		1,239	
LANCASTER, Osbert (1908-1986) British					
wc/d	2	3,132	1,392	1,566	1,740
LANCASTER, Percy (1878-1951) British					
oil	1	2,002		2,002	
wc/d	1	2,100		2,100	
LANCE, George (1802-1864) British					
oil	3	20,194	2,538	2,538	15,100
LANCERAY, Eugène Alexandro (1848-1886) Russian					
3D	13	60,097	1,855	3,200	9,274
LANCHARD, A (19th C) French					
oil	1	3,273		3,273	
LANCKOW, L (19th C) German					
oil	1	3,269		3,269	
LANCRET, Nicolas (1690-1743) French					
oil	3	787,273	7,273	140,000	640,000
wc/d	4	21,711	4,200	5,256	7,000
LANDALUZE, Victor Patricio (1828-1889) Cuban/Spanish					
wc/d	1	4,500		4,500	
LANDAU, Zygmunt (1898-1962) Polish					
oil	1	1,489		1,489	
LANDEAU, Remy E (1859-1931) French					
oil	2	13,824	1,500	6,912	12,324
LANDELLE, Charles Zacharie (1812-1908) French					
oil	5	75,847	1,033	3,307	65,000
LANDENBERGER, Christian (1862-1927) German					
oil	4	20,878	2,469	5,796	6,818
LANDER, John St Helier (1869-1944) British					
oil	3	9,187	2,400	2,669	4,118
LANDERER, Albert (1816-1893) Swiss					
oil	1	2,587		2,587	
LANDERS, Sean (1962-) German					
oil	1	40,000		40,000	
LANDERSET, Ernest de (1832-1907) French					
wc/d	1	1,038		1,038	
LANDERSET, Joseph de (1753-1824) German					
wc/d	1	1,359		1,359	
LANDERT, Josef (1912-) German					
oil	1	2,019		2,019	
LANDI, Bruno (1941-) Italian					
oil	3	3,609	1,109	1,164	1,336
LANDI, Ricardo Verdugo (1871-1930) Spanish					
oil	1	2,075		2,075	

Name	No.	Total Sales Value	Prices lowest	Prices median	highest
LANDINI, Andrea (1847-?) Italian					
oil	1	42,000		42,000	
LANDINI, Jacopo (1297-1358) Italian					
oil	1	142,235		142,235	
LANDOLT, Otto (1889-1951) Swiss					
oil	1	1,094		1,094	
LANDOLT, Salomon (1741-1818) Swiss					
oil	1	1,195		1,195	
wc/d	1	4,064		4,064	
LANDOWSKI, Paul Maximilien (1875-1961) French					
3D	3	44,729	1,085	13,268	30,376
LANDSEER, Sir Edwin (1802-1873) British					
oil	6	948,080	21,750	36,465	743,600
wc/d	6	43,238	2,686	5,854	15,730
LANDT, Frants (1885-1976) Danish					
oil	2	2,550	1,259	1,275	1,291
LANDUYT, Octave (1922-) Belgian					
oil	1	1,305		1,305	
wc/d	1	3,282		3,282	
LANDY, Art (1903-) American					
wc/d	1	1,000		1,000	
LANE, Abigail (1967-) British					
3D	1	9,060		9,060	
wc/d	1	8,758		8,758	
LANE, Fitz Hugh (1804-1865) American					
oil	3	4,380,000	270,000	510,000	3,600,000
LANFANT DE METZ (1814-1892) French					
oil	1	3,003		3,003	
LANFANT DE METZ, François Louis (1814-1892) French					
oil	6	22,293	2,250	2,766	8,649
LANFRANCO, Giovanni (1582-1647) Italian					
oil	2	51,460	25,000	25,730	26,460
wc/d	1	8,305		8,305	
LANG, A (19th C) German					
oil	3	4,387	1,241	1,452	1,694
LANG, Albert (1847-1933) German					
oil	1	1,685		1,685	
LANG, Gary (20th C) American					
oil	10	20,200	1,100	1,650	4,000
LANG, Hans (1898-1971) Austrian					
oil	1	1,923		1,923	
LANG, Heinrich (1838-1891) German					
oil	1	1,963		1,963	
LANG, Leslie W (fl.1909-1937) British					
wc/d	1	1,080		1,080	
LANG, Louis (1814-1893) German					
oil	1	1,139		1,139	
LANGASKENS, Maurice (1884-1946) Belgian					
oil	4	7,357	1,019	1,916	2,507
wc/d	1	2,976		2,976	
LANGDON, B (?) British					
oil	1	1,022		1,022	
LANGE, Curt (19th C) German					
oil	1	1,228		1,228	
LANGE, Johann (18/19th C) German					
oil	1	2,262		2,262	
LANGE, Julius (1817-1878) German					
oil	2	4,921	1,966	2,461	2,955
LANGE, Karl (1884-?) German					
oil	1	1,077		1,077	

Name	No.	Total Sales Value	lowest	Prices median	highest
LANGE, Karl Ernst (1887-) German					
oil	1	2,048		2,048	
LANGENDYK, Jan Anthonie (1780-1818) Dutch					
wc/d	1	1,963		1,963	
LANGENHOEFFEL, Johann Joseph Friedrich (1750-1805) German					
oil	1	2,991		2,991	
LANGER, Otto Richard (1878-?) German					
3D	1	1,861		1,861	
LANGER, Viggo (1860-1942) Danish					
oil	8	13,128	1,008	1,506	3,000
LANGER, Wilhelm (1869-?) Austrian					
oil	1	1,219		1,219	
LANGEROCK, Henri (1830-1915) Belgian					
oil	2	12,339	4,339	6,170	8,000
LANGEVELD, Frans (1877-1939) Dutch					
oil	5	33,202	1,395	2,717	20,000
LANGEVIN, Claude (1942-) Canadian					
oil	13	22,060	1,040	1,436	2,966
LANGEWEG, Ger (1891-1970) Dutch					
oil	7	24,258	1,221	3,707	4,797
wc/d	1	1,090		1,090	
LANGHAMMER, Arthur (1854-1901) German					
oil	1	4,966		4,966	
LANGHAMMER, Carl (1868-?) German					
oil	1	1,073		1,073	
LANGKO, Dietrich (1819-1896) German					
oil	1	2,245		2,245	
LANGLANDS and BELL (20th C) British					
3D	1	16,610		16,610	
LANGLET, Alexander (1870-1953) Swedish					
oil	2	2,696	1,247	1,348	1,449
LANGLEY, Edward M (1870-1949) American					
oil	1	1,000		1,000	
LANGLEY, Walter (1852-1922) British					
oil	1	30,000		30,000	
wc/d	17	231,988	1,027	9,750	58,000
LANGLEY, William (fl.1880-1920) British					
oil	5	5,934	1,048	1,136	1,359
LANGLOIS, H W (?) ?					
oil	1	1,852		1,852	
LANGLOIS, J (19th C) British					
oil	1	4,800		4,800	
LANGLOIS, L (19th C) French					
3D	1	1,359		1,359	
LANGLOIS, Mark W (fl.1862-1873) British					
oil	5	9,710	1,305	1,883	3,300
LANGLOIS, T (?) ?					
oil	1	2,147		2,147	
LANGMAID, Rowland (1897-1956) British					
oil	1	1,200		1,200	
wc/d	1	2,114		2,114	
LANJANI, Morteza Ibn Mohamed Hossein El-Mussavi (1877-) Iranian					
oil	1	3,894		3,894	
LANNICIONI (?) ?					
oil	1	1,355		1,355	
LANOE, Alphonse (1926-) Swiss					
oil	1	1,355		1,355	
LANOUE, Felix Hippolyte (1812-1872) French					
wc/d	1	1,021		1,021	

Name	No.	Total Sales Value	Prices lowest	median	highest
LANSIL, Walter Franklin (1846-1925) American					
oil	2	6,950	2,200	3,475	4,750
LANSKOY, Andre (1902-1976) Russian/French					
oil	42	390,547	1,228	7,392	42,245
wc/d	30	79,442	1,094	2,472	5,172
LANSON, Alfred Desire (1851-1898) French					
3D	3	20,511	1,756	3,655	15,100
LANSYER, Emmanuel (1835-1893) French					
oil	2	8,577	3,793	4,289	4,784
LANTARA, Simon Mathurin (1729-1778) French					
oil	2	11,227	4,655	5,614	6,572
wc/d	2	2,933	1,400	1,467	1,533
LANTOINE, F (1876-c.1955) French					
oil	1	1,523		1,523	
LANTOINE, Fernand (1876-c.1955) French					
oil	5	48,957	1,908	3,222	24,488
LANYON, Peter (1918-1964) British					
oil	1	24,000		24,000	
wc/d	7	84,671	3,432	9,750	30,000
LANZA, Giovanni (1827-1889) Italian					
wc/d	2	5,943	1,110	2,972	4,833
LANZA, Luigi (19th C) Italian					
oil	2	10,148	4,898	5,074	5,250
LANZA, Vicenzo (1822-1902) Italian					
wc/d	2	39,420	4,380	19,710	35,040
LANZIROTI, Antonio Giovanni (1839-?) Italian					
3D	1	16,905		16,905	
LAPARRA, William (1873-1920) French					
oil	1	1,519		1,519	
LAPAYESE DEL RIO, Jose (1926-2000) Spanish					
oil	3	5,405	1,122	1,709	2,574
LAPEHINE, J (20th C) French					
oil	1	3,249		3,249	
LAPEINERE, Huissier (19th C) ?					
oil	1	2,145		2,145	
LAPERRIERE, Gaston de (1848-?) French					
oil	2	8,394	3,894	4,197	4,500
LAPICQUE, Charles (1898-1988) French					
oil	43	424,819	1,018	5,647	73,066
wc/d	16	27,186	1,003	1,576	3,009
LAPIERRE-RENOUARD, Paul Marie (1854-?) French					
oil	1	4,000		4,000	
LAPINI, Cesare (1848-?) Italian					
3D	3	16,188	2,000	5,688	8,500
LAPINO, Marco (?) ?					
oil	1	1,003		1,003	
LAPIRA (?) Italian					
wc/d	2	3,391	1,100	1,696	2,291
LAPIRA, P (?) Italian					
wc/d	1	6,019		6,019	
LAPIS, Gaetano (1706-1758) Rumanian					
oil	2	2,952	1,459	1,476	1,493
LAPITO, Louis Auguste (1803-1874) French					
oil	1	13,272		13,272	
LAPLAGNE, Guillaume (19th C) French					
3D	4	38,154	9,224	9,224	10,482
LAPORTE, E (19th C) French					
3D	3	5,249	1,401	1,567	2,281

Name	No.	Total Sales Value	lowest	Prices median	highest
LAPORTE, Emile (1858-1907) French					
3D	3	6,203	1,350	1,860	2,993
LAPORTE, Émile Henri (1841-1919) French					
3D	1	5,896		5,896	
LAPORTE, G H (1799-1873) German					
oil	1	7,514		7,514	
LAPORTE, George Henry (1799-1873) German					
oil	1	55,300		55,300	
LAPORTE, Georges (1926-2000) French					
oil	9	14,880	1,016	1,586	3,251
LAPORTE, John (1761-1839) British					
oil	1	9,724		9,724	
wc/d	2	2,845	1,365	1,423	1,480
LAPORTE-BLAIRSY, Leo (1865-1923) French					
3D	1	4,673		4,673	
LAPOSTOLET, Charles (1824-1890) French					
wc/d	1	1,018		1,018	
LAPOUJADE, Robert (1921-) French					
oil	1	1,033		1,033	
LAPRADE, Pierre (1875-1932) French					
oil	4	16,673	2,046	3,560	7,507
LAQUY, Willem Joseph (1738-1798) German					
oil	1	10,919		10,919	
wc/d	1	2,414		2,414	
LARA, Antonio (?) ?					
oil	1	2,794		2,794	
LARA, Clever (?) ?					
oil	3	3,650	1,000	1,300	1,350
LARA, Ernest (1870-?) British					
oil	1	3,289		3,289	
LARA, Georgina (fl.1862-1871) British					
oil	5	27,087	1,924	5,495	10,875
LARCHE, Raoul (1860-1912) French					
3D	11	175,926	1,005	3,625	88,200
LARCHER, Émile (19th C) French					
oil	1	3,200		3,200	
LARGE, George (1936-) British					
oil	1	1,349		1,349	
LARGILLIERE, Nicolas de (1656-1746) French					
oil	10	340,456	4,814	33,000	97,340
LARI, Pietro (19th C) Italian					
oil	1	3,669		3,669	
LARIONOV, Mikhail (1881-1964) Russian					
oil	3	58,977	4,108	7,097	47,772
wc/d	9	38,975	1,006	2,457	16,379
LARIVE-GODEFROY, Pierre Louis de (1735-1817) Swiss					
oil	3	38,079	3,988	10,938	23,153
LARMON, Kevin (1955-) American					
oil	1	2,000		2,000	
LAROCHE, Ernesto (1879-1940) Uruguayan					
oil	1	1,450		1,450	
LARPENTEUR, Balthasar Charles (18th C) French					
oil	1	1,791		1,791	
LARRAZ, Julio (1944-) Cuban					
3D	2	125,000	55,000	62,500	70,000
oil	2	170,000	60,000	85,000	110,000
wc/d	1	2,600		2,600	
LARREGIEU, Fulbert Pierre (?-1886) French					
3D	1	6,480		6,480	

Name	No.	Total Sales Value	Prices lowest	median	highest
LARROCHA GONZALEZ, Jose (1850-1933) Spanish					
oil	2	5,018	1,126	2,509	3,892
LARSEN, Adolph (1856-1942) Danish					
oil	1	1,073		1,073	
LARSEN, Alfred (1860-1946) Danish					
oil	1	1,026		1,026	
LARSEN, Carl Christian (1853-1910) Austrian					
oil	1	1,153		1,153	
LARSEN, Emanuel (1823-1859) Danish					
oil	4	20,021	1,763	2,675	12,908
LARSEN, Emanuel and NEUMANN, Carl (19th C) Danish					
oil	1	9,000		9,000	
LARSEN, Johannes (1867-1961) Danish					
oil	13	61,890	1,008	3,379	22,638
LARSEN, Jorn (1926-) Danish					
oil	1	1,056		1,056	
LARSEN, Karl (1897-1977) Danish					
oil	1	1,153		1,153	
LARSEN, Knud (1865-1922) Danish					
oil	1	1,023		1,023	
LARSEN, Oscar (1882-1972) Austrian					
oil	4	6,153	1,038	1,038	3,039
LARSSON, Carl (1853-1919) Swedish					
oil	3	260,014	3,520	84,372	172,122
wc/d	8	955,610	6,208	44,216	424,340
LARSSON, Hans (1910-1973) Swedish					
oil	1	1,328		1,328	
LARSSON, Marcus (1825-1864) Swedish					
oil	5	21,240	2,015	3,404	8,706
LARTIGUE, Dany (1921-) French					
oil	1	1,626		1,626	
LARUE, Lucien de (1925-) French					
oil	2	3,100	1,400	1,550	1,700
LARUS, Eliane (1944-) French					
oil	1	1,069		1,069	
LARUSDOTTIR, Karolina (1943) ?					
oil	1	1,510		1,510	
LARWEY, H (19th C) ?					
oil	1	3,000		3,000	
LARY, Roland (1855-1933) Dutch					
oil	2	2,659	1,291	1,330	1,368
LASALLE, Charles (1894-1958) American					
wc/d	1	2,000		2,000	
LASAR, Charles (1856-1936) American					
oil	1	6,500		6,500	
LASCAUX, Elie (1888-1969) French					
oil	1	1,018		1,018	
LASCH, Carl (1822-1888) German					
oil	1	1,216		1,216	
LASCH, Hermann (1861-?) German					
wc/d	1	1,436		1,436	
LASCHIEZE-REY, Henri (1927-1974) French					
oil	1	2,884		2,884	
LASKE, Oskar (1874-1951) Austrian					
oil	1	5,100		5,100	
wc/d	1	3,300		3,300	
LASKER, Jonathan (1948-) American					
oil	3	80,920	8,500	9,000	63,420
wc/d	1	2,064		2,064	

Name	No.	Total Sales Value	Prices lowest	median	highest
LASKY, Bessie (1890-?) American					
oil	1	1,300		1,300	
LASKY, L (19th C) French					
oil	1	1,073		1,073	
LASSALLE, Louis Simon (1810-) French					
oil	1	11,376		11,376	
LASSBROOK, L (19/20th C) ?					
oil	1	1,700		1,700	
LASSENCE, Paul de (1886-1962) Belgian					
oil	1	1,021		1,021	
LASZLO DE LOMBOS, Philip Alexius de (1869-1937) British					
oil	1	5,214		5,214	
wc/d	1	2,030		2,030	
LASZLO, de (19/20th C) ?					
oil	1	3,988		3,988	
LATAPIE, Louis (1891-1972) French					
oil	9	19,113	1,083	1,897	4,519
LATASTER, Ger (1920-) Dutch					
oil	4	13,282	1,901	2,662	6,057
wc/d	1	2,802		2,802	
LATHAM, Molly M (c.1900-1987) British					
oil	3	6,315	1,470	2,145	2,700
LATHANGUE, Henry Herbert (1859-1929) British					
oil	2	702,600	181,200	351,300	521,400
LATHROP, William Langson (1859-1938) American					
oil	1	5,250		5,250	
LATIMER, Lorenzo Palmer (1857-1941) American					
wc/d	2	5,750	2,250	2,875	3,500
LATOIX, Gaspard (fl.1882-1903) British					
oil	1	6,000		6,000	
LATORRE, Rafael (1872-) Spanish					
oil	1	3,091		3,091	
LATOUCHE, Gaston de (1854-1913) French					
oil	4	158,636	2,213	15,666	125,092
wc/d	1	35,000		35,000	
LATOUR, Maurice Quentin de (1704-1788) French					
wc/d	1	5,549		5,549	
LAUDATI, Raffaele (1864-1941) Italian					
oil	1	1,058		1,058	
LAUDER, Charles James (1841-1920) British					
oil	2	8,238	2,211	4,119	6,027
wc/d	3	8,024	1,976	3,045	3,045
LAUDY, Jean (1877-1956) Belgian					
oil	7	14,003	1,275	1,490	5,284
LAUER, Josef (1818-1881) Austrian					
oil	1	15,800		15,800	
wc/d	1	4,274		4,274	
LAUGE (1861-1944) French					
oil	1	1,342		1,342	
LAUGE, Achille (1861-1944) French					
oil	9	458,023	5,819	12,227	334,584
wc/d	1	3,565		3,565	
LAUGEE, Georges (1853-?) French					
oil	2	17,924	2,924	8,962	15,000
LAUNAY, E de (19th C) French					
oil	1	4,133		4,133	
LAUNOIS, Jean (1898-1942) French					
wc/d	3	6,703	1,515	2,594	2,594
LAUPHEIMER, Anton (1848-1927) German					
oil	2	22,211	9,029	11,106	13,182

Name	No.	Total Sales Value	Prices lowest	Prices median	highest
LAUR, Marie Yvonne (1879-1943) French					
oil	3	37,970	2,670	15,800	19,500
LAURE, Jules (1806-1861) French					
oil	1	2,320		2,320	
LAURENCE, Sydney Mortimer (1865-1940) American					
oil	15	244,592	2,592	11,000	50,000
wc/d	1	17,000		17,000	
LAURENCIN, Marie (1885-1956) French					
oil	24	1,527,824	6,092	50,000	234,050
wc/d	96	561,008	1,022	3,359	24,826
LAURENS, A (19th C) ?					
oil	1	1,354		1,354	
LAURENS, Henri (1885-1954) French					
3D	6	903,160	30,200	66,450	580,000
wc/d	7	208,748	3,770	13,911	145,000
LAURENS, Jean Pierre (1875-1932) French					
oil	1	1,283		1,283	
LAURENS, Jules Joseph Augustin (1825-1901) French					
oil	1	56,487		56,487	
wc/d	1	5,840		5,840	
LAURENT (?) ?					
3D	1	1,193		1,193	
LAURENT, Ernest Joseph (1859-1929) French					
wc/d	2	3,748	1,092	1,874	2,656
LAURENT, G H (20th C) French					
3D	1	1,290		1,290	
LAURENT, Henri Adolphe Louis (19th C) French					
oil	1	26,000		26,000	
LAURENT, Jean (20th C) French					
oil	1	1,050		1,050	
LAURENT, Jean Émile (1906-) French					
oil	1	6,490		6,490	
LAURENT-DESROUSSEAUX, Henry Alphonse Louis (1862-1906) French					
oil	1	3,630		3,630	
LAURENTI, Cesare (1854-1937) Italian					
oil	1	5,808		5,808	
LAURET, Emmanuel Joseph (1809-1882) French					
wc/d	3	6,406	1,240	1,791	3,375
LAURET, François (1820-1868) French					
oil	2	4,629	2,170	2,315	2,459
LAUREUS, Alexander (1783-1823) Finnish					
oil	1	3,622		3,622	
LAURI, Filippo (1623-1694) Italian					
oil	1	6,048		6,048	
LAURITZ, Jack (20th C) American					
oil	1	1,000		1,000	
LAURITZ, Paul (1889-1975) American					
oil	8	31,350	2,100	3,125	7,500
LAUTERBURG, Martin (1891-1960) Swiss					
oil	2	2,991	1,242	1,496	1,749
LAUTERS, Paul (1806-1876) Belgian					
wc/d	1	1,275		1,275	
LAUTTER, E R (18th C) Austrian					
oil	1	6,831		6,831	
LAUVERGNE, Barthelemy (1805-1871) French					
wc/d	1	1,914		1,914	
LAUVERNAY-PETITJEAN, Jeanne (1875-1955) French					
oil	2	2,992	1,210	1,496	1,782

Name	No.	Total Sales Value	Prices lowest	median	highest
LAUVRAY, Abel (1870-1950) French					
oil	6	14,724	1,033	2,774	3,574
LAUX, August (1847-1921) American					
oil	4	15,575	2,500	3,788	5,500
LAUZERO, Albert (1909-) French					
oil	1	14,632		14,632	
LAVAL, Fernand (1886-1966) French					
oil	1	1,186		1,186	
LAVALLEE, Geeraert de (17th C) Flemish					
oil	4	48,935	5,800	8,074	26,988
LAVALLEE-POUSSIN, Étienne de (1733-1793) French					
wc/d	1	1,971		1,971	
LAVATER, Johann Kaspar (1741-1801) Swiss					
wc/d	1	1,519		1,519	
LAVAULT, Albert Tibule Furcy de (19th C) French					
oil	1	11,000		11,000	
LAVERGNE (?) ?					
3D	2	6,299	1,589	3,150	4,710
LAVERNE, Philip Kelvin (20th C) ?					
3D	1	1,500		1,500	
LAVERY, Sir John (1856-1941) British					
oil	25	3,854,798	4,736	59,200	1,332,000
LAVES, Werner (1903-1972) German					
oil	1	4,109		4,109	
LAVIE, Raffi (1937-) Israeli					
oil	3	10,200	1,000	1,700	7,500
wc/d	1	3,400		3,400	
LAVIEILLE, Eugène (1820-1889) French					
oil	5	15,148	1,263	2,924	5,686
LAVIER, Bertrand (1949-) French					
oil	1	4,800		4,800	
LAVILLE, Joy (1923-) British					
oil	1	4,000		4,000	
LAVRILLIER, Gaston Andre (1885-1987) French					
wc/d	1	1,232		1,232	
LAVROFF (1895-?) Russian					
3D	1	1,313		1,313	
wc/d	1	1,749		1,749	
LAVROFF, G (1895-?) Russian					
3D	1	2,276		2,276	
LAVROFF, Georges (1895-?) Russian					
3D	3	9,753	1,143	2,250	6,360
LAW, Andrew (fl.1895-1940) British					
oil	1	4,266		4,266	
LAW, Bhawani Charan (1880-1946) Indian					
wc/d	1	2,600		2,600	
LAWES, Harold (fl.1890`s) British					
wc/d	2	2,388	1,193	1,194	1,195
LAWLER, Louise (1947-) American					
oil	1	15,000		15,000	
LAWLEY, Douglas (1906-1971) Canadian					
oil	3	3,676	1,175	1,175	1,306
LAWRENCE, E (19th C) British					
oil	2	3,914	1,256	1,957	2,658
LAWRENCE, G (19/20th C) British					
oil	1	1,480		1,480	
LAWRENCE, J (19/20th C) ?					
oil	1	5,500		5,500	

Name	No.	Total Sales Value	Prices lowest	Prices median	highest
LAWRENCE, Jacob (1917-2000) American					
oil	1	88,000		88,000	
wc/d	1	62,500		62,500	
LAWRENCE, John C (19th C) British					
oil	1	9,295		9,295	
LAWRENCE, Sir Thomas (1769-1830) British					
oil	6	379,020	19,750	61,935	128,700
wc/d	4	29,438	3,768	8,305	9,060
LAWRENCE, Sir Thomas (school) (1769-1830) British					
oil	1	1,600		1,600	
LAWRENSON, Edward Louis (1868-1940) British					
oil	1	1,580		1,580	
LAWSON, Cecil Gordon (1851-1882) British					
oil	1	2,556		2,556	
LAWSON, Ernest (1873-1939) American					
oil	12	553,400	2,400	25,500	260,000
LAWSON, J F (?) British?					
oil	1	1,410		1,410	
LAWSON, Sonia (1934-) British					
oil	3	4,100	1,208	1,382	1,510
wc/d	1	1,178		1,178	
LAYS, Jean Pierre (1825-1887) French					
oil	2	60,000	28,000	30,000	32,000
LAZARE-LEVY (?) ?					
oil	1	1,947		1,947	
LAZERGES, Jean Raymond Hippolyte (1817-1887) French					
oil	2	14,710	6,444	7,355	8,266
LAZERGES, Paul Jean Baptiste (1845-1902) French					
oil	4	33,669	2,333	4,713	21,910
LAZZARI, Sebastiano (18th C) Italian					
oil	1	20,000		20,000	
LAZZARINI, Gregorio (1655-1730) Italian					
oil	1	15,000		15,000	
LAZZARO, Walter (1914-1989) Italian					
oil	1	4,582		4,582	
LAZZELL, Blanche (1878-1956) American					
oil	1	19,000		19,000	
LDOKOV, Boris Petrovich (1929-) Russian					
oil	1	2,205		2,205	
LE PHO (1907-) Vietnamese/French					
oil	15	100,938	1,100	7,000	12,000
LEADER, Benjamin Williams (1831-1923) British					
oil	25	605,377	1,800	6,500	180,000
LEADER, Charles (19th C?) British?					
oil	1	1,185		1,185	
LEADER, Stanley (?) British					
oil	1	1,817		1,817	
LEANDRE, Charles (1862-1930) French					
wc/d	4	13,615	1,532	2,985	6,113
LEAR, Edward (1812-1888) British					
oil	2	81,690	24,310	40,845	57,380
wc/d	29	194,655	1,392	5,652	33,180
LEAR, John (20th C) American					
oil	1	1,400		1,400	
wc/d	1	1,600		1,600	
LEATHAM, William J (fl.1840-1855) British					
oil	1	3,823		3,823	
LEAVER, C (19th C) British					
oil	1	3,912		3,912	

Name	No.	Total Sales Value	lowest	Prices median	highest
LEAVER, Charles (19th C) British					
oil	3	13,662	2,523	5,293	5,846
LEAVER, Noel Harry (1889-1951) British					
wc/d	16	41,282	1,021	2,263	7,584
LEAVERS, Lucy A (fl.1887-1898) British					
oil	1	3,200		3,200	
LEAVITT, Edward C (1842-1904) American					
oil	6	22,550	1,600	3,225	7,250
LEBARON-DESVES, Augusta (1804-?) French					
wc/d	1	1,471		1,471	
LEBASQUE, H (1865-1937) French					
oil	1	8,270		8,270	
LEBASQUE, Henri (1865-1937) French					
oil	46	2,092,951	1,959	35,680	188,049
wc/d	20	94,981	1,451	3,800	13,575
LEBDUSKA, Lawrence (1894-1966) American					
oil	3	5,000	1,000	1,000	3,000
LEBEDEV, Vladimir V (1891-1967) Russian					
oil	1	1,486		1,486	
wc/d	1	1,486		1,486	
LEBEDJEV, Klawdij (1852-1916) Russian					
oil	1	4,200		4,200	
LEBEL, Edmond (1834-1909) French					
oil	1	2,272		2,272	
LEBEL, Jean Jacques (1936-) French					
oil	1	5,267		5,267	
wc/d	1	5,633		5,633	
LEBENSTEIN, Jan (1930-) Polish/French					
wc/d	1	1,107		1,107	
LEBLANC, Lee (1913-1983) American					
oil	1	7,000		7,000	
LEBLANC, Walter (1932-1986) Belgian					
oil	3	11,123	1,327	4,926	4,926
wc/d	1	4,721		4,721	
LEBOURG, Albert (1849-1928) French					
oil	39	759,106	1,807	18,000	51,100
wc/d	12	20,177	1,038	1,257	4,368
LEBOURGEOIS, Gaston Étienne (1880-1956) French					
3D	1	6,128		6,128	
LEBRATO, Aurelio (1944-) Uruguayan					
3D	1	1,200		1,200	
LEBRET, Frans (1820-1909) Dutch					
oil	1	6,978		6,978	
LEBRUN (?) ?					
oil	1	4,500		4,500	
LEBRUN, A (?) ?					
oil	1	2,030		2,030	
LEBRUN, Charles (1619-1690) French					
oil	1	3,993		3,993	
wc/d	3	69,300	1,300	18,000	50,000
LEBRUN, Christopher (1951-) British					
oil	1	14,000		14,000	
LEBRUN, Henriette Perrard (19th C) French					
oil	1	3,500		3,500	
LEBRUN, L J (19/20th C) French?					
oil	1	1,452		1,452	
LEBRUN, Marcel (19/20th C) French?					
oil	1	16,000		16,000	
LEBRUN, Rico (1900-1964) American/Italian					
wc/d	1	7,000		7,000	

Name	No.	Total Sales Value	lowest	Prices median	highest
LEBRUN, Theodore (19th C) French					
oil	1	24,000		24,000	
LEBSCHE, Karl-August (1800-1877) Polish					
oil	1	3,000		3,000	
LECHERTIER (?) ?					
3D	1	6,520		6,520	
LECHESNE, Auguste (19th C) French					
3D	1	4,089		4,089	
LECHESNE, Auguste Jean Baptiste (c.1815-1888) French					
3D	1	3,975		3,975	
LECKE, Ferdinand (19/20th C) German					
oil	1	3,275		3,275	
LECLERC DES GOBELINS, Sebastian (1734-1785) French					
oil	1	10,205		10,205	
LECLERC, Sebastien (elder) (1637-1714) French					
wc/d	3	14,651	3,624	5,027	6,000
LECOINTE, Charles Joseph (1824-1886) French					
wc/d	1	1,018		1,018	
LECOMTE DU NOUY, Jean Jules Antoine (1842-1923) French					
oil	4	87,199	2,707	14,746	55,000
LECOMTE, Alice (19/20th C) French					
oil	1	1,018		1,018	
LECOMTE, Émile (1866-1938) Belgian					
oil	1	1,542		1,542	
LECOMTE, Hippolyte (1781-1857) French					
oil	2	16,586	7,824	8,293	8,762
LECOMTE, Paul (1842-1920) French					
oil	3	4,962	1,050	1,700	2,212
wc/d	1	2,610		2,610	
LECOMTE, Paul Émile (1877-1950) French					
oil	7	32,429	1,456	2,918	13,623
wc/d	2	3,979	1,659	1,990	2,320
LECOSSOIS, Victor (1897-1976) Belgian					
oil	1	1,651		1,651	
LECOUFLET, Jean Claude (1944-) French					
3D	1	1,259		1,259	
LECOURTIER, Prosper (1855-1924) French					
3D	5	17,953	1,313	2,880	7,009
LECUONA, Antonio Maria de (1831-1907) Spanish					
oil	1	16,381		16,381	
LEDERER, Richard (1848-1923) Hungarian					
oil	1	1,226		1,226	
LEDOUX, Jeanne Philiberte (1767-1840) French					
oil	1	9,580		9,580	
LEDRAY, Charles (1960-) American					
3D	1	14,000		14,000	
LEDRU (?) French					
3D	1	3,761		3,761	
LEDRU, Auguste (1860-1902) French					
3D	1	2,000		2,000	
LEDUC, A (?) French					
oil	1	1,789		1,789	
LEDUC, Arthur Jacques (1848-1918) French					
3D	2	6,918	3,105	3,459	3,813
LEDUC, Fernand (1916-) Canadian					
wc/d	1	1,055		1,055	
LEDUC, Ozias (1864-1955) Canadian					
oil	6	70,045	1,490	4,026	53,139

Name	No.	Total Sales Value	lowest	Prices median	highest
LEDUC, Paul (1876-1943) Belgian					
oil	14	133,178	3,140	5,944	25,685
LEE, Anthony (?-1769) British					
oil	1	20,720		20,720	
LEE, Bertha Stringer (1873-1937) American					
oil	2	7,500	2,000	3,750	5,500
LEE, Doris (1905-1983) American					
oil	1	3,100		3,100	
LEE, F R (1798-1879) British					
oil	1	1,125		1,125	
LEE, Frederick Richard (1798-1879) British					
oil	2	5,853	1,420	2,927	4,433
LEE-HANKEY, William (1869-1952) British					
oil	10	62,112	1,435	6,357	12,000
wc/d	5	14,882	1,435	2,414	5,434
LEE-SMITH, Hughie (1915-1999) American					
oil	2	24,250	2,250	12,125	22,000
LEEB-LUNDBERG, Gustav Leo Valdemar (1880-1927) Swedish					
oil	1	1,054		1,054	
LEECH, John (1817-1864) British					
oil	1	3,476		3,476	
LEECH, William John (1881-1968) Irish					
oil	1	133,200		133,200	
LEEFLANG, Arie (1906-1956) Dutch					
oil	1	1,021		1,021	
LEEKE, Ferdinand (1859-1923) German					
oil	5	12,028	1,472	2,600	3,575
LEEMANS, Johannes (1633-1688) Dutch					
oil	1	8,570		8,570	
LEEMANS, T (18th C) British					
oil	2	11,583	5,148	5,792	6,435
LEEMANS, Thomas (18th C) British					
oil	1	6,080		6,080	
LEEMPOELS, Jef (1867-?) Belgian					
oil	4	5,889	1,109	1,441	1,898
LEEMPUTTEN, Cornelis van (1841-1902) Belgian					
oil	8	39,827	1,215	3,259	13,000
LEEMPUTTEN, Cornelis van and KOEKKOEK, Hendrik Pieter (19th C) Belgian/Dutch					
oil	1	16,000		16,000	
LEEMPUTTEN, Frans van (1850-1914) Belgian					
oil	6	19,626	1,079	3,325	5,739
LEEMPUTTEN, Jef Louis van (1865-1948) Belgian					
oil	6	23,165	1,001	1,671	11,091
LEEN, Willem van (1753-1825) Dutch					
oil	1	16,610		16,610	
LEENE, Jules van de (1887-1962) Belgian					
oil	2	3,015	1,338	1,508	1,677
wc/d	1	1,903		1,903	
LEEPIN, Robert (1884-1967) ?					
oil	1	1,906		1,906	
LEES, Derwent (1885-1931) British					
oil	1	12,750		12,750	
LEEUW, Adrian de (19th C) Belgian					
oil	1	5,356		5,356	
LEEUW, Alexis de (fl.1848-1883) Belgian					
oil	9	23,703	1,109	2,400	4,528
LEEUW, Bert de (1926-) Belgian					
oil	1	1,898		1,898	

Name	No.	Total Sales Value	lowest	Prices median	highest
LEEUWEN, H van (19/20th C) Dutch					
oil	1	8,000		8,000	
LEEUWEN, Henk van (1890-1972) Dutch					
oil	3	4,269	1,150	1,231	1,888
LEEWENS, Will (1923-) Dutch					
oil	4	8,265	1,584	2,048	2,586
LEFEBRE, Wilhelm (1873-1974) German					
oil	1	1,290		1,290	
LEFEBVRE, Georges (19th C) French					
oil	1	6,000		6,000	
LEFEBVRE, Jules Joseph (1836-1911) French					
wc/d	1	3,500		3,500	
LEFEBVRE, Madeleine (19/20th C) ?					
oil	1	1,593		1,593	
LEFEBVRE, Maurice Jean (1873-1954) Belgian					
oil	1	3,407		3,407	
LEFEBVRE, Valentin (c.1642-1680) Flemish					
oil	1	16,379		16,379	
LEFEVRE, Robert Jacques François (1755-1830) French					
oil	1	17,000		17,000	
LEFF, Rita (1907-) American					
wc/d	1	1,200		1,200	
LEFFLER, Robert (1811-1853) Swedish					
oil	1	1,445		1,445	
LEFORT, Alexandre (1854-?) French					
oil	1	2,400		2,400	
LEFORT, Jean (1875-1954) French					
oil	1	1,400		1,400	
LEFRANC, Roland (20th C) French					
oil	1	1,113		1,113	
LEGA, Silvestro (1826-1895) Italian					
oil	1	16,793		16,793	
LEGAGNEUR, Jean Claude (?) Haitian					
oil	1	1,463		1,463	
LEGAT, Léon (1829-?) French					
oil	1	18,000		18,000	
LEGENDRE, M (20th C) French?					
oil	1	1,378		1,378	
LEGER, Fernand (1881-1955) French					
3D	6	277,000	22,000	40,000	75,000
oil	17	9,936,253	14,195	304,500	2,300,000
wc/d	44	1,873,082	2,000	21,636	249,150
LEGGETT, Alexander (1848-1884) British					
oil	1	2,698		2,698	
LEGILLON, Jean François (1739-1797) Flemish					
oil	1	3,020		3,020	
LEGNANI, Stefano Maria (1660-1715) Italian					
oil	1	11,195		11,195	
LEGNER, Johan C W (1859-1932) Dutch					
oil	1	1,377		1,377	
LEGORA, Giovanni Cappa (1887-1970) Italian					
oil	3	4,475	1,318	1,318	1,839
LEGOUT-GERARD (1856-1924) French					
oil	1	11,407		11,407	
LEGOUT-GERARD, Fernand (1856-1924) French					
oil	15	109,170	1,500	7,578	13,895
LEGRAIN, Pierre (1888-1929) French					
wc/d	1	6,128		6,128	

Name	No.	Total Sales Value	lowest	Prices median	highest
LEGRAND, J (17/18th C) French					
oil	1	2,100		2,100	
LEGRAND, Jenny (19th C) French					
oil	1	1,571		1,571	
LEGRAND, Louis Auguste Mathieu (1863-1951) French					
oil	1	7,788		7,788	
wc/d	4	14,594	1,211	4,117	5,150
LEGRAND, Marcelo (1961-) Uruguayan					
wc/d	1	1,000		1,000	
LEGROS, Alphonse (1837-1911) French					
wc/d	1	1,963		1,963	
LEGUEULT, Raymond (1898-1971) French					
oil	3	28,599	8,116	10,329	10,329
wc/d	2	4,135	1,996	2,068	2,139
LEGULUARD, Leon (19th C) ?					
oil	1	7,668		7,668	
LEHMAN, Irving (20th C) American					
oil	1	1,500		1,500	
LEHMANN, Olga (fl.1932-1933) British					
oil	1	2,130		2,130	
LEHMANN, Rudolf (1819-1905) German					
oil	1	45,268		45,268	
LEHMANN, Wilhelm Ludwig (1861-1932) Swiss					
oil	1	1,823		1,823	
LEHMANN-LEONHARD, W (1877-1954) German					
oil	1	1,606		1,606	
LEHMBRUCK, Wilhelm (1881-1919) German					
3D	5	363,290	19,417	57,554	129,600
LEHNEN, Jacob (1803-1847) German					
oil	1	17,665		17,665	
LEHNERT, Hildegard (1857-?) German					
oil	1	2,796		2,796	
LEHR, Adam (1853-1924) American					
oil	1	1,300		1,300	
LEIBER, Otto Ferdinand (1878-1958) German					
oil	1	1,077		1,077	
LEIBL, Wilhelm (1844-1900) German					
oil	1	12,461		12,461	
LEICKERT, C (1818-1907) Belgian					
oil	1	1,508		1,508	
LEICKERT, Charles (1818-1907) Belgian					
oil	23	437,485	1,603	17,444	48,000
wc/d	1	3,922		3,922	
LEIDEN SCHOOL, 18th C Dutch					
wc/d	1	2,692		2,692	
LEIDERSTAM, Matts (1956-) Swedish					
oil	1	1,497		1,497	
LEIDL, Anton (20th C) German					
oil	1	2,414		2,414	
LEIGH, William R (1866-1955) American					
oil	10	917,000	11,000	60,000	220,000
LEIGHTON, Alfred Crocker (1901-1965) British					
oil	1	1,306		1,306	
wc/d	1	2,467		2,467	
LEIGHTON, Edmund Blair (1853-1922) British					
oil	5	1,506,600	8,060	175,890	966,400
LEIGHTON, F (19/20th C) ?					
wc/d	1	2,703		2,703	

Name	No.	Total Sales Value	lowest	Prices median	highest
LEIGHTON, Kathryn Woodman (1876-1952) American					
oil	2	3,950	1,200	1,975	2,750
LEIGHTON, Lord Frederic (1830-1896) British					
3D	1	7,550		7,550	
oil	4	1,967,577	4,750	75,414	1,812,000
wc/d	2	7,011	2,811	3,506	4,200
LEIGHTON, Scott (1847-1898) American					
oil	6	7,300	1,000	1,100	1,900
LEINBERGER, Hans (16th C) German					
3D	1	3,591		3,591	
LEINWEBER, Heinrich (1836-1908) German					
oil	1	19,095		19,095	
LEIRNER, Jac (1961-) Brazilian					
3D	1	18,000		18,000	
LEIRNER, Nelson (1932-) Brazilian					
wc/d	1	16,000		16,000	
LEIRO, Francisco (1957-) Spanish					
3D	1	19,875		19,875	
LEISTIKOW, Walter (1865-1908) Russian					
oil	5	55,825	2,300	5,611	33,099
wc/d	1	1,877		1,877	
LEISZ, M B (?) ?					
oil	1	1,200		1,200	
LEITCH, Richard Principal (?-1882) British					
wc/d	1	1,304		1,304	
LEITCH, William Leighton (1804-1883) British					
oil	1	1,740		1,740	
wc/d	9	24,130	1,144	1,430	10,296
LEITH-ROSS, Harry (1886-1973) American					
oil	1	2,600		2,600	
wc/d	1	1,100		1,100	
LEITHAUSER, Alfred (1898-1979) German					
oil	1	2,184		2,184	
LEITHNER VON SCHWATZ, Johann Josef (18th C) German					
3D	1	10,872		10,872	
LEITNER, Heinrich (1842-1913) Austrian					
oil	1	1,655		1,655	
LEITNER, Robert (1888-?) Austrian					
oil	1	2,718		2,718	
LEIVA, Nicolas (1958-) Argentinian					
oil	3	46,000	7,000	13,000	26,000
LEJEUNE, A A (18/19th C) French					
wc/d	1	22,000		22,000	
LEJEUNE, N (?) ?					
oil	1	1,022		1,022	
LEK, Hans van der (1936-) Dutch					
oil	1	1,093		1,093	
LELEE, Leopold (1872-1947) French					
wc/d	1	2,815		2,815	
LELLI, Giovan Battista (1828-1887) Italian					
oil	1	3,344		3,344	
LELLOUCHE, Jules (1903-1963) French					
oil	1	1,173		1,173	
LELLOUCHE, Ofer (1947-) Israeli					
oil	1	12,000		12,000	
LELOIR, Alexandre Louis (1843-1884) French					
wc/d	2	14,940	1,800	7,470	13,140
LELOIR, Maurice (1853-1940) French					
wc/d	4	7,243	1,259	1,695	2,557

Name	No.	Total Sales Value	lowest	Prices median	highest
LELONG (17/19th C) French					
oil	1	9,482		9,482	
wc/d	5	33,344	2,960	4,144	11,325
LELONG, Paul (19th C) French					
wc/d	2	8,220	3,419	4,110	4,801
LELU, Pierre (1741-1810) French					
wc/d	2	4,479	1,501	2,240	2,978
LELY, Sir Peter (1618-1680) British					
oil	9	198,430	3,486	15,730	72,480
LELY, Sir Peter (school) (1618-1680) British					
oil	3	10,075	3,000	3,160	3,915
LEMAIRE (?) French					
oil	1	1,099		1,099	
LEMAIRE, Casimir (19/20th C) French					
oil	1	2,698		2,698	
LEMAIRE, Jean (1598-1659) French					
oil	2	125,869	19,109	62,935	106,760
wc/d	1	1,029		1,029	
LEMAIRE, Madeleine (1845-1928) French					
oil	1	20,000		20,000	
wc/d	4	8,051	1,430	1,799	3,000
LEMAIRE, R (19/20th C) ?					
wc/d	1	2,800		2,800	
LEMAIRE, V (19th C) ?					
oil	1	1,058		1,058	
LEMAITRE, Albert (1886-1975) Belgian					
oil	2	2,226	1,006	1,113	1,220
LEMAITRE, Andre (1909-) French					
oil	1	1,244		1,244	
LEMAITRE, Andre and Ivanna (20th C) French					
wc/d	1	1,354		1,354	
LEMAITRE, Gustave (19th C) French					
oil	1	1,971		1,971	
LEMAITRE, Léon (1850-1905) French					
oil	1	1,691		1,691	
LEMAITRE, Maurice (1926-) French					
oil	6	10,000	1,297	1,577	2,112
LEMAITRE, Maurice (1929-) French					
oil	3	6,074	1,218	2,278	2,578
LEMAITRE, Nathanael (1831-1897) French					
oil	1	1,179		1,179	
LEMAN, Ulrich (19/20th C) German					
wc/d	1	2,100		2,100	
LEMANN, Ulrich (fl.1960s) ?					
wc/d	1	1,275		1,275	
LEMARCHAND, David (1674-1726) French					
3D	2	18,877	7,852	9,439	11,025
LEMARQUIER, Charles Paul Alfred (19th C) French					
3D	1	1,409		1,409	
LEMAY, Robert (20th C) Canadian					
oil	1	2,000		2,000	
LEMBERGER, Georg (c.1490-c.1540) German					
oil	1	57,380		57,380	
LEMENS, Balthasar van (1637-1704) Flemish					
oil	1	3,182		3,182	
LEMEUNIER, Basile (1852-?) French					
oil	1	1,600		1,600	
LEMIEUX, Annette (1957-) American					
oil	1	2,400		2,400	

Name	No.	Total Sales Value	Prices lowest	median	highest
LEMIEUX, Jean Paul (1904-1990) Canadian					
oil	5	222,114	3,650	8,628	159,910
LEMIRE, Charles Gabriel (1741-1827) French					
3D	1	2,587		2,587	
LEMIRE, Sophie (1785-?) French					
oil	1	16,000		16,000	
LEMMEN, Georges (1865-1916) Belgian					
oil	6	42,132	1,557	6,390	13,663
wc/d	4	8,787	1,078	2,389	2,932
LEMMENS, E (19th C) French					
oil	1	1,320		1,320	
LEMMENS, Theophile Victor Émile (1821-1867) French					
oil	3	8,820	1,709	2,883	4,228
LEMMERS, Georges (1871-1944) Belgian					
oil	4	11,311	1,885	2,331	4,765
LEMOINE, Marie Victoire (1754-1820) French					
oil	1	12,000		12,000	
LEMON, Arthur (1850-1912) British					
oil	1	4,108		4,108	
LEMOS, Luis (20th C) French?					
oil	1	1,298		1,298	
LEMOYNE, François (1688-1737) French					
3D	1	1,115		1,115	
oil	1	8,123		8,123	
LEMOYNE, Jean Baptiste (elder) (c.1681-1731) French					
3D	1	53,231		53,231	
LEMOYNE, Jean Baptiste (younger) (1704-1778) French					
3D	1	21,662		21,662	
LEMPEREUR, Edmond (1876-1909) French					
oil	1	1,142		1,142	
LEMPICKA, Tamara de (1898-1980) Polish					
oil	5	180,298	8,000	27,298	80,000
LENAERTS, Leon (19th C) Belgian					
oil	1	1,605		1,605	
LENAIL, Marie Joseph Ernest (19th C) French					
oil	1	1,083		1,083	
LENAIN BROTHERS (17th C) French					
oil	1	4,116		4,116	
LENAIN, Mathieu (1607-1677) French					
oil	1	110,000		110,000	
LENARDI, Giovan Battista (1656-1704) Italian					
oil	1	22,650		22,650	
LENBACH, Franz von (1836-1904) German					
oil	11	63,476	1,082	5,623	15,131
wc/d	3	4,484	1,413	1,427	1,644
LENCK, Albert (1857-1915) German?					
oil	1	3,218		3,218	
LENEPVEU, Jules Eugène (1819-1898) French					
oil	1	1,250		1,250	
LENGO Y MARTINEZ, Horacio (1840-1890) Spanish					
oil	1	1,859		1,859	
LENK, Franz (1898-1968) German					
oil	6	81,503	6,147	12,505	27,774
wc/d	5	15,384	1,089	2,045	7,776
LENK, Kaspar Thomas (1933-) German					
3D	1	1,211		1,211	
LENK, Thomas (1933-) German					
3D	1	1,207		1,207	

Name	No.	Total Sales Value	Prices lowest	Prices median	highest
LENKIEWICZ, R O (1941-) British/Jewish					
oil	9	66,015	1,450	5,655	17,520
LENKIEWICZ, Robert O (1941-) British/Jewish					
oil	12	25,055	1,003	1,881	3,021
LENOIR, Charles Amable (1861-?) French					
oil	1	10,000		10,000	
LENOIR, E (19th C) French					
oil	1	2,112		2,112	
LENOIR, Felix G (?) ?					
oil	1	1,600		1,600	
LENOIR, M (?) French					
oil	1	1,103		1,103	
LENOIR, Maurice (20th C) French					
oil	2	6,313	1,641	3,157	4,672
LENOIR, Paul Marie (?-1881) French					
oil	1	1,700		1,700	
LENOIR, Pierre (1879-?) French					
3D	1	10,154		10,154	
LENORDEZ, Pierre (19th C) French					
3D	5	19,514	2,840	3,456	5,530
LENS, Andries (1739-1822) Flemish					
oil	1	1,007		1,007	
LENS, Hendrik (19/20th C) Belgian					
oil	1	2,600		2,600	
LENTREIN, Jules (20th C) Belgian?					
oil	2	4,205	1,196	2,103	3,009
LENZ, Alfred David (1872-1926) American					
3D	1	2,250		2,250	
LENZ, Maximilien (1860-1948) Austrian					
oil	1	2,437		2,437	
LEON Y ESCOSURA, Ignacio de (1834-1901) Spanish					
oil	1	1,298		1,298	
LEON, Achille (19th C) Continental					
oil	1	1,450		1,450	
LEON, Carlos (1948-) Spanish					
oil	1	1,967		1,967	
LEON, Ernesto (1956-) Venezuelan					
wc/d	1	1,245		1,245	
LEON, M (1838-1865) Dutch					
oil	1	1,136		1,136	
LEONARD, A (19th C) French					
3D	2	12,416	2,416	6,208	10,000
LEONARD, Agathan (1841-?) French					
3D	4	107,466	1,300	18,278	69,610
LEONARD, E (19/20th C) French					
oil	1	3,300		3,300	
LEONARD, George H (1869-) American					
oil	1	2,000		2,000	
LEONARD, George M (c.1826-?) American					
oil	1	2,800		2,800	
LEONARD, Jacques (?) Belgian					
oil	1	1,048		1,048	
LEONARD, Patrick (1918-) British					
oil	3	20,610	2,850	8,880	8,880
LEONARDI, A (19th C) Italian					
oil	1	2,281		2,281	
LEONARDO DA PISA, Ranieri di (16th C) Italian					
oil	1	100,000		100,000	

Name	No.	Total Sales Value	lowest	Prices median	highest
LEONARDO DA VINCI (school) (1452-1519) Italian					
wc/d	1	4,197		4,197	
LEONE, Colle (19th C) Italian					
oil	1	3,256		3,256	
LEONE, John (20th C) American					
oil	1	2,300		2,300	
LEONE, Romolo (19th C) French					
oil	2	4,363	1,153	2,182	3,210
LEONEL (19th C) ?					
oil	1	3,265		3,265	
LEONHARD, Johannes (1858-1913) German					
wc/d	1	3,317		3,317	
LEONI, Ottavio (1587-1630) Italian					
oil	1	3,020		3,020	
wc/d	2	10,334	4,874	5,167	5,460
LEOPOLD, Warren F (20th C) American					
oil	1	2,100		2,100	
LEOTARD, Alice (20th C) Belgian					
oil	1	1,273		1,273	
LEPAGE, Celine (1882-1928) French					
3D	2	42,145	2,676	21,073	39,469
LEPAGE, P M (20th C) French					
oil	1	1,446		1,446	
LEPAPE, George (1887-1971) French					
oil	1	1,337		1,337	
LEPCKE, Ferdinand (1866-1909) German					
3D	2	3,804	1,108	1,902	2,696
LEPERE, Auguste (1849-1918) French					
oil	1	5,819		5,819	
wc/d	1	1,139		1,139	
LEPETIT (19th C) French					
oil	1	1,797		1,797	
LEPICIE, Michel Nicolas Bernard (1735-1784) French					
wc/d	4	18,862	1,029	4,728	8,378
LEPIE, Ferdinand (1824-1883) Czechoslovakian					
oil	1	1,227		1,227	
LEPINARD, Paul (20th C) Swiss					
oil	2	4,313	1,864	2,157	2,449
LEPINE, Joseph Louis Francois (1867-1943) French					
oil	2	2,946	1,296	1,473	1,650
LEPINE, Stanislas (1835-1892) French					
oil	7	133,552	2,525	10,774	55,870
L'EPLATTENIER, Charles (1874-1946) Swiss					
oil	3	26,255	2,146	5,247	18,862
wc/d	1	1,399		1,399	
LEPOITTEVIN, Eugène (1806-1870) French					
oil	3	17,576	2,031	3,943	11,602
LEPOITTEVIN, Louis (1847-1909) French					
oil	1	3,768		3,768	
LEPPIEN, Jean (1910-1991) German					
oil	4	10,735	1,350	1,655	6,076
wc/d	3	3,462	1,019	1,157	1,286
LEPRI, Stanislao (1905-1980) Italian					
oil	1	1,317		1,317	
wc/d	1	1,300		1,300	
LEPRIN, Marcel (1891-1933) French					
oil	11	64,742	1,463	6,416	8,462
LEPRINCE, Auguste Xavier (1799-1826) French					
oil	4	42,901	4,752	7,075	24,000

Name	No.	Total Sales Value	lowest	Prices median	highest
LEPRINCE, J B (1734-1781) French					
oil	1	34,443		34,443	
LEPRINCE, Jean Baptiste (1734-1781) French					
oil	1	4,990		4,990	
wc/d	3	6,941	1,200	1,241	4,500
LEPRINCE, Jean Baptiste (school) (1734-1781) French					
oil	1	2,100		2,100	
LEPRINCE, Robert Leopold (1800-1847) French					
oil	1	1,154		1,154	
LEPSIUS, Sabine (1864-?) German					
oil	2	2,583	1,164	1,292	1,419
LERFELDT, Hans Henrik (1946-1990) Danish					
oil	2	2,643	1,159	1,322	1,484
wc/d	3	4,078	1,129	1,380	1,569
LERGAARD, Niels (1893-1982) Danish					
oil	5	19,634	1,051	3,400	6,574
LERICHE (18/19th C) ?					
oil	2	29,518	4,716	14,759	24,802
LERMITE, Jean Pierre (1920-1977) French					
wc/d	1	6,776		6,776	
LEROUX, Auguste (1871-1954) French					
oil	1	2,707		2,707	
LEROUX, Gaston (1854-1942) French					
3D	3	19,711	1,211	8,500	10,000
LEROUX, Georges (1877-1957) French					
oil	1	5,836		5,836	
LEROY DE LIANCOURT, François (1741-1835) French					
wc/d	2	5,484	2,400	2,742	3,084
LEROY, Étienne (1828-?) French					
oil	1	1,489		1,489	
LEROY, Eugène (1910-) French					
oil	4	30,416	4,064	8,542	9,268
LEROY, Joseph Francois (1768-1829) French					
wc/d	1	2,182		2,182	
LEROY, Jules (?-c.1920) French					
oil	11	33,922	1,254	2,757	6,320
LEROY, Patrick (1948-) French					
oil	2	2,214	1,084	1,107	1,130
LEROY, Paul Alexandre Alfred (1860-1942) French					
oil	1	1,800		1,800	
LEROY, Sylvie (20th C) French					
oil	2	9,418	4,231	4,709	5,187
LESAGE, Augustin (1876-1954) French					
oil	2	41,315	8,728	20,658	32,587
LESELLIER (20th C) ?					
oil	1	2,156		2,156	
LESIEUR (20th C) French					
oil	1	1,923		1,923	
LESIEUR, Pierre (1922-) French					
oil	10	17,148	1,019	1,519	3,116
LESKER, Hans (1879-1914) German					
oil	1	2,277		2,277	
LESKOY, J (19th C) ?					
oil	1	5,292		5,292	
LESLIE, Charles (19th C) British					
oil	12	29,001	1,005	1,761	8,532
LESLIE, Charles Robert (1794-1859) British					
oil	1	7,150		7,150	

Name	No.	Total Sales Value	Prices lowest	median	highest
LESLIE, G (19th C) American					
oil	1	2,250		2,250	
LESLIE, George Dunlop (1835-1921) British					
oil	1	44,330		44,330	
LESLIE, John (1822-1916) British					
oil	1	1,027		1,027	
LESOURD-BEAUREGARD, Ange Louis Guillaume (1800-1885) French					
oil	3	55,453	7,000	10,953	37,500
LESPINASSE, Charles (19/20th C) French					
oil	1	1,283		1,283	
LESPINASSE, Louis Nicolas de (1734-1808) French					
wc/d	2	54,489	13,290	27,245	41,199
LESREL, Adolphe Alexandre (1839-1929) French					
oil	7	312,436	7,008	12,000	220,000
LESSARD, Real (20th C) ?					
oil	1	13,915		13,915	
LESSEPS, Jules de (19th C) French?					
wc/d	1	3,245		3,245	
LESSI, Tito (1858-1917) Italian					
oil	2	19,086	4,000	9,543	15,086
LESSIEUX, Ernest Louis (1848-1925) French					
wc/d	2	3,768	1,727	1,884	2,041
LESSIEUX, Louis Ernest (1874-1925) French					
wc/d	1	1,586		1,586	
LESSING, Karl Friedrich (1808-1880) German					
oil	4	25,548	2,561	6,011	10,965
wc/d	1	1,759		1,759	
LESSING, Konrad Ludwig (1852-1916) German					
oil	2	2,553	1,090	1,277	1,463
LESSORE, Therese (1884-1945) French					
oil	2	4,591	1,431	2,296	3,160
LESTER, Leonard (1876-?) American/British					
oil	1	4,000		4,000	
LESTER, William Lewis (1910-1991) American					
oil	1	1,900		1,900	
LESUEUR, Pierre Étienne (18th C) French					
oil	1	33,847		33,847	
LESUR, Henri Victor (1863-1900) French					
oil	1	3,791		3,791	
LETELLIER (?) French					
oil	1	24,000		24,000	
LETENDRE, Rita (1928-) Canadian					
oil	2	3,084	1,057	1,542	2,027
LETH, Harald (1899-1986) Danish					
oil	1	1,025		1,025	
LETIN, Jacques Ninet de (1597-1661) French					
oil	1	12,000		12,000	
LETO, Antonino (1844-1913) Italian					
oil	3	25,408	3,577	3,956	17,875
LETSCH, Louis (1856-?) German					
oil	1	1,001		1,001	
LETTL, Wolfgang (1919-) German					
oil	1	1,550		1,550	
LETURCQ, Arnaud (1961-) French					
oil	2	22,325	5,192	11,163	17,133
LEU, August (1852-1876) German					
oil	1	8,218		8,218	
LEU, August Wilhelm (1819-1897) German					
oil	3	17,990	1,708	3,552	12,730

Name	No.	Total Sales Value	lowest	Prices median	highest
LEU, Oscar (1864-1942) German					
oil	1	1,000		1,000	
LEU, Otto (1855-1922) German					
oil	1	4,661		4,661	
LEUB, Fr de (19/20th C) ?					
oil	1	3,040		3,040	
LEUERS, Jeanette (20th C) ?					
oil	1	1,800		1,800	
LEUPPI, Leo Peter (1893-1972) Swiss					
oil	3	21,841	2,390	7,073	12,378
wc/d	1	1,115		1,115	
LEURS, J (?) ?					
oil	1	1,025		1,025	
LEURS, J K (19th C) Dutch					
oil	1	1,483		1,483	
LEURS, Johannes Karel (1865-1938) Dutch					
oil	3	3,813	1,154	1,179	1,480
LEUSDEN, Willem van (1886-?) Dutch					
oil	1	1,724		1,724	
wc/d	1	4,357		4,357	
LEUTERITZ, Franz Wilhelm (1817-1902) German					
oil	1	10,010		10,010	
LEUTERITZ, Paul (1867-1919) German					
oil	1	3,591		3,591	
LEUUS, Jesus (1931-) Mexican					
oil	1	1,100		1,100	
LEUZE-HIRSCHFELD, Emmy (1884-?) Austrian					
oil	1	1,102		1,102	
LEVALLOIS, Pierre Ernest (19th C) French					
oil	1	4,345		4,345	
LEVANBERGH, P (?) ?					
oil	1	1,131		1,131	
LEVANON, Mordechai (1901-1968) Israeli					
oil	5	30,800	3,400	6,500	10,500
wc/d	4	6,900	1,400	1,600	2,200
LEVASSEUR, Henri (1853-1934) French					
3D	4	17,111	1,244	1,654	12,560
LEVASSEUR, Leon (19/20th C) French					
oil	1	2,563		2,563	
LEVENTSEV, Nikolai (1930-) Russian					
oil	1	2,700		2,700	
LEVEQUE, Auguste (1866-1921) Belgian					
oil	2	4,891	1,459	2,446	3,432
LEVER, Charles (19/20th C) British					
oil	1	5,112		5,112	
LEVER, Richard Hayley (1876-1958) American					
oil	13	59,065	1,000	4,350	16,000
wc/d	6	10,100	1,100	1,300	3,500
LEVERD, René (1872-1938) French					
oil	1	1,106		1,106	
wc/d	3	3,411	1,019	1,083	1,309
LEVERE, Paul (19th C) French					
oil	1	1,164		1,164	
LEVI, Basil (1878-1954) Russian					
oil	2	3,473	1,359	1,737	2,114
LEVI, Carlo (1902-1975) Italian					
oil	12	36,308	1,077	2,664	6,309
LEVIER, Charles (1920-) French					
oil	4	6,600	1,000	1,650	2,300

Name	No.	Total Sales Value	lowest	Prices median	highest
LEVIGNE, Theodore (1848-1912) French					
oil	8	22,442	1,003	3,040	3,764
LEVINE, Sherrie (1947-) American					
wc/d	3	18,000	6,000	6,000	6,000
LEVIS, Maurice (1860-1940) French					
oil	11	42,389	2,190	3,791	5,703
wc/d	1	1,408		1,408	
LEVIS, Max (1863-?) German					
oil	1	5,056		5,056	
wc/d	1	1,818		1,818	
LEVITAN, Isaac Ilyitch (1860-1900) Russian					
oil	4	291,906	2,066	9,020	271,800
wc/d	1	31,020		31,020	
LEVORATI, Guido (1888-1960) Italian					
oil	1	1,379		1,379	
LEVRAC-TOURNIERES, Robert (1667-1752) French					
oil	2	25,670	5,733	12,835	19,937
LEVREAU, Georges (1867-?) French					
oil	1	2,750		2,750	
LEVREL, René (1900-1981) French					
oil	1	1,119		1,119	
LEVRERO, Beppe (1901-1986) Italian					
oil	1	1,877		1,877	
LEVY, Charles (19th C) French					
3D	1	1,764		1,764	
LEVY, Charles-Octave (?-1899) French					
wc/d	1	3,056		3,056	
LEVY, Émile (1826-1890) French					
oil	1	10,000		10,000	
LEVY, Henri Leopold (1840-1904) French					
oil	1	2,799		2,799	
LEVY, Moses (1885-1968) Italian					
oil	3	10,799	1,568	3,917	5,314
LEVY, Ra'anan (1954-) Israeli					
wc/d	4	8,900	1,800	2,150	2,800
LEVY, Rudolf (1875-1943) German					
oil	1	10,380		10,380	
wc/d	1	2,472		2,472	
LEVY, S (19th C) ?					
oil	1	1,305		1,305	
LEVY-DHURMER, Lucien (1865-1953) French					
wc/d	4	53,644	1,760	13,611	24,662
LEWIN, Stephen (fl.1890-1910) British					
oil	3	20,718	5,500	5,738	9,480
LEWINDON, Ron (20th C) British					
oil	1	1,562		1,562	
LEWIS, Charles (1753-1795) British					
oil	1	1,095		1,095	
LEWIS, Charles James (1830-1892) British					
oil	1	4,400		4,400	
wc/d	3	7,251	1,144	1,817	4,290
LEWIS, Cyril Arthur (1903-) British/American					
oil	1	1,100		1,100	
LEWIS, Edmonia (1843-?) American					
3D	2	120,000	55,000	60,000	65,000
LEWIS, Edmund Darch (1835-1910) American					
oil	8	52,050	1,100	3,425	18,000
wc/d	11	33,100	1,000	2,000	13,000
LEWIS, George Robert (1782-1871) British					
wc/d	1	12,584		12,584	

Name	No.	Total Sales Value	Prices lowest	median	highest
LEWIS, Harry Emerson (1892-1958) American					
oil	3	4,500	1,000	1,000	2,500
LEWIS, J (?) ?					
oil	1	1,000		1,000	
LEWIS, Jeanette Maxfield (1894-1982) American					
oil	3	12,250	2,500	4,250	5,500
LEWIS, John Frederick (1805-1876) British					
oil	2	242,440	68,640	121,220	173,800
wc/d	7	34,742	1,034	4,004	10,570
LEWIS, Josephine M (1865-1959) American					
oil	1	6,000		6,000	
LEWIS, L (19th C) British					
wc/d	1	1,170		1,170	
LEWIS, Martin (1881-1962) American					
wc/d	1	2,200		2,200	
LEWIS, Maud (1903-1970) Canadian					
oil	14	41,919	1,759	2,843	4,978
wc/d	1	2,270		2,270	
LEWIS, Percy Wyndham (1882-1957) British					
oil	2	97,500	46,500	48,750	51,000
wc/d	9	91,469	1,193	6,435	25,740
LEWIS, William Lee (?) American?					
oil	1	1,000		1,000	
LEWITT, Sol (1928-) American					
3D	11	269,633	2,073	24,160	65,000
oil	1	1,352		1,352	
wc/d	23	86,471	1,068	2,420	20,300
LEX, Isidore (?) ?					
oil	1	23,552		23,552	
LEY, Hans Christian Clausen (1828-1875) Danish					
oil	1	1,763		1,763	
LEY, Sophie (1859-1918) German					
oil	2	7,548	1,355	3,774	6,193
LEYDE, Otto (1835-1897) German					
wc/d	1	1,359		1,359	
LEYDEN, Ernest van (1892-1969) Dutch					
oil	1	3,233		3,233	
LEYENDECKER, J C (1874-1951) American					
oil	1	37,000		37,000	
LEYENDECKER, Joseph C (1874-1951) American					
oil	6	226,250	4,500	43,750	70,000
LEYGUE, Eugène (1813-1877) French					
oil	1	1,300		1,300	
LEYMAN, Alfred (1856-1933) British					
oil	1	1,015		1,015	
wc/d	2	3,078	1,422	1,539	1,656
LEYMARIE, Hippolyte (1809-1844) French					
oil	1	1,168		1,168	
LEYS, Baron Hendrik (1815-1869) Belgian					
oil	4	13,952	1,075	3,468	5,941
wc/d	1	1,083		1,083	
LEYSTER, Judith (1600-1660) Dutch					
oil	1	63,420		63,420	
LHARDY Y GARRIGUES, Agustin (1848-1918) Spanish					
oil	3	25,031	2,529	2,810	19,692
L'HERMINEZ, Theo (1921-) Dutch					
oil	2	4,741	1,724	2,371	3,017
LHERMITTE, Léon (1844-1925) French					
oil	7	1,670,199	23,199	65,000	850,000
wc/d	19	198,951	1,383	8,728	26,000

Name	No.	Total Sales Value	lowest	Prices median	highest
L'HOEST, Engelbert (1919-) Dutch					
wc/d	1	1,293		1,293	
LHOTE, Andre (1885-1962) French					
oil	51	1,047,996	3,512	12,000	140,000
wc/d	21	85,333	1,426	3,832	8,700
LI KERAN (1907-1989) Chinese					
wc/d	1	6,000		6,000	
LIAUSU, Camille (1894-1975) French					
oil	1	2,357		2,357	
LIBALT, Gottfried (fl.1649-1666) Dutch					
oil	1	35,280		35,280	
LIBERICH, K (?) Russian					
3D	1	8,305		8,305	
LIBERMAN, Alexander (1912-) American					
3D	3	13,700	3,200	4,000	6,500
LIBERT, Georg Emil (1820-1908) Danish					
oil	2	4,154	1,071	2,077	3,083
LICATA, Riccardo (1929-) Italian					
oil	10	20,470	1,070	1,760	4,692
wc/d	2	8,488	4,159	4,244	4,329
LICHTENBERGER, Hermann Julius (?-1897) German					
oil	1	22,500		22,500	
LICHTENSTEIN, Roy (1923-1997) American					
3D	9	1,021,447	1,745	21,000	550,000
oil	7	2,552,000	7,000	290,000	750,000
wc/d	10	804,298	13,000	27,590	530,000
LICINI, Osvaldo (1894-1958) Italian					
oil	2	105,875	49,151	52,938	56,724
wc/d	3	15,095	3,927	5,161	6,007
LIDDELL, T Hodgson (1860-1925) British					
wc/d	1	1,193		1,193	
LIDDELL, William F (19/20th C) British					
wc/d	1	1,740		1,740	
LIDDERDALE, Charles Sillem (1831-1895) British					
oil	10	57,605	1,809	4,388	15,100
wc/d	2	7,710	1,500	3,855	6,210
LIDDERDALE, Charles Sillem and WARDLE, Arthur (19/20th C) British					
oil	1	8,305		8,305	
LIDWINE (20th C) ?					
wc/d	1	1,460		1,460	
LIE, Jonas (1880-1940) American					
oil	7	129,650	1,100	16,500	50,000
LIEBERMANN, Ernst (1869-1960) German					
oil	4	5,714	1,288	1,391	1,644
LIEBERMANN, Ferdinand (1883-1941) German					
3D	1	3,677		3,677	
LIEBERMANN, Max (1847-1935) German					
oil	17	3,795,119	14,400	75,690	1,087,540
wc/d	21	223,925	1,009	3,500	61,470
LIEBSCHER, Adolf (1857-?) Czechoslovakian					
oil	1	2,500		2,500	
LIEGI, Ulvi (1860-1939) Italian					
oil	5	28,803	1,848	3,900	12,708
LIENDER, Jacobus van (1696-1759) Flemish					
wc/d	1	1,414		1,414	
LIENDER, Pieter Jan van (1727-1779) Dutch					
oil	2	34,091	15,909	17,046	18,182
LIER, Adolf (1826-1882) German					
oil	6	21,010	1,906	2,813	6,479

Name	No.	Total Sales Value	lowest	Prices median	highest
LIERNUR, Willem Adriaan Alexander (1856-1917) Dutch					
oil	1	4,208		4,208	
LIEROW, Anny (1879-?) Swiss					
oil	1	1,108		1,108	
LIES, Jozef H (1821-1865) Belgian					
oil	2	2,575	1,198	1,288	1,377
LIESEGANG, Helmut (1858-1945) German					
oil	3	7,064	1,330	2,234	3,500
LIESKE, Karl (1816-1878) German					
oil	1	1,364		1,364	
LIESTE, Cornelis (1817-1861) Dutch					
oil	3	12,978	3,796	4,591	4,591
LIEVENS, Jan (1607-1674) Dutch					
oil	1	28,723		28,723	
LIEVIN, Jacques (1850-?) French					
oil	3	7,544	1,337	2,437	3,770
wc/d	1	9,433		9,433	
LIEXANDER, A (19th C) Continental					
oil	1	1,550		1,550	
LIEZEN-MAYER, Alexander von (1839-1898) Austrian					
oil	1	1,704		1,704	
LIFSHITZ, Uri (1936-) Israeli					
oil	3	8,600	1,400	3,000	4,200
wc/d	1	1,400		1,400	
LIGABUE, Antonio (1899-1965) Italian					
oil	1	27,727		27,727	
LIGER, F (19/20th C) French					
oil	1	2,600		2,600	
LIGER-HIDALGO, T (20th C) Spanish					
oil	1	10,220		10,220	
LIGNY, Charles and ROBBE, Louis (19th C) Belgian					
oil	1	3,472		3,472	
LIGON, Glenn (1960-) American					
oil	3	77,000	8,500	22,500	46,000
LIGORIO, Pirro (1513-1583) Italian					
wc/d	2	17,362	2,669	8,681	14,693
LIGOZZI, Jacopo (1547-1632) Italian					
wc/d	1	35,000		35,000	
LIGTELIJN, Evert Jan (1893-1977) Dutch					
oil	2	3,552	1,180	1,776	2,372
LIGURIAN SCHOOL, 15th C Italian					
oil	1	15,000		15,000	
LILANGA DI NYAMA, Georges (1944-) African					
oil	1	1,745		1,745	
LILJEBLADH, Birgitta (1924-) Swedish					
oil	2	2,091	1,037	1,046	1,054
LILJEFORS, Bruno (1860-1939) Swedish					
oil	42	940,744	2,503	13,805	109,810
wc/d	1	3,105		3,105	
LILJEFORS, Lindorm (1909-1985) Swedish					
oil	31	54,271	1,087	1,552	4,080
LILLIS, Richard (20th C) American					
oil	1	3,250		3,250	
LILLONI, Umberto (1898-1980) Italian					
oil	11	85,417	4,852	6,545	12,617
wc/d	1	3,743		3,743	
LILLYWHITE, Raphael (1891-1958) American					
oil	2	6,200	1,700	3,100	4,500

Name	No.	Total Sales Value	lowest	Prices median	highest
LIMBACH, Hans Jorg (1928-1990) Swiss					
3D	1	11,146		11,146	
LIMBORCH, Hendrik van (1681-1759) Dutch					
oil	2	29,550	7,550	14,775	22,000
LIMNELL, Per Emanuel (1764-1861) Swedish					
oil	1	1,373		1,373	
LIMOGES SCHOOL, 13th C French					
3D	1	27,156		27,156	
LIMOSIN, Leonard (c.1505-c.1575) French					
wc/d	1	494,602		494,602	
LIMOUSE, Roger (1894-1990) French					
oil	6	12,897	1,570	1,950	3,064
LIMPERT, Heinrich (1858-1938) German					
oil	1	1,250		1,250	
LIN FENGMIAN (1900-1991) Chinese					
wc/d	3	51,000	13,500	16,500	21,000
LINARES FERNANDEZ, Juan Idalgo (1880-?) Spanish					
oil	2	6,000	3,000	3,000	3,000
LINCKE, Karl Ludwig (1822-1888) German					
oil	1	4,518		4,518	
LIND, Christian Georg von (1800-1856) Danish					
oil	1	1,906		1,906	
LINDAU (19th C) ?					
oil	1	1,491		1,491	
LINDAU, Dietrich Wilhelm (1799-1862) German					
oil	1	2,786		2,786	
wc/d	2	4,831	1,891	2,416	2,940
LINDBERG, Alf (1905-1990) Swedish					
oil	1	1,143		1,143	
LINDBERG, Frans (1858-1944) Swedish					
oil	1	2,691		2,691	
LINDBERG, Gustaf (1852-1932) Swedish					
3D	2	3,199	1,129	1,600	2,070
LINDBERG, Harald (1901-1976) Swedish					
oil	2	2,418	1,094	1,209	1,324
LINDBERG, Maria (1958-) Swedish					
wc/d	1	2,995		2,995	
LINDBERG, Stig (1916-1982) Swedish					
wc/d	1	1,706		1,706	
LINDE, G van der (18th C) Dutch					
oil	1	1,869		1,869	
LINDE, Jan van der (1864-1945) Dutch					
oil	3	3,587	1,080	1,132	1,375
LINDE, Johan van de (1887-1956) Dutch					
oil	1	3,540		3,540	
LINDE, Ossip L (?-1940) American					
oil	1	1,175		1,175	
LINDE-WALTHER, Heinrich Eduard (1868-1939) German					
oil	1	2,097		2,097	
LINDEGREN, Amalia (1814-1891) Swedish					
oil	1	1,204		1,204	
LINDELL, Lage (1920-1980) Swedish					
oil	5	21,607	1,505	2,721	8,542
wc/d	3	7,679	1,555	1,756	4,368
LINDEMAN, Emil (1864-c.1945) Polish					
oil	1	1,374		1,374	
LINDEMANN, Kai (1931-) Danish					
oil	2	3,322	1,177	1,661	2,145

Name	No.	Total Sales Value	lowest	Prices median	highest
LINDEMANN-FROMMEL, Karl (1819-1891) German					
oil	1	18,894		18,894	
wc/d	1	1,259		1,259	
LINDEMANN-FROMMEL, Manfred (1852-?) German					
oil	1	17,726		17,726	
LINDEN, Helge (1897-1971) Swedish					
oil	2	3,148	1,407	1,574	1,741
LINDENAU, Martin (20th C) French					
oil	1	1,204		1,204	
LINDERUM, Richard (1851-?) German					
oil	1	1,123		1,123	
LINDFORS, Evert (1927-) Swedish					
3D	1	1,558		1,558	
LINDH, Bror (1877-1941) Swedish					
oil	3	6,788	1,483	2,032	3,273
LINDHOLM, Berndt (1841-1914) Finnish					
oil	10	158,165	3,950	10,764	37,750
LINDI (1904-1991) Swiss					
oil	1	2,565		2,565	
LINDLAR, Johann Wilhelm (1816-1896) German					
oil	2	9,047	2,129	4,524	6,918
LINDNER, Ernest (1897-1988) Canadian					
wc/d	3	13,069	1,034	5,224	6,811
LINDNER, Peter Moffat (1854-1949) British					
oil	1	7,008		7,008	
LINDNER, Richard (1901-1978) American/German					
3D	1	3,342		3,342	
wc/d	6	27,412	1,382	1,951	16,000
LINDO, F (18th C) British					
oil	1	1,849		1,849	
LINDQVIST, Axel Hjalmar (1843-1917) Swedish					
oil	2	3,137	1,105	1,569	2,032
LINDQVIST, Herman (1868-1923) Swedish					
oil	1	4,176		4,176	
LINDSAY, Norman Alfred Williams (1879-1969) Australian					
wc/d	1	17,000		17,000	
LINDSAY, Percy (1870-1952) Australian					
oil	1	3,557		3,557	
LINDSAY, Sir Coutts (1824-1907) British					
oil	1	1,296		1,296	
LINDSEY, N (fl.1880-1920) American?					
oil	1	5,500		5,500	
LINDSTRAND, Vicke (1904-1983) Swedish					
oil	1	3,819		3,819	
LINDSTROM, Arvid Mauritz (1849-1923) Swedish					
oil	2	6,013	2,013	3,007	4,000
LINDSTROM, Bengt (1925-) Swedish					
oil	61	185,154	1,021	2,434	10,329
wc/d	2	2,563	1,206	1,282	1,357
LINDSTROM, Carl Jacob (19th C) Swedish					
wc/d	1	3,499		3,499	
LINDSTROM, Rikard (1882-1943) Swedish					
oil	2	3,810	1,136	1,905	2,674
LINER, Carl (1914-1997) Swiss					
oil	50	291,127	1,210	5,830	18,656
wc/d	14	34,078	1,089	2,246	4,373
LINER, Carl August (1871-1946) Swiss					
oil	6	63,003	1,839	6,062	33,543
wc/d	3	10,182	1,677	3,790	4,715

Name	No.	Total Sales Value	Prices lowest	median	highest
LINES, Samuel (1778-1863) British					
oil	1	9,724		9,724	
LINGELBACH, Johannes (1622-1674) Dutch					
oil	2	25,230	12,000	12,615	13,230
LINGELBACH, Johannes (school) (1622-1674) Dutch					
oil	2	18,718	7,901	9,359	10,817
LINGENFELDER, Eugen (1862-?) German					
oil	1	1,500		1,500	
LINGUET, Henri (fl.1881-1914) French					
oil	1	6,900		6,900	
LINGWOOD, Edward J (fl.1884-1904) British					
oil	1	6,450		6,450	
LINKENS, Wilfred (19th C) ?					
oil	1	1,731		1,731	
LINNELL, James Thomas (1826-1905) British					
oil	1	68,640		68,640	
LINNELL, John (1792-1882) British					
oil	9	97,842	1,287	8,030	23,925
LINNELL, William (1826-1910) British					
oil	1	1,296		1,296	
LINNIG, Egidius (1821-1860) Belgian					
oil	3	10,679	1,259	3,904	5,516
LINNIG, Willem (19th C) Belgian					
oil	2	2,298	1,149	1,149	1,149
LINNIG, Willem (elder) (1819-1885) Belgian					
oil	2	10,263	1,564	5,132	8,699
LINNIG, Willem (younger) (1842-1890) Belgian					
oil	2	9,967	1,981	4,984	7,986
LINNQVIST, Hilding (1891-1984) Swedish					
oil	12	93,305	1,909	5,232	29,483
wc/d	2	3,990	1,180	1,995	2,810
LINO, Gustave (1893-?) ?					
oil	3	19,354	3,222	7,110	9,022
wc/d	1	1,804		1,804	
LINS, Adolf (1856-1927) German					
oil	7	32,517	1,122	4,492	8,000
LINT, Giacomo van (1723-1790) Italian					
oil	3	296,950	7,350	25,000	264,600
LINT, Hendrik van (1684-1763) Flemish					
oil	2	19,276	7,850	9,638	11,426
LINT, Louis van (1909-1986) Belgian					
oil	1	8,508		8,508	
wc/d	2	2,434	1,107	1,217	1,327
LINT, Peter van (1609-1690) Flemish					
oil	4	130,988	15,319	23,950	67,769
LINTHORST, Jacobus (1745-1815) Dutch					
oil	1	135,900		135,900	
LINTON, William (1791-1876) British					
oil	1	2,487		2,487	
LINTZ, Ferdinand Ernst (1833-1909) Dutch					
oil	1	3,097		3,097	
LION CACHET, Carel Adolphe (1864-1945) Dutch					
oil	1	1,215		1,215	
LIONE, Andrea di (1596-1675) Italian					
oil	2	26,281	11,007	13,141	15,274
LIONEL, Percy (?) British					
oil	1	1,435		1,435	
LIOTARD, Jean-Étienne (1702-1789) Swiss					
oil	1	80,850		80,850	

Name	No.	Total Sales Value	lowest	Prices median	highest
wc/d	2	107,248	5,024	53,624	102,224
LIOZU, G (19/20th C) ?					
oil	1	2,062		2,062	
LIPCHITZ, Jacques (1891-1973) French					
3D	7	1,251,448	1,800	7,000	660,000
oil	1	47,772		47,772	
wc/d	2	4,254	2,047	2,127	2,207
LIPCHYTZ, Samuel (20th C) French					
3D	2	5,332	1,104	2,666	4,228
LIPHART, Ernest Friedrich von (1847-1934) Russian					
oil	1	16,000		16,000	
LIPINSKI, Hypolit (1846-1884) Czechoslovakian					
oil	1	1,514		1,514	
LIPP, Maren (1926-) German					
3D	1	1,365		1,365	
LIPPI, Filippino (1457-1504) Italian					
oil	1	906,000		906,000	
LIPPINCOTT, William H (1849-1920) American					
oil	2	29,685	9,685	14,843	20,000
LIPPMANN, Karl Friedrich (1858-?) German					
oil	1	1,079		1,079	
LIPSON, G S (1905-1992) American					
oil	1	1,600		1,600	
LIRA, Armando (1903-1959) Chilean					
oil	1	1,290		1,290	
LIRA, Pedro (19th C) Chilean					
oil	1	5,840		5,840	
LISA, Esteban (1895-1983) Argentinian					
wc/d	1	2,000		2,000	
LISA, Mario (1908-1992) Italian					
oil	2	3,126	1,379	1,563	1,747
LISCHKA, Reinhold (1881-1949) German					
oil	2	6,785	2,316	3,393	4,469
LISHANSKY, Batya (1901-1992) Israeli					
oil	3	4,000	1,100	1,400	1,500
LISIEWSKA, Anna Dorothea (1721-1782) German					
oil	2	7,302	2,078	3,651	5,224
LISMER, Arthur (1885-1969) Canadian					
oil	10	79,780	3,667	6,569	14,601
wc/d	4	5,177	1,007	1,043	2,085
LISMONDE, Jules (1908-) Belgian					
wc/d	1	2,783		2,783	
LISS, Jan (c.1595-1629) Dutch					
oil	1	6,142		6,142	
LISSAC, Pierre (1878-) French					
wc/d	1	1,653		1,653	
LISSE, Dirck van der (?-1669) Dutch					
oil	1	4,536		4,536	
LISSITZKY, El (1890-1941) Russian					
wc/d	1	91,421		91,421	
LISZT (20th C) American					
oil	1	1,200		1,200	
LIT, Jan van (19th C) ?					
oil	1	1,773		1,773	
LITTLE, A Platte (19th C) American					
oil	1	1,300		1,300	
LITTLE, George Léon (fl.1884-1926) British					
oil	1	1,278		1,278	

Name	No.	Total Sales Value	lowest	Prices median	highest
LITTLE, John C (1928-) Canadian					
oil	8	16,665	1,016	2,254	3,171
LITTLE, Norman (20th C) British					
oil	2	2,625	1,200	1,313	1,425
LITTLECHILD, George (20th C) North American					
wc/d	1	1,427		1,427	
LITTLEWOOD, Edward (20th C) British					
oil	1	1,027		1,027	
LITTROW, Leo von (1860-1914) Austrian					
oil	4	8,240	1,526	2,046	2,623
LITVINOVSKY, Pinchas (1894-1985) Israeli					
wc/d	1	12,000		12,000	
LITZINGER, Dorothea M (1889-1925) American					
oil	1	2,800		2,800	
LIVEMONT, Privat (1861-1936) Belgian					
oil	3	4,887	1,054	1,677	2,156
wc/d	2	2,244	1,100	1,122	1,144
LIVENS, H (19th C) British?					
oil	1	1,207		1,207	
LIVENS, Henry (19th C) British					
oil	3	8,827	1,500	3,034	4,293
LIVENS, Horace Mann (1862-1936) British					
oil	1	2,212		2,212	
LIVESAY, Richard (1753-1823) British					
oil	1	1,580		1,580	
LIZARDO, Luis (1956-) Venezuelan					
oil	1	2,200		2,200	
LIZCANO Y ESTEBAN, Angel (1846-1929) Spanish					
oil	5	81,706	1,573	5,227	46,204
LJUBA (1934-) Yugoslavian					
oil	12	56,065	1,446	3,828	11,682
LJUNGBERG, Sven (1913-) Swedish					
oil	2	2,442	1,152	1,221	1,290
LJUNGGREN, Reinhold (1920-) Swedish					
oil	1	2,073		2,073	
wc/d	1	2,394		2,394	
LJUNGQUIST, Birger (1898-1965) Swedish					
oil	4	4,651	1,037	1,148	1,318
wc/d	1	1,708		1,708	
LLANECES, Jose (1863-1919) Spanish					
oil	5	41,225	1,013	9,480	11,100
LLEWELLYN, Sir William (1858-1941) British					
wc/d	1	1,406		1,406	
LLIMONA, Rafael (1896-1957) Spanish					
oil	1	7,073		7,073	
LLOPIS, Carlos Ruano (1878-1950) Spanish					
oil	2	6,040	2,158	3,020	3,882
LLORENS ARTIGAS, Josep and MIRO, Joan (20th C) Spanish					
oil	1	85,000		85,000	
wc/d	1	58,188		58,188	
LLORENS Y DIAZ, F (1874-1948) Spanish					
oil	2	3,011	1,124	1,506	1,887
LLORENS Y DIAZ, Francisco (1874-1948) Spanish					
oil	1	11,615		11,615	
LLOYD, Edward (19th C) British					
oil	4	10,246	1,963	2,492	3,300
LLOYD, James (1905-1974) British					
wc/d	1	1,350		1,350	

Name	No.	Total Sales Value	lowest	Prices median	highest
LLOYD, R Malcolm (fl.1879-1907) British					
wc/d	4	6,857	1,027	1,790	2,250
LLOYD, T Ivester (1873-1942) British					
oil	6	14,829	1,130	2,365	3,775
wc/d	3	7,255	1,057	2,700	3,498
LLOYD, Thomas James (1849-1910) British					
oil	2	7,592	1,256	3,796	6,336
wc/d	2	10,428	1,133	5,214	9,295
LLOYD, W Stuart (fl.1875-1929) British					
oil	4	15,554	2,054	3,225	7,050
wc/d	9	20,993	1,296	2,054	4,440
LLULL, Jose Pinelo (1861-1922) Spanish					
oil	3	14,499	3,835	5,065	5,599
LLUNA, Juan (1933-) Spanish					
oil	1	1,144		1,144	
LO MEDICO, Thomas Gaetano (1904-1985) American					
3D	1	4,200		4,200	
LOAN, Dorothy van (1904-1999) American					
oil	5	11,450	1,750	2,400	3,000
LOBBEDEZ, Charles-Auguste-Romain (1825-1882) French					
oil	3	15,953	1,309	6,023	8,621
LOBEL-RICHE, Almery (1880-1950) French					
wc/d	1	1,092		1,092	
LOBO, Balthazar (1910-1993) Spanish					
3D	1	27,640		27,640	
wc/d	2	2,022	1,010	1,011	1,012
LOBRE, Maurice (1862-1951) French					
oil	1	1,200		1,200	
LOCATELLI, Andrea (1693-1741) Italian					
oil	6	210,838	10,268	29,683	81,540
wc/d	1	1,400		1,400	
LOCATELLI, Giovan Francesco (1810-1882) Italian					
oil	1	10,000		10,000	
LOCATELLI, Romualdo (1905-1943) Italian					
oil	4	20,835	3,349	5,542	6,403
LOCHER, Carl (1851-1915) Danish					
oil	16	40,511	1,033	1,897	7,149
LOCHER, I (19th C) British?					
oil	1	8,360		8,360	
LOCHER, Thomas (1956-) American					
oil	1	3,250		3,250	
LOCHHEAD, John (1866-1921) British					
oil	2	11,660	1,510	5,830	10,150
LOCHHEAD, Kenneth (1926-) Canadian					
wc/d	1	1,567		1,567	
LOCHORE, Brad (1960-) New Zealander					
oil	2	17,125	5,800	8,563	11,325
LOCKHART, William Ewart (1846-1900) British					
oil	1	33,350		33,350	
LOCKWOOD, John Ward (1894-1963) American					
oil	1	2,200		2,200	
LODEIRO, Jose Telmo (1931-) Spanish					
oil	1	2,076		2,076	
LODER OF BATH, Edwin (1827-1885) British					
oil	2	2,811	1,178	1,406	1,633
LODER OF BATH, James (1784-1860) British					
oil	2	5,796	1,896	2,898	3,900
LODGE, George Edward (1860-1954) British					
oil	4	12,716	1,410	3,285	4,736
wc/d	2	3,252	1,500	1,626	1,752

Name	No.	Total Sales Value	lowest	Prices median	highest
LODOLA, Marco (1955-) Italian					
wc/d	2	2,882	1,047	1,441	1,835
LOEB, Sidonia (1871-1944) American					
oil	2	2,400	1,000	1,200	1,400
LOEBER, Lou (1894-1983) Dutch					
oil	7	23,865	1,940	3,233	5,603
LOEFFLER, Gisella (1900-) American/Austrian					
oil	1	3,000		3,000	
LOEMANS, Alexander François (c.1816-1898) American/French					
oil	5	26,367	1,100	1,567	19,000
LOENEN, Cor van (1942-) Dutch					
oil	1	2,366		2,366	
LOESCH, Ernst (1860-?) German					
wc/d	1	1,355		1,355	
LOESCHIN, Herman (?-1872) German					
oil	1	7,295		7,295	
LOEW, Michael (1907-1985) American					
oil	1	9,000		9,000	
LOFDAHL, Eva (1953-) Swedish					
3D	1	1,382		1,382	
LOFFLER, August (1822-1866) German					
oil	1	3,498		3,498	
wc/d	3	6,200	1,694	2,178	2,328
LOFFLER, Franz Karl (1875-1955) German					
oil	3	3,784	1,183	1,183	1,418
LOFGREN, Clara (1843-1923) Swedish					
oil	1	1,306		1,306	
LOGAN, Maurice (1886-1977) American					
oil	2	55,000	5,000	27,500	50,000
wc/d	2	2,500	1,000	1,250	1,500
LOGHADES, Leonie de (1859-?) French					
wc/d	1	1,241		1,241	
LOGSDAIL, William (1859-1944) British					
oil	1	7,065		7,065	
LOHEZ, Yves (20th C) French					
3D	2	3,550	1,750	1,775	1,800
LOHMANN VAN DER FEER LADER, Else (1897-1984) German					
oil	1	1,963		1,963	
LOHMANN, Franz (19th C) German					
oil	1	1,000		1,000	
LOHMANN, Mogens (1918-1985) Danish					
oil	5	15,082	1,689	3,258	3,740
LOHR, August (1843-1919) German					
wc/d	1	4,410		4,410	
LOHR, Franz (1874-1918) German					
3D	1	1,159		1,159	
LOHSE, Richard Paul (1902-1988) Swiss					
oil	1	6,512		6,512	
LOHSE-WACHTLER, Elfriede (1899-1940) German					
wc/d	1	54,720		54,720	
LOIR, Luigi (1845-1916) French					
oil	10	244,824	4,095	23,876	58,000
wc/d	2	9,674	2,109	4,837	7,565
LOIR, Nicolas (1624-1679) French					
oil	2	20,314	1,329	10,157	18,985
LOISEAU, Gustave (1865-1935) French					
oil	44	2,297,223	2,800	45,735	150,000
LOISEAU-ROUSSEAU, Paul Louis Émile (1861-1927) French					
3D	1	5,187		5,187	

Name	No.	Total Sales Value	lowest	Prices median	highest
LOISELLE, René (?) ?					
oil	1	1,268		1,268	
LOJACONO, Francesco (1841-1915) Italian					
oil	6	116,374	5,723	12,063	55,300
LOKHORST, Dirk van (1818-1893) Dutch					
oil	1	1,414		1,414	
LOKHORST, Jan van (1837-?) Dutch					
oil	1	2,397		2,397	
LOMAX, John Arthur (1857-1923) British					
oil	10	81,024	1,034	8,175	13,500
LOMBARD SCHOOL, 15th C Italian					
3D	1	134,012		134,012	
LOMBARD SCHOOL, 16th C Italian					
oil	3	37,973	3,235	5,338	29,400
LOMBARD SCHOOL, 16th/17th C Italian					
oil	1	7,248		7,248	
LOMBARD SCHOOL, 17th C Italian					
oil	18	188,205	2,293	3,919	87,354
LOMBARD SCHOOL, 18th C Italian					
oil	5	26,828	4,812	5,064	7,095
LOMBARD SCHOOL, 18th/19th C Italian					
wc/d	1	7,407		7,407	
LOMBARD SCHOOL, 19th C Italian					
oil	1	8,087		8,087	
LOMBARD, F (19th C) French					
oil	1	3,555		3,555	
LOMEITTERE, L de (19th C) French					
oil	1	2,267		2,267	
LOMI, Aurelio (1556-1622) Italian					
oil	1	28,690		28,690	
LOMI, Giovanni (1889-1969) Italian					
oil	9	19,005	1,026	2,008	3,567
LOMIKINE, Konstantin (1924-1992) Russian					
wc/d	1	1,080		1,080	
LOMMEN, Wilhelm (1838-1895) German					
oil	1	3,365		3,365	
LONBLAD, Emilia (1865-1946) Swedish					
oil	2	2,049	1,016	1,025	1,033
LONCIN, L (19/20th C) ?					
oil	1	1,057		1,057	
LONDONIO, Francesco (1723-1783) Italian					
oil	2	27,175	5,823	13,588	21,352
LONE WOLF (1882-?) American					
oil	1	2,500		2,500	
LONG, Charles (19th C) British					
3D	1	14,000		14,000	
LONG, Edwin (1829-1891) British					
oil	4	955,500	7,500	124,000	700,000
LONG, Harry (20th C) American					
oil	1	2,500		2,500	
LONG, L (?) ?					
oil	1	1,341		1,341	
LONG, Richard (1945-) British					
wc/d	2	4,069	1,804	2,035	2,265
LONG, Sydney (1871-1955) Australian					
wc/d	1	2,067		2,067	
LONGANESI, Leo (1905-1957) Italian					
oil	1	3,697		3,697	

Name	No.	Total Sales Value	lowest	Prices median	highest
LONGARETTI, Trento (1916-) Italian					
oil	4	8,217	1,366	1,486	3,879
LONGCHAMP, Henriette de (19th C) French					
oil	1	2,900		2,900	
LONGHI, Alessandro (1733-1813) Italian					
oil	1	5,499		5,499	
LONGHI, Luca (1507-1580) Italian					
oil	3	57,985	6,645	19,630	31,710
LONGHI, Pietro (1702-1785) Italian					
oil	2	71,659	12,859	35,830	58,800
wc/d	1	18,120		18,120	
LONGHI, Pietro (school) (1702-1785) Italian					
oil	1	5,131		5,131	
LONGLEY, Stanislaus Soutten (1894-c.1967) British					
wc/d	1	3,146		3,146	
LONGMAID, William (fl.1886-1909) British					
oil	1	1,570		1,570	
LONGO, Robert (1953-) American					
wc/d	1	5,500		5,500	
LONGOBARDI, Casimiro (20th C) ?					
oil	1	2,047		2,047	
LONGONI, Baldassare (1876-1956) Italian					
oil	1	16,793		16,793	
LONGPRE, Paul de (1855-1911) American/French					
wc/d	3	26,500	5,500	6,000	15,000
LONGPRE, Raoul de (19/20th C) American					
wc/d	7	64,457	3,381	6,000	24,000
LONGSTAFF, Sir John (1861-1941) Australian					
oil	1	2,718		2,718	
LONGSTAFFE, Edgar (1849-1912) British					
oil	2	3,427	1,425	1,714	2,002
LONZA, Antonio (1846-?) Italian					
oil	4	29,411	3,207	7,262	11,680
LOO, Amedee van (1719-1795) French					
oil	2	48,108	22,108	24,054	26,000
LOO, Carle van (1705-1765) French					
oil	1	250,000		250,000	
wc/d	6	176,608	1,094	3,871	112,013
LOO, Frans van (1708-1732) Flemish					
oil	1	3,210		3,210	
LOO, Jacob van (1614-1670) Dutch					
oil	1	14,002		14,002	
LOO, Jean Baptiste van (1684-1745) French					
oil	1	2,730		2,730	
LOO, Jules Cesar Denis van (1743-1821) French					
oil	1	13,435		13,435	
LOO, Louis-Michel van (1707-1771) French					
oil	4	251,401	12,401	59,500	120,000
LOO, Pieter van (1731-1784) Dutch					
wc/d	1	1,154		1,154	
LOO, van (school) (?) ?					
oil	1	2,613		2,613	
LOOF, Aurel de (1901-) ?					
oil	2	3,689	1,593	1,845	2,096
LOOMIS, Andrew (1892-1959) American					
oil	3	11,937	1,437	3,500	7,000
LOON, Theodoor van (c.1585-c.1667) Flemish					
oil	1	6,142		6,142	

Name	No.	Total Sales Value	lowest	Prices median	highest
LOOS, Friedrich (1797-1890) Austrian					
oil	2	21,767	9,805	10,884	11,962
wc/d	1	1,730		1,730	
LOOS, Henry (19/20th C) Belgian					
oil	1	9,880		9,880	
LOOS, John F (19th C) Belgian					
oil	1	4,560		4,560	
LOOSCHEN, Hans (1859-1923) German					
oil	1	1,783		1,783	
LOOSE, Basile de (1809-1885) Dutch					
oil	6	120,469	2,820	6,251	58,934
LOOTEN, Jan (1618-1681) Dutch					
oil	1	6,048		6,048	
LOOTZ, Eva (1940-) ?					
oil	1	1,450		1,450	
LOOY, Jacobus van (1855-1930) Dutch					
oil	1	9,961		9,961	
wc/d	1	1,585		1,585	
LOOY, Jan van (1882-1971) Belgian					
oil	1	3,351		3,351	
LOOYMANS, Romain (1864-1914) Belgian					
oil	1	1,885		1,885	
LOOZ-CORSWAREM, Walter de (1874-?) German					
oil	1	1,366		1,366	
LOPEZ CANCIO, Mariana (1909-1996) Spanish					
oil	1	1,297		1,297	
LOPEZ ENGUIDANOS, Jose (1760-1812) Spanish					
oil	1	19,110		19,110	
LOPEZ GARCIA, Ezequiel (1940-) Spanish					
oil	1	1,063		1,063	
LOPEZ LEAO DE LAGUNA, Baruch (1864-1943) Dutch					
oil	1	2,200		2,200	
LOPEZ MENDEZ, Luis Alfredo (1901-) Venezuelan					
oil	6	15,960	1,270	2,570	4,310
LOPEZ MEZQUITA, Jose Maria (1883-1954) Spanish					
oil	3	18,292	1,768	5,378	11,146
LOPEZ PIQUER, Luis (1802-1865) Spanish					
wc/d	1	1,282		1,282	
LOPEZ RUIZ, Antonio (1935-) Spanish					
oil	1	2,359		2,359	
LOPEZ Y PORTANA, Vicente (1772-1850) Spanish					
oil	3	8,649	1,936	2,370	4,343
wc/d	1	3,134		3,134	
LOPEZ, Gasparo (1650-1732) Italian					
oil	4	62,333	7,418	15,458	24,000
LOPEZ, Viveana (20th C) American					
oil	1	2,200		2,200	
LOPEZ-CABRERA, Ricardo (1866-1950) Spanish					
oil	5	11,970	1,388	2,758	3,000
LOPEZ-CURVAL, Catherine (1954-) French					
oil	1	3,870		3,870	
LORAN, Erle (1905-) American					
oil	2	5,850	1,100	2,925	4,750
wc/d	1	2,750		2,750	
LORCA, Federico Garcia (1899-1936) Spanish					
wc/d	2	5,537	2,109	2,769	3,428
LORCHER, Alfred (1875-1962) ?					
3D	2	4,038	1,600	2,019	2,438

Name	No.	Total Sales Value	Prices lowest	median	highest
LORD, Andrew (20th C) American					
3D	1	8,500		8,500	
LORD, W (19th C) American?					
oil	1	1,800		1,800	
LORDON, Pierre Jerome (1780-1838) French					
oil	1	1,263		1,263	
LORENTSON, Waldemar (1899-1982) Swedish					
oil	24	80,061	1,088	2,231	17,060
LORENTZ, A J (1813-?) French					
oil	1	1,350		1,350	
LORENTZEN, C A (1746-1828) Danish					
oil	3	9,056	1,311	2,383	5,362
LORENTZON, Wald (20th C) French?					
oil	1	8,127		8,127	
LORENZ, Ernest (1872-?) German					
oil	1	2,455		2,455	
LORENZ, Richard (1858-1915) German					
oil	3	187,500	20,000	47,500	120,000
LORENZALE SUGRANES, Claudio (1815-1889) Spanish					
oil	1	1,665		1,665	
LORENZL, J (1892-1950) Austrian					
3D	2	4,668	1,170	2,334	3,498
LORENZL, Josef (1892-1950) Austrian					
3D	8	18,064	1,079	2,112	4,530
LORIAN, Dolia (20th C) American?					
oil	1	1,400		1,400	
LORIMER, John Henry (1856-1936) British					
oil	3	110,808	2,058	43,500	65,250
LORIOL, Albert Francisque Michel (1882-?) French					
oil	1	1,164		1,164	
LORJOU, Bernard (1908-1986) French					
oil	9	51,442	1,328	4,205	19,090
wc/d	2	5,207	2,073	2,604	3,134
LORMIER, J (?) French					
3D	2	10,109	1,287	5,055	8,822
LORRAINE SCHOOL, 17th C French					
wc/d	1	3,322		3,322	
LORTEL, Leberecht (c.1818-1901) French					
oil	2	8,369	2,333	4,185	6,036
LORY, Gabriel Ludwig (1763-1840) Swiss					
wc/d	3	11,302	1,815	3,790	5,697
LOS, Waldemar (1849-1888) Polish					
oil	2	42,740	14,300	21,370	28,440
LOTH, Johann Karl (1632-1698) German					
oil	3	30,633	3,791	12,054	14,788
LOTH, Wilhelm (1920-1993) German					
3D	3	8,839	2,656	2,723	3,460
LOTICHIUS, Ernst (19th C) German					
oil	1	2,500		2,500	
LOTIRON, Robert (1886-1966) French					
oil	8	18,071	1,092	1,945	3,764
LOTT, Frederick Tully (fl.1852-1879) British					
oil	2	3,245	1,600	1,623	1,645
LOTTER, Heinrich (1875-1941) German					
oil	4	12,815	2,273	2,875	4,792
LOTTIER, Louis (1815-1892) French					
oil	1	3,616		3,616	
LOUBERE, Roger Lambert (20th C) French?					
oil	1	1,338		1,338	

Name	No.	Total Sales Value	lowest	Prices median	highest
LOUCHE, Constant (19/20th C) French					
oil	1	1,168		1,168	
LOUCHET, Paul-François (1854-1936) French					
oil	1	2,726		2,726	
LOUD, Arthur Bertram (1863-1930) British					
oil	1	1,800		1,800	
LOUDER, C J (?) ?					
wc/d	1	1,500		1,500	
LOUDERBACK, Walt (1887-1941) American					
oil	4	26,050	1,800	5,125	14,000
LOUDON, Terence (fl.1921-1940) British					
oil	1	2,465		2,465	
LOUGHEED, Robert Elmer (1910-1982) Canadian					
oil	3	13,500	2,500	4,200	6,800
LOUIS, Morris (1912-1962) American					
oil	4	1,230,000	190,000	330,000	380,000
LOUISIANA SCHOOL, 19th C American					
wc/d	1	5,000		5,000	
LOUND, Thomas (1802-1861) British					
oil	1	6,040		6,040	
LOUPPE, Leo (1869-?) French					
oil	1	2,212		2,212	
LOUPPE, Marguerite (c.1902-) French					
oil	1	1,510		1,510	
LOUSLAUD (20th C) French?					
3D	1	4,770		4,770	
LOUTHERBOURG, Jacques Philippe de II (1740-1812) French					
oil	4	26,323	3,024	4,650	14,000
wc/d	1	8,580		8,580	
LOUTREUIL, Maurice (1885-1925) French					
oil	2	9,193	2,424	4,597	6,769
LOUVRIER, Maurice (1878-1954) French					
oil	2	3,873	1,338	1,937	2,535
LOUYOT, Edmond (19th C) German					
oil	3	3,800	1,000	1,100	1,700
LOVATI, Augusto (1816-) Italian					
oil	1	3,427		3,427	
LOVATTI, E Augusto (1816-?) Italian					
oil	1	2,710		2,710	
LOVATTI, Matteo (1861-?) Italian					
oil	1	7,590		7,590	
LOVE, George Paterson (1887-?) American					
oil	1	1,300		1,300	
LOVE, Ralph (1907-) American					
oil	1	3,000		3,000	
LOVEGROVE, W (20th C) British					
3D	1	1,207		1,207	
LOVELL, Tom (1909-1997) American					
oil	8	308,300	2,600	11,000	210,000
wc/d	6	24,500	1,000	4,250	8,500
LOVERIDGE, Clinton (19th C) British					
oil	4	14,950	1,300	3,325	7,000
LOVERING, Ida R (fl.1881-1903) British					
wc/d	1	5,880		5,880	
LOVEROFF, Frederick Nicholas (1894-1959) Canadian					
oil	4	8,670	1,110	1,591	4,379
LOVESEY, Roderick (1944-) British					
oil	1	1,216		1,216	

Name	No.	Total Sales Value	lowest	Prices median	highest
LOVET-LORSKI, Boris (1894-1973) Russian/American					
3D	3	31,200	1,200	13,000	17,000
LOW, Bet (?) British					
oil	1	2,567		2,567	
LOW, Will Hicock (1853-1932) American					
oil	2	3,650	1,400	1,825	2,250
LOW, William Gilman (19/20th C) American					
oil	1	1,750		1,750	
LOWCOCK, Charles Frederick (fl.1878-1922) British					
oil	2	17,305	8,305	8,653	9,000
LOWELL, Milton H (1848-1927) American					
oil	1	1,300		1,300	
LOWENSBERG, Verena (1912-1986) Swiss					
oil	1	3,848		3,848	
LOWENSTERN, Christian Ludwig von (1701-1754) German					
oil	1	1,373		1,373	
LOWENTHAL, Emil (1835-1895) German					
oil	1	2,581		2,581	
LOWER RHINE SCHOOL, 16th C German					
3D	1	31,281		31,281	
LOWITH, Wilhelm (1861-1932) Austrian					
oil	1	1,226		1,226	
LOWNDES, Alan (1921-1978) British					
oil	5	19,317	1,533	4,500	5,100
LOWRY, L S (1887-1976) British					
wc/d	4	21,623	2,288	4,005	11,325
LOWRY, Laurence Stephen (1887-1976) British					
oil	35	4,131,757	2,592	63,450	679,500
wc/d	43	807,471	2,826	15,510	59,220
LOWRY, Laurence Stephen and RILEY, Harold (20th C) British					
wc/d	1	13,500		13,500	
LOXTON, John S (1903-1971) Australian					
oil	1	1,050		1,050	
LOYEUX, Charles Antoine Joseph (1823-1893) French					
oil	1	7,215		7,215	
LOZANO SANCHIS, Francisco (1912-2000) Spanish					
oil	2	8,539	3,194	4,270	5,345
wc/d	1	1,779		1,779	
LOZANO, Francisco (20th C) Spanish					
oil	3	20,486	3,194	7,857	9,435
LU JIAHE (20th C) Chinese					
wc/d	1	2,300		2,300	
LUBBERS, Adriaan (1892-1954) Dutch					
oil	3	19,355	4,000	6,734	8,621
LUBBERS, Holger (1850-1931) Danish					
oil	6	15,741	1,153	2,200	6,440
LUBEN, Adolf (1837-1905) German					
oil	1	1,124		1,124	
LUBIN, Arieh (1897-1980) Israeli					
oil	1	4,200		4,200	
wc/d	1	1,500		1,500	
LUBITCH, Ossip (1896-1986) French					
oil	2	5,300	1,900	2,650	3,400
LUBSCHITZ, John Leopold (1858-1941) Danish					
oil	1	1,191		1,191	
LUCA, G de (19/20th C) Italian					
3D	1	1,494		1,494	
LUCA, Giuseppe de (19th C) Italian					
3D	1	1,318		1,318	

Name	No.	Total Sales Value	Prices lowest	Prices median	highest
LUCAS Y PADILLA, Eugenio (1824-1870) Spanish					
oil	1	14,600		14,600	
wc/d	1	1,547		1,547	
LUCAS Y VILLAAMIL, Eugenio (1858-1918) Spanish					
oil	7	86,334	1,918	8,299	30,020
LUCAS, Albert Durer (1828-1918) British					
oil	3	7,330	1,480	1,500	4,350
LUCAS, Arthur (fl.1881-1893) British					
wc/d	1	1,628		1,628	
LUCAS, Auger (1685-1765) French					
oil	1	6,401		6,401	
LUCAS, August Georg Friedrich (1803-1863) German					
oil	1	44,858		44,858	
wc/d	1	1,951		1,951	
LUCAS, F H (19th C) ?					
oil	1	1,872		1,872	
LUCAS, Henry Frederick Lucas (?-1943) British					
oil	10	22,949	1,208	2,308	3,480
LUCAS, J D (19th C) British					
oil	1	1,917		1,917	
LUCAS, Jean (1823-?) French					
oil	1	12,000		12,000	
LUCAS, John (1807-1874) British					
oil	1	8,758		8,758	
LUCAS, John Seymour (1849-1923) British					
oil	5	11,979	1,072	2,983	3,432
LUCAS, John Templeton (1836-1880) British					
oil	2	3,906	1,650	1,953	2,256
LUCAS, Sarah (1962-) British					
3D	2	72,320	24,000	36,160	48,320
wc/d	1	2,800		2,800	
LUCAS, W (19/20th C) ?					
wc/d	1	1,800		1,800	
LUCAS, Wilhelm (1884-1918) German					
oil	4	14,920	2,500	3,831	4,758
LUCAS, William (1840-1895) British					
wc/d	1	2,190		2,190	
LUCAS-ROBIQUET, Marie Aimee (1858-1959) French					
oil	2	99,399	2,735	49,700	96,664
LUCASSEN, Reinier (1939-) Dutch					
oil	2	8,189	3,879	4,095	4,310
wc/d	1	1,207		1,207	
LUCCHESI, Andrea Carlo (1860-1924) British					
3D	1	1,275		1,275	
LUCCHESI, Bruno (1926-) American					
3D	1	1,500		1,500	
oil	1	1,000		1,000	
LUCCHESI, Giorgio (1855-1941) Italian					
oil	2	21,585	1,763	10,793	19,822
LUCE (?) ?					
3D	1	2,288		2,288	
oil	1	1,640		1,640	
LUCE, Frederic (1896-1974) French					
oil	1	2,852		2,852	
wc/d	1	2,852		2,852	
LUCE, M (1858-1941) French					
oil	1	9,981		9,981	
LUCE, Maximilien (1858-1941) French					
oil	155	1,837,653	1,056	5,703	160,000
wc/d	2	2,115	1,003	1,058	1,112

Name	No.	Total Sales Value	lowest	Prices median	highest
LUCE, Molly (1896-1986) American					
oil	1	1,300		1,300	
LUCEBERT (1924-1994) Dutch					
oil	9	85,848	1,933	5,942	28,017
wc/d	13	41,084	1,115	2,971	10,258
LUCIANI, Ascanio (1621-1706) Italian					
oil	1	4,407		4,407	
LUCIANI, Giovanni Batta (19th C) Italian					
oil	1	1,800		1,800	
LUCINI, Giovanni Battista (1639-1686) Italian					
oil	1	10,570		10,570	
LUCIONI, Luigi (1900-1988) American					
oil	5	36,850	2,100	7,500	11,000
wc/d	2	5,500	1,900	2,750	3,600
LUCIUS, S (19th C) ?					
oil	1	1,500		1,500	
LUCKEROTH, Jupp (1919-1993) German					
wc/d	2	3,221	1,442	1,611	1,779
LUCKHARDT, Karl (1886-?) German					
oil	1	1,197		1,197	
LUCKNOW SCHOOL, 18th C Indian					
wc/d	1	3,327		3,327	
LUCKX, Frans (1802-1849) Belgian					
oil	1	11,091		11,091	
LUCOP, T (19th C) British?					
oil	1	1,617		1,617	
LUCOP, Thomas (19th C) British?					
oil	1	1,287		1,287	
LUCY, Adrien (?-1875) French					
oil	1	7,432		7,432	
LUDDERS, Hinrich P (1826-1897) German?					
wc/d	1	1,151		1,151	
LUDECKE, Karl (1897-1956) German					
3D	1	1,687		1,687	
LUDECKE-CLEVE, August (1868-1957) German					
oil	2	4,793	2,061	2,397	2,732
LUDICKE, Marianne (1919-) German					
3D	1	1,202		1,202	
LUDLOW, Henry Stephen (1861-?) British					
oil	1	1,008		1,008	
LUDOVICI, Albert (1820-1894) British					
oil	1	3,575		3,575	
LUDOVICO -19th C (19th C) Spanish					
oil	1	3,292		3,292	
LUEGER, Michael (1804-1883) German					
oil	2	7,558	3,240	3,779	4,318
wc/d	1	1,262		1,262	
LUENA (?) ?					
3D	1	1,672		1,672	
LUFAF, M (?) ?					
3D	1	1,831		1,831	
LUGARDON, Albert (1827-1909) French					
oil	3	5,846	1,073	1,129	3,644
LUGATTO, G (19/20th C) ?					
oil	1	1,106		1,106	
LUGINBUHL, Bernhard (1929-) Swiss					
3D	2	27,406	9,723	13,703	17,683
LUGO, Emil (1840-1902) German					
oil	2	15,407	6,934	7,704	8,473

Name	No.	Total Sales Value	lowest	Prices median	highest
LUGRIS GONZALEZ, Urbano (1908-1973) Spanish					
wc/d	1	1,249		1,249	
LUGRIS VADILLO, Urbano (1942-) Spanish					
oil	5	9,900	1,038	1,744	3,892
LUIGI, L (?) Italian?					
oil	1	1,489		1,489	
LUIGI, Ludovico de (1933-) Italian					
3D	1	1,800		1,800	
LUIGI, P (19th C) ?					
oil	1	5,700		5,700	
LUIGINI, Ferdinand-Jean (1870-1943) French					
wc/d	1	1,712		1,712	
LUINO, Bernardino (1951-) Italian					
oil	1	3,515		3,515	
LUKE, Alexandra (20th C) Canadian					
wc/d	1	1,032		1,032	
LUKE, John (1906-1975) British					
oil	1	54,000		54,000	
LUKER, Ada (fl.1900) British					
oil	1	1,420		1,420	
LUKER, William (jnr) (1867-1951) British					
oil	3	18,630	3,950	3,950	10,730
LUKER, William (1828-1905) British					
oil	1	1,200		1,200	
LUKESCH, Hans (1867-?) Austrian					
oil	1	4,046		4,046	
LUKITS, Theodore Nikolai (1897-1992) American					
oil	1	2,250		2,250	
wc/d	1	2,750		2,750	
LUKS, George (1867-1933) American					
oil	5	179,000	12,000	17,000	85,000
LUMIS, Harriet Randall (1870-1953) American					
oil	2	83,250	3,250	41,625	80,000
LUNA Y NOVICIO, Juan (1857-1900) Spanish					
oil	1	1,588		1,588	
LUNA, Mariano (19th C) Italian					
wc/d	1	2,114		2,114	
LUNAR, Emerio Dario (1940-1990) Venezuelan					
oil	1	1,300		1,300	
LUND, Aage (fl.1918) Danish?					
oil	1	1,637		1,637	
LUND, Bernt (1812-1885) Norwegian					
oil	1	1,216		1,216	
LUND, Carl Ove Julian (1857-1936) Danish					
oil	1	1,207		1,207	
LUND, F C (1826-1901) Danish					
oil	3	3,308	1,008	1,044	1,256
LUND, Frederik Christian (1826-1901) Danish					
oil	3	11,180	1,613	1,689	7,878
LUND, Henrik (1879-1935) Norwegian					
oil	1	1,318		1,318	
LUND, Johan Ludvig (1777-1867) Danish					
oil	1	3,922		3,922	
LUND, V (19th C) Danish					
oil	1	2,204		2,204	
LUNDBERG, Gustaf (1695-1786) Swedish					
wc/d	2	12,266	4,140	6,133	8,126
LUNDBERG, Robert (1861-1903) Swedish					
oil	1	4,140		4,140	

Name	No.	Total Sales Value	lowest	Prices median	highest
LUNDBERG, Sture (1900-1930) Swedish					
oil	2	7,746	1,013	3,873	6,733
wc/d	1	1,204		1,204	
LUNDBOHM, Sixten (1895-1982) Swedish					
oil	2	2,614	1,207	1,307	1,407
LUNDBYE, J T (1818-1848) Danish					
wc/d	1	1,077		1,077	
LUNDBYE, Johan Thomas (1818-1848) Danish					
oil	5	83,072	2,194	10,161	38,103
wc/d	2	2,780	1,288	1,390	1,492
LUNDE, Anders (1809-1886) Danish					
oil	3	6,561	1,430	1,765	3,366
LUNDEBERG, Helen (1908-) American					
oil	1	3,000		3,000	
LUNDEGARD, Justus (1860-1924) Swedish					
oil	1	1,440		1,440	
LUNDENS, Gerrit (1622-1677) Dutch					
oil	1	18,857		18,857	
LUNDGREN, Egron Sillif (1815-1875) Swedish					
oil	4	19,337	1,087	3,249	11,752
wc/d	4	8,069	1,136	1,914	3,105
LUNDGREN, Tyra (1897-1979) Swedish					
3D	1	1,507		1,507	
oil	1	2,451		2,451	
LUNDGREN, Vilgodt (1849-1911) Swedish					
oil	1	2,747		2,747	
LUNDH, Theodor (1812-1896) Swedish					
oil	1	4,554		4,554	
LUNDMARK, Leon (1875-?) American					
oil	1	1,100		1,100	
LUNDQUIST, Evert (1904-1994) Swedish					
oil	40	259,535	1,104	3,718	33,665
LUNDQVIST, John (1882-1972) Swedish					
3D	1	7,990		7,990	
LUNDSTROM, Knut (1892-1945) Swedish					
oil	2	27,077	1,806	13,539	25,271
LUNDSTROM, Vilhelm (1893-1950) Danish					
oil	7	118,753	3,587	17,471	34,867
LUNIOT, Edmond-Louis (1851-?) French					
oil	1	1,687		1,687	
LUNS, Huib (1881-1942) Dutch					
oil	1	1,171		1,171	
LUNY, T (1759-1837) British					
oil	1	2,044		2,044	
LUNY, Thomas (1759-1837) British					
oil	14	168,380	2,709	7,791	37,180
LUPERTZ, Markus (1941-) Czechoslovakian					
3D	2	38,494	14,706	19,247	23,788
oil	5	43,518	1,363	1,942	32,439
wc/d	7	22,627	1,122	3,233	6,040
LUPIANEZ Y CARRASCO, Jose (1864-1933) Spanish					
oil	2	6,759	3,020	3,380	3,739
LUPIANEZ, Jose (?) Spanish					
oil	2	2,810	1,405	1,405	1,405
LUPO, Alessandro (1876-1953) Italian					
oil	7	45,511	1,017	3,515	18,455
LUPPEN, Gerard Josef Adrian van (1834-1891) Belgian					
oil	4	11,067	1,541	2,365	4,753
LURCAT, Andre (20th C) French?					
oil	1	7,040		7,040	

Name	No.	Total Sales Value	lowest	Prices median	highest
LURCAT, Jean (1892-1966) French					
oil	11	157,426	3,222	12,801	39,954
wc/d	9	26,588	1,463	2,394	5,343
LUSSENBURGH, Johannes (1889-1975) Dutch					
oil	1	1,807		1,807	
LUTHER, Adolf (1912-1990) German					
3D	5	13,368	1,311	2,524	5,190
LUTHER, Adolf and UECKER, Gunter (20th C) German					
3D	1	11,821		11,821	
LUTHI, Urs (1947-) Swiss					
oil	1	1,894		1,894	
LUTHY, Oskar Wilhelm (1882-1945) Swiss					
oil	2	4,715	1,473	2,358	3,242
LUTI, Benedetto (1666-1724) Italian					
oil	1	5,875		5,875	
wc/d	4	292,599	8,039	42,280	200,000
LUTKEN, Mathias (1841-1905) Danish					
oil	1	1,016		1,016	
LUTSCHER, Fernand (19th C) French					
oil	1	5,848		5,848	
LUTTEROTH, Ascan (1842-1923) German					
oil	4	11,334	1,366	2,546	4,877
LUTTICHUYS, Isaak (1616-1673) Dutch					
oil	1	6,772		6,772	
LUTTICHUYS, Simon (1610-1662) Dutch					
oil	2	236,097	22,727	118,049	213,370
LUTYENS, Charles Augustus Henry (1829-1915) British					
oil	5	10,099	1,184	1,350	4,290
LUTZ, Rudolf (1895-1955) German					
oil	1	2,056		2,056	
LUXARDO, Lazzaro (1865-1949) Italian					
oil	1	1,028		1,028	
LUXORO, Tammar (1825-1899) Italian					
oil	1	5,273		5,273	
LUYKEN, Jan (1649-1712) Dutch					
wc/d	3	6,678	1,571	1,964	3,143
LUYKX, Christiaan (1623-c.1653) Flemish					
oil	1	24,000		24,000	
LUYT, A (20th C) Dutch					
oil	1	1,782		1,782	
LUYTEN, Henri (1859-1945) Belgian					
oil	3	5,762	1,103	1,800	2,859
LUZRO, A (19th C) Italian					
wc/d	1	1,057		1,057	
LUZURIAGA, Juan Ramon (1938-) Spanish					
oil	7	7,722	1,006	1,068	1,398
LUZZO, Anthony (1855-1907) Italian?					
wc/d	1	1,716		1,716	
LYALL, Laura Adeline (1860-1930) Canadian					
oil	1	2,522		2,522	
LYBAERT, T M F (1848-1927) Belgian					
oil	1	1,191		1,191	
LYBAERT, Theophile Marie Françoise (1848-1927) Belgian					
oil	1	6,028		6,028	
LYLE, David (19th C) British					
oil	1	4,560		4,560	
LYMAN, John Goodwin (1886-1967) Canadian					
oil	5	10,826	1,599	2,079	2,762
wc/d	2	3,859	1,007	1,930	2,852

Name	No.	Total Sales Value	lowest	Prices median	highest
LYMBURNER, Francis (1916-1972) Australian					
oil	1	1,343		1,343	
LYNAS-GRAY, John Abernethy (1869-?) British					
wc/d	1	1,812		1,812	
LYNCH, Albert (1851-?) Peruvian					
oil	4	104,631	1,831	23,900	55,000
wc/d	1	2,979		2,979	
LYNCH, O (20th C) French					
oil	1	1,869		1,869	
LYNDE, Raymond (?) British?					
oil	2	19,832	4,736	9,916	15,096
LYNE, Michael (1912-1989) British					
oil	4	33,167	1,027	6,450	19,240
LYNEN, Amedee (1852-1938) Belgian					
oil	1	2,426		2,426	
LYNN, John (fl.1826-1838) British					
oil	4	103,150	9,000	28,955	36,240
LYNTON, Henry S (19/20th C) British					
oil	1	1,034		1,034	
LYON, C de (?-1574) Flemish					
oil	1	1,251		1,251	
LYON, Harold (1930-) Canadian					
oil	1	1,698		1,698	
LYON, John Howard (?-1921) British					
oil	2	5,619	2,115	2,810	3,504
LYRE, Adolphe la (1850-1935) French					
oil	5	60,741	1,309	2,791	47,878
LYSENKO, Andrei (1916-) Russian					
oil	2	3,161	1,250	1,581	1,911
LYTENS, Gysbrecht (17th C) Flemish					
oil	2	55,391	4,320	27,696	51,071
LYTH, Harald (1937-) Swedish					
oil	1	1,104		1,104	
wc/d	1	7,863		7,863	
LYTRAS, Nicolas (1883-1927) Greek					
oil	1	51,100		51,100	
LYTZEN, Niels Aagaard (1826-1890) Danish					
oil	1	2,628		2,628	
MA TSE LIN (20th C) ?					
wc/d	1	1,654		1,654	
MAAR, Dora (1909-1997) French					
oil	1	1,329		1,329	
MAAREL, Marinus van der (1857-1921) Dutch					
oil	2	8,716	2,216	4,358	6,500
MAAS MOSEN, Nancy (20th C) American					
oil	1	2,072		2,072	
MAAS, Christian (1951-) ?					
3D	2	3,406	1,065	1,703	2,341
MAAS, Dirck (1659-1717) Dutch					
oil	2	28,317	5,317	14,159	23,000
MAAS, Ernst (1904-1971) Swiss					
oil	1	2,013		2,013	
MAAS, Harry (1906-) Dutch					
oil	4	9,682	1,149	2,116	4,302
MAAS, Paul (1890-1962) Belgian					
oil	6	10,267	1,222	1,634	2,568
wc/d	1	1,065		1,065	
MAASS, David (20th C) American					
oil	2	31,000	15,000	15,500	16,000

Name	No.	Total Sales Value	lowest	Prices median	highest
MAASS, Johann Gottfried (19th C) German					
oil	1	2,255		2,255	
MAATEN, Jacob Jan van der (1820-1879) Dutch					
oil	3	42,310	4,293	16,069	21,948
MAATSCH, Thilo (1900-1983) German					
oil	1	1,992		1,992	
MACALA, Abel (?) South African					
3D	1	1,185		1,185	
MACALLUM, Hamilton (1841-1896) British					
oil	3	15,319	2,774	4,089	8,456
wc/d	1	1,115		1,115	
MACARA, Andrew (1944-) British					
oil	3	4,067	1,185	1,422	1,460
MACARRON, Ricardo (1926-) Spanish					
oil	1	1,505		1,505	
MACAVOY, Edouard (1905-1991) French					
oil	2	3,852	1,567	1,926	2,285
MACBETH, Robert Walker (1848-1910) British					
oil	2	4,141	1,441	2,071	2,700
MACBETH-RAEBURN, Henry (1860-1947) British					
oil	1	1,264		1,264	
MACBRIDE, William (1856-1913) British					
oil	2	10,541	1,001	5,271	9,540
MACBRYDE, Robert (1913-1966) British					
oil	1	9,425		9,425	
MACCABE, Gladys (1918-) Irish					
oil	4	9,035	1,015	1,994	4,032
MACCARI, Mino (1898-1989) Italian					
oil	19	76,464	1,396	3,273	9,384
wc/d	2	3,821	1,447	1,911	2,374
MACCHIATI, Serafino (1860-1916) Italian					
oil	21	61,361	1,070	2,676	6,689
wc/d	1	2,230		2,230	
MACCIO, Romulo (1931-) Argentinian					
oil	3	46,000	12,000	15,000	19,000
MACCO, Georg (1863-1933) German					
oil	4	19,087	1,823	5,281	6,702
MACDONALD, Arthur (fl.1897-1940) British					
wc/d	1	1,480		1,480	
MACDONALD, J E H (1873-1932) Canadian					
oil	3	38,589	6,711	10,067	21,811
MACDONALD, J Tim (19/20th C) British					
wc/d	2	3,848	1,628	1,924	2,220
MACDONALD, James Edward Hervey (1873-1932) Canadian					
oil	21	220,440	2,257	7,300	51,171
wc/d	1	2,239		2,239	
MACDONALD, James W G (1897-1960) Canadian					
oil	2	8,849	2,349	4,425	6,500
MACDONALD, John Blake (1829-1901) British					
oil	2	7,880	1,016	3,940	6,864
MACDONALD, Manly Edward (1889-1971) Canadian					
oil	6	14,144	1,219	2,185	4,474
MACDONALD, R (20th C) American					
3D	1	1,700		1,700	
MACDONALD, Richard (20th C) British					
oil	1	1,573		1,573	
MACDONALD, W Alister (fl.1893-1910) British					
wc/d	3	3,709	1,144	1,144	1,342

Name	No.	Total Sales Value	lowest	Prices median	highest
MACDONALD-WRIGHT, Stanton (1890-1973) American					
oil	2	20,500	7,500	10,250	13,000
wc/d	2	10,700	4,200	5,350	6,500
MACE, John Edmund (1889-?) British					
oil	2	3,854	1,014	1,927	2,840
MACGEORGE, William Stewart (1861-1931) British					
oil	5	198,336	8,216	39,150	90,520
MACGINNIS, Robert E (1926-) American					
oil	2	6,200	1,700	3,100	4,500
wc/d	2	15,500	6,500	7,750	9,000
MACGOUN, Hannah C Preston (1864-1913) British					
wc/d	1	2,132		2,132	
MACGREGOR, Harry (fl.1894-1934) British					
oil	2	6,842	1,622	3,421	5,220
MACH, David (1956-) British					
3D	1	7,248		7,248	
wc/d	1	1,200		1,200	
MACHARD, Jules Louis (1839-1900) French					
oil	2	11,290	4,290	5,645	7,000
wc/d	1	2,060		2,060	
MACHELL, Reginald (fl.1881-1900) British					
oil	1	4,424		4,424	
MACHEN, William H (1832-1911) American					
oil	3	4,600	1,200	1,200	2,200
MACHEREN, Philip van (17th C) Dutch					
oil	1	10,800		10,800	
MACHOLD, Jorge (1940-) German					
3D	1	2,472		2,472	
MACINTOSH, John Macintosh (1847-1913) British					
oil	1	1,399		1,399	
MACINTYRE, James (1926-) British					
wc/d	3	4,724	1,570	1,570	1,584
MACK, Heinz (1931-) German					
3D	7	26,310	1,282	2,618	8,192
oil	1	38,926		38,926	
MACKAY, Thomas (19/20th C) British					
wc/d	2	4,064	1,776	2,032	2,288
MACKE, August (1887-1914) German					
oil	5	4,762,232	16,088	230,400	3,744,000
wc/d	6	141,224	4,500	13,804	65,988
MACKE, Helmuth (1891-1936) German					
wc/d	2	4,013	1,877	2,007	2,136
MACKELDEY, Karl Bernhard (1826-1890) German					
wc/d	1	2,336		2,336	
MACKENNAL, Sir Edgar Bertram (1863-1931) Australian					
3D	1	4,228		4,228	
MACKENSEN, Fritz (1866-?) German					
oil	2	8,409	2,045	4,205	6,364
wc/d	2	5,365	2,195	2,683	3,170
MACKENZIE, Alexander (1923-) British					
oil	3	18,652	1,872	5,530	11,250
MACKENZIE, Frederick (1787-1854) British					
wc/d	1	1,580		1,580	
MACKENZIE, J Hamilton (1875-1926) British					
oil	1	1,441		1,441	
MACKENZIE, Marie Henrie (1878-1961) Dutch					
oil	3	15,679	3,442	4,087	8,150
wc/d	1	1,416		1,416	
MACKENZIE, William G (?-1925) British					
oil	1	3,021		3,021	

Name	No.	Total Sales Value	lowest	Prices median	highest
MACKEPRANG, Adolf (1833-1911) Danish					
oil	8	43,090	1,454	2,364	17,872
MACKIE, Charles H (1862-1920) British					
oil	2	5,667	1,752	2,834	3,915
wc/d	1	1,544		1,544	
MACKIE, Kathleen Isabella (1899-1996) Irish?					
oil	1	2,368		2,368	
MACKIE, Peter R M (1867-1959) British					
oil	2	6,525	2,465	3,263	4,060
MACKINTOSH, Charles Rennie (1868-1928) British					
wc/d	3	45,260	5,840	17,520	21,900
MACKLOTH, Johann (fl.1876-1894) Austrian?					
oil	1	1,308		1,308	
MACKNIGHT, Dodge (1860-1950) American					
wc/d	1	2,600		2,600	
MACKOWIAK, Erwin (1926-) Belgian					
oil	2	2,902	1,231	1,451	1,671
MACKRILL, Martyn (1961-) British					
oil	2	47,996	8,476	23,998	39,520
wc/d	5	19,000	2,002	3,423	6,683
MACLAREN, Walter (fl.1869-1893) British					
oil	2	8,333	4,105	4,167	4,228
MACLEAY, McNeil (19th C) British					
oil	2	6,844	1,314	3,422	5,530
MACLEOD, Pegi Nichol (1904-1949) Canadian					
oil	1	7,300		7,300	
MACLET, Elisee (1881-1962) French					
oil	54	204,891	1,018	3,798	15,711
wc/d	1	1,591		1,591	
MACLISE, Daniel (1806-1870) British/Irish					
wc/d	1	2,960		2,960	
MACMASTER (19th C) British					
oil	1	3,400		3,400	
MACMIADHACHAIN, Padraig (20th C) Irish					
oil	2	2,515	1,065	1,258	1,450
MACMONNIES, Frederick William (1863-1937) American					
3D	3	133,500	8,500	15,000	110,000
oil	1	22,000		22,000	
MACMONNIES, Mary Fairchild (1858-1946) American					
oil	1	1,600		1,600	
MACNAB, Peter (?-1900) British					
oil	2	7,100	1,988	3,550	5,112
MACNEE, Robert Russell (1880-1952) British					
oil	3	14,753	1,359	3,969	9,425
MACNEIL, Hermon Atkins (1866-1947) American					
3D	1	50,000		50,000	
MACOUILLARD, Louis (1913-1987) American					
wc/d	1	2,500		2,500	
MACPHERSON, John and FAULKNER, John (19th C) British					
wc/d	1	3,900		3,900	
MACQUOID, Percy (1852-1925) British					
wc/d	1	1,106		1,106	
MACQUOID, Thomas (1820-1912) British					
wc/d	2	5,944	1,492	2,972	4,452
MACRAE, Elmer (1875-1953) American					
oil	1	4,000		4,000	
wc/d	1	1,700		1,700	
MACRAE, Emma Fordyce (1887-1974) American					
oil	2	8,200	1,700	4,100	6,500

Name	No.	Total Sales Value	Prices lowest	median	highest
MACREAU, Michel (1935-) French					
oil	3	6,032	1,615	1,928	2,489
MACRITCHIE, Alexina (fl.1885-1932) British					
wc/d	1	1,667		1,667	
MACTAGGART, Sir William (1903-1981) British					
oil	7	57,901	4,380	6,174	17,064
MACWHIRTER, John (1839-1911) British					
oil	8	55,026	2,198	7,034	10,950
wc/d	3	4,039	1,264	1,275	1,500
MACY, William Ferdinand (1852-1901) American					
oil	1	2,900		2,900	
MACY, William Starbuck (1853-1945) American					
oil	1	6,000		6,000	
MADDOX, Conroy (1912-) British					
oil	1	2,852		2,852	
MADELAIN, G (1867-1944) French					
oil	2	4,896	2,051	2,448	2,845
MADELAIN, Gustave (1867-1944) French					
oil	10	22,495	1,318	2,004	3,990
MADELINE, Paul (1863-1920) French					
oil	15	94,499	2,166	4,753	26,185
MADER, Karin (1910-1973) Dutch					
oil	1	1,585		1,585	
MADIOL, Adrien Jean (1845-1892) Dutch					
oil	2	5,767	1,167	2,884	4,600
MADOU, Jean Baptiste (1796-1877) Belgian					
oil	2	14,892	3,192	7,446	11,700
MADRASSI, Luca (1848-1919) Italian					
3D	3	9,368	1,418	1,450	6,500
MADRASSI, Ludovic Lucien (1881-1956) French					
oil	1	2,835		2,835	
MADRAZO Y GARRETA, Raimundo de (1841-1920) Spanish					
oil	12	915,273	2,184	23,806	250,000
MADRAZO Y GARRETA, Ricardo de (1852-1917) Spanish					
oil	1	97,790		97,790	
MADRID SCHOOL, 17th C Spanish					
oil	2	8,437	3,260	4,219	5,177
MADRIGALI, Olynthe (20th C) ?					
oil	1	2,204		2,204	
MADSEN, A P (1822-1911) Danish					
oil	1	1,140		1,140	
MADSEN, C F (19/20th C) Danish					
oil	1	1,020		1,020	
MADSEN, Otto (1882-) American					
oil	1	1,400		1,400	
MADYOL, Jacques (1871-1950) Belgian					
oil	4	10,950	1,019	1,852	6,228
MAEDA, Josaku (1926-) Japanese					
oil	2	13,410	4,350	6,705	9,060
MAEDA, Seison (1885-1977) Japanese					
wc/d	2	760,000	280,000	380,000	480,000
MAEGHT, Jos de (1865-1954) Belgian					
3D	1	1,668		1,668	
MAELLA, Mariano Salvador de (1739-1819) Spanish					
oil	2	58,537	11,396	29,269	47,141
wc/d	2	5,525	1,582	2,763	3,943
MAENTEL, Jacob (1763-1863) American					
wc/d	1	29,000		29,000	

Name	No.	Total Sales Value	lowest	Prices median	highest
MAERTENS, Medard (1875-1940) Belgian					
oil	1	1,585		1,585	
wc/d	1	1,171		1,171	
MAES, Eugène Remy (1849-1931) Belgian					
oil	2	7,971	1,725	3,986	6,246
MAES, Godfried (1649-1700) Flemish					
wc/d	1	1,375		1,375	
MAES, Henri (19th C) Belgian					
oil	1	1,000		1,000	
MAES, Jacques (1905-1968) Belgian					
oil	1	1,030		1,030	
MAES, Jan (1876-1974) Belgian					
oil	1	1,459		1,459	
MAES, Jan Baptist Lodewyck (1794-1856) Flemish					
oil	2	26,820	8,700	13,410	18,120
MAES, Nicolaes (1632-1693) Dutch					
oil	11	165,756	1,702	5,507	100,000
wc/d	1	7,857		7,857	
MAES, Nicolaes (school) (1632-1693) Dutch					
oil	1	17,830		17,830	
MAESMIEZ, G (?) ?					
oil	1	1,450		1,450	
MAESTOSI, F (19th C?) Italian					
oil	1	11,325		11,325	
MAESTRI, Michelangelo (?-1812) Italian					
oil	1	2,799		2,799	
wc/d	4	33,523	2,820	4,275	21,980
MAETA, Kanji (1896-1930) Japanese					
oil	1	95,000		95,000	
MAETERLINCK, L (1846-1926) Belgian					
oil	1	3,630		3,630	
MAETZEL, Emil (1877-1955) German					
wc/d	1	1,845		1,845	
MAETZEL-JOHANNSEN, Dorothea (1886-1930) German					
oil	1	1,319		1,319	
MAEZTU, Gustavo de (1887-1947) Spanish					
oil	3	35,066	7,244	9,555	18,267
wc/d	1	1,355		1,355	
MAFAI, Antonietta Raphael (1900-1975) Italian					
3D	1	6,028		6,028	
MAFAI, Mario (1902-1965) Italian					
oil	2	19,387	9,002	9,694	10,385
wc/d	2	3,353	1,553	1,677	1,800
MAGAFAN, Ethel (1916-) American					
oil	1	1,800		1,800	
MAGANZA, Alessandro (1556-1630) Italian					
wc/d	1	4,530		4,530	
MAGAZZINI, Salvatore (1955-) Italian					
oil	3	3,759	1,017	1,336	1,406
MAGGI, Cesare (1881-1961) Italian					
oil	10	91,224	1,098	7,871	21,957
MAGGIONE, Piero (1931-1995) Italian					
oil	1	1,359		1,359	
wc/d	1	2,241		2,241	
MAGGIORANI, Luigi (19th C) Italian					
wc/d	1	1,122		1,122	
MAGGIOTTO, Domenico (1713-1794) Italian					
oil	2	18,312	6,792	9,156	11,520
MAGGIOTTO, Francesco (1750-1805) Italian					
oil	1	3,857		3,857	

Name	No.	Total Sales Value	Prices lowest	median	highest
MAGGS, John Charles (1819-1896) British					
oil	6	24,058	1,400	3,449	7,172
MAGNASCO, Alessandro (1667-1749) Italian					
oil	7	294,956	4,604	31,720	140,000
wc/d	1	9,815		9,815	
MAGNASCO, Alessandro and PERUZZINI, Anton Francesco (17/18th C) Italian					
oil	2	109,702	48,320	54,851	61,382
MAGNASCO, Stefano (1635-1681) Italian					
oil	1	15,700		15,700	
MAGNE, Desire Alfred (1855-1936) French					
oil	3	9,937	1,092	4,495	4,495
MAGNELLI, Alberto (1888-1971) Italian					
oil	3	82,562	6,327	25,485	50,750
wc/d	13	81,386	1,159	5,624	11,929
MAGNI, Giuseppe (1869-1956) Italian					
oil	1	2,172		2,172	
MAGNI, Pietro (1816-1877) Italian					
3D	1	105,700		105,700	
MAGNIN, Pierre (20th C) French?					
oil	1	1,311		1,311	
MAGNUS, Camille (1850-?) French					
oil	6	15,378	1,329	2,260	4,283
MAGRITTE, René (1898-1967) Belgian					
3D	1	232,000		232,000	
oil	10	6,988,800	286,900	546,700	1,800,000
wc/d	18	2,412,536	1,661	82,375	700,000
MAGUIRE, Cecil (20th C) British					
oil	7	20,562	1,233	3,454	4,710
MAGUIRE, Robert (1921-) American					
oil	3	5,000	1,200	1,500	2,300
MAHLKNECHT, Edmund (1820-1903) Austrian					
oil	1	3,993		3,993	
MAHN, Richard (1866-?) German					
oil	3	3,978	1,151	1,151	1,676
MAHONEY, James Owen (1907-1987) American					
oil	1	2,000		2,000	
MAHU, Cornelis (1613-1689) Flemish					
oil	3	210,460	4,082	95,543	110,835
MAHU, Victor (?-1700) Flemish					
oil	1	11,760		11,760	
MAI THU (1906-1980) Vietnamese					
oil	1	9,118		9,118	
wc/d	1	8,933		8,933	
MAI-THU (20th C) ?					
wc/d	3	3,943	1,056	1,197	1,690
MAIDMENT, Henry (19/20th C) British					
oil	8	13,155	1,144	1,630	2,840
MAIDMENT, T (1871-?) British					
wc/d	1	3,002		3,002	
MAIGRET, Jacobus Adrianus (1812-1893) Dutch					
oil	1	2,107		2,107	
MAILLARD, Émile (1846-?) French					
oil	2	7,850	3,600	3,925	4,250
MAILLART, Diogene Ulysse Napoleon (1840-1926) French					
oil	3	11,538	2,016	3,412	6,110
MAILLAUD, Fernand (1863-1948) French					
oil	13	31,582	1,088	2,037	4,655
MAILLOL, Aristide (1861-1944) French					
3D	21	7,601,101	12,000	57,500	2,800,000
wc/d	22	175,266	2,271	4,848	33,390

Name	No.	Total Sales Value	lowest	Prices median	highest
MAINCENT, Gustave (1850-1887) French					
oil	2	5,158	1,063	2,579	4,095
MAINELLA, Raffaele (1858-1907) Italian					
oil	1	1,399		1,399	
wc/d	1	1,030		1,030	
MAINERI, Giovanni Francesco (15th C) Italian					
oil	1	95,000		95,000	
MAINOLFI, Luigi (1948-) Italian					
3D	3	15,603	1,571	1,833	12,199
MAINSSIEUX, Lucien (1885-1958) French					
oil	1	1,422		1,422	
MAINZ, Paul Meyer (?) ?					
oil	1	1,442		1,442	
MAIRAGHI, Clemente (1889-1962) Italian					
oil	1	1,845		1,845	
MAIRE, Andre (1898-1985) French					
oil	1	1,037		1,037	
wc/d	4	6,237	1,365	1,413	2,047
MAIROVICH, Zvi (1911-1973) Israeli					
oil	5	7,300	1,000	1,600	1,800
wc/d	4	14,400	1,800	2,800	7,000
MAISTRE, Louis (1862-?) French					
wc/d	1	3,778		3,778	
MAISTRE, Roy de (1894-1968) Australian					
oil	3	15,742	1,998	3,976	9,768
MAITLAND, Paul (1869-1909) British					
oil	5	48,606	6,952	8,520	13,395
MAJOR, Ernest (1864-1935) American					
oil	1	7,000		7,000	
MAJOR, Henry A (fl.1859-1873) British					
oil	1	4,228		4,228	
MAJOR, Theodore (1908-) British					
oil	1	3,575		3,575	
MAJOREL, Fernand (1898-1965) French					
oil	1	1,103		1,103	
MAJORELLE, J (20th C) French					
oil	1	7,733		7,733	
MAJORELLE, Jacques (1886-1962) French					
oil	8	201,462	4,124	21,782	56,709
wc/d	12	538,076	4,932	30,288	220,438
MAKAROV, Ivan Kozmich (1822-1897) Russian					
oil	1	7,248		7,248	
MAKART, Hans (1840-1884) Austrian					
oil	6	317,816	3,303	18,004	223,200
wc/d	1	11,192		11,192	
MAKELA, Jukka (1949-) Finnish					
oil	1	1,613		1,613	
MAKELA, Marika (1947-) Finnish					
oil	1	2,880		2,880	
MAKOBYKYN, K H (19th C) ?					
oil	1	1,669		1,669	
MAKOKIAN, Vartan (1869-1937) Armenian					
oil	2	4,856	2,200	2,428	2,656
MAKOVSKY, Konstantin (1839-1915) Russian					
oil	12	413,174	3,102	16,815	107,160
wc/d	3	13,265	2,265	3,950	7,050
MAKOVSKY, Vladimir (1846-1920) Russian					
oil	4	62,220	1,200	13,590	33,840
wc/d	6	36,023	1,128	5,176	11,280

Name	No.	Total Sales Value	Prices lowest	median	highest
MAKOWSKI, Tade (1882-1932) Polish					
oil	1	8,106		8,106	
wc/d	1	14,216		14,216	
MAKS, Cornelis Johannes (1876-1967) Dutch					
oil	7	81,657	3,763	10,299	29,709
wc/d	3	11,687	2,052	3,169	6,466
MAKSIMOV, Vasili Maksimovich (1844-1911) Russian					
oil	1	1,963		1,963	
MALACREA, Francesco (1812-1886) Italian					
oil	2	6,915	3,338	3,458	3,577
MALAGOLI, Francesco (18th C) Italian					
oil	1	28,260		28,260	
MALANCA, Jose (1897-1967) Argentinian					
oil	1	3,200		3,200	
MALATESTA, Adeodato (1806-1891) Italian					
oil	1	17,138		17,138	
MALAVAL, Robert (1937-1980) French					
3D	2	18,385	5,418	9,193	12,967
oil	7	12,936	1,092	1,440	4,504
wc/d	6	12,485	1,028	1,409	5,841
MALBON, William (1805-1877) British					
oil	3	11,966	1,074	3,456	7,436
MALCHAIR, John Baptiste (1731-1817) British					
wc/d	13	53,152	1,359	2,718	13,590
MALCZEWSKI, Rafal (1892-1965) Polish					
oil	3	4,548	1,445	1,445	1,634
MALDARELLI, Federico (1826-1893) Italian					
oil	1	13,453		13,453	
MALDONADO, Manuel (20th C) Italian?					
oil	1	2,332		2,332	
MALEAS, Constantine (1879-1928) Greek					
oil	1	13,140		13,140	
MALEHERBE, William (1884-1952) French					
oil	1	1,900		1,900	
MALERMAN, Josef (1908-) German?					
oil	1	1,365		1,365	
MALESCI, Giovanni (1884-1969) Italian					
oil	2	3,529	1,236	1,765	2,293
MALESPINA, Louis Ferdinand (1874-1940) French					
oil	5	10,370	1,405	1,663	3,793
MALET, Albert (1905-1986) French					
oil	7	11,809	1,233	1,619	2,197
MALEVICH, Kasimir (1878-1935) Russian					
oil	1	15,500,000		15,500,000	
wc/d	2	94,533	30,000	47,267	64,533
MALFAIT, Hubert (1898-1971) Belgian					
oil	6	56,546	1,567	8,514	19,815
wc/d	1	1,903		1,903	
MALFRAY, Charles Alexandre (1887-1940) French					
3D	1	7,040		7,040	
MALFROY (19/20th C) French					
oil	1	3,549		3,549	
MALFROY, Charles (1862-1918) French					
oil	1	3,588		3,588	
MALFROY, Henry (1895-1944) French					
oil	8	21,336	1,287	2,561	4,097
MALGATI, A (19th C) Italian					
3D	1	2,117		2,117	
MALHERBE, William (1884-1951) French					
oil	7	14,499	1,282	1,800	3,365

Name	No.	Total Sales Value	lowest	Prices median	highest
MALI SCHOOL					
3D	1	31,824		31,824	
MALI, Christian (1832-1906) German					
oil	8	74,143	2,248	7,920	21,895
MALIAVINE, Philippe (1869-1940) Russian					
oil	5	102,199	3,899	6,500	67,680
wc/d	14	51,237	1,208	3,525	9,870
MALINCONICO, Nicola (1654-1721) Italian					
oil	1	16,048		16,048	
MALINOWSKY, Lise (1957-) Danish					
oil	3	4,798	1,192	1,412	2,194
MALIOUTIN, Serge (1859-1937) Russian					
oil	1	4,228		4,228	
MALISSARD, Georges (1877-1942) French					
3D	3	13,762	2,826	3,871	7,065
MALKINE, Georges (1898-1970) French					
oil	1	35,218		35,218	
MALKOWSKY, Heiner (1920-1988) German					
oil	1	4,037		4,037	
wc/d	1	1,413		1,413	
MALLE, Charles (1935-) French					
oil	8	12,766	1,141	1,194	3,327
MALLEBRANCHE (1790-1838) French					
oil	1	2,182		2,182	
MALLEBRANCHE, Louis-Claude (1790-1838) French					
oil	4	9,856	1,298	2,674	3,210
MALLET, Jean Baptiste (1759-1835) French					
oil	4	25,289	4,424	6,508	7,850
wc/d	3	33,724	2,702	9,022	22,000
MALLINA, Erich (1873-1954) Austrian					
wc/d	1	2,458		2,458	
MALLO, Cristino (1905-) Spanish?					
3D	1	7,550		7,550	
MALLOL SUAZO, Josep M (1910-1986) Spanish					
oil	5	26,523	1,858	2,384	13,938
MALMSTROM, August (1829-1901) Swedish					
oil	2	19,207	2,277	9,604	16,930
MALONEY, Martin (1961-C) British					
oil	1	3,775		3,775	
MALPIERI, T (19/20th C) Italian					
3D	1	1,600		1,600	
MALSKAT, Lothar (1913-1988) German					
wc/d	1	3,901		3,901	
MALTA, Eduardo (20th C) American?					
oil	1	1,337		1,337	
MALTESE SCHOOL, 19th C					
oil	1	3,750		3,750	
MALTESE, Jean Pierre (1946-) French					
oil	1	2,487		2,487	
MALTON, Thomas (jnr) (1748-1804) British					
wc/d	1	1,776		1,776	
MALVA (?) ?					
oil	1	2,000		2,000	
MAMBOR, Renato (1936-) Italian					
wc/d	1	1,688		1,688	
MAMBOUR, Auguste (1896-1968) Belgian					
oil	7	65,778	2,674	8,207	25,509
wc/d	4	5,672	1,266	1,299	1,797

Name	No.	Total Sales Value	lowest	Prices median	highest
MAMMEN, Jeanne (1890-1976) German					
wc/d	4	93,600	15,840	23,040	31,680
MAMPASO, Manuel (1924-) Spanish					
oil	1	1,479		1,479	
MAMVURA, A N (20th C) ?					
3D	1	1,179		1,179	
MAN-RAY (1890-1976) American					
3D	19	336,871	1,888	3,879	210,250
oil	5	600,632	30,000	43,500	391,500
wc/d	12	161,276	2,900	5,451	55,100
MANAGO (20th C) French					
oil	1	2,962		2,962	
MANAGO, Vincent (1880-1936) French					
oil	5	10,668	1,300	2,363	2,466
MANAI, Piero (1951-1988) Italian					
wc/d	1	1,516		1,516	
MANANOS, Asterio (1861-1935) Spanish					
oil	1	4,052		4,052	
MANARA, Horace de (1802-?) Italian					
oil	1	5,569		5,569	
MANARESI, Ugo (1851-1917) Italian					
oil	2	4,577	1,275	2,289	3,302
MANCADAN, Jacobus Sibrandi (1602-1680) Dutch					
oil	1	24,160		24,160	
wc/d	1	1,963		1,963	
MANCINI, Antonio (1852-1930) Italian					
oil	9	268,247	2,400	31,281	59,614
wc/d	2	4,201	1,201	2,101	3,000
MANCINI, Carlo (1829-1910) Italian					
oil	1	5,236		5,236	
MANCINI, F (18/19th C) Italian					
oil	1	2,000		2,000	
MANCINI, Francesco (18/19th C) Italian					
oil	3	15,668	1,835	1,908	11,925
wc/d	1	3,761		3,761	
MANCINI, Francesco (1829-1905) Italian					
oil	1	2,800		2,800	
MANCOBA, Sonja Ferlov (1911-1984) Danish					
3D	4	21,607	2,375	4,998	9,237
MANDELBERG, Johan Edvard (1730-1786) Danish					
oil	1	11,287		11,287	
MANDER, W H (fl.1880-1922) British					
oil	1	2,686		2,686	
MANDER, William Henry (fl.1880-1922) British					
oil	8	42,304	1,278	5,012	12,155
MANDL, Franz Xaver (1800-?) German					
oil	1	1,162		1,162	
MANDL, Josef (1874-?) German					
oil	6	12,800	1,266	1,477	5,626
MANDRUP, Peter (1949-) Danish					
oil	2	2,562	1,025	1,281	1,537
MANE KATZ (1894-1962) French					
3D	2	6,058	2,741	3,029	3,317
oil	32	425,173	1,693	9,280	65,000
wc/d	8	18,866	1,073	1,845	4,832
MANERA, Domenico (19th C) Italian					
3D	1	17,498		17,498	
MANERA, Enrico (1947-) Italian					
oil	2	2,713	1,248	1,357	1,465
wc/d	1	1,359		1,359	

Name	No.	Total Sales Value	lowest	Prices median	highest
MANES, Antonin (1784-1843) Czechoslovakian					
oil	1	9,470		9,470	
MANESSIER, Alfred (1911-1993) French					
oil	4	65,872	3,847	10,925	40,176
wc/d	3	8,317	1,355	1,510	5,452
MANET, Edouard (1832-1883) French					
oil	1	19,000,000		19,000,000	
wc/d	3	12,228	2,800	3,609	5,819
MANFREDI, Alberto (1930-) Italian					
oil	1	1,070		1,070	
MANGE, Joseph-Julien (1866-c.1935) French					
oil	2	4,144	1,910	2,072	2,234
MANGLARD, Adrien (1695-1760) French					
oil	2	285,300	45,300	142,650	240,000
wc/d	1	4,364		4,364	
MANGO, Leonardo (1843-?) Italian					
oil	1	32,221		32,221	
MANGOLD, Burkard (1873-1950) Swiss					
wc/d	1	1,096		1,096	
MANGOLD, Josef (1884-1942) German					
wc/d	1	1,853		1,853	
MANGOLD, Robert (1937-) American					
oil	3	54,800	3,800	11,000	40,000
wc/d	3	29,990	6,490	6,500	17,000
MANGOLD, Sylvia (1938-) American					
oil	1	7,000		7,000	
MANGUIN, Henri (1874-1949) French					
oil	18	486,472	2,208	21,621	60,755
wc/d	9	50,160	2,500	4,085	15,772
MANIRAKA, G Razana (19/20th C) ?					
oil	1	1,677		1,677	
MANKES, Jan (1889-1920) Dutch					
oil	3	214,302	51,724	75,431	87,147
MANLY, Eleanor E (fl.1875-1898) British					
oil	1	12,560		12,560	
MANN, Alexander (1853-1908) British					
oil	4	7,743	1,413	1,815	2,700
MANN, James Scrimgeour (1883-1946) British					
wc/d	1	1,575		1,575	
MANN, Joshua Hargrave Sams (?-1886) British					
oil	1	2,054		2,054	
MANNCHEN, Adolf (1860-1920) German					
wc/d	1	1,077		1,077	
MANNERS, William (fl.1885-c.1910) British					
oil	4	6,184	1,380	1,550	1,704
wc/d	6	11,714	1,022	1,904	2,698
MANNHEIM, Jean (1863-1945) American/German					
oil	5	18,700	1,100	3,250	7,500
MANNING, Westley (1868-1954) British					
oil	1	1,219		1,219	
MANNO, Francesco (1752-1831) Italian					
oil	1	16,610		16,610	
MANNUCCI, Cipriano (1882-1970) Italian					
oil	3	5,313	1,297	1,959	2,057
MANOLO (1872-1945) Spanish					
3D	9	25,820	1,846	2,951	3,992
wc/d	2	2,153	1,057	1,077	1,096
MANOYEZ, F (?) French					
oil	1	5,841		5,841	

Name	No.	Total Sales Value	lowest	Prices median	highest
MANRIQUE, Cesar (1920-1992) Spanish					
oil	1	8,604		8,604	
wc/d	2	7,334	3,432	3,667	3,902
MANSER, Albert (1937-) Swiss					
oil	3	6,984	2,124	2,236	2,624
MANSER, Josef (20th C) German					
oil	1	4,901		4,901	
MANSFELD, Josef (1819-1894) Austrian					
oil	4	11,065	1,600	2,400	4,665
MANSFIELD, Louise (1876-?) American					
oil	3	3,835	1,224	1,233	1,378
MANSHIP, Paul Howard (1885-1966) American					
3D	11	2,916,000	16,000	140,000	850,000
MANSKIRCH, Bernhard Gottfried (1736-1817) German					
oil	1	2,849		2,849	
MANSKIRCH, Franz Joseph (1770-1830) German					
oil	1	7,924		7,924	
MANSON, James Bolivar (1879-1945) British					
oil	3	9,704	2,400	2,880	4,424
MANSOUROFF, Paul (1896-1983) French					
oil	3	10,876	3,274	3,412	4,190
wc/d	1	1,068		1,068	
MANSSON, Per (1896-1949) Swedish					
oil	2	6,824	2,208	3,412	4,616
MANSUROFF, Pavel (1896-1984) Russian					
wc/d	1	1,476		1,476	
MANTEGAZZA, Giacomo (1853-1920) Italian					
oil	2	8,737	1,863	4,369	6,874
MANTEUFFEL, Julie (19th C) Swedish?					
oil	1	2,799		2,799	
MANTOVANI, Guido (1916-) Italian					
oil	1	2,799		2,799	
MANTUA SCHOOL, 16th C Italian					
oil	1	43,790		43,790	
wc/d	1	21,895		21,895	
MANTYNEN, Jussi (1886-1978) Finnish					
3D	4	11,356	2,173	2,554	4,051
MANUEL, Victor (1897-1969) Cuban					
oil	3	45,000	10,000	17,000	18,000
MANZ, Emil (1880-1945) German					
3D	1	1,667		1,667	
MANZANA-PISSARRO (1871-1961) French					
oil	1	5,500		5,500	
MANZANA-PISSARRO, Georges (1871-1961) French					
oil	3	20,104	2,493	6,509	11,102
wc/d	1	1,111		1,111	
MANZONE, Giuseppe (1887-1983) Italian					
oil	2	6,705	2,395	3,353	4,310
MANZONI, Piero (1933-1963) Italian					
3D	5	113,050	8,650	23,200	31,900
oil	2	116,730	31,214	58,365	85,516
wc/d	10	1,628,721	3,938	106,475	609,000
MANZU, Giacomo (1908-1991) Italian					
3D	6	946,200	23,000	98,600	551,000
wc/d	4	8,026	1,182	1,574	3,697
MANZUOLI, Tommaso D'Antonio (1536-1571) Italian					
wc/d	1	28,000		28,000	
MARA, Pol (1920-1998) Belgian					
oil	6	15,914	2,089	2,605	3,523
wc/d	1	1,906		1,906	

Name	No.	Total Sales Value	Prices lowest	median	highest
MARAIS, Adolphe Charles (1856-1940) French					
oil	3	31,914	2,114	2,800	27,000
MARAIS-MILTON, V (1872-1968) French					
oil	2	27,311	10,759	13,656	16,552
wc/d	1	5,565		5,565	
MARAIS-MILTON, Victor (1872-1968) French					
oil	7	90,846	5,598	9,300	35,750
MARANIELLO, Giuseppe (1945-) Italian					
3D	1	2,426		2,426	
wc/d	1	3,381		3,381	
MARANTA, Vincenzo (1871-1956) Italian					
oil	1	1,379		1,379	
MARASCO, Antonio (1886-1975) Italian					
oil	1	3,542		3,542	
MARASTONI, Giuseppe (1834-1895) Italian					
oil	1	2,592		2,592	
MARATTA, Carlo (1625-1713) Italian					
oil	3	851,780	1,780	250,000	600,000
wc/d	5	55,467	2,000	6,342	36,240
MARAZZANI, Agostino (1853-1914) Italian					
3D	1	4,530		4,530	
MARC, Franz (1880-1916) German					
3D	1	33,099		33,099	
oil	1	86,400		86,400	
wc/d	9	243,419	12,294	25,920	45,300
MARC, J A (?) French					
wc/d	1	1,179		1,179	
MARC, Jean Auguste (1818-1886) French					
wc/d	1	1,179		1,179	
MARC, Robert (1943-1993) French					
oil	3	14,082	4,423	4,699	4,960
MARC, Wilhelm (1839-1907) German					
oil	1	1,227		1,227	
MARCA-RELLI, Conrad (1913-2000) American					
oil	6	44,697	3,397	5,900	16,000
wc/d	1	2,000		2,000	
MARCED FURIO, Jose (1896-) Spanish					
oil	1	1,140		1,140	
MARCEL-BERONNEAU, Pierre Amedee (1869-1937) French					
oil	1	5,633		5,633	
MARCEL-CLEMENT, Amedee Julien (1873-?) French					
oil	4	42,386	1,008	7,957	25,464
wc/d	1	2,920		2,920	
MARCEL-LEBRUN (20th C) French					
oil	1	2,139		2,139	
MARCEL-LENOIR (1872-1931) French					
wc/d	1	1,329		1,329	
MARCELLI, Giorgio (19th C) Italian					
oil	1	12,400		12,400	
MARCETTE, Alexandre (1853-1929) Belgian					
oil	1	1,416		1,416	
MARCETTE, Henri (1824-1890) Belgian					
oil	1	1,044		1,044	
MARCH, Giovanni (1894-?) Tunisian					
oil	2	4,076	1,873	2,038	2,203
MARCHAIS DES GENTILS (19th C) French					
oil	1	4,308		4,308	
MARCHAND, A (1907-) French					
oil	1	2,812		2,812	

Name	No.	Total Sales Value	lowest	Prices median	highest
MARCHAND, Andre (1907-1998) French					
oil	12	28,232	1,033	2,286	4,064
wc/d	1	1,152		1,152	
MARCHAND, Jean Hippolyte (1883-1940) French					
oil	4	92,415	1,185	8,080	75,070
MARCHAND, John N (1875-1921) American					
oil	1	2,500		2,500	
MARCHANT, J (?) ?					
oil	1	1,027		1,027	
MARCHANT, Jean (1808-1864) Belgian					
oil	1	25,000		25,000	
MARCHES SCHOOL, 15th C Italian					
oil	1	27,720		27,720	
MARCHETTI, Ludovico (1853-1909) Italian					
wc/d	3	8,772	2,500	2,500	3,766
MARCHIGIAN SCHOOL, 15th C Italian					
oil	1	12,960		12,960	
MARCHIS, Domenico de (c.1655-c.1718) Italian					
oil	1	9,792		9,792	
MARCIUS-SIMONS, Pinky (1867-1909) American					
oil	1	4,567		4,567	
MARCKE DE LUMMEN, Émile van (1827-1890) French					
oil	3	10,107	2,000	3,607	4,500
MARCKE DE LUMMEN, Jean van (1875-1918) French					
wc/d	1	1,625		1,625	
MARCKE, van (19/20th C?) ?					
oil	1	5,565		5,565	
MARCKS, Alexander (1864-1909) German					
oil	1	6,500		6,500	
MARCKS, Gerhard (1889-1981) German					
3D	20	158,986	2,011	5,644	33,099
MARCLAY, Christian (20th C) American					
wc/d	1	6,000		6,000	
MARCOLA, Marco (1740-1793) Italian					
oil	1	4,153		4,153	
MARCOTTE, Marie Antoinette (1869-1929) French					
oil	1	1,122		1,122	
MARCOUSSIS, Louis (1883-1941) French					
oil	10	577,811	15,605	35,358	151,504
wc/d	2	5,775	1,425	2,888	4,350
MARCUS, Kaete Ephraim (1892-1970) Israeli					
3D	1	4,400		4,400	
oil	4	15,400	2,600	3,900	5,000
wc/d	1	1,200		1,200	
MARCUS, Otto (1863-?) German					
oil	1	4,924		4,924	
MARCUSE, Rudolf (1878-?) German					
3D	2	4,868	1,510	2,434	3,358
MARDEN, Brice (1938-) American					
oil	3	3,185,000	85,000	1,400,000	1,700,000
wc/d	5	254,000	22,000	38,000	100,000
MARE, Georges le (1866-1942) French					
wc/d	1	3,867		3,867	
MARECHAL, Charles (1801-1887) French					
oil	1	5,582		5,582	
MAREELS, Maurice (1893-1975) Belgian					
oil	1	1,050		1,050	
MAREES, Hans von (1837-1887) German					
oil	1	12,975		12,975	
wc/d	2	24,400	8,491	12,200	15,909

Name	No.	Total Sales Value	lowest	Prices median	highest
MAREMBERT, Jean (c.1900-1968) French					
oil	1	3,048		3,048	
wc/d	2	3,766	1,365	1,883	2,401
MARESCA, E (?) ?					
oil	1	3,180		3,180	
MAREVNA, Marie (1892-1984) Russian					
oil	4	88,361	2,343	3,009	80,000
MARFAING, Andre (1925-1987) French					
oil	12	50,802	1,031	4,237	7,765
wc/d	3	5,736	1,033	1,426	3,277
MARGANTIN, Louis (1900-) French					
oil	1	7,956		7,956	
MARGAT, Andre (1903-) French					
wc/d	3	4,583	1,237	1,298	2,048
MARGETSON, William Henry (1861-1940) British					
oil	1	5,500		5,500	
MARGETTS, Mary (fl.1841-1886) British					
wc/d	1	2,574		2,574	
MARGULIES, Joseph (1896-1984) American					
oil	2	5,550	1,300	2,775	4,250
wc/d	1	34,000		34,000	
MARGUOT (20th C) ?					
3D	1	3,882		3,882	
MARIA, Nicola de (1954-) Italian					
oil	6	164,802	12,835	25,776	45,300
wc/d	10	49,135	1,359	3,281	10,049
MARIANI, Carlo Maria (1931-) Italian					
oil	3	47,230	7,200	16,000	24,030
wc/d	5	16,943	1,230	4,000	6,050
MARIANI, Emilio (20th C) Italian					
oil	1	1,314		1,314	
MARIANI, Mario (1907-) Italian					
oil	1	2,200		2,200	
MARIANI, Pompeo (1857-1927) Italian					
oil	11	78,131	3,076	7,236	13,473
wc/d	7	10,182	1,036	1,480	1,628
MARIANO (19th C) Italian?					
oil	1	3,245		3,245	
MARIE, Adrien Emmanuel (1848-1891) French					
oil	2	13,098	5,848	6,549	7,250
MARIE, Jacques (19/20th C) French					
oil	1	1,672		1,672	
MARIESCHI, Michele (1696-1743) Italian					
oil	2	64,680	27,930	32,340	36,750
wc/d	1	2,618		2,618	
MARIESCHI, Michele (school) (1696-1743) Italian					
oil	2	11,000	5,000	5,500	6,000
MARIESHI, P (?) Italian					
oil	1	1,110		1,110	
MARIL, Herman (1908-1986) American					
oil	2	3,600	1,600	1,800	2,000
MARILHAT, Prosper (1811-1847) French					
oil	2	413,603	4,803	206,802	408,800
MARIN (?) ?					
3D	1	3,270		3,270	
MARIN MARIE (1901-1987) French					
wc/d	2	14,588	5,111	7,294	9,477
MARIN RAMOS, Eustaquio (1873-1959) Spanish					
oil	2	6,699	1,151	3,350	5,548

Name	No.	Total Sales Value	lowest	Prices median	highest
MARIN, Augusto (1922-) Puerto Rican					
oil	1	4,000		4,000	
MARIN, Émile (1876-?) French					
wc/d	3	3,387	1,129	1,129	1,129
MARIN, Enrique (1876-?) Spanish					
wc/d	2	3,739	1,852	1,870	1,887
MARIN, Giovanni (20th C) Italian					
oil	1	4,108		4,108	
MARIN, Javier (1962-) Mexican					
3D	1	18,000		18,000	
MARIN, John (1870-1953) American					
oil	2	630,000	80,000	315,000	550,000
wc/d	19	645,000	4,500	24,000	160,000
MARIN, Joseph Charles (1759-1834) French					
3D	1	20,064		20,064	
MARIN, Marie (?) French?					
wc/d	2	12,873	1,300	6,437	11,573
MARINARI, Onorio (1627-1715) Italian					
oil	1	20,580		20,580	
MARINELLI, Fuse (20th C) Italian					
3D	1	2,434		2,434	
MARINI, A (?) Italian					
oil	1	26,080		26,080	
MARINI, Antonio Maria (1668-1725) Italian					
oil	1	8,727		8,727	
MARINI, Marino (1901-1980) Italian					
3D	9	1,698,987	15,950	87,267	812,000
oil	6	1,386,804	13,933	97,835	664,400
wc/d	18	307,701	2,791	11,369	62,000
MARINO, Armando (1968-) Cuban					
oil	2	19,000	8,000	9,500	11,000
MARINUS, Ferdinand Joseph Bernard (1808-1890) Belgian					
oil	3	12,952	1,220	2,097	9,635
MARIO, A (19th C) Italian					
oil	1	1,200		1,200	
MARIO, Alessandro E (19th C) Italian					
oil	1	1,800		1,800	
MARIOTON, E (1854-1925) French					
3D	1	1,668		1,668	
MARIOTON, Eugène (1854-1925) French					
3D	12	35,202	1,198	2,446	6,255
MARIS, Ferdinand Johannes Jacobus (1873-1935) Dutch					
wc/d	1	3,693		3,693	
MARIS, Jacob (1837-1899) Dutch					
oil	8	135,782	2,732	6,689	63,649
wc/d	1	14,851		14,851	
MARIS, Matthijs (1839-1917) Dutch					
oil	1	2,065		2,065	
MARIS, Simon (1873-1935) Dutch					
oil	12	31,524	1,061	2,028	8,722
MARIS, W (1844-1910) Dutch					
oil	1	1,179		1,179	
MARIS, Willem (1844-1910) Dutch					
oil	11	71,902	1,530	4,208	21,000
wc/d	1	1,959		1,959	
MARISALDI, Elena Falco (1902-1086) Italian					
oil	3	4,086	1,192	1,192	1,597
MARISCAL, Javier (1950-) Spanish					
oil	2	2,937	1,055	1,469	1,882

Name	No.	Total Sales Value	lowest	Prices median	highest
MARISOL (1930-) American/Venezulean					
3D	1	80,000		80,000	
MARISTANY, Luis (20th C) Uruguayan					
oil	1	1,500		1,500	
MARK, Lajos (1867-1942) Hungarian					
oil	2	7,317	1,185	3,659	6,132
MARKES, Albert Ernest (1865-1901) British					
wc/d	1	1,141		1,141	
MARKES, Richmond (19th C) British					
wc/d	2	2,263	1,108	1,132	1,155
MARKHAM, Kyra (1891-1967) American					
oil	1	2,750		2,750	
MARKHAM, R C (?) British?					
oil	1	1,213		1,213	
MARKO, Andreas (1824-1895) Austrian					
oil	5	31,263	3,265	5,888	9,500
MARKO, C (1902-1986) ?					
oil	1	7,266		7,266	
MARKO, Henry (1855-1921) Italian					
oil	5	9,780	1,240	1,517	3,054
MARKO, Karl (19th C) Hungarian					
oil	2	8,142	1,020	4,071	7,122
MARKO, Karl (elder) (1791-1860) Hungarian					
oil	3	17,172	1,833	3,893	11,446
MARKO, Karl (younger) (1822-1891) Hungarian					
oil	2	3,558	1,412	1,779	2,146
MARKOFF, Natacha (1911-) Russian					
oil	2	5,647	1,514	2,824	4,133
MARKONI, K (19th C) Italian					
wc/d	2	4,904	2,452	2,452	2,452
MARKS, Claude (19th C) ?					
wc/d	1	1,200		1,200	
MARKS, George (fl.1876-1922) British					
wc/d	1	4,500		4,500	
MARKS, Henry Stacy (1829-1898) British					
oil	1	57,000		57,000	
MARKUS, Ans (1947-) Dutch					
oil	2	5,783	1,030	2,892	4,753
MARLATT, H Irving (1860-1929) American					
oil	1	1,300		1,300	
MARLE, Felix del (1889-1952) French					
wc/d	1	1,993		1,993	
MARLIER, Philippe de (c.1573-1668) Flemish					
oil	2	108,290	33,220	54,145	75,070
MARLLY, Petrus (19th C) French?					
oil	1	1,288		1,288	
MARLOW, William (1740-1813) British					
oil	1	1,590		1,590	
MARLY, E (19th C) French					
wc/d	1	1,547		1,547	
MARNEFFE, Ernest (1866-1921) Belgian					
oil	1	1,877		1,877	
MARNIERRE, G de la (?) French					
oil	1	2,730		2,730	
MARNY, Paul (1829-1914) British					
wc/d	9	17,441	1,564	1,988	2,250
MAROHN, Ferdinand (19th C) French					
oil	1	5,510		5,510	
wc/d	1	1,334		1,334	

Name	No.	Total Sales Value	Prices lowest	median	highest
MAROLD, Ludwig (1865-1898) Czechoslovakian					
wc/d	1	7,976		7,976	
MARON, Anton von (1733-1808) Austrian					
oil	1	3,738		3,738	
MARONIEZ, Georges Philibert Charles (1865-1933) French					
oil	4	6,847	1,002	1,826	2,193
MARQUARD, Otto (1881-?) German					
oil	3	7,285	1,294	1,438	4,553
MARQUES, Guilherme d'Oliveira (1887-?) ?					
oil	1	1,677		1,677	
MARQUET (1875-1947) French					
3D	1	6,421		6,421	
wc/d	1	3,707		3,707	
MARQUET, Albert (1875-1947) French					
oil	28	2,611,262	20,300	54,360	320,000
wc/d	20	86,031	1,228	2,944	17,490
MARQUET, René-Paul (1875-?) French					
3D	1	1,259		1,259	
MARR, Joseph Heinrich Ludwig (1807-1871) German					
oil	2	23,810	1,364	11,905	22,446
MARRABLE, Madeline Frances (?-1916) British					
wc/d	1	1,294		1,294	
MARRANI, A (19/20th C) ?					
wc/d	1	1,513		1,513	
MARREL, Jacob (1614-1681) Dutch					
wc/d	1	300,766		300,766	
MARSA CASAS, Javier (1944-) Spanish					
wc/d	1	3,226		3,226	
MARSH, Edwin W (fl.1915-1939) British					
oil	1	1,349		1,349	
MARSH, Reginald (1898-1954) American					
oil	10	338,500	1,000	8,500	170,000
wc/d	23	684,250	3,250	13,000	260,000
MARSHAL, Alexander (17th C) British					
wc/d	2	35,788	10,048	17,894	25,740
MARSHALL, Ben (1767-1835) British					
oil	1	20,720		20,720	
MARSHALL, Clark S (1882-?) American					
oil	1	10,000		10,000	
MARSHALL, Clark Summers (1861-1944) American					
oil	1	2,300		2,300	
MARSHALL, Frank H (1866-1934) American					
oil	2	4,850	1,600	2,425	3,250
MARSHALL, Herbert Menzies (1841-1913) British					
oil	1	1,160		1,160	
wc/d	5	13,526	1,103	3,473	3,718
MARSHALL, John Miller (fl.1881-1927) British					
wc/d	1	1,287		1,287	
MARSHALL, Lambert (1810-1870) British					
oil	1	8,140		8,140	
MARSHALL, Roberto Angelo Kittermaster (1849-1902) British					
wc/d	5	7,934	1,193	1,359	2,130
MARSTRAND, Wilhelm (1810-1873) Danish					
oil	15	231,839	1,072	7,100	116,013
wc/d	1	1,059		1,059	
MARTEL, Jan and Joel (1896-1966) French					
3D	5	28,040	2,457	4,082	11,970
MARTEL, Paul (1879-1944) Belgian					
wc/d	1	1,382		1,382	

Name	No.	Total Sales Value	lowest	Prices median	highest
MARTELL, K L (20th C) American					
3D	1	2,212		2,212	
MARTELLY, John S de (1903-1979) American					
oil	2	13,200	2,200	6,600	11,000
MARTEN, Elliot H (fl.1886-1910) British					
wc/d	1	1,073		1,073	
MARTENS, Conrad (1801-1878) Australian					
wc/d	1	1,029		1,029	
MARTENS, Henry (?-1860) British					
oil	1	1,336		1,336	
wc/d	1	1,001		1,001	
MARTENS, Willy (1856-1927) Dutch					
oil	2	4,240	1,093	2,120	3,147
wc/d	1	14,365		14,365	
MARTI Y ALSINA, Ramon (1826-1894) Spanish					
oil	2	9,448	1,344	4,724	8,104
MARTIN (?) ?					
wc/d	1	3,797		3,797	
MARTIN GIMENEZ, Juan (1855-1901) Spanish					
oil	1	1,396		1,396	
MARTIN REBOLLO, Tomas (1858-1919) Spanish					
oil	6	7,509	1,008	1,097	2,113
MARTIN, Agnes (1912-) American/Canadian					
oil	2	1,370,000	70,000	685,000	1,300,000
wc/d	7	2,231,000	39,000	190,000	1,100,000
MARTIN, Angel (20th C) Spanish					
oil	1	1,168		1,168	
MARTIN, Anson A (fl.1840-1861) British					
oil	1	4,200		4,200	
MARTIN, David (1736-1798) British					
oil	2	7,328	2,323	3,664	5,005
MARTIN, Elias (1739-1818) Swedish					
oil	2	22,297	6,772	11,149	15,525
wc/d	4	14,076	2,173	3,202	5,500
MARTIN, Étienne (1913-1995) French					
3D	1	12,110		12,110	
MARTIN, Eugène-Louis (1880-1954) Swiss					
oil	1	1,033		1,033	
MARTIN, Fletcher (1904-1979) American					
oil	3	25,200	2,500	2,700	20,000
MARTIN, Gilbert (19th C) ?					
oil	2	8,964	1,214	4,482	7,750
MARTIN, Henri (1860-1943) French					
oil	44	3,122,841	3,152	60,711	211,400
wc/d	1	1,549		1,549	
MARTIN, Henry (1835-1908) British					
oil	2	4,021	1,413	2,011	2,608
MARTIN, Homer D (1836-1897) American					
oil	3	24,300	1,300	3,000	20,000
MARTIN, I R (19th C) ?					
oil	1	1,700		1,700	
MARTIN, J (?) ?					
oil	2	2,400	1,100	1,200	1,300
MARTIN, Jacques (1844-1919) French					
oil	3	8,276	1,740	1,740	4,784
MARTIN, Jason (1970-) British					
oil	3	58,885	15,000	15,950	27,935
MARTIN, Jean Baptiste (1659-1735) French					
oil	3	71,043	10,000	25,670	35,373

Name	No.	Total Sales Value	lowest	Prices median	highest
MARTIN, Johan Fredrik (1755-1816) Swedish					
wc/d	1	2,709		2,709	
MARTIN, John (1789-1854) British					
wc/d	2	30,888	3,718	15,444	27,170
MARTIN, Kenneth (1905-) British					
oil	1	5,640		5,640	
MARTIN, Maurice (1894-1978) French					
oil	2	3,305	1,382	1,653	1,923
MARTIN, Pierre Denis (1663-1742) French					
oil	1	7,295		7,295	
MARTIN, Sylvester (fl.1856-1906) British					
oil	2	2,637	1,287	1,319	1,350
MARTIN, Thomas Mower (1838-1934) Canadian					
oil	3	11,070	1,000	2,920	7,150
wc/d	1	1,244		1,244	
MARTIN, W (?) ?					
oil	1	1,500		1,500	
MARTIN, William Alison (c.1878-1936) British					
oil	1	1,896		1,896	
MARTIN-AMORBACH, Oskar (20th C) German					
oil	1	1,609		1,609	
MARTIN-FERRIERES, Jac (1893-1972) French					
oil	14	76,807	1,178	3,750	17,000
MARTIN-GOURDAULT, Marie (1880-1938) French					
oil	1	8,266		8,266	
MARTIN-KAVEL, François (1861-1918) French					
oil	3	31,020	2,000	9,000	20,020
MARTINA, Umberto (1880-c.1945) Italian					
oil	1	5,373		5,373	
MARTINE, Martine (1932-) French					
oil	3	9,928	2,716	3,139	4,073
MARTINEAU, Antoon Pieter Johan (1926-) Dutch					
oil	2	2,772	1,386	1,386	1,386
MARTINEAU, Edith (1842-1909) British					
wc/d	2	8,305	3,300	4,153	5,005
MARTINEAU, Emilly (19/20th C) French					
oil	1	4,205		4,205	
MARTINELLI, Ezio (1913-1980) American					
3D	1	1,600		1,600	
MARTINETTI, Maria (1864-?) Italian					
wc/d	1	3,428		3,428	
MARTINEZ (19th C) French					
oil	1	2,126		2,126	
MARTINEZ ALCOVER, Manuel (1927-) Spanish					
oil	1	3,432		3,432	
MARTINEZ CHECA, Fernando (?) Spanish					
oil	2	2,044	1,022	1,022	1,022
MARTINEZ DE LA VEGA, Joaquin (1846-1905) Spanish					
wc/d	1	1,137		1,137	
MARTINEZ DE LEON, Andres (1895-1978) Spanish					
oil	1	1,344		1,344	
MARTINEZ DIAZ, Rafael (1915-1991) Spanish					
oil	3	6,756	1,778	1,887	3,091
MARTINEZ HOWARD, Julio (1932-1999) Spanish					
oil	6	8,700	1,400	1,400	1,600
wc/d	1	1,700		1,700	
MARTINEZ MOYANO, Sebastian (1956-) Spanish					
oil	1	1,320		1,320	

Name	No.	Total Sales Value	lowest	Prices median	highest
MARTINEZ NOVILLO, Cirilo (1921-) Spanish					
oil	2	6,763	2,964	3,382	3,799
MARTINEZ ORTIZ, Nicolas (1907-1990) Spanish					
oil	3	19,566	3,764	6,660	9,142
MARTINEZ RIBES, Jose (1912-1995) Spanish					
oil	1	1,125		1,125	
MARTINEZ TARRASSO, Casimiro (1900-1980) Spanish					
oil	1	6,991		6,991	
MARTINEZ VAZQUEZ, Eduardo (1886-1971) Spanish					
oil	4	13,191	1,173	3,106	5,807
MARTINEZ, Alfredo Ramos (1872-1946) Mexican					
wc/d	1	26,000		26,000	
MARTINEZ, Domingo (fl.1688-1749) Spanish					
oil	1	6,903		6,903	
MARTINEZ, F (?) Spanish					
3D	1	1,353		1,353	
MARTINEZ, F E (?) ?					
oil	2	5,778	2,628	2,889	3,150
MARTINEZ, Pedro Antonio (1886-?) Spanish					
oil	1	2,151		2,151	
MARTINEZ, Prospero (1885-1966) Venezuelan					
oil	2	4,520	2,200	2,260	2,320
MARTINEZ, Raoul (1876-1973) Dutch					
oil	3	4,824	1,396	1,396	1,979
MARTINEZ, Ricardo (1918-) Mexican					
oil	3	78,000	5,000	28,000	45,000
MARTINEZ, Xavier (1869-1943) American					
oil	3	19,700	1,200	7,500	11,000
MARTINI (?) ?					
oil	1	1,204		1,204	
MARTINI, Alberto (1876-1954) Italian					
wc/d	3	18,915	2,184	4,443	12,288
MARTINI, Arturo (1889-1947) Italian					
3D	3	338,301	12,132	75,713	250,456
oil	1	5,176		5,176	
MARTINI, Enrico (1898-?) Italian					
3D	1	1,500		1,500	
MARTINI, Joseph de (1896-?) American					
oil	3	8,350	1,400	2,750	4,200
MARTINI, Reno (1917-) Italian					
3D	1	1,253		1,253	
wc/d	1	1,253		1,253	
MARTINO, Antonio Pietro (1902-1989) American					
oil	6	26,500	1,500	3,250	10,000
MARTINO, Edoardo (1838-1912) Italian					
oil	5	59,612	2,100	4,832	36,480
wc/d	1	1,141		1,141	
MARTINO, Giovanni di (1870-1935) Italian					
3D	1	1,047		1,047	
MARTINOL, E (19th C) French					
oil	1	2,300		2,300	
MARTINOTTI, Evangelista Giovanni (1634-1694) Italian					
oil	1	2,972		2,972	
MARTINS, Antonio P (?) ?					
oil	1	7,000		7,000	
MARTORELL, Jose (19th C) Spanish					
oil	1	3,194		3,194	
MARTORI, Gino (1951-) Italian					
oil	1	1,307		1,307	

Name	No.	Total Sales Value	lowest	Prices median	highest
MARTSEN, Jan (younger) (1609-c.1647) Flemish					
oil	2	14,535	6,615	7,268	7,920
MARUSCELLI, Paolo (17th C) Italian					
wc/d	1	2,416		2,416	
MARUSSIG, Guido (1885-1938) Italian					
oil	1	1,835		1,835	
MARUSSIG, Piero (1879-1937) Italian					
oil	5	66,646	6,761	13,963	21,817
MARVAL, Jacqueline (1866-1932) French					
oil	2	11,975	1,056	5,988	10,919
MARX, Alphonse (19/20th C) French					
oil	2	16,981	7,700	8,491	9,281
MARX, Ernst Bernhard (1864-?) German					
oil	1	7,642		7,642	
MARX, Franz (1889-1960) German					
oil	1	1,307		1,307	
MARX, Gustav (1855-1928) German					
oil	1	2,699		2,699	
MARX, Maurice Roger (1872-?) French					
3D	1	2,218		2,218	
MARXEN, Herbert (1900-1954) German					
oil	1	5,760		5,760	
MARXER, Alfred (1876-1945) Swiss					
oil	2	3,713	1,793	1,857	1,920
MARYAN, Burstein Pinchas (1927-1977) American					
oil	2	13,273	5,317	6,637	7,956
wc/d	1	1,328		1,328	
MARZELLE, Jean (1916-) French					
oil	2	3,229	1,505	1,615	1,724
MARZIN, Alfred (20th C) French					
oil	1	1,050		1,050	
MAS Y FONDEVILA, Arcadio (1852-1934) Spanish					
oil	2	16,407	1,588	8,204	14,819
wc/d	1	4,646		4,646	
MAS, Felix (20th C) Spanish					
oil	1	2,960		2,960	
MASCARINI, Giuseppe (1877-?) Italian					
oil	1	2,831		2,831	
MASCART, Gustave (1834-1914) French					
oil	11	27,245	1,118	1,659	9,870
MASEREEL, Frans (1889-1972) Belgian					
oil	15	110,750	1,048	6,056	31,680
wc/d	13	33,036	1,219	1,609	6,560
MASI, A (19/20th C) Italian					
3D	1	1,931		1,931	
MASIDE, Carlos (1897-1958) Spanish					
wc/d	1	4,878		4,878	
MASKELL, Christopher M (1846-1933) British					
oil	1	3,053		3,053	
MASON, Barry (1927-) British					
oil	4	8,220	1,435	2,034	2,718
MASON, Emily Florence (1870-?) British					
oil	1	1,994		1,994	
MASON, Frank H (1876-1965) British					
oil	7	20,552	1,193	3,150	6,248
wc/d	18	40,059	1,080	2,063	5,396
MASON, Roy M (1886-1972) American					
oil	2	4,800	1,800	2,400	3,000
wc/d	5	19,650	1,900	4,000	5,500

Name	No.	Total Sales Value	lowest	Prices median	highest
MASON, William Henry (fl.1858-1885) British					
oil	1	1,141		1,141	
MASON, William Sanford (1824-1864) American					
wc/d	1	1,500		1,500	
MASRELIEZ, Louis (1748-1810) Swedish					
wc/d	3	8,241	2,010	2,211	4,020
MASRIERA Y MANOVENS, Francisco (1842-1902) Spanish					
oil	2	16,934	2,714	8,467	14,220
MASRIERA Y MANOVENS, Jose (1841-1912) Spanish					
oil	1	2,519		2,519	
MASSANI, Paolo (19th C) Italian					
oil	1	1,644		1,644	
MASSANI, Pompeo (1850-1920) Italian					
oil	3	17,896	1,896	7,000	9,000
MASSART, J (?) Belgian?					
oil	1	1,220		1,220	
MASSAUX, Léon Charles (1845-1926) Belgian					
oil	1	3,359		3,359	
MASSE, C (?) French					
3D	1	1,264		1,264	
MASSE, Jean Baptiste (1687-1767) French					
wc/d	1	1,297		1,297	
MASSE, Jean Eugène Julien (1856-1950) French					
oil	2	4,800	2,000	2,400	2,800
MASSINI, A (?) Italian					
oil	1	1,273		1,273	
MASSON DE TOURBET, Louis (20th C) French?					
wc/d	1	3,351		3,351	
MASSON, Andre (1896-1987) French					
3D	7	87,291	2,416	3,775	45,000
oil	13	430,659	14,519	25,670	86,791
wc/d	16	71,186	1,447	3,699	11,682
MASSON, Clovis (1838-1913) French					
3D	2	4,800	1,300	2,400	3,500
MASSON, Henri L (1907-1996) Canadian					
oil	12	22,060	1,057	1,603	3,198
MASSON, J E (1871-1932) French					
3D	1	3,150		3,150	
MASSON, Jules-Edmond (1871-1932) French					
3D	2	4,901	1,159	2,451	3,742
MASSOT, Firmin (1766-1849) Swiss					
oil	1	143,450		143,450	
wc/d	1	7,000		7,000	
MASTAGLIO, F D (fl.1860-1900) German					
oil	1	7,500		7,500	
MASTENBROEK, Albert (20th C) Belgian					
oil	3	7,939	2,298	2,507	3,134
MASTENBROEK, Johann Hendrik van (1875-1945) Dutch					
oil	6	71,214	3,226	10,396	27,500
wc/d	5	18,151	1,454	1,970	7,244
MASTER OF 1416 (15th C) Italian					
oil	2	157,810	59,660	78,905	98,150
MASTER OF 1540 (16th C) Dutch					
oil	1	20,000		20,000	
MASTER OF BORGO ALLA COLLINA (?) ?					
oil	1	60,400		60,400	
MASTER OF CHARLES OF DURAZZO (?) ?					
oil	1	63,420		63,420	

Name	No.	Total Sales Value	lowest	Prices median	highest
MASTER OF FRANKFURT (c.1490-1515) Dutch					
oil	2	256,700	60,400	128,350	196,300
MASTER OF GUSTROW (16th C) Belgian					
oil	1	37,750		37,750	
MASTER OF LIGURIA (16th C) Italian					
oil	1	189,662		189,662	
MASTER OF MARRADI (15th C) Italian					
oil	1	18,484		18,484	
MASTER OF PEREA (fl.1490-1505) Spanish					
oil	1	105,513		105,513	
MASTER OF PORTIUNCULA (15th C) Spanish					
oil	1	44,678		44,678	
MASTER OF PRATO CAPRICCI (18th C) Italian					
wc/d	1	4,800		4,800	
MASTER OF SAINT IVO (14th C) Italian					
oil	1	53,862		53,862	
MASTER OF SANTA VERDIANA (14th C) Italian					
oil	2	108,983	30,200	54,492	78,783
MASTER OF SHELDON (fl.1580-1610) British					
oil	1	22,880		22,880	
MASTER OF THE ACQUAVELLA STILL LIFE (17th C) Italian					
oil	1	800,000		800,000	
MASTER OF THE BEFFI TRIPTYCH (15th C) Italian					
oil	1	49,980		49,980	
MASTER OF THE CAMPANA CASSONI (?) Italian?					
oil	1	9,966		9,966	
MASTER OF THE CARNATIONS (15th C) Italian					
oil	1	19,411		19,411	
MASTER OF THE COBURG ROUNDELS (15th C) German					
wc/d	1	2,700		2,700	
MASTER OF THE DEATH OF SAINT NICHOLAS OF MUNSTER (15th C) ?					
oil	1	3,200,000		3,200,000	
MASTER OF THE EGMONT ALBUMS (?) ?					
wc/d	1	18,875		18,875	
MASTER OF THE FEMALE HALF LENGTHS (16th C) Flemish					
oil	2	307,600	117,600	153,800	190,000
MASTER OF THE FIESOLE EPIPHANY (15th C) Italian					
oil	2	57,040	22,500	28,520	34,540
MASTER OF THE GROTESQUE VASES (17th C) Italian					
oil	1	66,189		66,189	
MASTER OF THE GUARDESCHI FLOWERS (18th C) Italian					
oil	1	11,925		11,925	
MASTER OF THE HARTFORD STILL LIFE (17th C) ?					
oil	1	60,342		60,342	
MASTER OF THE HOLY BLOOD (16th C) Flemish					
oil	1	60,000		60,000	
MASTER OF THE ILSUNG MADONNA (15th C) German					
oil	1	26,816		26,816	
MASTER OF THE JOHNSON NATIVITY (15th C) Italian					
oil	1	5,738		5,738	
MASTER OF THE KRESS LANDSCAPES (16th C) Italian					
oil	2	122,225	12,225	61,113	110,000
MASTER OF THE LANGMATT FOUNDATION VIEW (fl.1740-1770) Italian					
oil	7	425,012	28,260	43,200	120,800
MASTER OF THE LEGEND OF SAINT CATHERINE (fl.1470-1500) Belgian					
oil	1	150,000		150,000	
MASTER OF THE LIECHTENSTEIN ADORATION (16th C) Swiss					
wc/d	1	7,248		7,248	

Name	No.	Total Sales Value	lowest	Prices median	highest
MASTER OF THE MADONNA DELLA MISERICORDIA (14th C) Italian					
oil	2	165,941	81,893	82,971	84,048
MASTER OF THE MADONNA LAZZARONE (15th C) Italian					
oil	1	94,824		94,824	
MASTER OF THE MAGDALEN LEGEND (15th C) Flemish					
oil	2	878,000	425,000	439,000	453,000
MASTER OF THE MISERICORDIA (15th C) Italian					
oil	1	45,000		45,000	
MASTER OF THE PARROT (16th C) Flemish					
oil	1	76,701		76,701	
MASTER OF THE PAU SUPPER AT EMMAUS (17th C) Italian?					
oil	1	13,680		13,680	
MASTER OF THE PONTEROSSO MADONNA (16th C) Italian					
oil	1	67,495		67,495	
MASTER OF THE PRODIGAL SON (16th C) Flemish					
oil	1	24,620		24,620	
MASTER OF THE RETABLE OF THE SANTOS JUANES (16th C) Spanish					
oil	1	9,771		9,771	
MASTER OF THE TURKISH SCENES (17th C) ?					
oil	1	45,093		45,093	
MASTERS, Edwin (19th C) British					
oil	2	5,424	1,420	2,712	4,004
MASTROIANNI, Umberto (1910-1998) Italian					
3D	6	18,184	1,681	2,924	5,305
oil	1	2,990		2,990	
wc/d	3	5,341	1,173	1,178	2,990
MASUI, Paul Auguste (1888-1981) Luxembourger					
oil	1	3,825		3,825	
MASURE, Jules (1819-1910) French					
oil	1	1,166		1,166	
MASUREL, Johannes Engel (1826-1915) Dutch					
oil	1	2,960		2,960	
MASWIENS, Joseph (1828-1880) Belgian					
oil	3	11,913	1,450	3,593	6,870
MASYK, Volodymir (20th C) Russian					
oil	1	3,528		3,528	
MATANIA, F (1881-1963) Italian					
wc/d	1	1,115		1,115	
MATANIA, Fortunino (1881-1963) Italian					
oil	4	16,256	2,646	4,050	5,510
wc/d	2	9,650	1,510	4,825	8,140
MATARE, Ewald (1887-1965) German					
3D	9	325,489	4,427	16,436	129,755
wc/d	4	23,685	2,656	5,645	9,740
MATE, Olga (20th C) ?					
3D	1	1,396		1,396	
MATEGOT, Mathieu (1910-) French					
wc/d	1	1,710		1,710	
MATEO CHARRIS, Angel (1962-) Spanish					
oil	1	1,265		1,265	
MATEOS, Francisco (1894-1976) Spanish					
oil	2	12,805	4,936	6,403	7,869
wc/d	1	1,056		1,056	
MATES, J (?) ?					
oil	1	1,128		1,128	
MATES, Juan (c.1370-1431) Spanish					
oil	1	55,000		55,000	
MATHEU, Leonel (1967-) Cuban					
wc/d	1	2,000		2,000	

Name	No.	Total Sales Value	lowest	Prices median	highest
MATHEWSON, Frank Convers (1862-1941) American					
wc/d	1	1,400		1,400	
MATHEY, Paul (1844-1929) French					
oil	1	1,400		1,400	
MATHEY, Paul (1891-1972) Swiss					
oil	2	4,028	1,179	2,014	2,849
MATHIESEN, Egon (1907-1976) Danish					
oil	1	1,095		1,095	
MATHIESON, W (?) ?					
oil	1	1,264		1,264	
MATHIEU, Georges (1921-) French					
oil	25	319,523	2,112	10,813	47,735
wc/d	12	32,874	1,353	2,761	5,088
MATHIEU, Paul (1872-1932) Belgian					
oil	14	69,666	1,585	4,669	11,772
MATHIEU-MEUSNIER, Roland (1824-1876) French					
3D	1	1,400		1,400	
MATHIS, Leonie (1883-1952) Argentinian					
wc/d	1	5,200		5,200	
MATILLA Y MARINA, Segundo (1862-1937) Spanish					
oil	8	21,811	1,821	2,589	4,683
wc/d	1	2,090		2,090	
MATINO, Vittorio (20th C) Italian					
oil	1	3,294		3,294	
MATISSE, Camille (20th C) French					
oil	1	2,500		2,500	
MATISSE, Henri (1869-1954) French					
3D	4	13,084,750	79,750	127,500	12,750,000
oil	8	31,340,203	3,400	2,031,473	15,500,000
wc/d	44	7,129,464	7,550	54,984	2,450,000
MATIUSHIN, Mikhail V (1861-1934) Russian					
wc/d	1	9,815		9,815	
MATSCH, Franz von (1861-1942) Austrian					
oil	2	48,313	13,000	24,157	35,313
MATSCHINSKY-DENNINGHOFF, Brigitte and Martin (20th C) German					
3D	4	21,599	2,391	5,398	8,412
MATSUMOTO, Shunsuke (1912-1948) Japanese					
oil	1	45,000		45,000	
MATTA (1911-) Chilean					
3D	1	4,424		4,424	
oil	29	1,308,551	10,335	22,070	220,000
wc/d	15	403,859	2,730	10,329	137,750
MATTA, Federica (20th C) ?					
3D	1	1,459		1,459	
wc/d	1	1,408		1,408	
MATTEIS, Francesco de (1852-?) Italian					
3D	1	3,808		3,808	
MATTEIS, Paolo de (1662-1728) Italian					
oil	3	47,015	3,020	16,697	27,298
MATTENHEIMER, Albin (1823-?) German					
oil	1	1,347		1,347	
MATTENHEIMER, Andreas Theodor (1752-1810) German					
oil	1	4,091		4,091	
MATTENHEIMER, Theodor (younger) (1787-1856) German					
oil	1	9,481		9,481	
MATTERN, Walter (20th C) American					
oil	1	3,750		3,750	
MATTHEWS, George Bagby (1857-1944) American					
oil	1	2,000		2,000	

Name	No.	Total Sales Value	lowest	Prices median	highest
MATTHEWS, James (19th C) British					
wc/d	3	6,168	1,776	2,072	2,320
MATTHEWS, Marmaduke (1837-1913) Canadian					
wc/d	1	1,327		1,327	
MATTHEWS, Terry O (1931-) British					
3D	1	2,016		2,016	
MATTHEY DE CATUS (?) ?					
oil	1	2,883		2,883	
MATTHEY, Julien (19/20th C) French?					
oil	1	2,184		2,184	
MATTHIESEN, Emma (20th C) Danish					
3D	1	1,177		1,177	
MATTHIEU, Georg David (1737-1776) German					
oil	1	55,000		55,000	
MATTHISON, William (fl.1883-1923) British					
wc/d	2	2,228	1,058	1,114	1,170
MATTIA, Traverso (19th C) Continental					
oil	1	4,000		4,000	
MATTINEN, Seppo (1930-) Finnish					
oil	1	1,473		1,473	
MATTINSON, William (?) British					
wc/d	1	1,326		1,326	
MATTIOLI, Carlo (1911-1994) Italian					
oil	2	30,673	7,984	15,337	22,689
wc/d	2	7,429	3,441	3,715	3,988
MATTIOLI, Silvio (1929-) Swiss					
3D	1	2,406		2,406	
MATTO (20th C) ?					
3D	1	1,812		1,812	
MATTO, Francisco (1911-1995) Uruguayan					
oil	5	16,679	1,012	4,390	5,177
MATTON, Arsene (1873-1933) Belgian					
3D	1	2,382		2,382	
MATULKA, Jan (1890-1972) American					
oil	2	48,000	20,000	24,000	28,000
wc/d	4	24,100	1,800	3,650	15,000
MATUSHEVSKI, Yuri (1930-1999) Russian					
oil	3	3,686	1,029	1,334	1,334
MAUCH, Richard (1874-1921) Austrian					
oil	1	6,678		6,678	
MAUFRA, Maxime (1861-1918) French					
oil	15	319,691	1,228	18,000	75,000
wc/d	11	25,400	1,167	2,279	3,791
MAUGERI, Concetto (1919-1951) Italian					
oil	1	2,099		2,099	
MAUGIN, E (?) ?					
oil	1	1,103		1,103	
MAULETTI, P Jean (19th C) Italian					
wc/d	1	4,500		4,500	
MAULWURF, Hans (19th C) German					
oil	1	1,024		1,024	
MAURER, Alfred H (1868-1932) American					
oil	2	100,000	50,000	50,000	50,000
wc/d	1	4,283		4,283	
MAURER, H (?) ?					
oil	1	1,387		1,387	
MAURIER, Georges du (1834-1896) French					
wc/d	2	11,782	1,057	5,891	10,725

Name	No.	Total Sales Value	lowest	Prices median	highest
MAURIN, Charles (1856-1914) French					
wc/d	6	10,530	1,164	1,713	2,579
MAURIN, Georges (1874-?) German					
3D	1	2,972		2,972	
MAURUS, Hans (1901-1942) German					
oil	3	4,313	1,145	1,483	1,685
MAURUS, Henriette (1854-?) Austrian					
oil	1	1,635		1,635	
MAURY, Georges Saveur (1872-?) French					
oil	1	4,471		4,471	
MAUVE, Anton (1838-1888) Dutch					
oil	4	60,040	1,748	8,104	42,084
wc/d	2	5,092	2,546	2,546	2,546
MAUVE, Anton Rudolf (1876-1962) Dutch					
oil	3	5,839	1,377	1,709	2,753
MAUZAISSE, Jean Baptiste (1784-1844) French					
wc/d	1	4,975		4,975	
MAX, Gabriel von (1840-1915) Czechoslovakian					
oil	2	10,588	3,388	5,294	7,200
MAX, Peter (1937-) American/German					
oil	1	3,400		3,400	
MAXENCE, Edgard (1871-1954) French					
oil	4	12,950	1,302	3,424	4,801
wc/d	1	1,311		1,311	
MAXFIELD, Clara (1879-1959) American					
wc/d	1	1,900		1,900	
MAXON, Wilhelm G (1894-?) German					
oil	1	1,079		1,079	
MAXWELL, Donald (1877-1936) British					
oil	1	5,688		5,688	
MAXWELL, John (1905-1962) British					
oil	1	7,975		7,975	
MAY, Henrietta Mabel (1884-1971) Canadian					
oil	2	8,632	1,632	4,316	7,000
MAY, Olivier le (1734-1797) French					
oil	1	30,667		30,667	
wc/d	1	1,233		1,233	
MAYAUX, Philippe (20th C) French					
oil	1	1,543		1,543	
MAYBURGER, Josef (1813-1908) Austrian					
oil	3	16,891	1,329	4,837	10,725
MAYER, Albrecht (1875-1952) Swiss					
oil	1	1,139		1,139	
MAYER, Auguste (19th C) French					
wc/d	2	4,582	1,702	2,291	2,880
MAYER, Casper (1871-1931) American/German					
3D	1	3,500		3,500	
MAYER, Johann Nepomuk (1805-1866) Austrian					
oil	1	1,942		1,942	
MAYER, Peter Bela (1888-?) American					
oil	1	9,500		9,500	
MAYER, Ralph (1898-1979) American					
oil	3	26,500	7,000	10,000	10,000
MAYERHOFER, A (20th C) German/Austrian					
oil	1	2,696		2,696	
MAYEUR, Adrien le (1844-1923) Belgian					
oil	1	1,831		1,831	
MAYEUR, Jean le (1880-1958) Belgian					
oil	2	44,599	9,008	22,300	35,591

Name	No.	Total Sales Value	lowest	Prices median	highest
wc/d	3	5,368	1,561	1,855	1,952
MAYNARD, G (?) ?					
oil	1	1,444		1,444	
MAYNARD, George Willoughby (1843-1923) American					
wc/d	1	1,300		1,300	
MAYNE, Henry (1891-1975) Swedish					
oil	1	1,016		1,016	
MAYNE, Jean (19th C) Belgian					
oil	2	8,859	2,648	4,430	6,211
MAYODON, Jean (1893-1967) French					
oil	1	11,347		11,347	
MAYON, L (19th C) ?					
wc/d	1	1,570		1,570	
MAYOR, Hannah (1871-1947) British					
wc/d	1	1,278		1,278	
MAYR-GRAZ, Karl (1850-1929) German					
oil	1	4,732		4,732	
MAYRHOFER, Johann Nepomuk (1764-1832) Austrian					
oil	1	31,680		31,680	
MAYRSHOFER, Max (1875-1950) German					
oil	2	2,222	1,089	1,111	1,133
MAZE, Paul (1887-1979) French					
oil	11	44,473	1,087	2,025	10,744
wc/d	20	53,992	1,029	2,310	7,800
MAZEROLLE, Alexis Joseph (1826-1889) French					
oil	1	1,900		1,900	
MAZO, Juan Bautista Martinez del (1612-1667) Spanish					
oil	1	19,871		19,871	
MAZUMDAR, Hemen (1894-1943) Indian					
oil	3	81,500	4,500	35,000	42,000
wc/d	3	11,930	2,880	4,050	5,000
MAZUMDAR, Kshistindranath (1891-1975) Indian					
wc/d	1	5,700		5,700	
MAZUROWSKI, Wiktor (1859-1944) Polish					
oil	1	4,530		4,530	
MAZZANOVICH, Lawrence (1872-1946) American					
oil	1	14,000		14,000	
MAZZELLA, E (?) ?					
oil	1	6,401		6,401	
MAZZETTI, Emo (1870-1955) Italian					
oil	2	11,354	3,500	5,677	7,854
MAZZOLA (15th C) Italian					
wc/d	1	1,586		1,586	
MAZZOLA, Francesco (1503-1540) Italian					
wc/d	3	142,040	13,000	47,500	81,540
MAZZOLA, Giuseppe (1748-1838) Italian					
oil	2	12,670	1,773	6,335	10,897
MAZZOLA, J (19th C) Italian?					
oil	1	4,770		4,770	
MAZZOLINI, G (1806-1876) Italian					
oil	1	1,347		1,347	
MAZZOLINI, Giuseppe (1806-1876) Italian					
oil	2	9,169	3,669	4,585	5,500
MAZZON, Galliano (1896-1978) Italian					
oil	1	1,800		1,800	
MAZZONI, Achille (19th C) Italian					
oil	1	1,272		1,272	
MAZZONI, Sebastiano (?-1683) Italian					
oil	1	38,220		38,220	

Name	No.	Total Sales Value	Prices lowest	median	highest
MBUNO, Kivuthi (1947-) African					
wc/d	1	1,222		1,222	
McALPINE, William (19th C) British					
oil	1	4,238		4,238	
McAULEY, Charles (1910-1999) British					
oil	16	51,318	1,305	3,179	5,966
McAULIFFE, James J (1848-1921) American					
oil	1	4,500		4,500	
McBEY, James (1883-1959) British					
oil	4	21,594	1,500	5,922	8,250
wc/d	5	12,021	1,026	1,323	5,880
McCABE, Gladys (?) ?					
oil	1	1,264		1,264	
McCAIG, Norman J (1929-) Irish					
oil	7	8,820	1,080	1,233	1,450
McCAIN, Buck (20th C) American					
3D	1	1,900		1,900	
McCALL, Charles (1907-1989) British					
oil	5	8,155	1,026	1,580	2,370
McCALL, Robert (1919-) American					
oil	1	6,000		6,000	
McCALL, William (fl.1818-1837) British					
oil	1	1,510		1,510	
McCALLION, W J (19/20th C) British					
oil	1	1,885		1,885	
McCALLUM, Andrew (1821-1902) British					
oil	2	5,506	1,884	2,753	3,622
McCAMPAS, V de (18/19th C) ?					
oil	1	2,300		2,300	
McCANN, Gerald Patrick (1916-) American					
oil	1	1,000		1,000	
McCARTAN, Edward (1879-1947) American					
3D	2	755,000	55,000	377,500	700,000
McCARTHY, Frank (1924-) American					
oil	4	122,500	8,500	9,500	95,000
McCARTHY, Paul (1945-) British					
wc/d	1	16,610		16,610	
McCAY, Winsor (1869-1934) American					
wc/d	2	68,000	30,000	34,000	38,000
McCLEARY, Bonnie (20th C) American					
3D	1	5,500		5,500	
McCLELLAND, Suzanne (1953-) American					
oil	1	4,000		4,000	
McCLOSKEY, Alberta Binford (1863-1911) American					
oil	1	42,500		42,500	
McCLURE (20th C) Canadian/American					
3D	1	4,200		4,200	
McCLURE, David (1926-1998) British					
oil	11	53,783	1,133	3,190	13,870
wc/d	2	2,942	1,057	1,471	1,885
McCOLLUM, Allan (1944-) American					
3D	1	2,444		2,444	
wc/d	4	52,850	8,500	10,850	22,650
McCOMAS, Eugenia Frances (1886-1982) American					
oil	1	1,100		1,100	
McCOMAS, Francis (1874-1938) American					
wc/d	1	7,000		7,000	
McCONNELL, George (1852-1929) American					
oil	1	1,100		1,100	

Name	No.	Total Sales Value	lowest	Prices median	highest
McCONNICO, Hilton (20th C) ?					
wc/d	1	1,549		1,549	
McCORD, George (1848-1909) American					
oil	8	40,750	1,200	2,900	16,000
McCORMACK, Selma (?) British?					
3D	1	1,305		1,305	
McCORMICK, Arthur David (1860-1943) British					
oil	1	2,282		2,282	
wc/d	4	5,464	1,216	1,335	1,510
McCOUCH, Gordon Mallet (1885-1956) American					
oil	2	9,614	3,537	4,807	6,077
McCOY, Ann Wyeth (20th C) American					
wc/d	1	4,000		4,000	
McCOY, Wilton Guy (1902-1986) American					
oil	2	3,600	1,000	1,800	2,600
McCRACKEN, James (20th C) American					
oil	3	6,300	1,500	2,100	2,700
McCRACKEN, John (1934-) American					
3D	5	87,000	5,000	17,000	30,000
McCREA, Harold Wellington (1887-1969) Canadian					
oil	1	2,031		2,031	
McCROSSAN, Mary (?-1934) British					
oil	1	9,164		9,164	
McCULLAM, W L (19th C) British					
oil	1	4,350		4,350	
McCULLOCH, Horatio (1805-1867) British					
oil	5	17,006	1,200	1,974	7,592
McDONALD, Madeline M (fl.1896-1903) British					
oil	1	2,205		2,205	
McDONNELL, Hector (1947-) British					
oil	1	2,465		2,465	
McDOWELL, William (fl.1919-1928) British					
wc/d	1	1,617		1,617	
McDUFF, Frederick H (1931-) American					
oil	1	2,600		2,600	
McELCHERAN, William (1927-) Canadian					
3D	4	26,532	1,652	7,323	10,619
McENTEE, Jervis (1828-1891) American					
oil	3	20,500	1,000	7,000	12,500
McEVOY, Ambrose (1878-1927) British					
oil	1	1,450		1,450	
wc/d	1	3,792		3,792	
McEVOY, William (fl.1858-1880) Irish					
oil	1	1,034		1,034	
McEWAN, Mary B (fl.1890-1891) British					
oil	1	1,080		1,080	
McEWAN, Tom (1846-1914) British					
oil	3	8,136	1,544	2,212	4,380
McEWEN, Jean (1923-1999) Canadian					
oil	2	7,473	3,650	3,737	3,823
wc/d	1	1,240		1,240	
McEWEN, Rory (1932-1982) British					
wc/d	1	1,103		1,103	
McEWEN, Walter (1860-1943) American					
oil	3	128,000	26,000	32,000	70,000
McFADYEN, Jock (1950-) British					
wc/d	1	2,130		2,130	
McFEE, Henry Lee (1886-1953) American					
oil	1	5,000		5,000	

Name	No.	Total Sales Value	lowest	Prices median	highest
McGARRY, Philip (1955-) British					
oil	4	10,582	2,556	2,610	2,698
McGEEHAN, Jessie M (fl.1892-1913) British					
oil	3	13,053	2,205	4,380	6,468
wc/d	1	1,296		1,296	
McGHIE, John (1867-1952) British					
oil	6	25,288	1,264	4,266	7,800
McGLADDERY, Anne (?) British?					
3D	1	1,440		1,440	
McGLYNN, Thomas A (1878-1966) American					
oil	1	15,000		15,000	
McGONIGAL, Maurice (1900-1979) British					
oil	2	10,360	4,736	5,180	5,624
McGORAN, K (1932-1990) British					
wc/d	1	2,700		2,700	
McGORAN, Kieran (1932-1990) British					
wc/d	9	22,325	1,368	2,983	3,454
McGRATH, James P (fl.1897) British					
oil	1	2,600		2,600	
McGREGOR, Robert (1848-1922) British					
oil	4	66,679	5,224	15,398	30,660
McGREGOR, W H (20th C) British					
wc/d	1	1,431		1,431	
McGUINNESS, Norah (1903-1980) British					
oil	2	22,940	6,660	11,470	16,280
wc/d	1	1,988		1,988	
McIAN, Robert Ronald (1803-1856) British					
oil	1	14,600		14,600	
McINNIS, Robert (1942-) Canadian					
oil	2	2,819	1,141	1,410	1,678
McINTYRE, Donald (1923-) British					
oil	18	34,260	1,193	1,540	4,108
McINTYRE, J (19th C) British					
oil	1	1,430		1,430	
McINTYRE, James (fl.1867-1898) British					
oil	1	1,287		1,287	
McINTYRE, Joseph Wrightson (fl.1866-1888) British					
oil	6	39,857	2,512	4,923	15,015
wc/d	1	1,027		1,027	
McINTYRE, Keith (1959-) British					
oil	1	2,340		2,340	
McINTYRE, Robert Finlay (fl.1892-1897) British					
oil	5	8,114	1,008	1,368	3,002
McKAY, Thomas Hope (fl.1900-1930) British					
oil	1	1,510		1,510	
McKAY, William Darling (1844-1924) British					
oil	6	45,777	2,190	4,014	27,930
McKEAN, Lorne (?) ?					
3D	1	9,734		9,734	
McKELVEY, Frank (1895-1974) Irish					
oil	14	253,467	2,700	11,690	100,640
wc/d	5	12,351	1,885	2,186	3,600
McKENZIE, J W (fl.1888-1890) British					
oil	1	2,230		2,230	
McKENZIE, Robert Tait (1867-1938) American					
3D	2	15,320	4,320	7,660	11,000
McKEWAN, David Hall (c.1816-1875) British					
wc/d	3	4,119	1,099	1,304	1,716

Name	No.	Total Sales Value	lowest	Prices median	highest
McKINSTRY, George A (fl.1875-1885) American					
oil	1	3,800		3,800	
McKNIGHT, Thomas (?) ?					
wc/d	1	1,600		1,600	
McLAUGHLIN, John (1898-1976) American					
oil	2	26,000	4,000	13,000	22,000
McLAURIN, Duncan (1884-1921) British					
oil	1	2,940		2,940	
McLEA, John Watson (19th C) British					
oil	1	1,648		1,648	
McLEAN, Jack Lee (1924-) Canadian					
oil	1	1,306		1,306	
McLEAN, James Augustus (1904-1989) American					
oil	8	33,000	1,000	3,100	14,000
wc/d	1	1,700		1,700	
McLELLAN, Alexander Matheson (1872-1957) British					
wc/d	1	3,926		3,926	
McMASTER, James (1856-1913) British					
wc/d	1	1,896		1,896	
McMEIN, Neysa (1890-1949) American					
wc/d	1	11,000		11,000	
McNAB, Ian (1944-) British					
oil	1	4,060		4,060	
McNAIR, Duncan (20th C) British					
oil	1	1,100		1,100	
McNEIL, George (1908-1995) American					
oil	1	1,800		1,800	
McNICOLL, Helen Galloway (1879-1915) Canadian					
oil	1	15,143		15,143	
McSWINEY, Eugène (1866-?) British					
oil	1	2,000		2,000	
McTAGGART, William (1835-1910) British					
oil	7	281,960	6,794	20,300	146,000
wc/d	6	37,568	2,370	3,634	14,500
McWILLIAM, F E (1909-1992) British					
3D	1	8,000		8,000	
McWILLIAM, Frederick Edward (1909-1992) British					
3D	2	21,793	7,975	10,897	13,818
MEACCI, Ricciardo (1856-?) Italian					
wc/d	4	11,388	1,508	2,652	4,576
MEADE, Arthur (1863-1948) British					
oil	2	2,212	1,087	1,106	1,125
MEADE-KING, Eric (1911-) British					
wc/d	4	4,994	1,011	1,317	1,359
MEADMORE, Clement (1929-) American/Australian					
3D	1	7,500		7,500	
MEADOWS, A J (1843-1907) British					
oil	1	2,250		2,250	
MEADOWS, Arthur Joseph (1843-1907) British					
oil	14	98,974	3,432	7,448	11,165
MEADOWS, Edwin L (fl.1854-1872) British					
oil	1	3,454		3,454	
MEADOWS, Gordon Arthur (1868-?) British					
oil	1	2,370		2,370	
MEADOWS, James (19th C) British					
oil	3	17,037	4,082	6,520	6,520
MEADOWS, James Edwin (1828-1888) British					
oil	8	52,499	2,234	5,110	12,155

Name	No.	Total Sales Value	lowest	Prices median	highest
MEADOWS, William (fl.1870-1895) British					
oil	8	32,040	1,106	4,063	6,908
MEARS, George (1865-1910) British					
oil	1	1,549		1,549	
MECHAU, Jakob Wilhelm (1745-1808) German					
oil	1	4,098		4,098	
wc/d	1	1,133		1,133	
MECHELN SCHOOL, 16th C German					
3D	1	17,301		17,301	
MECKLENBURG, Ludwig (1820-1882) German					
oil	2	9,435	3,925	4,718	5,510
MECKSEPER, Friedrich (1936-) German?					
wc/d	1	2,404		2,404	
MEDARD, Eugène (1847-1897) French					
oil	1	4,400		4,400	
MEDARD, Jules Ferdinand (c.1853-1927) French					
oil	1	5,892		5,892	
MEDINA SERRANO, Antonio (1944-) Spanish					
oil	1	3,091		3,091	
MEDINA VERA, Inocenzio (1876-1917) Spanish					
wc/d	1	1,161		1,161	
MEDINA, Antonio (19th C) Spanish					
oil	2	9,034	1,943	4,517	7,091
MEDINA, Enrique (?) ?					
oil	1	1,100		1,100	
MEDINA, Sir John (1659-1710) British					
oil	1	7,500		7,500	
MEDIZ-PELIKAN, Emilie (1861-1908) Austrian					
oil	1	1,341		1,341	
MEDLEY, Robert (1905-) British					
oil	2	5,358	1,974	2,679	3,384
MEDLYCOTT, Sir Hubert (1841-1920) British					
wc/d	2	4,011	1,580	2,006	2,431
MEEGAN, Walter (1859-1944) British					
oil	4	6,787	1,106	1,261	3,160
MEEGEREN, Han van (1889-1947) Dutch					
oil	2	2,397	1,106	1,199	1,291
wc/d	1	1,902		1,902	
MEEKER, Joseph R (1827-1889) American					
oil	4	44,250	1,500	8,875	25,000
MEER, Barend van der (1659-?) Dutch					
oil	1	13,649		13,649	
MEERTS (1923-1978) Belgian?					
oil	1	1,234		1,234	
MEERTS, Frans (1836-1896) Belgian					
oil	2	5,925	2,025	2,963	3,900
MEESER, Lillian B (1864-1942) American					
oil	1	3,500		3,500	
MEESTER DE BETZENBROECK, Raymond de (1904-1995) Belgian					
3D	10	28,777	1,066	2,689	6,468
MEESTERS, Dirk (1899-1950) British					
oil	1	2,038		2,038	
MEGANCK, J (19th C) German					
oil	1	1,358		1,358	
MEGANCK, Renier (1637-1690) Belgian					
oil	1	2,045		2,045	
MEGONDOFF, Isabell B (19th C) ?					
wc/d	1	1,222		1,222	

Name	No.	Total Sales Value	lowest	Prices median	highest
MEHEUT, François (?) French					
3D	1	7,785		7,785	
MEHEUT, Maryvonne (20th C) French					
oil	1	1,347		1,347	
MEHEUT, Mathurin (1882-1958) French					
oil	5	17,478	1,083	1,516	7,974
wc/d	14	32,468	1,103	1,759	5,145
MEHTA, Tyeb (1925-) Indian					
oil	1	13,000		13,000	
MEI, Paolo (19th C) Italian					
oil	2	5,127	1,552	2,564	3,575
MEIDNER, Ludwig (1884-1966) German					
oil	1	7,084		7,084	
wc/d	15	605,104	1,063	8,511	208,800
MEIER, Bodo (1949-) German					
oil	1	1,634		1,634	
MEIER, Bruno (1905-1967) Swiss					
oil	1	1,591		1,591	
MEIER, Paul Louis (1950-) Swiss					
3D	1	1,006		1,006	
MEIFREN Y ROIG, Eliseo (1859-1940) Spanish					
oil	9	205,240	1,137	29,345	33,320
MEIJI DYNASTY (19th C) Japanese					
3D	15	69,357	2,656	3,643	14,000
wc/d	2	9,576	4,263	4,788	5,313
MEILI, Conrad (1895-1969) Swiss					
oil	2	2,758	1,129	1,379	1,629
wc/d	1	1,611		1,611	
MEINERI, Guido (1869-1944) Italian					
oil	1	1,241		1,241	
MEINERS, Claas Hendrik (1819-1894) Dutch					
oil	2	2,374	1,061	1,187	1,313
MEINERS, Piet (1857-1903) Dutch					
wc/d	1	4,208		4,208	
MEINERT, Frederike (19th C) German					
oil	1	1,761		1,761	
MEINHARD, Fritz (1910-) German					
oil	1	1,026		1,026	
MEINZOLT, Georg (1863-1945) German					
oil	1	1,900		1,900	
MEIREN, Jan Baptist van der (1664-1708) Flemish					
oil	1	3,125		3,125	
MEIRHANS, Joseph (1890-1981) American					
oil	1	1,550		1,550	
MEISEL, Ernst (1838-1895) German					
oil	1	32,500		32,500	
MEISENBACH, Karl (1898-1976) German					
oil	1	3,323		3,323	
MEISSER, Leonhard (1902-1977) Swiss					
oil	1	2,286		2,286	
MEISSNER, Adolf Ernst (1837-1902) German					
oil	1	2,697		2,697	
MEISSONIER, J L E (1815-1891) French					
oil	1	12,000		12,000	
MEISSONIER, Jean Louis Ernest (1815-1891) French					
3D	2	27,885	12,185	13,943	15,700
oil	8	228,057	1,800	4,275	180,000
wc/d	2	2,715	1,047	1,358	1,668
MEISSONIER, Jean Louis Ernest (school) (1815-1891) French					
oil	1	4,673		4,673	

Name	No.	Total Sales Value	lowest	Prices median	highest
MEISSONNIER, Joseph (1864-1943) French					
oil	1	1,537		1,537	
MEISTERMANN, Georg (1911-1990) German					
oil	7	107,546	2,850	8,650	41,616
wc/d	2	3,317	1,154	1,659	2,163
MEJIAZ, Mauro (1930-) Venezuelan					
oil	1	3,370		3,370	
MEKKINK, Johan (1904-) Dutch					
oil	2	20,489	3,248	10,245	17,241
MELBOURNE, H (18th C) British					
oil	1	1,285		1,285	
MELBYE, Anton (1818-1875) Danish					
oil	16	63,215	1,160	2,345	14,893
MELBYE, Wilhelm (1824-1882) Danish					
oil	5	20,643	2,145	3,819	5,643
MELCHER, G (20th C) ?					
oil	1	1,079		1,079	
MELCHER, Gaspare Otto (1945-) Swiss					
oil	1	1,598		1,598	
MELCHERS, Gari (1860-1932) American					
oil	1	14,000		14,000	
MELCHERT, Adolf (19th C) Danish					
oil	1	2,500		2,500	
MELCHUS, H (20th C) German?					
oil	1	2,133		2,133	
MELENDEZ, Gerardo (1856-?) Spanish					
oil	1	2,636		2,636	
MELINGUE, Étienne Marin (1808-1875) French					
3D	1	2,160		2,160	
MELLE (1908-1976) Dutch					
oil	1	6,466		6,466	
wc/d	1	6,034		6,034	
MELLE, Henri van (1859-1930) Belgian					
oil	1	1,530		1,530	
MELLERUP, Tage (1910-1988) Danish					
oil	1	1,278		1,278	
MELLERY, Xavier (1845-1921) Belgian					
oil	1	4,067		4,067	
MELLON, Campbell (1876-1955) British					
oil	7	26,552	1,240	2,703	9,425
MELLOR, Everett W (1878-1965) British					
oil	1	2,030		2,030	
wc/d	1	1,562		1,562	
MELLOR, Joseph (fl.1850-1885) British					
oil	1	1,335		1,335	
MELLOR, William (1851-1931) British					
oil	54	313,649	1,233	5,073	23,550
MELONI, Gino (1905-) Italian					
oil	1	1,397		1,397	
MELOT (19th C) Belgian					
3D	1	1,668		1,668	
MELOTTI, Fausto (1901-1986) Italian					
3D	6	172,114	2,025	23,522	63,800
oil	1	2,656		2,656	
wc/d	1	4,125		4,125	
MELROSE, Andrew (1836-1901) American					
oil	2	12,750	2,750	6,375	10,000
MELTSNER, Paul R (1905-1966) American					
oil	1	1,300		1,300	

Name	No.	Total Sales Value	lowest	Prices median	highest
MELTZER, Anna Elkan (20th C) American					
oil	1	9,000		9,000	
MELTZOFF, Stanley (1917-) American					
oil	1	1,300		1,300	
MELVILLE, Arthur (1858-1904) British					
oil	5	36,450	1,422	2,628	15,800
wc/d	1	29,000		29,000	
MELVILLE, Harden Sidney (fl.1837-1881) British					
oil	3	5,488	1,144	1,800	2,544
MENA, Daniel (1945-) French?					
oil	26	38,038	1,026	1,300	2,964
MENABONI, Athos (1895-?) ?					
oil	2	5,200	1,200	2,600	4,000
MENAGEOT, François Guillaume (1744-1816) French					
oil	1	12,502		12,502	
MENARD, Emile René (1862-1930) French					
oil	4	15,720	2,488	3,616	6,000
wc/d	3	9,456	1,233	1,885	6,338
MENARD, René-Joseph (1827-1887) French					
oil	1	5,398		5,398	
MENASSE, L (?) ?					
oil	1	1,471		1,471	
MENATO, Giuseppe (1876-1962) Italian					
oil	2	11,237	3,440	5,619	7,797
MENCHAUSEN-LABRIOLA, Frieda (1861-?) German					
oil	1	1,096		1,096	
MENDEL, Franz (1807-1876) German					
oil	1	1,200		1,200	
MENDELSON, Marc (1915-) Belgian					
oil	2	14,915	2,239	7,458	12,676
wc/d	8	13,340	1,288	1,610	2,502
MENDEZ BRINGA, Narciso (1868-1933) Spanish					
wc/d	1	1,278		1,278	
MENDEZ OSUNA, Elbano (20th C) Venezuelan					
oil	1	2,240		2,240	
MENDIVE, Manuel (1944-) Cuban					
3D	1	3,000		3,000	
oil	5	36,028	1,902	2,224	19,000
wc/d	3	6,191	1,756	1,927	2,508
MENDJISKY (20th C) ?					
oil	1	1,824		1,824	
MENDJISKY, Serge (1929-) French					
oil	5	8,754	1,024	1,313	3,456
MENDLIK, Oscar Johan Alfred (1871-1963) Hungarian/Dutch					
oil	1	2,173		2,173	
MENDOZE, Robert (20th C) ?					
oil	1	1,200		1,200	
MENE, P J (1810-1879) French					
3D	8	30,719	1,500	3,584	7,830
MENE, Pierre Jules (1810-1879) French					
3D	70	424,470	1,047	3,299	54,950
MENEGHELLI, E (?) ?					
oil	2	2,759	1,281	1,380	1,478
MENEGHELLI, Enrico (19th C) Italian					
oil	4	25,832	1,582	5,625	13,000
MENEGHETTI, Renato (1947-) Italian					
wc/d	3	18,476	4,368	5,006	9,102
MENESCARDI, Giustino (18th C) Italian					
oil	2	20,940	7,350	10,470	13,590

Name	No.	Total Sales Value	lowest	Prices median	highest
MENESES OSORIO, Francisco (1630-1705) Spanish					
oil	1	2,500		2,500	
MENEVILLE (19/20th C) French					
3D	1	2,600		2,600	
MENGATTI, J (20th C) Swiss?					
oil	1	1,283		1,283	
MENGE, Charles (1920-) ?					
oil	1	2,824		2,824	
MENGIN, Charles Auguste (1853-1933) French					
3D	1	1,196		1,196	
MENGIN, Paul Eugène (1853-1937) French					
3D	2	4,255	1,634	2,128	2,621
MENGOTTI, Enrique (1899-1988) Spanish					
oil	1	2,640		2,640	
MENGS, Anton Raphael (1728-1779) German					
oil	2	77,911	37,644	38,956	40,267
MENGUY, Frederic (1927-) French					
oil	2	5,352	1,152	2,676	4,200
MENINSKY, Bernard (1891-1950) British					
oil	6	27,447	1,050	2,729	13,345
wc/d	4	12,895	1,287	2,804	6,000
MENKEN, Johann Heinrich (1766-1834) German					
oil	3	4,090	1,136	1,136	1,818
MENKES, Zygmunt (1896-1986) Polish					
oil	6	30,080	2,854	4,750	7,726
MENN, Barthelemy (1815-1893) Swiss					
oil	3	7,329	1,633	2,431	3,265
MENN, Charles Louis (1822-1894) French					
3D	1	1,021		1,021	
MENNET, Louis (1829-1875) Swiss					
oil	1	1,108		1,108	
MENNYEY, Francesco (1889-1950) Italian					
oil	1	1,098		1,098	
MENON, Anjolie Ela (1940-) Indian					
oil	2	30,000	15,000	15,000	15,000
MENPES, Mortimer L (1860-1938) British					
oil	2	11,741	2,627	5,871	9,114
wc/d	5	10,492	1,051	1,875	3,476
MENS, Isidorus Maria Cornelis van (1890-1985) Belgian					
oil	4	12,080	1,055	3,600	3,825
wc/d	1	1,314		1,314	
MENSAQUE Y ALVARADO, Antonio (19th C) Spanish					
oil	1	1,452		1,452	
MENSE, Carlo (1886-1965) German					
oil	1	6,098		6,098	
wc/d	1	1,138		1,138	
MENSION, Cornelis Jan (1882-1950) Dutch					
oil	1	1,873		1,873	
MENTA, Edouard (1858-1915) Swiss/French					
oil	2	3,341	1,153	1,671	2,188
MENTELER, Franz Thaddaus I (1712-1789) Swiss					
oil	1	1,945		1,945	
MENTELER, Franz Thaddaus II (1751-1794) Swiss					
oil	1	2,674		2,674	
MENTOR (?) ?					
oil	1	1,048		1,048	
MENTOR, Blasco (1918-) Spanish					
oil	8	18,196	1,297	1,847	3,655

Name	No.	Total Sales Value	lowest	Prices median	highest
MENYAYEV, Sergei (1953-) Russian					
oil	1	1,058		1,058	
MENZEL, Adolph (1815-1905) German					
3D	1	1,700		1,700	
wc/d	21	511,349	1,187	14,185	125,429
MENZIES, William A (fl.1886-1911) British					
oil	1	11,360		11,360	
MENZIO, Francesco (1899-1979) Italian					
oil	3	10,716	1,664	4,311	4,741
MENZLER, Wilhelm (1846-1926) German					
oil	1	30,000		30,000	
MERANO, Giovanni Battista (1632-c.1698) Italian					
oil	1	13,710		13,710	
MERARD, Pierre (fl.1763-1800) French					
3D	1	10,080		10,080	
MERCADANTE, Biagio (1893-?) Italian					
oil	1	2,621		2,621	
MERCADE VERGES, Jaume (1922-) Spanish					
oil	1	2,711		2,711	
MERCADE, Jaime (1889-1967) Spanish					
oil	3	9,728	2,017	2,406	5,305
MERCADE, Jordi (1923-) Spanish					
oil	1	1,120		1,120	
MERCHI, Gaetano (1747-1823) Italian					
3D	1	2,436		2,436	
MERCIE, Marius Jean Antonin (1845-1916) French					
3D	13	133,687	1,620	4,396	48,000
MERCIER, Philippe (1689-1760) French					
oil	5	157,780	7,550	27,180	83,050
MERCKAERT, Jules (1872-1924) Belgian					
oil	2	2,869	1,089	1,435	1,780
MERCKER, Erich (1891-1973) German					
oil	5	7,147	1,138	1,552	1,593
MERCULIANO, Giacomo (1859-1935) French					
3D	1	1,501		1,501	
MERDY, Jean le (1928-) French					
oil	1	2,177		2,177	
MEREDITH, John (1933-) Canadian					
oil	1	2,655		2,655	
MEREGAEM, E (19th C) ?					
oil	1	4,750		4,750	
MERIAN, Maria Sibylla (1647-1717) German					
wc/d	1	7,925		7,925	
MERIAN, Matthaus (17th C) Swiss					
wc/d	1	7,071		7,071	
MERIAN, Matthaus (elder) (1593-1650) Swiss					
wc/d	1	2,648		2,648	
MERIDA, Carlos (1891-1984) Guatemalan					
oil	1	8,359		8,359	
wc/d	5	21,850	2,200	2,750	10,000
MERIEL-BUSSY, Andre (1902-1985) French					
oil	1	1,929		1,929	
MERIGS, A R (19th C) French					
oil	1	1,019		1,019	
MERIMEE, Jean Francois Leonor (1757-1836) French					
wc/d	1	1,547		1,547	
MERION, René (19/20th C) ?					
oil	1	1,133		1,133	

Name	No.	Total Sales Value	lowest	Prices median	highest
MERKER, Max (1861-1928) German					
oil	2	2,422	1,184	1,211	1,238
MERKESTEYN, Gerrit Arnoldus van (1825-1858) Dutch					
oil	1	1,530		1,530	
MERLE, Hughes (1823-1881) French					
oil	1	15,730		15,730	
MERLIN, Daniel (1861-1933) French					
oil	1	2,747		2,747	
MERLO, Camillo (20th C) ?					
oil	1	1,318		1,318	
MERLO, Metello (1886-1964) Italian					
oil	3	4,628	1,098	1,651	1,879
MERME, Charles (19th C) French					
oil	1	2,928		2,928	
MERODE, Carl von (1853-1909) Austrian					
oil	1	1,473		1,473	
MERON, C (19th C?) ?					
oil	1	1,700		1,700	
MERRICK, Arthur T (20th C) American					
oil	1	2,700		2,700	
MERRIFIELD, Tom (1932-) Australian					
3D	2	6,134	2,186	3,067	3,948
MERRILD, Knud (1894-1954) Danish					
oil	1	3,254		3,254	
MERRYFIELD, Tom (20th C) British					
oil	1	1,250		1,250	
MERSON, Luc-Olivier (1846-1920) French					
wc/d	1	13,422		13,422	
MERSSEMAN, Auguste Joseph Marie de (1808-1879) French					
oil	1	5,360		5,360	
MERTENS, A (19/20th C) Belgian?					
3D	1	1,424		1,424	
MERTENS, Charles (1865-1919) Belgian					
oil	1	1,308		1,308	
MERTZ, H (19th C) German?					
oil	1	3,142		3,142	
MERTZ, Johann Cornelius (1819-1891) Dutch					
oil	2	3,977	1,885	1,989	2,092
MERWART, Paul (1855-1902) Polish					
oil	1	6,285		6,285	
MERZ, Gerhard (1947-) German					
oil	1	5,000		5,000	
MERZ, Karl (1890-1970) German					
oil	1	1,932		1,932	
MERZ, Mario (1925-) Italian					
oil	3	101,982	4,832	31,900	65,250
wc/d	3	21,131	3,460	8,290	9,381
MES, Hans (1938-) Dutch					
oil	1	1,386		1,386	
MESCHERSKY, Arsenii Ivanovich (1834-1902) Russian					
oil	3	12,210	2,820	3,750	5,640
MESDAG VAN HOUTEN, Sientje (1834-1909) Dutch					
oil	1	4,924		4,924	
wc/d	1	2,134		2,134	
MESDAG, Hendrik-Willem (1831-1915) Dutch					
oil	13	1,038,701	1,358	59,977	203,676
wc/d	6	72,878	3,396	11,934	21,216
MESDAG, Taco (1829-1902) Dutch					
oil	1	1,721		1,721	

Name	No.	Total Sales Value	lowest	Prices median	highest
MESEGUER, Jose (1900-1957) Spanish					
oil	1	1,444		1,444	
MESGRINY, Claude François Auguste de (1836-1884) French					
oil	1	13,000		13,000	
MESLY, David (20th C) ?					
3D	1	2,170		2,170	
MESNAGER, Jerome (1961-) French					
oil	2	5,211	1,283	2,606	3,928
MESNIER (19/20th C) French					
oil	1	6,004		6,004	
MESNIL, Andre (20th C) French					
oil	1	1,049		1,049	
MESSAGER, Annette (1943-) French					
oil	1	21,827		21,827	
wc/d	1	1,654		1,654	
MESSAGIER, Jean (1920-1999) French					
oil	6	20,395	1,383	2,879	6,911
wc/d	1	1,033		1,033	
MESSEG, Aharon (1942-) Israeli					
oil	8	35,050	1,100	3,750	9,000
MESSICK, Ben (1901-1981) American					
oil	1	3,500		3,500	
MESSINA, Francesco (1900-1995) Italian					
3D	9	84,494	1,396	7,373	24,080
wc/d	1	1,080		1,080	
MESSINA, Lillo (1941-) Italian					
oil	1	2,038		2,038	
MESTERHAZY, Kalman (1857-1898) Hungarian					
oil	1	1,500		1,500	
MESTROVIC, Ivan (1883-1962) American/Yugoslavian					
3D	1	3,000		3,000	
METCALF, Conger (1914-1998) American					
oil	1	3,000		3,000	
METCALF, Eliab (1785-1834) American					
oil	2	13,000	6,000	6,500	7,000
METCALF, Willard Leroy (1858-1925) American					
oil	3	247,000	17,000	50,000	180,000
METEYARD, Sidney Harold (1868-1947) British					
wc/d	1	10,010		10,010	
METEYARD, Thomas B (1865-1928) American					
oil	1	3,750		3,750	
METHUEN, Lord (1886-1974) British					
oil	2	3,925	1,081	1,963	2,844
METROFANOV, Sergei (20th C) American					
oil	2	16,000	6,000	8,000	10,000
METSU, Gabriel (1629-1667) Dutch					
oil	1	380,000		380,000	
METSYS, Quentin (1466-1530) Flemish					
oil	1	9,194		9,194	
METTLING, Louis (1847-1904) French					
oil	1	1,476		1,476	
METZ, Friedrich (1820-1901) German					
oil	1	2,420		2,420	
METZ, Johann Martin (1717-1790) German					
oil	1	7,956		7,956	
METZEL, Olaf (1952-) German					
3D	2	3,980	1,709	1,990	2,271
METZINGER, Jean (1883-1956) French					
oil	17	1,339,178	10,570	37,750	550,000

Name	No.	Total Sales Value	lowest	Prices median	highest
wc/d	2	18,466	2,992	9,233	15,474
METZLER, Kurt Laurenz (1941-) Swiss					
3D	2	19,639	4,839	9,820	14,800
MEUCCI, Michelangelo (19th C) Italian					
oil	4	14,097	1,283	3,407	6,000
MEULEN, A (19th C) Dutch					
oil	1	1,000		1,000	
MEULEN, Adam Frans van der (1632-1690) Flemish					
oil	4	241,625	3,750	18,938	200,000
wc/d	2	6,440	2,718	3,220	3,722
MEULEN, Edmond van der (1841-1905) Belgian					
oil	1	4,507		4,507	
MEULENAERE, Pierre Joseph (20th C) ?					
oil	1	3,180		3,180	
MEULENER, Pieter (1602-1654) Dutch					
oil	5	97,217	4,116	9,554	57,380
MEUNIER, Andre-Jacques (18th C) French					
wc/d	1	3,870		3,870	
MEUNIER, Constantin (1831-1905) Belgian					
3D	10	43,622	1,216	3,429	11,008
oil	4	20,666	1,582	4,177	10,730
MEUNIER, Philippe (1655-1734) French					
oil	1	31,400		31,400	
wc/d	2	17,158	8,500	8,579	8,658
MEURER, Charles A (1865-1955) American					
oil	1	6,500		6,500	
MEURS, Harmen (1891-1964) Dutch					
oil	6	23,526	1,481	2,264	12,513
MEVIUS, Hermann (1820-1864) German					
wc/d	1	1,026		1,026	
MEWAR SCHOOL, 17th C Indian					
wc/d	1	3,300		3,300	
MEWAR SCHOOL, 18th C Indian					
wc/d	1	1,500		1,500	
MEXICAN SCHOOL					
oil	1	4,033		4,033	
MEY, Jos de (20th C) Belgian					
oil	1	1,317		1,317	
MEYER VON BREMEN, Johann Georg (1813-1886) German					
oil	9	109,074	2,869	7,742	40,000
wc/d	1	1,136		1,136	
MEYER, A A de (19th C) Dutch					
oil	1	3,681		3,681	
MEYER, Carl Vilhelm (1870-1938) Danish					
oil	3	7,544	2,058	2,711	2,775
MEYER, Christophe (20th C) ?					
oil	2	2,156	1,070	1,078	1,086
MEYER, Claus (1856-1919) German					
oil	1	4,463		4,463	
MEYER, Émile (19th C) French					
oil	1	18,000		18,000	
MEYER, Emmy (1866-1940) German					
oil	1	1,796		1,796	
MEYER, Felicia (1913-) American					
oil	1	1,300		1,300	
MEYER, Hendrik de (17/18th C) Dutch					
oil	1	3,028		3,028	
MEYER, Hendrik de I (1600-1690) Dutch					
oil	2	10,746	2,950	5,373	7,796

Name	No.	Total Sales Value	lowest	Prices median	highest
MEYER, Hendrik de II (1737-1793) Dutch					
wc/d	1	1,768		1,768	
MEYER, Henk (1894-?) Dutch					
oil	1	1,268		1,268	
MEYER, Johan Hendrik Louis (1809-1866) Dutch					
oil	1	12,273		12,273	
MEYER, Jurgen (1945-) German					
oil	1	2,811		2,811	
MEYER, Lazare (19th C) French?					
oil	1	6,530		6,530	
MEYER, Maurice de (1911-) Belgian					
oil	2	2,210	1,053	1,105	1,157
MEYER, Rolf (1913-) Swiss					
oil	1	1,139		1,139	
MEYER, Siri (1898-?) Swedish					
wc/d	1	3,822		3,822	
MEYER-AMDEN, Otto (1885-1933) Swiss					
oil	1	6,653		6,653	
MEYER-BASEL, Carl Theodor (1860-1932) Swiss					
oil	1	1,468		1,468	
MEYER-ELBING, Oscar (1866-?) German					
oil	1	2,320		2,320	
MEYER-MORINGEN, Helene (1898-1958) German					
oil	1	1,226		1,226	
MEYER-WISMAR, Ferdinand (1833-1917) German					
oil	2	9,706	2,206	4,853	7,500
MEYER-ZIMMERMANN, Georg (1814-1895) Swiss					
oil	1	1,355		1,355	
MEYERHEIM, Friedrich Edouard (1808-1879) German					
oil	2	17,916	8,825	8,958	9,091
MEYERHEIM, Paul Friedrich (1842-1915) German					
oil	5	39,560	1,729	2,960	27,413
wc/d	1	2,837		2,837	
MEYERHEIM, Paul Wilhelm (19th C) German					
oil	3	5,609	1,355	2,048	2,206
MEYERHEIM, Robert (19th C) German					
wc/d	1	1,080		1,080	
MEYERHEIM, Wilhelm Alexander (1815-1882) German					
oil	4	23,918	3,147	5,516	9,740
MEYERING, Albert (1645-1714) Dutch					
wc/d	1	1,419		1,419	
MEYEROWITZ, William (1887-1981) American					
oil	1	2,200		2,200	
MEYERS, Isidore (1836-1917) Belgian					
oil	1	1,553		1,553	
MEYERS, Robert (1919-1970) American					
wc/d	1	2,750		2,750	
MEYNIER, Charles (1768-1832) French					
wc/d	1	7,385		7,385	
MEYS, Marcel (fl.1880-1901) French					
oil	1	1,312		1,312	
MEZA, Guillermo (1917-) Mexican					
oil	1	1,700		1,700	
MEZGER, Anton (18th C) Swiss					
wc/d	1	1,155		1,155	
MIAHLE, F (1800-1868) French					
oil	1	1,006		1,006	
MIASOYEDOV, Grigori Grigorievich (1834-1911) Russian					
oil	1	67,950		67,950	

Name	No.	Total Sales Value	Prices lowest	median	highest
MICAELLES, Ruggero (1898-1976) Italian					
oil	2	3,211	1,338	1,606	1,873
MICALI, Giuseppe (19th C) Italian					
oil	1	2,197		2,197	
MICBERTH, Sotere (?) ?					
3D	1	2,025		2,025	
MICCINI, Eugenio (20th C) Italian					
wc/d	2	5,563	2,182	2,782	3,381
MICH, Jean T (1871-1919) Luxembourger					
3D	1	1,282		1,282	
MICHA, Maurice Jean (1890-1969) Belgian					
oil	2	2,569	1,016	1,285	1,553
MICHAEL, Loui (1933-) Scandinavian					
oil	1	2,200		2,200	
MICHALLON, Achille Etna (1796-1822) French					
oil	2	173,721	3,721	86,861	170,000
MICHAU, Theobald (1676-1765) Flemish					
oil	6	240,456	1,340	36,659	84,011
MICHAUX, Henri (1899-1984) Belgian					
oil	8	69,907	3,931	6,940	18,563
wc/d	29	140,097	1,815	4,657	9,554
MICHAUX, John (1876-1956) Belgian					
3D	1	1,087		1,087	
oil	2	4,681	2,135	2,341	2,546
MICHEL (?) ?					
oil	1	2,268		2,268	
MICHEL, C (19th C) French/Belgian					
3D	1	1,547		1,547	
MICHEL, Charles (19th C) French/Belgian					
oil	1	1,097		1,097	
MICHEL, Georges (1763-1843) French					
oil	2	8,735	1,267	4,368	7,468
wc/d	1	2,384		2,384	
MICHEL, Robert (1897-1983) German					
wc/d	2	22,282	7,282	11,141	15,000
MICHELACCI, Luigi (?) Italian					
oil	1	2,007		2,007	
MICHELANGELO (1475-1564) Italian					
wc/d	1	11,174,001		11,174,001	
MICHELANGELO (school) (1475-1564) Italian					
wc/d	1	4,750		4,750	
MICHELENA, Arturo (1863-1898) Venezuelan					
wc/d	1	3,370		3,370	
MICHELET, Georges (19/20th C) French					
oil	1	34,443		34,443	
MICHELETTI, Mario (1892-?) Italian					
oil	3	4,532	1,338	1,497	1,697
MICHETTI, Francesco Paolo (1851-1929) Italian					
oil	9	83,778	1,516	7,069	20,066
wc/d	4	6,899	1,055	1,523	2,799
MICHIE, David (1928-) British					
oil	2	3,100	1,520	1,550	1,580
MICHIE, James Coutts (1861-1919) British					
oil	1	1,716		1,716	
MICHIE, John D (fl.1864-1892) British					
oil	1	1,600		1,600	
MICHIELS, Robert (1933-) Belgian					
3D	1	2,146		2,146	

Name	No.	Total Sales Value	lowest	Prices median	highest
MICHONZE, Gregoire (1902-1982) French					
oil	2	3,841	1,918	1,921	1,923
MIDDEL, Maurits van (1886-?) Belgian					
oil	1	1,211		1,211	
MIDDENDORF, Helmut (1953-) German					
oil	6	35,833	3,244	6,358	10,000
wc/d	4	23,804	1,211	4,204	14,185
MIDDLE RHINE SCHOOL, 15th C German					
3D	1	5,363		5,363	
MIDDLETON, Colin (1910-1983) British					
oil	9	63,873	1,125	5,338	19,240
wc/d	3	5,727	1,152	1,275	3,300
MIDDLETON, John (1828-1856) British					
wc/d	1	9,295		9,295	
MIDDLETON, Sam (1927-) American					
wc/d	1	1,293		1,293	
MIDWOOD, William Henry (fl.1867-1871) British					
oil	3	9,688	1,659	3,453	4,576
MIDY, A (19/20th C) French					
wc/d	1	2,980		2,980	
MIDY, Arthur (1887-1944) French					
oil	2	3,383	1,179	1,692	2,204
MIDY, Theophile Adolphe (1821-?) French					
wc/d	1	1,232		1,232	
MIEDEMA, Rein (1835-1912) Dutch					
oil	1	1,483		1,483	
MIEDUCH, Dan (1947-) American					
oil	1	30,000		30,000	
MIEGHEM, Eugène van (1875-1930) Belgian					
oil	14	129,800	1,180	5,117	29,247
wc/d	49	147,952	1,045	1,552	23,727
MIEL, Jan (1599-1663) Flemish					
wc/d	1	1,208		1,208	
MIEL, Jan (school) (1599-1663) Flemish					
oil	1	4,374		4,374	
MIELUNSKI, M (19/20th C) ?					
oil	1	1,634		1,634	
MIENSE, Jan (c.1610-1668) Dutch					
oil	1	17,776		17,776	
MIERAS, J P (20th C) Dutch?					
oil	1	2,399		2,399	
MIEREVELT, Michiel Jans van (1567-1641) Dutch					
oil	2	22,315	8,635	11,158	13,680
MIERIS, Frans van (elder) (1635-1681) Dutch					
oil	1	575,000		575,000	
MIERIS, Willem van (1662-1747) Dutch					
oil	4	501,500	3,460	111,520	275,000
wc/d	1	3,689		3,689	
MIERLO, Eugène Victor Joseph van (1880-1972) Belgian					
oil	1	3,003		3,003	
MIETH, Hugo (1865-?) German					
oil	2	3,474	1,224	1,737	2,250
MIGLIARA, Giovanni (1785-1837) Italian					
oil	2	32,660	12,080	16,330	20,580
wc/d	3	11,872	2,328	3,202	6,342
MIGLIARO, Vincenzo (1858-1938) Italian					
oil	3	18,411	1,180	1,431	15,800
wc/d	1	2,182		2,182	
MIGNARD, Nicolas (1606-1668) French					
oil	2	120,449	38,000	60,225	82,449

Name	No.	Total Sales Value	lowest	Prices median	highest
wc/d	3	7,593	1,139	1,197	5,257
MIGNARD, Paul (c.1638-1691) French					
oil	1	4,305		4,305	
MIGNARD, Pierre (17/18th C) French					
oil	1	16,610		16,610	
MIGNECO, Giuseppe (1908-1997) Italian					
oil	12	128,782	2,232	8,415	25,656
wc/d	3	4,150	1,173	1,434	1,543
MIGNON, Abraham (1640-1679) German					
oil	1	875,800		875,800	
MIGNON, L (19/20th C) ?					
3D	1	1,593		1,593	
MIGNON, Léon (1847-1898) Belgian					
3D	3	4,423	1,220	1,486	1,717
MIGNON, Lucien (1865-1944) French					
oil	4	8,264	1,460	1,902	3,000
MIKESCH, Fritzi (1853-1891) Austrian					
oil	2	16,500	8,000	8,250	8,500
MIKLOS, Gustave (1888-1967) French					
3D	1	11,766		11,766	
wc/d	3	8,893	2,062	2,062	4,769
MIKLOS, Gustave and SCHMIED, Francois Louis (20th C) French/Swiss					
wc/d	3	12,729	3,564	3,637	5,528
MIKULICZ-BREYER, Isabella von (1887-1973) Czechoslovakian					
oil	1	2,915		2,915	
MILANESE SCHOOL, 16th C Italian					
oil	2	56,924	8,024	28,462	48,900
MILANESE SCHOOL, 17th C Italian					
oil	1	4,655		4,655	
MILANI, Aureliano (1675-1749) Italian					
wc/d	1	1,470		1,470	
MILANI, H (20th C) Italian					
3D	1	1,750		1,750	
MILANI, Umberto (1912-1969) Italian					
oil	3	9,100	1,447	2,912	4,741
MILBURN, Oliver (1883-1934) American					
oil	2	9,000	4,000	4,500	5,000
MILEHAM, Harry Robert (1873-1957) British					
oil	1	5,145		5,145	
MILES, J R (20th C?) Australian?					
oil	1	1,763		1,763	
MILES, John (?) British?					
oil	1	12,324		12,324	
MILES, Thomas Rose (fl.1869-1906) British					
oil	11	43,429	1,208	2,512	15,000
MILEY, R A (19th C) British					
oil	1	3,146		3,146	
MILHAZES, Beatriz (1960-) Brazilian					
wc/d	1	1,800		1,800	
MILIADIS, Stelios (1881-1965) Greek					
oil	1	5,256		5,256	
MILICH, Simon Levy Gimond (20th C) French					
oil	1	2,762		2,762	
MILLAIS, Raoul (1901-) British					
oil	3	13,435	1,502	1,573	10,360
MILLAIS, Sir John Everett (1829-1896) British					
oil	5	1,974,600	31,600	211,400	1,208,000
MILLAN FERRIZ, Emilio (19th C) Spanish					
oil	1	1,026		1,026	

Name	No.	Total Sales Value	lowest	Prices median	highest
MILLAR, Addison T (1860-1913) American					
oil	7	94,803	1,900	6,000	44,088
wc/d	2	6,300	3,000	3,150	3,300
MILLAR, James (18th C) British					
oil	1	4,228		4,228	
wc/d	1	3,160		3,160	
MILLARD, Daryl (20th C) American					
oil	1	1,500		1,500	
MILLARES, Manolo (1926-1972) Spanish					
oil	7	166,001	5,010	17,257	62,273
wc/d	3	72,796	8,745	9,724	54,327
MILLER, Alfred Jacob (1810-1874) American					
oil	1	46,000		46,000	
wc/d	3	59,750	2,000	2,750	55,000
MILLER, Charles Keith (19th C) British					
oil	5	21,971	1,216	4,228	9,880
MILLER, Frederick (19th C) British					
wc/d	1	1,884		1,884	
MILLER, G W (19th C) British					
oil	2	2,583	1,073	1,292	1,510
MILLER, George (fl.1827-1853) British					
oil	1	11,000		11,000	
MILLER, H G (?) American					
oil	1	1,176		1,176	
MILLER, Iris Marie Andrew (1881-?) American					
oil	2	2,100	1,000	1,050	1,100
MILLER, J (?) British					
oil	1	1,900		1,900	
MILLER, James (18-20th C) British					
wc/d	1	2,256		2,256	
MILLER, John (1911-1975) British					
oil	2	5,184	2,340	2,592	2,844
MILLER, John (fl.1876-1890) British					
oil	1	1,975		1,975	
MILLER, John (1931-) British					
oil	3	6,188	1,008	2,160	3,020
MILLER, John (1893-1975) British					
oil	2	2,294	1,147	1,147	1,147
MILLER, Mildred Bunting (1892-?) American					
oil	1	2,000		2,000	
MILLER, Ralph Davison (1858-1946) American					
oil	1	1,500		1,500	
MILLER, Richard E (1875-1943) American					
oil	7	1,455,000	10,000	55,000	600,000
MILLER, Roy (1938-) British					
oil	5	6,422	1,057	1,284	1,661
MILLER, Thomas Oxley (1854-1909) American					
oil	1	4,000		4,000	
MILLER, William G (fl.1891-1908) British					
wc/d	2	12,197	1,050	6,099	11,147
MILLER, William Rickarby (1818-1893) American					
oil	3	54,800	2,800	12,000	40,000
wc/d	1	2,000		2,000	
MILLER-DIFLO, Otto (1878-1949) German					
oil	1	1,007		1,007	
MILLES, Carl (1875-1955) Swedish/American					
3D	24	278,852	1,146	4,347	76,588
MILLES, Ruth (1873-1955) Swedish					
3D	3	4,697	1,126	1,656	1,915

Name	No.	Total Sales Value	lowest	Prices median	highest
MILLESON, Royal Hill (1849-1926) American					
oil	1	2,000		2,000	
MILLET, Francisque II (school) (1666-1723) French					
oil	1	2,360		2,360	
MILLET, Jean Baptiste (1831-1906) French					
wc/d	1	2,000		2,000	
MILLET, Jean François (1814-1875) French					
oil	4	447,200	7,200	40,000	360,000
wc/d	16	262,439	1,185	4,025	90,000
MILLIKEN, James W (fl.1887-1930) British					
wc/d	1	1,181		1,181	
MILLIKEN, Robert W (1920-) British					
wc/d	1	1,450		1,450	
MILLION, Joseph (1861-1931) French					
oil	1	1,305		1,305	
MILLNER, Karl (1825-1894) German					
oil	8	19,745	1,288	2,222	4,210
MILLNER, William Edward (1849-1885) British					
oil	1	5,720		5,720	
MILNE, David Brown (1882-1953) Canadian					
oil	2	46,738	1,044	23,369	45,694
wc/d	6	103,449	8,628	19,165	23,892
MILNE, J M (?) British					
oil	1	5,292		5,292	
MILNE, Joe (fl.1905-1908) British					
oil	3	7,866	1,029	3,045	3,792
MILNE, John Maclaughlan (1885-1957) British					
oil	5	47,966	4,116	9,165	16,060
wc/d	1	1,431		1,431	
MILNE, Joseph (1861-1911) British					
oil	3	13,226	2,920	5,056	5,250
MILNE, William (19/20th C) British					
oil	2	3,388	1,650	1,694	1,738
MILNE, William Watt (fl.1900-1915) British					
oil	10	37,480	1,029	2,431	11,680
MILO, Jean (1906-1993) Belgian					
oil	1	1,916		1,916	
wc/d	2	2,939	1,278	1,470	1,661
MILON, J (20th C) French					
oil	1	1,272		1,272	
MILOVITCH, Tanasko (1900-) American/Yugoslavian					
oil	1	1,600		1,600	
MILROY, Lisa (1959-) Canadian					
oil	5	59,260	3,000	13,590	17,000
MILTHON (20th C) French?					
3D	1	1,710		1,710	
MILTON-JENSEN, C (1855-1928) Danish					
oil	2	2,559	1,132	1,280	1,427
MILTON-JENSEN, Carl (1855-1928) Danish					
oil	1	1,272		1,272	
MIMNAUGH, Terry (20th C) American					
oil	1	16,000		16,000	
MIMON, S (?) Spanish					
oil	1	1,026		1,026	
MIMRAN, Patrick (1956-) American?					
wc/d	1	60,000		60,000	
MIN, Jaap (1914-1987) Dutch					
oil	3	13,116	2,341	4,741	6,034

Name	No.	Total Sales Value	lowest	Prices median	highest
MINARDI, Tommaso (1787-1871) Italian					
wc/d	1	2,200		2,200	
MIND, Gottfried (1768-1814) Swiss					
wc/d	1	3,546		3,546	
MINDERHOUT, Hendrik van (1632-1696) Dutch					
oil	2	36,755	10,570	18,378	26,185
MINDERMANN, J H (1872-1959) German					
oil	1	2,994		2,994	
MINERBI, Arrigo (1881-1960) Italian					
3D	1	9,890		9,890	
MINET, Louis Émile (?-1920) French					
oil	1	1,503		1,503	
MING DYNASTY Chinese					
wc/d	1	9,000		9,000	
MINGORANCE ACIEN, Manuel (1920-) Spanish					
oil	3	4,147	1,287	1,430	1,430
MINGORANCE, Juan E (1906-1976) Spanish					
oil	1	1,200		1,200	
MINGUZZI, Luciano (1911-) Italian					
oil	1	2,676		2,676	
MINNE, George (1866-1941) Belgian					
3D	7	43,754	1,429	4,178	19,032
wc/d	6	20,709	1,640	3,095	6,717
MINNE, Jean Louis (?) ?					
oil	1	1,668		1,668	
MINNEBO, Hubert (1940-) Belgian					
3D	1	10,483		10,483	
MINOR, Robert Crannell (1839-1904) American					
oil	1	2,300		2,300	
MINSHULL, R T (fl.1866-1885) British					
oil	1	3,796		3,796	
MINTCHINE, Abraham (1898-1931) Russian					
oil	1	2,213		2,213	
MINTON, John (1917-1957) British					
oil	1	1,132		1,132	
wc/d	3	9,034	1,716	3,600	3,718
MIOLA, Camillo (1840-1919) Italian					
oil	1	1,149		1,149	
MIOLIN (?) French					
3D	1	2,884		2,884	
MION, Luigi (19th C) Italian					
oil	1	1,049		1,049	
MIOTTE, Jean (1926-) French					
oil	5	13,897	1,180	3,076	4,132
MIR Y TRINXET, Joaquin (1873-1940) Spanish					
oil	9	533,666	6,078	17,257	330,000
MIRA, Alfred S (20th C) American					
oil	7	57,150	3,700	5,500	19,000
MIRA, Victor (1949-) Spanish					
oil	6	14,042	1,282	1,882	4,225
wc/d	1	1,149		1,149	
MIRABELLA, Saro (20th C) Italian					
oil	2	5,411	2,239	2,706	3,172
MIRABENT Y CATELL, Jose (1831-1899) Spanish					
oil	1	7,706		7,706	
MIRAGLIA, Ermogene (1907-1964) Italian					
oil	1	2,182		2,182	
MIRALDA, Antoni (1942-) Spanish					
3D	1	1,224		1,224	

Name	No.	Total Sales Value	Prices lowest	median	highest
MIRALLES DARMANIN, Jose (1851-?) Spanish					
oil	4	56,661	1,278	8,105	39,173
MIRALLES, Enrique (19/20th C) Spanish					
oil	1	1,895		1,895	
MIRALLES, Francisco (1848-1901) Spanish					
oil	3	77,462	6,490	25,389	45,583
wc/d	1	1,452		1,452	
MIRANDA Y RENDON, Manuel (19th C) Spanish					
oil	1	7,857		7,857	
MIRKO (1910-1969) Italian					
oil	1	1,242		1,242	
MIRO ARGENTER, Joaquim (1849-1914) Argentinian					
oil	2	3,889	1,249	1,945	2,640
MIRO, Joachim (1875-1941) Spanish					
oil	6	33,227	2,108	5,919	8,181
MIRO, Joan (1893-1983) Spanish					
3D	9	1,374,007	7,877	48,320	500,000
oil	10	5,577,635	9,000	410,000	1,500,000
wc/d	45	3,965,597	1,212	21,854	1,900,000
MIRZA, Bashir (1941-2000) Indian					
wc/d	1	3,000		3,000	
MISAO, Yokoyama (1920-1973) Japanese					
wc/d	1	40,000		40,000	
MISSONI, Ottavio (20th C) Italian?					
wc/d	1	1,165		1,165	
MISZFELDT, Heinrich (1872-?) German					
3D	1	1,982		1,982	
MITCHELL OF MARYPORT, William (c.1806-1900) British					
oil	2	6,000	1,500	3,000	4,500
MITCHELL, Alfred R (1888-1972) American					
oil	13	118,000	3,500	7,500	24,000
MITCHELL, Arthur (181864-1954) American					
oil	1	1,100		1,100	
MITCHELL, Denis (1912-1993) British					
3D	1	1,444		1,444	
MITCHELL, Gordon K (20th C) British					
oil	1	2,160		2,160	
MITCHELL, J A (1845-?) American					
oil	1	18,590		18,590	
MITCHELL, Janet (1912-1998) Canadian					
oil	2	3,016	1,200	1,508	1,816
wc/d	1	1,567		1,567	
MITCHELL, Joan (1926-1992) American					
oil	8	1,539,000	16,000	106,500	750,000
wc/d	2	16,836	3,836	8,418	13,000
MITCHELL, John (1838-1926) British					
wc/d	1	1,197		1,197	
MITCHELL, John Campbell (1862-1922) British					
oil	1	1,029		1,029	
wc/d	1	7,250		7,250	
MITCHELL, Philip (1814-1896) British					
wc/d	1	1,200		1,200	
MITCHELL, Thomas (1735-1790) British					
oil	1	6,435		6,435	
MITCHELL, William (fl.1880-1903) British					
oil	1	1,233		1,233	
MITCHELL, William Frederick (1845-1914) British					
wc/d	1	1,141		1,141	
MITFORD, Robert (20th C) American?					
wc/d	1	1,500		1,500	

Name	No.	Total Sales Value	lowest	Prices median	highest
MITORAJ, Igor (20th C) ?					
3D	1	1,482		1,482	
wc/d	1	1,129		1,129	
MITSUARI (19th C) Japanese					
3D	1	6,198		6,198	
MITTERFELLNER, A (1912-1972) German					
oil	2	3,872	1,936	1,936	1,936
MITTERFELLNER, Andreas (1912-1972) German					
oil	1	1,007		1,007	
MITTERTREINER, Johannes Jacobus (1851-1890) Dutch					
oil	1	3,443		3,443	
MITTEY, Joseph (1853-1936) Swiss?					
wc/d	1	1,709		1,709	
MIXON, A (17th C) German					
oil	1	4,874		4,874	
MIYAJIMA, Tatsuo (1957) Japanese					
3D	2	24,080	12,000	12,040	12,080
MIYAMOTO, Saburo (1905-1974) Japanese					
oil	2	113,000	38,000	56,500	75,000
MIYAO (?) Japanese					
3D	1	11,283		11,283	
MIZEN, Frederic Kimball (1888-1964) American					
oil	2	8,500	3,500	4,250	5,000
wc/d	1	1,400		1,400	
MNIZECK, Andre Vandalin (?-1905) French					
oil	1	5,164		5,164	
MOAL, Jean le (1909-) French					
oil	9	38,871	2,240	3,274	7,524
MOCK, Jhr Johannes (1800-1884) Dutch					
oil	1	3,707		3,707	
MODELL, Elisabeth (1820-1865) Austrian					
oil	1	1,309		1,309	
MODERAT D'OTEMAR, Marie Adolphe (19th C) French					
oil	1	2,408		2,408	
MODERN SCHOOL					
wc/d	1	6,401		6,401	
MODERSOHN, Otto (1865-1943) German					
oil	16	347,506	8,650	15,592	86,503
MODERSOHN-BECKER, Paula (1876-1907) German					
wc/d	3	11,625	1,496	2,564	7,565
MODESITT, John (1955-) American					
oil	3	7,750	2,500	2,500	2,750
MODIGLIANI, Amedeo (1884-1920) Italian					
3D	1	13,659		13,659	
oil	8	37,300,000	1,500,000	3,550,000	14,200,000
wc/d	22	1,825,181	7,200	38,327	550,000
MODROW, Fritz (1888-) German					
oil	1	1,026		1,026	
MOEBIUS (20th C) French					
wc/d	3	4,599	1,168	1,387	2,044
MOEBUS, Peter (1954-) German					
oil	2	4,398	2,184	2,199	2,214
MOELLER, Louis C (1855-1930) American					
oil	6	38,550	3,000	5,400	13,000
MOER, Jean Baptiste van (1819-1884) Belgian					
oil	3	7,396	1,030	2,431	3,935
MOERENHOUT, Edouard Joris (1801-?) Belgian					
oil	1	2,575		2,575	

Name	No.	Total Sales Value	lowest	Prices median	highest
MOERENHOUT, Edward (19th C) Belgian					
oil	2	3,747	1,179	1,874	2,568
MOERENHOUT, Joseph Jodocus (1801-1874) Belgian					
oil	1	27,581		27,581	
MOERMAN, Albert Edouard (1808-1856) Belgian					
oil	1	23,586		23,586	
MOERMAN, Johannes Lodewyk (1850-1896) Flemish					
oil	1	2,366		2,366	
MOESCHLIN, Walter J (1902-1961) Swiss					
oil	2	3,612	1,362	1,806	2,250
MOEST, Hermann (1868-1945) German					
oil	1	8,218		8,218	
MOEYAERT, Nicolaes Cornelisz (1592-1655) Dutch					
oil	1	8,820		8,820	
MOFFAT, O (20th C) British					
oil	1	1,001		1,001	
MOFFETT, Donald (?) American?					
oil	1	4,250		4,250	
MOGFORD OF EXETER, Thomas (1809-1868) British					
oil	1	11,850		11,850	
MOGFORD, John (1821-1885) British					
oil	2	5,136	1,924	2,568	3,212
wc/d	9	28,230	1,138	2,002	9,724
MOGGIOLI, Umberto (1886-1919) Italian					
oil	1	30,499		30,499	
wc/d	1	2,033		2,033	
MOGHUL SCHOOL, 17th C Indian					
oil	2	73,000	28,000	36,500	45,000
wc/d	3	13,108	3,745	3,745	5,618
MOGHUL SCHOOL, 18th C Indian					
wc/d	3	10,969	2,675	2,943	5,351
MOGUILEVSKI, Leonid (1931-) Russian					
3D	1	1,000		1,000	
MOHLER, Gustave Jean Louis (1836-?) French					
oil	1	13,000		13,000	
MOHN, Victor Paul (1842-1911) German					
oil	1	18,940		18,940	
MOHOLY-NAGY, Laszlo (1895-1946) American/Hungarian					
oil	2	1,015,500	34,000	507,750	981,500
wc/d	12	108,751	1,092	2,572	42,500
MOHR, K (19/20th C) German					
oil	1	1,700		1,700	
MOHRMANN, John Henry (1857-1916) American					
oil	4	19,938	1,931	4,292	9,424
MOIGNIEZ, Jules (1835-1894) French					
3D	23	64,393	1,095	2,200	9,000
MOILLIET, Louis (1880-1962) Swiss					
wc/d	7	40,316	3,327	4,858	9,723
MOILLON, Louise (1609-1696) French					
oil	1	83,050		83,050	
MOIRIGNOT, Edmond (1913-) French					
3D	3	8,236	1,237	2,572	4,427
MOISELET, Gabriel (1885-1961) French					
oil	1	4,838		4,838	
MOISES, Julio (1888-1968) Spanish					
oil	1	1,582		1,582	
MOISNIEZ, G (?) ?					
oil	1	1,081		1,081	

Name	No.	Total Sales Value	Prices lowest	median	highest
MOISSET, Raymond (1906-) French					
oil	1	1,663		1,663	
MOITTE, Alexandre (1750-1828) French					
wc/d	1	3,750		3,750	
MOITTE, Jean Guillaume (1746-1810) French					
wc/d	3	21,461	6,000	7,156	8,305
MOJA, Frederico (1802-1885) Italian					
oil	3	25,989	5,224	9,227	11,538
MOKADY, Moshe (1902-1975) Israeli					
oil	9	185,600	1,900	9,000	70,000
wc/d	2	42,200	2,200	21,100	40,000
MOL, Gerrit (1869-1961) Dutch					
oil	1	1,078		1,078	
MOL, Leo (1915-) Canadian					
3D	1	3,068		3,068	
MOLA, Jean Baptiste (1616-1661) Italian/French					
oil	1	3,871		3,871	
MOLA, Pier Francesco (1612-1666) Italian					
oil	1	2,220		2,220	
wc/d	7	60,386	1,481	7,550	17,365
MOLA, Pier Francesco (school) (1612-1666) Italian					
oil	1	4,666		4,666	
MOLANUS, Mattheus (?-1645) Dutch					
oil	1	12,866		12,866	
MOLE, John Henry (1814-1886) British					
wc/d	9	28,893	1,044	1,800	8,294
MOLENAAR, Johannes Petrus (1914-) Dutch					
oil	1	1,100		1,100	
MOLENAER, Bartholomeus (1612-1650) Dutch					
oil	2	35,073	10,828	17,537	24,245
MOLENAER, Jan Jacobz (1654-?) Dutch					
oil	1	2,166		2,166	
MOLENAER, Jan Miense (1610-1668) Dutch					
oil	15	184,700	1,182	4,500	40,000
MOLENAER, Klaes (1630-1676) Dutch					
oil	6	63,482	2,617	9,598	21,571
MOLERO, Antonio (1945-) ?					
oil	1	1,687		1,687	
MOLES, Francisco (19/20th C) Spanish					
oil	1	3,087		3,087	
MOLEZUN SUAREZ, Manuel (1920-) Spanish					
wc/d	1	1,453		1,453	
MOLFENTER, Hans (1884-?) German					
oil	3	3,910	1,009	1,387	1,514
wc/d	4	7,267	1,009	1,363	3,533
MOLIN, Oreste da (1856-1921) Italian					
oil	2	5,844	2,500	2,922	3,344
MOLINA CAMPOS, Florencio (1891-1959) Argentinian					
oil	1	12,500		12,500	
MOLINA NUNEZ, Emilio (20th C) Spanish					
oil	1	1,639		1,639	
MOLINA, Juan Jose (20th C) South American?					
oil	1	1,720		1,720	
MOLINARI, Antonio (school) (?-1648) Italian					
oil	1	17,453		17,453	
MOLINARI, Guido (19th C) Italian					
oil	2	24,707	4,797	12,354	19,910
MOLINARO, Giacomo (1834-1901) Italian					
oil	1	1,376		1,376	

Name	No.	Total Sales Value	lowest	Prices median	highest
MOLINARY, Andre (1847-1915) American					
oil	1	3,500		3,500	
MOLINO, Walter (1915-1997) Italian					
oil	1	1,877		1,877	
MOLL, Carl (1861-1945) Austrian					
oil	2	99,779	30,000	49,890	69,779
MOLL, Evert (1878-1955) Dutch					
oil	22	46,089	1,061	1,712	4,683
MOLL, Marg (1884-1977) German					
3D	2	3,127	1,282	1,564	1,845
MOLL, Oskar (1875-1947) German					
oil	5	70,235	7,785	10,680	20,805
wc/d	3	23,368	6,620	8,010	8,738
MOLLARI, Mario Miguel (1930-) Argentinian					
oil	1	1,600		1,600	
MOLLBACK, Christian (1853-1921) Danish					
oil	3	29,448	2,065	2,383	25,000
MOLLENHAUER, Ernst (1892-1963) German					
oil	1	16,505		16,505	
MOLLER, Carl Henrik Koch (1845-1920) Danish					
oil	1	1,044		1,044	
MOLLER, J P (1783-1854) Danish					
oil	2	2,628	1,044	1,314	1,584
MOLLER, Jens Peter (1783-1854) Danish					
oil	4	21,772	1,207	5,178	10,209
MOLLER, Johan Frederik (1797-1871) Danish					
oil	1	1,484		1,484	
MOLLER, Olivia Holm (1875-1970) Danish					
oil	1	1,211		1,211	
MOLLET, L A (?) ?					
oil	1	4,926		4,926	
MOLLICA, Achille (19th C) Italian					
oil	3	49,305	3,160	4,145	42,000
MOLLICA, Emanuell (19th C) Italian					
oil	1	1,057		1,057	
MOLLIET, Clemence (19th C) French					
oil	1	4,000		4,000	
MOLLINGER, Alexander (1836-1867) Dutch					
oil	1	2,869		2,869	
MOLNAR, Rezes C (20th C) Hungarian					
oil	1	1,400		1,400	
MOLS, N P (1859-1921) Danish					
oil	4	10,084	1,511	2,461	3,652
MOLS, Niels Pedersen (1859-1921) Danish					
oil	1	1,026		1,026	
MOLS, Robert (1848-1903) Belgian					
oil	2	4,954	2,328	2,477	2,626
MOLSTED, Chr (1862-1930) Danish					
oil	6	25,511	1,140	3,845	7,149
MOLTENI, Giuseppe (1800-1867) Italian					
oil	1	17,965		17,965	
MOLTINO, Francis (1818-1874) British					
oil	2	4,280	1,430	2,140	2,850
MOLYN, Petrus Marius (1819-1849) Belgian					
oil	1	1,380		1,380	
MOLYN, Pieter (1595-1661) Dutch					
oil	2	22,301	7,386	11,151	14,915
wc/d	6	108,081	9,060	17,843	28,000

Name	No.	Total Sales Value	lowest	Prices median	highest
MOLYNEUX, Edward (1896-?) American					
oil	1	1,199		1,199	
MOLZAHN, Johannes (1892-1965) German					
wc/d	1	16,868		16,868	
MOMEN, Karl (1935-) Swedish					
3D	1	2,412		2,412	
MOMMERS, Hendrik (1623-1693) Dutch					
oil	2	15,087	3,087	7,544	12,000
MOMPER, Frans de (1603-1660) Flemish					
oil	1	5,142		5,142	
MOMPER, Jan de (16/17th C) Flemish					
oil	4	64,858	7,920	10,388	36,163
MOMPER, Joos de (1564-1635) Flemish					
oil	3	145,874	14,673	32,928	98,273
MOMPER, Joos de (school) (1564-1635) Flemish					
oil	1	13,248		13,248	
MOMPER, Philips de (elder) (1598-1634) Flemish					
oil	1	7,820		7,820	
MOMPER, Philips de (younger) (c.1610-1675) Flemish					
oil	1	10,205		10,205	
MOMPO, Manolo (20th C) Spanish					
oil	2	24,974	9,687	12,487	15,287
MOMPOU, Joseph (1888-1969) Spanish					
wc/d	1	1,016		1,016	
MONA, Domenico (c.1550-1602) Italian					
wc/d	1	2,265		2,265	
MONACA, Alberto la (1862-1936) Italian					
wc/d	1	2,523		2,523	
MONACA, Francis la (1882-1937) Italian					
3D	1	1,659		1,659	
MONACA, la (?) ?					
3D	1	3,500		3,500	
MONACHESI, Sante (1910-1991) Italian					
oil	9	17,883	1,055	1,833	4,363
wc/d	1	1,877		1,877	
MONALDI, Paolo (18th C) Italian					
oil	2	42,000	9,500	21,000	32,500
MONAMY, Peter (1689-1749) British					
oil	9	168,638	4,530	15,200	38,610
MONASTERIOS, Rafael (1884-1961) Venezuelan					
oil	1	3,000		3,000	
MONCADA CALVACHE, Jose (1895-) Spanish					
oil	2	6,968	3,484	3,484	3,484
MONCEL DE PERRIN, Count Alphonse de (1866-1930) French					
3D	1	1,375		1,375	
MONCHABLON, Jean Ferdinand (1855-1904) French					
oil	1	1,380		1,380	
MONDINEN, E (1872-?) French					
oil	1	3,120		3,120	
MONDINO, Aldo (1938-) Italian					
oil	3	3,511	1,134	1,134	1,222
MONDO, Domenico (1717-1806) Italian					
wc/d	3	9,924	1,468	1,661	6,795
MONDOLONI, Jules Frank (20th C) French					
wc/d	1	1,500		1,500	
MONDRIAAN, Frits (1853-1932) Dutch					
oil	1	1,795		1,795	
MONDRIAN, P (1872-1944) Dutch					
oil	1	232,759		232,759	

Name	No.	Total Sales Value	lowest	Prices median	highest
MONDRIAN, Piet (1872-1944) Dutch					
oil	2	283,974	27,729	141,987	256,245
wc/d	2	337,759	107,759	168,880	230,000
MONDZAIN, Simon François Stanislas (1890-1979) French					
oil	1	1,567		1,567	
MONET, Claude (1840-1926) French					
oil	25	118,858,001	650,000	2,250,000	22,000,000
wc/d	3	570,000	170,000	180,000	220,000
MONEY, Fred (1882-1956) French					
oil	1	3,791		3,791	
MONFORT, Octavianus (fl.17th C) Italian					
oil	4	85,563	5,064	8,706	63,087
MONFORT, Octavianus (school) (fl.17th C) Italian					
oil	2	3,720	1,848	1,860	1,872
MONFREID, Georges Daniel de (1856-1929) French					
3D	1	13,533		13,533	
oil	3	15,383	2,112	5,280	7,991
MONGIN, Antoine Pierre (1761-1827) French					
wc/d	2	50,063	3,275	25,032	46,788
MONGINOT, Charles (1825-1900) French					
oil	2	21,120	8,250	10,560	12,870
wc/d	1	1,197		1,197	
MONGINOT, Charlotte (1872-?) French					
3D	1	1,761		1,761	
MONGOLIAN SCHOOL, 17th C					
wc/d	1	3,412		3,412	
MONI, Louis de (1698-1771) Dutch					
oil	2	15,242	2,682	7,621	12,560
MONIC, Daniel (1948-) ?					
3D	1	1,177		1,177	
MONIER, Pierre (1641-1703) French					
wc/d	1	5,285		5,285	
MONINOT, Bernard (20th C) French					
wc/d	2	5,210	2,259	2,605	2,951
MONKS, John Austin Sands (1850-1917) American					
oil	2	2,219	1,076	1,110	1,143
MONLEON Y TORRES, Raphael (1847-1900) Spanish					
wc/d	1	1,709		1,709	
MONNICKENDAM, Martin (1874-1943) Dutch					
oil	1	1,724		1,724	
wc/d	1	2,970		2,970	
MONNIER, Charles (1837-1875) Swiss					
oil	1	1,253		1,253	
MONNINGTON, Sir Walter Thomas (1903-1976) British					
oil	1	3,666		3,666	
MONNOT, Maurice Louis (1869-?) French					
oil	1	1,291		1,291	
MONNOYER (17/18th C) French					
oil	1	3,263		3,263	
MONNOYER, Jean Baptiste (1636-1699) French					
oil	6	235,734	8,500	33,717	80,000
MONNOYER, Jean Baptiste (school) (1636-1699) French					
oil	1	2,400		2,400	
MONOGRAMMIST A G (?) ?					
oil	1	24,990		24,990	
MONOGRAMMIST A G F (?) ?					
oil	1	1,225		1,225	
MONOGRAMMIST A H (?) ?					
oil	1	2,693		2,693	

Name	No.	Total Sales Value	Prices lowest	Prices median	highest
MONOGRAMMIST A J H (?) ?					
oil	1	9,491		9,491	
MONOGRAMMIST A V (?) ?					
oil	1	1,472		1,472	
MONOGRAMMIST B B (?) ?					
oil	1	33,022		33,022	
MONOGRAMMIST C B (?) ?					
oil	1	2,724		2,724	
MONOGRAMMIST C H (?) ?					
oil	1	2,023		2,023	
MONOGRAMMIST C L (?) ?					
oil	1	1,475		1,475	
MONOGRAMMIST C R (?) ?					
oil	1	1,090		1,090	
MONOGRAMMIST C V (?) ?					
oil	1	3,596		3,596	
MONOGRAMMIST C W (?) ?					
oil	1	2,963		2,963	
MONOGRAMMIST E (?) ?					
oil	1	1,765		1,765	
MONOGRAMMIST E B (?) ?					
oil	2	4,390	2,058	2,195	2,332
MONOGRAMMIST E B L (?) ?					
oil	1	8,356		8,356	
MONOGRAMMIST E F (?) ?					
oil	1	1,088		1,088	
MONOGRAMMIST E G (?) ?					
oil	1	1,734		1,734	
MONOGRAMMIST E J (?) ?					
oil	1	3,596		3,596	
MONOGRAMMIST E K (?) ?					
oil	1	1,251		1,251	
MONOGRAMMIST E L (?) ?					
oil	1	1,573		1,573	
MONOGRAMMIST E M (?) ?					
oil	1	1,412		1,412	
MONOGRAMMIST E M B (?) ?					
oil	1	6,379		6,379	
MONOGRAMMIST E.R (?) ?					
oil	1	1,581		1,581	
MONOGRAMMIST E W (?) ?					
oil	1	2,273		2,273	
MONOGRAMMIST E Z S (?) ?					
oil	1	1,428		1,428	
MONOGRAMMIST F B (?) ?					
oil	1	4,843		4,843	
MONOGRAMMIST F C (?) ?					
oil	1	1,848		1,848	
MONOGRAMMIST F H (?) ?					
oil	1	1,073		1,073	
MONOGRAMMIST F L (?) ?					
wc/d	1	1,160		1,160	
MONOGRAMMIST F S (?) ?					
oil	1	1,811		1,811	
MONOGRAMMIST G (?) ?					
oil	1	1,177		1,177	
MONOGRAMMIST G H B (?) ?					
oil	2	2,506	1,253	1,253	1,253

Name	No.	Total Sales Value	lowest	Prices median	highest
MONOGRAMMIST G P (?) ? oil	1	1,734		1,734	
MONOGRAMMIST G S (?) ? oil	2	10,317	1,288	5,159	9,029
MONOGRAMMIST H A (?) ? oil	1	5,697		5,697	
MONOGRAMMIST H B (?) ? oil	2	9,394	4,000	4,697	5,394
MONOGRAMMIST H C (?) ? oil	1	1,634		1,634	
MONOGRAMMIST H D K E (?) ? oil	1	2,186		2,186	
MONOGRAMMIST H K (?) ? oil	2	3,955	1,483	1,978	2,472
MONOGRAMMIST H O (?) ? 3D	1	1,065		1,065	
MONOGRAMMIST H S (?) ? oil	2	21,088	2,857	10,544	18,231
MONOGRAMMIST I C (?) ? wc/d	1	1,452		1,452	
MONOGRAMMIST I M (?) ? oil	1	1,982		1,982	
MONOGRAMMIST I V (?) ? oil	2	3,823	1,227	1,912	2,596
MONOGRAMMIST I Z (?) ? 3D	1	2,165		2,165	
MONOGRAMMIST J C (?) ? oil	1	12,751		12,751	
MONOGRAMMIST J M (?) ? oil	1	3,004		3,004	
MONOGRAMMIST J N (?) ? oil	1	2,257		2,257	
MONOGRAMMIST J V (?) ? oil	2	7,866	1,090	3,933	6,776
MONOGRAMMIST K F R (?) ? oil	1	1,455		1,455	
MONOGRAMMIST K ST (?) ? oil	1	2,248		2,248	
MONOGRAMMIST L E (?) ? oil	1	3,872		3,872	
MONOGRAMMIST L F (?) ? oil	1	1,290		1,290	
MONOGRAMMIST L G R (?) ? wc/d	1	2,972		2,972	
MONOGRAMMIST L G Y (?) ? oil	1	1,749		1,749	
MONOGRAMMIST L K (?) ? oil	1	1,110		1,110	
MONOGRAMMIST L S (?) ? oil	1	1,727		1,727	
MONOGRAMMIST M (?) ? oil	1	2,091		2,091	
MONOGRAMMIST M A (?) ? oil	2	2,803	1,298	1,402	1,505
MONOGRAMMIST M B (?) ? oil	3	15,938	3,404	5,184	7,350
MONOGRAMMIST M S (?) ? oil	1	2,500		2,500	

Name	No.	Total Sales Value	lowest	Prices median	highest
MONOGRAMMIST N P (?) ?					
oil	1	4,824		4,824	
MONOGRAMMIST N R (?) ?					
oil	1	1,321		1,321	
MONOGRAMMIST N S (?) ?					
oil	1	1,349		1,349	
MONOGRAMMIST N Z (?) ?					
oil	1	2,724		2,724	
MONOGRAMMIST O D C (?) ?					
oil	1	1,449		1,449	
MONOGRAMMIST O P (?) ?					
oil	1	4,840		4,840	
MONOGRAMMIST P B (?) ?					
oil	1	2,713		2,713	
MONOGRAMMIST P I E (?) ?					
oil	1	1,662		1,662	
MONOGRAMMIST P L (?) ?					
wc/d	1	1,966		1,966	
MONOGRAMMIST P V A (?) ?					
oil	1	9,157		9,157	
MONOGRAMMIST P V B (?) ?					
oil	1	1,157		1,157	
MONOGRAMMIST R A (?) ?					
oil	1	1,595		1,595	
MONOGRAMMIST R D G (18th C) ?					
oil	1	2,040		2,040	
MONOGRAMMIST R R (?) ?					
oil	1	2,279		2,279	
MONOGRAMMIST V A (?) ?					
oil	1	1,720		1,720	
MONOGRAMMIST V M (?) ?					
oil	1	2,212		2,212	
MONOGRAMMIST V O (?) ?					
oil	1	1,247		1,247	
MONOGRAMMIST W B (?) ?					
oil	1	1,702		1,702	
MONOGRAMMIST W D (?) ?					
oil	1	17,346		17,346	
MONOGRAMMIST W H (?) ?					
oil	1	4,953		4,953	
MONOGRAMMIST W W (?) ?					
oil	1	1,310		1,310	
MONORY, Jacques (1924-) French					
oil	9	65,214	2,172	7,129	15,051
MONSANTO, Bernardo (?) ?					
oil	1	1,045		1,045	
MONSTED, Peder (1859-1941) Danish					
oil	124	1,958,182	1,211	7,519	165,426
wc/d	1	1,191		1,191	
MONTAG, Carl (1880-1956) Swiss					
oil	2	5,339	2,510	2,670	2,829
MONTAGNE, Louis (1879-1960) French					
oil	2	5,474	2,062	2,737	3,412
MONTAGUE, Alfred (fl.1832-1883) British					
oil	14	36,431	1,133	2,432	5,760
wc/d	1	1,506		1,506	
MONTALD, Constant (1862-1944) Belgian					
oil	5	32,340	1,765	4,880	12,842
wc/d	5	25,740	1,259	5,565	7,705

Name	No.	Total Sales Value	Prices lowest	median	highest
MONTALIER, M (19th C) French					
oil	1	1,900		1,900	
MONTAN, Anders (1846-1917) Swedish					
oil	4	9,554	1,039	1,646	5,224
MONTANARI, Giuseppe (1889-?) Italian					
oil	2	20,795	9,242	10,398	11,553
MONTANARINI, Luigi (1906-1998) Italian					
oil	2	3,534	1,134	1,767	2,400
MONTANI, Carlo Giuseppe (1868-1936) Italian					
oil	1	1,240		1,240	
MONTANIER, Francis (1895-1974) French					
wc/d	1	1,326		1,326	
MONTARDIER (19th C) French					
wc/d	1	2,047		2,047	
MONTARLOT, M (19th C) French					
oil	1	1,378		1,378	
MONTASSIER, Henri (1880-1946) French					
oil	1	1,091		1,091	
MONTEFUSCO, Vincenzo (19th C) Italian					
wc/d	1	1,142		1,142	
MONTELATICI, Francesco (1600-1661) Italian					
wc/d	1	7,475		7,475	
MONTEMEZZO, Antonio (1841-1898) German					
oil	3	8,750	1,210	1,731	5,809
MONTEN, Dietrich (1799-1843) German					
oil	2	5,478	1,863	2,739	3,615
MONTENARD, Frederic (1849-1926) French					
oil	2	7,619	3,219	3,810	4,400
MONTENEGRO CAPELL, Jose (1855-1924) Spanish					
oil	2	2,590	1,056	1,295	1,534
MONTENEGRO, Roberto (1881-1968) Mexican					
wc/d	1	2,178		2,178	
MONTERO, Manuel (?) Spanish?					
oil	1	1,249		1,249	
MONTES, B (19th C) Spanish					
oil	1	1,588		1,588	
MONTES, Jose (?) Uruguayan?					
oil	1	1,000		1,000	
MONTEYNE, Roland (1932-) Belgian					
3D	1	1,231		1,231	
MONTEZIN, Pierre Eugène (1874-1946) French					
oil	33	464,189	2,119	10,150	57,500
wc/d	6	11,035	1,538	1,886	2,066
MONTFORT, Antoine Alphonse (1802-1884) French					
wc/d	1	4,133		4,133	
MONTFORT, Franz van (1889-1980) Belgian					
oil	3	4,191	1,045	1,452	1,694
MONTHOLON, François de (1856-1940) French					
oil	3	18,864	1,146	4,718	13,000
MONTI, Cesare (1891-1952) Italian					
oil	1	2,003		2,003	
MONTI, Francesco (1646-1712) Italian					
oil	1	15,100		15,100	
wc/d	1	5,145		5,145	
MONTI, Francesco (1685-1768) Italian					
oil	1	15,700		15,700	
MONTI, Giovanni (1779-1844) Italian					
oil	1	1,590		1,590	

Name	No.	Total Sales Value	Prices lowest	median	highest
MONTI, Nicola (1780-1854) Italian					
oil	1	4,183		4,183	
MONTI, V (19/20th C) Italian					
oil	3	3,582	1,162	1,162	1,258
MONTICELLI, Adolphe (1824-1886) French					
oil	20	250,267	3,102	8,495	48,479
MONTIEL, Jonio (?) South American					
3D	1	7,000		7,000	
MONTIGNY, Jules Léon (1847-1899) Belgian					
oil	3	6,975	1,975	1,975	2,917
MONTINI, Umberto (1897-1978) Italian					
oil	1	1,294		1,294	
MONTJOYE (18th C) French					
wc/d	1	2,686		2,686	
MONTPEZAT, Henri d'Ainecy Comte de (1817-1859) French					
oil	1	22,940		22,940	
MONTZAIGLE, Edgard (1867-?) French					
wc/d	1	14,000		14,000	
MONVOISIN, Raymond Auguste Quinsac de (1794-1870) French					
oil	1	34,554		34,554	
MONVOISIN, S (20th C) French					
oil	1	2,525		2,525	
MONZON, Uria (1929-1996) Spanish					
oil	1	4,496		4,496	
MOODY, Barbara (20th C) American					
oil	2	2,700	1,300	1,350	1,400
MOODY, Fannie (fl.1885-1897) British					
oil	3	21,486	2,850	6,636	12,000
wc/d	1	1,500		1,500	
MOODY, John Charles (1884-1962) British					
wc/d	2	2,332	1,036	1,166	1,296
MOOR, Carel de (1656-1738) Dutch					
oil	1	2,211		2,211	
MOOR, Karl (1904-1991) Swiss					
oil	1	1,049		1,049	
MOOR, Pieter Cornelis de (1866-1953) Dutch					
oil	1	1,807		1,807	
MOORE OF IPSWICH, George (?) British					
oil	1	2,385		2,385	
MOORE OF IPSWICH, John (1820-1902) British					
oil	7	40,687	1,544	6,600	10,570
MOORE, A Harvey (?-1905) British					
oil	1	3,454		3,454	
MOORE, Abel Buel (19th C) American					
oil	1	3,750		3,750	
MOORE, Albert Joseph (1841-1893) British					
oil	1	58,630		58,630	
wc/d	1	5,700		5,700	
MOORE, Barlow (fl.1863-1891) British					
oil	1	1,915		1,915	
wc/d	2	4,381	1,284	2,191	3,097
MOORE, Benson Bond (1882-1974) American					
oil	1	1,400		1,400	
MOORE, Claude T S (1853-1901) British					
oil	1	7,865		7,865	
MOORE, G (19/20th C) ?					
oil	1	1,343		1,343	
MOORE, H (19/20th C) British?					
3D	1	7,000		7,000	

Name	No.	Total Sales Value	lowest	Prices median	highest
oil	1	1,136		1,136	
MOORE, Henry O M (1898-1986) British					
3D	41	3,264,149	7,500	30,000	480,000
wc/d	26	800,592	8,635	15,730	210,000
MOORE, Henry R A (1831-1895) British					
oil	7	26,323	1,109	3,000	9,424
wc/d	3	5,110	1,106	1,430	2,574
MOORE, John (19th C) British					
oil	1	1,430		1,430	
MOORE, Nelson Augustus (1823-1902) American					
oil	1	4,200		4,200	
MOORE, R H (19th C) British					
oil	1	9,815		9,815	
MOORE, Robert (?) ?					
oil	1	1,420		1,420	
MOORE, Ronald (?) British					
oil	1	1,015		1,015	
MOORE, Rubens Arthur (fl.1881-1920) British					
oil	1	3,021		3,021	
MOORE, T C (1827-1901) British					
oil	1	1,088		1,088	
MOORMANS, Franz (1832-1893) Dutch					
oil	1	4,260		4,260	
MOOS, Joseph von (1859-1939) Swiss					
oil	2	3,076	1,025	1,538	2,051
MOOS, Max von (1903-1979) Swiss					
oil	7	43,868	1,115	3,219	17,928
MOOSBRUGGER, Josef (1810-1869) German					
oil	1	1,366		1,366	
MOR, Antonis (1519-1575) Dutch					
oil	1	15,000		15,000	
MORA, Francis Luis (1874-1940) American					
oil	4	22,400	1,200	3,600	14,000
wc/d	1	1,573		1,573	
MORACH, Otto (1887-1973) Swiss					
oil	4	85,161	8,252	20,224	36,462
wc/d	1	1,195		1,195	
MORAGAS Y TORRAS, Tomas (1837-1906) Spanish					
wc/d	1	10,220		10,220	
MORAIN (19th C) French					
oil	1	4,500		4,500	
MORALES, Armando (1927-) Nicaraguan					
oil	7	479,164	12,000	48,000	220,000
MORALES, Dario (1944-1988) Colombian					
3D	1	39,000		39,000	
wc/d	1	22,000		22,000	
MORALES, Eduardo (c.1869-1938) Cuban					
oil	4	14,500	2,000	3,500	5,500
MORALES, Juan Antonio (19/20th C) Spanish					
oil	1	4,570		4,570	
MORALES, Luis de (c.1509-1586) Spanish					
oil	3	1,305,966	290,366	411,600	604,000
MORALES, Rodolfo (1925-) Mexican					
oil	1	10,000		10,000	
MORALT, Willy (1884-1947) German					
oil	10	73,018	3,596	7,006	12,587
wc/d	3	4,197	1,259	1,455	1,483
MORAN, E Percy (1862-1935) American					
oil	1	1,500		1,500	

Name	No.	Total Sales Value	lowest	Prices median	highest
MORAN, Edward (1829-1901) American					
oil	16	262,446	2,646	16,500	35,000
wc/d	1	1,500		1,500	
MORAN, Jose Luis (1924-) Spanish					
oil	1	1,287		1,287	
MORAN, Leon (1864-1941) American					
oil	1	1,000		1,000	
MORAN, Peter (1841-1914) American					
oil	1	16,000		16,000	
MORAN, Thomas (1837-1926) American					
oil	9	1,276,000	21,000	40,000	950,000
wc/d	5	742,100	2,600	45,000	500,000
MORANDI, Giorgio (1890-1964) Italian					
oil	14	5,098,728	108,750	248,210	1,102,000
wc/d	6	107,236	4,501	16,803	32,661
MORANDINI, Francesco (1544-1597) Italian					
wc/d	1	2,400		2,400	
MORANDIS, Gino (1915-) Italian					
oil	1	1,376		1,376	
MORANDO, Pietro (1892-1980) Italian					
oil	9	22,956	1,359	1,971	4,741
wc/d	1	1,078		1,078	
MORANI, Vincenzo (1809-1870) Italian					
wc/d	1	1,001		1,001	
MORANT, L (?) ?					
oil	1	5,748		5,748	
MORAS, Walter (1856-1925) German					
oil	2	5,202	2,425	2,601	2,777
MORAT, Johann Martin (1805-1867) German					
wc/d	1	1,734		1,734	
MORBELLI, Angelo (1853-1919) Italian					
oil	7	196,756	4,363	28,436	62,973
wc/d	1	84,848		84,848	
MORBELLI, Marc (1936-) French					
3D	2	2,760	1,242	1,380	1,518
MORCHAIN, Paul-Bernard (1876-1938) French					
oil	3	6,612	1,895	2,030	2,687
MORCILLO RAYA, Gabriel (1888-1973) Spanish					
oil	1	2,301		2,301	
MORDT, Gustav (1826-1856) Norwegian					
oil	1	1,627		1,627	
MORE, Jacob (1740-1793) British					
oil	2	24,589	9,889	12,295	14,700
wc/d	1	3,791		3,791	
MORE, Paul le (1863-1914) French					
oil	2	3,928	1,789	1,964	2,139
MOREAU (?) French					
3D	1	4,290		4,290	
MOREAU DE TOURS, Georges (1848-1901) French					
oil	1	2,500		2,500	
MOREAU, A (?) French					
3D	2	4,744	1,422	2,372	3,322
MOREAU, Adrien (1843-1906) French					
oil	2	57,981	9,981	28,991	48,000
MOREAU, Auguste (19th C) French					
3D	19	53,906	1,053	2,662	6,795
MOREAU, Auguste Louis Mathurin (1834-1917) French					
3D	2	10,380	4,728	5,190	5,652
MOREAU, François Hippolyte (19th C) French					
3D	4	14,249	1,712	3,309	5,920

Name	No.	Total Sales Value	Prices lowest	median	highest
MOREAU, Gustave (1826-1898) French					
wc/d	1	789,600		789,600	
MOREAU, H (19/20th C) French					
3D	1	1,884		1,884	
MOREAU, Henri (1869-1943) Belgian					
oil	4	11,346	1,210	1,946	6,244
MOREAU, Hippolite (19th C) French					
3D	2	9,917	4,914	4,959	5,003
MOREAU, Hippolyte François (1832-1927) French					
3D	4	8,935	1,321	2,309	2,997
MOREAU, J (19th C) French					
oil	1	2,340		2,340	
MOREAU, Jean Michel (younger) (1741-1814) French					
wc/d	4	63,319	1,434	4,205	53,475
MOREAU, Leon (19th C) French					
oil	1	1,095		1,095	
MOREAU, Louis Gabriel (1740-1806) French					
oil	3	20,491	2,662	6,000	11,829
wc/d	5	69,009	1,382	6,795	28,000
MOREAU, Mathurin (1822-1912) French					
3D	40	151,521	1,110	3,146	10,942
MOREAU, Max (1902-1992) Belgian					
oil	6	23,913	1,065	2,418	11,682
MOREAU-NELATON, Étienne (1859-1927) French					
wc/d	1	1,608		1,608	
MOREAU-VAUTHIER, Edme Augustin Jean (1831-1893) French					
3D	3	10,846	3,190	3,574	4,082
MOREAU-VAUTHIER, Paul (1871-?) French					
3D	1	2,146		2,146	
MOREL FATIO, Antoine Léon (1810-1871) French					
oil	2	4,490	1,511	2,245	2,979
MOREL, Jan Evert II (1835-1905) Dutch					
oil	5	14,862	1,377	2,732	5,000
MOREL, Willem F A I Vaarzon (1868-1955) Dutch					
oil	1	3,664		3,664	
MORELLET, François (1926-) French					
oil	2	13,794	6,466	6,897	7,328
wc/d	3	10,492	2,458	3,342	4,692
MORELLI, Domenico (1826-1901) Italian					
oil	2	8,661	1,335	4,331	7,326
MORELLI, E (19/20th C) Italian					
oil	1	1,374		1,374	
MORELLI, F (1768-1830) French					
oil	2	3,124	1,057	1,562	2,067
MORELLI, L (?) Italian					
3D	1	1,726		1,726	
MORENI, Mattia (1920-1999) Italian					
oil	3	24,593	6,794	7,909	9,890
wc/d	3	6,512	1,340	1,877	3,295
MORENNA, G (?) Italian					
oil	1	1,152		1,152	
MORENO VILLA, Jose (1887-1960) Spanish					
wc/d	2	3,765	1,748	1,883	2,017
MORENO, Jean Philip (1906-) ?					
oil	1	5,214		5,214	
MORENO, Michel (1945-) French					
wc/d	1	1,716		1,716	
MORERA Y GALICIA, Jaime (1854-1927) Spanish					
oil	1	4,152		4,152	

Name	No.	Total Sales Value	lowest	Prices median	highest
MORET, Henry (1856-1913) French					
oil	17	878,871	7,582	45,000	95,000
MORETH (18th C) French					
wc/d	1	6,142		6,142	
MORETTI, Alessandro (18th C) Italian					
wc/d	1	4,704		4,704	
MORETTI, Antonio (?) Italian					
oil	1	1,371		1,371	
MORETTI, G R (?) Italian					
wc/d	1	1,290		1,290	
MORETTI, Lucien Philippe (1922-) French					
oil	1	1,970		1,970	
wc/d	3	4,187	1,196	1,263	1,728
MORETTI, Professor R (?) Italian?					
wc/d	1	1,548		1,548	
MORETTI, Raymond (1931-) French					
wc/d	7	9,378	1,056	1,179	1,769
MORGAN, Charlotte E (1867-1947) American					
oil	1	1,700		1,700	
MORGAN, Franklin Townsend (1883-?) American					
oil	1	4,000		4,000	
MORGAN, Frederick (1856-1927) British					
oil	8	2,121,900	29,000	170,000	880,000
wc/d	1	6,750		6,750	
MORGAN, Gladys B (1899-?) American					
oil	1	1,400		1,400	
MORGAN, J (19/20th C) British					
oil	1	1,435		1,435	
MORGAN, Jenny (20th C) British					
oil	1	2,736		2,736	
MORGAN, John (1823-1886) British					
oil	4	195,431	2,961	20,735	151,000
MORGAN, Mary de Neale (1868-1948) American					
oil	2	24,000	7,000	12,000	17,000
MORGAN, Matthew Somerville (1839-1890) American/British					
oil	1	57,200		57,200	
MORGAN, P (19th C) French					
oil	1	2,596		2,596	
MORGAN, Robert F (1929-) American					
oil	1	5,000		5,000	
MORGAN, W (?) ?					
oil	1	1,010		1,010	
MORGAN, Walter Jenks (1847-1924) British					
oil	1	1,501		1,501	
MORGAN, William (1826-1900) American					
oil	2	19,000	8,000	9,500	11,000
MORGENSTERN, Christian (1805-1867) German					
oil	2	98,414	7,260	49,207	91,154
wc/d	1	2,878		2,878	
MORGENSTERN, Friedrich Ernst (1853-1919) German					
oil	1	1,138		1,138	
MORGENSTERN, Johann Ludwig Ernst (1738-1819) German					
oil	1	32,340		32,340	
MORGENSTERN, Karl (1811-1893) German					
oil	4	30,879	2,273	8,248	12,110
MORGENSTERN, Karl Ernst (1847-1928) German					
oil	1	2,942		2,942	
MORGENSTERNE MUNTHE, Gerhard (1875-1927) Dutch					
oil	14	86,701	1,723	4,923	15,610

Name	No.	Total Sales Value	Prices lowest	median	highest
MORGENTHALER, Ernst (1887-1962) Swiss					
oil	10	28,219	1,154	1,965	7,292
MORGNER, Wilhelm (1891-1917) German					
wc/d	3	8,387	1,899	3,028	3,460
MORI, Mariko (1967-) American					
3D	1	30,200		30,200	
MORI, Neno (1898-1970) Italian					
oil	2	3,883	1,671	1,942	2,212
MORIER, David (1705-1770) Swiss					
oil	2	24,739	11,154	12,370	13,585
MORILLO FERRADAS, Jose (1853-1920) Spanish					
oil	1	4,314		4,314	
MORIN, Claude (1932-) French					
3D	1	9,283		9,283	
MORIN, Edmond (1824-1882) French					
wc/d	1	1,197		1,197	
MORIN, Louis (1855-?) French					
oil	1	5,699		5,699	
MORINIERE, de la (19th C) French					
oil	1	1,595		1,595	
MORIS, R (18th C) Dutch					
wc/d	1	1,624		1,624	
MORISOT, Berthe (1841-1895) French					
oil	7	5,970,261	25,000	250,000	4,000,000
wc/d	3	36,334	5,819	13,515	17,000
MORISOT, Edma (19th C) French					
oil	1	1,227		1,227	
MORITZ, Fritz (1922-) German					
oil	1	2,249		2,249	
MORITZ, Goth (?) ?					
oil	1	1,109		1,109	
MORLAN, Dorothy (20th C) American					
oil	1	1,100		1,100	
MORLAND, George (1763-1804) British					
oil	18	161,158	1,080	4,753	60,000
wc/d	4	4,851	1,050	1,201	1,352
MORLAND, Henry Robert (c.1719-1797) British					
oil	1	18,590		18,590	
MORLEY (?) British?					
oil	1	2,400		2,400	
MORLEY, Harry (1881-1943) British					
oil	8	32,074	1,738	3,081	9,480
MORLEY, Henry (1869-1937) British					
oil	2	4,354	1,340	2,177	3,014
MORLEY, Malcolm (1931-) British					
oil	4	369,000	14,000	70,000	215,000
wc/d	3	28,000	2,500	7,500	18,000
MORLEY, Thomas W (1859-1925) British					
wc/d	1	1,027		1,027	
MORLOTTI, Ennio (1910-1992) Italian					
oil	7	199,780	4,951	11,591	72,500
wc/d	4	9,864	1,408	2,471	3,515
MORNARD, Henri (?) ?					
oil	1	2,783		2,783	
MORNER, Stellan (1896-1979) Swedish					
oil	25	66,803	1,034	2,310	6,733
wc/d	1	1,278		1,278	
MORNY, Paul (?) ?					
wc/d	1	1,088		1,088	

Name	No.	Total Sales Value	lowest	Prices median	highest
MORODER, Josef Theodor (1846-1939) Austrian					
oil	1	4,114		4,114	
MORONEY, Ken (1949-) British					
oil	9	12,514	1,043	1,248	2,567
MORONI, Giovan Battista (1525-1578) Italian					
oil	1	256,700		256,700	
MOROSINI, George (?-1882) Irish					
wc/d	1	1,963		1,963	
MOROT, Aime (1850-1913) French					
oil	1	66,360		66,360	
MORPHY, Garrett (?-1715) British					
oil	1	41,440		41,440	
MORRAW (20th C) European					
oil	1	1,430		1,430	
MORREL, Luis (?) Spanish					
oil	1	1,425		1,425	
MORRELL, Wayne (1923-) American					
oil	4	7,300	1,200	1,750	2,600
MORREN, Georges (1868-1941) Belgian					
oil	2	14,976	6,849	7,488	8,127
MORRICE, James Wilson (1865-1924) Canadian					
oil	8	190,684	2,196	14,758	87,444
MORRIS, Alfred (19th C) British					
oil	2	6,110	2,920	3,055	3,190
MORRIS, C E (20th C) ?					
oil	1	2,385		2,385	
MORRIS, Cedric (1889-1982) British					
oil	12	85,429	1,200	7,500	12,000
MORRIS, Charles (19th C) British					
oil	1	1,240		1,240	
MORRIS, Edmund Montague (1871-1913) Canadian					
oil	1	3,115		3,115	
MORRIS, Franklin E (20th C) American					
oil	1	2,000		2,000	
MORRIS, H (19th C) British					
oil	1	1,362		1,362	
MORRIS, J (19th C) British					
oil	1	2,000		2,000	
MORRIS, J C (19th C) British					
oil	1	4,576		4,576	
MORRIS, J W (19th C) British					
oil	1	1,173		1,173	
MORRIS, John (19th C) British					
oil	6	33,447	2,039	2,774	14,000
MORRIS, Kathleen (1893-1986) Canadian					
oil	3	25,910	1,354	10,619	13,937
MORRIS, Margaret (1891-1980) British					
oil	3	15,720	2,920	5,840	6,960
MORRIS, Philip Richard (1838-1902) British					
oil	5	40,719	4,000	7,900	14,915
MORRIS, Robert (1931-) American					
3D	1	26,000		26,000	
oil	1	7,500		7,500	
MORRIS, Sarah (1967-) American					
oil	2	21,060	9,060	10,530	12,000
MORRIS, Thomas (18/19th C) British					
oil	1	1,704		1,704	
MORRIS, William C (20th C) American					
oil	1	1,100		1,100	

Name	No.	Total Sales Value	lowest	Prices median	highest
MORRISH, Sydney S (fl.1852-1894) British					
oil	1	2,664		2,664	
MORRISON, James (1932-) British					
oil	5	21,977	1,064	5,372	8,030
MORRISSEAU, Norval (1930-) Canadian					
oil	3	4,742	1,170	1,270	2,302
MORROCCO, Alberto (1917-1998) British					
oil	7	122,748	6,424	10,150	58,000
MORROCCO, Léon (1942-) Australian					
oil	1	4,350		4,350	
wc/d	1	6,132		6,132	
MORSE, C Roy (20th C) American					
oil	2	2,500	1,100	1,250	1,400
MORSE, Jonathan Bradley (1834-1898) American					
oil	1	1,000		1,000	
MORSE, Samuel F B (1791-1872) American					
oil	1	1,100		1,100	
MORSING, Ivar (1919-) Swedish					
oil	6	16,855	1,114	2,130	6,623
MORSTADT, Anna (1874-?) Czechoslovakian					
oil	1	16,874		16,874	
MORSZOECK, Heinz (1961-) German					
oil	1	1,125		1,125	
MORTEL, Jan (1650-1719) Dutch					
oil	1	16,500		16,500	
MORTELMANS, F (19/20th C) Belgian					
oil	2	25,655	9,103	12,828	16,552
MORTELMANS, Frans (1865-c.1936) Belgian					
oil	8	71,743	1,480	7,570	22,182
MORTENSEN, Richard (1910-1994) Danish					
3D	1	1,689		1,689	
oil	8	183,585	1,623	17,263	56,672
wc/d	3	7,825	1,056	2,655	4,114
MORTIER, Antoine (1908-1998) Belgian					
oil	9	45,348	2,610	3,760	9,401
wc/d	7	15,591	1,462	1,776	3,134
MORTIMER, G (19/20th C) ?					
oil	1	1,238		1,238	
MORTIMER, John Hamilton (1740-1779) British					
wc/d	1	4,116		4,116	
MORTIMER, Lewis (20th C) British					
wc/d	1	1,184		1,184	
MORTIMER, Thomas (?) British					
wc/d	1	1,304		1,304	
MORTON (?) ?					
oil	1	4,225		4,225	
MORTON, Andrew (1802-1845) British					
oil	1	1,585		1,585	
MORTON, Thomas Corsan (1859-1928) British					
oil	1	1,296		1,296	
MORTON-JOHNSON, Francis (1878-1931) French					
oil	1	3,992		3,992	
MOSCA, Lorenzo (?-1789) Italian					
3D	1	2,854		2,854	
MOSCARDO, Jose (1953-) Spanish					
oil	3	7,230	2,026	2,515	2,689
MOSCARDO, Ramon (1953-) Spanish					
wc/d	1	1,824		1,824	

Name	No.	Total Sales Value	Prices lowest	median	highest
MOSCHER, Jacob van (fl.1635-1655) Dutch					
oil	1	6,379		6,379	
MOSER, Amy (1873-?) British/Swiss					
oil	1	1,179		1,179	
MOSER, Julius (1808-?) German					
3D	1	1,981		1,981	
MOSER, Oswald (1874-1953) British					
wc/d	1	1,027		1,027	
MOSER, Wilfried (1914-1997) Swiss					
oil	6	20,665	1,505	3,431	5,920
wc/d	1	1,338		1,338	
MOSES, Anna Mary Robertson (Grandma) (1860-1961) American					
oil	14	684,000	15,000	43,750	100,000
MOSES, Ed (1926-) American					
oil	3	16,500	3,000	6,500	7,000
wc/d	1	4,250		4,250	
MOSES, Forrest K (1893-1974) American					
oil	1	2,000		2,000	
MOSES, Walter Farrington (1874-?) ?					
oil	1	1,000		1,000	
MOSLER, Henry (1841-1920) American					
oil	2	18,250	4,250	9,125	14,000
MOSNIER, Jean Laurent (1743-1808) French					
oil	2	65,000	15,000	32,500	50,000
MOSS, Charles Eugène (1860-1901) Canadian					
oil	1	3,250		3,250	
MOSS, Marlow (1890-1958) British					
oil	2	56,250	24,560	28,125	31,690
MOSSA, Alexis (1844-1926) French					
wc/d	3	3,560	1,094	1,211	1,255
MOSSA, Gustave Adolf (1883-1971) French					
oil	1	18,330		18,330	
wc/d	5	16,225	1,286	2,852	5,703
MOSSES, Alexander (1793-1837) British					
oil	1	1,500		1,500	
MOSSET, Olivier (1944-) Swiss					
oil	2	10,184	3,987	5,092	6,197
MOSTAERT, Gillis (elder) (1534-1598) Flemish					
oil	1	5,745		5,745	
MOSTERT, David (1952-) South African					
3D	1	1,406		1,406	
MOSTYN, Tom (1864-1930) British					
oil	9	22,322	1,136	2,496	4,077
MOTA Y MORALES, Vicente (19/20th C) Spanish					
oil	2	2,090	1,045	1,045	1,045
MOTE, George William (1832-1909) British					
oil	2	7,050	3,300	3,525	3,750
MOTELEY, Jules Georges (1865-1923) French					
oil	2	4,090	1,690	2,045	2,400
MOTHERWELL, Robert (1915-1991) American					
oil	10	391,000	11,000	26,000	80,000
wc/d	5	47,063	5,738	6,825	19,000
MOTLEY, Wilton (19/20th C) British					
oil	1	2,431		2,431	
MOTSCH, A (20th C) German?					
oil	1	1,055		1,055	
MOTTA, Raffaellino (1550-1578) Italian					
wc/d	2	96,450	45,110	48,225	51,340

Name	No.	Total Sales Value	lowest	Prices median	highest
MOTTET, Johann Daniel (1754-1822) Swiss					
oil	1	1,733		1,733	
MOTTRAM, Charles Sim (fl.1880-1919) British					
wc/d	1	1,343		1,343	
MOTZER, August Ferdinand (1844-) Austrian					
oil	1	20,777		20,777	
MOUALLA, Fikret (1903-1967) Turkish					
oil	14	104,849	1,179	5,253	22,634
wc/d	33	279,348	1,047	2,619	46,515
MOUCHERON, Frederic de (1633-1686) Dutch					
oil	3	15,834	2,918	5,334	7,582
wc/d	1	1,886		1,886	
MOUCHERON, Isaac de (1667-1744) Dutch					
oil	1	19,791		19,791	
wc/d	2	9,107	4,000	4,554	5,107
MOUCHOT, Louis Hippolyte (1846-1893) French					
oil	3	28,585	1,885	4,200	22,500
MOUFFE, Michel (1957-) Belgian					
wc/d	1	6,795		6,795	
MOUILLOT, Marcel (1889-1972) French					
oil	1	1,605		1,605	
MOUKHINA, Vera Ignatievna (1889-1953) Russian					
wc/d	1	1,812		1,812	
MOULD, John (20th C) British					
oil	1	1,133		1,133	
MOULIN, Hippolyte (1832-1884) French					
3D	1	2,300		2,300	
MOULTHROP, Reuben (1763-1814) American					
oil	1	13,000		13,000	
MOUNCEY, William (1852-1901) British					
oil	4	17,358	3,003	4,640	5,075
MOUNT, William Sidney (1807-1868) American					
oil	5	441,000	14,000	22,000	350,000
MOUNTFORT, B (19th C) British					
oil	1	1,092		1,092	
MOURET, Achille Ernest (19/20th C) French					
oil	1	5,530		5,530	
MOURIER-PETERSEN, Christian (1858-1945) Danish					
oil	1	40,509		40,509	
MOUSSEAU, Jean Paul (1927-1991) Canadian					
oil	1	2,239		2,239	
MOUTTE, Jean Joseph Marie Alphonse (1840-1913) French					
oil	1	4,095		4,095	
MOYADAR, P (?) Spanish					
oil	1	6,769		6,769	
MOYERS, John (1958-) American					
oil	1	2,000		2,000	
MOYES, F (19th C) ?					
oil	1	1,037		1,037	
MOYNET, Jean Pierre (1819-1876) French					
oil	1	5,056		5,056	
MOYNIHAN, Rodrigo (1910-) British					
oil	1	7,920		7,920	
MOZELLI (19/20th C) Italian					
oil	1	1,731		1,731	
MOZIN, Charles Louis (1806-1862) French					
oil	5	20,743	1,200	4,189	6,401
wc/d	2	4,305	1,817	2,153	2,488

Name	No.	Total Sales Value	lowest	Prices median	highest
MUBIN, Othon (1924-1981) Turkish					
oil	2	3,057	1,329	1,529	1,728
MUCHA, Alphonse (1860-1939) Czechoslovakian					
oil	3	326,500	2,000	4,500	320,000
wc/d	7	214,112	1,591	3,286	160,000
MUCHE, Georg (1895-1987) German					
oil	1	12,396		12,396	
MUCKE, Carl Emil (1847-1923) German					
oil	1	1,596		1,596	
MUCKLEY, William Jabez (1837-1905) British					
oil	1	4,350		4,350	
wc/d	1	2,980		2,980	
MUEHLHAUS, Daniel (1907-1981) Dutch					
oil	1	4,301		4,301	
MUELLER-GRAF, Egon (20th C) German					
oil	1	1,463		1,463	
MUENIER, Jules Alexis (1863-1942) French					
oil	1	3,797		3,797	
MUFF, Orla (1903-1984) Danish					
oil	1	1,060		1,060	
MUGHAL SCHOOL, 16th C Asian					
oil	1	15,000		15,000	
MUGHAL SCHOOL, 17th C Asian					
wc/d	1	10,200		10,200	
MUGHAL SCHOOL, 18th C Asian					
oil	2	16,000	6,000	8,000	10,000
MUHL, Roger (1929-) French					
oil	9	28,810	1,479	3,041	5,551
MUHLENEN, Max von (1903-1971) Swiss					
oil	2	12,243	2,915	6,122	9,328
MUHLENFELD, L (19th C) ?					
oil	1	1,975		1,975	
MUHLENFELD, Otto (1871-1907) American					
oil	1	7,000		7,000	
MUHLENHAUPT, Kurt (1921-) German					
oil	1	1,349		1,349	
MUHLENWEG, Elisabeth (1910-1961) Austrian					
oil	2	2,396	1,054	1,198	1,342
MUHLHAN, Adolf (1886-?) German					
oil	1	1,529		1,529	
MUHLIG, Bernard (1829-1910) German					
oil	4	6,539	1,162	1,679	2,020
MUHLIG, Hugo (1854-1929) German					
oil	12	125,090	1,506	7,012	41,708
wc/d	2	3,906	1,455	1,953	2,451
MUHLIG, Meno (1823-1873) German					
oil	1	4,000		4,000	
MUHLTHALER, Helene von (19th C) German					
wc/d	1	2,070		2,070	
MUIJSENBERG, Toon van den (1901-1967) Dutch					
oil	1	2,155		2,155	
MUIRHEAD, John (1863-1927) British					
oil	1	2,431		2,431	
MUKERY, Roma (1910-) Italian					
wc/d	1	7,000		7,000	
MUKHERJEE, Benode Behari (1904-1980) Indian					
oil	1	3,750		3,750	
wc/d	2	5,448	2,448	2,724	3,000

Name	No.	Total Sales Value	lowest	Prices median	highest
MULDERS, Marc (1958-) Dutch					
oil	2	11,207	3,448	5,604	7,759
MULDERS, R (?) Belgian?					
oil	2	2,115	1,006	1,058	1,109
MULET-CLAVER, Vincent (1895-?) Spanish					
oil	1	2,624		2,624	
MULFORD, Stockton (1886-?) American?					
oil	1	2,700		2,700	
MULHAUPT, Frederick J (1871-1938) American					
oil	4	46,350	2,100	6,125	32,000
MULHOLLAND, St Clair A (19th C) British					
oil	2	4,611	1,272	2,306	3,339
MULIER, Pieter (17th C) Dutch					
oil	1	3,147		3,147	
MULIER, Pieter (school) (17th C) Dutch					
oil	1	6,923		6,923	
MULIER, Pieter (younger) (1637-1701) Dutch					
oil	1	13,345		13,345	
MULLER (?) ?					
oil	1	1,251		1,251	
MULLER, A (19/20th C) ?					
oil	1	1,800		1,800	
MULLER, Adam August (1811-1844) Danish					
oil	1	2,383		2,383	
MULLER, Adolf (19th C) Hungarian					
oil	1	1,841		1,841	
MULLER, Albert (1897-1926) Swiss					
oil	1	1,210		1,210	
wc/d	8	35,853	1,338	2,132	10,938
MULLER, Alexander (1872-1935) American					
oil	1	5,000		5,000	
MULLER, Alfredo (1869-1940) Italian					
oil	1	5,723		5,723	
MULLER, Archibald Herman (1878-1952) Indian					
oil	2	14,450	6,200	7,225	8,250
MULLER, Charles (19th C) French					
3D	1	2,854		2,854	
MULLER, E (20th C) German					
oil	2	6,482	2,245	3,241	4,237
MULLER, Emil (1924-) Swiss					
oil	1	1,066		1,066	
MULLER, Emma von (1859-1925) Austrian					
oil	3	3,288	1,058	1,091	1,139
MULLER, Erich Martin (1888-1972) German					
oil	2	3,808	1,152	1,904	2,656
wc/d	1	3,206		3,206	
MULLER, Eugène Robert (19th C) French					
wc/d	1	2,508		2,508	
MULLER, Franz (1843-1929) German					
oil	1	6,570		6,570	
MULLER, Fritz (19th C) German					
oil	3	12,222	1,000	1,000	10,222
MULLER, Giovanni (20th C) Swiss					
oil	1	4,800		4,800	
MULLER, Hans (?) German					
3D	1	1,072		1,072	
MULLER, Heinrich (19/20th C) ?					
oil	1	1,269		1,269	

Name	No.	Total Sales Value	lowest	Prices median	highest
MULLER, J W (19th C) German					
oil	1	2,099		2,099	
MULLER, Jacques (1930-) Belgian					
oil	1	1,313		1,313	
MULLER, Johann Georg (1913-1986) German					
oil	7	92,743	5,825	12,975	21,779
wc/d	2	19,727	9,709	9,864	10,018
MULLER, Johannes (19/20th C) German?					
oil	1	4,781		4,781	
MULLER, Josef Felix (1955-) Swiss					
3D	1	5,920		5,920	
oil	1	1,115		1,115	
MULLER, Leopold Carl (1834-1892) German					
oil	1	10,762		10,762	
MULLER, Moritz (jnr) (20th C) German					
oil	1	1,228		1,228	
MULLER, Moritz (snr) (1841-1899) German					
oil	3	4,352	1,349	1,407	1,596
MULLER, Moritz Karl Friedrich (1807-1865) German					
oil	3	15,939	1,772	2,922	11,245
MULLER, Otto (1874-1930) German					
3D	1	9,723		9,723	
wc/d	3	92,261	8,937	18,447	64,877
MULLER, Peter Paul (1853-?) German					
oil	2	2,242	1,065	1,121	1,177
MULLER, R (?) ?					
oil	1	4,004		4,004	
MULLER, Richard (1874-1954) Austrian					
oil	1	6,534		6,534	
wc/d	2	3,532	1,168	1,766	2,364
MULLER, Robert (1920-) Swiss					
3D	2	3,789	1,066	1,895	2,723
wc/d	1	1,823		1,823	
MULLER, Robert Antoine (19th C) British					
oil	2	3,206	1,256	1,603	1,950
MULLER, Rudolph (1802-1885) Swiss					
wc/d	4	10,279	1,422	2,093	4,672
MULLER, Severin (1964-) Swiss					
3D	1	2,131		2,131	
MULLER, William James (1812-1845) British					
oil	10	77,949	1,898	3,240	27,935
wc/d	5	20,305	1,144	3,476	9,295
MULLER-BECK, H (20th C) German?					
oil	1	1,282		1,282	
MULLER-BRESLAU, Georg (1856-1911) German					
oil	1	2,328		2,328	
MULLER-BRITTNAU, Willy (1938-) Swiss					
oil	1	3,256		3,256	
MULLER-CORNELIUS, Ludwig (1864-1946) German					
oil	7	13,428	1,091	1,694	4,210
MULLER-KAEMPFF, Paul (1861-1941) German					
oil	7	27,789	1,743	4,424	5,883
MULLER-KURZWELLY, Konrad Alexander (1855-1914) German					
oil	2	10,732	2,641	5,366	8,091
MULLER-LINGKE, Albert (1844-?) German					
oil	2	3,876	1,694	1,938	2,182
MULLER-SCHNUTTENBACH, Hans (1889-1975) German					
oil	2	3,544	1,366	1,772	2,178
wc/d	1	2,277		2,277	

Name	No.	Total Sales Value	lowest	Prices median	highest
MULLER-WERLAU, Peter Paul (1864-1945) German					
oil	2	3,203	1,505	1,602	1,698
MULLER-WISCHIN, Anton (1865-1949) German					
oil	1	1,089		1,089	
MULLEY, Oskar (1891-1949) Austrian					
oil	11	61,819	1,227	6,379	12,878
wc/d	3	5,699	1,273	1,727	2,699
MULLICAN, Matt (1951-) American					
oil	2	8,250	1,000	4,125	7,250
MULREADY, Augustus E (fl.1863-1905) British					
oil	6	36,107	1,700	2,780	20,410
MULTSCHER, Hans (1400-1467) German					
3D	1	21,375		21,375	
MULVAD, Emma (1838-1903) Danish					
oil	3	12,230	2,320	2,613	7,297
MULVEY, Joseph P (19/20th C) American					
oil	1	1,500		1,500	
MUMPRECHT, Walter Rudolf (1918-) Swiss					
oil	1	3,148		3,148	
wc/d	2	4,630	1,242	2,315	3,388
MUNARI, Bruno (1907-) Italian					
oil	1	8,331		8,331	
MUNARI, Cristoforo (1667-1720) Italian					
oil	1	55,994		55,994	
MUNCASTER, Claude (1903-1974) British					
oil	1	1,200		1,200	
wc/d	1	1,001		1,001	
MUNCH, Edvard (1863-1944) Norwegian					
oil	3	901,020	127,190	160,000	613,830
wc/d	2	47,792	8,532	23,896	39,260
MUNCH, Otto (1885-1965) Swiss					
3D	1	1,244		1,244	
MUNCH, William (20th C) American					
wc/d	1	1,800		1,800	
MUNCHAUSEN, August van (20th C) ?					
wc/d	1	9,750		9,750	
MUNDARAY, Ismael (1952-) Venezuelan					
oil	1	1,150		1,150	
MUNDELL, J (1818-1875) British					
oil	2	2,493	1,113	1,247	1,380
MUNDO, Ignasi (1918-) Spanish					
oil	1	1,344		1,344	
MUNDT, Caroline Emilie (1849-1922) Danish					
oil	4	9,672	1,342	1,665	5,000
MUNDY, Henry (1919-) British					
oil	1	2,205		2,205	
MUNGER, Anne Wells (1862-1945) American					
oil	2	15,250	3,250	7,625	12,000
MUNGER, Gilbert (1837-1903) American					
oil	1	10,010		10,010	
MUNICH SCHOOL, 19th C German					
oil	1	2,955		2,955	
wc/d	1	3,000		3,000	
MUNICH SCHOOL, 19th/20th C German					
oil	1	2,697		2,697	
MUNICH SCHOOL, 20th C German					
oil	1	2,727		2,727	
MUNIZ, Vik (1961-) ?					
oil	1	2,600		2,600	

Name	No.	Total Sales Value	lowest	Prices median	highest
MUNKACSY (1844-1900) Hungarian					
oil	1	1,452		1,452	
MUNKACSY, Mihaly Lieb (1844-1900) Hungarian					
oil	7	218,222	9,480	18,821	75,000
MUNNIK, Henk (1912-1997) Dutch					
oil	1	1,639		1,639	
MUNNINGER, Ludwig (20th C) German					
oil	4	20,750	3,500	5,625	6,250
MUNNINGS, Charles (19th C) British					
oil	1	2,800		2,800	
MUNNINGS, Sir Alfred (1878-1959) British					
oil	26	10,830,151	7,900	201,000	2,750,000
wc/d	15	319,231	1,131	5,720	105,000
MUNNO, Giovanni di (20th C) ?					
oil	1	1,060		1,060	
MUNNS, John Bernard (1869-1942) British					
oil	1	3,750		3,750	
MUNOZ RUBIO (19th C) Spanish					
oil	1	8,000		8,000	
MUNOZ RUBIO, Ramon (19th C) Spanish					
oil	2	6,828	2,523	3,414	4,305
wc/d	1	1,068		1,068	
MUNOZ Y CUESTA, Domingo (1850-1912) Spanish					
oil	2	48,546	24,000	24,273	24,546
MUNOZ Y LUCENA, Tomas (1860-1943) Spanish					
oil	2	12,433	2,654	6,217	9,779
MUNOZ, Ana Maria (1947-) Spanish					
oil	1	1,859		1,859	
MUNOZ, Godofredo Ortega (1905-1982) Spanish					
oil	2	28,540	13,875	14,270	14,665
MUNOZ, Juan (1953-) Spanish					
3D	3	93,191	7,250	34,601	51,340
MUNOZ, Lucio (1929-1998) Spanish					
oil	3	44,885	8,000	14,030	22,855
wc/d	2	34,143	6,268	17,072	27,875
MUNOZ-DEGRAIN, Antoine (1843-1924) French					
oil	7	113,242	2,528	8,418	66,602
MUNOZ-VERA, Guillermo (1949-) Chilean					
oil	5	365,124	28,124	45,000	190,000
wc/d	4	21,511	2,184	5,630	8,067
MUNRO, Alexander Graham (fl.1923-1940) British					
oil	1	3,020		3,020	
MUNRO, Peter (1954-) British					
oil	2	3,473	1,208	1,737	2,265
MUNS, Luis Muntane (1899-1989) Spanish					
oil	1	1,621		1,621	
MUNSELL, Albert Henry (1858-?) American					
oil	1	1,000		1,000	
MUNSTER, Claud (19th C) ?					
oil	1	1,323		1,323	
MUNSTERFELD, F (?) ?					
oil	2	4,403	1,700	2,202	2,703
MUNSTERHJELM, Ali (1873-1944) Finnish					
oil	3	9,392	2,007	2,458	4,927
MUNSTERHJELM, Hjalmar (1840-1905) Finnish					
oil	1	7,584		7,584	
MUNTANOLA, Manuel (1931-1992) Spanish					
oil	1	1,523		1,523	

Name	No.	Total Sales Value	lowest	Prices median	highest
MUNTER, Gabriele (1877-1962) German					
oil	15	1,634,021	8,854	37,827	600,000
wc/d	3	26,430	2,320	5,663	18,447
MUNTHE, Ludvig (1841-1896) Norwegian					
oil	10	50,910	1,306	3,619	15,168
MUNTHE-NORSTEDT, Anna (1854-1936) Swedish					
oil	3	10,762	1,648	4,353	4,761
MUNTTER, E (19/20th C) German					
oil	1	1,823		1,823	
MUNZER, Adolf (1870-1952) German					
oil	2	2,532	1,238	1,266	1,294
MUNZO, Alfredo (19/20th C) Austrian					
oil	1	3,000		3,000	
MURA, Francesco de (1696-1782) Italian					
oil	10	102,891	3,375	6,609	32,340
MURA, Francesco de (school) (1696-1782) Italian					
oil	1	2,417		2,417	
MURADO, Antonio (20th C) Spanish					
oil	2	2,664	1,103	1,332	1,561
MURAKAMI, Takashi (1962-) Japanese					
3D	1	1,900		1,900	
MURATENY, Emile (?) French?					
oil	1	1,891		1,891	
MURCH, Walter (1907-1967) American/Canadian					
oil	1	1,750		1,750	
MURER, A (1922-1985) Italian					
3D	1	1,998		1,998	
MURER, Christoph (1558-1614) Swiss					
wc/d	1	5,444		5,444	
MURI, Roland (1959-) Swiss					
oil	1	3,323		3,323	
MURILLO BRACHO, Jose Maria (1827-1882) Spanish					
oil	1	3,831		3,831	
MURILLO, Bartolome Esteban (1618-1682) Spanish					
oil	2	216,244	1,480	108,122	214,764
MURILLO, Bartolome Esteban (school) (1618-1682) Spanish					
oil	2	5,824	2,250	2,912	3,574
MURPHY, Ada Clifford (19/20th C) American					
oil	1	3,800		3,800	
MURPHY, Christopher (jnr) (1902-1969) American					
oil	1	1,750		1,750	
MURPHY, Herman Dudley (1867-1945) American					
oil	2	17,000	5,000	8,500	12,000
wc/d	1	1,500		1,500	
MURPHY, J Francis (1853-1921) American					
oil	11	79,600	1,200	5,500	24,000
MURPHY, Noel (?) Irish?					
oil	1	1,727		1,727	
MURRAY, Charles Fairfax (1849-1919) British					
oil	1	1,343		1,343	
MURRAY, David (19th C) British?					
oil	1	3,634		3,634	
MURRAY, Eben H (fl.1880-1886) British					
oil	1	4,200		4,200	
MURRAY, Elizabeth (1940-) American					
3D	1	35,000		35,000	
oil	1	52,000		52,000	
wc/d	2	13,200	3,200	6,600	10,000

Name	No.	Total Sales Value	Prices lowest	median	highest
MURRAY, G (19th C) ?					
oil	1	1,216		1,216	
MURRAY, H (fl.1850-1860) British					
wc/d	2	2,200	1,000	1,100	1,200
MURRAY, J (?) British?					
oil	2	4,964	1,189	2,482	3,775
MURRAY, Sir David (1849-1933) British					
oil	7	41,903	1,296	3,925	20,020
MURRAY, Waldo (20th C) American					
oil	1	1,300		1,300	
MURRAY, William (19th C) British					
oil	1	10,500		10,500	
MUS, Italo (1892-1967) Italian					
oil	2	42,562	7,631	21,281	34,931
MUSCHAMP, F Sydney (1851-1929) British					
oil	5	40,315	1,390	3,210	23,700
MUSCHAMP, Francis (fl.1865-1885) British					
oil	1	1,776		1,776	
MUSCHAMP, W (19th C) British					
oil	1	1,300		1,300	
MUSCHER, Michel van (?) Belgian?					
oil	1	2,662		2,662	
MUSIC, Zoran (1909-) Italian					
oil	15	315,479	1,853	16,945	87,267
wc/d	18	50,681	1,003	2,099	8,534
MUSIN, A (19/20th C) Belgian					
oil	1	1,095		1,095	
MUSIN, Auguste (1852-1920) Belgian					
oil	9	35,197	1,103	3,531	9,300
MUSIN, François Etienne (1820-1888) Belgian					
oil	10	82,257	1,253	6,437	20,334
MUSIN, Maurice (1939-) Belgian					
oil	4	5,521	1,253	1,413	1,442
MUSSCHER, Michiel van (1645-1705) Dutch					
oil	1	33,220		33,220	
MUSSINI, Cesare (1804-1879) Italian					
oil	1	4,830		4,830	
MUSSO, Carlo (1907-1968) Italian					
oil	4	10,812	1,318	2,569	4,357
MUTANE, Luis (1899-) ?					
oil	1	7,932		7,932	
MUTER, Mela (1886-1967) French					
oil	24	171,937	1,752	6,660	18,447
MUTRIE, Annie Feray (1826-1893) British					
oil	1	7,900		7,900	
wc/d	1	1,738		1,738	
MUTRIE, Martha Darley (1824-1885) British					
oil	1	7,100		7,100	
wc/d	1	1,659		1,659	
MUTZNER, Sammys (1869-1958) Rumanian					
oil	1	2,090		2,090	
MUTZNER, Samuel (1886-?) Rumanian					
oil	1	2,315		2,315	
MUUKKA, Elias (1853-1938) Finnish					
oil	1	2,829		2,829	
MUXART, Jaime (1922-) Spanish					
oil	2	3,183	1,405	1,592	1,778
MUYDEN, Alfred van (1818-1898) Swiss					
oil	3	13,236	1,700	2,105	9,431

Name	No.	Total Sales Value	lowest	Prices median	highest
MUYS, Nicolaes (1740-1808) Dutch					
oil	1	57,380		57,380	
MUZZIOLI, Giovanni (1854-1894) Italian					
oil	2	136,821	11,821	68,411	125,000
MY, Hieronymus van der (1687-1761) Dutch					
oil	1	36,000		36,000	
MYERS, Frank Harmon (1899-1956) American					
oil	3	11,050	1,800	2,750	6,500
MYERS, Harry (1886-1961) American					
oil	1	1,600		1,600	
MYERS, Jerome (1867-c.1941) American					
oil	4	67,700	1,700	18,000	30,000
MYGATT, Robertson K (1861-1919) American					
oil	2	4,700	1,200	2,350	3,500
MYN, Francis van der (1719-1783) Dutch					
oil	1	6,750		6,750	
MYN, Herman van der (1684-1741) Dutch					
oil	2	28,968	3,768	14,484	25,200
MYRAH, Newman (1921-) Canadian					
oil	1	8,000		8,000	
MYTENS, Daniel (17th C) Dutch					
oil	1	57,380		57,380	
MYTENS, Martin (school) (17/18th C) Dutch/Swedish					
oil	1	3,500		3,500	
MYTENS, Martin I (1648-1736) Dutch					
oil	1	5,643		5,643	
MYTENS, Martin II (1695-1770) Swedish					
oil	3	21,656	2,689	8,762	10,205
NABERT, Wilhelm (1830-1904) German					
oil	2	4,142	1,765	2,071	2,377
NACKAERTS, Frans (1884-?) Belgian					
wc/d	1	2,427		2,427	
NADAL, Carlos (1917-1998) Spanish					
oil	8	98,585	4,108	10,363	27,180
wc/d	2	4,204	1,630	2,102	2,574
NADELMAN, Elie (1882-1946) American/Polish					
3D	4	531,000	25,000	118,000	270,000
wc/d	2	28,500	4,500	14,250	24,000
NAFTEL, Isabel (fl.1862-1891) British					
wc/d	1	3,718		3,718	
NAFTEL, Maud (1856-1890) British					
wc/d	4	12,460	1,924	2,900	4,736
NAFTEL, Paul Jacob (1817-1891) British					
wc/d	2	4,424	1,896	2,212	2,528
NAGANO, M (19th C) Japanese					
oil	1	7,214		7,214	
NAGEL, Otto (1894-1967) German					
oil	1	1,349		1,349	
NAGELE, Reinhold (1884-1972) German					
oil	2	9,776	1,932	4,888	7,844
NAGERA, Asuncion (19th C) Spanish					
oil	1	3,853		3,853	
NAGI, D (19th C) Italian?					
3D	1	12,960		12,960	
NAGORNOV, Vladislav (1974-) Russian					
oil	3	3,741	1,056	1,185	1,500
NAGTEGAAL, Jan (1920-) Dutch					
oil	1	1,000		1,000	

Name	No.	Total Sales Value	lowest	Prices median	highest
NAGY, Ernest de (?) ?					
oil	1	1,000		1,000	
NAGY, Vilmos (1874-1953) Hungarian					
oil	1	1,352		1,352	
NAIGELE, Jan van de (20th C) ?					
oil	1	2,000		2,000	
NAIGEON, Jean Guillaume Elzidor (1797-1867) French					
oil	1	4,499		4,499	
NAILOR, Gerald (1917-1952) American					
wc/d	3	11,800	1,800	3,000	7,000
NAIRN, Margaret (20th C) British					
wc/d	1	1,298		1,298	
NAIVEU, Matthys (1647-1721) Dutch					
oil	2	623,177	5,777	311,589	617,400
NAKAGAWA, Kazumasa (1893-1991) Japanese					
oil	1	32,000		32,000	
NAKAJIMA, Chinami (1945-) Japanese					
wc/d	2	220,000	90,000	110,000	130,000
NAKAMURA, Naondo (20th C) Japanese					
wc/d	2	3,143	1,343	1,572	1,800
NAKIAN, Reuben (1897-1986) American					
3D	1	3,200		3,200	
wc/d	1	3,250		3,250	
NAKKEN, W C (1835-1926) Dutch					
oil	1	1,057		1,057	
NAKKEN, Willem Carel (1835-1926) Dutch					
oil	8	39,492	1,641	3,348	11,478
wc/d	4	8,883	1,641	2,149	2,944
NALDINI, Giovan Battista (1537-1591) Italian					
oil	1	2,406		2,406	
wc/d	1	27,180		27,180	
NALLARD, Louis (1918-) French					
wc/d	2	2,586	1,293	1,293	1,293
NAM GREB (19/20th C) Austrian					
3D	2	7,144	3,000	3,572	4,144
NAM, Jacques (1881-1974) French					
3D	4	14,288	2,634	3,523	4,609
oil	2	4,800	1,891	2,400	2,909
NAMATJIRA, Albert (1902-1959) Australian					
wc/d	1	1,470		1,470	
NAMUR, Franz (1877-?) French					
oil	1	2,518		2,518	
NANI, Giacomo (1701-1770) Italian					
oil	1	91,140		91,140	
NANIN (19/20th C) Italian?					
3D	1	1,459		1,459	
NANNI, Giovanni (1487-1564) Italian					
wc/d	1	75,500		75,500	
NANNINGA, Dirk Berend (1868-1954) Dutch					
oil	1	1,259		1,259	
NANNINGA, Jaap (1904-1962) Dutch					
oil	2	4,374	1,205	2,187	3,169
wc/d	3	10,334	1,901	3,283	5,150
NANSKY (20th C) ?					
wc/d	1	1,326		1,326	
NAONDO, Nakamuro (20th C) Japanese					
oil	1	1,091		1,091	
NAPIER, George (fl.1850-1860s) British					
oil	1	14,300		14,300	

Name	No.	Total Sales Value	lowest	Prices median	highest
NAPPER, John (1916-) British					
wc/d	1	2,686		2,686	
NAPPI, Rudy (20th C) American					
oil	1	4,500		4,500	
NAQQASH, Mohammad (20th C) Iranian					
oil	1	1,933		1,933	
NAQSH, Jamil (1938-) Indian					
wc/d	1	1,950		1,950	
NARA, Yoshimoto (1959-) American?					
wc/d	1	1,900		1,900	
NARANJO, Eduardo (1944-) Spanish					
oil	1	2,323		2,323	
NARAY, Aurel (1883-1948) Hungarian					
oil	1	1,000		1,000	
NARCISSUS (?) ?					
3D	1	1,687		1,687	
NARDI, Enrico (1864-?) Italian					
wc/d	1	3,000		3,000	
NARDO, Mariotto di (14/15th C) Italian					
oil	1	83,557		83,557	
NARJOT, Ernest (1826-1898) American					
oil	1	22,500		22,500	
NARLET, J (?) French					
wc/d	1	1,082		1,082	
NARVAEZ, Francisco (1905-1982) Venezuelan					
3D	1	2,870		2,870	
oil	2	8,330	3,590	4,165	4,740
NARVAIZA RUBIO, Alejandro and RUBIO DALMATI, Alejandro (?) Spanish					
oil	1	2,689		2,689	
NARVARTE (?) Spanish					
oil	1	1,344		1,344	
NASCIMBENE (20th C) Italian					
oil	1	2,038		2,038	
NASH, David (1945-) British					
3D	2	8,285	3,000	4,143	5,285
wc/d	1	1,221		1,221	
NASH, Eustace (1886-?) British					
oil	1	1,208		1,208	
NASH, Frederick (1782-1856) British					
wc/d	5	16,787	1,422	1,859	7,500
NASH, John (1893-1977) British					
oil	5	45,680	3,160	10,270	13,500
wc/d	6	22,096	1,269	3,576	5,700
NASH, Joseph (1808-1878) British					
wc/d	2	4,083	1,223	2,042	2,860
NASH, Paul (1889-1946) British					
wc/d	10	113,484	1,450	8,370	40,040
NASH, Thomas (1891-1968) British					
oil	1	3,625		3,625	
NASI, G (19th C) Italian					
oil	1	1,400		1,400	
NASMYTH, Alexander (1758-1840) British					
oil	3	21,231	4,740	7,008	9,483
NASMYTH, Anne (1793-?) British					
oil	1	2,370		2,370	
NASMYTH, Charlotte (1804-1884) British					
oil	1	5,000		5,000	
NASMYTH, Jane (1788-1867) British					
oil	2	6,968	1,168	3,484	5,800

Name	No.	Total Sales Value	lowest	Prices median	highest
NASMYTH, Patrick (1787-1831) British					
oil	7	48,127	1,850	5,841	12,870
NAST, Gustave Louis (1826-?) French					
3D	1	41,466		41,466	
NAT, Willem Hendrik van der (1864-1929) Dutch					
oil	7	24,386	1,257	3,317	5,073
NATALI, Renato (1883-1979) Italian					
oil	34	89,304	1,249	2,824	5,351
NATHAN, M H (fl.1885-1886) British					
oil	1	13,000		13,000	
NATHAN, Max (1880-1952) Danish					
oil	1	1,134		1,134	
NATHE, Christoph (1753-1806) German					
wc/d	1	2,506		2,506	
NATIVI, Gualtiero (1921-1997) Italian					
oil	8	12,080	1,032	1,453	2,077
wc/d	1	1,978		1,978	
NATKIN, Robert (1930-) American					
oil	6	19,850	2,400	3,200	4,250
NATOIRE, Charles-Joseph (1700-1777) French					
wc/d	8	54,719	1,176	5,207	18,120
NATON, Avraham (1906-1959) Israeli					
oil	1	3,200		3,200	
NATTIER, Jean Marc (1685-1766) French					
oil	3	805,000	105,000	120,000	580,000
NATTIER, Jean Marc (school) (1685-1766) French					
oil	1	5,000		5,000	
NATTINI, Amos (1892-?) Italian					
oil	2	14,836	7,418	7,418	7,418
NATTINO, Girolamo (19th C) Italian					
oil	1	2,110		2,110	
NATTINO, Vittorio (1890-1971) Italian					
oil	1	1,379		1,379	
NATTRESS, George (fl.1866-1888) British					
wc/d	2	7,150	3,575	3,575	3,575
NAUEN, Heinrich (1880-1941) German					
oil	1	14,000		14,000	
NAUEN, Paul (1859-1932) German					
wc/d	1	1,328		1,328	
NAULO, William (fl.1820-1860) French?					
oil	1	2,000		2,000	
NAUMAN, Bruce (1941-) American					
3D	8	1,619,000	19,000	190,000	420,000
oil	1	12,000		12,000	
wc/d	4	140,100	15,000	21,500	82,000
NAVARRO LLORENS, Jose (1867-1923) Spanish					
oil	6	82,430	1,604	11,117	37,500
NAVARRO, Enrique (20th C) Spanish					
oil	1	2,251		2,251	
NAVARRO, Jose (19th C) Spanish					
oil	1	65,523		65,523	
NAVARRO, Roman (1854-1928) Spanish					
wc/d	1	1,467		1,467	
NAVASCUES, Jose Maria (1944-) Spanish					
oil	1	1,709		1,709	
wc/d	1	2,422		2,422	
NAVAZIO, Walter de (1887-1921) Argentinian					
oil	1	9,000		9,000	

Name	No.	Total Sales Value	lowest	Prices median	highest
NAVEZ, Arthur (1881-1931) Belgian					
oil	1	4,271		4,271	
NAVEZ, François Joseph (1787-1869) Belgian					
oil	1	4,294		4,294	
NAVEZ, Léon (1900-1967) Belgian					
oil	2	4,334	1,437	2,167	2,897
NAVIASKY, Philip (1894-1983) British					
oil	2	2,649	1,199	1,325	1,450
NAVLET, Joseph (1821-1889) French					
oil	3	7,541	1,298	2,148	4,095
NAY, Ernst Wilhelm (1902-1968) German					
oil	5	462,032	15,571	80,383	203,884
wc/d	12	259,820	4,728	24,061	31,141
NAZARENE SCHOOL German					
oil	2	8,386	3,386	4,193	5,000
NEAL, James (1918-) British					
oil	3	3,986	1,027	1,074	1,885
NEALE, Edward (19/20th C) British					
oil	1	4,452		4,452	
NEAPOLITAN SCHOOL					
wc/d	1	3,289		3,289	
NEAPOLITAN SCHOOL, 17/18th C					
oil	1	35,373		35,373	
NEAPOLITAN SCHOOL, 17th C					
3D	2	35,879	2,451	17,940	33,428
oil	16	177,134	2,285	5,940	59,812
NEAPOLITAN SCHOOL, 18/19th C					
oil	1	3,183		3,183	
NEAPOLITAN SCHOOL, 18th C					
3D	2	13,429	6,591	6,715	6,838
oil	14	117,737	3,428	6,042	22,050
wc/d	1	5,091		5,091	
NEAPOLITAN SCHOOL, 19/20th C					
oil	1	6,320		6,320	
NEAPOLITAN SCHOOL, 19th C					
3D	1	3,102		3,102	
oil	11	66,007	2,182	3,295	28,182
wc/d	15	124,834	2,856	4,394	45,300
NEAPOLITAN SCHOOL, 20th C					
oil	2	7,856	2,861	3,928	4,995
wc/d	2	4,576	1,716	2,288	2,860
NEAVE, Vincent (20th C) British					
oil	2	6,840	3,040	3,420	3,800
NEBBIA, Cesare (1536-1614) Italian					
oil	1	16,511		16,511	
wc/d	2	4,011	1,691	2,006	2,320
NEBEKER, Bill (20th C) American					
3D	1	16,000		16,000	
NEBEL, Friedrich Joseph Adolf (1818-1892) German					
oil	1	1,382		1,382	
NEBEL, Kay Heinrich (1888-1953) German					
oil	1	4,059		4,059	
NEBEL, Otto (1892-1975) German					
wc/d	3	5,633	1,468	1,560	2,605
NEBOT, Balthasar (18th C) British					
oil	1	14,798		14,798	
NECK, Jan van (1635-1714) Dutch					
oil	2	23,250	7,550	11,625	15,700
NEDER, Johann Michael (1807-1882) Austrian					
oil	1	28,909		28,909	

Name	No.	Total Sales Value	lowest	Prices median	highest
NEDERGAARD, Niels (20th C) Scandinavian					
wc/d	1	1,247		1,247	
NEEDHAM, William (19th C) British					
oil	1	7,436		7,436	
NEEFFS, Pieter (16/17th C) Flemish					
oil	1	6,049		6,049	
NEEFFS, Pieter (elder) (1578-1658) Flemish					
oil	1	18,720		18,720	
NEEFFS, Pieter (school) (16/17th C) Flemish					
oil	1	5,281		5,281	
NEEFFS, Pieter (younger) (1620-1675) Flemish					
oil	1	41,160		41,160	
NEEFS, Pieter III (17th C?) Flemish					
oil	2	17,453	3,791	8,727	13,662
NEER, A van der (17th C) Dutch					
oil	1	1,738		1,738	
NEER, Aert van der (1603-1677) Dutch					
oil	3	355,682	5,682	100,000	250,000
NEFF, Timoleon Karl (1805-1876) Russian					
oil	1	22,650		22,650	
NEFKENS, Martinus Jacobus (1866-1941) Dutch					
oil	2	2,470	1,221	1,235	1,249
NEGRI, Mario (1916-) Italian					
3D	5	16,902	1,756	2,028	7,000
NEGRI, Pietro (c.1591-1661) Italian					
oil	1	37,750		37,750	
NEGULESCU, Jean (1900-1993) Rumanian/American					
wc/d	1	1,800		1,800	
NEHER, Michael (1798-1876) German					
oil	1	34,890		34,890	
NEILAND, Brendan (1941-) British					
oil	1	1,570		1,570	
NEILLOT, Louis (1898-1973) French					
oil	1	1,354		1,354	
wc/d	1	1,085		1,085	
NEJAD, Mehmed (1923-1994) Turkish					
oil	1	2,757		2,757	
NELLENS, Roger (1937-) Belgian					
oil	3	5,222	1,671	1,671	1,880
NELLIUS, Martinus (fl.1670-1706) Dutch					
oil	3	53,347	10,607	21,600	21,600
NELSON, A (18th C) British					
3D	1	1,161		1,161	
NELSON, Alphonse Henri (1854-?) French					
3D	2	2,379	1,048	1,190	1,331
NELSON, E M (20th C) British					
oil	1	2,200		2,200	
NELSON, Ernest Bruce (1888-1952) American					
oil	1	5,000		5,000	
NELSON, Joan (1958-) American					
oil	5	31,500	2,500	7,000	9,000
NEMES, Endre (1909-1985) Hungarian					
oil	8	19,046	1,204	2,453	4,616
wc/d	1	1,190		1,190	
NEMES-LAMPERTH, Jozsef (1891-1924) Hungarian					
wc/d	1	1,612		1,612	
NEMETHY, Albert (1920-) American					
oil	1	1,150		1,150	

Name	No.	Total Sales Value	Prices lowest	median	highest
NEMOURS, Aurelie (1910-) French					
oil	1	16,719		16,719	
NEMUKHIN, Vladimir (1925-) Russian					
oil	2	6,092	1,580	3,046	4,512
NEO-CLASSICAL FRENCH SCHOOL					
wc/d	1	3,322		3,322	
NEO-CLASSICAL FRENCH SCHOOL, 19th C					
3D	2	17,757	2,743	8,879	15,014
NEO-CLASSICAL SCHOOL					
3D	1	15,034		15,034	
NEO-CLASSICAL SCHOOL, 18th C					
3D	3	36,858	5,712	13,131	18,015
oil	4	56,498	3,264	9,209	34,817
NEO-CLASSICAL SCHOOL, 19th C					
3D	1	44,341		44,341	
oil	1	26,605		26,605	
NEOGRADY, Antal (1861-1942) Hungarian					
oil	3	4,300	1,000	1,200	2,100
NEOGRADY, Laszlo (1896-1962) Hungarian					
oil	9	18,977	1,027	1,800	4,530
NEPALESE SCHOOL, 18th C					
3D	1	3,822		3,822	
NEPALESE SCHOOL, 19th C					
wc/d	1	3,950		3,950	
NEPVEU, Eugene Charles Frederic (1819-?) French					
oil	1	1,897		1,897	
NERI, Paul (19/20th C) ?					
oil	1	3,222		3,222	
NERLY, Friedrich (19th C) Italian/Austrian					
oil	1	44,954		44,954	
wc/d	2	4,689	2,020	2,345	2,669
NERLY, Friedrich (younger) (1824-1919) Italian					
oil	3	25,414	2,054	8,760	14,600
NERUD, Josef Karl (1900-1982) German					
wc/d	1	2,960		2,960	
NESBITT, Frances E (1864-1934) British					
wc/d	1	2,114		2,114	
NESBITT, Jackson Lee (1913-) American					
oil	2	11,200	2,200	5,600	9,000
wc/d	2	3,400	1,200	1,700	2,200
NESBITT, John (1831-1904) British					
oil	1	1,911		1,911	
NESBITT, Lowell (1933-1993) American					
oil	4	13,718	1,478	3,390	5,460
NESCH, Rolf (1893-1975) Norwegian					
oil	4	64,705	2,019	5,392	51,902
NESFIELD, William Andrews (1793-1881) British					
wc/d	1	4,424		4,424	
NESHAT, Shirin (1957-) American					
wc/d	4	88,500	7,500	19,500	42,000
NESPOLO, Ugo (1941-) Italian					
oil	13	33,363	1,361	2,426	5,934
wc/d	2	5,721	1,220	2,861	4,501
NESSELTHALER, Andreas (?-1821) Austrian					
oil	1	9,060		9,060	
NESSI, Marie Lucie (1900-1992) French					
oil	1	1,500		1,500	
NESTE, Alfred van (1874-1969) Belgian					
oil	2	4,076	1,787	2,038	2,289

Name	No.	Total Sales Value	lowest	Prices median	highest
NESTEROV, Mikhail Vasilievich (1862-1942) Russian					
oil	1	25,380		25,380	
NESTEROV, O (19/20th C) Russian					
oil	1	4,408		4,408	
NETER, Laurentius de (1600-?) German					
oil	2	30,380	4,710	15,190	25,670
NETHERLANDISH SCHOOL, 15th C					
oil	1	30,000		30,000	
NETHERLANDISH SCHOOL, 16th C					
3D	1	6,040		6,040	
oil	6	86,311	4,896	13,103	27,360
NETHERLANDISH SCHOOL, 16th/17th C					
3D	1	26,412		26,412	
NETHERLANDISH SCHOOL, 17th C					
3D	1	6,342		6,342	
oil	6	29,671	2,944	5,275	6,870
NETHERLANDISH SCHOOL, 17th/18th C					
oil	2	6,204	3,017	3,102	3,187
NETHERLANDISH SCHOOL, 18th C					
3D	1	9,224		9,224	
oil	5	23,921	2,273	4,907	6,934
NETHERLANDISH SCHOOL, 18th/19th C					
oil	1	3,864		3,864	
NETHERLANDISH SCHOOL, 19th C					
3D	1	2,935		2,935	
NETHERLANDISH SCHOOL, 19th/20th C					
oil	1	4,661		4,661	
NETO, Ernesto (1964-) Brazilian					
3D	2	34,000	4,000	17,000	30,000
NETSCHER, Caspar (1639-1684) Dutch					
oil	3	7,715	1,324	2,611	3,780
NETSCHER, Constantyn (1668-1723) Dutch					
oil	2	10,986	3,600	5,493	7,386
NETSCHER, Constantyn (school) (1668-1723) Dutch					
oil	1	3,800		3,800	
NETTLESHIP, John Trivett (1847-1902) British					
wc/d	1	1,278		1,278	
NEUBERT, Ludwig (1846-1892) German					
oil	2	2,719	1,259	1,360	1,460
NEUCKENS, P J (19th C) Belgian					
oil	1	1,328		1,328	
NEUDECKER, Mariele (1965-) German					
3D	1	4,530		4,530	
NEUENSCHWANDER, Albert (1902-1984) Swiss					
oil	2	2,520	1,129	1,260	1,391
NEUFCHATEL, Nicolas (1527-1590) Flemish					
oil	1	1,189		1,189	
NEUGEBAUER, Rudolf (1892-?) German					
oil	1	1,128		1,128	
NEUHAUS, Werner (1897-1934) Swiss					
oil	1	1,166		1,166	
NEUHUYS, Albert (1844-1914) Dutch					
oil	6	18,922	1,506	3,327	4,436
wc/d	5	40,801	5,516	9,480	10,270
NEUJEAN, Arnold Bernard (1887-1959) Dutch					
oil	2	2,656	1,207	1,328	1,449
NEUMAN, Johan Heinrich (1819-1898) German					
oil	1	1,020		1,020	

Name	No.	Total Sales Value	lowest	Prices median	highest
NEUMANN (?) ?					
oil	1	1,788		1,788	
NEUMANN, Carl (1833-1891) Danish					
oil	4	6,669	1,043	1,653	2,320
NEUMANN, F (?) German?					
oil	1	1,288		1,288	
NEUMANN, Johan (1860-1940) Danish					
oil	8	12,581	1,016	1,259	3,359
NEUMANN, Max (1949-) German					
oil	1	1,539		1,539	
wc/d	1	1,165		1,165	
NEUQUELMAN, Lucien (1909-1988) French					
oil	2	4,473	1,151	2,237	3,322
NEUSCHUL, Ernest (1895-1968) Austrian					
oil	1	5,760		5,760	
NEUSER, L A William (1833-1902) German/American					
oil	1	4,200		4,200	
NEUSTATTER, Ludwig (1829-1899) German					
oil	1	5,500		5,500	
NEUVILLE, Alphonse Marie de (1835-1885) French					
oil	1	1,154		1,154	
NEVELSON, Louise (1899-1988) American					
3D	18	412,984	3,000	15,500	130,000
wc/d	4	12,766	2,000	2,528	5,710
NEVILLE, Edward (?) British					
wc/d	1	1,269		1,269	
NEVINSON, Christopher Richard Wynne (1889-1946) British					
oil	5	310,016	1,406	5,372	257,400
NEW ENGLAND SCHOOL, 19th C American					
oil	3	28,000	4,500	4,500	19,000
wc/d	4	78,750	3,750	7,500	60,000
NEWBERY, Francis H (1855-1946) British					
oil	1	3,243		3,243	
NEWBOLT, John (fl.1868) British					
oil	1	8,584		8,584	
NEWBURY, Francis Henry (1885-1946) British					
oil	1	91,140		91,140	
NEWBY, J H (19th C) British					
oil	1	1,001		1,001	
NEWCOMB, Mary (1922-) British					
oil	4	164,320	34,760	37,920	53,720
wc/d	1	1,152		1,152	
NEWCOMBE, Frederick Clive (1847-1894) British					
oil	1	2,145		2,145	
NEWCOMBE, William John Bertram (1907-1969) Canadian					
oil	1	1,208		1,208	
wc/d	2	6,593	2,926	3,297	3,667
NEWELL, George Glenn (1870-1947) American					
oil	1	5,000		5,000	
NEWELL, Peter Shead Hersey (1862-1924) American					
wc/d	2	6,200	3,000	3,100	3,200
NEWEY, H F (1858-1933) British					
oil	1	1,413		1,413	
NEWMAN, Henry Roderick (c.1833-1918) American					
wc/d	2	50,000	22,000	25,000	28,000
NEWMAN, Milton R (20th C) American					
oil	1	4,750		4,750	
NEWMAN, Robert Loftin (1827-1912) American					
oil	1	8,000		8,000	

Name	No.	Total Sales Value	lowest	Prices median	highest
NEWMAN, Vicky (20th C) ?					
oil	1	1,300		1,300	
NEWSON, Marc (1963-) Australian					
3D	1	90,000		90,000	
NEWTON, Algernon (1880-1968) British					
oil	2	3,177	1,305	1,589	1,872
wc/d	1	2,400		2,400	
NEWTON, G E (19th C) British					
oil	1	1,304		1,304	
NEWTON, Gilbert Stuart (1794-1835) British					
oil	1	4,716		4,716	
NEWTON, Lilias Torrance (1896-1980) Canadian					
oil	1	1,336		1,336	
NEWTON, Sir William John (1785-1869) British					
oil	1	2,657		2,657	
NEYLAND, Harry A (1877-1958) American					
oil	1	1,650		1,650	
NEYLIES, J H (?) French?					
oil	1	5,500		5,500	
NEYLIS (19th C) French					
oil	1	2,634		2,634	
NEYMARK, Gustave (1850-?) French					
oil	2	2,506	1,000	1,253	1,506
NEYN, Pieter de (1597-1639) Dutch					
oil	1	12,560		12,560	
NEYTS, Gillis (1623-1687) Flemish					
oil	1	5,106		5,106	
wc/d	1	1,068		1,068	
NHLENGETHWA, Sam (1955-) South African					
oil	1	2,350		2,350	
NIBBRIG, Ferdinand Hart (1866-1915) Dutch					
oil	2	11,488	5,546	5,744	5,942
NIBBS, Richard Henry (1816-1893) British					
oil	7	57,439	1,963	7,500	16,590
wc/d	4	4,658	1,027	1,158	1,316
NIBLETT, Gary (1943-) American					
oil	1	17,000		17,000	
NICAES, Christian (20th C) Belgian					
3D	1	1,810		1,810	
NICCOLO, Pasqualino di (?) Italian					
oil	1	80,850		80,850	
NICHOLAS, J T (20th C) American					
oil	1	5,500		5,500	
NICHOLAS, Thomas (20th C) American					
oil	1	1,400		1,400	
NICHOLL, Agnes Rose (1842-c.1892) British					
wc/d	2	6,064	1,008	3,032	5,056
NICHOLL, Andrew (1804-1886) British					
wc/d	9	89,563	2,669	6,660	26,640
NICHOLLS, Burr H (1848-1915) American					
oil	2	13,500	5,500	6,750	8,000
NICHOLLS, John E (fl.1922-1955) British					
oil	2	5,103	2,100	2,552	3,003
NICHOLS, Carroll Leja (1882-?) American					
oil	1	2,500		2,500	
NICHOLS, Henry Hobart (1869-1962) American					
oil	1	3,000		3,000	
NICHOLSON, Ben (1894-1982) British					
oil	13	686,606	13,968	42,280	143,450

Name	No.	Total Sales Value	Prices lowest	Prices median	highest
wc/d	4	54,725	6,750	10,938	26,100
NICHOLSON, Charles A (19th C) ?					
wc/d	1	1,727		1,727	
NICHOLSON, D (19th C) British					
oil	1	1,988		1,988	
NICHOLSON, Edward H (1901-1966) American					
oil	1	1,200		1,200	
NICHOLSON, Francis (1753-1844) British					
wc/d	6	24,908	1,011	2,791	9,480
NICHOLSON, George W (1832-1912) American					
oil	9	26,650	1,400	2,700	4,750
NICHOLSON, John H (1911-1988) British					
wc/d	1	1,001		1,001	
NICHOLSON, John Millar (fl.1877-1888) British					
wc/d	1	1,502		1,502	
NICHOLSON, Kate (20th C) ?					
oil	2	6,040	2,265	3,020	3,775
NICHOLSON, Lillie May (1884-1964) American					
oil	1	1,500		1,500	
NICHOLSON, Sir William (1872-1949) British					
oil	5	415,388	5,688	36,660	232,500
wc/d	1	3,002		3,002	
NICHOLSON, Winifred (1893-1981) British					
oil	5	122,190	7,500	20,540	53,650
wc/d	3	17,094	2,400	5,530	9,164
NICKEL, Hans (1916-1986) German					
oil	4	7,360	1,397	1,841	2,282
NICKELE, Isaak van (?-1703) Dutch					
oil	1	18,120		18,120	
NICKERSON, Reginald E (1915-) American					
oil	2	11,000	5,500	5,500	5,500
NICOL, Erskine (1825-1904) British					
oil	6	55,884	4,134	6,090	22,050
wc/d	1	1,963		1,963	
NICOLAAS, Joep (1897-?) Dutch					
oil	1	1,171		1,171	
NICOLAIDES, Kimon (1892-1938) American					
oil	2	4,850	1,600	2,425	3,250
NICOLAU, Francisco Sebastian (1956-) Spanish					
wc/d	1	1,040		1,040	
NICOLAUS, Martin (1870-1945) German					
oil	1	1,564		1,564	
NICOLET, P (18th C) French					
oil	1	20,425		20,425	
NICOLL, Marion Florence (1909-1985) Canadian					
oil	2	4,865	1,502	2,433	3,363
wc/d	1	1,330		1,330	
NICOLLE, Victor Jean (1754-1826) French					
wc/d	20	81,263	1,241	2,977	9,528
NIEDMANN, August Heinrich (1826-1910) German					
oil	1	24,534		24,534	
NIEHAUS, Kaspar (1889-1974) Dutch					
oil	1	2,802		2,802	
NIELSEN, Amaldus Clarin (1838-1932) Norwegian					
oil	1	2,096		2,096	
NIELSEN, Ejnar (1872-1956) Danish					
oil	2	3,545	1,162	1,773	2,383
NIELSEN, Helge (1893-1980) Danish					
oil	1	1,150		1,150	

Name	No.	Total Sales Value	lowest	Prices median	highest
NIELSEN, Jais (1885-1961) Danish					
oil	4	19,211	1,170	1,990	14,061
wc/d	1	2,183		2,183	
NIELSEN, Kai (1882-1924) Danish					
3D	4	6,244	1,020	1,523	2,178
NIELSEN, Kay (1886-1957) Danish					
wc/d	3	46,866	1,133	5,733	40,000
NIELSEN, Kehnet (1947-) Danish					
oil	6	9,044	1,162	1,527	2,007
NIELSEN, Knud (1916-) Danish					
oil	16	34,320	1,056	1,306	6,662
NIELSEN, Poul (1920-1998) Danish					
oil	1	1,170		1,170	
NIEMANN, E J (1813-1876) British					
oil	1	1,110		1,110	
NIEMANN, Edmund John (1813-1876) British					
oil	19	59,975	1,145	2,400	12,640
NIEMANN, Edward H (fl.1863-1887) British					
oil	7	15,468	1,027	1,950	4,060
NIEMEYER, Jo (1946-) German					
3D	2	4,738	1,951	2,369	2,787
NIEMEYER, John Henry (1839-1932) American					
oil	1	1,200		1,200	
NIERMAN, Leonardo (1932-) Mexican					
oil	3	7,450	1,700	2,500	3,250
NIESTLE, Henry (1876-1966) Swiss					
oil	1	2,178		2,178	
NIESTLE, Jean Bloe (1884-1942) German					
oil	1	22,062		22,062	
NIETO, Leonardo Alenza (1807-1845) Spanish					
oil	2	37,318	17,677	18,659	19,641
NIETO, Rodolfo (1936-1988) Mexican					
oil	1	2,440		2,440	
NIETSCHE, Paul (fl.1930s) British					
oil	2	4,210	1,350	2,105	2,860
NIEULANDT, Adriaen van (16/17th C) Flemish/Dutch					
oil	1	5,075		5,075	
NIEULANDT, Willem van (16/17th C) Flemish					
oil	1	2,948		2,948	
wc/d	1	2,431		2,431	
NIEUWENHOVEN, Willem van (1879-?) Dutch					
oil	3	5,561	1,358	2,052	2,151
NIEUWENHUYS, Johannes (1922-1986) Dutch					
oil	1	7,130		7,130	
wc/d	1	1,724		1,724	
NIEUWENHUYSE, Jean Walther van (1900-1980) Belgian					
oil	1	4,898		4,898	
NIEUWERKERKE, Comte de Alfred-Emilien (1811-1892) French					
3D	1	5,189		5,189	
NIEWEG, Jaap (1877-1955) Dutch					
oil	1	7,900		7,900	
NIGG, Joseph (1782-1863) Austrian					
oil	1	25,000		25,000	
NIGHTINGALE, Basil (1864-1940) British					
oil	1	1,088		1,088	
wc/d	6	13,485	1,000	1,403	4,710
NIGHTINGALE, Robert (1815-1895) British					
oil	2	42,750	15,750	21,375	27,000

Name	No.	Total Sales Value	lowest	Prices median	highest
NIGRO, Mario (1917-1992) Italian					
oil	3	9,190	1,894	2,949	4,347
NIKEL, Lea (1918-) Israeli					
oil	7	51,100	1,100	4,000	28,000
NIKKO, Bonsai Loki (?) Oriental?					
wc/d	1	6,500		6,500	
NILSON, Johann Esaias (1721-1788) German					
wc/d	1	2,595		2,595	
NILSON, K G (1942-) Swedish					
oil	1	1,278		1,278	
NILSON, Karl Gustaf (1942-) Swedish					
oil	1	2,948		2,948	
NILSON, Severin (1846-1918) Swedish					
oil	45	175,944	1,054	2,110	18,630
wc/d	2	2,373	1,117	1,187	1,256
NILSSON, Axel (1889-1981) Swedish					
oil	19	84,493	1,310	2,208	24,586
wc/d	2	3,918	1,959	1,959	1,959
NILSSON, Gunnar (1904-1995) Swedish					
3D	1	3,265		3,265	
NILSSON, Lars (1956-) Swedish					
wc/d	1	1,656		1,656	
NILSSON, Nils (1901-1949) Swedish					
oil	6	20,984	1,318	3,182	5,985
NILSSON, Olof (1868-1956) Swedish					
oil	4	6,927	1,442	1,760	2,077
NILSSON, Vera (1888-1979) Swedish					
oil	9	96,203	1,337	5,441	39,176
wc/d	1	6,006		6,006	
NILUS, Pjotr Alexandrowitsch (1869-1943) Russian					
oil	5	37,564	4,832	6,204	11,325
NINAS, Paul (1903-1964) American					
oil	1	2,000		2,000	
NINO, Carmelo (20th C) South American					
oil	1	1,045		1,045	
NISBET, Pollock (1848-1922) British					
oil	3	4,462	1,152	1,510	1,800
NISBET, Robert Buchan (1857-1942) British					
oil	3	8,789	1,889	2,115	4,785
NISBET, Robert H (1879-1961) American					
oil	1	5,250		5,250	
NISINI, G (19th C) Italian					
3D	1	33,785		33,785	
NISS, Thorvald (1842-1905) Danish					
oil	10	21,555	1,008	1,750	6,961
NITSCH, Hermann (1938-) Austrian					
oil	6	45,777	1,089	3,570	19,923
wc/d	1	3,552		3,552	
NITSCH, Richard (1866-?) German					
oil	4	5,195	1,002	1,280	1,634
NITTIS, Giuseppe de (1846-1884) Italian					
oil	3	49,517	1,450	11,376	36,691
wc/d	1	3,790		3,790	
NIVELT, Roger (1899-1962) French					
oil	1	1,677		1,677	
NIVEN, Margaret Graeme (1906-) British					
oil	1	3,268		3,268	
NIVIAKSIAK (1918-1959) North American					
3D	1	2,246		2,246	

Name	No.	Total Sales Value	lowest	Prices median	highest
NIXON, Nils (1912-1998) Swedish					
oil	1	1,126		1,126	
NKUMANDA, Jackson (1948-) South African					
wc/d	1	1,262		1,262	
NOBELE, Henri de (c.1820-1870) Belgian					
oil	1	4,215		4,215	
NOBILI, Riccardo (1859-?) Italian					
oil	1	23,000		23,000	
NOBLE, J (19/20th C) British					
oil	1	1,922		1,922	
NOBLE, James Campbell (1846-1913) British					
oil	4	21,344	2,370	5,244	8,486
NOBLE, John Sargeant (1848-1896) British					
oil	3	165,159	5,400	37,960	121,799
NOBLE, Paul (1963-) British					
wc/d	2	12,986	6,040	6,493	6,946
NOBLE, Richard (19th C) British					
oil	1	1,800		1,800	
NOBLE, Richard Pratchett (fl.1830-1861) British					
wc/d	1	1,026		1,026	
NOBLE, Robert (1857-1917) British					
oil	3	5,773	1,510	1,617	2,646
NOCI, Arturo (1875-1953) Italian					
oil	1	9,810		9,810	
wc/d	1	1,800		1,800	
NOCK, L F (20th C) American					
3D	2	6,200	3,000	3,100	3,200
NOCKEN, Wilhelm Theodor (1830-1905) German					
oil	1	1,124		1,124	
NODE, Charles (1811-1886) French					
oil	1	5,403		5,403	
NOEL, Alexandre Jean (1752-1834) French					
oil	1	8,085		8,085	
wc/d	4	52,182	2,680	8,372	32,758
NOEL, Georges (1924-) French					
oil	8	33,884	1,289	3,599	7,950
wc/d	7	15,995	1,765	2,506	2,567
NOEL, Hippolyte (1828-1902) French					
oil	1	1,086		1,086	
NOEL, J A (1815-1881) French					
wc/d	1	2,957		2,957	
NOEL, J B (19/20th C) British					
oil	1	1,138		1,138	
NOEL, John Bates (fl.1893-1909) British					
oil	3	7,213	1,272	1,570	4,371
NOEL, Jules (1815-1881) French					
oil	13	80,033	1,486	5,312	15,500
wc/d	1	1,342		1,342	
NOEL, Louis (?) French					
3D	1	7,274		7,274	
NOEL, Matthias Joseph de (1782-1849) German					
wc/d	1	4,273		4,273	
NOEL, Peter Paul Joseph (1789-1822) Belgian					
oil	1	6,064		6,064	
NOEL, Pol (?) French					
oil	2	2,862	1,102	1,431	1,760
NOELSMITH, Thomas (fl.1889-1900) British					
wc/d	1	2,000		2,000	

Name	No.	Total Sales Value	Prices lowest	Prices median	highest
NOERR, Julius (1827-1897) German					
oil	5	25,792	1,227	4,046	12,099
NOGARI, Giuseppe (1699-1763) Italian					
oil	3	39,697	12,080	12,617	15,000
NOGUCHI, Isamu (1904-1988) American					
3D	5	1,525,000	40,000	350,000	580,000
NOIRE, Maxime (1861-1927) French					
oil	7	10,630	1,031	1,289	2,341
NOIROT, Émile (1853-1924) French					
oil	1	1,501		1,501	
NOLAN, Sidney (1917-1992) Australian					
oil	6	171,445	1,692	8,511	108,750
NOLAND, Kenneth (1924-) American					
oil	11	941,140	3,000	15,000	720,000
wc/d	1	1,450		1,450	
NOLDE, Emil (1867-1956) German					
oil	5	1,565,369	26,364	345,600	720,000
wc/d	31	2,181,027	3,460	52,270	174,757
NOLHAC, Charles (20th C) French					
oil	1	1,598		1,598	
NOLKEN, Franz (1884-1918) German					
oil	3	40,010	3,128	16,077	20,805
wc/d	1	1,125		1,125	
NOLL, Alexandre (1890-1970) French					
3D	5	62,304	6,128	9,827	23,844
oil	1	1,228		1,228	
NOLL, David (20th C) American					
oil	3	8,000	2,000	2,600	3,400
wc/d	2	4,400	2,200	2,200	2,200
NOLLET, Paul (1911-1996) Belgian					
oil	1	1,317		1,317	
NOLTEE, Cornelis (1903-1967) Dutch					
oil	51	148,246	1,101	1,967	7,244
NOMELLINI, Plinio (1866-1943) Italian					
oil	2	73,444	9,061	36,722	64,383
NONELL Y MONTURIOL, Isidro (1873-1911) Spanish					
oil	4	405,393	6,212	94,591	210,000
wc/d	4	8,396	1,092	1,345	4,614
NONNENBRUCH, Max (1857-1922) German					
oil	2	34,167	13,840	17,084	20,327
NONNOTTE, Donat (1708-1785) French					
oil	2	32,406	2,406	16,203	30,000
NOORDE, Cornelis van (1731-1795) Dutch					
wc/d	2	3,143	1,257	1,572	1,886
NOORDIJK, Willem Frederik (1887-1970) Dutch					
oil	1	1,071		1,071	
NOORT, A C van (1914-) Dutch					
oil	1	1,214		1,214	
NOORT, Adrianus Cornelis van (1914-) Dutch					
oil	2	2,884	1,093	1,442	1,791
NOORT, Jan van (16-18th C) Dutch					
oil	1	8,640		8,640	
NOORT, Pieter van (1602-1648) Dutch					
oil	2	14,747	2,667	7,374	12,080
NOOTEBOOM, Jacobus Hendricus Johannes (1811-1878) Dutch					
oil	1	1,079		1,079	
NORBERG, Hildegard (1844-1917) Swedish					
oil	1	1,221		1,221	
NORBERTO (1927-) Italian					
oil	3	10,055	2,099	2,892	5,064

Name	No.	Total Sales Value	lowest	Prices median	highest
NORBLIN DE LA GOURDAINE, Jean Pierre (1745-1830) French					
oil	1	5,534		5,534	
wc/d	3	81,660	2,546	18,000	61,114
NORBLIN DE LA GOURDAINE, Sebastien Louis Guillaume (1796-1884) French					
wc/d	1	5,216		5,216	
NORDAU, Maxa (20th C) French					
oil	1	2,200		2,200	
NORDBERG, Olle (1905-1986) Swedish					
oil	1	1,212		1,212	
NORDELL, Carl J (1885-1934) American					
oil	1	3,000		3,000	
NORDEN, R van (?) ?					
oil	1	1,144		1,144	
NORDENBERG, Bengt (1822-1902) Swedish					
oil	9	149,494	1,341	4,265	92,113
wc/d	1	1,088		1,088	
NORDENBERG, Hendrick (1857-1928) Swedish					
oil	3	6,892	1,500	2,277	3,115
NORDFELDT, B J O (1878-1955) American					
oil	1	3,500		3,500	
wc/d	3	4,400	1,000	1,400	2,000
NORDFELDT, Bror Julius Olsson (1878-1955) American					
oil	3	16,500	3,500	5,000	8,000
NORDGREN, Anna (1847-1916) Swedish					
oil	2	18,298	1,138	9,149	17,160
NORDGREN, Axel (1828-1888) Swedish					
oil	4	18,495	1,035	2,094	13,272
NORDGREN, Wilhelm (1804-1857) Swedish					
oil	1	1,656		1,656	
NORDIN, Alice (1871-1948) Swedish					
3D	2	3,933	1,449	1,967	2,484
NORDLING, Adolf (1840-1888) Swedish					
oil	1	1,524		1,524	
NORDSTROM, Karl (1855-1923) Swedish					
oil	3	9,070	1,204	2,484	5,382
wc/d	1	1,088		1,088	
NORDT, J F C (18/19th C) German					
wc/d	1	1,105		1,105	
NOREAU, Francine (20th C) American					
oil	1	1,009		1,009	
NORELIUS, Einar (1900-1984) Danish					
wc/d	1	1,400		1,400	
NORGA, S (?) Continental					
3D	2	5,757	1,257	2,879	4,500
NORGARD, Lars (1956-) Danish					
oil	1	2,707		2,707	
NORIE, Orlando (1832-1901) British					
wc/d	12	25,757	1,008	1,395	5,720
NORIERI, Auguste (1860-1898) American					
oil	1	2,800		2,800	
NORMANN, A (1848-1918) Norwegian					
oil	1	1,798		1,798	
NORMANN, Adelsteen (1848-1918) Norwegian					
oil	12	103,520	1,088	3,945	46,215
NORMIL, Andre (1934-) Haitian					
oil	1	1,289		1,289	
NORRIS, Hugh L (fl.1882-1904) British					
wc/d	1	1,431		1,431	

Name	No.	Total Sales Value	Prices lowest	median	highest
NORRMAN, Herman (1864-1906) Swedish					
oil	2	4,249	1,138	2,125	3,111
NORSTEDT, Reinhold (1843-1911) Swedish					
oil	1	1,032		1,032	
NORTH EUROPEAN SCHOOL, 15th/16th C					
oil	1	2,927		2,927	
NORTH EUROPEAN SCHOOL, 16th C					
3D	1	42,309		42,309	
NORTH EUROPEAN SCHOOL, 17th C					
oil	2	8,173	2,542	4,087	5,631
NORTH EUROPEAN SCHOOL, 18th C					
3D	1	11,407		11,407	
oil	1	5,323		5,323	
NORTH GERMAN SCHOOL, 18th C					
wc/d	1	2,395		2,395	
NORTH ITALIAN SCHOOL					
oil	1	5,382		5,382	
wc/d	1	3,800		3,800	
NORTH ITALIAN SCHOOL, 15th C					
oil	1	19,000		19,000	
NORTH ITALIAN SCHOOL, 15th/16th C					
3D	1	7,550		7,550	
NORTH ITALIAN SCHOOL, 16th C					
oil	5	190,965	5,050	13,590	126,840
NORTH ITALIAN SCHOOL, 16th/17th C					
3D	1	5,436		5,436	
oil	1	6,912		6,912	
NORTH ITALIAN SCHOOL, 17th C					
oil	7	113,076	3,792	13,965	37,295
wc/d	1	4,750		4,750	
NORTH ITALIAN SCHOOL, 18th C					
3D	2	6,835	3,368	3,418	3,467
oil	10	118,746	2,880	6,610	36,000
NORTH ITALIAN SCHOOL, 19th C					
3D	2	35,569	7,335	17,785	28,234
NORTH, John William (1842-1924) British					
oil	2	44,240	8,690	22,120	35,550
wc/d	4	59,724	4,424	15,010	25,280
NORTHCOTE, James (1746-1831) British					
oil	2	4,950	1,000	2,475	3,950
NORTHERN SCHOOL, 18th C					
oil	1	4,800		4,800	
NORTHERN SCHOOL, 19th C					
oil	1	4,000		4,000	
NORTHERN WEY DYNASTY Chinese					
3D	1	37,500		37,500	
NORTON, Benjamin Cam (1835-1900) British					
oil	2	7,942	2,400	3,971	5,542
NORTON, Elizabeth (1887-?) American					
3D	1	3,000		3,000	
NORTON, Louis Doyle (1867-?) American					
wc/d	1	1,000		1,000	
NORTON, W E (1843-1916) American					
oil	1	3,100		3,100	
NORTON, William Edward (1843-1916) American					
oil	5	30,400	2,400	4,000	14,500
NORWEGIAN SCHOOL, 19th/20th C					
oil	1	2,854		2,854	
NOTENBOOM, B (?) Dutch					
oil	1	1,179		1,179	

Name	No.	Total Sales Value	lowest	Prices median	highest
NOTER, David de (1825-1875) Belgian					
oil	3	62,456	1,066	6,090	55,300
NOTER, Pierre François de (1779-1843) Belgian					
oil	2	9,148	2,820	4,574	6,328
NOTERMAN, Emmanuel (1808-1863) Flemish					
oil	2	10,336	2,928	5,168	7,408
NOTERMAN, Zacharias (1820-1890) German					
oil	10	35,662	1,597	3,161	6,844
NOTT, Raymond (1888-1948) American					
oil	1	1,300		1,300	
NOTTE, Emilio (1891-1982) Italian					
oil	1	2,705		2,705	
wc/d	1	2,315		2,315	
NOURISSON, René (c.1610-c.1650) French					
oil	1	105,840		105,840	
NOURSE, Elizabeth (1859-1938) American					
oil	2	22,500	4,500	11,250	18,000
wc/d	4	62,400	1,900	7,750	45,000
NOUVEAU, Henri (1901-1959) Rumanian					
oil	2	3,790	1,728	1,895	2,062
NOVATI, Cesare Calchi (1858-1939) Italian					
oil	1	3,338		3,338	
NOVATI, Marco (1895-?) Italian					
oil	15	58,402	1,180	3,441	10,322
NOVELIERS, Pierre (?-1618) Flemish					
oil	1	34,540		34,540	
NOVELLI, Gastone (1925-1968) Italian					
oil	1	94,250		94,250	
wc/d	2	92,885	44,363	46,443	48,522
NOVELLI, Pietro (1603-1647) Italian					
oil	3	67,192	5,962	20,410	40,820
NOVELLI, Pietro Antonio (1729-1804) Italian					
wc/d	4	11,334	1,933	2,175	5,000
NOVO, Stefano (1862-?) Italian					
oil	1	2,860		2,860	
NOVOA, Leopoldo (1929-) Uruguayan					
oil	1	3,764		3,764	
wc/d	1	1,427		1,427	
NOWAK, Ernst (1853-1919) Austrian					
oil	4	9,885	1,000	1,818	5,250
NOWEY, A (19th C) British?					
oil	1	1,276		1,276	
NOWEY, Adolf (19th C) British?					
oil	1	1,820		1,820	
NOWEY, D (19th C) ?					
oil	1	2,005		2,005	
NOYER, Philippe (1917-) French					
oil	5	7,214	1,100	1,100	2,114
wc/d	1	1,197		1,197	
NOYES, George L (1864-1951) Canadian					
oil	3	20,950	2,200	3,750	15,000
NTIRO, Sam (1923-) Tanzanian					
oil	1	1,269		1,269	
NUCARA, Renzo (1948-) Italian					
3D	1	1,032		1,032	
NUCKEL, Otto (1888-1956) German					
oil	3	27,808	6,212	6,212	15,245
NUCUM, Edgar S (20th C) British?					
oil	3	4,147	1,001	1,573	1,573

Name	No.	Total Sales Value	lowest	Prices median	highest
NUDERSCHER, Frank (1880-1959) American					
oil	1	1,900		1,900	
NUESCH, Johann Jakob (1845-1895) Swiss					
oil	1	2,924		2,924	
NUGLISCH, Friedrich Christian (18/19th C) German					
oil	1	3,412		3,412	
NUMA, Pierre (19th C) French					
wc/d	1	1,091		1,091	
NUMAN, Hermanus (1744-1820) Dutch					
wc/d	1	3,143		3,143	
NUNAMAKER, Kenneth R (1890-1957) American					
oil	2	29,000	13,000	14,500	16,000
NUNEZ LOSADA, Francisco (1889-1973) Spanish					
oil	2	10,574	4,646	5,287	5,928
NUNZIO (20th C) American					
3D	1	5,796		5,796	
wc/d	1	8,509		8,509	
NUREMBERG SCHOOL, 15th C German					
oil	1	9,821		9,821	
NUREMBERG SCHOOL, 15th/16th C German					
3D	1	32,357		32,357	
NUREMBERG SCHOOL, 16th C German					
oil	1	18,046		18,046	
NUSSBAUM, Felix (1904-1944) German					
oil	3	1,979,523	97,087	298,436	1,584,000
NUSSBAUM, Jacob (1873-1936) German					
oil	1	1,108		1,108	
NUSSBAUMER, Hans (1920-1985) Swiss					
oil	1	1,866		1,866	
NUTTER, William Henry (1821-1872) British					
wc/d	2	6,300	2,550	3,150	3,750
NUVOLONE, Carlo Francesco (1608-1665) Italian					
oil	3	45,671	5,861	14,690	25,120
NUVOLONE, Giuseppe (1619-1703) Italian					
oil	1	18,840		18,840	
NUVOLONE, Panfilo (school) (c.1581-1651) Italian					
oil	1	5,774		5,774	
NUYEN, W J J (1813-1839) Dutch					
oil	1	12,413		12,413	
NUZZI, Mario (1603-1673) Italian					
oil	7	278,203	2,940	27,180	100,379
NYBOE, Friis (1869-1929) Danish					
oil	3	4,250	1,207	1,256	1,787
NYBORG, Peter (1937-) Danish					
oil	2	3,050	1,000	1,525	2,050
NYE, Edgar (1879-1943) American					
oil	1	1,400		1,400	
NYFELLER, Albert (1883-1969) German					
oil	2	5,419	2,595	2,710	2,824
NYILASY, Sandor (1873-?) Hungarian					
oil	1	2,265		2,265	
NYL-FROSCH, Marie (1857-1914) German					
oil	1	5,500		5,500	
NYMAN, Ingrid Vang (1916-1959) Swedish					
wc/d	1	7,336		7,336	
NYMAN, Olle (1909-1999) Swedish					
oil	3	4,526	1,360	1,558	1,608
NYROP, Borge (1881-1948) Danish					
oil	3	4,989	1,071	1,311	2,607

Name	No.	Total Sales Value	lowest	Prices median	highest
NYS, Alexis (20th C) Belgian					
oil	1	1,015		1,015	
NYSTROM, Jenny (1854-1946) Swedish					
oil	5	50,728	1,524	4,243	38,689
wc/d	29	121,357	1,056	2,691	19,147
OAKES, A T (c.1826-1886) American					
oil	1	1,000		1,000	
OAKES, John Wright (1820-1887) British					
oil	2	8,277	1,413	4,139	6,864
OAKLEY, J (19th C) British					
oil	1	1,200		1,200	
OAKLEY, Octavius (1800-1867) British					
wc/d	2	10,475	2,610	5,238	7,865
OAKLEY, Thornton (1881-1953) American					
wc/d	1	3,500		3,500	
OAKLEY, Violet (1874-1961) American					
wc/d	2	40,900	2,900	20,450	38,000
OBER, A (19th C) Russian					
3D	1	1,102		1,102	
OBERHAUSER, Emanuel (19/20th C) Austrian					
oil	2	13,431	4,431	6,716	9,000
OBERMAN, Anthony (1781-1845) Dutch					
oil	4	25,097	2,355	3,076	16,590
OBERTEUFFER, George (1878-1940) American					
oil	1	5,500		5,500	
OBIOLS DELGADO, Mariano (19th C) Spanish					
oil	1	2,439		2,439	
OBJOY, el (19th C) ?					
oil	1	7,586		7,586	
OBREGON, Alejandro (1920-1992) Colombian					
oil	1	110,000		110,000	
OBREGON, Roberto (20th C) South American					
3D	1	6,500		6,500	
O'BRIEN, Dermod (1865-1945) British					
oil	2	12,876	4,736	6,438	8,140
O'BRIEN, Frank Morgan (1877-1919) American					
oil	1	3,600		3,600	
O'BRIEN, John (1834-1904) British					
oil	1	1,919		1,919	
O'BRIEN, Lucius Richard (1832-1899) Canadian					
wc/d	4	12,003	1,306	1,699	7,300
OCAMPO, Manuel (1965-) ?					
3D	1	2,000		2,000	
oil	5	36,700	1,700	8,000	11,000
wc/d	1	1,447		1,447	
OCHOA Y MADRAZO, Raphael de (1858-?) Spanish					
oil	1	2,031		2,031	
wc/d	1	5,257		5,257	
OCHTERVELT, Jacob (1635-?) Dutch					
oil	1	24,000		24,000	
OCHTMAN, Dorothy (1892-1971) American					
oil	1	3,000		3,000	
OCHTMAN, Leonard (1854-1934) American					
oil	4	30,300	3,300	4,500	18,000
O'CONNOR, Andrew (jnr) (1874-1941) American					
3D	1	13,320		13,320	
O'CONNOR, Christopher (20th C) American?					
oil	1	1,940		1,940	

Name	No.	Total Sales Value	lowest	Prices median	highest
O'CONNOR, Henri (20th C) American					
wc/d	1	1,200		1,200	
O'CONNOR, James Arthur (1792-1841) British					
oil	8	96,414	1,100	10,116	25,670
wc/d	1	1,896		1,896	
O'CONOR, Roderic (1860-1940) Irish					
oil	8	1,731,334	19,035	155,870	480,000
wc/d	3	3,854	1,110	1,350	1,394
OCTAVIEN, François (1695-1732) French					
oil	1	60,400		60,400	
ODDIE, Walter M (1808-1865) American					
oil	1	17,000		17,000	
ODELMARK, Frans Wilhelm (1849-1937) Swedish					
oil	19	57,119	1,003	1,806	10,428
wc/d	3	5,305	1,306	1,809	2,190
ODIER, Jacques (1853-1930) Swiss					
oil	1	2,026		2,026	
ODIN, Blanche (1865-?) French					
wc/d	1	1,433		1,433	
O'DONOGHUE, Hughie (1953-) British					
wc/d	1	1,422		1,422	
OEFFELE-PIEKARSKI, Franz Ignaz (1721-1797) Polish					
oil	1	5,538		5,538	
OEHLEN, Albert (1954-) German					
oil	1	55,000		55,000	
OEHLEN, Markus (1956-) German					
oil	1	1,650		1,650	
wc/d	2	5,484	1,942	2,742	3,542
OEHMICHEN, Hugo (1843-1933) German					
oil	4	37,592	1,766	9,817	16,193
OELTJEN-KASIMIR, Elsa (19/20th C) European					
oil	1	1,196		1,196	
OEMBERG, C van (1824-1901) ?					
3D	1	3,853		3,853	
OEPTS, Willem Anthonie (1904-1988) Dutch					
oil	11	35,917	1,379	3,233	6,034
OER, P van (?) ?					
oil	1	4,114		4,114	
OERDER, Frans (1866-1944) Dutch					
oil	3	8,339	1,291	1,886	5,162
OERI, Hans Jakob (1782-1868) Swiss					
wc/d	1	6,015		6,015	
OERTLI, Max (1921-) Swiss					
oil	2	3,522	1,006	1,761	2,516
OESCH, Albert Sebastian (1893-1920) Swiss					
wc/d	1	6,685		6,685	
OESTERLEY, Carl August Heinrich Ferdinand (1839-1930) German					
oil	1	1,822		1,822	
OFEN, Michael van (1956-) ?					
oil	1	2,396		2,396	
OFFERMANS, Tony Lodewyk George (1854-1911) Dutch					
oil	1	2,360		2,360	
OFILI, Chris (1968-) British					
oil	2	183,000	78,000	91,500	105,000
wc/d	3	12,850	1,650	2,200	9,000
OGDEN, Reverend J Williams (?) ?					
oil	1	2,219		2,219	
OGE, Pierre Marie François (1849-1913) French					
3D	1	1,600		1,600	

Name	No.	Total Sales Value	lowest	Prices median	highest
OGGIONO, Marco (1470-1530) Italian					
oil	4	481,171	13,994	46,089	375,000
OGILVIE, John Clinton (1838-1900) American					
oil	1	6,000		6,000	
OGILVIE, William Abernethy (1901-1989) Canadian					
oil	2	2,265	1,062	1,133	1,203
O'GORMAN, Juan (1905-1982) Mexican					
oil	1	120,000		120,000	
wc/d	1	4,500		4,500	
OGUISS, Takanari (1901-1986) Japanese					
oil	9	485,345	5,769	66,400	120,000
wc/d	1	6,090		6,090	
OGUNDELE, Rufus (1946-1996) Nigerian					
oil	1	1,410		1,410	
O'HARA, Helen (fl.1881-1908) British					
wc/d	4	9,933	1,305	2,139	4,350
OHASHI, Yutaka (1923-) American/Japanese					
oil	1	1,400		1,400	
OHL, Fritz (1904-1976) Dutch					
oil	1	2,029		2,029	
OHLSEN, Jeppe Madsen (1891-1948) Danish					
oil	2	6,436	1,756	3,218	4,680
OHLSEN, Theodor (1855-?) German					
oil	1	1,136		1,136	
OHLSON, Alfred (1868-1940) Swedish					
3D	1	1,278		1,278	
OKADA, Kenzo (1902-1982) American/Japanese					
wc/d	1	5,400		5,400	
OKADA, Saburosuke (1869-1939) Japanese					
oil	1	30,285		30,285	
O'KEEFFE, Georgia (1887-1986) American					
oil	1	700,000		700,000	
wc/d	2	95,000	20,000	47,500	75,000
O'KELLY, Aloysius (1853-1929) Irish					
oil	1	9,620		9,620	
OKULICK, John (1947-) American					
3D	1	7,000		7,000	
OLABARRIETA, Manuel (1932-) Spanish					
oil	1	1,467		1,467	
OLAFSON, Tove (1909-1992) Danish					
3D	2	2,655	1,039	1,328	1,616
OLALDE, Gaston (1925-) Uruguayan					
3D	1	1,035		1,035	
wc/d	1	1,035		1,035	
OLATUNDE, Asiru (1918-1993) Nigerian					
3D	2	6,345	2,115	3,173	4,230
OLDE, Hans (younger) (1895-1987) German					
oil	1	2,136		2,136	
OLDENBURG, Claes (1929-) American					
3D	16	465,864	1,200	5,750	180,000
oil	2	33,000	14,000	16,500	19,000
wc/d	4	145,000	11,500	25,500	82,500
OLDENDORP, Christian Johann (1772-?) German					
oil	1	2,437		2,437	
OLDEROCK, Max (1895-1972) German					
oil	1	1,073		1,073	
wc/d	1	2,194		2,194	
OLDEWELT, Ferdinand Gustaaf Willem (1857-1935) Dutch					
wc/d	1	1,888		1,888	

Name	No.	Total Sales Value	lowest	Prices median	highest
OLDFIELD, Otis (1890-1969) American					
oil	1	5,000		5,000	
OLEG, Kedria (20th C) ?					
3D	1	6,578		6,578	
OLGYAI, Viktor (1870-1929) Hungarian					
oil	1	1,045		1,045	
OLINDO, Giovanni (fl.1900-1940) Italian					
oil	1	7,500		7,500	
OLINSKY, Ivan G (1878-1962) American					
oil	5	48,700	3,700	5,500	27,000
wc/d	1	10,000		10,000	
OLINSKY, Tosca (?) ?					
oil	1	1,000		1,000	
OLITSKI, Jules (1922-) American/Russian					
oil	3	10,907	1,500	1,900	7,507
OLIVA, Pedro Pablo (1949-) Cuban					
oil	1	7,500		7,500	
OLIVARES VELENCIAGA, Juan Benito (1909-) Spanish					
oil	2	2,770	1,201	1,385	1,569
OLIVARES, Alfonso (19/20th C) Spanish					
oil	1	5,551		5,551	
OLIVE, Ceferi (1907-1995) Spanish					
wc/d	3	3,575	1,037	1,086	1,452
OLIVE, Jean Baptiste (1848-1936) French					
oil	7	170,387	5,460	24,841	51,063
OLIVEIRA, Nathan (1928-) American					
3D	1	25,000		25,000	
oil	1	40,000		40,000	
wc/d	2	18,500	5,500	9,250	13,000
OLIVER Y AZNAR, Mariano (1863-1927) Spanish					
oil	1	2,793		2,793	
OLIVER, Alfred (?) ?					
oil	1	1,278		1,278	
OLIVER, Julie Ford (20th C) British/American					
oil	1	1,350		1,350	
OLIVER, Myron (1891-1967) American					
oil	1	3,250		3,250	
OLIVER, William (fl.1867-1882) British					
oil	3	9,581	1,144	2,717	5,720
OLIVER, William (early 19th C) (1805-1853) British					
oil	2	11,118	1,823	5,559	9,295
OLIVER, William (late 19th C) (fl.1865-1897) British					
oil	5	24,942	1,413	3,713	12,000
OLIVERO, Matteo (1879-1932) Italian					
oil	2	49,880	3,669	24,940	46,211
OLIVIE-BON, Léon (1863-1901) French					
oil	1	12,000		12,000	
OLIVIER (?) ?					
wc/d	1	3,126		3,126	
OLIVIER, Friedrich (1791-1859) German					
wc/d	2	8,356	4,178	4,178	4,178
OLIVIER, Michel Barthelemy (1712-1784) French					
oil	1	4,368		4,368	
wc/d	2	10,388	2,265	5,194	8,123
OLIVIERO, Ettore Pistoletto (1898-1981) Italian					
oil	1	1,758		1,758	
OLLEROS Y QUINTANA, Blas (1851-1919) Italian					
oil	1	1,167		1,167	

Name	No.	Total Sales Value	lowest	Prices median	highest
OLLERS, Edvin (1888-1959) Swedish					
oil	1	3,111		3,111	
OLLIER, L (19/20th C) French?					
oil	1	1,298		1,298	
OLLILA, Yrjo (1887-1932) Finnish					
oil	1	2,394		2,394	
OLMEDO, Cristobal (1957-) Spanish					
oil	1	1,597		1,597	
OLMO, Gregorio del (1921-1977) Spanish					
oil	1	1,900		1,900	
OLOFSSON, Pierre (1921-1996) Swedish					
oil	3	8,915	1,802	2,107	5,006
wc/d	3	4,919	1,204	1,204	2,511
OLRICK, Henrik Benedikt (1830-1890) Danish					
oil	2	9,077	3,526	4,539	5,551
OLRIK, Balder (1966-) Danish					
oil	2	5,830	1,602	2,915	4,228
wc/d	1	3,587		3,587	
OLSEN, Alfred (1854-1932) Danish					
oil	2	3,496	1,276	1,748	2,220
OLSEN, Carl (1818-1878) Danish					
oil	3	9,515	1,490	2,025	6,000
OLSEN, Chr Benjamin (1873-1935) Danish					
oil	9	24,186	1,207	1,672	7,296
OLSEN, Gudmund (1913-1985) Danish					
oil	2	2,606	1,211	1,303	1,395
OLSEN, Jorgen Peter (1815-1869) Danish					
wc/d	1	1,160		1,160	
OLSOMMER, Charles Clos (1883-1966) Swiss					
wc/d	2	5,254	1,866	2,627	3,388
OLSON, Axel (1899-1986) Swedish					
oil	23	90,596	1,013	2,417	21,074
wc/d	2	8,712	1,868	4,356	6,844
OLSON, Bengt (1930-) Swedish					
oil	1	1,741		1,741	
OLSON, Eric H (1909-1996) Swedish					
3D	1	2,730		2,730	
OLSON, Erik (1901-1986) Swedish					
oil	17	136,147	1,070	3,809	38,218
wc/d	1	1,310		1,310	
OLSON, Gary (1946-) Canadian					
oil	1	1,379		1,379	
OLSON, Victor (20th C) American					
oil	1	1,800		1,800	
OLSSON, Emil (1890-1964) Scandinavian					
oil	1	2,839		2,839	
OLSSON, Julius (1864-1942) British					
oil	11	38,394	1,000	3,101	12,640
OLSSON, Sigvard (1936-) Swedish					
wc/d	1	1,204		1,204	
OLSSON-HAGALUND, Olle (1904-1972) Swedish					
oil	10	243,246	3,832	20,744	42,147
wc/d	1	8,541		8,541	
OLSTED, P (1824-1887) Danish					
oil	1	1,196		1,196	
OLSZEWSKI, Karl Ewald (1884-?) Rumanian					
oil	1	1,963		1,963	
O'LYNCH OF TOWN, Karl (1869-1942) German					
oil	5	12,165	1,519	1,823	4,840

Name	No.	Total Sales Value	lowest	Prices median	highest
O'MALLEY, Tony (1913-) British					
oil	1	14,060		14,060	
wc/d	2	9,008	1,208	4,504	7,800
OMAPPENIZ (20th C) ?					
oil	1	2,358		2,358	
O'MEARA, Frank (1853-1888) British					
oil	1	74,000		74,000	
OMERTH, Georges (fl.1895-1925) French					
3D	1	1,605		1,605	
OMICCIOLI, Giovanni (1901-1975) Italian					
oil	11	22,277	1,047	1,736	4,582
wc/d	2	2,946	1,352	1,473	1,594
OMMEGANCK (18/19th C) Flemish					
oil	1	3,322		3,322	
OMMEGANCK, Balthasar Paul (1755-1826) Flemish					
oil	4	9,518	1,136	1,817	4,748
ONDERDONK, Julian (1882-1922) American					
oil	1	6,500		6,500	
ONDERDONK, Robert Jenkins (1853-1917) American					
oil	1	3,250		3,250	
O'NEILL, Daniel (1920-1974) British					
oil	13	274,900	5,180	14,060	88,800
wc/d	2	4,672	2,160	2,336	2,512
O'NEILL, George Bernard (1827-1917) British					
oil	4	86,031	17,270	20,500	27,761
O'NEILL, Henry (1798-1880) British					
oil	1	12,625		12,625	
wc/d	1	1,272		1,272	
O'NEILL, Henry Nelson (1817-1880) British					
oil	4	1,289,615	12,155	261,230	755,000
ONLEY, Toni (1928-) Canadian					
oil	1	1,419		1,419	
ONNES, Harm Henrick Kamerlingh (1893-1985) Dutch					
oil	9	24,072	1,032	2,163	5,507
wc/d	2	2,401	1,180	1,201	1,221
ONOFRE COTTO, Pedro (17th C) Spanish					
oil	1	13,675		13,675	
ONOFRI, Crescenzio (1632-1698) Italian					
oil	1	6,093		6,093	
ONSI, Omar (1901-1969) Lebanese					
oil	1	5,155		5,155	
ONTANI, Luigi (1943-) Italian					
wc/d	1	2,836		2,836	
ONTANON FERNANDEZ, Santiago (1903-1989) Spanish					
wc/d	4	4,064	1,016	1,016	1,016
OOLEN, Adriaen van (?-1694) Dutch					
oil	1	31,680		31,680	
OORSCHOT, Dorus van (1910-1989) Dutch					
oil	1	1,100		1,100	
OORT, Hendrik van (1775-1847) Dutch					
oil	1	3,395		3,395	
OOST, Jacques van (elder) (1601-1671) Belgian					
oil	1	50,000		50,000	
OOSTEN, Izaack van (1613-1661) Flemish					
oil	2	163,500	67,950	81,750	95,550
OPALKA, Roman (1931-) Polish					
oil	1	42,280		42,280	
wc/d	1	5,190		5,190	
OPDENHOFF, George Willem (1807-1873) Dutch					
oil	7	74,040	1,200	8,604	26,781

Name	No.	Total Sales Value	lowest	Prices median	highest
OPHEY, Walter (1882-1930) German					
oil	1	27,184		27,184	
wc/d	3	9,239	1,482	2,223	5,534
OPIE, Edward (1810-1894) British					
oil	1	1,872		1,872	
OPIE, John (1761-1807) British					
oil	3	18,966	3,692	4,530	10,744
OPIE, Julian (1958-) British					
3D	1	3,500		3,500	
OPISSO SALA, Ricardo (1880-1960) Spanish					
wc/d	1	6,328		6,328	
OPISSO, Alfredo (1907-1980) Spanish					
oil	3	6,810	1,186	2,740	2,884
wc/d	1	1,140		1,140	
OPISSO, Ricardo (1880-1966) Spanish					
wc/d	2	3,240	1,334	1,620	1,906
OPPEL, Lisel (1897-1960) German					
oil	2	15,953	6,198	7,977	9,755
OPPENHEIM, Dennis (1938-) American					
oil	1	1,157		1,157	
wc/d	1	3,797		3,797	
OPPENHEIM, Meret (1913-1986) Swiss					
3D	1	12,154		12,154	
wc/d	1	3,707		3,707	
OPPENHEIMER, Charles (1875-1961) British					
oil	1	4,640		4,640	
wc/d	1	2,592		2,592	
OPPENHEIMER, Jonny (1923-) Swedish					
oil	2	3,635	1,673	1,818	1,962
OPPENHEIMER, Josef (1876-1966) German					
oil	2	3,921	1,320	1,961	2,601
OPPENHEIMER, Max (1885-1954) Austrian					
oil	1	19,765		19,765	
OPPENOORTH, Willem (1847-1905) Dutch					
oil	2	3,185	1,249	1,593	1,936
OPPI, Ubaldo (1889-1942) Italian					
oil	1	21,352		21,352	
wc/d	2	6,524	2,511	3,262	4,013
OPSOMER, I (1878-1967) Belgian					
oil	1	1,413		1,413	
OPSOMER, Isidore (1878-1967) Belgian					
oil	4	15,045	1,037	3,422	7,165
ORANT, Marthe (1874-1953) French					
oil	6	7,851	1,037	1,240	1,713
ORAZI, Manuel (19/20th C) French					
oil	1	3,099		3,099	
wc/d	5	13,058	1,107	2,582	3,836
ORCHARDSON, Sir William Quiller (1832-1910) British					
oil	1	8,250		8,250	
ORECHNIKOV, Viktor (1904-1987) Russian					
oil	1	4,998		4,998	
ORFEI, Orfeo (19th C) Italian					
oil	1	3,435		3,435	
ORGAN, Bryan (1935-) British					
oil	2	3,092	1,136	1,546	1,956
ORGANIA, V (19th C) Italian					
oil	1	2,406		2,406	
ORI, Luciano (1928-) Italian					
wc/d	1	1,745		1,745	

Name	No.	Total Sales Value	Prices lowest	median	highest
ORIANI, Pippo (1909-1972) Italian					
oil	3	10,854	1,382	3,927	5,545
ORIENTAL SCHOOL					
oil	2	7,239	2,981	3,620	4,258
ORIENTAL SCHOOL, 18th C					
oil	1	6,717		6,717	
wc/d	1	2,578		2,578	
ORIENTAL SCHOOL, 19th C					
oil	7	114,146	4,409	5,841	61,865
ORIENTAL SCHOOL, 20th C					
oil	1	5,235		5,235	
ORIENTALIST SCHOOL, 19th C					
oil	1	9,735		9,735	
ORIENTALIST SCHOOL, 19th/20th C					
oil	1	20,119		20,119	
ORLEY, Richard van (1663-1732) Flemish					
wc/d	1	1,298		1,298	
ORLIK, Emil (1870-1932) Czechoslovakian					
oil	3	26,881	2,523	2,732	21,626
ORLOFF, Chana (1888-1968) French					
3D	9	125,242	1,964	16,033	27,599
ORLOFF, J (18th C) Russian					
oil	1	2,373		2,373	
ORLOWSKI, Alexander (1777-1832) Polish					
wc/d	1	1,797		1,797	
ORMAOLEA, Jose Antonio (1912-) Spanish					
oil	1	1,846		1,846	
ORME, E (?) British?					
oil	1	1,454		1,454	
ORME, E Anthony (?) British?					
wc/d	1	1,363		1,363	
OROSCHAKOFF, Haralampi (1955-) ?					
oil	2	6,100	1,775	3,050	4,325
OROZCO, Gabriel (1962-) Mexican					
3D	2	110,000	35,000	55,000	75,000
ORPEN, Sir William (1878-1931) Irish					
oil	2	81,400	39,960	40,700	41,440
wc/d	12	151,893	1,065	5,402	85,840
ORR, Eric (20th C) American					
oil	1	3,000		3,000	
wc/d	1	1,037		1,037	
ORRENTE, Pedro (1570-1644) Spanish					
oil	3	49,370	14,518	16,285	18,567
ORROCK, James (1829-1913) British					
wc/d	2	3,170	1,185	1,585	1,985
ORSELLI, Arturo (19th C) Italian					
oil	1	5,180		5,180	
ORSI, Carlo (19th C) Italian					
oil	1	10,000		10,000	
ORSI, Lelio (1511-1587) Italian					
wc/d	2	6,763	2,836	3,382	3,927
ORTEGA, J (19/20th C) Spanish					
oil	1	1,047		1,047	
ORTEGA, Jose (1921-1990) Spanish					
oil	2	9,318	1,130	4,659	8,188
ORTH, Emil Cordius Heinrich (1833-1919) Danish					
oil	1	1,787		1,787	
ORTIS (20th C) Continental					
3D	1	1,264		1,264	

Name	No.	Total Sales Value	lowest	Prices median	highest
ORTIZ DE ZARATE (20th C) ?					
oil	1	1,641		1,641	
ORTIZ DE ZARATE, Manuel (1886-1946) French					
oil	5	11,413	1,355	1,927	3,985
ORTIZ, Angeles (1895-1984) Spanish					
oil	1	6,136		6,136	
ORTIZ, Dario (1968-) Colombian					
oil	1	20,000		20,000	
ORTIZ, J (19th C) Spanish					
3D	1	1,228		1,228	
ORTIZ, Manuel Angeles (1895-1984) Spanish					
oil	1	1,553		1,553	
wc/d	2	3,666	1,509	1,833	2,157
ORTLIEB, Friedrich (1839-1909) German					
oil	2	2,935	1,341	1,468	1,594
ORTMANS, François-Auguste (1827-1884) French					
oil	3	8,394	1,196	2,730	4,468
wc/d	1	4,800		4,800	
ORTNER, F (19/20th C) Austrian					
oil	1	2,664		2,664	
ORTOLANI, Augusto (1873-?) Italian					
oil	1	4,905		4,905	
ORTUNO, Roberto (1953-) Spanish					
oil	1	1,404		1,404	
ORTVAD, Erik (1917-) Danish					
oil	1	7,100		7,100	
ORUP, Bengt (1916-1996) Swedish					
oil	1	1,524		1,524	
OS, George Jacobus Johannes van (younger) (1805-1841) Dutch					
wc/d	1	9,947		9,947	
OS, Georgius Jacobus Johannes van (1782-1861) Dutch					
oil	4	43,185	1,358	11,414	19,000
wc/d	2	9,647	3,816	4,824	5,831
OS, Jan van (1744-1808) Dutch					
oil	8	1,142,710	24,000	108,045	360,000
OS, Pieter Frederik van (1808-1860) Dutch					
oil	3	10,197	2,667	2,667	4,863
OS, Pieter Gerardus van (1776-1839) Dutch					
oil	5	45,803	3,122	5,162	27,581
OS, Tony van (1886-1945) Belgian					
oil	3	5,331	1,064	1,182	3,085
OS, van (18th C) Dutch					
oil	1	4,714		4,714	
OS-DELHEZ, Hendrik van (1880-1976) Dutch					
oil	1	1,483		1,483	
OSBECK, J (1898-1938) German					
oil	1	1,364		1,364	
OSBERT, Alphonse (1857-1939) French					
oil	2	10,065	1,337	5,033	8,728
wc/d	2	11,374	4,801	5,687	6,573
OSBOLLE, H (19/20th C) ?					
oil	1	1,324		1,324	
OSBORNE, James (1940-1992) British					
3D	8	17,622	1,239	2,119	3,480
OSBORNE, Walter (1859-1903) Irish					
oil	3	673,400	22,200	207,200	444,000
OSBORNE, William (1823-1901) Irish					
oil	1	17,760		17,760	

Name	No.	Total Sales Value	Prices lowest	median	highest
O'SHEE, G E (19/20th C) British					
oil	1	1,896		1,896	
O'SICKEY, Joseph B (20th C) American					
oil	1	9,000		9,000	
OSSANI, Alessandro (fl.1857-1888) British					
oil	1	1,208		1,208	
OSSLUND, Helmer (1866-1938) Swedish					
oil	34	227,571	1,005	2,462	36,224
wc/d	3	12,456	2,197	4,616	5,643
OSSORIO, Alfonso (1916-1990) American					
wc/d	2	21,322	3,322	10,661	18,000
OSSWALD, Fritz (1878-1966) Swiss					
oil	3	8,881	1,094	1,935	5,852
OSSWALD-TOPPI, Margherita (1897-1971) Italian					
oil	3	4,195	1,003	1,228	1,964
OST, Alfred (1884-1945) Belgian					
oil	2	3,342	1,671	1,671	1,671
wc/d	1	3,085		3,085	
OSTADE, Adriaen van (1610-1684) Dutch					
oil	5	472,237	1,450	28,260	382,200
wc/d	2	29,304	3,768	14,652	25,536
OSTADE, Isaac van (1621-1649) Dutch					
oil	1	1,479,800		1,479,800	
wc/d	1	1,100		1,100	
OSTENDARP, Carl (1961-) American?					
wc/d	1	5,000		5,000	
OSTERLIND, Allan (1855-1938) Swedish					
oil	2	4,804	1,558	2,402	3,246
OSTERLIND, Anders (1887-1960) French					
oil	3	3,902	1,168	1,309	1,425
OSTERLUND, Herman (1873-1964) Swedish					
oil	2	3,032	1,213	1,516	1,819
OSTERMAN, Elvine (1908-) Swedish?					
oil	1	1,156		1,156	
OSTERSETZER, C (1865-1914) Austrian					
oil	2	3,513	1,350	1,757	2,163
OSTERSETZER, Carl (1865-1914) Austrian					
oil	6	9,724	1,026	1,668	2,158
OSTHAUS, Edmund H (1858-1928) American					
oil	4	156,600	1,600	40,000	75,000
wc/d	8	82,450	2,200	10,000	19,000
OSTLUND, Manne (1904-1957) Scandinavian					
oil	1	2,613		2,613	
wc/d	1	1,005		1,005	
OSTRANDER, William C (1858-) American					
wc/d	1	1,900		1,900	
OSTY, Hari (20th C) ?					
wc/d	1	1,355		1,355	
OSWALD, C W (fl.1892) British					
oil	4	6,791	1,065	1,599	2,400
OTERMIN Y GARCIA BUSTAMANTE, Agustin (1870-1926) Spanish					
oil	1	1,026		1,026	
OTERO ABELEDO LAXEIRO, Jose (1908-1996) Spanish					
oil	11	84,683	1,613	7,024	20,812
wc/d	11	18,340	1,003	1,427	4,302
OTERO, Alejandro (1921-1990) Venezuelan					
wc/d	3	12,975	1,450	5,015	6,510
OTERO, Carlos (1886-1977) Venezuelan					
oil	2	6,200	1,170	3,100	5,030

Name	No.	Total Sales Value	Prices lowest	median	highest
OTERO, Manuel (?-1875) Spanish					
wc/d	2	2,329	1,035	1,165	1,294
OTHONIEL, Jean Michel (1964-) French					
3D	1	3,666		3,666	
OTIS, George Demont (1877-1962) American					
oil	6	44,500	3,750	6,250	13,000
OTT, Johann Nepomuk (1804-1870) Swiss					
oil	3	21,583	5,674	6,818	9,091
OTTE, C (?) German					
oil	1	1,273		1,273	
OTTE, William Louis (1871-1957) American					
oil	3	10,400	1,400	2,500	6,500
wc/d	3	11,750	2,250	3,500	6,000
OTTENFELD, Rudolf Ritter von (1856-1913) Italian					
oil	1	14,220		14,220	
OTTENHEIM, J (?) ?					
oil	1	1,350		1,350	
OTTERBEEK, Jacobus Hermanus (1839-1902) Dutch					
wc/d	1	1,721		1,721	
OTTERNESS, Tom (1952-) American					
3D	4	38,450	1,650	4,400	28,000
OTTESEN, Otto Didrik (1816-1892) Danish					
oil	6	43,542	2,923	3,912	24,554
OTTEWELL, Benjamin John (fl.1885-1930) British					
wc/d	1	1,256		1,256	
OTTMANN, Henri (1877-1927) French					
oil	6	18,693	1,244	3,006	5,821
OTTO, Heinrich (1858-1923) German					
oil	1	2,200		2,200	
OTTO, Waldemar (1929-) Polish					
3D	1	1,408		1,408	
OUBORG, Piet (1893-1956) Dutch					
oil	1	1,188		1,188	
wc/d	3	26,049	2,773	6,897	16,379
OUDART, Paul Louis (1796-1850) French					
wc/d	5	17,382	2,897	3,292	4,214
OUDENHAVEN, T van (19th C) ?					
oil	2	7,000	3,500	3,500	3,500
OUDERRA, Pierre van der (1841-1915) Belgian					
oil	7	41,148	1,109	5,270	13,000
OUDES, Dirk (1895-1969) Dutch					
oil	1	2,802		2,802	
OUDINOT, Achille (1820-1891) Flemish					
oil	1	6,000		6,000	
OUDOT, Georges (20th C) French					
3D	1	1,567		1,567	
OUDOT, Roland (1897-1981) French					
oil	21	70,007	1,039	2,626	9,399
OUDRY, Jacques-Charles (1720-1778) French					
oil	1	16,000		16,000	
wc/d	1	1,021		1,021	
OUDRY, Jean Baptiste (1686-1755) French					
oil	10	2,833,156	35,779	215,000	1,208,000
wc/d	8	54,338	1,812	4,029	15,000
OUDRY, Jean Baptiste (school) (1686-1755) French					
oil	2	23,726	3,418	11,863	20,308
OULESS, Philip J (1817-1885) British					
oil	2	13,633	1,073	6,817	12,560

Name	No.	Total Sales Value	lowest	Prices median	highest
OULINE (20th C) ?					
3D	1	1,224		1,224	
OULTON, Therese (1953-) British					
oil	1	2,718		2,718	
OURSLER, Tony (1957-) American					
3D	3	106,784	12,284	32,500	62,000
OUTCAULT, Richard F (1863-1928) American					
wc/d	1	8,500		8,500	
OUTER, Nestor (1865-1923) Belgian					
wc/d	1	2,069		2,069	
OUTERBRIDGE, Paul (jnr) (1896-1958) American					
wc/d	1	3,250		3,250	
OUTIN, Pierre (1840-1899) French					
oil	2	72,885	20,385	36,443	52,500
OUVRIE, Justin (1806-1879) French					
oil	3	11,335	1,728	3,098	6,509
wc/d	5	14,939	1,326	3,011	5,367
OVADYAHU, Samuel (1892-1963) Israeli					
oil	6	23,700	2,500	4,000	5,600
wc/d	1	1,200		1,200	
OVENDEN, F W (fl.1834-1843) British					
oil	1	3,040		3,040	
OVENS, Jurgen (1623-1678) German					
oil	1	20,182		20,182	
OVERBECK, Johann Friedrich (1789-1869) German					
wc/d	1	27,500		27,500	
OVERBEEK, Gijsbertus Johannes van (1882-1947) Dutch					
oil	4	5,202	1,067	1,125	1,886
OVERBEEK, Leendert (1752-1815) Dutch					
wc/d	1	2,946		2,946	
OVERBEEK, Olaf Cleofas van (1946-) Dutch					
oil	1	5,942		5,942	
OVERMAN, Gerard (1855-1906) Dutch					
oil	1	1,231		1,231	
OWEN, Joel (20th C) British					
oil	1	1,296		1,296	
OWEN, Robert Emmett (1878-1957) American					
oil	6	17,550	1,300	2,825	5,200
OWEN, Samuel (1768-1857) British					
wc/d	5	16,732	2,574	2,860	5,434
OWEN, Vera H (20th C) American					
oil	1	1,500		1,500	
OWEN, William (1769-1825) British					
oil	2	10,235	1,600	5,118	8,635
OWENS, Laura (1970-) American					
oil	1	7,500		7,500	
OYELAMI, Muraina (1940-) African					
oil	1	1,269		1,269	
OYENS, David (1842-1902) Flemish					
oil	4	15,920	1,449	3,387	7,697
wc/d	1	1,836		1,836	
OYENS, Pierre (1842-1894) Flemish					
oil	1	14,538		14,538	
OZANNE (18th C) French					
oil	1	1,164		1,164	
OZANNE, Nicolas Marie (1728-1811) French					
oil	1	8,189		8,189	
wc/d	1	8,003		8,003	

Name	No.	Total Sales Value	lowest	Prices median	highest
OZANNE, Pierre (1737-1813) French					
wc/d	1	2,389		2,389	
OZENFANT, Amedee (1886-1966) French					
oil	4	44,307	7,123	9,332	18,521
OZOLS, Auseklis (1941-) American/Latvian					
oil	2	9,000	4,500	4,500	4,500
PAAL, Ladislas de (1846-1879) Hungarian					
oil	3	74,860	1,150	12,109	61,601
PAALEN, Wolfgang (1905-1959) Austrian					
wc/d	1	5,646		5,646	
PAANANEN, Robert (?) Canadian?					
oil	1	1,012		1,012	
PAAPE (20th C) ?					
wc/d	1	3,067		3,067	
PABLO, Julio de (1917-) Spanish					
oil	1	1,122		1,122	
PABLOS MERCEDES, Gomez (20th C) ?					
oil	1	1,267		1,267	
PACE, Achille (1923-) Italian					
oil	1	2,025		2,025	
PACE, Nicholas (1957-) British					
oil	1	1,924		1,924	
PACHECO RIVAS, Julio (1953-) Venezuelan					
oil	1	2,150		2,150	
PACHECO, Francisco (1564-1654) Spanish					
oil	1	61,361		61,361	
wc/d	1	15,670		15,670	
PACHER, Ferdinand (1852-1911) German					
wc/d	1	1,182		1,182	
PACINI, Santi (18th C) Italian					
oil	1	1,300		1,300	
PACINO DA BUONAGUIDA (14th C) Italian					
oil	1	158,231		158,231	
PADAMSEE, Akbar (1928-) Indian					
oil	5	47,566	2,416	11,000	18,000
PADDAY, Charles Murray (1868-1954) British					
oil	1	19,500		19,500	
PADILLA, J (18th C) Mexican					
oil	1	3,343		3,343	
PADUA SCHOOL, 17th C Italian					
3D	1	3,932		3,932	
PADUA, Paul Matthias (1903-1981) Austrian					
oil	6	31,879	1,184	3,029	17,068
wc/d	1	1,077		1,077	
PAEDE, Paul (1868-1929) German					
oil	6	10,734	1,033	1,594	2,740
PAEFFGEN, C O (20th C) German					
3D	1	2,396		2,396	
oil	1	11,619		11,619	
wc/d	4	5,357	1,068	1,174	1,942
PAEFFGEN, Claes Otto (20th C) German					
oil	1	9,615		9,615	
PAELINCK, Joseph (1781-1839) Belgian					
oil	1	24,000		24,000	
PAERELS, Willem (1878-1962) Belgian/Dutch					
oil	8	37,190	1,188	4,681	10,677
PAESCHKE, Paul (1875-1943) German					
wc/d	1	6,034		6,034	

Name	No.	Total Sales Value	lowest	Prices median	highest
PAEZ VILARO, Jorge (20th C) Uruguayan					
oil	1	3,800		3,800	
PAEZ, Jose de (1720-?) Mexican					
oil	2	32,314	15,263	16,157	17,051
PAGANI, Paolo (1661-1716) Italian					
wc/d	1	2,567		2,567	
PAGANO, Michele (1697-1732) Italian					
oil	1	10,090		10,090	
PAGE, Edward A (1850-1928) American					
oil	1	1,800		1,800	
PAGE, Henry Maurice (fl.1878-1890) British					
oil	1	3,318		3,318	
PAGEOT-ROUSSEAUX, Lucienne (20th C) French					
oil	1	1,167		1,167	
PAGES, Jules Eugene (1867-1946) American					
oil	3	41,000	12,000	13,000	16,000
PAGLIANO, Eleuterio (1826-1903) Italian					
wc/d	1	2,064		2,064	
PAGLIARA, A (19th C) Italian					
oil	1	4,990		4,990	
PAGLIEI, Gioacchino (?-1896) Italian					
oil	1	40,000		40,000	
PAGLIER, B G da (?-1896) Italian					
oil	1	5,024		5,024	
PAGLIOLICO, Romolo (1878-1962) Italian					
oil	1	1,517		1,517	
PAGNI, Ferruccio (1866-1935) Italian					
oil	1	1,147		1,147	
PAGNI, Ricardo (1936-) Italian					
3D	1	1,694		1,694	
PAGUENAUD, Jean-Louis (1876-1952) French					
oil	1	44,132		44,132	
PAI, Laxman (1926-) Indian					
oil	1	2,250		2,250	
PAICE, George (1854-1925) British					
oil	4	7,108	1,478	1,788	2,054
PAIK, Nam June (1932-) American/Korean					
3D	6	114,945	1,782	15,406	45,300
wc/d	3	65,911	1,078	11,602	53,231
PAIL, Edouard (1851-1916) French					
oil	2	6,262	2,628	3,131	3,634
PAILLARD, Henri (1844-1912) French					
oil	1	2,077		2,077	
PAILLER, Henri (20th C) French					
oil	1	1,916		1,916	
PAILLET, Charles (1871-?) French					
3D	4	8,505	1,000	1,881	3,744
PAILLOU, Peter (snr) (fl.1744-1784) British					
wc/d	1	8,460		8,460	
PAILOS, Manuel (1917-) Uruguayan					
oil	6	17,970	1,000	2,900	6,120
wc/d	2	6,300	1,300	3,150	5,000
PAINE, May (1873-) American					
oil	1	1,800		1,800	
PAJAU, F (18th C) ?					
3D	1	10,445		10,445	
PAJER-GARTEGEN, Robert (1866-1944) Austrian					
oil	1	6,828		6,828	

Name	No.	Total Sales Value	lowest	Prices median	highest
PAJETTA, Guido (20th C) Italian					
oil	1	3,284		3,284	
PAJETTA, Pietro (1845-1911) Italian					
oil	1	6,000		6,000	
PAJOT, Émile Paul (1870-1930) French					
oil	3	5,117	1,595	1,661	1,861
wc/d	3	6,557	2,140	2,191	2,226
PAJOT, Gilbert (?) French					
wc/d	1	2,006		2,006	
PAJOU, Augustin (1730-1809) French					
wc/d	2	3,322	1,558	1,661	1,764
PAJOU, Jacques Augustin Catherine (1766-1828) French					
oil	1	3,750		3,750	
wc/d	1	6,196		6,196	
PAL, Fried (1914-) Hungarian					
oil	8	17,500	1,200	1,900	4,000
PAL, Motilal (fl.1918-1920) Indian					
oil	1	15,000		15,000	
PALACIOS, Joaquin Vaquero (1900-1998) Spanish					
oil	3	24,117	3,372	9,990	10,755
PALADE BONNAL, Felicie (19th C) French					
oil	1	3,692		3,692	
PALADINI, Vinicio (1902-1971) Italian					
oil	2	5,565	1,440	2,783	4,125
wc/d	1	2,669		2,669	
PALADINO, Mimmo (1948-) Italian					
3D	2	27,145	12,835	13,573	14,310
oil	8	146,388	2,051	20,302	33,220
wc/d	9	26,597	1,184	2,567	5,920
PALAMEDES, Anthonie (1601-1673) Dutch					
oil	4	29,540	5,129	7,496	9,420
PALANTI, Giuseppe (1881-1946) Italian					
oil	1	1,946		1,946	
PALAU Y FERRE, Matias (20th C) Spanish					
oil	1	4,355		4,355	
PALAZUELO, Pablo (1916-) Spanish					
wc/d	1	9,204		9,204	
PALAZZOLO, Carl (20th C) ?					
oil	1	3,500		3,500	
PALDI, Israel (1892-1979) Israeli					
oil	5	117,600	2,200	6,200	66,000
PALENCIA, Benjamin (1894-1980) Spanish					
oil	15	249,689	1,687	12,662	62,426
wc/d	25	56,447	1,001	1,887	6,745
PALERMO, Blinky (1943-1977) German					
oil	2	416,700	160,000	208,350	256,700
PALEZIEUX, Gerard (1919-) Swiss					
wc/d	1	1,864		1,864	
PALIN, William Mainwaring (1862-1947) British					
oil	1	1,258		1,258	
PALING, Johannes Jacobus (1844-1892) Dutch					
oil	1	2,600		2,600	
PALINGH, Isaak (1630-1719) Dutch					
oil	1	50,000		50,000	
PALIZZI, Filippo (1818-1899) Italian					
oil	2	98,386	16,000	49,193	82,386
wc/d	1	1,222		1,222	
PALIZZI, G (1812-1888) Italian					
oil	1	5,994		5,994	

Name	No.	Total Sales Value	lowest	Prices median	highest
PALIZZI, Giuseppe (1812-1888) Italian					
oil	4	35,010	2,523	9,090	14,307
PALIZZI, Nicola (1820-1870) Italian					
oil	1	1,959		1,959	
PALLANDT, Charlotte van (1898-1997) Dutch					
3D	14	59,529	1,293	3,233	12,069
PALLARES Y ALLUSTANTE, Joaquin (1853-1935) Spanish					
oil	8	92,769	2,021	4,896	33,723
PALLIERE, Armand Julien (1784-1862) French					
wc/d	1	1,273		1,273	
PALLIERE, Jean Léon (1823-1887) Brazilian/French					
wc/d	2	46,981	19,288	23,491	27,693
PALLIK, Bela (1845-1908) Hungarian					
oil	1	1,064		1,064	
PALLMANN, Gotz (1908-1966) German					
oil	6	20,636	1,346	2,887	6,373
PALLMANN, Kurt (1886-?) German					
oil	1	1,397		1,397	
PALLYA, C (19/20th C) Hungarian					
oil	1	2,107		2,107	
PALM, Anna (1859-1924) Swedish					
oil	1	2,154		2,154	
wc/d	16	37,389	1,016	1,541	9,832
PALM, Gustaf Wilhelm (1810-1890) Swedish					
oil	6	36,838	2,032	5,692	14,069
PALM, Otto (?) Austrian					
oil	1	1,430		1,430	
PALM, Torsten (1875-1934) Swedish					
oil	1	1,809		1,809	
PALMA, J (il Giovane) (1544-1628) Italian					
oil	1	6,373		6,373	
PALMA, Jacopo (16/17th C) Italian					
oil	1	3,234		3,234	
PALMA, Jacopo (il Giovane) (1544-1628) Italian					
oil	1	23,323		23,323	
wc/d	7	23,997	1,510	3,738	5,500
PALMAROLI Y GONZALEZ, Vicente (1834-1896) Spanish					
oil	1	5,739		5,739	
PALMAROLI, Vicente (?) Spanish					
oil	1	30,389		30,389	
PALMEIRO, Jose (1903-1984) Spanish					
oil	20	52,142	1,130	1,771	16,132
PALMER (?) ?					
oil	1	3,250		3,250	
PALMER, Harry Sutton (1854-1933) British					
wc/d	28	84,882	1,094	2,382	7,900
PALMER, Herbert Sidney (1881-1970) Canadian					
oil	4	6,127	1,151	1,540	1,896
PALMER, James Lynwood (1868-1941) British					
oil	3	9,435	1,147	3,200	5,088
wc/d	1	8,000		8,000	
PALMER, Pauline (1867-1938) American					
oil	2	6,750	1,250	3,375	5,500
PALMER, Samuel (1805-1881) British					
oil	1	328,900		328,900	
wc/d	1	1,020,000		1,020,000	
PALMER, Sutton (1854-1935) British					
wc/d	3	9,938	2,718	3,020	4,200

Name	No.	Total Sales Value	lowest	Prices median	highest
PALMER, Walter L (1854-1932) American					
oil	3	73,554	4,554	29,000	40,000
wc/d	2	19,250	7,250	9,625	12,000
PALMERO DE GREGORIO, Alfredo (1901-1991) Spanish					
oil	7	17,243	1,318	2,151	4,062
PALMERO, Maestro (1901-1991) Spanish					
oil	3	7,792	1,394	2,445	3,953
PALMEZZANO, Marco (1458-1539) Italian					
oil	1	18,840		18,840	
PALMIE, Charles (1863-1911) German					
oil	2	7,649	2,779	3,825	4,870
PALMIERI, Francesco (16th C) Italian					
wc/d	1	2,469		2,469	
PALMIERI, Pietro Giacomo (?-c.1819) Italian					
wc/d	1	1,481		1,481	
PALMORE, Tom (1944-) American					
oil	1	2,000		2,000	
PAMBOUJIAN, Gerard (1941-) French					
oil	1	1,902		1,902	
PAN, Jean Louis (1943-) French					
wc/d	1	1,568		1,568	
PAN, Marta (1923-) Hungarian/ French					
3D	1	2,992		2,992	
PANABAKER, Frank S (1904-1992) Canadian					
oil	1	2,275		2,275	
PANAMERENKO (1940-) Belgian					
3D	1	9,491		9,491	
wc/d	2	8,356	4,178	4,178	4,178
PANCKOUCKE, Ernestine (1784-1860) French					
wc/d	1	1,210		1,210	
PANCOAST, Morris Hall (1877-?) American					
oil	5	13,100	1,600	2,000	4,500
PANDIT, S M (?) Indian					
wc/d	1	2,880		2,880	
PANERAI, Ruggero (1862-1923) Italian					
oil	2	9,578	1,106	4,789	8,472
PANETTI, Domenico (1460-c.1513) Italian					
oil	2	33,625	9,625	16,813	24,000
PANINI (school) (18/19th C) Italian					
oil	1	4,544		4,544	
PANINI, Francesco (18th C) Italian					
wc/d	1	30,200		30,200	
PANINI, Giovanni Paolo (1691-1765) Italian					
oil	4	413,648	24,746	114,451	160,000
wc/d	5	44,257	1,178	5,236	25,670
PANINI, Giovanni Paolo (school) (1691-1765) Italian					
oil	2	28,600	4,600	14,300	24,000
PANITZSCH, Robert (1879-1949) German/Danish					
oil	6	13,282	1,008	1,683	4,873
PANKO, William (1892-1948) Canadian/Austrian					
wc/d	1	1,678		1,678	
PANKOK, Bernhard (1872-1943) German					
oil	2	6,108	2,926	3,054	3,182
PANKOK, Otto (1893-1966) German					
3D	1	2,396		2,396	
wc/d	1	4,111		4,111	
PANN, Abel (1883-1963) Israeli/Latvian					
wc/d	2	8,527	3,027	4,264	5,500

Name	No.	Total Sales Value	lowest	Prices median	highest
PANSINI, Edoardo (1886-1968) Italian					
oil	1	1,130		1,130	
PANTAZIS, Pericles (1849-1884) Greek					
oil	1	4,938		4,938	
wc/d	1	5,840		5,840	
PANTON, Lawrence Arthur Colley (1894-1954) Canadian					
oil	5	7,480	1,062	1,261	2,323
PANTON, Verner (1926-1999) ?					
3D	1	24,000		24,000	
PANTORBA, Bernardino de (1896-1990) Spanish					
oil	2	7,363	3,301	3,682	4,062
PANZA, Giovanni (1894-1989) Italian					
oil	7	22,763	1,600	2,549	8,250
PAOLETTI, Antonio (1834-1912) Italian					
oil	5	64,768	2,500	9,000	28,000
PAOLETTI, Rodolfo (1866-1940) Italian					
oil	3	6,470	1,155	2,311	3,004
PAOLINI, Giulio (1940-) Italian					
3D	1	58,000		58,000	
oil	1	24,915		24,915	
wc/d	1	3,376		3,376	
PAOLOZZI, Eduardo (1924-) British					
3D	2	52,941	3,641	26,471	49,300
oil	1	3,750		3,750	
wc/d	2	7,615	1,015	3,808	6,600
PAOLUCCI, Enrico (?) Italian					
oil	1	5,240		5,240	
PAP, Emil (1884-?) Hungarian					
oil	10	29,961	1,100	2,505	6,912
PAPALOUCAS, Spyros (1892-1957) Greek					
oil	1	4,380		4,380	
PAPALUCA, L (20th C) Italian					
wc/d	1	2,860		2,860	
PAPALUCA, Louis (20th C) Italian					
wc/d	6	13,455	1,386	2,318	3,000
PAPART, Max (1911-1994) French					
oil	6	11,844	1,408	2,077	2,541
wc/d	3	5,044	1,012	1,461	2,571
PAPAZOFF, Georges (1894-1972) Bulgarian					
oil	4	8,817	1,031	2,426	2,935
PAPE, Eduard (1817-1905) German					
oil	2	5,366	2,364	2,683	3,002
PAPE, Emile (?) ?					
oil	1	1,000		1,000	
PAPE, William (1859-1920) German					
oil	1	2,396		2,396	
PAPENDRECHT, Jan Hoynck van (1858-1933) Dutch					
oil	2	21,444	3,622	10,722	17,822
PAPETY, Dominique Louis (1815-1849) French					
wc/d	1	1,141		1,141	
PAPPELENDAM, Laura van (20th C) American					
oil	1	4,000		4,000	
PAPPERITZ, Fritz Georg (1846-1918) German					
oil	1	8,420		8,420	
PAQUEAU, Gaston (19th C) French					
oil	1	2,874		2,874	
PAQUIN, Pauline (1952-) Canadian					
oil	1	1,632		1,632	
PARADIES, Herman Cornelis Adolf (1883-1966) Dutch					
wc/d	2	9,205	3,365	4,603	5,840

Name	No.	Total Sales Value	lowest	Prices median	highest
PARANT, Louis Bertin (1768-1851) French					
wc/d	1	2,439		2,439	
PARAVASINI, C (?) ?					
3D	1	1,427		1,427	
PARAVISINI, Christine (20th C) ?					
3D	1	1,418		1,418	
PARC, Julio le (1928-) Argentinian					
oil	1	3,515		3,515	
PARDI, Gian Franco (1933-) Italian					
3D	1	1,318		1,318	
PARDO, Mercedes (1922-) South American					
oil	2	3,100	1,340	1,550	1,760
PARDON (19/20th C) ?					
3D	1	2,306		2,306	
PAREDES, Vicenta de (1857-1903) Spanish					
oil	2	13,864	4,140	6,932	9,724
PAREDES, Vicente Garcia de (1845-1903) Spanish					
oil	1	5,078		5,078	
PARELLE, M-A (18th C) French					
oil	1	24,000		24,000	
PARENT, Aubert Henri Joseph (1753-1835) French					
3D	1	13,590		13,590	
PARENT, Roger (1881-1985) French					
oil	3	19,667	1,712	3,400	14,555
PARESCE, Renato (1886-1937) Italian					
oil	3	40,782	9,599	13,607	17,576
PARESSANT, Jules (?) French					
oil	9	18,831	1,110	1,895	3,995
PARET Y ALCAZAR, Luis (1746-1799) Spanish					
oil	2	126,336	6,336	63,168	120,000
wc/d	1	8,629		8,629	
PARIS, Camille Adrien (1834-1901) French					
oil	1	2,678		2,678	
PARIS, Pierre-Adrien (1745-1819) French					
wc/d	1	38,939		38,939	
PARIS, René (1881-1970) French					
3D	2	6,925	3,275	3,463	3,650
PARIS, Roland (1894-?) French					
3D	2	7,906	2,717	3,953	5,189
PARIS, Walter (1842-1906) American/British					
wc/d	5	12,500	1,300	1,700	5,500
PARISON, Gaston (1889-?) French					
oil	1	3,773		3,773	
PARK, David (1911-1960) American					
oil	3	489,000	9,000	30,000	450,000
wc/d	2	77,800	2,800	38,900	75,000
PARK, H Morley (fl.1884-1895) British					
oil	1	2,940		2,940	
PARK, John Anthony (1880-1962) British					
oil	22	102,262	1,029	4,424	8,584
PARK, Leonard (?) British?					
oil	1	1,763		1,763	
PARK, Madeleine (1891-1960) American					
3D	7	14,900	1,500	2,000	3,600
PARK, Stuart (1862-1933) British					
oil	18	53,913	1,551	2,849	5,800
PARKER, Bill (1922-) American					
oil	2	2,178	1,056	1,089	1,122

Name	No.	Total Sales Value	Prices lowest	median	highest
PARKER, Daniel (20th C) American					
3D	1	20,000		20,000	
PARKER, George Waller (1888-1957) American					
oil	1	2,000		2,000	
PARKER, Henry (19/20th C) British					
oil	1	4,710		4,710	
PARKER, Henry H (1858-1930) British					
oil	16	134,283	1,650	8,893	17,202
wc/d	4	7,007	1,176	1,716	2,400
PARKER, Henry Perlee (1795-1873) British					
oil	1	1,888		1,888	
PARKER, J M (19th C) British?					
oil	1	1,184		1,184	
PARKER, Lawton S (1868-1954) American					
oil	3	75,800	1,800	24,000	50,000
PARKER, Ray (1922-1990) American					
oil	1	3,500		3,500	
PARKMAN, Alfred Edward (1852-?) British					
wc/d	1	1,133		1,133	
PARLBER, Samuel (19th C) British					
wc/d	1	2,054		2,054	
PARMA SCHOOL, 17th C Italian					
oil	2	23,710	4,710	11,855	19,000
PARMENTIER, Jacques (1658-1730) French					
oil	2	17,806	6,816	8,903	10,990
PARMENTIER, Pol (20th C) Belgian					
oil	2	3,069	1,278	1,535	1,791
PARMESAN (school) (16th C) Italian					
wc/d	1	3,473		3,473	
PARMIGGIANI, Claudio (1943-) Italian					
3D	1	13,775		13,775	
oil	2	20,312	2,912	10,156	17,400
PARPAN, Ferdinand (1902-) French					
3D	3	4,804	1,317	1,317	2,170
PARR, Frank (?) British					
wc/d	1	1,411		1,411	
PARR, Nuna (1949-) North American					
3D	2	12,582	5,200	6,291	7,382
PARRA, Gines (1895-1960) Spanish					
oil	14	49,355	1,076	2,847	10,375
wc/d	4	5,165	1,161	1,269	1,467
PARRA, Miguel (1784-1846) Spanish					
oil	1	10,546		10,546	
PARRENS, Louis (1904-) French					
oil	1	1,015		1,015	
PARRISH, Maxfield (1870-1966) American					
oil	4	704,500	32,000	141,250	390,000
PARRISH, Stephen (1846-1938) American					
oil	1	3,000		3,000	
PARROCEL, Charles (1688-1752) French					
wc/d	2	8,998	1,998	4,499	7,000
PARROCEL, Étienne (1696-1776) French					
oil	1	4,422		4,422	
wc/d	1	1,600		1,600	
PARROCEL, Étienne Antoine (1817-1899) French					
oil	1	1,168		1,168	
PARROCEL, Joseph (1646-1704) French					
wc/d	1	1,727		1,727	

Name	No.	Total Sales Value	Prices lowest	median	highest
PARROCEL, Joseph François (1704-1781) French					
wc/d	1	1,099		1,099	
PARROW, Karin (1900-1986) Swedish					
oil	10	26,047	1,260	2,223	6,230
PARS, William (1742-1782) British					
wc/d	1	1,352		1,352	
PARSHALL, Douglas (1899-1990) American					
oil	1	4,600		4,600	
PARSONS, Alfred William (1847-1920) British					
oil	1	2,610		2,610	
wc/d	2	8,224	3,289	4,112	4,935
PARSONS, Arthur Wilde (1854-1931) British					
oil	5	16,483	1,065	3,600	5,738
wc/d	2	3,566	1,340	1,783	2,226
PARSONS, Beatrice (1870-1955) British					
wc/d	16	56,397	1,160	3,850	7,722
PARSONS, Betty (1900-1982) American					
3D	1	1,500		1,500	
PARSONS, Max (19/20th C) British?					
oil	1	1,136		1,136	
PARSONS, Orrin Sheldon (1866-1943) American					
oil	4	12,900	1,900	3,000	5,000
PARTENHEIMER, Jurgen (1947-) German					
wc/d	2	4,428	2,214	2,214	2,214
PARTHENIS, Constantine (1878-1967) Greek					
oil	3	158,880	8,500	40,880	109,500
wc/d	3	20,030	5,500	6,500	8,030
PARTIKEL, Alfred (1888-1946) German					
oil	1	3,317		3,317	
PARTINGTON, Richard Langtry (1868-1929) American/British					
oil	1	2,500		2,500	
PARTON, Arthur (1842-1914) American					
oil	5	28,000	2,500	4,000	12,000
PARTON, Ernest (1845-1933) British					
oil	6	19,842	1,050	2,118	9,500
PARTRIDGE, J C (19th C) British					
oil	1	1,287		1,287	
PARTURIER, Marcel (1901-) French					
oil	9	11,733	1,047	1,112	2,357
PASCAL, Paul (1832-1903) French					
wc/d	8	15,526	1,000	1,361	3,481
PASCALI, Pino (1935-1968) Italian					
3D	1	203,000		203,000	
oil	7	17,213	1,427	2,182	3,601
wc/d	7	21,186	1,338	2,475	5,851
PASCH, Clemens (1910-) Swiss					
3D	1	1,442		1,442	
PASCH, Johan (elder) (1706-1769) Swedish					
wc/d	1	1,035		1,035	
PASCH, Lorens (younger) (1733-1805) Swedish					
oil	3	31,303	4,215	4,515	22,573
PASCH, Ulrika (1735-1796) Swedish					
oil	1	11,964		11,964	
PASCHKE, Ed (1939-) American					
oil	2	18,500	5,500	9,250	13,000
PASCIN (1885-1930) American/Bulgarian					
wc/d	1	1,168		1,168	
PASCIN, Jules (1885-1930) American/Bulgarian					
oil	6	372,914	38,000	57,500	100,000
wc/d	35	109,789	1,069	2,957	6,525

Name	No.	Total Sales Value	lowest	Prices median	highest
PASCUAL RODES, Ivo (1883-1949) Spanish					
oil	1	6,078		6,078	
PASINELLI, Lorenzo (1629-1700) Italian					
oil	1	39,250		39,250	
PASINETTI, Antonio (1863-1940) Italian					
oil	1	1,784		1,784	
PASINI, Alberto (1826-1899) Italian					
oil	12	1,083,908	6,591	48,750	292,000
wc/d	2	12,170	2,080	6,085	10,090
PASMORE, Daniel (19th C) British					
oil	1	1,545		1,545	
wc/d	1	2,416		2,416	
PASMORE, Daniel (jnr) (1829-1891) British					
oil	1	2,052		2,052	
PASMORE, F G (jnr) (fl.1875-1884) British					
oil	1	1,776		1,776	
PASMORE, Frederick George (jnr) (fl.1875-1884) British					
oil	1	2,400		2,400	
PASMORE, John F (1820-1871) British					
oil	1	2,550		2,550	
wc/d	1	1,133		1,133	
PASMORE, Victor (1908-1998) British					
3D	3	35,554	2,842	12,972	19,740
oil	2	69,450	30,450	34,725	39,000
wc/d	3	11,389	2,100	3,744	5,545
PASQUA, Philippe (20th C) French					
oil	1	12,212		12,212	
wc/d	1	8,470		8,470	
PASQUIER, Noel (20th C) French					
wc/d	1	5,192		5,192	
PASSAGE, Comte Arthur Marie Gabriel du (1838-1909) French					
3D	5	39,992	2,634	6,912	19,000
PASSAROTTI, Bartolomeo (1529-1592) Italian					
oil	1	26,364		26,364	
wc/d	2	23,000	7,000	11,500	16,000
PASSE, Chrispijn van de (younger) (1594-1670) Dutch					
wc/d	1	1,470		1,470	
PASSEBON, Pierre (20th C) French					
wc/d	1	1,408		1,408	
PASSEY, Charles H (fl.1870-1885) British					
oil	2	2,737	1,350	1,369	1,387
PASSINI (19/20th C) Italian					
oil	1	1,981		1,981	
PASSINI, Johann Ludwig (1832-1903) Austrian					
wc/d	1	60,900		60,900	
PASTEGA, Luigi (1858-1927) Italian					
oil	2	11,946	5,000	5,973	6,946
PASTOR CALPENA, Vicente (20th C) Spanish					
wc/d	2	3,361	1,652	1,681	1,709
PASTOUR, Louis (1876-1948) French					
oil	2	2,010	1,000	1,005	1,010
PASTUR, Arnold (19th C) ?					
oil	1	1,655		1,655	
PATA, Cherubino (1827-1899) French					
oil	2	19,498	1,378	9,749	18,120
PATANIA, Giuseppe (1780-1852) Italian					
oil	1	17,555		17,555	
PATEL, Antoine Pierre (younger) (1648-1707) French					
wc/d	2	4,012	2,006	2,006	2,006

Name	No.	Total Sales Value	lowest	Prices median	highest
PATEL, Homi B (1928-) Indian					
oil	1	1,440		1,440	
PATEL, Kirti (?) ?					
3D	2	2,580	1,032	1,290	1,548
PATEL, Pierre (elder) (1605-1676) French					
wc/d	1	3,375		3,375	
PATELLIERE, Amedee de la (1890-1932) French					
oil	5	10,529	1,196	2,392	2,924
wc/d	2	2,685	1,196	1,343	1,489
PATEMANT, A (19/20th C) ?					
oil	1	1,501		1,501	
PATER, Jean Baptiste (1695-1736) French					
oil	4	848,958	1,908	203,025	441,000
wc/d	1	4,511		4,511	
PATER, Jean Baptiste (school) (1695-1736) French					
oil	1	4,629		4,629	
PATERNOTTE, C (?) Belgian?					
3D	1	1,007		1,007	
PATERSON, Caroline (fl.1880`s) British					
wc/d	1	4,452		4,452	
PATERSON, Hamish (1890-1955) British					
oil	3	24,308	2,528	4,380	17,400
PATERSON, James (1854-1932) British					
oil	6	28,511	1,450	4,289	10,990
wc/d	6	25,249	1,764	3,412	9,052
PATHEMONT, Elie (20th C) ?					
oil	1	1,425		1,425	
PATIGIAN, Haig (1876-1950) American					
3D	1	5,250		5,250	
PATINO, Anton (1957-) Spanish					
oil	2	4,505	1,547	2,253	2,958
PATON, Frank (1856-1909) British					
oil	2	9,435	1,570	4,718	7,865
PATON, L (?) ?					
oil	1	1,630		1,630	
PATON, Richard (1717-1791) British					
oil	2	23,039	1,144	11,520	21,895
PATON, Sir Joseph Noel (1821-1901) British					
oil	3	108,490	13,590	36,500	58,400
PATON, Waller Hugh (1828-1895) British					
oil	3	141,280	21,900	41,470	77,910
wc/d	5	8,687	1,001	1,480	2,920
PATOUX, Émile (1893-1985) Belgian					
oil	1	3,103		3,103	
PATRICK, Ann (1937-) British					
oil	1	1,450		1,450	
PATRICK, Emily (?) British?					
oil	2	9,480	4,582	4,740	4,898
PATRICK, James McIntosh (1907-1998) British					
oil	3	38,294	6,194	13,140	18,960
wc/d	7	32,406	1,050	4,380	7,300
PATROIS, Isidore (1815-1884) French					
oil	1	3,160		3,160	
PATRONE, Virginia (1950-) Uruguayan					
oil	1	1,500		1,500	
PATTEIN, Cesar (19/20th C) French					
oil	1	6,653		6,653	
PATTERSON, Alexander (20th C) British					
oil	1	1,752		1,752	

Name	No.	Total Sales Value	lowest	Prices median	highest
PATTERSON, Howard Ashman (1891-?) American					
oil	1	10,000		10,000	
PATTERSON, Margaret Jordan (1867-1950) American					
oil	1	2,500		2,500	
wc/d	2	2,900	1,300	1,450	1,600
PATTERSON, Neil (1947-) Canadian					
oil	1	3,027		3,027	
PATTERSON, Robert (1898-) American					
wc/d	1	2,800		2,800	
PAUELSEN, Erik (1749-1790) Danish					
oil	1	2,079		2,079	
PAUL, Ernst Wilhelm (1856-?) German					
oil	1	2,550		2,550	
PAUL, Jeremy (1954-) British					
oil	3	13,436	4,260	4,260	4,736
PAUL, John (19th C) British					
oil	1	11,440		11,440	
PAUL, Joseph (1804-1887) British					
oil	4	16,064	1,000	3,215	8,635
PAUL, Maurice (1889-1965) Dutch					
oil	2	3,664	1,078	1,832	2,586
PAULI, Fritz (1891-1968) Swiss					
oil	1	2,652		2,652	
PAULI, Georg (1855-1935) Swedish					
oil	14	129,535	1,106	2,433	54,412
wc/d	2	21,414	2,370	10,707	19,044
PAULI, Hanna (1864-1940) Swedish					
oil	4	13,261	1,204	1,578	8,901
PAULIN, Paul (19/20th C) French					
3D	1	1,297		1,297	
PAULMAN, Joseph (19th C) British					
oil	5	10,598	1,063	1,888	3,816
PAULSEN, Fritz (1838-1898) German					
oil	2	9,134	3,414	4,567	5,720
PAULSEN, Ingwer (1883-?) German					
oil	1	1,581		1,581	
PAULSEN, Julius (1860-1940) Danish					
oil	13	29,207	1,073	1,816	4,933
PAULUCCI, Enrico (1901-1999) Italian					
oil	19	86,191	1,121	2,967	23,106
wc/d	3	3,821	1,173	1,173	1,475
PAULUS, L (20th C) ?					
oil	1	3,657		3,657	
PAULUS, Pierre (1881-1959) Belgian					
oil	5	33,221	1,505	6,211	11,449
PAULY, F (19th C) ?					
oil	1	1,238		1,238	
PAUPION, Eduard (1854-1912) French					
oil	1	10,242		10,242	
PAUQUET, H (19th C) French					
wc/d	1	1,344		1,344	
PAUQUET, Hippolyte Louis Emile (1797-?) French					
wc/d	1	1,752		1,752	
PAUSINGER, Clemens von (1855-1936) German					
oil	1	10,049		10,049	
PAUSINGER, Franz von (1839-1915) German					
oil	1	1,839		1,839	
wc/d	1	1,227		1,227	

Name	No.	Total Sales Value	lowest	Prices median	highest
PAUTROT (19th C) French					
3D	2	3,966	1,302	1,983	2,664
PAUTROT, Ferdinand (1832-1874) French					
3D	4	13,965	2,100	3,773	4,320
PAUW, Paul de (1910-1961) ?					
oil	1	2,306		2,306	
PAUW, Robert de (1842-1914) Belgian					
oil	1	14,372		14,372	
PAUWELS, Jos (1818-1876) Belgian					
oil	16	31,735	1,065	1,406	4,672
PAUWELS, Maximilien (fl.1643-1661) Belgian					
oil	1	13,590		13,590	
PAVAN, Angelo (1893-1945) Italian					
oil	1	1,138		1,138	
PAVIL, Elie Anatole (1873-1948) French					
oil	15	37,025	1,175	2,212	5,281
wc/d	1	1,626		1,626	
PAVLIKEVICH, J (19/20th C) Russian					
wc/d	1	1,752		1,752	
PAVLOS (1930-) Greek					
3D	2	4,664	1,672	2,332	2,992
wc/d	1	10,625		10,625	
PAVLOS, Paul (1930-) Greek					
3D	1	1,638		1,638	
PAVLYUK, Nikolai (1901-1980) Russian					
oil	1	1,470		1,470	
PAVY, Philippe (1860-?) French					
oil	2	13,104	1,424	6,552	11,680
PAWLE, John (1915-) British					
oil	3	3,474	1,026	1,184	1,264
PAXSON, Edgar S (1852-1919) American					
oil	4	90,500	5,500	20,000	45,000
wc/d	3	34,500	4,500	10,000	20,000
PAXTON, William A (20th C) American					
oil	2	3,650	1,400	1,825	2,250
PAXTON, William McGregor (1869-1941) American					
oil	2	90,000	10,000	45,000	80,000
PAYNE, Charles Johnson (1884-1967) British					
wc/d	16	36,377	1,080	1,568	4,082
PAYNE, David (19th C) British					
oil	4	12,193	1,570	3,107	4,410
PAYNE, Edgar (1882-1947) American					
oil	17	456,500	2,500	18,000	90,000
wc/d	1	2,250		2,250	
PAYNE, Elsie Palmer (1884-1971) American					
oil	1	7,000		7,000	
PAYNE, W (18/19th C) British					
oil	1	1,800		1,800	
PAYNE, William (1760-1830) British					
oil	1	3,283		3,283	
wc/d	4	7,751	1,144	1,780	2,983
PAYTON, J (19th C) British					
oil	1	2,538		2,538	
PAYZANT, Charles (1898-1980) American/Canadian					
wc/d	1	1,400		1,400	
PAZ, Joseph de (18th C) Spanish					
oil	1	11,512		11,512	
PEABODY, Ruth (1898-1967) American					
oil	1	7,000		7,000	

Name	No.	Total Sales Value	lowest	Prices median	highest
PEAK, Bob (1928-1992) American					
wc/d	4	9,550	1,800	2,000	3,750
PEAKE, Mervyn (1911-1968) British					
oil	3	6,269	1,500	2,100	2,669
wc/d	1	3,432		3,432	
PEALE, James (elder) (1749-1831) American					
oil	1	4,000		4,000	
PEALE, Mary Jane (1827-1902) American					
oil	1	8,500		8,500	
PEALE, Rembrandt (1778-1860) American					
oil	2	222,000	42,000	111,000	180,000
PEALE, Rubens (1784-1865) American					
oil	1	57,500		57,500	
PEARCE, Bryan (1929-) British					
oil	1	4,230		4,230	
wc/d	1	2,755		2,755	
PEARCE, Charles Sprague (1851-1914) American					
oil	3	30,067	4,669	5,398	20,000
PEARLSTEIN, Philip (1924-) American					
wc/d	1	1,400		1,400	
PEARS, Charles (1873-1958) British					
oil	8	52,564	1,034	5,750	19,760
PEARSALL, Mike (?-1997) American					
wc/d	2	2,700	1,300	1,350	1,400
PEARSE, M H (19th C) British					
oil	1	1,170		1,170	
PEARSON (?) ?					
oil	1	2,000		2,000	
PEARSON, Constance (1886-1970) British					
wc/d	1	2,028		2,028	
PEARSON, Cornelius (1805-1891) British					
wc/d	2	2,973	1,144	1,487	1,829
PEARSON, Fred (?) British					
wc/d	1	1,875		1,875	
PEARSON, J (19th C) British					
oil	1	1,352		1,352	
PEARSON, John (19th C) British					
wc/d	1	2,288		2,288	
PEARSON, Marguerite S (1898-1978) American					
oil	7	34,200	1,200	1,700	13,000
PEARSON, Robert (?-1891) American					
oil	1	1,200		1,200	
PEARSON, William Henry (19/20th C) British					
wc/d	1	1,144		1,144	
PECHAUBES, Eugène (1890-1967) French					
oil	6	11,155	1,239	1,580	2,753
PECHEUR, Anne-Marie (20th C) French					
oil	1	1,097		1,097	
PECHMANN, Carl Heinrich von (1826-1905) German					
oil	1	3,552		3,552	
PECHSTEIN, Max (1881-1955) German					
oil	8	1,707,718	30,276	183,600	547,200
wc/d	21	227,715	1,496	12,543	30,388
PECRUS, Charles (1826-1907) French					
oil	9	27,320	1,097	2,437	6,416
PECSI-PILCH, Dezso (1888-1949) Hungarian					
oil	1	1,352		1,352	
PECZELY, Anton (1891-?) Hungarian					
oil	1	1,500		1,500	

Name	No.	Total Sales Value	lowest	Prices median	highest
PEDDER, John (1850-1929) British					
wc/d	2	2,932	1,216	1,466	1,716
PEDERSEN, Carl-Henning (1913-1993) Danish					
3D	2	3,360	1,648	1,680	1,712
oil	5	83,785	6,271	12,812	38,437
wc/d	11	19,662	1,033	1,787	2,562
PEDERSEN, Finn (1944-) Danish					
oil	3	3,482	1,046	1,220	1,220
PEDERSEN, Hugo Vilfred (1870-1959) Danish					
oil	5	7,095	1,027	1,207	2,343
PEDERSEN, Ole (1856-1898) Danish					
oil	1	1,291		1,291	
PEDERSEN, Thorolf (1858-1942) Danish					
oil	3	16,337	1,430	3,531	11,376
PEDERSEN, Viggo (1854-1926) Danish					
oil	11	23,278	1,026	1,256	8,789
PEDERSOLI, P (19th C) Italian					
oil	1	12,000		12,000	
PEDRETTI, Antonio (1950-) Italian					
oil	1	1,479		1,479	
PEEL, James (1811-1906) British					
oil	9	29,569	1,139	2,280	10,010
PEEL, Paul (1861-1892) Canadian					
oil	3	270,890	23,500	119,462	127,928
wc/d	1	151,000		151,000	
PEELE, James (1847-1905) Australian					
oil	1	2,703		2,703	
PEETERS, Eugene (19th C) American					
oil	1	1,500		1,500	
PEETERS, Gillis (1612-1653) Flemish					
oil	2	31,180	4,720	15,590	26,460
PEETERS, Jan (1624-1680) Flemish					
oil	1	38,220		38,220	
PEETERS, Jozef (1895-1960) Belgian					
oil	2	2,310	1,099	1,155	1,211
wc/d	1	1,797		1,797	
PEGG, William Quaker (1775-1851) British					
oil	1	1,600		1,600	
PEGOT-OGIER, Jean Bertrand (1877-1915) French					
oil	13	46,130	1,240	3,238	7,000
wc/d	2	3,903	1,354	1,952	2,549
PEGURIER, Auguste (1856-1936) French					
wc/d	1	1,018		1,018	
PEHRSON, Karl Axel (1921-) Swedish					
oil	14	43,399	2,129	2,562	6,552
wc/d	1	1,529		1,529	
PEIFFER, Auguste Joseph (1832-c.1879) French					
3D	2	3,627	1,623	1,814	2,004
PEIFFER, Engelbert Joseph (1830-1896) German					
3D	1	1,580		1,580	
PEIFFER-WATENPHUL, Max (1896-1976) German					
oil	4	92,569	18,769	21,978	29,844
PEINADO, Joaquin (1898-1975) Spanish					
oil	4	30,202	3,484	6,637	13,444
wc/d	4	8,262	1,069	1,564	4,065
PEIPERS, Eugène Friedrich (1805-1885) German					
oil	1	2,212		2,212	
PEIRCE, Waldo (1884-1970) American					
oil	3	11,200	1,800	4,200	5,200

Name	No.	Total Sales Value	lowest	Prices median	highest
PEIRE, Luc (1916-1994) Belgian					
oil	6	20,818	1,871	2,929	6,438
PEISER, Kurt (1887-1962) Belgian					
oil	12	27,784	1,073	1,467	6,587
wc/d	1	2,911		2,911	
PEIXOTTO, George da Maduro (1862-1937) American					
oil	1	5,500		5,500	
PELAEZ, Amelia (1897-1968) Cuban					
oil	2	154,596	54,596	77,298	100,000
wc/d	4	60,704	2,704	16,000	26,000
PELAEZ, Juan (1881-1937) Argentinian					
oil	1	1,777		1,777	
PELAYO FERNANDEZ, Eduardo (c.1850-?) Spanish					
oil	2	9,040	4,228	4,520	4,812
PELAYO, Eduardo (1901-) Spanish					
oil	2	3,965	1,298	1,983	2,667
PELAYO, Orlando (1920-1990) Spanish					
oil	4	8,495	1,229	2,154	2,958
wc/d	1	1,943		1,943	
PELEGRIN, Santiago (1885-1954) Spanish					
oil	2	12,896	1,967	6,448	10,929
PELEZ, Fernand (1843-1913) French					
oil	2	2,271	1,038	1,136	1,233
PELGROM, Jacobus (1811-1861) Dutch					
oil	1	2,332		2,332	
PELHAM, James II (1800-1874) British					
wc/d	1	2,646		2,646	
PELHAM, Thomas Kent (fl.1860-1891) British					
oil	2	4,917	2,200	2,459	2,717
PELISSIER, D (20th C) Italian					
oil	1	1,248		1,248	
PELL, Jacob (1900-) American					
oil	1	1,000		1,000	
PELLAN, Alfred (1906-1988) Canadian					
oil	4	39,769	1,400	6,434	25,502
wc/d	3	11,891	3,378	3,378	5,108
PELLEGRIN, Honore (1800-1870) French					
wc/d	1	1,809		1,809	
PELLEGRIN, Jacques (1944-) French					
oil	1	1,128		1,128	
PELLEGRINI, Alfred Heinrich (1881-1958) Swiss					
oil	3	10,096	2,333	3,342	4,421
PELLEGRINI, Carlo (1839-1889) Italian					
wc/d	1	1,103		1,103	
PELLEGRINI, Carlos Enrique (1800-1875) Argentinian					
wc/d	1	1,500		1,500	
PELLEGRINI, Domenico (1759-1840) Italian					
oil	1	12,156		12,156	
PELLEGRINI, Giacomo Antonio (18th C) Austrian					
oil	1	14,700		14,700	
wc/d	1	1,812		1,812	
PELLEGRINI, Giovanni Antonio (1675-1741) Italian					
oil	2	57,747	26,000	28,874	31,747
wc/d	1	1,621		1,621	
PELLEGRINI, Riccardo (1863-1934) Italian					
oil	13	86,481	1,355	2,861	32,500
wc/d	3	6,020	1,281	1,784	2,955
PELLEGRINO, Oscar (1947-) Venezuelan					
wc/d	1	1,440		1,440	

Name	No.	Total Sales Value	lowest	Prices median	highest
PELLERIER, Maurice (1875-?) French					
oil	1	1,625		1,625	
PELLETIER, Auguste (fl.1800-1847) French					
wc/d	4	59,255	13,168	13,168	19,751
PELLETIER, Jules (19th C) French					
oil	1	4,265		4,265	
PELLETIER, Pierre-Jacques (1869-1931) French					
wc/d	1	1,056		1,056	
PELLICCIOTTI, Tito (1872-1943) Italian					
oil	7	16,328	1,497	1,835	5,516
PELLICER, Rafael (1906-1963) Spanish					
oil	1	1,630		1,630	
PELLIZZA DA VOLPEDO, Giuseppe (1868-1907) Italian					
oil	1	13,863		13,863	
PELOUSE, Léon Germain (1838-1891) French					
oil	7	20,935	1,196	1,861	7,500
PELT, A van (1815-1895) Dutch					
oil	1	2,015		2,015	
PELUCHE, Amable Elisabeth (1781-1850) French					
oil	1	8,106		8,106	
PELUSO, Francesco (1836-?) Italian					
oil	5	21,157	2,215	4,424	5,869
PELUZZI, Eso (1894-1985) Italian					
oil	1	2,636		2,636	
PEMBERTON, Sophie T (1869-1959) British					
oil	1	2,516		2,516	
PEMPER, Alvaro (1965-) Uruguayan					
wc/d	1	3,000		3,000	
PENA Y MUNOZ, Maximino (1863-1940) Spanish					
oil	4	10,958	1,870	1,956	5,177
wc/d	2	4,605	1,405	2,303	3,200
PENA, Angel (1949-) Venezuelan					
oil	1	1,080		1,080	
PENA, Maximino (?) Spanish					
oil	1	1,144		1,144	
wc/d	2	4,083	2,002	2,042	2,081
PENAGOS ZALABARDO, Rafael de (1889-1954) Spanish					
oil	2	14,070	2,565	7,035	11,505
wc/d	2	2,062	1,027	1,031	1,035
PENALBA, Alicia (1918-1982) Argentinian					
3D	5	26,110	1,671	3,857	9,735
PENASSE, Paul (19/20th C) French					
oil	1	2,755		2,755	
PENCK, A R (1939-) German					
3D	2	2,918	1,188	1,459	1,730
oil	8	130,583	4,350	14,228	40,000
wc/d	5	16,263	1,311	2,330	8,579
PENDER, Jack (1918-1998) British					
oil	1	1,176		1,176	
PENDINI, Fulvio (1907-1975) Italian					
oil	1	1,427		1,427	
PENDL, Erwin (1875-?) Austrian					
wc/d	1	2,114		2,114	
PENE DU BOIS, Guy (1884-1958) American					
oil	4	334,300	1,300	46,500	240,000
wc/d	1	1,400		1,400	
PENFOLD, Frank C (1849-1920) American					
oil	1	4,250		4,250	
PENKOAT, Pierre (1945-) French					
oil	1	1,690		1,690	

Name	No.	Total Sales Value	lowest	Prices median	highest
PENNACHINI, Domenico (1860-?) Italian					
wc/d	1	1,200		1,200	
PENNASILICO, Giuseppe (1861-1940) Italian					
oil	3	5,357	1,376	1,835	2,146
PENNE, Olivier de (1831-1897) French					
oil	7	44,647	1,690	5,000	16,500
wc/d	2	3,689	1,117	1,845	2,572
PENNELL, Harry (19th C) British					
oil	3	6,517	1,541	1,875	3,101
PENNELL, Henry (1879-1934) British					
oil	1	2,000		2,000	
PENNELL, Joseph (1860-1926) American					
wc/d	1	3,200		3,200	
PENNI, Luca (1500-1556) Italian					
oil	1	6,239		6,239	
PENNIMAN, John Ritto (1782-1841) American					
oil	1	4,750		4,750	
PENNSYLVANIA SCHOOL, 19th C American					
wc/d	3	28,500	2,500	5,000	21,000
PENONE, Giuseppe (1947-) Italian					
3D	1	21,750		21,750	
wc/d	1	1,068		1,068	
PENOT, Albert Joseph (19th C) French					
oil	1	1,872		1,872	
PENOT, Jean Vallette (1710-1777) French					
oil	3	192,000	27,000	60,000	105,000
PENROSE, Sir Roland (1900-1984) British					
wc/d	2	2,863	1,063	1,432	1,800
PENSON, James (1814-1907) British					
wc/d	1	1,661		1,661	
PENTON, Howard (20th C) British					
wc/d	1	1,113		1,113	
PEPI, Vincent (1926-) American					
oil	1	2,800		2,800	
PEPIN, Edouard (1853-?) French					
3D	1	1,331		1,331	
PEPLOE, Denis (1914-) British					
oil	1	3,171		3,171	
PEPLOE, Samuel John (1871-1935) British					
oil	9	481,770	8,760	43,800	175,200
PEPPER, Beverly (1924-) American					
3D	2	18,200	4,200	9,100	14,000
PEPYN, Marten (1575-1642) Flemish					
oil	3	50,912	7,056	19,696	24,160
PERAIRE, Paul Emmanuel (1829-1893) French					
oil	3	14,655	1,106	4,299	9,250
PERALTA DEL CAMPO, Francisco (1837-1897) Spanish					
wc/d	1	1,022		1,022	
PERBANDT, Carl von (1832-1911) American					
oil	1	4,000		4,000	
PERBOYRE, Paul Emile Léon (19th C) French					
oil	2	7,978	2,137	3,989	5,841
PERCEVAL, Don Louis (1908-1979) American					
oil	2	27,000	2,000	13,500	25,000
PERCIER, Charles (1764-1838) French					
wc/d	8	50,137	2,356	4,582	19,375
PERCIVAL, Bessie (fl.1885-1891) British					
oil	1	2,900		2,900	

Name	No.	Total Sales Value	Prices lowest	median	highest
PERCIVAL, T S (?) ?					
oil	2	3,136	1,178	1,568	1,958
PERCY, Arthur (1886-1976) Swedish					
oil	4	8,913	1,457	1,872	3,713
PERCY, Herbert Sidney (fl.1880-1903) British					
oil	4	5,993	1,100	1,263	2,368
PERCY, Samuel (1750-1820) British					
3D	1	7,850		7,850	
PERCY, Sidney Richard (1821-1886) British					
oil	21	922,772	2,130	17,160	189,600
PERDIKIDIS (20th C) Greek					
oil	1	2,628		2,628	
PERE, Jean Baptiste le (1761-1844) French?					
wc/d	1	10,000		10,000	
PEREDA, Antonio de (1599-1669) Spanish					
oil	1	25,079		25,079	
PERELLI, Achille (1822-1891) American/Italian					
oil	1	4,300		4,300	
wc/d	1	1,400		1,400	
PERETTI, Achille (1857-1923) American					
oil	1	2,250		2,250	
PEREZ DE VILLAAMIL, Genaro (1807-1854) Spanish					
oil	6	358,867	4,886	22,305	218,384
wc/d	1	2,589		2,589	
PEREZ GIL, Jose (1918-1998) Spanish					
oil	2	8,890	1,013	4,445	7,877
PEREZ MUNOZ, Julian (1927-) Spanish					
oil	1	1,334		1,334	
PEREZ, Alonzo (fl.1893-1914) Spanish					
oil	2	8,425	1,625	4,213	6,800
PEREZ, Augusto (1929-) Italian					
3D	1	3,491		3,491	
PEREZ, Bartolomeo (1634-1693) Spanish					
oil	2	153,905	72,480	76,953	81,425
PEREZ, Mario (1960-) Argentinian					
oil	2	48,000	24,000	24,000	24,000
PERI, Lucien (1880-1948) French					
oil	1	1,693		1,693	
PERIGAL, A (19th C) British					
oil	1	8,216		8,216	
PERIGAL, Arthur (jnr) (1816-1884) British					
oil	2	3,545	1,080	1,773	2,465
PERIGNON, Alexis Nicolas (elder) (1726-1782) French					
wc/d	1	4,024		4,024	
PERILLI, Achille (1927-) Italian					
oil	3	22,711	4,951	7,618	10,142
wc/d	8	32,231	1,724	2,123	13,503
PERIN, Alfred Henri (1798-1874) French					
wc/d	1	1,455		1,455	
PERIS BRELL, Julio (1866-1944) Spanish					
oil	1	2,033		2,033	
PERIS MARCO, Vicente (1943-) Spanish					
oil	3	19,090	4,571	5,915	8,604
PERJONS, Per Hilding (1911-) Swedish?					
oil	1	1,039		1,039	
PERKINS (20th C) American					
wc/d	1	1,500		1,500	
PERKINS, David J (1936-) British					
oil	2	3,550	1,420	1,775	2,130

Name	No.	Total Sales Value	lowest	Prices median	highest
PERKINS, Granville (1830-1895) American					
oil	4	21,400	1,900	5,000	9,500
PERLBERG, Friedrich (1848-1921) German					
oil	3	15,778	5,009	5,009	5,760
PERLMUTTER, Jack (1920-) American					
oil	1	1,000		1,000	
PERMAN, Louise E (1854-1921) British					
oil	2	10,266	4,134	5,133	6,132
PERMEKE (20th C) Belgian					
wc/d	1	13,447		13,447	
PERMEKE, Constant (1886-1952) Belgian					
oil	9	57,385	2,135	5,695	14,983
wc/d	10	84,709	1,391	5,920	17,795
PERMEKE, Hendrik Lodewyk (1849-1912) Belgian					
oil	1	4,178		4,178	
PERMEKE, Joopie (1938-) Belgian					
3D	1	1,462		1,462	
PERMEKE, Paul (1918-1990) Belgian					
oil	10	19,108	1,236	1,814	2,859
PERNELLE, Ernest (1870-?) French					
oil	1	1,104		1,104	
PERNES, Leo (19/20th C) ?					
oil	1	1,446		1,446	
PERNET, Alexandre (19th C) French					
wc/d	1	2,166		2,166	
PERNET, Jean Henry Alexandre (1763-?) French					
wc/d	3	10,121	1,000	1,812	7,309
PEROT, Luc (1922-1985) Belgian					
oil	1	1,068		1,068	
PEROT-CANET (19th C) French					
oil	1	7,172		7,172	
PERRACHON, Andre (1827-1909) French					
oil	1	28,835		28,835	
PERRAULT-HARRY, Emile (1878-1938) French					
3D	1	2,826		2,826	
PERRET, Aime (1847-1927) French					
oil	6	30,241	1,132	4,396	10,000
PERREY, Louis (1856-?) French					
oil	1	2,642		2,642	
PERREZ, Sophie (19th C) ?					
oil	1	1,193		1,193	
PERRI, Frank (20th C) American					
oil	2	2,800	1,000	1,400	1,800
PERRIE, Bertha Eversfield (1868-1921) American					
oil	1	2,000		2,000	
PERRIER, Alexandre (1862-1936) Swiss					
oil	2	6,608	1,481	3,304	5,127
PERRON, C (20th C) Continental					
oil	1	1,323		1,323	
PERRONEAU, Jean Baptiste (1715-1783) French					
oil	1	28,000		28,000	
wc/d	1	5,819		5,819	
PERROT, Ferdinand (1808-1841) French					
oil	1	3,243		3,243	
PERRY, Enoch Wood (1831-1915) American					
oil	1	12,000		12,000	
PERRY, Lilla Cabot (1848-1933) American					
oil	1	12,000		12,000	

Name	No.	Total Sales Value	Prices lowest	median	highest
PERRY, Roland Hinton (1870-1949) American					
3D	2	3,500	1,700	1,750	1,800
PERSHAKOV, Alexander Feodorovitch (1843-?) Russian?					
oil	1	7,010		7,010	
PERSIAN SCHOOL, 16th/17th C					
wc/d	1	5,497		5,497	
PERSIAN SCHOOL, 17th C					
wc/d	2	11,236	5,618	5,618	5,618
PERSIAN SCHOOL, 19th C					
3D	1	6,490		6,490	
oil	1	12,266		12,266	
PERSOGLIA, Franz von (1852-1912) Austrian					
oil	4	20,248	2,010	5,169	7,901
PERSON, Henri (1876-1926) French					
wc/d	2	3,387	1,175	1,694	2,212
PERSSON, Peter Adolf (1862-1914) Swedish					
oil	5	10,768	1,747	2,194	2,575
PERSSON, Ragnar (1905-1993) Swedish					
oil	42	132,829	1,091	2,312	16,925
PERUGINI, Charles Edward (1839-1918) British					
oil	1	10,010		10,010	
PERUVIAN COLONIAL SCHOOL, 18th C					
3D	1	13,928		13,928	
PERUZZI, Osvaldo (1907-) Italian					
wc/d	1	1,440		1,440	
PERUZZINI, Antonio Francesco (1668-?) Italian					
oil	1	24,000		24,000	
PESARO, Cesare (19th C) Italian					
oil	1	1,500		1,500	
PESCE, Gaetano (1939-) ?					
3D	6	138,475	12,325	17,425	55,000
PESCHAUBES, Eugene (1890-1967) French?					
oil	1	1,010		1,010	
PESCHKE, Christian (1946-) German					
3D	2	12,043	4,169	6,022	7,874
oil	2	4,030	1,525	2,015	2,505
PESELLINO, Francesco (1422-1457) Italian					
oil	1	482,738		482,738	
PESENTI, Domenico (1843-1918) Italian					
oil	1	2,844		2,844	
PESKE, Jean (1870-1949) French					
oil	3	9,042	2,036	2,948	4,058
PESNE, Antoine (1683-1757) French					
oil	1	8,546		8,546	
PESSERS, Henriette (1899-?) Dutch					
oil	1	2,581		2,581	
PETER, Axel (1863-1942) Swedish					
oil	3	6,399	1,345	1,758	3,296
PETER, Victor (1840-1918) French					
3D	1	1,638		1,638	
PETER, Wenzel Johann (1742-1829) Austrian					
oil	1	18,424		18,424	
PETERELLE, Adolphe (1874-1947) French					
oil	3	5,841	1,282	1,995	2,564
PETERS (?) ?					
oil	1	2,259		2,259	
PETERS, Anna (1843-1926) German					
oil	14	62,983	1,341	3,371	11,385

Name	No.	Total Sales Value	lowest	Prices median	highest
PETERS, Carl W (1897-1988) American					
oil	5	19,250	3,000	4,000	5,250
PETERS, Charles Rollo (1862-1928) American					
oil	2	12,250	4,250	6,125	8,000
PETERS, E (19th C) ?					
oil	1	5,909		5,909	
PETERS, Herbert (1925-) German?					
3D	1	2,145		2,145	
PETERS, Matthew William (1742-1814) British					
oil	3	74,870	1,600	32,500	40,770
PETERS, Otto (1858-1908) Austrian					
oil	1	5,075		5,075	
PETERS, Pieter Francis (1818-1903) Dutch					
oil	8	31,180	1,290	2,658	9,083
wc/d	2	3,625	1,167	1,813	2,458
PETERS, Pietronella (1848-1924) German					
oil	4	22,473	2,212	3,846	12,570
PETERS, Udo (1884-1964) German					
oil	1	1,366		1,366	
PETERSEN, Anna (1845-1910) Danish					
oil	1	8,119		8,119	
PETERSEN, Armand (1891-1969) Swiss/French					
3D	18	73,979	1,127	3,243	10,714
PETERSEN, Edvard (1841-1911) Danish					
oil	5	23,809	1,033	2,900	12,263
PETERSEN, Emmanuel Aage (1894-1948) Danish					
oil	10	15,315	1,039	1,544	2,172
PETERSEN, H (19th C) ?					
oil	1	1,160		1,160	
PETERSEN, Hans Gyde (1862-1943) Danish					
oil	1	1,427		1,427	
PETERSEN, Hans Ritter von (1850-1914) German					
oil	1	2,572		2,572	
PETERSEN, Jakob (1774-1854) Danish					
oil	1	8,305		8,305	
wc/d	3	8,694	2,201	3,040	3,453
PETERSEN, Johan Erik Chr (1839-1874) Danish					
oil	1	10,000		10,000	
PETERSEN, Lorenz (1803-1870) German					
oil	2	8,520	4,145	4,260	4,375
PETERSEN, Lorenz and HOLM, Peter Christian (19th C) German					
oil	2	6,490	1,658	3,245	4,832
PETERSEN, Olaf (20th C) Norwegian					
oil	1	4,500		4,500	
PETERSEN, Robert Storm (1882-1949) Danish					
wc/d	2	2,901	1,087	1,451	1,814
PETERSEN, Roland (1926-) American					
oil	3	43,500	7,500	16,000	20,000
PETERSEN, Sophus (1837-1904) Danish					
oil	3	18,506	1,588	8,340	8,578
PETERSEN, Stefan Viggo (1891-1965) Danish					
oil	1	1,443		1,443	
PETERSEN, Vilhelm (1812-1880) Danish					
oil	3	12,527	1,192	4,786	6,549
PETERSON, Jane (1876-1965) American					
oil	20	722,741	2,000	10,875	200,000
wc/d	16	187,800	1,000	3,600	37,000
PETERSON, Martin (fl.1933) American					
oil	1	2,800		2,800	

Name	No.	Total Sales Value	lowest	Prices median	highest
PETERSON, Roger Tory (1908-1996) American					
wc/d	1	1,908		1,908	
PETERSON, Roland (1926-) American					
oil	2	15,600	4,600	7,800	11,000
PETERSSON, Axel (1868-1925) Swedish					
3D	12	55,121	1,524	3,791	9,932
PETHER, Abraham (1756-1812) British					
oil	2	7,990	2,556	3,995	5,434
PETHER, Henry (fl.1828-1865) British					
oil	2	33,260	6,080	16,630	27,180
PETHER, Sebastian (1790-1844) British					
oil	3	6,501	1,413	1,704	3,384
PETILLION, Jules (1845-1899) French					
oil	5	32,756	1,557	7,129	13,000
PETIT, B le (17th C) Dutch					
oil	1	4,030		4,030	
PETIT, Charles (19th C) French?					
oil	3	14,400	2,610	4,250	7,540
PETIT, Eugène (1839-1886) French					
oil	4	20,954	1,661	4,907	9,480
PETIT, Eugène Joseph (1845-?) French					
oil	4	8,167	1,474	2,010	2,674
PETIT-GERARD, Pierre (1852-?) French					
oil	1	1,729		1,729	
PETITI, Filiberto (1845-1924) Italian					
oil	2	7,344	2,299	3,672	5,045
PETITJEAN, E (1844-1925) French					
oil	1	3,031		3,031	
PETITJEAN, Edmond (1844-1925) French					
oil	25	131,627	1,354	3,917	22,000
PETITJEAN, Hippolyte (1854-1929) French					
oil	5	53,126	3,283	5,733	22,650
wc/d	1	3,000		3,000	
PETITJEAN, Victor (19/20th C) French?					
oil	1	2,667		2,667	
PETITOT, Joseph (1771-?) French					
oil	1	1,418		1,418	
wc/d	1	1,215		1,215	
PETITPIERRE, Petra (1905-1959) Swiss					
oil	2	2,685	1,211	1,343	1,474
PETLEY, Roy (1951-) British					
oil	4	7,035	1,057	1,857	2,370
PETLEY-JONES, Llewellyn (1908-1986) Canadian					
oil	3	5,437	1,279	2,079	2,079
PETO, John F (1854-1907) American					
oil	3	47,000	5,000	10,000	32,000
PETRASSI, Luigi (1868-1948) Italian					
oil	2	2,792	1,134	1,396	1,658
PETRELLA DA BOLOGNA, Vittorio (1886-1951) Italian					
oil	1	1,098		1,098	
PETRI, P (?) ?					
oil	1	1,300		1,300	
PETRIE, George (1790-1866) British					
wc/d	1	3,432		3,432	
PETRIE, Graham (1859-1940) British					
oil	1	1,224		1,224	
PETRILLI, Professor A (19th C) Italian					
3D	1	2,000		2,000	

Name	No.	Total Sales Value	lowest	Prices median	highest
PETRINI (?) Italian					
oil	2	4,772	2,054	2,386	2,718
PETRINI, Giuseppe Antonio (1677-1758) Italian					
oil	2	36,274	3,054	18,137	33,220
PETRITSKY, Anatoli (1895-1964) Russian					
oil	1	11,650		11,650	
PETROV-VODKIN, Kuzma (1878-1939) Russian					
wc/d	2	17,156	5,076	8,578	12,080
PETROVICHEV, Piotr Ivanovich (1874-1947) Russian					
oil	2	3,322	1,057	1,661	2,265
PETRUOLO, Salvatore (1857-1946) Italian					
oil	4	17,535	1,494	3,252	9,538
wc/d	1	1,493		1,493	
PETTENELLA, E (19th C) ?					
3D	1	1,835		1,835	
PETTENKOFEN, August von (1822-1889) Austrian					
oil	3	58,913	10,500	21,000	27,413
wc/d	1	2,764		2,764	
PETTER, Franz Xaver (1791-1866) Austrian					
oil	3	48,630	11,962	15,734	20,934
PETTERSEN, Arvid (1943-) Norwegian					
oil	3	6,181	1,054	1,671	3,456
PETTERSON, Johan (1957-) Swedish					
oil	1	1,081		1,081	
PETTIBON, Raymond (1957-) American					
oil	2	29,000	12,000	14,500	17,000
wc/d	8	20,550	1,600	2,375	3,800
PETTIBONE, Richard (1938-) American					
oil	2	84,500	2,000	42,250	82,500
PETTIBONE, Shirley (20th C) American?					
oil	1	2,200		2,200	
PETTIE, John (1839-1893) British					
oil	1	1,208		1,208	
PETTINGALE, W E (19/20th C) British					
oil	1	1,332		1,332	
PETTITT, Charles (19th C) British					
oil	1	1,291		1,291	
PETTITT, George (1831-1863) British					
oil	2	8,969	2,669	4,485	6,300
PETTITT, J A Coniston (19/20th C) British					
oil	1	1,323		1,323	
PETTITT, Joseph Paul (?-1882) British					
oil	3	16,184	2,914	3,975	9,295
PETTITT, Wilfred Stanley (1904-) British					
oil	1	1,199		1,199	
PETTRICH, Ferdinand Friedrich August (1798-1872) German					
3D	1	22,000		22,000	
PETZHOLDT, Fritz (1805-1838) Danish					
oil	3	11,750	1,574	2,159	8,017
PETZOLD, Werner (20th C) German?					
oil	2	3,456	1,462	1,728	1,994
PEVERELLI, Cesare (1922-2000) Italian					
oil	3	4,051	1,018	1,249	1,784
wc/d	1	1,571		1,571	
PEVERNAGIE, Erik (1939-) Belgian					
oil	11	37,341	3,029	3,372	3,796
wc/d	5	16,205	2,925	3,239	3,678
PEVERNAGIE, Louis (1904-1970) Belgian					
oil	3	8,377	1,716	3,359	3,359

Name	No.	Total Sales Value	Prices lowest	median	highest
PEVSNER, Antoine (1886-1962) Russian					
oil	1	108,871		108,871	
wc/d	2	11,825	5,841	5,913	5,984
PEYNET, Raymond (1908-) French					
wc/d	1	1,291		1,291	
PEYNOT, Émile Edmond (1850-1932) French					
3D	2	59,600	14,600	29,800	45,000
PEYRAUD, Frank Charles (1858-1948) American					
oil	2	5,400	1,900	2,700	3,500
PEYRE, Raphael (1872-1949) French					
3D	3	27,273	1,353	11,520	14,400
PEYRISSAC, Jean (1895-1974) French					
3D	2	12,213	5,143	6,107	7,070
oil	1	4,976		4,976	
wc/d	4	12,404	1,197	3,592	4,024
PEYRO-URREA, Juan (1847-1924) Spanish					
oil	1	17,000		17,000	
PEYTON, Bertha S Menzler (1871-1950) American					
oil	1	27,500		27,500	
PEYTON, Elizabeth (1965-) American					
oil	2	81,000	21,000	40,500	60,000
wc/d	1	9,000		9,000	
PEZOUS, Jean (1815-1885) French					
oil	1	2,921		2,921	
PEZZINO, Antonio (20th C) South American					
oil	2	2,750	1,300	1,375	1,450
PEZZO, Lucio del (1933-) Italian					
3D	2	18,623	1,223	9,312	17,400
oil	3	4,749	1,170	1,731	1,848
wc/d	2	5,239	1,099	2,620	4,140
PFAHLER, Karl Georg (1926-) German					
oil	4	19,390	1,742	4,698	8,252
wc/d	2	5,206	2,178	2,603	3,028
PFANNENSTIEL, Rudolf (1888-1979) German					
oil	1	1,708		1,708	
PFEFFERKORN, Felix Samuel (1945-) German					
oil	10	15,115	1,001	1,512	1,911
PFEIFFER, Francois Joseph (jnr) (1778-1835) Dutch					
wc/d	1	2,056		2,056	
PFEIFFER, Wilhelm (1822-1891) German					
oil	3	3,767	1,215	1,276	1,276
PFEILER, Maximilian (18th C) German					
oil	1	8,000		8,000	
PFISTER, Albert (1884-?) Swiss					
oil	1	3,342		3,342	
PFORR, Johann Georg (1745-1798) German					
oil	1	6,651		6,651	
PFUND, Alois (1876-1946) Austrian					
oil	1	1,079		1,079	
PFUND, Roger (1943-) Swiss					
oil	1	2,552		2,552	
PFYFFER, Niklaus (1836-1908) Swiss					
oil	1	1,139		1,139	
PHADNIS, H M (?) Indian					
wc/d	1	1,650		1,650	
PHELAN, Charles T (1840-?) American					
oil	2	3,016	1,016	1,508	2,000
PHELPS, William Preston (1848-1923) American					
oil	6	25,200	1,300	2,950	11,000

Name	No.	Total Sales Value	lowest	Prices median	highest
PHILIP, James George (?) British					
wc/d	2	3,225	1,110	1,613	2,115
PHILIP, John (?) British?					
oil	1	1,184		1,184	
PHILIPAULT, Julie (1780-1834) French					
oil	1	13,742		13,742	
PHILIPP, Robert (1895-1981) American					
oil	9	27,100	1,200	2,600	6,000
PHILIPPE (?) French					
3D	1	3,000		3,000	
PHILIPPE, P (19/20th C) French					
3D	2	16,445	7,150	8,223	9,295
PHILIPPE, Paul (fl.1920-1929) French					
3D	3	35,741	3,972	14,903	16,866
oil	1	1,929		1,929	
PHILIPPEAU, Karel Frans (1825-1897) Dutch					
oil	1	1,500		1,500	
PHILIPPET, Léon (1843-1906) Belgian					
oil	1	3,134		3,134	
PHILIPPOT, Karl Ludwig (1801-1859) French					
oil	1	2,700		2,700	
PHILIPPOTEAUX, Henri Felix Emmanuel (1815-1884) French					
oil	1	61,421		61,421	
wc/d	1	1,854		1,854	
PHILIPPOTEAUX, Paul Dominique (1846-?) American					
oil	1	4,582		4,582	
wc/d	1	3,104		3,104	
PHILIPS, Charles (1708-1747) British					
oil	1	37,750		37,750	
PHILIPS, F A (19/20th C) British					
oil	1	1,133		1,133	
PHILIPS, G W F (19th C) ?					
oil	1	1,349		1,349	
PHILIPS, Richard (1681-1741) British					
oil	1	8,820		8,820	
PHILIPSEN, Theodor (1840-1920) Danish					
3D	1	2,668		2,668	
oil	11	25,146	1,191	2,566	3,480
wc/d	1	1,700		1,700	
PHILIPSEN, Victor (1841-1907) French					
oil	1	1,549		1,549	
PHILIPSON, Robin (1916-1992) British					
oil	14	194,145	5,214	6,738	55,480
wc/d	3	20,570	1,976	9,480	9,480
PHILLIP, John (1817-1867) British					
oil	4	31,530	1,885	4,673	20,300
PHILLIP, John and ANSDELL, Richard (19th C) British					
oil	1	14,220		14,220	
PHILLIPPE (fl.1900-1930) French					
3D	1	13,585		13,585	
PHILLIPPE, P (fl.1900-1930) French					
wc/d	1	1,146		1,146	
PHILLIPS, Ammi (1787-1865) American					
oil	3	30,000	6,000	7,000	17,000
PHILLIPS, Bert G (1868-1956) American					
oil	2	14,000	6,500	7,000	7,500
wc/d	1	32,500		32,500	
PHILLIPS, Harriet (fl.1840-1860) British					
oil	1	2,160		2,160	

Name	No.	Total Sales Value	lowest	Prices median	highest
PHILLIPS, John Campbell (1873-1949) American					
oil	1	1,100		1,100	
PHILLIPS, Peter (1939-) British					
oil	2	3,256	1,480	1,628	1,776
wc/d	1	1,560		1,560	
PHILLIPS, S George (20th C) American					
oil	2	6,000	2,500	3,000	3,500
PHILLIPS, Tom (1937-) British					
oil	1	6,795		6,795	
PHILLIPS, W J (1884-1963) American/Canadian					
wc/d	1	2,190		2,190	
PHILLIPS, Walter Joseph (1884-1963) American/Canadian					
wc/d	7	51,140	3,700	6,530	11,351
PHILLOTT, Constance (1842-1931) British					
wc/d	2	14,729	6,435	7,365	8,294
PHILP, James George (1816-1885) British					
oil	1	1,193		1,193	
PHILPOT, Glyn (1884-1937) British					
oil	12	183,045	2,030	6,162	63,200
wc/d	1	2,370		2,370	
PHIPPEN, George (1915-1966) American					
oil	1	1,650		1,650	
PIACENTINO, Gianni (1945-) Italian					
3D	2	9,692	2,898	4,846	6,794
PIACENZA, Carlo (1814-1887) Italian					
oil	2	4,394	1,758	2,197	2,636
PIACESI, Walter (1929-) Italian					
oil	8	13,313	1,126	1,541	2,693
PIANA, Giuseppe Ferdinando (1864-1958) Italian					
oil	2	13,295	1,802	6,648	11,493
PIANCA, Giuseppe Antonio (1703-1757) Italian					
oil	1	4,083		4,083	
PIANE, Giovanni Maria delle (1660-1745) Italian					
oil	2	34,046	13,649	17,023	20,397
PIAT, Frederic Eugène (1827-1903) French					
3D	1	1,595		1,595	
PIATTI, Antonio (1875-1962) Italian					
oil	5	15,056	1,605	2,676	5,504
PIATTOLI, Giuseppe (fl.1785-1807) Italian					
wc/d	2	21,152	5,880	10,576	15,272
PIAUBERT, Jean (1900-) French					
oil	6	7,587	1,009	1,355	1,442
wc/d	3	4,174	1,309	1,309	1,556
PIAZZA, A (?) Italian					
3D	1	3,500		3,500	
PIAZZA, Calisto (1505-1561) Italian					
oil	1	117,600		117,600	
PIAZZETTA, Giambattista (1682-1754) Italian					
oil	2	33,883	12,495	16,942	21,388
wc/d	6	154,372	8,188	21,895	60,400
PIAZZETTA, Giambattista (school) (1682-1754) Italian					
oil	1	2,732		2,732	
PIAZZONI, Gottardo (1872-1945) American/Swiss					
oil	1	3,000		3,000	
PICABIA, Francis (1878-1953) French					
oil	20	1,791,016	8,698	39,260	460,000
wc/d	25	630,367	2,658	8,639	170,000
PICARD, Georges (1857-?) French?					
oil	2	12,763	1,514	6,382	11,249
wc/d	1	1,370		1,370	

Name	No.	Total Sales Value	Prices lowest	median	highest
PICARD, Louis (1861-?) French					
oil	1	10,000		10,000	
PICART LE DOUX, Charles (1881-1959) French					
oil	2	2,859	1,113	1,430	1,746
PICART, Jean Michel (1600-1682) Flemish					
oil	1	85,000		85,000	
PICASSO (20th C) Spanish					
3D	1	2,115		2,115	
wc/d	1	1,911		1,911	
PICASSO, Pablo (1881-1973) Spanish					
3D	64	5,271,358	1,355	8,338	2,265,000
oil	32	138,890,305	2,905	975,650	50,000,000
wc/d	119	7,963,751	1,160	37,156	470,000
PICAULT, E (1839-1915) French					
3D	3	7,517	1,862	2,025	3,630
PICAULT, Émile (1839-1915) French					
3D	18	54,549	1,045	1,494	16,000
PICCIOLI, M (20th C) Italian					
3D	1	1,584		1,584	
PICHAT, Olivier (1820-1912) French					
oil	1	1,504		1,504	
PICHETTE, James (1920-1996) French					
oil	4	6,543	1,033	1,436	2,638
wc/d	2	2,135	1,028	1,068	1,107
PICHHADZE, Meir (1955-) Israeli					
oil	4	19,700	1,300	5,200	8,000
PICHLER, Antonio (1802-?) Italian					
3D	1	4,374		4,374	
PICHON, Charles (20th C) French					
wc/d	1	2,190		2,190	
PICHOT GIRONES, Ramon Antonio (1872-1925) Spanish					
oil	2	4,239	2,081	2,120	2,158
PICHOT, Ramon (1924-1996) Spanish					
oil	6	26,293	1,400	4,689	6,189
PICK, Anton (1840-?) Austrian					
oil	1	1,796		1,796	
PICKARDT, Ernst (1876-1931) German					
oil	1	2,272		2,272	
PICKERING, Henry (18th C) British					
oil	1	13,156		13,156	
PICKERING, Joseph Langsdale (1845-1912) British					
oil	2	5,188	2,485	2,594	2,703
PICKERSGILL, Henry William (1782-1875) British					
oil	2	4,920	1,937	2,460	2,983
PICKETT, M S (19th C) British					
wc/d	1	1,160		1,160	
PICKNELL, William Lamb (1854-1897) American					
oil	2	70,000	32,000	35,000	38,000
PICOT (?) ?					
oil	1	2,166		2,166	
PICOU (?) French					
oil	1	3,992		3,992	
PICOU, Henri Pierre (1824-1895) French					
oil	2	33,000	14,000	16,500	19,000
PICQUE, Charles (1799-1869) Belgian					
oil	1	13,753		13,753	
PICZECK, F (19th C) ?					
oil	1	2,844		2,844	

Name	No.	Total Sales Value	lowest	Prices median	highest
PIDDING, Henry James (1797-1864) British					
oil	2	42,280	12,080	21,140	30,200
PIDELASERRA BRIAS, Marian (1877-1946) Spanish					
oil	2	2,520	1,257	1,260	1,263
PIECK, Anton (1895-1987) Dutch					
oil	1	10,903		10,903	
PIEDMONTESE SCHOOL, 16th C Italian					
oil	1	10,435		10,435	
PIEDMONTESE SCHOOL, 17th C Italian					
oil	1	5,184		5,184	
PIEDMONTESE SCHOOL, 17th/18th C Italian					
oil	1	4,621		4,621	
PIEDMONTESE SCHOOL, 18th C Italian					
oil	7	89,824	6,403	9,117	33,220
PIEDMONTESE SCHOOL, 19th C Italian					
3D	1	61,126		61,126	
PIELER, F X (1879-1952) Austrian					
oil	1	2,100		2,100	
PIELER, Franz Xaver (1879-1952) Austrian					
oil	2	12,476	3,872	6,238	8,604
PIENE, Otto (1928-) German					
oil	7	35,171	1,328	4,728	11,650
wc/d	6	19,822	1,081	2,145	7,597
PIEPENHAGEN, August (1791-1868) Polish					
oil	1	6,479		6,479	
PIEPHO, Karl (1869-1920) German					
oil	1	1,065		1,065	
PIERACCINI, E (?) Italian					
wc/d	1	1,236		1,236	
PIERCE, Charles Franklin (1844-1920) American					
oil	1	1,900		1,900	
PIERDON, François (1821-1904) French					
oil	1	2,653		2,653	
PIERNEEF, Jacob Hendrik (1886-1957) South African					
oil	1	38,160		38,160	
PIERON, Henry (19th C) French					
oil	2	3,394	1,488	1,697	1,906
PIERRAKOS, Alkis (1920-) ?					
oil	4	5,348	1,273	1,337	1,401
PIERRAT, Nicolas-Constant (1829-1910) French					
oil	2	3,246	1,623	1,623	1,623
PIERRE and GILLES (20th C) French					
oil	1	5,312		5,312	
PIERRE, Andre (1914-) Haitian					
oil	1	1,900		1,900	
PIERRE, Jean Baptiste Marie (1713-1789) French					
oil	3	82,524	17,524	25,000	40,000
PIERSON, Jack (1960-) American					
3D	4	153,500	16,000	36,250	65,000
oil	1	16,000		16,000	
wc/d	2	13,500	3,500	6,750	10,000
PIET, Fernand (1869-1942) French					
oil	2	4,497	1,354	2,249	3,143
PIETERS, E (1856-1932) Dutch					
oil	1	4,345		4,345	
PIETERS, Evert (1856-1932) Dutch					
oil	18	135,572	1,553	5,975	20,890
PIETRI, Pietro Antonio de (1663-1716) Italian					
wc/d	1	1,208		1,208	

Name	No.	Total Sales Value	Prices lowest	median	highest
PIETRI, Pietro Michele de (19th C) Italian					
wc/d	1	1,492		1,492	
PIETRO DI DOMENICO (1457-?) Italian					
oil	1	42,762		42,762	
PIETRO DI FRANCESCO DEGLI ORIOLI (1458-1496) Italian					
oil	2	240,240	30,240	120,120	210,000
PIETRO DI RUFFOLO (15th C) Italian					
oil	1	13,000		13,000	
PIETSCHMANN, Max (1865-?) German					
oil	1	1,723		1,723	
PIETTE, Ludovic (1826-1877) French					
oil	1	3,987		3,987	
PIETZSCH, Richard (1872-1960) German					
oil	1	1,277		1,277	
PIFFARD, Harold (fl.1895-1899) British					
oil	4	14,402	1,208	3,747	5,700
PIFFARD, Henry (1850-?) British					
oil	1	1,470		1,470	
PIFFARETTI, Bernard (20th C) French					
oil	2	6,820	2,707	3,410	4,113
PIGEON, Maurice (19/20th C) French?					
oil	1	2,140		2,140	
PIGHLEIN, Elimar Ulrich Bruno (1848-1894) German					
oil	2	8,051	1,364	4,026	6,687
PIGNATELLI, Ercole (1935-) Italian					
oil	1	2,542		2,542	
PIGNATELLI, Luca (1962-) Italian					
wc/d	1	10,191		10,191	
PIGNON, Edouard (1905-1993) French					
oil	12	76,468	1,355	4,298	22,353
wc/d	30	62,002	1,027	2,266	3,793
PIGNON-ERNEST, Ernest (1942-) French					
wc/d	2	3,222	1,056	1,611	2,166
PIGNONE, Joseph (20th C) American					
wc/d	1	2,600		2,600	
PIGNONI, Simone (1614-1698) Italian					
oil	1	10,570		10,570	
PIGNOTTI, Lamberto (20th C) Italian					
wc/d	1	1,964		1,964	
PIGOTT, Charles (1863-c.1940) British					
wc/d	1	1,110		1,110	
PIGOTT, W H (19th C) British					
wc/d	1	2,198		2,198	
PIGOTT, William Henry (c.1835-1901) British					
wc/d	1	1,185		1,185	
PIGUET, Jean Louis (1944-) Swiss					
oil	2	2,299	1,016	1,150	1,283
PIKE, Sidney (fl.1880-1901) British					
oil	3	8,276	1,963	1,963	4,350
wc/d	2	2,356	1,178	1,178	1,178
PIKE, William H (1846-1908) British					
oil	2	3,675	1,800	1,838	1,875
wc/d	3	7,929	1,963	2,669	3,297
PILET, Léon (1839-1916) French					
3D	1	1,711		1,711	
PILKINGTON, Penelope (?) British					
oil	1	1,323		1,323	
PILLE, Charles Henri (1844-1897) French					
wc/d	1	1,018		1,018	

Name	No.	Total Sales Value	Prices lowest	median	highest
PILLEMENT, Jean (1728-1808) French					
oil	4	82,918	2,218	11,833	57,034
wc/d	8	75,018	1,911	4,750	45,300
PILLET, Edgar (1912-1996) French					
oil	2	4,576	2,199	2,288	2,377
wc/d	2	2,709	1,283	1,355	1,426
PILNY, Otto (1866-1936) Swiss					
oil	11	299,732	2,004	11,388	93,149
PILO, Carl Gustaf (1712-1792) Swedish					
oil	3	41,217	6,924	15,000	19,293
PILO, Carl Gustaf (school) (1712-1792) Swedish					
oil	1	2,519		2,519	
PILON, E Agathe (19th C) French					
oil	1	28,000		28,000	
PILON, Germain (1535-1590) French					
3D	1	724,800		724,800	
PILOT, Robert Wakeham (1898-1967) Canadian					
oil	15	181,941	2,201	6,305	66,368
PILOTY, Karl Theodor von (1824-1886) German					
oil	3	5,314	1,594	1,800	1,920
PILS, Isidore (1813-1875) French					
oil	3	25,439	1,933	7,506	16,000
wc/d	3	35,323	1,655	5,657	28,011
PILZ, Otto (1876-1934) German					
3D	1	6,034		6,034	
oil	1	2,918		2,918	
PIMM, William Edwin (1863-1952) British					
oil	1	1,590		1,590	
PINA, Alfredo (1887-1966) Italian					
3D	5	19,553	1,994	3,003	6,178
PINAL, Fernand (1881-1958) French					
oil	2	2,715	1,047	1,358	1,668
PINATEL, R (19/20th C) French?					
oil	1	2,921		2,921	
PINAZO, Ignacio (?) ?					
oil	1	3,775		3,775	
wc/d	1	3,239		3,239	
PINCEMIN, Jean-Pierre (1944-) French					
oil	12	116,500	2,483	8,689	23,144
wc/d	3	18,366	3,351	7,123	7,892
PINCHART, Émile Auguste (1842-1924) French					
oil	2	11,974	4,673	5,987	7,301
PINCHON, Robert Antoine (1886-1943) French					
oil	8	75,533	4,345	7,039	21,052
wc/d	1	3,210		3,210	
PINDON, H Pillard (19th C) ?					
wc/d	1	2,220		2,220	
PINE, Robert Edge (1742-1788) British					
oil	1	7,500		7,500	
PINEDA, Jose (19th C) ?					
oil	1	2,389		2,389	
PINEDA-MONTON, Miguel (?) Spanish					
oil	1	5,372		5,372	
PINEDO, Émile (1840-1916) French					
3D	4	7,506	1,300	1,831	2,544
PINEL DE GRANDCHAMP, Louis-Émile (1831-1894) French					
oil	4	84,811	10,311	14,750	45,000
wc/d	1	1,022		1,022	
PINELLI, Achille (19th C) Italian					
wc/d	1	4,740		4,740	

Name	No.	Total Sales Value	Prices lowest	median	highest
PINELLI, Auguste de (1823-1890) French					
oil	1	36,088		36,088	
PINELLI, Bartolomeo (1781-1835) Italian					
wc/d	5	9,673	1,240	1,547	2,861
PINERA Y PEREZ, Juan (?-1878) Spanish					
oil	1	1,368		1,368	
PINGGERA, H (1900-) Italian					
oil	1	4,800		4,800	
PINGGERA, Heinz (1900-) Italian					
oil	1	5,000		5,000	
PINGRET, Charles (?) French?					
oil	1	2,105		2,105	
PINGRET, E H T (1788-1875) French					
oil	1	1,066		1,066	
PINGRET, Edouard Henri Theophile (1788-1875) French					
oil	3	21,018	3,418	3,418	14,000
PINHEIRO, Oscar (19/20th C) Portuguese					
oil	1	4,084		4,084	
PINOLE Y RODRIGUEZ, Nicanor (1877-?) Spanish					
oil	1	1,943		1,943	
PINOS, Juan (1862-1910) Spanish					
oil	2	4,063	1,509	2,032	2,554
PINOT, Albert (1875-1962) Belgian					
oil	1	1,120		1,120	
PINTO, Abdon (?-1918) Venezuelan					
oil	1	2,390		2,390	
PINTURICCHIO, Bernardino (1454-1513) Italian					
oil	1	5,000		5,000	
PIOLA, Domenico (17/18th C) Italian					
wc/d	6	26,066	1,056	2,864	12,080
PIOLA, Domenico (elder) (1627-1703) Italian					
wc/d	1	1,510		1,510	
PIOLA, Paolo Gerolamo (1666-1724) Italian					
wc/d	2	2,813	1,061	1,407	1,752
PIOT, Adolphe (1850-1910) French					
oil	3	16,600	1,100	4,500	11,000
PIOT, Jacques Samuel Louis (1743-1812) Swiss					
oil	1	3,797		3,797	
PIOTROWSKI, Antoni (1853-1924) Polish					
oil	1	6,743		6,743	
PIPAL, Viktor (1887-1971) Austrian					
oil	1	1,700		1,700	
PIPER, J (1903-1992) British					
wc/d	1	3,450		3,450	
PIPER, John (1903-1992) British					
oil	7	49,247	3,384	7,000	13,430
wc/d	49	256,406	1,092	3,666	23,700
PIPPAL, Hans Robert (1915-) Austrian					
oil	1	1,608		1,608	
PIPPEL, Otto (1878-1960) German					
oil	24	91,700	1,045	2,500	11,385
PIPPIG, Heiko (1951-) German					
oil	3	5,857	1,463	1,514	2,880
wc/d	1	2,184		2,184	
PIRA (1954-) ?					
3D	1	15,287		15,287	
PIRA, Gioacchino la (19th C) Italian					
wc/d	3	13,552	3,732	4,168	5,652

Name	No.	Total Sales Value	lowest	Prices median	highest
PIRANDELLO, Fausto (1899-1975) Italian					
oil	4	215,819	14,835	53,177	94,630
wc/d	6	11,058	1,244	1,893	2,170
PIRANESI, Giovan Battista (1720-1778) Italian					
wc/d	1	70,000		70,000	
PIRE, Ferdinand (1943-) Belgian					
wc/d	4	10,813	1,185	1,380	6,868
PIRE, Marcel (1913-1981) Belgian					
oil	2	13,045	1,306	6,523	11,739
PIRES, Yves (1958-) French					
3D	6	8,797	1,096	1,246	2,676
PIRIE, Sir George (1863-1946) British					
oil	3	13,631	1,176	1,430	11,025
PIRKHERT, Alfred V (1887-1971) Yugoslavian					
oil	1	1,880		1,880	
PIRNGRUBER, Ottilie (19th c) ?					
oil	1	3,002		3,002	
PIROLA, René (1879-1912) French					
oil	1	1,896		1,896	
PIRON, Léon (1899-1962) Belgian					
oil	5	60,224	10,863	12,315	13,341
PIRONIN, Hortense (20th C) French					
oil	1	1,500		1,500	
PISANI, Gianni (1935-) Italian					
oil	1	2,960		2,960	
PISANI, Vettor (1938-) Italian					
wc/d	1	1,745		1,745	
PISANO, Giovanni (1875-1954) Italian					
oil	3	6,412	1,198	1,996	3,218
PISANO, Gustavo (1877-?) Italian					
oil	1	1,142		1,142	
PISIS, Filippo de (1896-1956) Italian					
3D	1	2,440		2,440	
oil	26	543,357	4,310	17,026	39,813
wc/d	10	30,827	1,249	2,055	6,435
PISKUNOV, V (1833-?) Russian					
oil	1	11,325		11,325	
PISSARRO, Camille (1830-1903) French					
oil	19	19,078,515	3,200	755,000	3,000,000
wc/d	37	3,402,453	2,679	11,600	1,750,000
PISSARRO, Claude (1935-) French					
oil	6	22,728	1,524	3,585	6,971
wc/d	2	7,329	1,329	3,665	6,000
PISSARRO, Lucien (1863-1944) British/French					
oil	6	259,515	20,410	48,000	60,630
wc/d	3	8,983	2,793	3,000	3,190
PISSARRO, Ludovic Rodo (1878-1952) French					
oil	11	21,087	1,047	1,440	3,339
PISSARRO, Paul Émile (1884-1972) French					
oil	9	26,333	1,476	3,000	5,192
wc/d	4	8,747	1,000	2,013	3,721
PISTOLETTO, Michelangelo (1933-) Italian					
oil	2	68,536	7,636	34,268	60,900
wc/d	2	36,964	1,964	18,482	35,000
PISTOR, Hermann (1832-?) German					
oil	1	2,544		2,544	
PISTORIUS, Eduard (1796-1862) German					
oil	1	14,500		14,500	
PITCHER, Neville Sotheby (20th C) British					
oil	3	6,035	1,200	1,738	3,097

Name	No.	Total Sales Value	lowest	Prices median	highest
PITHAWALLA, Manchershaw (1872-1937) Indian					
oil	1	7,200		7,200	
PITLOO, Antonio Sminck (1791-1837) Dutch					
oil	1	12,936		12,936	
PITMAN, John (19th C) British					
oil	1	3,432		3,432	
PITOCCHI, Matteo de (17th C) Italian					
oil	1	6,545		6,545	
PITT, William (19th C) British					
oil	6	22,010	1,059	1,774	9,940
PITTALUGA (19/20th C) Italian					
3D	1	3,710		3,710	
PITTARA, Carlo (1836-1890) Italian					
oil	1	5,131		5,131	
PITTMAN, Hobson (c.1899-1972) American					
wc/d	1	1,300		1,300	
PITTMAN, Lari (1952-) American					
oil	2	88,000	40,000	44,000	48,000
PITTO, Giacomo (1872-?) Italian					
oil	1	1,204		1,204	
PITTO, Guiseppe (1857-1928) Italian					
oil	1	1,721		1,721	
PITTONI, Giovanni Battista (younger) (1687-1767) Italian					
oil	2	266,000	52,850	133,000	213,150
PIZARRO, Cecilio (19th C) Spanish					
oil	1	1,204		1,204	
PIZZALA, P (19th C) Polish					
oil	1	4,250		4,250	
PIZZANI, Jorge (1949-) Venezuelan					
oil	1	1,150		1,150	
PIZZI CANNELLA, Piero (1955-) Italian					
oil	2	9,014	2,033	4,507	6,981
wc/d	1	5,787		5,787	
PIZZI, Carlo (19th C) Italian					
oil	1	18,000		18,000	
PIZZOLATTO, Eugenio (19th C) Italian					
oil	1	3,586		3,586	
PLA Y GALLARDO, Cecilio (1860-1934) Spanish					
oil	10	111,688	1,140	4,363	39,480
wc/d	1	1,299		1,299	
PLA Y RUBIO, Alberto (1867-1929) Spanish					
oil	2	10,506	2,506	5,253	8,000
PLAATZER VAN DER HULL, Hubert Willem (1810-c.1848) Dutch					
oil	1	1,875		1,875	
PLAGEMANN, Arnold (1826-1862) Swedish					
oil	3	3,914	1,304	1,304	1,306
PLAGEMANN, Augusta (1799-1888) Swedish					
oil	1	3,813		3,813	
PLAISANT, F (19th C) ?					
oil	1	3,375		3,375	
PLANCHON, Hippolyte (19th C) French					
oil	1	20,000		20,000	
PLANELLS, Angel (1902-1989) Spanish					
oil	1	1,807		1,807	
PLANES, Jose (20th C) Spanish					
3D	3	7,364	1,479	2,420	3,465
PLANGG, Werner (1933-1994) American					
oil	1	7,500		7,500	

Name	No.	Total Sales Value	lowest	Prices median	highest
PLANQUETTE, Felix (1873-1964) French					
oil	1	2,259		2,259	
PLANSON, Andre (1898-1981) French					
oil	11	23,288	1,139	1,963	4,124
wc/d	4	6,552	1,103	1,201	3,048
PLANSON, Joseph Alphonse (1799-?) French					
oil	1	1,329		1,329	
PLAS, Lourentius (1828-1888) Dutch					
oil	1	1,101		1,101	
PLAS, Nicholaas van der (1954-) Dutch					
oil	1	1,300		1,300	
PLAS, Pieter (1810-1853) Dutch					
oil	1	2,052		2,052	
PLASENCIA, Casto (1846-1890) Spanish					
oil	2	7,159	2,557	3,580	4,602
PLATE, Anna (1871-1941) German					
oil	1	1,364		1,364	
PLATNER, Ferdinand von (1824-1896) Italian					
oil	1	3,428		3,428	
PLATSCHEK, Hans (1923-) German					
wc/d	1	1,081		1,081	
PLATT, James C (?-1882) American					
oil	1	3,000		3,000	
PLATTEEL, Jean (fl.1839-1867) Belgian					
oil	1	4,260		4,260	
PLATTEMONTAGNE, Nicolas de (c.1631-1706) French					
wc/d	1	2,000		2,000	
PLATTNER, Karl (1919-1987) Austrian					
oil	3	61,692	3,928	16,636	41,128
PLATZ, Ernst Heinrich (1867-1940) German					
oil	1	2,917		2,917	
PLATZER, Johann Georg (1704-1761) Austrian					
oil	3	521,322	27,872	143,450	350,000
PLAUZEAU, Alfred (1875-1918) French					
oil	1	1,273		1,273	
PLAYFAIR, James Charles (fl.1865-1878) British					
wc/d	1	1,335		1,335	
PLAZZOTTA, Enzo (1921-1981) Italian					
3D	5	51,508	1,228	3,800	38,480
PLE, Henri Honore (1853-1922) French					
3D	1	5,624		5,624	
PLEISSNER, Ogden M (1905-1983) American					
oil	1	22,500		22,500	
wc/d	4	67,000	9,000	14,000	30,000
PLENSA, Jaume (1955-) Spanish					
3D	2	12,591	4,641	6,296	7,950
wc/d	7	23,909	1,365	3,565	4,848
PLESSEN, Hans Wilhelm (19th C) German					
oil	1	1,496		1,496	
PLESSI, Fabrizio (1940-) Italian					
wc/d	1	1,527		1,527	
PLEUER, Hermann (1863-1911) German					
oil	2	5,303	1,341	2,652	3,962
PLEYSIER, A (1809-1879) Dutch					
oil	1	2,250		2,250	
PLEYSIER, Ary (1809-1879) Dutch					
oil	2	6,810	2,151	3,405	4,659
PLISNIER, A (19/20th C) ?					
3D	1	1,501		1,501	

Name	No.	Total Sales Value	lowest	Prices median	highest
PLOMTEUX, Leopold (1920-) Belgian					
oil	1	4,436		4,436	
PLOSKY, Jonas (1940-) British					
oil	1	1,080		1,080	
PLOTNIKOFF, Vladimir Alexandrovitch (1866-?) Russian					
wc/d	1	2,255		2,255	
PLUCHART, Henri Eugène (1835-1898) French					
oil	1	3,582		3,582	
PLUM, Poul August (1815-1876) Danish					
oil	1	2,453		2,453	
PLUMMER, William Henry (1839-?) American					
oil	1	1,900		1,900	
PLUMOT, Andre (1829-1906) Belgian					
oil	3	23,665	2,904	7,008	13,753
POBBIATI, Mario (1887-?) Italian					
oil	5	15,762	2,463	3,448	3,448
POBOGENSKY, Wjatscheslaw (1943-) Russian					
oil	1	1,895		1,895	
POCOCK (?) British					
oil	1	3,016		3,016	
POCOCK, Nicholas (1740-1821) British					
oil	2	18,155	5,285	9,078	12,870
wc/d	7	23,491	1,290	3,234	6,594
PODCHERNIKOFF, Alexis Angelo (1912-1987) American					
oil	1	2,000		2,000	
PODCHERNIKOFF, Alexis M (1886-1933) American/Russian					
oil	1	5,500		5,500	
PODESTI, Vincenzo (1812-1897) Italian					
oil	1	9,312		9,312	
POEL, Egbert van der (1621-1664) Dutch					
oil	5	70,376	2,355	7,767	33,458
POELENBURGH, Cornelis van (1586-1667) Dutch					
oil	7	171,950	3,388	12,835	65,000
wc/d	1	2,000		2,000	
POELS, Albert (1903-1984) Belgian					
3D	1	1,891		1,891	
POERSON, Charles (1609-1667) French					
oil	1	105,700		105,700	
POERTZEL, Otto (1876-?) German					
3D	4	37,696	2,116	9,890	15,800
POESCHMANN, Rudolf (1878-1954) German					
oil	1	3,442		3,442	
POETOU, Emile François (1885-1975) Belgian					
3D	2	5,472	1,824	2,736	3,648
POETZELBERGER, Oswald (1893-?) German					
oil	1	1,981		1,981	
POGANY, Willy (1882-1956) American					
oil	1	1,900		1,900	
wc/d	1	1,088		1,088	
POGGENBEEK, Geo (1853-1903) Dutch					
oil	3	15,352	1,503	4,514	9,335
wc/d	1	1,173		1,173	
POGLIAGHI, Ludovico (1857-1950) Italian					
oil	1	2,230		2,230	
POHL, Adolf Josef (1872-?) Austrian					
wc/d	1	1,431		1,431	
POHL, Edward Henry (1874-1956) American					
wc/d	1	1,200		1,200	

Name	No.	Total Sales Value	lowest	Prices median	highest
POHLE, Hermann (1831-1901) German					
oil	1	1,981		1,981	
POHLE, Léon (1841-1908) German					
oil	1	4,046		4,046	
POHLE, Rudolf (1837-?) German					
3D	1	1,684		1,684	
POILLEUX-SAINT-ANGE, Georges Louis (19th C) French					
oil	1	11,296		11,296	
POINGDESTRE, Charles H (?-1905) British					
oil	1	1,950		1,950	
POINT, Armand (1860-1932) French					
oil	2	11,772	2,772	5,886	9,000
wc/d	2	2,197	1,000	1,099	1,197
POIRIER, Jacques (1942-) Canadian					
oil	2	20,254	1,828	10,127	18,426
POIRIER, Paul (?-1895) French					
oil	1	1,350		1,350	
POISSON, Pierre (18/19th C) French					
3D	1	3,582		3,582	
POISSON, Pierre Marie (1876-1953) French					
3D	1	1,314		1,314	
POITEVIN (?) ?					
3D	1	2,127		2,127	
POITEVIN, Philippe (1831-1907) French					
3D	1	1,221		1,221	
POITTEVIN, Eugene Modeste le (1806-1870) French					
oil	1	3,322		3,322	
POIVRET, Jean-Luc (1950-) French					
3D	1	1,180		1,180	
oil	1	1,370		1,370	
wc/d	1	1,222		1,222	
POKITONOV, Ivan (1850-1923) Russian					
oil	1	14,805		14,805	
POLACK, E Ferdinand (19/20th C) ?					
wc/d	1	2,480		2,480	
POLAK, D (19th C) Dutch					
oil	1	2,753		2,753	
POLASTRI, Constantin (1933-) ?					
oil	1	2,578		2,578	
POLEDNE, F (1873-1932) Austrian					
wc/d	1	1,050		1,050	
POLEDNE, Franz (1873-1932) Austrian					
wc/d	1	2,950		2,950	
POLELONEMA, Otis (1902-) American					
wc/d	1	2,250		2,250	
POLENOV, Vassili (1844-1927) Russian					
oil	1	23,970		23,970	
POLEO, Hector (1918-) Venezuelan					
oil	1	1,830		1,830	
wc/d	1	4,180		4,180	
POLESELLO, Rogelio (1939-) Argentinian					
oil	1	1,000		1,000	
POLI, Fabio de (1947-) Italian					
oil	1	1,964		1,964	
POLI, Jacques (1938-) French					
oil	1	1,160		1,160	
POLIAKOFF, Serge (1906-1969) Russian					
oil	17	1,690,695	19,928	53,625	362,400
wc/d	20	332,245	6,000	16,042	30,450

Name	No.	Total Sales Value	lowest	Prices median	highest
POLIDORI, Anna Maria (20th C) Italian					
3D	1	3,374		3,374	
POLIDORO DA CARAVAGGIO (1492-1543) Italian					
wc/d	1	9,060		9,060	
POLIDORO DA CARAVAGGIO (school) (1492-1543) Italian					
wc/d	1	1,100		1,100	
POLIZZI, Franco (20th C) Italian					
oil	2	3,872	1,773	1,936	2,099
POLKE, Sigmar (1941-) German					
oil	12	2,825,040	9,740	92,500	1,500,000
wc/d	22	484,708	2,580	13,571	211,400
POLL, Herbert van der (1877-1963) Dutch					
wc/d	1	1,184		1,184	
POLLARD, S G (19th C) British					
oil	1	7,584		7,584	
POLLENTINE, Alfred (fl.1861-1880) British					
oil	20	117,704	1,516	3,051	23,550
POLLET, J (?) ?					
oil	1	2,628		2,628	
POLLET, Joseph Michel-Ange (1814-1870) French					
3D	2	7,479	1,793	3,740	5,686
POLLINI, Cesare (1560-1630) Italian					
wc/d	1	30,200		30,200	
POLLITT, Albert (fl.1889-1920) British					
wc/d	1	1,200		1,200	
POLLOCK, Jackson (1912-1956) American					
oil	1	600,000		600,000	
wc/d	2	13,500	3,500	6,750	10,000
POLLONERA, Carlo (c.1849-1923) Italian					
oil	2	8,689	1,793	4,345	6,896
POLLONI, Silvio (20th C) Italian					
oil	1	1,126		1,126	
POLOWSKI (19th C) ?					
oil	1	2,826		2,826	
POMA, Silvio (1840-1932) Italian					
oil	4	25,795	1,848	2,500	18,947
POMARDI, Simone (1760-1830) Italian					
wc/d	1	2,574		2,574	
POMAREDE, Leon D (c.1807-1892) American/French					
oil	1	2,500		2,500	
POMEROY, Frederick William (1856-1924) British					
3D	1	17,280		17,280	
POMI, Alessandro (1890-?) Italian					
oil	1	4,682		4,682	
POMMEREULLE, Daniel (1937-) French					
3D	1	2,259		2,259	
POMODORO, Arnaldo (1926-) Italian					
3D	14	497,352	2,912	23,621	137,750
POMODORO, Gio (1930-) Italian					
3D	5	56,889	1,758	9,481	34,207
wc/d	1	3,882		3,882	
POMPA, Gaetano (1928-) Italian					
3D	1	1,964		1,964	
POMPE, Walter (1707-1777) Flemish					
3D	2	23,734	7,098	11,867	16,636
POMPON, François (1855-1933) French					
3D	28	395,964	2,370	9,091	54,870
PONC, Joan (1927-1984) Spanish					
wc/d	4	9,908	1,613	1,937	4,421

Name	No.	Total Sales Value	lowest	Prices median	highest
PONCE DE LEON, Angel (20th C) South American					
oil	1	3,500		3,500	
PONCE DE LEON, Fidelio (1896-1957) Cuban					
oil	1	5,000		5,000	
PONCET, Jean Baptiste (1827-1901) French					
oil	3	3,545	1,096	1,096	1,353
PONEMONE, Scott (1949-) ?					
wc/d	1	4,991		4,991	
PONOMARENKO, Mikhail (1958-) Russian					
oil	1	1,367		1,367	
PONS, Louis (20th C) ?					
3D	1	1,003		1,003	
wc/d	2	4,745	1,196	2,373	3,549
PONSEN, Tunis (1891-1968) American					
oil	2	6,000	3,000	3,000	3,000
PONSIOEN, Johannes Bernardus (1900-1969) Dutch					
oil	1	5,669		5,669	
PONSON, Luc Raphael (1835-1904) French					
oil	1	1,153		1,153	
PONTHUS-CINIER, Antoine (1812-1885) French					
oil	3	20,813	6,043	7,447	7,447
PONTICELLI, G (19th C) Italian					
oil	1	2,230		2,230	
PONTOY (20th C) French					
oil	1	1,843		1,843	
PONTOY, Henri Jean (1888-1969) French					
oil	15	69,494	1,053	3,867	11,033
wc/d	9	29,775	1,102	2,755	7,578
PONZONE, Matteo (1586-1664) Italian					
oil	1	41,630		41,630	
POOLE, Horatio Nelson (1884-1949) American					
oil	1	23,000		23,000	
POOLE, James (1804-1886) British					
oil	1	2,646		2,646	
POOLE, Paul Falconer (1807-1879) British					
oil	4	15,327	1,693	2,527	8,580
wc/d	2	3,118	1,343	1,559	1,775
POOR, Henry Varnum (1888-1970) American					
oil	1	14,000		14,000	
POORTEN, Hendrik Josef Franciscus van der (1789-1874) Belgian					
oil	1	3,500		3,500	
POORTEN, Jacobus Johannes van (1841-1914) German					
oil	2	9,027	3,187	4,514	5,840
POORTER, Willem de (1608-1648) Dutch					
oil	1	132,300		132,300	
POOT, Rik (1924-) Belgian					
3D	2	3,812	1,610	1,906	2,202
POOTER, Bernard de (1883-?) Belgian					
oil	1	3,146		3,146	
POOTER, Frans de (1898-1987) Belgian					
oil	1	1,111		1,111	
POPE, Alexander (1849-1924) American					
oil	3	104,000	2,000	22,000	80,000
POPHILLAT, Jean Pierre (20th C) French					
oil	1	1,084		1,084	
POPINEAU, E (20th C) French					
3D	1	1,714		1,714	
POPPE, D (19th C) American?					
oil	1	1,400		1,400	

Name	No.	Total Sales Value	lowest	Prices median	highest
POPPEL, Peter van (1945-) Dutch					
oil	1	4,957		4,957	
PORACCIA, Piero (1893-1965) Italian/French					
oil	1	1,267		1,267	
PORAY, Stanislaus (1888-1948) American					
oil	3	6,900	1,000	1,700	4,200
PORBUCHRAI, Yehuda (1949-) Israeli?					
oil	1	6,500		6,500	
PORCELLIS, Jan (16/17th C) Dutch					
oil	1	14,362		14,362	
PORCELLIS, Jan I (1584-1632) Dutch					
oil	1	30,000		30,000	
PORCELLIS, Julius (1610-1645) Dutch					
oil	2	59,704	29,464	29,852	30,240
POREAU, Oswald (1877-1955) Belgian					
oil	3	3,260	1,043	1,043	1,149
PORET, Xavier de (19th C) Swiss					
wc/d	1	1,525		1,525	
PORGES, Clara (1879-?) Swiss					
oil	1	4,081		4,081	
wc/d	5	12,026	1,632	1,749	3,552
PORION, Charles (1814-?) French					
oil	1	16,301		16,301	
PORPORA, Paolo (1617-1673) Italian					
oil	1	95,000		95,000	
PORTAELS, Jean François (1818-1895) Belgian					
oil	5	17,322	1,442	1,950	9,752
wc/d	1	1,567		1,567	
PORTAIL, Jacques Andre (1695-1759) French					
wc/d	1	1,935		1,935	
PORTELLI, Carlo (?-1574) Italian					
oil	2	233,450	90,000	116,725	143,450
PORTENAART, Jeanne (1911-1991) Belgian					
oil	1	1,343		1,343	
PORTER, C E (1847-1923) American					
oil	2	7,250	3,250	3,625	4,000
PORTER, Charles E (1847-1923) American					
oil	1	2,100		2,100	
PORTER, Fairfield (1907-1975) American					
oil	3	350,000	30,000	120,000	200,000
PORTER, Sir Robert Kerr (1777-1842) British					
oil	1	1,413		1,413	
PORTIELJE, Edward Antoon (1861-1949) Belgian					
oil	26	258,115	1,111	10,500	19,000
PORTIELJE, Gerard (1856-1929) Belgian					
oil	12	221,184	1,139	16,077	48,620
PORTIELJE, Jon Frederik Pieter (1829-1908) Belgian/Dutch					
oil	6	49,378	1,873	5,429	22,955
PORTOCARRERO, René (1912-1986) Cuban					
oil	5	99,000	5,000	15,000	42,000
wc/d	4	34,031	2,031	8,000	16,000
PORTUGUESE SCHOOL, 16th C					
oil	1	32,340		32,340	
PORTUGUESE SCHOOL, 17th C					
3D	1	4,325		4,325	
PORTUGUESE SCHOOL, 18th C					
oil	1	32,600		32,600	
PORTUGUESE SCHOOL, 19th C					
oil	1	4,242		4,242	

Name	No.	Total Sales Value	lowest	Prices median	highest
PORTUGUESE SCHOOL, 20th C					
oil	1	2,813		2,813	
PORTWAY, Douglas (1922-1993) South African					
oil	2	4,594	1,896	2,297	2,698
POSADA, Manuel (19th C) South American					
oil	1	2,862		2,862	
POSCH, Alexander (1890-?) German					
oil	1	2,926		2,926	
POSCHINGER, Richard von (1839-1915) German					
oil	2	13,240	3,760	6,620	9,480
POSE, Eduard Wilhelm (1812-1878) German					
oil	2	4,735	1,495	2,368	3,240
POSILLIPO SCHOOL, 19th C Italian					
oil	4	13,752	2,844	3,054	4,800
POSLIN (18th C) ?					
wc/d	1	6,000		6,000	
POSSART, Felix (1837-1928) German					
oil	5	13,163	1,373	1,933	5,844
POSSENTI, Antonio (1933-) Italian					
oil	13	25,204	1,121	1,710	3,754
POST, Eduard C (1827-1882) German					
oil	1	5,000		5,000	
POST, Frans (1612-1680) Dutch					
oil	1	2,600,000		2,600,000	
POST, William Merritt (1856-1935) American					
oil	3	19,000	3,000	6,000	10,000
POSTEL, Jules (1867-1955) Belgian					
oil	2	2,571	1,234	1,286	1,337
POSTELLE, Germain (19th C) French					
oil	1	1,606		1,606	
POSTIGLIONE, Luca (1876-1936) Italian					
oil	2	10,187	4,698	5,094	5,489
POSTIGLIONE, Salvatore (1861-1906) Italian					
oil	1	7,418		7,418	
POT, Hendrick Gerritsz (1585-1657) Dutch					
oil	1	5,142		5,142	
POTEMONT, Adolphe Theodore (1828-1883) French					
oil	1	2,495		2,495	
POTHAST, Bernard (1882-1966) Dutch/Belgian					
oil	10	178,513	1,914	19,816	34,760
POTHAST, Willem Frederik Alfons (1877-1917) Dutch					
oil	1	4,143		4,143	
POTRONAT, Lucien (1889-?) French					
oil	2	3,833	1,233	1,917	2,600
POTT, Laslett John (1837-1898) British					
oil	1	6,532		6,532	
POTTER, Adolphe (1835-1911) Swiss					
oil	1	2,979		2,979	
POTTER, Agnes (1892-?) American					
oil	1	1,100		1,100	
POTTER, Louis McClellan (1873-1912) American					
3D	1	4,000		4,000	
POTTER, Mary (1900-1981) British					
oil	18	129,467	2,400	6,809	16,920
POTTER, Maurice (1865-1898) Swiss					
oil	1	2,859		2,859	
POTTER, Paulus (1625-1654) Dutch					
oil	1	6,934		6,934	

Name	No.	Total Sales Value	Prices lowest	median	highest
POTTER, Pieter Symonsz (1597-1652) Dutch					
oil	1	3,872		3,872	
POTTER, William J (1883-1934) American					
oil	1	2,300		2,300	
POTTHAST, Edward Henry (1857-1927) American					
oil	5	335,000	7,000	18,000	280,000
POTTHOF, Hans (1911-) Swiss					
oil	4	18,802	3,748	4,563	5,929
POTTNER, Emil (1872-?) German					
oil	1	4,250		4,250	
POTUYL, Hendrik (17th C) Dutch					
oil	1	2,408		2,408	
POUCHON, Charles (1814-1882) French					
oil	1	2,277		2,277	
POUGNY, Jean (1894-1956) French					
oil	6	22,390	1,397	2,684	7,232
wc/d	3	12,252	2,292	2,951	7,009
POUILLY, de (?) French					
3D	1	3,520		3,520	
POULSEN, Axel (1887-1972) Danish					
3D	1	57,935		57,935	
POULTON, James (19th C) British					
oil	1	1,649		1,649	
POUMEYROL, Jean-Marie (1945-) French					
oil	4	17,980	2,712	4,425	6,419
POUNOT, C (19th C) British?					
oil	1	1,087		1,087	
POURCELLY, Jean Baptiste (18/19th C) French					
wc/d	2	4,719	1,947	2,360	2,772
POURTAU, Léon (1868-1898) French					
oil	2	48,413	7,643	24,207	40,770
POUSETTE-DART, Richard (1916-1992) American					
oil	2	122,700	2,700	61,350	120,000
wc/d	2	6,500	2,500	3,250	4,000
POUSSIN, Nicolas (1594-1665) French					
oil	2	120,994	5,534	60,497	115,460
wc/d	1	27,180		27,180	
POUSSIN, Nicolas (school) (1594-1665) French					
oil	1	2,900		2,900	
POWELL, Alfred (fl.1870-1901) British					
wc/d	2	3,403	1,628	1,702	1,775
POWELL, Arthur J E (1864-1956) American					
oil	1	3,750		3,750	
POWELL, Charles Martin (1775-1824) British					
oil	3	18,822	5,216	6,006	7,600
POWELL, F (?) British?					
wc/d	1	1,131		1,131	
POWELL, Lucien Whiting (1846-1930) American					
oil	3	7,000	1,700	1,800	3,500
wc/d	1	2,700		2,700	
POWELL, Samuel K (?) British?					
wc/d	1	1,216		1,216	
POWELL, William E (19/20th C) British					
wc/d	1	3,575		3,575	
POWER, Harold Septimus (1878-1951) New Zealander					
oil	2	27,380	8,140	13,690	19,240
POWNALL, Gilbert Anthony (fl.1903-1938) British					
oil	1	1,670		1,670	

Name	No.	Total Sales Value	lowest	Prices median	highest
POY DALMAU, Emilio (1876-1933) Spanish					
oil	1	1,629		1,629	
POYNTER, Sir Edward John (1836-1919) British					
wc/d	5	16,005	2,232	2,700	4,800
POZZATI, Concetto (1935-) Italian					
wc/d	1	1,745		1,745	
POZZI, C (18th C) Italian					
wc/d	1	4,228		4,228	
POZZI, Pippo (1910-1999) Italian					
oil	1	1,971		1,971	
POZZI, U (?) Italian					
3D	1	3,917		3,917	
POZZI, Walter (1911-1989) Italian					
oil	1	1,078		1,078	
PRABHA, B (20th C) Indian					
oil	1	4,500		4,500	
PRACHENSKY, Markus (1932-) Austrian					
oil	2	17,607	5,313	8,804	12,294
PRADA, Carlo (1884-1960) Italian					
oil	2	7,467	1,533	3,734	5,934
PRADA, Carlos (1944-) Venezuelan					
3D	2	3,540	1,340	1,770	2,200
PRADIER, J J (1792-1852) French/Swiss					
3D	1	1,186		1,186	
PRADIER, Jean Jacques (1792-1852) French/Swiss					
3D	15	51,528	1,139	2,713	7,400
PRADILLA GONZALEZ, Miguel (1884-) Spanish					
oil	3	5,072	1,266	1,547	2,259
PRADILLA Y ORTIZ, Francisco (1848-1921) Spanish					
oil	3	8,626	2,391	3,140	3,140
wc/d	3	30,038	3,943	9,000	17,095
PRADILLA, Francisco (1840-1921) Spanish					
oil	1	11,224		11,224	
wc/d	2	14,381	6,903	7,191	7,478
PRADILLA, Miguel (?) Spanish					
oil	1	3,419		3,419	
PRAETERE, Edmond Joseph de (1826-1888) Belgian					
oil	1	4,807		4,807	
PRAGER, Heinz Gunter (1944-) German					
3D	1	3,320		3,320	
PRAMPOLINI, Enrico (1894-1956) Italian					
oil	3	53,582	4,853	10,472	38,257
wc/d	1	32,955		32,955	
PRANGEY (?) French?					
oil	1	3,559		3,559	
PRASAD, Jaggu (1963-) Indian					
wc/d	2	2,664	1,036	1,332	1,628
PRASSINOS (1916-1985) Turkish					
wc/d	1	1,711		1,711	
PRASSINOS, Mario (1916-1985) Turkish					
oil	2	5,351	2,535	2,676	2,816
PRATELLA, Ada (19th C) Italian					
oil	2	3,402	1,494	1,701	1,908
PRATELLA, Attilio (1856-1949) Italian					
oil	23	230,651	1,297	9,425	24,167
wc/d	1	11,000		11,000	
PRATELLA, Fausto (1888-1948) Italian					
oil	4	24,039	2,453	3,376	14,835

Name	No.	Total Sales Value	lowest	Prices median	highest
PRATERE, Edmond Joseph de (1826-1888) Belgian					
oil	1	13,200		13,200	
PRATERE, Henri de (1815-1890) Belgian					
oil	1	2,624		2,624	
PRATSCHKE, Wanda (1939-) German					
3D	1	1,346		1,346	
PRATT (20th C) ?					
wc/d	1	13,872		13,872	
PRATT, Henry Cheever (1803-1880) American					
oil	1	25,000		25,000	
PRATT, Henry Lark (1805-1873) British					
oil	1	3,243		3,243	
PRATT, William (1855-1936) British					
oil	2	14,230	1,180	7,115	13,050
PRAX, Valentine (1899-1981) French					
oil	9	34,453	1,756	3,515	8,700
PREAULT, Auguste (1809-1879) French					
3D	1	34,730		34,730	
PREAULX, Michel François (fl.1796-1827) French					
wc/d	1	9,500		9,500	
PREDA, Ambrogio (1839-1906) Italian					
oil	1	9,911		9,911	
PREDA, Carlo (17th C) Italian					
oil	1	9,381		9,381	
PREETORIUS, Willy (1882-?) German					
oil	1	1,136		1,136	
PREGO, Manuel (1915-1986) Spanish					
wc/d	1	1,168		1,168	
PREHN, A (19th C) ?					
oil	1	1,386		1,386	
PREISS, F (1882-1943) German					
3D	10	76,772	1,435	6,494	13,590
PREISS, Ferdinand (1882-1943) German					
3D	21	212,597	1,828	8,030	27,650
PRELL, Hermann (1854-1922) German					
oil	1	3,962		3,962	
PRELLER, Friedrich Johann Christian Ernst (1804-1878) German					
oil	2	15,747	4,782	7,874	10,965
PRELLER, Louis Friedrich (1838-1901) German					
oil	5	8,619	1,231	1,891	1,979
PRELLER, R U (?) ?					
oil	1	1,981		1,981	
PREM, Heimrad (1934-1978) German					
oil	4	14,524	1,254	2,752	7,767
wc/d	1	8,192		8,192	
PREMAZZI, L (19th C) Italian					
wc/d	1	1,500		1,500	
PREMAZZI, Ludwig (1814-1891) Russian					
oil	1	6,320		6,320	
PRENDERGAST, Maurice (1859-1924) American					
oil	3	325,000	35,000	50,000	240,000
wc/d	5	2,445,000	95,000	340,000	1,500,000
PRENDONI, Attilio (1875-1942) Italian					
3D	1	1,926		1,926	
PRENTICE, Levi Wells (1851-1935) American					
oil	8	121,500	7,000	12,000	28,000
PRENTZEL, Hans (1880-1956) German					
oil	2	3,084	1,465	1,542	1,619

Name	No.	Total Sales Value	lowest	Prices median	highest
PRESS, Friedrich (1904-1990) German					
3D	2	8,121	3,445	4,061	4,676
PRESSMANE, Joseph (1904-1967) French					
oil	1	14,000		14,000	
PRESTON, T (19th C) ?					
oil	1	2,000		2,000	
PRESTON, W F (?) ?					
oil	1	1,590		1,590	
PRETE, Juan del (1897-1987) Argentinian					
wc/d	1	5,000		5,000	
PRETRE, Jean Gabriel (fl.1800-1840) French					
wc/d	10	39,767	2,897	4,082	4,214
PREUDHOMME, Jerome (1732-1795) French					
oil	1	3,491		3,491	
PREUSS, Emil (19th C) German					
oil	1	1,100		1,100	
PREUSSE, August (1908-1942) German					
oil	1	4,870		4,870	
PREUSSER, Robert Ormerod (1919-) American					
oil	1	2,500		2,500	
PREVAL, Christiane de (1876-?) French					
oil	1	2,800		2,800	
PREVERT, Jacques (20th C) French					
oil	2	6,380	3,038	3,190	3,342
wc/d	3	9,396	1,063	3,190	5,143
PREVIATI, Gaetano (1852-1920) Italian					
oil	5	77,301	11,250	12,363	26,598
wc/d	3	7,593	1,773	2,857	2,963
PREVILLE, Andree (20th C) French					
wc/d	1	1,160		1,160	
PREVOST, Jean Louis (1760-1810) French					
oil	1	2,740		2,740	
PREVOST, Nicolas (19th C) French					
oil	1	5,236		5,236	
PREVOST-RITTER, Jean Henri Marie (1810-1898) Swiss					
oil	1	2,972		2,972	
PREVOT, E (19th C) French					
wc/d	1	4,062		4,062	
PREVOT, Maria (19th C) French					
oil	1	4,400		4,400	
PREVOT-VALERI, Andre (1890-1930) French					
oil	1	1,750		1,750	
PREY, J Z (1744-1823) Dutch					
oil	1	34,339		34,339	
PREYER, Emilie (1849-1930) German					
oil	2	96,000	48,000	48,000	48,000
PREYER, Johann Wilhelm (1803-1889) German					
oil	1	28,000		28,000	
PREZIOSI, Amadeo (1816-1882) Italian					
wc/d	7	31,235	1,352	4,770	10,220
PRIANICHNIKOFF, Ilarion Michailovitch (1840-1894) Russian					
oil	1	19,740		19,740	
PRICE, Clark Kelly (20th C) American					
oil	1	16,000		16,000	
PRICE, George (1901-1995) American					
wc/d	2	3,400	1,600	1,700	1,800
PRICE, J (?) ?					
oil	1	1,050		1,050	

Name	No.	Total Sales Value	lowest	Prices median	highest
PRICE, Julius Mendes (1857-1924) British					
oil	2	6,370	1,400	3,185	4,970
PRICE, Norman Mills (1877-1951) American					
oil	1	6,000		6,000	
wc/d	1	1,400		1,400	
PRIECHENFRIED, Alois (1867-1953) German					
oil	5	22,672	1,454	1,661	16,000
PRIECHENFRIED, G Kalla (20th C) German					
oil	1	5,400		5,400	
PRIEM, Maurice (?) Belgian					
3D	1	3,703		3,703	
PRIESS, F (?) ?					
3D	1	4,851		4,851	
PRIEST, H (20th C) British					
wc/d	1	1,872		1,872	
PRIESTMAN, Arnold (1854-1925) British					
oil	1	1,349		1,349	
PRIESTMAN, Bertram (1868-1951) British					
oil	3	11,472	1,128	2,844	7,500
PRIESTMAN, Peter Walter (1868-1951) American					
oil	1	1,900		1,900	
PRIETO, César (1882-1976) Venezuelan					
oil	1	1,610		1,610	
PRIETO, Gregorio (1899-1992) Spanish					
oil	1	1,760		1,760	
PRIETO, Jeronimo (1941-) Spanish					
oil	1	2,301		2,301	
PRIETO, Manuel Jimenez (1849-?) Spanish					
oil	1	26,133		26,133	
PRIETO, Monique (1962-) American					
oil	2	34,000	12,000	17,000	22,000
PRIKING, Franz (1927-1979) French					
oil	29	69,486	1,443	2,406	4,543
wc/d	1	1,171		1,171	
PRIMATICCIO, Francesco (school) (1504-1570) French					
wc/d	1	1,998		1,998	
PRIMAVESI, Georg (1776-1855) German					
oil	1	2,608		2,608	
PRINCE FEDERICO CESI (1585-1630) Italian					
wc/d	1	8,500		8,500	
PRINCE, Richard (1949-) Canadian					
oil	6	258,640	10,000	26,250	90,000
wc/d	1	12,000		12,000	
PRINCE, William Meade (1893-1951) American					
oil	1	4,250		4,250	
PRINCESS MARIA PILAR OF BAVARIA (1891-1987) German					
oil	2	3,105	1,190	1,553	1,915
wc/d	2	2,070	1,035	1,035	1,035
PRINCESS MATHILDE BONAPARTE (1820-1908) French					
wc/d	1	2,112		2,112	
PRINCESS WILHELMINE FREDERIKE SOPHIE (18/19th C) German					
wc/d	1	3,076		3,076	
PRINCETEAU, René (1844-1914) French					
oil	1	3,093		3,093	
PRINET, René-Xavier (1861-1946) French					
oil	18	91,567	1,224	3,151	20,953
wc/d	3	5,735	1,482	2,062	2,191
PRINGLE, J B (fl.1870-1900) British					
oil	1	2,940		2,940	

Name	No.	Total Sales Value	lowest	Prices median	highest
PRINGLE, James (19th C) British					
oil	1	1,573		1,573	
PRINNER, Anton (1902-1983) French					
3D	2	9,770	4,242	4,885	5,528
PRINS, Arturo (1972-) Argentinian					
wc/d	1	1,357		1,357	
PRINS, Ferdinand de (1859-1908) Belgian					
oil	1	2,531		2,531	
PRINS, Pierre (1838-1913) French					
oil	3	3,995	1,095	1,100	1,800
wc/d	8	14,521	1,154	1,606	3,533
PRINSEP, James (1799-1840) British					
wc/d	1	2,844		2,844	
PRINSEP, Valentine Cameron (1838-1904) British					
oil	2	57,150	7,850	28,575	49,300
PRINSSAY, Madame (18/19th C) French					
oil	1	230,000		230,000	
PRINZ, Bernhard (1953-) German					
3D	1	1,262		1,262	
PRIOR HAMBLEN SCHOOL, 19th C American					
oil	4	102,000	8,500	25,500	42,500
PRIOR, William Matthew (1806-1873) American					
oil	1	2,400		2,400	
PRITCHARD, G Thompson (1878-1962) American					
oil	2	4,800	2,000	2,400	2,800
PRITCHETT, Edward (fl.1828-1864) British					
oil	13	224,320	2,431	11,060	40,040
PRITT, Thomas (fl.1861-1864) British					
oil	1	2,703		2,703	
PRITTIE, Edward (1851-1882) Irish					
oil	1	2,960		2,960	
PRITZSCHE, M (20th C) ?					
3D	1	1,300		1,300	
PRIVAT, Colette (1935-) French					
oil	1	1,300		1,300	
PRIVAT, Gilbert Auguste (1892-1969) French					
3D	1	2,897		2,897	
PRIVATO, Cosimo (1899-1971) Italian					
oil	4	4,699	1,070	1,190	1,249
PRIVER, Aharon (20th C) Israeli?					
3D	1	1,450		1,450	
PRIZEMAN, E K (19th C) ?					
oil	1	1,812		1,812	
PROBST, Carl (1854-1924) Austrian					
oil	1	13,868		13,868	
PROBST, Thorwald (1886-1948) American					
oil	2	2,800	1,100	1,400	1,700
PROBSTHAYN, Carl (1770-1818) Danish					
oil	1	4,170		4,170	
PROCACCINI, Camillo (1546-1629) Italian					
wc/d	4	6,069	1,086	1,359	2,265
PROCACCINI, Giulio Cesare (1570-1625) Italian					
wc/d	1	16,000		16,000	
PROCKTOR, Patrick (1936-) British					
oil	2	5,168	1,692	2,584	3,476
wc/d	2	2,501	1,001	1,251	1,500
PROCTER, Dod (1892-1972) British					
oil	7	124,293	7,248	11,325	58,500

Name	No.	Total Sales Value	lowest	Prices median	highest
PROCTER, Ernest (1886-1935) British					
oil	2	105,612	6,912	52,806	98,700
wc/d	1	1,340		1,340	
PROCTOR, Adam E (1864-1913) British					
oil	4	25,260	1,304	3,296	17,365
PROCTOR, Alexander Phimister (1862-1950) American					
3D	2	21,500	8,500	10,750	13,000
wc/d	2	3,000	1,100	1,500	1,900
PROCTOR, Charles E (20th C) American					
oil	1	1,000		1,000	
PRODAN, Auriel (20th C) German					
oil	6	9,000	1,000	1,500	2,200
PROIETTI, Norberto (1927-) Italian					
oil	6	16,463	1,484	2,530	4,363
PROKOFIEFF, Dimitrij (?-1944) Russian					
oil	1	1,178		1,178	
PROLSS, Friedrich Anton Otto (1855-?) German					
oil	1	1,251		1,251	
PRONK, Cornelis (1691-1759) Dutch					
wc/d	1	1,571		1,571	
PROOST, Alfons (1880-1957) Belgian					
oil	3	7,461	1,358	1,358	4,745
PROOYEN, Albert Jurardus van (1834-1898) Dutch					
oil	2	7,458	2,366	3,729	5,092
PROSA, Alfredo (1884-?) Italian					
oil	1	6,701		6,701	
PROSALENTIS, Emilios (1859-1926) Greek					
oil	3	28,178	7,008	8,760	12,410
PROSDOCINI, A (1852-?) Italian					
wc/d	1	3,900		3,900	
PROSDOCINI, Alberto (1852-?) Italian					
wc/d	3	8,480	1,106	3,476	3,898
PROSPER, Pierre Louis (?) Haitian					
oil	1	1,244		1,244	
PROSSER, George Frederick (fl.1828-1868) British					
wc/d	2	7,279	1,988	3,640	5,291
PROST, Léon Henri (1874-1959) French					
oil	1	1,056		1,056	
PROST, Maurice (1894-?) French					
3D	9	49,560	2,844	4,711	8,754
PROTHEAU (19th C) French					
3D	1	10,765		10,765	
PROTTI, Alfredo (1882-1949) Italian					
oil	1	16,468		16,468	
PROUDFOOT, James (20th C) British					
oil	1	1,738		1,738	
PROUDFOOT, William (19th C?) British?					
oil	1	3,575		3,575	
PROUST, A (?) French					
oil	1	1,378		1,378	
PROUT, John Skinner (1806-1876) British					
wc/d	1	1,606		1,606	
PROUT, Margaret Fisher (1875-1963) British					
oil	6	10,769	1,106	1,742	2,397
PROUT, Samuel (1783-1852) British					
wc/d	7	45,048	1,144	1,573	34,320
PROUT, Samuel Gillespie (1822-1911) British					
wc/d	1	1,200		1,200	

Name	No.	Total Sales Value	lowest	Prices median	highest
PROUVE, Victor (1858-1943) French					
oil	2	3,482	1,367	1,741	2,115
wc/d	1	2,842		2,842	
PROUVEUR, Jean Francois (1646-1697) French					
oil	1	1,354		1,354	
PROVIS, Alfred (19th C) British					
oil	4	16,620	3,312	4,169	4,970
PROVOST, A le (19th C) French					
wc/d	1	9,500		9,500	
PROVOST, Jan (15/16th C) Flemish					
oil	1	78,052		78,052	
PROWETT, James C (?-1946) British					
oil	2	3,558	1,500	1,779	2,058
PRUCHA, Gustav (1875-1952) Austrian					
oil	4	6,804	1,073	1,435	2,862
PRUDHON, Pierre Paul (1758-1823) French					
oil	1	2,007		2,007	
wc/d	2	9,430	4,339	4,715	5,091
PRULAY, R de (19th C) French					
oil	1	2,918		2,918	
PRUNA, Pedro (1904-1977) Spanish					
oil	4	64,159	3,764	14,065	32,266
wc/d	2	2,339	1,157	1,170	1,182
PRYDE, James (1869-1941) British					
oil	2	31,086	5,586	15,543	25,500
wc/d	2	5,320	2,130	2,660	3,190
PRYN, Harald (1891-1968) Danish					
oil	6	11,681	1,068	1,654	3,848
PRYTHERCH, Thomas (1864-?) British					
wc/d	1	1,207		1,207	
PSEUDO FARDELLA (17th C) Italian					
oil	2	179,407	7,000	89,704	172,407
PSEUDO ROESTRAETEN (17th C) ?					
oil	1	15,000		15,000	
PUCCI, Silvio (1892-?) Italian					
oil	1	1,714		1,714	
PUCCINI, Mario (1869-1920) Italian					
oil	2	23,034	6,875	11,517	16,159
PUCHI, Francisco (20th C) South American					
oil	1	1,460		1,460	
PUDLICH, Robert (1905-1962) German					
oil	3	14,564	1,282	6,198	7,084
PUDOR, Wilhelm (1814-1845) German					
oil	1	1,618		1,618	
PUECH, Denis (1854-1942) French					
3D	2	16,900	1,216	8,450	15,684
PUEEHMAGRE, Louis (19th C) French					
wc/d	1	1,180		1,180	
PUENTE, Rogelio (1936-1996) Cuban					
oil	3	11,595	2,108	3,764	5,723
PUEYRREDON, Prilidiano (1823-1870) Argentinian					
oil	1	120,000		120,000	
PUGA, Antonio (1602-1648) Spanish					
oil	1	28,542		28,542	
PUGET, Pierre (1620-1694) French					
oil	2	100,674	2,524	50,337	98,150
PUGH, David (1946-1994) Canadian					
oil	6	7,952	1,076	1,326	1,547

Name	No.	Total Sales Value	lowest	Prices median	highest
PUGHE, Buddig Anwylini (1857-?) British					
wc/d	1	1,184		1,184	
PUGI (19th C) Italian					
3D	2	6,453	1,437	3,227	5,016
PUGLISI, Giuseppe (1965-) Italian					
oil	1	1,399		1,399	
PUHONNY, Victor (1838-1909) Polish					
oil	1	1,283		1,283	
PUIG, August (1929-1999) Spanish					
oil	1	1,388		1,388	
PUIG-RODA, Gabriel (1865-1919) Spanish					
oil	1	16,028		16,028	
PUIGAUDEAU, Fernand du (1866-1930) French					
oil	17	482,106	4,413	28,145	57,000
wc/d	2	17,039	4,200	8,520	12,839
PUIGDENGOLAS BARELLA, Jose (1906-1987) Spanish					
oil	3	17,988	3,372	6,006	8,610
PUIGMARTI, Xavier (20th C) French					
oil	1	2,604		2,604	
PUJOL DE GUASTAVINO, Clement (1850-1905) French					
oil	2	24,209	10,000	12,105	14,209
PUJOL, Adrian (20th C) South American					
oil	1	1,940		1,940	
PUJOL, Alexandre Denis Abel de (1787-1861) French					
wc/d	1	1,617		1,617	
PULLER, John Anthony (fl.1821-1867) British					
oil	4	29,206	1,106	7,258	13,585
PUN WOO (?) Oriental					
oil	2	24,500	9,500	12,250	15,000
PUNJAB SCHOOL, 19th C Indian					
wc/d	1	42,000		42,000	
PUPINI, Biagio (16th C) Italian					
wc/d	1	8,000		8,000	
PURDY, Donald (1924-) American					
oil	2	5,400	1,900	2,700	3,500
PURGAU, Franz Michael Siegmund von (17/18th C) Austrian					
oil	1	5,601		5,601	
PURICELLI, Giuseppe (1862-1894) Italian					
oil	1	5,351		5,351	
PURIFICATO, Domenico (1915-1984) Italian					
oil	4	9,165	1,571	2,351	2,893
wc/d	5	6,355	1,026	1,222	1,640
PURRMANN, Hans (1880-1966) German					
oil	14	912,413	7,084	64,210	139,858
wc/d	15	51,432	1,282	1,756	18,447
PURVIS, T G (fl.1900-1910) British					
oil	1	2,119		2,119	
PURY, Edmond-Jean de (1845-1911) Swiss					
oil	1	3,038		3,038	
PURYEAR, Martin (1941-) American					
3D	1	440,000		440,000	
PURYGIN, Leonid (1951-) Russian					
oil	2	11,844	4,512	5,922	7,332
PUSHMAN, Hovsep (1877-1966) American					
oil	4	106,500	9,500	27,500	42,000
PUSOLE, Pierluigi (1963-) Italian					
oil	1	1,747		1,747	
wc/d	1	1,543		1,543	

Name	No.	Total Sales Value	lowest	Prices median	highest
PUTHOD, Dolores (1934-) Italian					
oil	1	1,408		1,408	
PUTHUFF, Hanson Duvall (1875-1972) American					
oil	6	94,750	2,250	13,000	32,500
PUTNAM, Arthur (1873-1930) American					
3D	1	9,000		9,000	
PUTTER, Pieter de (1600-1659) Dutch					
oil	2	7,254	2,646	3,627	4,608
PUTTNER, Josef Carl Berthold (1821-1881) Austrian					
oil	1	1,788		1,788	
PUTZ, Leo (1869-1940) German					
oil	.11	434,079	6,831	25,523	136,615
PUTZHOFEN-HAMBUCHEN, Paul (19/20th C) German					
oil	2	2,317	1,117	1,159	1,200
PUVIS DE CHAVANNES, Pierre (1824-1898) French					
wc/d	4	22,304	2,182	4,466	11,190
PUY, Jean (1876-1960) French					
oil	8	49,730	1,973	3,166	20,599
wc/d	1	1,567		1,567	
PUYENBROECK, Vital van (1906-) Belgian					
oil	1	1,300		1,300	
PUYL, Louis François Gerard van der (1750-1824) Dutch					
oil	1	1,179		1,179	
PUYT, A (?) ?					
3D	1	7,594		7,594	
PYE, William (fl.1881-1908) British					
oil	1	2,718		2,718	
PYK, Madeleine (1934-) Swedish					
oil	15	25,303	1,004	1,632	2,612
wc/d	2	2,628	1,131	1,314	1,497
PYLE, Howard (1853-1911) American					
oil	3	133,000	16,000	32,000	85,000
wc/d	1	5,500		5,500	
PYNACKER, Adam (1622-1673) Dutch					
oil	4	230,924	4,599	43,960	138,405
PYNAS, Jan (1583-1631) Dutch					
wc/d	1	1,510		1,510	
PYNE, Ganesh (1937-) Indian					
oil	1	24,000		24,000	
wc/d	13	38,540	1,440	1,950	6,000
PYNE, George (1800-1884) British					
wc/d	1	1,073		1,073	
PYNE, James Baker (1800-1870) British					
oil	4	11,843	1,467	2,988	4,400
wc/d	2	5,370	2,370	2,685	3,000
PYNE, Robert Lorraine (19th C) American					
oil	2	2,900	1,100	1,450	1,800
QAJAR SCHOOL, 19th C Persian					
3D	1	9,554		9,554	
oil	2	65,092	31,823	32,546	33,269
QING DYNASTY Chinese					
wc/d	2	56,211	5,211	28,106	51,000
QUADAL, Martin Ferdinand (1736-1811) Austrian					
oil	2	6,752	3,002	3,376	3,750
QUAEDVLIEG, Carel Max Gerlach Anton (1823-1874) Dutch					
oil	1	44,000		44,000	
QUAGLIA, Carlo (1907-1970) Italian					
oil	1	1,800		1,800	
QUAGLIO, Domenico (younger) (1787-1837) German					
oil	4	57,507	2,182	11,464	32,397

Name	No.	Total Sales Value	lowest	Prices median	highest
wc/d	2	2,103	1,040	1,052	1,063
QUAGLIO, Franz (1844-1920) German					
oil	5	14,174	2,439	2,926	3,273
QUAGLIO, Lorenzo (18/19th C) German					
oil	4	90,165	3,987	24,258	37,662
wc/d	1	10,191		10,191	
QUARTERLY, Arthur (19th C) British					
wc/d	1	2,000		2,000	
QUARTLEY, Arthur (1839-1886) American					
oil	2	16,200	1,800	8,100	14,400
QUARTO, Andrea (1959-) Italian					
oil	1	1,078		1,078	
QUARTREMAIN, William Wells (fl.1906-1908) British					
wc/d	1	1,225		1,225	
QUAST, Pieter (1606-1647) Dutch					
oil	1	7,500		7,500	
wc/d	2	3,729	1,719	1,865	2,010
QUAYLE, E Christian (fl.1894-1921) British					
wc/d	3	8,826	1,026	2,184	5,616
QUEEN OF DENMARK, Louise (1817-1898) Danish					
oil	1	6,729		6,729	
QUEEN OF DENMARK, Margrethe II (1940-) Danish					
wc/d	3	36,363	6,741	12,879	16,743
QUELLINUS, Erasmus II (1607-1678) Flemish					
oil	3	86,799	8,711	9,060	69,028
QUELLINUS, Jan Erasmus (1634-1715) Flemish					
oil	1	4,777		4,777	
QUENTIN, Bernard (1923-) French					
wc/d	1	1,711		1,711	
QUERFURT, August (1696-1761) German					
oil	3	20,637	4,862	7,850	7,925
QUERNER, Curt (1904-1976) German					
wc/d	4	6,347	1,456	1,537	1,818
QUESADA, Jaime (1937-) Spanish					
oil	1	1,507		1,507	
wc/d	1	1,124		1,124	
QUESADAS, Augusto Manuel (19th C) Spanish					
oil	1	3,372		3,372	
QUESNE, Fernand le (1856-?) French					
oil	1	1,263		1,263	
QUILLIVIC, René (1879-?) French					
3D	3	11,643	3,249	3,791	4,603
oil	1	1,218		1,218	
QUILP (?) ?					
oil	1	7,850		7,850	
QUILP, W (19th C) British ?					
oil	1	2,718		2,718	
QUINAUX, Joseph (1822-1895) Belgian					
oil	3	4,261	1,288	1,288	1,668
QUINCY, Edmund (1903-) American					
oil	1	5,000		5,000	
QUINONES, Lee (20th C) ?					
oil	1	3,500		3,500	
QUINQUAUD, Anna (1890-1984) French					
3D	2	8,837	4,274	4,419	4,563
QUINQUELA MARTIN, Benito (1890-1977) Argentinian					
oil	2	37,000	15,000	18,500	22,000
wc/d	4	23,146	1,653	5,236	11,022

Name	No.	Total Sales Value	lowest	Prices median	highest
QUINTANA CASTILLO, Manuel (1928-) Venezuelan					
oil	4	4,755	1,130	1,195	1,235
wc/d	1	1,005		1,005	
QUINTANA, Carlos (1966-) Cuban					
oil	1	8,500		8,500	
QUINTANILLA, Luis (1893-1978) Spanish					
oil	1	2,171		2,171	
QUINTE, Lothar (1923-) German					
oil	3	5,234	1,525	1,525	2,184
QUINTERO, Daniel (19/20th C) ?					
wc/d	1	3,053		3,053	
QUINTON, Clement (1851-?) French					
oil	1	1,285		1,285	
QUINTON, H (19th C) British					
oil	1	22,500		22,500	
QUIROS, Antonio (18th C) Spanish					
oil	1	5,058		5,058	
QUISPEL, Matthys (1805-1858) Dutch					
oil	1	1,913		1,913	
QUITON, Eugene (19th C) French?					
3D	1	6,248		6,248	
QUITTNER, Rudolf (1872-1910) Austrian					
oil	1	11,850		11,850	
QUITTON, Edovard (1842-1934) Belgian					
oil	2	4,991	1,442	2,496	3,549
QUIZET, Alphonse (1885-1955) French					
oil	11	27,766	1,088	2,063	6,094
QUOST, Ernest (1844-1931) French					
oil	2	29,265	3,425	14,633	25,840
QUOYAVEMA, Riley (?) ?					
wc/d	1	3,250		3,250	
RAAB (19th C) ?					
oil	1	8,500		8,500	
RAADAL, Erik (1905-1941) Danish					
oil	4	11,242	1,803	3,020	3,477
RAADSIG, Peter (1806-1882) Danish					
oil	6	12,393	1,033	1,919	3,132
RAAPHORST, Cornelis (1875-1954) Dutch					
oil	14	72,735	1,744	3,747	12,678
RAAY, Jean Jozef Frans van (1898-1974) Dutch					
oil	1	3,737		3,737	
RABA, Manuel (1928-1983) Spanish					
wc/d	1	2,110		2,110	
RABE, Max (19/20th C) German					
oil	1	2,708		2,708	
RABERTI, Albert (19th C) ?					
oil	1	2,304		2,304	
RABES, Max (1868-1944) Austrian					
oil	5	20,383	1,006	2,448	10,634
RABIER, Benjamin Armand (1869-1939) French					
wc/d	1	1,606		1,606	
RABIN, Sam (1903-) British					
oil	2	5,822	1,846	2,911	3,976
RABINE, Oskar (1928-) Russian					
oil	1	5,358		5,358	
wc/d	1	3,950		3,950	
RABUS, Carl (1898-1974) German					
oil	1	1,117		1,117	

Name	No.	Total Sales Value	lowest	Prices median	highest
RABUZIN, Ivan (1919-) Yugoslavian					
oil	1	5,647		5,647	
RACIM, Mohammed (1896-1975) Algerian					
wc/d	1	5,155		5,155	
RACIM, Omar (1883-1958) ?					
wc/d	1	3,797		3,797	
RACINE, E (?) ?					
oil	2	4,271	2,023	2,136	2,248
RACITI, Mario (1934-) Italian					
oil	1	1,229		1,229	
wc/d	1	1,440		1,440	
RACKHAM, Arthur (1867-1939) British					
wc/d	5	97,980	2,700	19,000	34,000
RACROIX (?) American?					
oil	1	15,410		15,410	
RADECKER, Antoon (1887-1960) Dutch					
3D	1	1,386		1,386	
RADECKER, J (20th C) Dutch					
3D	1	9,366		9,366	
RADECKER, John (1885-1956) Dutch					
3D	7	203,890	4,310	17,241	129,310
oil	1	5,172		5,172	
RADEMAKER, Abraham (1675-1735) Dutch					
wc/d	1	1,133		1,133	
RADERSCHEIDT, Anton (1892-1970) German					
oil	7	33,699	1,307	3,629	10,625
wc/d	5	33,863	2,404	5,227	14,374
RADFORD, Edward (1831-1920) British					
wc/d	2	6,880	2,590	3,440	4,290
RADICE, Mario (1900-1987) Italian					
oil	4	34,579	3,397	9,675	11,833
wc/d	2	2,705	1,256	1,353	1,449
RADLER, Max (1904-1971) German					
oil	1	31,680		31,680	
RADZIWILL, Franz (1895-1983) German					
oil	7	504,418	7,354	36,764	182,945
wc/d	12	42,095	1,073	1,977	11,172
RAE, Barbara (1943-) British					
wc/d	2	6,453	1,397	3,227	5,056
RAE, Fiona (1963-) British					
oil	3	25,268	1,208	9,060	15,000
RAE, Henrietta (1859-1928) British					
oil	3	759,068	2,512	12,956	743,600
RAE, John (1882-?) American					
wc/d	1	1,500		1,500	
RAEBURN, Sir Henry (1756-1823) British					
oil	6	183,084	8,758	26,110	70,000
RAEMAEKERS, Louis (1869-1956) Dutch					
oil	1	1,490		1,490	
RAETZ, Markus (1941-) Swiss					
3D	2	15,392	2,960	7,696	12,432
wc/d	8	30,517	1,694	2,177	10,194
RAETZ, Pierre (1941-) German?					
wc/d	1	5,565		5,565	
RAETZER, Hellmuth (1838-1909) German					
oil	1	1,694		1,694	
RAEV, Vasili Egorovich (1808-1871) Russian					
oil	1	72,500		72,500	
RAFFAEL, Joseph (1933-) American					
oil	1	13,000		13,000	

Name	No.	Total Sales Value	lowest	Prices median	highest
wc/d	2	11,800	4,800	5,900	7,000
RAFFAELE, Ambrogio (1860-1928) Italian					
oil	1	3,076		3,076	
RAFFAELLI (?) ?					
oil	1	5,418		5,418	
RAFFAELLI, Jean François (1850-1924) French					
oil	15	331,345	3,644	14,250	90,000
wc/d	1	4,089		4,089	
RAFFALT, Ignaz (1800-1857) Austrian					
oil	2	6,700	2,500	3,350	4,200
RAFFEINER, Emmanuel (1881-1923) Austrian					
oil	1	1,081		1,081	
RAFFET, Auguste-Marie (1804-1860) French					
oil	1	2,182		2,182	
RAFFIN, Andre (1927-) French					
oil	1	1,074		1,074	
RAFOLS CULLERES, Alberto (1892-) Spanish					
oil	1	1,129		1,129	
RAFTERY, Ted (1938-) Canadian					
oil	1	1,045		1,045	
RAGIONE, Raffaele (1851-1925) Italian					
oil	3	39,493	11,446	13,500	14,547
RAGOT, Jules (19th C) French					
oil	2	9,382	1,936	4,691	7,446
RAGUENET, Nicolas (18th C) French					
wc/d	1	5,436		5,436	
RAHIMAN, Abalal (c.1856-1931) Indian					
wc/d	1	6,750		6,750	
RAHN-HIRZEL, Eduard (1801-1851) Swiss					
oil	1	5,010		5,010	
RAIGHASSE, P (20th C) French					
oil	1	2,127		2,127	
RAIGHASSE, Pierre (20th C) French					
oil	1	2,500		2,500	
RAIMONDI, Aldo (1902-) Italian					
wc/d	1	1,478		1,478	
RAIMONDI, Marcantonio (school) (c.1480-c.1527) Italian					
wc/d	1	6,934		6,934	
RAIMONDI, R (19th C) Italian					
wc/d	1	1,169		1,169	
RAINBEAUX, F (19th C) ?					
oil	2	7,335	2,119	3,668	5,216
RAINER (19/20th C) ?					
oil	1	1,894		1,894	
RAINER, Arnulf (1929-) Austrian					
oil	5	71,683	4,228	10,194	32,622
wc/d	7	30,187	1,543	4,427	5,340
RAINERI, Carlo Antonio (18th C) Italian					
oil	1	5,418		5,418	
RAINERI, Francesco Maria (1703-1785) Italian					
oil	1	27,421		27,421	
RAISSIGUIER, Paul Emile Felix (1851-1932) French					
3D	1	1,233		1,233	
RAJASTHAN SCHOOL, 17th C Indian					
oil	1	3,500		3,500	
RAJASTHAN SCHOOL, 18th C Indian					
oil	1	3,800		3,800	
RAJASTHAN SCHOOL, 19th C Indian					
oil	1	5,500		5,500	

Name	No.	Total Sales Value	Prices lowest	median	highest
RAJLICH, Thomas (1940-) Czechoslovakian					
oil	1	5,942		5,942	
RALLI, Theodore Jacques (1852-1909) Greek					
oil	2	50,750	20,300	25,375	30,450
RAMAH, Henri (1887-1947) Belgian					
oil	3	7,213	1,030	1,180	5,003
wc/d	1	13,949		13,949	
RAMASSO, Marco (1964-) Italian					
oil	8	16,652	1,408	1,858	3,218
RAMBERG, Johann Heinrich (1763-1840) German					
wc/d	1	1,359		1,359	
RAMBERG, Ulf (1935-) Swedish					
oil	2	6,239	2,308	3,120	3,931
wc/d	2	4,515	2,107	2,258	2,408
RAMBOLD, Karl (19th C) Austrian					
oil	1	1,080		1,080	
RAMBOUX, Johann Anton Alban (1790-1866) German					
wc/d	1	3,205		3,205	
RAME, Louis (1877-1927) French					
oil	1	3,782		3,782	
RAMIN, G (19th C) Scandinavian?					
oil	1	1,787		1,787	
RAMIREZ SANCHEZ, Manuel (1886-1961) Spanish					
oil	1	3,653		3,653	
RAMIREZ, Martin (1895-1963) Mexican					
wc/d	1	24,000		24,000	
RAMIREZ-IBANEZ, Manuel (1856-1925) Spanish					
oil	1	1,397		1,397	
RAMIS, Julio (1909-1990) Spanish					
oil	1	2,933		2,933	
wc/d	1	1,778		1,778	
RAMOS ARTAL, Manuel (19th C) Spanish					
oil	6	18,861	1,140	2,630	6,838
RAMOS, Domingo (1894-1967) Cuban					
oil	2	27,500	7,500	13,750	20,000
RAMOS, F (?) ?					
wc/d	1	1,706		1,706	
RAMOS, Julio (1868-?) Portuguese					
oil	1	6,328		6,328	
RAMOS, Mel (1935-) American					
oil	2	75,000	30,000	37,500	45,000
RAMOS, Rodolfo (1937-) Argentinian					
wc/d	1	1,200		1,200	
RAMOS, Theodore (19th C) ?					
oil	1	2,550		2,550	
RAMSAY, Allan (1713-1784) British					
oil	3	166,070	21,750	34,320	110,000
RAMSAY, Allan (fl.1880-1920) British					
oil	1	5,110		5,110	
RANCILLAC, Bernard (1931-) French					
oil	5	24,534	1,854	3,085	12,894
wc/d	2	3,034	1,180	1,517	1,854
RANCILLAC, Jean Jules Paul (1934-) French					
wc/d	2	3,096	1,205	1,548	1,891
RANCOULET, Ernest (19th C) French					
3D	3	11,714	1,234	3,480	7,000
RANDAL, Frank (fl.1887-1901) British					
wc/d	3	3,697	1,015	1,015	1,667

Name	No.	Total Sales Value	lowest	Prices median	highest
RANDIVOSON, A (20th C) ?					
3D	1	1,342		1,342	
RANEM, Mohammed (1925-) Algerian					
wc/d	1	1,289		1,289	
RANFTL, Johann Matthias (1805-1854) Austrian					
oil	2	40,845	17,445	20,423	23,400
RANGER, Henry Ward (1858-1916) American					
oil	1	1,800		1,800	
wc/d	1	1,200		1,200	
RANIERI, Aristide de (19/20th C) Italian					
3D	1	3,379		3,379	
RANK, William (20th C) American					
wc/d	7	15,000	1,500	1,700	3,300
RANKLEY, Alfred (1819-1872) British					
oil	3	8,036	1,716	3,160	3,160
RANSON, E (20th C) ?					
wc/d	1	1,629		1,629	
RANSON, Elie Miller (19/20th C) ?					
oil	1	3,144		3,144	
RANSON, Paul (1864-1909) French					
oil	1	15,100		15,100	
wc/d	3	6,996	1,418	2,232	3,346
RANSON, Rose von (1895-?) German					
3D	1	2,587		2,587	
RANSY, Jean (1910-1991) Belgian					
oil	2	4,137	1,668	2,069	2,469
RANUCCI, Giuseppe (18th C) Italian					
oil	1	9,000		9,000	
RANVIER-CHARTIER, Lucie (1867-1932) French					
oil	1	1,160		1,160	
RANWELL, William (fl.1830-1843) British					
wc/d	1	4,290		4,290	
RANZONI, Daniele (1843-1889) Italian					
wc/d	1	12,784		12,784	
RAOUX, Albert (19th C) French					
oil	2	5,357	2,674	2,679	2,683
RAOUX, Jean (1677-1734) French					
oil	2	38,840	18,840	19,420	20,000
RAPACKI, Jozef (1871-1929) Polish					
oil	2	4,234	1,769	2,117	2,465
RAPHAEL (school) (1483-1520) Italian					
wc/d	1	3,491		3,491	
RAPHAEL (1483-1520) Italian					
oil	1	550,000		550,000	
RAPHAEL, Joseph (1869-1950) American					
oil	6	390,450	1,268	5,207	350,000
wc/d	5	7,713	1,132	1,585	2,264
RAPOUS, Michele Antonio (1733-1819) Italian					
oil	1	29,265		29,265	
RAPPARD, Anton Gerhard Alexander van (1858-1892) Dutch					
oil	1	3,607		3,607	
RASCH, Heinrich (1840-1913) German					
oil	1	1,500		1,500	
RASCHEN, Henry (1854-1937) German/American					
oil	1	1,000		1,000	
RASENBERGER, Alfred (1885-1949) German					
oil	1	1,107		1,107	
RASER, Pierre (20th C) French					
oil	2	4,523	2,043	2,262	2,480

Name	No.	Total Sales Value	Prices lowest	median	highest
RASHLEIGH, Kate (20th C) British					
wc/d	1	1,200		1,200	
RASMUSSEN, Anna (1879-1963) Danish					
oil	1	1,421		1,421	
RASMUSSEN, Carl (1831-1903) Danish					
oil	1	1,634		1,634	
RASMUSSEN, Georg Anton (1842-1914) Norwegian					
oil	6	20,741	1,049	3,740	5,688
RASMUSSEN, I E C (1841-1893) Danish					
oil	2	2,673	1,143	1,337	1,530
RASMUSSEN, Jens Erik Carl (1841-1893) Danish					
oil	4	18,209	2,264	4,341	7,264
RASMUSSEN, N P (1847-1918) Danish					
oil	1	2,169		2,169	
RASMUSSEN, Niels Peter (1847-1918) Danish					
oil	2	2,258	1,030	1,129	1,228
RASMUSSEN, Thorvald (1850-1919) Danish					
oil	1	1,863		1,863	
RASMUSSEN, Tonning (1936-) Danish					
oil	1	1,071		1,071	
RASSENFOSSE, Armand (1862-1934) Belgian					
oil	4	13,645	2,575	3,193	4,684
wc/d	6	37,241	1,331	4,161	19,977
RASSILI (19th C) Italian					
oil	1	1,273		1,273	
RASTRUP, Lars (1862-1949) Danish					
oil	1	1,311		1,311	
RATY, Albert (1889-1970) Belgian					
oil	9	48,886	1,597	3,853	12,819
RAU, Emil (1858-1937) German					
oil	9	35,314	1,226	2,158	9,906
RAU, Martin Friedrich (1858-?) German					
oil	1	2,000		2,000	
RAUCH, Johann Nepomuk (1804-1847) Austrian					
oil	2	26,038	4,984	13,019	21,054
RAUDNITZ, Albert (1814-1899) German					
oil	1	5,441		5,441	
RAUECKER, Theodor (1854-1940) German					
oil	2	8,706	2,206	4,353	6,500
RAUHWERGER, Jan (1942-) Israeli					
wc/d	1	2,600		2,600	
RAUPP, Karl (1837-1918) German					
oil	5	88,154	1,570	9,328	50,000
RAUSCHENBERG, Robert (1925-) American					
3D	12	332,760	1,414	5,000	180,000
oil	6	952,590	13,590	35,000	800,000
wc/d	19	1,181,308	1,215	30,000	425,000
RAUSCHER, Johann Albrecht Friedrich (1754-1808) German					
wc/d	1	10,194		10,194	
RAVEEL, Roger (1921-) Belgian					
oil	4	58,525	5,794	12,416	27,899
wc/d	9	43,257	2,610	5,172	6,685
RAVEL, Edouard-John E (1847-1920) Swiss					
oil	1	6,000		6,000	
wc/d	1	5,756		5,756	
RAVEN, Ernst von (1816-1890) German					
oil	1	1,963		1,963	
RAVEN, John Samuel (1829-1877) British					
oil	1	48,980		48,980	

Name	No.	Total Sales Value	lowest	Prices median	highest
RAVEN, Samuel (1775-1847) British					
oil	1	1,247		1,247	
RAVENSTEIN, Paul von (1854-1938) German					
oil	1	3,316		3,316	
RAVENSWAAY, Adriana van (1816-1872) Dutch					
oil	2	17,506	1,506	8,753	16,000
RAVENSWAAY, Jan van (1789-1869) Dutch					
oil	2	6,396	2,546	3,198	3,850
RAVESTEYN, Dirck de Quade van (fl.1589-1619) Dutch					
oil	2	123,186	14,466	61,593	108,720
RAVET, Victor (1840-?) Belgian					
oil	2	4,866	1,366	2,433	3,500
RAVIER, Auguste François (1814-1895) French					
oil	10	25,731	1,365	2,430	3,894
wc/d	7	20,596	1,096	2,994	4,278
RAVLIN, Grace (1885-1956) American					
oil	1	1,200		1,200	
RAWCLIFFE, John (19th C) ?					
oil	1	1,956		1,956	
RAWLINGS, Leo (1918-1984) British					
wc/d	1	3,180		3,180	
RAWNSLEY, David (?) ?					
3D	1	2,220		2,220	
RAWSON, Carl W (1884-1970) American					
oil	2	5,850	2,600	2,925	3,250
RAY, Charles (1953-) American					
3D	2	2,800,000	800,000	1,400,000	2,000,000
RAY, Shyamal Dutta (1934-) Indian					
wc/d	1	1,125		1,125	
RAYA-SORKINE (1936-) French					
oil	3	10,243	1,918	2,484	5,841
RAYMOND (?) ?					
oil	1	1,462		1,462	
RAYMOND, Marie (1908-1988) French					
oil	1	2,526		2,526	
RAYNAUD, A (20th C) French					
oil	1	1,273		1,273	
RAYNAUD, Aurelien (1970-) French					
3D	1	2,556		2,556	
oil	1	8,520		8,520	
RAYNAUD, Jean Pierre (1939-) French					
3D	5	29,206	1,171	5,460	12,758
wc/d	2	5,328	1,460	2,664	3,868
RAYNAUD, Patrick (1946-) French					
3D	1	1,671		1,671	
RAYNER, Louise (1832-1924) British					
wc/d	6	61,407	1,264	4,457	28,800
RAYNER, Samuel (?-1874) British					
wc/d	1	1,160		1,160	
RAYO, Omar (1928-) Colombian					
oil	2	2,885	1,125	1,443	1,760
RAYPER, Ernesto (1840-1873) Italian					
oil	1	5,598		5,598	
RAYSKI, Ferdinand von (1807-1890) German					
oil	1	3,240		3,240	
RAYSSE, Martial (1936-) French					
3D	1	23,476		23,476	
oil	5	42,209	1,302	2,047	31,710
wc/d	2	8,356	2,571	4,178	5,785

Name	No.	Total Sales Value	lowest	Prices median	highest
RAZA, Sayed Haider (1922-) Indian					
oil	3	20,650	2,600	4,050	14,000
wc/d	1	2,160		2,160	
RAZUMOV, Konstantin (1961-) Russian					
oil	35	98,082	1,008	2,160	7,500
READ, Catherine (1723-1778) British					
wc/d	2	14,291	5,127	7,146	9,164
READ, Matthias (1669-1747) British					
oil	1	14,300		14,300	
READ, Thomas Buchanan (1822-1872) American					
oil	1	9,250		9,250	
READER, William (17th C) British					
oil	2	25,764	9,391	12,882	16,373
REALFONSO, Tommaso (18th C) Italian					
oil	1	19,110		19,110	
REAM, Carducius Plantagenet (1837-1917) American					
oil	4	32,000	2,250	2,875	24,000
REAM, Morston C (1840-1898) American					
oil	3	18,500	5,000	5,500	8,000
REBELL, Joseph (1787-1828) Austrian					
oil	2	27,414	12,461	13,707	14,953
REBER, John (1857-1938) American					
3D	1	9,000		9,000	
REBEYROLLE, Paul (1926-) French					
oil	5	41,717	1,496	9,224	17,524
wc/d	2	3,003	1,180	1,502	1,823
REBOLLEDO CORREA, Benito (1880-1964) Chilean					
oil	1	9,480		9,480	
REBRY, Gaston (1933-) Canadian					
oil	7	16,745	1,045	1,977	4,243
RECCO, Elena (17th C) Italian					
oil	1	12,678		12,678	
RECCO, Giuseppe (1634-1695) Italian					
oil	1	45,300		45,300	
RECHLIN, Karl (1804-1882) German					
oil	1	4,800		4,800	
RECIO Y GIL, Enrique (1860-?) Spanish					
oil	1	1,020		1,020	
RECKELBUS, L (19/20th C) Belgian					
wc/d	1	1,324		1,324	
RECKELBUS, Louis (1864-1958) Belgian					
wc/d	1	1,259		1,259	
RECKNAGL, Theodor (19th C) German					
oil	1	1,586		1,586	
REDELSPERGER, Charles Louis Emile Jacques (19/20th C) French					
wc/d	1	2,400		2,400	
REDER, Bernard (1897-1963) Israeli					
oil	1	5,200		5,200	
REDER, Christian (1656-1729) German					
oil	1	5,249		5,249	
REDER-BROILI, Franz (1854-1918) German					
oil	2	5,121	1,250	2,561	3,871
REDFIELD, Edward (1869-1965) American					
oil	5	772,000	27,000	180,000	320,000
REDFIELD, Heloise Guillou (1883-?) American					
wc/d	1	1,700		1,700	
REDGATE, Arthur W (fl.1880-1906) British					
oil	4	6,474	1,095	1,677	2,054

Name	No.	Total Sales Value	lowest	Prices median	highest
REDGRAVE, Richard (1804-1888) British					
oil	1	20,020		20,020	
REDI, B (19th C) German?					
oil	1	1,288		1,288	
REDIG, Laurent Herman (1822-1861) Dutch					
oil	2	6,507	3,131	3,254	3,376
REDKOVSKY, A (19th C) Russian					
oil	1	21,150		21,150	
REDMAYNE, N J (fl.1894-1896) British					
oil	1	1,011		1,011	
REDMOND, Granville (1871-1935) American					
oil	13	1,139,250	4,750	32,000	380,000
REDMORE, Edward King (1860-1941) British					
oil	5	6,765	1,015	1,385	1,921
REDMORE, Henry (1820-1887) British					
oil	12	140,367	2,074	10,280	33,220
REDON, Odilon (1840-1916) French					
oil	8	1,502,484	28,000	69,684	700,000
wc/d	14	2,983,750	14,896	41,000	850,000
REDONDELA, Agustin (1922-) Spanish					
oil	7	55,816	1,700	8,325	13,444
wc/d	3	12,872	1,964	1,967	8,941
REDOUTE, Antoine Ferdinand (1756-1809) Flemish					
oil	1	3,473		3,473	
REDOUTE, Henri Joseph (1766-1852) French					
wc/d	1	1,728		1,728	
REDOUTE, Pierre Joseph (1759-1840) French					
wc/d	7	401,004	7,624	12,365	302,000
REDPATH, Anne (1895-1965) British					
oil	17	357,407	5,738	18,644	59,860
wc/d	8	63,079	4,380	8,611	10,875
REDTWITZ, A (19th C) German					
oil	1	3,900		3,900	
REDUZZI, C (?) ?					
3D	1	1,207		1,207	
REEB, David (1952-) Israeli					
oil	3	12,150	1,150	5,000	6,000
REED, David (1946-) American					
oil	1	1,100		1,100	
REED, Marjorie (1915-) American					
oil	3	6,050	1,600	1,700	2,750
REEDE, W van (19th C) ?					
oil	1	3,250		3,250	
REEKERS, Hendrik (1815-1854) Dutch					
oil	1	331,800		331,800	
REEKERS, Johannes (jnr) (1824-1895) Dutch					
oil	2	5,065	2,004	2,533	3,061
REES, Otto van (1884-1957) Dutch					
oil	2	8,715	2,773	4,358	5,942
REES, William E (20th C) British					
oil	2	2,449	1,027	1,225	1,422
REEVES, Claude (fl.1900) British					
oil	2	8,585	2,265	4,293	6,320
REEVES, Richard Stone (20th C) American					
oil	3	12,000	3,800	4,000	4,200
REGEMORTER, Ignatius Josephus van (1785-1873) Flemish					
oil	3	9,476	2,404	3,160	3,912
REGEMORTER, P van (18/19th C) Flemish					
oil	2	20,097	9,930	10,049	10,167

Name	No.	Total Sales Value	lowest	Prices median	highest
REGEMORTER, Petrus Johannes van (1755-1830) Flemish					
oil	1	4,431		4,431	
REGGIANI, Mauro (1897-1980) Italian					
oil	7	50,752	4,424	9,093	9,093
wc/d	1	1,098		1,098	
REGGIANINI, Vittorio (1858-1939) Italian					
oil	4	382,346	15,096	53,625	260,000
REGILD, Carsten (1941-1992) Swedish					
wc/d	1	1,325		1,325	
REGINA, Guido la (1909-) Italian					
oil	1	3,397		3,397	
REGNART, Lucien Franc (19th C) French					
oil	1	1,903		1,903	
REGNAULT DE MAULMAIN, Émile (1836-1897) French					
oil	1	39,420		39,420	
REGNAULT, Baron Jean Baptiste (1754-1829) French					
oil	2	38,114	3,114	19,057	35,000
wc/d	1	2,233		2,233	
REGNAULT, Henri (1843-1871) French					
oil	2	11,991	4,377	5,996	7,614
REGNIER (?) ?					
oil	1	4,506		4,506	
REGO, Paula (1935-) Portuguese					
wc/d	1	15,800		15,800	
REGOYOS, Dario de (1857-1913) Spanish					
oil	5	242,789	28,061	48,895	90,545
wc/d	1	8,451		8,451	
REGTEREN ALTENA, Marie E van (1868-1958) Dutch					
oil	2	8,603	3,622	4,302	4,981
REH, Theodore (1845-1918) Belgian					
oil	1	6,410		6,410	
REHDER, Julius Christian (1861-?) German					
oil	3	5,107	1,270	1,564	2,273
REHN, Frank Knox Morton (1848-1914) American					
oil	1	2,000		2,000	
REHNBERG, Hakan (1953-) Swedish					
oil	1	1,278		1,278	
REIBENSTEIN, F (18th C) French					
wc/d	1	1,054		1,054	
REICH, Adolf (1887-1963) Austrian					
oil	1	2,862		2,862	
REICHEL, Hans (1892-1958) German					
wc/d	3	6,132	1,607	1,899	2,626
REICHENBACH, Eugen (1840-1926) German					
oil	1	1,124		1,124	
REICHENBACH, F W (19th C) German					
oil	1	1,092		1,092	
REICHERT, Carl (1836-1918) Austrian					
oil	8	65,463	2,023	3,950	29,862
REICHMANN, Vilem (1908-) ?					
wc/d	1	1,918		1,918	
REID, Archibald David (1844-1908) British					
oil	4	10,806	1,147	3,160	3,339
REID, Flora MacDonald (fl.1880-1938) British					
oil	2	11,844	2,940	5,922	8,904
REID, George Agnew (1860-1947) Canadian					
oil	1	1,693		1,693	
REID, George Ogilvy (1851-1928) British					
oil	1	2,041		2,041	

Name	No.	Total Sales Value	Prices lowest	median	highest
wc/d	1	1,294		1,294	
REID, John Robertson (1851-1926) British					
oil	7	20,547	1,008	2,800	5,680
wc/d	1	1,081		1,081	
REID, Nano (1905-1981) Irish					
oil	1	7,200		7,200	
REID, Robert (1862-1929) American					
oil	3	70,000	12,000	20,000	38,000
REID, Robert Payton (1859-1945) British					
oil	1	13,050		13,050	
REID, Sir George (1841-1913) British					
oil	1	4,116		4,116	
REID, Stephen (1873-1948) British					
oil	3	15,416	1,510	3,256	10,650
REIFFEL, Charles (1862-1942) American					
oil	4	58,250	3,750	11,000	32,500
wc/d	2	4,850	2,250	2,425	2,600
REIFFENSTEIN, Carl Theodore (1820-1893) German					
wc/d	1	1,282		1,282	
REIGL, Judit (1923-) Hungarian					
oil	2	2,434	1,180	1,217	1,254
REILLE, Karl (1886-1975) French					
oil	1	3,943		3,943	
wc/d	7	27,473	2,065	3,987	6,194
REIMANS, Richard (1882-?) Belgian					
oil	1	1,244		1,244	
REINA, Antonio (?) ?					
oil	1	22,055		22,055	
REINAGLE, Philip (1749-1833) British					
oil	1	35,750		35,750	
REINAGLE, Ramsay Richard (1775-1862) British					
oil	5	34,373	2,370	4,544	19,110
wc/d	2	5,716	2,556	2,858	3,160
REINDEL, Edna (1900-1990) American					
oil	2	5,250	2,000	2,625	3,250
REINER, Wenzel Lorenz (1686-1743) Austrian					
wc/d	1	1,317		1,317	
REINHARD, Josef (1749-1824) Swiss					
oil	1	3,133		3,133	
REINHARDT, Ad (1913-1967) American					
oil	2	539,270	39,270	269,635	500,000
wc/d	1	32,000		32,000	
REINHARDT, Louis (?-1870) German					
oil	2	2,706	1,000	1,353	1,706
REINHARDT, Siegfried (1925-1984) American					
oil	4	7,550	1,600	1,825	2,300
wc/d	1	4,000		4,000	
REINHARDT, Wilhelm (1815-1881) German					
oil	1	1,854		1,854	
REINHART, Benjamin Franklin (1829-1885) American					
oil	2	37,113	1,113	18,557	36,000
REINHART, Johann Christian (1761-1847) German					
wc/d	2	5,238	2,033	2,619	3,205
REINHART, Joseph (1749-1829) Swiss					
oil	2	3,825	1,519	1,913	2,306
REINHOLD, Friedrich Philipp (1779-1840) German					
oil	1	2,595		2,595	
wc/d	1	1,125		1,125	
REINHOLD, Heinrich (1788-1825) Austrian					
oil	1	17,445		17,445	

Name	No.	Total Sales Value	Prices lowest	median	highest
REINIGER, Otto (1863-1909) German					
oil	3	4,096	1,139	1,347	1,610
REINIKE, Charles Henry (1906-1983) American					
wc/d	3	4,300	1,000	1,600	1,700
REINKEN, Margarethe von (1877-1962) German					
oil	1	3,409		3,409	
REIS, M G (19th C) ?					
oil	1	4,564		4,564	
REISER, Carl (1877-1950) German					
oil	1	3,244		3,244	
REISMAN, Ori (1924-1991) Israeli					
oil	2	88,000	30,000	44,000	58,000
REISS (?) ?					
3D	1	2,200		2,200	
REISS, Fritz (1857-1916) German					
oil	3	5,202	1,212	1,995	1,995
REISS, Fritz Winold (1886-1953) American/German					
oil	1	170,000		170,000	
REISS, Lionel S (1894-1929) American/Austrian					
oil	1	3,000		3,000	
REISZ, Hermann (1865-?) Austrian					
oil	1	1,036		1,036	
REITER, Johann Baptist (1813-1890) Austrian					
oil	1	12,461		12,461	
RELYEA, Charles M (1863-?) American					
oil	1	4,250		4,250	
REMBRANDT (1606-1669) Dutch					
oil	1	26,460,000		26,460,000	
wc/d	4	6,100,475	150,475	1,275,000	3,400,000
REMBRANDT (school) (1606-1669) Dutch					
oil	3	11,391	2,220	4,171	5,000
wc/d	1	2,062		2,062	
REMENICK, Seymour (1923-) American					
oil	1	1,400		1,400	
REMINGTON, Frederic (1861-1909) American					
3D	6	1,170,324	2,824	97,500	750,000
oil	2	250,000	120,000	125,000	130,000
wc/d	11	258,500	4,000	20,000	70,000
REMOND, Jean Charles Joseph (1795-1875) French					
oil	3	11,396	1,297	2,302	7,797
REMPRECHT, J K (19/20th C) German					
oil	1	1,100		1,100	
RENARD, A (19th C) ?					
oil	1	1,087		1,087	
RENARD, Stephen J (1947-) British					
oil	6	61,591	2,128	6,103	32,000
RENAUDIN, Alfred (1866-1944) French					
oil	1	3,597		3,597	
wc/d	1	1,354		1,354	
RENAULT, Andre (20th C) ?					
oil	1	1,314		1,314	
RENAULT, Luigi P (1845-c.1910) Italian					
wc/d	1	1,057		1,057	
RENAULT-DES-GRAVIERS, Victor J (?-1905) French					
oil	1	2,595		2,595	
RENDA, Giuseppe (1859-1939) Italian					
3D	2	2,740	1,318	1,370	1,422
RENDELL (20th C) ?					
oil	1	1,020		1,020	

Name	No.	Total Sales Value	lowest	Prices median	highest
RENDON (20th C) ?					
oil	1	1,895		1,895	
RENE, Jean Jacques (1943-) French					
oil	3	6,208	1,021	1,092	4,095
RENEFER (1879-1957) French					
oil	1	1,378		1,378	
RENGIFO, Cesar (1915-1980) Venezuelan					
oil	1	2,180		2,180	
RENI, Guido (1575-1642) Italian					
oil	2	90,081	43,940	45,041	46,141
wc/d	1	22,000		22,000	
RENNIE, George Melvin (1874-1953) British					
oil	1	6,090		6,090	
RENOIR, Pierre Auguste (1841-1919) French					
3D	7	124,697	3,200	11,015	50,627
oil	78	46,739,121	16,843	185,600	8,000,000
wc/d	12	2,226,438	11,113	78,366	1,200,000
RENOIR, Pierre Auguste and GUINO, Richard (19/20th C) French					
3D	1	4,500		4,500	
RENOIR, Pierre Auguste and MOREL, Louis (19/20th C) French					
3D	1	12,000		12,000	
RENOUARD, Antoine Eugene (1835-1921) French					
wc/d	1	1,470		1,470	
RENOUX, Charles (1795-1846) French					
oil	1	1,018		1,018	
RENOUX, Jules Ernest (1863-1932) French					
oil	1	1,251		1,251	
RENQVIST, Torsten (1924-) Swedish					
oil	3	4,729	1,306	1,638	1,785
RENSHAW, Alice (fl.1880-1890) British					
oil	1	1,420		1,420	
RENTZING, F (19/20th C) ?					
oil	1	1,075		1,075	
RENUCCI, Renuccio (1880-1947) Italian					
oil	3	4,719	1,427	1,508	1,784
REOL, Marie Marguerite (1880-1963) French					
oil	2	3,299	1,286	1,650	2,013
REOL, Martine (?) French					
oil	1	1,929		1,929	
REPIN, Ilia (1844-1930) Russian					
oil	6	108,653	1,138	9,815	67,950
wc/d	11	55,605	1,410	5,285	11,325
REQUICHOT, Bernard (1929-1961) French					
oil	3	7,861	1,263	3,276	3,322
RESCALLI, Don Angelo (1884-c.1956) Italian					
oil	4	5,862	1,152	1,439	1,833
RESCHREITER, Rudolf (1868-?) German					
wc/d	1	1,065		1,065	
RESINO, Jose Luis (1950-) Spanish					
oil	1	1,173		1,173	
RESNICK, Milton (1917-) American					
oil	2	26,400	1,400	13,200	25,000
RESSENDI, Romero (19/20th C) Spanish					
oil	1	2,045		2,045	
RESTORI, M M (19th C) ?					
oil	1	1,100		1,100	
RESTOUT, Jean (school) (17/18th C) French					
oil	1	1,459		1,459	

Name	No.	Total Sales Value	Prices lowest	Prices median	highest
RETH, Alfred (1884-1966) French					
3D	1	2,459		2,459	
oil	7	20,348	1,098	2,062	6,042
wc/d	6	11,360	1,289	1,983	2,457
RETHEL, Alfred (1816-1859) German					
wc/d	1	1,419		1,419	
RETS, Jean (1910-1998) Belgian					
wc/d	1	2,440		2,440	
RETT, Gustav (1889-1969) German					
oil	1	2,018		2,018	
RETTICH, Karl Lorenz (1841-1904) German					
oil	1	1,966		1,966	
REULEN, Gerrant (19/20th C) German?					
oil	1	1,064		1,064	
REUTER, Erich Fritz (1911-1997) German					
3D	1	2,076		2,076	
REUTER, Fritz (1895-?) German					
oil	1	2,214		2,214	
REUTER, I (?) ?					
oil	1	1,560		1,560	
REUTER, Josef (19th C) ?					
oil	1	4,050		4,050	
REUTERSWARD, Carl Fredrik (1934-) Swedish					
3D	2	7,824	2,910	3,912	4,914
oil	4	8,781	1,327	1,717	4,020
wc/d	1	1,094		1,094	
REVEL, Gabriel (1642-1712) French					
oil	1	9,483		9,483	
REVELLO DE TORO, Felix (1926-) Spanish					
oil	1	3,739		3,739	
REVENGA SANCHO, Maria (1901-) Spanish					
oil	1	1,076		1,076	
REVERON, Armando (1889-1954) Venezuelan					
oil	2	146,000	26,000	73,000	120,000
REVILL, C H (19th C) British					
oil	1	1,491		1,491	
REVILLE, H Whittaker (fl.1881-1903) British					
oil	1	5,400		5,400	
REVILLIOD, Horace Ernest (1811-1858) ?					
oil	1	5,677		5,677	
REVOIL, Pierre (1776-1842) French					
oil	1	28,930		28,930	
REY, Beatriz (1939-) Spanish					
oil	2	2,439	1,041	1,220	1,398
REYCEND, Enrico (1855-1928) Italian					
oil	2	58,660	8,584	29,330	50,076
REYL-HANISCH, Herbert von (1898-1937) Austrian					
oil	1	11,502		11,502	
REYMANN, J (19/20th C) French					
oil	1	4,172		4,172	
REYMOND, Carlos (1884-1970) French					
oil	1	2,628		2,628	
REYMOND, Casimir (1893-1969) Swiss					
oil	1	1,166		1,166	
REYNA, Antonio Maria de (1859-1937) Spanish					
oil	17	320,619	1,870	19,500	42,000
wc/d	1	1,058		1,058	
REYNAUD, F (1825-1909) French					
oil	1	1,196		1,196	

Name	No.	Total Sales Value	lowest	Prices median	highest
REYNAUD, Marius (19th C) French					
oil	2	5,621	2,452	2,811	3,169
REYNI, Ingalvur av (1920-) Icelandic					
oil	1	1,586		1,586	
REYNOLDS, Alan (1926-) British					
wc/d	5	16,849	1,065	2,250	6,000
REYNOLDS, Frank (?-1895) British					
wc/d	1	1,740		1,740	
REYNOLDS, J F (19th C) ?					
oil	1	1,600		1,600	
REYNOLDS, Sir Joshua (1723-1792) British					
oil	8	2,467,935	17,000	27,953	2,265,000
REYNOLDS, Sir Joshua (school) (1723-1792) British					
oil	2	14,500	2,500	7,250	12,000
REYNOLDS, Walter G (fl.1859-1885) British					
oil	1	2,145		2,145	
REYNTJENS, Henrich Engelbert (1817-1900) Dutch					
oil	3	9,578	2,086	2,265	5,227
REYSSCHOOT, Peter Jan van (1702-1772) Flemish					
oil	1	16,246		16,246	
REZIA, Felice A (fl.1866-1902) British					
oil	4	6,528	1,422	1,447	2,212
RHAI, Aritz (19/20th C) ?					
oil	1	1,131		1,131	
RHAYE, Yves (1936-1995) Belgian					
3D	1	1,455		1,455	
RHEAD, George Woolliscroft (1855-1920) British					
oil	1	3,600		3,600	
RHEAM, Henry Meynell (1859-1920) British					
oil	1	2,002		2,002	
wc/d	7	77,583	1,034	6,996	36,240
RHEAUME, Jeanne (1915-) Canadian					
oil	1	2,043		2,043	
RHEIN, Fritz (1873-1948) German					
oil	1	1,355		1,355	
RHINE SCHOOL, 18th C German					
oil	4	10,841	1,557	2,480	4,325
RHINE SCHOOL, 19th C German					
oil	1	3,210		3,210	
RHODES, John (1809-1842) British					
oil	1	1,026		1,026	
RHOMBERG, Hanno (1820-1869) German					
oil	2	8,900	1,471	4,450	7,429
RHOMBERG, Joseph Anton (1786-1855) German					
oil	2	2,295	1,019	1,148	1,276
RHYS, Oliver (fl.1876-1895) British					
oil	4	31,792	1,500	6,146	18,000
RIABOUCHINSKY (20th C) ?					
3D	1	1,676		1,676	
RIBAK, Louis (1902-1979) American					
oil	1	1,400		1,400	
RIBALTA, Francesco (1565-1628) Spanish					
oil	1	1,139		1,139	
RIBARZ, Rudolf (1848-1904) Austrian					
oil	1	8,972		8,972	
RIBAS MONTENEGRO, Federico (1890-1952) Spanish					
wc/d	1	1,002		1,002	
RIBAULT, Julie (1789-) French					
oil	1	1,028		1,028	

Name	No.	Total Sales Value	lowest	Prices median	highest
RIBAUPIERRE, François de (1886-?) Swiss					
wc/d	1	6,212		6,212	
RIBCOWSKY, Dey de (1880-1936) American/Bulgarian					
oil	4	7,000	1,100	1,200	3,500
RIBEIRO, Alceu (1919-) Uruguayan					
oil	4	6,900	1,100	1,500	2,800
RIBEIRO, Edgardo (1921-) Uruguayan					
oil	3	3,700	1,000	1,300	1,400
RIBERA, Francisco (1907-) Spanish					
oil	2	4,059	1,688	2,030	2,371
RIBERA, Juan Vicente de (fl.1703-1725) Spanish					
oil	1	12,017		12,017	
RIBERA, Jusepe de (1588-1656) Spanish					
oil	2	342,456	142,456	171,228	200,000
RIBERA, Jusepe de (school) (1588-1656) Spanish					
oil	1	24,000		24,000	
RIBERA, Pierre (1867-1932) French					
oil	1	1,045		1,045	
RIBERA, Roman (1848-1935) Spanish					
wc/d	1	1,583		1,583	
RIBERO, Elena del (1952-) Spanish					
oil	2	9,700	3,200	4,850	6,500
RIBOT, Germain Theodore (1845-1893) French					
oil	4	25,292	2,920	6,686	9,000
RIBOT, Theodule (1823-1891) French					
oil	3	18,348	2,600	2,600	13,140
RICARD (?) French					
oil	1	1,800		1,800	
RICARD-CORDINGLEY, Georges (1873-1939) French					
oil	2	3,921	1,619	1,961	2,302
RICARDI, G (?) ?					
oil	1	2,955		2,955	
RICCARDI, Lia (?) Italian					
oil	1	1,478		1,478	
RICCARDI, Luigi (1808-1877) French?					
oil	1	1,109		1,109	
RICCHI, Pietro (1605-1675) Italian					
oil	1	10,570		10,570	
RICCI da NOVARA, Giovanni Battista (1537-1627) Italian					
wc/d	1	4,000		4,000	
RICCI, A (19/20th C) Italian					
oil	1	3,000		3,000	
RICCI, Arturo (1854-?) Italian					
oil	4	369,117	1,408	67,530	232,650
RICCI, F (1608-1685) Spanish					
oil	1	12,000		12,000	
RICCI, Francisco (1608-1685) Spanish					
oil	1	12,000		12,000	
RICCI, Giuseppe (19/20th C) Italian					
oil	1	3,992		3,992	
RICCI, Marco (1676-1729) Italian					
oil	8	488,947	9,815	48,750	205,800
RICCI, Pio (?-1919) Italian					
oil	5	34,264	1,964	6,300	12,000
RICCI, Sebastiano (1659-1734) Italian					
oil	4	441,040	13,090	63,975	300,000
RICCIARDI (?) Italian					
oil	1	1,716		1,716	

Name	No.	Total Sales Value	lowest	Prices median	highest
RICCIARDI, Caesar A (1892-?) American					
oil	1	1,600		1,600	
RICCIARDI, Oscar (1864-1935) Italian					
oil	11	28,001	1,088	2,549	4,203
RICCIO, Andrea (1470-1532) Italian					
3D	4	40,431	4,305	6,021	24,084
RICCITELLI, Domenico (1881-?) American/Italian					
oil	1	1,000		1,000	
RICE, Anne Estelle (1879-1959) American					
oil	1	3,770		3,770	
RICE, Henry Webster (1853-1934) American					
wc/d	2	2,800	1,300	1,400	1,500
RICE-PEREIRA, Irene (1907-1971) American					
oil	2	7,900	2,900	3,950	5,000
wc/d	3	5,000	1,100	2,000	2,000
RICH, John Hubbard (1876-1954) American					
oil	3	17,000	2,500	7,000	7,500
RICHARD (?) ?					
oil	2	2,775	1,342	1,388	1,433
RICHARD, Alexandre Louis Marie Theodore (1782-1859) French					
oil	2	11,343	2,843	5,672	8,500
RICHARD, Alfred Pierre (?-1884) French					
3D	2	4,378	1,024	2,189	3,354
RICHARD, Jim (1943-) American					
oil	1	12,000		12,000	
RICHARD, P (?) ?					
oil	1	8,500		8,500	
RICHARD, P J (20th C) French					
oil	1	1,210		1,210	
RICHARD, René (1895-1982) Canadian					
oil	3	6,981	1,850	2,287	2,844
RICHARD, S T (?) ?					
oil	1	1,106		1,106	
RICHARDE, Ludvig (1862-1929) Swedish					
oil	1	1,474		1,474	
RICHARDS, Ceri (1903-1971) British					
oil	2	25,375	10,875	12,688	14,500
wc/d	5	14,876	1,500	3,456	3,926
RICHARDS, Charles (1906-1992) American					
oil	4	7,000	1,300	1,750	2,200
RICHARDS, Frank (1863-1935) British					
wc/d	1	2,205		2,205	
RICHARDS, Frederick de Berg (1822-1903) American					
oil	1	3,000		3,000	
RICHARDS, John Inigo (?-1810) British					
wc/d	1	1,661		1,661	
RICHARDS, L (19th C) British					
oil	1	1,304		1,304	
RICHARDS, Richard Peter (1840-1877) British					
wc/d	1	1,238		1,238	
RICHARDS, Thomas Addison (1820-1900) American					
oil	2	26,100	1,100	13,050	25,000
RICHARDS, Thomas Miles (jnr) (19th C) British					
wc/d	1	2,120		2,120	
RICHARDS, W (19th C) British					
oil	3	3,178	1,008	1,057	1,113
RICHARDS, W T (1833-1905) American					
oil	2	8,900	1,900	4,450	7,000

Name	No.	Total Sales Value	Prices lowest	Prices median	highest
RICHARDS, William (?) ?					
oil	1	1,391		1,391	
RICHARDS, William Trost (1833-1905) American					
oil	16	650,500	3,500	29,000	100,000
wc/d	9	151,250	6,000	9,250	50,000
RICHARDSON, Edward (1810-1874) British					
wc/d	4	9,344	1,624	1,712	4,290
RICHARDSON, Frederic Stuart (1855-1934) British					
oil	2	3,752	1,480	1,876	2,272
RICHARDSON, John Isaac (1836-1913) British					
wc/d	2	3,398	1,208	1,699	2,190
RICHARDSON, Jonathan (snr) (1665-1745) British					
oil	1	3,718		3,718	
RICHARDSON, T M (snr) (1784-1848) British					
wc/d	1	1,027		1,027	
RICHARDSON, Theodore J (1855-1914) American					
wc/d	3	23,900	2,200	3,700	18,000
RICHARDSON, Thomas Miles (jnr) (1813-1890) British					
wc/d	19	65,820	1,287	2,567	12,584
RICHARDSON, Thomas Miles (snr) (1784-1848) British					
oil	1	54,340		54,340	
wc/d	2	3,631	1,057	1,816	2,574
RICHARDSON, Volney A (1880-1950) American					
oil	1	3,750		3,750	
RICHARDSON, William (19th C) British					
oil	1	1,846		1,846	
RICHARDT, Ferdinand (1819-1895) Danish					
oil	5	20,292	1,300	4,641	6,712
RICHE, Louis (1877-1949) French					
3D	3	16,146	1,700	3,456	10,990
RICHE, le (18/19th C) French					
oil	1	2,750		2,750	
RICHEBE, Horace (1871-1958) French					
oil	1	6,838		6,838	
RICHER, Paul M L Pierre (1849-1933) French					
3D	1	1,191		1,191	
RICHERT, Charles Henry (1880-?) American					
oil	1	2,600		2,600	
RICHET, Léon (1847-1907) French					
oil	22	146,321	1,138	5,235	16,000
RICHETTE, C (?) Belgian?					
oil	1	3,216		3,216	
RICHIER, Germaine (1904-1959) French					
3D	6	225,981	1,945	12,807	105,700
RICHIR, Herman (1866-1942) Belgian					
oil	5	9,241	1,549	2,025	2,025
RICHMOND, George (1809-1896) British					
wc/d	1	2,718		2,718	
RICHMOND, Leonard (?-1965) British					
oil	1	5,928		5,928	
RICHTER, Adolf (1794-?) German					
oil	1	1,604		1,604	
RICHTER, Edouard Frederic Wilhelm (1844-1913) French					
oil	7	298,286	4,740	40,000	102,000
RICHTER, F (1774-1863) German					
3D	1	1,472		1,472	
RICHTER, Gerhard (1932-) German					
3D	1	30,200		30,200	
oil	47	15,236,281	3,883	36,240	4,500,000

Name	No.	Total Sales Value	lowest	Prices median	highest
wc/d	3	30,665	2,265	11,000	17,400
RICHTER, Giovanni (18th C) Italian					
oil	2	178,032	36,092	89,016	141,940
RICHTER, Gustav Karl (1823-1884) German					
oil	2	10,102	3,102	5,051	7,000
RICHTER, H (?) ?					
oil	2	10,390	1,740	5,195	8,650
RICHTER, Hans (1888-1975) German					
oil	1	2,836		2,836	
wc/d	1	1,115		1,115	
RICHTER, Henry Leopold (1870-1960) American					
oil	2	7,000	2,500	3,500	4,500
RICHTER, Herbert Davis (1874-1955) British					
oil	11	40,297	1,125	2,940	13,500
RICHTER, Ludwig Adrian (1803-1884) German					
oil	1	314,215		314,215	
wc/d	1	3,643		3,643	
RICHTER, Luisa (20th C) Latin American					
wc/d	1	1,005		1,005	
RICHTER, O (?) ?					
wc/d	1	1,408		1,408	
RICHTER, Wilhelm (1824-1892) Austrian					
oil	1	1,001		1,001	
RICHTER-BERLIN, Heinrich (1884-1981) German					
oil	1	3,448		3,448	
RICHTERS, Marius (1878-1955) Dutch					
oil	1	1,454		1,454	
RICHY, J (?) ?					
oil	1	1,264		1,264	
RICKETTS, Charles Robert (fl.1868-1874) British					
oil	1	1,440		1,440	
RICKEY, George (1907-) American					
3D	9	336,919	6,294	24,000	104,026
RICKMAN, Philip (1891-1982) British					
wc/d	1	2,700		2,700	
RICKS, James (fl.1868-1894) British					
oil	1	2,607		2,607	
RICO Y CEJUDO, Jose (1864-?) Spanish					
oil	2	16,138	1,918	8,069	14,220
wc/d	3	12,847	1,173	1,320	10,354
RICO Y ORTEGA, Martin (1833-1908) Spanish					
oil	7	227,706	5,000	22,000	90,000
wc/d	2	4,519	2,184	2,260	2,335
RICOIS, François Edme (1795-1881) French					
oil	1	6,769		6,769	
RIDDEL, James (1858-1928) British					
oil	5	12,686	1,029	1,544	5,292
RIDDELL, W H (?) British					
wc/d	2	2,844	1,264	1,422	1,580
RIDER, Arthur G (1886-1975) American					
oil	4	91,250	4,750	12,000	62,500
wc/d	1	3,200		3,200	
RIDER, H Orne (1860-?) American					
oil	1	1,100		1,100	
RIDINGER, Johann Elias (1698-1767) German					
wc/d	2	3,644	1,644	1,822	2,000
RIDOLA, Mario (1890-?) Italian					
oil	2	45,773	6,346	22,887	39,427

Name	No.	Total Sales Value	lowest	Prices median	highest
RIECK, E (19th C) German					
wc/d	1	1,178		1,178	
RIECK, Emil (1852-?) German					
wc/d	1	1,094		1,094	
RIECKE, George (1848-1924) ?					
oil	2	2,700	1,200	1,350	1,500
RIEDEL, August (1799-1883) German					
oil	3	39,636	3,750	11,962	23,924
RIEDER, H (19th C) ?					
3D	1	1,073		1,073	
RIEDER, Marcel (1852-?) French					
oil	5	11,082	1,069	2,210	3,944
RIEGEN, Nicolaas (1827-1889) Dutch					
oil	6	42,232	1,924	4,293	16,124
RIEGER, Albert (1834-1905) Austrian					
oil	4	5,233	1,001	1,344	1,545
RIELLY, James (1956-) ?					
oil	1	5,800		5,800	
RIEMSDYK, Barthold Willem Floris van (1850-1942) Dutch					
oil	1	4,000		4,000	
RIEPER, August (1865-1940) German					
oil	1	1,427		1,427	
RIES, Ignacio de (1612-1661) Spanish					
oil	1	24,200		24,200	
RIESENBERG, Sidney (1885-?) American					
oil	2	8,500	3,000	4,250	5,500
RIESENER, Henri François (1767-1828) French					
oil	1	2,718		2,718	
RIESTRA, Adolfo (1944-1989) Mexican					
3D	1	18,000		18,000	
RIET, Jan van (1948-) Belgian					
wc/d	1	4,271		4,271	
RIETER, Heinrich (1751-1818) Swiss					
oil	1	13,788		13,788	
RIETH, Paul (1871-1925) German					
oil	3	4,044	1,072	1,486	1,486
RIETSCHEL, Ernst Wilhelm (1824-1860) German					
oil	1	27,740		27,740	
RIETSCHOTEN, Hermann van (1883-1962) German?					
oil	1	1,455		1,455	
RIFKA, Judy (20th C) ?					
oil	1	3,000		3,000	
RIGA, H (?) Hungary					
oil	1	1,064		1,064	
RIGAUD, Hyacinthe (1659-1743) French					
oil	4	78,019	9,019	19,500	30,000
RIGAUD, Jean (1912-1999) French					
oil	2	2,968	1,222	1,484	1,746
RIGAUD, John Francis (1742-1810) British					
oil	1	3,219		3,219	
RIGAUD, Pierre Gaston (1874-?) French					
oil	3	6,250	1,387	1,463	3,400
RIGAUT (?) French?					
oil	1	1,459		1,459	
RIGAUT, A (20th C) French?					
oil	1	1,817		1,817	
RIGET, Karl Age (1933-2001) Danish					
oil	1	1,025		1,025	

Name	No.	Total Sales Value	Prices lowest	median	highest
RIGG, Arthur H (1868-1947) British					
oil	2	3,497	1,697	1,749	1,800
RIGG, Ernest Higgins (1868-1947) British					
oil	10	31,672	1,022	1,917	9,750
RIGGS, Robert (1896-1970) American					
oil	2	142,500	32,500	71,250	110,000
RIGHETTI, Guido (1875-1958) Italian					
3D	4	8,669	1,244	2,221	2,983
RIGNANO, Vittorio (1860-1916) Italian					
oil	1	5,000		5,000	
RIGNY, Alfred (20th C) French					
oil	1	1,000		1,000	
RIGOLOT, Albert (1862-1932) French					
oil	5	28,713	1,341	4,200	15,500
RIJ-ROUSSEAU, Jeanne (1870-1956) French					
oil	1	2,900		2,900	
RIJK, Anna Francisca de (1834-1889) Dutch					
oil	2	4,341	2,159	2,171	2,182
RIJK, James de (1806-1882) Dutch					
oil	2	7,923	2,667	3,962	5,256
RIJKELIJKHUYSEN, Hermanus Jan Hendrik (1813-1883) Dutch					
oil	1	1,454		1,454	
RILEY (?) ?					
oil	1	3,171		3,171	
RILEY, Bernard (1915-1984) American?					
oil	1	1,500		1,500	
RILEY, Bridget (1931-1984) British					
oil	2	233,150	95,400	116,575	137,750
wc/d	1	7,150		7,150	
RILEY, Harold (1934-) British					
wc/d	1	1,359		1,359	
RILEY, John (1646-1691) British					
oil	3	46,888	4,004	9,664	33,220
RILEY, Kenneth (1919-) American					
oil	1	10,000		10,000	
RIMINI, G (19th C) Italian					
oil	2	2,907	1,425	1,454	1,482
RIMPATTA DA BOLOGNA, Antonio (16th C) Italian					
oil	1	36,882		36,882	
RINALDI, Claudio (19th C) Italian					
oil	1	4,898		4,898	
RINALDI, Francesco (18th C) Italian					
wc/d	1	1,100		1,100	
RINALDI, M (?) Italian					
oil	1	1,250		1,250	
RING, Laurits Andersen (1854-1933) Danish					
oil	14	84,172	1,850	4,776	23,235
wc/d	1	40,605		40,605	
RING, Ole (1902-1972) Danish					
oil	20	31,605	1,072	1,311	3,336
RING, Pieter de (1615-1660) Dutch					
oil	1	21,792		21,792	
RINGE, Niels (1791-1854) Danish					
wc/d	1	1,345		1,345	
RINGEL D'ILLZACH, Jean Desire (1847-1916) French					
3D	1	2,259		2,259	
RINK, Paulus Philippus (1861-1903) Dutch					
wc/d	2	3,971	1,293	1,986	2,678

Name	No.	Total Sales Value	Prices lowest	Prices median	highest
RIOPELLE, Jean-Paul (1923-) Canadian					
oil	20	843,653	5,973	36,507	166,100
wc/d	11	74,651	2,750	6,346	18,546
RIOS, Luigi da (1844-1892) Italian					
oil	1	9,096		9,096	
RIOU, Louis (20th C) French					
oil	1	1,676		1,676	
RIP, Willem C (1856-1922) Dutch					
oil	4	10,833	1,327	1,527	6,453
wc/d	2	3,571	1,506	1,786	2,065
RIPARI, Virgilio (1843-1902) Italian					
oil	2	42,774	3,032	21,387	39,742
wc/d	1	2,566		2,566	
RIPLEY, Aiden Lassell (1896-1969) American					
oil	2	68,000	34,000	34,000	34,000
wc/d	4	56,500	9,000	14,250	19,000
RIPOLLES, Juan (1932-) Spanish					
oil	1	2,279		2,279	
RIPPL-RONAI, Jozsef (1861-1927) Hungarian					
oil	1	4,791		4,791	
wc/d	3	15,770	3,537	4,403	7,830
RISEGARI, Silvio (19th C) Italian					
wc/d	1	1,088		1,088	
RISS, Thomas (1871-1959) Austrian					
oil	4	8,559	1,331	2,137	2,955
RISSA (1938-) German					
oil	1	5,009		5,009	
wc/d	1	2,831		2,831	
RIST, Pipilotti (1962-) German					
3D	3	168,157	2,457	60,000	105,700
RITCHIE, John (fl.1841-1875) British					
oil	1	7,500		7,500	
RITCHIE, Matthew (20th C) American?					
wc/d	1	1,850		1,850	
RITMAN, Louis (1889-1963) American/Russian					
oil	3	395,000	5,000	150,000	240,000
RITSCHEL, William (1864-1949) American					
oil	5	56,750	2,250	8,000	24,000
wc/d	1	3,000		3,000	
RITSCHL, Otto (1885-1976) German					
oil	2	7,767	2,670	3,884	5,097
RITSEMA, Coba (1876-1961) Dutch					
oil	3	16,412	1,561	6,789	8,062
RITSEMA, Jacob Coenraad (1869-1943) Dutch					
oil	1	1,132		1,132	
RITTENBERG, Henry R (1879-1969) American					
oil	1	2,774		2,774	
RITTER, Anne Gregory (1868-1929) American					
oil	1	2,700		2,700	
RITTER, Caspar (1861-1923) German					
oil	2	10,840	1,019	5,420	9,821
RITTER, Paul (elder) (1829-1907) German					
oil	1	2,500		2,500	
RITZ, Raphael (1829-1894) Swiss					
oil	3	15,338	2,915	5,647	6,776
RITZ, Valentine (18th C) British					
oil	1	1,139		1,139	
RITZBERGER, Albert (1853-1915) German					
oil	1	1,920		1,920	

Name	No.	Total Sales Value	lowest	Prices median	highest
RITZENHOFEN, Hubert (1879-1961) Dutch					
oil	2	4,564	1,075	2,282	3,489
RIVA, Guiseppe (19th C) Italian					
wc/d	1	1,900		1,900	
RIVA, J (19th C) Italian					
wc/d	1	1,400		1,400	
RIVALTA, Augusto (1838-1925) Italian					
3D	1	1,159		1,159	
RIVAROLI, Giuseppe (1885-1943) Italian					
oil	2	4,573	1,800	2,287	2,773
RIVAS, Antonio (19th C) Italian					
oil	1	4,000		4,000	
RIVAS, Bárbaro (1893-1967) Venezuelan					
oil	1	4,630		4,630	
RIVAUD, Eugene (19th C) French					
oil	1	7,100		7,100	
RIVELLES GUILLEN, Juan (1896-) Spanish					
oil	1	1,245		1,245	
RIVERA, Diego (1886-1957) Mexican					
oil	4	782,000	12,000	60,000	650,000
wc/d	15	144,705	1,600	8,000	26,000
RIVERA, Manuel (1927-1995) Spanish					
3D	2	29,297	13,066	14,649	16,231
oil	5	51,013	1,994	11,440	18,822
wc/d	4	44,477	1,397	13,508	16,064
RIVERA, Oscar Garcia (1915-1971) Cuban					
oil	3	18,500	2,000	2,500	14,000
RIVERS, A Montague (19/20th C) British					
wc/d	1	1,144		1,144	
RIVERS, Larry (1923-) American					
oil	3	155,000	20,000	65,000	70,000
wc/d	7	39,132	1,162	2,400	13,000
RIVERS, Leopold (1852-1905) British					
oil	3	5,935	1,510	1,670	2,755
wc/d	1	1,272		1,272	
RIVEY, Arsene-Hippolyte (1838-1903) French					
oil	1	2,854		2,854	
RIVIERE, Adriaan de la (1857-1941) Dutch					
oil	5	9,227	1,179	1,472	3,143
RIVIERE, Briton (1840-1920) British					
oil	1	6,750		6,750	
wc/d	1	2,002		2,002	
RIVIERE, Charles (1848-1920) French					
oil	3	18,171	1,170	3,802	13,199
RIVIERE, Henri (1864-1951) French					
oil	1	1,510		1,510	
wc/d	4	14,031	1,281	2,144	8,462
RIVIERE, Henry Parsons (1811-1888) British					
oil	1	1,396		1,396	
RIVIERE, Hugh Goldwin (1869-1956) British					
oil	1	15,072		15,072	
RIVIERE, Theodore (1857-1912) French					
3D	3	16,416	2,647	3,385	10,384
RIVOIRE (?) French					
wc/d	1	5,111		5,111	
RIVOIRE, François (1842-1919) French					
wc/d	3	5,871	1,043	1,056	3,772
RIVOIRE, Raymond (1884-1966) French					
3D	3	7,900	1,843	2,370	3,687

Name	No.	Total Sales Value	lowest	Prices median	highest
RIX, Julian (1850-1903) American					
oil	4	10,750	1,000	2,375	5,000
RIZZO, A (20th C) Italian?					
oil	1	2,400		2,400	
RIZZO, Pippo (1897-1964) Italian					
oil	1	1,773		1,773	
RIZZONI, Alexandre (1836-1902) Russian					
wc/d	2	15,095	7,065	7,548	8,030
ROBART, R G (18th C) Dutch					
oil	1	18,046		18,046	
ROBB, William George (1872-1940) British					
oil	2	2,827	1,232	1,414	1,595
ROBBE, Henri (1807-1899) Belgian					
oil	1	1,456		1,456	
ROBBE, Louis (1806-1887) Belgian					
oil	10	21,375	1,020	2,188	3,586
ROBBE, Manuel (1872-1936) French					
oil	1	4,000		4,000	
ROBBINS, Bruce (20th C) American					
3D	1	3,641		3,641	
ROBBINS, Horace Wolcott (1842-1904) American					
oil	1	14,000		14,000	
ROBERT, Alphonse (1807-1880) French?					
oil	1	9,113		9,113	
ROBERT, Ernst Friedrich Ferdinand (1763-1843) German					
oil	1	2,163		2,163	
ROBERT, Henry (1881-1961) French					
wc/d	1	1,976		1,976	
ROBERT, Hubert (1733-1808) French					
oil	19	2,903,127	25,000	100,000	389,863
wc/d	20	407,061	1,099	10,823	140,000
ROBERT, Leo Paul Samuel (1851-1923) Swiss					
wc/d	1	4,664		4,664	
ROBERT, Leopold-Louis (1794-1835) French					
oil	2	13,396	1,242	6,698	12,154
ROBERT, Louis Valentin Elias (1821-1874) French					
3D	1	5,192		5,192	
ROBERT, Nicolas (1614-1685) French					
wc/d	28	176,815	2,634	5,070	20,410
ROBERT, Philippe (1881-1930) Swiss					
oil	2	4,835	1,920	2,418	2,915
wc/d	1	1,129		1,129	
ROBERT, Theophile (1879-1954) Swiss					
oil	4	8,908	1,516	2,202	2,988
ROBERT-FLEURY, Tony (1837-1912) French					
oil	1	5,500		5,500	
ROBERTS, Arthur Spencer (1920-) British					
wc/d	2	6,996	2,556	3,498	4,440
ROBERTS, Carl (20th C) South African					
3D	1	2,130		2,130	
ROBERTS, David (1796-1864) British					
oil	9	108,128	2,115	4,672	40,600
wc/d	14	180,984	1,050	8,058	91,520
ROBERTS, Edwin (1840-1917) British					
oil	4	25,958	2,700	7,129	9,000
ROBERTS, Elizabeth W (1871-1927) American					
oil	1	2,900		2,900	
ROBERTS, F W (19th C) ?					
oil	1	1,400		1,400	

Name	No.	Total Sales Value	lowest	Prices median	highest
ROBERTS, James (fl.1858-1876) British					
oil	1	2,355		2,355	
ROBERTS, James (19th C) French					
wc/d	1	2,820		2,820	
ROBERTS, Julie (1963-) American					
oil	3	27,208	2,188	3,020	22,000
ROBERTS, Ray (20th C) American					
oil	2	6,900	1,400	3,450	5,500
ROBERTS, Thomas (1748-1778) Irish					
oil	1	606,800		606,800	
ROBERTS, Thomas E (1820-1901) British					
oil	1	11,775		11,775	
ROBERTS, William (1895-1980) British					
oil	1	46,500		46,500	
wc/d	10	42,010	1,692	3,549	7,975
ROBERTS, William Goodridge (1904-1974) Canadian					
oil	27	135,711	1,327	3,264	19,583
wc/d	3	4,664	1,240	1,300	2,124
ROBERTSON, Anne MacKinne (20th C) American					
wc/d	1	2,600		2,600	
ROBERTSON, Charles (1844-1891) British					
wc/d	2	7,901	1,859	3,951	6,042
ROBERTSON, Charles Kay (fl.1888-1931) British					
oil	1	7,592		7,592	
ROBERTSON, George (1748-1788) British					
wc/d	1	5,840		5,840	
ROBERTSON, James Downie (1931-) British					
oil	2	2,532	1,092	1,266	1,440
ROBERTSON, Samuel (1868-1943) Canadian					
oil	1	1,483		1,483	
ROBERTSON, Suze (1856-1922) Dutch					
oil	7	27,377	1,358	2,970	8,417
wc/d	1	1,526		1,526	
ROBERTSON, Tom (1850-1947) British					
oil	1	1,113		1,113	
ROBICHON, Jules Paul Victor (19/20th C) French					
oil	1	6,208		6,208	
ROBIE, Jean Baptiste (1821-1910) Belgian					
oil	6	146,849	1,797	19,035	72,680
ROBIN, Georges (19/20th C) French					
oil	3	3,292	1,000	1,073	1,219
ROBINEAU-SALLARD, Ferdinand Desire (1823-1870) French					
oil	1	2,872		2,872	
ROBINET, Gustave Paul (elder) (1845-1932) French					
oil	4	11,150	1,719	2,653	4,126
ROBINS, Jane (19th C) British					
oil	1	5,922		5,922	
ROBINS, Thomas (younger) (1745-1806) British					
wc/d	3	22,214	3,624	9,295	9,295
ROBINS, Thomas Sewell (1814-1880) British					
oil	1	8,965		8,965	
wc/d	7	23,796	1,650	2,860	6,435
ROBINSON, Albert Henry (1881-1956) Canadian					
oil	2	13,975	6,175	6,988	7,800
ROBINSON, Alexander (1867-1952) American					
oil	2	2,277	1,097	1,139	1,180
ROBINSON, Charles (1870-1937) British					
oil	1	4,452		4,452	
wc/d	1	6,300		6,300	

Name	No.	Total Sales Value	lowest	Prices median	highest
ROBINSON, Chas Dorman (1847-1933) American					
oil	4	14,500	2,000	2,750	7,000
ROBINSON, Hal (1875-1933) American					
oil	3	6,050	1,250	1,300	3,500
ROBINSON, Harry W (fl.1899-1907) British					
oil	1	1,151		1,151	
ROBINSON, M F (20th C) American					
oil	1	1,400		1,400	
ROBINSON, Markey (1918-1997) Irish					
oil	9	54,046	2,368	5,920	11,840
wc/d	13	44,324	1,088	1,584	11,440
ROBINSON, Theodore (1852-1896) American					
oil	4	1,215,000	20,000	287,500	620,000
wc/d	2	23,089	8,500	11,545	14,589
ROBINSON, Thomas (?-1810) British					
oil	1	3,750		3,750	
ROBINSON, William Heath (1872-1944) British					
wc/d	4	11,371	1,510	2,515	4,832
ROBINSON, William S (1861-1945) American					
oil	1	2,800		2,800	
ROBJENT, Richard (1937-) British					
wc/d	1	1,573		1,573	
ROBSON, George Fennel (1788-1833) British					
wc/d	4	39,013	1,099	3,947	30,020
ROBUS, Hugo (1885-1964) American					
3D	2	10,000	5,000	5,000	5,000
ROBUS, J F (?) ?					
oil	1	4,684		4,684	
ROCA GISBERT (20th C) Spanish					
wc/d	1	1,705		1,705	
ROCA SASTRE, Jose (1928-1997) Spanish					
oil	3	23,243	2,958	7,626	12,659
ROCA, Junn (1948-) American					
oil	2	3,400	1,500	1,700	1,900
ROCCA, Michele (1670-1751) Italian					
oil	2	14,783	6,660	7,392	8,123
ROCCA, della (17/18th C) Italian					
oil	1	5,624		5,624	
ROCCATAGLIATA, Niccolo (16/17th C) Italian					
3D	1	4,915		4,915	
ROCCATAGLIATA, Sebastiano (17th C) Italian					
3D	1	21,551		21,551	
ROCCHI, Francesco de (1902-1978) Italian					
oil	2	11,765	4,833	5,883	6,932
ROCHA, Joaquim Manoel da (1727-1786) Portuguese					
oil	1	34,000		34,000	
ROCHARD, I (20th C) French					
3D	1	1,124		1,124	
ROCHARD, Irenee (1906-1984) French					
3D	3	11,342	2,041	3,021	6,280
ROCHAT, Willy (1920-) Swiss					
oil	1	4,930		4,930	
ROCHE, Alexander (1861-1921) British					
oil	2	6,045	1,305	3,023	4,740
ROCHE, Marcel (1890-1959) French					
oil	1	6,769		6,769	
ROCHEGROSSE, Georges (1859-1938) French					
oil	7	145,742	2,567	12,114	54,516

Name	No.	Total Sales Value	lowest	Prices median	highest
ROCHELT AMANN, Juan Jose (20th C) Spanish					
oil	1	3,380		3,380	
ROCHER, Charles (1890-1962) French					
oil	2	4,930	2,320	2,465	2,610
ROCHOLL, Theodor (1854-1933) German					
oil	2	4,966	1,730	2,483	3,236
ROCHUSSEN, Charles (1814-1894) Dutch					
oil	1	2,595		2,595	
wc/d	1	5,516		5,516	
ROCKLINE, Vera (1896-1934) American					
oil	2	19,149	2,394	9,575	16,755
ROCKMORE, Noel (1928-1995) American					
oil	5	10,750	1,200	1,900	4,250
ROCKWELL, Augustus (1822-1882) American					
oil	1	15,000		15,000	
ROCKWELL, Norman (1894-1978) American					
oil	11	791,000	4,000	65,000	190,000
wc/d	3	44,000	7,000	9,000	28,000
ROCQUEMONT, Eugène (1805-?) French					
oil	1	1,728		1,728	
RODA, Antonio (1921-1970) Spanish					
oil	1	8,000		8,000	
RODA, Leonardo (1868-1933) Italian					
oil	18	61,636	1,468	2,557	7,735
RODAKOWSKI, Henryk (1823-1894) Polish					
oil	1	9,194		9,194	
RODDE, Karl Gustav (1830-1906) German					
oil	1	1,366		1,366	
RODDE, Michel (1913-) French					
oil	2	2,680	1,278	1,340	1,402
RODE, E (19th C) French					
oil	1	2,248		2,248	
RODECK, Karl (1841-1909) Dutch					
oil	2	3,133	1,033	1,567	2,100
RODETTI, A (19th C) Italian					
oil	1	5,500		5,500	
RODEWALD, Fred (20th C) American					
wc/d	1	2,600		2,600	
RODIEUX, Maurice (1876-1927) Swiss					
wc/d	1	2,320		2,320	
RODIN, A (1840-1917) French					
3D	1	1,700		1,700	
RODIN, Auguste (1840-1917) French					
3D	75	13,583,167	2,084	39,260	2,500,000
oil	1	15,274		15,274	
wc/d	8	244,404	3,750	20,040	84,373
RODRIGUE, George (20th C) American					
oil	2	13,750	5,750	6,875	8,000
RODRIGUEZ BONOME, Santiango (1901-?) Spanish					
3D	1	5,184		5,184	
RODRIGUEZ BRONCHU, Salvador (1912-) Spanish					
oil	1	1,294		1,294	
RODRIGUEZ CASTELAO, Alfonso (1886-1950) Spanish					
wc/d	2	5,703	1,326	2,852	4,377
RODRIGUEZ DE LOSADA, Jose Maria (1826-1896) Spanish					
oil	1	10,755		10,755	
RODRIGUEZ ETCHART, Severo (1864-?) South American					
oil	1	33,899		33,899	

Name	No.	Total Sales Value	Prices lowest	median	highest
RODRIGUEZ SAN CLEMENT (19/20th C) Spanish					
oil	2	2,919	1,115	1,460	1,804
RODRIGUEZ SANCHEZ CLEMENT, Francisco (1893-1968) Spanish					
oil	5	8,523	1,425	1,687	1,904
RODRIGUEZ, Guillermo (20th C) Uruguayan?					
oil	1	1,400		1,400	
RODRIGUEZ, Mariano (1912-1990) Cuban					
oil	1	18,000		18,000	
RODRIGUEZ, Ruben (1955-) ?					
oil	1	1,509		1,509	
RODRIGUEZ, Victor (1970-) Mexican					
oil	2	18,000	5,000	9,000	13,000
RODRIK, Paul (19/20th C) Canadian					
oil	2	2,920	1,261	1,460	1,659
ROE, Clarence (?-1909) British					
oil	5	8,155	1,100	1,372	2,385
ROE, Robert Ernest (fl.1860-1880) British					
oil	10	106,498	1,001	5,533	57,380
wc/d	2	4,101	1,829	2,051	2,272
ROE, Robert Henry (1822-1905) British					
oil	1	2,291		2,291	
ROEBER, Ernst (1849-1915) German					
oil	1	2,000		2,000	
ROECKER, Henry Leon (1860-1941) American					
oil	1	1,200		1,200	
ROED, Jorgen (1808-1888) Danish					
oil	3	3,616	1,085	1,101	1,430
ROEDE, Jan (1914-) Dutch					
oil	7	25,929	1,981	3,879	6,034
ROEDER, Cyriakus (c.1560-1598) German					
oil	1	5,652		5,652	
ROEDER, Emy (1890-1971) German					
3D	1	9,948		9,948	
ROEDER, Francois (19th C) French					
oil	1	5,119		5,119	
ROEDER, Max (1866-1947) German					
oil	2	3,274	1,366	1,637	1,908
ROEDERSTEIN, Ottilie Wilhelmine (1859-1937) Swiss					
oil	2	4,036	1,615	2,018	2,421
ROEGGE, Wilhelm (jnr) (1870-1947) German					
oil	2	3,399	1,560	1,700	1,839
ROEGGE, Wilhelm (snr) (1829-1908) German					
oil	1	2,696		2,696	
ROEHN, Jean Alphonse (1799-1864) French					
oil	3	46,520	1,800	12,220	32,500
ROELANT, Edward (?-1883) Belgian					
oil	1	3,950		3,950	
ROELOFS, Albert (1877-1920) Dutch					
oil	4	47,868	2,360	10,025	25,459
ROELOFS, Willem (1822-1897) Dutch					
oil	9	215,627	1,534	10,608	110,324
ROELOFS, Willem Elisa (1874-1940) Dutch					
oil	1	4,591		4,591	
wc/d	1	1,377		1,377	
ROELOFSZ, Charles (1897-1962) Dutch					
oil	1	1,268		1,268	
ROERICH, Nikolai Konstantinovitch (1874-1947) American/Russian					
oil	2	72,300	30,000	36,150	42,300
wc/d	2	23,624	3,624	11,812	20,000

Name	No.	Total Sales Value	lowest	Prices median	highest
ROESE, Eckart (1959-) German					
oil	1	1,298		1,298	
ROESEN, Severin (fl.1848-1872) American/German					
oil	6	405,000	22,500	75,000	100,000
ROESEN, Severin (school) (fl.1848-1872) American/German					
oil	1	8,750		8,750	
ROESLER, Franz Ettore (1845-1907) Italian					
wc/d	1	2,898		2,898	
ROESSINGH, Louis Albert (1873-1951) Dutch/Belgian					
oil	5	9,883	1,259	1,671	2,847
ROESSLER, Georg (1861-1925) German					
oil	1	1,100		1,100	
ROESTRATEN, Pieter Gerritsz van (1630-1700) Dutch					
oil	1	41,399		41,399	
ROFFIAEN, Jean François (1820-1898) Belgian					
oil	11	43,293	1,103	3,087	10,211
ROFFLER, Mario (20th C) Swiss					
oil	2	2,884	1,269	1,442	1,615
ROGANEAU, François-Maurice (1883-1974) French					
oil	1	1,579		1,579	
ROGER, Emili Bosch (1894-1980) Spanish					
oil	1	6,006		6,006	
ROGER, Suzanne (1898-1986) French					
oil	1	1,267		1,267	
ROGERS, Claude (1907-1979) British					
oil	1	2,808		2,808	
ROGERS, Frank Whiting (1854-?) American					
oil	2	5,169	1,919	2,585	3,250
ROGERS, Howard (1932-) American					
oil	1	5,500		5,500	
ROGERS, Otto Donald (20th C) Canadian					
oil	1	3,027		3,027	
ROGERS, Philip Hutchins (1794-1853) British					
oil	1	2,748		2,748	
ROGERS, Thomas (19th C) British					
oil	1	1,800		1,800	
ROGERS, William P (fl.1842-1872) British					
oil	1	2,300		2,300	
ROGET, John Lewis (1828-1908) British					
wc/d	1	1,716		1,716	
ROGGE, Adalbert (1861-?) German					
oil	1	3,778		3,778	
ROGGE, Theodor (1854-?) German					
wc/d	1	1,200		1,200	
ROGGE, Wilhelm (1829-1908) German					
oil	1	1,346		1,346	
ROGHMAN, Roeland (1597-1686) Dutch					
wc/d	1	37,321		37,321	
ROGIER, Camille (19th C) French					
oil	1	9,666		9,666	
wc/d	2	2,554	1,038	1,277	1,516
ROGNONI, Angelo (1896-1957) Italian					
oil	1	2,025		2,025	
wc/d	4	12,906	2,475	3,032	4,368
ROGNONI, Franco (1913-1999) Italian					
oil	5	8,447	1,109	1,698	2,160
wc/d	2	3,408	1,034	1,704	2,374
ROHDE, Fredrik (1816-1886) Danish					
oil	7	15,900	1,291	2,025	3,873

Name	No.	Total Sales Value	lowest	Prices median	highest
ROHDE, Johan (1856-1935) Danish					
oil	3	3,284	1,030	1,159	1,159
ROHL, Karl Peter (1890-1975) German					
wc/d	1	4,530		4,530	
ROHLFS, Christian (1849-1938) German					
oil	14	548,612	4,356	28,420	116,779
wc/d	15	320,841	2,364	13,000	61,470
ROHNER, Georges (1913-2000) French					
oil	6	21,985	1,053	1,707	12,997
ROIDKIN, Rene (18th C) German					
wc/d	1	3,205		3,205	
ROIDOT, Henri (1877-1960) Belgian					
oil	5	17,940	1,111	2,199	9,852
ROIG (20th C) ?					
oil	1	2,610		2,610	
ROIG GUTIERREZ, Francisco (1882-1958) Spanish					
oil	2	3,712	1,856	1,856	1,856
ROIG Y SOLER (19/20th C) Spanish					
oil	1	10,415		10,415	
ROIG Y SOLER, Juan (1852-1909) Spanish					
oil	3	23,477	3,831	7,000	12,646
ROING, Johan (1958-) German					
3D	1	1,211		1,211	
ROJAS, Carlos (1933-) Colombian					
oil	1	15,000		15,000	
ROJAS, Elmar (1938-) Guatemalan					
oil	1	20,000		20,000	
ROJKA, Fritz (1878-1939) Austrian					
oil	1	1,073		1,073	
ROKA, Charles Antonio (1912-) Scandinavian?					
oil	1	1,382		1,382	
ROKACHEVSKY, Afanasy Efimovich (1830-1901) Russian					
oil	1	6,040		6,040	
ROKLINE, Vera (1896-1938) ?					
oil	1	4,377		4,377	
ROLAND DE LA PORTE, Henri Horace (1724-1793) French					
oil	1	7,500		7,500	
ROLARD, François Laurent (1842-1912) French					
3D	1	1,522		1,522	
ROLDAN, Enrique (19th C) Spanish					
oil	2	6,714	1,714	3,357	5,000
ROLFE, Henry Leonidas (fl.1847-1881) British					
oil	1	8,000		8,000	
ROLING, Gerard Victor Alphons (1904-1981) Dutch					
oil	2	21,734	9,056	10,867	12,678
ROLLA, Adolfo Giuseppe (1899-1967) Italian					
oil	1	1,468		1,468	
ROLLAND, Auguste (1797-1859) French					
oil	1	1,788		1,788	
ROLLAND, Benjamin de (1777-1855) French					
oil	1	11,671		11,671	
ROLLE, A (19th C) ?					
3D	1	3,140		3,140	
ROLLE, August H O (1875-1941) American					
oil	2	3,300	1,500	1,650	1,800
ROLLI, Vincenzo (?) Italian?					
oil	1	1,885		1,885	
ROLLINS, I (19/20th C) ?					
oil	1	1,400		1,400	

Name	No.	Total Sales Value	Prices lowest	median	highest
ROLLINS, Warren E (1861-1962) American					
oil	3	26,700	2,200	3,500	21,000
ROLLOF, Ulf (1961-) Swedish					
wc/d	1	1,497		1,497	
ROLSHOVEN, Julius (1858-1930) American					
oil	2	3,100	1,100	1,550	2,000
ROMAGNOLI, Giovanni (20th C) Italian?					
oil	1	4,800		4,800	
ROMAGNONI, Bepi (1930-1964) Italian					
wc/d	3	12,526	1,497	4,394	6,635
ROMAKO, Anton (1832-1889) Austrian					
oil	3	57,274	4,740	20,934	31,600
ROMAN SCHOOL Italian					
3D	1	14,182		14,182	
ROMAN SCHOOL, 14th C Italian					
oil	1	17,640		17,640	
ROMAN SCHOOL, 16th C Italian					
oil	3	15,204	3,898	3,898	7,350
wc/d	1	8,526		8,526	
ROMAN SCHOOL, 16th/17th C Italian					
3D	1	5,776		5,776	
oil	1	22,650		22,650	
ROMAN SCHOOL, 17th C Italian					
3D	6	79,025	3,322	10,590	34,730
oil	42	535,279	2,201	7,055	105,700
wc/d	2	10,426	3,926	5,213	6,500
ROMAN SCHOOL, 17th/18th C Italian					
3D	3	55,991	5,880	6,210	43,901
oil	4	43,378	2,752	5,193	30,240
ROMAN SCHOOL, 18th C Italian					
3D	7	198,582	7,250	27,727	67,468
oil	32	332,689	2,269	6,393	53,380
wc/d	1	3,020		3,020	
ROMAN SCHOOL, 19th C Italian					
3D	1	10,198		10,198	
oil	1	2,448		2,448	
wc/d	1	4,586		4,586	
ROMAN SCHOOL, 1st C Italian					
3D	1	35,913		35,913	
ROMANACH, Leopoldo (1862-1951) Cuban					
oil	3	26,067	1,567	6,500	18,000
ROMANELLI, Giovanni Francesco (1610-1662) Italian					
oil	1	24,767		24,767	
wc/d	2	13,337	6,500	6,669	6,837
ROMANELLI, Giovanni Francesco (school) (1610-1662) Italian					
oil	1	3,500		3,500	
ROMANELLI, P (1812-1887) Italian					
3D	1	4,500		4,500	
ROMANELLI, Pasquale (1812-1887) Italian					
3D	1	15,100		15,100	
ROMANELLI, Raffaelo (1856-1920) Italian					
3D	2	48,543	13,543	24,272	35,000
ROMANG, Johann Franz (1777-?) Swiss					
wc/d	1	1,709		1,709	
ROMANI, Juana (1869-1924) Italian					
oil	1	10,000		10,000	
ROMANI, Romolo (1884-1916) Italian					
wc/d	2	3,194	1,262	1,597	1,932
ROMANINO, Girolamo (1484-1562) Italian					
oil	1	116,468		116,468	

Name	No.	Total Sales Value	Prices lowest	median	highest
ROMANO (?) Italian					
oil	1	2,166		2,166	
ROMANO, Daniela (1947-) Italian					
oil	1	7,758		7,758	
ROMANO, Elio (1906-1996) Italian					
oil	1	1,773		1,773	
ROMANO, Emanuel Glicen (1897-1984) Italian/American					
oil	1	3,000		3,000	
ROMANO, Giulio (1499-1546) Italian					
oil	1	28,000		28,000	
wc/d	2	27,531	1,861	13,766	25,670
ROMANO, Giulio (school) (1499-1546) Italian					
oil	1	3,200		3,200	
ROMANTIC SCHOOL, 19th C					
oil	1	9,016		9,016	
ROMANY, Adele (1769-1846) French					
oil	1	20,160		20,160	
ROMBAUX, Egide (1865-?) Belgian					
3D	1	1,630		1,630	
ROMBERG DE VAUCORBEIL, Maurice (1862-1943) French					
oil	1	5,929		5,929	
wc/d	2	3,362	1,558	1,681	1,804
ROMBOUTS, Gillis (1630-1678) Dutch					
oil	1	12,080		12,080	
ROMBOUTS, Salomon (17th C) Dutch					
oil	2	7,673	3,744	3,837	3,929
ROMBOUTS, Theodor (1597-1637) Flemish					
oil	1	17,976		17,976	
ROMEK, Arpad (1883-?) Hungarian					
oil	1	1,099		1,099	
ROMERO DE TORRES, Enrique (1876-1956) Spanish					
oil	1	1,278		1,278	
ROMERO DE TORRES, Julio (1879-1930) Spanish					
oil	2	618,895	48,895	309,448	570,000
ROMERO RESSENDI, Baldomero (1922-1977) Spanish					
oil	4	8,607	1,210	2,131	3,136
ROMERO Y BARROS, Rafael (1833-1895) Spanish					
oil	2	23,600	3,146	11,800	20,454
ROMERO Y ESCALANTE, Juan de Sevilla (1643-1695) Spanish					
oil	1	8,181		8,181	
ROMERO Y LOPEZ, Jose Maria (c.1815-1880) Spanish					
oil	2	3,738	1,699	1,869	2,039
ROMERO, Juan (?) Spanish					
oil	1	2,288		2,288	
ROMERO, Rafael (19th C) Spanish					
oil	1	5,495		5,495	
ROMEYN, Willem (1624-1694) Dutch					
oil	1	6,679		6,679	
ROMITI, Gino (1881-1967) Italian					
oil	7	18,389	1,145	1,435	5,723
ROMITI, Sergio (1928-) Italian					
oil	6	47,020	3,601	7,673	11,864
ROMNEY, George (1734-1802) British					
oil	16	304,993	1,440	8,095	114,400
RONAY, Marcel (1910-) German					
oil	1	11,520		11,520	
RONCALLI, Cristoforo (1552-1626) Italian					
wc/d	3	8,644	2,182	3,140	3,322

Name	No.	Total Sales Value	lowest	Prices median	highest
RONCHETTI, Torres (19th C) ?					
oil	1	4,839		4,839	
RONDA, Omar (1947-) Italian					
3D	1	1,783		1,783	
oil	1	1,484		1,484	
RONDANI, Francesco (1490-1550) Italian					
oil	1	10,474		10,474	
RONDAS, Willi (20th C) British					
oil	1	1,264		1,264	
RONDEL, Frederick (1826-1892) American					
oil	2	6,750	3,000	3,375	3,750
RONNER, Alfred Jean (1851-1901) Belgian					
oil	1	1,071		1,071	
RONNER, Henriette (1821-1909) Dutch					
oil	24	692,897	1,951	7,900	210,000
wc/d	4	10,971	1,880	2,502	4,087
RONTINI, Ferruccio (1893-1964) Italian					
oil	3	3,924	1,115	1,204	1,605
ROOBJEE, Pjeroo (1945-) Belgian					
oil	1	1,180		1,180	
ROOD, John (1902-) Greek/American					
3D	2	4,900	2,100	2,450	2,800
ROOKE, Thomas Matthew (1842-1942) British					
wc/d	4	20,010	1,400	1,440	15,730
ROOKER, Michael Angelo (1743-1801) British					
wc/d	4	10,733	1,173	1,445	6,636
ROONEY, Mick (1944-) British					
oil	1	5,640		5,640	
ROOS, C G (17th C) ?					
oil	1	4,544		4,544	
ROOS, Cajetan (1690-1770) Italian					
oil	4	19,527	2,793	4,592	7,550
ROOS, Jacob (1682-?) Italian					
oil	2	2,926	1,463	1,463	1,463
ROOS, Johann Heinrich (1631-1685) German					
oil	5	65,846	1,154	3,893	40,770
ROOS, Johann Melchior (1659-1731) German					
oil	3	19,932	3,856	4,162	11,914
ROOS, Peter (1850-?) American					
oil	1	2,500		2,500	
ROOS, Philipp Peter (1657-1706) German					
oil	8	98,408	3,744	8,007	25,120
ROOSE, Charles van (1883-1960) Belgian					
oil	1	2,635		2,635	
ROOSENBOOM, Albert (1845-1875) Belgian					
oil	3	9,639	1,048	4,000	4,591
ROOSENBOOM, Margaretha (1843-1896) Dutch					
oil	2	2,893	1,395	1,447	1,498
wc/d	1	12,243		12,243	
ROOSENBOOM, Nicolaas Johannes (1805-1880) Dutch					
oil	8	171,763	2,264	9,487	94,800
ROOSKENS, Anton (1906-1976) Dutch					
oil	4	20,832	1,814	4,558	9,903
wc/d	6	15,206	1,268	2,570	3,367
ROOSVAAL-KALLSTENIUS, Gerda (1864-1939) Swedish					
oil	1	1,587		1,587	
ROOTIUS, Jakobus (1644-1681) Dutch					
oil	1	33,556		33,556	

Name	No.	Total Sales Value	lowest	Prices median	highest
ROOVER, Ferdinand de (19th C) Belgian					
oil	1	1,331		1,331	
ROPE, George Thomas (1846-1929) British					
oil	2	7,327	1,027	3,664	6,300
ROPELE, Walter (1934-) Swiss					
oil	8	14,703	1,580	1,827	2,127
ROPP, van (19th C) ?					
oil	1	2,449		2,449	
ROPS, Felicien (1833-1898) Belgian					
wc/d	6	12,759	1,241	1,502	3,782
ROQUE, Joannis de la (17th C) French?					
wc/d	1	1,130		1,130	
ROQUEPLAN, Camille (1803-1855) French					
wc/d	1	1,020		1,020	
RORBYE, Martinus (1803-1848) Danish					
oil	4	666,076	5,004	68,036	525,000
wc/d	3	10,418	1,270	3,480	5,668
ROS Y GUELL, Antonio (1873-1957) Spanish					
oil	1	1,388		1,388	
ROSA, A (?) ?					
oil	1	1,026		1,026	
ROSA, Buddy di (20th C) ?					
3D	2	3,783	1,455	1,892	2,328
ROSA, Herve di (1959-) French					
3D	2	8,641	4,219	4,321	4,422
oil	18	73,035	1,003	1,867	14,018
wc/d	3	17,086	5,133	5,822	6,131
ROSA, Pacecco di (1600-1654) Italian					
oil	1	36,473		36,473	
ROSA, Raffaele de (1940-) Italian					
oil	3	5,033	1,286	1,495	2,252
ROSA, Richard di (1963-) French					
3D	1	1,928		1,928	
oil	1	2,357		2,357	
wc/d	1	3,098		3,098	
ROSA, Salvator (1615-1673) Italian					
oil	5	144,803	3,800	12,080	61,740
wc/d	7	46,993	1,891	6,342	16,610
ROSA, Salvator (school) (1615-1673) Italian					
oil	5	28,429	2,281	4,083	14,000
ROSA, Saverio dalla (1745-1821) Italian					
oil	1	10,166		10,166	
ROSAI, Ottone (1895-1957) Italian					
oil	11	248,632	5,401	14,835	75,050
wc/d	7	17,258	1,170	2,170	4,610
ROSALES, Eduardo (1836-1873) Spanish					
oil	4	44,458	1,224	5,647	31,940
wc/d	1	1,028		1,028	
ROSANDIC, Toma (1876-?) Yugoslavian					
3D	1	6,897		6,897	
ROSATI, G (1858-1917) Italian					
oil	1	4,777		4,777	
ROSATI, Giulio (1858-1917) Italian					
wc/d	9	184,938	7,248	18,000	35,000
ROSCH, Carl (1884-?) German					
oil	6	21,127	1,424	2,292	8,945
wc/d	1	1,398		1,398	
ROSCOE, S G Williams (1852-c.1922) British					
wc/d	2	3,029	1,170	1,515	1,859

Name	No.	Total Sales Value	Prices lowest	median	highest
ROSE, Alexandre Auguste (19th C) French					
oil	1	1,793		1,793	
ROSE, Carl (1903-1971) American					
wc/d	1	1,100		1,100	
ROSE, D (20th C) American					
oil	1	1,000		1,000	
ROSE, Georges (1895-?) French					
wc/d	1	1,411		1,411	
ROSE, Guy (1867-1925) American					
oil	3	552,000	32,000	120,000	400,000
ROSE, Julius (1828-1911) German					
oil	3	7,299	1,026	1,273	5,000
ROSE, Manuel (1872-1961) Uruguayan					
oil	4	26,400	1,000	1,450	22,500
ROSE, Ted (20th C) American?					
wc/d	3	6,300	1,300	2,250	2,750
ROSEBEE (20th C) American					
oil	3	5,000	1,500	1,600	1,900
ROSELAND, Harry (1868-1950) American					
oil	5	67,600	3,600	10,000	26,000
ROSELL, A (1858-1922) British					
oil	3	7,522	1,287	2,465	3,770
ROSELL, Alexander (1859-1922) British					
oil	2	3,377	1,389	1,689	1,988
ROSELLI, Carlo (1939-) Italian					
oil	4	5,317	1,088	1,176	1,877
ROSELLINO, Antonio (1427-1479) Italian					
3D	1	193,957		193,957	
ROSEMEIER, Alexander Coenraad (1888-1992) Italian					
oil	1	1,093		1,093	
ROSEN, Ernest (1877-1926) American					
oil	1	2,500		2,500	
ROSEN, Georg von (1843-1923) Swedish					
wc/d	1	8,924		8,924	
ROSENBERG, Edward (1858-1934) Swedish					
oil	2	2,512	1,206	1,256	1,306
ROSENFELD, Alexander (20th C) American					
oil	1	1,400		1,400	
ROSENHAUER, Theodor (1901-1996) German					
oil	3	22,080	6,098	6,098	9,583
ROSENKRANTZ, Anna (19/20th C) Danish					
oil	2	2,142	1,008	1,071	1,134
ROSENKRANZ, Johann Heinrich Jacob Christian (1801-1851) German					
oil	1	2,273		2,273	
ROSENQUIST, James (1933-) American					
3D	1	80,000		80,000	
oil	10	750,700	12,000	50,000	256,700
wc/d	4	35,000	1,500	7,250	19,000
ROSENSOHN, Lennart (1918-1994) Swedish					
oil	1	2,837		2,837	
ROSENSTAND, Emil (1852-1932) German					
wc/d	1	7,500		7,500	
ROSENSTAND, Vilhelm (1838-1915) Danish					
oil	5	9,608	1,259	1,889	3,098
ROSENSTOCK, Isidore (1880-1956) French					
wc/d	1	1,028		1,028	
ROSENTHAL, Doris (20th C) American					
oil	1	1,700		1,700	

Name	No.	Total Sales Value	lowest	Prices median	highest
ROSENTHAL, Toby Edward (1849-1917) American					
oil	1	1,108		1,108	
ROSENTHALIS, Moshe (1922-) Israeli					
oil	2	6,400	1,600	3,200	4,800
ROSIER, Amedee (1831-1898) French					
oil	6	22,157	1,305	3,680	6,473
ROSLIN, Alexander (1718-1793) Swedish					
oil	3	83,785	16,370	24,526	42,889
ROSOMAN, Leonard (1913-) British					
oil	2	10,605	2,850	5,303	7,755
wc/d	1	2,212		2,212	
ROSS, Alex (1909-1990) American					
wc/d	1	1,700		1,700	
ROSS, Christian Meyer (1843-1904) Norwegian					
oil	1	9,000		9,000	
ROSS, Isabel (20th C) American					
oil	2	8,900	2,400	4,450	6,500
ROSS, Joseph Thorburn (1849-1903) British					
oil	1	2,163		2,163	
ROSS, Robert Thorburn (1816-1876) British					
wc/d	1	2,900		2,900	
ROSS, Sir William Charles (1794-1860) British					
oil	1	3,900		3,900	
ROSSANO, Federico (1835-1912) Italian					
oil	3	27,765	2,453	5,246	20,066
ROSSEELS, J (19th C) Flemish					
oil	1	1,773		1,773	
ROSSELLI, Cosimo (1439-1507) Italian					
oil	1	7,550		7,550	
ROSSELLI, Matteo (1578-1650) Italian					
oil	1	10,570		10,570	
wc/d	2	12,806	1,481	6,403	11,325
ROSSERT, Paul (1851-1918) French					
oil	2	6,976	1,476	3,488	5,500
ROSSETTI, Dante Gabriel (1828-1882) British					
wc/d	7	4,239,061	7,441	157,300	3,624,000
ROSSI (?) ?					
3D	1	3,000		3,000	
ROSSI, Alberto (1858-1936) Italian					
oil	5	23,639	3,743	4,750	5,776
wc/d	1	3,327		3,327	
ROSSI, Aldo (1931-) Italian?					
wc/d	1	1,724		1,724	
ROSSI, Alexander M (fl.1870-1905) British					
oil	1	14,500		14,500	
ROSSI, Giovan Battista (fl.1749-1782) Italian					
oil	1	17,000		17,000	
ROSSI, Giuseppe (19th C) Italian					
oil	1	26,448		26,448	
ROSSI, Lucius (1846-1913) French					
oil	5	71,399	1,354	16,675	30,000
wc/d	1	4,350		4,350	
ROSSI, Luigi (1853-1923) Swiss					
oil	5	23,807	1,207	2,293	16,326
wc/d	1	1,400		1,400	
ROSSI, Roberto (1896-1957) Argentinian					
oil	1	1,600		1,600	
ROSSLER, Ludwig Christian Friedrich Wilhelm (1842-1910) German					
oil	1	5,006		5,006	

Name	No.	Total Sales Value	lowest	Prices median	highest
ROSSLER, Rudolf (1864-?) Austrian					
oil	1	1,355		1,355	
ROSSO, Mino (1904-1963) Italian					
3D	1	7,244		7,244	
ROSSUM DU CHATTEL, Fredericus Jacobus van (1856-1917) Dutch					
oil	2	22,617	7,314	11,309	15,303
wc/d	4	6,988	1,249	1,869	2,002
ROSSUM, Jan van (1630-1673) Dutch					
oil	2	11,079	2,872	5,540	8,207
ROST, Johannes (1816-1859) Dutch					
oil	1	1,268		1,268	
ROSTEL, Agathe (fl.1871-1893) German					
oil	1	60,000		60,000	
ROSTRUP-BOYESEN, Peter (1882-1952) Danish					
oil	6	8,414	1,072	1,162	2,026
ROTA, Cesare (1848-1885) Italian					
oil	1	1,619		1,619	
ROTA, G (1777-1821) Italian					
oil	1	4,413		4,413	
ROTARI, Pietro (1707-1762) Italian					
oil	7	182,606	5,364	25,000	45,815
wc/d	1	8,305		8,305	
ROTARI, Pietro (school) (1707-1762) Italian					
oil	1	2,720		2,720	
ROTELLA, Mimmo (1918-) Italian					
oil	3	9,275	1,632	3,623	4,020
wc/d	20	158,506	1,359	2,402	87,000
ROTH, Dieter (1930-1998) German					
3D	10	94,128	1,282	4,005	42,538
oil	2	7,854	3,000	3,927	4,854
wc/d	10	55,243	1,072	2,334	14,585
ROTH, Dieter and Bjorn (20th C) German					
3D	1	1,063		1,063	
oil	1	11,840		11,840	
wc/d	1	2,333		2,333	
ROTH, Dieter and RAINER, Arnulf (20th C) German/Austrian					
wc/d	1	2,917		2,917	
ROTH, George (?) British					
oil	1	3,472		3,472	
ROTH, George Andries (1809-1887) Dutch					
oil	2	15,686	5,739	7,843	9,947
ROTH, Philipp (1841-1921) German					
oil	5	26,551	1,734	3,372	10,725
ROTHBORT, Samuel (1882-1971) American					
oil	3	11,000	1,200	2,800	7,000
ROTHENBERG, Susan (1945-) American					
oil	3	297,000	42,000	125,000	130,000
wc/d	1	15,000		15,000	
ROTHENSTEIN, Michael (1908-1994) British					
wc/d	1	1,368		1,368	
ROTHKO, Mark (1903-1970) American					
oil	4	27,000,000	1,000,000	6,500,000	13,000,000
wc/d	3	54,640	4,640	12,000	38,000
ROTHSTEN, Carl Abraham (1826-1877) Swedish					
oil	4	21,276	1,073	3,892	12,420
ROTIG, G F (1873-1961) French					
wc/d	1	1,160		1,160	
ROTIG, Georges Frederic (1873-1961) French					
oil	7	20,393	1,355	2,957	3,988
wc/d	7	11,636	1,047	1,451	2,979

Name	No.	Total Sales Value	lowest	Prices median	highest
ROTTA, Antonio (1828-1903) Italian					
oil	2	12,964	5,934	6,482	7,030
ROTTA, Silvio Giulio (1853-1913) Italian					
oil	1	3,992		3,992	
ROTTEKEN, Carl Johann Friedrich Adolf (1831-1900) German					
oil	1	17,188		17,188	
ROTTIERS, Bernard Eugene Antoine (1771-1858) Belgian					
wc/d	1	2,718		2,718	
ROTTMANN, Carl (1798-1850) German					
oil	3	104,670	1,882	23,040	79,748
wc/d	2	2,968	1,196	1,484	1,772
ROTTMANN, Leopold (1812-1881) German					
oil	1	1,219		1,219	
ROTTMANN, Mozart (1874-?) Hungarian					
oil	1	4,681		4,681	
ROUAN, François (1943-) French					
oil	1	19,109		19,109	
wc/d	1	2,656		2,656	
ROUART, Ernest (1874-1942) French					
wc/d	1	8,872		8,872	
ROUAULT, Georges (1871-1958) French					
oil	9	749,635	11,000	71,550	212,925
wc/d	8	297,863	2,081	25,375	130,000
ROUBAUD, Franz (1856-1928) Russian					
oil	10	61,489	2,155	6,154	16,500
ROUBAUD, Jean Baptiste (1871-?) French					
oil	1	1,375		1,375	
ROUBTZOFF, Alexandre (1884-1949) French?					
oil	7	69,825	1,168	4,822	33,748
ROUBY, Alfred (1849-1909) French					
oil	3	5,431	1,043	2,047	2,341
ROUFOSSE, Charles Joseph (1853-1901) French					
3D	1	2,826		2,826	
ROUGELET, Benedict (1834-1894) French					
3D	1	1,363		1,363	
ROUGEMONT, Guy de (1935-) French					
3D	1	1,028		1,028	
wc/d	1	2,535		2,535	
ROUGEMONT, Philippe de (1891-1965) Swedish					
oil	1	2,800		2,800	
ROUGET, Eliane (20th C) ?					
oil	1	3,144		3,144	
ROUILLARD, Pierre Louis (1820-1881) French					
3D	1	1,350		1,350	
ROUILLIET, Nicolas Amaranthe (1810-1889) French					
oil	1	1,015		1,015	
ROULET, Henry (1915-) Swiss					
oil	1	1,924		1,924	
ROULIN, Felix (1931-) Belgian					
3D	1	2,298		2,298	
ROULLET, Gaston (1847-1925) French					
oil	4	8,607	1,160	2,167	3,114
wc/d	1	1,314		1,314	
ROUSAUD, Aristide (1868-1946) French					
3D	1	2,951		2,951	
ROUSSE, Frank (fl.1897-1915) British					
wc/d	15	31,554	1,027	1,276	5,304
ROUSSEAU (?) ?					
3D	1	1,742		1,742	

Name	No.	Total Sales Value	lowest	Prices median	highest
ROUSSEAU, Adrien (19th C) French					
oil	1	1,317		1,317	
ROUSSEAU, Albert (1908-1982) Canadian					
oil	3	3,580	1,083	1,216	1,281
ROUSSEAU, Camille (?) French?					
oil	1	1,035		1,035	
ROUSSEAU, Emmanuel (19th C) French					
oil	1	1,822		1,822	
ROUSSEAU, Gabriel (20th C) French					
wc/d	3	10,903	3,115	3,634	4,154
ROUSSEAU, Helen (1896-1992) American					
oil	2	10,500	3,500	5,250	7,000
ROUSSEAU, Henri Emilien (1875-1933) French					
oil	7	57,382	1,516	8,955	16,533
wc/d	2	24,533	8,470	12,267	16,063
ROUSSEAU, Henri Julien Felix (1844-1910) French					
oil	1	150,139		150,139	
wc/d	1	36,240		36,240	
ROUSSEAU, Nicolas (19th C) French					
oil	1	1,650		1,650	
ROUSSEAU, Philippe (1816-1887) French					
oil	5	52,995	1,190	3,097	42,432
ROUSSEAU, Theodore (1812-1867) French					
oil	10	525,455	1,081	12,964	320,000
wc/d	10	72,079	1,001	3,564	24,730
ROUSSEAU, Victor (1865-1954) Belgian					
3D	3	11,719	2,826	4,398	4,495
ROUSSEL, Alphonse (1829-1868) French					
oil	1	10,512		10,512	
ROUSSEL, Charles-Emanuel-Joseph (1861-1936) French					
oil	3	8,634	1,313	2,200	5,121
ROUSSEL, Ker Xavier (1867-1944) French					
oil	3	26,797	5,800	7,254	13,743
wc/d	1	4,282		4,282	
ROUSSEL, Marie (fl.1894-95) American					
oil	1	3,250		3,250	
ROUSSEL, Pierre (1927-1995) French					
oil	1	2,800		2,800	
ROUSSEL, Theodore (1847-1926) British					
oil	2	9,425	4,350	4,713	5,075
ROUSSIN, Georges (1854-?) French					
wc/d	1	1,254		1,254	
ROUSSIN, Victor (1812-c.1900) French					
oil	1	3,627		3,627	
ROUVIERE, Charles Claude Etienne (1866-1924) French					
oil	2	9,927	1,927	4,964	8,000
ROUX, Andre Paul le (1870-?) French					
oil	1	5,221		5,221	
ROUX, Antoine (elder) (1765-1835) French					
wc/d	7	35,776	2,077	4,543	9,500
ROUX, Carl (1826-1894) German					
oil	1	1,471		1,471	
ROUX, Constant (1865-1929) French					
3D	2	5,270	2,578	2,635	2,692
ROUX, François Geoffroy (1811-1882) French					
wc/d	11	56,099	1,082	4,283	10,384
ROUX, Frederic (1805-1874) French					
wc/d	2	15,274	2,943	7,637	12,331

Name	No.	Total Sales Value	Prices lowest	median	highest
ROUX, Gerard (1946-) French					
oil	1	1,200		1,200	
ROUX, Joseph Ange Antoine (1765-1835) French					
wc/d	1	1,812		1,812	
ROUX, Louis (1817-1903) French					
wc/d	2	3,094	1,084	1,547	2,010
ROUX, Polidore (1792-1833) French					
oil	1	16,610		16,610	
ROUX-CHAMPION, Joseph Victor (1871-1953) French					
oil	1	2,336		2,336	
ROVATS, K (19th C) ?					
oil	1	3,796		3,796	
ROVERE (19th C) ?					
wc/d	1	4,154		4,154	
ROVERE, Giovanni Battista della (1561-c.1630) Italian					
wc/d	1	1,481		1,481	
ROVERS, Jos (1893-1976) Dutch					
oil	2	2,451	1,093	1,226	1,358
ROWBOTHAM, Charles (1856-1921) British					
wc/d	18	43,239	1,036	1,846	7,436
ROWBOTHAM, Thomas Charles Leeson (1823-1875) British					
wc/d	6	10,229	1,460	1,460	2,145
ROWDEN, Thomas (1842-1926) British					
wc/d	10	15,117	1,001	1,310	2,416
ROWE, E Arthur (1863-1922) British					
wc/d	4	10,733	1,332	2,925	3,552
ROWE, Tom Trythall (1856-?) British					
oil	1	5,966		5,966	
ROWLANDSON, George Derville (1861-?) British					
oil	4	23,436	2,114	5,965	9,815
ROWLANDSON, Thomas (1756-1827) British					
wc/d	37	119,775	1,001	2,669	10,868
ROY, Dolf van (1858-1943) Belgian					
oil	1	1,149		1,149	
ROY, Jamini (1887-1972) Indian					
oil	1	3,600		3,600	
wc/d	6	20,928	1,350	2,739	7,800
ROY, Jean Baptiste de (1759-1839) Belgian					
oil	2	13,356	6,291	6,678	7,065
ROY, Louis George Eleonor (1862-1907) French					
wc/d	4	13,704	1,127	1,415	9,748
ROY, Marius (1833-?) French					
oil	1	1,600		1,600	
ROY, Pierre (1880-1950) Italian					
oil	2	67,900	31,900	33,950	36,000
ROY, Pranay Ranjan (1909-) Indian					
wc/d	2	17,280	8,640	8,640	8,640
ROY, Proshanto (1908-1973) Indian					
wc/d	6	24,648	2,880	3,384	6,000
ROY-AUDY, Jean Baptiste (1778-c.1848) Canadian					
oil	1	22,719		22,719	
ROYBET, Ferdinand (1840-1920) French					
oil	12	99,190	2,249	7,701	26,000
ROYER, Leon Jules Alphonse le (1858-1939) French					
oil	1	2,407		2,407	
ROYER, Lionel-Noel (1852-1926) French					
oil	3	18,102	1,227	6,000	10,875
ROYET, Henri (19/20th C) French					
oil	1	1,024		1,024	

Name	No.	Total Sales Value	lowest	Prices median	highest
ROYLE, Herbert (1870-1958) British					
oil	16	93,765	1,015	6,658	9,480
ROZ, Andre (1897-?) French					
oil	1	1,129		1,129	
ROZE, Emile (?) ?					
oil	1	1,021		1,021	
ROZEN, George (1895-1973) American					
oil	2	5,800	1,800	2,900	4,000
ROZEN, Jerome (20th C) American					
oil	1	4,250		4,250	
ROZIER, Dominique Hubert (1840-1901) French					
oil	1	1,354		1,354	
ROZIER, Jules (1821-1882) French					
oil	5	13,611	1,154	1,867	4,673
RUABON, Dennis (19/20th C) ?					
3D	1	6,216		6,216	
RUBELLI, Giuseppe de (1844-1916) Italian					
oil	1	1,367		1,367	
RUBENS (school) (1577-1640) Flemish					
oil	2	11,989	5,398	5,995	6,591
RUBENS, Sir Peter Paul (1577-1640) Flemish					
oil	4	14,053,000	425,000	3,064,000	7,500,000
wc/d	2	47,500	15,000	23,750	32,500
RUBIN, Reuven (1893-1974) Israeli					
oil	14	958,000	14,000	67,500	210,000
wc/d	7	28,456	1,200	4,000	6,500
RUBIO, Louis (1795-1882) Italian					
oil	2	11,164	2,164	5,582	9,000
RUBY, Claire (20th C) American					
oil	3	6,800	1,100	1,700	4,000
RUCKER, Robert (1932-) American					
oil	3	8,800	1,600	1,700	5,500
RUCKRIEM, Ulrich (1938-) German					
3D	1	16,981		16,981	
RUDBERG, Gustav (1915-1994) Swedish					
oil	28	82,696	1,088	2,583	6,468
RUDDER, I de (1855-?) Belgian					
3D	1	1,210		1,210	
RUDE, François (1784-1855) French					
3D	2	8,524	3,239	4,262	5,285
RUDE, Olaf (1886-1957) Danish					
oil	15	50,851	1,129	2,308	13,947
RUDELL, Carl (1852-1920) German					
oil	1	1,341		1,341	
wc/d	8	20,851	1,251	1,954	7,360
RUDENSKOLD, Thure Gabriel (1799-1878) Swedish					
oil	1	7,336		7,336	
RUDGE, Bradford (1805-1885) British					
wc/d	1	2,574		2,574	
RUDISUHLI, Eduard (1875-1938) Swiss					
oil	2	3,805	1,131	1,903	2,674
RUDISUHLI, Hermann (1864-1945) Swiss					
oil	3	8,247	1,184	2,158	4,905
RUDISUHLI, Jakob Lorenz (1835-1918) Swiss					
oil	1	1,283		1,283	
RUDY, Durs (1766-1843) American					
wc/d	1	10,000		10,000	
RUE, Louis-Felix de la (1731-1765) French					
wc/d	2	3,916	1,800	1,958	2,116

Name	No.	Total Sales Value	lowest	Prices median	highest
RUEDA, Gerardo (1926-) Spanish					
3D	1	4,065		4,065	
oil	3	28,628	1,144	10,227	17,257
wc/d	3	3,162	1,007	1,045	1,110
RUETER, Georg (1875-1966) Dutch					
oil	52	144,600	1,011	2,185	7,744
RUETER, Gerarda (1904-1993) Dutch					
3D	2	3,235	1,213	1,618	2,022
RUFFINI, Napoleone (?) ?					
3D	1	3,014		3,014	
RUFS, Josef (19th C) Swiss					
oil	1	1,215		1,215	
RUGENDAS, Georg Philipp (17/18th C) German					
oil	1	9,890		9,890	
RUGENDAS, Georg Philipp I (1666-1742) German					
oil	4	48,423	11,364	11,364	14,331
RUGENDAS, Johann Moritz (1802-1858) German					
oil	4	95,813	11,831	24,491	35,000
RUGGERI, Piero (1930-) Italian					
oil	5	15,781	1,115	1,484	7,294
RUGGERO, R (?) Italian					
oil	1	2,836		2,836	
RUIBAL, Mercedes (1928-) Spanish					
oil	2	3,926	1,873	1,963	2,053
RUITH, Horace van (1839-1923) British					
wc/d	1	1,480		1,480	
RUIZ ANGLADA, Martin (1929-) Spanish					
oil	1	1,956		1,956	
RUIZ LUNA, Justo (1865-1926) Spanish					
oil	4	8,966	1,866	2,301	2,498
wc/d	1	1,125		1,125	
RUIZ MELERO (19th C) Spanish					
oil	1	3,146		3,146	
RUIZ MORALES (19/20th C) Spanish					
oil	1	2,669		2,669	
RUIZ SANCHEZ MORALES, Manuel (1853-1922) Spanish					
wc/d	1	1,358		1,358	
RUIZ, Manolo Pipo (1925-) Spanish					
wc/d	1	1,439		1,439	
RUIZ, Tomasso (18th C) Spanish					
oil	1	47,100		47,100	
RUIZ-PIPO, Manolo (1929-) Spanish					
wc/d	1	1,638		1,638	
RUL, Henri (1862-1942) Belgian					
oil	2	9,993	2,463	4,997	7,530
RULLMANN, Ludwig (1765-1822) German					
wc/d	1	2,191		2,191	
RUMLER-SIUCHNINSKI, Friedrich (1884-?) German					
oil	1	1,268		1,268	
RUMP, Godfred (1816-1880) Danish					
oil	2	9,164	3,207	4,582	5,957
RUMPF, Philipp (1821-1896) German					
oil	2	40,169	11,131	20,085	29,038
RUNDT, Carl Ludwig (1802-1868) German					
oil	2	4,026	1,730	2,013	2,296
RUNGE, Julius Friedrich Ludwig (1843-1922) German					
oil	2	5,597	1,274	2,799	4,323
RUNGIUS, Carl (1869-1959) American/German					
oil	8	950,000	27,500	92,500	230,000

Name	No.	Total Sales Value	lowest	Prices median	highest
RUOPPOLO, Giuseppe (1639-1710) Italian					
oil	2	143,622	65,283	71,811	78,339
RUPERT, Johan Christian (c.1600-1654) German					
oil	1	5,127		5,127	
RUPERTI, K (?) ?					
oil	1	5,220		5,220	
RUPPERT, Otto von (1841-?) German					
oil	2	2,142	1,020	1,071	1,122
RUPPRECHT, Wilhelm (19th C) German					
oil	1	2,600		2,600	
RUSCHA, Edward (1937-) American					
oil	8	562,000	15,000	50,000	220,000
wc/d	11	314,400	10,000	22,000	95,000
RUSCHI, Francesco (17th C) Italian					
oil	1	120,000		120,000	
RUSELL, A S (?) ?					
oil	1	3,021		3,021	
RUSH, Olive (1873-1966) American					
oil	1	2,100		2,100	
wc/d	1	3,000		3,000	
RUSHBURY, Sir Henry (1889-1968) British					
wc/d	1	1,184		1,184	
RUSHTON, J (19th C) British?					
oil	1	1,191		1,191	
RUSHTON, William Charles (1860-1921) British					
oil	2	2,670	1,278	1,335	1,392
wc/d	1	1,278		1,278	
RUSINOL, Santiago (1861-1931) Spanish					
oil	5	275,114	9,601	69,688	98,599
RUSKIN, John (1819-1900) British					
wc/d	11	113,189	1,950	11,060	42,900
RUSS, Ad (19th C) ?					
oil	1	5,127		5,127	
RUSS, Robert (1847-1922) Austrian					
oil	1	11,615		11,615	
RUSSEL, Theodore (1614-1689) British					
oil	1	12,870		12,870	
RUSSELL, Charles M (1864-1926) American					
3D	10	142,550	2,000	11,500	50,000
oil	4	975,000	25,000	175,000	600,000
wc/d	15	1,502,000	13,000	35,000	1,000,000
RUSSELL, George (1867-1935) Irish					
oil	7	139,627	4,239	9,588	53,280
RUSSELL, Gyrth (1892-1970) Canadian					
oil	4	8,256	1,300	1,603	3,750
RUSSELL, J (18th C) British					
wc/d	9	292,044	4,800	12,324	142,200
RUSSELL, James (fl.1878-1887) British					
oil	1	1,128		1,128	
RUSSELL, John (1745-1806) British					
oil	1	3,000		3,000	
wc/d	7	31,038	1,500	3,454	10,500
RUSSELL, John (fl.1869-1918) British					
oil	1	1,500		1,500	
RUSSELL, John B (19/20th C) British					
oil	1	1,600		1,600	
RUSSELL, John Bucknell (1819-1893) British					
oil	2	19,204	4,704	9,602	14,500
RUSSELL, John Wentworth (1879-1959) Canadian					
oil	2	2,642	1,306	1,321	1,336

Name	No.	Total Sales Value	lowest	Prices median	highest
RUSSELL, Morgan (1886-1953) American					
oil	4	96,506	1,756	7,375	80,000
RUSSELL, Moses B (1810-1884) American					
oil	1	4,250		4,250	
RUSSIAN SCHOOL, 18th C					
oil	2	8,947	4,135	4,474	4,812
RUSSIAN SCHOOL, 18th/19th C					
oil	1	5,936		5,936	
RUSSIAN SCHOOL, 19th C					
3D	2	4,776	2,339	2,388	2,437
oil	12	77,363	2,697	5,717	14,183
wc/d	1	8,001		8,001	
RUSSIAN SCHOOL, 19th/20th C					
oil	1	2,273		2,273	
RUSSIAN SCHOOL, 20th C					
wc/d	1	3,146		3,146	
RUST, Johan Adolph (1828-1915) Dutch					
oil	4	52,415	5,739	12,817	21,042
RUSTIN, Jean (1928-) French					
oil	1	6,676		6,676	
RUSZKOWSKI, Zdzislaw (1907-1990) Polish					
oil	3	4,194	1,050	1,560	1,584
RUTH, Jan de (20th C) ?					
oil	1	1,100		1,100	
RUTHART, Karl Andreas (1630-1703) German					
oil	2	78,932	3,432	39,466	75,500
RUTHERFORD, Harry (1903-) British					
oil	1	1,425		1,425	
RUTHS, Amelie (1871-1956) German					
oil	1	1,598		1,598	
RUTHS, Valentin (1825-1905) German					
oil	6	52,998	2,745	4,486	22,429
RUTILI, Charles (20th C) French?					
oil	1	1,103		1,103	
RUTS, F (19th C) German					
oil	1	1,740		1,740	
RUYSDAEL, Jacob Salomonsz van (1630-1681) Dutch					
oil	4	77,830	7,850	16,615	36,750
RUYSDAEL, Jacob van (1628-1682) Dutch					
oil	7	1,903,600	6,500	250,000	528,500
RUYSDAEL, Salomon van (1600-1670) Dutch					
oil	2	72,497	33,237	36,249	39,260
RUYSSEVELT, Jozef van (1941-1985) Belgian					
wc/d	1	1,281		1,281	
RUYTEN, Jan Michael (1813-1881) Belgian					
oil	3	23,487	2,440	7,098	13,949
RUYTENBACH, E (17th C) Dutch					
oil	1	2,595		2,595	
RUYTINX, Alfred (1871-?) Belgian					
oil	2	11,172	3,559	5,586	7,613
RYAN, Anne (1889-1954) American					
wc/d	1	2,500		2,500	
RYBACK, Issachar (1897-1935) Russian					
oil	2	7,200	1,200	3,600	6,000
wc/d	1	2,066		2,066	
RYBERG, Hulda (1836-1924) Swedish?					
oil	1	1,507		1,507	
RYBKOWSKI, Tadeusz (1848-1926) Polish					
oil	1	15,100		15,100	

Name	No.	Total Sales Value	Prices lowest	Prices median	highest
RYCKAERT, David III (1612-1661) Flemish					
oil	3	34,010	5,880	8,500	19,630
RYCKAERT, Marten (1587-1631) Flemish					
oil	3	115,974	14,739	20,385	80,850
RYCKX, Nicolaes (1637-?) Flemish					
oil	1	20,410		20,410	
RYD, Carl (1883-1958) Swedish					
oil	1	1,708		1,708	
RYDBERG, Gustaf (1835-1933) Swedish					
oil	6	27,960	1,105	3,210	10,395
RYDER, Chauncey F (1868-1949) American					
oil	6	32,000	2,500	5,625	7,500
RYDER, R T (20th C) British?					
oil	1	1,133		1,133	
RYLAARSDAM, Jan (1911-) Dutch					
oil	1	2,257		2,257	
RYLAND, Henry (1856-1924) British					
wc/d	2	15,940	4,500	7,970	11,440
RYLANDER, H C (1939-) Danish					
oil	1	1,000		1,000	
RYLOV, Arkadij (1870-1939) Russian					
oil	1	3,322		3,322	
RYMAN, Robert (1930-) American					
3D	1	80,000		80,000	
oil	3	635,000	45,000	240,000	350,000
wc/d	4	435,000	25,000	70,000	270,000
RYNENBURG, Nicolaes (1716-1776) Dutch					
oil	1	6,155		6,155	
RYSBRACK, Pieter (1655-1729) Flemish					
oil	2	28,081	4,379	14,041	23,702
RYSBRACK, Pieter Andreas (1690-1748) Flemish					
oil	2	39,250	17,270	19,625	21,980
RYSSELBERGHE, Theo van (1862-1926) Belgian					
oil	11	522,517	1,305	23,366	151,000
wc/d	5	46,876	1,481	5,220	30,893
RYSWYCK, Edward van (1871-?) Belgian					
oil	3	12,921	3,480	4,515	4,926
RYSWYCK, T van (?) ?					
3D	1	4,267		4,267	
RYSWYCK, Thierry van (20th C) Belgian					
3D	4	12,805	1,996	3,084	4,641
RYUKI (19th C) Japanese					
3D	1	12,396		12,396	
SAABYE, Svend (1913-) Danish					
oil	4	8,433	1,430	1,812	3,379
SAADA, Henri (1906-1976) Tunisian					
wc/d	2	2,392	1,168	1,196	1,224
SAAL, Georg (1818-1870) German					
oil	1	12,225		12,225	
SAALBORN, Louis (1890-1957) Dutch					
oil	1	1,724		1,724	
SAARINEN, Yrjo (1899-1958) Finnish					
oil	1	2,967		2,967	
SABALI, V (?) ?					
oil	1	1,184		1,184	
SABATELLI, Luigi (1772-1850) Italian					
wc/d	2	5,152	1,275	2,576	3,877
SABATER, Daniel (1888-1951) Spanish					
oil	4	6,676	1,012	1,405	2,854

Name	No.	Total Sales Value	lowest	Prices median	highest
SABATER, Manuel (19th C) Spanish					
oil	1	1,030		1,030	
SABATINI, Andrea (1487-1530) Italian					
oil	1	4,320		4,320	
SABATINI, Luigi (19th C) Italian					
oil	1	2,618		2,618	
SABAVALA, Jehangir (1922-) Indian					
oil	2	22,500	6,000	11,250	16,500
SABBAGH, Georges (1887-1951) French					
oil	4	9,983	1,979	2,396	3,213
SABLET, François Jean (1745-1819) French/Swiss					
oil	1	8,367		8,367	
SABY, Bernard (20th C) French?					
oil	2	4,722	1,918	2,361	2,804
SACCOROTTI, Oscar (1898-) Italian					
oil	1	1,063		1,063	
SACHAROFF, Olga (1889-1969) Russian					
oil	3	44,421	8,822	10,257	25,342
SACHERI, Giuseppe (1863-1950) Italian					
oil	3	16,281	1,149	3,686	11,446
wc/d	1	1,533		1,533	
SACHS, Michael (1837-1893) German					
oil	3	21,217	1,988	2,229	17,000
SACHS, Tom (1966-) American					
3D	1	13,000		13,000	
SACHSEN SCHOOL, 17th C Swiss					
oil	1	2,915		2,915	
SADEE, Philippe (1837-1904) Dutch					
oil	5	233,570	11,881	28,694	127,190
SADEQUAIN (1930-1987) Indian					
wc/d	1	2,250		2,250	
SADKOWSKI, Alex (1934-) Swiss					
oil	1	1,059		1,059	
wc/d	2	2,372	1,073	1,186	1,299
SADLER (?) British					
wc/d	1	2,500		2,500	
SADLER, Walter Dendy (1854-1923) British					
oil	7	235,490	1,959	3,744	175,000
SADLER, William (18/19th C) British					
oil	1	4,198		4,198	
SADLER, William (jnr) (1782-1839) British					
oil	1	35,520		35,520	
SAEDELEER, Valerius de (1867-1941) Belgian					
oil	7	88,718	2,480	8,356	36,944
wc/d	2	3,274	1,483	1,637	1,791
SAEKI, Yuzo (1898-1928) Japanese					
oil	3	1,580,000	380,000	550,000	650,000
SAENE, Maurice van (1919-) Belgian					
oil	1	1,231		1,231	
SAETTI, Bruno (1902-1984) Italian					
oil	6	15,648	1,159	1,628	7,618
SAEYS, Jakob Ferdinand (1658-1725) Flemish					
oil	1	18,999		18,999	
SAEZ, Martin (1923-1989) Spanish					
oil	1	1,353		1,353	
SAFAVID SCHOOL, 16th C Persian					
wc/d	1	7,377		7,377	
SAFTLEVEN, Cornelis (1607-1681) Dutch					
wc/d	4	27,843	1,493	5,625	15,100

Name	No.	Total Sales Value	lowest	Prices median	highest
SAFTLEVEN, Herman (1609-1685) Dutch					
oil	6	156,225	1,133	16,554	75,500
wc/d	1	1,375		1,375	
SAGE, Henry James (1868-1953) British					
oil	1	1,650		1,650	
SAGER-NELSON, Olof (1868-1896) Swedish					
oil	1	30,471		30,471	
SAGEWKA, Ernst (1883-1959) German					
oil	2	7,851	3,606	3,926	4,245
SAGRESTANI, Giovanni Camillo (1660-1731) Italian					
oil	3	33,342	3,168	6,624	23,550
SAILLEFON, B (19th C) French					
wc/d	1	1,401		1,401	
SAILMAKER, Isaac (1633-1721) British					
oil	1	6,795		6,795	
SAIN, Edouard Alexandre (1830-1910) French					
oil	1	1,633		1,633	
SAIN, Paul Jean Marie (1853-1908) French					
oil	4	10,734	1,427	2,029	5,250
ST JOHN, E (19th C) British					
oil	1	1,001		1,001	
wc/d	1	1,410		1,410	
ST JOHN, Edwin (19th C) British					
wc/d	2	2,313	1,057	1,157	1,256
ST JOHN-JONES, Herbert (fl.1905-1923) British					
oil	1	1,970		1,970	
SAINT-AUBIN, Augustin de (1736-1807) French					
wc/d	2	2,718	1,359	1,359	1,359
SAINT-AUBIN, Gabriel de (1724-1780) French					
wc/d	6	104,150	2,909	14,519	42,187
SAINT-DELIS, Henri de (1878-1949) French					
wc/d	7	16,611	1,196	2,031	4,132
SAINT-DELIS, René de (1877-1958) French					
oil	1	1,002		1,002	
SAINT-FLEURANT, Louisianne (1924-) Haitian					
oil	1	1,112		1,112	
SAINT-JEAN, Simon (1808-1860) French					
oil	1	20,444		20,444	
SAINT-LAURENT, Yves (1936-) French					
wc/d	1	3,500		3,500	
SAINT-LOUIS, Blaise (20th C) Haitian					
oil	1	5,929		5,929	
SAINT-MARCEAUX, René (1845-1915) French					
3D	3	8,770	1,196	2,512	5,062
SAINT-MARCEL, Edme de (1819-1890) French					
wc/d	1	1,425		1,425	
SAINT-MICHEL, Joseph de (fl.1756-1776) French					
wc/d	1	1,382		1,382	
SAINT-OURS, Jean-Pierre (1752-1809) Swiss					
wc/d	1	6,645		6,645	
SAINT-PHALLE, Niki de (1930-) French					
3D	33	683,969	2,197	12,280	141,405
wc/d	6	35,620	1,885	4,809	14,500
SAINT-PIERRE, Gaston Casimir (1833-1916) French					
oil	1	8,250		8,250	
SAINTHILL, Loudon (1919-1969) Australian					
wc/d	1	1,481		1,481	
SAINTIN, Henri (1846-1899) French					
oil	1	8,000		8,000	

Name	No.	Total Sales Value	lowest	Prices median	highest
SAINTIN, Jules Émile (1829-1894) French					
oil	1	26,781		26,781	
SAINVILLE, Armand de (19th C) French					
oil	1	3,365		3,365	
SAINZ Y SAINZ, Casimiro (1853-1898) Spanish					
oil	5	56,984	2,279	2,862	45,711
SAINZ, E (20th C) Spanish					
oil	1	1,040		1,040	
SAIVE, Jean Baptiste de (1540-1624) Flemish					
oil	1	80,000		80,000	
SAIVE, Jean de II (1597-?) Flemish					
oil	1	453,000		453,000	
SALA Y FRANCES, Emilio (1850-1910) Spanish					
oil	7	120,111	1,684	2,786	63,000
SALA, Eugène de (1899-1987) Danish					
oil	1	4,847		4,847	
SALA, Josep (?) Spanish					
oil	1	1,067		1,067	
SALA, Juan (1867-1918) Spanish					
oil	1	8,391		8,391	
SALA, Paolo (1859-1929) Italian					
oil	5	32,632	1,594	7,000	11,085
wc/d	5	9,280	1,224	1,848	2,932
SALABET, Jean (20th C) French					
oil	2	10,400	1,400	5,200	9,000
SALAS, Tito (1888-1974) Venezuelan					
oil	1	12,930		12,930	
SALATHE, Friedrich (1793-1860) French					
wc/d	1	11,000		11,000	
SALAVERRIA, Elias (1883-1952) Spanish					
oil	2	5,123	2,235	2,562	2,888
SALAZAR Y MENDOZA, Jose Francisco (school) (18/19th C) Mexican					
oil	1	2,750		2,750	
SALAZAR, Francisco (1937-) French/Venezuelian					
oil	1	1,650		1,650	
SALCES, Manuel (19th C) Spanish					
oil	1	1,266		1,266	
SALDANA, Il Pescador (19th C) Spanish					
oil	1	1,790		1,790	
SALEH, Raden (1807-1880) Javanese					
oil	1	19,142		19,142	
SALEMME, Attilio (1911-1955) American					
oil	1	14,000		14,000	
SALENDRE, Georges (20th C) French					
3D	1	5,673		5,673	
SALENTIN, Hubert (1822-1910) German					
oil	1	19,663		19,663	
SALERNO, Charles (1916-) American					
3D	1	2,000		2,000	
SALERO, Lugh (20th C) ?					
3D	1	2,860		2,860	
SALES, Francisco (1905-1976) Spanish					
oil	3	3,745	1,010	1,122	1,613
SALIETTI, Alberto (1892-1961) Italian					
oil	3	20,553	3,515	7,127	9,911
SALIGER, Ivo (1894-1975) Austrian					
oil	1	1,330		1,330	
SALIM, Abdallah (1958-) ?					
3D	1	3,441		3,441	

Name	No.	Total Sales Value	lowest	Prices median	highest
SALIMBENI, Ventura (1568-1613) Italian					
wc/d	1	12,244		12,244	
SALINAS, Pablo (1871-1946) Spanish					
oil	8	307,910	4,491	24,250	116,000
SALINAS, Porfirio (1910-1972) American					
oil	3	28,000	5,000	7,000	16,000
SALINI, Tommaso (1575-1625) Italian					
oil	3	209,256	41,160	84,048	84,048
SALINI, Tommaso (school) (1575-1625) Italian					
oil	1	64,634		64,634	
SALIOLA, Antonio (20th C) Italian					
wc/d	1	1,456		1,456	
SALIS, Pierre de (1827-1919) Swiss					
oil	1	1,228		1,228	
SALISBURY, Frank O (1874-1962) British					
oil	2	4,086	1,350	2,043	2,736
wc/d	1	1,595		1,595	
SALLE, David (1952-) American					
oil	9	634,760	2,500	40,000	210,000
wc/d	2	8,332	3,500	4,166	4,832
SALLES-WAGNER, Jules (1814-1898) French					
oil	1	7,030		7,030	
SALM, Adriaan (fl.1708-1720) Dutch					
wc/d	2	200,000	100,000	100,000	100,000
SALME, Lambert (19th C) Belgian					
oil	1	7,837		7,837	
SALMON, John Cuthbert (1844-1917) British					
wc/d	1	1,846		1,846	
SALMON, Robert (1775-1844) American					
oil	8	152,229	7,500	17,500	35,000
SALMON, Robert (school) (1775-1844) American					
oil	1	2,900		2,900	
SALMON, Theodore Frederic (1811-1876) French					
oil	2	3,380	1,059	1,690	2,321
SALMSON, Fred (1941-) Swedish?					
oil	1	1,004		1,004	
SALMSON, Hugo (1844-1894) Swedish					
oil	3	17,505	2,394	6,831	8,280
wc/d	1	2,088		2,088	
SALMSON, Jean Jules (1823-1902) French					
3D	1	3,250		3,250	
SALOKIVI, Santeri (1886-1940) Finnish					
oil	2	6,962	2,747	3,481	4,215
SALOME (1954-) German					
oil	10	74,489	2,649	7,828	14,185
SALT, James (19th C) British					
oil	6	24,649	1,884	4,598	5,680
SALTER, William Philip (fl.1847-1851) British					
oil	1	2,355		2,355	
SALTI, Giulio (1899-?) Italian					
oil	2	2,399	1,126	1,200	1,273
SALTINI, Pietro (1839-1908) Italian					
oil	1	5,000		5,000	
SALTO, Axel (1889-1961) Danish					
wc/d	1	1,211		1,211	
SALTOFT, Edvard Anders (1883-1939) Danish					
oil	1	1,922		1,922	
SALTZMAN, William (1916-) American					
oil	1	3,250		3,250	

Name	No.	Total Sales Value	lowest	Prices median	highest
SALVAT, François (1892-1976) French					
oil	1	1,167		1,167	
SALVIATI, Francesco (1510-1563) Italian					
wc/d	2	83,310	3,310	41,655	80,000
SALVIATI, Giovanni (1881-?) Italian					
wc/d	1	1,526		1,526	
SALVIATI, Giuseppe Porta (c.1520-1573) Italian					
wc/d	1	98,150		98,150	
SALVO (1947-) Italian					
3D	3	6,648	1,941	2,038	2,669
oil	18	124,652	1,571	4,258	30,543
SAMACCHINI, Orazio (1532-1577) Italian					
wc/d	1	12,080		12,080	
SAMARTZIS, George (1868-?) ?					
wc/d	1	1,110		1,110	
SAMBA, Cheri (1956-) Zairean					
oil	5	13,750	1,253	1,358	6,406
SAMBROOK, Russell (20th C) American?					
oil	2	11,250	4,250	5,625	7,000
SAMLICKI, Marcin (1878-1945) Polish					
oil	1	1,014		1,014	
SAMMONS, Carl (1888-1968) American					
oil	4	7,600	1,100	1,550	3,400
wc/d	1	1,900		1,900	
SAMONOFF (?) Russian					
3D	1	4,619		4,619	
SAMPLE, Paul (1896-1974) American					
oil	1	8,000		8,000	
wc/d	1	1,700		1,700	
SAMPSON, Alden (1853-?) American					
oil	1	1,800		1,800	
SAMSON, E (?) ?					
3D	1	1,111		1,111	
SAMUELSON, Ulrik (1935-) Swedish					
oil	4	19,050	2,419	4,630	7,372
wc/d	1	2,304		2,304	
SAMVELLIS, Z (18/19th C) ?					
oil	1	5,883		5,883	
SAN JOSE, Francisco (1919-1981) Spanish					
oil	5	10,664	1,087	1,829	3,764
SAN-YU (1901-1966) Chinese					
wc/d	4	8,312	1,228	2,092	2,900
SANCHEZ LAREDO, Miguel (1969-) Spanish					
oil	1	1,008		1,008	
SANCHEZ, Andres (16th/17th C) Spanish					
oil	1	6,660		6,660	
SANCHEZ, Edgar (1940-) Venezuelan					
oil	2	12,140	1,140	6,070	11,000
SANCHEZ, Tomas (1948-) Cuban					
oil	6	416,000	22,000	26,000	280,000
SANCHEZ, Trino (1968-) Venezuelan					
oil	3	41,500	7,500	14,000	20,000
SANCHEZ-PERRIER, Emilio (1855-1907) Spanish					
oil	2	34,000	12,000	17,000	22,000
SANCHIZ Y QUESADA, Joaquin (19th C) Spanish					
oil	1	1,017		1,017	
SANCHO, Jose (1924-) Spanish					
oil	2	4,714	1,186	2,357	3,528

Name	No.	Total Sales Value	lowest	Prices median	highest
SAND, George (1804-1876) French					
wc/d	1	3,380		3,380	
SANDALINAS, Joan (1903-1991) Spanish					
oil	9	12,956	1,016	1,537	1,887
SANDBACK, Fred (1943-) American					
oil	1	1,400		1,400	
wc/d	1	1,117		1,117	
SANDBERG, Johan Gustaf (1782-1854) Swedish					
oil	4	9,817	1,850	2,134	3,700
SANDBERG, Ragnar (1902-1972) Swedish					
oil	15	151,987	1,254	5,419	40,265
wc/d	4	11,270	1,415	2,730	4,395
SANDBY, Paul (1730-1809) British					
oil	1	4,576		4,576	
wc/d	14	158,905	1,027	2,148	50,050
SANDELS, Gosta (1877-1919) Swedish					
oil	5	86,595	1,747	4,415	39,694
SANDER, Sherry Salari (1941-) American					
3D	1	6,000		6,000	
SANDER-PLUMP, Agnes (1888-1980) German					
oil	1	1,463		1,463	
SANDERS, Christopher (1905-1991) British					
oil	1	2,465		2,465	
SANDERS, George (1774-1846) British					
oil	1	19,875		19,875	
SANDERSON, Robert (fl.1858-1908) British					
oil	1	1,425		1,425	
SANDERSON-WELLS, John (1872-1955) British					
oil	9	38,611	1,800	3,322	7,500
SANDHAM, Henry (1842-1910) Canadian					
wc/d	1	1,800		1,800	
SANDOZ (19th C) ?					
3D	1	1,813		1,813	
SANDOZ, A (19/20th C) ?					
oil	1	1,237		1,237	
SANDOZ, Edouard-Marcel (1881-1971) Swiss					
3D	19	106,492	1,290	3,183	20,474
SANDROCK, Leonhard (1867-?) German					
oil	6	16,640	1,311	2,475	5,267
SANDRUCCI, G (19th C) Italian					
oil	1	1,800		1,800	
SANDS, Frederick (?) ?					
oil	1	1,275		1,275	
SANDSTEDE, Kurt (1907-) German					
oil	1	1,154		1,154	
SANDSTROM, Anders (1933-) Swedish					
3D	1	1,005		1,005	
SANDZEN, Birger (1871-1954) American/Swedish					
oil	9	393,500	17,000	37,500	120,000
SANGO (?) ?					
3D	1	1,032		1,032	
SANGSTER, Alfred (fl.1904-1914) British					
oil	1	12,000		12,000	
SANI, A (19/20th C) Italian					
oil	1	12,000		12,000	
SANI, Alessandro (19/20th C) Italian					
oil	4	20,112	2,900	4,856	7,500
SANI, David (19/20th C) Italian					
oil	1	3,976		3,976	

Name	No.	Total Sales Value	Prices lowest	median	highest
SANQUIRICO, Pio (1847-1900) Italian					
oil	1	19,635		19,635	
SANS CORBELLA, Tomas (1869-1911) Spanish					
oil	1	1,557		1,557	
SANT, James (1820-1916) British					
oil	6	27,607	1,264	4,263	7,474
SANTA COLOMA, Emmanuel de (1826-1886) French					
oil	1	6,000		6,000	
SANTA MARIA, Marceliano (19/20th C) Spanish					
oil	4	39,980	6,078	7,536	18,456
SANTACROCE (15/16th C) Italian					
oil	1	36,509		36,509	
SANTACROCE, Francesco Rizzo da (15/16th C) Italian					
oil	1	36,724		36,724	
SANTARELLI, Andria (1935-) French					
oil	1	1,283		1,283	
SANTERRE, Jean Baptiste (1651-1717) French					
oil	1	2,416		2,416	
SANTIAGO, Carlos de (20th C) South American					
oil	1	3,600		3,600	
SANTIAGO, Paula (1969-) Mexican					
3D	1	6,500		6,500	
SANTIAGO, Santiago de (1925-) Spanish					
3D	1	4,062		4,062	
SANTILARI, Joseph (20th C) ?					
wc/d	1	1,267		1,267	
SANTOLONI, Felice (?) Italian					
wc/d	1	3,922		3,922	
SANTOMASO, Giuseppe (1907-1990) Italian					
oil	6	114,353	2,624	9,709	65,250
wc/d	8	56,112	1,670	3,878	23,294
SANTORO, Francesco Raffaello (1844-1927) Italian					
oil	1	4,000		4,000	
SANTORO, Rubens (1859-1942) Italian					
oil	9	405,592	7,500	39,150	85,000
wc/d	1	13,500		13,500	
SANVISENS, Ramon (1917-1987) Spanish					
oil	2	4,515	1,393	2,258	3,122
SANVITO, E (19th C) Italian					
3D	2	2,752	1,376	1,376	1,376
SANZ DE SANTOS, Santos (20th C) Spanish					
oil	1	2,730		2,730	
SANZ MAGALLON, Jose Luis (1926-) Spanish					
oil	1	1,069		1,069	
SANZEL, Felix (1829-1883) French					
3D	1	1,200		1,200	
SAORIN BOX, Pedro Antonio (1944-) Spanish					
3D	1	2,476		2,476	
SAPP, Allen (1929-) Canadian					
oil	15	24,915	1,182	1,678	2,350
SARACENI, Carlo (1585-1620) Italian					
oil	1	324,930		324,930	
SARARIN, M (?) ?					
oil	1	1,329		1,329	
SARAZIN DE BELMONT, Louise Josephine (1790-1870) French					
oil	1	6,121		6,121	
SARDELLI, Trafeli (?) Italian?					
3D	1	3,561		3,561	

Name	No.	Total Sales Value	lowest	Prices median	highest
SARDEN, L (18th C) British?					
oil	1	1,012		1,012	
SARDESAI, N R (?) ?					
wc/d	1	1,152		1,152	
SARDI, Jean (1947-) French					
oil	5	7,076	1,160	1,317	1,756
SARG, Tony (1880-?) American					
wc/d	3	3,594	1,027	1,178	1,389
SARGENT, J S (1856-1925) American/British					
3D	1	6,000		6,000	
wc/d	1	7,000		7,000	
SARGENT, John Singer (1856-1925) British/American					
oil	4	1,552,317	62,317	270,000	950,000
wc/d	10	986,549	30,000	44,250	350,000
SARGENT, Paul Turner (1880-1946) American					
oil	3	4,400	1,400	1,500	1,500
SARGENT, Walter (1868-1927) American					
oil	1	2,400		2,400	
SARIAN, Martiros (1880-1972) Armenian					
oil	1	21,140		21,140	
wc/d	1	9,870		9,870	
SARKIS, Zabunyan (20th C) ?					
wc/d	1	1,028		1,028	
SARKISIAN, Sarkis (1909-1977) American					
oil	3	5,000	1,100	1,400	2,500
SARKISSOFF, Maurice (1882-1946) Swiss					
3D	1	1,373		1,373	
SARMENTO, Juliao (1948-) Portuguese					
oil	1	35,000		35,000	
wc/d	3	34,000	4,000	10,000	20,000
SARNARI, Franco (1933-) Italian					
oil	1	2,426		2,426	
SARNOFF, Arthur (20th C) ?					
oil	1	1,000		1,000	
SAROYAN, William (1908-1981) American					
oil	1	2,500		2,500	
SARRAZIN, Jean Baptiste (18th C) French					
oil	1	5,581		5,581	
SARTEEL, Léon (1882-1942) Belgian					
3D	1	2,025		2,025	
SARTELLE, Herbert (1885-1955) American					
oil	1	1,000		1,000	
SARTO, Andrea del (1487-1530) Italian					
oil	2	1,002,099	2,099	501,050	1,000,000
SARTORIO, Giulio Aristide (1861-1932) Italian					
wc/d	1	1,208		1,208	
SARTORIUS, G W (19/20th C) British					
oil	1	2,265		2,265	
SARTORIUS, John Nott (1759-1828) British					
oil	9	116,929	2,869	12,580	27,180
SARTORIUS, Virginie de (1828-?) Belgian					
oil	1	3,147		3,147	
SASSENBROUCK, Achille van (1886-1979) Belgian					
oil	6	11,118	1,013	1,743	2,859
SASSOFERRATO (1609-1685) Italian					
oil	10	222,129	1,856	12,628	63,420
SASSU, Aligi (1912-2000) Italian					
3D	2	8,079	1,689	4,040	6,390
oil	8	132,908	4,741	13,250	32,348
wc/d	4	13,089	1,088	2,741	6,520

Name	No.	Total Sales Value	lowest	Prices median	highest
SATRUSTEGUI, Rafael (1960-) Spanish					
oil	1	2,758		2,758	
SATTLER, Hubert (1817-1904) Austrian					
oil	3	7,331	1,028	1,228	5,075
SATUR, Edmond Byrne de (?) ?					
oil	1	1,001		1,001	
SAUBER, Robert (1868-1936) British					
oil	5	25,206	3,040	4,108	10,000
SAUER, Walter (1889-1972) Belgian					
wc/d	6	17,785	1,358	2,440	6,438
SAUERBRUCH, Hans (1910-) German					
oil	1	1,125		1,125	
SAUERWEID, Alexander (1783-1844) Russian					
wc/d	1	2,002		2,002	
SAUERWEIN, Frank P (1871-1910) American					
wc/d	3	8,600	1,100	3,500	4,000
SAUERWEIN, W V (20th C) American					
oil	1	1,300		1,300	
SAUL, A (?) ?					
3D	1	1,452		1,452	
SAUL, G (19th C) Italian					
3D	1	17,934		17,934	
SAUL, Peter (1934-) American					
oil	2	9,022	3,867	4,511	5,155
wc/d	2	6,056	2,780	3,028	3,276
SAULO, Georges Ernest (1865-?) French					
3D	1	2,250		2,250	
SAUNIER, Charlotte (19th C) French					
oil	1	5,455		5,455	
SAUNIER, Noel (1847-1890) French					
oil	2	10,604	2,000	5,302	8,604
SAUPIQUE, Georges Laurent (1889-?) French					
3D	1	644,424		644,424	
SAURA, Antonio (1930-1998) Spanish					
oil	16	385,568	2,200	18,971	71,550
wc/d	12	140,385	2,535	5,324	65,842
SAURFELT, Leonard (19th C) French					
oil	2	3,466	1,166	1,733	2,300
SAUSSE, Honore (1891-1936) French					
3D	1	1,365		1,365	
SAUTER, Aloys (1952-) ?					
oil	1	1,168		1,168	
SAUTEUR, Claude le (1926-) Canadian					
oil	1	3,007		3,007	
SAUTHIER, Claude (1929-) Swiss					
oil	2	3,025	1,049	1,513	1,976
SAUTTER, Walter (1911-1991) Swiss					
oil	2	3,673	1,632	1,837	2,041
SAUVAGE, Arsene (19th C) French					
oil	3	5,641	1,221	2,139	2,281
SAUVAGE, François Phillippe (19th C) French					
oil	1	4,030		4,030	
SAUVAIGO, Martin (19/20th C) ?					
oil	1	2,775		2,775	
SAUVAN, Philippe (1698-1789) French					
wc/d	1	1,676		1,676	
SAUZAY, Adrien Jacques (1841-1928) French					
oil	2	11,422	1,422	5,711	10,000

Name	No.	Total Sales Value	lowest	Prices median	highest
SAVAGE, Anne (1896-1971) Canadian					
oil	1	2,522		2,522	
SAVAGE, Edward (1761-1817) American					
oil	1	650,000		650,000	
SAVAGE, Eugene (1883-1978) American					
oil	1	2,600		2,600	
SAVERY, Jacob (16/17th C) Dutch					
oil	1	377,500		377,500	
SAVERY, Roeland (1576-1639) Dutch					
oil	6	420,339	3,412	14,244	332,200
SAVERYS, Albert (1886-1964) Belgian					
oil	20	242,157	4,327	10,004	28,202
wc/d	5	9,585	1,167	1,761	2,662
SAVI, Alfredo (1881-1958) Italian					
oil	1	1,149		1,149	
SAVIGNY (?) French					
oil	1	2,281		2,281	
SAVIGNY, G (?) French					
oil	1	1,891		1,891	
SAVIN, Maurice (1894-1973) French					
oil	6	16,038	1,168	2,000	5,301
SAVINI, Alfonso (1836-1908) Italian					
oil	1	9,815		9,815	
SAVINIO, Alberto (1891-1952) Italian					
oil	1	75,645		75,645	
wc/d	2	29,647	13,503	14,824	16,144
SAVINIO, Ruggero (1934-) Italian					
oil	1	2,197		2,197	
SAVOIA, Achille (1842-1886) Italian					
oil	1	3,567		3,567	
SAWYERS, Lilian Dorothy (fl.1928-1934) British					
oil	1	1,087		1,087	
SAWYIER, Paul (1865-1917) American					
oil	1	55,000		55,000	
SAXON, Charles (1920-1088) American					
wc/d	1	1,900		1,900	
SAY, Frederick Richard (c.1827-1860) British					
oil	3	8,663	1,287	2,800	4,576
SAYAGO, Adolfo (1963-) Uruguayan					
oil	1	2,300		2,300	
SAYNE, Comtesse de (19th C) French					
wc/d	1	2,159		2,159	
SAYRE, Fred Grayson (1879-1938) American					
oil	6	34,900	1,300	2,975	22,000
SAYVE, Auguste de (19/20th C) French?					
oil	1	2,618		2,618	
SCACCIATI, Andrea (1642-1704) Italian					
oil	1	18,999		18,999	
SCAGLIA, Michele (1859-1918) Italian					
oil	1	1,098		1,098	
SCALA, Vincenzo (19th C) Italian					
oil	1	22,296		22,296	
SCALBERT, Jules (1851-?) French					
wc/d	1	3,404		3,404	
SCANAVINO, Emilio (1922-1986) Italian					
3D	1	1,527		1,527	
oil	15	112,156	1,309	5,401	24,954
wc/d	3	6,678	1,877	2,052	2,749

Name	No.	Total Sales Value	lowest	Prices median	highest
SCANDINAVIAN SCHOOL, 17th C					
3D	1	3,394		3,394	
SCANDINAVIAN SCHOOL, 18th C					
oil	3	12,494	3,000	3,614	5,880
SCANDINAVIAN SCHOOL, 19th C					
oil	1	7,850		7,850	
SCANNEL, Edith M S (fl.1880-1921) British					
oil	1	2,230		2,230	
SCARBOROUGH, Frederick W (fl.1896-1939) British					
wc/d	5	32,437	1,092	6,040	11,440
SCARBROUGH, Frank William (fl.1896-1939) British					
oil	1	4,440		4,440	
wc/d	8	21,535	1,413	2,414	5,700
SCARCELLINO, Ippolito (1551-1620) Italian					
oil	1	10,290		10,290	
SCARFE, Gerald (1936-) British					
wc/d	7	43,149	1,057	7,975	11,600
SCARLETT, Rolph (1889-1984) American					
oil	1	2,000		2,000	
SCARPA, Riccardo (1905-) Italian					
3D	4	8,590	1,760	1,901	3,028
SCARPITTA, Salvatore (1919-) American					
3D	1	4,800		4,800	
oil	1	10,000		10,000	
wc/d	1	49,300		49,300	
SCARVELLI, Spyridon (1868-1942) Greek					
oil	1	8,000		8,000	
SCARVILLA, F (20th C) ?					
oil	1	1,200		1,200	
SCATIZZI, Sergio (1918-) Italian					
oil	2	2,693	1,175	1,347	1,518
SCAUFLAIRE, Edgar (1893-1960) Belgian					
oil	2	4,864	1,542	2,432	3,322
wc/d	1	1,533		1,533	
SCHAAN, Paul (19/20th C) French					
oil	2	13,000	5,500	6,500	7,500
SCHAAP, Hendrik (1878-1955) Dutch					
wc/d	1	1,414		1,414	
SCHACHT, Rudolf (1900-1974) German					
oil	3	4,602	1,196	1,330	2,076
SCHACHTEL, Hans (19th C) German					
oil	1	1,772		1,772	
SCHACKWITZ, Michael (1956-) German					
oil	1	2,396		2,396	
wc/d	1	2,732		2,732	
SCHAD, Christian (1894-1982) German					
wc/d	2	11,581	2,941	5,791	8,640
SCHAD, Paul (fl.1887) German					
oil	1	6,687		6,687	
SCHAD-ROSSA, Paul (1862-1916) German					
oil	2	2,892	1,092	1,446	1,800
SCHAEFELS, Hendrik Frans (1827-1904) Belgian					
oil	2	37,242	16,552	18,621	20,690
SCHAEFELS, Hendrik Raphael (1785-1857) Belgian					
oil	2	10,869	1,996	5,435	8,873
SCHAEFER, Carl Fellman (1903-) Canadian					
oil	3	13,908	3,318	4,550	6,040
wc/d	2	4,444	1,682	2,222	2,762
SCHAEFFER, August (1833-1916) Austrian					
oil	2	5,841	1,727	2,921	4,114

Name	No.	Total Sales Value	lowest	Prices median	highest
SCHAEFFER, Henri (1900-1975) French					
oil	1	1,516		1,516	
SCHAEFFER, Mead (1898-1980) American					
oil	2	19,900	2,900	9,950	17,000
SCHAEFLER, Fritz (1888-1954) German					
oil	1	1,650		1,650	
wc/d	1	2,111		2,111	
SCHAEKER, W and STARKE, N (?) ?					
oil	1	2,440		2,440	
SCHAEP, Henri Adolphe (1826-1870) Dutch					
oil	7	95,368	4,405	7,186	49,864
SCHAFER, A (?) ?					
wc/d	1	1,249		1,249	
SCHAFER, F F (1839-1927) American					
oil	1	1,900		1,900	
SCHAFER, Frederick Ferdinand (1839-1927) American					
oil	4	12,600	1,500	3,300	4,500
SCHAFER, H (19th C) British/French					
oil	3	4,186	1,080	1,500	1,606
SCHAFER, Henry (19th C) British/French					
oil	15	38,384	1,177	2,044	5,100
wc/d	1	2,512		2,512	
SCHAFER, Henry Thomas (19/20th C) British					
oil	1	1,625		1,625	
wc/d	1	1,413		1,413	
SCHAFER, M (?) ?					
wc/d	1	1,232		1,232	
SCHAFER, Roland Maria (1974-) German					
wc/d	1	1,211		1,211	
SCHAFFER, Adalbert (1815-1871) Hungarian					
oil	1	3,200		3,200	
SCHAFFROTH, Johann Stanislaus (1766-1851) German					
wc/d	1	4,582		4,582	
SCHAGEN, Gerbrand Frederik van (1880-1968) Dutch					
oil	1	1,103		1,103	
SCHALCKEN, Godfried (1643-1706) Dutch					
oil	4	1,103,334	17,234	155,550	775,000
SCHALDACH, William J (1896-?) American					
wc/d	1	2,250		2,250	
SCHALKEN, Leonard (19/20th C) ?					
wc/d	1	1,160		1,160	
SCHALL, Jean Frederic (1752-1825) French					
oil	1	3,500		3,500	
SCHAMBERG, Morton Livingston (1881-1918) American					
wc/d	1	75,000		75,000	
SCHAMPHELEER, Edmond de (1824-1899) Belgian					
oil	5	24,608	1,305	1,926	12,388
SCHANTZ, Philip von (1928-1998) Swedish					
oil	1	12,420		12,420	
wc/d	1	1,088		1,088	
SCHANZ, Heinz (1927-) German					
oil	1	2,364		2,364	
SCHAPER, Friedrich (1869-1956) German					
oil	2	3,299	1,117	1,650	2,182
SCHAPER, Fritz Hugo Wilhelm (1841-1919) German					
3D	1	1,526		1,526	
SCHAPER, H (1853-1911) German					
oil	1	3,823		3,823	

Name	No.	Total Sales Value	Prices lowest	Prices median	highest
SCHAPER, Herman (1853-1911) German					
oil	1	6,783		6,783	
SCHARER, Hans (1927-1997) Swiss					
oil	3	4,120	1,066	1,480	1,574
SCHARF, Kenny (1958-) American					
oil	7	123,555	3,000	8,555	68,000
SCHARFF, William (1886-1959) Danish					
oil	3	4,140	1,044	1,270	1,826
SCHARL, Josef (1896-1954) German					
oil	6	136,410	1,591	21,453	57,600
wc/d	3	3,706	1,073	1,268	1,365
SCHARRATH, Karl (1870-1907) German					
3D	1	6,934		6,934	
SCHATT, Michaele Andrea (20th C) ?					
wc/d	1	1,476		1,476	
SCHATZ, Arnold (1929-) German					
oil	1	1,251		1,251	
SCHATZ, M (20th C) German					
oil	1	1,295		1,295	
SCHATZ, Manfred (1925-) German					
oil	3	6,400	1,032	1,936	3,432
SCHAUFER, Henry Troy (19th C) ?					
oil	1	20,000		20,000	
SCHAUMANN, Wilhelm Heinrich (1841-1893) German					
oil	1	1,027		1,027	
SCHAUSS, Ferdinand (1832-1916) German					
oil	1	9,480		9,480	
SCHEERBOOM, Andries (1832-1880) Dutch					
oil	3	9,609	1,562	3,180	4,867
SCHEFFEL, Johan Hendrik (1690-1781) Swedish					
oil	1	2,285		2,285	
SCHEFFER, Ary (1795-1858) French					
oil	4	18,157	1,146	4,506	8,000
SCHEFFER, Henri (1798-1862) French					
oil	1	8,001		8,001	
SCHEFFER, Johann Bernard Baptiste (1765-1809) German					
oil	1	1,873		1,873	
SCHEFFER, Robert (1859-?) Austrian					
oil	1	5,500		5,500	
SCHEGGI, C (19th C) Italian					
3D	2	3,713	1,300	1,857	2,413
SCHEGGI, Paolo (1940-1971) Italian					
wc/d	1	2,967		2,967	
SCHEIBER, Hugo (1873-1950) Hungarian					
oil	2	26,681	9,401	13,341	17,280
wc/d	4	10,378	1,225	2,878	3,397
SCHEINER, Jakob (1821-1911) German					
wc/d	1	4,700		4,700	
SCHEINER, Wilhelm (1852-1922) German					
wc/d	2	8,760	1,923	4,380	6,837
SCHEINHAMMER, Otto (1897-1982) German					
oil	1	1,165		1,165	
SCHEINS, Karl Ludwig (1808-1879) German					
oil	2	6,828	1,923	3,414	4,905
SCHEITS, Matthias (1640-1700) German					
oil	1	7,218		7,218	
wc/d	2	2,076	1,038	1,038	1,038
SCHELCK, Maurice (1906-1978) Belgian					
oil	5	16,606	1,092	1,306	7,082

Name	No.	Total Sales Value	lowest	Prices median	highest
SCHELFHOUT (19/20th C) Dutch					
oil	1	3,751		3,751	
SCHELFHOUT, Andreas (1787-1870) Dutch					
oil	15	843,695	14,747	36,346	213,878
wc/d	4	19,934	2,065	4,267	9,335
SCHELFHOUT, Andreas (school) (1787-1870) Dutch					
oil	1	6,321		6,321	
SCHELLENBERG, Johann Rudolf (1740-1806) German					
wc/d	1	3,586		3,586	
SCHELLENBERGER, Daniel (19th C) American					
wc/d	1	75,000		75,000	
SCHELLER, Christoph (16th C) German					
3D	1	13,868		13,868	
SCHELLINCKS, Daniel (school) (1627-1701) Dutch					
oil	1	4,312		4,312	
SCHELLINGER, Hans (1905-) German					
oil	2	2,942	1,079	1,471	1,863
SCHELLINKS, Willem (1627-1678) Dutch					
oil	4	24,624	3,693	6,313	8,305
SCHENCK, August Friedrich Albrecht (1828-1901) Danish					
oil	2	5,355	2,165	2,678	3,190
SCHENDEL, Bernardus van (1649-1709) Dutch					
oil	1	6,615		6,615	
SCHENDEL, Mira (1919-1988) Brazilian					
oil	2	40,000	12,000	20,000	28,000
wc/d	1	30,000		30,000	
SCHENDEL, Petrus van (1806-1870) Belgian					
oil	7	338,530	6,256	43,500	127,600
SCHENEAU, Johann Eleazar (1737-1807) German					
oil	1	8,843		8,843	
SCHENK, Karl (1905-1973) Swiss					
oil	8	14,495	1,242	1,607	2,541
SCHENKEL, Jan Jacob (1829-1900) Dutch					
oil	1	7,214		7,214	
SCHENONE PUIG, Dolcey (?) Uruguayan?					
oil	1	1,600		1,600	
SCHEPP, Auguste (1846-1905) German					
oil	1	2,917		2,917	
SCHERER, Hermann (1893-1927) Swiss					
wc/d	2	10,084	4,254	5,042	5,830
SCHERF, Louis (1870-1955) German					
3D	1	2,371		2,371	
SCHERFIG, Hans (1905-1979) Danish					
oil	9	47,693	1,583	3,487	20,500
wc/d	2	2,869	1,162	1,435	1,707
SCHERMAN, Tony (1950-) Canadian?					
oil	1	9,860		9,860	
wc/d	2	5,795	2,275	2,898	3,520
SCHERMER, Cornelis (1824-1915) Dutch					
oil	3	9,108	1,414	3,760	3,934
SCHERRER, Jean Jacques (19th C) French					
oil	1	1,244		1,244	
SCHERREWITZ, Johan (1868-1951) Dutch					
oil	19	179,237	2,573	7,500	29,842
SCHETKY, John Christian (1778-1874) British					
oil	3	110,230	9,060	37,750	63,420
wc/d	3	11,459	2,445	3,146	5,868
SCHEUCHZER, Wilhelm (1803-1866) Swiss					
oil	3	8,906	1,215	1,481	6,210
wc/d	2	2,412	1,072	1,206	1,340

Name	No.	Total Sales Value	lowest	Prices median	highest
SCHEUERER, Julius (1859-1913) German					
oil	17	37,775	1,276	2,039	4,458
SCHEUERER, Otto (1862-1934) German					
oil	6	10,198	1,090	1,699	2,277
SCHEUERMANN, Carl Georg (1803-1859) Danish					
oil	1	1,322		1,322	
SCHEUREN, Caspar Johann Nepomuk (1810-1887) German					
oil	1	9,000		9,000	
SCHIAMINOSSI, Raffaello (c.1529-1622) Italian					
wc/d	1	1,234		1,234	
SCHIAVONI, Natale (1777-1858) Italian					
oil	1	2,033		2,033	
SCHICK, Carl (1826-1873) German					
oil	1	1,341		1,341	
SCHICK, Christian Gottlieb (1776-1812) German					
oil	1	120,000		120,000	
SCHIDER, Fritz (1846-1907) Austrian					
oil	4	6,628	1,296	1,620	2,093
SCHIDONE, Bartolomeo (1578-1615) Italian					
oil	1	19,110		19,110	
SCHIEDGES, Peter Paulus (1812-1876) Dutch					
oil	5	18,073	2,360	2,753	6,634
SCHIELE, Egon (1890-1918) Austrian					
oil	1	9,360,001		9,360,001	
wc/d	9	3,579,819	41,000	210,000	1,250,000
SCHIERTZ, Franz Wilhelm (1813-1887) German					
oil	1	3,217		3,217	
SCHIESS, Ernst Traugott (1872-1919) Swiss					
oil	1	1,033		1,033	
SCHIESS, Hans Rudolf (1904-1978) Swiss					
oil	1	2,229		2,229	
SCHIESS, Traugott (1834-1869) Swiss					
oil	3	5,080	1,337	1,798	1,945
SCHIESTL, Matthaus (1869-1939) German					
wc/d	1	1,231		1,231	
SCHIFANO, Mario (1934-1998) Italian					
oil	17	168,350	1,180	4,206	87,000
wc/d	44	248,022	1,017	3,491	48,609
SCHIFFER, Anton (1811-1876) Austrian					
oil	2	27,912	13,956	13,956	13,956
SCHIFFER, Ethel Bennett (1879-?) American					
oil	1	1,268		1,268	
SCHIFFERLE, Claudia (1955-) Swiss					
3D	1	1,338		1,338	
oil	1	1,226		1,226	
SCHIFFMANN, Jost Joseph Niklaus (1822-1883) Swiss					
oil	1	3,831		3,831	
SCHIKKINGER, Frans (1838-1902) Dutch					
wc/d	2	2,082	1,021	1,041	1,061
SCHILBACH, Johann Heinrich (1798-1851) German					
oil	3	48,246	1,553	7,767	38,926
SCHILDER, Andrei Nikolaevich (1861-1919) Russian					
oil	1	10,872		10,872	
SCHILKIN, Mikael (1900-1962) Finnish/Russian					
3D	1	1,627		1,627	
SCHILLING, Erich (1885-1945) German					
wc/d	2	3,091	1,455	1,546	1,636
SCHILT, Martinus (1867-1921) Dutch					
wc/d	1	1,657		1,657	

Name	No.	Total Sales Value	Prices lowest	median	highest
SCHILTER, Hans (1911-1988) Swiss					
wc/d	1	1,538		1,538	
SCHIMON, Ferdinand (1797-1852) German					
oil	1	1,496		1,496	
SCHINDLER, Albert (1805-1861) Austrian					
oil	1	1,863		1,863	
SCHINDLER, Johann Josef (1777-1836) Austrian					
oil	1	1,043		1,043	
SCHINDLER, Osmar (1869-1927) German					
wc/d	1	1,486		1,486	
SCHINNAGL, Maximilian Joseph (1697-1762) German					
oil	1	32,351		32,351	
SCHINZ, Caspar (1804-1848) Swiss					
wc/d	1	1,250		1,250	
SCHIOLER, Inge (1908-1971) Swedish					
oil	34	429,266	1,719	6,760	45,862
wc/d	9	16,474	1,004	1,708	2,637
SCHIONNING, Constance (19/20th C) Danish					
oil	1	1,259		1,259	
SCHIOTT, August (1823-1895) Danish					
oil	2	55,909	3,401	27,955	52,508
SCHIOTTZ-JENSEN, N F (1855-1941) Danish					
oil	2	4,131	1,033	2,066	3,098
SCHIOTTZ-JENSEN, Niels F (1855-1941) Danish					
oil	3	29,674	1,896	12,537	15,241
SCHIPPERS, Joseph (1868-1950) Belgian					
oil	3	32,870	1,780	11,228	19,862
SCHIRM, Carl Cowen (1852-1928) German					
oil	1	1,481		1,481	
SCHIRMER, Johann Wilhelm (1807-1863) German					
oil	3	17,254	4,326	4,953	7,975
wc/d	1	1,817		1,817	
SCHIRREN, Ferdinand (1872-1944) Belgian					
oil	1	3,812		3,812	
wc/d	5	16,363	1,898	2,790	5,457
SCHJERFBECK, Helene (1862-1946) Finnish					
oil	2	199,807	79,007	99,904	120,800
wc/d	1	4,761		4,761	
SCHLAGETER, Karl (1894-?) Swiss					
oil	2	4,842	1,139	2,421	3,703
SCHLATTER, Ernst Emil (1883-1954) Swiss					
oil	2	3,382	1,516	1,691	1,866
SCHLEEH, Hans (1928-) Canadian					
3D	1	1,599		1,599	
SCHLEICH, August (1814-1865) German					
oil	1	1,057		1,057	
SCHLEICH, Eduard (19th C) German					
oil	3	10,489	1,364	3,725	5,400
SCHLEICH, Eduard (elder) (1812-1874) German					
oil	3	27,530	3,182	11,887	12,461
SCHLEICH, Eduard (younger) (1853-1893) German					
oil	1	2,243		2,243	
SCHLEICH, Robert (1845-1934) German					
oil	9	42,681	1,552	3,872	10,965
SCHLEICHER, Carl (19th C) Austrian					
oil	1	1,200		1,200	
SCHLEINITZ, Max (?-1935) German					
oil	1	4,554		4,554	

Name	No.	Total Sales Value	lowest	Prices median	highest
SCHLEISNER, C A (1810-1882) Danish					
oil	4	6,513	1,162	1,516	2,320
SCHLEISNER, Christian Andreas (1810-1882) Danish					
oil	2	5,242	2,549	2,621	2,693
SCHLEMMER, Oskar (1888-1943) German					
oil	2	592,563	2,163	296,282	590,400
wc/d	2	101,989	10,380	50,995	91,609
SCHLESINGER, Felix (1833-1910) German					
oil	4	30,374	3,480	6,672	13,551
SCHLESINGER, Henri-Guillaume (1814-1893) French					
oil	2	28,084	7,150	14,042	20,934
SCHLESINGER, Samuel (1896-1952) Israeli					
oil	1	3,770		3,770	
SCHLICHTER, Rudolf (1890-1955) German					
oil	1	43,200		43,200	
wc/d	22	149,387	2,128	5,201	18,914
SCHLICHTING CARLSEN, Carl (1852-1903) Danish					
oil	1	1,549		1,549	
SCHLIECKER, August Eduard (1833-1911) German					
oil	2	15,389	2,850	7,695	12,539
SCHLITT, Heinrich (1849-1923) German					
oil	2	4,485	2,206	2,243	2,279
wc/d	1	1,211		1,211	
SCHLOBACH, Willy (1865-1951) Belgian					
oil	2	21,314	3,609	10,657	17,705
SCHLOESSER, Carl (1832-1914) German					
oil	1	3,530		3,530	
SCHLOGL, Josef von (1851-?) Austrian					
oil	2	12,224	1,259	6,112	10,965
SCHLOMKA, Alfred (19/20th C) Hungarian					
oil	2	5,713	1,580	2,857	4,133
SCHLOSSER, Gerard (1931-) French					
oil	4	35,026	7,586	8,802	9,836
wc/d	1	1,374		1,374	
SCHLOTTER, Eberhard (1921-) German?					
wc/d	1	1,154		1,154	
SCHMALIX, Hubert (1952-) Austrian					
oil	3	8,393	2,117	2,878	3,398
SCHMALZ, Herbert Gustave (1856-1935) British					
oil	2	72,566	3,926	36,283	68,640
SCHMEDTGEN, William H (1862-1936) American					
oil	1	2,750		2,750	
SCHMID, David Alois (1791-1861) Swiss					
wc/d	2	11,452	2,124	5,726	9,328
SCHMID, Henri (1924-) Swiss					
oil	4	6,218	1,323	1,455	1,985
SCHMID, R (?) ?					
oil	1	1,151		1,151	
SCHMID, Richard (20th C) American					
oil	2	121,750	1,750	60,875	120,000
SCHMID, Wilhelm (1892-1971) Swiss					
oil	6	19,925	1,003	2,241	7,663
SCHMIDT, Adolf (19th C) German					
oil	1	2,662		2,662	
SCHMIDT, Albert (1883-1970) Swiss					
oil	1	3,703		3,703	
wc/d	1	1,359		1,359	
SCHMIDT, Alexander (1842-1903) Danish					
oil	1	2,023		2,023	

Name	No.	Total Sales Value	lowest	Prices median	highest
SCHMIDT, Carl (1885-1969) American					
oil	3	7,900	1,100	1,300	5,500
SCHMIDT, Christian (1835-?) German					
oil	1	9,000		9,000	
SCHMIDT, Christian Friedrich (18/19th C) American					
3D	1	9,500		9,500	
SCHMIDT, Eduard (19/20th C) German					
oil	2	4,444	1,994	2,222	2,450
SCHMIDT, Edward (20th C) American?					
wc/d	1	6,820		6,820	
SCHMIDT, Harold von (1893-1982) American					
oil	1	18,000		18,000	
wc/d	1	4,250		4,250	
SCHMIDT, Johann Martin (1718-1801) German					
wc/d	1	3,727		3,727	
SCHMIDT, Leonhard (1892-1978) German					
wc/d	2	2,523	1,009	1,262	1,514
SCHMIDT, Lucien Louis J B (1825-1891) French					
oil	2	12,218	4,274	6,109	7,944
SCHMIDT, Matthias (1749-1823) German					
oil	1	2,519		2,519	
SCHMIDT, Max (1818-1901) German					
oil	1	3,546		3,546	
SCHMIDT, Robert (1863-1927) German					
oil	1	1,211		1,211	
SCHMIDT, Theodor (1855-?) German					
oil	1	4,200		4,200	
SCHMIDT, Willem Hendrik (1809-1849) Dutch					
oil	1	1,093		1,093	
SCHMIDT-CASSEL, G (1867-?) German					
3D	1	2,114		2,114	
SCHMIDT-FELING (19/20th C) German					
3D	1	3,792		3,792	
SCHMIDT-FELING, J (1895-1930) German					
3D	1	1,394		1,394	
SCHMIDT-HAMBURG, Robert (1885-1963) German					
oil	1	1,251		1,251	
SCHMIDT-HOFER (19/20th C) German					
3D	1	2,000		2,000	
SCHMIDT-KESTNER, Erich (1877-?) German					
3D	3	6,872	2,206	2,273	2,393
SCHMIDT-PHISELDECH, Carl von (1853-1917) Danish					
oil	2	2,197	1,030	1,099	1,167
SCHMIDT-ROTTLUFF, Karl (1884-1976) German					
3D	1	19,480		19,480	
oil	4	511,055	75,969	132,431	170,224
wc/d	21	408,886	1,182	11,492	55,859
SCHMIED, François Louis (1873-?) Swiss					
wc/d	1	3,098		3,098	
SCHMIEGELOW, Pedro Ernst Johann (1863-?) German					
oil	1	1,616		1,616	
SCHMIERMANN, J (19th C) Dutch					
oil	1	1,449		1,449	
SCHMITT, A C (19th C) ?					
oil	1	5,500		5,500	
SCHMITT, Albert Felix (1873-?) American?					
oil	1	7,000		7,000	
SCHMITT, Paul (1856-1902) French					
oil	2	8,019	2,519	4,010	5,500

Name	No.	Total Sales Value	lowest	Prices median	highest
SCHMITT, Wilhelm (1831-1891) German					
oil	1	1,040		1,040	
SCHMITZ, Ernst (1859-1917) German					
oil	2	3,977	1,133	1,989	2,844
SCHMITZ, Guido (?) ?					
oil	1	1,359		1,359	
SCHMITZ, Hans (1886-1977) German					
3D	1	1,384		1,384	
SCHMITZ, Jean Paul (19th C) German					
oil	1	1,065		1,065	
SCHMITZ, Johann Jacob (1724-1810) German					
oil	1	20,634		20,634	
SCHMITZBERGER, Josef (1851-?) German					
oil	5	14,058	1,073	1,364	6,624
SCHMUTZER, Ferdinand (1833-1915) Austrian					
oil	1	1,615		1,615	
SCHMUTZLER, Leopold (1864-1941) German					
oil	5	52,274	1,349	3,648	40,000
SCHNABEL, Julian (1951-) American					
oil	16	848,787	3,500	44,693	140,000
SCHNARRENBERGER, Wilhelm (1892-?) German					
oil	2	6,817	2,419	3,409	4,398
SCHNAUDER, Richard George (1886-1956) German					
3D	1	1,145		1,145	
SCHNEIDER, Carlos (1889-1932) Swiss					
oil	1	1,565		1,565	
wc/d	2	2,508	1,166	1,254	1,342
SCHNEIDER, Caspar (1753-1839) German					
oil	1	7,183		7,183	
SCHNEIDER, Georg (1759-1842) German					
oil	1	1,852		1,852	
SCHNEIDER, Georg August (1842-1872) Norwegian					
oil	1	1,963		1,963	
SCHNEIDER, Gerard (1896-1986) Swiss					
oil	37	227,125	1,329	4,709	20,675
wc/d	14	28,859	1,069	1,516	5,165
SCHNEIDER, Gerhard (1842-1873) Norwegian					
oil	1	1,495		1,495	
SCHNEIDER, Johann Jakob (1822-1889) Swiss					
wc/d	1	4,800		4,800	
SCHNEIDER, Max (20th C) German					
oil	1	1,377		1,377	
SCHNEIDER, Otto Henry (1865-1950) American					
oil	3	28,000	4,000	9,000	15,000
SCHNEIDER, W (19/20th C) ?					
oil	1	3,796		3,796	
SCHNEIDER-BLUMBERG, Bernhard (1881-1956) German					
wc/d	2	2,999	1,375	1,500	1,624
SCHNIER, Jacques (1898-1988) American					
3D	1	3,250		3,250	
SCHNORR VON CAROLSFELD, Julius (1794-1872) German					
wc/d	2	58,486	4,126	29,243	54,360
SCHNORR VON CAROLSFELD, Ludwig (1788-1853) Austrian					
oil	2	43,362	10,965	21,681	32,397
SCHNUG, Leo (1878-1933) French					
wc/d	1	8,250		8,250	
SCHNURINGER, M J (?) ?					
oil	1	1,287		1,287	

Name	No.	Total Sales Value	lowest	Prices median	highest
SCHNYDER, Albert (1898-1989) German					
oil	12	74,671	2,988	6,334	11,859
SCHOBEL, Georg (1860-?) German					
oil	1	2,105		2,105	
SCHODL, Max (1834-1921) Austrian					
oil	1	1,500		1,500	
SCHOEFFT, August Theodor (1809-1888) Hungarian					
oil	1	3,775		3,775	
SCHOELLHORN, Hans Karl (1892-1983) Swiss					
oil	2	3,615	1,283	1,808	2,332
SCHOENBECK, Albert (19th C) German					
oil	1	6,620		6,620	
SCHOENEWERK, Alexandre (1820-1885) French					
3D	3	8,241	1,979	2,440	3,822
SCHOEVAERDTS, Mathys (c.1665-1723) Flemish					
oil	3	311,162	6,148	35,014	270,000
SCHOFFMANN, Maria (19/20th C) ?					
oil	1	1,222		1,222	
SCHOFIELD, John William (?-1944) British					
oil	1	1,272		1,272	
SCHOFIELD, Kershaw (1872-1941) British					
oil	2	2,838	1,021	1,419	1,817
SCHOFIELD, Walter Elmer (1867-1944) American					
oil	12	271,188	6,000	14,500	59,000
SCHOGGI, C (?) Italian					
3D	1	1,091		1,091	
SCHOLANDER, Fredrik (1816-1881) Swedish					
oil	1	3,047		3,047	
wc/d	2	3,392	1,360	1,696	2,032
SCHOLDERER, Otto (1834-1902) German					
oil	1	4,486		4,486	
SCHOLZ, Georg (1890-1945) German					
oil	1	259,200		259,200	
SCHOLZ, Max (1855-?) German					
oil	2	4,627	1,900	2,314	2,727
SCHOLZ, Werner (1898-1982) German					
oil	4	24,188	4,854	6,092	7,150
wc/d	1	1,698		1,698	
SCHON, Andreas (1955-) German?					
oil	1	5,190		5,190	
SCHON, Friedrich Wilhelm (1810-1868) German					
oil	1	3,657		3,657	
SCHONBERGER, Alfred Karl Julius Otto von (1845-?) German					
oil	1	1,133		1,133	
SCHONCHEN, Leopold (1855-1935) German					
oil	1	1,463		1,463	
SCHONLEBER, Gustav (1851-1917) German					
oil	9	40,187	2,111	4,210	8,754
SCHONN, Alois (1826-1897) Austrian					
oil	2	14,778	1,636	7,389	13,142
SCHONROCK, Julius (1835-?) German					
oil	2	4,226	1,226	2,113	3,000
SCHONZEIT, Ben (1942-) American					
oil	1	1,068		1,068	
SCHOONHOVEN, Jan J (1914-1994) Dutch					
oil	2	4,984	1,188	2,492	3,796
wc/d	20	45,507	1,078	1,875	6,466
SCHOONOVER, Frank E (1877-1972) American					
oil	6	377,000	5,000	26,500	250,000

Name	No.	Total Sales Value	Prices lowest	median	highest
SCHOOTEN, Floris van (1590-1657) Dutch					
oil	2	65,037	20,037	32,519	45,000
SCHOPIN, Frederic Henri (1804-1880) French					
oil	1	1,090		1,090	
SCHORER, Hans Friedrich (17th C) German					
wc/d	2	4,983	1,200	2,492	3,783
SCHORK, Hans (1849-?) Austrian					
3D	1	2,618		2,618	
SCHOT, Francina Louise (1816-1894) Dutch					
oil	1	21,042		21,042	
SCHOTEL, Anthonie Pieter (1890-1958) Dutch					
oil	3	11,415	2,758	3,925	4,732
SCHOTEL, Jan Christianus (1787-1838) Dutch					
oil	3	47,356	5,334	6,709	35,313
wc/d	2	28,615	4,612	14,308	24,003
SCHOTEL, Petrus Jan (1808-1865) Dutch					
oil	2	9,889	2,122	4,945	7,767
wc/d	3	8,812	1,488	3,395	3,929
SCHOTH, A (1859-1906) German					
oil	3	5,193	1,501	1,573	2,119
SCHOTZ, Benno (1891-1984) British					
3D	1	1,950		1,950	
SCHOU, Ludvig Abelin (1838-1867) Danish					
oil	4	24,975	1,810	3,515	16,136
SCHOU, Peter Johan (1863-1934) Danish					
oil	1	3,000		3,000	
SCHOU, Sigurd (1875-1944) Danish					
oil	1	1,073		1,073	
SCHOUMAN, Aert (1710-1792) Dutch					
oil	1	38,000		38,000	
wc/d	3	7,072	1,179	2,357	3,536
SCHOUMAN, Martinus (1770-1848) Dutch					
oil	1	3,489		3,489	
wc/d	1	3,892		3,892	
SCHOUTEN, Henry (1864-1927) Belgian					
oil	40	101,330	1,008	1,792	22,066
SCHOUTEN, Henry and Paul (19/20th C) Belgian					
oil	1	1,278		1,278	
SCHOUTEN, Paul (1860-1922) Belgian					
oil	3	4,042	1,191	1,220	1,631
SCHOVELIN, Axel Thorsen (1827-1893) Danish					
oil	3	5,811	1,104	2,324	2,383
SCHOYERER, Josef (1844-1923) German					
oil	6	18,094	1,079	2,421	7,744
SCHRADER-VELGEN, Carl Hans (1876-1945) German					
oil	1	3,596		3,596	
SCHRAEGLE, Gustav Peter Franz (1867-?) German					
oil	1	1,276		1,276	
SCHRAG, Karl (1912-1995) American/German					
oil	2	6,500	1,000	3,250	5,500
wc/d	1	3,800		3,800	
SCHRAM, Alois Hans (1864-1919) Austrian					
oil	3	19,048	1,387	6,411	11,250
wc/d	1	6,320		6,320	
SCHRAMM-ZITTAU, Rudolf (1874-1950) German					
oil	3	11,573	1,210	1,863	8,500
SCHRANZ (?) ?					
wc/d	1	1,988		1,988	
SCHRANZ, Anton (1769-1839) Austrian					
oil	2	88,910	31,710	44,455	57,200

Name	No.	Total Sales Value	lowest	Prices median	highest
SCHRANZ, Anton (younger) (1801-?) Austrian					
oil	1	29,200		29,200	
SCHRECKENGOST, Victor (1906-) American					
wc/d	3	4,600	1,100	1,100	2,400
SCHREIBER (?) ?					
oil	1	2,182		2,182	
SCHREIBER, Charles Baptiste (1845-1903) French					
oil	1	1,012		1,012	
SCHREIBER, Georges (1904-1977) American					
wc/d	1	2,200		2,200	
SCHREIBER, Hugo (19/20th C) ?					
wc/d	2	2,937	1,237	1,469	1,700
SCHREUER, Wilhelm (1866-1933) German					
oil	1	1,229		1,229	
wc/d	5	8,695	1,081	1,619	2,458
SCHREYER, Adolf (1828-1899) German					
oil	10	345,312	2,549	13,591	120,000
wc/d	1	1,306		1,306	
SCHREYER, Franz (1858-?) German					
oil	1	4,076		4,076	
SCHREYER, Wilhelm (1890-?) Dutch					
oil	1	3,485		3,485	
SCHREYVOGEL, Charles (1861-1912) American					
wc/d	1	10,000		10,000	
SCHRIECK, Otto Marseus van (1619-1678) Dutch					
oil	3	108,345	12,835	20,510	75,000
SCHRIEK, Daniel van der (19th C) Belgian					
oil	1	7,326		7,326	
SCHRIKKEL, Louis (1902-) Dutch					
oil	2	11,200	3,872	5,600	7,328
wc/d	2	6,633	1,030	3,317	5,603
SCHRIMPF, Georg (1889-1938) German					
wc/d	1	2,330		2,330	
SCHRODER, Albert Friedrich (1854-1939) German					
oil	1	1,600		1,600	
SCHRODER, Poul (1894-1957) Danish					
oil	1	1,046		1,046	
SCHRODER, Sierk (1903-) Dutch					
wc/d	1	2,179		2,179	
SCHRODER, Theodor (19th C) German					
oil	1	1,882		1,882	
SCHRODER-SONNENSTERN, Friedrich (1892-1982) German					
wc/d	1	4,758		4,758	
SCHROEDER, Louis Jean Desire (1828-1898) French					
3D	2	19,614	7,586	9,807	12,028
SCHROETER, Paul (1866-?) German					
oil	2	3,727	1,545	1,864	2,182
SCHROTER, Wilhelm (1849-1904) German					
oil	4	10,069	1,347	1,861	5,000
SCHROTTER, A von (1856-1935) Austrian					
oil	1	1,573		1,573	
SCHROTZBERG, Franz (1811-1889) Austrian					
oil	1	1,630		1,630	
SCHRYVER, Louis Marie de (1862-1942) French					
oil	3	26,068	1,329	4,739	20,000
SCHUBACK, Emil Gottlieb (1820-1902) German					
oil	1	2,273		2,273	
SCHUBERT, Otto (1892-1970) German					
oil	1	1,226		1,226	

Name	No.	Total Sales Value	lowest	Prices median	highest
SCHUCH, A (19/20th C) German					
oil	1	18,960		18,960	
SCHUCH, Carl (1846-1903) Austrian					
oil	4	236,526	9,968	69,779	89,716
SCHUCH, Karl (1846-1903) Austrian					
oil	1	1,800		1,800	
SCHUCH, Werner Wilhelm Gustav (1843-1918) German					
oil	3	19,749	2,277	6,998	10,474
SCHUCKER, James (20th C) American					
oil	1	2,000		2,000	
SCHUER, Theodorus Cornelisz van der (1628-1707) Dutch					
oil	1	15,700		15,700	
SCHUFFENECKER, Claude Émile (1851-1934) French					
oil	2	37,512	10,559	18,756	26,953
wc/d	3	7,806	1,240	2,341	4,225
SCHUHMACHER, Wim (1894-1986) Dutch					
oil	7	209,108	8,621	28,017	79,224
wc/d	2	38,793	4,310	19,397	34,483
SCHUL, Adrien (?) French?					
oil	1	5,848		5,848	
SCHULLER, Joseph Carl Paul (19th C) French					
oil	1	9,000		9,000	
SCHULMAN, David (1881-1966) Dutch					
oil	3	6,838	1,205	1,530	4,103
SCHULT, Hans Jurgen (1939-) German					
3D	1	1,311		1,311	
wc/d	1	1,463		1,463	
SCHULTEN, Arnold (1809-1874) German					
oil	1	7,476		7,476	
SCHULTS, Jane (19th C) ?					
oil	1	1,103		1,103	
SCHULTZ, Bernard (20th C) ?					
wc/d	1	1,240		1,240	
SCHULTZ, C (19th C) German					
oil	1	5,285		5,285	
SCHULTZ, George F (1869-?) American					
oil	1	1,600		1,600	
SCHULTZ, Ludwig (19th C) German					
oil	1	2,476		2,476	
SCHULTZ-RIGA, Emil (1872-?) German					
oil	1	1,251		1,251	
SCHULTZBERG, Anshelm (1862-1945) Swedish					
oil	29	89,228	1,005	2,534	10,552
SCHULTZE, Bernard (1915-) German					
3D	3	14,634	1,822	3,821	8,991
oil	9	78,335	2,681	7,084	15,938
wc/d	13	39,658	1,003	2,155	10,680
SCHULTZE, Carl (1856-1935) German					
oil	2	7,460	3,250	3,730	4,210
SCHULTZE, Robert (1828-?) German					
oil	1	1,788		1,788	
SCHULTZENHEIM, Ida von (1859-1940) Swedish					
oil	2	4,221	1,005	2,111	3,216
SCHULY, Adrian (20th C) ?					
oil	1	1,000		1,000	
SCHULZ, Adolph R (1869-1963) American					
oil	1	4,000		4,000	
SCHULZ, Adrien (1851-1931) French					
oil	3	5,341	1,063	1,063	3,215

Name	No.	Total Sales Value	Prices lowest	median	highest
SCHULZ, Charles M (1922-2000) American					
wc/d	5	47,500	6,000	10,000	13,000
SCHULZ, Ella (19/20th C) ?					
oil	1	2,382		2,382	
SCHULZ, Friedrich (1823-1875) German					
oil	1	1,162		1,162	
SCHULZ, Robert (1928-1978) American					
oil	2	5,250	2,000	2,625	3,250
SCHULZ, Walter (1895-1918) American					
oil	1	7,000		7,000	
SCHULZ-MATAN, Walter (1889-?) German					
oil	2	14,077	1,117	7,039	12,960
SCHULZ-STRADTMANN, Otto (1892-1960) German					
oil	3	3,795	1,073	1,208	1,514
SCHULZE, Andreas (1955-) German					
oil	1	10,194		10,194	
SCHULZE, Horst (?) ?					
oil	1	1,002		1,002	
SCHUMACHER, Carl Georg (1797-1869) German					
oil	1	4,655		4,655	
SCHUMACHER, Emil (1912-1999) German					
oil	4	147,375	16,550	21,140	88,545
wc/d	6	194,643	1,240	18,621	111,719
SCHUMACHER, Ernst (1905-1963) German					
oil	1	1,771		1,771	
SCHUMACHER, Harald (1836-1912) Danish					
oil	1	1,878		1,878	
SCHUMANN, Christian (1970-) American					
oil	3	96,000	18,000	38,000	40,000
SCHUPPEN, Jacob van (1670-1751) Dutch					
oil	2	57,563	26,530	28,782	31,033
SCHURCH, Johann Robert (1895-1941) Swiss					
oil	2	10,415	1,574	5,208	8,841
wc/d	2	2,289	1,105	1,145	1,184
SCHURR, Claude (1920-) French					
oil	2	2,236	1,032	1,118	1,204
SCHUSTER, Donna (1883-1953) American					
oil	1	16,000		16,000	
SCHUSTER, Karl Maria (1871-1953) Austrian					
oil	1	2,750		2,750	
SCHUSTER, Ludwig (1820-1873) Austrian					
oil	1	1,300		1,300	
SCHUSTER, Ludwig Albrecht (1824-1905) German					
oil	1	1,981		1,981	
SCHUT, Cornelis (17th C) Flemish					
oil	1	6,181		6,181	
SCHUTT, Franz (1908-) German					
wc/d	1	2,160		2,160	
SCHUTTE, Thomas (1954-) German					
3D	1	54,360		54,360	
wc/d	3	17,971	1,771	4,200	12,000
SCHUTZ, Christian Georg (18/19th C) German					
oil	2	34,057	5,944	17,029	28,113
SCHUTZ, Christian Georg (school) (18/19th C) German					
oil	1	3,988		3,988	
SCHUTZ, Christian Georg I (1718-1791) German					
oil	3	36,229	9,060	10,990	16,179
SCHUTZ, Christian Georg II (1758-1823) German					
oil	2	37,366	18,166	18,683	19,200

Name	No.	Total Sales Value	lowest	Prices median	highest
wc/d	2	2,826	1,182	1,413	1,644
SCHUTZ, Heinrich (1875-?) German					
oil	1	1,073		1,073	
SCHUTZ, Jan Frederik (1817-1888) Dutch					
oil	3	11,652	1,729	2,099	7,824
SCHUTZ, Johann Georg (1755-1813) German					
wc/d	2	3,574	1,309	1,787	2,265
SCHUTZ, Johannes (20th C) Swiss					
oil	2	3,973	1,785	1,987	2,188
SCHUTZ, Willem Joannes (1854-1933) Dutch					
wc/d	1	2,360		2,360	
SCHUTZE, Wilhelm (1840-1898) German					
oil	3	9,459	1,823	1,936	5,700
SCHUYFF, Peter (1958-) Dutch					
oil	1	1,100		1,100	
SCHUZ, Theodor (1830-1900) German					
oil	1	5,920		5,920	
SCHWAB, Elmer P (?) ?					
oil	2	4,500	1,500	2,250	3,000
SCHWABE, Hans Alwin (1878-1940) Swiss					
oil	1	1,129		1,129	
SCHWALBE, Ole (1929-1990) Danish					
3D	1	3,017		3,017	
oil	31	96,144	1,056	2,293	11,876
SCHWAMMBERGER, Hildegard (1950-) German					
oil	1	2,595		2,595	
SCHWAN, H (19th C) German					
oil	1	1,729		1,729	
SCHWARTZ, Andrew T (1867-1942) American					
oil	1	1,600		1,600	
SCHWARTZ, Davis F (1879-1969) American					
oil	2	3,450	1,200	1,725	2,250
SCHWARTZ, Frans (1850-1917) Danish					
oil	2	3,838	1,097	1,919	2,741
SCHWARTZ, Lester (20th C) American					
wc/d	1	1,000		1,000	
SCHWARTZ, Mommie (1876-1942) Dutch					
oil	2	16,869	7,386	8,435	9,483
SCHWARTZ, William S (1896-1977) American					
oil	1	30,000		30,000	
wc/d	3	9,400	2,800	3,000	3,600
SCHWARTZMAN, Rosi (1947-) Peruvian					
oil	1	4,000		4,000	
SCHWARZER, Bernd (1954-) German					
oil	2	5,415	1,514	2,708	3,901
wc/d	1	5,128		5,128	
SCHWEGLER, Xaver (1832-1902) Swiss					
oil	1	4,102		4,102	
SCHWEICH, Karl (1823-1898) German					
wc/d	1	4,874		4,874	
SCHWEIRING, Conrad (1916-1986) American					
oil	1	5,000		5,000	
SCHWEITZER, Alfred (1882-?) German					
oil	1	1,099		1,099	
SCHWEITZER, Cajetan (1844-1913) German					
oil	1	2,476		2,476	
SCHWENDY, Albert (1820-1902) German					
oil	1	2,414		2,414	

Name	No.	Total Sales Value	lowest	Prices median	highest
SCHWENINGER, Carl (elder) (1818-1887) Austrian					
oil	2	3,275	1,591	1,638	1,684
SCHWENINGER, Carl (younger) (1854-1903) Austrian					
oil	1	15,824		15,824	
SCHWENINGER, Rosa (19th C?) German?					
oil	1	1,349		1,349	
SCHWERIN, Amelie von (1819-1897) Swedish					
oil	3	5,428	1,104	1,105	3,219
SCHWERIN, Ludwig (1897-1983) Israeli					
oil	1	1,800		1,800	
SCHWICHTENBERG, Martel (1896-1945) German					
oil	1	25,920		25,920	
SCHWIEGER-UELZEN, Heinrich (1902-) German					
oil	1	1,471		1,471	
SCHWIND, Moritz von (1804-1871) Austrian					
oil	1	30,000		30,000	
wc/d	2	6,692	1,165	3,346	5,527
SCHWINGER, A (19/20th C) Austrian					
oil	1	4,500		4,500	
SCHWITTERS, Kurt (1887-1948) German					
oil	2	78,682	3,182	39,341	75,500
wc/d	14	971,030	31,900	52,380	120,000
SCHYL, Jules (1893-1977) Swedish					
oil	14	31,666	1,054	1,923	3,914
wc/d	1	1,155		1,155	
SCIALOJA, Toti (1914-1998) Italian					
oil	3	10,438	2,250	3,273	4,915
wc/d	2	2,542	1,004	1,271	1,538
SCILTIAN, Gregorio (1900-1985) Russian					
oil	4	47,996	6,981	12,015	16,985
wc/d	1	4,236		4,236	
SCIPIONE (1904-1933) Italian					
wc/d	2	8,198	3,376	4,099	4,822
SCIUTI, Giuseppi (1835-1911) Italian					
oil	3	16,590	3,732	5,861	6,997
SCKELL, Ludwig (1833-1912) German					
oil	8	36,401	2,377	3,495	12,267
SCOGNAMIGLIO, Cavaliero Antonio (19th C) Italian					
oil	1	4,381		4,381	
SCOLART, A (19th C) ?					
oil	1	6,421		6,421	
SCOMPARINI, Eugenio (1845-1913) Italian					
oil	1	3,363		3,363	
SCOPA, Simoneto (18th C) Italian					
oil	1	2,314		2,314	
SCOPPA, Giuseppe (19th C) Italian					
wc/d	2	4,190	2,002	2,095	2,188
SCOPPA, Raimondo (1820-?) Italian					
oil	1	4,451		4,451	
SCOPPETTA, Pietro (1863-1920) Italian					
oil	8	97,947	2,836	8,745	28,561
wc/d	1	1,780		1,780	
SCOPPOLA, A (20th C) Italian					
wc/d	1	1,413		1,413	
SCOREL, Jan van (1495-1562) Dutch					
wc/d	1	67,950		67,950	
SCORIEL, Jean Baptiste (1883-?) Belgian					
oil	2	2,251	1,107	1,126	1,144
SCORZA, Sinibaldo (1589-1631) Italian					
oil	1	4,052		4,052	

Name	No.	Total Sales Value	lowest	Prices median	highest
SCOTT, Adam Sheriff (1887-1980) Canadian					
oil	2	4,039	1,384	2,020	2,655
SCOTT, Clyde Eugene (1884-1959) American					
oil	2	7,250	2,250	3,625	5,000
SCOTT, David (1806-1849) British					
oil	1	5,439		5,439	
SCOTT, Eric (20th C) ?					
oil	1	1,481		1,481	
SCOTT, Georges Bertin (1873-1942) French					
oil	1	3,137		3,137	
SCOTT, Henry (1911-1966) British					
oil	17	91,087	2,445	4,500	12,000
SCOTT, John (19th C) British					
oil	5	61,060	3,575	8,410	22,650
wc/d	1	1,269		1,269	
SCOTT, John W (1907-1987) American					
wc/d	1	3,000		3,000	
SCOTT, Robert (1958-) British					
oil	1	2,736		2,736	
SCOTT, Sir Peter (1909-1989) British					
oil	5	16,522	1,350	3,021	6,636
SCOTT, Thomas Jefferson (19th C) ?					
oil	1	2,600		2,600	
SCOTT, Tom (1854-1927) British					
oil	1	1,812		1,812	
wc/d	12	49,787	1,580	3,715	7,268
SCOTT, William (1913-1989) British					
oil	6	348,360	36,660	58,200	82,500
wc/d	4	30,965	4,290	6,450	13,775
SCOTT, William Bell (1811-1890) British					
wc/d	3	10,286	1,145	2,145	6,996
SCOTT, Winfield Lionel (c.1839-?) American					
oil	1	2,000		2,000	
SCOTTISH SCHOOL, 19th C					
oil	1	3,020		3,020	
SCOUEZEC, Maurice le (1881-1940) French					
oil	5	23,238	2,112	4,062	7,040
wc/d	6	11,956	1,110	1,802	3,926
SCRAGGS, J (19th C) British					
oil	2	2,973	1,088	1,487	1,885
SCRIVENER, Henry A (1842-1906) ?					
wc/d	1	1,195		1,195	
SCRIVER, Robert Macfie (1914-1999) American					
3D	1	7,000		7,000	
SCRIVO (1942-) Belgian?					
oil	2	7,443	2,847	3,722	4,596
SCROCCO, Virginia Tomescu (19th C) Italian					
oil	1	1,854		1,854	
SCROPPO, Filippo (1910-1993) Italian					
oil	1	1,800		1,800	
SCROUVENS, Cesar (1884-) Belgian					
3D	1	1,996		1,996	
SCUDDER, James Long (1836-1881) American					
oil	2	29,000	11,000	14,500	18,000
SCUDDER, Janet (1873-1940) American					
3D	1	7,000		7,000	
SCUFFI, Marcello (1948-) Italian					
oil	14	22,350	1,014	1,338	3,144

Name	No.	Total Sales Value	Prices lowest	median	highest
SCULLY, Harry (?-1935) British					
wc/d	2	6,380	2,465	3,190	3,915
SCULLY, Sean (1946-) American/Irish					
oil	2	102,000	32,000	51,000	70,000
SCULTHORPE, Peter (1948-) American					
wc/d	1	14,500		14,500	
SEAGO, Edward (1910-1974) British					
oil	54	1,025,192	4,200	14,925	82,537
wc/d	6	30,295	1,073	4,669	9,000
SEAL, Jogesh Chander (1895-1926) Indian					
oil	2	39,500	7,500	19,750	32,000
SEALY, Colin (1900-1976) British					
oil	1	2,869		2,869	
wc/d	1	1,404		1,404	
SEARLE, Ronald (1920-) British					
wc/d	41	118,305	1,057	2,416	8,700
SEARLE, W (19th C) British?					
oil	1	2,983		2,983	
SEBA, Sigfried Shalom (1897-1975) Israeli					
wc/d	2	3,800	1,000	1,900	2,800
SEBEN, Henri van (1825-1913) Belgian					
oil	3	11,367	2,207	2,900	6,260
SEBILLE, Albert (1874-1953) French					
oil	1	1,167		1,167	
SEBIRE, Gaston (1920-) French					
oil	7	9,891	1,070	1,196	2,350
SEBREGTS, L (20th C) Belgian					
wc/d	1	1,188		1,188	
SECKHAM, Violet Thorne (fl.1909-1923) British					
oil	1	1,284		1,284	
SECOLA, A (?) Italian					
oil	1	2,400		2,400	
SECURE, Alfred de (?) ?					
oil	1	2,385		2,385	
SEDELMAYER, Joseph Anton (1797-1863) German					
oil	1	4,271		4,271	
SEDELMAYER, Martin (1766-1799) Austrian					
wc/d	7	98,022	11,532	14,415	14,415
SEDGELEY, Peter (1930-) British					
3D	1	1,481		1,481	
oil	1	2,609		2,609	
SEDGLEY, Peter (1930-) British					
wc/d	1	3,625		3,625	
SEDLACEK, Stephan (19/20th C) Austrian					
oil	5	15,405	2,100	3,212	3,948
SEDRAC, Serge (1878-1974) French					
oil	1	1,410		1,410	
SEEGER, Hermann (1857-1920) German					
oil	3	20,896	4,507	6,169	10,220
SEEHAUS, Paul Adolf (1891-1919) German					
oil	1	35,418		35,418	
SEEKATZ, Johann Conrad (1719-1768) German					
oil	9	102,478	3,143	12,849	21,268
SEEL, Adolf (1829-1907) German					
oil	1	3,826		3,826	
SEEL, Johann Richard (1819-1875) German					
oil	1	1,019		1,019	
SEEMAN, Enoch (17/18th C) German/Polish					
oil	4	31,161	2,574	7,144	14,300

Name	No.	Total Sales Value	lowest	Prices median	highest
SEEREY-LESTER, John (1945-) British					
oil	2	4,936	2,272	2,468	2,664
SEEVAGEN, Lucien (1887-1959) French					
oil	1	1,083		1,083	
SEGAL, Arthur (1875-1944) Rumanian					
oil	7	177,986	4,794	11,000	90,000
wc/d	2	28,849	10,849	14,425	18,000
SEGAL, George (1924-2000) American					
3D	4	601,900	1,900	140,000	320,000
wc/d	1	2,976		2,976	
SEGAL, Simon (1898-1969) French					
oil	4	8,458	1,428	2,161	2,709
SEGANTINI, Giovanni (1858-1899) Italian					
oil	6	516,005	7,500	30,669	321,377
wc/d	3	49,475	5,797	20,101	23,577
SEGANTINI, Gottardo (1882-1974) Italian					
oil	10	179,110	1,309	16,324	54,692
SEGER, E (1868-1939) German					
3D	2	6,288	1,578	3,144	4,710
SEGER, Ernst (1868-1939) German					
3D	8	36,162	1,751	3,863	9,315
SEGERS, Adrien (1876-1950) Belgian					
oil	1	4,319		4,319	
SEGERS, Maria (1922-1979) ?					
oil	1	1,419		1,419	
SEGEWITZ, Eugen (1878-?) German					
oil	1	2,000		2,000	
SEGHERS, Corneille (1814-1875) Belgian					
oil	1	2,648		2,648	
SEGHERS, Daniel (1590-1661) Flemish					
oil	2	448,119	95,319	224,060	352,800
SEGNA DI BONAVENTURA (fl.1298-1326) Italian					
oil	1	57,380		57,380	
SEGOFFIN, Victor (1867-1925) French					
3D	1	19,245		19,245	
SEGONI, Alcide (1847-1894) Italian					
oil	1	20,000		20,000	
SEGRELLES, Eustaquio (1936-) Spanish					
oil	11	33,708	1,008	2,082	7,784
SEGRELLES, Jose (1885-1969) Spanish					
oil	2	6,200	1,013	3,100	5,187
wc/d	1	1,638		1,638	
SEGRI, Ernst (19th C) ?					
3D	1	4,380		4,380	
SEGUI, Antonio (1934-) Argentinian					
oil	2	20,738	3,738	10,369	17,000
wc/d	8	23,601	1,690	2,486	4,986
SEGUIN, Armand (1869-1903) French					
oil	1	1,499		1,499	
SEIBEZZI, Fioravante (1906-1975) Italian					
oil	2	3,232	1,561	1,616	1,671
SEIDEL, A (1820-1904) German					
oil	2	3,316	1,658	1,658	1,658
SEIDEL, August (1820-1904) German					
oil	8	28,647	1,080	3,369	8,511
SEIFERT, Alfred (1850-1901) Czechoslovakian					
oil	3	17,620	1,850	3,770	12,000
SEIFERT, V H (1870-1953) German					
3D	1	1,727		1,727	

Name	No.	Total Sales Value	lowest	Prices median	highest
SEIFERT, Victor Heinrich (1870-1953) German					
3D	4	7,347	1,377	1,632	2,683
SEIFF, P J (18th C) German?					
wc/d	1	1,196		1,196	
SEIGNAC, Guillaume (1870-1924) French					
oil	8	242,853	5,680	18,875	80,000
SEIGNAC, Paul (1826-1904) French					
oil	2	20,020	3,020	10,010	17,000
SEIGNEMARTIN, Jean (1848-1875) French					
oil	2	3,737	1,804	1,869	1,933
SEIJO Y RUBIO, Jose (1881-1970) Spanish					
oil	1	7,244		7,244	
SEILER, Carl Wilhelm Anton (1846-1921) German					
oil	4	13,909	1,551	3,019	6,285
SEILER, Joseph Albert (19th C) Austrian					
oil	1	1,268		1,268	
SEITS, J (20th C) ?					
wc/d	1	1,189		1,189	
SEITZ (?) ?					
3D	1	2,278		2,278	
SEITZ, Anton (1829-1900) German					
oil	3	10,515	1,800	4,359	4,359
SEITZ, Gustav (1906-1969) German					
3D	9	45,972	1,182	3,883	15,053
wc/d	1	1,550		1,550	
SEITZ, Johann (?-c.1812) Austrian					
oil	1	14,361		14,361	
SEITZ, Maximilian (1811-1869) German					
oil	1	1,812		1,812	
SEITZ, Otto (1846-1912) German					
oil	1	2,130		2,130	
SEIZ, Max Eugen (1927-) German					
3D	1	1,068		1,068	
SEJOURNE, Bernard (1945-) Haitian					
oil	1	4,829		4,829	
SEKRET, Valery (1950-) Russian					
oil	4	7,929	1,263	2,133	2,400
SEKULA, Sonja (1918-1963) American/Swiss					
oil	1	2,486		2,486	
SEKULIC, Sava (20th C) ?					
oil	1	1,615		1,615	
SELBY, Charles E (1857-1920) American?					
oil	1	2,000		2,000	
SELBY, Prideaux John (1788-1867) British					
oil	1	6,864		6,864	
wc/d	2	5,200	1,000	2,600	4,200
SELDEN, Henry Bill (1886-1934) American					
oil	2	2,380	1,180	1,190	1,200
SELDEN, Roger (1945-) American					
wc/d	1	1,964		1,964	
SELDER, Bjorn (1940-) Swedish					
3D	1	1,306		1,306	
SELIGMANN, Kurt (1900-1962) American/Swiss					
oil	3	31,582	5,000	8,500	18,082
wc/d	6	22,062	1,800	2,800	8,500
SELINGER, Emily H McGary (1848-1927) American					
oil	3	5,750	1,200	1,300	3,250
SELL, Christian (elder) (1831-1883) German					
oil	2	4,728	1,347	2,364	3,381

Name	No.	Total Sales Value	lowest	Prices median	highest
SELL, Christian (younger) (1854-1925) German					
oil	2	2,955	1,384	1,478	1,571
SELLAIO, Arcangelo Jacopo del (1478-1531) Italian					
oil	1	113,250		113,250	
SELLAIO, Jacopo del (1441-1493) Italian					
oil	1	151,793		151,793	
SELLENATI, H (19th C) ?					
oil	1	1,311		1,311	
SELLENATI, J (?) Italian					
oil	1	1,800		1,800	
SELLEY, Lyndsey (20th C) British					
oil	2	5,822	1,136	2,911	4,686
SELLMAYR, Ludwig (1834-1901) German					
oil	1	1,798		1,798	
SELMERSHEIM-DESGRANGE, Jeanne (1877-1958) French					
oil	1	3,627		3,627	
SELOUS, Henry Courtney (1811-1890) British					
oil	1	2,800		2,800	
SELREGTS, L (?) Belgian?					
oil	1	1,257		1,257	
SELTZER, Olaf C (1877-1957) American					
oil	6	173,500	7,000	28,500	50,000
wc/d	3	64,500	4,500	22,500	37,500
SELTZER, William S (1955-) American					
wc/d	1	3,800		3,800	
SELVATICO, Lino (1872-1924) Italian					
oil	1	4,357		4,357	
SELVE, W (19/20th C) German					
oil	1	1,095		1,095	
SEMEGHINI, Pio (1878-1964) Italian					
oil	3	13,143	3,882	3,956	5,305
SEMENOWSKY, Eisman (19th C) French					
oil	7	28,319	1,349	2,800	11,060
SEMENTA, Eugenio (1902-1958) Italian					
oil	1	1,484		1,484	
SEMPERE, Eusebio (1924-) Spanish					
oil	1	5,460		5,460	
SEMPILL, Joseph (19th C) British					
oil	1	2,280		2,280	
SEMSER, Charles (1922-) American					
3D	1	15,027		15,027	
SEN, Sushil (?) Indian					
wc/d	3	3,750	1,050	1,050	1,650
SENAPE, Antonio (?) Italian					
wc/d	4	20,752	3,491	5,233	6,795
SENAVE, Jacques Albert (1758-1829) Belgian					
oil	1	5,929		5,929	
SENECHAL DE KERDREORET, Gustave Edouard le (1840-1920) French					
oil	2	21,434	6,780	10,717	14,654
SENEQUIER, Jules (1821-1846) French					
oil	1	16,048		16,048	
SENET, Rafael (1856-1926) Spanish					
oil	6	97,916	1,266	18,531	22,855
SENFF, Adolf (1785-1863) German					
oil	1	13,759		13,759	
SENIOR, Mark (1864-1927) British					
oil	9	87,878	3,322	7,952	17,750
SENISE, Daniel (1955-) Brazilian					
oil	2	26,000	12,000	13,000	14,000

Name	No.	Total Sales Value	lowest	Prices median	highest
SENNWALD, Max (20th C) German					
oil	1	1,001		1,001	
SEOANE, Luis (1910-1979) Argentinian					
oil	7	37,462	1,739	4,423	11,788
wc/d	1	1,010		1,010	
SEPESHY, Zoltan L (1898-1974) American					
oil	5	17,450	1,800	3,400	5,500
SEPHTON, George Harcourt (fl.1885-1923) British					
oil	1	2,484		2,484	
SERADOUR, Guy (1922-) French					
oil	3	10,296	2,195	2,572	5,529
SERAPHINE DE SENLIS (1864-1942) French					
oil	1	5,142		5,142	
SERDOBBEL, G (19th C) ?					
oil	1	1,896		1,896	
SEREBRIAKOV, Alexander (1907-1994) Russian					
oil	1	3,222		3,222	
SEREBRIAKOVA, Zinaida (1884-1967) Russian					
oil	2	151,000	75,500	75,500	75,500
wc/d	2	61,232	4,832	30,616	56,400
SERENIUS (18th C) ?					
oil	1	6,003		6,003	
SERGE, M (19/20th C) French					
oil	1	16,533		16,533	
SERGEL, Johan Tobias (1740-1814) Swedish					
wc/d	2	41,353	1,088	20,677	40,265
SERGER, Frederick B (1889-1965) American					
oil	2	8,189	3,879	4,095	4,310
SERIN, Harmen (1678-1765) Flemish					
oil	2	7,176	3,413	3,588	3,763
SERNA, Ismael de la (1897-1968) Spanish					
oil	51	288,678	1,012	3,183	31,824
wc/d	7	15,914	1,084	1,493	6,774
SERNEELS, Clement (1912-1991) Belgian					
oil	4	6,834	1,258	1,782	2,012
SEROV, Valentin Alexandrovitch (1865-1911) Russian					
wc/d	1	4,228		4,228	
SERPAN (20th C) ?					
oil	3	3,708	1,141	1,141	1,426
SERRA CASTELLET, Francisco (1909-) Spanish					
oil	1	3,642		3,642	
SERRA Y AUQUE, Enrico (1859-1918) Spanish					
oil	5	17,102	2,071	2,397	7,300
SERRA Y FARNES, Pedro (1890-1974) Spanish					
oil	1	1,144		1,144	
SERRA, Andreu (20th C) Spanish					
oil	1	1,186		1,186	
SERRA, Richard (1939-) American					
3D	4	498,150	40,000	119,075	220,000
oil	5	208,440	5,190	44,000	65,000
wc/d	1	7,785		7,785	
SERRA, Rosa (1944-) Dutch					
3D	2	12,047	5,150	6,024	6,897
SERRALUNGA, Luigi (1880-1940) Italian					
oil	1	3,194		3,194	
SERRANO RUEDA, Santiago (20th C) Spanish					
wc/d	1	2,194		2,194	
SERRANO, Andres (1950-) American					
oil	1	20,445		20,445	

Name	No.	Total Sales Value	lowest	Prices median	highest
SERRASANTA, Jose (1916-) Argentinian					
oil	3	7,671	1,010	1,731	4,930
SERRES, Antony (1828-1898) French					
oil	1	1,073		1,073	
SERRES, Dominic (1722-1793) British					
oil	4	97,580	1,385	18,498	59,200
wc/d	3	7,707	1,558	2,860	3,289
SERRES, Dominic Michael (fl.1783-1804) British					
wc/d	2	5,148	2,574	2,574	2,574
SERRES, John Thomas (1759-1825) British					
oil	5	82,430	2,700	13,590	43,768
wc/d	1	3,700		3,700	
SERRITELLI, Giovanni (19th C) Italian					
oil	3	53,546	1,049	16,218	36,279
SERRURE, Auguste (1825-1903) Flemish					
oil	4	29,982	2,147	2,858	22,120
SERSTE, P (?) ?					
3D	1	1,174		1,174	
SERT Y BADIA, Jose Maria (1876-1945) Spanish					
oil	4	39,809	2,301	5,573	26,363
SERT, Henri (1938-1964) French					
oil	2	2,425	1,097	1,213	1,328
SERUSIER, Paul (1863-1927) French					
oil	7	93,738	4,409	12,899	30,000
wc/d	4	56,440	4,409	7,104	37,823
SERVAES, Albert (1883-1966) Belgian					
oil	4	31,392	1,321	6,387	17,298
wc/d	5	23,299	1,506	1,936	14,627
SERVANDONI, Jean Nicolas (1695-1766) French					
oil	1	2,921		2,921	
SERVEAU, Clement (1886-1972) French					
oil	9	58,615	1,320	1,910	19,798
wc/d	3	4,487	1,320	1,451	1,716
SERVIN, Amedee (1829-1885) French					
oil	1	5,748		5,748	
SESSA, Aldo (20th C) Italian					
wc/d	1	3,000		3,000	
SESSIONS, James (1882-1962) American					
wc/d	2	3,700	1,200	1,850	2,500
SESSLER, Alfred (1909-1963) American					
oil	1	5,000		5,000	
SESSO, Kato (1872-1928) Japanese					
wc/d	1	2,878		2,878	
SETHER, Gulbrand (1869-1910) Norwegian/American					
oil	1	2,700		2,700	
SETKOWICZ, Adam (1875-1945) Polish					
oil	2	3,355	1,374	1,678	1,981
SETON-CARR, Heywood Walter (1859-?) British					
wc/d	1	1,749		1,749	
SETTI, Ercole (16th C) Italian					
wc/d	2	19,103	1,103	9,552	18,000
SETTLE, W F (1821-1897) British					
oil	1	1,985		1,985	
SETTLE, William F (1821-1897) British					
oil	1	11,520		11,520	
wc/d	2	3,641	1,057	1,821	2,584
SEUPHOR, Michel (1901-1999) Belgian					
wc/d	1	1,033		1,033	
SEURAT, Georges (1859-1891) French					
oil	1	1,000,000		1,000,000	

Name	No.	Total Sales Value	lowest	Prices median	highest
wc/d	2	34,000	8,000	17,000	26,000
SEUSS, Dr (1904-1991) American					
wc/d	2	16,750	3,750	8,375	13,000
SEVAGIN, Dmitrii (1974-) Russian					
oil	1	1,076		1,076	
SEVEN-SEVEN, Twins (1944-) Nigerian					
wc/d	3	4,301	1,128	1,340	1,833
SEVER, Michail Ivanovich (20th C) Russian					
oil	1	3,000		3,000	
SEVERDONCK, Franz van (1809-1889) Belgian					
oil	17	48,565	1,500	1,972	7,900
SEVERDONCK, Joseph van (1819-1905) Belgian					
oil	1	2,574		2,574	
SEVEREN, Dan van (1927-) Belgian					
oil	2	3,134	1,567	1,567	1,567
wc/d	1	3,648		3,648	
SEVERINI, Gino (1883-1966) Italian					
3D	2	35,140	14,000	17,570	21,140
oil	15	1,331,180	2,703	43,634	362,500
wc/d	16	704,707	1,575	7,400	231,445
SEVERN, Joseph Arthur Palliser (1842-1931) British					
wc/d	2	2,973	1,343	1,487	1,630
SEVERN, Walter (1830-1904) British					
wc/d	1	1,264		1,264	
SEVESO, Pompilio (1877-1949) Italian					
oil	1	2,289		2,289	
SEVILLANO, Angel (20th C) Spanish					
oil	4	6,837	1,055	1,634	2,515
SEVILLE SCHOOL, 17th C Spanish					
3D	1	4,843		4,843	
oil	1	2,675		2,675	
SEVILLE SCHOOL, 19th C Spanish					
3D	1	7,978		7,978	
oil	2	10,738	5,113	5,369	5,625
SEVIN, Lucille (20th C) French					
3D	1	4,424		4,424	
SEVIN, Pierre Paul (1650-1710) French					
wc/d	1	1,727		1,727	
SEYLBERGH, Jacques van den (1884-1960) Belgian					
wc/d	2	3,179	1,562	1,590	1,617
SEYLER, Julius (1873-1958) German					
oil	15	36,043	1,082	2,198	4,457
SEYMOUR, James (1702-1752) British					
oil	2	679,500	135,900	339,750	543,600
wc/d	2	7,061	1,055	3,531	6,006
SEYMOUR, Tom (19th C) British					
oil	2	2,852	1,335	1,426	1,517
SEYPPEL, Carl Maria (1847-1913) German					
oil	1	2,699		2,699	
SEYSSAUD, René (1867-1952) French					
oil	5	26,896	2,626	6,674	7,916
SEZANNE, Enrico (1864-1945) Italian					
oil	1	1,450		1,450	
SGARBY, Hector (?) ?					
oil	1	1,300		1,300	
SHAACK, J S C (18th C) Dutch					
oil	1	5,181		5,181	
SHACKLETON, John (18th C) British					
oil	1	135,900		135,900	

Name	No.	Total Sales Value	Prices lowest	median	highest
SHACKLETON, Keith (1923-) British					
oil	4	6,962	1,278	1,848	1,988
SHADBOLT, Jack (1909-1998) Canadian					
oil	2	29,126	6,376	14,563	22,750
wc/d	12	68,709	1,300	3,176	15,436
SHAEFER, S R (19/20th C) Continental					
oil	1	2,500		2,500	
SHAFER, Henry Thomas (1854-?) British					
oil	1	4,400		4,400	
SHAFER, Laura A (1866-1940) American					
oil	1	2,500		2,500	
SHAH, Somalal (1905-1994) Indian					
wc/d	1	1,125		1,125	
SHAHN, Ben (1898-1969) American					
oil	1	11,000		11,000	
wc/d	4	10,400	1,100	2,650	4,000
SHAHN, Ben and ZIEBOLZ, Herbert (20th C) American/German					
wc/d	1	1,456		1,456	
SHAKUNTALA (20th C) Indian					
wc/d	1	2,850		2,850	
SHALDERS, George (1826-1873) British					
oil	3	7,448	1,088	2,130	4,230
wc/d	3	9,737	1,628	3,498	4,611
SHANE, Frederick (1907-) American					
oil	1	1,300		1,300	
SHANKS, Duncan F (1937-) British					
oil	1	4,350		4,350	
SHANKS, William Somerville (1864-1951) British					
oil	3	26,013	1,233	1,580	23,200
SHANNON, Sir James Jebusa (1862-1923) British/American					
oil	2	77,796	1,956	38,898	75,840
SHAPIRO, Joel (1941-) American					
3D	4	125,000	15,000	32,500	45,000
wc/d	4	56,002	4,002	11,000	30,000
SHAPLAND, John (1865-1929) British					
wc/d	1	1,074		1,074	
SHAPLEIGH, Frank Henry (1842-1906) American					
oil	3	19,750	3,500	7,250	9,000
SHAPOSHNIKOV, Boris V (1890-1956) ?					
oil	1	6,098		6,098	
SHARP, Dorothea (1874-1955) British					
oil	26	651,791	4,680	12,815	148,812
SHARP, Joseph Henry (1859-1953) American					
oil	13	720,200	1,100	47,500	210,000
SHARP, Louis H (1875-1946) American					
oil	1	4,000		4,000	
SHARPE, Caroline (?) ?					
wc/d	1	3,454		3,454	
SHARPE, Eliza (1796-1874) British					
wc/d	1	1,130		1,130	
SHARROCK, Joan (1946-) British					
oil	2	2,320	1,136	1,160	1,184
SHATTUCK, Aaron Draper (1832-1928) American					
oil	2	11,250	5,250	5,625	6,000
SHAW, Arthur Winter (1869-1948) British					
oil	1	1,252		1,252	
wc/d	2	5,072	2,072	2,536	3,000
SHAW, Charles Green (1892-1974) American					
oil	5	45,000	1,000	6,000	30,000

Name	No.	Total Sales Value	lowest	Prices median	highest
SHAW, Charles L (19th C) British					
oil	1	2,826		2,826	
SHAW, George (1843-1915) British					
oil	1	1,100		1,100	
SHAW, J H (19th C) British					
oil	1	1,352		1,352	
SHAW, Jim (1952-) American					
wc/d	1	3,750		3,750	
SHAW, John Byam (1872-1919) British					
oil	3	26,855	5,338	8,580	12,937
wc/d	1	4,200		4,200	
SHAW, M (?) ?					
oil	1	1,988		1,988	
SHAW, Richard (1941-) American					
3D	1	3,000		3,000	
SHAW, Walter (1851-1933) British					
oil	1	4,089		4,089	
SHAWCROSS, Neal (1940-) British					
wc/d	1	1,595		1,595	
SHAWE, George (1915-1995) ?					
oil	1	1,200		1,200	
SHAYER, Charles (c.1826-1914) British					
oil	2	15,800	7,900	7,900	7,900
SHAYER, Charles and Henry and SHAYER, William (snr) (19th C) British					
oil	1	18,000		18,000	
SHAYER, H (19th C) British					
oil	1	2,382		2,382	
SHAYER, W (19th C) British					
oil	1	3,528		3,528	
SHAYER, William (snr) (1787-1879) British					
oil	22	162,840	1,084	6,139	20,000
SHAYER, William J (1811-1892) British					
oil	5	38,822	1,884	2,900	20,000
SHEARBON, Andrew (fl.1868) British					
oil	1	2,343		2,343	
SHEARER, Christopher H (1840-1926) American					
oil	13	49,000	1,000	4,000	7,000
SHEARER, James Elliot (1858-?) British					
wc/d	1	1,168		1,168	
SHEE, Sir Martin Archer (1769-1850) British					
oil	3	31,735	3,775	7,550	20,410
SHEELER, Charles (1883-1965) American					
oil	1	340,000		340,000	
wc/d	1	31,000		31,000	
SHEETS, Millard (1907-1989) American					
oil	3	28,000	7,000	8,000	13,000
wc/d	5	18,250	2,000	3,500	6,500
SHEETS, Nan (c.1889-1976) American					
oil	1	5,200		5,200	
SHEFFIELD, George (1839-1892) British					
wc/d	2	5,846	2,370	2,923	3,476
SHEINKMAN, Mark (1963-) American					
wc/d	4	6,400	1,400	1,650	1,700
SHELESNYAK, Henry (20th C) Israeli					
wc/d	1	5,500		5,500	
SHELLEY, John (1938-) British					
oil	1	3,456		3,456	
SHELTON, Peter (1951-) American					
3D	1	12,000		12,000	

Name	No.	Total Sales Value	lowest	Prices median	highest
SHEMI, Menachem (1896-1951) Israeli					
oil	2	61,000	21,000	30,500	40,000
SHEMI, Yehiel (1922-) Israeli					
3D	3	72,000	8,000	24,000	40,000
oil	1	7,000		7,000	
SHEPARD, E H (1879-1976) British					
wc/d	1	4,320		4,320	
SHEPARD, Ernest Howard (1879-1976) British					
wc/d	6	119,140	1,813	12,986	63,420
SHEPHERD, David (1931-) British					
oil	16	295,518	1,422	16,500	55,000
wc/d	1	2,567		2,567	
SHEPHERD, Ernest Howard (1879-?) British					
wc/d	2	35,000	16,000	17,500	19,000
SHEPHERD, F N (19th C) British					
wc/d	1	2,700		2,700	
SHEPHERD, George (19th C) British					
wc/d	1	3,003		3,003	
SHEPHERD, George Sydney (1784-1858) British					
wc/d	4	21,865	1,716	6,142	7,865
SHEPHERD, J H S (19th C) British					
oil	1	1,008		1,008	
SHEPHERD, Thomas Hosmer (1792-1864) British					
wc/d	2	2,717	1,001	1,359	1,716
SHEPPARD, Charlotte Lillian (?-1925) British					
oil	1	6,500		6,500	
SHEPPARD, Peter Clapham (1882-1965) Canadian					
oil	3	6,442	1,044	2,611	2,787
SHEPPARD, Warren W (1858-1937) American					
oil	5	53,000	4,500	5,500	20,000
SHERBINOVSKY, Dmitri Anfimovitch (19/20th C) Russian?					
oil	1	4,731		4,731	
SHERINGHAM, George (1884-1937) British					
wc/d	1	1,154		1,154	
SHERLOCK, Marjorie (1897-1973) British					
oil	1	1,776		1,776	
SHERLOCK, William P (1780-?) British					
oil	1	1,900		1,900	
SHERMAN (20th C) American					
oil	1	2,250		2,250	
SHERMAN, Cindy (1954-) American					
3D	1	3,763		3,763	
oil	1	22,500		22,500	
SHERRIFF-SCOTT, Adam (1887-1980) Canadian					
oil	1	1,604		1,604	
SHERRIN, D (19/20th C) British					
oil	1	1,500		1,500	
SHERRIN, Daniel (1868-1940) British					
oil	26	52,796	1,000	1,456	7,250
SHERRIN, John (1819-1896) British					
wc/d	1	1,971		1,971	
SHERRIN, Reginald D (1891-1971) British					
oil	1	1,060		1,060	
SHERRING (?) British?					
oil	1	1,825		1,825	
SHERWAN, Earl (20th C) American					
wc/d	1	1,400		1,400	
SHERWOOD, Walter J (1865-?) American					
oil	1	2,200		2,200	

Name	No.	Total Sales Value	lowest	Prices median	highest
SHI, Carle (20th C) American?					
oil	1	1,430		1,430	
SHIELDS, Frederic (1833-1911) British					
wc/d	1	20,020		20,020	
SHIELS, William (1785-1857) British					
oil	1	7,300		7,300	
SHIGERU, Aoki (1882-1911) Japanese					
oil	1	190,000		190,000	
SHIKALIEV, Rahman (20th C) Russian					
oil	1	1,136		1,136	
SHIKHOV, R (19th C) Russian?					
oil	1	6,040		6,040	
SHIKLER, Aaron (1922-) American					
wc/d	1	5,000		5,000	
SHIMADA, Hiroyoshi (1948-) French/Japanese					
oil	1	1,100		1,100	
SHINN, Everett (1876-1953) American					
oil	6	402,500	20,000	66,250	110,000
wc/d	5	274,700	2,200	20,000	170,000
SHINODA, Toko (1913-) Japanese					
wc/d	1	1,400		1,400	
SHIPHAM, Benjamin (1806-1872) British					
oil	1	2,664		2,664	
SHIRLAW, Walter (1838-1909) American					
oil	3	6,100	1,100	2,000	3,000
SHIRLEY, Henry (19th C) British					
oil	1	3,180		3,180	
SHISHKIN, Ivan Ivanovich (1832-1898) Russian					
oil	3	329,390	18,330	39,260	271,800
wc/d	3	27,550	1,500	2,080	23,970
SHOESMITH, Kenneth Denton (1890-1939) British					
wc/d	1	3,600		3,600	
SHONBORN, John Lewis (1852-1931) Hungarian					
oil	2	6,896	3,029	3,448	3,867
SHOR, Zvi (1898-1979) Israeli					
oil	3	3,850	1,150	1,200	1,500
SHORLON, J (19th C) British					
oil	1	1,100		1,100	
SHORT, Frederick Golden (1863-1936) British					
oil	11	15,805	1,057	1,422	2,212
SHORT, Richard (1841-1916) British					
oil	1	1,341		1,341	
SHOTEI, Watanabe (1851-1918) Chinese					
wc/d	1	1,500		1,500	
SHRADY, Henry M (1871-1922) American					
3D	1	9,750		9,750	
SHRESHTHA, Laxman (1939-) Indian					
oil	1	2,160		2,160	
SHUKHAEV, Vasili (1887-1972) Russian					
oil	1	14,100		14,100	
SHUKLIN, Vitaly (1970-) Russian					
oil	2	4,050	1,800	2,025	2,250
SHULZ, Ada Walter (1870-1928) American					
oil	3	197,500	32,500	85,000	85,000
SHULZ, Adolph Robert (1869-1963) American					
oil	1	19,000		19,000	
SHUNKO, Waki (1887-?) Japanese					
wc/d	1	1,958		1,958	

Name	No.	Total Sales Value	lowest	Prices median	highest
SI CHEN YUAN (1912-1974) ?					
oil	1	1,900		1,900	
SIAULE, Agathe (19th C) French					
oil	1	3,655		3,655	
SIBBONS, Gudron (?) ?					
oil	1	1,502		1,502	
SIBERDT, Eugène (1851-1931) Belgian					
oil	1	5,177		5,177	
SIBERECHTS, Jan (1627-1703) Flemish					
oil	1	600,600		600,600	
SIBERG, J (19th C) ?					
oil	1	2,377		2,377	
SIBLEY, Frederick T (19th C) British					
oil	1	1,144		1,144	
SICARD, Charles (19th C) French					
oil	1	1,000		1,000	
SICHEL, Nathaniel (1843-1907) German					
oil	3	5,397	1,430	1,694	2,273
SICILIA, Jose Maria (1954-) Spanish					
oil	6	55,204	6,036	7,287	17,000
wc/d	2	56,280	23,009	28,140	33,271
SICILIAN SCHOOL, 18th C					
wc/d	1	24,576		24,576	
SICKERT (?) ?					
oil	1	1,450		1,450	
SICKERT, Walter Richard (1860-1942) British					
oil	9	323,855	4,320	26,100	84,600
wc/d	5	12,860	1,233	1,450	4,495
SIDANER, Henri le (1862-1939) French					
oil	28	3,635,843	3,582	65,000	573,800
wc/d	6	56,276	2,211	4,388	28,367
SIDDAL, Elizabeth (1834-1862) British					
wc/d	1	6,864		6,864	
SIDOLI, Pacifico (1868-?) Italian					
wc/d	1	1,830		1,830	
SIDORENKO, Sergei (1968-) Russian					
oil	1	1,728		1,728	
SIDOUX, P (?) ?					
oil	1	2,948		2,948	
SIEBERG, Johannes (1893-1874) Dutch					
oil	1	5,363		5,363	
SIECK, Rudolf (1877-1957) German					
wc/d	1	1,242		1,242	
SIEFFERT, Paul (1874-1957) French					
oil	8	51,473	2,370	4,034	24,000
SIEGARD, Par (1877-1961) Swedish					
oil	1	3,613		3,613	
SIEGEN, August (19th C) German					
oil	17	68,382	1,716	3,000	8,690
SIEGERT, Eugen (c.1858-1906) German					
oil	1	2,267		2,267	
SIEGRIEST, Louis Bassi (1899-1989) American					
oil	1	65,000		65,000	
SIEMER, Christian (1874-1940) American					
oil	4	18,100	1,100	4,750	7,500
SIEMIRADZKI, Hendrik (1843-1902) Polish					
oil	1	265,000		265,000	
SIENESE SCHOOL, 13th/14th C Italian					
oil	1	10,362		10,362	

Name	No.	Total Sales Value	lowest	Prices median	highest
SIENESE SCHOOL, 14th C Italian					
oil	1	4,489		4,489	
wc/d	1	4,399		4,399	
SIENESE SCHOOL, 16th C Italian					
3D	1	17,204		17,204	
oil	2	88,217	43,102	44,109	45,115
wc/d	1	5,024		5,024	
SIENESE SCHOOL, 16th/17th C Italian					
oil	1	8,305		8,305	
SIENESE SCHOOL, 17th C Italian					
3D	2	21,026	7,163	10,513	13,863
oil	4	59,786	2,869	7,664	41,590
SIERICH, Ludwig Casimir (1834-1919) Dutch					
oil	1	1,698		1,698	
SIERON, Maurice (20th C) Belgian					
oil	1	1,374		1,374	
SIEVANEN, Jaakko (1932-) Finnish					
wc/d	1	1,195		1,195	
SIGALON, Xavier (1787-1837) French					
oil	1	2,866		2,866	
SIGARD, Eliahu (1901-1975) Israeli					
oil	2	3,000	1,100	1,500	1,900
SIGMUND, B D (fl.1880-1904) British					
wc/d	1	1,241		1,241	
SIGMUND, Benjamin D (fl.1880-1904) British					
wc/d	3	6,932	1,030	3,002	3,002
SIGNAC, Paul (1863-1935) French					
oil	9	1,387,009	6,055	85,000	550,000
wc/d	41	714,654	2,308	15,000	115,000
SIGNOL, Emile (1804-1892) French					
oil	1	1,800		1,800	
SIGNORET-LEDIEU, Lucie (1858-1904) French					
3D	1	4,559		4,559	
SIGNORI, Carlo Sergio (c.1906-) Italian					
3D	2	5,658	2,622	2,829	3,036
SIGNORINI (?) Italian					
oil	1	5,236		5,236	
SIGNORINI, Giovanni (1808-1864) Italian					
wc/d	1	1,493		1,493	
SIGNORINI, Giuseppe (1857-1932) Italian					
wc/d	7	28,901	1,000	4,108	10,000
SIGNORINI, Telemaco (1835-1901) Italian					
oil	5	185,934	2,100	15,168	138,330
SIGNOVERT, Jean (1919-1981) French					
oil	1	3,966		3,966	
SIGRIST, Kurt (1943-) Swiss?					
3D	1	5,746		5,746	
SIGVARD, Rune (1907-1942) Swedish					
oil	1	1,725		1,725	
SIKANDER, Shahzia (1969-) American?					
wc/d	3	13,500	3,000	3,000	7,500
SILBERT, Jose (19/20th C) ?					
wc/d	1	3,764		3,764	
SILBERT, Max (1871-?) French					
oil	1	3,322		3,322	
SILCOCK, H (?) British					
oil	1	2,567		2,567	
SILEIKIS, Michael Justin (1893-?) American/Lithuanian					
oil	1	1,300		1,300	

Name	No.	Total Sales Value		Prices	
			lowest	median	highest
SILLEN, Herman (1857-1908) Swedish					
oil	5	102,579	1,612	25,732	38,939
SILO, Adam (1674-1772) Dutch					
oil	3	60,793	13,739	23,527	23,527
SILVA MAVIGNIER, Almir da (1925-) Brazilian					
3D	1	1,456		1,456	
oil	1	11,688		11,688	
SILVA, Francis Augustus (1835-1886) American					
oil	5	394,800	9,800	60,000	160,000
SILVA, William P (1859-1948) American					
oil	4	12,850	2,500	3,075	4,200
SILVAIN, Christian (1950-) Belgian					
oil	1	6,692		6,692	
wc/d	2	2,966	1,424	1,483	1,542
SILVEN, Jakob (1851-1924) Swedish					
oil	3	5,105	1,097	1,756	2,252
SILVERA, P (19th C) Spanish					
oil	1	1,283		1,283	
SILVERMAN, Burton (1928-) American					
wc/d	1	2,100		2,100	
SILVESTRE, Louis (17/18th C) French					
oil	3	114,400	9,000	45,000	60,400
SILVESTRE, Paul (1884-?) French					
3D	1	1,817		1,817	
SIMA, Joseph (1891-1971) Czechoslovakian					
oil	4	33,502	4,298	5,048	19,109
wc/d	2	4,932	2,067	2,466	2,865
SIMARD, Claude A (1943-) Canadian					
oil	2	3,068	1,110	1,534	1,958
SIMBARI, Nicola (1927-) Italian					
oil	4	12,807	1,691	2,308	6,500
SIMBERG, Hugo (1873-1917) Finnish					
oil	1	39,260		39,260	
SIMKIN, Richard (1840-1926) British					
wc/d	6	11,089	1,050	1,445	3,575
SIMM, Franz Xaver (1853-1918) Austrian					
oil	2	12,412	3,775	6,206	8,637
wc/d	1	2,370		2,370	
SIMMET, Illa (?) German					
oil	2	4,167	1,961	2,084	2,206
SIMMLER, Wilhelm (1840-1914) German					
oil	1	19,031		19,031	
SIMMONS, Gary (1964-) American					
wc/d	2	6,250	2,500	3,125	3,750
SIMMONS, J Deane (fl.1882-1889) British					
wc/d	1	1,650		1,650	
SIMMS, G H (fl.1864-1865) British					
oil	1	1,350		1,350	
SIMOLDI, A (20th C) Italian?					
oil	1	1,136		1,136	
SIMON (?) ?					
oil	1	2,139		2,139	
SIMON, Émile (1890-1976) French					
oil	3	6,751	1,033	1,791	3,927
SIMON, François (1818-1896) French					
oil	1	1,971		1,971	
SIMON, Hermann Gustave (1846-1895) American					
oil	1	2,600		2,600	

Name	No.	Total Sales Value	lowest	Prices median	highest
SIMON, Lucien (1861-1945) French					
oil	5	20,849	1,819	2,572	7,666
wc/d	2	6,115	1,791	3,058	4,324
SIMON, Paul (1892-1979) French					
3D	1	1,313		1,313	
SIMON, Yohanan (1905-1976) Israeli					
oil	5	63,921	3,800	6,000	40,000
wc/d	9	31,806	1,000	2,200	14,500
SIMONE, A de (19/20th C) Italian					
oil	2	6,326	3,146	3,163	3,180
wc/d	9	23,848	1,057	2,265	4,832
SIMONE, Alfredo de (19/20th C) Italian					
oil	1	9,500		9,500	
wc/d	2	6,967	3,192	3,484	3,775
SIMONE, D (?) Italian					
wc/d	1	1,051		1,051	
SIMONE, Tommaso de (19th C) Italian					
oil	5	31,108	2,567	6,600	9,060
wc/d	2	2,738	1,320	1,369	1,418
SIMONE, de (19/20th C) Italian					
wc/d	4	11,418	1,386	2,542	4,949
SIMONET, L A (19th C) French					
wc/d	1	1,047		1,047	
SIMONETTI, Amedeo (1874-1922) Italian					
oil	1	2,250		2,250	
wc/d	3	33,520	7,000	9,000	17,520
SIMONETTI, Attilio (1843-1925) Italian					
oil	1	2,003		2,003	
SIMONETTI, Ettore (19th C) Italian					
wc/d	3	76,750	12,750	28,000	36,000
SIMONI, Alfredo de (19th C) Italian					
oil	1	5,500		5,500	
SIMONI, Gustavo (1846-1926) Italian					
oil	2	36,036	11,237	18,018	24,799
wc/d	1	24,000		24,000	
SIMONIDY, Michel (1870-1933) Rumanian					
oil	1	2,712		2,712	
SIMONIN, Victor (1877-1946) Belgian					
oil	3	4,888	1,298	1,405	2,185
SIMONINI, Francesco (1686-1753) Italian					
oil	3	68,719	8,630	18,840	41,249
wc/d	3	10,102	1,191	3,020	5,891
SIMONS, Franz (1855-1919) Belgian					
oil	4	5,463	1,120	1,149	2,045
SIMONS, Michiel (?-1673) Dutch					
oil	3	180,000	10,000	70,000	100,000
SIMONSEN, Niels (1807-1885) Danish					
oil	1	1,637		1,637	
SIMONSEN, Simon (1841-1928) Danish					
oil	19	94,296	1,300	2,689	16,373
SIMONSON, David (1831-1896) German					
oil	1	2,453		2,453	
SIMONSSON, Birger (1883-1938) Swedish					
oil	6	9,379	1,054	1,356	3,015
SIMONSSON, Konrad (1843-1916) Swedish					
oil	1	2,110		2,110	
SIMONY, Stefan (1860-1950) Austrian					
oil	1	7,500		7,500	
SIMOV, Viktor Andreevich (1858-1935) Russian					
oil	1	3,020		3,020	

Name	No.	Total Sales Value	lowest	Prices median	highest
SIMPSON (?) British					
oil	1	1,584		1,584	
SIMPSON, Charles (20th C) British					
oil	1	1,800		1,800	
wc/d	1	1,661		1,661	
SIMPSON, Charles Walter (1885-1971) British					
oil	10	126,164	1,201	5,675	50,560
wc/d	6	17,494	2,265	2,905	3,454
SIMPSON, Jackson (?) ?					
wc/d	1	1,430		1,430	
SIMPSON, John (1782-1847) British					
oil	2	6,776	3,300	3,388	3,476
SIMPSON, R (?) British					
oil	1	1,113		1,113	
SIMPSON, William (1823-1899) British					
wc/d	4	36,781	2,385	8,198	18,000
SIMS, Charles (1873-1926) British					
oil	3	7,072	1,110	1,612	4,350
wc/d	1	1,404		1,404	
SINCLAIR, Alexander Garden (1859-1930) British					
oil	1	3,915		3,915	
SINCLAIR, Irving (1895-1969) American					
oil	2	9,798	3,750	4,899	6,048
SINCLAIR, M (19th C) British					
oil	2	3,515	1,073	1,758	2,442
SINCLAIR, Max (fl.1890-1910) British					
oil	1	1,502		1,502	
SINDING, Knud (1875-1946) Danish					
oil	3	4,751	1,191	1,385	2,175
SINDING, Otto Ludvig (1842-1909) Norwegian					
oil	4	10,381	1,431	2,608	3,735
SINDING, Paul (?) Scandinavian					
oil	1	2,280		2,280	
SINDING, Stephan (1846-1922) Norwegian					
3D	2	8,559	3,715	4,280	4,844
SINDING-LARSEN, Kristoffer (1873-1948) Norwegian					
oil	1	1,008		1,008	
SINEMUS, Willem Frederik (1903-1987) Dutch					
wc/d	1	3,233		3,233	
SINGER, Clyde (1908-) American					
oil	1	1,400		1,400	
wc/d	1	1,000		1,000	
SINGER, William Henry (jnr) (1868-1943) American					
oil	2	5,547	2,400	2,774	3,147
SINGH, Sobha (1901-) Indian					
wc/d	1	12,240		12,240	
SINGIER, Gustave (1909-1985) French					
oil	6	141,629	5,460	16,862	54,360
wc/d	5	10,581	1,386	1,611	3,594
SINHA, Satish (1893-1965) Indian					
oil	1	1,440		1,440	
SINIBALDO (?) Italian					
oil	1	1,273		1,273	
SINS, Ad (19/20th C) ?					
oil	1	5,393		5,393	
SINTENIS, Renée (1888-1965) German					
3D	23	198,097	2,163	6,956	23,169
SIQUEIROS, David (1896-1974) Mexican					
oil	4	331,224	11,224	75,000	170,000
wc/d	2	89,000	24,000	44,500	65,000

Name	No.	Total Sales Value	lowest	Prices median	highest
SIRANI, Elisabetta (1638-1665) Italian					
oil	2	58,000	28,000	29,000	30,000
wc/d	2	2,666	1,086	1,333	1,580
SIRANI, Giovanni Andrea (1610-1670) Italian					
oil	2	103,007	20,452	51,504	82,555
SIRIOTOLARINI (?) Italian					
3D	1	9,981		9,981	
SIRKS, Jan (1885-1938) Dutch					
oil	1	1,273		1,273	
SIRONI, Mario (1885-1961) Italian					
oil	34	658,881	1,047	10,447	82,904
wc/d	20	88,124	1,134	3,374	19,773
SISLEY, Alfred (1839-1899) French					
oil	14	12,406,800	260,000	489,150	3,200,000
wc/d	2	96,628	46,000	48,314	50,628
SISMORE, Charles Porter (20th C) British					
oil	2	5,935	1,359	2,968	4,576
SISQUELLA, Alfredo (1900-1964) Spanish					
oil	1	2,904		2,904	
SISSON, Laurence P (1928-) American					
oil	2	5,350	1,100	2,675	4,250
wc/d	1	2,500		2,500	
SITE, Mino delle (1914-1996) Italian					
oil	2	15,271	2,669	7,636	12,602
SITTE, Willi (1921-) German?					
oil	1	3,575		3,575	
SIVERS, Clara von (1854-1924) German					
oil	1	8,604		8,604	
SIVILLA TORRES, Emili (19th C) Spanish					
oil	1	3,194		3,194	
SJAMAAR, Pieter Geerard (1819-1876) Dutch					
oil	4	8,653	1,641	2,006	3,000
SJOBERG, Axel (1866-1950) Swedish					
oil	3	4,742	1,362	1,732	1,732
wc/d	1	1,055		1,055	
SJOHOLM, Charles (1933-) Swedish					
oil	1	1,671		1,671	
SJOSTRAND, Carl Gustaf (19th C) Swedish					
oil	1	1,587		1,587	
SKADE, Fritz (1898-1971) German					
wc/d	1	2,160		2,160	
SKAGERFORS, Olle (1920-1997) Swedish					
wc/d	3	6,938	1,360	1,759	3,819
SKALL (20th C) French					
3D	1	2,314		2,314	
SKANBERG, Carl (1850-1883) Swedish					
oil	5	8,135	1,108	1,501	2,822
SKARBINA, Franz (1849-1910) German					
oil	1	18,155		18,155	
wc/d	4	45,536	3,900	12,168	17,301
SKEAPING, John (1901-1980) British					
wc/d	3	5,882	1,570	1,896	2,416
SKELL, L (1843-1905) German					
oil	1	3,636		3,636	
SKEMP, Robert Oliver (1907-1979) American					
oil	1	2,100		2,100	
SKLAR, Dorothy (20th C) American					
oil	1	2,500		2,500	
SKLAVOS, Yerassimos (1927-1967) Greek					
3D	1	2,964		2,964	

Name	No.	Total Sales Value	Prices lowest	median	highest
SKOLD, Otte (1894-1958) Swedish					
oil	5	20,339	1,959	2,511	10,049
wc/d	2	8,302	3,385	4,151	4,917
SKOU, Sigurd (1878-1929) American					
oil	1	10,500		10,500	
SKOVGAARD, Joakim (1856-1933) Danish					
oil	1	1,622		1,622	
SKOVGAARD, Niels (1858-1938) Danish					
oil	2	6,642	1,073	3,321	5,569
SKOVGAARD, P C (1817-1875) Danish					
oil	2	6,417	1,889	3,209	4,528
SKOVGAARD, Peter Christian (1817-1875) Danish					
oil	4	19,791	1,399	4,846	8,701
SKOVGAARD, Suzette Cathrine Holten (1863-1937) Danish					
oil	1	1,342		1,342	
SKRAMSTAD, Ludwig (1855-1912) Norwegian					
oil	2	5,086	1,099	2,543	3,987
SKREBER, Dirk (20th C) German					
oil	1	10,813		10,813	
SKREDSVIG, Christian (1854-1924) Norwegian					
oil	1	7,513		7,513	
SKULASON, Thorvaldur (1906-1984) Icelandic					
oil	2	8,709	3,035	4,355	5,674
SKUM, Nils Nilsson (1872-1951) Swedish					
oil	1	5,659		5,659	
wc/d	6	7,436	1,005	1,146	1,656
SLABBINCK, Rik (1914-1991) Belgian					
oil	16	45,005	1,019	1,857	8,067
wc/d	1	1,294		1,294	
SLATER, C H (fl.1867) British					
oil	1	1,704		1,704	
SLATER, J F (1857-1937) British					
oil	1	1,329		1,329	
SLATER, John Falconar (1857-1937) British					
oil	12	26,085	1,088	1,564	5,652
wc/d	2	2,900	1,015	1,450	1,885
SLEATOR, James Sinton (1889-1950) British					
oil	1	1,440		1,440	
SLEIGH, Bernard (1872-1954) British					
oil	1	6,006		6,006	
SLEVOGT, Max (1868-1932) German					
oil	5	381,038	14,953	59,811	172,800
wc/d	5	6,413	1,081	1,229	1,644
SLEWINSKY, Wladyslaw (1854-1918) Polish					
oil	1	38,000		38,000	
SLINGELANDT, Pieter van (1640-1691) Dutch					
oil	1	35,280		35,280	
SLIPPER, Gary P (1934-) Canadian					
oil	1	1,436		1,436	
SLOAN, George (1864-?) American					
oil	1	6,000		6,000	
SLOAN, John (1871-1951) American					
oil	4	2,124,000	16,000	54,000	2,000,000
wc/d	1	3,800		3,800	
SLOANE, Eric (1910-1985) American					
oil	12	133,300	1,300	9,500	25,000
SLOCOMBE, Edward (1850-?) British					
wc/d	1	1,950		1,950	
SLOTT-MOLLER, Agnes (1862-1937) Danish					
oil	4	9,040	1,133	1,372	5,163

Name	No.	Total Sales Value	lowest	Prices median	highest
SLOTT-MOLLER, Harald (1864-1937) Danish					
oil	4	54,169	1,192	8,617	35,744
SLOUN, Frank van (1879-1938) American					
oil	1	12,500		12,500	
SLUITER, Willy (1873-1949) Dutch					
oil	7	36,073	1,291	1,721	25,459
wc/d	8	21,469	1,231	2,200	5,516
SLUYS, Theo van (19th C) Belgian					
oil	3	15,037	2,537	4,500	8,000
SLUYTERS, Jan (1881-1957) Dutch					
oil	7	154,396	8,715	19,014	47,414
wc/d	13	63,001	1,180	3,233	15,845
SLY, F (fl.1642) ?					
oil	1	3,456		3,456	
SMALL, Florence (c.1860-1933) British					
oil	2	10,226	3,076	5,113	7,150
SMARGIASSI, Gabriele (1798-1882) Italian					
oil	2	3,138	1,230	1,569	1,908
SMART, R Borlase (1881-1947) British					
oil	1	5,688		5,688	
SMEERS, Frans (1873-1960) Belgian					
oil	18	46,633	1,070	1,495	9,404
wc/d	3	7,737	1,898	1,986	3,853
SMEETS, Yves (1961-) Belgian					
oil	1	1,043		1,043	
SMELLIE, John (?-1925) British					
oil	1	46,400		46,400	
SMET, Gustave de (1877-1943) Belgian					
oil	6	94,686	2,373	15,673	31,690
SMET, Léon de (1881-1966) Belgian					
oil	10	103,543	1,145	8,113	30,200
wc/d	1	2,621		2,621	
SMETHAM-JONES, G W (fl.1887-1893) British					
wc/d	1	1,896		1,896	
SMETS, L (19th C) Dutch					
oil	1	3,385		3,385	
SMETS, Louis (19th C) Belgian					
oil	2	40,770	15,950	20,385	24,820
SMIDTH, Hans (1839-1917) Danish					
oil	13	27,346	1,044	1,678	6,553
SMIGIELSKI, Wladislaw Konrad (1908-1999) British/Polish					
oil	2	2,371	1,164	1,186	1,207
SMILLIE, George H (1840-1921) American					
oil	6	65,400	2,100	10,500	24,000
wc/d	2	9,000	3,500	4,500	5,500
SMILLIE, Helen Sheldon Jacobs (1854-1926) American					
wc/d	1	2,000		2,000	
SMILLIE, James David (1833-1909) American					
oil	2	12,500	5,500	6,250	7,000
SMIRNOV, Serguei (1954-) Russian					
oil	2	3,121	1,068	1,561	2,053
SMIT, Derk (20th C) Dutch/American					
oil	1	2,600		2,600	
SMITH OF CHICHESTER, George (1714-1776) British					
oil	1	2,574		2,574	
SMITH, A (?) ?					
oil	1	1,533		1,533	
SMITH, Alexis (1949-) American					
wc/d	1	4,500		4,500	

Name	No.	Total Sales Value	lowest	Prices median	highest
SMITH, Alfred H (1953-) French					
oil	2	3,740	1,168	1,870	2,572
SMITH, Alice Ravenel Huger (1876-1945) American					
wc/d	1	56,000		56,000	
SMITH, Arthur Reginald (1871-1934) British					
wc/d	3	5,316	1,704	1,716	1,896
SMITH, Brett (20th C) American					
oil	1	20,000		20,000	
SMITH, Bryce (19th C) ?					
oil	1	1,554		1,554	
SMITH, Campbell Lindsay (1915-) British					
oil	1	2,812		2,812	
SMITH, Carlton A (1853-1946) British					
oil	4	63,307	1,817	15,730	30,030
wc/d	7	66,208	1,924	4,794	18,460
SMITH, Cary (1955-) American					
oil	3	6,843	1,200	2,000	3,643
SMITH, Charles L A (1871-1937) American					
oil	1	4,500		4,500	
SMITH, David (1906-1965) American					
3D	1	180,000		180,000	
oil	2	14,000	6,000	7,000	8,000
SMITH, David (1920-1998) British					
oil	5	10,491	1,072	1,800	4,424
SMITH, E Boyd (1860-1943) American					
oil	1	16,000		16,000	
SMITH, Edith Agnes (1867-1954) Canadian					
oil	1	1,567		1,567	
SMITH, Edward Gregory (1880-1961) American					
oil	1	7,000		7,000	
SMITH, Eileen Laurence (19/20th C) British					
wc/d	1	3,834		3,834	
SMITH, Ernest Browning (1866-1951) American					
oil	1	1,500		1,500	
SMITH, Francis (20th C) ?					
oil	4	66,719	9,554	12,049	33,068
wc/d	2	10,378	1,506	5,189	8,872
SMITH, Francis Hopkinson (1838-1915) American					
wc/d	5	17,550	2,000	3,750	5,500
SMITH, Frank Hill (1841-1904) American					
oil	1	4,600		4,600	
SMITH, Frank L (19th C) American					
3D	1	25,000		25,000	
SMITH, Frank Vining (1879-1967) American					
oil	2	18,000	3,000	9,000	15,000
wc/d	1	2,067		2,067	
SMITH, Frederick Carl (1868-1955) American					
oil	2	3,300	1,500	1,650	1,800
SMITH, George (1829-1901) British					
oil	4	53,850	4,350	10,530	28,440
SMITH, George (1870-1934) British					
oil	10	29,063	1,000	2,971	5,800
wc/d	1	1,050		1,050	
SMITH, Gordon Appelby (1919-) Canadian					
oil	4	9,509	1,143	2,233	3,900
SMITH, H Hilliard (1871-1948) American					
oil	1	1,700		1,700	
SMITH, Hassel (1915-) American					
oil	1	12,000		12,000	

Name	No.	Total Sales Value	lowest	Prices median	highest
SMITH, Henry Pember (1854-1907) American					
oil	11	57,541	1,760	4,400	13,500
wc/d	1	9,000		9,000	
SMITH, Hobbe (1862-1942) Dutch					
oil	8	32,588	1,431	4,040	6,789
SMITH, J A (19th C) ?					
oil	1	2,649		2,649	
SMITH, J B (18/19th C) British					
oil	2	15,500	6,000	7,750	9,500
SMITH, J Christopher (1891-1943) American					
oil	3	6,800	1,000	1,800	4,000
SMITH, Jack (1928-) British					
oil	2	4,205	1,450	2,103	2,755
SMITH, Jack W (1873-1949) American					
oil	9	166,000	3,000	7,500	100,000
SMITH, James Burrell (1824-1897) British					
oil	1	4,293		4,293	
wc/d	5	10,437	1,230	1,430	4,290
SMITH, James Whittet (19th C) British					
oil	1	1,144		1,144	
wc/d	1	1,859		1,859	
SMITH, Jeremy (1946-) Canadian					
oil	1	17,256		17,256	
SMITH, John (fl.1854-1876) British					
wc/d	1	1,392		1,392	
SMITH, John Brandon (fl.1859-1884) British					
oil	7	42,257	1,435	7,110	11,060
SMITH, John Guthrie Spence (1880-1951) British					
oil	2	4,816	1,896	2,408	2,920
SMITH, John Rubens (1775-1849) British/American					
oil	1	8,000		8,000	
SMITH, John Warwick (1749-1831) British					
wc/d	5	7,578	1,184	1,539	1,812
SMITH, Jori (1907-) Canadian					
oil	1	2,878		2,878	
SMITH, Kiki (1954-) American					
3D	3	265,000	40,000	65,000	160,000
wc/d	1	1,500		1,500	
SMITH, Langdon (1870-1959) American					
oil	1	1,400		1,400	
wc/d	2	2,300	1,000	1,150	1,300
SMITH, Leon Polk (1906-) American					
wc/d	1	4,500		4,500	
SMITH, Leslie (19/20th C) ?					
oil	1	5,500		5,500	
SMITH, Madeline (19/20th C) French					
wc/d	1	4,062		4,062	
SMITH, Marshall (20th C) American					
oil	1	3,250		3,250	
SMITH, May Ferris (1871-?) American					
oil	1	2,400		2,400	
SMITH, Miller (fl.1885-1920) British					
wc/d	1	1,380		1,380	
SMITH, Nicholas (20th C) British					
wc/d	1	1,065		1,065	
SMITH, Philip Wilton (fl.1892-1907) British					
oil	1	1,138		1,138	
SMITH, Ray (1959-) American					
oil	2	6,949	2,949	3,475	4,000

Name	No.	Total Sales Value	lowest	Prices median	highest
SMITH, Reginald (1855-1925) British					
oil	1	1,950		1,950	
SMITH, Richard (1931-) British					
oil	2	2,886	1,014	1,443	1,872
SMITH, Richard J (1955-) British					
oil	1	1,573		1,573	
SMITH, Russell (1812-1896) American					
oil	5	26,800	1,300	3,000	17,000
SMITH, Sir Matthew (1879-1959) British					
oil	7	199,330	11,280	27,550	43,500
wc/d	5	13,188	1,199	1,988	4,740
SMITH, Stephen Catterson (19/20th C) British					
oil	1	2,000		2,000	
SMITH, Stephen Catterson (elder) (1806-1872) British					
oil	1	1,362		1,362	
SMITH, Thomas Lochlan (1835-1884) American					
oil	1	3,500		3,500	
SMITH, Tony (1912-1980) American					
3D	1	4,800		4,800	
SMITH, W (?) ?					
oil	1	2,750		2,750	
SMITH, Wallace Herndon (1901-) American					
oil	2	3,200	1,000	1,600	2,200
SMITH, William (18/19th C) ?					
oil	1	3,000		3,000	
SMITH, William H (fl.1863-1880) British					
oil	1	1,152		1,152	
SMITH, William Harding (1848-1922) British					
wc/d	1	1,200		1,200	
SMITH, Xanthus (1838-1929) American					
oil	1	7,000		7,000	
wc/d	1	2,000		2,000	
SMITH-HALD, Frithjof (1846-1903) Norwegian					
oil	1	5,000		5,000	
SMITHEMAN, S Francis (20th C) British					
oil	2	9,861	4,576	4,931	5,285
SMITHERS, Collier (fl.1892-1936) British					
oil	1	4,640		4,640	
SMITHSON, Robert (1938-1973) American					
3D	1	75,500		75,500	
wc/d	2	24,340	3,200	12,170	21,140
SMITS, Jakob (1856-1928) Belgian					
oil	1	61,162		61,162	
wc/d	6	17,248	1,075	3,060	5,710
SMITS, Jan Gerard (1823-1910) Dutch					
oil	3	7,335	1,607	2,546	3,182
SMITZ, Gaspar (1635-1707) Dutch					
oil	1	12,420		12,420	
SMOLDERS, Pol (1921-1997) Belgian					
oil	1	1,996		1,996	
SMOORENBERG, Dirk (1883-1960) Dutch					
oil	13	87,239	1,936	6,023	12,046
SMOUT, Lucas (younger) (1671-1713) Flemish					
oil	1	2,400		2,400	
SMYTH, E R (?) ?					
oil	1	1,300		1,300	
SMYTH, Norman (20th C) Irish					
oil	1	1,305		1,305	

Name	No.	Total Sales Value	Prices lowest	Prices median	highest
SMYTHE (?) British					
oil	1	3,341		3,341	
SMYTHE, Ansdele (19/20th C) British					
oil	1	3,260		3,260	
SMYTHE, E R (19th C) British					
oil	1	1,397		1,397	
SMYTHE, Edward Robert (1810-1899) British					
oil	5	24,518	1,020	2,265	10,570
SMYTHE, Eugene Leslie (1857-1932) American					
oil	1	1,600		1,600	
SMYTHE, Leslie (19th C) British					
oil	1	1,350		1,350	
SMYTHE, Lionel Percy (1839-1913) British					
oil	1	9,230		9,230	
SMYTHE, Thomas (1825-1906) British					
oil	12	85,998	1,189	6,040	21,808
SNAPE, Martin (fl.1874-1901) British					
wc/d	2	2,290	1,106	1,145	1,184
SNAPE, William H (fl.1885-1892) British					
oil	1	19,575		19,575	
SNAYERS, Peeter (1592-1666) Flemish					
oil	1	22,987		22,987	
SNELL, Henry Bayley (1858-1943) American					
oil	1	6,000		6,000	
SNELLINCK, Cornelis (?-1669) Dutch					
oil	1	10,205		10,205	
SNIDOW, Gordon (1936-) British					
wc/d	1	19,000		19,000	
SNIJDERS, Christiaan (1881-1943) Dutch					
oil	1	3,707		3,707	
SNOECK, Jacques (1881-1921) Dutch					
oil	2	3,373	1,256	1,687	2,117
SNOW, Michael (1929-) Canadian					
wc/d	1	1,002		1,002	
SNYDER, Bladen Tasker (1864-1923) American					
oil	1	2,100		2,100	
SNYDER, Joan (1940-) American					
oil	1	22,000		22,000	
SNYDER, William Henry (1829-1910) American					
oil	1	3,750		3,750	
SNYDER, William McKendree (1848-1930) American					
oil	1	10,000		10,000	
SNYDERS, Christiaan Pieter (1904-) Dutch					
oil	1	1,286		1,286	
SNYDERS, F (1579-1657) Dutch					
oil	1	2,136		2,136	
SNYDERS, Frans (1579-1657) Dutch					
oil	2	24,136	10,799	12,068	13,337
wc/d	3	10,155	1,553	1,923	6,679
SNYDERS, Frans (school) (1579-1657) Dutch					
oil	2	52,569	10,569	26,285	42,000
SNYERS, Pieter (1681-1752) Flemish					
oil	2	20,154	8,665	10,077	11,489
SOARES, Valeska (1957-) Brazilian					
3D	2	13,500	4,500	6,750	9,000
SOBRADO, Pedro (1936-) Spanish					
oil	5	7,979	1,068	1,726	1,887
SOBRILE, Giuseppe (1879-1956) Italian					
oil	4	38,403	1,714	5,163	26,364

Name	No.	Total Sales Value	lowest	Prices median	highest
SOBRINO, Carlos (1927-) Argentinian					
oil	1	2,231		2,231	
SOCHACZEWSKI, Alexander (1843-1923) Polish					
oil	1	2,703		2,703	
SOCKWELL, Carroll (20th C) American					
wc/d	1	1,900		1,900	
SOCO (20th C) ?					
oil	1	1,428		1,428	
SODAR, Franz (1827-1899) Belgian					
oil	1	13,140		13,140	
SODERGREN, Sigfrid (1920-) Swedish					
oil	1	5,678		5,678	
SODRING, Frederik (1809-1862) Danish					
oil	3	18,223	1,850	8,252	8,252
SOER, Chris (1882-1961) Dutch					
oil	4	7,065	1,179	1,310	3,267
SOEST, Gerard van (c.1637-1681) British					
oil	3	15,627	1,963	4,500	9,164
SOEST, Louis W van (1867-1948) Dutch					
oil	6	12,673	1,160	2,065	3,147
SOEST, Pierre Gerardus Cornelis van (1930-) Dutch					
oil	1	1,205		1,205	
SOETE, Pierre de (20th C) Belgian					
3D	1	1,793		1,793	
SOFFICI, Ardengo (1879-1964) Italian					
oil	6	175,126	10,676	22,484	80,722
SOHLBERG, Harald (1869-1935) Norwegian					
oil	1	64,385		64,385	
SOHN, Carl Ferdinand (1805-1867) German					
oil	1	4,091		4,091	
SOHN, Carl Rudolf (1845-1908) German					
oil	1	25,000		25,000	
SOHN, Paul Eduard Richard (1834-1912) German					
oil	1	13,000		13,000	
SOHN-RETHEL, Alfred (1875-?) German					
wc/d	1	1,089		1,089	
SOISEL, Gaston (19th C) French					
oil	1	3,283		3,283	
SOJO, Alberto (?) ?					
oil	1	1,932		1,932	
SOLANO, Pablo (20th C) Spanish?					
wc/d	1	16,778		16,778	
SOLANO, Susana (1946-) Spanish					
3D	1	5,428		5,428	
SOLARI, Achille (1835-?) Italian					
oil	3	7,427	2,077	2,200	3,150
SOLARI, Luis A (1918-) Uruguayan					
oil	1	3,100		3,100	
SOLARIO, Andrea (1460-1522) Italian					
oil	1	260,000		260,000	
SOLAZZO, Mario (1944-) Italian					
oil	1	2,570		2,570	
SOLDATI, Atanasio (1896-1953) Italian					
oil	3	29,419	1,833	3,151	24,435
SOLDENHOFF, Alexander Leo (1882-1951) Swiss					
oil	2	6,680	2,429	3,340	4,251
SOLDINI, Arnaldo (1862-1936) Italian					
oil	1	3,493		3,493	

Name	No.	Total Sales Value	Prices lowest	Prices median	Prices highest
SOLE JORBA, Vicenc (1904-1949) Spanish					
oil	1	1,800		1,800	
SOLE, Giovan Gioseffo dal (1654-1719) Italian					
oil	2	59,095	4,095	29,548	55,000
SOLENGHI, Giuseppe (1879-1944) Italian					
oil	5	8,177	1,187	1,478	2,473
SOLER, Domingo (20th C) Spanish					
oil	1	3,164		3,164	
SOLER, Juan (20th C) Spanish					
oil	6	10,822	1,083	1,713	2,844
SOLI, Gaylord (?) American?					
oil	1	1,100		1,100	
SOLIMENA, Francesco (1657-1747) Italian					
oil	2	88,445	10,800	44,223	77,645
SOLIMENA, Francesco (school) (1657-1747) Italian					
oil	3	27,083	6,610	6,746	13,727
SOLIN, Timo (1947-) Swedish					
3D	3	4,057	1,088	1,440	1,529
SOLIVA, Louis (19/20th C) French					
3D	1	2,827		2,827	
SOLLENATI, J (19th C) German					
oil	1	1,002		1,002	
SOLLIER, Henri Alexandre (1886-?) French					
oil	7	13,226	1,102	1,860	2,618
wc/d	2	3,238	1,309	1,619	1,929
SOLLMANN, Paul (1886-) German					
wc/d	1	3,775		3,775	
SOLMAN, Joseph (1909-) American					
oil	1	4,200		4,200	
wc/d	2	2,300	1,100	1,150	1,200
SOLOMATKIN, Leonid Ivanovitch (1837-1883) Russian					
oil	1	24,675		24,675	
SOLOMON, Rebecca (1832-1886) British					
oil	1	22,500		22,500	
SOLOMONS, Estella Frances (1882-1968) Irish					
oil	1	5,920		5,920	
SOMAINI, Francesco (20th C) ?					
3D	1	1,318		1,318	
SOMER, Paul van I (school) (c.1577-1621) Flemish					
oil	1	4,000		4,000	
SOMERS, Francine (1923-) Belgian					
oil	2	2,390	1,048	1,195	1,342
SOMERS, Louis (1813-1880) Belgian					
oil	1	7,111		7,111	
SOMERSCALES, Thomas (1842-1927) British					
oil	6	257,190	15,000	34,200	98,800
SOMERSET, Richard Gay (1848-1928) British					
oil	1	2,750		2,750	
SOMERVILLE, Edith Oenone (1858-1949) British					
oil	1	3,318		3,318	
SOMERVILLE, Peggy (1918-1975) British					
oil	3	16,437	1,323	6,000	9,114
wc/d	3	7,321	1,294	2,205	3,822
SOMERVILLE, Stuart (1908-1983) British					
oil	1	1,030		1,030	
SOMM, Henry (1844-1907) French					
wc/d	3	5,244	1,200	1,585	2,459
SOMME, Theophile (1871-1952) French					
3D	1	1,947		1,947	

Name	No.	Total Sales Value	lowest	Prices median	highest
SOMMER, Alice (1898-1982) German					
oil	1	10,080		10,080	
wc/d	1	2,880		2,880	
SOMMER, Ferdinand (1822-1901) Swiss					
oil	3	6,322	1,210	1,694	3,418
SOMMER, Georg (19th C) German					
oil	1	1,775		1,775	
SOMMER, Harald (1930-) German?					
oil	1	1,374		1,374	
wc/d	2	2,328	1,164	1,164	1,164
SOMMER, William (1867-1949) American					
oil	1	5,350		5,350	
wc/d	6	12,115	1,000	1,853	3,900
SOMOV, Konstantin (1869-1939) Russian					
wc/d	3	47,236	3,205	3,205	40,770
SOMVILLE, Roger (1923-) Belgian					
oil	1	5,749		5,749	
wc/d	5	8,294	1,278	1,780	1,926
SONDERBORG, Karl Horst (20th C) German					
oil	1	27,006		27,006	
wc/d	3	13,103	1,284	2,435	9,384
SONDERBORG, Kurt R H (1923-) Danish					
oil	3	22,514	4,545	8,512	9,457
wc/d	4	20,668	1,537	3,531	12,069
SONDERGAARD, Jens (1895-1957) Danish					
oil	11	40,435	1,524	2,812	10,387
SONDERLAND, Fritz (1836-1896) German					
oil	3	15,707	2,152	3,545	10,010
SONDERMANN, Heinrich (fl.1850) German					
oil	1	2,991		2,991	
SONDERMANN, Hermann (1832-1901) German					
oil	1	1,684		1,684	
SONDHEIM, Maier Salomon (1806-?) German					
oil	1	1,128		1,128	
SONJE, Jan Gabrielsz (1625-1707) Dutch					
oil	2	26,012	4,032	13,006	21,980
SONNE, Jorgen Valentin (1801-1890) Danish					
oil	2	6,690	2,695	3,345	3,995
SONNTAG, William L (1822-1900) American					
oil	6	82,250	5,250	10,500	25,000
wc/d	2	5,200	1,600	2,600	3,600
SONNTAG, William L (jnr) (1869-?) American					
wc/d	1	2,000		2,000	
SONREL, Elisabeth (1874-1953) French					
oil	1	65,000		65,000	
wc/d	4	23,259	1,902	5,698	9,961
SOOLMAKER, Jan Frans (1635-1685) Flemish					
oil	1	4,758		4,758	
SOONIUS, Louis (1883-1956) Dutch					
oil	3	14,357	2,163	3,283	8,911
wc/d	2	2,814	1,093	1,407	1,721
SOPER, Eileen A (1905-1990) British					
oil	1	4,050		4,050	
SOPER, Thomas James (1836-1890) British					
oil	1	2,000		2,000	
SOPPERA, Hans (1900-1963) Swiss					
oil	1	1,016		1,016	
SORBI, Raffaello (1844-1931) Italian					
oil	9	226,952	2,007	6,109	162,150

Name	No.	Total Sales Value		Prices
			lowest	median	highest
SOREN, John Johnston (?-1889) American					
oil	1	3,000		3,000	
SORENSEN, C F (1818-1879) Danish					
oil	6	11,938	1,678	1,943	2,380
wc/d	1	2,085		2,085	
SORENSEN, Carl Frederick (1818-1879) Danish					
oil	17	157,750	1,569	9,036	36,144
SORENSEN, Eiler (1869-1953) Danish					
oil	1	3,119		3,119	
SORENSEN, Henrik (1882-1962) Norwegian					
oil	1	1,558		1,558	
SORENSEN, Jacobus Lorenz (1812-1857) Dutch					
oil	1	2,717		2,717	
SORENSEN, Jens (1887-1953) Danish					
oil	1	1,096		1,096	
SORENSEN, Jens Flemming (1933-) Danish					
3D	1	2,492		2,492	
SORENSEN, L (?) Scandinavian					
oil	1	1,190		1,190	
SORESSI, Alfredo (1897-?) Italian					
oil	1	2,808		2,808	
SORGH, Hendrik Martensz (1611-1670) Dutch					
oil	4	221,134	14,130	53,502	100,000
SORIA AEDO, Francisco (1898-?) Spanish					
oil	2	41,516	20,758	20,758	20,758
SORINE, Saveli (1878-1953) Russian					
oil	1	56,400		56,400	
SOROLLA Y BASTIDA, Joaquin (1863-1923) Spanish					
oil	24	2,828,100	3,114	21,551	720,000
wc/d	2	3,121	1,412	1,561	1,709
SORTET, Paul (1905-1966) Belgian					
oil	2	3,144	1,467	1,572	1,677
SORTFELDT, Sohn (?) ?					
oil	1	1,061		1,061	
SORTIS, Eduardo de (1861-?) Italian					
3D	1	2,307		2,307	
SORVIG, Frederich Martin (1823-1892) Norwegian					
oil	1	3,574		3,574	
wc/d	1	2,668		2,668	
SOSNO, Sacha (1937-) French					
3D	1	1,382		1,382	
SOSSON, L (20th C) French					
3D	2	6,538	3,180	3,269	3,358
SOSSON, Louis (20th C) French					
3D	1	1,751		1,751	
SOTO, Jesus Rafael (1923-) Venezuelan					
3D	22	158,205	1,253	2,755	25,030
oil	4	58,582	2,120	9,231	38,000
SOTO, Rafael Fernandez de (1915-1984) Spanish					
3D	1	1,253		1,253	
SOTO, Raphael de (1904-1987) ?					
oil	1	5,000		5,000	
SOTOMAYOR Y ZARAGOZA, Fernando (1875-1960) Spanish					
oil	7	67,007	4,914	6,991	21,295
SOTTER, George William (1879-1953) American					
oil	1	9,000		9,000	
wc/d	1	1,500		1,500	
SOTTSASS, Ettore (20th C) ?					
3D	4	63,700	6,525	15,588	26,000

Name	No.	Total Sales Value	Prices lowest	median	highest
SOUCHON, Marian Sims (1870-1954) American					
oil	1	6,250		6,250	
SOUDEIKINE, Sergei (1883-1946) Russian					
oil	2	5,750	2,250	2,875	3,500
wc/d	1	1,900		1,900	
SOUDIER, Jane le (?) ?					
3D	1	1,030		1,030	
SOUILLET, Georges François (1861-1957) French					
oil	1	3,576		3,576	
SOUKOP, Willi (1907-1995) British					
3D	1	1,368		1,368	
SOULACROIX (1825-1879) French					
oil	1	284,400		284,400	
SOULACROIX, Frederic (1825-1879) French					
oil	6	274,870	12,870	36,500	95,000
SOULAGES, Pierre (1919-) French					
oil	8	1,117,229	81,356	115,224	286,900
wc/d	1	31,801		31,801	
SOULEN, Henry James (1888-1965) American					
oil	1	3,000		3,000	
SOURGEN, Jean Roger (?) French?					
oil	1	1,278		1,278	
SOUSA, Joaquin Pedro de (1818-1878) Portuguese					
oil	2	9,171	3,545	4,586	5,626
SOUTER, John Bulloch (1890-1972) British					
oil	1	1,470		1,470	
SOUTH AMERICAN SCHOOL					
oil	1	2,674		2,674	
SOUTH AMERICAN SCHOOL, 19th C					
oil	1	3,140		3,140	
SOUTH AMERICAN SCHOOL, 20th C					
oil	1	3,000		3,000	
SOUTH EUROPEAN SCHOOL, 17th C					
oil	1	38,872		38,872	
SOUTH GERMAN SCHOOL, 15th C					
oil	2	17,472	4,238	8,736	13,234
SOUTH GERMAN SCHOOL, 15th/16th C					
3D	2	35,485	15,100	17,743	20,385
SOUTH GERMAN SCHOOL, 16th C					
3D	7	54,100	2,727	3,964	30,200
oil	3	10,952	3,020	3,456	4,476
SOUTH GERMAN SCHOOL, 16th/17th C					
3D	1	2,273		2,273	
SOUTH GERMAN SCHOOL, 17th C					
3D	12	73,617	2,215	5,357	12,495
oil	2	8,085	3,182	4,043	4,903
SOUTH GERMAN SCHOOL, 18th C					
3D	13	51,233	2,234	3,028	9,091
oil	6	48,118	2,273	2,879	31,894
SOUTH GERMAN SCHOOL, 19th C					
3D	1	13,956		13,956	
SOUTH ITALIAN SCHOOL, 19th C					
oil	2	8,326	3,815	4,163	4,511
SOUTHALL, Joseph Edward (1861-1944) British					
oil	1	9,653		9,653	
wc/d	1	6,594		6,594	
SOUTHERN AMERICAN SCHOOL, 19th C					
oil	1	3,250		3,250	
SOUTHERN DUTCH SCHOOL, 17th C					
3D	1	2,960		2,960	

Name	No.	Total Sales Value	lowest	Prices median	highest
SOUTHERN FRENCH SCHOOL, 15th C					
3D	1	3,460		3,460	
SOUTHGATE, Frank (1872-1916) British					
wc/d	2	5,073	1,173	2,537	3,900
SOUTINE, Chaim (1893-1943) Russian					
oil	5	653,500	42,500	140,000	180,000
wc/d	4	5,818	1,210	1,210	2,188
SOUTMAN, Pieter Claesz (1580-1657) Dutch					
oil	1	16,000		16,000	
SOUTO, Arturo (1901-1964) Spanish					
oil	2	16,656	2,138	8,328	14,518
wc/d	10	26,053	1,430	2,989	3,938
SOUTTER, Louis (1871-1942) Swiss					
oil	1	45,968		45,968	
wc/d	6	485,964	2,202	53,049	205,645
SOUVERBIE, Jean (1891-1981) French					
oil	8	88,737	1,448	5,257	31,393
wc/d	2	5,999	2,012	3,000	3,987
SOUZA, Francis Newton (1924-) British/Indian					
oil	12	48,233	2,272	3,406	9,300
wc/d	3	6,834	1,136	2,698	3,000
SOUZA-PINTO, Jose Giulio (1856-1939) Portuguese					
oil	4	34,137	7,522	7,811	10,993
SOWERBY, John G (fl.1876-1914) British					
wc/d	2	5,335	2,175	2,668	3,160
SOWERBY, Millicent (1878-1967) British					
wc/d	1	4,740		4,740	
SOYA-JENSEN, Carl Martin (1860-1912) Danish					
wc/d	1	2,038		2,038	
SOYER, Moses (1899-1974) American					
oil	5	10,400	1,000	1,600	4,000
wc/d	1	1,000		1,000	
SOYER, Raphael (1899-1987) American					
oil	9	56,100	1,300	5,000	15,000
wc/d	6	14,300	1,100	1,300	6,500
SPADINI, Armando (1883-1925) Italian					
oil	1	36,969		36,969	
wc/d	1	1,959		1,959	
SPADINO, Bartolomeo (18th C) Italian					
oil	1	12,560		12,560	
SPADINO, Giovanni Paolo (17th C) Italian					
oil	3	90,639	19,249	19,940	51,450
SPAGNOLA, G (fl.1900-1940) Italian					
oil	2	16,500	8,000	8,250	8,500
SPAGNULO, Giuseppe (1936-) Italian					
3D	2	13,167	5,313	6,584	7,854
SPAHN, Victor (20th C) French					
oil	1	1,659		1,659	
SPALLETTI, Ettore (1940-) Italian					
wc/d	1	12,080		12,080	
SPALTHOF, Jan Philip (fl.1700-1724) Flemish					
oil	1	6,660		6,660	
SPANG, Frederick A (1834-1891) American					
oil	1	2,300		2,300	
SPANG, Tillie Neville (fl.1890-1939) American					
oil	1	1,500		1,500	
SPANGENBERG, Paul (1843-1918) German					
oil	1	3,575		3,575	
SPANISH COLONIAL SCHOOL, 17th C					
oil	2	7,734	3,234	3,867	4,500

Name	No.	Total Sales Value	lowest	Prices median	highest
SPANISH COLONIAL SCHOOL, 18th C					
oil	1	17,280		17,280	
SPANISH COLONIAL SCHOOL, 18th/19th C					
3D	1	3,000		3,000	
SPANISH FORGER (fl.1890-1920) Spanish					
oil	1	3,856		3,856	
SPANISH SCHOOL					
3D	1	3,028		3,028	
oil	2	8,728	2,813	4,364	5,915
SPANISH SCHOOL, 14th C					
3D	1	23,325		23,325	
SPANISH SCHOOL, 15th C					
3D	2	30,727	10,435	15,364	20,292
oil	1	4,710		4,710	
SPANISH SCHOOL, 16th C					
3D	7	97,455	2,854	6,421	46,037
oil	4	29,200	3,451	6,947	11,855
wc/d	2	9,100	3,600	4,550	5,500
SPANISH SCHOOL, 16th/17th C					
3D	1	4,050		4,050	
SPANISH SCHOOL, 17th C					
3D	11	78,693	3,630	6,015	18,484
oil	34	462,970	2,400	4,100	161,066
wc/d	2	16,530	4,530	8,265	12,000
SPANISH SCHOOL, 17th/18th C					
3D	1	3,681		3,681	
oil	4	13,944	2,959	3,582	3,822
SPANISH SCHOOL, 18th C					
3D	2	8,853	3,276	4,427	5,577
oil	16	255,761	1,147	7,030	91,140
SPANISH SCHOOL, 19th C					
oil	15	77,705	2,920	3,934	8,880
wc/d	2	10,559	3,520	5,280	7,039
SPANISH SCHOOL, 19th/20th C					
oil	1	5,000		5,000	
SPANISH SCHOOL, 20th C					
3D	1	4,062		4,062	
oil	4	16,178	3,320	3,496	5,866
SPANISH-FLEMISH SCHOOL, 16th C					
3D	1	15,016		15,016	
oil	1	8,820		8,820	
SPANISH-FLEMISH SCHOOL, 17th C					
oil	3	16,971	2,876	4,710	9,385
SPANISH-PHILIPPINO SCHOOL, 18th C					
3D	2	54,636	4,396	27,318	50,240
SPANO, R (19th C) Italian?					
oil	1	2,400		2,400	
SPANO, Raffaello (1817-?) Italian					
oil	2	3,652	1,427	1,826	2,225
SPARE, Austin Osman (1888-1956) British					
wc/d	3	4,962	1,422	1,800	1,800
SPARKES, Catherine Adelaide (1842-?) British					
oil	1	30,020		30,020	
SPARKS, Herbert Blande (fl.1892-1893) British					
oil	1	2,982		2,982	
wc/d	1	1,727		1,727	
SPARKS, Nathaniel (1880-?) British					
wc/d	1	1,184		1,184	
SPARKS, Will (1862-1937) American					
oil	4	16,500	1,200	3,650	8,000

Name	No.	Total Sales Value	Prices lowest	Prices median	highest
SPAT, Gabriel (1890-1967) French					
oil	1	2,600		2,600	
SPAZZAPAN, Luigi (1890-1958) Italian					
oil	5	25,419	1,833	5,141	9,706
wc/d	4	5,792	1,078	1,419	1,877
SPEAR, Ruskin (1911-1990) British					
oil	17	91,369	1,136	3,969	26,790
wc/d	1	1,326		1,326	
SPEED, Harold (1872-1957) British					
oil	3	4,325	1,150	1,300	1,875
SPEELMAN, Adriana Gerarda (1801-1847) Dutch					
oil	1	2,988		2,988	
SPEICHER, Eugene (1883-1962) American					
oil	2	9,500	1,500	4,750	8,000
SPELMAN, John A (1880-1941) American					
oil	1	1,500		1,500	
SPENCE, Percy Frederick Seaton (1868-1933) Australian					
oil	1	2,499		2,499	
SPENCE, Thomas Ralph (1855-1903) British					
oil	2	16,000	4,000	8,000	12,000
SPENCELAYH, Charles (1865-1958) British					
oil	11	392,473	1,924	19,500	99,660
wc/d	2	20,461	1,586	10,231	18,875
SPENCER (?) ?					
oil	1	1,471		1,471	
SPENCER, Gilbert (1892-1979) British					
wc/d	1	7,200		7,200	
SPENCER, John C (19/20th C) American					
oil	1	1,900		1,900	
SPENCER, Lilly Martin (school) (1822-1902) American					
oil	1	4,250		4,250	
SPENCER, Niles (1893-1952) American					
oil	1	6,000		6,000	
SPENCER, Richard B (fl.1840-1870) British					
oil	5	33,229	2,100	4,530	15,485
SPENCER, Robert (1879-1931) American					
oil	2	76,000	30,000	38,000	46,000
SPENCER, Sir Stanley (1891-1959) British					
oil	3	241,590	3,300	62,040	176,250
wc/d	6	35,016	1,800	6,207	10,500
SPERL, Johann (1840-1914) German					
oil	5	70,221	2,807	3,987	54,483
SPERLI, Johann Jakob (1770-1841) Swiss					
wc/d	1	1,299		1,299	
SPERLING, Heinrich (1844-1924) German					
oil	5	42,208	1,885	3,187	29,000
SPERMAN, L (19th C) Continental					
oil	1	3,400		3,400	
SPERRY, Josephine (fl.1910-c.1949) American					
oil	1	1,600		1,600	
SPETHMANN, Albert (1894-?) German					
oil	1	1,936		1,936	
SPIEGEL, Johann II (1748-1823) Austrian					
oil	1	1,320		1,320	
SPIEKERMANN, Thorsten (1964-) ?					
oil	1	1,557		1,557	
SPIELMANN, Oscar (1901-1974) Austrian					
oil	2	3,390	1,586	1,695	1,804

Name	No.	Total Sales Value	lowest	Prices median	highest
SPIERS, B W (fl.1875-1893) British					
wc/d	1	3,816		3,816	
SPIERS, Benjamin Walter (fl.1875-1893) British					
wc/d	1	2,376		2,376	
SPIERS, Richard Phene (1838-1916) British					
wc/d	3	5,972	1,021	2,355	2,596
SPIES, S (19th C) Scandinavian?					
oil	1	1,162		1,162	
SPILBERG, Johann (1619-1690) German					
wc/d	1	7,644		7,644	
SPILIMBERGO, Adriano (1908-1975) Italian					
oil	4	11,018	1,475	1,884	5,776
SPILLAR, Karel (1871-1939) Czechoslovakian					
oil	1	1,028		1,028	
SPILLIAERT, Francois (?) Belgian					
wc/d	1	2,463		2,463	
SPILLIAERT, L (1881-1946) Belgian					
wc/d	1	59,283		59,283	
SPILLIAERT, Léon (1881-1946) Belgian					
oil	1	13,103		13,103	
wc/d	28	362,586	1,561	7,846	54,652
SPILMAN, Hendrik (1721-1784) Dutch					
wc/d	1	1,179		1,179	
SPILSBURY, Maria (1777-c.1823) British					
oil	1	2,771		2,771	
SPIN, Jacob (1806-1885) Dutch					
wc/d	3	5,532	1,100	2,052	2,380
SPINKS, Thomas (19th C) British					
oil	6	16,729	1,420	2,230	5,724
SPINNY, Guillaume Jean Joseph de (1721-1785) Flemish					
oil	1	1,994		1,994	
SPIRO, Eugen (1874-1972) German					
oil	13	40,020	1,009	2,564	6,897
SPIRO, Georges (1909-1994) French					
oil	7	12,605	1,200	1,746	2,764
wc/d	1	3,564		3,564	
SPITZER, Walter (1927-) Polish					
oil	3	5,255	1,106	1,440	2,709
SPITZWEG, Carl (1808-1885) German					
oil	12	1,427,491	5,448	31,291	1,078,899
wc/d	5	10,017	1,298	1,920	2,811
SPLIETH, Heinrich Joseph (1842-1894) German					
3D	1	1,618		1,618	
SPLITGERBER, August (1844-1918) German					
oil	2	5,737	1,139	2,869	4,598
SPODE, Samuel (19th C) British					
oil	3	19,006	2,288	3,718	13,000
SPOERER, Eduard (1841-1898) German					
oil	1	1,458		1,458	
SPOERRI, Daniel (1930-) Swiss					
3D	11	62,724	1,155	4,144	16,581
wc/d	1	5,825		5,825	
SPOHLER, J J C (1837-1923) Dutch					
oil	1	11,000		11,000	
SPOHLER, Jan Jacob (1811-1866) Dutch					
oil	18	357,807	1,358	11,441	85,320
SPOHLER, Jan Jacob Coenraad (1837-1923) Dutch					
oil	8	51,920	1,358	5,013	16,973

Name	No.	Total Sales Value	lowest	Prices median	highest
SPOHLER, Johannes Franciscus (1853-1894) Dutch					
oil	5	63,540	2,179	10,117	25,280
SPOONER, Arthur (1873-1962) British					
oil	5	12,940	1,145	2,370	5,056
SPORRI, Eduard (1901-1995) Swiss					
3D	7	16,856	1,074	1,412	4,604
SPOTTER, Paul (20th C) German?					
oil	1	1,251		1,251	
SPRAGUE, Edith (fl.1883-1903) British					
oil	1	2,567		2,567	
SPRINCHORN, Carl (1887-1971) American					
oil	1	35,000		35,000	
wc/d	2	4,600	1,000	2,300	3,600
SPRING, Alfons (1843-1908) German					
oil	2	10,023	1,387	5,012	8,636
SPRINGER, C (1817-1891) Dutch					
oil	1	1,658		1,658	
SPRINGER, Cornelis (1817-1891) Dutch					
oil	9	1,245,065	1,300	150,100	351,979
wc/d	4	79,105	6,121	22,702	27,581
SPRINGOLO, Nino (1886-?) Italian					
oil	3	11,318	3,195	3,441	4,682
SPRONKEN, Arthur (1930-) Dutch					
3D	1	16,379		16,379	
SPROTTE, Siegward (1913-) German					
oil	5	12,279	1,117	1,820	4,916
wc/d	8	12,043	1,211	1,477	1,942
SPRUANCE, Benton (1904-1967) American					
wc/d	1	1,500		1,500	
SPRUNGLIN, Niklaus (1725-1802) Swiss					
wc/d	1	2,279		2,279	
SPURLING, Jack (1870-1933) British					
wc/d	1	12,225		12,225	
SPYROPOULOS, Jannis (1912-1990) Greek					
oil	4	36,020	1,560	5,550	23,360
SQUILLANTINI, Remo (1920-1996) Italian					
oil	19	92,076	1,784	4,945	6,470
wc/d	1	1,848		1,848	
SQUIRE, Geoffrey (20th C) British					
oil	1	1,431		1,431	
SQUIRRELL, Leonard (1893-1979) British					
oil	2	2,561	1,232	1,281	1,329
wc/d	4	6,137	1,020	1,209	2,700
ST JOHN GOGARTY, Brenda (fl.1920-1940) ?					
3D	1	4,440		4,440	
STAATEN, L van (19th C) Dutch					
wc/d	3	4,111	1,343	1,343	1,425
STAATEN, Louis van (19th C) Dutch					
wc/d	8	9,236	1,021	1,071	1,343
STABLI, Adolf (1842-1901) Swiss					
oil	6	12,339	1,228	1,932	3,242
STACEY, Anna Lee (1871-1943) American					
oil	3	4,200	1,000	1,400	1,800
STACEY, Walter S (1846-1929) British					
wc/d	1	1,001		1,001	
STACK, J (19th C) ?					
oil	1	1,307		1,307	
STACK, Josef Magnus (1812-1868) Swedish					
oil	2	4,625	1,034	2,313	3,591

Name	No.	Total Sales Value	Prices lowest	Prices median	highest
STAD, Willem (1873-1959) Dutch					
wc/d	1	1,414		1,414	
STADELHOFER, Helmut (?) German					
oil	4	5,230	1,035	1,206	1,783
STADEMANN, Adolf (1824-1895) German					
oil	16	56,784	1,471	3,480	6,364
STADENAR, A (?) ?					
oil	1	1,107		1,107	
STADLER, Toni (1888-1982) German					
3D	2	6,442	2,186	3,221	4,256
oil	1	2,472		2,472	
STADLER, Toni von (1850-1917) Austrian					
oil	2	8,916	2,173	4,458	6,743
STAEHR-NIELSEN, Erik (1890-1921) Danish					
oil	1	1,674		1,674	
STAEL, Nicolas de (1914-1955) French					
oil	3	1,558,265	51,421	156,844	1,350,000
wc/d	5	94,181	1,286	20,568	32,500
STAETS, Hendrik (fl.1643-1659) Dutch?					
oil	1	3,768		3,768	
STAGER, Balz (1861-1937) Swiss					
oil	6	15,630	1,129	2,377	5,247
STAGLIANO, Arturo (1870-1936) Italian					
oil	1	4,239		4,239	
STAGURA, Albert (1866-1947) German					
wc/d	4	12,519	1,483	2,390	6,256
STAHL, Benjamin Albert (1910-1987) American					
oil	1	9,000		9,000	
STAHL, Friedrich (1863-1940) German					
oil	3	27,165	3,650	10,875	12,640
STAHLY, François (1911-) French					
3D	1	1,659		1,659	
STAIGER, Otto (1894-) Swiss					
oil	1	4,715		4,715	
STAINTON, G (fl.1860-1890) British					
oil	2	7,335	1,793	3,668	5,542
STAINTON, George (fl.1860-1890) British					
oil	5	10,993	1,022	1,862	4,560
wc/d	2	2,288	1,001	1,144	1,287
STAITE, Harriet (fl.1895-1903) British					
oil	1	2,226		2,226	
STALBEMT, Adriaen van (1580-1662) Flemish					
oil	3	180,260	47,040	47,143	86,077
STALBOM, Johan (1712-1777) Swedish					
oil	1	1,656		1,656	
STALLAERT, Joseph (1825-1903) Belgian					
oil	1	2,246		2,246	
STALLER, Gerard Johan (1880-1956) Dutch					
oil	2	4,984	1,291	2,492	3,693
wc/d	1	2,796		2,796	
STAMMBACH, Eugen (1876-1966) German					
oil	3	4,431	1,189	1,276	1,966
STAMOS, Theodoros (1922-1997) American					
oil	14	116,609	1,000	5,914	19,000
wc/d	1	1,006		1,006	
STAMPFLI, Peter (1937-) Swiss					
wc/d	1	2,057		2,057	
STAMPFLI, Pierre Victor (1916-1975) Swiss					
oil	1	1,139		1,139	

Name	No.	Total Sales Value	Prices lowest	median	highest
STANCHI, Giovanni (c.1645-?) Italian					
oil	2	115,049	9,349	57,525	105,700
STANCHI, Nicolo (1623-1690) Italian					
oil	1	6,764		6,764	
STANCLIFF, J W (1814-1879) American					
oil	1	1,600		1,600	
STANCZAK, Julian (1928-) American/Polish					
oil	2	2,200	1,000	1,100	1,200
STANDING, H W (19/20th C) British					
wc/d	3	4,656	1,001	1,287	2,368
STANDING, William (20th C) American					
oil	1	2,600		2,600	
STANESBY, Alexander (1832-1916) British					
oil	1	2,698		2,698	
STANFIELD, Clarkson (1793-1867) British					
oil	8	74,469	1,963	2,699	27,170
wc/d	4	8,252	1,110	1,457	4,228
STANFIELD, George Clarkson (1828-1878) British					
oil	3	21,992	3,918	8,584	9,490
STANGE, Bernhard (1807-1880) German					
oil	2	14,532	2,071	7,266	12,461
STANHOPE, Elmer H (1907-1956) American					
oil	1	1,300		1,300	
STANIER, H (19th C) British					
wc/d	1	1,248		1,248	
STANIER, Henry (?-1892) British					
wc/d	8	19,267	1,006	2,885	3,171
STANILAND, Charles (1838-1916) British					
wc/d	2	7,865	3,003	3,933	4,862
STANISLAWSKI, Jan (1860-1907) Polish					
oil	3	19,285	2,127	8,690	8,690
STANKIEWICZ, Zofia (1862-) Polish					
oil	1	5,840		5,840	
STANLEY, Archer (19th C) British					
wc/d	1	2,500		2,500	
STANLEY, Caleb Robert (1795-1868) British					
oil	1	9,000		9,000	
STANLEY, Robert (20th C) American					
oil	1	1,800		1,800	
STANNARD OF BEDFORD, Emily (1875-1907) British					
wc/d	1	1,154		1,154	
STANNARD, Alexander Molyneux (1878-1975) British					
wc/d	2	2,227	1,043	1,114	1,184
STANNARD, Alfred (1806-1889) British					
oil	3	12,016	1,703	4,273	6,040
STANNARD, Alfred George (1828-1885) British					
wc/d	1	1,501		1,501	
STANNARD, Eloise Harriet (c.1828-1915) British					
oil	9	111,582	5,625	10,205	30,000
STANNARD, Henry (1844-1920) British					
wc/d	1	2,370		2,370	
STANNARD, Henry Sylvester (1870-1951) British					
oil	1	1,668		1,668	
wc/d	29	81,605	1,066	2,145	5,922
STANNARD, Lilian (1877-1944) British					
wc/d	14	77,757	1,300	3,950	17,270
STANNARD, Theresa Sylvester (1898-1947) British					
wc/d	5	12,899	1,145	2,198	3,816

Name	No.	Total Sales Value	lowest	Prices median	highest
STANNUS, Anthony Carey (fl.1862-1910) British					
wc/d	1	3,925		3,925	
STANZANI, Emilio (1906-1977) Swiss					
3D	1	1,684		1,684	
STANZIONE, Massimo (1585-1656) Italian					
oil	1	51,340		51,340	
STAPLES, Sir Robert Ponsonby (1853-1943) British					
oil	2	6,835	2,700	3,418	4,135
STAPPERS, J (?) ?					
oil	1	1,066		1,066	
STAPPERS, Julien (1875-1960) Belgian					
oil	11	29,400	1,015	1,545	6,179
STARCKE, Richard (1864-1945) German					
oil	1	1,995		1,995	
STARENS, J D (19th C) Belgian					
oil	1	6,876		6,876	
STARITSKY, Anna (1908-1981) French					
oil	2	2,750	1,179	1,375	1,571
STARK, James (1794-1859) British					
oil	23	475,873	1,065	11,925	72,480
STARK, Karl (1921-) Austrian					
wc/d	5	10,604	1,078	1,207	3,879
STARK, Otto (1859-1926) American					
wc/d	1	2,300		2,300	
STARKENBORGH, Jacobus Nicolas Tjarda van (1822-1895) Dutch					
oil	1	16,069		16,069	
STARKENBORGH, Willem Tjarda van (1823-1885) Dutch					
oil	1	3,768		3,768	
STARKER, Erwin (1872-1938) German					
oil	2	2,664	1,178	1,332	1,486
STARKWEATHER, William Edward (1879-1969) American					
oil	2	4,780	2,100	2,390	2,680
wc/d	1	1,300		1,300	
STARLING, Albert (fl.1878-1922) British					
oil	1	10,150		10,150	
STARN TWINS (1961-) American					
3D	1	7,000		7,000	
STASIO, Stefano di (1948-) Italian					
oil	1	1,964		1,964	
STAUDACHER, Hans (1923-) Swiss					
oil	2	10,641	4,721	5,321	5,920
wc/d	2	4,948	1,820	2,474	3,128
STAUDACHER, Vitus (1850-1925) German					
oil	5	21,644	1,227	1,994	9,305
STAUDER, Jacob Carl (1694-1756) Swiss					
oil	1	3,500		3,500	
STAUFFER, Fred (1892-1980) Swiss					
oil	8	13,897	1,049	1,314	4,373
STAVROWSKY, Oleg (20th C) American					
oil	1	14,000		14,000	
STAZEWSKI, Henryk (1894-?) Polish					
oil	3	5,887	1,682	1,727	2,478
STEAD, Fred (1863-1940) British					
oil	1	3,834		3,834	
STEARNS, Junius Brutus (1810-1885) American					
oil	1	1,100		1,100	
STEELE, E (19/20th C) British					
oil	2	4,070	1,670	2,035	2,400

Name	No.	Total Sales Value	Prices lowest	median	highest
STEELE, Edwin (19th C) British					
oil	1	1,037		1,037	
STEELE, Theodore Clement (1847-1926) American					
oil	3	48,000	3,000	21,000	24,000
STEELINK, Willem (jnr) (1856-1928) Dutch					
oil	1	4,327		4,327	
STEELL, David George (1856-1930) British					
oil	1	1,340		1,340	
STEELL, Gourlay (1819-1894) British					
oil	1	1,650		1,650	
STEEN, Jan (c.1626-1679) Dutch					
oil	4	403,320	63,420	99,950	140,000
STEENBERGEN, Albert (1814-1900) Dutch					
wc/d	1	1,011		1,011	
STEENE, van den (19th C) Belgian					
oil	1	10,647		10,647	
STEENWYCK, Harmen van (1612-1656) Dutch					
oil	2	39,247	12,557	19,624	26,690
STEENWYCK, Hendrik van (younger) (1580-1649) Flemish					
oil	1	18,000		18,000	
STEER, Philip Wilson (1860-1942) British					
oil	4	185,955	4,515	34,320	112,800
wc/d	2	2,146	1,036	1,073	1,110
STEFANONI, Tino (1937-) Italian					
oil	2	3,948	1,941	1,974	2,007
STEFANOWICZ, Karol (19/20th C) Polish					
oil	1	1,035		1,035	
STEFANSSEN, Jon (1881-1962) Icelandic					
oil	1	6,379		6,379	
STEFFAN, Johann Gottfried (1815-1905) Swiss					
oil	8	64,124	1,733	6,004	23,092
STEFFANI, Luigi (1827-1898) Italian					
oil	1	5,440		5,440	
STEFFELAAR, Cornelis (1795-1861) Dutch					
oil	2	3,933	1,180	1,967	2,753
STEFFELAAR, Nicolaas (1852-1918) Dutch					
wc/d	1	1,526		1,526	
STEFFEN, Eduard (19th C) Austrian					
oil	2	2,194	1,097	1,097	1,097
STEFFEN, Walter Arnold (1924-1982) Swiss					
oil	1	1,474		1,474	
STEFFENINI, Ottavio (1889-1971) Italian					
oil	1	1,845		1,845	
STEFFENSEN, Hans Voigt (1941-) Danish					
oil	1	1,095		1,095	
STEFFENSEN, Poul (1866-1923) Danish					
oil	7	13,482	1,220	1,624	3,275
STEFFGEN, Heinrich (19th C) German					
oil	1	1,717		1,717	
STEGER, Milly (1881-1948) German					
wc/d	1	1,495		1,495	
STEGMANN, Franz (1831-1892) German					
oil	1	4,500		4,500	
STEICHEN, Edward J (1879-1973) American					
oil	1	75,000		75,000	
STEIG, William (1907-) American					
wc/d	1	1,800		1,800	
STEIGER, Robert von (1856-1941) Swiss					
oil	1	1,139		1,139	

Name	No.	Total Sales Value	lowest	Prices median	highest
STEIN, Georges (1870-?) French					
oil	6	49,194	4,253	7,430	16,000
wc/d	3	14,771	1,774	5,497	7,500
STEIN, Henri (?) ?					
oil	2	3,764	1,687	1,882	2,077
STEINACH, Anton Victor Alexander (1819-1891) German					
oil	1	2,184		2,184	
STEINACKER, Alfred (1838-1914) Austrian					
oil	1	1,047		1,047	
STEINBACH, Eduard (1878-?) German					
oil	2	4,351	2,081	2,176	2,270
STEINBACH, Haim (1944-) American					
3D	3	26,000	5,000	9,000	12,000
STEINBERG, Saul (1914-) American					
wc/d	7	61,836	1,680	7,500	18,000
STEINER, L (?) ?					
3D	1	1,800		1,800	
STEINFELD, Franz (1787-1868) Austrian					
oil	1	3,596		3,596	
STEINFELD, Wilhelm (1816-1854) Austrian					
oil	1	3,987		3,987	
STEINHARDT, Jakob (1887-1968) Israeli					
oil	4	239,500	9,500	12,500	205,000
wc/d	3	21,160	1,000	8,640	11,520
STEINHAUSER, Adolph Georg Gustav (1825-1858) German					
3D	1	36,000		36,000	
STEINHEIL, Adolphe Charles Edouard (1850-1908) French					
oil	1	1,864		1,864	
STEINHEIL, Charles August (1814-1885) French					
oil	2	13,570	1,570	6,785	12,000
STEINKOPF, Julius (1815-1892) German					
oil	1	16,800		16,800	
STEINLE, Edward Jakob von (1810-1886) Austrian/German					
wc/d	1	4,178		4,178	
STEINLEN, Theophile Alexandre (1859-1923) Swiss					
3D	2	15,052	2,033	7,526	13,019
oil	2	3,365	1,455	1,683	1,910
wc/d	29	136,351	1,000	3,028	20,630
STEINMETZ, Antonie Johan Marinus (1867-1950) Dutch					
oil	1	1,327		1,327	
STEINMETZ-NORIS, Fritz (1860-?) German					
oil	2	4,017	1,500	2,009	2,517
STEIR, Pat (1940-) American					
oil	2	28,000	7,000	14,000	21,000
STEKETEE, Sallie Hall (1882-) American					
oil	1	4,500		4,500	
STELLA, Frank (1936-) American					
3D	8	449,857	25,000	57,500	90,000
oil	7	549,310	10,000	40,000	260,000
wc/d	3	1,318,000	8,000	10,000	1,300,000
STELLA, Guglielmo (1828-1888) Italian					
oil	1	9,061		9,061	
STELLA, Jacques de (1596-1657) French					
oil	1	9,362		9,362	
wc/d	2	23,994	4,364	11,997	19,630
STELLA, Joseph (1877-1946) American					
oil	6	62,400	1,300	2,700	30,000
wc/d	3	38,800	1,800	2,000	35,000
STELLETSKY, Dimitri (1875-1947) Russian					
wc/d	3	9,815	1,057	3,020	5,738

Name	No.	Total Sales Value	lowest	Prices median	highest
STEMATSKY, Avigdor (1908-1989) Israeli					
wc/d	5	19,800	1,000	1,600	14,000
STEN, John (1879-1922) Swedish					
oil	1	2,822		2,822	
STENGEL, George J (1872-1937) American					
oil	1	4,750		4,750	
STENN, Henri (20th C) ?					
oil	1	1,244		1,244	
STENNER, Hermann (1891-1914) German					
wc/d	1	2,308		2,308	
STENVILL, E (?) ?					
oil	1	1,952		1,952	
STEPAN, Bohumil (1913-1985) ?					
oil	1	1,019		1,019	
STEPHAN, A (?) ?					
oil	1	2,950		2,950	
STEPHAN, August (1868-1936) Austrian					
oil	1	1,100		1,100	
STEPHANOFF, F P (1788-1860) British					
oil	1	1,152		1,152	
STEPHANOFF, Francis Philip (1788-1860) British					
oil	1	2,355		2,355	
STEPHANOFF, James (1787-1874) British					
wc/d	1	2,198		2,198	
STEPHENS, Christopher (1974-) British					
oil	1	1,110		1,110	
STEPHENSON, Lionel Macdonald (1854-1907) Canadian					
oil	2	3,451	1,327	1,726	2,124
STEPPE, Romain (1859-1927) Belgian					
oil	14	21,637	1,003	1,412	2,690
STERCHI, Eda Elizabeth (1885-?) American					
oil	13	97,950	1,600	2,900	30,000
wc/d	1	3,000		3,000	
STERKENBURG, Piet (20th C) Dutch					
oil	1	1,375		1,375	
STERL, Robert Hermann (1867-1932) German					
oil	4	4,428	1,107	1,107	1,107
wc/d	1	1,600		1,600	
STERLING, Marc (1898-?) Russian					
oil	1	1,273		1,273	
STERN, Anton Alois (1827-1924) Austrian					
oil	1	1,510		1,510	
STERN, Ignaz (1680-1748) German					
oil	3	28,242	5,099	7,091	16,052
STERN, Max (1872-?) German					
oil	3	17,259	1,341	1,341	14,518
STERNBERG, Harry (1904-) American					
oil	1	12,000		12,000	
STERNER, Albert Edward (1863-1946) American					
wc/d	1	1,300		1,300	
STERRE DE JONG, Jacobus (1866-1920) Dutch					
oil	1	1,168		1,168	
STERRY, Carl (1861-?) German					
oil	1	11,881		11,881	
STETSON (19th C) American					
oil	1	2,000		2,000	
STETSON, Charles Walter (1858-1911) American					
oil	2	3,100	1,000	1,550	2,100

Name	No.	Total Sales Value	lowest	Prices median	highest
STETTLER, Marthe (1870-1945) Swiss					
oil	3	33,150	3,418	14,732	15,000
STEUBEN, Carl (1788-1856) German					
oil	1	5,483		5,483	
STEUERWALDT, Wilhelm I (1791-1863) German					
oil	1	4,728		4,728	
STEUERWALDT, Wilhelm II (1815-1871) German					
oil	1	5,009		5,009	
STEVENS, Agapit (1849-1917) Belgian					
oil	2	4,843	1,180	2,422	3,663
STEVENS, Aime (1879-?) Belgian					
oil	1	2,342		2,342	
STEVENS, Albert George (1863-1925) British					
wc/d	1	2,627		2,627	
STEVENS, Alfred (1823-1906) Belgian					
oil	17	302,844	1,625	4,669	220,000
wc/d	2	4,017	1,234	2,009	2,783
STEVENS, Alfred (school) (1823-1906) Belgian					
oil	1	11,000		11,000	
STEVENS, Alfred George (1817-1875) British					
wc/d	1	1,539		1,539	
STEVENS, Gustav Max (1871-1946) German					
oil	2	2,946	1,269	1,473	1,677
STEVENS, Joseph (1819-1892) Belgian					
oil	2	17,120	1,120	8,560	16,000
STEVENS, Pieter (1567-1624) Flemish					
wc/d	1	4,000		4,000	
STEVENS, René (1858-1937) Belgian					
oil	1	2,054		2,054	
STEVENS, Will Henry (1881-1949) American					
oil	2	21,000	10,000	10,500	11,000
wc/d	1	1,400		1,400	
STEVENS, William Lester (1888-1969) American					
oil	11	33,300	1,400	2,600	7,500
wc/d	1	3,000		3,000	
STEVENSON, M G (?) ?					
oil	1	5,528		5,528	
STEVENSON, Robert Macaulay (1860-1952) British					
oil	2	3,504	1,502	1,752	2,002
STEVER, Jorge (1940-) German					
oil	1	1,590		1,590	
wc/d	1	1,000		1,000	
STEVNS, Niels Larsen (1864-1941) Danish					
oil	5	13,797	2,306	2,324	3,459
wc/d	1	1,666		1,666	
STEWART, F A (1877-1945) British					
wc/d	1	1,500		1,500	
STEWART, Frank Algernon (1877-1945) British					
wc/d	5	11,598	1,128	2,550	3,045
STEWART, James Lawson (fl.1883-1889) British					
wc/d	3	11,252	1,034	1,352	8,866
STEWART, John (19/20th C) British					
oil	2	2,321	1,057	1,161	1,264
wc/d	2	7,660	3,432	3,830	4,228
STEWART, Julius L (1855-1919) American					
oil	3	54,021	9,500	16,521	28,000
STEWART, Kerry (1965-) British					
3D	2	20,600	7,550	10,300	13,050
STEWART, Mary (1773-1849) British					
wc/d	1	1,208		1,208	

Name	No.	Total Sales Value	lowest	Prices median	highest
STEWART-WATT, Eva (?) Irish?					
oil	2	5,965	2,341	2,983	3,624
STEZAKER, John (20th C) ?					
wc/d	1	4,262		4,262	
STHELIN, D (18th C) ?					
wc/d	1	3,500		3,500	
STICHT, Albert (20th C) German					
oil	1	2,157		2,157	
STICKS, George Blackie (1843-1900) British					
oil	11	23,483	1,118	1,888	4,396
STICKS, Harry (1867-1938) British					
oil	2	3,234	1,193	1,617	2,041
STIEGLITZ, Edward (19/20th C) American					
oil	2	14,000	3,000	7,000	11,000
STIELER, Joseph Karl (1781-1858) German					
oil	2	27,599	12,080	13,800	15,519
STIELER, Maximilian (1825-1897) German					
oil	1	1,882		1,882	
STIEPEVICH, Vincent G (1841-1910) Russian					
oil	1	9,666		9,666	
wc/d	1	3,150		3,150	
STIFTER, Moritz (1857-1905) Austrian					
oil	1	3,950		3,950	
STILKE, Hermann Anton (1803-1860) German					
oil	1	9,464		9,464	
STILL, Clyfford (1904-1980) American					
oil	2	1,630,000	80,000	815,000	1,550,000
STILLMAN, Marie Spartali (1844-1927) British					
wc/d	2	84,480	33,000	42,240	51,480
STINGEL, Rudolf (1956-) Austrian					
oil	1	8,000		8,000	
wc/d	1	4,310		4,310	
STINTON, James (1870-1961) British					
wc/d	4	9,954	1,185	1,425	5,920
STIRNBRAND, Franz Seraph (1788-1882) Austrian					
oil	2	3,881	1,430	1,941	2,451
STIVERS, Don (20th C) American					
oil	2	11,000	5,000	5,500	6,000
STOBBAERTS, Jan (1838-1914) Belgian					
oil	1	3,489		3,489	
STOBBAERTS, Pieter (1865-1948) Belgian					
oil	1	3,647		3,647	
STOBWASSER, Gustav (19th C) German					
oil	1	4,782		4,782	
STOCK, H (19th C) ?					
oil	1	5,006		5,006	
STOCK, Henry John (1853-1930) British					
oil	1	4,000		4,000	
STOCK, Joseph Whiting (1815-1855) American					
oil	1	12,500		12,500	
STOCKER, Carlotta (1921-1972) Swiss					
oil	1	2,842		2,842	
STOCKER, Daniel (1865-1957) German					
3D	1	1,894		1,894	
STOCKFLETH, J (19th C) German?					
oil	1	2,107		2,107	
STOCKHAUSEN, Friedemann von (1945-) German					
oil	1	1,933		1,933	

Name	No.	Total Sales Value	lowest	Prices median	highest
STOCKHOLDER, Jessica (1959-) American					
3D	2	26,000	11,000	13,000	15,000
STOCKLEIN, Christian (1741-1795) Swiss					
oil	2	8,394	3,000	4,197	5,394
STOCKMANN (19th C) German?					
oil	3	5,073	1,257	1,796	2,020
STOCKS, Arthur (1846-1889) British					
oil	2	13,164	2,664	6,582	10,500
STOCKS, Minna (1846-1928) German					
oil	1	1,499		1,499	
STOCQUART, Ildephonse (1819-1889) Belgian					
oil	2	6,987	1,664	3,494	5,323
STODDARD, Alice Kent (1893-1976) American					
oil	5	11,300	1,200	1,850	3,500
STODDART, Frances (fl.1837-1867) British					
oil	1	3,528		3,528	
STODDART, Margaret Olrog (1865-1934) New Zealander					
wc/d	1	1,359		1,359	
STOECKL, Rupert (1923-) German					
wc/d	1	1,519		1,519	
STOECKLI, Paul (1906-1992) Swiss					
oil	3	8,219	1,672	3,315	3,315
wc/d	2	3,158	1,560	1,579	1,598
STOECKLIN, Niklaus (1896-1982) Swiss					
oil	3	72,521	12,967	23,092	36,462
wc/d	1	1,300		1,300	
STOFF, Alois (1846-?) Austrian					
oil	1	1,422		1,422	
STOFFE, Jan van der (1611-1682) Dutch					
oil	1	5,962		5,962	
STOFFLER, Friedrich (fl.1811-1848) German					
oil	1	1,684		1,684	
STOHR, A (19th C) ?					
oil	1	1,900		1,900	
STÖHRER, Walter (1937-) German					
oil	2	20,471	1,505	10,236	18,966
wc/d	12	30,404	1,088	2,074	6,294
STOILOFF, Constantin (1850-1924) Austrian/Russian					
oil	11	30,476	1,128	2,158	8,578
STOITZNER, Carl (1866-1943) Austrian					
oil	1	2,000		2,000	
STOITZNER, Constantin (1863-1934) Austrian					
oil	1	1,171		1,171	
STOITZNER, Josef (1884-1951) Austrian					
oil	1	3,133		3,133	
STOJANOW, C (19th C) Russian					
oil	1	2,128		2,128	
STOJANOW, Pjotr (fl.1887-1894) Russian					
oil	1	2,114		2,114	
STOJAROV, Vladimir (1926-1973) Russian					
oil	1	3,000		3,000	
STOK, Jacobus van der (1795-1864) Dutch					
oil	5	81,519	4,396	17,822	29,000
STOKEL, Johann M (20th C) Austrian					
oil	1	1,073		1,073	
STOKES, Adrian (1854-1935) British					
oil	2	5,075	2,030	2,538	3,045
STOKES, George Vernon (1873-1954) British					
wc/d	1	1,463		1,463	

Name	No.	Total Sales Value	lowest	Prices median	highest
STOKES, Marianne (1855-1927) British					
oil	2	23,570	10,570	11,785	13,000
STOKES, Thomas P (1934-) American					
oil	1	1,284		1,284	
STOKVIS, Hendrik (1768-1823) Flemish					
oil	1	1,375		1,375	
STOLZ, Ignaz (younger) (1868-?) Austrian					
oil	1	1,133		1,133	
STOMPS, Louise (1900-1988) German					
3D	2	2,000	1,000	1,000	1,000
STONE, A (19th C) British?					
oil	1	1,074		1,074	
STONE, Don (1929-) American					
wc/d	1	1,100		1,100	
STONE, Frank (1800-1859) British					
oil	1	5,651		5,651	
STONE, G (?) ?					
oil	2	3,871	1,304	1,936	2,567
STONE, Marcus (1840-1921) British					
oil	2	23,184	1,963	11,592	21,221
STONE, R (fl.1900) British					
oil	2	10,296	1,296	5,148	9,000
STONE, Rudolf (19/20th C) British					
oil	5	19,226	1,435	2,869	6,795
STONE, Sarah (18th C) ?					
wc/d	3	17,729	3,000	5,005	9,724
STONE, William (19/20th C) British					
oil	3	4,361	1,034	1,551	1,776
STOOP, Maerten (1620-1647) Dutch					
oil	1	45,300		45,300	
STOOPENDAAL, Mosse (1901-1948) Swedish					
oil	34	99,616	1,133	2,229	9,142
wc/d	1	1,006		1,006	
STOOPS, Herbert Morton (1887-1948) American					
oil	1	1,800		1,800	
STOOTER, Cornelis Leonardsz (1602-1655) Dutch					
oil	1	2,826		2,826	
STORCH, Karl (elder) (1864-1954) German					
oil	1	1,956		1,956	
STORCHLIN, Johann Josef (?-1778) Swiss					
wc/d	1	1,208		1,208	
STORCK, Abraham (c.1635-c.1710) Dutch					
oil	14	1,869,686	28,357	91,725	604,000
STORCK, Jacob (1641-1687) Dutch					
oil	3	69,719	11,339	20,973	37,407
wc/d	1	1,253		1,253	
STORER, Charles (1817-1907) American					
oil	1	6,500		6,500	
STORER, Johann Christoph (1611-1671) Swiss					
wc/d	1	49,830		49,830	
STOREY, G A (1834-1919) British					
oil	1	6,240		6,240	
STOREY, George Adolphus (1834-1919) British					
oil	3	15,118	3,408	4,710	7,000
STORK-KRUYFF, Anna Maria (1870-1946) Dutch					
oil	1	5,000		5,000	
STORM VAN S'GRAVENSANDE, Jacob Jan Julius (1824-1900) Dutch					
oil	1	1,061		1,061	

Name	No.	Total Sales Value	lowest	Prices median	highest
STORM, Juan (1927-) Uruguayan					
oil	6	16,100	1,800	2,800	3,600
STORRS, John (1885-1956) American					
3D	1	7,000		7,000	
oil	1	30,000		30,000	
STORTENBEKER, Pieter (1828-1898) Dutch					
wc/d	1	1,964		1,964	
STORY, George H (1835-1923) American					
oil	1	7,500		7,500	
STORY, Julian Russell (1850-1919) American					
oil	1	11,060		11,060	
STORY, William Wetmore (1819-1895) American					
3D	1	10,362		10,362	
STOTHARD, Thomas (1755-1834) British					
oil	2	11,843	1,099	5,922	10,744
wc/d	1	1,232		1,232	
STOTT OF OLDHAM, William (1857-1900) British					
wc/d	1	2,574		2,574	
STOTT, Edward (1859-1918) British					
oil	1	4,935		4,935	
wc/d	1	3,289		3,289	
STOUF, Jean Baptiste (1742-1826) French					
3D	1	90,053		90,053	
STOWARD, F (19th C) ?					
oil	1	1,021		1,021	
STOWER, Willy (1864-1931) German					
wc/d	1	1,657		1,657	
STOWITTS, Hubert (20th C) American					
oil	1	2,400		2,400	
STRACHAN, Claude (1865-1929) British					
oil	1	1,160		1,160	
wc/d	9	55,242	1,272	2,397	17,490
STRAET, Jan van der (1523-1605) Flemish					
wc/d	2	37,611	5,111	18,806	32,500
STRAETEN, George van der (1856-1928) Belgian					
3D	3	4,170	1,278	1,287	1,605
STRAETEN, Lea van der (1929-) Belgian					
oil	1	1,310		1,310	
STRAETEN, van der (?) ?					
3D	1	1,331		1,331	
STRANDMAN, Otto (1871-1960) Swedish					
3D	1	1,671		1,671	
STRANG, Ray C (1893-1957) American					
oil	2	5,500	2,500	2,750	3,000
STRANG, William (1859-1921) British					
wc/d	1	1,258		1,258	
STRANGE, William le (1782-1846) British					
oil	1	1,300		1,300	
STRANOVER, Tobias (1684-1735) Czechoslovakian					
oil	1	5,880		5,880	
STRASSER (?) ?					
3D	1	1,896		1,896	
STRATEN, Henri van (20th C) Belgian					
3D	1	1,241		1,241	
oil	2	3,760	1,880	1,880	1,880
STRATFORD, F (19/20th C) British					
oil	1	1,343		1,343	
STRATHMANN, Carl (1866-?) German					
oil	1	1,684		1,684	
wc/d	3	9,289	1,658	1,822	5,809

Name	No.	Total Sales Value	lowest	Prices median	highest
STRATTEN, van der (?) ?					
3D	1	1,500		1,500	
STRAUB, Johann Baptist (1704-1784) German					
3D	1	5,000		5,000	
STRAUBE, William (1871-1954) German					
oil	1	1,202		1,202	
STRAUBINGER, Klaus (1839-?) German					
oil	3	7,109	1,716	2,206	3,187
wc/d	1	1,716		1,716	
STRAUCH, Lorenz (1554-1630) German					
oil	1	10,379		10,379	
STRAUCH, Lothar (1907-1991) German					
3D	1	1,038		1,038	
STRAUMANN, Max (20th C) ?					
3D	1	1,028		1,028	
STRAUS, Meyer (1831-1905) American/German					
oil	2	5,750	2,500	2,875	3,250
wc/d	1	1,000		1,000	
STRAUSS, Andre (1885-1971) French					
oil	1	1,422		1,422	
STRAYER, Paul (1885-?) American					
oil	1	2,400		2,400	
STREATOR, Harold A (1861-1926) American					
oil	1	1,500		1,500	
STREBEL, Fritz (1920-) Swiss					
oil	2	3,073	1,228	1,537	1,845
STREBELLE, Rodolphe (1880-1959) Belgian					
oil	1	8,155		8,155	
STRECHINE, Stephanie de (1858-?) German					
oil	1	1,080		1,080	
STRECKENBACH, Max T (1865-1936) German					
oil	7	23,518	1,219	3,128	6,371
STRECKER, Emil (1841-1925) German					
oil	1	6,340		6,340	
STRECKER, Paul (1900-1950) German					
oil	1	4,758		4,758	
STRECKER, Wilhelm Friedrich (1795-1857) German					
oil	1	5,127		5,127	
STREECK, Jurriaen van (1632-1687) Dutch					
oil	1	26,690		26,690	
STREEFKERK, Carl August (1884-1968) Dutch					
oil	2	3,951	1,585	1,976	2,366
STREET, Robert (1796-1865) American					
oil	2	2,900	1,200	1,450	1,700
STREETON, Sir Arthur Ernest (1867-1943) Australian					
wc/d	1	1,988		1,988	
STREICHMAN, Yehezkel (1906-1993) Israeli					
oil	1	100,000		100,000	
wc/d	9	38,805	1,500	3,200	14,000
STREIT, Robert (1883-1957) Austrian					
oil	1	1,073		1,073	
STREITT, F (1839-1890) Polish					
oil	1	3,219		3,219	
STREITT, Franciszek (1839-1890) Polish					
oil	1	7,975		7,975	
STREMPEL, Horst (1904-1975) German					
oil	1	1,545		1,545	
STRESOR, Henri (?-1679) French					
oil	1	6,342		6,342	

Name	No.	Total Sales Value	Prices lowest	median	highest
STREVENS, John (1902-1990) British					
oil	3	4,490	1,136	1,650	1,704
STRICH-CHAPELL, Walter (1877-1960) German					
oil	8	12,219	1,000	1,352	2,776
STRICK, Pieter (18th C) Dutch					
oil	1	4,321		4,321	
STRICKLER, Kaspar Jacob (1906-1976) Swiss					
oil	1	1,880		1,880	
STRINDBERG, August (1849-1912) Swedish					
oil	1	248,394		248,394	
STRITSKI, Christoph (1694-1753) Polish					
3D	1	5,495		5,495	
STROEBEL, Johann Anthonie Balthasar (1821-1905) Dutch					
oil	3	19,292	1,559	4,424	13,309
STROHLING, Peter Eduard (1768-1826) Russian					
oil	1	48,638		48,638	
STROMBERG, Julia (1851-1920) Swedish					
oil	1	1,034		1,034	
STROMEYER, Helene Marie (1834-1924) German					
oil	1	1,136		1,136	
STRONG, C E (19th C) British					
oil	1	1,214		1,214	
STRONG, Elizabeth (1855-1941) American					
oil	1	4,000		4,000	
STRONG, Ray Stanford (1905-) American					
oil	2	2,900	1,300	1,450	1,600
STROUDLEY, James (1906-1985) British					
oil	22	48,175	1,027	1,527	10,270
wc/d	1	2,385		2,385	
STROZZI, Bernardo (1581-1644) Italian					
oil	4	150,294	10,772	39,561	60,400
STRUBE, Adolf (1881-?) German					
oil	1	1,072		1,072	
STRUBE, Hermann (1879-?) German					
oil	1	1,296		1,296	
STRUBE, Jan (20th C) Dutch					
oil	1	2,773		2,773	
STRUBIN, Robert (1897-1965) Swiss					
wc/d	1	3,038		3,038	
STRUCK, Hermann (1876-1944) German					
oil	1	8,000		8,000	
wc/d	4	4,600	1,000	1,200	1,200
STRUTT, Alfred William (1856-1924) British					
oil	2	54,435	6,435	27,218	48,000
wc/d	4	5,950	1,034	1,386	2,145
STRUTT, Jacob George (1784-1867) British					
oil	1	10,570		10,570	
STRUTT, William (1826-1915) British					
wc/d	1	12,750		12,750	
STRUTZEL, Otto (1855-1930) German					
oil	7	25,856	1,152	3,027	7,800
wc/d	2	3,786	1,262	1,893	2,524
STRUYKEN, Peter (1939-) Dutch					
oil	1	3,233		3,233	
STRY, Abraham van (18/19th C) Dutch					
oil	1	21,911		21,911	
STRY, Abraham van (elder) (1753-1826) Dutch					
oil	1	30,774		30,774	

Name	No.	Total Sales Value	Prices lowest	median	highest
STRY, Jacob van (1756-1815) Dutch					
wc/d	3	12,733	1,179	2,554	9,000
STRY, van (18/19th C) Dutch					
oil	2	4,439	1,279	2,220	3,160
STRYBOS, J (?) ?					
oil	1	4,067		4,067	
STRYDONCK, Guillaume van (1861-1937) Belgian					
oil	1	5,431		5,431	
STUART, Alexander Charles (1831-1898) American					
oil	1	4,200		4,200	
STUART, Ernest (fl.1889-1903) British					
wc/d	1	2,265		2,265	
STUART, Gilbert (1755-1828) American					
oil	2	20,500	7,500	10,250	13,000
STUART, J (1713-1788) British					
wc/d	1	5,148		5,148	
STUART, Michelle (1940-) American					
wc/d	1	3,000		3,000	
STUART, R (?) ?					
oil	1	1,095		1,095	
STUART, R Easton (fl.1890-1940) British					
oil	1	1,068		1,068	
STUART, W (19th C) British					
oil	1	1,270		1,270	
STUART, W E D (19th C) British					
oil	2	11,231	2,531	5,616	8,700
STUART, William E D (fl.1846-1858) British					
oil	2	99,330	15,730	49,665	83,600
STUART-WATT, Eva (?) Irish					
oil	2	2,275	1,123	1,138	1,152
STUBBE, Gaby (20th C) German					
wc/d	1	1,065		1,065	
STUBBENDORF, A (?) ?					
oil	1	1,126		1,126	
STUBBS, George (1724-1806) British					
oil	2	6,746,000	3,171,000	3,373,000	3,575,000
STUBBS, J Woodhouse (c.1865-c.1909) British					
wc/d	1	1,021		1,021	
STUBBS, Ralph (1820-1880) British					
oil	1	2,567		2,567	
STUBBS, W P (1842-1909) American					
oil	1	15,500		15,500	
STUBBS, William P (1842-1909) American					
oil	5	43,250	3,000	5,000	22,500
STUBER, Dedrick B (1878-1954) American					
oil	6	26,350	2,200	3,625	7,500
STUCK, Franz von (1863-1928) German					
3D	6	81,316	5,465	12,285	22,650
oil	4	83,143	6,831	21,111	34,091
wc/d	5	50,077	1,644	8,532	24,160
STUCKGOLD, Stanislaw (1868-1933) Polish					
oil	1	11,650		11,650	
STUEMPFIG, Walter (1914-1970) American/German					
oil	1	3,200		3,200	
STUHLMULLER, K (1858-1930) German					
oil	1	3,086		3,086	
STUHLMULLER, Karl (1858-1930) German					
oil	6	52,045	3,575	7,500	14,519

Name	No.	Total Sales Value	lowest	Prices median	highest
STUHR, Johann Georg (c.1640-1721) German					
oil	1	4,410		4,410	
STULL, Henry (1851-1913) American					
oil	3	27,500	7,500	8,000	12,000
STUMPF, Wilhelm (1873-1928) German					
oil	1	2,084		2,084	
STUPAR, Marko (20th C) ?					
wc/d	1	1,486		1,486	
STURGESS, John (19th C) British					
wc/d	1	1,000		1,000	
STURLA, Michel (19/20th C) ?					
oil	2	3,207	1,160	1,604	2,047
STURM, Helmut (1932-) German					
oil	1	1,483		1,483	
wc/d	1	1,138		1,138	
STURM, Justin (1899-) American					
3D	1	1,900		1,900	
STURSA, Jan (1880-1925) Czechoslovakian					
3D	1	1,573		1,573	
STURTEVANT, Elaine (1926-) American					
wc/d	1	35,000		35,000	
STURZENEGGER, Hans (1875-1943) Swiss					
oil	2	3,727	1,807	1,864	1,920
STUTTERHEIM, Lodewyk Philippus (1873-1943) Dutch					
oil	2	3,713	1,132	1,857	2,581
STUVEN, Ernst (1660-1712) German					
oil	1	27,180		27,180	
STUYTS (?) Belgian					
oil	1	6,655		6,655	
STYKA, Adam (1890-c.1970) French					
oil	7	81,347	6,275	12,412	16,755
STYKA, Jan (1858-1925) French					
oil	1	9,500		9,500	
STYKA, Tade (1889-1954) French					
oil	2	11,871	4,511	5,936	7,360
STYLE, Ann (?) British?					
wc/d	1	1,133		1,133	
SUAREZ PEREGRIN, Jose (1908-) Spanish					
oil	1	1,221		1,221	
SUAREZ, Antonio (1923-) Spanish					
oil	1	1,405		1,405	
SUBERCASEAUX ERAZURIZ, Pedro (1881-1956) Chilean					
oil	1	1,269		1,269	
SUCASAS, Alfonso (20th C) Spanish					
oil	6	16,091	1,452	2,215	5,378
wc/d	1	2,707		2,707	
SUCH, William T (fl.1847-1857) British					
oil	1	2,145		2,145	
SUCHY, Maria Antonia (19th C) ?					
oil	1	26,460		26,460	
SUDA, Kunitaro (1891-1961) Japanese					
oil	1	45,000		45,000	
SUDDABY, Rowland (1912-1973) British					
oil	6	14,794	1,050	1,787	5,640
wc/d	5	16,029	1,036	2,175	6,345
SUDEIKIN, Sergei Yurievich (1882-1946) Russian					
oil	1	4,228		4,228	
SUDKOVSKY, Rufin (1850-1885) Russian					
oil	1	5,285		5,285	

Name	No.	Total Sales Value	lowest	Prices median	highest
SUDRE, Pierre (?) French					
oil	1	1,246		1,246	
SUGAI, Kumi (1919-1996) Japanese					
oil	4	95,489	3,246	22,513	47,218
wc/d	5	16,033	2,256	2,804	4,481
SUGHI, Alberto (1928-) Italian					
oil	11	50,923	1,017	3,498	14,835
SUGIYAMA, Yasushi (1909-1993) Japanese					
wc/d	1	48,000		48,000	
SUHRLANDT, Carl (1828-1919) German					
oil	1	2,718		2,718	
SUHRLANDT, Johann Heinrich (1742-1827) German					
oil	1	15,971		15,971	
SUISSE, Gaston (20th C) ?					
oil	1	3,067		3,067	
wc/d	13	43,742	1,091	2,791	7,149
SUKER, Arthur (1857-?) British					
wc/d	1	1,630		1,630	
SUKHODOLSKY, Pyotr Alexandrovich (19th C) Russian					
oil	1	15,100		15,100	
SUKKERT, Adolf (19th C) German					
oil	1	7,183		7,183	
SULLIVAN, William Holmes (?-1908) British					
oil	1	2,400		2,400	
SULLY, Thomas (1783-1872) American/British					
oil	8	131,660	3,000	12,000	45,000
wc/d	1	7,500		7,500	
SULTAN, Donald (1951-) American					
oil	3	50,000	11,000	14,000	25,000
wc/d	3	17,270	4,770	6,000	6,500
SUMIDA, Gregory (20th C) American?					
oil	1	8,000		8,000	
SUMMERS E ISERN, Ricardo (1908-1995) Spanish					
oil	2	3,806	1,829	1,903	1,977
SUNDBERG, Christine (1837-1892) Swedish					
oil	2	6,772	2,425	3,386	4,347
SUNDBLOM, Haddon Hubbard (1899-1976) American					
oil	5	200,450	2,700	19,000	140,000
SUNDERLAND, Thomas (1744-1828) British					
wc/d	3	6,230	1,113	2,567	2,567
SUNDT-HANSEN, Carl (1841-1907) Norwegian					
oil	1	27,088		27,088	
SUNER ADRALL, Francisco (?) Spanish					
oil	1	2,210		2,210	
SUNESSON, Stina (1925-1998) Swedish					
wc/d	6	14,672	1,088	1,814	5,037
SUNYER, Joachim (1875-1956) Spanish					
oil	3	54,250	1,597	15,263	37,390
wc/d	1	3,064		3,064	
SUPERSTUDIO (20th C) Italian					
3D	1	21,750		21,750	
SURAND, Gustave (1860-1937) French					
oil	2	14,826	1,326	7,413	13,500
SURBEK, Victor (1885-1975) Swiss					
oil	2	3,848	1,749	1,924	2,099
SURDI, Luigi (1897-1959) Italian					
oil	1	1,134		1,134	
SUREDA, Andre (1872-1930) French					
oil	3	10,125	1,947	2,207	5,971
wc/d	4	9,086	1,314	2,280	3,213

Name	No.	Total Sales Value	Prices lowest	median	highest
SURGEY, J B (fl.1851-1883) British					
wc/d	1	1,001		1,001	
SURIE, Jacoba (1879-1970) Dutch					
oil	2	3,819	1,061	1,910	2,758
SURIKOV, Vasilii Ivanovich (1848-1916) Russian					
wc/d	1	5,358		5,358	
SURREY, Philip Henry (1910-1990) Canadian					
oil	6	20,958	1,858	3,447	6,201
SURTEL, Paul (1893-1985) French					
oil	1	1,405		1,405	
SURVAGE, Leopold (1879-1968) French					
oil	18	406,870	1,482	13,916	94,025
wc/d	16	33,590	1,178	1,823	3,836
SUSEMIHL, Johann Theodor (1772-?) German					
oil	1	9,305		9,305	
SUSTERMANS, Justus (1597-1681) Flemish					
oil	1	5,000		5,000	
SUSTRIS, Friedrich (1540-1599) Dutch					
wc/d	1	3,926		3,926	
SUTCLIFFE, T (19th C) British					
wc/d	1	2,686		2,686	
SUTER, August (1887-1965) Swiss					
3D	2	7,296	2,840	3,648	4,456
SUTER, Jakob (1805-1874) Swiss					
wc/d	4	6,591	1,028	1,456	2,652
SUTHERLAND, George Mowbray (fl.1861-1866) British					
wc/d	1	2,512		2,512	
SUTHERLAND, Graham (1903-1980) British					
oil	3	26,660	4,200	10,546	11,914
wc/d	34	427,406	2,960	8,690	47,400
SUTTER, Jules de (1895-1970) Belgian					
oil	3	8,047	1,180	1,931	4,936
SUTTERBY, Rod (1955-) British					
oil	2	6,738	3,020	3,369	3,718
wc/d	2	2,420	1,133	1,210	1,287
SUTTON, Philip (1928-) British					
oil	6	24,992	2,184	4,275	6,480
SUVERO, Mark di (1933-) American					
3D	3	189,000	14,000	25,000	150,000
oil	3	3,600	1,200	1,200	1,200
SUYDAM, James Augustus (1819-1865) American					
oil	1	50,000		50,000	
SUZOR-COTE, Marc-Aurele de Foy (1869-1937) Canadian					
3D	6	64,569	3,270	7,550	31,982
oil	3	56,720	2,350	12,793	41,577
wc/d	5	36,572	1,652	4,181	13,937
SVANBERG, Max Walter (1912-1995) Swedish					
wc/d	8	29,075	1,154	2,165	9,576
SVANLUND, Josef (20th C) Swedish					
oil	1	1,190		1,190	
SVEDBERG, Lena (1946-1972) Swedish					
wc/d	2	4,057	1,147	2,029	2,910
SVEINSDOTTIR, Juliana (1889-1966) Icelandic					
oil	2	5,263	1,932	2,632	3,331
SVENDSEN, Svend (1864-1934) Norwegian/American					
oil	1	1,300		1,300	
SVENSSON, Christian Fredrik (1834-1909) Swedish					
oil	6	15,246	1,126	2,027	5,054
SVENSSON, Gunnar (1892-1977) Swedish					
oil	1	1,859		1,859	

Name	No.	Total Sales Value	lowest	Prices median	highest
SVENSSON, Otto H (20th C) Scandinavian					
oil	1	1,016		1,016	
SVENSSON, Roland (1910-) Swedish					
oil	2	37,608	5,441	18,804	32,167
wc/d	4	8,097	1,442	1,641	3,374
SVENSSON, Wiking (1915-1979) Swedish					
oil	1	1,260		1,260	
SVERTSCHKOFF, Nicolas Gregorovitch (1817-1898) Russian					
oil	3	37,800	3,723	4,467	29,610
SVIRIDOV, Sergei (1964-) Russian					
oil	1	1,185		1,185	
SWABIAN SCHOOL, 16th C German					
oil	1	33,760		33,760	
SWABIAN SCHOOL, 18th C German					
3D	1	3,367		3,367	
SWAEN, Hugo (1825-1910) Dutch					
oil	1	1,373		1,373	
SWAGEMAKERS, Theo (1898-1994) Dutch					
oil	1	1,721		1,721	
SWAGERS, Frans (1756-1836) Dutch					
oil	5	85,288	8,754	10,702	42,500
SWAINE, Francis (1740-1782) British					
oil	9	289,756	1,597	9,724	177,600
SWAISH, Frederick George (?-1931) British					
oil	1	1,590		1,590	
SWAMINATHAN, Jagdish (1928-) Indian					
oil	4	44,340	8,640	10,320	15,000
SWAN, Cuthbert Edmund (1870-1931) British					
wc/d	3	4,512	1,036	1,278	2,198
SWANE, Christine (1876-1960) Danish					
oil	4	7,840	1,270	1,554	3,462
SWANE, Sigurd (1879-1973) Danish					
oil	4	7,715	1,087	1,369	3,891
SWANEVELT, Herman van (1600-1655) Dutch					
oil	7	130,057	1,628	14,927	59,660
wc/d	2	8,881	3,143	4,441	5,738
SWANWICK, Betty (1915-1989) British					
wc/d	1	1,144		1,144	
SWANWICK, Harold (1866-1929) British					
wc/d	2	4,280	1,100	2,140	3,180
SWANZY, Mary (1882-1978) Irish					
oil	2	10,100	2,700	5,050	7,400
SWATSLEY, John (1937-) American					
oil	1	3,700		3,700	
SWEBACH, Bernard Edouard (1800-1870) French					
oil	2	12,724	6,092	6,362	6,632
wc/d	1	2,680		2,680	
SWEBACH-DESFONTAINES, Jacques François (1769-1823) French					
oil	6	42,604	1,630	2,951	18,153
wc/d	1	2,320		2,320	
SWEDISH SCHOOL, 18th C					
oil	2	15,019	5,659	7,510	9,360
SWEDISH SCHOOL, 18th/19th C					
oil	1	4,161		4,161	
SWEDISH SCHOOL, 19th C					
oil	1	5,886		5,886	
SWEDLUND, Pelle (1865-1947) Swedish					
oil	1	3,061		3,061	

Name	No.	Total Sales Value	lowest	Prices median	highest
SWEERTS, Michiel (1624-1664) Dutch					
oil	1	5,378		5,378	
SWEET, W H (20th C) British					
wc/d	1	1,806		1,806	
SWEET, Walter H (1889-1943) British					
wc/d	1	1,580		1,580	
SWENNEN, Walter (20th C) ?					
oil	2	4,349	1,502	2,175	2,847
SWETOHKOFF, George de (19/20th C) ?					
oil	1	1,000		1,000	
SWIESZEWSKI, A (1839-1895) Polish					
oil	1	1,200		1,200	
SWIESZEWSKI, Alexander (1839-1895) Polish					
oil	1	4,200		4,200	
SWIFT, Edmund (jnr) (19th C) British					
oil	1	1,072		1,072	
SWIFT, John Warkup (1815-1869) British					
oil	2	4,560	2,115	2,280	2,445
SWINBURNE, Edward (1765-1847) British					
wc/d	1	1,287		1,287	
SWINNERTON, James G (1875-1974) American					
oil	1	3,000		3,000	
SWINSTEAD, George Hillyard (1860-1926) British					
oil	1	14,490		14,490	
SWISS SCHOOL, 16th C					
wc/d	1	61,098		61,098	
SWISS SCHOOL, 17th C					
wc/d	1	4,536		4,536	
SWISS SCHOOL, 18th C					
oil	4	25,245	3,418	5,748	10,331
SWISS SCHOOL, 19th C					
oil	6	51,871	1,166	6,670	25,724
SWOBODA, Rudolf (elder) (1819-1859) Austrian					
oil	1	6,300		6,300	
SWYNCOP, Philippe (1878-1949) Belgian					
oil	6	17,578	1,273	2,592	6,246
wc/d	2	3,342	1,671	1,671	1,671
SWYNNERTON, Annie (1844-1933) British					
oil	1	4,710		4,710	
SYBERG, Anna Louise Brigitte (1870-1914) Danish					
wc/d	1	4,040		4,040	
SYBERG, Fritz (1862-1939) Danish					
oil	13	20,737	1,001	1,353	3,683
SYCHKOV, Feodor Vasilievich (1870-1958) Russian					
oil	3	47,861	4,228	20,368	23,265
SYDNEY, Berenice (1944-1983) British?					
oil	4	10,602	1,500	3,000	3,300
SYER, J (19th C) British					
oil	1	2,397		2,397	
SYER, John (1815-1885) British					
oil	6	13,293	1,022	2,273	3,691
SYKES, Charles (20th C) British					
3D	2	8,750	2,750	4,375	6,000
oil	1	1,659		1,659	
SYLVESTER, Frederick Oakes (1869-1915) American					
oil	4	7,500	1,100	1,850	2,700
SYLVESTRE, Paul (?) French					
3D	1	2,320		2,320	

Name	No.	Total Sales Value	Prices lowest	median	highest
SYMONDS, Richard (1969-) British					
oil	1	2,130		2,130	
wc/d	1	1,846		1,846	
SYMONDS, William Robert (1851-1934) British					
oil	1	5,434		5,434	
SYMONS, George Gardner (1863-1930) American					
oil	9	56,350	2,400	3,800	16,000
SYMONS, William Christian (1845-1911) British					
oil	1	18,684		18,684	
SYS, Maurice (1880-1972) Belgian					
oil	4	64,456	4,957	10,718	38,063
wc/d	1	3,359		3,359	
SZAFRAN, Sam (1930-) French					
oil	1	11,826		11,826	
wc/d	1	1,443		1,443	
SZANKOWSKI, Boleslaw von (1873-1953) Polish					
oil	2	3,646	1,193	1,823	2,453
SZANTHO, Maria (1898-1984) Hungarian					
oil	10	13,636	1,133	1,236	1,728
SZCEZESNY, Stefan (1951-) German					
oil	1	1,366		1,366	
SZCZEBLEWSKI, V (19th C) European					
3D	1	1,829		1,829	
SZEKELY, Bertalan (1835-1910) Hungarian					
oil	1	81,780		81,780	
SZEWCZENKO, Konstanty (1909-) Czechoslovakian					
oil	1	1,077		1,077	
SZYK, Arthur (1894-1951) Polish					
wc/d	3	4,700	1,000	1,100	2,600
SZYMANSKI, Rolf (1928-) German					
3D	1	1,262		1,262	
SZYSZLO, Fernando de (1925-) Peruvian					
wc/d	1	3,000		3,000	
TAAFFE, Philip (1955-) American					
oil	2	138,350	10,000	69,175	128,350
TAANMAN, Jacob (1836-1923) Dutch					
oil	2	2,326	1,067	1,163	1,259
TABACCHI, Odoardo (1831-1905) Italian					
3D	3	4,811	1,297	1,727	1,787
TABARY, E (19th C) French					
oil	1	4,000		4,000	
TABERSON (?) ?					
3D	1	13,680		13,680	
TABLADA DE DIEGO, Lope (1903-1974) Spanish					
oil	2	4,857	2,045	2,429	2,812
TABNER, Len (1936-) British					
oil	1	1,580		1,580	
wc/d	1	1,659		1,659	
TABUCHI, Yasse (1921-) Japanese					
oil	3	7,605	1,430	2,040	4,135
TABUENA, Romeo (1921-) Mexican					
oil	1	1,306		1,306	
TABUSSO, Francesco (1930-) Italian					
oil	2	2,947	1,422	1,474	1,525
TACCONE, Innocenzio (1575-?) Italian					
oil	1	35,000		35,000	
TACLA, Jorge (1958-) Chilean					
oil	1	15,000		15,000	

Name	No.	Total Sales Value	Prices lowest	median	highest
TADEMA-GROENEVELD, Thamine Henriette Bartholde Jacoba (1871-1938) Dutch					
oil	1	2,573		2,573	
TADEUSZ, Norbert (1940-) ?					
oil	3	13,575	4,109	4,109	5,340
wc/d	2	3,596	1,072	1,798	2,524
TADINI, Emilio (1927-) Italian					
oil	7	14,171	1,293	1,780	4,459
TAEUBER-ARP, Sophie (1889-1943) Swiss					
wc/d	1	16,000		16,000	
TAFLINGER, Elmer E (1891-?) American					
oil	1	4,250		4,250	
TAFURI, Clemente (1903-1971) Italian					
oil	4	27,830	2,217	7,389	10,836
TAFURI, Raffaele (1857-1929) Italian					
oil	1	12,000		12,000	
TAG, Georges (?) French?					
3D	1	2,302		2,302	
TAGGART, Lucy M (20th C) American					
wc/d	1	3,000		3,000	
TAGGART, Richard T (1904-) American					
oil	1	1,300		1,300	
TAGGER, Siona (1900-1988) Israeli					
wc/d	1	4,600		4,600	
TAGLIABUE, Carlo Costantino (1880-1960) Italian					
oil	3	7,568	1,427	1,784	4,357
TAGLIAPIETRA, J (19th C) Italian					
oil	1	10,938		10,938	
TAGORE, Abanindranath (1871-1951) Indian					
wc/d	1	3,300		3,300	
TAGORE, Gaganendranath (1867-1938) Indian					
wc/d	4	10,575	1,800	2,363	4,050
TAGORE, Rabindra Nath (1861-1941) Indian					
wc/d	4	26,180	4,050	6,025	10,080
TAILHARDAT, Vincent (1970-) French					
oil	1	2,708		2,708	
TAILLASSON, Jean Joseph (1745-1809) French					
oil	1	13,345		13,345	
wc/d	1	4,364		4,364	
TAILLEUX, Francis (1913-) French					
oil	2	2,779	1,278	1,390	1,501
TAIT, Arthur Fitzwilliam (1819-1905) American					
oil	10	228,500	6,500	11,250	80,000
TAKEUCHI, Seiho and TOMIOKA, Tessai (19/20th C) Japanese					
wc/d	1	1,904		1,904	
TAKIS (1925-) Greek					
3D	3	16,515	3,342	5,460	7,713
TAL COAT, Pierre (1905-1985) French					
oil	15	64,467	1,289	3,689	14,461
wc/d	5	6,156	1,028	1,197	1,549
TALBOYS, Agnes Augusta (fl.1920) British					
oil	3	19,288	2,288	8,500	8,500
TALLONE, Cesare (1853-1919) Italian					
oil	1	1,376		1,376	
TALMAGE, Algernon (1871-1939) British					
oil	1	1,510		1,510	
TALPINO, Enea (c.1558-1626) Italian					
wc/d	1	1,383		1,383	
TALWINSKI, Igor (1907-) Polish					
oil	2	3,139	1,264	1,570	1,875

Name	No.	Total Sales Value	lowest	Prices median	highest
TAMAGNI, Vincenzo (1492-1530) Italian					
oil	1	6,366		6,366	
TAMAYO, Rufino (1899-1991) Mexican					
oil	6	1,580,000	85,000	205,000	650,000
wc/d	3	57,800	1,800	26,000	30,000
TAMBURI, Orfeo (1910-1994) Italian					
oil	14	44,273	1,061	2,744	6,278
wc/d	1	1,262		1,262	
TAMBURINI, Arnaldo (1843-?) Italian					
oil	5	27,206	1,200	4,398	11,000
TAMM, F W (1658-1724) German					
oil	1	4,782		4,782	
TAMM, Franz Werner (1658-1724) German					
oil	6	73,305	2,736	8,952	27,180
TAN, Pierre le (1950-) French					
wc/d	3	4,873	1,141	1,690	2,042
TANABE, Takao (1926-) Canadian					
oil	3	14,895	1,371	4,896	8,628
TANAKA, Akira (1918-) Japanese					
oil	3	12,941	1,769	2,211	8,961
TANAKA, Yasushi (1886-?) Japanese					
oil	3	9,074	1,501	2,525	5,048
TANCREDI (1927-1964) Italian					
oil	1	38,580		38,580	
wc/d	4	83,482	8,735	19,904	34,940
TANCREDI, Parmeggiani (1927-1964) Italian					
wc/d	1	7,394		7,394	
TANG DYNASTY (8th C) Chinese					
3D	1	8,218		8,218	
TANG HAIWEN (1929-1991) Chinese					
wc/d	1	1,349		1,349	
TANGER, F (19th C) French					
oil	1	31,600		31,600	
TANGUY, Morel de (?) ?					
oil	1	5,528		5,528	
TANGUY, Yves (1900-1955) American/French					
oil	7	2,594,000	87,000	332,200	724,800
wc/d	7	271,430	2,571	12,855	87,000
TANJORE SCHOOL, 19th C Indian					
wc/d	1	2,730		2,730	
TANK, Heinrich Friedrich (1808-1872) German					
oil	2	17,323	2,472	8,662	14,851
TANNAES, Marie (1854-1939) Norwegian					
oil	1	1,549		1,549	
TANNER, E L (19/20th C) British?					
oil	1	1,278		1,278	
TANNER, Ethel L (fl.1907-1919) British					
oil	1	2,002		2,002	
TANNER, Henry Ossawa (1859-1937) American					
oil	1	1,895		1,895	
TANNERT, Volker (1955-) German					
oil	1	4,854		4,854	
TANNHEIMER, Willi (1940-) German					
3D	2	5,979	1,063	2,990	4,916
TANNING, Dorothea (1910-) American					
oil	1	26,000		26,000	
TANOUX, Adrien Henri (1865-1923) French					
oil	6	23,235	1,963	4,404	5,075

Name	No.	Total Sales Value	lowest	Prices median	highest
TANREI, Araki (1857-1931) Japanese					
wc/d	1	1,063		1,063	
TANSEY, Mark (1949-) American					
oil	1	90,000		90,000	
wc/d	2	16,270	6,270	8,135	10,000
TANSLEY, Eric (20th C) ?					
oil	1	1,761		1,761	
TANYU, Kano (1602-1674) Japanese					
wc/d	1	5,313		5,313	
TANZI, Léon Louis Antoine (1846-1913) French					
oil	1	1,717		1,717	
TAPIE DE CELEYRAN, Michel (20th C) French					
oil	2	5,596	2,320	2,798	3,276
TAPIES, Antonio (1923-) Spanish					
oil	13	1,408,530	8,067	39,260	406,000
wc/d	17	821,963	1,320	14,683	453,000
TAPLIN, Guy (1939-) British					
3D	12	72,274	1,269	2,193	21,750
TAPPERT, Georg (1880-1957) German					
oil	6	166,224	7,360	22,836	54,064
wc/d	4	7,621	1,262	1,791	2,777
TAQUOY, Maurice (20th C) French					
wc/d	2	5,610	2,707	2,805	2,903
TARABELLA, Viliano (20th C) ?					
3D	1	1,003		1,003	
TARANOW, Michail A (1909-1973) Russian?					
oil	1	3,336		3,336	
TARANTINO, Giuseppe (1916-) Italian					
3D	1	1,548		1,548	
TARAVAL, Hugues (1729-1785) French					
oil	3	86,944	2,944	4,000	80,000
TARAVAL, Louis Gustave (1738-1794) French					
wc/d	1	4,832		4,832	
TARBELL, Edmund C (1862-1938) American					
oil	2	512,500	32,500	256,250	480,000
wc/d	1	2,800		2,800	
TARDIEU, Jean Charles (1765-1830) French					
oil	1	14,465		14,465	
TARDIEU, L (20th C) ?					
oil	1	2,342		2,342	
TARDIEU, Victor François (1870-1937) French					
oil	1	2,730		2,730	
TARENGHI, Enrico (1848-?) Italian					
wc/d	3	13,573	3,200	4,673	5,700
TARGETT, Thomas G (fl.1869-1879) British					
oil	1	1,160		1,160	
TARIN, Ben (20th C) ?					
wc/d	1	1,200		1,200	
TARKHOFF, Nicolas (1871-1930) Russian					
oil	4	23,687	2,757	4,665	11,600
wc/d	1	1,607		1,607	
TARRANT, Margaret Winifred (1888-1959) British					
wc/d	2	3,907	1,833	1,954	2,074
TARRANT, Percy (fl.1881-1930) British					
oil	1	2,475		2,475	
TASLITZKY, Boris (1911-) French					
oil	1	4,422		4,422	
TASSAERT, Octave (1800-1874) French					
oil	2	2,769	1,309	1,385	1,460

Name	No.	Total Sales Value	lowest	Prices median	highest
TASSEL, Jean (1608-1667) French					
oil	1	8,555		8,555	
TASSEL, Jean (school) (1608-1667) French					
oil	1	1,100		1,100	
TASSI, Agostino (1565-1644) Italian					
wc/d	2	8,773	1,773	4,387	7,000
TATAFIORE, Ernesto (1943-) Italian					
oil	1	1,104		1,104	
wc/d	1	1,165		1,165	
TATAH, Djamel (20th C) ?					
oil	4	11,503	1,197	1,633	7,041
TATOSSIAN, Armand (20th C) Canadian					
oil	8	11,143	1,044	1,394	2,089
TAUBE, Eugen (1860-1913) Finnish					
oil	1	3,618		3,618	
TAUBE, Evert (1890-1975) Scandinavian					
oil	1	1,706		1,706	
TAUBERT, Gerhard (1928-) German					
oil	1	2,811		2,811	
TAUNAY, Nicolas Antoine (1755-1830) French					
oil	3	17,348	1,218	3,000	13,130
wc/d	1	1,655		1,655	
TAUPIN, Jules (1863-1932) French					
oil	2	5,474	1,998	2,737	3,476
TAUTENHAYN, Josef (19/20th C) Austrian					
3D	1	2,311		2,311	
TAVELLA, Carlo Antonio (1668-1738) Italian					
oil	1	6,545		6,545	
TAVENRAAT, Johannes (1809-1881) Dutch					
oil	1	1,268		1,268	
TAVERNER, William (1703-1772) British					
wc/d	1	2,250		2,250	
TAVERNIER, Andrea (1858-1932) Italian					
oil	4	105,821	10,978	13,738	67,367
wc/d	1	3,100		3,100	
TAVERNIER, Armand (1899-1991) Belgian					
oil	4	7,726	1,191	1,600	3,335
TAVERNIER, Jules (1844-1899) French					
oil	1	2,750		2,750	
TAVERNIER, Paul (1852-?) French					
oil	2	11,852	2,852	5,926	9,000
TAYLER, Albert Chevallier (1862-1925) British					
oil	7	58,351	1,570	5,700	25,000
TAYLER, D (?) ?					
oil	1	1,500		1,500	
TAYLER, John Frederick (1802-1889) British					
wc/d	2	3,555	1,410	1,778	2,145
TAYLER, Norman E (1843-1915) British					
wc/d	1	2,400		2,400	
TAYLOR, Charles (19th C) British					
wc/d	2	3,808	1,305	1,904	2,503
TAYLOR, Charles (jnr) (fl.1841-1883) British					
wc/d	3	6,622	1,043	1,787	3,792
TAYLOR, E (?) ?					
wc/d	1	1,099		1,099	
TAYLOR, Edward R (1838-1912) British					
oil	1	5,056		5,056	
TAYLOR, Frederick Bourchier (1906-1987) Canadian					
oil	3	5,530	1,187	1,625	2,718

Name	No.	Total Sales Value	lowest	Prices median	highest
wc/d	1	1,200		1,200	
TAYLOR, George T (1838-1913) Canadian					
wc/d	1	2,397		2,397	
TAYLOR, Henry White (1899-1943) American					
oil	1	10,000		10,000	
TAYLOR, J Fraser (19th C) British					
oil	1	5,436		5,436	
TAYLOR, Leonard Campbell (1874-1963) British					
oil	4	41,199	1,510	4,045	31,600
TAYLOR, Robert (19th C) British					
oil	1	1,500		1,500	
TAYLOR, Rolla S (1874-1929) American					
oil	2	4,000	1,000	2,000	3,000
TAYLOR, S (19th C) British					
oil	1	2,370		2,370	
TAYLOR, W (?) ?					
wc/d	1	1,271		1,271	
TCHELITCHEV, Pavel (1898-1957) American/Russian					
oil	3	18,284	2,852	3,432	12,000
wc/d	2	3,700	1,200	1,850	2,500
TCHISTOVSKI, Lew (1902-) Russian					
oil	1	1,053		1,053	
wc/d	1	1,053		1,053	
TCHORZEWSKI, Jerzy (1928-) Polish					
oil	2	10,000	4,750	5,000	5,250
TCHOUMAKOFF, Theodore (1823-1911) Russian					
oil	1	1,511		1,511	
TEAGUE, Donald (1897-1991) American					
wc/d	4	20,750	3,000	4,875	8,000
TEDESCO-HOFFMANN, Julia (1843-?) Italian					
oil	1	2,110		2,110	
wc/d	1	2,693		2,693	
TEED, Douglas Arthur (1864-1929) American					
oil	5	12,600	1,900	2,200	3,250
TEERLINK, Abraham (1776-1857) Dutch					
oil	3	51,840	8,420	8,420	35,000
TEGNER, Christian Martin (1803-1881) Danish					
oil	1	2,645		2,645	
TEGNER, Rudolph (1873-1950) Danish					
3D	2	2,526	1,156	1,263	1,370
TEIBLER, Cenci (?) ?					
oil	1	3,000		3,000	
TEIXEIRA DE MATTOS, Joseph (1892-1971) Dutch					
oil	1	6,466		6,466	
TEJERA, Angel (?) ?					
oil	4	4,650	1,000	1,125	1,400
TELARIK, A (?) ?					
oil	1	2,548		2,548	
TELEMAQUE, Herve (1937-) Haitian					
oil	9	89,093	1,133	8,309	23,868
wc/d	4	16,004	3,173	4,123	4,585
TELLER, Grif (20th C) American					
oil	2	39,000	15,000	19,500	24,000
TELLIER, Raymond (1897-1985) French					
oil	3	6,137	1,154	1,761	3,222
TEMMAM, Muhammed (1915-1988) Algerian					
wc/d	1	4,511		4,511	
TEMPESTA, Antonio (1555-1630) Italian					
oil	1	44,640		44,640	

Name	No.	Total Sales Value	lowest	Prices median	highest
wc/d	1	1,000		1,000	
TEMPESTI, Giovanni Battista (c.1732-1804) Italian					
oil	1	3,165		3,165	
TEMPLE, Hans (1857-1931) Austrian					
oil	3	61,250	2,000	8,500	50,750
TEMPLE, Ruth Anderson (1884-1939) American					
oil	1	4,750		4,750	
TEMPLIN, Victor (1920-1994) Russian					
oil	12	15,555	1,060	1,176	1,778
TEN BERGE, Bernardus Gerardus (1825-1875) Dutch					
oil	2	2,700	1,350	1,350	1,350
TEN BOSCH, Lena Cornelia (1890-1945) Dutch					
oil	1	4,452		4,452	
TEN CATE, Hendrik Gerrit (1803-1856) Dutch					
oil	2	32,236	5,056	16,118	27,180
wc/d	1	1,282		1,282	
TEN CATE, Johannes Marinus (1859-1896) Dutch					
wc/d	2	3,197	1,075	1,599	2,122
TEN CATE, Pieter (1868-1937) Dutch					
oil	1	1,148		1,148	
TEN CATE, Siebe Johannes (1858-1908) Dutch					
oil	1	2,073		2,073	
wc/d	2	2,620	1,267	1,310	1,353
TEN KATE, Herman (1822-1891) Dutch					
oil	6	21,132	1,477	3,634	5,500
wc/d	6	22,822	1,180	3,934	5,889
TEN KATE, Jan Jacob Lodewijk (1850-1929) Dutch					
oil	2	14,566	2,790	7,283	11,776
TEN KATE, Johan Mari (1831-1910) Dutch					
oil	6	85,706	1,179	15,994	27,581
wc/d	5	17,618	1,377	2,850	5,941
TENER, René (1846-1925) French					
oil	2	4,174	1,782	2,087	2,392
TENGGREN, Gustaf Adolf (1896-1981) Swedish					
wc/d	3	18,822	1,863	1,959	15,000
TENIERS (school) (17th C) Flemish					
wc/d	1	1,452		1,452	
TENIERS, D (younger) (1610-1690) Flemish					
oil	1	100,000		100,000	
TENIERS, David (elder) (1582-1649) Flemish					
oil	1	22,650		22,650	
TENIERS, David (younger) (1610-1690) Flemish					
oil	12	968,001	8,000	83,520	181,200
wc/d	4	19,751	1,470	2,266	13,750
TENIERS, David (younger-school) (1610-1690) Flemish					
oil	1	5,099		5,099	
TENNANT, J (?) British					
oil	1	1,359		1,359	
TENNANT, John F (1796-1872) British					
oil	5	45,247	4,740	6,750	20,540
TENNANT, Lady Emma (1943-) British					
wc/d	2	8,400	4,200	4,200	4,200
TENNIEL, John (1820-1914) British					
wc/d	1	1,284		1,284	
TENRE, Henry (1864-1924) French					
oil	1	8,532		8,532	
TEPLER, Samuel (1918-) Israeli					
oil	3	3,800	1,000	1,000	1,800

Name	No.	Total Sales Value	lowest	Prices median	highest
TEPPER, Saul (1899-1987) American					
oil	1	7,000		7,000	
TER MEULEN, Frans Pieter (1843-1927) Dutch					
oil	3	4,980	1,000	1,313	2,667
TERBORCH, Gerard (1617-1681) Dutch					
oil	4	81,469	7,000	15,185	44,100
TERECHKOVITCH, Costia (1902-1978) French					
oil	9	52,411	2,508	4,097	13,403
wc/d	9	19,028	1,459	1,995	2,835
TERESZCZUK, P (20th C) Austrian					
3D	1	2,718		2,718	
TERESZCZUK, Paul (20th C) Austrian					
3D	1	2,288		2,288	
TERESZCZUK, Peter (fl.1895-1925) Austrian					
3D	1	1,585		1,585	
TERLIKOWSKI, Vladimir de (1873-1951) Polish					
oil	12	29,807	1,194	2,128	4,716
TERLOUW, Kees (1890-1948) Dutch					
oil	5	8,440	1,313	1,902	1,902
TERMOTE, Albert (1887-?) Dutch					
3D	1	1,723		1,723	
TERNANTE-LEMAIRE, Amedee de (19th C) French					
oil	1	3,438		3,438	
TERNI, A L (?) Italian					
oil	3	5,513	1,299	1,662	2,552
TERPNING, Howard A (1927-) American					
oil	6	488,000	3,000	85,000	130,000
wc/d	1	1,600		1,600	
TERPNING, Susan (20th C) American					
oil	1	10,000		10,000	
TERRADES, Matias (1903-) Spanish					
oil	1	2,964		2,964	
TERRIS, John (1865-1914) British					
oil	1	2,370		2,370	
wc/d	1	3,950		3,950	
TERRUELLA, Joaquim (1891-1957) Spanish					
oil	11	62,922	1,056	2,420	18,284
TERRUSO, Saverio (1939-) Italian					
oil	17	27,923	1,017	1,408	2,938
TERRY, Henry (fl.1879-1920) British					
wc/d	2	2,765	1,027	1,383	1,738
TERRY, Joseph Alfred (1872-1939) British					
oil	1	1,008		1,008	
TERWEI, Wilhelm (1875-1946) German?					
oil	2	2,354	1,079	1,177	1,275
TERWESTEN, Augustin (17/18th C) Dutch					
oil	1	12,960		12,960	
TERWESTEN, Matheus (1670-1757) Dutch					
oil	1	3,685		3,685	
TERWEY, Jan Pieter (1883-1965) Dutch					
oil	2	2,098	1,049	1,049	1,049
TESHIGAHARA, Sofu (1900-) Japanese					
wc/d	3	15,227	2,155	5,150	7,922
TESSIER, Pierre-Léon (19th C) French					
oil	1	4,361		4,361	
TESSON, Louis (19th C) French					
wc/d	1	1,365		1,365	
TESTAS, Willem de Famars (1834-1896) Dutch					
oil	1	1,477		1,477	

Name	No.	Total Sales Value	lowest	Prices median	highest
wc/d	1	1,358		1,358	
TESTI, Arnolfo (1913-) Italian					
oil	1	2,217		2,217	
TESTU, Pierre (19/20th C) French					
oil	3	5,065	1,560	1,804	1,804
TETAR VAN ELVEN (19/20th C) Dutch					
oil	1	2,385		2,385	
TETAR VAN ELVEN, Jan Baptist (1805-1889) Dutch					
oil	1	2,487		2,487	
TETAR VAN ELVEN, Pierre Henri Theodore (1828-1908) Dutch					
oil	1	33,000		33,000	
wc/d	1	3,375		3,375	
TEUCHERT, Karoly (1886-1926) Hungarian					
oil	1	8,880		8,880	
TEUFNER, Gustav (19th C) ?					
oil	1	2,708		2,708	
TEUPKEN, D A (19th C) Dutch					
wc/d	1	1,907		1,907	
TEUSCH, Dieter (1940-) German					
3D	1	1,699		1,699	
TEVET, Nachum (1946-) Israeli					
3D	1	10,000		10,000	
TEW, Justin (1969-) British					
oil	2	2,678	1,258	1,339	1,420
TEXIER, Richard (1955-) French					
oil	1	7,302		7,302	
wc/d	1	1,069		1,069	
THABARD, Adolphe Martial (1831-1905) French					
3D	2	5,324	2,178	2,662	3,146
THAETER, Julius Caesar (1804-1870) German					
wc/d	1	1,229		1,229	
THALINGER, E Oscar (1885-?) American					
oil	1	2,800		2,800	
THAMM, Adolf (1859-1925) German					
oil	1	1,294		1,294	
THANS, G (19th C) Dutch					
oil	1	1,067		1,067	
THARRATS, Juan Jose (1918-) Spanish					
oil	2	2,340	1,160	1,170	1,180
THAULOW, Fritz (1847-1906) Norwegian					
oil	9	340,389	1,195	25,271	170,640
wc/d	1	32,997		32,997	
THAXTER, Edward R (?-1881) American					
3D	1	1,400		1,400	
THAYAHT, Ernesto (1893-1959) Italian					
wc/d	1	1,671		1,671	
THAYER, Abbott H (1849-1921) American					
oil	1	2,200		2,200	
THEED, William (younger) (1804-1891) British					
3D	1	2,302		2,302	
THEGERSTROM, Robert (1857-1919) Swedish					
oil	1	1,749		1,749	
wc/d	1	2,494		2,494	
THELANDER, Par Gunnar (1936-) Swedish					
oil	5	17,390	1,583	2,613	5,460
THELIE, Georges (19/20th C) German					
oil	1	2,431		2,431	
THELIN, Janine (1916-) Swiss					
oil	1	1,516		1,516	

Name	No.	Total Sales Value	lowest	Prices median	highest
THELWELL, Norman (1923-) British					
wc/d	3	4,812	1,275	1,287	2,250
THEODORE, Gerard (1829-1895) Belgian					
oil	1	6,057		6,057	
THEOFILOS (1867-1934) Greek					
oil	1	7,300		7,300	
THERIAT, Charles James (1860-1934) American					
oil	2	13,084	5,500	6,542	7,584
THERKILDSEN, Michael (1850-1925) Danish					
oil	1	1,937		1,937	
THERRIEN, Robert (1947-) American					
3D	1	55,000		55,000	
wc/d	1	4,500		4,500	
THESSEL, Anton Moritz (1830-1873) German					
oil	1	1,450		1,450	
THEUNINCK, Walter (1941-) Belgian					
oil	1	1,068		1,068	
THEUS, Jeremiah (1720-1774) American					
oil	2	41,040	4,800	20,520	36,240
THEVENET (?) ?					
oil	1	1,378		1,378	
THEVENET, Louis (1874-1930) Belgian					
oil	9	69,937	1,927	6,644	20,039
THEVENET, Pierre (1870-1937) Belgian					
oil	2	2,512	1,142	1,256	1,370
THEYS, Ivan (1936-) Belgian					
oil	2	5,807	2,790	2,904	3,017
THIBAULT, Jean Thomas (1757-1826) French					
wc/d	1	2,084		2,084	
THIBESART, Raymond (1874-?) French					
oil	1	1,222		1,222	
THIBON DE LIBIAN, Valentin (1889-1931) Argentinian					
oil	1	170,000		170,000	
THIEBAUD, Wayne (1920-) American					
oil	5	1,260,000	80,000	280,000	350,000
wc/d	3	112,000	8,000	14,000	90,000
THIELEMANN, Alfred (1883-?) German					
oil	1	1,341		1,341	
THIELEN, Jan Philips van (1618-1667) Flemish					
oil	3	180,713	11,429	44,334	124,950
THIELER, Fred (1916-1999) German					
oil	5	28,995	2,913	5,809	8,192
wc/d	12	60,557	1,366	4,373	13,067
THIEMANN, Carl (1881-1966) German					
wc/d	1	1,365		1,365	
THIEME, Anthony (1888-1954) American/Dutch					
oil	12	150,400	5,400	10,000	28,000
wc/d	2	3,600	1,700	1,800	1,900
THIEME, Theodor (1823-1901) German					
oil	1	1,208		1,208	
THIEMER, Ivan (20th C) ?					
3D	1	6,390		6,390	
THIER, Barend Hendrik (1751-1814) Dutch					
oil	2	5,667	1,257	2,834	4,410
THIERRY, Joseph François Desire (1812-1866) French					
wc/d	1	9,698		9,698	
THIERSCH, Ludwig (1825-1909) German					
oil	1	1,811		1,811	

Name	No.	Total Sales Value	lowest	Prices median	highest
THIJSEN, Carolus Johannes (1867-1917) Dutch					
oil	1	2,581		2,581	
THIRION, Victor Charles (1833-1878) French					
oil	2	51,091	21,091	25,546	30,000
THIRTLE, John (1777-1839) British					
wc/d	2	13,013	2,717	6,507	10,296
THOLEN, Willem Bastiaan (1860-1931) Dutch					
oil	16	51,458	1,224	1,904	19,129
wc/d	2	11,979	4,143	5,990	7,836
THOLENAAR, Theodore Ludwig (19th C) Dutch/French					
3D	1	1,442		1,442	
THOLER, Raymond (1859-?) French					
oil	1	6,000		6,000	
THOM, J C (1835-1898) American					
oil	1	15,000		15,000	
THOM, James Crawford (1835-1898) American					
oil	3	10,980	1,700	4,530	4,750
wc/d	1	1,800		1,800	
THOMA, Emil (1869-?) Swiss					
oil	1	1,002		1,002	
THOMA, H (1839-1924) German					
oil	1	1,000		1,000	
THOMA, Hans (1839-1924) German					
oil	8	109,496	4,903	10,633	23,924
wc/d	4	5,034	1,040	1,175	1,644
THOMA, Josef (1828-1899) Austrian					
oil	11	25,378	1,210	2,245	4,705
THOMA-HOEFELE, Carl (1866-1923) Swiss					
oil	1	2,564		2,564	
THOMAS, A (19/20th C) American					
oil	1	1,168		1,168	
THOMAS, Alma Woolsey (1896-1978) American					
oil	1	26,000		26,000	
THOMAS, Charles (1857-1892) French					
oil	1	7,000		7,000	
THOMAS, David (?) British					
oil	1	3,432		3,432	
THOMAS, Fanny E (fl.1880) British					
wc/d	1	1,463		1,463	
THOMAS, Henri Joseph (1878-1972) Belgian					
oil	9	53,415	1,157	1,911	28,686
wc/d	1	1,420		1,420	
THOMAS, M (?) ?					
oil	1	4,077		4,077	
THOMAS, Margaret (1916-) British					
oil	3	3,987	1,184	1,425	1,425
THOMAS, Mark (19/20th C) Belgian					
3D	1	1,974		1,974	
THOMAS, Norman Millet (1915-) American					
oil	1	1,800		1,800	
THOMAS, Paul (1859-?) French					
oil	1	1,100		1,100	
THOMAS, Pieter Hendrik (1814-1866) Dutch					
oil	2	4,597	1,057	2,299	3,540
THOMAS, Robert Strickland (1787-1853) British					
oil	2	21,510	10,010	10,755	11,500
THOMAS, Stephen Seymour (1868-1956) American					
oil	1	1,100		1,100	

Name	No.	Total Sales Value	Prices lowest	median	highest
THOMAS, T (19th C) British					
oil	1	1,200		1,200	
THOMAS, Thomas (19th C) British					
oil	1	3,171		3,171	
THOMAS, William Barton (1877-1947) British					
wc/d	1	1,264		1,264	
THOMASCH (?) ?					
3D	1	1,012		1,012	
THOMASSIN, Desire (1858-1933) Austrian					
oil	21	84,922	1,246	3,864	9,470
THOME, Verner (1878-1953) Finnish					
oil	1	1,538		1,538	
THOMING, Frederik Christian (1802-1873) Danish					
oil	2	16,541	4,984	8,271	11,557
THOMIRE, Pierre Philippe (1751-1843) French					
3D	1	8,000		8,000	
THOMKINS, Andre (1930-1985) Swiss					
3D	1	1,215		1,215	
oil	1	2,214		2,214	
wc/d	2	2,310	1,155	1,155	1,155
THOMON, Thomas de (1754-1813) French					
wc/d	1	1,397		1,397	
THOMOPOULOS, Epaminondas (1878-1974) Greek					
oil	2	24,510	5,530	12,255	18,980
THOMPSON, Albert (1853-?) American					
oil	1	3,000		3,000	
THOMPSON, Bob (1937-1966) American					
oil	4	56,200	4,200	13,000	26,000
THOMPSON, Edward H (1866-1949) British					
wc/d	12	17,970	1,027	1,351	2,492
THOMPSON, G (?) ?					
oil	2	2,335	1,057	1,168	1,278
THOMPSON, Harry (19th C) British					
oil	1	7,000		7,000	
THOMPSON, Kim (1963-) British					
oil	1	2,130		2,130	
THOMPSON, Mark (1812-1875) British					
oil	1	9,940		9,940	
THOMPSON, Ralph (20th C) British					
wc/d	1	1,480		1,480	
THOMPSON, Steve (20th C) British					
oil	1	1,036		1,036	
THOMPSON, Tim (20th C) British					
oil	2	7,264	2,700	3,632	4,564
THOMS, Ernst (20th C) German					
wc/d	1	1,553		1,553	
THOMSEN, August Carl Wilhelm (1813-1886) Danish					
oil	1	7,481		7,481	
THOMSEN, Carl (1847-1912) Danish					
oil	1	1,269		1,269	
THOMSEN, Emma Augusta (1822-1897) Danish					
oil	3	41,429	1,420	3,485	36,524
THOMSEN, F G (1819-1891) Danish					
oil	1	1,818		1,818	
THOMSEN, Frederik Gotfred (1819-1891) Danish					
oil	1	6,320		6,320	
THOMSEN, Jorgen (1905-1959) Danish					
oil	1	1,586		1,586	

Name	No.	Total Sales Value	lowest	Prices median	highest
THOMSEN, Pauline (1858-1931) Danish					
oil	1	1,810		1,810	
THOMSEN, René (1897-1976) French					
oil	1	3,245		3,245	
THOMSON OF DUDDINGTON, Rev John (1778-1840) British					
oil	2	3,430	1,110	1,715	2,320
THOMSON, Adam Bruce (1885-1976) British					
oil	2	13,050	5,800	6,525	7,250
wc/d	1	3,675		3,675	
THOMSON, Captain (19th C) British					
oil	1	3,020		3,020	
THOMSON, Carl Christian Frederik Jakob (1847-1912) Danish					
oil	3	5,040	1,071	1,110	2,859
THOMSON, George (1868-1965) Canadian					
oil	1	1,240		1,240	
THOMSON, Henry (1773-1843) British					
oil	1	7,399		7,399	
THOMSON, Henry Grinnell (1850-1939) American					
oil	1	1,000		1,000	
THOMSON, I Beatrice (20th C) ?					
oil	1	1,065		1,065	
THOMSON, John Murray (1885-1974) British					
oil	1	1,200		1,200	
THOMSON, Tom (1877-1917) Canadian					
oil	3	133,950	21,125	53,094	59,731
THOMSON, William (1927-1990) British					
oil	1	1,306		1,306	
THON, William (1916-) American					
oil	1	4,500		4,500	
THONY, Eduard (1866-1950) German					
oil	1	1,268		1,268	
wc/d	9	13,859	1,138	1,650	2,280
THONY, Wilhelm (1888-1949) Austrian					
3D	1	40,909		40,909	
oil	1	56,741		56,741	
wc/d	4	36,165	2,184	6,178	21,626
THORAK, Josef (1889-1952) Austrian					
3D	2	4,457	1,384	2,229	3,073
THORBURN, Archibald (1860-1935) British					
wc/d	61	891,581	1,144	12,640	71,040
THOREL, F (19th C) French					
oil	1	3,097		3,097	
THOREN, Esaias (1901-1981) Swedish					
oil	28	61,346	1,005	1,633	7,425
wc/d	3	7,935	1,134	1,783	5,018
THOREN, Otto von (1828-1889) Austrian					
oil	1	2,179		2,179	
THORENFELD, Anton Erik (1839-1907) Danish					
oil	2	3,516	1,083	1,758	2,433
THORLAKSON, Benedikt Thoarinn Benedikt (1867-1924) Icelandic					
oil	1	1,740		1,740	
THORLEIFSSON, Jon (1891-1961) Icelandic					
oil	1	1,507		1,507	
THORN PRIKKER, Jan (1868-1932) Dutch					
oil	1	4,870		4,870	
THORNAM, Emmy (1852-1935) Danish					
oil	2	2,341	1,134	1,171	1,207
THORNAM, Ludovica (1853-1896) Danish					
oil	1	2,324		2,324	

Name	No.	Total Sales Value	lowest	Prices median	highest
THORNE, Alfred (1850-1916) Swedish					
oil	5	10,351	1,099	2,201	3,216
THORNE, Angela (1911-) British					
oil	2	2,030	1,015	1,015	1,015
THORNHILL, Sir James (1675-1734) British					
wc/d	1	1,738		1,738	
THORNLEY, Hubert (19th C) British					
oil	4	14,674	1,885	3,787	5,216
THORNLEY, T (?) ?					
oil	1	1,288		1,288	
THORNLEY, William (19/20th C) British					
oil	40	183,663	1,001	3,900	13,050
wc/d	1	2,791		2,791	
THORNTON, R (?) British?					
wc/d	1	2,000		2,000	
THORNYCROFT, Ann (20th C) American					
oil	1	1,500		1,500	
THORNYCROFT, Hamo (1850-1925) British					
3D	4	28,623	2,100	7,749	11,025
THORRESTRUP, Christian (1823-1892) Danish					
oil	1	1,013		1,013	
THORS, J (19th C) British					
oil	1	1,058		1,058	
THORS, Joseph (fl.1863-1900) British					
oil	30	102,985	1,022	2,700	10,440
THORSTEINSSON, Gudmundur (1891-1924) Icelandic					
oil	2	4,498	1,558	2,249	2,940
THORVALDSEN, Bertel (1770-1844) Danish					
3D	2	3,484	1,160	1,742	2,324
THRASHER, Leslie (1889-1936) American					
oil	1	4,250		4,250	
THUILLIER, Pierre (1799-1858) French					
oil	1	10,220		10,220	
THULDEN, Theodor van (1606-1669) Dutch					
oil	1	21,140		21,140	
wc/d	1	2,000		2,000	
THULIN, Carl (1748-1808) Swedish					
wc/d	1	1,524		1,524	
THULSTRUP, William August (19th C) Danish					
wc/d	1	5,145		5,145	
THUMANN, Paul (1834-1908) German					
oil	1	1,658		1,658	
THUNMAN, Olof (1879-1944) Swedish					
wc/d	1	2,380		2,380	
THURAU, Friedrich (?-1888) German					
oil	1	8,665		8,665	
THURBER, James Grover (1894-1961) American					
wc/d	3	15,500	2,000	6,500	7,000
THURLBY, Frank (20th C) British?					
oil	1	4,004		4,004	
THURM, Willy (1880-1964) German					
oil	1	2,119		2,119	
THURMER, Joseph (1789-1833) German					
wc/d	2	10,201	4,534	5,101	5,667
THURNER, Gabriel Edouard (1840-1907) French					
oil	1	2,857		2,857	
THURSZ, Frederic Matys (1930-1992) German					
oil	1	56,227		56,227	

Name	No.	Total Sales Value	lowest	Prices median	highest
THYS, Gaston (1863-1893) French					
oil	1	1,600		1,600	
THYS, Susy Kathy (1936-) Swiss					
oil	1	1,166		1,166	
THYSEBAERT, Émile (1873-1962) Belgian					
oil	1	1,452		1,452	
TIBBLE, Geoffrey (1909-1952) British					
oil	1	3,925		3,925	
TIBETAN SCHOOL					
3D	1	22,614		22,614	
TIBETAN SCHOOL, 17th C					
wc/d	1	9,641		9,641	
TIBETAN SCHOOL, 18th C					
3D	1	4,241		4,241	
TIBETAN SCHOOL, 18th/19th C					
3D	2	83,135	3,135	41,568	80,000
TICHO, Anna (1894-1980) Israeli					
wc/d	4	43,361	2,361	9,500	22,000
TIDEMAND, Adolph (1814-1876) Norwegian					
oil	4	203,998	8,642	41,680	111,997
TIDEY, Alfred (1808-1892) British					
wc/d	1	1,060		1,060	
TIECHE, Adolf (1877-1957) Swiss					
wc/d	1	1,242		1,242	
TIEDJEN, Willy (1881-1950) German					
oil	6	9,658	1,240	1,551	2,151
TIEL, Quiryn Martinus Adrianus van (1900-1967) Dutch					
oil	2	7,867	2,717	3,934	5,150
TIELEMANS, Louis (1826-1856) Belgian					
oil	1	1,000		1,000	
TIEPOLO, Giovanni Battista (1696-1770) Italian					
oil	4	4,110,524	160,524	975,000	2,000,000
wc/d	19	504,354	1,700	9,815	100,000
TIEPOLO, Giovanni Domenico (1727-1804) Italian					
oil	3	370,120	48,320	48,320	271,800
wc/d	8	135,241	3,709	12,040	65,000
TIESENHAUSEN, Paul (1837-1876) German					
oil	1	1,966		1,966	
TIFFANY, Louis Comfort (1848-1933) American					
oil	1	55,000		55,000	
TIGER, Frans Johan (1849-1919) Finnish					
oil	1	1,813		1,813	
TIKHMENOV, Efim (19/20th C) Russian					
oil	1	4,228		4,228	
TILBORCH, Gillis van (c.1625-1678) Flemish					
oil	2	45,240	15,840	22,620	29,400
TILEMAN-PETERSEN, Christian (1874-1926) Danish					
oil	1	1,008		1,008	
TILL, Johann (jnr) (1827-1894) Austrian					
oil	1	1,475		1,475	
TILLBERG, Peter (1946-) Swedish					
oil	2	4,817	1,204	2,409	3,613
TILLEMANS, Peter (1684-1734) Flemish					
oil	4	79,233	4,832	13,201	48,000
TILSON, Joe (1928-) British					
oil	2	6,050	2,500	3,025	3,550
wc/d	1	5,436		5,436	
TIMEN, Frans (1883-1968) Swedish					
oil	1	1,345		1,345	

Name	No.	Total Sales Value	lowest	Prices median	highest
TIMMERMAHN (1942-) Swiss					
wc/d	1	1,066		1,066	
TIMMERMAHN, Peter Klein (1942-) Swiss					
oil	1	1,003		1,003	
TIMMERMANS, H (1858-1942) Belgian					
oil	2	4,878	2,069	2,439	2,809
TIMMERMANS, Jean (1899-1986) Belgian					
oil	1	4,861		4,861	
TIMMERMANS, Louis (1846-1910) French					
oil	7	31,873	1,000	3,407	8,760
TIMPE, Wil (1920-) American					
oil	2	4,250	1,500	2,125	2,750
TIMYM, William (20th C) British					
3D	1	1,136		1,136	
TINAYRE, Louis (1861-?) French					
oil	1	1,141		1,141	
TINDLE, David (1932-) British					
oil	7	19,346	1,080	1,800	6,300
wc/d	1	2,698		2,698	
TINEL, Pieter Frans (1895-1964) Belgian					
3D	1	1,065		1,065	
TING, Walasse (1929-1998) Chinese					
oil	5	18,055	2,694	2,789	5,381
wc/d	9	31,963	1,609	2,234	8,190
TINGQUA (fl.1840-1870) Chinese					
wc/d	1	1,600		1,600	
TINGUELY, Jean (1925-1991) Swiss					
3D	3	33,334	3,083	14,610	15,641
oil	7	34,734	2,057	4,144	9,717
wc/d	19	77,781	1,003	2,842	10,610
TINGUELY, Jean and AEPPLI, Eva (20th C) Swiss/French					
3D	1	7,258		7,258	
TINGUELY, Jean and SAINT PHALLE, Niki de (20th C) Swiss/American					
wc/d	1	1,121		1,121	
TINN, E T (19th C) British					
oil	1	1,198		1,198	
TINTHOFF, M (19th C) Swiss?					
oil	1	4,245		4,245	
TINTORETTO (school) (16/17th C) Italian					
oil	1	2,218		2,218	
TINTORETTO, Domenico (1560-1635) Italian					
oil	3	50,082	9,312	18,120	22,650
TINTORETTO, Jacopo (1518-1594) Italian					
oil	1	105,700		105,700	
TIPPETT, William Vivian (1833-1910) British					
oil	3	5,031	1,027	1,859	2,145
TIRADO Y CARDONA, Fernando (1862-1907) Spanish					
oil	1	1,918		1,918	
TIRATELLI, Aurelio (1842-1900) Italian					
oil	1	3,273		3,273	
TIRATELLI, Cesare (1864-1933) Italian					
oil	5	61,002	1,098	1,222	55,000
TIRAVANIJA, Rirkrit (1961-) American					
wc/d	1	8,000		8,000	
TIREFORT, J E (20th C) American?					
oil	1	3,700		3,700	
TIRELLI, Marco (1956-) Italian					
wc/d	2	3,323	1,359	1,662	1,964

Name	No.	Total Sales Value	lowest	Prices median	highest
TIREN, Gerda (1858-1928) Swedish					
wc/d	1	3,047		3,047	
TIREN, Johan (1853-1911) Swedish					
oil	3	17,894	3,942	5,913	8,039
wc/d	3	8,246	1,749	1,975	4,522
TIREN, Nils (1885-1935) Swedish					
wc/d	1	2,914		2,914	
TIRINNANZI, Nino (1923-) Italian					
oil	2	2,502	1,224	1,251	1,278
TIRONI, Francesco (?-1800) Italian					
oil	1	50,501		50,501	
wc/d	2	36,345	14,345	18,173	22,000
TISCHBEIN, Anton (1730-1804) German					
oil	2	57,870	12,570	28,935	45,300
TISCHBEIN, Anton Johann (1720-1784) German					
oil	1	3,168		3,168	
TISCHBEIN, Jakob (1725-1791) German					
oil	1	7,744		7,744	
TISCHBEIN, Johann Friedrich August (1750-1812) German					
oil	3	27,302	3,596	3,706	20,000
TISCHBEIN, Johann Heinrich (18th C) German					
wc/d	1	1,709		1,709	
TISCHBEIN, Johann Heinrich (elder) (1722-1789) German					
wc/d	3	4,171	1,229	1,471	1,471
TISCHBEIN, Johann Heinrich (younger) (1742-1808) German					
oil	1	9,727		9,727	
wc/d	1	1,229		1,229	
TISCHBEIN, Johann Heinrich Wilhelm (1751-1829) German					
wc/d	6	17,573	1,748	2,573	4,466
TISCHLER, Victor (1890-1951) Austrian					
oil	1	1,422		1,422	
TISIO, Benvenuto da Garofalo (1481-1559) Italian					
oil	1	60,400		60,400	
TISSOT, James Jacques Joseph (1836-1902) French					
oil	5	46,410	4,655	7,901	14,300
TITCOMB, Mary Bradish (1858-1927) American					
oil	1	20,000		20,000	
TITIAN (c.1488-1576) Italian					
oil	3	3,382,307	2,664	57,643	3,322,000
TITO, Ettore (1859-1941) Italian					
oil	3	51,628	15,272	17,308	19,048
TITUS, Earle A (20th C) American					
oil	1	1,300		1,300	
TITUS-CARMEL, Gerard (1942-) French					
oil	2	2,795	1,157	1,398	1,638
wc/d	2	5,202	2,190	2,601	3,012
TIVOLI, Serafino de (1826-1892) Italian					
oil	1	25,740		25,740	
TIXIER, Daniel (19/20th C) French					
oil	1	11,600		11,600	
TOBEEN, Felix-Elie (1880-1938) French					
oil	3	8,654	1,741	1,741	5,172
TOBEY, Mark (1890-1976) American					
oil	10	104,108	1,499	8,792	27,866
wc/d	14	81,657	1,408	5,032	12,000
TOBIASSE (?) ?					
oil	1	2,255		2,255	
TOBIASSE, Theo (1927-) Israeli					
oil	17	106,184	1,782	3,685	18,836
wc/d	11	35,358	1,038	2,137	7,256

Name	No.	Total Sales Value	Prices lowest	median	highest
TOBLER, Verena (20th C) Swiss					
oil	1	1,133		1,133	
TOCQUE, Louis (1696-1772) French					
oil	4	123,647	7,274	20,364	75,645
wc/d	1	8,024		8,024	
TOD, Joanne (20th C) Canadian					
wc/d	1	1,069		1,069	
TOD, Richard (fl.1901-1917) British					
oil	1	2,720		2,720	
TODD, Arthur Ralph Middleton (1891-c.1967) British					
oil	1	1,305		1,305	
TODD, Henry George (1846-1898) British					
oil	6	23,840	1,027	3,358	9,425
TODD, John George (fl.1875-1900) British					
oil	1	2,857		2,857	
TODD, R H (18th C) ?					
wc/d	2	3,002	1,501	1,501	1,501
TODD, Ralph (1856-1932) British					
oil	1	18,000		18,000	
wc/d	4	11,525	1,103	2,886	4,650
TODE, Knut Gustaf Waldemar (1859-1900) Swedish					
oil	1	1,973		1,973	
TODE, Waldemar (1859-1900) French					
oil	1	2,320		2,320	
TODESCHINI, Lucio (1892-1969) Italian					
oil	3	11,663	1,497	4,621	5,545
TODHUNTER, Francis Augustus (1884-1963) American					
oil	3	5,500	1,700	1,800	2,000
TOECHE, Karl Friedrich (1814-1890) German					
oil	1	1,632		1,632	
TOFANARI, Sirio (1886-?) Italian					
3D	2	17,505	8,085	8,753	9,420
TOFANO, Edouardo (1838-1920) Italian					
oil	2	45,623	17,623	22,812	28,000
wc/d	2	11,588	5,056	5,794	6,532
TOFFOLI (1907-1999) French					
oil	3	10,913	2,281	4,058	4,574
TOFFOLI, Louis (1907-1999) French					
oil	21	146,671	1,605	7,316	13,024
wc/d	7	20,976	1,012	2,394	5,317
TOFT, Albert (1862-1949) British					
3D	1	1,276		1,276	
TOGNI, Edoardo (1884-1962) Italian					
oil	1	5,099		5,099	
TOGORES, Jose de (1893-1970) Spanish					
oil	5	48,079	5,603	9,565	14,118
TOJETTI, Eduardo (1851-1930) American					
oil	2	3,800	1,400	1,900	2,400
TOJETTI, Virgilio (1851-1901) American					
oil	1	3,000		3,000	
TOJNER, Vibeke (20th C) ?					
oil	1	1,690		1,690	
TOL, Dominicus van (1635-1676) Dutch					
oil	2	77,704	9,905	38,852	67,799
TOLEDO, Alvaro (1965-) Spanish					
oil	1	1,263		1,263	
TOLEDO, Francisco (1940-) Mexican					
oil	1	400,000		400,000	
wc/d	14	330,300	1,200	22,000	75,000

Name	No.	Total Sales Value	lowest	Prices median	highest
TOLL, Emma (1847-1917) Swedish					
oil	1	2,691		2,691	
TOLLEY, Edward (fl.1848-1867) British					
oil	1	5,100		5,100	
TOLLIN, Ferdinand (1807-c.1860) Swedish					
wc/d	1	2,847		2,847	
TOM, Jan Bedys (1813-1894) Dutch					
oil	1	4,668		4,668	
wc/d	1	2,984		2,984	
TOM-PETERSEN, Peter (1861-1926) Danish					
oil	11	23,662	1,013	1,816	7,100
TOMA, Matthias Rudolf (1792-1869) Austrian					
oil	2	14,952	4,984	7,476	9,968
TOMANECK, Joseph (1889-?) American					
oil	4	8,900	1,800	2,200	2,700
TOMASELLI, Fred (1956-) American?					
3D	1	5,500		5,500	
oil	1	17,000		17,000	
TOMASELLO, Luis (1915-) Argentinian					
3D	1	1,211		1,211	
oil	1	2,066		2,066	
TOMEA, Fiorenzo (1910-1960) Italian					
oil	14	110,227	2,411	6,632	29,117
wc/d	1	1,309		1,309	
TOMEK (20th C) ?					
3D	1	1,455		1,455	
TOMINETTI, Achille (1848-1917) Italian					
oil	2	27,262	9,796	13,631	17,466
TOMINZ, Alfredo (1854-1936) Italian					
oil	1	7,089		7,089	
TOMKINS, William (1730-1792) British					
oil	1	31,710		31,710	
TOMLIN, Bradley Walker (1899-1953) American					
wc/d	1	7,500		7,500	
TOMMASI FERRONI, Riccardo (1934-2000) Italian					
oil	2	4,625	1,047	2,313	3,578
wc/d	1	1,456		1,456	
TOMMASI, Adolfo (1851-1933) Italian					
oil	2	21,962	8,584	10,981	13,378
TOMMASI, Angiolo (1858-1923) Italian					
oil	2	39,629	1,926	19,815	37,703
TOMMASI, Ghigo (1906-) Italian					
oil	1	1,077		1,077	
TOMMASI, Ludovico (1866-1941) Italian					
oil	9	26,090	1,331	2,440	6,653
wc/d	1	1,481		1,481	
TOMMASO (?) Italian					
oil	2	104,150	38,000	52,075	66,150
TOMME, Luca di (1330-1389) Italian					
oil	2	468,100	181,200	234,050	286,900
TOMSON, Clifton (1775-1828) British					
oil	1	2,145		2,145	
TONDINE, S (20th C) French?					
3D	1	2,062		2,062	
TONGE, Lammert van der (1871-1937) Dutch					
oil	3	9,896	1,600	2,052	6,244
TONGE, Robert (1823-1856) British					
oil	2	2,686	1,027	1,343	1,659
TONGEREN, Jan van (1897-1991) Dutch					
oil	3	29,529	3,169	4,808	21,552

Name	No.	Total Sales Value	lowest	Prices median	highest
TONK, Ernest (1889-1968) American					
oil	1	3,250		3,250	
wc/d	1	3,750		3,750	
TONKISS, Sam (20th C) British					
3D	1	4,740		4,740	
TONKS, Henry (1862-1937) British					
wc/d	1	2,844		2,844	
TONNANCOUR, Jacques de (1917-) Canadian					
oil	2	15,032	2,239	7,516	12,793
wc/d	2	2,788	1,062	1,394	1,726
TOORENVLIET, Jacob (1635-1719) Dutch					
oil	4	27,309	1,514	6,612	12,571
TOOROP, Charley (1891-1955) Dutch					
oil	2	213,362	15,086	106,681	198,276
TOOROP, Jan Th (1858-1928) Dutch					
oil	1	5,942		5,942	
wc/d	11	80,809	1,221	3,512	41,380
TOOTHAKER, Victor (?) American?					
wc/d	1	3,500		3,500	
TOPFFER, Adam (1766-1847) Swiss					
oil	1	47,154		47,154	
wc/d	2	11,055	3,884	5,528	7,171
TOPHAM, F W (1808-1877) British					
wc/d	3	11,963	1,233	3,335	7,395
TOPHAM, Francis William (1808-1877) British					
wc/d	1	2,700		2,700	
TOPHAM, Frank William Warwick (1838-1929) British					
oil	3	19,734	2,829	4,905	12,000
wc/d	1	2,250		2,250	
TOPKE, Dirk Antoon (jnr) (1828-1859) Dutch					
wc/d	3	7,463	2,160	2,357	2,946
TOPLIS, William A (fl.1875-1922) British					
wc/d	3	14,182	3,996	4,710	5,476
TOPOLSKI, Feliks (1907-1989) Polish					
wc/d	3	3,918	1,106	1,264	1,548
TOPOLSKI, Maciej (1907-1990) Polish					
oil	1	3,000		3,000	
TOPOR, Roland (1938-1997) French					
wc/d	2	2,125	1,059	1,063	1,066
TOPP, Arnold (1887-1945) German					
oil	2	97,815	33,981	48,908	63,834
wc/d	1	8,218		8,218	
TOPPELIUS, Woldemar (1858-1933) Russian					
oil	3	3,801	1,170	1,303	1,328
TORAL, Cristobal (1938-) Spanish					
oil	2	29,883	14,146	14,942	15,737
wc/d	3	8,079	2,498	2,806	2,806
TORDOIRE, Narcisse (1954-) Belgian					
oil	1	1,379		1,379	
TORELLI, L (19th C) Italian					
3D	1	1,467		1,467	
TORHAMN, Gunnar (1894-1955) Swedish					
oil	10	22,065	1,082	2,160	3,931
TORNA, Oscar (1842-1894) Swedish					
oil	7	16,974	1,206	1,318	8,831
TORNABUONI, Lorenzo (1934-) Italian					
oil	2	2,967	1,134	1,484	1,833
wc/d	1	1,222		1,222	
TORNAI, Gyula (1861-1928) Hungarian					
oil	5	151,627	4,339	7,975	119,415

Name	No.	Total Sales Value	lowest	Prices median	highest
TORNE ESQUIUS, Pere (1879-1936) Spanish					
oil	2	6,201	1,630	3,101	4,571
TORNEMAN, Axel (1880-1925) Swedish					
oil	2	14,196	3,276	7,098	10,920
TORNIOLI, Niccolo (17th C) Italian					
oil	1	25,878		25,878	
TORNOE, Wenzel (1844-1907) Danish					
oil	4	21,001	1,906	6,212	6,708
TORONI, Niele (1937-) French					
oil	2	17,277	7,974	8,639	9,303
TORRE, Flaminio (1621-1661) Italian					
oil	1	20,000		20,000	
TORRE, Giulio del (1856-1932) Italian					
oil	2	4,839	1,884	2,420	2,955
TORRE, Martin Nestor Fernandez de la (1888-1938) Spanish					
oil	1	9,142		9,142	
wc/d	2	10,176	3,816	5,088	6,360
TORRE, S del (19th C) ?					
oil	1	5,181		5,181	
TORREGIANI, Bartolomeo (1590-c.1675) Italian					
oil	2	25,844	9,268	12,922	16,576
TORRES FUSTER, Antonio (1874-1945) Spanish					
oil	3	24,660	1,687	3,260	19,713
TORRES MARTINEZ, Manuel (1901-1995) Spanish					
oil	1	1,738		1,738	
TORRES, Augusto (1913-1992) Uruguayan					
oil	10	39,400	2,400	3,950	5,800
TORRES, Horacio (1924-1976) Uruguayan					
oil	2	6,450	2,150	3,225	4,300
TORRES-GARCIA, Joaquin (1874-1949) Uruguayan					
oil	8	414,153	2,346	23,409	172,571
wc/d	5	63,378	6,300	7,788	25,413
TORRESCASSANA, Francisco (1845-1918) Spanish					
oil	1	2,595		2,595	
TORREY, Elliot Bouton (1867-1949) American					
oil	1	2,250		2,250	
TORRIGLIA, Giovanni Battista (1858-1937) Italian					
oil	1	90,000		90,000	
TORRINI, E (19th C) Italian					
oil	1	3,800		3,800	
TORROELLA, Ezequiel (1921-) Spanish					
oil	1	1,298		1,298	
TORSSLOW, Harald (1838-1909) Swedish					
oil	2	5,275	1,759	2,638	3,516
TOSA SCHOOL, 18th/19th C Japanese					
oil	1	4,500		4,500	
TOSCHI, Ermanno (1906-) Italian					
oil	1	3,549		3,549	
TOSI, Arturo (1871-1956) Italian					
oil	15	149,930	1,068	10,676	16,985
TOSINI, Michele (1503-1577) Italian					
oil	2	97,850	45,000	48,925	52,850
TOUCHAGUES, Louis (1893-1974) French					
wc/d	1	2,253		2,253	
TOUDOUZE, Edouard (1848-1907) French					
oil	1	43,000		43,000	
TOUDOUZE, Simon Alexandre (1850-1909) French					
oil	1	2,112		2,112	

Name	No.	Total Sales Value	lowest	Prices median	highest
TOULMOUCHE, Auguste (1829-1890) French					
oil	2	29,490	2,800	14,745	26,690
TOULOUSE-LAUTREC, Henri de (1864-1901) French					
oil	7	15,504,308	59,308	750,000	8,500,000
wc/d	12	577,697	1,748	14,293	280,000
TOUPIN, Fernand (1930-) Canadian					
oil	1	1,460		1,460	
TOURGUENEFF, Pierre Nicolas (1854-1912) Russian/French					
3D	1	1,570		1,570	
TOURILLON, Alfred Edouard (19th C) French					
oil	1	5,250		5,250	
TOURNACHON, Gaspard Felix (1820-1910) French					
wc/d	1	2,182		2,182	
TOURNEMINE, Charles Emile de (1812-1872) Italian					
oil	4	16,030	2,207	3,667	6,490
TOURNES, Étienne (1857-1931) French					
oil	1	2,824		2,824	
TOURNEUX, Eugène (1809-1867) French					
oil	1	1,349		1,349	
TOURSKY, G de (19/20th C) ?					
oil	1	6,200		6,200	
TOUSIGNANT, Claude (1932-) Canadian					
wc/d	1	1,022		1,022	
TOUSSAINT, Fernand (1873-1956) Belgian					
oil	33	267,245	1,088	6,620	25,074
wc/d	4	17,732	1,160	4,005	8,562
TOUTENEL, Lodewijk Jan Petrus (1819-1883) Belgian					
oil	1	1,615		1,615	
TOVAR, Ivan (1942-) Dominican					
oil	4	40,503	2,037	4,233	30,000
TOVEY, Brian (?) British?					
oil	1	3,160		3,160	
TOWN, Harold Barling (1924-1990) Canadian					
oil	2	12,050	5,973	6,025	6,077
wc/d	2	7,560	1,919	3,780	5,641
TOWNE, Charles (1763-1840) British					
oil	11	72,928	1,590	4,740	24,000
TOWNE, Francis (1740-1816) British					
wc/d	1	2,860		2,860	
TOWNLEY, Minnie (fl.1866-1899) British					
oil	1	2,556		2,556	
TOWNSEND, Arthur Louis (fl.1880-1912) British					
oil	2	3,585	1,359	1,793	2,226
TOWNSEND, H William (1940-) Canadian					
oil	1	1,437		1,437	
TOWNSEND, James (?) British					
oil	1	1,752		1,752	
TOXIC (1965-) American					
wc/d	1	1,527		1,527	
TOYEN, Marie Germinova (1902-1980) Czechoslovakian					
oil	1	1,167		1,167	
TOYNBEE, Lawrence L (1922-) British					
oil	1	4,640		4,640	
TOZER, H S (1864-c.1938) British					
wc/d	1	6,996		6,996	
TOZER, H Spernon (1864-c.1938) British					
oil	1	1,988		1,988	
wc/d	5	9,555	1,072	1,977	3,000

Name	No.	Total Sales Value	Prices lowest	median	highest
TOZZI, Mario (1895-1979) Italian					
oil	9	226,914	4,347	26,563	43,102
wc/d	2	6,785	3,076	3,393	3,709
TRACHSEL, Albert (1863-1929) Swiss					
oil	1	2,177		2,177	
wc/d	1	1,129		1,129	
TRAFFELET, Fritz (1897-1954) Swiss					
oil	2	2,437	1,195	1,219	1,242
TRAGARDH, Carl (1861-1899) Swedish					
oil	5	11,834	1,180	2,068	4,450
TRAIES, William (1789-1872) British					
oil	1	7,865		7,865	
TRAMPEDACH, Kurt (1943-) Danish					
3D	1	10,890		10,890	
oil	5	26,537	2,562	6,406	7,047
wc/d	3	11,785	1,511	4,637	5,637
TRAQUAIR, Phoebe Anna (1852-1936) British					
oil	3	38,978	7,268	13,590	18,120
TRATON, Marcel (?) French?					
oil	1	2,909		2,909	
TRAUTMANN, Johann Georg (1713-1769) German					
oil	3	7,925	2,000	2,880	3,045
TRAUTSCHOLD, Carl Friedrich Wilhelm (1815-1877) German					
wc/d	1	6,216		6,216	
TRAUTSCHOLD, Manfred (1854-?) German					
oil	1	14,000		14,000	
TRAUTTWEILLER, Stefanie von (1888-?) German					
oil	1	2,482		2,482	
TRAVER, Marion Gray (1892-?) American					
oil	1	1,400		1,400	
TRAVERSO, Mattia (1885-1956) Italian					
oil	1	1,862		1,862	
TRAVI, Antonio (1608-1665) Italian					
oil	1	5,880		5,880	
TRAVIES, Edouard (1809-?) French					
wc/d	23	119,167	1,975	4,345	10,534
TRAVIS, Paul Bough (1891-1975) American					
wc/d	1	1,200		1,200	
TRAYER, Jules (1824-1908) French					
oil	2	23,930	11,850	11,965	12,080
wc/d	2	3,887	1,422	1,944	2,465
TREACY, Liam (1934-) Irish					
oil	1	1,296		1,296	
TRECCANI, Ernesto (1920-1994) Italian					
oil	8	18,294	1,126	2,356	4,310
wc/d	1	1,347		1,347	
TREMLETT, David (1945-) British					
wc/d	2	10,934	2,862	5,467	8,072
TREMONT, Auguste (1893-?) Luxembourger					
3D	1	20,541		20,541	
TRENTI, Gerolamo (1828-1898) Italian					
oil	2	7,502	3,002	3,751	4,500
TRENTIN, Angelo (1850-1912) Austrian					
oil	1	1,500		1,500	
TRERY, L (19th C) ?					
oil	1	2,282		2,282	
TREU, Catherina (1743-1811) German					
oil	1	25,670		25,670	
TREU, Nicolaus (1734-1786) German					
oil	1	26,261		26,261	

Name	No.	Total Sales Value	Prices lowest	Prices median	Prices highest
TREVELYAN, Julian (1910-1989) British					
oil	15	144,047	1,580	9,000	27,650
wc/d	3	5,083	1,580	1,740	1,763
TREVISANI, Angelo (1669-1753) Italian					
wc/d	1	2,567		2,567	
TREVISANI, Francesco (1656-1746) Italian					
oil	2	39,660	9,420	19,830	30,240
wc/d	1	27,747		27,747	
TREVOR, Edward (19th C) British					
oil	2	9,559	2,175	4,780	7,384
TREVOR, Helen Mabel (1831-1900) British					
wc/d	1	12,080		12,080	
TRIBOUT, G (20th C) French?					
oil	1	5,840		5,840	
TRICKETT, John (1952-) British					
oil	1	1,200		1,200	
TRIEBNER, F P (20th C) German					
oil	1	1,000		1,000	
TRIER, Adeline (fl.1879-1903) British					
oil	1	3,692		3,692	
TRIER, Hann (1915-1999) German					
oil	5	42,689	3,676	7,039	18,914
wc/d	2	3,027	1,081	1,514	1,946
TRIPP, Jan Peter (1945-) German					
wc/d	1	1,708		1,708	
TRIPPEL, Albert Ludwig (1813-1854) German					
oil	1	2,306		2,306	
TRIRUM, Johannes Wouterus van (1924-) Dutch					
oil	1	1,021		1,021	
TRIVIDIC, Pierre le (1898-1960) French					
wc/d	1	1,222		1,222	
TRIVILINI, Armand (20th C) American					
oil	1	1,800		1,800	
TROCKEL, Rosemarie (1952-) German					
3D	1	42,000		42,000	
wc/d	5	31,013	2,047	3,322	19,000
TRODOUX, Henri Émile Adrien (19th C) French					
3D	1	1,300		1,300	
TROFELI, P M (20th C) ?					
3D	1	2,000		2,000	
TROFIMENKO, Boris (1919-) Russian					
oil	2	2,291	1,106	1,146	1,185
TROGER, Paul (1698-1762) Austrian					
wc/d	1	1,655		1,655	
TROIANI, Troiano (1885-1963) Argentinian					
3D	1	2,007		2,007	
TROIVAUX, Jean Baptiste Desire (1788-1860) French					
wc/d	1	1,125		1,125	
TROKES, Heinz (1913-1997) German					
oil	6	26,964	3,783	4,431	5,364
wc/d	3	3,634	1,019	1,196	1,419
TROMBADORI, Francesco (1886-1961) Italian					
oil	1	7,463		7,463	
TROMP, Jan Zoetelief (1872-1947) Dutch					
oil	5	85,872	1,505	20,314	26,781
TROMPIZ, Virgilio (1927-) Venezuelan					
oil	2	5,385	1,075	2,693	4,310
wc/d	1	1,370		1,370	
TROOD, William Henry Hamilton (1848-1899) British					
oil	3	38,904	4,350	12,054	22,500

Name	No.	Total Sales Value	Prices lowest	median	highest
TROOST, Cornelis (1697-1750) Dutch					
oil	1	15,701		15,701	
wc/d	1	4,838		4,838	
TROPININ, Vassili (1776-1857) Russian					
oil	1	1,669		1,669	
TROPPA, Girolamo (1636-1706) Italian					
oil	1	87,580		87,580	
TROSCHEL, Hans (1585-1628) German					
wc/d	1	1,964		1,964	
TROST, Carl (1811-1884) German					
wc/d	1	1,367		1,367	
TROTTER, John (fl.1756-1792) Irish					
oil	2	208,120	53,280	104,060	154,840
TROTTER, N H (1827-1898) American					
oil	1	2,100		2,100	
TROTTER, Newbold Hough (1827-1898) American					
oil	2	2,500	1,200	1,250	1,300
TROTZIG, Ulf (1925-) Norwegian					
oil	2	4,418	1,907	2,209	2,511
TROUBETZKOY, Prince Paolo (1866-1938) Russian					
3D	18	176,165	1,399	5,585	39,690
oil	1	4,357		4,357	
wc/d	1	2,057		2,057	
TROUILLE, Clovis (1889-1975) French					
oil	1	1,570		1,570	
TROUILLEBERT, Paul Desire (1829-1900) French					
oil	24	236,241	1,171	7,308	27,000
wc/d	3	4,018	1,130	1,130	1,688
TROVA, Ernest (1927-) American					
3D	2	5,400	2,400	2,700	3,000
TROWELL, O (19th C) ?					
oil	1	2,452		2,452	
TROXLER, Georges Alfons (1901-1990) Swiss					
oil	1	1,481		1,481	
TROY, François de (1645-1730) French					
oil	2	32,665	8,355	16,333	24,310
TROY, Jean François de (1679-1752) French					
oil	4	3,513,155	9,555	90,800	3,322,000
TROYEN, Rombout van (1605-c.1650) Dutch					
oil	2	12,198	5,159	6,099	7,039
TROYER, Prosper de (1880-1961) Belgian					
oil	3	5,306	1,128	2,089	2,089
TROYON, Constant (1810-1865) French					
oil	9	41,065	1,010	4,278	12,000
wc/d	1	1,923		1,923	
TRUBIANI, Valeriano (1937-) Italian					
3D	1	2,007		2,007	
TRUBNER, Wilhelm (1851-1917) German					
oil	4	50,968	3,792	13,361	20,455
TRUCHET, A (19/20th C) French					
oil	1	3,000		3,000	
TRUDEAU, Angus (1908-) Canadian?					
wc/d	1	1,354		1,354	
TRUELLE, Auguste (1818-1908) French					
oil	1	10,644		10,644	
TRUELSEN, Mathias Jacob Theodore (1836-1900) European					
wc/d	1	1,520		1,520	
TRUELSEN, Nis Nissen (1792-1862) Danish?					
wc/d	1	1,151		1,151	

Name	No.	Total Sales Value	lowest	Prices median	highest
TRUESDELL, Gaylord Sangston (1850-1899) American					
oil	1	4,250		4,250	
TRUMBULL, John (1756-1843) American					
oil	1	2,200		2,200	
TRUNINGER, Max (1910-1986) Swiss					
oil	1	1,129		1,129	
TRUPHEME, Andre François (1820-1888) French					
3D	2	13,200	1,200	6,600	12,000
TRUPHEMUS, Jacques (1922-) French					
oil	4	11,928	1,014	2,966	4,982
TRUPPE, Karl (1887-1959) Austrian					
oil	3	13,212	2,451	4,728	6,033
TRUSS, Jonathan (1960-) British					
oil	2	4,196	1,924	2,098	2,272
TRUSSEL, Alexander (1735-1824) Swiss					
oil	1	5,469		5,469	
TRUYEN, Johannes Paulus Franciscus (1928-) Dutch					
oil	1	1,981		1,981	
TRYGGELIN, Erik (1878-1962) Swedish					
oil	1	1,884		1,884	
TRYON, Dwight W (1849-1925) American					
oil	3	85,000	5,000	25,000	55,000
TSCHAGGENY, Edmond (1818-1873) Belgian					
oil	1	6,621		6,621	
TSCHAN, Rudolf (1848-1919) Swiss					
oil	1	1,049		1,049	
TSCHANG-YEUL KIM (1929-) Korean					
oil	1	35,000		35,000	
TSCHARNER, Johann Wilhelm von (1886-1946) Swiss					
oil	2	5,055	1,768	2,528	3,287
TSCHUDI, Rudolf (jnr) (1855-1923) American					
oil	1	2,000		2,000	
TSE-YE-MU (?) ?					
wc/d	1	1,500		1,500	
TSELKOV, Oleg (1934-) ?					
oil	2	5,267	1,053	2,634	4,214
TSINGOS, Thanos (1914-1965) Greek					
oil	10	88,962	2,924	3,893	40,880
TSIREH, Awa (1895-1955) American					
wc/d	2	11,000	5,000	5,500	6,000
TSOCLIS, Costa (1930-) Greek					
3D	3	11,166	1,668	4,278	5,220
TSUNEMITSU (19th C) Japanese					
3D	2	3,095	1,359	1,548	1,736
TUAILLON, Louis (1862-1919) German					
3D	1	5,340		5,340	
TUBBECKE, Paul (1848-1924) German					
oil	3	10,285	1,229	2,107	6,949
TUBKE, Werner (1929-) ?					
oil	2	52,485	17,022	26,243	35,463
wc/d	8	16,412	1,211	1,514	4,728
TUCKER, Allen (1866-1939) American					
oil	4	33,500	4,000	8,250	13,000
TUCKER, Arthur (1864-1929) British					
wc/d	2	2,254	1,110	1,127	1,144
TUCKER, Charles E (fl.1880-1904) British					
oil	1	10,990		10,990	
TUCKER, Frederick (fl.1880-1915) British					
wc/d	1	1,404		1,404	

Name	No.	Total Sales Value	lowest	Prices median	highest
TUDGAY, F (19th C) British					
oil	1	9,060		9,060	
TUDGAY, I (19th C) British					
oil	1	30,000		30,000	
TUERENHOUT, Jef van (1926-) Belgian					
oil	2	9,016	4,271	4,508	4,745
wc/d	1	2,089		2,089	
TUERLINCKX, Baudouin (20th C) Belgian					
3D	2	6,542	2,146	3,271	4,396
TUGEL, Otto (1892-1973) German					
wc/d	3	4,499	1,196	1,538	1,765
TUKE, Henry Scott (1858-1929) British					
oil	5	597,860	8,460	30,000	282,000
wc/d	13	77,134	1,139	5,285	10,998
TULL, Ebenezer (18th C) British					
oil	1	1,397		1,397	
TULLI, Wladimiro (1922-) Italian					
3D	1	1,142		1,142	
TUMARKIN, Igael (1933-) Israeli					
oil	3	16,274	4,000	5,000	7,274
wc/d	10	53,363	2,114	5,150	8,001
TUNGA (1952-) Brazilian					
3D	1	22,000		22,000	
TUNICA, Hermann August Theodor (1826-1907) German					
oil	1	1,169		1,169	
TUNNARD, John (1900-1971) British					
oil	1	33,840		33,840	
wc/d	2	5,832	1,800	2,916	4,032
TUNNICLIFFE, C F (1901-1979) British					
wc/d	1	1,580		1,580	
TUNNICLIFFE, Charles Frederick (1901-1979) British					
wc/d	6	22,774	1,950	2,519	10,368
TURCAN, Jean (1846-1895) French					
3D	1	1,500		1,500	
TURCATO, Giulio (1912-1995) Italian					
oil	20	71,488	2,230	2,902	8,680
wc/d	5	29,547	1,495	3,376	18,325
TURCHI, Alessandro (1578-1649) Italian					
oil	1	7,805		7,805	
TUREN, E van (?) ?					
oil	1	2,167		2,167	
TURIN SCHOOL, 17th C Italian					
wc/d	1	4,832		4,832	
TURIN SCHOOL, 18th C Italian					
oil	1	98,150		98,150	
TURINA Y AREAL, Joaquin (1847-1903) Spanish					
oil	1	9,555		9,555	
TURK, Lewis B de (1862-1933) American					
3D	1	3,500		3,500	
TURKI, Yahia (1903-1968) Tunisian					
oil	5	15,057	1,791	2,204	5,413
TURKISH SCHOOL, 18th C					
oil	1	15,120		15,120	
TURKISH SCHOOL, 19th C					
3D	1	5,192		5,192	
TURLETTI, Celestino (1845-1904) Italian					
oil	1	15,269		15,269	
TURNBULL, Andrew Watson (1874-?) British					
oil	1	3,001		3,001	

Name	No.	Total Sales Value	lowest	Prices median	highest
TURNBULL, William (1922-) British					
3D	2	61,050	13,050	30,525	48,000
TURNER (school) (?) ?					
oil	1	3,009		3,009	
TURNER OF OXFORD, William (1789-1862) British					
wc/d	5	86,409	2,700	4,290	60,400
TURNER, A (?) British					
oil	1	1,128		1,128	
TURNER, A M (1852-1932) British					
wc/d	1	1,100		1,100	
TURNER, C F (19th C) ?					
oil	1	1,800		1,800	
TURNER, Charles E (fl.1912-1919) British					
oil	1	7,632		7,632	
TURNER, Charles Henry (1848-?) American					
oil	1	6,260		6,260	
TURNER, Charles Yardley (1850-1918) American					
oil	1	4,000		4,000	
TURNER, Edward (19th C) British					
oil	1	4,740		4,740	
TURNER, Francis Calcraft (c.1782-1846) British					
oil	3	17,484	1,859	6,200	9,425
TURNER, Frank (fl.1866-1874) British					
oil	1	2,002		2,002	
TURNER, Frank James (fl.1863-1875) British					
oil	1	1,200		1,200	
TURNER, G (18/20th C) British					
oil	1	1,057		1,057	
TURNER, George (1843-1910) British					
oil	28	149,937	1,130	5,077	13,050
TURNER, Joseph Mallord William (1775-1851) British					
wc/d	13	641,625	4,290	17,696	271,800
TURNER, M A (19th C) American					
wc/d	1	1,800		1,800	
TURNER, Ross Sterling (1847-1915) American					
wc/d	1	3,750		3,750	
TURNER, W H M (fl.1850-1887) British					
oil	1	1,600		1,600	
TURNER, William Lakin (1867-1936) British					
oil	9	15,650	1,034	1,749	3,146
TURPIN DE CRISSE, Lancelot Theodore (1782-1859) French					
oil	1	32,000		32,000	
TURPIN, Pierre Jean Francois (1775-1840) French					
wc/d	4	4,380	1,095	1,095	1,095
TURRELL, James (1943-) American					
3D	1	100,000		100,000	
wc/d	1	7,000		7,000	
TURZAK, Charles (1899-?) American					
oil	1	2,300		2,300	
TUSCAN SCHOOL, 13th C Italian					
3D	1	81,893		81,893	
TUSCAN SCHOOL, 14th C Italian					
3D	1	301,711		301,711	
oil	2	40,690	15,700	20,345	24,990
TUSCAN SCHOOL, 15th C Italian					
3D	1	4,530		4,530	
oil	2	32,550	5,190	16,275	27,360
TUSCAN SCHOOL, 15th/16th C Italian					
3D	1	6,040		6,040	

Name	No.	Total Sales Value	Prices lowest	median	highest
oil	1	4,320		4,320	
TUSCAN SCHOOL, 16th C Italian					
3D	1	28,016		28,016	
oil	2	6,114	2,197	3,057	3,917
TUSCAN SCHOOL, 16th/17th C Italian					
3D	1	32,348		32,348	
TUSCAN SCHOOL, 17th C Italian					
3D	3	70,702	5,545	11,091	54,066
oil	4	31,415	2,752	4,105	20,454
TUSCAN SCHOOL, 18th C Italian					
oil	1	4,159		4,159	
TUSCAN SCHOOL, 19th C Italian					
oil	1	3,697		3,697	
TUSCHER, Charles Marc (1705-1751) German					
wc/d	1	2,800		2,800	
TUSEK, Mitja (1961-) Yugoslavian					
wc/d	1	4,228		4,228	
TUSET TUSET, Salvador (1883-1951) Spanish					
oil	1	2,689		2,689	
TUTTLE, Richard (1941-) American					
wc/d	4	16,894	3,394	4,350	4,800
TUTUNDJIAN, Léon (1905-1968) French/Armenian					
oil	1	3,689		3,689	
wc/d	6	10,150	1,021	1,377	3,190
TUXEN, Laurits (1853-1927) Danish					
oil	19	126,927	1,033	2,519	37,124
TUYMANS, Luc (1958-) Belgian					
oil	2	150,000	55,000	75,000	95,000
TUZINA, Gunter (1951-) German					
oil	1	1,341		1,341	
wc/d	1	1,341		1,341	
TVOROZHNIKOV, Ivan Ivanovich (1848-1919) Russian					
oil	1	5,134		5,134	
TWACHTMAN, John Henry (1853-1902) American					
oil	5	740,500	5,500	65,000	490,000
wc/d	1	2,800		2,800	
TWELLS, Arthur H (20th C) British					
oil	1	1,044		1,044	
TWOMBLY, Cy (1929-) American					
oil	10	5,041,900	60,000	253,450	2,600,000
wc/d	4	526,901	6,751	80,075	360,000
TWORKOV, Jack (1900-1982) American					
oil	3	79,000	21,000	21,000	36,000
TXILLIDA, Pedro (1952-) Spanish					
oil	1	1,967		1,967	
TYCK, Edward (1847-?) Belgian					
oil	1	1,906		1,906	
TYLER, Bayard Henry (1855-1931) American					
oil	2	3,800	1,400	1,900	2,400
TYLER, J G (1855-1931) American					
oil	2	3,450	1,700	1,725	1,750
TYLER, James Gale (1855-1931) American					
oil	8	28,100	1,000	2,000	15,000
TYLER, William R (1825-1896) American					
oil	1	1,978		1,978	
TYNDALE, Thomas Nicholson (1858-1936) British					
wc/d	2	2,338	1,160	1,169	1,178
TYNDALE, Walter (1855-1943) British					
wc/d	7	16,873	1,087	2,220	5,075

Name	No.	Total Sales Value	lowest	Prices median	highest
TYRAHN, Georg (1860-1917) German					
oil	1	1,355		1,355	
TYROLEAN SCHOOL, 15th C Austrian					
3D	1	7,785		7,785	
TYROLEAN SCHOOL, 16th C Austrian					
3D	1	9,625		9,625	
TYROLEAN SCHOOL, 17th C Austrian					
3D	1	2,727		2,727	
TYROLEAN SCHOOL, 18th C Austrian					
3D	2	6,823	3,187	3,412	3,636
oil	1	3,372		3,372	
TYRRELL, J J (?) British?					
wc/d	1	2,250		2,250	
TYSON, Carroll (1878-1956) American					
oil	1	16,000		16,000	
TYSON, Nicola (1960-) British					
wc/d	3	7,065	2,000	2,265	2,800
TYTGAT, Edgard (1879-1957) Belgian					
oil	3	64,672	4,684	9,239	50,749
wc/d	4	11,507	1,483	1,954	6,117
TYTGAT, Medard (1871-1948) Belgian					
oil	1	1,264		1,264	
TZAPOFF, Antoine (20th C) ?					
oil	1	2,964		2,964	
UBAC, Raoul (1910-1985) Belgian					
3D	2	6,739	2,957	3,370	3,782
oil	1	6,512		6,512	
UBBELOHDE, Otto (1867-1922) German					
oil	1	5,363		5,363	
wc/d	2	3,853	1,707	1,927	2,146
UBEDA, Augustin (1925-) Spanish					
oil	11	28,256	1,287	2,200	6,388
UBERTALLI, Romolo (1871-1928) Italian					
wc/d	1	2,794		2,794	
UBERTINI, Francesco (1494-1557) Italian					
oil	1	573,300		573,300	
UDALTSOVA, Nadezhda (1886-1961) Russian					
wc/d	4	16,157	2,265	3,775	6,342
UDEN, Lucas van (1595-1672) Flemish					
oil	2	39,190	12,500	19,595	26,690
UECKER, Gunther (1930-) German					
3D	2	52,749	9,515	26,375	43,234
oil	2	12,583	3,883	6,292	8,700
wc/d	3	5,408	1,129	1,379	2,900
UELLIGER, Karl (1920-1993) Swiss					
oil	6	14,329	1,632	2,112	3,498
UEMURA, Shoen (1875-1949) Japanese					
wc/d	1	190,000		190,000	
UFER, Walter (1876-1936) American					
oil	2	115,000	55,000	57,500	60,000
UGARD, R (19th C) British?					
oil	1	4,228		4,228	
UGARTE, Ignacio (1860-1914) Spanish					
oil	1	10,117		10,117	
UHDE, Fritz von (1848-1911) German					
oil	4	26,782	2,472	3,184	17,943
UHLIG, Max (1937-) German					
oil	2	10,337	3,244	5,169	7,093
UHLMAN, Fred (1901-1985) British					
oil	9	16,463	1,103	1,738	2,900

Name	No.	Total Sales Value	lowest	Prices median	highest
UHLMANN, Hans (1900-1975) German					
3D	2	25,518	10,380	12,759	15,138
wc/d	1	1,456		1,456	
UHRDIN, Sam (1886-1964) Swedish					
oil	10	26,618	1,242	2,905	4,140
UKIL, Sharada (19/20th C) Indian					
wc/d	1	4,050		4,050	
ULFSPARRE AF BROXVIK, Carl Gustaf (1790-1862) Swedish					
oil	2	4,295	2,018	2,148	2,277
ULFT, Jacob van der (1627-1689) Dutch					
wc/d	2	2,792	1,100	1,396	1,692
ULIVELLI, Cosimo (1625-1704) Italian					
wc/d	1	1,975		1,975	
ULLIK, Hugo (19/20th C) German					
oil	1	1,079		1,079	
ULLMANN, T (20th C) Austrian?					
3D	1	2,145		2,145	
ULLRICH, Josef (1815-1867) German					
oil	1	4,903		4,903	
ULTVEDT, Per Olof (1927-) Finnish					
3D	1	3,686		3,686	
UMBRIAN SCHOOL, 14th C Italian					
3D	1	120,685		120,685	
UMBRIAN SCHOOL, 15th C Italian					
oil	1	26,460		26,460	
UMBRIAN SCHOOL, 16th C Italian					
wc/d	1	3,000		3,000	
UMBRIAN SCHOOL, 17th/18th C Italian					
oil	1	18,630		18,630	
UMEHARA, Ryuzaburo (1888-1986) Japanese					
oil	3	320,000	65,000	95,000	160,000
UMGELTER, Hermann Ludwig (1891-1962) German					
oil	4	6,259	1,072	1,490	2,208
UNCETA Y LOPEZ, Marcelino de (1835-1905) Spanish					
oil	1	4,000		4,000	
UNCINI, Giuseppe (1929-) Italian					
3D	1	5,796		5,796	
oil	1	2,426		2,426	
UNDERWOOD, Léon (1890-1975) British					
3D	2	11,195	2,030	5,598	9,165
oil	1	4,350		4,350	
UNDERWOOD, Thomas Richard (1765-1836) British					
wc/d	1	1,358		1,358	
UNG-NO-LEE (1904-) Korean					
wc/d	1	4,314		4,314	
UNGER, Hans (1872-1936) German					
oil	1	1,734		1,734	
UNGERER, Tomi (1931-) ?					
wc/d	1	3,749		3,749	
UNGEWITTER, Hugo (1869-c.1944) German					
oil	1	1,471		1,471	
UNOLD, Max (1885-1964) German					
wc/d	1	1,211		1,211	
UNTERBERGER, Franz Richard (1838-1902) Belgian					
oil	11	454,092	1,273	43,500	98,150
UNTERBERGER, Michelangelo (1695-1758) Austrian					
oil	1	16,364		16,364	
UNWIN, Frances Mabelle (?) British?					
wc/d	1	1,533		1,533	

Name	No.	Total Sales Value	lowest	Prices median	highest
UPHOFF, Fritz (1890-1966) German					
oil	2	4,390	1,080	2,195	3,310
UPP, George (19th C) American					
oil	2	3,100	1,500	1,550	1,600
UPPER RHINE SCHOOL, 15th C					
oil	1	6,617		6,617	
UPPER RHINE SCHOOL, 16th C					
3D	2	38,378	6,920	19,189	31,458
oil	4	143,297	9,968	25,140	83,050
URBACH, Josef (1889-1973) German					
oil	1	2,404		2,404	
URBAHN, O (19th C) German					
oil	1	2,145		2,145	
URBAN, Hermann (1866-1946) German					
oil	1	1,241		1,241	
URCULO, Eduardo (1938-) Spanish					
oil	3	9,112	2,371	2,373	4,368
wc/d	1	1,056		1,056	
URECH-SEON, Rudolf (1876-1959) Swiss					
oil	1	1,059		1,059	
UREN, John C (1845-1932) British					
wc/d	2	3,637	1,749	1,819	1,888
URGELL, Ricardo (1874-1924) Spanish					
oil	1	1,630		1,630	
URI, Aviva (1927-1989) Israeli					
wc/d	3	8,400	1,200	2,200	5,000
URQUHART, Tony (1934-) Canadian					
oil	1	1,336		1,336	
URSULA (1921-) German					
oil	1	6,641		6,641	
URTIN, Paul François Marie (1874-1962) French					
oil	1	1,462		1,462	
URY, Lesser (1861-1931) German					
oil	12	376,831	3,448	19,797	108,754
wc/d	17	374,835	6,000	16,550	48,000
USELLINI, Gian Filippo (1903-1971) Italian					
oil	2	7,240	3,376	3,620	3,864
USIKOVA, Evdokia G (1913-) Russian					
oil	1	1,470		1,470	
USLE, Juan (1953-) Spanish					
oil	4	78,900	9,425	16,618	36,240
USSI, Stefano (1822-1901) Italian					
oil	1	15,179		15,179	
UTH, Max (1863-1914) German					
oil	1	3,310		3,310	
UTRECHT, Adriaen van (1599-1653) Flemish					
oil	2	53,752	9,792	26,876	43,960
UTRILLO, Maurice (1883-1955) French					
oil	50	3,804,278	14,563	63,067	293,454
wc/d	33	891,920	4,364	22,470	72,327
UTZON-FRANK, Ejnar (1888-1955) Danish					
3D	10	34,621	1,133	2,488	8,387
UVA, Cesare (19th C) Italian					
oil	1	1,250		1,250	
wc/d	2	6,664	1,300	3,332	5,364
UWINS, Thomas (1782-1857) British					
wc/d	1	4,424		4,424	
UYTEWAEL, Joachim (1566-1638) Dutch					
oil	1	7,930		7,930	
wc/d	1	21,821		21,821	

Name	No.	Total Sales Value	lowest	Prices median	highest
UYTTENBROECK, Moses van (1590-1648) Dutch					
oil	1	9,362		9,362	
UYTTERSCHAUT, Victor (1847-1917) Belgian					
wc/d	1	1,224		1,224	
VAARBERG, Johannes Christoffel (1825-1871) Dutch					
oil	2	7,814	1,025	3,907	6,789
VAARDT, Jan van der (1647-1721) Dutch					
oil	1	4,641		4,641	
VACCARI, Alfredo (1877-1933) Italian					
oil	1	2,957		2,957	
VACCARO, Andrea (c.1598-1670) Italian					
oil	1	13,759		13,759	
VACCARO, Nicola (c.1634-1709) Italian					
oil	3	32,471	5,386	9,815	17,270
VACCHI, Sergio (1925-) Italian					
oil	1	1,157		1,157	
VACHELL, B (19th C) ?					
oil	1	1,324		1,324	
VADDER, Lodewyk de (1605-1655) Flemish					
oil	1	4,195		4,195	
VADER, Hendrik (19/20th C) Belgian					
oil	1	1,855		1,855	
VADILLO, Francisco (?) Spanish?					
oil	5	8,080	1,320	1,580	1,940
VAERENBERGH, G van (19/20th C) Belgian					
3D	1	2,783		2,783	
VAERENBERGH, Georges van (19/20th C) Belgian					
3D	1	3,600		3,600	
VAERNEWIJCK, Lode van (20th C) Belgian					
oil	1	1,379		1,379	
VAES, Walter (1882-1958) Belgian					
oil	5	29,369	3,630	4,000	9,530
wc/d	2	3,538	1,635	1,769	1,903
VAGAGGINI, Memo (1892-1955) Italian					
oil	1	1,187		1,187	
VAGLIERI, Tino (1929-2000) Italian					
oil	3	5,125	1,081	1,449	2,595
VAGO, Valentino (1931-) Italian					
oil	1	1,201		1,201	
VAIKUNTAM, Thotha (1942-) Indian					
oil	1	2,400		2,400	
VAIL, Eugene Laurent (1857-1934) American/French					
oil	2	2,674	1,337	1,337	1,337
VAILLANT, Bernard (1632-1698) French					
wc/d	1	3,095		3,095	
VAISMAN, Meyer (1960-) American					
oil	1	12,000		12,000	
wc/d	3	28,100	1,600	8,500	18,000
VAL D'OSNE FOUNDRY (19th C) French					
3D	2	26,320	13,000	13,160	13,320
VAL, del (?) Spanish?					
oil	1	1,393		1,393	
VALADE, Jean (1709-1787) French					
wc/d	1	5,686		5,686	
VALADIE, Jean Baptiste (1933-) French					
oil	1	2,407		2,407	
VALADON, Suzanne (1865-1938) French					
oil	8	223,050	2,851	25,896	53,989
wc/d	7	65,317	3,629	6,358	29,000

Name	No.	Total Sales Value	lowest	Prices median	highest
VALANTIN, Paul (19th C) French					
oil	1	1,412		1,412	
VALCKENAERE, Leon Jules (1853-?) Belgian					
oil	1	1,337		1,337	
VALCKERT, Werner van den (1585-c.1655) Dutch					
oil	1	31,773		31,773	
VALDES, Lucas de (1661-1724) Spanish					
oil	1	2,842		2,842	
VALDES, Manuel (1942-) Spanish					
oil	2	65,459	24,200	32,730	41,259
wc/d	4	16,964	3,301	4,290	5,083
VALDIVIESO, Antonio (1918-2000) Spanish					
oil	1	2,259		2,259	
VALENCIA, Manuel (1856-1935) American					
oil	1	2,750		2,750	
VALENCIAN SCHOOL Spanish					
oil	1	3,003		3,003	
VALENCIAN SCHOOL, 16th C Spanish					
oil	2	39,779	10,379	19,890	29,400
VALENCIAN SCHOOL, 18th C Spanish					
oil	2	56,378	3,528	28,189	52,850
VALENCIENNES, Pierre Henri de (1750-1819) French					
wc/d	1	4,710		4,710	
VALENKAMPH, Theodor Victor Carl (1868-1924) American					
oil	1	2,700		2,700	
VALENSI, Henry (1883-1960) French					
oil	1	9,247		9,247	
VALENTA, Ludwig (1882-1943) Austrian					
oil	1	1,500		1,500	
VALENTI, Italo (1912-1995) Italian					
wc/d	1	1,203		1,203	
VALENTINI, Gottardo (1820-1884) Italian					
oil	2	4,550	2,077	2,275	2,473
VALENTINI, Walter (1912-1995) Italian					
wc/d	1	1,802		1,802	
VALENTINO, Gian Domenico (17th C) Italian					
oil	1	7,644		7,644	
VALENTINY, Janos (1842-1902) Hungarian					
oil	1	1,618		1,618	
VALERIO, Theodore (1819-1879) French					
wc/d	1	5,819		5,819	
VALERO, R (19/20th C) ?					
oil	1	1,400		1,400	
VALETTE, Adolphe (1861-1942) French					
oil	1	1,026		1,026	
VALETTE, Henri (19/20th C) French					
3D	2	2,925	1,287	1,463	1,638
VALETTE, Pierre Adolphe (1876-1942) French					
oil	7	20,995	2,054	2,920	4,266
VALINOTTI, Domenico (1889-1962) Italian					
oil	1	1,098		1,098	
VALK, Anna Maria Bernardina van der (1947-) Dutch					
oil	1	1,584		1,584	
VALK, Hendrik Jacobus (1897-1986) Dutch					
oil	3	13,578	3,448	3,664	6,466
VALKENBORCH, Frederick van (1570-1623) Flemish					
oil	2	35,560	3,077	17,780	32,483
VALKENBORCH, Lucas van and FLEGEL, Georg (16th C) Flemish/German					
oil	1	271,800		271,800	

Name	No.	Total Sales Value	lowest	Prices median	highest
VALKENBORCH, Martin van (1535-1612) Flemish					
oil	2	94,195	6,615	47,098	87,580
VALKENBURG, Hendrik (1826-1896) Dutch					
oil	2	8,259	4,088	4,130	4,171
wc/d	1	3,122		3,122	
VALLAYER-COSTER, Anne (1744-1818) French					
oil	2	31,754	3,754	15,877	28,000
wc/d	1	24,000		24,000	
VALLAYER-MOUTET, Pauline (19th C) French					
oil	2	8,413	3,663	4,207	4,750
VALLE, Giovan Battista (1843-1885) Italian?					
oil	1	2,426		2,426	
VALLEE, Étienne Maxime (19th C) French					
oil	1	8,000		8,000	
VALLEE, Ludovic (1864-1939) French					
oil	4	12,758	1,520	1,969	7,301
VALLELY, J B (1941-) British					
oil	3	11,386	3,432	3,432	4,500
VALLELY, John B (1941-) British					
oil	1	14,976		14,976	
VALLET, Edouard (1876-1929) Swiss					
oil	6	81,933	1,793	12,488	28,293
wc/d	2	3,381	1,632	1,691	1,749
VALLETTE, Henri (1877-1962) French					
3D	1	22,475		22,475	
VALLEY, Jonas Joseph la (1858-1930) American					
oil	2	3,100	1,100	1,550	2,000
VALLGREN, Ville (1855-1940) French					
3D	1	2,717		2,717	
VALLIN, Jacques Antoine (1760-1831) French					
oil	11	67,180	1,117	4,127	26,323
VALLIN, Jacques Antoine (school) (1760-1831) French					
oil	2	3,616	1,446	1,808	2,170
VALLMAN, Uno (1913-) Swedish					
oil	6	13,108	1,167	1,839	4,346
VALLMITJANA, Venancio (1850-1915) Spanish					
3D	1	1,573		1,573	
VALLORZ, Paolo (1931-) Italian					
oil	2	14,286	1,196	7,143	13,090
VALLOTTON, Felix (1865-1925) Swiss					
3D	1	10,237		10,237	
oil	30	5,658,124	8,367	41,885	1,473,577
wc/d	11	118,763	1,061	3,646	41,260
VALLS, Xavier (1923-) Spanish					
oil	2	9,054	4,124	4,527	4,930
VALMIER, Georges (1885-1937) French					
oil	6	461,190	13,560	65,815	160,000
wc/d	6	33,618	1,160	5,686	10,405
VALMONT, E (19th C) French					
oil	1	1,873		1,873	
VALMOR, G (19th C) Continental					
oil	1	1,200		1,200	
VALOIS, Jean François (1778-1853) Dutch					
wc/d	1	1,205		1,205	
VALORE, Lucie (1878-1965) Swiss					
wc/d	1	1,056		1,056	
VALTAT, Louis (1869-1952) French					
3D	8	20,986	1,140	2,280	4,673
oil	67	2,161,078	2,047	20,000	290,000
wc/d	23	68,014	1,180	2,361	12,822

Name	No.	Total Sales Value	lowest	Prices median	highest
VALTER, Frederick E (1850-1930) British					
oil	1	1,207		1,207	
VALTON (19/20th C) French					
3D	1	1,476		1,476	
VALTON, C (?) ?					
3D	2	5,371	1,621	2,686	3,750
VALTON, Charles (1851-1918) French					
3D	7	15,010	1,276	1,775	3,926
VANAISE, Gustaaf (1854-1902) Belgian					
oil	2	2,708	1,242	1,354	1,466
VANCE (20th C) French?					
wc/d	1	2,482		2,482	
VANCELLS, Joaquin (1866-1942) Spanish					
oil	1	2,406		2,406	
VANDEKERCKHOVE, Hans (1957-) Belgian					
oil	3	7,110	1,671	1,880	3,559
VANDENBERG, Philippe (1952-) Belgian?					
oil	2	5,014	2,507	2,507	2,507
VANDENBRANDEN, Guy (1926-) Belgian					
oil	1	1,144		1,144	
VANDERBANK, John (1694-1739) British					
oil	1	2,860		2,860	
wc/d	1	6,040		6,040	
VANDERCAM, Serge (1924-) Danish					
oil	1	2,859		2,859	
wc/d	1	2,373		2,373	
VANDERLICK, Armand (1897-1985) Belgian					
oil	2	6,777	2,747	3,389	4,030
VANDERSTATEN (?) ?					
3D	1	2,292		2,292	
VANDERVAEL, Armily (1908-) Belgian					
oil	1	1,102		1,102	
VANDEVERDONCK, Franz (19th C) Belgian					
oil	2	2,834	1,414	1,417	1,420
VANDIER, B (?) ?					
oil	1	2,550		2,550	
VANELLI, A (19/20th C) Italian					
3D	1	3,480		3,480	
VANETTI (19/20th C) Italian					
3D	1	5,285		5,285	
VANETTI, Antonio (19/20th C) Italian					
3D	1	4,250		4,250	
VANEVERDONCK, F (19th C) Belgian					
oil	1	2,207		2,207	
VANGI, Giuliano (1931-) Italian					
wc/d	1	1,994		1,994	
VANMOUR, Jan Baptiste (1671-1737) Flemish					
oil	2	84,897	2,233	42,449	82,664
VANNETTI, Angiolo (19/20th C) Italian					
3D	1	2,500		2,500	
VANNI, Francesco (c.1563-1610) Italian					
wc/d	1	3,775		3,775	
VANNI, Giovanni Battista (1599-1660) Italian					
wc/d	1	5,134		5,134	
VANNINI, Ottavio (1585-1643) Italian					
oil	1	27,720		27,720	
wc/d	2	9,060	3,775	4,530	5,285
VANNUCCIO, Francesco di (fl.1361-1388) Italian					
oil	1	43,102		43,102	

Name	No.	Total Sales Value	Prices lowest	median	highest
VANUFFEL, J (19/20th C) ?					
oil	1	1,113		1,113	
VANVITELLI, Luigi (1700-1773) Italian					
wc/d	1	1,273		1,273	
VAQUERO TURCIOS, Joaquin (1933-) Spanish					
oil	3	19,613	1,249	6,078	12,286
VARA, Enrique (?) Spanish					
oil	1	1,008		1,008	
VARAGNOLO, Mario (1901-1971) Italian					
oil	2	3,215	1,249	1,608	1,966
VAREJAO, Adriana (1964-) Brazilian					
oil	1	38,000		38,000	
VARELA, Abigail (1948-) Venezuelan					
3D	3	52,000	8,000	16,000	28,000
VARESE, Carlo (1903-) Italian					
oil	1	2,735		2,735	
VARGAS MACHUCA, Luis Martinez (1875-1929) Spanish					
oil	1	4,831		4,831	
VARGAS RUIZ, Guillermo (1910-1990) Spanish					
oil	1	1,977		1,977	
VARGAS, Alberto (20th C) American					
wc/d	1	26,000		26,000	
VARLA, Felix (20th C) French					
oil	2	2,710	1,355	1,355	1,355
VARLEY, Albert Fleetwood (1804-1876) British					
wc/d	1	1,661		1,661	
VARLEY, Cornelius (1781-1873) British					
wc/d	1	1,144		1,144	
VARLEY, Edgar J (1839-1888) British					
wc/d	1	2,860		2,860	
VARLEY, Frederick Horsman (1881-1969) Canadian/British					
oil	4	58,979	3,650	12,473	30,383
wc/d	4	6,164	1,000	1,504	2,157
VARLEY, John (1778-1842) British					
oil	1	4,347		4,347	
wc/d	28	94,020	1,001	2,850	9,750
VARLEY, John (jnr) (?-1899) British					
wc/d	3	7,859	1,400	3,003	3,456
VARLIN (1900-1977) Swiss					
oil	8	190,314	9,723	20,904	44,207
wc/d	3	5,658	1,153	1,512	2,993
VARLIN, Willy Guggenheim (1900-1977) Swiss					
oil	4	98,334	11,248	25,398	36,290
VARMA, Raja Ravi (1848-1906) Indian					
oil	4	123,000	20,000	30,500	42,000
VARMING, Hanne (20th C) Danish					
3D	1	1,360		1,360	
VARNI, Santo (1807-1885) Italian					
3D	1	1,471		1,471	
VARNIER, R (20th C) French					
3D	1	1,700		1,700	
VAROTARI, Alessandro (1588-1648) Italian					
oil	4	74,109	15,711	18,571	21,257
VARTANYAN, Gervasia (1927-) Armenian					
oil	1	2,058		2,058	
VASARELY (1908-1997) Hungarian					
wc/d	1	1,328		1,328	
VASARELY, Victor (1908-1997) Hungarian					
3D	5	13,499	1,289	1,942	5,340

Name	No.	Total Sales Value	Prices lowest	median	highest
oil	33	300,386	1,068	8,162	27,892
wc/d	10	36,157	1,312	2,740	9,815
VASARI, Giorgio (1511-1574) Italian					
oil	1	520,000		520,000	
wc/d	2	41,060	1,800	20,530	39,260
VASARRI, Emilio (19/20th C) Italian					
oil	1	21,000		21,000	
VASCOVI, A (?) Italian?					
oil	1	1,793		1,793	
VASILIEV, B N (19/20th C) Russian					
oil	1	4,530		4,530	
VASQUEZ BRITO, Ramón (1927-) Venezuelan					
oil	2	10,430	4,310	5,215	6,120
VASQUEZ DIAZ, Daniel (1882-1969) Spanish					
oil	7	154,031	2,786	32,762	41,259
wc/d	1	1,502		1,502	
VASQUEZ, Carlos (1869-1944) Spanish					
oil	2	3,965	1,298	1,983	2,667
wc/d	1	1,282		1,282	
VASS, Bela (1872-1934) Hungarian					
oil	1	1,200		1,200	
VASSALLO, Nicola (18/19th C) Italian					
3D	1	2,465		2,465	
VASSELIN, L E (19th C) French					
oil	1	2,707		2,707	
VASSELON, Marius (19th C) French					
oil	1	2,995		2,995	
VASSEUR, Adolphe (1836-1907) Belgian					
wc/d	1	5,452		5,452	
VASSILIEFF, Marie (1894-1955) Russian					
oil	3	162,025	7,025	25,000	130,000
wc/d	1	3,047		3,047	
VASSILIOU, Spyros (1902-1984) Greek					
oil	2	33,580	13,140	16,790	20,440
VASTAGH, Geza (1866-1919) Hungarian					
oil	3	12,484	1,704	1,843	8,937
VATTEN (19th C) ?					
oil	1	1,140		1,140	
VAUBOURGOIN, Thierry (1944-) French					
oil	1	1,532		1,532	
VAUCLEROY, P de (1892-1969) Belgian					
oil	1	1,016		1,016	
VAUCLEROY, Pierre de (1892-1969) Belgian					
oil	1	4,769		4,769	
VAUDECHAMP, Joseph (1790-1866) French					
oil	2	3,351	1,031	1,676	2,320
VAUDOYER, Laurent Thomas (1756-1846) French					
wc/d	1	3,624		3,624	
VAUDREUIL, Victoire (19th C) French?					
oil	1	1,440		1,440	
VAUGHAN, A G (fl.1846-1852) British					
wc/d	1	2,844		2,844	
VAUGHAN, Keith (1912-1974) British					
oil	3	13,650	2,400	4,500	6,750
wc/d	16	74,531	1,103	2,823	13,775
VAUTHIER, Pierre (1845-1916) French					
oil	1	6,500		6,500	
VAUTHRIN, Ernest Germain (20th C) French					
oil	2	2,442	1,064	1,221	1,378

Name	No.	Total Sales Value	lowest	Prices median	highest
VAUTIER, Andre (1861-1941) French					
oil	1	1,787		1,787	
VAUTIER, Benjamin (19/20th C) German/Swiss					
oil	12	49,979	1,047	2,321	12,154
wc/d	1	8,872		8,872	
VAUTIER, Benjamin (elder) (1829-1898) German					
oil	1	11,478		11,478	
VAUTIER, Otto (1863-1919) Swiss					
oil	5	9,947	1,089	1,935	2,849
wc/d	2	4,598	1,061	2,299	3,537
VAUVRAY (19th C) ?					
3D	1	2,339		2,339	
VAWTER, Will (1871-1941) American					
oil	2	36,000	11,000	18,000	25,000
VAY, Lodewyck (1630-c.1655) German					
oil	1	46,080		46,080	
VAYREDA CANADELL, Josep Maria (1932-) Spanish					
oil	3	6,167	1,716	2,163	2,288
VAZI, Sophia (20th C) ?					
3D	1	25,740		25,740	
VAZQUEZ DIAS, Daniel (1881-1969) Spanish					
oil	3	74,109	2,958	10,218	60,933
wc/d	1	1,758		1,758	
VAZQUEZ, Alberto (20th C) Spanish					
oil	1	4,346		4,346	
VAZQUEZ, Antonio (c.1485-1563) Spanish					
oil	1	28,690		28,690	
VAZQUEZ, Gloria (1944-) Spanish					
oil	1	1,688		1,688	
VEAL, George (19th C) British					
oil	1	16,000		16,000	
VECCHIA, Pietro della (1605-1678) Italian					
oil	3	179,481	5,831	60,400	113,250
wc/d	1	1,216		1,216	
VECCHIETTA (1405-1480) Italian					
3D	1	152,497		152,497	
VECELLIO, Francesco (1483-1559) Italian					
oil	1	16,241		16,241	
VEDANI, Michele (1874-?) Italian					
3D	1	1,468		1,468	
VEDEL, Herman (1875-1948) Danish					
oil	1	3,813		3,813	
VEDOVA, Emilio (1919-) Italian					
oil	4	241,771	3,743	28,389	181,250
wc/d	3	55,842	1,419	14,280	40,143
VEDOVA, Mario della (1958-) Italian					
oil	1	1,456		1,456	
VEEL, Armand le (1821-1905) French					
3D	2	11,290	5,040	5,645	6,250
VEEN, Gerardus van (17th C) Dutch					
wc/d	1	1,257		1,257	
VEEN, Karel van (1898-1988) Dutch					
oil	1	1,573		1,573	
VEEN, Otto van (1556-1629) Flemish					
oil	1	10,000		10,000	
wc/d	1	2,972		2,972	
VEEN, Pieter van (1875-1961) American					
oil	1	2,000		2,000	
VEGA Y MUNOZ, Pedro de (fl.1866-1882) Spanish					
oil	4	12,100	1,015	2,900	5,285

Name	No.	Total Sales Value	lowest	Prices median	highest
VEGA, Jose de la (19th C) Spanish					
oil	1	3,245		3,245	
VEILLON, Auguste-Louis (1834-1890) Swiss					
oil	8	19,368	1,133	2,216	4,862
VEITH, Eduard (1856-1925) Austrian					
oil	3	9,960	1,728	3,632	4,600
VEITH, Johann Philipp (1768-1837) German					
wc/d	1	11,650		11,650	
VELA ZANETTI, Jose (1913-1999) Spanish					
oil	2	20,811	8,711	10,406	12,100
wc/d	1	10,354		10,354	
VELARDE, Pablita (1918-) American					
wc/d	1	8,500		8,500	
VELASCO, Rosario de (?) Spanish					
oil	1	5,433		5,433	
VELASQUEZ, Diego Rodriguez de Silva y (school) (1599-1660) Spanish					
oil	2	11,970	5,500	5,985	6,470
VELASQUEZ, Jose Antonio (1906-1983) Honduran					
oil	2	7,000	3,000	3,500	4,000
VELAZQUEZ, Eugenio Lucas (1817-1870) Spanish					
oil	14	271,930	2,081	7,058	80,078
wc/d	2	3,357	1,344	1,679	2,013
VELDE, Adriaen van de (1636-1672) Dutch					
oil	3	43,365	5,000	6,996	31,369
VELDE, Bram van (1895-1981) Dutch					
oil	2	32,758	2,586	16,379	30,172
wc/d	3	63,438	1,297	3,951	58,190
VELDE, Esaias van de (1587-1630) Dutch					
oil	1	151,000		151,000	
wc/d	2	13,601	2,601	6,801	11,000
VELDE, Geer van (1898-c.1977) Dutch					
oil	8	115,704	2,253	15,984	25,748
wc/d	8	51,545	2,140	5,178	20,690
VELDE, Henry Clemens van de (1863-1957) Belgian					
oil	1	2,431		2,431	
VELDE, Jan Jansz van de (1620-1662) Dutch					
oil	1	80,850		80,850	
VELDE, Pieter van de (1634-1687) Flemish					
oil	3	41,150	9,106	12,080	19,964
VELDE, W van de (younger) (1633-1707) Dutch					
oil	1	1,015		1,015	
VELDE, Willem van de (elder-school) (1611-1693) Dutch					
oil	1	8,000		8,000	
VELDE, Willem van de (younger) (1633-1707) Dutch					
oil	2	2,675,400	617,400	1,337,700	2,058,000
wc/d	2	3,965	1,500	1,983	2,465
VELDE, Willem van de (younger-school) (1633-1707) Dutch					
oil	1	2,400		2,400	
VELDEN, Adrianus Dirk Blok van der (1913-) Dutch					
oil	1	1,180		1,180	
VELDEN, Petrus van der (1837-1915) New Zealander/Dutch					
wc/d	1	2,935		2,935	
VELICKOVIC (1935-) Yugoslavian					
wc/d	1	3,098		3,098	
VELICKOVIC, Vladimir (1935-) Yugoslavian					
oil	7	41,889	2,424	5,892	11,602
wc/d	11	16,640	1,047	1,355	2,886
VELLACOTT, Elizabeth (1905-) British					
oil	1	4,108		4,108	

Name	No.	Total Sales Value	Prices lowest	median	highest
VELLAN, Felice (1889-1976) Italian					
oil	2	2,159	1,061	1,080	1,098
VELTEN, Wilhelm (1847-1929) Russian					
oil	15	44,535	1,282	2,942	6,000
VELTZ, Ivan (1866-1926) Russian					
oil	1	14,805		14,805	
VENARD, Claude (1913-1999) French					
oil	27	63,455	1,053	2,006	4,884
VENET, Bernar (1941-) French					
3D	2	35,182	4,530	17,591	30,652
oil	2	10,949	2,500	5,475	8,449
wc/d	6	38,918	2,020	6,163	12,284
VENETIAN SCHOOL Italian					
3D	1	10,053		10,053	
oil	1	8,000		8,000	
VENETIAN SCHOOL, 15th C Italian					
3D	1	7,183		7,183	
oil	1	17,000		17,000	
VENETIAN SCHOOL, 16th C Italian					
3D	2	22,981	11,206	11,491	11,775
oil	5	49,513	3,000	6,528	27,839
wc/d	2	7,852	3,926	3,926	3,926
VENETIAN SCHOOL, 16th/17th C Italian					
oil	2	39,789	3,549	19,895	36,240
VENETIAN SCHOOL, 17th C Italian					
3D	2	15,170	6,390	7,585	8,780
oil	18	206,077	2,264	5,272	86,906
VENETIAN SCHOOL, 18th C Italian					
3D	4	87,370	5,466	16,206	49,492
oil	24	461,730	2,440	7,225	90,909
VENETIAN SCHOOL, 18th/19th C Italian					
3D	1	5,466		5,466	
VENETIAN SCHOOL, 19th C Italian					
3D	4	35,110	2,733	6,189	20,000
oil	2	13,308	6,490	6,654	6,818
wc/d	1	11,347		11,347	
VENETIAN SCHOOL, 20th C Italian					
oil	1	5,500		5,500	
VENETO SCHOOL, 16th C Italian					
oil	6	38,500	2,217	3,143	21,447
VENETO SCHOOL, 16th/17th C Italian					
oil	1	14,690		14,690	
VENETO SCHOOL, 17th C Italian					
3D	2	18,947	7,856	9,474	11,091
oil	6	33,441	3,004	4,865	9,173
VENETO SCHOOL, 18th C Italian					
3D	3	29,473	3,732	9,755	15,986
oil	15	155,032	2,981	6,421	32,348
VENETO SCHOOL, 19th C Italian					
3D	1	5,131		5,131	
oil	2	7,952	3,100	3,976	4,852
VENETO-CRETAN SCHOOL, 18th C Italian					
oil	2	5,462	2,546	2,731	2,916
VENETO-DALMATIAN SCHOOL, 14th C Italian					
3D	1	5,415		5,415	
VENETO-DALMATIAN SCHOOL, 17th C Italian					
oil	1	2,311		2,311	
VENEZUELAN SCHOOL, 18th C					
oil	1	3,500		3,500	
VENIG, Karl Bogdanovich (1830-1908) Russian					
oil	1	7,248		7,248	

Name	No.	Total Sales Value	lowest	Prices median	highest
VENNE, Adriaen Pietersz van de (1589-1662) Dutch					
oil	3	65,379	3,143	11,165	51,071
wc/d	1	8,643		8,643	
VENNE, Fritz van der (19/20th C) German					
oil	6	13,005	1,600	2,152	2,724
VENNE, Jan van de (1636-1672) Dutch					
oil	1	1,200		1,200	
VENNEMAN, Charles (1802-1875) Flemish					
oil	5	22,207	1,111	5,100	6,846
VENNEMAN, Rosa (19th C) Belgian					
oil	2	4,614	1,210	2,307	3,404
VENTAYOL, Juan (1911-) Uruguayan					
oil	2	4,100	1,100	2,050	3,000
wc/d	1	2,000		2,000	
VENTOSA, Josep (1897-1982) Spanish					
oil	1	2,335		2,335	
VERA, Cristino de (1931-) Spanish					
oil	3	15,265	3,642	5,708	5,915
VERA, Enrique (1886-1956) Spanish					
oil	10	24,251	1,030	2,262	6,735
VERBEECK, Henri Daniel (1817-1863) Flemish					
oil	1	11,313		11,313	
VERBOECKHOVEN, Eugène (1798-1881) Belgian					
oil	31	584,028	1,012	6,894	72,500
wc/d	2	6,409	2,700	3,205	3,709
VERBOECKHOVEN, Eugène and CAMPOTOSTO, Henry (19th C) Belgian					
oil	3	47,814	11,850	17,982	17,982
VERBOECKHOVEN, Louis (1802-1889) Belgian					
oil	12	61,149	1,091	4,581	13,616
VERBOOM, Adriaen (1628-1670) Dutch					
oil	3	75,437	18,857	27,180	29,400
wc/d	1	1,585		1,585	
VERBRUGGE, C (19/20th C) Continental					
oil	1	1,184		1,184	
VERBRUGGEN, Gaspar Pieter (17/18th C) Flemish					
oil	2	20,405	2,718	10,203	17,687
VERBRUGGEN, Gaspar Pieter II (1664-1730) Flemish					
oil	7	135,670	1,628	26,690	31,400
VERBRUGGHE, H (1886-1957) Belgian					
oil	1	1,760		1,760	
VERBURGH, Dionys (1655-1722) Dutch					
oil	1	3,200		3,200	
VERBURGH, Medard (1886-1957) Belgian					
oil	6	23,057	1,160	3,065	9,342
VERBURGH, Rutger (1678-?) Belgian					
oil	1	29,094		29,094	
VERCELLI, Giulio Romano (1871-1951) Italian					
oil	2	7,344	2,299	3,672	5,045
VERDES, Jose Luis (1933-) Spanish					
oil	1	2,594		2,594	
VERDEVOYE, E (19th C) French					
oil	1	1,229		1,229	
VERDIER, François (1651-1730) French					
wc/d	1	3,000		3,000	
VERDILHAN, Mathieu (1875-1928) French					
oil	6	37,125	1,549	5,460	12,822
wc/d	2	2,548	1,140	1,274	1,408
VERDOEL, Adriaan (1620-1695) Dutch					
oil	1	18,089		18,089	

Name	No.	Total Sales Value	lowest	Prices median	highest
VERDUSSEN, Jan Peeter (1700-1763) Flemish					
oil	6	79,705	5,418	10,195	28,004
VERDYEN, Eugène (1836-1903) Belgian					
oil	1	3,357		3,357	
VERELST, John (fl.1698-1734) Flemish					
oil	1	4,082		4,082	
VERELST, Pieter (c.1618-1668) Dutch					
oil	2	396,900	117,600	198,450	279,300
VERELST, Simon (1644-1721) Dutch					
oil	4	352,880	18,120	57,380	220,000
VERELST, Willem (?-c.1756) British					
oil	1	4,600		4,600	
VERENDAEL, Nicolas van (1640-1691) Flemish					
oil	2	211,950	31,400	105,975	180,550
VERESMITH, Daniel Albert (1861-1932) German					
oil	1	1,413		1,413	
VERESS, Zoltan (1868-1935) Hungarian					
oil	1	1,058		1,058	
VERETSHCHAGIN, Piotr (1836-1886) Russian					
oil	5	253,104	9,060	24,084	169,200
VERETSHCHAGIN, Vassily Petrovich (1835-1909) Russian					
oil	1	118,440		118,440	
VERETSHCHAGIN, Vassily Vasilievich (1842-1904) Russian					
oil	1	1,813		1,813	
wc/d	2	4,832	1,208	2,416	3,624
VEREYCKEN, Edouard (1893-1967) Belgian					
3D	1	1,287		1,287	
VERGARA Y XIMENO, Jose (1726-1799) Spanish					
oil	1	17,904		17,904	
VERHAECHT, Tobias (1561-1631) Flemish					
oil	2	37,130	13,130	18,565	24,000
wc/d	1	2,357		2,357	
VERHAEGEN, Fernand (1884-1976) Belgian					
oil	6	25,415	1,158	3,114	11,582
VERHAERT, Dirck (17th C) Dutch					
oil	1	151,000		151,000	
VERHAERT, Piet (1852-1908) Flemish					
oil	3	6,696	1,087	1,321	4,288
VERHAS (19/20th C) Belgian					
oil	1	2,966		2,966	
VERHAS, Frans (c.1827-1897) Belgian					
oil	1	9,323		9,323	
VERHAS, Jan Frans (1834-1896) Belgian					
oil	2	59,335	16,793	29,668	42,542
VERHEGGEN, Hendrik Frederik (1809-1883) Dutch					
oil	1	3,128		3,128	
VERHEYDEN, François (1806-1889) Belgian					
oil	4	8,178	1,543	1,855	2,925
VERHEYDEN, Isidore (1848-1905) Belgian					
oil	8	35,153	1,278	3,508	9,530
VERHEYDEN, Matthaeus (1700-1776) Dutch					
oil	1	17,234		17,234	
VERHEYEN, Jan Hendrik (1778-1846) Dutch					
oil	2	43,500	15,000	21,750	28,500
wc/d	1	2,617		2,617	
VERHEYEN, Jef (1932-) Belgian					
oil	2	16,921	3,128	8,461	13,793
VERHOESEN, Albertus (1806-1881) Dutch					
oil	12	29,561	1,259	2,434	3,962

Name	No.	Total Sales Value	lowest	Prices median	highest
VERHOESEN, M (19th C) Dutch					
oil	1	1,171		1,171	
VERHOEVEN-BALL, Adrien Joseph (1824-1882) Belgian					
oil	2	19,263	5,510	9,632	13,753
VERHORST, Andre (1889-1977) Dutch					
oil	1	1,377		1,377	
VERHOUTTE, Max (?) ?					
oil	1	3,987		3,987	
VERKOLJE, Jan (1650-1693) Dutch					
oil	2	33,059	8,218	16,530	24,841
wc/d	3	6,129	1,021	2,554	2,554
VERKOLJE, Nicolaes (1673-1746) Dutch					
oil	2	87,294	18,046	43,647	69,248
VERKOREN, Lucas (1888-1955) Dutch					
oil	1	2,264		2,264	
VERLAINE, H (?) ?					
oil	1	2,100		2,100	
VERLAINE, Paul Marie (1844-1896) French					
wc/d	1	13,096		13,096	
VERLAT, A (?) ?					
oil	1	2,109		2,109	
VERLAT, C M M (1824-1890) Belgian					
oil	1	4,637		4,637	
VERLAT, Charles Michel Maria (1824-1890) Belgian					
oil	2	2,404	1,145	1,202	1,259
VERLINDE, Claude (20th C) ?					
oil	1	1,298		1,298	
wc/d	1	2,122		2,122	
VERMEER OF HAARLEM, Jan (elder) (1628-1691) Dutch					
oil	1	10,000		10,000	
VERMEER OF HAARLEM, Jan (younger) (1656-1705) Dutch					
oil	1	5,623		5,623	
VERMEERSCH, Jose (1922-1997) Belgian					
3D	6	27,361	1,761	4,131	6,685
VERMEHREN, Gustav (1863-1931) Danish					
oil	2	4,146	1,826	2,073	2,320
VERMEHREN, Sophus (1866-1950) Danish					
oil	1	1,807		1,807	
VERMEIR, Alfons (1905-1994) Belgian					
oil	3	3,467	1,075	1,101	1,291
VERMEIRE, Geo (20th C) ?					
oil	1	1,145		1,145	
VERMEIRE, Jules (1885-?) Dutch					
3D	5	35,646	1,810	4,310	18,103
wc/d	2	2,156	1,078	1,078	1,078
VERMEULEN, Andreas Franciscus (1821-1884) Dutch					
oil	2	13,268	6,634	6,634	6,634
VERMEULEN, Andries (1763-1814) Dutch					
oil	5	37,680	3,000	7,850	12,960
wc/d	1	1,812		1,812	
VERMEULEN, P (20th C) Dutch					
oil	1	1,180		1,180	
VERMIGLIO, Giuseppe (16/17th C) Italian					
oil	2	57,612	6,500	28,806	51,112
VERMONT, Nicolae (1886-1932) Rumanian					
oil	1	1,365		1,365	
VERNAY, François (1821-1896) French					
oil	2	10,999	2,527	5,500	8,472

Name	No.	Total Sales Value	lowest	Prices median	highest
VERNER, Frederick Arthur (1836-1928) Canadian					
oil	2	20,255	9,636	10,128	10,619
wc/d	12	41,911	1,062	3,003	6,305
VERNET, Carle (1758-1836) French					
wc/d	5	13,013	1,273	1,947	5,093
VERNET, Horace (1789-1863) French					
oil	2	39,221	7,000	19,611	32,221
VERNET, Joseph (1714-1789) French					
oil	11	3,420,791	15,000	189,662	940,800
wc/d	4	12,795	1,489	2,029	7,248
VERNET, Joseph (school) (1714-1789) French					
oil	5	20,166	1,983	3,047	6,963
VERNET, Pierre Maria Joseph (1797-?) French					
oil	1	1,207		1,207	
VERNEUIL, J de (fl.c.1850-1870) ?					
oil	1	1,066		1,066	
VERNI, Arturo (1891-1960) Italian					
oil	1	1,242		1,242	
VERNON, Emile (19/20th C) British					
oil	5	97,364	7,000	18,615	37,700
VERNON, Jules (20th C) French					
oil	1	1,038		1,038	
VERNON, Paul (1796-1875) French					
oil	2	3,129	1,380	1,565	1,749
VERON, Alexandre Paul Joseph (1773-?) French					
wc/d	1	1,354		1,354	
VERON, Alexandre René (1826-1897) French					
oil	18	88,377	1,080	4,386	15,000
VERONA SCHOOL, 14th C Italian					
oil	1	42,000		42,000	
VERONE (20th C) Swiss					
oil	1	2,664		2,664	
VERONESE SCHOOL, 17th C Italian					
oil	2	11,469	2,940	5,735	8,529
VERONESE, Marco (1962-) Italian					
wc/d	1	1,088		1,088	
VERONESE, Paolo (1528-1588) Italian					
oil	1	87,351		87,351	
wc/d	4	74,500	7,000	15,000	37,500
VERONESE, Paolo (school) (1528-1588) Italian					
oil	1	19,500		19,500	
VERONESI, Luigi (1908-1998) Italian					
oil	6	52,877	2,912	6,670	24,606
wc/d	2	2,673	1,282	1,337	1,391
VERPOEKEN, Hendrik (1791-1869) Dutch					
oil	1	2,717		2,717	
VERRIER, Max le (19/20th C) Belgian					
3D	3	9,415	2,100	3,565	3,750
VERRYCK, Theodor (1734-1786) Dutch					
wc/d	1	1,253		1,253	
VERRYT, Dirk (17th C) Dutch					
wc/d	1	1,179		1,179	
VERSAILLE, H (?) ?					
oil	1	2,437		2,437	
VERSCHAFFELT, Edouard (1874-1955) Belgian					
oil	4	44,463	5,413	10,181	18,688
VERSCHUIER, Albregt (?-1680) Dutch					
oil	1	3,140		3,140	

Name	No.	Total Sales Value	lowest	Prices median	highest
VERSCHUIER, Lieve (1630-1686) Dutch					
oil	2	118,445	11,760	59,223	106,685
VERSCHUIER, Lieve (school) (1630-1686) Dutch					
oil	1	19,000		19,000	
VERSCHURING, Hendrik (1627-1690) Dutch					
oil	1	4,883		4,883	
VERSCHUUR, Cornelius (19th C) Dutch					
oil	1	2,175		2,175	
VERSCHUUR, W (snr) (1812-1874) Dutch					
oil	2	18,786	1,570	9,393	17,216
VERSCHUUR, Wouter (jnr) (1841-1936) Dutch					
oil	2	4,112	1,612	2,056	2,500
VERSCHUUR, Wouter (snr) (1812-1874) Dutch					
oil	18	935,535	2,667	26,425	165,486
wc/d	1	1,231		1,231	
VERSPRONCK, Jan (1597-1662) Dutch					
oil	2	143,050	60,000	71,525	83,050
VERSTEEGH, Michiel (1756-1843) Dutch					
oil	1	8,643		8,643	
VERSTER, Floris (1861-1927) Dutch					
oil	2	54,571	24,868	27,286	29,703
VERSTRAETE, L (?) Belgian					
oil	1	1,996		1,996	
VERSTRAETE, Theodore (1850-1907) Belgian					
oil	2	8,208	2,884	4,104	5,324
VERSTRAETEN, Edmond (1870-1956) Belgian					
oil	2	6,643	1,045	3,322	5,598
VERSTYNEN, Henri (1882-1940) Dutch					
oil	1	1,026		1,026	
VERTANGEN, Daniel (1598-1684) Dutch					
oil	6	53,199	5,009	8,180	15,330
VERTES, Marcel (1895-1961) French					
oil	1	4,000		4,000	
VERTIN, Petrus Gerardus (1819-1893) Dutch					
oil	19	122,785	1,951	5,463	12,730
VERTUNNI, Achille (1826-1897) Italian					
oil	1	8,275		8,275	
VERUDZI, L (?) ?					
oil	1	1,134		1,134	
VERVEER, Elchanon Leonardus (1826-1900) Dutch					
oil	2	15,506	2,200	7,753	13,306
VERVEER, Salomon Leonardus (1813-1876) Dutch					
oil	5	46,068	2,366	7,009	16,124
wc/d	3	6,938	1,377	1,530	4,031
VERVISCH, Jean (1896-1977) Belgian					
oil	1	1,278		1,278	
VERVLOET, Augustine (1806-?) Belgian					
oil	1	6,500		6,500	
VERVLOET, Frans (1795-1872) Dutch					
oil	4	99,463	1,058	3,383	91,640
VERWEE (?) Belgian					
oil	1	2,884		2,884	
VERWEE, Alfred Jacques (1838-1895) Belgian					
oil	2	4,448	1,537	2,224	2,911
VERWEE, Charles Louis (?-1882) Belgian					
oil	1	28,000		28,000	
VERWEE, Louis Pierre (1807-1877) Belgian					
oil	3	16,220	2,030	2,270	11,920

Name	No.	Total Sales Value	lowest	Prices median	highest
VERWER, Justus (c.1626-c.1688) Dutch					
oil	1	9,420		9,420	
VERWEY, Kees (1900-1995) Dutch					
oil	2	10,992	2,371	5,496	8,621
wc/d	3	6,115	1,132	2,181	2,802
VERWY, Kees (1900-1995) Dutch					
wc/d	1	1,386		1,386	
VESIN, Jaroslav Fr Julius (1859-1915) Bulgarian					
oil	3	24,801	2,681	10,795	11,325
VESPIGNANI, Renzo (1924-) Italian					
oil	4	28,955	4,276	5,809	13,061
wc/d	3	7,176	1,932	2,346	2,898
VESTER, Willem (1824-1871) Dutch					
oil	3	28,256	4,178	8,486	15,592
VETH, Jan (1864-1925) Dutch					
oil	1	2,224		2,224	
VETTER, Charles (1858-1936) German					
oil	3	11,881	1,214	4,356	6,311
VETTER, Jean (1820-1900) French					
oil	1	1,031		1,031	
VETTRIANO, Jack (1954-) British					
oil	12	210,779	3,950	14,703	38,220
VETTURALI, Gaetano (18th C) Italian					
oil	1	19,411		19,411	
VEYOLS, G (?) ?					
oil	1	4,082		4,082	
VEYRASSAT, Jules Jacques (1828-1893) French					
oil	10	107,692	1,032	5,634	36,000
wc/d	1	1,050		1,050	
VIALLAT, Claude (1936-) French					
oil	7	50,038	2,361	6,572	13,723
wc/d	3	13,710	1,460	1,933	10,317
VIANELLI, Achille (1803-1894) Italian					
oil	1	65,000		65,000	
wc/d	10	24,810	1,043	2,051	5,351
VIANELLO, C (19th C) Italian?					
oil	1	3,703		3,703	
VIANELLO, Cesare (19th C) Italian					
oil	1	2,752		2,752	
VIANI, Alberto (1906-1989) Italian					
3D	1	4,159		4,159	
VIANI, Lorenzo (1882-1936) Italian					
oil	1	22,689		22,689	
wc/d	3	6,988	1,032	1,745	4,211
VIAVANT, George L (1872-1925) American					
wc/d	1	2,400		2,400	
VIBERT (?) ?					
3D	1	7,064		7,064	
VIBERT, Jean Georges (1840-1902) French					
oil	4	67,690	1,690	18,000	30,000
VICCHIO, Giulio da (1925-) Italian					
oil	1	1,978		1,978	
VICENTE, Eduardo (1909-1968) Spanish					
oil	3	7,744	2,457	2,529	2,758
wc/d	1	1,022		1,022	
VICENTE, Esteban (1906-) American/Spanish					
oil	1	22,500		22,500	
VICENTE, Victoria (1650-1712) Italian					
oil	1	13,539		13,539	

Name	No.	Total Sales Value	lowest	Prices median	highest
VICENZINO, Giuseppe (17/18th C) Italian					
oil	1	11,602		11,602	
VICHI, F (19th C) Italian					
3D	2	11,659	1,385	5,830	10,274
VICHI, Ferdinando (19th C) Italian					
3D	2	17,873	2,773	8,937	15,100
VICKERS, A H (fl.1853-1907) British					
oil	2	3,354	1,164	1,677	2,190
VICKERS, Alfred (19th C) British					
oil	9	23,391	1,016	1,704	5,720
VICKERS, Alfred (snr) (1786-1868) British					
oil	2	3,198	1,460	1,599	1,738
VICKERS, Alfred Gomersal (1810-1837) British					
wc/d	1	1,193		1,193	
VICKERS, Alfred H (fl.1853-1907) British					
oil	9	17,849	1,136	1,500	5,056
VICKERS, Charles (19th C) British					
oil	1	1,500		1,500	
VICTORIAN SCHOOL, 19th C British					
oil	1	11,760		11,760	
VICTORS, Jan (1620-1676) Dutch					
oil	2	33,201	14,361	16,601	18,840
VICTORYNS, Anthonie (1612-1655) Flemish					
oil	1	11,295		11,295	
VIDA, Gabor (1937-) Hungarian					
oil	1	6,831		6,831	
VIDAL, Emeric Essex (1791-1861) British					
wc/d	1	20,580		20,580	
VIDAL, Eugène (19/20th C) French					
oil	1	9,000		9,000	
VIDAL, Louis (1754-1807) French					
oil	1	18,720		18,720	
VIDAL, Vincent (1811-1887) French					
oil	1	2,774		2,774	
VIEG, Dieter (1958-) German					
oil	1	3,219		3,219	
VIEGENER, Eberhard (19/20th C) German					
oil	4	5,612	1,001	1,260	2,091
wc/d	3	7,214	1,427	2,662	3,125
VIEGERS, Bernardus Petrus (1886-1947) Dutch					
oil	15	36,229	1,180	1,573	4,981
VIEILLEVOYE, Barthelemy Josef (1788-1855) Belgian					
oil	2	9,524	3,566	4,762	5,958
VIEIRA DA SILVA, Maria Elena (1908-1992) French/Portuguese					
oil	12	1,363,210	52,573	109,360	205,674
wc/d	9	136,364	4,279	16,610	24,347
VIELLE, P della (19th C) ?					
oil	1	1,454		1,454	
VIEN, Joseph Marie (1716-1809) French					
oil	3	66,983	6,983	10,000	50,000
wc/d	1	1,142		1,142	
VIEN, Marie Therese (1738-1805) French					
wc/d	1	9,827		9,827	
VIENNESE SCHOOL, 20th C Austrian					
3D	1	1,215		1,215	
VIERGE, Daniel (1851-1904) Spanish					
wc/d	3	6,391	1,151	1,151	4,089
VIERIN, Emmanuel (1869-1954) Belgian					
oil	2	5,294	1,101	2,647	4,193

Name	No.	Total Sales Value	lowest	Prices median	highest
VIERTEL, I (19th C) ?					
3D	1	8,978		8,978	
VIERTHALER, Johann (1869-?) German					
3D	1	1,220		1,220	
VIGAS, Oswaldo (1926-) Venezuelan					
3D	1	4,100		4,100	
oil	2	4,820	1,100	2,410	3,720
wc/d	1	1,465		1,465	
VIGEE, Louis (1715-1767) French					
wc/d	1	6,110		6,110	
VIGEE-LEBRUN, Marie Louise Elisabeth (1755-1842) French					
oil	3	306,285	6,285	120,000	180,000
wc/d	2	38,929	18,120	19,465	20,809
VIGEE-LEBRUN, Marie Louise Elisabeth (school) (1755-1842) French					
wc/d	1	11,461		11,461	
VIGER DU VIGNEAU, Jean Louis Victor (1819-1879) French					
oil	1	11,600		11,600	
VIGHI, Coriolano (1846-1905) Italian					
wc/d	1	3,190		3,190	
VIGIER, Philbert (1636-1719) French					
3D	1	4,500		4,500	
VIGNALI, Jacopo (1592-1664) Italian					
oil	1	39,279		39,279	
wc/d	2	263,042	6,342	131,521	256,700
VIGNANI, Giuseppe (1932-) Italian					
oil	1	2,252		2,252	
VIGNE, Edouard de (1808-1866) Belgian					
oil	3	10,647	1,275	2,997	6,375
VIGNE, Paul de (1843-1901) Belgian					
3D	1	4,281		4,281	
VIGNOLES, Andre (?) ?					
oil	3	5,500	1,500	1,800	2,200
VIGNON, Claude (1593-1670) French					
wc/d	1	12,244		12,244	
VIGNON, Victor Alfred Paul (1847-1909) French					
oil	8	48,024	1,327	5,814	10,712
VIGO, Nanda (20th C) Italian					
3D	1	15,950		15,950	
VIGON, Jacques (20th C) French?					
oil	1	1,267		1,267	
VIJAIWARGIYA, Ram Gopal (1905-) Indian					
wc/d	1	3,600		3,600	
VIKAS, K (1875-1934) Austrian					
oil	1	1,122		1,122	
VILA Y PRADES, Jose (1873-1930) Spanish					
oil	1	1,282		1,282	
VILA Y PRADES, Julio (1873-1930) Spanish					
oil	3	26,673	2,670	3,003	21,000
VILALLONGA, Jesus Carlos de (1927-) Canadian					
oil	1	1,759		1,759	
VILATO, Javier (1921-) French					
3D	1	1,742		1,742	
oil	4	6,739	1,088	1,876	1,918
VILBOUX, Alain (20th C) French					
oil	2	4,376	2,188	2,188	2,188
VILLA, Émile (19th C) French					
oil	1	72,680		72,680	
VILLA, Miguel (1901-1988) Spanish					
oil	5	46,877	6,453	8,547	15,813

Name	No.	Total Sales Value	lowest	Prices median	highest
VILLANIS, E (19th C) French					
3D	2	3,217	1,491	1,609	1,726
VILLANIS, Emmanuele (19th C) Italian					
3D	4	11,254	1,033	1,871	6,480
VILLAPAREDES, Esteban (1933-) Venezuelan					
oil	2	2,810	1,090	1,405	1,720
VILLAR, Isabel (?) Spanish?					
oil	1	2,468		2,468	
VILLEGAS Y CORDERO, Jose (1848-1922) Spanish					
oil	6	113,891	3,791	15,879	34,514
VILLEGAS Y CORDERO, Ricardo (1852-?) Spanish					
oil	1	9,779		9,779	
VILLEGLE, Jacques de la (1926-) French					
oil	1	1,137		1,137	
wc/d	16	106,374	1,501	4,409	21,396
VILLENEUVE, Gabriel (19th C) French					
oil	1	2,708		2,708	
VILLEON, Emmanuel de la (1858-1944) French					
oil	18	81,306	1,069	3,713	15,000
VILLERET, François Etienne (1800-1866) French					
wc/d	2	9,403	3,802	4,702	5,601
VILLERS, Jacob de (1616-1667) Dutch					
oil	1	27,180		27,180	
VILLON, Jacques (1875-1963) French					
oil	6	58,750	1,579	5,622	34,716
wc/d	13	43,710	1,106	2,200	14,000
VIMAZ, A (20th C) ?					
oil	1	9,815		9,815	
VINCENT, Charles (fl.1820-1860) British					
oil	1	2,500		2,500	
VINCENT, François Andre (1746-1816) French					
oil	3	94,192	10,990	13,376	69,826
wc/d	7	224,707	1,673	15,334	92,157
VINCENT, George (1796-c.1831) British					
oil	3	13,057	3,167	4,380	5,510
VINCENT, Harry A (1864-1931) American					
oil	1	6,500		6,500	
VINCENT, J (19th C) ?					
oil	2	3,160	1,264	1,580	1,896
VINCENT, Jean (20th C) French?					
oil	1	1,891		1,891	
VINCENT-ANGLADE, Henri (19th C) French					
oil	1	2,207		2,207	
VINCK, Franz (1827-1903) Belgian					
oil	4	10,302	1,761	2,483	3,576
VINCK, Jan (17th C) Dutch					
oil	1	10,329		10,329	
VINCK, Joseph (1900-1979) Belgian					
oil	2	4,065	1,275	2,033	2,790
VINCKEBOONS, David (1576-1629) Flemish					
oil	6	372,494	22,568	61,516	90,454
wc/d	2	12,965	6,286	6,483	6,679
VINCKEBOONS, David (school) (1576-1629) Flemish					
oil	1	11,000		11,000	
VINCKENS, P (19th C) Belgian					
oil	1	2,100		2,100	
VINCOTTE, Thomas (1850-1925) Belgian					
3D	1	1,385		1,385	

Name	No.	Total Sales Value	Prices lowest	median	highest
VINDFELDT, Ejnar (1905-1953) Danish					
wc/d	1	1,160		1,160	
VINE OF COLCHESTER, John (1809-1867) British					
oil	1	3,480		3,480	
VINEA, Francesco (1845-1902) Italian					
oil	5	49,925	4,000	8,690	22,000
wc/d	1	1,309		1,309	
VINES, Hernando (1904-1993) Spanish					
oil	16	65,671	1,221	2,532	14,048
wc/d	3	7,429	2,118	2,118	3,047
VINIEGRA Y LASSO, Salvador (1862-1915) Spanish					
oil	2	9,971	4,440	4,986	5,531
VINNEN, Carl (1863-1922) German					
oil	4	45,253	1,734	7,574	28,371
VINOGRADOV, Sergei Arsenevich (1869-1938) Russian					
oil	1	1,025		1,025	
VINTILESCU, Maria Manuela (1959-) ?					
oil	1	1,671		1,671	
VINTON, Frederick Porter (1846-1911) American					
oil	1	2,800		2,800	
VINZIO, Giulio Cesare (1881-1940) Italian					
oil	1	2,836		2,836	
VINZMAN, Josef Osip (1848-1909) Russian					
oil	1	7,550		7,550	
VIOLA, Manuel (1919-1987) Spanish					
oil	16	57,049	1,045	1,760	11,615
wc/d	1	1,026		1,026	
VIOLLET LE DUC, Victor (1848-1901) French					
oil	1	3,500		3,500	
VIOLLET-LE-DUC, Eugène (1814-1879) French					
wc/d	1	15,055		15,055	
VIOLLIER, Jean (1896-1985) Swiss					
oil	6	13,746	1,084	1,491	6,645
VION, Maguy de (1894-1980) French					
oil	1	1,307		1,307	
VIRBICKY, A (19/20th C) ?					
oil	1	2,544		2,544	
VIRNICH, Thomas (1957-) German					
3D	2	2,676	1,220	1,338	1,456
VIRULY, Willem (1604-1677) Dutch					
oil	1	3,892		3,892	
VISCA, Jorge (1920-) Uruguayan					
oil	1	1,000		1,000	
VISCA, Rodolfo (1939-) Uruguayan					
oil	2	2,450	1,050	1,225	1,400
VISCONTI, Adolfo Ferraguti (1850-1924) Italian					
oil	3	19,115	4,558	7,163	7,394
VISCONTI, Francois (19th C) French?					
oil	1	3,498		3,498	
VISCONTI, Louis Tullius Joachim (19th C) ?					
wc/d	1	1,256		1,256	
VISCONTI, V (?) Italian					
oil	1	2,463		2,463	
VISENTINI, Antonio (1688-1782) Italian					
wc/d	2	7,497	2,205	3,749	5,292
VISKI, Janos (1891-?) Hungarian					
oil	1	1,300		1,300	
VISO, Nicola (18th C) Italian					
oil	2	28,142	13,345	14,071	14,797

Name	No.	Total Sales Value	Prices lowest	median	highest
VISSER, Carel (1928-) Dutch					
3D	5	35,683	5,172	5,942	10,345
wc/d	3	12,453	2,971	4,741	4,741
VISSER, Tjipke (1876-1955) Dutch					
3D	1	1,810		1,810	
VITA, Miguel de (?) ?					
oil	1	1,500		1,500	
VITA, Wilhelm (1846-1919) Austrian					
oil	1	29,200		29,200	
VITAL, Edgar (1883-?) Swiss					
oil	1	1,581		1,581	
VITAL, Not (1948-) American					
oil	1	4,715		4,715	
VITALE, Carlo (1902-) Italian					
oil	1	2,523		2,523	
VITALE, F (19th C) Italian					
oil	1	1,595		1,595	
VITALIS, Macario (1898-?) Philippino					
oil	1	1,740		1,740	
VITALONI, Michael (1967-) Italian					
3D	1	5,964		5,964	
VITALONI, Michelle (20th C) ?					
3D	1	1,859		1,859	
VITI, Guisto (19th C) Italian					
3D	1	3,975		3,975	
VITO, Camillo de (19th C) Italian					
oil	1	3,292		3,292	
wc/d	1	4,396		4,396	
VITRINGA, Wigerus (1657-1721) Dutch					
oil	1	11,325		11,325	
wc/d	1	1,767		1,767	
VITTORI, Carlo (1881-1943) Italian					
oil	1	3,004		3,004	
wc/d	1	1,617		1,617	
VIUDES, Vincente (1916-) Spanish?					
wc/d	1	1,650		1,650	
VIVANCOS (20th C) Spanish					
oil	1	1,386		1,386	
VIVIAN (19th C) Italian					
oil	1	7,452		7,452	
VIVIAN, J (19th C) British					
oil	3	22,311	4,710	6,090	11,511
VIVIAN, Miss J (fl.1869-1877) British					
oil	1	3,289		3,289	
VIVIEN, Joseph (1657-1735) French					
wc/d	1	8,000		8,000	
VIVIEN, Narcisse (19th C) French					
wc/d	1	1,755		1,755	
VIVIN, Louis (1861-1936) French					
oil	1	1,947		1,947	
VIZKELETY, E (1819-1895) Hungarian					
oil	1	1,300		1,300	
VIZZOTTO-ALBERTI, Giuseppe (1862-1931) Italian					
wc/d	2	11,403	2,230	5,702	9,173
VLAMINCK, Maurice de (1876-1958) French					
oil	74	5,713,232	12,080	45,850	430,000
wc/d	23	379,464	1,800	15,274	55,279
VLECK, Natalie van (1901-1981) American					
oil	3	7,450	2,000	2,200	3,250

Name	No.	Total Sales Value	lowest	Prices median	highest
VLEUGHELS, Nicolas (1668-1737) French					
oil	1	1,653		1,653	
VLIEGER, Simon de (1600-1653) Dutch					
oil	2	55,220	14,400	27,610	40,820
wc/d	2	8,163	2,270	4,082	5,893
VLIET, Hendrik Cornelisz van der (1611-1675) Dutch					
oil	3	44,025	11,025	16,000	17,000
VLIET, Jan Joris van (17th C) Dutch					
oil	1	1,687		1,687	
VLIET, Willem van der (1584-1642) Dutch					
oil	1	20,000		20,000	
VLOORS, Émile (1871-1952) Belgian					
oil	1	2,254		2,254	
VOELCKER, Gottfried Wilhelm (1775-1849) German					
oil	2	70,701	31,824	35,351	38,877
VOERMAN, Jan (jnr) (1890-1976) Dutch					
oil	10	33,258	2,179	3,283	4,981
wc/d	1	1,268		1,268	
VOERMAN, Jan (snr) (1857-1941) Dutch					
oil	1	1,573		1,573	
wc/d	1	1,171		1,171	
VOET, Jacob Ferdinand (1639-c.1700) Flemish					
oil	4	21,575	3,265	5,682	6,946
VOET, Jacob Ferdinand (school) (1639-c.1700) Flemish					
oil	1	2,593		2,593	
VOGEL VON VOGELSTEIN, Carl Christian (1788-1868) German					
oil	1	37,382		37,382	
VOGEL, Bernard (1683-1737) German					
wc/d	1	1,609		1,609	
VOGEL, Cornelis Jan de (1824-1879) Flemish					
oil	5	33,143	1,268	5,724	11,881
VOGEL, Hannes (1938-) Swiss					
oil	1	3,315		3,315	
VOGEL, Ludwig (1788-1879) Swiss					
oil	2	4,253	1,967	2,127	2,286
VOGELER, Heinrich (1872-1942) German					
oil	2	224,288	54,064	112,144	170,224
wc/d	1	1,028		1,028	
VOGELS, Guillaume (1836-1896) Belgian					
oil	3	17,814	1,620	8,060	8,134
VOGLER, Paul (1852-1904) French					
oil	7	55,967	1,448	3,520	22,795
VOGT, Louis Charles (1864-?) American					
wc/d	1	5,500		5,500	
VOGT, Victor (19th C) ?					
oil	1	2,250		2,250	
VOIGT, Bruno (1912-1989) German					
oil	1	4,320		4,320	
wc/d	7	32,976	2,304	4,032	9,360
VOIGT, Franz Wilhelm (1867-?) German					
oil	1	1,162		1,162	
VOIGT, Leigh (1943-) South African					
oil	1	2,556		2,556	
VOILLE, Jean (1744-1796) French					
oil	2	18,677	4,073	9,339	14,604
VOIRIN, Jules Antoine (1833-1898) French					
oil	1	8,904		8,904	
VOIS, A de (1631-1680) Flemish					
oil	1	1,000		1,000	

Name	No.	Total Sales Value	Prices lowest	median	highest
VOISIN, Gerard (20th C) French					
3D	1	1,152		1,152	
VOLAIRE, Pierre Jacques (1729-1802) French					
oil	3	375,000	35,000	70,000	270,000
wc/d	4	6,766	1,096	1,804	2,062
VOLANG, Jean (?) ?					
oil	2	3,927	1,177	1,964	2,750
VOLCKER, Robert (1854-1924) German					
oil	1	1,461		1,461	
VOLK, Leonard Wells (1828-1895) American					
3D	1	1,600		1,600	
VOLKEL, Reinhold (19/20th C) Austrian					
wc/d	1	1,966		1,966	
VOLKERS, Emil (1831-1905) German					
oil	8	24,715	1,981	2,680	5,809
VOLKERT, Edward Charles (1871-1935) American					
oil	2	6,350	1,600	3,175	4,750
VOLKHART, Max (1848-1935) German					
oil	1	29,905		29,905	
VOLKMANN, Hans Richard von (1860-1927) German					
oil	12	25,498	1,268	1,882	4,361
VOLKMAR, Charles (1841-1914) American					
oil	1	1,400		1,400	
VOLKOV, Efim Efimovich (1844-1920) Russian					
oil	1	1,195		1,195	
VOLL, Christoph (1897-1939) German					
3D	1	15,495		15,495	
VOLLENWEIDER, Johann Gustav (1852-1919) Swiss					
oil	1	1,215		1,215	
VOLLERDT, Johann Christian (1708-1769) German					
oil	2	41,847	5,000	20,924	36,847
VOLLET, Henri Émile (1861-1945) French					
oil	2	3,339	1,579	1,670	1,760
VOLLMER, Adolf Friedrich (1806-1875) German					
oil	1	1,278		1,278	
VOLLON, Alexis (1865-1945) French					
oil	5	30,874	2,031	3,647	11,850
VOLLON, Antoine (1833-1900) French					
oil	10	103,069	1,933	4,931	38,000
VOLLON, M (19/20th C) French					
oil	1	5,548		5,548	
VOLLWEIDER, Johann Jakob (1834-1891) German					
oil	1	1,900		1,900	
VOLMAR, Georg (1770-1831) German					
oil	1	5,766		5,766	
wc/d	1	13,147		13,147	
VOLPE, Alessandro la (1820-1887) Italian					
oil	4	44,998	1,055	8,382	27,180
VOLPE, Angiolo (20th C) ?					
oil	1	1,115		1,115	
VOLPE, Vincenzo (1855-1929) Italian					
oil	2	5,065	1,065	2,533	4,000
wc/d	1	2,225		2,225	
VOLPENGO, Amedeo Ghesio (1847-1889) British					
oil	1	9,173		9,173	
VOLTERRA (16th C) Italian					
oil	1	13,000		13,000	
VOLTI, Antoniucci (1915-1990) French					
3D	7	130,713	4,832	17,359	40,532

Name	No.	Total Sales Value	lowest	Prices median	highest
wc/d	13	31,823	1,010	2,618	4,189
VOLTZ, Friedrich (1817-1886) German					
oil	16	93,755	1,145	2,150	18,648
wc/d	1	1,798		1,798	
VOLTZ, Ludwig (1825-1911) German					
oil	3	5,722	1,364	1,634	2,724
VOLZ, Herman (1904-1990) American					
oil	2	3,100	1,500	1,550	1,600
VOLZ, Hermann (1814-1894) German					
oil	4	13,683	2,059	3,584	4,457
VOLZ, Wilhelm (1855-1901) German					
oil	1	7,264		7,264	
VONLANTHEN, Louis (1889-1937) Swiss					
oil	2	8,821	1,242	4,411	7,579
VONNOH, Bessie Potter (1872-1955) American					
3D	2	11,000	3,500	5,500	7,500
VONNOH, Robert (1858-1933) American					
oil	2	19,000	9,000	9,500	10,000
VONTILLIUS, Jeppe (1915-1994) Danish					
oil	1	1,743		1,743	
VOOGD, Hendrik (1766-1839) Dutch					
oil	1	2,378		2,378	
VOORDECKER, François (19th C) Flemish					
oil	1	1,037		1,037	
VOORDEN, August Willem van (1881-1921) Dutch					
oil	2	9,925	2,181	4,963	7,744
VOORZAAT, Theo (1938-) Dutch					
oil	1	1,379		1,379	
VORDEMBERGE, Friedrich (1897-1980) German					
oil	1	1,550		1,550	
VORGANG, Paul (1860-1927) German					
oil	1	1,961		1,961	
VORST, Joseph Paul (1897-1947) American/German					
oil	1	2,000		2,000	
wc/d	1	1,100		1,100	
VORST, Tony van de (20th C) Dutch					
3D	1	2,586		2,586	
VOS, Christoffel Albertus (1813-1877) Dutch					
oil	1	2,206		2,206	
VOS, Cornelis de (1585-1651) Flemish					
wc/d	1	9,892		9,892	
VOS, Eddy de (1950-) Belgian					
oil	2	2,090	1,045	1,045	1,045
VOS, Maria (1824-1906) Dutch					
oil	1	7,269		7,269	
wc/d	1	1,071		1,071	
VOS, Martin de (1532-1603) Flemish					
oil	1	58,800		58,800	
wc/d	2	3,312	1,500	1,656	1,812
VOS, Martin de (school) (1532-1603) Flemish					
oil	1	1,442		1,442	
VOS, Paul de (1596-1678) Flemish					
oil	1	84,711		84,711	
VOS, Simon de (1603-1676) Flemish					
oil	4	49,026	3,418	6,593	32,423
VOS, Vincent de (1829-1875) Belgian					
oil	3	18,472	2,440	3,097	12,935
VOSBERG, Heinrich (1833-1891) German					
oil	2	3,273	1,364	1,637	1,909

Name	No.	Total Sales Value	Prices lowest	median	highest
VOSS, Frank B (1880-1953) American					
oil	7	62,750	4,250	5,000	24,000
VOSS, Jan (1936-) German					
3D	1	1,419		1,419	
oil	10	50,831	1,511	4,148	10,890
wc/d	1	1,690		1,690	
VOSSARD, J (20th C) ?					
oil	1	2,904		2,904	
VOSTELL, Wolf (1932-) German					
wc/d	4	9,963	1,788	2,538	3,099
VOUET, Simon (1590-1649) French					
oil	1	362,400		362,400	
wc/d	2	20,385	9,815	10,193	10,570
VOULKOS, Peter (1924-) American					
3D	1	8,500		8,500	
VOULLEMIER, Anne Nicole (1796-1886) French					
wc/d	1	1,173		1,173	
VOYET, Jacques (1927-) French					
oil	1	2,200		2,200	
VRANCX, Sebastian (1573-1647) Flemish					
oil	2	272,700	16,000	136,350	256,700
VRBOVA, M (20th C) Czechoslovakian					
oil	2	2,833	1,273	1,417	1,560
VRBOVA, Miloslava (20th C) Czechoslovakian					
oil	1	1,700		1,700	
VREEDENBORGH, H (20th C) Dutch?					
wc/d	1	4,152		4,152	
VREEDENBURGH, Cornelis (1880-1946) Dutch					
oil	7	68,706	2,366	12,325	15,000
wc/d	1	1,377		1,377	
VREEDENBURGH, Herman (1887-1956) Dutch					
oil	1	2,052		2,052	
VREESE, Godefroid (1861-1941) Belgian					
3D	4	7,457	1,068	1,598	3,194
VRIENDT, Juliaan de (1842-1935) Belgian					
oil	2	69,691	15,971	34,846	53,720
VRIENS, Antoine (1902-1987) Belgian					
3D	2	5,159	1,687	2,580	3,472
VRIES, Abraham de (1590-c.1662) Dutch					
oil	1	48,000		48,000	
VRIES, Dick de (1948-) Dutch					
oil	1	1,716		1,716	
VRIES, Hans Vredeman de (1527-1604) Flemish					
oil	1	42,107		42,107	
VRIES, Herman de (1931-) Dutch					
oil	1	2,184		2,184	
VRIES, Paul Vredeman de (1567-c.1630) Flemish					
oil	1	32,000		32,000	
VRIES, Roelof van (1631-1681) Dutch					
oil	6	29,273	1,407	4,491	10,290
VRIESLANDER, John Jack (1879-1957) German					
wc/d	3	12,051	2,191	3,158	6,702
VROLYK, Adrianus Jacobus (1834-1862) Dutch					
oil	3	43,300	9,384	9,756	24,160
VROLYK, Jan (1845-1894) Dutch					
wc/d	1	1,964		1,964	
VROUTOS, Georgios (1843-1908) Greek					
3D	1	75,920		75,920	

Name	No.	Total Sales Value	lowest	Prices median	highest
VRYZAKIS, Theodor (1814-1878) Greek					
oil	1	73,000		73,000	
VU CAO DAM (1908-) Vietnamese					
oil	5	39,738	1,400	2,708	27,484
VU, Yannick (20th C) French					
oil	1	1,433		1,433	
VUCHT, Jan van der (1603-1637) Dutch					
oil	1	5,966		5,966	
VUIDARS, J (19th C) French					
oil	1	9,500		9,500	
VUILLARD (1868-1940) French					
oil	2	245,000	120,000	122,500	125,000
wc/d	2	104,000	32,000	52,000	72,000
VUILLARD, Edouard (1868-1940) French					
oil	14	6,348,868	10,875	151,880	2,700,000
wc/d	16	2,424,667	2,718	22,925	1,000,000
VUILLEMENOT (19th C) French					
oil	1	3,389		3,389	
VUILLIER, Gaston Charles (1847-1915) French					
oil	1	1,166		1,166	
VULLIAMY, Gerard (1909-) French					
oil	1	2,656		2,656	
VUUREN, Jan van (1871-1941) Dutch					
oil	4	9,430	1,205	2,102	4,021
VYGH, Arent (18th C) Dutch					
oil	1	4,456		4,456	
VYLBRIEF, Ernst (1934-) Dutch					
oil	1	1,268		1,268	
VYLDER, C de (19th C) Dutch					
oil	1	5,530		5,530	
WAAGEN (19th C) German					
3D	1	3,067		3,067	
WAAGEN, Adalbert (1833-1898) German					
oil	1	1,692		1,692	
WAAGEN, Arthur (19th C) French					
3D	5	45,486	2,800	6,702	18,875
WAANDERS, Franciscus Bernardus (1809-1880) Dutch					
oil	1	1,483		1,483	
WAANO-GANO, Joe (1906-) American					
oil	1	1,200		1,200	
WAAS, H (19th C) American?					
oil	1	1,300		1,300	
WAAS, Maurice A (19th C) American?					
oil	1	2,300		2,300	
WAAY, Nicolaas van der (1855-1936) Dutch					
oil	2	23,463	11,662	11,732	11,801
wc/d	1	14,538		14,538	
WABEL, Henry (1889-1981) Swiss					
oil	1	1,384		1,384	
WACHSMUTH, Maximilian (1859-1912) German					
oil	1	1,397		1,397	
WACHTEL, Elmer (1864-1929) American					
oil	5	42,250	2,250	9,500	12,000
WACHTEL, Marion K (1876-1954) American					
oil	8	80,000	3,000	6,500	28,000
wc/d	1	28,000		28,000	
WACHTEL, Wilhelm (1875-1942) German					
wc/d	1	1,449		1,449	

Name	No.	Total Sales Value	lowest	Prices median	highest
WACHTER, Eberhard (1762-1852) German					
oil	2	15,909	7,727	7,955	8,182
WACHTMEISTER, Rosina (20th C) German?					
wc/d	2	2,524	1,262	1,262	1,262
WACKER, Rudolf (1893-1939) Austrian					
oil	3	209,543	65,518	69,961	74,064
wc/d	1	3,106		3,106	
WADE, George Edward (1853-1933) British					
3D	2	4,290	2,100	2,145	2,190
WADE, Jonathan (1960-) British					
oil	5	7,903	1,050	1,349	2,844
WADSWORTH, Adelaide (1844-1928) American					
wc/d	1	2,400		2,400	
WADSWORTH, Edward (1889-1949) British					
oil	1	33,000		33,000	
wc/d	1	4,500		4,500	
WADSWORTH, Frank R (1874-1905) American					
oil	1	4,250		4,250	
WADSWORTH, Wedworth (1846-?) American					
wc/d	1	1,000		1,000	
WAEFELAERTS, Marten (1748-1799) Flemish					
oil	1	1,391		1,391	
WAEL, Cornelis de (1592-1667) Flemish					
oil	1	17,293		17,293	
wc/d	1	2,114		2,114	
WAENTIG, Walter (1881-?) German					
oil	4	8,402	1,917	2,045	2,396
WAERHERT, Arthur de (20th C) Belgian?					
oil	1	1,210		1,210	
WAGEMAKER, Jaap (1906-1972) Dutch					
oil	3	32,318	3,448	4,310	24,560
wc/d	5	36,424	2,581	7,130	10,345
WAGEMANS, Maurice (1877-1927) Belgian					
oil	3	12,089	1,075	3,849	7,165
WAGENHALS, Katherine (1883-?) American					
oil	1	1,300		1,300	
WAGENSCHOEN, Franz Xaver (1726-1790) Austrian					
wc/d	1	1,818		1,818	
WAGNER, A (20th C) German					
wc/d	1	2,311		2,311	
WAGNER, Carl (1796-1857) German					
wc/d	1	1,457		1,457	
WAGNER, Erich (1890-1974) Austrian					
wc/d	1	2,926		2,926	
WAGNER, Ferdinand (19/20th C) German					
oil	1	5,682		5,682	
WAGNER, Ferdinand (jnr) (1847-1927) German					
oil	1	23,059		23,059	
WAGNER, Fred (1864-1940) American					
oil	2	9,750	4,250	4,875	5,500
WAGNER, Fritz (1872-1948) Swiss					
oil	13	89,816	3,189	6,709	14,300
WAGNER, H (fl.1890) German?					
oil	2	5,227	1,027	2,614	4,200
WAGNER, Hans Johann (1866-1940) Austrian					
oil	1	1,186		1,186	
WAGNER, Hans Jorg (1930-) German					
wc/d	1	1,219		1,219	

Name	No.	Total Sales Value	Prices lowest	median	highest
WAGNER, Johann Peter (1730-1809) German					
3D	1	6,292		6,292	
WAGNER, Jules (1818-?) German					
oil	2	7,891	2,300	3,946	5,591
WAGNER, K (?) ?					
oil	1	2,085		2,085	
WAGNER, Karl (1864-?) Austrian/German					
oil	5	9,891	1,000	1,961	3,800
WAGNER, L (19th C) German?					
oil	1	2,000		2,000	
WAGNER, Otto (1803-1861) German					
wc/d	1	3,665		3,665	
WAGNER, Paul Hermann (1852-?) German					
oil	2	10,916	2,926	5,458	7,990
WAGNER, Pierre (1897-?) French					
oil	1	1,392		1,392	
WAGNER-HOHENBERG, Josef (1870-1939) German					
oil	4	12,231	2,010	2,657	4,907
WAGONER, Harry B (19/20th C) American					
oil	1	1,400		1,400	
WAHL, Johann Friedrich (1719-?) German					
oil	1	3,379		3,379	
WAHLBERG, Alfred (1834-1906) Swedish					
oil	7	35,960	1,242	2,176	14,069
wc/d	1	1,016		1,016	
WAHLBERG, Ulf (1938-) Swedish					
oil	1	2,184		2,184	
WAHLE, Friedrich (1863-1927) German					
oil	1	1,629		1,629	
WAHLGREN, Anders (1861-1928) Swedish					
oil	1	1,011		1,011	
WAHLQVIST, Ehrnfried (1814-1895) Swedish					
oil	6	11,091	1,035	1,278	4,228
WAHLROOS, Dora (1870-1947) Finnish					
oil	1	1,950		1,950	
WAHLSTROM, Charlotte (1849-1924) Swedish					
oil	3	4,452	1,242	1,306	1,904
WAHS, R (20th C) ?					
oil	1	1,077		1,077	
WAIDEYOORN, W (?) ?					
oil	1	1,326		1,326	
WAIN, Louis (1860-1939) British					
wc/d	36	135,712	1,001	2,860	12,750
WAINEWRIGHT, Thomas Francis (19th C) British					
oil	2	4,294	1,034	2,147	3,260
wc/d	3	7,365	2,041	2,574	2,750
WAINWRIGHT, W J (1855-1931) British					
wc/d	1	2,212		2,212	
WAINWRIGHT, William John (1855-1931) British					
oil	1	9,230		9,230	
WAIS, Alfred (1905-) German					
oil	1	2,777		2,777	
WAITE, Edward Wilkins (fl.1878-1927) British					
oil	7	105,261	2,422	9,000	40,820
WAITE, James Clarke (1832-1921) British					
oil	2	10,444	2,414	5,222	8,030
WAITE, John (19th C) British					
oil	1	1,900		1,900	

Name	No.	Total Sales Value	lowest	Prices median	highest
WAITE, Robert Thorne (1842-1935) British					
wc/d	5	21,982	1,208	2,320	10,725
WAKEFORD, Edward (1914-1973) British					
oil	1	1,103		1,103	
WAKELIN, Roland Shakespeare (1887-1971) Australian					
oil	1	1,670		1,670	
WALBOURN, Ernest (1872-1927) British					
oil	25	130,577	1,100	4,620	10,725
WALCH, Charles (1896-1948) French					
oil	4	17,034	1,442	2,886	9,821
wc/d	2	2,849	1,211	1,425	1,638
WALCH, Thomas (1867-1843) Austrian					
oil	2	3,680	1,407	1,840	2,273
WALCOT, William (1874-1943) British					
oil	1	5,738		5,738	
wc/d	1	3,322		3,322	
WALDBERG, Isabelle (1917-) French?					
3D	5	25,740	3,979	4,641	7,842
WALDBURGER, J B (1924-) Swiss					
oil	1	2,449		2,449	
WALDE, Alfons (1891-1958) Austrian					
oil	5	258,611	15,800	43,200	100,000
WALDEK, H (?) ?					
oil	2	5,550	1,050	2,775	4,500
WALDEN, Lionel (1861-1933) American					
oil	2	7,751	1,431	3,876	6,320
WALDMULLER, Ferdinand Georg (1793-1865) Austrian					
oil	10	456,468	5,247	14,953	249,211
WALDORP, Antonie (1803-1866) Dutch					
oil	3	30,615	1,898	6,717	22,000
WALDORP, Jan Gerard (1740-?) Dutch					
oil	1	3,142		3,142	
WALE, John Porter (1860-1920) British					
wc/d	3	4,762	1,125	1,125	2,512
WALKER, Charles J (fl.1860-1870) British					
oil	1	4,290		4,290	
WALKER, Dame Ethel (1861-1951) British					
oil	7	17,167	1,264	1,482	5,145
wc/d	1	1,500		1,500	
WALKER, Henry Oliver (1843-1929) American					
oil	1	4,000		4,000	
WALKER, Horatio (1858-1938) Canadian					
oil	3	18,872	5,549	5,973	7,350
WALKER, J F (1825-1906) British					
oil	1	32,560		32,560	
WALKER, James Alexander (1841-1898) British					
oil	1	14,250		14,250	
WALKER, James Crampton (20th C) Irish					
oil	2	3,625	1,305	1,813	2,320
WALKER, John (1939-) British					
oil	2	10,192	1,692	5,096	8,500
WALKER, John Eaton (fl.1855-1866) British					
oil	1	1,000		1,000	
WALKER, Kara (1969-) American					
wc/d	2	32,000	15,000	16,000	17,000
WALKER, William Aiken (1838-1921) American					
oil	23	190,000	3,000	9,000	14,000
WALKOWITZ, Abraham (1878-1965) American/Russian					
oil	2	8,500	1,500	4,250	7,000

Name	No.	Total Sales Value	Prices lowest	median	highest
wc/d	9	33,200	1,000	2,600	15,000
WALL PERNE, Joseph van de (1877-1941) Dutch					
oil	1	8,197		8,197	
WALL, A Bryan (1861-1935) American					
oil	2	2,200	1,100	1,100	1,100
WALL, E (19th C) British					
oil	1	1,287		1,287	
WALL, W (?) ?					
oil	1	1,264		1,264	
WALL, William Archibald (1828-1875) British/American					
oil	2	4,860	1,700	2,430	3,160
WALL, William Coventry (1810-1886) American					
oil	1	6,500		6,500	
WALLACE, Harry (19th C) British					
oil	1	1,011		1,011	
WALLACE, John (19th C) British					
wc/d	1	3,456		3,456	
WALLACE, John (?-1903) British					
wc/d	1	1,045		1,045	
WALLAERT, Pierre Joseph (1753-1812) French					
oil	3	48,400	12,560	17,000	18,840
WALLANDER, Alf (1862-1914) Swedish					
3D	2	5,350	1,201	2,675	4,149
wc/d	1	2,857		2,857	
WALLANDER, Josef Wilhelm (1821-1888) Swedish					
oil	1	1,005		1,005	
WALLAT, Paul (1879-?) German					
oil	1	1,902		1,902	
WALLER, Frank (1842-1923) American					
oil	1	3,575		3,575	
WALLER, Samuel Edmund (1850-1903) British					
oil	1	3,718		3,718	
WALLERSTEIN, G (?) ?					
oil	1	3,905		3,905	
WALLET, Taf (1902-) Belgian					
oil	2	2,071	1,006	1,036	1,065
WALLIN, Anders (1953-) Swedish					
oil	1	1,229		1,229	
wc/d	1	1,555		1,555	
WALLINGER, Mark (1959-) British					
oil	2	49,075	20,385	24,538	28,690
WALLIS, Alfred (1855-1942) British					
oil	2	19,860	7,110	9,930	12,750
wc/d	2	22,510	9,750	11,255	12,760
WALLIS, J (?) British					
wc/d	1	1,231		1,231	
WALLNER, Thure (1888-1965) Swedish					
oil	15	43,072	1,197	1,759	9,029
WALLS, William (1860-1942) British					
oil	4	14,217	1,027	2,329	8,532
WALRAVEN, Jan (1827-?) Dutch					
oil	4	15,423	1,623	3,125	7,550
WALRECHT, Ben (1911-1980) Dutch					
oil	2	8,596	3,622	4,298	4,974
WALSCAPELLE, Jacob van (1644-1727) Dutch					
oil	1	37,196		37,196	
WALT DISNEY PRODUCTIONS (20th C) American					
wc/d	1	4,500		4,500	

Name	No.	Total Sales Value	lowest	Prices median	highest
WALT DISNEY STUDIOS (20th C) American					
wc/d	1	2,000		2,000	
WALTENSPERGER, Charles (1870-1931) American					
oil	2	3,600	1,400	1,800	2,200
WALTER, F (?) British?					
oil	1	1,224		1,224	
WALTER, Joseph (1783-1856) British					
oil	2	18,665	7,865	9,333	10,800
WALTER, Martha (1875-1976) American					
oil	11	193,800	3,000	6,000	46,000
wc/d	4	19,200	4,000	5,000	5,200
WALTER-KURAU, Johann (1869-1932) German					
oil	1	1,162		1,162	
WALTERS, Curt (1958-) American					
oil	1	5,000		5,000	
WALTERS, Emile (1893-?) American					
oil	1	2,000		2,000	
WALTERS, G S (19th C) British					
oil	3	5,434	1,800	1,817	1,817
WALTERS, George Stanfield (1838-1924) British					
oil	2	13,050	1,800	6,525	11,250
wc/d	2	2,409	1,185	1,205	1,224
WALTERS, Miles (1774-1849) British					
oil	1	10,000		10,000	
WALTERS, Samuel (1811-1882) British					
oil	4	170,860	6,300	44,780	75,000
WALTHER, Karl (1905-) German					
oil	1	1,080		1,080	
WALTHER, L (?) French?					
3D	1	3,793		3,793	
WALTON, Constance (?-1960) British					
wc/d	2	4,731	2,175	2,366	2,556
WALTON, Frank (1840-1928) British					
oil	3	10,748	1,008	4,770	4,970
wc/d	3	5,780	1,138	2,226	2,416
WALTON, Joseph (c.1810-1879) British					
oil	1	1,580		1,580	
WALTRIN, Etienne (1890-1915) French					
3D	1	2,194		2,194	
WANDEL, Sigurd (1875-1947) Danish					
oil	1	2,979		2,979	
WANDESFORDE, Juan B (1817-1902) American					
oil	2	27,500	1,500	13,750	26,000
wc/d	1	2,200		2,200	
WANE, Harold (?-1900) British					
wc/d	1	1,073		1,073	
WANE, Richard (1852-1904) British					
oil	4	7,103	1,296	1,512	2,783
WANG YOUNG-TING (1950-) ?					
wc/d	1	1,134		1,134	
WANG, Aage (1879-1959) Danish					
oil	1	3,574		3,574	
WANING, Cornelis Anthony van (1861-1929) Dutch					
oil	3	12,255	1,291	2,790	8,174
WANING, Martin van (1889-1972) Dutch					
oil	1	2,163		2,163	
WANKIE, Wladyslaw (c.1860-1925) Polish					
oil	1	4,427		4,427	

Name	No.	Total Sales Value	lowest	Prices median	highest
WANKOWICZ, Valentin (1800-1842) Polish					
oil	1	4,085		4,085	
WANLESS, Harry (snr) (1873-1933) British					
wc/d	3	3,402	1,074	1,168	1,168
WANSLEBEN, Arthur (1861-1917) German					
oil	1	2,724		2,724	
WANTE, Ernest (1872-1960) Belgian					
oil	2	4,652	1,045	2,326	3,607
WANUM, Arie van (1733-1780) Dutch					
wc/d	1	1,271		1,271	
WAPPERS, Gustave (1803-1874) Belgian					
oil	4	11,608	1,253	2,627	5,102
WARB, Nicolaas (1906-1957) Dutch					
oil	1	2,107		2,107	
WARBURTON, Samuel (1874-1938) British					
oil	1	1,113		1,113	
WARD OF HULL, John (1798-1849) British					
oil	2	9,758	2,608	4,879	7,150
WARD, Arthur E (1863-1928) American					
oil	1	1,250		1,250	
WARD, Charles Caleb (c.1831-1896) American					
oil	1	2,603		2,603	
WARD, Charlotte (20th C) British					
wc/d	1	1,480		1,480	
WARD, Cyril (1863-1935) British					
wc/d	3	4,356	1,185	1,208	1,963
WARD, Edward Matthew (1816-1879) British					
oil	2	43,200	13,000	21,600	30,200
WARD, Henrietta Mary Ada (1832-1924) British					
oil	1	7,000		7,000	
WARD, J Q A (1830-1910) American					
3D	1	3,000		3,000	
WARD, James (1769-1859) British					
oil	5	247,612	7,000	16,610	131,560
wc/d	2	4,252	2,002	2,126	2,250
WARD, James Charles (fl.1830-1859) British					
oil	1	2,211		2,211	
WARD, John (1917-) British					
wc/d	2	2,510	1,170	1,255	1,340
WARD, John Quincy Adams (1830-1910) American					
3D	1	90,000		90,000	
WARD, Mary (fl.1828-1849) British					
wc/d	1	1,169		1,169	
WARD, Sarah Ann Henshaw (1809-?) American					
wc/d	2	10,000	5,000	5,000	5,000
WARD, Thomas (19th C) British					
oil	1	1,335		1,335	
WARD, V (20th C) British					
oil	1	1,200		1,200	
WARD, Vernon (1905-1985) British					
oil	5	7,350	1,036	1,269	2,120
WARD, William H (19th C) British					
oil	2	6,555	2,265	3,278	4,290
WARDLE, Arthur (1864-1947) British					
oil	8	63,070	3,020	6,184	14,250
wc/d	6	18,920	1,034	2,306	6,615
WARDLE, John Clifford (1907-) British					
oil	1	1,036		1,036	

Name	No.	Total Sales Value	lowest	Prices median	highest
WARDLEWORTH, J L (19th C) British					
oil	1	2,250		2,250	
WARHOL, Andy (1928-1987) American					
3D	3	130,783	14,715	31,068	85,000
oil	19	8,844,292	14,000	65,000	4,200,000
wc/d	82	22,257,717	1,124	90,810	4,000,000
WARING, R (19th C) ?					
oil	1	2,550		2,550	
WARING, W H (19/20th C) British					
oil	2	2,775	1,178	1,388	1,597
WARMINGTON, E A (19th C) British					
wc/d	1	1,258		1,258	
WARNE-BROWN, Alfred J (fl.1890-1900) British					
oil	1	1,022		1,022	
WARNER, Everett L (1877-1963) American					
oil	2	6,150	1,900	3,075	4,250
WARNER, Nell Walker (1891-1970) American					
oil	5	18,500	1,400	1,600	8,000
WARNIA-ZARZECKI, Joseph (1850-?) French					
oil	1	33,180		33,180	
WAROQUIER, Henry de (1881-1970) French					
oil	5	15,306	1,267	2,252	5,187
WARREN, Bonomi Edward (19th C) British					
wc/d	1	2,114		2,114	
WARREN, Edmund George (1834-1909) British					
oil	1	1,884		1,884	
wc/d	4	34,888	3,160	5,139	21,450
WARREN, Harold Broadfield (1859-1934) American					
wc/d	1	2,500		2,500	
WARSHAW, Lhorenze (20th C) American					
oil	1	1,000		1,000	
WARSHAWSKY, Abel George (1883-1962) American					
oil	1	10,000		10,000	
WASDAIL (18th C) British?					
oil	1	15,730		15,730	
WASHBURN, Cadwallader (1866-1965) American					
oil	1	13,000		13,000	
WASHBURN, Mary Nightingale (1861-1932) American					
oil	1	1,000		1,000	
WASHINGTON, Georges (1827-1910) French					
oil	15	201,702	4,555	12,331	21,174
wc/d	1	1,908		1,908	
WASILEWSKI, Czeslaw (1875-1946) Polish					
oil	1	2,445		2,445	
WASLEY, Frank (1848-1934) British					
oil	2	5,091	1,275	2,546	3,816
wc/d	2	3,777	1,332	1,889	2,445
WASMER, Erich (1915-1972) Swiss					
oil	1	1,694		1,694	
WASSE, Arthur (19th C) British					
oil	2	8,465	1,400	4,233	7,065
WASSENAAR, Willem Abraham (1873-1956) Dutch					
oil	1	1,405		1,405	
WATELET, Charles Joseph (1867-1954) Belgian					
oil	4	6,478	1,000	1,406	2,666
WATELET, Louis Étienne (1780-1866) French					
oil	1	2,957		2,957	
WATELIN, J E (?) ?					
oil	1	2,200		2,200	

Name	No.	Total Sales Value	lowest	Prices median	highest
WATELIN, Louis (1838-1907) French					
oil	4	8,750	1,263	2,311	2,866
WATERFORD, Louise (1818-1891) British					
wc/d	1	1,216		1,216	
WATERHOUSE, John William (1849-1917) British					
oil	4	11,618,001	143,000	1,204,000	9,060,001
WATERLOO, Anthonie (1609-1690) Flemish					
wc/d	3	13,168	1,418	2,750	9,000
WATERLOW, Sir Ernest Albert (1850-1919) British					
oil	4	11,724	1,232	2,876	4,740
wc/d	2	6,206	1,058	3,103	5,148
WATERMAN, Marcus (1834-1914) American					
oil	1	1,600		1,600	
WATERS, Billie (1896-1979) British					
oil	1	3,020		3,020	
WATERS, G W (19th C) ?					
oil	1	4,750		4,750	
WATERS, Kate (1964-) German					
oil	1	1,211		1,211	
WATERS, Susan (1823-1900) American					
oil	3	16,100	2,100	6,000	8,000
WATJEN, Otto von (1881-1942) German					
oil	3	5,415	1,350	1,800	2,265
WATKINS, Kenneth (1847-1933) New Zealander					
wc/d	1	1,352		1,352	
WATKINS, Susan (19th C) British					
oil	1	21,000		21,000	
WATKINS, William Reginald (1890-?) British/American					
oil	1	1,100		1,100	
WATMOUGH, Amos (fl.1884-1885) British					
oil	2	4,174	1,974	2,087	2,200
WATRIN, Étienne (19/20th C) ?					
3D	1	2,400		2,400	
WATROUS, Harry W (1857-1940) American					
oil	1	13,000		13,000	
WATSON, A W (?) British					
oil	1	5,214		5,214	
WATSON, Charles (19th C) British					
oil	1	13,490		13,490	
WATSON, Charles A (1857-1923) American					
oil	1	3,500		3,500	
WATSON, Geoffrey (fl.1920-1937) British					
oil	1	4,582		4,582	
WATSON, George Spencer (1869-1934) British					
oil	1	1,500		1,500	
WATSON, Harry (1871-1936) British					
oil	3	4,670	1,269	1,661	1,740
WATSON, Homer Ransford (1855-1936) Canadian					
oil	5	13,092	1,737	2,370	4,314
WATSON, John (early 20th C) British?					
oil	1	1,767		1,767	
WATSON, John Dawson (1832-1892) British					
oil	1	2,030		2,030	
wc/d	1	1,450		1,450	
WATSON, R (18th C) British					
oil	1	3,003		3,003	
WATSON, Robert (fl.1877-1920) British					
oil	19	92,479	1,444	4,260	13,870

Name	No.	Total Sales Value	Prices lowest	median	highest
WATSON, Robert (1865-1916) British					
oil	1	1,963		1,963	
WATSON, Robert F (1815-1885) British					
oil	1	6,320		6,320	
WATSON, S (?) ?					
oil	1	2,755		2,755	
WATSON, Sidney (19/20th C) British					
oil	1	3,816		3,816	
WATSON, W (19/20th C) British					
oil	1	5,819		5,819	
WATSON, Walter (19/20th C) American?					
oil	1	7,500		7,500	
WATSON, Walter J (1879-?) British					
oil	5	41,087	5,005	7,722	12,000
WATSON, William (19/20th C) British					
oil	5	24,304	3,432	4,380	6,952
WATSON, William (jnr) (?-1921) British					
oil	2	27,125	8,250	13,563	18,875
WATSON, William Henry (20th C) British					
oil	1	4,862		4,862	
WATT, Alison (1965-) British					
oil	1	9,480		9,480	
WATT, Elizabeth Mary (fl.1922-1940) British					
wc/d	2	2,444	1,160	1,222	1,284
WATT, Linnie (fl.1874-1908) British					
oil	1	2,021		2,021	
WATT, Millar (?) British					
oil	1	1,073		1,073	
WATT, W A (19th C) British					
oil	1	1,287		1,287	
WATTEAU (18/19th C) French					
oil	1	3,359		3,359	
WATTEAU DE LILLE, Louis Joseph (1731-1798) French					
oil	2	15,393	5,749	7,697	9,644
WATTEAU, François L J (1758-1823) French					
oil	1	5,841		5,841	
wc/d	1	14,345		14,345	
WATTEAU, Jean Antoine (1684-1721) French					
oil	2	3,235,162	1,162	1,617,581	3,234,000
wc/d	2	50,835	12,835	25,418	38,000
WATTENWYL, Peter von (1942-) Swiss					
3D	1	1,337		1,337	
oil	1	1,016		1,016	
WATTIER, Charles Émile (1800-1868) French					
wc/d	1	1,359		1,359	
WATTS, Arthur George (1883-1935) British					
wc/d	1	2,100		2,100	
WATTS, Frederick William (1800-1862) British					
oil	12	149,136	1,287	5,663	40,040
WATTS, George Frederick (1817-1904) British					
oil	1	120,800		120,800	
wc/d	2	6,474	2,574	3,237	3,900
WATTS, James T (1853-1930) British					
oil	2	9,703	1,013	4,852	8,690
wc/d	19	186,914	2,844	9,480	24,490
WATZELHAN, Carl (1867-1942) Austrian					
oil	1	2,200		2,200	
WATZKE, J (19th C) ?					
oil	1	2,055		2,055	

Name	No.	Total Sales Value	lowest	Prices median	highest
WAUD, Alfred Rudolf (1828-1891) American					
wc/d	1	16,000		16,000	
WAUER, William (1866-1962) German					
3D	5	14,613	2,049	2,265	5,282
WAUGH, Frederick J (1861-1940) American					
oil	10	85,570	1,500	7,375	22,000
wc/d	1	1,200		1,200	
WAUTERS, Camille (1856-1919) Belgian					
oil	1	1,371		1,371	
WAXSCHLUNGER, Johann Georg (18th C) German					
oil	1	1,000		1,000	
WAY, Andrew John Henry (1826-1888) American					
oil	2	13,000	4,000	6,500	9,000
WAY, Charles Jones (1834-1919) British					
wc/d	1	3,289		3,289	
WAYCOTT, Hedley (1865-1938) American					
oil	1	1,300		1,300	
WEATHERILL, George (1810-1890) British					
wc/d	21	86,778	1,404	4,212	7,550
WEATHERILL, Mary (1834-1913) British					
wc/d	2	8,028	3,045	4,014	4,983
WEATHERILL, Richard (1844-1913) British					
oil	4	20,767	1,812	5,424	8,164
WEATHERSTONE, Alfred C (fl.1888-1929) British					
wc/d	2	9,734	1,044	4,867	8,690
WEAVER, Thomas (1774-1843) British					
oil	3	11,685	1,661	5,024	5,024
WEBB, Archibald (jnr) (fl.1886-1892) British					
wc/d	1	1,520		1,520	
WEBB, Byron (19th C) British					
oil	1	3,770		3,770	
WEBB, Edward Walter (1810-1851) British					
oil	1	5,328		5,328	
WEBB, James (1825-1895) British					
oil	26	208,564	1,095	6,090	28,000
WEBB, Kenneth (1927-) British					
oil	2	3,480	1,125	1,740	2,355
WEBB, Octavius (fl.1880-1889) British					
oil	1	2,544		2,544	
WEBB, W (?) British					
oil	1	1,296		1,296	
WEBB, William (1790-1856) British					
oil	2	17,624	5,624	8,812	12,000
WEBB, William Edward (1862-1903) British					
oil	23	191,984	2,538	5,900	34,320
WEBBER (19th C) British					
oil	1	4,452		4,452	
WEBBER, John (1750-1793) British					
wc/d	1	23,520		23,520	
WEBBER, Wesley (1841-1914) American					
oil	6	10,600	1,200	1,850	2,200
WEBER, A (?) ?					
oil	2	2,446	1,090	1,223	1,356
WEBER, Adolf (1925-) Swiss					
oil	1	2,308		2,308	
WEBER, Alfred Charles (1862-1922) French					
wc/d	1	1,410		1,410	
WEBER, Andreas Paul (1893-1980) German					
wc/d	1	2,111		2,111	

Name	No.	Total Sales Value	lowest	Prices median	highest
WEBER, August (1817-1873) German					
oil	2	10,672	3,738	5,336	6,934
WEBER, C Phillip (1849-1921) American					
oil	1	1,300		1,300	
WEBER, Carl (1850-1921) American					
oil	3	3,700	1,200	1,200	1,300
wc/d	1	1,200		1,200	
WEBER, Evarist Adam (1887-?) German					
oil	1	1,597		1,597	
WEBER, Hugo (1918-1971) Swiss					
oil	1	17,683		17,683	
wc/d	1	1,302		1,302	
WEBER, J M (19th C) French					
oil	1	1,676		1,676	
WEBER, Joseph (1803-1881) German					
oil	1	4,326		4,326	
WEBER, M (?) ?					
oil	1	1,134		1,134	
WEBER, Max (1881-1961) American					
oil	4	26,000	3,500	6,500	9,500
wc/d	2	15,750	4,750	7,875	11,000
WEBER, Otis S (19th C) American					
oil	1	1,700		1,700	
WEBER, Otto (1832-1888) German					
wc/d	1	23,700		23,700	
WEBER, Paul (1823-1916) American/German					
oil	15	121,129	1,227	2,727	60,000
WEBER, Theodore (1838-1907) French					
oil	6	36,518	1,156	6,436	10,000
WEBER, Thomas (?) British?					
oil	1	7,150		7,150	
WEBER, Willy (1895-1959) German					
oil	1	1,658		1,658	
WEBER-TYROL, Hans Josef (1874-1957) Austrian					
oil	2	15,938	7,286	7,969	8,652
wc/d	1	1,220		1,220	
WEBSKY, Wolfgang von (1895-1992) German					
oil	1	1,081		1,081	
WEBSTER, George (19th C) British					
oil	6	86,928	10,010	14,450	20,385
WEBSTER, R Wellesley (19/20th C) British					
wc/d	1	1,103		1,103	
WEBSTER, Thomas (1800-1886) British					
oil	4	8,430	1,425	2,163	2,717
WEBSTER, Walter Ernest (1878-1959) British					
oil	4	7,263	1,500	1,639	2,485
wc/d	2	3,380	1,392	1,690	1,988
WEDEL, Nils (1897-1967) Swedish					
oil	1	14,551		14,551	
wc/d	1	1,507		1,507	
WEDER, Jakob (1906-) ?					
oil	1	4,518		4,518	
WEDIG, Gotthardt de (1583-1641) German					
wc/d	1	19,000		19,000	
WEDIN, Elof (1901-1983) American					
oil	1	1,600		1,600	
WEE, Robert (?) American?					
oil	1	1,300		1,300	
WEEBER, Eduard von (1834-1891) Austrian					
oil	1	2,243		2,243	

Name	No.	Total Sales Value	lowest	Prices median	highest
WEEDON, Augustus Walford (1838-1908) British					
wc/d	2	4,512	1,650	2,256	2,862
WEEKES, Henry (jnr) (?-c.1910) British					
oil	1	8,294		8,294	
WEEKES, William (fl.1864-1904) British					
oil	10	80,861	1,420	6,503	20,000
WEEKS, Edwin Lord (1849-1903) American					
oil	10	600,721	1,386	37,500	240,000
wc/d	1	5,250		5,250	
WEEKS, James (1922-1998) American					
oil	4	39,000	3,000	10,500	16,000
wc/d	1	1,000		1,000	
WEELE, Herman Johannes van der (1852-1930) Dutch					
oil	4	9,477	1,132	2,455	3,435
wc/d	1	1,727		1,727	
WEENIX, J B (1621-1663) Dutch					
oil	1	13,662		13,662	
WEENIX, Jan (1640-1719) Dutch					
oil	5	263,925	3,016	29,830	181,200
WEESOP (fl.1641-1649) British					
oil	1	18,590		18,590	
WEGENER, Gerda (1885-1940) Danish					
oil	3	40,797	3,098	18,960	18,960
wc/d	3	6,265	1,281	2,264	2,720
WEGERER, Julius (1886-1960) Austrian					
oil	1	2,648		2,648	
WEGMAN, William (1942-) American					
oil	1	2,593		2,593	
WEGMANN, Bertha (1847-1926) Danish					
oil	5	37,823	2,986	3,574	18,892
WEGNER, Erich (1899-1980) German					
wc/d	4	13,268	1,748	3,240	5,040
WEHLE, Johann Raphael (1848-1936) German					
oil	2	7,677	2,724	3,839	4,953
WEIDEMANN, Magnus (1880-?) German					
oil	2	4,936	1,068	2,468	3,868
WEIDENMANN, Johann Caspar (1805-1850) Swiss					
oil	1	2,334		2,334	
WEIDIG, Wilhelm Julius (1837-1918) Swedish					
oil	1	1,005		1,005	
WEIDNER, Joseph (1801-1870) Austrian					
oil	1	4,040		4,040	
WEIE, Edvard (1879-1943) Danish					
oil	9	115,667	1,511	8,717	37,510
WEIGAND, Konrad (1842-1897) German					
oil	1	2,145		2,145	
WEIGELE, Henry (1858-1927) French					
3D	1	110,000		110,000	
WEIGHT, Carel (1908-1997) British					
oil	21	118,011	1,060	3,692	22,500
WEIL, Lucien (?) French					
oil	1	1,625		1,625	
WEILAND, Johannes (1856-1909) Dutch					
oil	4	14,303	1,950	3,459	5,436
wc/d	2	4,617	1,483	2,309	3,134
WEILER, Milton C (1910-1974) American					
wc/d	2	9,500	4,500	4,750	5,000
WEIMAR, H W S (19/20th C) ?					
oil	1	21,190		21,190	

Name	No.	Total Sales Value	lowest	Prices median	highest
WEINBERGER, Anton (1843-1912) German					
oil	1	1,095		1,095	
WEINDORF, Paul Friedrich (1887-1965) American					
oil	1	1,100		1,100	
WEINER, Lawrence (1942-) American					
3D	1	19,000		19,000	
oil	1	18,000		18,000	
wc/d	1	7,500		7,500	
WEINER, R (19th C) ?					
oil	1	1,659		1,659	
WEINGART, Joachim (1895-1942) Polish					
oil	2	5,354	1,563	2,677	3,791
WEINMAN, Adolph Alexander (1870-1952) American					
3D	2	16,000	8,000	8,000	8,000
WEINRICH, Agnes (?-1946) American					
wc/d	1	1,600		1,600	
WEIR, J Alden (1852-1919) American					
oil	3	207,200	1,200	16,000	190,000
WEIR, John Ferguson (1841-1926) American					
oil	4	119,500	5,500	22,000	70,000
WEIR, Robert W (1803-1889) American					
oil	1	9,500		9,500	
WEIROTTER, Franz Edmund (1730-1771) Austrian					
wc/d	2	2,513	1,189	1,257	1,324
WEIRS, M (20th C) British					
wc/d	1	1,284		1,284	
WEISBECKER, Clement (20th C) American					
oil	1	1,900		1,900	
WEISBUCH, Claude (1927-) French					
oil	10	30,365	1,031	3,077	5,155
wc/d	5	6,689	1,024	1,474	1,496
WEISGERBER, Albert (1878-1915) German					
oil	2	12,953	1,788	6,477	11,165
wc/d	2	4,218	1,548	2,109	2,670
WEISGERBER, Carl (1891-?) German					
oil	1	1,551		1,551	
WEISKONIG, Werner (1907-1982) Swiss					
oil	2	4,584	1,789	2,292	2,795
WEISS, David (20th C) Swiss					
wc/d	2	2,230	1,115	1,115	1,115
WEISS, Hugh (1925-) American					
oil	1	1,150		1,150	
wc/d	1	1,056		1,056	
WEISS, Jose (1859-1919) British					
oil	1	2,167		2,167	
WEISS, Ludwig Caspar (1793-1867) German					
oil	1	3,244		3,244	
WEISS, Mary L (20th C) American					
oil	1	3,750		3,750	
WEISS, Olga (1853-1903) German					
oil	1	1,888		1,888	
WEISS, Peter (1916-1982) Swedish					
oil	1	1,136		1,136	
WEISSBORT, George (20th C) British?					
oil	3	17,472	2,340	6,552	8,580
wc/d	1	1,326		1,326	
WEISSENBRUCH, J H (1824-1903) Dutch					
wc/d	1	1,641		1,641	
WEISSENBRUCH, Jan (1822-1880) Dutch					
oil	2	19,271	6,365	9,636	12,906

Name	No.	Total Sales Value	lowest	Prices median	highest
wc/d	1	3,443		3,443	
WEISSENBRUCH, Jan Hendrik (1824-1903) Dutch					
oil	13	183,021	1,959	10,608	46,676
wc/d	4	129,930	20,368	28,000	53,562
WEISSENBRUCH, Willem (1864-1941) Dutch					
oil	3	29,670	1,268	2,943	25,459
WEISTLING, Morgan (20th C) American					
oil	1	8,000		8,000	
WEISZ, Adolphe (1868-?) French					
oil	1	18,875		18,875	
WEITBRECHT, L (?) ?					
oil	1	1,268		1,268	
WELCH, Ludmilla P (1867-1925) American					
oil	1	11,000		11,000	
WELCH, Thaddeus (1844-1919) American					
oil	6	69,250	2,500	11,500	24,000
WELLENS, Charles (1889-1958) Belgian					
oil	2	3,575	1,092	1,788	2,483
WELLENSTEIN, Walter (1898-1970) German					
oil	1	1,000		1,000	
WELLERSHAUS, Paul (1887-1976) German					
oil	2	3,640	1,456	1,820	2,184
WELLES, E F (19th C) British					
oil	1	3,948		3,948	
WELLINGS, William (fl.1778-1792) British					
wc/d	1	2,574		2,574	
WELLS, C H C (19/20th C) British					
oil	1	1,021		1,021	
WELLS, Henry Tanworth (1828-1903) British					
oil	1	2,114		2,114	
wc/d	1	7,150		7,150	
WELLS, Madeline Rachel (fl.1909-1940) British					
oil	1	4,640		4,640	
WELLS, William Page Atkinson (1871-1923) British					
oil	1	5,922		5,922	
wc/d	1	1,058		1,058	
WELSCH, Karl Friedrich Christian (1828-1904) German					
oil	1	10,500		10,500	
WEMAIRE, Pierre (1913-) Belgian					
oil	4	12,770	1,743	2,306	6,416
WENCKBACH, Ludwig Willem Reymert (1860-?) Dutch					
oil	1	1,231		1,231	
WENCKE, Sophie (1874-1963) German					
oil	2	4,982	1,324	2,491	3,658
WENDLBERGER, Wenzel Hermann (1882-?) German					
oil	1	1,803		1,803	
WENDLER, Friedrich Moritz (1814-1872) German					
oil	1	1,472		1,472	
WENDT, William (1865-1946) American					
oil	13	687,500	3,000	42,500	140,000
WENGLEIN, Adam (19th C) German					
oil	1	2,610		2,610	
WENGLEIN, Joseph (1845-1919) German					
oil	14	114,021	1,178	5,714	23,000
WENING, Rudolf (1893-1970) Swiss					
oil	1	2,559		2,559	
WENK, Albert (1863-1934) German					
oil	2	4,364	2,182	2,182	2,182

Name	No.	Total Sales Value	lowest	Prices median	highest
WENNERBERG, Brynolf (1823-1894) Swedish					
oil	3	4,870	1,133	1,551	2,186
WENNERBERG, Gunnar (1863-1914) Swedish					
oil	2	3,405	1,395	1,703	2,010
WENNERWALD, Emil (1859-1934) Danish					
oil	2	3,059	1,422	1,530	1,637
WENNING, Ype (1879-1959) Dutch					
oil	4	5,559	1,075	1,382	1,721
WENS, F (19th C) ?					
oil	1	1,305		1,305	
WENTSCHER, Julius (1842-1918) German					
oil	1	3,414		3,414	
WENZELL, Albert Beck (1864-1917) American					
oil	1	40,000		40,000	
WEREFKIN, Marianne von (1870-1938) Russian					
oil	3	73,344	4,737	20,063	48,544
wc/d	1	3,219		3,219	
WERLEN, Ludwig (1884-) Swiss					
oil	2	3,114	1,073	1,557	2,041
WERNER, Anton Alexander von (1843-1915) German					
oil	2	13,186	1,365	6,593	11,821
wc/d	1	1,081		1,081	
WERNER, B (?) ?					
oil	1	1,829		1,829	
WERNER, Carl (1808-1894) German					
oil	2	22,008	1,971	11,004	20,037
wc/d	2	3,475	1,539	1,738	1,936
WERNER, Fritz (1827-1908) German					
oil	2	2,844	1,100	1,422	1,744
WERNER, Gosta (1909-1989) Swedish					
oil	1	5,218		5,218	
WERNER, Hilding (1880-1944) Swedish					
oil	1	9,707		9,707	
WERNER, J N (19th C) ?					
oil	1	2,862		2,862	
WERNER, Joseph (1818-1887?) Austrian					
wc/d	2	241,400	1,400	120,700	240,000
WERNER, Lambert (1900-1983) Swedish					
oil	1	2,503		2,503	
WERNER, Reinhold (1842-1922) German					
oil	1	1,133		1,133	
WERNER, Theodor (1886-1969) German					
oil	11	73,971	1,514	5,190	17,083
wc/d	4	9,799	1,045	1,540	5,674
WERNER-BEHN, Hans (20th C) American					
oil	1	1,200		1,200	
WERSON, Jules (1884-) ?					
3D	1	2,011		2,011	
WERTHEIMER, Gustave (1847-1904) Austrian					
oil	2	6,273	2,961	3,137	3,312
WERTMULLER, Adolf Ulrik (1751-1811) Swedish					
oil	1	9,255		9,255	
WERY, Marthe (1930-) Belgian					
oil	1	1,120		1,120	
WESCOTT, Paul (1904-1970) American					
oil	1	1,300		1,300	
WESSEL, Bessie Hoover (1889-) American					
oil	1	22,000		22,000	

Name	No.	Total Sales Value	Prices lowest	median	highest
WESSEL, Manuel (1833-1907) Cuban					
oil	1	13,280		13,280	
wc/d	1	6,838		6,838	
WESSEL, Wilhelm (1904-1971) German					
oil	1	5,000		5,000	
WESSELING, Hendrik Jan (1881-1950) Dutch					
oil	1	1,313		1,313	
WESSELMANN (1931-) American					
oil	1	7,000		7,000	
WESSELMANN, Tom (1931-) American					
3D	5	106,780	1,780	16,000	41,000
oil	15	495,995	9,163	22,253	130,000
wc/d	44	466,454	1,048	4,791	120,000
WESSON, Edward (1910-1983) British					
oil	1	1,113		1,113	
wc/d	1	2,288		2,288	
WEST, Benjamin (1738-1820) British/American					
oil	1	10,570		10,570	
wc/d	1	2,574		2,574	
WEST, David (1868-1936) British					
wc/d	5	11,509	1,250	2,352	3,002
WEST, Franz (1947-) Austrian					
3D	2	11,262	1,262	5,631	10,000
WEST, R (?) ?					
oil	1	1,082		1,082	
WEST, Richard Whately (1848-1905) British					
oil	1	1,651		1,651	
WESTALL, A (?) British					
oil	1	1,133		1,133	
WESTALL, Richard (1765-1836) British					
oil	3	11,284	3,048	4,200	4,200
WESTCHILOFF, Constantin (1877-1945) Russian					
oil	1	2,000		2,000	
wc/d	1	5,738		5,738	
WESTENBERG, Pieter George (1791-1873) Dutch					
oil	1	2,052		2,052	
WESTENDORP-OSIECK, Betsy (1880-1968) Dutch					
oil	1	1,635		1,635	
WESTERBEEK, Cornelis (1844-1903) Dutch					
oil	8	26,739	2,487	3,309	5,110
WESTERFROLKE, Paul (1886-1975) German					
oil	1	1,058		1,058	
WESTERIK, Jacobus (1924-) Dutch					
wc/d	8	18,143	1,188	1,581	4,741
WESTFELT-EGGERTZ, Ingeborg (1855-1936) Swedish					
oil	2	4,237	1,190	2,119	3,047
WESTMACOTT, James Sherwood (1823-1900) British					
3D	1	8,250		8,250	
WESTMAN, Edvard (1865-1917) Swedish					
oil	1	19,777		19,777	
WESTMAN, Sven Reinhold (1887-1962) Swedish					
oil	1	3,076		3,076	
WESTON, W P (1879-1967) Canadian					
oil	4	50,635	2,349	5,688	36,911
wc/d	1	1,625		1,625	
WESTON, William Percy (1879-1967) Canadian					
oil	2	40,100	1,100	20,050	39,000
WESTPHAL, Frits (1804-1844) Danish					
oil	1	1,787		1,787	

Name	No.	Total Sales Value	lowest	Prices median	highest
WESTPHALIA SCHOOL, 17th/18th C German					
3D	1	2,539		2,539	
WET, Jacob Jacobsz de (1640-1697) Dutch					
oil	2	10,225	2,145	5,113	8,080
WET, Jacob de (1610-1671) Dutch					
oil	6	35,553	2,866	4,269	12,080
WETERING DE ROOY, Johann Embrosius van de (1877-1972) Dutch					
oil	5	8,855	1,149	1,721	2,581
WETHERBEE, George Faulkner (1851-1920) American					
oil	2	14,570	6,670	7,285	7,900
WETZEL, Johann Jakob (1781-1834) Swiss					
wc/d	2	4,876	2,311	2,438	2,565
WEVER, A de (1836-?) Belgian					
3D	1	7,165		7,165	
WEVER, Auguste de (1836-?) Belgian					
3D	1	1,145		1,145	
WEWERKA, Stefan (1928-) German					
wc/d	1	2,214		2,214	
WEX, Adalbert (1867-?) German					
oil	1	1,136		1,136	
WEX, Willibald (1831-1892) German					
oil	1	1,200		1,200	
WEXLER, Jacob (1912-) Israeli					
oil	1	1,050		1,050	
WEYDE, Julius (1822-1860) German					
oil	1	2,619		2,619	
WEYDEN, Harry van der (1868-?) American					
oil	1	1,617		1,617	
WEYER, Jacob (c.1620-1670) German					
wc/d	2	2,986	1,493	1,493	1,493
WEYER, Matthias (1620-1690) German					
wc/d	1	1,208		1,208	
WEYERS, Berend Wolter (1866-1949) Dutch					
oil	1	1,071		1,071	
WEYL, Max (1837-1914) American/German					
oil	3	4,900	1,500	1,600	1,800
WEYNS, Jan Harm (1864-1945) Dutch					
oil	2	3,211	1,514	1,606	1,697
WEYSSER, Karl (1833-1904) German					
oil	1	2,639		2,639	
WEYTS, Carolus (1828-1875) Belgian					
oil	1	6,864		6,864	
WHAITE, Henry Clarence (1828-1912) British					
oil	1	2,750		2,750	
WHAITE, James (19th C) British					
wc/d	1	1,144		1,144	
WHALE, Robert Reginald (1805-1887) Canadian					
oil	2	3,913	1,354	1,957	2,559
WHANKI, Kim (1913-1974) Korean					
oil	5	159,000	27,000	33,000	35,000
WHATLEY, Henry (1824-1901) British					
wc/d	1	1,738		1,738	
WHEALE, Ivan Trevor (?) Canadian					
oil	1	1,170		1,170	
WHEATLEY, Francis (1747-1801) British					
oil	3	345,966	7,100	8,866	330,000
wc/d	2	7,188	1,500	3,594	5,688
WHEELER, Alfred (1852-1932) British					
oil	13	54,711	1,428	3,718	8,965

Name	No.	Total Sales Value	Prices lowest	median	highest
WHEELER, Hughlette (1901-1954) American					
3D	1	4,000		4,000	
WHEELER, John Arnold (1821-1903) British					
oil	13	33,270	1,284	2,200	6,250
WHEELER, Walter Herbert (1878-1960) British					
oil	1	1,424		1,424	
WHEELER, William R (1832-1895) American					
oil	1	3,500		3,500	
WHEELWRIGHT, Roland (1870-1955) British					
oil	2	2,718	1,359	1,359	1,359
WHELDON, James (1830-1895) British					
oil	1	14,000		14,000	
WHIPPLE, John (19th C) British					
oil	1	3,076		3,076	
WHISTLER, James Abbott McNeill (1834-1903) American					
oil	1	2,600,000		2,600,000	
wc/d	4	218,450	4,350	22,050	170,000
WHISTLER, Rex (1905-1944) British					
wc/d	2	10,560	2,610	5,280	7,950
WHITAKER, Frederic (1891-?) American					
wc/d	1	1,600		1,600	
WHITAKER, George William (1841-1916) American					
oil	5	10,100	1,200	2,200	2,800
WHITCOMB, Jon (1906-1988) American					
oil	1	2,600		2,600	
wc/d	1	4,000		4,000	
WHITCOMBE, Thomas (1760-c.1824) British					
oil	5	169,474	7,584	28,690	85,840
WHITE, Alice (19/20th C) British					
wc/d	2	2,414	1,136	1,207	1,278
WHITE, Arthur (1865-1953) British					
oil	4	4,483	1,001	1,097	1,208
wc/d	1	1,586		1,586	
WHITE, Edith (1855-1946) American					
oil	5	18,250	2,500	3,500	4,750
WHITE, Ethelbert (1891-1972) British					
oil	8	17,967	1,109	1,682	5,510
WHITE, G (?) British					
oil	1	1,420		1,420	
WHITE, H M (?) British?					
3D	1	1,573		1,573	
WHITE, J Talmage (1833-1907) British					
wc/d	1	18,000		18,000	
WHITE, John (1851-1933) British					
wc/d	14	26,671	1,027	1,501	3,180
WHITE, Orrin A (1883-1969) American					
oil	6	43,300	1,800	6,500	14,000
WHITE, Sydney Watts (fl.1892-1917) British					
oil	1	1,114		1,114	
WHITE, Valentino (?) ?					
oil	3	4,004	1,016	1,318	1,670
WHITEHAND, Michael J (1941-) British					
oil	11	33,089	1,208	3,000	4,727
WHITEHEAD, Frederick (1853-1938) British					
oil	2	3,743	1,327	1,872	2,416
WHITEHEAD, Michael J (20th C) British					
oil	1	1,144		1,144	
WHITEREAD, Rachel (1953-) British					
3D	4	119,500	3,500	23,000	70,000

Name	No.	Total Sales Value	lowest	Prices median	highest
wc/d	2	85,000	25,000	42,500	60,000
WHITESIDE, Frank Reed (1866-1929) American					
oil	2	2,500	1,200	1,250	1,300
WHITFIELD, H (19th C) British					
oil	1	1,136		1,136	
WHITFORD, Richard (19th C) British					
oil	2	10,217	2,352	5,109	7,865
WHITING, Frederick (1874-1962) British					
oil	1	1,193		1,193	
wc/d	1	1,963		1,963	
WHITING, Henry W (19th C) American					
oil	1	2,250		2,250	
WHITMORE, Coby (1913-) American					
wc/d	1	3,500		3,500	
WHITTINGTON, William G (fl.1904-1914) British					
wc/d	1	1,977		1,977	
WHITTLE, Thomas (19th C) British					
oil	1	2,458		2,458	
WHITTLE, Thomas (jnr) (19th C) British					
oil	4	4,997	1,022	1,278	1,420
WHITTLE, Thomas (snr) (19th C) British					
oil	1	4,000		4,000	
WHITTREDGE, Worthington (1820-1910) American					
oil	7	154,500	3,000	20,000	40,000
WHITWORTH, Charles H (fl.1875-1913) British					
oil	1	2,432		2,432	
WHORF, John (1903-1959) American					
wc/d	13	75,900	1,600	5,100	20,000
WHYDALE, Ernest Herbert (1886-1952) British					
oil	1	2,160		2,160	
WHYMPER, Charles (1853-1941) British					
oil	1	1,435		1,435	
wc/d	3	6,087	1,661	1,859	2,567
WHYMPER, Frederick (1838-1901) Canadian/British					
wc/d	1	3,356		3,356	
WHYMPER, Josiah Wood (1813-1903) British					
wc/d	3	4,498	1,145	1,208	2,145
WHYTE, Duncan McGregor (1866-1953) British					
oil	1	5,075		5,075	
WHYTE, Nicholas (19th C) American					
oil	1	2,500		2,500	
WHYTE-HOLDICH, W (fl.1878-1893) British					
oil	1	1,898		1,898	
WIBERG, Harald (1908-1986) Swedish					
oil	5	10,572	1,635	1,923	2,582
wc/d	2	2,400	1,095	1,200	1,305
WICHFELD, H (19th C) ?					
oil	1	1,259		1,259	
WICHMANN, Christian (1958-) German					
3D	1	1,068		1,068	
WICHMANN, Johannes (1854-?) German					
oil	1	5,250		5,250	
WICHMANN, Peter (1706-1769) Danish					
oil	1	1,430		1,430	
WICKENDEN, Robert J (1861-1931) American/British					
oil	4	7,338	1,000	1,700	2,938
WICKEY, Harry (1892-) American					
3D	1	6,500		6,500	

Name	No.	Total Sales Value	Prices lowest	median	highest
WIDFORSS, Gunnar M (1879-1934) American					
wc/d	6	193,000	4,000	22,500	105,000
WIDGERY, Frederick John (1861-1942) British					
oil	2	4,205	1,450	2,103	2,755
wc/d	39	67,393	1,011	1,500	3,476
WIDGERY, T (?) British					
wc/d	1	2,114		2,114	
WIDGERY, W (1822-1893) British					
oil	1	1,110		1,110	
WIDGERY, William (1822-1893) British					
oil	3	19,042	1,021	3,021	15,000
wc/d	4	6,239	1,169	1,429	2,212
WIDMAN, Bruno (1930-) Uruguayan					
oil	8	11,865	1,000	1,310	2,395
WIDMER, Hans (1872-1925) Swiss					
oil	2	6,414	2,624	3,207	3,790
WIDOFF, Anders (1953-) Swedish					
oil	1	6,523		6,523	
WIEGAND, Charmion von (1899-1983) American					
wc/d	2	29,500	3,500	14,750	26,000
WIEGAND, Gustave (1870-1957) American					
oil	3	8,750	1,750	3,200	3,800
WIEGANDT, Bernhard (1851-1918) German					
oil	1	1,079		1,079	
WIEGERS, Jan (1893-1959) Dutch					
oil	1	1,293		1,293	
WIEGHEM, Joseph Nan (19th C) ?					
oil	1	1,332		1,332	
WIEGHORST, Olaf (1899-1988) American					
oil	10	220,900	2,800	15,000	67,000
wc/d	8	34,200	2,700	3,750	7,500
WIEGMAN, Matthieu (1886-1971) Dutch					
oil	4	14,410	1,293	3,047	7,024
wc/d	1	1,358		1,358	
WIEHL, Franz (fl.1837-1858) Austrian					
oil	1	1,096		1,096	
WIELAND, Dow (20th C) American					
wc/d	1	1,100		1,100	
WIELAND, Hans Beat (1867-1945) Swiss					
oil	2	2,472	1,073	1,236	1,399
WIELANDT, Manuel (1863-1922) German					
oil	1	3,630		3,630	
WIEMANS, Andries (1826-?) Dutch					
oil	1	3,826		3,826	
WIEMKEN, Walter Kurt (1907-1940) Swiss					
oil	1	16,576		16,576	
wc/d	1	1,580		1,580	
WIEN, S (20th C) ?					
3D	1	1,687		1,687	
WIERINGEN, Cornelis Claesz van (1580-1633) Dutch					
oil	1	73,500		73,500	
wc/d	1	35,357		35,357	
WIERSMA, Ids (1878-1965) Dutch					
oil	1	6,887		6,887	
WIERTZ, Antonie (1806-1865) Belgian					
oil	1	11,091		11,091	
WIERUSZ-KOWALSKI, Alfred von (1849-1915) Polish					
oil	7	271,810	9,805	20,000	147,311
WIESCHEBRINK, Franz (1818-1884) German					
oil	2	16,348	5,398	8,174	10,950

Name	No.	Total Sales Value	lowest	Prices median	highest
WIESELTHIER, Vally (1885-?) Austrian					
3D	1	2,100		2,100	
WIETHASE, E (20th C) Belgian					
oil	1	18,621		18,621	
WIETHASE, Edgard (1881-1965) Belgian					
oil	2	11,997	1,514	5,999	10,483
WIGAND, Albert (1890-1978) German					
oil	1	1,709		1,709	
WIGAND, Balthasar (1771-1846) Austrian					
wc/d	3	4,920	1,189	1,823	1,908
WIGAND, Balthasar (school) (1771-1846) Austrian					
wc/d	1	4,530		4,530	
WIGERT, Hans (1932-) Swedish					
oil	8	18,741	1,004	1,504	6,552
WIGG, Charles Mayes (1889-1969) British					
wc/d	1	1,205		1,205	
WIGGERS, Dirk (1866-1933) Dutch					
oil	4	5,025	1,061	1,240	1,485
WIGGERS, Karel (1916-1989) Dutch					
oil	2	12,716	4,095	6,358	8,621
WIGGINS, Carleton (1848-1932) American					
oil	6	17,750	1,000	3,100	4,750
WIGGINS, Guy A (20th C) American					
oil	1	14,000		14,000	
WIGGINS, Guy Carleton (1883-1962) American					
oil	30	1,087,900	1,900	28,000	110,000
WIGMANA, Gerard (1637-1741) Dutch					
oil	2	21,403	9,323	10,702	12,080
WIHLBORG, Gerhard (1897-1982) Swedish					
oil	3	3,918	1,063	1,180	1,675
WIHLEN (?) ?					
oil	1	3,720		3,720	
WIIG-HANSEN, Svend (1922-1997) Danish					
3D	1	1,537		1,537	
oil	1	2,050		2,050	
WIJCKAERT, Maurice (1923-1996) Belgian					
oil	1	6,169		6,169	
WIJNBERG, Nicolaas (1918-) Dutch					
oil	1	2,065		2,065	
WIJNGAERDT, Piet van (1873-1964) Dutch					
oil	12	20,236	1,073	1,506	3,902
WIKSTROM, Bror Anders (1854-1909) American/Swedish					
oil	1	2,000		2,000	
WILBERG, Christian (1839-1882) German					
oil	1	10,220		10,220	
WILCOX, Jim (20th C) American					
oil	1	10,000		10,000	
WILCOX, Leslie A (1904-) British					
oil	2	2,287	1,015	1,144	1,272
WILCOXSON, Frederick John (fl.1899) British					
3D	1	3,848		3,848	
WILD, Carel Frederik Louis de (1870-1922) Dutch					
oil	1	1,075		1,075	
WILD, Charles (1781-1835) British					
wc/d	1	2,794		2,794	
WILD, Frank Percy (1861-1950) British					
oil	1	1,133		1,133	
WILD, Hamilton Gibbs (1827-1884) American					
oil	1	3,750		3,750	

Name	No.	Total Sales Value	Prices lowest	median	highest
WILDA, Charles (1854-1907) Austrian					
oil	2	6,080	1,408	3,040	4,672
WILDE, David (1931-) British					
oil	1	1,812		1,812	
WILDE, Samuel de (1748-1832) British					
oil	1	1,057		1,057	
WILDENS, Jan (1586-1653) Flemish					
oil	3	69,668	13,000	17,277	39,391
wc/d	1	11,000		11,000	
WILDER, Andre (1871-1965) French					
oil	1	3,950		3,950	
WILDER, Tom Milton (1876-?) American					
oil	1	2,100		2,100	
WILES, Irving Ramsey (1861-1948) American					
oil	6	229,250	5,750	16,000	140,000
wc/d	1	1,200		1,200	
WILFERT, F (19th C) ?					
oil	1	1,450		1,450	
WILHELM, A L (20th C) American					
oil	1	1,700		1,700	
WILHELM, Roy (1895-1954) American					
oil	1	2,900		2,900	
WILHELMS, Carl (1889-1953) Finnish					
3D	1	1,039		1,039	
WILHELMSON, Carl (1866-1928) Swedish					
oil	16	500,643	1,044	7,070	293,454
wc/d	3	6,638	1,608	1,608	3,415
WILHJELM, Johannes (1868-1938) Danish					
oil	2	10,107	1,291	5,054	8,816
WILKE, Paul Ernst (1894-1972) German					
oil	4	7,907	1,364	1,565	3,414
WILKENSON, Michael (20th C) American?					
3D	1	2,750		2,750	
WILKIE, Sir David (1785-1841) British					
oil	4	292,267	1,738	2,265	286,000
wc/d	3	4,762	1,144	1,588	2,030
WILKIN, Eloise (1904-1987) American					
wc/d	1	6,000		6,000	
WILKINS, John (fl.1794-1853) British					
oil	1	6,435		6,435	
WILKINSON, Arthur (?) Australian					
wc/d	4	6,695	1,000	1,702	2,291
WILKINSON, Edward (fl.1882-1904) British					
wc/d	1	7,436		7,436	
WILKINSON, Ellis (fl.1874-1890) British					
oil	1	2,700		2,700	
WILKINSON, Henry (19/20th C) British					
oil	1	1,199		1,199	
WILKINSON, Norman (1878-1971) British					
oil	10	38,216	1,108	3,322	9,620
WILKS, M C (1910-1984) British					
oil	2	4,605	2,250	2,303	2,355
WILKS, Maurice C (1910-1984) British					
oil	23	78,854	1,368	2,880	6,912
wc/d	5	11,738	1,378	2,368	3,256
WILL (20th C) French?					
wc/d	1	7,593		7,593	
WILLAERT, Ferdinand (1861-1938) Belgian					
oil	4	13,707	1,391	2,733	6,760

Name	No.	Total Sales Value	Prices lowest	median	highest
WILLAERT, Joseph (20th C) ?					
oil	1	1,073		1,073	
WILLAERTS, Adam (1577-1669) Dutch					
oil	2	168,617	67,950	84,309	100,667
WILLAERTS, Isaac (1620-1693) Dutch					
oil	3	110,240	4,840	45,000	60,400
WILLARD, Archibald M (1836-1918) American					
oil	1	1,800		1,800	
WILLARST, Adam Edvard de (1693-1752) Danish					
wc/d	1	5,262		5,262	
WILLE, August von (1829-1887) German					
oil	1	1,936		1,936	
WILLE, Clara von (1838-1883) German					
oil	2	3,008	1,390	1,504	1,618
WILLE, Fritz von (1860-1941) German					
oil	8	62,966	3,415	6,216	13,406
WILLE, Pierre-Alexandre (1748-1821) French					
wc/d	3	5,432	1,200	1,611	2,621
WILLEBOIRTS, Thomas (1614-1654) Flemish					
oil	1	51,479		51,479	
WILLEMS, Florent (1823-1905) Belgian					
oil	2	4,861	2,037	2,431	2,824
WILLEMSEN, Willem Jan (1866-1914) Dutch					
oil	1	2,678		2,678	
WILLEMSENS, Abraham (fl.1627-1672) Flemish?					
oil	1	11,347		11,347	
WILLERUP, Oscar (1864-1931) German					
wc/d	1	3,614		3,614	
WILLETT, Arthur (c.1857-1918) British					
wc/d	2	2,866	1,128	1,433	1,738
WILLIAMS OF PLYMOUTH, William (1808-1895) British					
oil	3	11,052	1,368	4,004	5,680
WILLIAMS, A (?) ?					
wc/d	1	1,000		1,000	
WILLIAMS, Albert (1922-) British					
oil	2	2,408	1,133	1,204	1,275
WILLIAMS, Alexander (1846-1930) British					
oil	3	3,847	1,145	1,359	1,359
WILLIAMS, Alfred Walter (1824-1905) British					
oil	1	1,606		1,606	
WILLIAMS, Col E A (19th C) British					
wc/d	1	7,222		7,222	
WILLIAMS, Dwight (1856-?) American					
oil	1	1,600		1,600	
WILLIAMS, E (1782-1855) British					
oil	3	4,865	1,015	1,250	2,600
wc/d	1	1,011		1,011	
WILLIAMS, Edward (1782-1855) British					
oil	5	44,562	1,704	6,006	20,020
WILLIAMS, Edward Charles (1807-1881) British					
oil	6	45,196	2,320	4,335	15,730
WILLIAMS, Esther (1907-) American					
oil	1	4,500		4,500	
WILLIAMS, Frederick Ballard (1871-1956) American					
oil	2	4,800	1,600	2,400	3,200
WILLIAMS, Frederick Dickenson (1829-1915) American					
oil	1	1,200		1,200	
WILLIAMS, Frederick Ronald (1927-1982) Australian					
wc/d	1	1,305		1,305	

Name	No.	Total Sales Value	Prices lowest	median	highest
WILLIAMS, G F (?) British?					
oil	1	1,043		1,043	
WILLIAMS, Garth M (1912-) American					
wc/d	1	18,000		18,000	
WILLIAMS, George Augustus (1814-1901) British					
oil	4	14,868	1,924	4,200	4,544
WILLIAMS, Jerry (1943-) American					
3D	1	1,376		1,376	
WILLIAMS, John Haynes (1836-1908) British					
oil	2	13,586	3,716	6,793	9,870
wc/d	1	4,800		4,800	
WILLIAMS, Kyffin (1918-) British					
oil	7	51,490	4,205	5,292	13,500
wc/d	2	4,096	1,846	2,048	2,250
WILLIAMS, Margaret Lindsay (?-1960) British					
oil	1	7,850		7,850	
WILLIAMS, Mildred Emerson (1892-) American					
oil	1	20,000		20,000	
WILLIAMS, Penry (1798-1885) British					
oil	3	33,770	3,020	9,750	21,000
WILLIAMS, Pownall Toker (fl.1872-1897) British					
wc/d	1	1,133		1,133	
WILLIAMS, Sue (1954-) American					
oil	8	234,677	4,777	34,050	48,000
wc/d	1	10,000		10,000	
WILLIAMS, Terrick (1860-1936) British					
oil	8	71,524	2,184	6,138	31,600
wc/d	2	4,490	1,058	2,245	3,432
WILLIAMS, Thomas (fl.1831-1850) British					
oil	1	2,512		2,512	
WILLIAMS, W (1835-1906) British					
oil	1	1,323		1,323	
WILLIAMS, W (19th C) British					
oil	1	1,139		1,139	
WILLIAMS, Walter (1835-1906) British					
oil	9	39,234	1,216	3,768	8,120
WILLIAMS, Walter (19th C) British					
oil	2	3,200	1,600	1,600	1,600
WILLIAMS, Walter (fl.1841-1876) British					
oil	3	24,625	6,000	6,300	12,325
WILLIAMS, Walter Heath (19th C) British					
oil	3	10,817	1,425	4,530	4,862
WILLIAMS, Warren (1863-1918) British					
wc/d	24	53,413	1,008	2,014	6,795
WILLIAMS, William (fl.1758-1797) British					
oil	4	43,140	4,260	8,000	22,880
WILLIAMS-LYOUNS, Herbert (1863-?) British					
oil	1	1,500		1,500	
WILLIAMSON, Albert Curtis (?) Canadian?					
oil	1	1,354		1,354	
WILLIAMSON, D (19th C) British					
oil	1	1,287		1,287	
WILLIAMSON, Frederick (c.1835-1900) British					
wc/d	6	15,036	1,027	1,569	5,005
WILLIAMSON, J (?) ?					
oil	1	2,840		2,840	
WILLIAMSON, James (1899-1978) American					
wc/d	1	1,600		1,600	

Name	No.	Total Sales Value	lowest	Prices median	highest
WILLIAMSON, John (fl.1891-1895) British					
oil	1	1,804		1,804	
WILLIAMSON, Laurie (1932-) British					
oil	1	2,100		2,100	
WILLIAMSON, William Henry (1820-1883) British					
oil	5	8,941	1,001	1,343	3,861
WILLICH, Caesar (1825-1886) German					
oil	1	8,420		8,420	
WILLIGEN, Christina Abigael van der (1850-1932) Dutch					
oil	1	1,364		1,364	
WILLIKENS, Ben (1939-) German					
oil	1	1,923		1,923	
WILLINGES, Johann (c.1560-1625) German					
wc/d	1	3,000		3,000	
WILLINK, Carel (1900-1979) Dutch					
oil	3	146,552	34,483	43,103	68,966
WILLIS, A (?) British?					
oil	1	2,862		2,862	
WILLIS, Charles (20th C) British					
oil	2	3,634	1,590	1,817	2,044
WILLIS, Henry Brittan (1810-1884) British					
oil	1	3,300		3,300	
wc/d	1	2,516		2,516	
WILLIS, J (?) British					
oil	1	2,250		2,250	
WILLIS, J R (1876-?) American					
oil	2	3,450	1,200	1,725	2,250
WILLIS, John Christopher Temple (1900-1969) British					
oil	1	2,500		2,500	
WILLIS, Thomas (1850-1912) American					
oil	1	15,000		15,000	
wc/d	1	13,000		13,000	
WILLROIDER, Josef (1838-1915) Austrian					
oil	3	9,648	1,727	2,811	5,110
WILLROIDER, Ludwig (1845-1910) German					
oil	7	24,493	1,135	2,229	11,520
WILLSHER, Brian (1930-) British					
3D	1	1,650		1,650	
WILLUMSEN, J F (1863-1958) Danish					
oil	1	1,129		1,129	
wc/d	3	6,809	1,023	2,208	3,578
WILLUMSEN, Jens Ferdinand (1863-1958) Danish					
oil	2	16,714	3,606	8,357	13,108
WILMARTH, Christopher (1943-1987) American					
3D	1	55,000		55,000	
WILMARTH, Lemuel Everett (1835-1918) American					
oil	1	2,500		2,500	
WILMS, Joseph (1814-1892) German					
oil	1	5,000		5,000	
WILS, Lydia (1924-) Belgian					
oil	1	1,109		1,109	
WILSON, Andrew (1780-1848) British					
wc/d	1	1,580		1,580	
WILSON, Charles Edward (1854-1941) British					
wc/d	3	28,726	8,250	9,322	11,154
WILSON, David Forrester (1873-1950) British					
oil	2	7,787	2,370	3,894	5,417
WILSON, Eric (1960-) British					
oil	2	5,860	1,420	2,930	4,440

Name	No.	Total Sales Value	lowest	Prices median	highest
WILSON, Frank Avray (1914-) British					
oil	3	6,877	1,099	1,278	4,500
WILSON, Hugh Cameron (1885-?) British					
oil	1	1,185		1,185	
WILSON, J (?) British					
oil	3	6,646	1,434	2,212	3,000
WILSON, John (1774-1855) British					
oil	7	19,964	1,136	2,860	5,285
WILSON, John H (?) British					
oil	1	5,434		5,434	
WILSON, John J (1836-1903) British					
oil	1	2,860		2,860	
WILSON, John James (1818-1875) British					
oil	7	26,533	1,430	3,423	7,540
WILSON, Mortimer (1906-1996) American					
oil	3	8,700	1,700	2,000	5,000
WILSON, P MacGregor (?-1960) British					
oil	1	1,125		1,125	
wc/d	1	1,043		1,043	
WILSON, Patten (1868-1928) British					
wc/d	3	6,142	1,184	2,442	2,516
WILSON, Richard (1714-1782) British					
oil	4	76,722	1,027	15,198	45,300
WILSON, Richard (school) (1714-1782) British					
oil	1	3,000		3,000	
WILSON, Samuel Henry (?) British					
wc/d	1	2,869		2,869	
WILSON, Scottie (1889-1972) British					
wc/d	1	1,248		1,248	
WILSON, Sol (1896-1974) American/Polish					
oil	1	1,000		1,000	
WILSON, Thomas (19th C) British					
oil	1	2,669		2,669	
WILSON, Thomas Robert (19th C) British					
oil	1	3,500		3,500	
WILSON, William (1905-1972) British					
wc/d	1	3,770		3,770	
WILSON, William Heath (1849-1927) British					
oil	1	1,824		1,824	
WILT, Hans (1867-1917) Austrian					
oil	1	3,948		3,948	
WILT, Thomas van der (1659-1733) Dutch					
oil	1	7,920		7,920	
WILTZ, Arnold (1889-1937) American/German					
oil	1	1,924		1,924	
WIMBUSH, Henry B (fl.1881-1904) British					
wc/d	1	1,117		1,117	
WIMMER, Konrad (1844-1905) German					
oil	6	15,493	1,345	2,664	3,962
WIMMER, Rudolf (1849-1915) German					
oil	1	2,472		2,472	
WIMPERIS, Edmund Morison (1835-1900) British					
oil	4	11,982	1,649	2,917	4,500
wc/d	2	2,501	1,021	1,251	1,480
WINCK, Johann Amandus (1748-1817) German					
oil	4	68,242	7,532	16,850	27,010
WINCK, Willibald (1867-1932) German					
oil	1	4,091		4,091	

Name	No.	Total Sales Value	lowest	Prices median	highest
WINDER, D H (fl.1880-1920) British					
oil	1	1,008		1,008	
WINDMAIER, Anton (1840-1896) German					
oil	4	9,270	1,653	2,412	2,794
WINDRED, W (19/20th C) British					
oil	1	1,628		1,628	
WINDT, Chris van der (1877-1952) Dutch					
oil	4	15,725	2,030	3,513	6,670
wc/d	4	13,041	1,171	2,087	7,697
WINGATE, Sir James Lawton (1846-1924) British					
oil	11	23,260	1,057	2,320	3,625
WINGERT, Edward Oswald (1864-?) American					
oil	1	4,750		4,750	
WINGFIELD, J D (1809-1872) British					
oil	1	1,278		1,278	
WINGFIELD, James Digman (1809-1872) British					
oil	3	20,996	3,300	6,636	11,060
WINKFIELD, Frederick A (fl.1873-1920) British					
oil	1	3,260		3,260	
wc/d	1	4,576		4,576	
WINKLER, Woldemar (1902-) German					
oil	1	1,202		1,202	
WINNER, William E (1815-1883) American					
oil	1	3,000		3,000	
WINSLOW, John (20th C) American					
oil	1	1,600		1,600	
WINSTANLEY, Henry (19th C) British					
oil	1	1,800		1,800	
WINSTANLEY, W (18th C) British					
oil	1	5,110		5,110	
WINT, Peter de (1784-1849) British					
oil	1	11,850		11,850	
wc/d	20	133,545	1,287	3,884	34,320
WINTER, Abraham Hendrik (1800-1861) Dutch					
oil	1	2,942		2,942	
WINTER, Andrew (1893-1958) American					
oil	1	4,000		4,000	
WINTER, Fritz (1905-1976) German					
oil	19	242,356	1,483	9,876	29,090
wc/d	8	52,568	1,181	2,678	28,113
WINTER, Heinrich (1843-1911) German					
oil	3	8,088	1,211	2,453	4,424
WINTER, Heinz (19/20th C) ?					
oil	1	3,300		3,300	
WINTER, Hendrik de (1717-1790) Dutch					
wc/d	1	1,111		1,111	
WINTER, Janus de (1882-1951) Dutch					
oil	1	2,093		2,093	
WINTER, Ludovicus de (1819-1900) Belgian					
oil	1	5,720		5,720	
WINTER, Robert (19/20th C) British					
wc/d	1	1,359		1,359	
WINTER, William Tatton (1855-1928) British					
wc/d	2	4,006	1,590	2,003	2,416
WINTERHALTER, Franz Xavier (1806-1873) German					
oil	2	45,913	6,640	22,957	39,273
wc/d	1	3,867		3,867	
WINTERHALTER, Franz Xavier (school) (1806-1873) German					
oil	1	3,498		3,498	

Name	No.	Total Sales Value	lowest	Prices median	highest
WINTERHALTER, Joseph (elder) (1702-1769) Austrian					
wc/d	1	1,419		1,419	
WINTERLIN, Anton (1805-1894) Swiss					
oil	1	3,671		3,671	
wc/d	1	2,076		2,076	
WINTERS, Robin (1950-) American					
3D	1	1,474		1,474	
WINTERS, Terry (1949-) American					
oil	2	200,000	65,000	100,000	135,000
wc/d	2	19,500	9,500	9,750	10,000
WINTHER, Frederick Julius August (1853-1916) Danish					
oil	1	1,026		1,026	
WINTHER, Richard (1926-) Danish					
3D	1	2,819		2,819	
WINTOUR, John Crawford (1825-1882) British					
oil	2	6,960	3,480	3,480	3,480
WINTTER, Joseph Georg (1751-1789) German					
oil	1	3,213		3,213	
WINTZ, Guillaume (1823-1899) French					
oil	2	4,072	1,702	2,036	2,370
WINTZ, Raymond (1884-?) French					
oil	2	3,014	1,313	1,507	1,701
WIRBEL, Veronique (1950-1990) French					
oil	4	9,696	1,751	2,368	3,210
WIRDOCK, P (19th C) British					
oil	1	1,699		1,699	
WIRGMAN, Charles (1832-1891) British					
oil	1	4,500		4,500	
WIRSING, Adam Louis (1733-1797) German					
wc/d	1	1,600		1,600	
WIRTH, H (20th C) ?					
oil	1	1,193		1,193	
WIRTH, Henri (1869-1947) French					
oil	1	1,196		1,196	
WISINGER-FLORIAN, Olga (1844-1926) Austrian					
oil	1	3,312		3,312	
WISLICENUS, Max (1861-1957) German					
oil	2	3,076	1,367	1,538	1,709
WISSEL, Abraham van der (1865-1926) Dutch					
oil	1	1,343		1,343	
WISSEL, Adolf (1894-1973) German					
oil	2	4,395	1,366	2,198	3,029
WISSING, Willem (1653-1687) Dutch					
oil	2	151,610	70,070	75,805	81,540
WIT, Frans de (1942-) Dutch					
oil	1	1,405		1,405	
WIT, Jacob de (1695-1754) Dutch					
oil	2	20,917	3,647	10,459	17,270
wc/d	5	9,012	1,128	1,323	3,143
WIT, Petrus Josephus de (1816-1870) Flemish					
oil	1	3,744		3,744	
WIT, Prosper Joseph de (c.1862-c.1951) Belgian					
oil	1	1,981		1,981	
WITDOECK, Petrus Josephus (1803-1840) Flemish					
oil	1	9,157		9,157	
WITHAM, J (19th C) British					
oil	1	3,040		3,040	
WITHERINGTON, W F (1785-1865) British					
oil	1	1,050		1,050	

Name	No.	Total Sales Value	lowest	Prices median	highest
WITHERINGTON, William Frederick (1785-1865) British					
oil	2	8,300	3,500	4,150	4,800
WITHOOS, Alida (1660-1715) Dutch					
oil	1	9,243		9,243	
WITHOOS, Matthias (1627-1703) Dutch					
oil	1	4,655		4,655	
wc/d	1	4,584		4,584	
WITHOOS, Pieter (1654-1693) Dutch					
wc/d	2	3,311	1,019	1,656	2,292
WITJENS, Willem (1884-1962) Dutch					
oil	1	1,268		1,268	
WITKOWSKI, Karl (1860-1910) American					
oil	2	7,210	1,210	3,605	6,000
WITSCHI, Hans (1954-) Swiss					
oil	1	2,215		2,215	
WITSEN, Willem (1860-1923) Dutch					
wc/d	2	18,753	3,902	9,377	14,851
WITT, John Henry (1840-1901) American					
oil	2	8,684	2,184	4,342	6,500
WITTE, Emanuel de (1617-1692) Dutch					
oil	2	361,200	44,100	180,600	317,100
WITTE, Gaspar de (1624-1681) Flemish					
oil	1	26,000		26,000	
WITTEL, Gaspar van (1653-1736) Dutch					
oil	2	644,867	51,810	322,434	593,057
wc/d	1	7,248		7,248	
WITTENBERG, Jan (1886-1963) Dutch					
oil	1	15,845		15,845	
WITTERWULGHE, Joseph (1883-1967) Belgian					
3D	2	3,138	1,358	1,569	1,780
WITTIG, Bartholomaus (1613-1684) German					
oil	2	5,628	1,584	2,814	4,044
WITTLICH, Josef (1903-1982) ?					
wc/d	1	1,262		1,262	
WITTMACK, Edgar Franklin (1894-1956) American					
oil	2	8,000	4,000	4,000	4,000
WITTS, E G (?) ?					
oil	1	18,980		18,980	
WOCHER, Johann Friedrich Thaddaeus (1726-1799) Swiss					
oil	1	2,163		2,163	
WOCHER, Tiberius Dominikus (1728-1799) Swiss					
oil	2	17,330	1,242	8,665	16,088
WODICK, Edmund (1817-1886) German					
oil	1	6,000		6,000	
WOELFLE, Arthur William (1873-1936) American					
oil	1	7,000		7,000	
WOERFFEL, Samonoff (?) Russian					
3D	1	3,000		3,000	
WOESTIJNE, Gustave van de (1881-1947) Belgian					
oil	3	412,198	62,693	107,473	242,032
wc/d	1	63,632		63,632	
WOGE, Daniel (?) ?					
oil	1	3,846		3,846	
WOHNER, Louis (1888-?) German					
oil	2	4,137	1,537	2,069	2,600
WOLBERS, Dirk (1890-1957) Dutch					
3D	1	2,586		2,586	
WOLCK, Nikolaus (1887-1950) German					
oil	2	15,712	1,412	7,856	14,300

Name	No.	Total Sales Value	lowest	Prices median	highest
WOLDE, Paul (1885-?) German?					
oil	1	1,400		1,400	
WOLEVER, Adeleine (1886-?) American					
oil	1	8,000		8,000	
WOLF, Albert (1863-?) German					
wc/d	1	1,238		1,238	
WOLF, Anne (20th C) French?					
3D	1	1,092		1,092	
WOLF, Caspar (1735-1798) Swiss					
oil	3	90,028	16,345	34,183	39,500
WOLF, Franz Xaver (1896-1989) Austrian					
oil	5	28,241	1,034	3,900	12,750
WOLF, Georg (1882-1962) German					
oil	4	5,309	1,095	1,323	1,569
WOLF, Gustav (1887-1947) German					
oil	1	1,129		1,129	
WOLF, Joseph (1820-1899) German					
wc/d	1	1,065		1,065	
WOLF, W (?) ?					
oil	1	1,264		1,264	
WOLF, Yelva (1842-1914) Danish					
oil	1	1,682		1,682	
WOLFAERTS, Artus (1581-c.1641) Flemish					
oil	1	6,521		6,521	
WOLFE, Edward (1897-1982) British					
oil	4	12,866	1,106	3,030	5,700
wc/d	1	1,397		1,397	
WOLFE, George (1834-1890) British					
wc/d	1	1,029		1,029	
WOLFE, Wallace de (20th C) ?					
oil	1	2,100		2,100	
WOLFERS, Philippe (1858-1929) Belgian					
3D	1	85,083		85,083	
WOLFF, Emil (1802-1879) German					
3D	1	10,360		10,360	
WOLFF, Eugen (1873-1937) German					
oil	4	8,466	1,258	1,595	4,019
WOLFF, Gustav H (1863-1935) American/German					
oil	1	1,600		1,600	
WOLFF, Jose (1884-1964) Belgian					
oil	5	7,777	1,021	1,553	2,222
WOLFLE, Franz Xavier (1887-1972) German					
oil	2	3,628	1,355	1,814	2,273
WOLFLI, Adolf (1864-1930) Swiss					
wc/d	8	78,170	6,956	9,829	14,146
WOLFRAM, Joseph (19th C) Austrian					
oil	1	1,094		1,094	
WOLFROM, Friedrich Ernst (1857-?) German					
oil	1	4,098		4,098	
WOLFS, Hubert (1899-1937) Belgian					
oil	2	7,830	3,559	3,915	4,271
WOLFSEN, Aleijda (1648-1690) Dutch					
oil	1	5,760		5,760	
WOLGERS, Dan (1955-) Swedish					
wc/d	1	4,723		4,723	
WOLK, William (1951-) American					
oil	1	1,215		1,215	
WOLLHEIM, Gert (1894-1974) German/American					
oil	1	1,788		1,788	

Name	No.	Total Sales Value	lowest	Prices median	highest
wc/d	1	10,800		10,800	
WOLMARK, Alfred (1877-1961) British					
oil	19	101,133	1,057	5,510	19,035
WOLS, Wolfgang (1913-1951) German					
wc/d	10	192,696	4,481	20,300	29,567
WOLSTENHOLME, Dean (snr) (1757-1837) British					
oil	1	5,000		5,000	
WOLTER, Hendrik Jan (1873-1952) Dutch					
oil	10	86,611	1,970	6,474	30,172
wc/d	2	9,711	1,090	4,856	8,621
WOLTERS, Eugène (1844-1905) Belgian					
oil	3	5,803	1,702	1,913	2,188
WOLVECAMP, Theo (1925-1992) Dutch					
oil	1	10,776		10,776	
WOLVENS, Henri Victor (1896-1977) Belgian					
oil	5	28,223	1,761	4,527	13,103
WONNER, Paul (1920-) American					
oil	3	64,500	2,500	30,000	32,000
wc/d	2	14,000	2,000	7,000	12,000
WOO, Jade Fon (1911-1983) American					
wc/d	2	2,500	1,000	1,250	1,500
WOOD, Charles Bernard (20th C) British					
oil	1	1,193		1,193	
WOOD, Charles Haigh (1856-1927) British					
oil	3	21,905	3,000	6,750	12,155
WOOD, Christopher (1901-1930) British					
oil	3	154,920	37,920	42,000	75,000
wc/d	5	18,948	1,988	3,102	7,540
WOOD, Donald (20th C) British					
oil	2	5,486	1,510	2,743	3,976
WOOD, Edgar Thomas (1860-1935) British					
oil	2	4,320	1,872	2,160	2,448
WOOD, Eleanor Stuart (fl.1876-1910) British					
oil	1	1,480		1,480	
WOOD, Frank Watson (1862-1953) British					
oil	2	7,324	1,044	3,662	6,280
wc/d	4	16,204	1,057	2,924	9,300
WOOD, G (?) British					
oil	1	4,710		4,710	
WOOD, Grant (1892-1942) American					
3D	1	65,000		65,000	
oil	2	245,000	115,000	122,500	130,000
wc/d	1	140,000		140,000	
WOOD, Hunter (19/20th C) American					
oil	1	3,000		3,000	
WOOD, John T (1845-1919) American					
oil	1	1,800		1,800	
WOOD, Lawson (1878-1957) British					
wc/d	2	4,005	1,740	2,003	2,265
WOOD, Lewis John (1813-1901) British					
oil	2	6,028	2,920	3,014	3,108
WOOD, Robert W (1889-1979) American					
oil	9	37,100	2,400	3,750	6,000
WOOD, Thomas Waterman (1823-1903) American					
oil	1	27,000		27,000	
wc/d	2	10,887	4,000	5,444	6,887
WOOD, William Thomas (1877-1958) British					
oil	1	1,924		1,924	
WOODBURY, Charles (1864-1940) American					
oil	3	20,100	4,600	5,500	10,000

Name	No.	Total Sales Value	Prices lowest	median	highest
WOODFORDE, Samuel (1763-1817) British					
oil	1	2,250		2,250	
WOODHOUSE, William (1857-1939) British					
oil	6	60,559	1,200	5,685	34,320
wc/d	3	4,627	1,133	1,661	1,833
WOODLOCK, David (1842-1929) British					
wc/d	8	18,380	1,140	2,006	4,576
WOODS, Albert (1871-1944) British					
oil	1	1,885		1,885	
WOODS, Henry (1846-1921) British					
oil	2	6,350	2,000	3,175	4,350
WOODVILLE, Richard Caton (jnr) (1856-1927) British					
oil	3	135,810	6,500	24,310	105,000
WOODVILLE, William Caton (1884-?) British					
oil	1	1,027		1,027	
WOODWARD (?) ?					
oil	1	4,100		4,100	
WOODWARD, Ellsworth (1861-1939) American					
oil	2	10,200	1,200	5,100	9,000
WOODWARD, George Moutard (1760-1809) British					
wc/d	1	1,073		1,073	
WOODWARD, Mabel (1877-1945) American					
oil	1	1,100		1,100	
WOODWARD, Robert Strong (1885-1960) American					
oil	1	2,000		2,000	
WOODWARD, Stanley W (1890-1970) American					
oil	3	6,100	1,000	2,000	3,100
WOODWARD, Thomas (1801-1852) British					
oil	1	3,926		3,926	
WOODWARD, William (1859-1939) American					
oil	4	41,000	9,000	10,250	11,500
wc/d	2	7,400	2,400	3,700	5,000
WOOG, J (?) ?					
oil	1	1,793		1,793	
WOOL, Christopher (1955-) American					
oil	7	262,130	2,730	30,000	80,000
wc/d	2	330,000	55,000	165,000	275,000
WOOLFE, Annette Marguerite Shipper (1889-?) American					
oil	1	1,700		1,700	
WOOLLETT, Henry (19th C) British					
oil	2	15,574	2,574	7,787	13,000
WOOLLEY, Virginia (1884-1971) American					
oil	1	3,750		3,750	
WOOLMER, Alfred Joseph (1805-1892) British					
oil	4	7,776	1,230	1,398	3,750
WOOSTER, Austin C (19/20th C) American					
oil	1	2,250		2,250	
WOOTTON, Frank (1911-1998) British					
oil	1	1,510		1,510	
WOPFNER, Joseph (1843-1927) Austrian					
oil	12	93,213	1,483	4,989	24,534
WORES, Theodore (1859-1939) American					
oil	7	50,200	1,700	8,000	11,000
WORKMAN, Harold (1897-1975) British					
oil	1	3,600		3,600	
WORMS, Jules (1832-1924) French					
oil	5	68,530	3,500	15,000	20,440
wc/d	1	2,580		2,580	

Name	No.	Total Sales Value	lowest	Prices median	highest
WORMS, Roger (1907-1980) French					
oil	1	1,106		1,106	
WORN, Walter (1901-1963) German					
oil	1	5,128		5,128	
wc/d	1	4,542		4,542	
WOROBIEFF, Maxim (1787-1855) Russian					
wc/d	1	22,154		22,154	
WORRELL, Abraham Bruiningh van (1787-1823) Dutch					
oil	2	8,203	2,122	4,102	6,081
WORSEL, Troels (1950-) Danish					
oil	1	1,666		1,666	
WORSEY, Thomas (1829-1875) British					
oil	4	9,324	1,332	1,776	4,440
WORSLEY, Charles N (c.1850-1923) New Zealander					
oil	1	1,156		1,156	
WORTH, Leslie Charles (1923-) British					
wc/d	1	1,800		1,800	
WOSTRY, Carlo (1865-?) Italian					
oil	1	32,120		32,120	
WOTRUBA, Fritz (1907-1975) Austrian					
3D	2	9,503	1,047	4,752	8,456
WOU, Claes Claesz (1592-1665) Dutch					
oil	1	4,710		4,710	
WOUTERMAERTENS, Edouard (1819-1897) Belgian					
oil	1	2,049		2,049	
WOUTERS, H (?) Belgian?					
oil	1	1,165		1,165	
WOUTERS, Rik (1882-1916) Belgian					
3D	2	5,222	1,389	2,611	3,833
wc/d	5	18,057	1,944	4,478	4,507
WOUWERMAN, Philips (1619-1668) Dutch					
oil	8	800,605	5,000	48,055	411,600
WOUWERMAN, Philips (school) (1619-1668) Dutch					
oil	1	4,953		4,953	
wc/d	1	1,538		1,538	
WOUWERMAN, Pieter (1623-1682) Dutch					
oil	7	105,096	3,675	14,518	37,232
WRAMPE, Fritz (1893-1934) German					
3D	1	3,981		3,981	
WRAY, Ellen (fl.1852) British					
oil	1	1,963		1,963	
WRBA, Georg (1872-1939) German					
3D	1	2,396		2,396	
WRIGHT OF DERBY, Joseph (1734-1797) British					
oil	5	250,920	6,750	30,000	120,000
wc/d	1	300,300		300,300	
WRIGHT, Charles Lennox (1876-?) American					
oil	1	5,000		5,000	
WRIGHT, Ferdinand von (1822-1906) Finnish					
oil	2	114,697	13,972	57,349	100,725
WRIGHT, George (1860-1942) British					
oil	8	76,558	4,532	8,275	21,140
WRIGHT, George Hand (1873-1951) American					
oil	1	5,000		5,000	
WRIGHT, Gilbert Scott (1880-1958) British					
oil	3	32,340	7,000	11,840	13,500
WRIGHT, John Michael (1617-1694) British					
oil	2	467,500	29,600	233,750	437,900

Name	No.	Total Sales Value	lowest	Prices median	highest
WRIGHT, Margaret Isobel (1884-1957) British					
wc/d	1	1,199		1,199	
WRIGHT, Richard Henry (1857-1930) British					
wc/d	1	1,320		1,320	
WRIGHT, Robert W (fl.1880-1900) British					
oil	1	1,908		1,908	
WRIGHT, Rufus (1832-?) American					
oil	1	1,600		1,600	
WRIGHT, Thomas (1792-1849) British					
oil	1	1,386		1,386	
WRIGHT, William (?) British					
oil	1	1,000		1,000	
WRINCH, Mary Evelyn (1877-1969) Canadian					
oil	2	4,514	2,257	2,257	2,257
WROBLEWSKI, Constantin (1868-1939) Russian					
oil	1	5,640		5,640	
WTBIXHO, O (20th C) Russian					
wc/d	1	1,807		1,807	
WUCHERER, Fritz (1873-1948) Swiss					
oil	6	15,590	1,276	2,193	4,661
wc/d	2	3,249	1,374	1,625	1,875
WUERMER, Carl (1900-1982) American					
oil	7	32,150	2,400	5,000	6,500
WUERPEL, Edmund H (1866-1958) American					
oil	4	5,700	1,300	1,400	1,600
WULFING, Karl (1812-1871) German					
oil	1	1,288		1,288	
WUNDERLICH, Hermann (1835-1915) German					
oil	2	2,418	1,132	1,209	1,286
WUNDERLICH, Paul (1927-) German					
3D	10	18,924	1,157	1,679	4,356
oil	4	22,082	1,514	3,234	14,101
wc/d	5	15,809	1,717	2,194	7,478
WUNDERWALD, Gustav (1882-1945) German					
oil	2	90,989	1,709	45,495	89,280
wc/d	1	1,410		1,410	
WUNNENBERG, Walther (1818-1900) German					
oil	1	1,364		1,364	
WUNSCH, Marie (1862-1898) German					
oil	3	18,500	2,000	7,500	9,000
WURBEL, Franz (1822-1900) Austrian					
oil	1	31,688		31,688	
WURTH, Xavier (1869-1933) Belgian					
oil	4	6,678	1,198	1,463	2,555
WURTZEN, Carl (1825-1880) Danish					
oil	1	2,645		2,645	
WUST, Johann Heinrich (1741-1821) Swiss					
oil	1	6,574		6,574	
WUSTLICH, Otto (1818-1886) German					
oil	1	3,525		3,525	
WUSTMANN, Gustav (1873-1939) German					
oil	1	1,275		1,275	
WUTHRICH, Marianne (1931-) Swiss					
oil	1	2,449		2,449	
WUTKY, Michael (1739-1823) Austrian					
oil	2	71,538	26,000	35,769	45,538
WUTTKE, Carl (1849-1927) German					
oil	2	11,617	1,238	5,809	10,379

Name	No.	Total Sales Value	lowest	Prices median	highest
WYANT, Alexander H (1836-1892) American					
oil	14	69,511	1,800	3,500	16,000
WYATT, Benjamin Dean (1775-1850) British					
wc/d	1	18,000		18,000	
WYBURD, Francis John (1826-?) British					
oil	1	22,000		22,000	
WYCK, Jan (1640-1702) Dutch					
oil	4	62,073	3,622	13,496	31,460
WYCK, Thomas (1616-1677) Dutch					
oil	1	32,340		32,340	
wc/d	1	1,298		1,298	
WYCKAERT, Maurice (1923-1996) Belgian					
oil	9	50,185	1,389	6,432	8,394
WYDEVELD, Arnoud (19th C) Dutch					
oil	1	11,500		11,500	
WYDOOGEN, N M (19th C) Dutch					
oil	2	2,475	1,100	1,238	1,375
WYETH, Andrew (1917-) American					
oil	2	895,000	95,000	447,500	800,000
wc/d	16	2,685,000	12,000	147,500	670,000
WYETH, Henriette (1907-1997) American					
oil	1	11,000		11,000	
WYETH, James (1946-) American					
oil	1	150,000		150,000	
wc/d	1	60,000		60,000	
WYETH, Newell Convers (1882-1945) American					
oil	13	2,610,000	55,000	180,000	570,000
wc/d	1	2,200		2,200	
WYGRZYWALSKI, Feliks (1875-1944) Polish					
oil	2	8,428	1,128	4,214	7,300
wc/d	1	2,052		2,052	
WYK, Charles van (1875-1917) Dutch					
3D	1	6,976		6,976	
oil	1	1,782		1,782	
WYK, Henri van (1833-?) Dutch					
oil	2	4,009	1,309	2,005	2,700
WYL, Jakob von (1586-c.1619) Swiss					
oil	1	6,685		6,685	
WYLAND (1956-) American					
3D	1	5,500		5,500	
WYLD, William (1806-1889) British					
oil	1	2,067		2,067	
wc/d	16	54,026	1,329	3,646	4,946
WYLER, Otto (1887-1965) Swiss					
oil	1	1,412		1,412	
WYLIE, Robert (?) British?					
oil	1	5,000		5,000	
WYLLIE, W L (1851-1931) British					
wc/d	1	3,344		3,344	
WYLLIE, William Lionel (1851-1931) British					
oil	2	56,800	13,000	28,400	43,800
wc/d	19	71,329	1,068	3,600	6,194
WYNANTS, Ferdinand (1887-1955) Belgian?					
3D	1	1,488		1,488	
WYNANTS, Jan (1630-1684) Dutch					
oil	3	38,972	5,738	7,510	25,724
WYNGAARD, L (?) ?					
oil	1	1,424		1,424	
WYNGAERDT, Anthonie Jacobus van (1808-1887) Dutch					
oil	7	48,837	1,200	4,745	17,380

Name	No.	Total Sales Value	lowest	Prices median	highest
WYNGAERDT, Petrus Theodorus van (1816-1893) Dutch					
oil	3	4,199	1,030	1,358	1,811
WYNN, Kenneth (1922-) British?					
oil	1	20,000		20,000	
WYNNE, David (1926-) British					
3D	2	20,775	10,200	10,388	10,575
WYNTER, Bryan (1915-1975) British					
oil	3	18,120	1,170	8,250	8,700
WYRSCH, Johann Melchior (1732-1798) Swiss					
oil	2	17,823	4,558	8,912	13,265
WYSMULLER, J H (1855-1925) Dutch					
oil	1	1,305		1,305	
WYSMULLER, Jan Hillebrand (1855-1925) Dutch					
oil	8	27,818	1,149	1,492	11,881
WYSPIANSKI, Stanislas (1869-1907) Polish					
wc/d	1	2,513		2,513	
WYTSMAN, Juliette (1866-1925) Belgian					
oil	4	50,739	1,485	8,493	32,269
wc/d	1	1,931		1,931	
WYTSMAN, R (1860-1927) Belgian					
oil	1	2,837		2,837	
WYTSMAN, Rodolphe (1860-1927) Belgian					
oil	7	48,113	1,310	5,062	15,673
WYWIORSKY, Michal (1861-1926) Polish					
oil	2	20,500	7,500	10,250	13,000
XAM (1915-) Spanish					
wc/d	2	4,292	1,920	2,146	2,372
XUAREB, A (18th C) ?					
oil	1	20,580		20,580	
XUAREZ, Juan Rodriguez (1675-c.1728) Mexican					
oil	1	5,550		5,550	
XUL SOLAR, Alejandro (1887-1963) Argentinian					
3D	1	50,000		50,000	
wc/d	2	80,000	30,000	40,000	50,000
XYLANDER, Wilhelm (1840-1913) Danish					
oil	1	1,105		1,105	
YAGUE, Cesar (1948-) Spanish					
oil	1	2,076		2,076	
YAKOVLEV, Vladimir (1934-) Russian					
wc/d	1	3,666		3,666	
YAMAGUCHI, Kaoru (1907-1968) Japanese					
oil	2	120,000	35,000	60,000	85,000
YAN PEI MING (1960-) ?					
oil	5	113,461	12,284	23,609	36,509
YAN, Robert (c.1901-) French					
oil	1	1,106		1,106	
YANAGI, Yukinori (1959-) ?					
wc/d	1	15,000		15,000	
YANEZ, Ferrando (fl.1506-1560) Spanish					
wc/d	1	13,590		13,590	
YANKEL (1920-) French					
oil	1	2,389		2,389	
YANKEL, Jacques (1920-) French					
oil	1	2,334		2,334	
YAOUANC, Alain le (c.1940-) French					
oil	1	1,476		1,476	
wc/d	1	1,395		1,395	
YARNOLD, G B (19th C) British					
oil	1	1,431		1,431	

Name	No.	Total Sales Value	lowest	Prices median	highest
YARNOLD, Joseph W (19th C) British					
oil	1	1,320		1,320	
YARROW-JONES, Ernest (1872-1951) British					
oil	1	2,686		2,686	
YARWOOD, Walter Hawley (1917-) Canadian					
oil	1	1,759		1,759	
YATES, Cullen (1866-1945) American					
oil	2	8,300	1,800	4,150	6,500
YATES, Fred (1922-) British					
oil	16	33,915	1,065	1,747	5,928
YATES, Frederic (1854-1919) British					
oil	2	6,627	3,102	3,314	3,525
YATES, Gideon (19th C) British					
wc/d	2	3,195	1,287	1,598	1,908
YATES, Thomas (?-1796) British					
oil	3	6,435	1,430	2,288	2,717
wc/d	1	1,580		1,580	
YATES, W (?) ?					
oil	1	1,050		1,050	
YATMAN, William Hamilton (1819-1897) British					
wc/d	1	1,661		1,661	
YEAMES, William Frederick (1835-1918) British					
oil	1	1,287		1,287	
YEATS, Jack Butler (1871-1957) Irish/British					
oil	13	3,254,610	29,610	136,160	1,258,000
wc/d	15	215,998	1,106	5,920	47,360
YEATS, William Butler (1865-1939) Irish					
oil	2	11,544	2,664	5,772	8,880
YEGOROV, Andrei (1878-1954) Russian					
oil	1	1,195		1,195	
YELLAND, Raymond D (1848-1900) American					
oil	3	20,250	2,750	5,500	12,000
YELTSEVA, Dina (1965-) Russian					
oil	2	2,250	1,050	1,125	1,200
YENS, Karl Julius Heinrich (1868-1945) American					
oil	3	5,350	1,200	1,400	2,750
YEPES, Tomas (1600-1674) Spanish					
oil	2	1,799,977	588,000	899,989	1,211,977
YERMOLOV, Pavel (1971-) Russian					
oil	3	3,292	1,027	1,185	1,185
YGLESIAS, Vincent Philip (1845-1911) German					
oil	2	3,938	1,650	1,969	2,288
YOAQUA (19th C) Chinese					
oil	1	3,100		3,100	
YOHN, Frederick Caffrey (1875-1933) American					
oil	2	7,000	3,000	3,500	4,000
YOKOI, Teruko (1924-) Japanese					
wc/d	1	1,049		1,049	
YOKOYAMA, Taikan (1868-1958) Japanese					
oil	1	150,000		150,000	
wc/d	2	61,831	6,831	30,916	55,000
YON, Edmond (1836-1897) French					
oil	3	4,405	1,283	1,317	1,805
YONG, Joe de (1894-1975) American					
oil	1	13,000		13,000	
YONGE, Antoni de (17th C) Dutch					
oil	1	4,500		4,500	
YOORS, Eugene (1879-1977) Belgian					
oil	2	13,410	1,210	6,705	12,200

Name	No.	Total Sales Value	lowest	Prices median	highest
YORKE, W H (19th C) British					
oil	1	3,083		3,083	
YORKE, William Henry (19th C) British					
oil	1	9,454		9,454	
YORKE, William Hoard (fl.1858-1903) British					
oil	3	25,065	6,525	9,540	9,540
YOSHIDA, Hiroshi (1876-1950) Japanese					
wc/d	1	2,500		2,500	
YOUNG, Alexander (1865-1923) British					
oil	6	12,652	1,359	2,457	2,528
YOUNG, Charles Morris (1869-1964) American					
oil	9	48,900	2,000	6,000	8,000
YOUNG, Florence Upson (1872-1964) American					
oil	1	2,500		2,500	
YOUNG, John (19th C) British					
oil	1	10,570		10,570	
YOUNG, John Tobias (fl.1811-1822) British					
oil	2	20,320	8,880	10,160	11,440
YOUNG, Mahonri (1877-1957) American					
wc/d	3	10,900	3,400	3,500	4,000
YOUNG, William S (fl.1850-1870) American					
oil	1	3,250		3,250	
YOUNGBLOOD, Nat (20th C) American					
wc/d	1	6,500		6,500	
YOUON, Konstantin (1875-1958) Russian					
oil	2	16,308	1,963	8,154	14,345
wc/d	2	5,334	2,416	2,667	2,918
YSERN Y ALIE, Pedro (1876-1946) Spanish					
oil	1	1,168		1,168	
YSLAIRE (20th C) ?					
wc/d	1	3,505		3,505	
YUAN-MING DYNASTY Chinese					
wc/d	1	9,000		9,000	
YULE, William James (19th C) British					
oil	1	8,250		8,250	
YUSKAVAGE, Lisa (1962-) American?					
wc/d	1	6,500		6,500	
YUZBASIYAN, Arto (1948-) Canadian					
oil	1	3,318		3,318	
YVARAL (1934-) French					
oil	2	2,715	1,166	1,358	1,549
YVON, Adolphe (1817-1893) French					
oil	1	5,455		5,455	
ZAAK, Gustav (1845-?) German					
oil	2	13,631	2,031	6,816	11,600
ZABALETA, Rafael (1907-1960) Spanish					
oil	5	326,182	24,194	64,533	123,651
wc/d	4	12,836	1,827	3,688	4,004
ZABEHLITZKY, Alois (1883-1969) Austrian					
oil	1	2,282		2,282	
ZABILETZKY, Alois (1883-1962) ?					
oil	1	4,768		4,768	
ZABOROV, Boris (1937-) ?					
oil	2	8,969	1,928	4,485	7,041
ZACH (?) ?					
3D	1	4,004		4,004	
ZACH, B (1891-?) Austrian					
3D	1	3,322		3,322	

Name	No.	Total Sales Value	lowest	Prices median	highest
ZACH, Bruno (1891-?) Austrian					
3D	5	12,271	1,144	2,355	3,624
ZACHMANN, Max (1892-1917) German					
wc/d	2	7,266	1,427	3,633	5,839
ZACHO, Christian (1843-1913) Danish					
oil	21	62,525	1,131	2,324	12,000
ZACHRISSON, Axel (1884-1944) Swedish					
oil	2	2,651	1,240	1,326	1,411
ZACK, Bruno (20th C) ?					
3D	1	2,044		2,044	
ZACK, Léon (1892-1980) Russian					
oil	13	36,697	1,002	2,951	5,582
ZADEMACK, Siegfried (1952-) German					
oil	1	1,600		1,600	
ZADIG, William (1884-1952) Swedish					
3D	1	1,197		1,197	
ZADKINE, Ossip (1890-1967) French					
3D	22	1,306,498	8,548	39,127	244,238
wc/d	18	138,037	1,092	4,828	21,905
ZAGO, Erma (1880-1942) Italian					
oil	6	15,533	1,379	1,862	4,390
ZAGO, Luigi (1894-1952) Italian					
oil	1	1,221		1,221	
ZAHND, J (1854-1934) Swiss					
oil	1	1,309		1,309	
ZAHND, Johann (1854-1934) Swiss					
oil	4	13,512	1,049	2,945	6,574
ZAHNDLER, Johann Georg (1877-1954) Swiss					
wc/d	1	6,574		6,574	
ZAHRTMANN, Kristian (1843-1917) Danish					
oil	9	32,390	1,097	3,023	7,487
ZAIRIS, Emmanuel (1876-1948) Greek					
oil	1	12,410		12,410	
ZAIS, Giuseppe (1709-1784) Italian					
oil	1	42,390		42,390	
wc/d	1	3,969		3,969	
ZAJAC, Jack (1929-) American					
3D	1	2,500		2,500	
ZAJICEK, Carl Wenzel (1860-1923) Austrian					
wc/d	1	4,061		4,061	
ZAJICEK, Karl (1879-?) Austrian					
wc/d	2	3,337	1,422	1,669	1,915
ZAKANITCH, Robert (1935-) American					
oil	2	3,679	1,500	1,840	2,179
ZALCE, Alfredo (1908-) Mexican					
oil	1	1,800		1,800	
ZALEZ, Ernesto (20th C) ?					
oil	1	1,720		1,720	
ZALIND, J (20th C) Italian					
oil	1	5,700		5,700	
ZALLO, S (19th C) ?					
wc/d	1	1,580		1,580	
ZAMACOIS Y ZABALA, Eduardo (1842-1871) Spanish					
oil	1	3,000		3,000	
ZAMBELETTI, Ludovico (1881-1966) Italian					
oil	1	2,225		2,225	
ZAMORANO, Ricardo (1922-) Spanish					
oil	2	2,802	1,320	1,401	1,482

Name	No.	Total Sales Value	lowest	Prices median	highest
ZAMPIGHI, Eugenio (1859-1944) Italian					
oil	17	422,919	6,000	18,000	113,286
wc/d	3	13,792	3,000	4,750	6,042
ZANCHI, Antonio (1631-1722) Italian					
oil	2	52,920	8,820	26,460	44,100
wc/d	1	18,000		18,000	
ZANDLEVEN, Jan Adam (1868-1923) Dutch					
oil	3	7,648	1,294	3,011	3,343
ZANDOMENEGHI, Federico (1841-1917) Italian					
oil	2	256,306	76,306	128,153	180,000
wc/d	2	23,892	1,298	11,946	22,594
ZANETTI, Antonio Maria (elder) (1680-1757) Italian					
wc/d	1	3,624		3,624	
ZANGS, Herbert (1924-) German					
oil	2	3,279	1,045	1,640	2,234
wc/d	6	10,277	1,117	1,473	3,000
ZANGUIDI, Jacopo (1544-1574) Italian					
oil	1	87,580		87,580	
wc/d	2	158,050	75,000	79,025	83,050
ZANICHELLI, Bruno (1963-1990) Italian					
oil	1	3,154		3,154	
ZANIN (19th C) Italian					
oil	1	7,163		7,163	
ZANIN, Francesco (19th C) Italian					
oil	1	1,641		1,641	
ZANKOVSKII, Ilia Nikolaevich (1843-1917) Russian					
oil	3	27,688	4,228	9,870	13,590
ZANNONI, Giuseppe (1849-1903) Italian					
oil	1	3,038		3,038	
ZANUTTO, Renzo (1909-1979) Italian					
oil	1	1,475		1,475	
ZAO-WOU-KI (1920-) Chinese					
oil	11	852,028	30,288	50,000	252,507
wc/d	13	98,073	1,215	6,552	14,786
ZARDO, Alberto (1876-1959) Italian					
oil	1	2,661		2,661	
ZARING, Louise E (c.1875-c.1945) American					
oil	3	16,500	4,200	4,800	7,500
ZARITSKY, Joseph (1891-1985) Israeli					
oil	1	34,000		34,000	
wc/d	10	164,700	4,200	13,500	35,000
ZARRAGA, Angel (1886-1946) Mexican					
oil	6	352,270	8,001	18,635	260,000
wc/d	2	3,506	1,463	1,753	2,043
ZARUBIN, Viktor Ivanovich (1866-1928) Russian					
oil	2	11,457	2,397	5,729	9,060
ZATZKA, Hans (1859-1949) Austrian					
oil	8	228,224	1,093	15,388	120,800
ZAUGG, Remy (1943-) Swiss					
oil	1	3,646		3,646	
ZAULI, Carlo (20th C) Italian					
3D	1	1,231		1,231	
ZAWADZKY, Margarete von (1889-) German					
oil	1	1,569		1,569	
ZEE, Jan van der (1898-1988) Dutch					
wc/d	1	4,357		4,357	
ZEEMAN (1623-1667) Dutch					
oil	1	30,200		30,200	
ZEITTER, John Christian (?-1862) British					
oil	1	1,185		1,185	

Name	No.	Total Sales Value	lowest	Prices median	highest
ZELENINE, Edouard (1938-) British					
wc/d	1	3,948		3,948	
ZELGER, Jakob Joseph (1812-1885) Swiss					
oil	5	18,788	1,823	3,038	5,951
ZELLER, Hans Arnold (1897-1983) Swiss					
oil	10	92,526	1,935	4,892	27,953
ZELLER, Johann Baptist (1877-1959) Swiss					
oil	1	11,789		11,789	
ZELLER, Johann Conrad (1807-1856) Swiss					
oil	1	4,518		4,518	
ZELONI, R (?) Italian?					
oil	2	3,158	1,500	1,579	1,658
ZENDEJAS, Miguel Jeronimo (19/20th C) Latin American					
oil	1	3,260		3,260	
ZENDER, Rudolf (1901-1988) Swiss					
oil	4	4,776	1,028	1,233	1,283
ZENETZIS, Vasilis (1935-) Greek					
oil	2	4,088	1,460	2,044	2,628
ZENIL, Nahum B (1947-) Mexican					
wc/d	1	11,000		11,000	
ZENKER, Flora (1876-?) ?					
oil	1	4,361		4,361	
ZERMATI, J (20th C) Italian					
oil	2	2,500	1,027	1,250	1,473
ZERMATI, Jules (20th C) Italian					
oil	1	1,600		1,600	
ZETSCHE, Eduard (1844-1927) Austrian					
oil	1	2,370		2,370	
ZETTERBERG, Nisse (1910-1986) Swedish					
oil	1	1,039		1,039	
ZEUGER, Martin Leon (1734-c.1780) Swiss					
oil	1	2,552		2,552	
ZEVENBERGHEN, Georges van (1877-1968) Belgian					
oil	2	3,105	1,281	1,553	1,824
ZEWY, Karl (1855-1929) Austrian					
oil	1	20,540		20,540	
ZEYSS, Julie (19th C) German?					
oil	1	2,958		2,958	
ZEZZOS, Alessandro (1848-1914) Italian					
oil	1	19,000		19,000	
wc/d	2	6,985	3,139	3,493	3,846
ZHANG DAQIAN (1899-1983) Chinese					
wc/d	1	22,000		22,000	
ZHEZHER, Anatoli (1937-) Russian					
oil	1	5,586		5,586	
ZHU DE-QUN (1922) Chinese					
wc/d	1	3,259		3,259	
ZIC, Zivko (1924-) American					
oil	1	4,200		4,200	
ZICK, Januarius (1730-1797) German					
oil	1	5,448		5,448	
ZICKENDRAHT, Bernhard (1854-1937) German					
oil	1	2,324		2,324	
ZIEBOLZ, Herbert (1903-1985) American?					
wc/d	3	7,436	1,417	2,831	3,188
ZIEGLAR, Frederick (20th C) ?					
3D	1	1,700		1,700	
ZIEGLER, Eustace Paul (1881-1969) American					
oil	2	12,500	3,000	6,250	9,500

Name	No.	Total Sales Value	lowest	Prices median	highest
ZIEGLER, Richard (1891-1992) German					
oil	7	387,360	4,032	12,240	216,000
wc/d	1	1,728		1,728	
ZIEM (1821-1911) French					
oil	1	1,430		1,430	
ZIEM, Felix (1821-1911) French					
oil	31	531,761	2,184	13,553	50,480
wc/d	4	30,658	1,970	2,540	23,609
ZIERMANN, Carl (1850-1881) German					
oil	1	3,000		3,000	
ZIGAINA, Giuseppe (1924-) Italian					
oil	3	13,365	4,276	4,363	4,726
ZILLE, Heinrich (1858-1929) German					
oil	2	36,132	2,151	18,066	33,981
wc/d	14	111,236	1,009	4,493	36,764
ZILLEN, J W (1824-1870) Danish					
oil	1	1,549		1,549	
ZILLER (?) ?					
oil	1	3,292		3,292	
ZIMMER, Bernd (1948-) German					
oil	6	40,578	3,287	7,267	10,847
wc/d	1	1,891		1,891	
ZIMMER, Hans Peter (1936-1992) German					
oil	1	1,211		1,211	
wc/d	1	18,181		18,181	
ZIMMER, Wilhelm Carl August (1853-1937) German					
oil	2	38,726	15,726	19,363	23,000
ZIMMERMAN, Frederick A (1886-1974) American					
oil	1	3,750		3,750	
ZIMMERMAN, Theodore (20th C) British					
wc/d	4	6,806	1,088	1,809	2,100
ZIMMERMANN, Albert (1809-1888) German					
oil	4	11,665	1,981	3,044	3,596
ZIMMERMANN, August Albert (1808-1888) German					
oil	1	17,000		17,000	
ZIMMERMANN, August Richard (1820-1872) German					
oil	1	12,000		12,000	
ZIMMERMANN, Carl (1863-1930) German					
oil	3	5,808	1,276	2,136	2,396
ZIMMERMANN, Ernst (1898-1966) German					
oil	1	1,182		1,182	
ZIMMERMANN, Friedrich (1823-1884) German					
oil	1	3,069		3,069	
ZIMMERMANN, Friedrich August (1805-1876) German					
oil	1	1,898		1,898	
ZIMMERMANN, J F (18th C) ?					
oil	1	2,696		2,696	
ZIMMERMANN, Max (1811-1878) German					
oil	2	4,744	1,108	2,372	3,636
ZIMMERMANN, Peter (1956-) German					
oil	1	6,040		6,040	
ZIMMERMANN, Richard (1820-1875) German					
oil	2	3,665	1,483	1,833	2,182
ZINGG, Adrian (1734-1816) Swiss					
oil	1	1,289		1,289	
wc/d	6	19,011	2,111	2,700	5,677
ZINGG, Jules (1882-1942) French					
oil	9	40,099	2,526	3,910	8,123
wc/d	3	8,218	2,552	2,552	3,114

Name	No.	Total Sales Value	Prices lowest	median	highest
ZINGONI, Aurelio (1853-1922) Italian					
oil	1	1,631		1,631	
ZINKEISEN, Anna (1901-1976) British					
oil	7	27,243	1,199	3,300	6,480
ZINKEISEN, Doris (1898-1991) British					
oil	16	67,235	1,050	3,526	11,280
wc/d	1	3,792		3,792	
ZITMAN, Cornelis (1926-) Dutch/Venezuelan					
3D	1	7,700		7,700	
ZITTEL, Andrea (1965-) American					
wc/d	1	4,500		4,500	
ZIVERI, Alberto (1908-1990) Italian					
oil	5	13,526	1,440	2,411	5,236
ZO, Henri (1873-1933) French					
oil	4	24,618	2,750	3,585	14,642
ZOBEL, Benjamin (1762-1831) German					
wc/d	1	3,770		3,770	
ZOBEL, Fernando (1924-1987) Spanish					
oil	7	33,328	1,773	3,382	14,928
ZOBERNIG, Heimo (1958-) ?					
wc/d	1	3,320		3,320	
ZOBOLI, Giacomo (1682-1757) Italian					
oil	1	3,482		3,482	
ZOCCHI, Emilio (1835-1913) Italian					
3D	1	7,350		7,350	
ZOCCHI, Giuseppe (1711-1767) Italian					
wc/d	1	10,183		10,183	
ZOCCHI, Guglielmo (1874-?) Italian					
oil	2	36,000	16,000	18,000	20,000
ZOELLY, Paul (1896-1971) Swiss					
oil	1	3,848		3,848	
ZOFF, Alfred (1852-1927) Austrian					
oil	5	19,101	1,341	3,964	6,776
ZOFFANY, Johann (1733-1810) British					
oil	1	20,540		20,540	
ZOFFOLI, Andreas (19th C) Italian					
oil	1	2,000		2,000	
ZOFFOLI, Angelo (fl.1860-1910) Italian					
oil	2	39,365	17,365	19,683	22,000
ZOFFOLI, Giovanni (18th C) Italian					
3D	1	4,410		4,410	
ZOLL, Kilian (1818-1860) Swedish					
oil	3	7,598	2,110	2,110	3,312
ZOLLA, Venanzio (1880-1961) Italian					
oil	1	2,566		2,566	
ZOMMER, Richard Karlovich (1866-1939) Russian					
oil	4	17,541	1,130	4,431	7,550
ZOMPINI, Gaetano (1700-1778) Italian					
oil	1	21,997		21,997	
wc/d	1	3,000		3,000	
ZON, Jacob (1872-1932) Dutch					
oil	1	1,224		1,224	
ZONARO, Fausto (1854-1929) Italian					
oil	8	624,396	1,258	21,603	390,000
ZOPPI, Antonio (1860-1926) Italian					
oil	2	4,086	1,750	2,043	2,336
ZORACH, Marguerite (1887-1968) American					
oil	4	102,500	3,500	17,000	65,000
wc/d	1	20,000		20,000	

Name	No.	Total Sales Value	Prices lowest	median	highest
ZORACH, William (1887-1966) American					
3D	3	58,000	7,000	16,000	35,000
wc/d	9	52,400	1,600	3,800	13,000
ZORILLA DE SAN MARTIN, Jose Luis (1891-?) Uruguayan					
3D	1	3,100		3,100	
ZORIO, Gilberto (1944-) Italian					
3D	1	26,100		26,100	
ZORKOCZY, Gyula (1873-1932) Hungarian					
oil	1	1,000		1,000	
ZORN, Anders (1860-1920) Swedish					
3D	1	19,093		19,093	
oil	9	2,403,347	41,399	269,094	677,201
wc/d	7	169,304	1,759	22,573	54,412
ZORNES, Milford (1908-) American					
oil	1	1,200		1,200	
wc/d	3	6,000	1,400	1,600	3,000
ZUBER, Henri (1844-1909) French					
oil	1	1,160		1,160	
ZUBER-BUHLER, Fritz (1822-1896) Swiss					
oil	2	181,783	1,783	90,892	180,000
wc/d	1	1,016		1,016	
ZUBIAURRE, Ramon de (1882-1969) Spanish					
oil	4	51,607	3,691	7,308	33,301
ZUBIAURRE, Valentin de (1879-1963) Spanish					
oil	2	48,085	15,819	24,043	32,266
ZUBTSOV, Sergei (1972-) Russian					
oil	3	3,425	1,050	1,055	1,320
ZUCCARELLI, Francesco (1702-1788) Italian					
oil	3	304,899	37,119	117,780	150,000
wc/d	5	46,062	2,646	7,550	25,670
ZUCCARO, Federico (1540-1609) Italian					
wc/d	2	40,335	12,835	20,168	27,500
ZUCCARO, Taddeo (1529-1566) Italian					
wc/d	3	124,442	20,000	40,000	64,442
ZUCCHERI, Luigi (1904-1974) Italian					
oil	1	3,121		3,121	
ZUCCHI, Jacopo (c.1541-1590) Italian					
wc/d	1	1,528		1,528	
ZUCHORS, W (19/20th C) ?					
oil	1	9,176		9,176	
ZUCKERBERG, Stanley (1919-1995) American					
oil	1	3,000		3,000	
ZUGEL, Heinrich von (1850-1941) German					
oil	14	163,951	1,136	10,218	27,241
wc/d	1	1,183		1,183	
ZUGEL, Wilhelm (1876-1950) German					
3D	3	4,836	1,307	1,307	2,215
ZUGNO, Francesco (1709-1787) Italian					
oil	1	5,633		5,633	
wc/d	2	2,776	1,176	1,388	1,600
ZUHR, Hugo (1895-1971) Swedish					
oil	16	32,809	1,305	1,826	4,415
ZUILL, Abbie Luella (1856-1921) American					
oil	1	7,000		7,000	
ZUILL, Alice I (19th C) American					
oil	1	1,200		1,200	
ZULOAGA, Elisa Elvira (1900-1980) South American?					
oil	2	3,480	1,720	1,740	1,760
ZULOAGA, Ignacio (1870-1945) Spanish					
oil	6	319,319	1,994	36,750	135,000

Name	No.	Total Sales Value	lowest	Prices median	highest
ZUMBUSCH, Ludwig von (1861-1927) German					
oil	2	4,180	1,708	2,090	2,472
ZUMEL, Nelson (?) ?					
wc/d	1	1,526		1,526	
ZUND, Robert (1827-1909) Swiss					
oil	14	215,666	1,641	6,126	48,615
wc/d	2	4,964	1,196	2,482	3,768
ZUNIGA, Francisco (1913-1998) Costa Rican					
3D	5	192,500	9,500	35,000	70,000
oil	3	42,500	3,500	4,000	35,000
wc/d	7	39,000	2,000	5,500	10,000
ZUPPINGER, Ernst Theodor (1875-1948) Swiss					
oil	1	1,139		1,139	
ZUR NEDDEN, Julius von (1824-?) German					
oil	1	1,072		1,072	
ZURBARAN, Francisco (1598-1664) Spanish					
oil	3	546,300	80,000	196,300	270,000
ZURBARAN, Juan de (1620-1649) Spanish					
oil	1	129,065		129,065	
ZURKINDEN, Irene (1909-1987) Swiss					
oil	6	20,090	1,211	2,320	9,035
wc/d	3	4,397	1,016	1,016	2,332
ZUSH (1946-) Spanish					
oil	1	1,318		1,318	
wc/d	3	4,147	1,055	1,344	1,748
ZUZARREN, C G (1873-1927) ?					
oil	1	1,154		1,154	
ZWAAN, Cornelisz C (1882-1964) Dutch					
oil	1	10,500		10,500	
ZWAN, Kazimierz (1792-1858) Polish					
oil	1	2,211		2,211	
ZWART, Arie (1903-1981) Dutch					
oil	13	22,096	1,075	1,585	3,622
ZWART, Willem de (1862-1931) Dutch					
oil	7	47,014	1,358	3,819	19,095
wc/d	7	23,886	1,358	2,546	10,258
ZWEIGBERGK, Bo Eison von (1897-1940) Swedish					
oil	2	20,344	4,020	10,172	16,324
wc/d	1	3,591		3,591	
ZWENGAUER, Anton (elder) (1810-1884) German					
oil	3	10,693	1,483	1,483	7,727
ZWERVER, Dolf (1932-) Dutch					
oil	1	4,957		4,957	
ZWICK, W (20th C) German					
3D	1	1,256		1,256	
ZWIETEN, Cornelis van (17th C) Dutch					
oil	1	21,140		21,140	
ZWILLER, Marie Augustin (1850-1939) French					
oil	6	27,571	1,978	4,050	10,500
ZYL, Ian van (1946-) South African					
oil	1	1,110		1,110	

Fifty Years of Art Auction Information

Art Sales Index Ltd has been providing reliable and accurate information on works of fine art that have sold at auction since 1968; we have accumulated considerable experience in this field.

Auction prices are in the public domain and can be considered a basis for determining the value of art.

This information is made available in a two volume hardcover book, published each fall, on CD ROM and now on the Internet. In the region of 145,000 lots are added to the database each year, which now contains more than 2.45 million entries.

A veritable mine of information and an important place to check if you collect, buy or sell art as prices are always changing.

An important feature is an authority database of 198,000 artist records, which represents 260,000 artist names that have featured at auction during this time.

For example: Mihail/Michail/Michel/Michael/Mikael Chemiakin all point to the same artist - Mikhail Chemiakin.

We are in the process of loading Christie's catalogues from 1920 to 1940 when many important paintings owned by the English aristocracy were bought by American collectors.

Old Masters were the favourites in those days; Impressionists hadn't been discovered and could sell for less than $5,000.

A recent entry to the database is "The Dream of Pope Sergius" by Rogier van der Weyden, which sold for $71,500 at the Mortimer Schiff sale in June 1938. In today's money, that's about $600,000 and it is still a record for this artist.

For more information, please contact us at the address below.

Art Sales Index Ltd
194 Thorpe Lea Road, Egham, Surrey, TW20 8HA, England
Tel: 011 44 1784 451145 Fax: 011 44 1784 451144
Email: info@art-sales-index.com
Internet: www.art-sales-index.com

HOUSE OF COLLECTIBLES SERIES

THE OFFICIAL PRICE GUIDES TO

Title	ISBN	Price	Author
Action Figures, 2nd ed.	0676601790	$21.95	Stuart Wells & Main Toys
Antique Clocks, 3rd ed.	0876375131	$12.00	Roy Erhardt
Antiques & Collectibles, 18th ed.	0676601855	$16.00	Rinker Enterprises
Beatles Records & Memorabilia, 2nd ed.	0676601812	$18.95	Perry Cox
Bottles, 13th ed.	0676601847	$17.95	Jim Megura
Civil War Collectibles, 2nd ed.	067660160X	$17.95	Richard Friz
Collectible Card Games	0676601456	$17.95	Tony Lee & Timothy Brown
Collecting Books, 4th ed.	0609807692	$18.00	Marie Tedford & Pat Goudey
Collector Knives, 13th ed.	0676601898	$17.95	C. Houston Price
Collector Plates, 7th ed.	0676601545	$19.95	Rinker Enterprises
Dinnerware of the 20th Century	0676600859	$29.95	Harry L. Rinker
Elvis Presley Records & Memorabilia, 2nd ed.	0676601413	$17.00	Jerry Osborne
Glassware, 3rd ed.	067660188X	$17.00	Mark Pickvet
Military Collectibles, 6th ed.	0676600522	$20.00	Richard Austin
Overstreet Comic Books, 31st ed.	0609808206	$22.00	Robert M. Overstreet
Overstreet Indian Arrowheads, 7th ed.	0609808699	$24.00	Robert M. Overstreet
Pottery & Porcelain, 8th ed.	0876378939	$18.00	Harvey Duke
Records 2001	0676601871	$25.95	Jerry Osborne
Rinker Collectibles, 4th ed.	0676601596	$19.95	Harry L. Rinker
R. L. Wilson Gun Collecting, 3rd ed.	0676601537	$24.95	R. L. Wilson
Silverware of the 20th Century	0676600867	$24.95	Harry L. Rinker
Star Wars Collectibles, 4th ed.	0876379951	$19.95	Sue Cornwell & Mike Kott
Stemware of the 20th Century	0676600840	$24.95	Harry L. Rinker
Vintage Fashion & Fabrics	0609808133	$17.00	Pamela Smith

THE OFFICIAL GUIDES TO

Title	ISBN	Price	Author
America's State Quarters	0609807706	$5.99	David L. Ganz
Coin Grading & Counterfeit Detection	0676600409	$29.95	Prof. Coin Grading Service
Flea Market Prices	0609807722	$14.95	Harry L. Rinker
How to Buy Jewelry Wholesale	067660126X	$10.95	Frank J. Adler
How to Make Money in Coins Right Now, 2nd ed.	0609807463	$14.95	Scott Travers
Official Directory to U.S. Flea Markets, 7th ed.	0676601901	$10.00	Kitty Werner
One-Minute Coin Expert, 4th ed.	0609807471	$7.99	Scott Travers

THE OFFICIAL BECKETT SPORTS CARDS PRICE GUIDES TO

Title	ISBN	Price	Author
Baseball Cards 2002, 21st ed.	0609807641	$7.99	Dr. James Beckett
Basketball Cards 2002, 11th ed.	0609808427	$6.99	Dr. James Beckett
Football Cards 2002, 21st ed.	0609808435	$7.99	Dr. James Beckett

THE OFFICIAL BLACKBOOK PRICE GUIDES TO

Title	ISBN	Price	Author
U.S. Coins 2002, 40th ed.	0676601731	$6.99	Marc & Tom Hudgeons
U.S. Paper Money 2002, 34th ed.	0676601677	$6.99	Marc & Tom Hudgeons
U.S. Postage Stamps 2002, 24th ed.	0676601707	$7.99	Marc & Tom Hudgeons
World Coins 2002, 5th ed.	0676601766	$7.99	Marc & Tom Hudgeons

Available in bookstores everywhere